PAUL AND THE FAITHFULNESS OF GOD

CHRISTIAN ORIGINS AND THE QUESTION OF GOD

PAUL AND THE FAITHFULNESS OF GOD

PARTS III and IV

N. T. Wright

University of St Andrews

SPCK

First published in Great Britain 2013

Society for Promoting Christian Knowledge,
36 Causton Street
London SW1P 4ST
www.spckpublishing.co.uk

British Library Cataloguing-in-Publication Data
A catalogue record for this book is available from the British Library

2-volume set ISBN 978–0–281–05555–5 (hardback)
2-volume set ISBN 978–0–281–05554–8 (paperback)
eBook ISBN 978–0–281–06756–5

Parts III and IV ISBN 978–0–281–07138–8 (hardback)
Parts III and IV ISBN 978–0–281–07140–1 (paperback)

NOT FOR INDIVIDUAL SALE

Typeset by Tom Wright, St Andrews, using *Nota Bene* software
First printed in Great Britain
Subsequently digitally printed in Great Britain

eBook by Data Standards Ltd, Frome, Somerset

Produced on paper from sustainable forests

For Richard Hays

a prince among exegetes
a jewel among friends

CONTENTS

BOOK I

Contents: Parts I and II xi
Preface xv

Part I PAUL AND HIS WORLD

1 Return of the Runaway? 3
2 Like Birds Hovering Overhead: the Faithfulness of the God of Israel 75
3 Athene and Her Owl: the Wisdom of the Greeks 197
4 A Cock for Asclepius: 'Religion' and 'Culture' in Paul's World 246
5 The Eagle Has Landed: Rome and the Challenge of Empire 279

Part II THE MINDSET OF THE APOSTLE

6 A Bird in the Hand? The Symbolic Praxis of Paul's World 351
7 The Plot, the Plan and the Storied Worldview 456
8 Five Signposts to the Apostolic Mindset 538

Bibliography for Parts I and II 572

BOOK II

Contents: Parts III and IV ix

Part III PAUL'S THEOLOGY

Introduction to Part III 609
9 The One God of Israel, Freshly Revealed 619
10 The People of God, Freshly Reworked 774
11 God's Future for the World, Freshly Imagined 1043

Part IV PAUL IN HISTORY

Introduction to Part IV 1269
12 The Lion and the Eagle: Paul in Caesar's Empire 1271
13 A Different Sacrifice: Paul and 'Religion' 1320
14 The Foolishness of God: Paul among the Philosophers 1354
15 To Know the Place for the First Time: Paul and His Jewish Context 1408
16 Signs of the New Creation: Paul's Aims and Achievements 1473

Full Bibliography of Works Referred to in Parts I–IV 1521
Indexes 1591

CONTENTS: PARTS III AND IV

Part III: PAUL'S THEOLOGY

Introduction to Part III 609

9 The One God of Israel, Freshly Revealed 619
1. First-Century Jewish 'Monotheism' 619
2. Paul's Reaffirmed Monotheism 634
   (i) Suffering for the One God 634
   (ii) Monotheism Reaffirmed: God the Creator, the Judge 638
   (iii) Monotheism in Practice: One God, Therefore One People 641
3. Monotheism Freshly Revealed (1): Jesus 644
   (i) Introduction: Paul and the 'Origin of Christology' 644
   (ii) Jesus and the God of Exodus, Return and Wisdom 656
      (a) Galatians 4.1–11 656
      (b) Romans 8.1–4 659
      (c) 1 Corinthians 8—10 661
      (d) Creation, Exodus and Wisdom: Colossians 1 670
      (e) 2 Corinthians 3 and 4 677
      (f) Philippians 2.6–11 680
      (g) Jesus and the Return of YHWH: Conclusion 689
   (iii) Jesus as Risen and Enthroned Messiah 690
      (a) Messiah and 'Son of God' 690
      (b) Jesus as *Kyrios*, Especially in Biblical Quotations 701
      (c) Romans 9.5: Does Paul Call Jesus 'God'? 707
4. Monotheism Freshly Revealed (2): the Spirit 709
   (i) Introduction 709
   (ii) The Spirit as the New Shekinah 711
   (iii) The Spirit and the New Exodus 717
   (iv) Monotheism and Spirit: Conclusion 727
5. Monotheism and the Single United Family: Ephesians 728
6. Revised Monotheism and the Kingdom of God: 1 Corinthians 15.20–8 733
7. The Dark Side of Revised Monotheism: the New Vision of Evil 737
   (i) Introduction: Jewish Monotheism and the 'Problem of Evil' 737
   (ii) 'Plight and Solution' in Paul's Theology 747
      (a) Introduction 747
      (b) The 'Plight' Revised (1): in the Light of the Cross 752
      (c) The 'Plight' Revised (2): in the Light of the Resurrection 756
      (d) The 'Plight' Revised (3): in the Light of the Spirit 758

(iii) The Problem of Romans 1.18—2.16 764
(iv) Monotheism and the Problem of Evil: Conclusion 771
8. Conclusion 772

10 The People of God, Freshly Reworked 774
1. Introduction 774
2. Israel and Its Purpose 783
(i) Adam and Abraham 783
(ii) Covenant, Law Court and 'Righteousness' 795
(iii) The Covenant Purpose: Through Israel to the World 804
3. Israel's Messiah as the Focus of Election 815
(i) Introduction: Jesus as the Messiah of Israel 815
(a) Introduction 815
(b) Jesus as Israel's Messiah 817
(c) Jesus as Israel's *Incorporative* Messiah 825
(d) Conclusion: Paul and Messiahship 835
(ii) Jesus as the *Faithful* Messiah of Israel: Romans 3 and 4 836
(iii) Jesus the Faithful Messiah and the Problem of Torah: Galatians 2—4 851
(a) Introduction 851
(b) Galatians 2.15–21 852
(c) Galatians 3.1—4.11 860
(α) Introduction 860
(β) Galatians 3.10–14 863
(γ) Galatians 3.15–18 868
(δ) Galatians 3.19–22 870
(ε) Galatians 3.23–9 873
(ζ) Galatians 4.1–11 876
(iv) Jesus as the Messiah through Whom God Has Reconciled the World 879
(a) 2 Corinthians 5.11—6.2 879
(b) Romans 5.6–21 885
(c) Romans 7.1—8.11 892
(v) Jesus the Messiah through Whom God's Love Holds His People Secure: Romans 8.31–9 902
(vi) The Messiah, the Hope of Israel, and the Torah: Conclusion 908
4. Election Reworked around the Spirit: the Messiah's Justified People 912
(i) Introduction 912
(ii) Election Redefined: Gospel and Spirit 914
(iii) Faith, Justification and the People of God 925
(a) The Shape of Justification 925
(b) Galatians 2.15—4.11 966
(c) 1 Corinthians 976
(d) 2 Corinthians 3 980
(e) Philippians 3.2–11 984
(f) Colossians 2 992
(g) Romans 3.21—4.25 995

(h) Romans 5—8 1007
(i) Conclusion: Justification in Christ, by Grace, through Faith, in the Present Time 1026
(j) What Then about Torah? 1032
5. Conclusion: Election Redefined 1038

11 God's Future for the World, Freshly Imagined 1043
1. Introduction 1043
2. Israel's God and the Story of Hope 1049
3. Hope Realized and Redefined 1061
(i) Through Jesus 1061
(ii) Through the Spirit 1074
4. Hope Still to Come – through Jesus and the Spirit 1078
5. Eschatology and Christian Living 1095
(i) Introduction 1095
(ii) Already in the New Age 1101
(iii) Not Yet Perfect: Inaugurated but Incomplete 1111
6. The Eschatological Challenge of Redefined Election 1128
(i) Introduction 1128
(ii) Galatians 4—6 1133
(iii) 1 Thessalonians 2 1151
(iv) Romans 9—11 1156
(a) Introduction 1156
(b) Exile, Justification, the Righteousness of God and Salvation: 10.1–17 1165
(c) The Surprised Gentiles and the Jealous Jews: 9.30–3; 10.18–21 1176
(d) Bearers of God's Strange Purpose: Romans 9.6–29 1181
(e) All Israel Shall Be Saved: Romans 11.1–32 1195
(α) Introduction to Romans 11 1195
(β) The Centre: 11.13–15 1197
(γ) 11.11–12 1206
(δ) 11.16–24 1211
(ε) 11.1–10 1222
(ζ) Romans 11.1–24: What Does Paul Envisage? 1229
(η) 'All Israel Shall Be Saved': 11.25–7 1231
(θ) Disobedience and Mercy for All: 11.28–32 1252
(ι) The End and the Beginning: 11.33–6 and 9.1–5 1256
7. Conclusion: Hope and Its Consequences 1258
(i) Introduction: Paul's Revised Hope 1258
(ii) The Effect of Paul's Theology 1259
(iii) Paul's Theology and His Three Worlds 1264

Part IV: PAUL IN HISTORY

Introduction to Part IV 1269

12 The Lion and the Eagle: Paul in Caesar's Empire 1271
1. Introduction 1271
2. Empire in Relation to Paul's Worldview and Theology 1277
3. Jesus Is Lord, and Therefore . . . 1284
   (i) Who Are the 'Rulers', and What Has Happened to Them? 1284
   (ii) The Apocalyptic, and Therefore Political, Triumph of God 1289
   (iii) Rising to Rule the Nations 1299
4. Paul and Caesar: Conclusion 1305

13 A Different Sacrifice: Paul and 'Religion' 1320
1. Introduction 1320
2. Paul among the Religions 1330
   (i) Introduction 1330
   (ii) Baptism: the Jesus-Shaped Exodus 1333
   (iii) The Living Sacrifice 1339
   (iv) The Breaking of Bread 1344
   (v) Prayer 1348
   (vi) Discerning the Way 1350
3. Paul and 'Religion': Conclusion 1352

14 The Foolishness of God: Paul among the Philosophers 1354
1. Introduction 1354
2. Paul's Questions to the Philosophers 1359
   (i) Introduction 1359
   (ii) 'Logic' and Epistemology 1362
   (iii) 'What There Is': Paul's Comments on 'Physics' 1367
   (iv) 'Ethics' 1371
3. Paul and the Stoics in Recent Study 1383
   (i) Introduction 1383
   (ii) Beyond the Engberg-Pedersen Divide? 1386
      (a) Exposition 1386
      (b) Critique 1392
4. Conclusion 1406

15 To Know the Place for the First Time: Paul and His Jewish Context 1408
1. Introduction 1408
2. Conversion, Call or Transformation? 1417
3. Paul and Jewish 'Identity' 1426
   (i) Introduction: the Question of 'Identity' 1426
   (ii) 'Like a Jew to the Jews'? 1434
   (iii) A 'Third Race'? 1443

4. Paul and Israel's Scriptures 1449
(i) Introduction 1449
(ii) Hermeneutics, Faith and the Faithfulness of God 1456
5. Conclusion 1471

16 Signs of the New Creation: Paul's Aims and Achievements 1473
1. Introduction 1473
2. Paul in Several Dimensions: the Ministry of Reconciliation 1484
3. Integration and Reconciliation 1504
4. Conclusion: Exalted Manna 1516

Full Bibliography of Works Referred to in Parts I–IV 1521
Abbreviations 1521
A Primary Sources 1527
B Secondary Literature 1532

Indexes 1591
Index of Ancient Sources 1591
1. Old Testament 1591
2. Apocrypha 1602
3. Pseudepigrapha 1603
4. Qumran 1606
5. Josephus 1606
6. Philo 1607
7. Rabbinic Works 1608
8. New Testament 1609
9. Christian and/or Gnostic Works 1629
10. Pagan Sources 1630
Index of Modern Authors 1635
Index of Selected Topics 1647

中 *Chū*

Medium

Straight downward through a rectangle
A swift bisecting bar
A stroke that likely started out
An arrow that pierces
Its target's 'medium', 'mid-point', 'midst'.
Definite line between
Refocusing our edge-lured minds.
Golden mean. Middle way.

Shot and follow-through.
A true shaft and singing arc.
Spot on. A bull's-eye.

The sign too for Middle Kingdom.
A centered self-belief:
All else east or west of China.
Assured parishioners.
Poet Kavanagh would have approved
How any dynasty
Knew the axis of everything
Drew a line through their world.

The place where it's at.
Middle of everywhere.
Arrow's *you are here.*

Micheal O'Siadhail

Part III

PAUL'S THEOLOGY

INTRODUCTION TO PART III

From worldview to theology. This is not, and should never be, an either/or distinction. My central argument in the present book is that when we analyze Paul's worldview we understand why his theology needed to be what it was. This works the other way round, too: when we analyze Paul's theology we understand better why his worldview was what it was – though of course, in a book, one cannot present both of these arguments sequentially. Worldview and theology go together in a chicken-and-egg sort of way, as opposed to a fish-and-chips sort of way. If, as some do, we replace 'worldview' with something like 'cosmology', we would see that this double reality, worldview plus theology, belongs on the same map as, say, Engberg-Pedersen's presentation of Stoicism (theology plus 'cosmology').[1] I find that usage inadequate and potentially confusing, but it is worth noting that I am doing something similar to those who employ it.

The hypothesis I shall now present, as the material centre of my argument, is that there is a way of understanding Paul's theology which does justice to the whole and the parts, to the multiple historical contexts within which Paul lived and the multiple social and ecclesial pressures and questions he faced – and, particularly, to the actual texts of the actual letters. Locating this overall aim within contemporary Pauline scholarship, I shall argue that this way of approaching him will draw together, and hold in a recognizably Pauline balance, the different strands or themes which have been highlighted and, all too often, played off against one another ('juristic', 'participationist', 'transformational', 'apocalyptic', 'covenantal' and 'salvation-historical' – and no doubt many more besides, including those old and potentially dualistic geometrical metaphors, 'vertical' and 'horizontal'). There are, no doubt, rough edges and craggy outcrops of thought here and there in Paul, as in any great thinker. But the inner coherence, not simply of a small central core, but of the large and broad sweep of his writing will emerge from the perspective I propose. This will constitute the major argument in its favour.

I shall repeatedly appeal to the *sequence of thought* in a letter as a whole, a section as a whole, a chapter or paragraph as a whole. I marvel at the extent to which this is often not done in works on Paul's theology or particular

[1] On ancient meanings of 'theology' see above, 216f., esp. n. 69.

aspects of it. I marvel in particular that many commentaries, which one might suppose to be committed to following the argument of the text they are studying, manage not to do that, but instead to treat a Pauline letter as if it were a collection of maxims, detached theological statements, plus occasional 'proofs from scripture' and the like.[2] I take it as axiomatic, on the contrary, that Paul deliberately laid out whole arguments, not just bits and pieces, miscellaneous *topoi* which just happen to turn up in these irrelevant 'contingent' contexts like oddly shaped pearls on an irrelevant string.[3] In any case, the point is that a thematic analysis of Paul's theological topics in themselves, and in their mutual interrelation, ought to enhance our appreciation of the flow of thought in his letters and their component parts, while also demonstrating coherence among themselves. The best argument in favour of the hypothesis is that this end is in fact achieved by this means. As Ernst Käsemann put it at the start of his great Romans commentary:

> Until I have proof to the contrary I proceed on the assumption that the text has a central concern and a remarkable inner logic that may no longer be entirely comprehensible to us.[4]

The first half of that statement (the assumption of a central concern and inner logic) constitutes the invitation to exegesis; the second half (the question of comprehensibility) constitutes its particular challenge. The study of Pauline theology is intended, at least in my own case, to contribute to the comprehensibility of the text's assumed 'central concern' and 'remarkable inner logic' by clarifying the underlying themes and concepts upon which Paul is drawing at any one time. And part of that clarifying, as will quickly become apparent, consists in recognizing that though there were 'many gods, many lords' in Paul's world, when he used the word *theos* he referred to the being he regarded as the one and only divinity, the creator, the one who had entered into covenant with Israel. That is why, in the present volume, I have been using the capital letter for the word 'God'.

My particular proposal in this Part has a simple outline, unfolding in three stages.

1. I take as the framework the three main elements of second-Temple Jewish 'theology', namely monotheism, election and eschatology. I am aware, as I have said before, that second-Temple Jews did not characteristically write works of systematic theology, but I am also aware that these three topics have a clear and well-known claim to summarize beliefs widely held at the

[2] A classic example of this is Betz 1979.

[3] I am reminded of Morna Hooker's famous remarks (Hooker 1972) about the way in which form critics, studying small 'units' of tradition strung together with no apparent regard for their mutual relationship, used to refer to such units as 'pearls on a string'. This, she said, was a typically masculine approach; any woman would know that the relative placing of the pearls was just as important as their individual value.

[4] Käsemann 1980 [1973], viii.

time.[5] I am equally aware that many essays in 'Pauline theology' have assumed that its central, dominant or even sole theme will be soteriology, and that my proposal may appear to be ignoring this and setting off in a quite different direction. However, as will become clear, I believe that the theme of 'election' is the best frame within which to understand Paul's soteriology, and that 'election' in turn is only properly understood within the larger frame of beliefs about the one God and the promised future (and the particular problem of evil which only emerges into full light once the reality of the one God has been glimpsed). Soteriology thus remains at the centre. Part of the strength of my proposal is, I believe, the clarity which it brings to the many debates which still buzz around Paul's exposition of salvation like bees around a hive.

Each of these topics – monotheism, election, eschatology – is of course controversial and complex in its own right in second-Temple Judaism, let alone in early Christianity.[6] But once we home in on what, more or less, these themes might have meant to a first-century Pharisee, we see not only that they do indeed shape Jewish thinking but that they form a tightly integrated whole: one God, one people of God, one future for Israel and the world. Each is kept in place by the others, and each is partly defined in relation to the others.

The first move in my overall hypothesis, then, is to propose that Paul remained a thoroughly Jewish thinker, and that these three topics substantially and satisfyingly cover the main things he was talking about and insisting upon, the central points upon which he drew when addressing the wide range of concerns which appear in his letters. This opening (theological) move is correlated with my basic (historical; an earlier generation would have said, 'religio-historical') assumption about where Paul stood in relation to the thought-worlds of his day. Like many other Jewish thinkers of his and other days, he radically revised and rethought his Jewish tradition (in his case, the viewpoint of a Pharisee) around a fresh understanding of the divine purposes, thus gaining a fresh hermeneutical principle. In other words, I proceed on the assumption that, however we describe what happened to Paul on the road to Damascus ('conversion'? 'call'?), its effect was not that he rejected everything about his Jewish life and thought and invented a new scheme, with or without borrowed non-Jewish elements, but that he thought through and transformed his existing Jewish worldview and theology in the light of the cataclysmic revelation that the crucified Jesus had been raised from the dead.[7] If this means that Paul held an 'apocalyptic' theology, so be it; though, over against some schemes that have claimed that title, what it means is that Paul remained, in his own mind at least, firmly

[5] See above, 179–93. It is noteworthy that, despite our other quite radical disagreements, Eisenbaum 2009 ch. 5 highlights the same three basic components: worship, Torah, redemption, where 'worship' focuses naturally on monotheism, 'Torah' on election and covenant, and 'redemption' on Israel's hope of new creation.

[6] See ch. 2 above.

[7] For the placing of this assumption within the history of scholarship on Paul, see *Interpreters*.

on the Jewish map. He did not, as many have wanted to believe, sweep that map off the table and replace it with something quite different, a fresh and essentially non-Jewish 'revelation'.

2. This brings us to the second stage of the hypothesis. I shall argue, in the case of each of these three central and correlated topics, that Paul rethought, reworked and reimagined them around Jesus the Messiah on the one hand and the spirit on the other.[8] As Wayne Meeks put it: 'the belief in the crucified Messiah introduces a new and controlling paradigm of God's mode of action.'[9] This hypothesis, of a christological and pneumatological reworking of the three central Jewish beliefs, will necessarily involve important sub-hypotheses about Jesus and the spirit: about Jesus as the personal revelation-in-action of Israel's God (in chapter 9); about Jesus' 'Messiahship' in Paul, and the relationship between that and Paul's view of Israel as the people of the one God (in chapter 10); about the spirit as the presence of the living God inhabiting the new temple (in chapter 9), and as the agent of covenant renewal (in chapter 10). Each of these, inevitably, will plunge us into topics which are often treated at monograph length in their own right, not least because they all correlate, in the treatment of 'election', with Paul's complex cluster of soteriological themes. There will not be room, of course, for such full treatment. But I hope that this framing of debates within the larger outline will nevertheless bring fresh clarity, and that the new proposals I advance will build on at least some of the strengths of recent scholarship.

There are, no doubt, other ways of lining up these dense, interlocking themes. I think this way has at least two important merits. First, it retains, and indeed emphasizes, Paul's location within second-Temple Judaism. Second, it highlights his serious and substantial reworking of traditional concepts.[10] When (for instance) he spoke about Jesus, or the spirit, or the law, or salvation, he was not freewheeling, inventing new ideas and foisting them on his readers. He was thinking through, in the light of the traditions (particularly the biblical traditions) he had inherited, what it meant to say that Israel's Messiah had been crucified and raised from the dead, and that the divine spirit had been poured out in a fresh way.

3. The third stage of the hypothesis is to demonstrate that this christologically and pneumatologically redefined complex of monotheism, election and eschatology was directed by Paul in three further ways, which we postpone to Part IV of the present book. I list them here in the reverse order in which they appear in that Part.

First, it was what drove and governed the main aims of his letter-writing. This activity, like Paul's praying and pastoral work themselves, was aimed at

[8] For an earlier, extremely brief, outline of this argument, see Wright 2005a [*Fresh Perspectives*], chs. 5, 6 and 7.

[9] Meeks 1983, 180. See too 168: 'For Paul himself, the central problem is not just to spell out the implications of monotheism, but to explain how the unified purpose of God through history could encompass the *novum* of a crucified Messiah.' That is exactly right, though I do not think that Meeks worked out fully the way in which Paul solved that problem.

[10] See Keck 1984, 231.

constructing and maintaining communities 'in the Messiah' across the world of first-century Turkey, Greece and Italy. It is important to note this here, in case it might appear that the real aim of all exegesis and historical or theological reconstruction, namely the understanding of Paul's letters themselves, had fallen out of sight. To the contrary: that is where it's all going. This is where the project finally comes in to land, in chapter 16.

Second, though, if Paul was indeed redefining the central beliefs of Second-Temple Judaism, we might expect to find, at least by implication, a running debate between him and others within that world, focused not least on how they were reading scripture. Sometimes, as in the controversy in Galatia, this debate emerges into the light of day (a very bright light, in that case, casting very large shadows). At other times it is more implicit than actual. But, as Francis Watson and others have shown, we can see in principle how Paul's reading of scripture stands in parallel to, and often in tension with, other readings taking place around the same time.[11] This involves another particular hypothesis, this time in relation to how Paul's reading of scripture actually works. Over against those who see it as atomistic or opportunistic, I follow those who see Paul dealing with the larger scriptural wholes from which he draws particular phrases and sentences, and particularly with the larger scriptural *narratives* which he wants his communities to inhabit for themselves.[12] This is the final element in the historical 'placing' of Paul, and it will occupy us in chapter 15, corresponding to chapter 2 in Part I.

Third, this christologically and pneumatologically redefined Jewish theology was in reasonably constant engagement, again sometimes explicitly and sometimes not, with the pagan world of Paul's day.[13] We will track this in the three stages we used in Part I: (a) Paul believed that the transforming power of his gospel upstaged the philosophers' quest, the pagan dream of a genuine humanness; (b) he articulated, and encouraged his churches to live with, a spirituality and *koinōnia*, again generated by the gospel, which he saw as the reality to which the 'religious' world of late antiquity obliquely pointed in its belief in suprahuman forces and intelligences which influenced and affected the ordinary world; (c) he believed that the universal lordship of Jesus, as Israel's true Messiah, upstaged the imperial dream of a single world-kingdom. I shall work through these themes, too, in reverse order, providing in Part IV a mirror image to the treatment in Part I. Thus chapter 12 deals with 'empire'; chapter 13 with 'religion'; and chapter 14 with 'philosophy'. In each case I choose, out of the plethora of modern studies, one or two particular conversation partners. This third part of the overall hypothesis – mapping out the ways in which the worldview and theology

[11] Watson 2004, e.g. 517; recently, cf. e.g. Moyise 2010.

[12] Against e.g. Tuckett 2000; Stanley 2004; Segal 2003, 164–7, speaking of 'Midrash to back up experience'. On all this see ch. 7 above, ch. 15 below, and the article in *Perspectives* ch. 32.

[13] Horrell 2005, 46 speaks of a 'broad consensus' on this point, but the legacy of Bultmann, with his attempt to derive early Christian ideas from pagan ones, lives on. See the remarks of Malherbe 1987, 32f.

of Parts II and III impacted on the contexts studied in Part I – forms a vital part of the overall argument.

One interesting reflection already follows from this. Paul was quite capable, as he says in 2 Corinthians 10.5, of 'taking every thought prisoner and making it obey the Messiah'. Like some of the Stoics, who could snatch 'Epicurean' or 'dualistic' concepts in order to show that in fact they supported their own position, Paul was quite capable of using language and ideas from the world of pagan philosophy in order to bring them, as it were, on side with his own project.[14] This in turn reflects an interesting emphasis which is often omitted: that Paul is at least implicitly, and occasionally explicitly, advocating the beginnings of a genuine 'public theology' – an aspiration far above the pragmatic reality of his tiny communities in the vast world of greco-roman antiquity, but a theme strongly hinted at in his attempt to create and sustain communities that were living the life of a genuine, God-reflecting humanness. Paul was, after all (to return to where we began), a full-blooded Jewish-style creational monotheist, which meant that in taking creation and humanness very seriously he held a view of redemption which affirmed the goodness of both rather than undermining it. The fact that humanness had been spoiled by idolatry did not mean that the divine plan of salvation involved the abandonment of humanness and its particular status and vocation. The fact that creation itself had been subjected to decay did not mean that the creator had given up on the vision of a good creation in need of renewal. For Paul, the gospel rendered people more human, not less, renewing the vocation of bearing the divine image, reflecting the divine wisdom into the rest of the world and reflecting the praises of creation back to its maker. This vision carried, from the start, strong and sometimes subversive meaning for real, public life.[15]

The result of all this (again, this will come in chapter 16) was the founding and maintaining of communities which, in terms of the first-century world of Diaspora Judaism, were bound to look extremely anomalous.[16] On the one hand, they would seem very Jewish, indeed 'conservatively' so. On the other hand, they would seem very 'assimilated', since they did not practise the customs and commandments that marked out Jews from their pagan neighbours. But these communities, Paul believed, possessed their own inner coherence, due to the freshly worked elements in the theology which he expounded, elements that were not bolted onto the outside of the parent Jewish theology as extraneous foreign bodies but were discerned to lie at the very heart of what that theology had most deeply affirmed.[17]

[14] See Gill 2003, 49; White 2003, 136.

[15] e.g. Phil. 1.27.

[16] See Barclay 1996, 381–95.

[17] This outflanks the implicit critique of scholars of ancient religion such as Rüpke 2007 [2001], ch. 5, who see 'Christian theology' as a second-century apologetic invention which became a weapon of political control for the new priestly caste. For Paul, 'theology' was the necessary activity if this community, with this worldview, was to survive, let alone flourish. Watson 2007 [1986], 26 rightly insists that to see Paul as 'thinker' is not enough unless we see that his thinking 'is at every point bound up with his action as founder of Christian communities'. Founder, yes; equally, maintainer, teacher, encourager.

The picture I have in mind of the hypothesis I am outlining can be sketched in terms of a rectangular box. As we look at this box from the front, we see the main elements of Jewish theology: monotheism, election and eschatology:

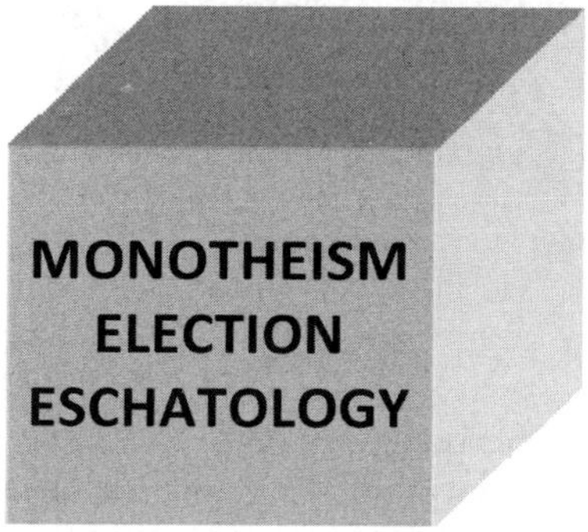

These three run, as it were, all the way through the box from front to back. As we look at the sides of the box, however, we see the two fresh themes which now redefine each of those three categories: Jesus the Messiah, the lord, and the spirit:

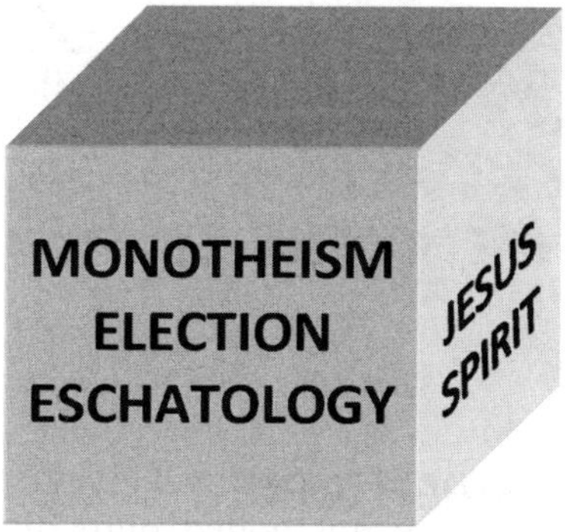

Again, these two run as it were all the way through from side to side, so that at every point in the content of the box we now have monotheism, election and eschatology redefined by Jesus and the spirit. Of course, Jesus and the spirit do not *replace* God the creator; somehow God the creator, already there of course at the heart of Jewish monotheism, is also there alongside the two new elements:

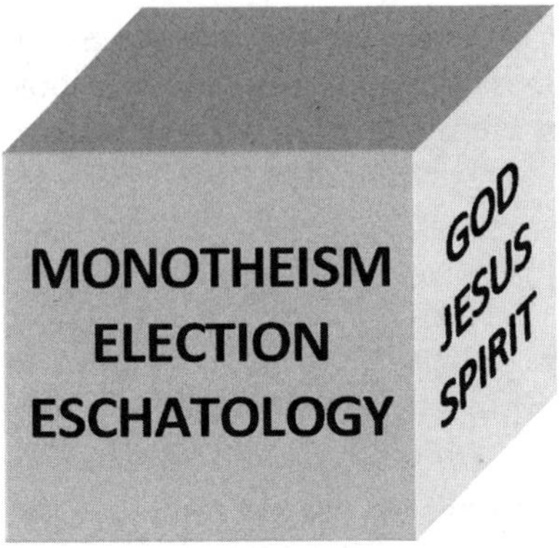

The base and the top of the box now come into play. The base is undoubtedly the Jewish Bible, foundational for Paul's thinking both traditional and creative. And the top is the world of paganism with which he found himself in constant engagement, sometimes in large but outflanking agreement, sometimes in sharp confrontation.

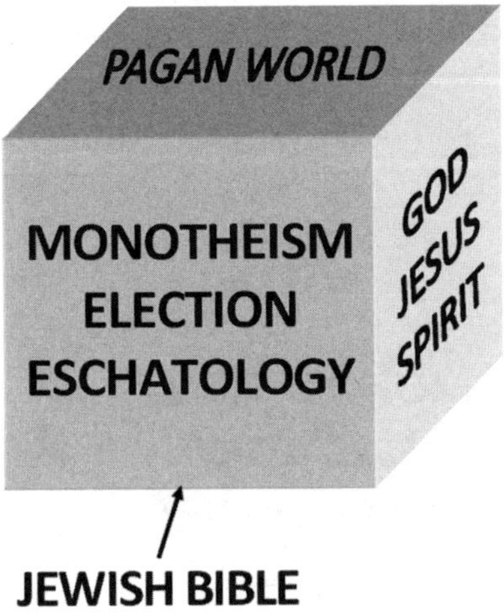

All this is of course complex, but necessarily so. Attempts to reduce that complexity in the pursuit of an easier comprehensibility are the equivalent of trying to make a model railway locomotive out of Playdough. Some parts may look familiar, but the train won't run down the track. The necessary complexity in question corresponds to the complexity of (a) the world(s) in which Paul lived, (b) the vocation he believed himself to have and particularly (c) the beliefs about the creator God and his purposes that formed the central material of his thinking. When we get these more or less right, the model locomotive will now work. We will find that Paul's various letters, our primary material, can be located comprehensibly and coherently somewhere within this box.

'Coherence' is after all what counts. We are not looking for the small-minded consistency which, though scorned by many Pauline scholars, is nevertheless wheeled out whenever they want to reject (say) Ephesians or 2 Thessalonians. We are looking for a larger consistency: this was, after all, a virtue prized by ancient Stoics as well as by some moderns.[18] Paul himself constantly urges his hearers to a 'consistency' of belief and life. We are looking for a coherence in which the different major themes, and their varied contextual expression, will be seen to offer mutual reinforcement even if not always expressed in precisely the same terminology.[19]

This hypothetical proposal, I submit, has strong initial plausibility. After the long years in which any 'explanation' of Paul's thinking was attractive so long as it did not involve much organic contact with Judaism, we are now much more attuned to thinking of him as a substantially Jewish figure and thinker, though this has meant that the problem has been rephrased: how did such a Jewish thinker manage to say things which sound, on occasion, so unJewish? My proposal addresses exactly this question. To see the shape of Jewish thought in the traditional terms of the one God, the one people of God, and the one future, and to see the coming of the Messiah and the giving of the spirit within that as the new defining point, is both to say, 'This is a very Jewish scheme' and 'This redefinition around Messiah and spirit is radical indeed.' (One might of course say exactly the same about the early Christian belief in Jesus' resurrection. That belief only made sense within the Jewish world, but it was something no Jew had imagined before, and it compelled radical revision of the things they *had* imagined before.[20]) To say all this sort of thing about tradition and redefinition is itself, I think, characteristically Jewish – and of course characteristically Pauline.

We should not be surprised to find that Paul was at his most world-challenging when he was at his most Jewish. The way I have drawn the 'box' of the different elements of Paul's thought indicates that he understood his radically reworked theology to be an account of the one God and the world, of Israel and the nations, of Jesus and his spirit-equipped people – an account which would address the wider non-Jewish world with news that, however apparently ridiculous and politically dangerous, could and would transform that world. Paul believed, after all, that with the crucified and risen Messiah the one God had tipped his hand, had drawn a line through the world, had placed a swift bisecting bar through the rectangular box, had refocused the edge-lured minds of the world onto this new strange centre.

[18] On 'consistency' as a Stoic aim: Gill 2003, 42; see Epict. *Disc.* 3.2.1–15; Schofield 2003b, 236.

[19] On Pauline 'consistency' see e.g. Horrell 2005; Sanders 1977, 518; 2008, 329; Achtemeier 1996; Beker 1980, e.g. 143 (where he says that only a 'consistent apocalyptic' will do); Roetzel 2003, 87 (his chapter 3 is entitled, provocatively, 'Paul as Organic Intellectual').

[20] So *RSG*, *passim*.

That is indeed how empires think. Paul believed in a different empire, a different *kind* of empire. He called it the kingdom of God.

And so to work. We begin with the centre of Jewish life and thought: the one creator God.

Chapter Nine

THE ONE GOD OF ISRAEL, FRESHLY REVEALED

1. First-Century Jewish 'Monotheism'

The word 'monotheism' has a dry, abstract sound, reminiscent of its origin in seventeenth-century European theology.[1] But if we want to know what believing in the One God of Israel would have meant to the young Saul of Tarsus, we have to look to a different context, not of philosophical speculation but of blood and breath, prayer and persecution, family and flesh. Roughly a century after Saul of Tarsus had gone off to do battle with the strange new sect of the Nazarenes on behalf of Israel's God and Torah, we find the last great teacher of Torah and Kingdom, Rabbi Akiba, on his way to torture and death for continuing to teach Torah in defiance of the Roman edict, and for his support of the bar-Kochba rebellion.

It was, explains the Talmud,

> the hour for the recital of the *Shema*. While they combed his flesh with iron combs, he was accepting upon himself the kingship of heaven [i.e. he was reciting the *Shema*].[2] His disciples said to him: Our teacher, even to this point? [i.e. Are you able still to pray the prayer while under such torture?] He said to them, 'All my days I have been troubled by this verse, "with all your soul", [which I interpret as] "even if he takes your soul". I said: When shall I have the opportunity of fulfilling this commandment? And now I finally have the opportunity to do so, shall I not fulfil it?' He prolonged the word *echad* [one], until he expired while saying it.[3]

In a parallel tradition, Akiba is asked by one of the Roman torturers why he was reciting the *Shema* as they were slowly killing him. He is even accused of being a sorcerer, since he appeared to feel no pain. He gives a similar explanation: up to now he has been able to love the Lord with all his might and his heart, but now the time has come to love him with his very life. He then continues to recite the prayer until he dies with '*adonai echad*', 'YHWH is one', on his lips.[4]

[1] On the origins and usefulness (or otherwise) of the term see esp. Macdonald 2003, 2004, with the discussion in Bauckham 2008/9, 62–71; Fredriksen 2007, 35–8; Moberly 2004. For this whole section, cf. *NTPG* 248–60, and above, ch. 2, esp. 179–93. Further bibliography in McGrath and Truex 2004; Hurtado 2010, 964.

[2] See above, 84, 179f.; and tBer 14b–15a.

[3] bBer. 61b. In some later traditions Akiba is seen as a villain, but this view does not seem widespread.

[4] jBer. 9.14b.

That is what 'monotheism' meant in the second-Temple period. That is how it functioned for the last great teacher of the stricter school of rabbinic thought, whose all-out commitment to God and Torah, and to the re-founding of the Jerusalem Temple (which had remained the focal point of the Jewish hope despite, or perhaps because of, Hadrian's decision to construct a pagan shrine on the site), led him to hail Simeon ben-Kosiba as 'son of the star, 'bar-Kochba', thus supporting the last great Jewish revolt.[5] That was a 'kingdom-of-God' movement, aimed at re-establishing the sovereignty of Israel's God, the creator, over the whole world, and especially over the Romans who were consolidating the victory of AD 70 by forbidding the very practices which defined Jewish life. As we saw earlier, the most intimate and personal way of 'taking on oneself the yoke of the kingdom of heaven' was the praying of the *Shema*, two or more times a day. Invoking YHWH as the 'one God' and determining to love him with mind, heart and *nephesh*, life itself, meant a total commitment to the sovereignty of this one God, the creator, the God of Israel, and a repudiation of all the idols of paganism and the cruel empires which served them. That is, more or less, the very heart of what 'monotheism' meant to a devout Jew of the period.[6]

Akiba's death came more or less seventy years after that of Paul (mid-130s as against mid-60s). If we go back roughly the same length of time before Paul's day, we find pious writers describing the 'zeal' of the Maccabees in ways which likewise evoked the 'monotheism' we may assume to have been that of Saul of Tarsus:

> Judas said to those who were with him, 'Do not fear their numbers or be afraid when they charge. Remember how our ancestors were saved at the Red Sea, when Pharaoh with his forces pursued them. And now, let us cry to Heaven, to see whether he will favour us and remember his covenant with our ancestors and crush this army before us today. Then all the Gentiles will know that there is one who redeems and saves Israel.'[7]

> O Lord, Lord God, Creator of all things, you are awe-inspiring and strong and just and merciful (*phoberos kai ischyros kai dikaios kai eleēmōn*), you alone are king and are kind (*ho monos basileus kai chrēstos*), you alone are bountiful, you alone are just and almighty and eternal (*ho monos chorēgos, ho monos dikaios kai pantocratōr kai aiōnios*). You rescue Israel from every evil; you chose the ancestors and consecrated them. Accept this sacrifice on behalf of all your people Israel and preserve your portion and make it holy. Gather together our scattered people, set free those who are slaves among the Gentiles, look on those who are rejected and despised, and let the Gentiles know that you are our God. Punish those who oppress and are insolent with pride. Plant your people in your holy place, as Moses promised.[8]

[5] On bar-Kochba cf. Schäfer 2003; Bloom 2010, ch. 16; Eshel 2010.

[6] Above, ch. 2, esp. 84f., 179–83. Despite considerable scholarly attention, the point of this monotheism had little to do with, and was in no way compromised by, belief in angels and other intermediate beings (see below on Paul's christology).

[7] 1 Macc. 4.8–11, cf. 4.30–3; 7.36–8.

[8] 2 Macc. 1.24–9. For the link of monotheism with the Temple, see 14.34–6. For the longer prayer of the high priest Simon, in similar terms, cf. 3 Macc. 2.1–21. On all this and more see Bickerman 1979.

Ho monos ... ho monos ... ho monos. 'Monotheism' indeed: neither a philosophical speculation nor an easy-going generalized religious supposition, but the clear, sharp, bright belief that Israel's God was the creator of all, unique among claimants to divinity in possessing all those specific attributes, in the middle of which we find the politically explosive one, *basileus*, 'king'. Monotheism and 'the kingdom of God' are here linked firmly, in the Maccabaean literature as in Akiba's day two hundred years later.[9] This is how zealous Jews, eager for God and the law, understood their God and their commitment to him. We have no reason to suppose it was any different for Saul of Tarsus. My contention throughout the present chapter is that what Saul came to believe about Jesus, and about the spirit, are best understood in terms of precisely this monotheism, freshly understood – or, as he would probably have said, freshly revealed. To understand this we must first recapitulate briefly how this monotheism was expressed at the time.

The zealous monotheism of the second-Temple period came to expression not least in a context of extreme suffering. The martyrs invoke the one true God, creator of all, who (they believe) will raise them from the dead. Thus, as we saw in chapter 2 above, the mother of the seven brothers whispers to her youngest son, giving him the theological encouragement he needs:

> I beg you, my child, to look at the heaven and the earth and see everything that is in them, and recognize that God made them out of things that did not exist. And in the same way the human race came into being. Do not fear this butcher, but prove worthy of your brothers.

And the young man himself answers the tyrant similarly:

> You have not yet escaped the judgment of the almighty, all-seeing God. For our brothers after enduring a brief suffering have drunk of ever-flowing life, under God's covenant; but you, by the judgment of God, will receive just punishment for your arrogance. I, like my brothers, give up body and life for the laws of our ancestors, appealing to God to show mercy soon to our nation and by trial and plagues to make you confess that he alone is God (*monos autos theos estin*), and through me and my brothers to bring to an end the wrath of the Almighty that has justly fallen on our whole nation.[10]

'That he alone is God': there we have it again. Israel's God, the creator, is the only suprahuman being worthy of the name 'God'. The compelling evidence of this will come in the form both of his rescue of Israel, if not *from* suffering and death, then *through* them at the final resurrection, and also of his eventual judgment on all those who, worshipping other gods, have behaved with arrogance, folly and cruelty. This is what 'monotheism' looks like on the ground of second-Temple Judaism.

That, of course, only increases the personal as well as the theological tension when things appear to be working out in very different ways. Thus

[9] I am assuming that 1 Macc. and 2 Macc., at least, are from the late second or early first century BC.
[10] 2 Macc. 7.28f., 35–8. See above, 179–81.

we find, in the aftermath of the terrible events of AD 70, the perplexed but still determined monotheism of *4 Ezra*:

> All this I have spoken before you, O Lord, because you have said that it was for us that you created this world. As for the other nations that have descended from Adam, you have said that they are nothing, and that they are like spittle, and you have compared their abundance to a drop from a bucket. And now, O Lord, these nations, which are reputed to be as nothing, domineer over us and devour us. But we your people, whom you have called your firstborn, only-begotten, zealous for you, and most dear, have been given into their hands. If the world has indeed been created for us, why do we not possess our world as an inheritance? How long will this be so?[11]

God the creator, God the God of Israel: this identification is both the source of the Israel-specific problem of theodicy and the ground of continuing hope for 'inheriting the world'.[12] That is the constant refrain, not least for those who believe themselves to be living in a continuing 'exile'. Their God is the true God, and his rescue of Israel will reveal that fact to the nations.[13]

The contrast between the living creator, Israel's God, and the 'gods' of the nations, is made sharply through portrayals such as the romance (if that is the right word) of *Joseph and Aseneth*.[14] Aseneth's prayer of repentance states the contrast as sharply as anything in Israel's scriptures themselves:

> And the Lord the God of the powerful Joseph, the Most High, hates all those who worship idols, because he is a jealous and terrible God toward all those who worship strange gods. Therefore he has come to hate me, too, because I worshipped dead and dumb idols, and blessed them, and ate from their sacrifices, and my mouth is defiled from their table, and I do not have the boldness to call on the Lord God of Heaven, the Most High, the Mighty One of the powerful Joseph, because my mouth is defiled from the sacrifices of the idols.
>
> But I have heard many saying that the God of the Hebrews is a true God, and a living God, and a merciful God, and compassionate and long-suffering and pitiful and gentle, and does not count the sin of a humble person, nor expose the lawless deeds of an afflicted person at the time of his affliction. Therefore I will take courage too and turn to him, and take refuge with him, and confess all my sins to him, and pour out my supplication before him . . .[15]

A very different kind of relationship between a Jew and a gentile is found in the book of Judith. There, the stunningly beautiful Jewish widow Judith tricks the pagan king Holofernes into thinking she might be sexually available, in order that, when he is thoroughly drunk in anticipation of his conquest, she can behead him and thus save the Jewish people from his army.

[11] *4 Ez.* 6.55–9; the passage immediately prior (6.38–54) consists of a full rehearsal of the story of creation, as in Gen. 1.1–26, climaxing with Adam as the ruler of all things (6.54). The equivalent train of thought is also seen in 3.4–36.

[12] On 'inheriting the world' see Rom. 4.13 with notes in Wright 2002 [*Romans*], 495f., and Ps. 2.8; and the discussion of Jewish 'empire' in 119–21 above.

[13] e.g. Bar. 2.11–15.

[14] I agree with those who consider this text to be Jewish rather than Christian. It cannot be dated with any precision but appears to be from the centuries immediately either side of the turn of the eras; see Kraemer 1998; Humphrey 2000.

[15] *JosAs* 11.7–11, tr. C. Burchard in Charlesworth 1985, 218f.

The heart of the book is Judith's prayer, in which classic second-Temple monotheism comes to glorious expression:

> You are the God of the lowly, helper of the oppressed, upholder of the weak, protector of the forsaken, saviour of those without hope. Please, please, God of my father, God of the heritage of Israel, Lord of heaven and earth, Creator of the waters, King of all your creation, hear my prayer! May my deceitful words [the words with which she will trick Holofernes] bring wound and bruise on those who have planned cruel things against your covenant, and against your sacred house, and against Mount Zion, and against the house your children possess. Let your whole nation and every tribe know and understand that you are God, the God of all power and might, and that there is no other who protects the people of Israel but you alone![16]

The trick works. Judith cuts off Holofernes's head and brings it back with her. The people congratulate her, and praise the one creator God for this deliverance.[17] This is second-Temple monotheism in action.

The same monotheism undergirds the warlike messianic hope expressed in the last two *Psalms of Solomon*:

> Lord, you are our king for evermore, for in you, O God, does our soul take pride.
> How long is the time of a person's life on the earth?
> As is his time, so also is his hope in him.
> But we hope in God our saviour, for the strength of our God is forever with mercy.
> And the kingdom of our God is forever over the nations in judgment.
> Lord, you chose David to be king over Israel,
> and swore to him about his descendants forever ...
> See, Lord, and raise up for them their king, the son of David,
> to rule over your servant Israel in the time known to you, O God ...
> May God dispatch his mercy to Israel;
> may he deliver us from the pollution of profane enemies;
> the Lord himself is our king forevermore.[18]
>
> O Lord, your mercy is upon the works of your hands forever.
> You show your goodness to Israel with a rich gift ...
> May God cleanse Israel for the day of mercy in blessing,
> for the appointed day when his Messiah will reign ...
> Our God is great and glorious, living in the highest heavens,
> who arranges the stars into orbits to mark time of the hours from day to day.[19]

Hundreds of other texts point in more or less the same direction. If what we loosely summarize as 'monotheism' is to be clarified in terms of the world of thought and practice we may safely ascribe to Saul of Tarsus, we should expect to find it, not in the realm of fine-tuned religious or philosophical speculation, not in debates about how many angels are permitted in the divine entourage before they compromise the divine unity, but in the sphere of Israel's aspirations, Israel's kingdom-of-God expectations. Monotheism of

[16] Jdth. 9.11–14.

[17] Congratulations: 13.17–20. The song of victory (16.1–17) echoes the song of Miriam in Ex. 15.1–18.

[18] *Pss. Sol.* 17.1–4, 21, 45f. (tr. R. B. Wright in Charlesworth 1985, 665–9).

[19] *Pss. Sol.* 18.1, 5, 10 (tr. R. B. Wright in Charlesworth 1985, 669).

the sort which fired Saul of Tarsus meant invoking God as creator and judge, and also as the God specifically of Israel, and doing this within a framework of actual events, including not least the fierce opposition by pagan tyrants, leading in some cases to torture and death. Jewish monotheism was rooted in prayer, particularly in praying of the *Shema*. To pray this prayer was not to make a subtle affirmation about the inner nature of the one God, but *to claim the sovereign rule of this one creator God* over the whole world, and to offer oneself in allegiance of mind, heart and life itself in the service of this God and this kingdom.

I begin with all this because it seems to me necessary, in view of recent scholarship, to shift the focus of discussion. It is of course important to be aware of the solid tradition of high-flown Jewish statements about the unity of God, such as we find in the *Letter of Aristeas*, in Philo and in Josephus.[20] But these are all couched in the framework of explaining Jewish belief to outsiders, and consequently in the language of quasi-philosophical reflection. They do not catch the vivid flavour and drama which the 'doctrine' had in real life (the very word 'doctrine' may throw some imaginations in the wrong direction, towards a dry dogma rather than a living faith and a socio-political agenda). Similarly, it is important to be aware that in the second-Temple period many Jews found themselves able to refer to a variety of (what we may call) intermediary figures who, acting on God's behalf or being greeted or hailed in such a capacity, might appear from some points of view to be themselves almost quasi-divine. Much work has been done in this area, but I agree with Richard Bauckham that it is of less significance for understanding Paul and the other early Christians than is sometimes thought.[21] Rather, the 'monotheism' that matters for our present concerns must be reimagined in the light of this tradition of zeal for God, for Israel, for the Torah, for God's kingdom. To get this straight is to place first-century Jewish monotheism back where it most securely belongs in the real life of the period. This is particularly so when we try to bring into focus the worldview and theology of a zealous first-century Pharisee.

It is no doubt an inestimably good thing that, in comparison with thirty or forty years ago, New Testament scholarship has begun to discuss the nature and meaning of first-century 'monotheism'. That was almost unheard of in the long winter of existentialist exegesis, where 'God' was more or less taken for granted (or, notoriously, subsumed under 'man').[22] When Nils Dahl published his now famous short essay on 'The One God of Jews and Gentiles', it stuck out: nobody else, much, had thought there was

[20] e.g. *Arist.* 132 (this is compatible with a relativized position in which all peoples in fact worship the same divinity that the Jews invoke, but merely call him by different names such as Zeus and Jove [*Arist.* 16]); Philo *Dec.* 65; Jos. *Ap.* 2.190–92; *Ant.* 3.91. See above, 266–70, 280 and e.g. Hurtado 2005, 111–33.

[21] See esp. Bauckham 2008/9, *passim*.

[22] As in Bultmann 1951–5, vol. 1 part 2: 'Every assertion about Christ is also an assertion about man and vice versa; and Paul's christology is simultaneously soteriology. Therefore, Paul's theology can best be treated as his doctrine of man ...' (1.191).

even a topic there worth discussing.[23] But it will be an even better thing that, having studied the complex arguments about quasi-divine mediator-figures and the like, we turn our attention back to the question of what zealous first-century Jews had in mind, and indeed in heart and life, when they thought, spoke, prayed and acted in relation to the one God whom they thus evoked day by day and hour by hour. And for that we need the line of actual history that runs from the Maccabees to Akiba, a line in which what we loosely call 'monotheism' was a matter, not of intellectual speculation and abstract discussion, but of life and death.[24]

This is all the more important if, as I have suggested already in line with the work of Wayne Meeks, the 'monotheism' we can ascribe to Paul the apostle played a significantly different role within his worldview, and the formation of his communities, from the role played by Jewish monotheism within the worldview Saul of Tarsus had held as a Pharisee. We are here approaching the very centre of the present book, the fulcrum around which the argument turns. Monotheism and its reframing is the arrow that pierces the mid-point of the target. We have looked at Paul's three worlds, and then at the worldview which he himself held and did his best to inculcate. We now make the major move through this mid-point to the cognate but quite different set of questions we call 'theology': beliefs about God, about the world, about humans, about Israel, about the future. I have already suggested that Paul's worldview was on the one hand very much like that of second-Temple Judaism, and on the other hand very different, and that if such an unusual and innovative worldview were to gain stability and coherence it would require rigorous fresh work on theology, particularly on the question of God and his faithfulness. That is where we are now going.

To be more explicit: the passages already quoted would be enough to indicate that this second-Temple monotheism played a very significant role within the worldview of a zealous Pharisee. It was the solid rock on which Jewish identity was built. But when, as we saw in chapter 5, the major symbolic praxis of that worldview (circumcision, food laws and so on) had been deemed *adiaphora*, 'indifferent', then 'theology', and particularly 'monotheism', needed to take on far more of the load in sustaining the worldview in its radically new form. This point can be sharpened further. If Paul's communities were going to be able to hold on to their very identity, to retain coherence and unity on the one hand and holiness and hope on the other, they needed to know who the God was in whom they were putting their trust, not as an armchair question for those who liked to muse about distant supernatural realities but as the day-to-day immediate lifeblood for those facing social, cultural and political challenges which could at any moment turn into a repeat performance of the persecution under Antiochus Epiphanes or an advance foretaste of Hadrian's crushing of the bar-Kochba rebellion. If Paul's communities were facing that kind of threat – and Paul

[23] Dahl 1977, 178–91. See too e.g. Young and Ford 1987, whose ch. 9 is entitled 'God and 2 Corinthians'.

[24] See Bauckham 2008/9, esp. at this point his chs. 2 and 3.

regularly implies that they were – then they needed to strengthen their resolve like the young brother in 2 Maccabees, to cling on to their faith like the author of the *Psalms of Solomon*, and, not least, to pray as Akiba would pray. They needed to be kingdom-of-God people, *Shema*-people, Jewish-style monotheists in a world of 'many gods, many lords'. They needed to be able to evoke the great bookending doctrines of creation and judgment, to tell the story of the God who was responsible for both and to know where they themselves came within that story. Only so could Paul's communities live as he believed they were called to live, as the *ekklēsia tou theou*, composed equally of Jews and gentiles but also defining themselves over against both those categories in and as a strange new entity.[25] They had to be the one-God people, but to be that people in a quite new way. A rethought theology had to arise to do the worldview-work previously done by the social and cultural boundary-markers. That is the challenge which drove Paul to some of his most breathtaking theological reformulations, which until recently have passed with little exegetical comment due to the fact that scholars were simply not asking the question in the way that, I am suggesting, it needs to be asked.[26]

The key thing about second-Temple monotheism was not, therefore, a particular proposal about the inner nature of the one God.[27] The substantial and fascinating discussions that have taken place over the last couple of decades about the role and status of 'intermediary' figures in Jewish thought – angels, patriarchs, 'wisdom' and so forth – seem to me mostly beside the point in a discussion of what 'monotheism' really meant in practice.[28] In particular, it is simply wrong-headed to suggest that such 'monotheism' might be compromised by a recognition of the existence of non-human powers or intelligences, whether good (angels) or evil (demons); it was no part of second-Temple monotheism to suggest that Israel's God was the only non-human intelligence existing in the cosmos.[29] (It is also very misleading to refer to such speculations about other non-human powers as 'dualism'; that would only obtain if one or more of them were equal and opposite to the one God.[30]) The first time we get a hint of 'monotheism'

[25] 1 Cor. 10.31f.; see above, 394f., and below, 1447–9.

[26] And as Meeks had suggested it should be asked. Recent studies of Paul's theology have indeed given some attention to 'God' in Paul's thought, but without highlighting this topic or in this way. Thus Schnelle 2005 [2003], 393f. is right to say, 'Jewish monotheism is the basis of the Pauline worldview', but his very brief treatment of Paul's development of the doctrine hardly allows the necessary perspectives to emerge. Dunn's brief though always interesting treatment (Dunn 1998, 27–50) likewise skates quickly over the material without delving into the way in which 'monotheism' related to the concrete issues of the day. Schreiner 2001, 18–35 provides a moving introduction on the centrality of God within Paul's thought but without coming close to the topic I am proposing as actually central not only to Paul's theological thinking but to his worldview.

[27] I am here close to the position of Bauckham 2008/9, in line with the position I first outlined in Wright 1986a ['Constraints'], 206–9, and followed particularly in Wright 1991 [*Climax*], ch. 6.

[28] See Rainbow 1991, critiquing Hurtado 1988; but see, much more fully, Hurtado 2003, with the discussion below. See too the critique of the whole category in Fredriksen 2007.

[29] Against e.g. Westerholm 2004, 363. Bauckham 2008/9, 99 points out that identifying 'demons' as standing behind 'idols' was 'a monotheistic commonplace' in the period.

[30] See *NTPG* 252–9.

being used to say 'therefore your speculations about the inner being of the one God are out of line' is actually in the reaction to Akiba himself, when he speculated that the 'thrones' in the heavenly scene in Daniel 7 were 'one for God, one for David', resulting in there being 'two powers in heaven'.[31] Akiba, as we saw, had a candidate in mind to sit on the second throne: he thought Simeon ben-Kosiba was the true 'son of David', and was hoping that now at last 'one like a son of man' would be exalted in exercising God's judgment over the last great 'beast'. But the strong likelihood is that Akiba's opponents were using the notion of God's oneness as a way of opposing him, not primarily on grounds of philosophical theology, but because they either disapproved of his revolutionary kingdom-of-God stance or disagreed with him about bar-Kochba's being Messiah. Or both.[32] I am not aware of evidence prior to this point, i.e. before around AD 130, that Jewish thinkers were debating questions to do with the inner being of the one God. When such debates happen, the best explanation is almost certainly that they were generated precisely in reaction to the Christian claims about Jesus.[33]

Interestingly, despite frequent scholarly assertions that the high status accorded to Jesus by the early Christians 'must have' caused difficulty for non-Christian Jews, there is actually no evidence of this throughout the first generation. Paul does not need to *argue* the points he makes about Jesus in dialogue with cautious Jewish monotheists who thought he was going too far. We see clearly into the heart of several controversies in his churches, including fierce debates with those who were insisting on some key aspects of the mainline Jewish worldview, but we never find Paul having to debate the massive affirmations he makes about Jesus. Granted what we shall see presently about the actual content of those affirmations, this absence of controversy itself tells us something, in retrospect as it were, about what 'Jewish monotheism' meant and did not mean in the period. And about how firmly Paul's belief about Jesus' identity *vis-à-vis* the one true God had already taken root, was already a given in early Christianity.

The main focus of Jewish monotheism in our period, then, looked not as it were inward, towards an analysis of the one God, but decidedly outward, to the relation of the one God to the world. Exploring the latter point will bring certain other features into focus. First, and foundational to everything else, when the Jewish monotheist looked at the world of creation, what he or she saw was a good cosmos made by a good God. The world of space, time and

[31] See bHag. 14a; cf. bSanh. 38a. The classic monograph is Segal 1977 (esp. here 47–50). A similar question is posed by *Ezek. Trag.* 68–82a, where Moses dreams of a remarkable scene (presumably derived from Dan. 7) of a man sitting on God's throne; this vision is then interpreted by Moses' father-in-law Jethro as referring to Moses himself (82b–89). Hurtado 1988, 57–9 regards this as an example of pre-Christian figures exercising 'divine agency'; Horbury 1998, 31 sees it, together with other passages ascribing at least royal significance to Moses, as indicating him as a messianic prototype.

[32] As Segal suggests, Akiba's apparent recantation of his 'two thrones' position, and the ascribing to him of a more abstract idea, that the two thrones represent two attributes of the one God (justice and grace), is almost certainly a way of sanitizing the tradition of the great man after the failure of the revolt.

[33] Philo might be considered an exception to this, with his proposal (influenced by Stoicism?) concerning a *deuteros theos*, a 'second god' (cf. *Quaest. Gen.* 2.62); but we have no evidence that his views were widely discussed at the time.

matter; the lights in the heavens and the creatures crawling on the ground; times and seasons, day and night, winter and summer, seedtime and harvest; the life-cycle of humans, beasts and plants, and the specific activities and functions concerning marriage, childbirth, food, drink, sleep, play, work, rest – all of these were good, and to be enjoyed in the proper ways at the proper times. To everything there was a season. To affirm the 'oneness' of Israel's God meant, in practical terms, a cheerful and guiltless partaking in and celebration of the world as a good gift to humans, a world full of strange beauty, massive power and silent song.[34] In particular, and following from the vocation of human beings to reflect God's wise order into the world, this kind of monotheism included the vocation to humans in general to bring God's justice to the world: justice is to human society what flourishing order is to the garden. It was thus, in principle, part of the inner structure of creational monotheism that humans should set up and run structures of governance, making and implementing laws, deciding cases, constantly working to bring a balance to God's world. Human government was a good thing: it was how the one God intended the world to be run. Human *judgment* was a good thing, the making of wise and proper decisions about what should and should not be done. In terms of society, anarchy would have been seen as threatening a return to *tohu wa-bohu*, the primeval chaos into which the creative act of the one God had brought order. The world, human life, including *ordered* human life: all of this was good and God-given. Evil was not an equal and opposite force to the one God. It was the corruption of the good creation, including the corruption of the human vocation to rule God's world.

Monotheism therefore meant, foundationally and scripturally, the renunciation of ontological dualism.[35] Renouncing the world itself, pretending it was a dark and gloomy place, complaining about the soul being imprisoned within a material body, or grumbling at the very existence of human rulers and power structures, was not part of that worldview.[36] There is, actually, no particular reason to suppose that very many first-century Jews were tempted in that direction, until the horrible failure of the bar-Kochba revolt drove some to stand their worldview on its head and to develop what we now know as gnosticism.[37] Granted the huge pressure first-century Jews were often under politically and culturally, the resistance to dualism is an indication of how strongly creational monotheism had soaked down into their hearts, minds and lives.

[34] cf. e.g. Pss. 19; 104; and indeed Job 26; 38–41.

[35] On types of dualism see *NTPG* 252–6.

[36] Again, Philo might be an exception; and cf. too Wis. 9.15, though how far one should press the latter is open to question. The rejection of 'grumbling', echoing the exodus narrative, is reflected also in Phil. 2.14–16.

[37] Again, one might cite the darker moods of Qumran, or *4 Ezra*, as counter-examples, but in both cases the goodness of creation remains basic. On the rise of gnosticism – and the current debates about everything to do with it, not least the term itself – see, as representatives of a much larger body of literature, e.g. King 2003; Williams 1996.

This celebration of creation, as part of classic second-Temple monotheism, could (as we saw earlier) be expressed in terms of God acting through his 'word' or his 'wisdom'. As is now generally recognized, this was never intended as a way of cunningly inventing, or claiming to discern, a second and separate divine being alongside the creator himself.[38] It was a way of putting the wind into a bottle, of speaking of the utterly transcendent and holy creator acting *here* and *now*, working first to create space, time and matter and then to sustain and direct them. It was a way of saying that when God created, he did so by speaking (i.e. highlighting his sovereignty: he didn't have to struggle or wrestle, but simply spoke and things happened[39]), and he did so wisely (i.e. highlighting the goodness of creation: it was not a foolish, pointless or random venture, but possessed proper order and beauty). We have already explored this, and merely need to remind ourselves of it as we move forwards.

This deep-level commitment to the goodness of the created order is the proper context for understanding what otherwise might be seen, and indeed has often been seen, as the negative stance which first-century Jewish monotheists took against idolatry and all that went with it. Much ink has been spilt, some of it quite helpfully, in clarifying the extent to which pre-Christian Judaism was in fact 'monotheist', and whether, from our late-modern perspective, this was even a good thing. Fortunately for the size of the present book, that is not our primary concern.[40] It may well be that ancient Israel was far less committed to the one God than we might have supposed from a surface-level reading of the Pentateuch, and that it was only with the experience of exile, and the slow, horrid realization of the kind of society generated and sustained by the worship of Bel and Nebo and their like, that the grand vision opened up, as we find it in Isaiah 40—55: YHWH as the absolutely only God, not just supreme over lesser divinities but gloriously alone, unique, all-powerful, majestic. Perhaps only then did the sense dawn on a surprised people that their God claimed the right to propose and dispose in the affairs of nations, to take up the isles like fine dust, to rescue muddled and still-rebellious Israel from captivity, to call up, commission and use a new pagan ruler within the divine covenantal purposes. Certainly after the exile we do not hear of the same problems which, according to the Deuteronomic historian with various prophets in support, had occurred again and again in the years of the monarchy.[41] Again, whether this was a

[38] Rightly, Bauckham 2008/9, 217 and elsewhere, against e.g. M. Barker and others.

[39] Ps. 33.8f. (with the consequent command to the nations to fear Israel's God); 147.15, 18 (again with the consequent distinction between Israel, as the people of this creator God, and the surrounding nations); 148.5f. (celebrating the whole of creation and, within that [148.14] the special status of Israel).

[40] See again e.g. MacDonald 2003; and the recent survey of Fretheim 2007.

[41] On the 'monotheism' of ancient Israel see the burgeoning literature surveyed in MacDonald 2003; Bauckham 2008/9, ch. 2. The point that needs to be made, as with similar points about early Christianity, is that we should expect, and not be surprised by, a tension between the actual practice and belief of members of the community and the principles enunciated by the scriptural writers. A variety of practice is actually presupposed by the texts in the Deuteronomic tradition which seek to curb such things; the problem here only arises if the scriptural writings are seen as 'authoritative' in their 'witness to the

good or bad thing – whether, in other words, the second-Temple commitment to monotheism was healthy, as Jews and Christians have mostly supposed, or unhealthy, as some postmodern moralists, naturally concerned about totalizing systems and their effects on human society and life, have suggested – is a different sort of question again.[42] So too is the matter of whether Isaiah 40—55 represents the eventual flowering of a generous, open-hearted, 'inclusive' monotheism such as we moderns can enthusiastically embrace, as opposed to the negative, exclusivist monotheism of some other texts, and whether that kind of 'progressive revelation' does any justice to the scriptural texts it seeks to use in support.[43] What matters for our purpose is to note, as with the line from the Maccabees to Akiba, that when first-century Jews thought of their God, when they committed themselves to his law, and above all when they prayed the *Shema* twice or more each day, they knew that they were opposed, in heart, mind and with the breath of life, to idols, to the making and worshipping of them, to the way of life that went with them and – not least – to the actual human beings and actual human systems whose lives revolved around 'the gods of the nations', their temples and their worship. To that extent, those recent writers are absolutely correct who have spoken of the monotheism of the period as 'exclusive'. It was, most emphatically, not a way of saying, as 'Aristeas' tried to say, that everybody, Israel included, worships the same divinity, but that they simply call this divinity by different names, YHWH here, Zeus there.[44] It was a way of saying what the Psalmist said, that the 'gods' of the nations are mere idols, and that it was YHWH who made the heavens; in other words, he didn't simply live in that house (heaven itself), he built it in the first place.

This is seen to spectacular effect in books like Daniel, which we know to have been a favourite in the first century. In the first half of the book, Daniel and his friends face challenge after challenge to their Jewish way of life, starting comparatively straightforwardly with the question of diet, but moving on rapidly to other demands, first that they worship the great image which the king has set up (chapter 3), and then that they pray to the king himself, and to him alone (chapter 6). The very phrase 'him alone' echoes so strongly with the normal claims of Jewish monotheism that we can see the clash coming.[45] Daniel's three friends refuse to worship the image, and are thrown into the fiery furnace (where, according to the apocryphal addition, they sing a great hymn about creation, inviting every aspect of the world to praise the creator: the best possible answer to the pagan challenge). Daniel, with his window open towards Jerusalem, goes on praying to the God of Israel, and is thrown into the den of lions. In each case, of course, they are

religious experience' of the time, as though the 'religious experience' was the main thing and the scriptures secondary. That is part of another debate.

[42] See the discussion in Moberly 2004; Bauckham 2008/9 ch. 2.

[43] See the discussion in e.g. Clements 1984.

[44] *Arist.* 16. For this kind of syncretism see the discussions at 216f., 268f., 275, 624.

[45] Bauckham 2008/9, 210 n. 67 lists several passages.

rescued, and in each case the king then acknowledges that Israel's God is the only true God.[46]

Stylized stories, of course. But again, if we want to know what monotheism looked like and felt like in the time of Saul of Tarsus, what people supposed it meant in practice, these will give us a strong clue. And, meanwhile, as in Isaiah 40—55, the great idolatrous empire is overthrown: Nebuchadnezzar loses his mind and his kingdom, Belshazzar his throne, and Darius acknowledges that Daniel's God is the only God and that his kingdom will never be destroyed. As with the constant refrain in the Maccabaean literature, pagan rulers who oppose the true God are brought crashing down from their proud eminence. All this then frames the visions of the second half of the book, in which 'Daniel' dreams dreams and sees visions which are themselves part of the outworking of the same monotheism: the four beasts in chapter 7 are four kingdoms, strongly reminiscent of the four parts of the statue in chapter 2, and the one God then sets up a kingdom which cannot be shaken.[47] Monotheism and the kingdom of God: here it is again. Kingdoms, and particularly empires, set up their signs of centered self-belief: the sign that means 'Medium' is also the sign for 'Middle Kingdom', with all else east or west of China. From the beginning, Jewish monotheism was a way of saying 'no' to this claim, whether from Egypt, Babylon, Greece, Syria, Rome or anywhere else, and a way of claiming instead (to the alarm of postmodernists who had imagined that the Jewish denunciation of pagan regimes would play out in support of an extreme laissez-faire relativism) that the God who made all the earth would set up his own kingdom, would draw his own line through the world, refocusing the edge-lured minds of his human creatures, in his own way and time.

Once again the Psalms bring all this into poetry. YHWH made the heavens and the earth; he is Israel's God; he will set his king in Zion, and will laugh at the nations who huff and puff all around. The Psalms repeat, over and over, the claim that Israel's God will judge the nations, indeed the whole world. Sometimes they suggest that the princes of the nations will come and join in the worship of this one God; sometimes, as in Isaiah 11, that God's Messiah will rule over them and bring justice to the ends of the earth. Always there is the note of celebration, even in sorrow and gloom. Jewish-style monotheism is seen to equally good effect in the darkness of Psalm 88 ('*You* have put lover and friend far from me') and in the royal glory of Psalm 89 ('His dominion shall be from the one sea to the other, from the River to the ends of the earth'); in the tub-thumping cheeriness of Psalm 136 ('Yea, and slew mighty kings, for his mercy endures for ever; Sihon, king of the Amorites, for his mercy endures for ever; and Og the king of Bashan, for his mercy endures for ever') and the utter desolation of Psalm 137 ('How shall

[46] Dan. 3, esp. vv. 28f.; 6, esp. vv. 26f. In between we have the scenes of Nebuchadnezzar's humiliation and acknowledgment of the one God (4, esp. vv. 34–7) and Belshazzar's feast, with a similar emphasis (5, esp. vv. 18, 21, 23).

[47] 2.44f.; 7.13f., 18, 26f.

we sing YHWH's song in a strange land?'). Monotheism intensifies the problems. A pagan would give a shrug of the shoulders and blame misfortune on a malevolent deity, perhaps bribed by an opponent. A dualist would blame it on The Dark Side. Those options are not open to the monotheist. But monotheism also regrounds hope: 'Have you not known? Have you not heard? YHWH is the everlasting God.'[48]

Within this world of belief, there was plenty of room for speculation about how precisely evil did its work. It appeared to be more than the sum total of human folly. Idolatry, it seemed, released forces, dark powers, into the world, which masqueraded under the names of gods and goddesses, and which could do real damage, but which were not on the same level as YHWH himself. The question of what precisely second-Temple Jews thought about such forces and powers, what kind of ontological status they assigned them, need not concern us in detail.[49] It is a red herring to ask whether belief in the possible existence of such powers in any way compromised the belief in the one God. That was always possible, of course; we see it in some later forms of syncretism and indeed in Jewish gnosticism. But, as with angels and other *benign* non-human intelligences and forces, so with demons and other *malevolent* non-human intelligences and forces. A belief in the reality of such things had nothing to do with 'monotheism' itself. The fact that there was one God did not entail any necessary conclusion about the existence or otherwise of other non-material beings. The discovery of protreptic amulets and similar objects at Qumran and elsewhere tells us, hardly to our surprise, that people who take seriously the existence of worlds beyond that of space, time and matter may well come to believe that these worlds are inhabited by creatures who may, or quite possibly may not, be kindly disposed towards them. They do nothing to undermine the claim of the same people to believe in one God, the creator, the God of Israel. It is precisely the dry Enlightenment Deism, not first-century Jewish monotheism, that scooped up all other non-spatio-temporal existences into the oneness of its 'monotheism'. In second-Temple monotheism, the fact that there was one God, utterly supreme, the only creator and governor of all, did not rule out the possibility of other inhabitants of the heavenly realm, but actually tended to entail that possibility.

If belief in the existence of lesser but still non-human powers did not undermine the strong belief in the *unity* of the one God, so too belief in the reality of demonic powers did not undermine the strong belief in the *goodness* of the one God. Such a belief merely reminds us, if we needed it, that believing in this God did not mean believing that everything in the world was just fine as it was, with no problems and nothing much to hope for. Anything but. Once again, monotheism intensifies the problems: Why is all this happening? And, once again, it offers a hard-won solution, demanding

[48] Isa. 40.28. The 'justice'/'covenant faithfulness' (*dikaiosynē*) of the one God is both the problem and the answer in the great prayer of Dan. 9; see above, 119f., 142–8.

[49] For this whole area see now A. T. Wright 2005.

patience and courage: YHWH's justice will triumph, his faithfulness will be revealed, and all flesh shall see his salvation.

This is what Richard Bauckham labels, helpfully, as 'eschatological monotheism'. YHWH will be one, and his name one.[50] I shall argue below that this eschatological focus, particularly when sharpened up (as we saw in chapter 2) in relation to the underlying exodus-narrative on the one hand and the closely related expectation of the return of Israel's God to Zion on the other, is the missing key to many current debates. This theme enables us to get to the heart of what Paul and other early Christians believed about both Jesus and the spirit, and enables us more particularly to understand why and how they came to that belief. The monotheism in which they were rooted was a belief in the God of the exodus, a God who (they believed) had abandoned Jerusalem at the time of the exile but who had promised to return in person to rescue his people and dwell in their midst. Early christology, I shall argue presently, was not a modification of pre-Christian Jewish beliefs about this or that mediator-figure. It was a radical concretization of pre-Christian Jewish beliefs about the one God, and particularly about what this one God had promised to *do*.

The people who lived and prayed this belief naturally formed a community whose commitment was reflected in practice. The goodness of creation, and YHWH's saving acts for Israel, were celebrated in festivals which were simultaneously agricultural and salvation-historical. The people were admonished to take great care to avoid the dangers of idolatry wherever they occurred. Questions have rightly been raised about the extent to which this teaching was effective in pre-exilic times, but it seems to have been more solidly observed in the second-Temple period. It is not hard to see how monotheism of this sort (as opposed to other sorts to which we shall return) generated and sustained such a community, and belonged closely with the world of symbolic praxis and narrative we studied in chapter 2. And it is idolatry, of course, together with the power of pagan empire built on that idolatry, that formed the basic monotheistic answer to the question, 'What's wrong?' The other obvious answers, that of the pagan or the dualist, were not open. The philosophical answers, that nothing could possibly be 'wrong' (Stoicism) or that things might not be as one might wish but one had to make the best of them (Epicureanism), were equally unsatisfactory. The Jewish monotheist, looking out on the world, understood evil to be the result of idolatry, not of an inherent badness within creation itself, and looked for the day when Israel's God would set up his kingdom of justice and peace. This kind of monotheism thus generated and sustained a view of God's people and God's future. The three together – monotheism, election and eschatology – formed then, as they form here in our exposition, the substructure of what it meant to be Israel, the people of this one true God.

[50] Zech. 14.9, the climax of a passage in which YHWH defeats all enemies and establishes his kingdom over all the earth (picking up 9.9f.). See esp. Bauckham 2008/9, 96f.

2. Paul's Reaffirmed Monotheism

(i) Suffering for the One God

The central claim of this chapter, and in a measure of this whole book, is that Paul clearly, solidly, skilfully and dramatically reworked exactly this 'monotheism' around Jesus the Messiah and also around the spirit. It is for the sake of Jesus, and in the power of the spirit, that Paul faces, and knows that his *ekklēsiai* are facing, the equivalent challenges to those faced by the Maccabees before him. Empires can tolerate people picking up funny religious ideas, adding another divinity to an already crowded pantheon, developing new styles of private spirituality. Empires thrive on religious relativism; the more gods the better, since the more there are the less likely they are to challenge the ruling ideology.[51] Indeed, as with the challenges to Daniel and his friends, it becomes easy for empires to suggest that actually all the intimations of immortality, all the hints of divine presence in the world, have now been drawn together in a fresh way in the new power that has emerged, whether that of Augustus in the first century or Hitler in the twentieth.[52] Before we look at the central and obvious passages where Paul appears to be redefining monotheism around Jesus the Messiah, we notice one or two passages where we hear the echo of the Maccabaean monotheists facing the pagan tyrants, and the advance echoes of Akiba himself:

> [28]We know, in fact, that God works all things together for good to those who love him, who are called according to his purpose. [29]Those he foreknew, you see, he also marked out in advance to be shaped according to the model of the image of his son, so that he might be the firstborn of a large family. [30]And those he marked out in advance, he also called; those he called, he also justified; those he justified, he also glorified.[53]

This is a dense but majestic statement of Jewish-style monotheism, summarizing the line of thought from Paul's preceding four chapters. But it gives rise to something even more, something utterly Jewish, utterly monotheistic, holding out against tyrants of every kind by holding on to the one true God:

> [31]What then shall we say to all this?
> If God is for us, who is against us?
> [32]God, after all, did not spare his own son; he gave him up for us all!
> How then will he not, with him, freely give all things to us?
> [33]Who will bring a charge against God's chosen ones?
> It is God who declares them in the right.
> [34]Who is going to condemn?
> It is the Messiah, Jesus, who has died, or rather has been raised;
> who is at God's right hand, and who also prays on our behalf!
> [35]Who shall separate us from the Messiah's love?

[51] The same is of course true of 'denominationalism' within the imperial world of the western Enlightenment; but that is another story.

[52] I am not suggesting, by this, the kind of exact analogy imagined by Syme 1939; see above, ch. 5.

[53] Rom. 8.28–30.

Suffering, or hardship, or persecution, or famine, or nakedness, or danger, or sword? [36]As the Bible says,

Because of you we are being killed all day long
We are regarded as sheep destined for slaughter.

[37]No: in all these things we are completely victorious through the one who loved us. [38]I am persuaded, you see, that neither death nor life, nor angels nor rulers, nor the present, nor the future, nor powers, [39]nor height nor depth nor any other creature will be able to separate us from the love of God in the Messiah, Jesus our lord.[54]

This passage is, I suppose, as well known as anything else in Paul, and rightly so. But its very familiarity may have blinded us to what might have been more obvious to some at least of its first hearers: that it constituted a victorious paean of praise to the one God, the creator and lord of all, the lifegiver, the one who rescues his people from the power of all tyrants, death itself included, and through their present suffering brings his new creation to birth and gives them new and glorious life within it. It is a glorious expression of second-Temple monotheism in the face of all the powers of the pagan world. The psalm from which Paul quotes in verse 36 is itself a classic monotheistic prayer, looking back to God's mighty acts of redemption, claiming God as 'king' and celebrating his name. We have not abandoned you, says the Psalmist, or been false to your covenant. We have been good monotheists:

If we had forgotten the name of our God,
or spread out our hands to a strange god,
would not God discover this?
For he knows the secrets of the heart.
Because of you we are being killed all day long,
and accounted as sheep for the slaughter.[55]

Paul, quoting the final two lines, appears to have had the larger context in mind all along. In verse 27 he had spoken of God 'searching the hearts' and thereby knowing 'the mind of the spirit', at work within God's people as they groan, longing for redemption.[56] The people he is describing in 8.18–27 are on their way to the 'inheritance' which is the whole renewed creation, and their present suffering is a sign of that, a sign that they are living already in the new world which is at violent odds with the present one. The whole passage in Romans 8 is monotheistic through and through, echoing the whole psalm, but instead of appealing to God to arise ('Get up! Why are you asleep? Stand up and help us!'[57]), it celebrates the fact that Jesus has *already* died and been raised, and on that basis it claims with confidence that the victory is already won.[58] And the people who enjoy that confidence are

[54] Rom. 8.31–9.

[55] Ps. 44.20–2.

[56] I owe this point originally, I believe, to Sylvia Keesmaat: see Keesmaat 1999, 128–33.

[57] 44.23, cf. 26.

[58] Rom. 8.34: The Messiah was raised, *egertheis*; Ps. 44 [LXX 43].24, *exegerthēti*; Rom. 8.34, he is at God's right hand; Ps. 44 [LXX 43].4, God's right hand rescued his people. These echoes go beyond those

precisely the people of the new monotheism, the renewed *Shema*: 'We know that God works all things together for good to those who love him, who are called according to his purpose.' Being 'called according to his purpose' is an obvious Israel-phrase; what we might miss, in the flurry of dramatic statement, is the echo that would be clear to anyone who prayed the prayer two or three times a day: *to those who love him*. 'Hear, O Israel, YHWH our God, YHWH is one, *and you shall love* YHWH *your God* ...' Here, half way between the Maccabees and Akiba, we find a monotheism as Jewish as theirs, as contested as theirs, as dangerous as theirs, as trusting as theirs, as *Shema*-based as theirs, and yet radically, breathtakingly different. The same God is now revealed as the father who sent the beloved son to die.[59] The same suffering is now understood in the light of the death of God's son. The same faith, hope and love; but now *at a different moment*: thc time of new creation, introduced by the resurrection of God's son.

We see the same thing in 2 Corinthians 4. Here, as part of his apologia for the nature of his apostleship, Paul goes back to the very beginning, to creation itself:

> the God who said 'let light shine out of darkness' has shone in our hearts, to produce the light of the knowledge of the glory of God in the face of Jesus the Messiah.[60]

Creation and new creation; the same God at work in both. 'The God of this world' may have blinded the minds of unbelievers, so that they will not see the light revealed by the Messiah, who is God's image (4.4). But new creation is happening anyway, even though those through whom it is being effected are

> under all kinds of pressure, but ... not crushed completely; we are at a loss, but not at our wits' end; [9]we are persecuted, but not abandoned; we are cast down, but not destroyed. [10]We always carry the deadness of Jesus about in the body, so that the life of Jesus may be revealed in our body. [11]Although we are still alive, you see, we are always being given over to death because of Jesus, so that the life of Jesus may be revealed in our mortal humanity.[61]

To be the people of the new creation, looking death in the face but claiming the power of the creator God: this is the kind of monotheism we saw in those ancient Jewish heroes. And again Paul quotes a psalm, this time the one we know as 116: 'I believed, and therefore I spoke.' Why? Perhaps because the whole psalm is about the Psalmist's steadfast loyalty to YHWH

plotted with pioneering insight by Hays 1989a, 57–63, though the echoes he already heard remain vital for any understanding of Paul's larger purposes.

[59] 8.32. The ancient context of this theme has been sensitively studied in Levenson 1993. Unfortunately, he repeats (210–19) several standard misconceptions of Paul.

[60] 2 Cor. 4.6.

[61] 2 Cor. 4.8–11.

(in other words, he has not gone wandering off after other gods), affirming his trust that YHWH will therefore bring him through his present distress.[62]

A further example of the same phenomenon – the pattern of second-Temple monotheism worked out through faithful witness to the one God of creation and covenant despite suffering at the hands of idolaters – is found in the letter to the Philippians. As we shall see, this letter contains, and indeed showcases, one of the most obvious and spectacular christological redefinitions of Jewish monotheism. But for the moment we highlight the Maccabees-to-Akiba line, and once again find Paul standing right in the middle of it:

> [14]There must be no grumbling and disputing in anything you do. [15]That way, nobody will be able to fault you, and you'll be pure and spotless children of God in the middle of a twisted and depraved generation. You are to shine among them like lights in the world, [16]clinging on to the word of life. That's what I will be proud of on the day of the Messiah. It will prove that I didn't run a useless race, or work to no purpose.
>
> [17]Yes: even if I am to be poured out like a drink-offering on the sacrifice and service of your faith, I shall celebrate, and celebrate jointly with you all. [18]In the same way, you should celebrate, yes, and celebrate with me.[63]

Like the Maccabaean martyrs, Paul sees his own potential death in sacrificial terms, related directly to God's purposes for his people.[64] And that people are to be the light-bearers in the midst of the dark pagan world – a point Paul then spells out in Philippians 3.17–21. The 'day' of liberation they look forward to is now, as we shall see in chapter 10, 'the day of the Messiah', rather than the ancient Israelite hope of the 'day of the lord'. But, granted that modification, we are still clearly in the same world.

The final example of the same point is in 1 Thessalonians, a letter which begins with a classic and uncompromising statement of second-Temple monotheism revised around the gospel:

> [9]They themselves tell the story of the kind of welcome we had from you, and how you turned to God from idols, to serve a living and true God, [10]and to wait for his son from heaven, whom he raised from the dead – Jesus, who delivers us from the coming fury.[65]

That is the context in which, once again, the note of suffering because of allegiance to the one God and his kingdom makes the sense it does, though this time there is a new, dark note. The persecuting opposition is now not merely pagans, it is the unbelieving Judaeans themselves:

[62] cf. too 2 Cor. 6.3–10, where the powerful catalogue of Paul's troubles is sandwiched between the Isaianic affirmation of 'the day of salvation' (6.2, quoting Isa. 49.8) and the appeal for God's holy people, his new Temple, to separate from idols (6.14—7.1, quoting Lev. 26.12; Isa. 52.11; 2 Sam. 7.14, with multiple other echoes of the monotheistic tradition).

[63] Phil. 2.14–17.

[64] cp. Col. 1.24–29. The cultic overtones here echo Bauckham's phrase, 'cultic monotheism'. For the Maccabaean echoes see e.g. *4 Macc.* 1.11; 6.28f.; 17.20–2.

[65] 1 Thess. 1.9f.

> [11]You know how, like a father to his own children, [12]we encouraged each of you, and strengthened you, and made it clear to you that you should behave in a manner worthy of the God who calls you into his own kingdom and glory.
>
> [13]So, therefore, we thank God constantly that when you received the word of God which you heard from us, you accepted it, not as the word of a mere human being but – as it really is! – the word of God which is at work in you believers. [14]For, my dear family, you came to copy God's assemblies in Judaea in the Messiah, Jesus. You suffered the same things from your own people as they did from those of the Judaeans [15]who killed the lord Jesus and the prophets, and who expelled us. They displease God; they oppose all people; [16]they forbid us to speak to the Gentiles so that they may be saved.[66]

How this works out we shall see later. But this quick glance at passages in a line from the Maccabees to Akiba shows that Paul knows the very practical meaning of monotheism: allegiance to the one God will mean persecution from the surrounding world. We must now look at the larger themes in which he reaffirms the basic structure of second-Temple monotheism, before then turning to the central point: the way in which he explicitly and dramatically reworks this monotheism around Jesus the Messiah.

(ii) Monotheism Reaffirmed: God the Creator, the Judge

Monotheism of the second-Temple Jewish kind, as we saw, was the belief not so much that there was one supernatural being rather than many, or that this God was a single and indivisible entity, but that the one true God was the creator of the world, supreme over all other orders of being, that he would be the judge of all, and that in between creation and final putting-to-rights he had a single purpose which arched its way over the multiple smaller stories of his creation and, not least, of Israel. This emphasis on the goodness of creation, on the single great story, and on the commitment of this God to put the world to rights at the last, are all strongly reaffirmed by Paul:

> [19]What can be known of God, you see, is plain to them, since God has made it plain to them. [20]Ever since the world was made, his eternal power and deity have been seen and known in the things he made.[67]
>
> But it can't be the case that God's word has failed![68]
>
> [33]O, the depth of the riches
> and the wisdom and knowledge of God!
> We cannot search his judgments,
> we cannot fathom his ways.
> [34]For 'who has known the mind of the Lord?
> Or who has given him counsel?
> [35]Who has given a gift to him

[66] 1 Thess. 2.11–16. On questions of interpolation in this passage see e.g. Fee 2009, 90–2; and below, 1152 n. 442.

[67] Rom. 1.19f.

[68] Rom. 9.6.

which needs to be repaid?'
[36]For from him, through him and to him are all things.
Glory to him for ever! Amen.[69]

[23]Each, however, in proper order. The Messiah rises as the first fruits; then those who belong to the Messiah will rise at the time of his royal arrival. [24]Then comes the end, the goal, when he hands over the kingly rule to God the father, when he has destroyed all rule and all authority and power. [25]He has to go on ruling, you see, until 'he has put all his enemies under his feet'. [26]Death is the last enemy to be destroyed, [27]because 'he has put all things in order under his feet'. But when it says that everything is put in order under him, it's obvious that this doesn't include the one who put everything in order under him. [28]No: when everything is put in order under him, then the son himself will be placed in proper order under the one who placed everything in order under him, so that God may be all in all.[70]

This strong creational emphasis provides the context for Paul's positive evaluation of the created order in such passages as 1 Corinthians 10.26, where, grounding the advice to eat whatever meat is sold in the open market, he quotes Psalm 24.1: 'the earth and its fullness belong to the lord'.[71] This belongs, too, with his emphasis in 1 Corinthians 7 on the goodness and God-givenness of marriage, and of sexual relations within marriage. He will argue the case for the possibility of a vocation to celibacy, but he is at pains to make clear that this has nothing whatever to do with a dualism that would reject the goodness of the created order.[72] This positive view of creation also explains the passages where Paul indicates that, even among pagans, there is a moral sense which will recognize the good behaviour of the Messiah's people and from which, in turn, one can even learn by example.[73] It is this, too, which enables Paul, exactly in line with at least one regular second-Temple viewpoint, to affirm the goodness and God-givenness of governments and authorities, even while (as it appears) reserving the right both to remind them of their God-given duty and to hold them to account in relation to it, and to proclaim energetically the ultimate sovereignty of the one God as revealed in his Messiah.[74]

In particular, we must note Paul's emphatic rejection of pagan idolatry. We have already seen his reminder to the Thessalonians that they 'turned to God from idols to serve a living and true God'. That remains basic. So, too, does the standard Jewish polemic against the pagan world which, through worshipping idols, has brought about the fracturing of its own image-bearing humanness:

[69] Rom. 11.33–6.

[70] 1 Cor. 15.23–8. Note especially the ref. to Ps. 110.1 in v. 25, and to Ps. 8.6 in v. 27.

[71] The same verse is quoted in tBer. 35a to indicate the importance of saying a blessing over food, since all belongs to God. According to mTam. 7.4, Ps. 24 was sung by the Levites in the Temple on the first day of every week. For the possible ref. here to Jesus as *kyrios* see below, 670.

[72] 1 Cor. 7.1–11; 25–40.

[73] e.g. Rom. 12.17; 14.18; 1 Cor. 5.1; 2 Cor. 8.21; Phil. 4.8. On this point see Horrell 2005, 266, 272.

[74] Rom. 13.1–7, on which see 1302–4 below.

[20]Ever since the world was made, his eternal power and deity have been seen and known in the things he made. As a result, they have no excuse: [21]they knew God, but didn't honour him as God or thank him. Instead, they learned to think in useless ways, and their unwise heart grew dark. [22]They declared themselves to be wise, but in fact they became foolish. [23]They swapped the glory of the immortal God for the likeness of the image of mortal humans – and of birds, animals and reptiles. [24]So God gave them up to uncleanness in the desires of their hearts, with the result that they dishonoured their bodies among themselves. [25]They swapped God's truth for a lie, and worshipped and served the creature rather than the creator, who is blessed for ever, Amen.[75]

[14]Therefore, my dear people, run away from idolatry. [15]I'm speaking as to intelligent people: you yourselves must weigh my words. [16]The cup of blessing which we bless is a sharing in the Messiah's blood, isn't it? The bread we break is a sharing in the Messiah's body, isn't it? [17]There is one loaf; well, then, there may be several of us, but we are one body, because we all share the one loaf.

[18]Consider ethnic Israel. Those who eat from the sacrifices share in the altar, don't they? [19]So what am I saying? That idol-food is real, or that an idol is a real being? [20]No: but when they offer sacrifices, they offer them to demons, not to God. And *I don't want you to be table-partners with demons.* [21]You can't drink the cup of the lord and the cup of demons. You can't share in the table of the lord and the table of demons. [22]Surely you don't want to provoke the lord to jealousy? We aren't stronger than him, are we?[76]

Here Paul stands exactly within the world, and one regular form of argumentation, of second-Temple Jews. The fact that there is one God means that idols – the actual supposed divinities, and their becoming present through a statue or image – are mere fictions, the creations of human imagination. But that doesn't mean that they are spiritually irrelevant. Demons, lurking in the shadows, masquerading behind the pomp and glory of pagan worship, will use these 'idols' to lure people away from the living God, and into a corrupting of their own genuine, image-bearing humanity. There is after all one 'image' of God, and that, for Paul, is Jesus the Messiah himself, the truly human one.[77] Those who are 'in the Messiah' are themselves to be renewed according to that 'image'.[78] And that affirmation is itself grounded, for Paul, in another central psalm, Psalm 8: 'God has put all things in subjection under his feet.'[79] This in turn points back to another denunciation of classic pagan behaviour, and to the typically Jewish claim that in the Messiah the one God will judge the world and rescue his people:

[18]You see, there are several people who behave as enemies of the cross of the Messiah. I told you about them often enough, and now I'm weeping as I say it again. [19]They are on the road to destruction; their stomach is their God, and they find glory in their own shame. All they ever think about is what's on the earth.

[20]We are citizens of heaven, you see, and we're eagerly waiting for the saviour, the lord, King Jesus, who is going to come from there. [21]Our present body is a shabby old thing, but he's going to transform it so that it's just like his glorious body. And he's going

[75] Rom. 1.20–5; nb. the close parallel in Wis. 12.23–7.

[76] 1 Cor. 10.14–22 (italics, of course, added). See below for the echoes of Ps. 24, then quoted explicitly in 10.26.

[77] 2 Cor. 4.4; Col. 1.15; see below.

[78] Rom. 8.29; Col. 3.10; Eph. 4.24.

[79] Ps. 8.6, referring back to Gen. 1.26–8; qu. by Paul in 1 Cor. 15.27; cf. Eph. 1.22.

to do this by the power which makes him able to bring everything into line under his authority.[80]

So Paul reaffirms the goodness and God-givenness of the created world, of food and drink, of marriage and sexuality, of political structures; the goodness and image-bearing vocation of human beings; the coming judgment at which the creator will put the world to rights, in line with the promises in the Psalms; the danger of idols and of the dehumanizing behaviour that results from worshipping them. He is, up and down, a classic second-Temple monotheist, and he must have been fully aware of the fact.

(iii) Monotheism in Practice: One God, Therefore One People

A further tell-tale sign of Paul's foundational commitment to his ancestral Jewish monotheism comes in a couple of short but crucial passages. In all of these we see Paul drawing on the basic monotheistic heritage to argue for the unity – not indeed of ethnic Israel, but for what he saw as the renewed people of God in the Messiah.

The first of these passages is in Romans 3.21–31. 'There is no distinction,' Paul insists in 3.23, echoing the point made in 1.17 and anticipating the parallel statement in 10.12–13. The preceding discussion, not least 2.1–16, indicates clearly enough that the 'distinction' which Paul is declaring to be irrelevant is that between Jew and gentile. In chapter 3 Paul continues with a statement, not of the universal lordship of Jesus, but of the universal state of sin: 'all sinned, and fell short of God's glory' (3.23). However, the monotheistically grounded unity of Jew and gentile returns to centre stage six verses later, when Paul is insisting, exactly as in 10.4–13, that justification by faith is the same for all, of whatever ethnic origin:

> 29Or does God belong only to Jews? Doesn't he belong to the nations as well? Yes, of course, to the nations as well, 30since God is one. He will make the declaration 'in the right' over the circumcised on the basis of faith, and over the uncircumcised through faith.[81]

This is one of Paul's most obvious evocations of the *Shema*. His point, echoing Zechariah 14.9, is that the unity of God himself grounds the unity of the community. And the community in question here consists of those marked out by *pistis*, 'faith', the faith which is the answering 'faith' to 'the faithfulness of the Messiah' in 3.22, which is itself the outworking of God's own faithfulness, his truthfulness and justice.[82] Here again we see the basic point of our present chapter: Jewish-style monotheism, rethought from top to

[80] Phil. 3.18–21. Note again the ref. to Ps. 8.6.

[81] Rom. 3.29f.

[82] On the confluence of the faithfulness, truthfulness and justice of God in Rom. 3 (3.3, 4, 5, 6, 7, 21) see below, 837–9, 995f.; and cf. *Perspectives* 503f.

bottom around the events concerning Jesus, is the necessary anchor for the radically revised worldview in which the united community, in its faith, worship and holiness, is the sole visible symbol.

Fascinatingly, when Paul speaks so powerfully of monotheism as the anchor of the worldview, he moves at once to Abraham, who within Jewish tradition (whatever the verdict of today's Old Testament historians!) was *the* monotheist par excellence. Abraham believed, declares Paul, in God as the lifegiver, the creator *ex nihilo*, giving this God the glory in a way in which pagan idolaters had not (1.16–25).[83] This kind of belief is precisely what we find in second-Temple monotheism, and Abraham modelled it, becoming 'the father of many nations' (4.17). Paul, throughout the chapter, is insisting that faith in 'the God who raised Jesus from the dead' is to be identified with this classic type of monotheism, and that this faith is the sole defining characteristic of the single family which God promised Abraham.[84] From here there is a straight line back to 10.1–13.

There is also a straight line to the close parallel in Galatians 3. Here the statement of monotheism comes at the heart of one of the densest and most difficult Pauline passages:

> [19]Why then the law? It was added because of transgressions, until the family should come to whom it had been promised. It was laid down by angels, at the hand of a mediator. [20]He, however, is not the mediator of the 'one' – but God is one![85]

I have argued at length elsewhere that this compressed statement belongs exactly within the argument that runs from 3.6 to 4.7, with climactic moments at 3.14, 18, 22 and 29.[86] This sequence of thought emphasizes the *singularity of the family* which God promised Abraham:

> [27]You see, every one of you who has been baptized into the Messiah has put on the Messiah. [28]There is no longer Jew or Greek; there is no longer slave or free; there is no 'male and female'; you are all one in the Messiah, Jesus.
>
> [29]And, if you belong to the Messiah, you are Abraham's family. You stand to inherit the promise.[87]

All one: Abraham's family, inheriting the promises; belonging to the Messiah. Those are the dominant themes. Meanwhile, as 3.10–14 makes clear, the Mosaic Torah had got in the way of this fulfilment;[88] and, as 3.15–18 insists, God still intends a single 'seed', which is *ho Christos*, the Messiah, the one who, as in 3.27, includes all his people in himself.[89] Once all this is grasped (which is difficult, because each move I have just made represents a

[83] cf. Wright 2002, 500.

[84] On Abraham see *Perspectives* ch. 33.

[85] Gal. 3.19f.

[86] *Climax* ch. 8.

[87] Gal. 3.27–9.

[88] See *Climax* ch. 7. The point is very close to that in Rom. 4.15: Torah brings wrath, but no Torah means no transgression.

[89] See *Perspectives* ch. 31.

point of view which scholarship has largely ignored, and the argument therefore has to be made inch by inch), the only difficulty in 3.19–20 is its characteristically Pauline overcompression. Here again, though, Paul is insisting that monotheism itself is the ground on which the single, united community stands. This claim confronts head on any attempt to divide the community again – which, in Galatians, refers to the work of the 'agitators', following the pattern of 'certain who came from James' to Antioch (2.12). To expand verses 19 and 20 only slightly, we might paraphrase to bring out the meaning:

> Why then did God give the Torah? It was added because of trespasses (because, in other words, Israel, the bearers of the promise, were themselves sinful), until the time came when the 'seed', the single promised seed which is the Messiah and his people, should arrive. The Torah was ordained through angels, by the hand of a mediator, in other words, through Moses. Moses, however, is not the mediator of the 'one', the 'single seed' promised to Abraham; but God is one, and therefore desires that single family.

This works perfectly with the condensed Greek and, more importantly, with Paul's larger argument, which then flows easily throughout the chapter – and reflects exactly what he says later in Romans 3 and 4.

Equally importantly, we have, once again, monotheism undergirding the single family, within the context of Abraham's faith in God's promise. This time, rather than emphasizing Abraham's faith in terms of his belief in God as creator *ex nihilo* and lifegiver, Paul emphasizes it in terms of the forthcoming exodus.[90] All humankind was enslaved, Jew as well as gentile. But God, in fulfilment of his promise and 'when the fullness of time arrived' (*hote de ēlthen to plērōma tou chronou*, 4.4), sent his son and his spirit to rescue the slaves and confer on them the status of 'sons'. The idea of the single plan now coming to fruition, as we saw earlier, is itself again an outflowing of monotheism: God has been in charge all along. And this fulfilment, just as in the original exodus, has constituted a fresh revelation of God's identity: 'now that you've come to know God – or, better, to be known *by* God', says Paul in 4.9.[91] The line of thought that runs all the way from Galatians 2.11 to 4.11, centred on the promises to Abraham as now fulfilled in the Messiah, thus constitutes a complex but powerful statement of radically revised second-Temple monotheism, presented as the foundation of the single family which, shorn of other worldview-symbols, urgently needs just this theological narrative of Abraham, exodus and Messiah for its foundation to be secure and its communal life stable.

All this is seen to excellent advantage in the entire letter to the Ephesians. But since the points to be made there depend on the exposition of Paul's revised monotheism in the next section of this chapter, we shall save them for later.

[90] Which, as Levenson 1993 has pointed out, is woven tightly into the Abraham-story in Gen.

[91] cf. 1 Cor. 8.1–3, a similar small-scale rhetorical point, but again within an argument explicitly grounded in Paul's revised monotheism.

3. Monotheism Freshly Revealed (1): Jesus

(i) Introduction: Paul and the 'Origin of Christology'

If Paul must have been aware that he was reaffirming the classic Jewish monotheism of his day, he must equally have been aware of the fact that he had redrawn this monotheism quite dramatically around Jesus himself.[92] This bold claim will be made good in what follows.

To understand how Paul came to speak of Jesus in the way he did, however, we need to set this question within the larger one: what did the earliest Christians say about Jesus, and why? Paul is regularly and rightly summoned as the first witness in the long-running debates about how the early Christians came to embrace and articulate their shocking belief in the 'divinity' of Jesus; and those larger debates have in turn exercised a powerful reflex action on the way he himself has been read. These matters are, rather obviously, at the centre of any investigation of 'Christian origins and the question of God'.

Early christology in general, with Pauline christology as a particular focus, has been a storm centre now for at least a generation. Significant shifts have taken place in the kinds of questions that are asked and the ways in which they are addressed. The older habit of studying the so-called 'christological titles' no longer holds; more attention is now paid, for reasons that will become clear, to minute analyses of second-Temple Jewish texts which might be thought to have a bearing on the topic.[93] The underlying question, though, remains in my view skewed by the assumptions of post-Enlightenment western discourse, in which the question as to whether Jesus was or was not 'divine' – and the sub-question of at what stage and in what terms did the first Christians come to think of him in that way – has become a kind of litmus test of the two competing 'orthodoxies' of the western world. The first, claiming the high ground of the Enlightenment, seeks to reduce Jesus to the status of a great teacher whose followers, some considerable time afterwards, tried to 'divinize' him. The second, claiming to speak for the Christian tradition, seeks to rehabilitate the 'divinity' of Jesus. Neither side has usually noticed that this question has been posed and addressed as though it could be detached from the equally important early Christian question to do with the coming of the 'kingdom of God' on earth as in heaven, which was after all the central message of the gospels and, arguably, a central underlying theme for Paul as well. Nor has either side paused to reflect on the effect this omission has had on the meanings of the words 'God' and 'divine' themselves. Nor, in particular, has either side appeared to notice that it is possible to give an 'orthodox' answer to the

[92] My own early reflections on this theme were helped by Kreitzer 1987. His work is reflected in some of what follows, though I have frequently differed from him, and in particular have brought out what seem to me important themes that he did not highlight.

[93] Perhaps the best known of the earlier title-based works is Cullmann 1963 [1957]; see too esp. Moule 1977.

question 'Was Jesus divine?', and to the sub-question 'When did the early Christians realize this?', while ignoring the dynamics of what this embodied God was actually up to. These vast and disturbing issues deserve fuller treatment, for which there is no space here. But we cannot proceed with this chapter without at least noting that the regular assumptions behind the ongoing debates are themselves in need of clarification if not correction. The fact that one can observe a storm centre does not mean that, so to speak, the storm is taking place in the right tea-cup.[94]

The question of what the early Christians thought about Jesus has slid to and fro along a hypothetical line co-ordinating two different axes: (a) how early was 'high christology'? (b) was it basically Jewish or non-Jewish? The working assumption has been that if the idea that Jesus was in some sense 'divine' only gradually dawned on the early Christians forty or more years after his lifetime, and within an essentially non-Jewish environment, it could be dismissed as a later and inauthentic development, whereas if the idea turned out to be early and Jewish the same could not be said, or not so easily. In terms of the misleading post-Enlightenment polarizations I mentioned a moment ago, this naturally means that the orthodoxy of the Enlightenment has wanted to see high christology as a late and non-Jewish development, and the responding would-be Christian orthodoxy has wanted to argue for a high christology that is both early and (in some sense) Jewish.

This whole uneasy debate urgently needs to be mapped on to two quite different ones, both of which rest on premises that ought now to be seen as dubious. First, there was a sea-change, some time in the middle of the twentieth century, in the evaluation of 'Jewish' and 'non-Jewish' ideas. Following Hegel and other Enlightenment thinkers, and combining that train of thought with a Lutheran reading of Paul in which 'Judaism' represented the wrong way of doing religion, 'Jewish' ideas were regarded as at best inadequate and at worst dangerous. The history-of-religions school a hundred years ago was eager, in its rejection of all things Jewish, to 'derive' Paul's view of Jesus from the pagan environment in which there were many *kyrioi*, 'lords': Jesus was simply a new one, a cult deity with certain specific features. Paul (on this view) purposely abandoned the Jewish category of 'Messiahship', since it would be incomprehensible to his pagan audience, and gave them something which made sense in their world. As a subcategory of this, many suggested that, with Caesar-worship on the rise in the eastern Mediterranean, Paul took some of the regular Caesar-language and applied it to Jesus. Such scholarship, represented in the early twentieth century by Bousset and Bultmann among others, was seeking to commend Christianity. It accidentally colluded with the long-running Jewish polemic in which, from at least Paul onwards, Christianity had become a form of paganism.[95]

[94] I have discussed these matters in a different context in Wright 2012a [*HGBK*[.

[95] cf. e.g. Schoeps 1961 [1959]; Maccoby 1986.

All this changed after the Second World War. In Pauline studies this was marked especially by W. D. Davies's groundbreaking book *Paul and Rabbinic Judaism*, helped on the one hand by excitement over the discovery of the Dead Sea Scrolls and on the other hand by a horrified dismay (and guilt?) over the disclosure of the holocaust.[96] Within the post-war mood, many have shown that Paul's language about Jesus remained rooted in his native Judaism, even though Judaism did not have a belief in a 'divine Messiah' or anything remotely like it. The texts which speak of or address Jesus as 'lord', *kyrios*, are not on this view borrowed from paganism; they are, in many cases, quotations from or allusions to Septuagintal passages where the word clearly denotes YHWH himself. At that point, as with the word *euangelion*, we have to reckon with *derivation* from ancient Jewish sources and *confrontation* with the pagan world around – something that history-of-religion study has always found difficult.

We shall return to these matters later; I only mention them here as an indication of the way things have changed quite radically. It is now in fact difficult, especially for non-Germans, to imagine the mindset in which older generations took it for granted that F. C. Baur had been right and that 'early Jewish' Christianity was something from which the movement had needed to escape, with Paul leading the break-out and being responsible for the all-important transformation and innovation. But it is harder still for scholars in whatever camp to escape the mood shared by both sides, in which the historical and cultural analysis of elements of a movement has been linked directly to evaluative assumptions, so that to show an idea to be 'Jewish' or 'non-Jewish' at once sends a signal that the idea in question is 'good' or 'bad'. The signals, as we have seen, can be switched this way and that, which calls their usefulness into question.

The second tendency has often been in tension with the first, but still exercises a powerful influence. Protestantism appealed over the head of later ecclesial developments to the fountain-head: to the Bible and the Fathers, against the medieval church. If one went back to the beginning, one would strip off folly and rediscover faith. With the Enlightenment, the 'bad period' was quietly extended: now, everything between the Bible and the Enlightenment itself was under judgment, and the Bible itself was picked apart for signs of a genuine early religion, whether that of Jesus himself or at least that of Paul. At the same time, Romanticism constantly implied that the 'primitive' form of any movement was the genuine, inspired article, the original vision which would fade over time as people moved from charisma to committees, from adoration to administration, from spontaneous and subversive spirituality to stable structures and a salaried sacerdotalism.

The newer history-of-religions movement, and the lingering Romanticism, have thus combined: for the last half century at least, to discover that something was 'Jewish' on the one hand, and that it was 'early' on the other, was to give it double praise. To discover that something called 'high

[96] Davies 1980 [1948].

christology' could be said to be both early and Jewish – the massively argued claim of, among others, the late great Tübingen scholar Martin Hengel – was to strike gold. It was enough to make people raise a flag, or at least a glass; to form new societies, or at least clubs.[97]

All this, of course, needs probing and questioning at various levels. Hengel was himself responsible for the dawning scholarly awareness that the Jewish world of the first century was itself hellenistic through and through, so that to do what some earlier generations had done and go looking for a pre-hellenistic, and indeed *non*-hellenistic, strand of primitive 'Jewish Christianity' was to search blindly in a dark room for a black cat that wasn't there in the first place.[98] And the fad for the 'primitive', which afflicted anthropology as much as theology, has likewise been challenged, as indeed the earlier liberal Protestants themselves challenged it, privileging supposedly 'primitive' *Pauline* Christianity over an earlier 'Jewish Christianity' (hence the attempted detection of 'pre-Pauline' formulae containing worryingly 'Jewish' notions like Davidic Messiahship or covenantal theology, which could then be put to one side) as much as over later supposedly deutero-Pauline 'developments' (hence the rejection of Ephesians).[99] In any case, the attempt to perform an essentially historical operation, i.e. the investigation of the dating and cultural setting of particular early Christian beliefs and motifs, was always at best an uneasy guide to the question of what might actually be true. Even if we came upon documents which demonstrated beyond a shadow of doubt that all Christians in the first decade of the movement believed most surely in a fully trinitarian theology, and believed that they could hold this view while remaining good Jews, that would be interesting but theologically inconclusive. Jewish thinkers would conclude that even the very early Christians were indeed deluded. Post-Enlightenment savants would sigh that the rot obviously set in even sooner than they had supposed.

About these things we cannot now speak in detail. I mention them only to show that the assumed foundations even of the questions that have been asked, let alone of the answers that have been given, ought themselves to be examined. However, none of this should cast a pall over the extraordinary achievements in recent decades, not only of Hengel but of other scholars, particularly Larry Hurtado and Richard Bauckham, who have done just as much as Hengel in their own ways to make it almost inconceivable that one would go back to the older days of Bousset and Bultmann (or even of Dunn, Casey and Vermes) by suggesting once more that people only began to think of Jesus as 'divine' after one or two generations, and (Casey and

[97] Though, sadly, the inscriptions on the coffee-mugs that were distributed among the members of the 'Early High Christology Club' (see Capes, DeConick, Bond, et al. 2007, ix) have themselves shown a tendency to fade over time. For the master's work see esp. Hengel 1976; 1983; 1995; 2006.

[98] Hengel 1974. See, more recently, the powerful and important essays of Meeks 2001 and Martin 2001, exposing the nineteenth-century roots of the constructs 'Judaism' and 'Hellenism' themselves.

[99] The obvious examples of 'pre-Pauline' material treated in this way are Rom. 1.3f.; 3.24–6 (or parts thereof). The exegetical effects of relativizing or setting aside, on the one hand, a solid epistolary introduction and, on the other, a dense climactic statement have been incalculable.

Vermes, but not Dunn) only after the early Christians had lost their grip on their Jewish heritage.[100] This story is now often told; indeed, it has become part of the miniature *Heilsgeschichte* of one branch of the discipline. The idea that a high christology must be late and non-Jewish has in fact been so widely rejected that a recent Jewish scholar, Daniel Boyarin, has swung round in the opposite direction, arguing that most if not all of the elements of early christology, not least the 'divinity' of the expected Messiah, were in fact present within pre-Christian Judaism itself.[101]

Even if such revisionist proposals were to be accepted – and my own view is that Boyarin has claimed much more than the texts will support – we would still have to recognize that the early Christians, already by the time of Paul, had articulated a belief in the 'divinity' of Jesus far more powerfully, and indeed poetically, than anyone had previously imagined. Paul can, in fact, assume his (very 'high') view of Jesus as a given. He never says, even to Corinth, 'How then can some of you be saying that Jesus was simply a wonderful human being and nothing more?' Nor does christology seem to be a point of contention between him and (say) the church in Jerusalem.[102] Despite regular assumptions and assertions, there is no historical evidence for an early 'Jewish Christianity' which (like the later 'Ebionites') denied any identification between Jesus and Israel's God.

All this tells us, from the start, that Paul's view of Jesus cannot have been simply the result of a private revelation. Even if his Damascus Road experience was indeed the moment when, and perhaps also the means by which, he himself arrived at the view that when one saw the face of Jesus one was looking at the glory of God, that was simply his own particular unconventional path to the goal which 'those who were "in the Messiah" before him' (as he puts it in Romans 16.7) had reached by other means. No: as with the summary of the gospel in 1 Corinthians 15.3–11, there is no good reason to suppose that Paul would not have said, of his view of Jesus within the reality of the one God, that 'whether it was me or them, that was the way we announced it, and that was the way you believed.'[103] But we still have to ask – indeed, this quick glance ahead at Paul compels us to ask: what was it exactly that pushed the early Christians in that direction? What was it that provided, if not a full pre-Christian anticipation of that early belief, nevertheless a pre-Christian set of ideas which could be catalysed, whether by Jesus himself, by his resurrection, or by his experienced presence in the early church, to produce the early high christology which is now regularly acknowledged not only in John's gospel, not only in Paul himself, but in

[100] See esp. Hurtado 2003; Bauckham 2008/9; Dunn 1980; Casey 1991; Vermes 1973 and frequently thereafter, including recently e.g. Vermes 2009; 2010.

[101] Boyarin 2012. A precursor of this kind of view was O'Neill 1995.

[102] Unless this be read into the question about 'another Jesus' in 2 Cor. 11.4, linked as it is to 'another gospel', with the parallel to the latter in Gal. 1.6–9. But this is highly speculative.

[103] 1 Cor. 15.11.

such passages as may reasonably be supposed to have taken shape before Paul incorporated them in his letters?[104]

This is the point at which the present chapter has a major new proposal to advance, and since space is limited I will have to take for granted most of the history of recent research which, in a fuller treatment, might be expected.[105] But we must at least note the high points.

An older view would have said that Jesus himself made it clear, by his use of 'son of man' language at least, that he was claiming some kind of equality or identity with Israel's God, and that the early church saw his resurrection as confirming that. I regard such a view as hopelessly short-circuited, though not entirely misleading or mistaken. Certainly without the personal impact of Jesus himself it is impossible seriously to imagine anyone inventing the christology which was already in place by the mid-50s.[106] Many have stressed in the last generation the point that would be obvious to the naked eye had it not been so obscured in the Bultmann school, namely that the impact of Jesus' own life, his personality, his words and deeds, not to mention the drama of his death and resurrection, were bound to have a continuing impact on those who had known him,[107] just as the friends of C. S. Lewis still bring out books of reminiscences about the great man forty or fifty years after his death, and people who worked with Winston Churchill during the war still dine out on their memories of his temper, his wit and his prodigious intake of alcohol. All this can, I think, be taken for granted – and with a large *a fortiori* to reflect the striking differences between those two great, but flawed, human beings and Jesus himself. But this still requires an account of how Jesus' teaching might have been heard and understood among Jews of his place and time, and how the early church found a matrix of thought within which to interpret what it remembered about him.

A second older view claimed that Paul's Damascus Road experience provided him, then and there, with the christological categories he proceeded to develop.[108] Again, there is I think more than a grain of truth in drawing attention to that extraordinary encounter as part of the formation of Paul's view of Jesus at least.[109] But those who have built most strongly at this point still have to invoke the Jewish categories which the pre-Christian Paul would have had in his head, and which were reconfigured by the experience.

[104] e.g. 1 Cor. 8.6; Phil. 2.6–11; Col. 1.15–20, on all of which see below.

[105] Among the flurry of important monographs and collections we note Horbury 1998; Eskola 2001; Stuckenbruck and North 2004; Lee 2005; Longenecker 2005; and the smaller debates between e.g. Hurtado 2005, McGrath 2009 and Dunn 2010. Towering over much of this is the massive and detailed exegetical work of Fee 2007. To engage properly with even these works, let alone the many others not even named here, would require a further book at least the size of the present one. I hope that my proposals in the present chapter will at least indicate where I think such a book might go, and – more important within the present volume, and usually ignored in single-issue monographs – how this vital topic integrates with the other major focal points of Paul's theology.

[106] This is the strong central point of Lee 2005, chs. 4 and 5. For my own treatment of Jesus' self-understanding see *JVG* ch. 13.

[107] This point is variously made by e.g. Moule 1977; Hengel 1983, xi, 178f.

[108] See esp. Kim 1981; and recently Churchill 2010.

[109] cf. *RSG* ch. 8.

And Paul's conversion can hardly account for christologies other than his own, whether those of the earliest pre-Pauline churches (unknown to us of course, but presumably in place before the Damascus Road event) or those of later movements such as those reflected in Hebrews or John.[110]

One of the two most important hypotheses which have been advanced in our own day is that of Larry Hurtado.[111] In his major assault on the older history-of-religions hypothesis represented by Bousset in particular, he proposes that it was *the sense and experience of the personal presence of the exalted Jesus*, in the way that one might expect to experience the presence of the living God, that led Jesus' earliest disciples first to worship him (without any sense of compromising their monotheism), then to re-read Israel's scriptures in such a way as to 'discover' him in passages which were about the One God, and then to develop ways of speaking about him in which this new, extraordinary belief was encapsulated. It was, to re-coin an older phrase, 'early Christian experience' of the risen lord in their midst that compelled them to the first stirrings of what would later become trinitarian and incarnational theology.[112]

Hurtado has thus argued at length for two interlocking points. First, the world of the pre-Christian Jews contained, in many different texts and movements, ideas about figures who were treated as quasi-divine: patriarchs (Enoch, Abraham, Moses), angels, possibly even a Messiah, and abstract entities such as 'wisdom'. Second, the early Christian experience of the presence of the risen and exalted Jesus in worship and prayer formed the context within which those pre-Christian Jewish ideas could come together and be formed into a new pattern. Led by their experience to think of Jesus in terms previously confined to the one God, and to worship him as such while continuing to think of themselves as monotheistic Jews, they drew on these various figures to cast this previously unimagined notion into language which claimed some coherence in itself and also some consistency with earlier Jewish patterns of thought and speech.[113]

I do not wish to challenge this view head on. Indeed, I am convinced that Hurtado is basically right in his presentation and analysis of the phenomena, which really do point to a central and major feature of the important early period, and really do rule out completely the hypotheses of Bousset and others which were so popular a hundred years ago and which still sometimes lurk behind the scholarly scenes.[114] But I have become convinced that there is still an element missing. Once we get that in place all kinds of things will come into focus which, without it, remain fuzzy.

[110] A further proposal in relation to a high christology in Paul was advanced by Moule 1977: that Paul's 'in Christ' language pointed to a view in which Jesus had become 'more than merely human'. I am not convinced that this is the best way to understand the phrase, on which see ch. 10 below.

[111] Hurtado 2003; and see the earlier statement in Hurtado 1988.

[112] On the appropriateness of using 'trinitarian' concepts and language in Paul cf. Gorman 2009, 109.

[113] See too the brief statement in Hurtado 1999a. An important set of studies of related themes is found in Newman, Davila and Lewis 1999.

[114] See Bousset 1970 [1913].

A different dimension within a similar argument has recently been offered by Chris Tilling.[115] He has pointed out in considerable detail that Paul's descriptions of the relationship between the early Christians and Jesus matches the scriptural descriptions of the relationship between Israel and the one God. 'The way Second Temple Judaism understood God as unique, namely through the God-relation pattern, was used by Paul to express the Christ-relation.'[116] This ought I believe to be factored in, alongside Hurtado's arguments, to any future statement of how Paul saw Jesus.

But the hypothesis I regard as even more important among recent explorations of early christology is that of Richard Bauckham, to which I have already referred several times. Bauckham rejects the attempt to discover pre-Christian Jewish 'anticipations' of incarnation in the figures of ancient patriarchs, leading angels or even a Messiah.[117] He draws out a wealth of biblical themes as they re-emerge in a wide range of New Testament writings, building in particular on his earlier work on Revelation in which he demonstrated the clear distinction between the fiercely monotheistic rejection of worship of angels and the taken-for-granted worship of 'God and the Lamb'.[118]

Bauckham's main proposal is that the New Testament, Paul included, offers a 'christology of "divine identity"' in which Jesus is included 'in the unique identity of this one God'.[119] He sets out clearly what he does and does not mean by 'identity', contrasting it with the notions of 'essence' or 'nature' that appear in later theology:

> Identity concerns *who* God is; nature concerns *what* God is or what divinity is ... If we wish to know in what Second Temple Judaism considered the uniqueness of the one God to consist, what distinguished God as unique from all other reality, including beings worshipped as gods by Gentiles, we must look not for a definition of divine nature but for ways of characterizing the unique divine identity.[120]

Israel's God disclosed himself, and his name, YHWH, in his covenant relationship with Israel, demonstrating not just *what* he was but *who* he was:

> The acts of God and the character description of God [in Exodus 34.6 and elsewhere] combine to indicate a consistent identity of the one who acts graciously towards his people and can be expected to do so. Through the consistency of his acts and character, the one called YHWH shows himself to be one and the same.[121]

115 Tilling 2012.

116 Tilling 2012, 256. Passages like Rom. 7.4–6; 2 Cor. 11.2, in which Paul envisages believers being 'married' to the Messiah, relate of course directly to the biblical theme of Israel as the bride of YHWH.

117 Bauckham 2008/9, 3–5, 13–16, 20, 221–32 (subsequent refs. to Bauckham are to this book unless otherwise noted). On pre-Christian divine Messiahship he argues, to my mind convincingly, against the proposals of Horbury 1998.

118 See e.g. Bauckham 1981; 1993, ch. 4 (contrasting e.g. Rev. 5.9–14 with 19.10; 22.8f.).

119 Bauckham 2008/9, 3.

120 Bauckham 2008/9, 7 (italics original).

121 Bauckham 2008/9, 8.

Israel's covenant God reveals, not least, that he is the sole creator of all things, the sole ruler of all things. This is sufficient to set this God apart from all other beings, who in the nature of the case are part of his creation, part of the world over which he rules. This naturally meant claiming exclusive worship; the various intermediary figures which flit through ancient literature, and which are sometimes claimed to be quasi-divine, do not sit on the divine throne, but rather stand before the one God in the position of servants, and (like the angels in Revelation) they explicitly reject worship.[122] The notions of the divine 'word' or 'wisdom', however, even if they come to be personified in later Jewish literature, are not to be thought of as created beings, or semi-divine entities 'occupying some ambiguous status between the One God and the rest of reality'. They are simply graphic ways of describing the one, unique God at work; 'they belong to the unique divine identity.'[123]

Bauckham's proposal is simple and striking: that

> the highest possible Christology – the inclusion of Jesus in the unique divine identity – was central to the faith of the early church even before any of the New Testament writings were written, since it occurs in all of them.

Nor did this require any backing away from ancient Jewish monotheism:

> ... this high Christology was entirely possible within the understanding of Jewish monotheism we have outlined. Novel as it was, it did not require any repudiation of the monotheistic faith which the first Christians axiomatically shared with all Jews. That Jewish monotheism and high Christology were in some way in tension is one of the prevalent illusions in this field that we must allow the texts to dispel.[124]

When we come to the texts, then, we discover something beyond the older and largely sterile debates between a 'functional' and an 'ontic' christology: a 'christology of divine identity'.[125] It is this that Bauckham then expounds in the writings of Paul.

Jewish Monotheism, he here clarifies, has three aspects: creational, eschatological and cultic. God is the sole creator; he will at the last establish his universal kingdom; and he and he alone is to be worshipped.[126] This launches Bauckham into a detailed, and necessarily technical, account of Paul's language about Jesus, from which he concludes that Paul, like the rest of early Christianity, unhesitatingly ascribed to Jesus precisely this triple

122 Bauckham, 15. Bauckham notes (16) that the 'son of man' figure in the 'parables of Enoch' constitutes the sole exception to this.

123 Bauckham, 17.

124 Bauckham, 19. That last remark alone deserves to be pinned up on the notice-boards of many a faculty of theology or biblical studies. See too 58: 'it was actually not Jewish but Greek philosophical categories which made it difficult to attribute true and full divinity to Jesus.' The Nicene and other creeds were thus a way, not of capitulating to Greek philosophy, but of resisting it, and reasserting, as best they could in the language available to them, the christological monotheism of the New Testament.

125 Bauckham, 30.

126 Bauckham, 184.

divine identity. He is the agent of creation; he is the one through whom all things are reconciled; he is to be worshipped.

With all of this I am in agreement. But there is one thing missing, and it is the burden of my song in this chapter to propose it and explain it. And it seems to me that when we do so all kinds of other evidence comes back into the picture to make an even larger, more comprehensive and satisfying whole.

The strength of Bauckham's position, I think, is his insistence that scholars have been looking in the wrong place. The question has been put in the form, Did Judaism have any figures – angels, mediators, messiahs, whatever – who were regarded in an 'exalted' fashion prior to the first century, so that there were Jewish categories available when someone came along whose followers wanted to find 'exalted' language to use of him? Quite apart from the apparently ad hoc nature of any such development, it seems unlikely that the entire early movement would scoop up the same language at the same time and would then make the same moves, out beyond such an initial identification, to a full early, high christology. That second move, in any case, remains very strange on such an account: exalted mediator-figures might be all very well, but they would still not explain the phenomena.

But to raise the question in this way is, I believe, to start at the wrong end. If the phenomenon to be explained is the fact that from extremely early on the followers of Jesus used language for him (and engaged in practices, such as worship, in which he was invoked) which might previously have been thought appropriate only for Israel's God, why should we not begin, not with 'exalted figures' who might as it were be assimilated into the one God, but with the One God himself? Did Judaism have any beliefs, stories, ideas *about God himself* upon which they might have drawn to say what they now wanted to say about Jesus?

The answer is: yes, they did. And this is where, in agreeing with Bauckham's positive proposal as far as it goes, I want to take a significant step beyond it to a point where a larger perspective altogether begins to emerge. Bauckham speaks of 'eschatological monotheism', but perhaps surprisingly does not develop it in this direction. Central to second-Temple monotheism was the belief we sketched in chapter 2: that *Israel's God, having abandoned Jerusalem and the Temple at the time of the Babylonian exile, would one day return.* He would return in person. He would return in glory. He would return to judge and save. He would return to bring about the new exodus, overthrowing the enemies that had enslaved his people. He would return to establish his glorious, tabernacling presence in their midst. He would return to rule over the whole world. *He would come back to be king.*[127] This act, still in the future from the perspective of the pre-Christian Jews, was a vital part of what they believed about 'divine identity'. And this

[127] On the return of YHWH to Zion see *JVG*, 615–24; and below, 1049–53. An important pointer in the direction I am taking here and elsewhere is Adams 2006. Adams relates the 'coming of God' texts to the parousia; I am proposing that they inform and underlie much of early christology and indeed pneumatology as a whole.

is the part that best explains not only Paul's view of Jesus but also that of the entire early church.[128] The long-awaited return of YHWH to Zion is, I suggest, the hidden clue to the origin of christology.

Devout Jews longed for that return. They saw it prophesied across the scriptures, and they prayed for its coming. Some such people, seeing the events concerning Jesus, deduced that it had happened. This is what, to their great surprise, it would look like when Israel's God returned to reign. Once more, the astonishing and unexpected apocalypse meant what it meant within the context of the long, dark story of second-Temple Judaism. Long before Paul dictated his first letter; long before the 'pre-Pauline' material, if such there was, took shape in the early worshipping community; before, even, the risen Jesus appeared to Paul on the road to Damascus, the early Christians believed that Israel's one God had returned in person. In the person of Jesus. The evidence for this proposal is found all over the New Testament, but especially of course in the letters of Paul, to which we shall shortly turn.

Notice, though, even at this stage, what follows. Whereas in the modern period people have come to the New Testament with the question of Jesus' 'divinity' as one of the uppermost worries in their mind, and have struggled to think of how a human being could come to be thought of as 'divine', for Jesus' first followers the question will have posed itself the other way round. It was not a matter of them pondering this or that human, angelic, perhaps quasi-divine figure, and then transferring such categories to Jesus in such a way as to move him up (so to speak) to the level of the one God. It was a matter of them pondering the promises of the one God whose identity, as Bauckham has rightly stressed, was made clear in the scriptures, and wondering what it would look like when he returned to Zion, when he came back to judge the world and rescue his people, when he did again what he had done at the exodus. Not for nothing had Jesus chosen Passover as the moment for his decisive action, and his decisive Passion. It was then a matter of Jesus' followers coming to believe that in him, and supremely in his death and resurrection – the resurrection, of course, revealing that the death was itself to be radically re-evaluated – Israel's God had done what he had long promised. He had returned to be king. He had 'visited' his people and 'redeemed' them.[129] He had returned to dwell in the midst of his people. Jesus had done what God had said he and he alone would do. Early christology did not begin, I suggest, as a strange new belief based on memories of earlier Jewish language for mediator-figures, or even on the strong sense of Jesus' personal presence during worship and prayer, important though that was as well. The former was not, I think, relevant, and the latter

[128] Bauckham 2008/9, 232 draws back from making any proposals as to how the very earliest christology began. It must, he says, 'have been a response to the unique events that brought the early Christian movement into existence'. This needs, he concludes, 'further investigation and reflection', an invitation to which the present chapter, in part, offers the beginnings of a response.

[129] Lk. 1.68; 7.16; 19.44. In 24.21 the two on the road to Emmaus spoke of hoping that Jesus would be the one 'to redeem Israel'; but in Isa. 41.14; 43.14f.; 44.6, 24 and many other passages YHWH himself is the expected 'redeemer' of his people.

was, I suggest, important but essentially secondary. The most important thing was that in his life, death and resurrection Jesus had accomplished the new exodus, had done in person what Israel's God had said he would do in person. He had inaugurated God's kingdom on earth as in heaven. Scholars have spent too long looking for pre-Christian Jewish ideas about human figures, angels or other intermediaries. What matters is the pre-Christian Jewish ideas about Israel's God. *Jesus' first followers found themselves not only (as it were) permitted to use God-language for Jesus, but compelled to use Jesus-language for the one God.*

All this, as I say, seems to have taken place before Paul ever put pen to paper. But it is in his letters that it emerges as already fully formed. It explodes into life, claiming to be the newly revealed form of ancient Jewish monotheism. It is, in particular, exodus-theology, which means a rich and dense combination of themes: sacrifice, redemption from slavery, the fresh revelation of YHWH's name, the giving of Torah, the personal presence of the divine glory in the pillar of cloud and fire and then in the newly constructed tabernacle. And it is return-to-Zion theology, not as a separate idea but as the necessary post-exilic focus of the exodus-hope, as in Ezekiel or Isaiah 40—66, Zechariah or Malachi: YHWH would return to the Temple, as he came down to Egypt to rescue his people, as he consented to dwell in the tabernacle even after Israel's sin. And the theme of YHWH's return itself opens up to reveal the strand which most recent interpreters have seen as important for New Testament christology but without understanding why, or what it meant. The one place in all of second-Temple literature where someone tried to suggest that Israel's God had perhaps returned to the Temple after all was Ben-Sirach 24. *And there the mode of the 'return' was the figure of Wisdom.* Wisdom had been sent from on high to 'tabernacle' on the holy mount, and there to be known through Torah. As the Wisdom of Solomon saw so clearly, it was the divine 'wisdom', responsible for the exodus itself, that was to be invoked by Israel's king as the key requirement for his promised worldwide rule. 'Wisdom-christology' is not part of a random ransacking of miscellaneous quasi-divine abstractions. It is one way in which some second-Temple Jews, and then many early Christians, spoke of the strange and unexpected return of Israel's God. And it was also one way in which some second-Temple Jews, and then many early Christians, spoke of the commissioning and equipment of the coming king. Here is the very centre of the early Christian innovation. Nobody, so far as I am aware, joined these particular threads together before Jesus. The events concerning Jesus compelled the first Christians to do just that. Paul reflects that joining of threads – indeed, he celebrates it and takes it forward in several giant leaps – but he did not invent the idea.

All these themes, then, lead into one another, spill over into one another, presuppose one another, interact with one another: exodus, redemption, tabernacle, presence, return, wisdom, kingship. The more we understand the second-Temple belief in the *eschatological monotheism* at the heart of the divine identity, the better we can see how the first Christians came at once to regard Jesus in the way they did, and the better we can see how Paul could draw on that already established belief at several decisive points in his writings.

It is high time, then, to examine the key texts.

(ii) Jesus and the God of Exodus, Return and Wisdom

(a) Galatians 4.1–11

If we look in Paul's letters for signs of an exodus-theology (or, to be more precise, a 'new-exodus' theology), one natural place to begin is a dense and pivotal section at the heart of Galatians, the first eleven verses of chapter 4:

> Let me put it like this. As long as the heir is a child, he is no different from a slave – even if, in fact, he is master of everything! He is kept under guardians and stewards until the time set by his father.
>
> Well, it's like that with us. When we were children, we were kept in 'slavery' under the 'elements of the world'. But when the fullness of time arrived, God sent out his son, born of a woman, born under the law, so that he might redeem those under the law, so that we might receive adoption as sons.
>
> And, because you are sons, God sent out the spirit of his son into our hearts, calling out 'Abba, father!' So you are no longer a slave, but a son! And, if you're a son, you are an heir, through God.
>
> However, at that stage you didn't know God, and so you were enslaved to beings that, in their proper nature, are not gods. But now that you've come to know God – or, better, to be known *by* God – how can you turn back again to that weak and poverty-stricken line-up of elements that you want to serve all over again? You are observing days, and months, and seasons, and years! I am afraid for you; perhaps my hard work with you is all going to be wasted.

Anyone familiar with second-Temple Jewish writing, with its complex webs of allusion and echo, will recognize at once that this is indeed a compact exodus-story.[130] Here is a group of slaves; here is the sovereign God, acting 'in the fullness of time'; he redeems the slaves, and addresses them as his 'sons'. Every element of this rings with exodus-echoes. But there is more. As we have seen, one of the other central elements in the exodus-narrative is the personal presence of Israel's God, acting dramatically to rescue his people, to lead them on their journey and ultimately to live in their midst in the tabernacle; and the promise of this personal presence was one of the ultimate back reference points for the second-Temple hope that this same God, having abandoned the Temple at the time of the Babylonian exile, would return at last to Zion. The 'sending' both of the unique 'son' and then of the 'spirit of the son' echoes the 'sending' of wisdom to dwell in the midst of Israel, as the mode by which, in Ben-Sirach, Israel's God was to come back and dwell in the Temple at last. Paul does not here join those particu-

[130] See e.g. Keesmaat 1999, chs. 5, 6.

lar dots, but as we shall see later it is central to his understanding of the spirit that, by its 'indwelling' within believers, the spirit constitutes the tabernacling presence of Israel's God, on the analogy of the pillar of cloud and fire accompanying the Israelites on their wilderness journey.

In case there should be any doubt on the question, Paul continues with several further echoes of the exodus. Those now redeemed and addressed as 'sons' are 'heirs', like Israel in the wilderness on the way to their 'inheritance'. They have been rescued from a former life of ignorance, through the revealing of the one true God, just like the Israelites in Exodus 4. Paul uses in verse 8 the word for 'you were enslaved', *edouleusate*, which was used to describe the same point in Genesis 15.13 – from the chapter which he was expounding through most of the previous chapter in Galatians. And the warning he issues in verses 8 and 9 reflects exactly the challenge faced again and again in the story of the people in the wilderness: how can you think of going back to slavery, of making a run for it back to Egypt?[131] He is doing his best, in other words, to place the present predicament and puzzlement of the Galatian Christians on to the well-known map of the exodus narrative, in order to draw the moral: don't go back to slavery, but go on to your inheritance, led by that indwelling divine presence. (This, of course, is more fully set out in Romans 8, to which we shall return presently.)

What does this tell us about Paul's revision of a second-Temple monotheism of eschatological divine identity? First, if this is indeed an exodus-narrative it is, by definition, a statement of one of the foundation stories of all Jewish monotheism. It was at the exodus that Israel's God revealed his covenant faithfulness and saving power. Paul is clear that, as with the Israelites in Exodus 3.13–15 and elsewhere, the events concerning Jesus and the spirit have constituted a fresh and full revelation of who the one God actually is. The key phrase is at the start of verse 9: 'now that you've come to know God – or, better, to be known *by* God . . .' In other words, the events concerning Jesus and the spirit have unveiled the true God in such a way that, so far from being a celestial object available as it were for inspection, he is the one who has taken the initiative in 'knowing', establishing a mutual relationship with, the Galatians.

But the God who is thus establishing this 'knowing' is defined precisely, in terms echoing the wisdom-traditions and hence the promise of YHWH's strange return, as the God who sent the son and who now sends the spirit of the son. Paul sketches in verses 8–9 a typically Jewish contrast between the true God and the pagan gods; but the true God here is the son-sending, spirit-sending God.

This then draws the eye back once more to verse 4, and to the central but multivalent image of Jesus as the 'son'. The context makes it clear that one of the obvious overtones is of Israel as God's 'son'; that is why, when the 'spirit of the son' is sent in turn, those in whom the spirit comes to dwell are

[131] See e.g. Num. 14.1–4; Neh. 9.17.

constituted as, themselves, 'sons'.[132] But at this point we meet, converging in a way that we shall have to examine more closely later on, the equally clear overtone of the 'son' as Messiah. If there was any doubt, the close parallel in Romans 8 once more clarifies the matter, since the themes of son of God/Messiah and inheritance are joined through the strong allusion to Psalm 2.7–8:

> I will tell of the decree of YHWH:
> He said to me, 'You are my son; today I have begotten you.
> Ask of me, and I will make the nations your heritage (*tēn klēronomian sou*)
> and the ends of the earth your possession.'

The Jesus of Galatians 4.4 is thus *both* the representative of God's people *and* the Davidic Messiah – which, as I shall explain later, is hardly accidental. But the context indicates that there is something more as well.

The phrase 'son of God' was not used in the pre-Christian Jewish world, so far as we know, for anyone thought to be a human embodiment of Israel's God – for the very good reason that such people did not exist. But I suggest that we have here, at or near the very start of the theological writing of the early church, the move which points on to the later usage in which 'son of God' straightforwardly and univocally denotes 'the incarnate one'. This is in fact a gross short-circuiting of a much more complex line of thought, and regularly results in an almost docetic reading of Paul. The phrase 'son of God' did not, in his day, mean 'the divine incarnate one'. But here in Galatians 4 it *comes* to mean that, by the explicit joining together of (a) the new-exodus theme in which Israel's God returns at last to deliver his people (and is now warning them against returning to Egypt!), (b) the wisdom-theme in which the wise presence of Israel's God is 'sent' to dwell among the people and to redeem them, (c) the new-revelation-of-God theme, with the one God made known in action as the son-sender and the spirit-sender, and then not least (d) the Messiah theme, in which the *Christos* who has been prominent in the letter up to this point is now referred to, not least in order to bring out the force of the exodus-story, as 'son of God', in keeping with the classic passages of Psalm 2.7, 2 Samuel 7.14, and Psalm 89.26–7.[133] The Jesus who is spoken of in Galatians 4.4 is thus not only Israel's Messiah and the representative of the new-exodus people; he is the embodiment of the one God, returning as promised to rescue his people. This is a christology of divine identity, specifically of exodus-shaped and then Messiah-shaped eschatological monotheism.[134]

We shall return to Galatians 4 later, to inspect the way the spirit fills out the same picture. For the moment we move on to the even more complex and dense parallel passage, Romans 8.1–4.

[132] Gal. 4.7 with 3.26; the echo is of Ex. 4.22f.; cf. Jer. 31.9.

[133] On the Messiahship of Jesus in Gal. cf. *Perspectives*, ch. 31.

[134] On the integration of 'Messiah'-categories at this point see below, 690–701.

(b) Romans 8.1–4

I have argued elsewhere that Romans 6—8 as a whole constitutes (among other things) a massive retelling of the exodus-narrative. It takes us on the journey through the water by which the slaves are set free (chapter 6), up to the mountain where the Torah is given, with its attendant paradox in that it simultaneously (a) invites Israel to keep it and so find life and (b) confronts Israel with the fact of indwelling sin (chapter 7), and then on the homeward march to the 'inheritance', again with sombre warnings about not wanting to go back to Egypt:

> You didn't receive a spirit of slavery, did you, to go back again into a state of fear? But you received the spirit of sonship, in whom we call out 'Abba, father!' When that happens, it is the spirit itself giving supporting witness to what our own spirit is saying, that we are God's children. And if we're children, we are also heirs: heirs of God, and fellow heirs with the Messiah, as long as we suffer with him so that we may also be glorified with him.[135]

Here the echoes of Psalm 2 are clear, anchoring the passage in between the exodus-story and the promise of the coming king who will be given the whole world, the whole created order, as his *klēronomia*, his 'inheritance'. This is, in other words, new-exodus theology, in a freshly messianic mode, once more placing the church on the map at the point where the people are being led through the desert by the personal presence of the one God. This has particular relevance to Paul's understanding of the spirit, as we shall see later on.

But it is with the christological redefinition of monotheism that we are primarily concerned at the moment, and here, as in Galatians, we find in 8.1–4 a further rich and complex statement of who Jesus is and what he has done – or, more specifically, what the one God has done in and through and as Jesus. The first two verses of the chapter constitute what broadcasters call a 'tease', a dense and provocative statement of what is then to be explained:

> So, therefore, there is no condemnation for those in the Messiah, Jesus! Why not? Because the law of the spirit of life in the Messiah, Jesus, released you from the law of sin and death.[136]

Then, as is his wont, Paul spells out what he means, explaining what has happened at the heart of the gospel events. This, as I have often told students, is one of his most central summaries:

> For God has done what the law (being weak because of human flesh) was incapable of doing. God sent his own son in the likeness of sinful flesh, and as a sin-offering; and, right there in the flesh, he condemned sin. This was in order that the right and proper verdict of

[135] Rom. 8.15–17.

[136] Rom. 8.1–2. On this passage see the discussions in Wright 1991 [*Climax*], ch. 10, and 2002 [*Romans*], 573–7.

> the law could be fulfilled in us, as we live not according to the flesh but according to the spirit.[137]

'God sent his own son': here again we have the wisdom-motif, the 'sending' of the one who is God's own second self, drawing together the language of Messiahship ('son of God') and the language of 'wisdom' which, through the fictive person of Solomon, itself already belonged closely with the idea of kingship.

The Wisdom of Solomon, in fact, offers its own complex meditation on themes very closely related to Romans 8. I am not suggesting that Paul got the ideas from there, only that the parallel themes are remarkable in themselves. The opening six chapters of Wisdom portray the 'wicked' who kill the 'righteous', but who are then confronted with divine judgment, and with the presence of the resurrected 'righteous' themselves, who are shown to be 'sons of God', with an inheritance among the holy ones (5.5). This leads in chapter 6 to an extended warning to the rulers of the earth, which is strongly reminiscent of Psalm 2.10 ('Now therefore, O kings, be wise; be warned, O rulers of the earth'). Wisdom is what earth's rulers require, and Solomon is there to testify that he gained it through his prayer (7.1–22). Wisdom is indeed 'a spotless mirror of the working of God, and an image of his goodness' (7.26), so that rulers who gain her are enabled to act wisely in their governing of peoples. The heart of Solomon's reported prayer is the request for 'wisdom' to be sent forth to enable him to do God's will. It is a pregnant poem, full of resonances both with Israel's ancient scriptures and with the early Christian writings:

> With you is wisdom, she who knows your works
> and was present when you made the world;
> she understands what is pleasing in your sight
> and what is right according to your commandments.
> Send her forth from the holy heavens,
> and from the throne of your glory send her,
> that she may labour at my side
> and that I may learn what is pleasing to you.
> For she knows and understands all things
> and she will guide me wisely in my actions
> and guard me with her glory.
> Then my works will be acceptable
> and I shall judge your people justly,
> and shall be worthy of the throne (Greek *thronōn*, 'thrones' plural) of my father.
> For who can learn the counsel of God?
> Or who can discern what the Lord wills? . . .
> Who has learned your counsel,
> unless you have given wisdom
> and sent your holy spirit from on high?[138]

137 Rom. 8.3–4.

138 Wis. 9.9–13, 17.

There are so many Pauline echoes here that it would be tedious to tabulate them all, and in any case my purpose here is to move on rapidly having made the point; for the book turns at once to the long retelling of the story of the human race and more especially of Israel, and all in terms of the guiding and leading of Wisdom. The concluding ten chapters consist mostly of a lengthy account of the exodus itself, with attendant meditations on the wickedness of both Egyptian and Canaanite idolaters, and indeed on idol-worship in general, and on the benefits of belonging to God's people and on trusting and obeying him alone. Those who thus obey Israel's God, the creator, will be acknowledged as 'God's son' (18.13). Here we have exactly that combination of themes of which we have spoken: exodus, redemption, wisdom and kingship, with the implied reader encouraged to remain faithful to Israel's one God and to trust that the deliverance he accomplished in the past will occur again, decisively, in the future.

This is exactly what we find in Romans 6—8 as a whole, so that although the word 'wisdom' does not occur we should not hesitate to see the same idea behind the 'sending of the son' in 8.3. The link with Torah-fulfilment provides another clue.[139] The detail of the task allotted to the messianic and divine son will be studied in the next chapter. Here we simply note that again, in one of Paul's most decisive and definitive sections, we find a classic monotheistic account of divine identity, radically revised around the fresh revelation of the death and resurrection of the Messiah.

Romans 8.1–4 is not, of course, detachable from 8.5–11, and we shall return to that in a later section of the present chapter. It is also closely cognate with Romans 10.6–13, to which again we shall return later. But for the moment we move on to another passage in which Paul evokes the exodus-narrative in order to locate the church on the map at the point where the people are in danger of disastrous rebellion.

(c) 1 Corinthians 8—10

It has recently been customary, and for good reason, to examine 1 Corinthians 8.6 as one of the key texts in which Paul's christologically revised monotheism comes to sharp and startling expression.[140] But in fact the entire section of the letter, addressing the question of how to live as a loyal follower of Jesus within the world of pagan culture, resonates at several points with the theme of monotheism and its revision, so that there is something to be said for seeing 8.6, like Romans 1.3–4 in relation to the rest of Romans, as a dense opening christological statement to be worked out in practice in what follows. Exactly as with the Jewish 'monotheism' of divine identity, this monotheism is both *creational* and *cultic*: the whole passage insists on the goodness of the present creation, and also on the need to be

[139] On the fulfilment of Torah, here and elsewhere, see below, 1036f.

[140] See my earlier statement in Wright 1986a ['Constraints'], 204–9; Wright 1991 [*Climax*], ch. 6.

sure one is worshipping the one God and him alone, avoiding the snares of pagan idolatry wherever they may appear. And the whole passage, in particular, is *eschatological*. The church is the people 'upon whom the ends of the ages have come' (10.11). It evokes, centrally to the argument, the great exodus-narrative: Paul's exposition of his own apostolic 'freedom' in chapter 9 is meant as an illustration of the 'freedom' in the Messiah which the Christians are to enjoy, but just as he says elsewhere the freedom that results from the Passover-event must not be followed by licentious or rebellious behaviour in the wilderness (10.1–13). The context is different, the tone of voice is different, but theologically and exegetically we are here on the same ground as in Galatians 4 (and indeed the exposition of freedom in Galatians 5) or Romans 8.

And it is of course in this context – the exodus, the wilderness journeys and the anticipated entry into the 'inheritance' – that the Pentateuch provides the prayer which summed up what monotheism meant for Jews in the ancient world and to this day. It is a prayer of loyalty to the one God when surrounded by pagan temptations. The prayer is dense and notoriously difficult to translate, just as Paul's reformulation of it is dense and resists easy rendering:

> *shema' israēl* YHWH *elohēnu* YHWH *echad*
> *w'ahabtha eth* YHWH *eloheka becol lebabka ubecol naphsheka ubecol m'odeka.*
>
> Hear, O Israel: YHWH is our God, YHWH alone.[141]
> You shall love YHWH your God with all your heart, and with all your soul, and with all your might.[142]

This is the natural place for a first-century Jew to begin when thinking of how one should behave within a surrounding pagan culture.

This passage must have been as dear to Saul of Tarsus as it was a hundred years later to Akiba. But what Paul the apostle – or someone else before him – has done with this famous prayer is utterly breathtaking. This central, decisive, sharply focused prayer of loyalty to the one God has been restated *so as to include Jesus at its very heart.*

It is a measure of the dramatic shift that has come over contemporary New Testament scholarship in the last generation that this conclusion, which was hardly even noticed thirty or forty years ago, now seems

[141] NRSV mg. offers alternatives (here substituting YHWH for NRSV 'the LORD'): 'YHWH our God is one YHWH' or 'YHWH is our God, YHWH is one.' Cf. RV: 'the LORD our God is one LORD,' with mg. alternatives (a) 'the LORD our God, the LORD is one,' (b) 'the LORD is our God, the LORD is one' and (c) 'the LORD is our God, the LORD alone.'

[142] Dt. 6.4f.

unavoidable and central to our understanding of Paul's christology.[143] But even among those who now see this point there is room for further exploration, not least in terms of the way in which the revised (Paul might say clarified and strengthened) monotheism functions in relation to the central worldview-symbol of the new movement, the one community itself and the way in which its common life was to be ordered. Here, in parallel with Philippians 2 (see below), we see how it is that theology (fresh, prayerful, scripturally rooted thinking about the one God, and about Jesus within that picture) sustains the vision of the one community, under pressure on every side yet finding the way forward precisely through this activity.

First, though, the basic point, in case it has still not been grasped. We have seen how central the *Shema* was for second-Temple Jewish monotheists. It was an acted sign that spoke of this 'monotheism' not as an abstract dogma (the evolutionary goal of the 'theisms' imagined by Enlightenment philosophers), but as the deeply personal reality that evoked the deeply personal response of prayer, love and allegiance. Personal: but also cosmic. To pray the *Shema* was to embrace the yoke of God's kingdom, to commit oneself to God's purposes on earth as in heaven, whatever it might cost. It was to invoke, and declare one's loyalty to, the one God who had revealed himself in action at the exodus and was now giving his people their inheritance. Paul uses the *Shema* in this passage in exactly this way, not as a detached statement of a dogma, not as a 'spiritual' aside, not simply in order to swat away the 'many "gods" and many "lords"' of the previous verse,[144] but in order to be the foundation for the community which is living, or which Paul is teaching to live, as the kingdom-people in the midst of the pagan world. (As we shall see presently, it is fascinating that one of Paul's rare explicit mentions of God's kingdom occurs at the relevant point in the parallel discussion in Romans.[145]) But the *Shema* as he uses it here is the redefined *Shema*. It has Jesus, and not least the *crucified* Jesus, at its centre: the cross is not mentioned explicitly in the revised prayer, but as soon as Paul applies the prayer to the challenge facing the community, it becomes apparent that he is assuming it there. And the underlying point should be clear, once we recognize the exodus-context of the original prayer and the new-exodus context of Paul's argument in 1 Corinthians 8—10. Just as the exodus was launched by the coming of Israel's God in person to rescue his people, so the new exodus has been launched by the long-awaited return of this same God *in and as Jesus himself*. Paul's use of the *Shema* here is, to

[143] See the refs. above in n. 100. It is noticeable that neither Fee 1987 nor Barrett 1971b [1957], ad loc., draw attention to the echo of the *Shema*; contrast e.g. Fitzmyer 2008, 342f. (Fitzmyer 343 also helpfully compares Dt. 10.17). See other discussions noted in Bauckham 2008/9, 211 n. 69; and cp. e.g. Hays 1997, 139f.; Waaler 2008; Lincicum 2010, 138–40. Lincicum quotes Lindemann 2000, 188, describing 1 Cor. 8.1–6 as 'one of the theologically most important texts in the Corpus Paulinum', a verdict the present chapter endorses and if anything amplifies. The reading of this text which I and others now take is still resisted by e.g. Dunn 2010, 108f. (noting that in Dunn 1980, 180 he had taken the other view!); McGrath 2009, 38–45.

[144] As Dunn now suggests (see previous note).

[145] Rom. 14.17. See too the highly compressed use of monotheism in the service of the single, united community in Gal. 3.20.

repeat, not a detached dogmatic aside or maxim to be drawn on in a pragmatic ethical argument, but a statement of eschatological and monotheistic divine identity. This is what it looked like when Israel's God came back at last.

How does this work out? The Greek form of the prayer, in the Septuagint of Deuteronomy 6.4 which most Jews across the Diaspora would say day by day, stands thus:

akoue Israēl	Hear, Israel
kyrios ho theos hēmon	YHWH our God
kyrios heis estin.	YHWH is one.

And the prayer continues, 'And you shall love YHWH your God with all your heart, with all your *psychē*, and with all your power.'[146]

If there is ever any doubt about scriptural allusions and echoes in Paul, there should be none here.[147] Faced with a classic question about how to navigate the choppy waters of a pagan environment with its idols and temples, the obvious place to start is with second-Temple monotheism; and one of the easiest ways of referring to that belief would be through a reference to the *Shema*. The basic point for a follower of Jesus in a world full of idols was simple: 'We are monotheists, not pagan polytheists.' The *Shema*-based allusions and echoes gather momentum from three verses back. First, 'if anybody loves God' (verse 3); then 'no God but one' (verse 4); then, as the rhetorical climax, verses 5 and 6. Here is the key verse with its build-up:

> 4So when it comes to food that has been offered to idols, we know that 'idols are nothing in the world', and that 'there is no God but one'. 5Yes, indeed: there may be many so-called 'gods', whether in heaven or on earth, just as there are many 'gods' and many 'lords'. 6But for us
>
> There is one God, the father,
> from whom are all things, and we to him;
> and one lord, Jesus the Messiah,
> through whom are all things, and we through him.[148]

This is already dense. 'We to him' and 'we through him' are initially puzzling. But actually the Greek is even denser:

all' hēmin	but for us

[146] Dt. 6.5. *Psychē* is of course regularly translated 'soul'; but, as the Akiba incident shows (above, 619f.), it was understood, translating *nephesh*, to mean 'life'.

[147] Dunn's alternative proposal is now that v. 6 was simply formed as a response to 'gods many and lords many' in v. 5. The high probability is that it was the other way round: that because Paul was getting ready to quote his revised *Shema* (already alluded to a few verses earlier), he phrased his description of the surrounding pagan religious context as a kind of advance echo.

[148] In my published translation I have expanded the two somewhat dense lines of verse 6 to 'from whom are all things, and we live to him and for him' and 'through whom are all things, and we live through him'. The addition of 'live' is an attempt to make the English sound less odd, and the addition of 'and for him' is designed to bring out a fuller meaning of *eis auton*: not just 'motion towards', but 'purpose'. See e.g. Thiselton 2000, 636, with God as 'the goal of our existence'.

heis theos ho patēr,	one God the father,
ex hou ta panta	from whom all things
kai hēmeis eis auton	and we to him
kai heis kyrios Iēsous Christos,	and one lord Jesus Messiah,
di'hou ta panta	through whom all things
kai hēmeis di'autou.	and we through him.

There are, in fact, no verbs in the entire formula (just as there were none in the opening lines of the *Shema* itself), but Paul and his hearers would hardly need them. They would understand 'there is', as in the earlier translation, and 'are', repeated, in the two main lines: '*there is* one God the father, from whom *are* all things and we *are* to him, and one lord Jesus Messiah, through whom *are* all things and we *are* through him.'

Even that might be thought somewhat obscure. Perhaps we should gloss the first main line with 'and we *belong* to him', though the bare 'to him' seems to mean more than 'belonging': something more like 'we exist in relation to him', 'we live towards him'. Perhaps, in the second line, we should reckon with something more explicit in relation to the saving work of the Messiah: not just 'and we *live* through him' but 'and we *have been saved* through him'.[149] Or perhaps these are precisely the sort of limiting moves that we should not make. Perhaps the formula was deliberately evocative and mysterious.[150]

We do not need to decide these questions for our present purpose, since the real shock of the passage is of course simply the expansion of the *Shema* to include Jesus within it. The fact that Paul can do what he has done here in verse 6, without explanation or justification, speaks volumes for the theological revolution that *had already taken place*, which as I (and Bauckham, and others) have said seems by this stage to be uncontroversially part of the Christian landscape. Paul is going to argue at length for positions that would be difficult and controversial for the Corinthians to grasp; he sees no need to argue for, or even explain any further, the astonishing theological claim of verse 6. We may even guess that Paul, accustomed since childhood to pray the *Shema* at regular hours, had himself now been praying it and teaching others to pray it in this new fashion, perhaps for several years, invoking the kingdom of Jesus the Messiah as the present instantiation of the kingdom of God the father, as in 1 Corinthians 15.20–8.

[149] This would not mean *replacing* a creational role with soteriology. The commentaries now routinely discuss the proposal of Murphy-O'Connor 1978 to that effect (see e.g. Thiselton 2000, 635f.; Fitzmyer 2008, 343), and just as routinely refute it.

[150] I am reminded of Jonathan Sacks's observation (Sacks 2011, 41–7) that Hebrew thought, with its right-brain emphasis on right-to-left script and originally without vowels, is open-ended, inviting the reader to inhabit the text afresh, unlike left-to-right languages in which everything needs spelling out by the logical left brain. Without buying completely into an absolutized right-brain/left-brain split (see Wright 2012b ['Imagining the Kingdom'], 396–8), let alone an absolutized Hebrew/Greek division, there is nevertheless an important point here about the necessary openness of both the *Shema* and Paul's reworking of it.

The force of the revision is obvious. What Paul has done (or what someone else has done, which Paul is here quoting) is to separate out *theos* and *kyrios*, 'God' and 'lord', in the original prayer, adding brief explanations: 'God' is glossed with 'the father', with the further phrase about God as source and goal of everything, ourselves included, and 'lord' is glossed with 'Jesus Messiah', with the further phrase about Jesus as the means of everything, the one through whom all was made, ourselves included. 'One God (the father), one lord (Jesus Messiah).' A small step for the language; a giant leap for the theology. Jesus is not a 'second God': that would abrogate monotheism entirely. He is not a semi-divine intermediate figure. He is the one in whom the identity of Israel's God is revealed, so that one cannot now speak of this God without thinking of Jesus, or of Jesus without thinking of the one God, the creator, Israel's God.

The context, and the way the chapter and the whole discussion flows out from here, rubs in the point. In a world of 'many gods and many lords', with idols on every street and 'tainted' idol-meat in every market, the point of the statement is that 'For us there is One.' To have said, or implied, 'For us there are Two,' would have meant, 'We are simply a new, curiously restricted, form of paganism'; whereas Paul, throughout the letter, is claiming to be standing on the ground of Jewish-style monotheism over against the pagan world. The long argument which begins here, and carries on to the end of chapter 10, develops exactly this point.

In particular, the way Paul moves into that argument shows that verse 6 is not just a flourish, a decorative allusion to a tradition, but is designed as the driving force for what follows. There is one God, one lord ... therefore pagan idols, the gods and goddesses in the pantheon (including, of course, the emperor and his family, whose cult was flourishing at Corinth as elsewhere), were non-existent. Caligula, Claudius, Nero and the rest did of course 'exist'. They were, or had been, people in the real world. The point was that they claimed to be divine, but were not so in fact. As 'divinities' they were non-existent. Paul will later say that when pagans invoke idols they are worshipping demons, lesser non-physical, supranatural entities; but the idols themselves, invoked by their devotees as divine, are a deceitful sham.[151] The result is dramatic: food that has been offered to these non-gods and non-lords is simply food. Nothing of major theological, cultic or sociological relevance has actually happened to it. A follower of the one God, one lord can eat it with a clear conscience. That is the point Paul makes more or less at once in chapter 8, and to which he will return in chapter 10.

Now we see what it means to say that second-Temple monotheism, reworked in this fashion in accordance with the new-exodus belief that Israel's God has returned at last in and as Jesus, anchors the key worldview-symbol, the single community of the Messiah's followers. The revised *Shema* sustains both the *unity* and the *holiness* of the community. The starting

[151] On this point see Rowe 2005a, 308f.

point, addressing the question of holiness (should one eat 'tainted' food?), is that people who understand this robust redefined monotheism can have a clear conscience in eating anything they like. The 'gods' are hollow nonentities; don't worry about them. Holiness will not be compromised if you eat. But what about unity? What about those whose conscience is not yet clear on these matters, but is rather, in Paul's manner of speaking, 'weak'? And what about those with a 'strong' conscience who find themselves in the same community as the 'weak'? Answer: think through what it means that *the monotheism upon which the worldview now rests has the crucified Messiah at its centre.* As we shall see in Philippians 2, the cross stands at the heart of the revelation of the one God, and hence at the heart of the worldview. If, on the basis of this rediscovered 'monotheism', believers go ahead and eat despite the scruples of the person with a 'weak conscience', they will be spurning the very inner nature of that same 'monotheism'. The Messiah's death is thus not simply a convenient way for God to deal with sins. It reflects the heart and character of the one true God, and that reflection must shine through the life of the community that invokes this one God, one lord. Otherwise, if 'you', with 'knowledge' of this one God, one lord, go ahead and eat despite the weaker fellow-believer, 'you' may encourage such a person back into genuine idolatry:

> [11]And so, you see, the weak person – a brother or sister for whom the Messiah died! – is then destroyed by your 'knowledge'. [12]That means you'll be sinning against your brother or sister, and attacking their weak conscience; and in doing this you'll be sinning against the Messiah.[152]

The revolution in theology is thus not simply the inclusion of Jesus within the *Shema*, but the inclusion of *the crucified Messiah* at that point. Here is the ultimate 'scandal', as in 1 Corinthians 1.23; but not to recognize this point, and not to act upon it, will be the new 'scandal', the thing that will trip up the 'weaker sibling'.[153] Choose your 'scandal', Paul seems to be saying: either the scandal of a crucified Messiah, or the scandal of a destroyed fellow-believer. The cross at the heart of God means the cross at the heart of the worldview-symbol which is the united and holy family itself. All this follows directly from the belief in inaugurated-eschatological monotheism, the belief that Israel's God has returned in the person of Jesus.

This vital move, the direct consequence of the revised *Shema*, does not leave behind the Jewish context in which, as we saw, to pray the *Shema* is to invoke and commit oneself to God's kingdom. In the very similar passage in Romans 14, where Paul has once again been using an essentially monotheistic argument to ground his appeal to regard food, drink and holy days as 'things indifferent', he explains:

[152] 1 Cor. 8.11f.

[153] 8.13, using the verb *skandalizō* twice, two out of Paul's four uses (cf. Rom. 14.21 in a similar context; also 2 Cor. 11.29).

> [17]God's kingdom, you see, isn't about food and drink, but about justice, peace, and joy in the holy spirit. [18]Anyone who serves the Messiah like this pleases God and deserves respect from other people.[154]

In other words, Paul sees the community of those who live by the rule of the one God, one lord – which is the community of the crucified Messiah, defined by him in his death and resurrection (14.9) – as the community in and through whom God's sovereign rule is coming to birth. To pray the revised *Shema*, just as much as the ancient one, was to take upon oneself the yoke of the kingdom. Putting 1 Corinthians 8 together with Romans 14, we can say that for Paul those who pray the *Shema* in the new way are thereby committed to the sovereign rule of the one true God coming true through the victory of Jesus the Messiah on the cross in the past, and through the victory he will win over all enemies, including death itself, in the future (1 Corinthians 15.20–8). In between those two victories, however, there will be a third: the quiet but significant victory which comes about as members of his family learn to live, not by insisting on their rights, but by looking out for one another's needs and consciences. This is how the community will learn to live together as the united and holy people of God, which is Paul's principal aim at so many points: by the prayerful understanding, with renewed minds, of the identity of the one God, one lord.

This sends us back to 1 Corinthians 8—10, this time to the conclusion of the long argument.[155] Paul has spent chapter 9 explaining his own apostolic practice of 'freedom', of knowing what his 'rights' are and then not insisting on them, in order to ground his appeal to the 'strong' that they should not insist on theirs. He then moves, in chapter 10, to a serious warning against idolatry – perhaps knowing that some will be tempted to say that they are 'strong' because they want to be 'allowed' to flirt once more with idolatry and the behaviour that goes with it. Not so, he says: you are the new-exodus people (10.1–13), the people upon whom 'the ends of the ages have come' (10.11).[156] You must learn from the mistakes of the first exodus-people; you must discover what it means that the Rock is the Messiah (10.4).[157] And this means that, for the 'strong' as well, there must be none of the false logic that draws from 'monotheism' the conclusion that, since idols don't exist, one might as well visit their temples from time to time. Paul does not draw back an inch from his basic principle, which he grounds in scripture: 'The earth and its fullness belong to the lord.' The opening line of Psalm 24 gives as clear a statement of creational monotheism as one could wish, providing

[154] Rom. 14.17f.

[155] Treating chs. 8—10 as a single argument of 73 verses means that it is significantly longer even than ch. 15, with its 58.

[156] See above, 552 n. 62.

[157] Paul seems to be understanding the 'rock' from which the Israelites drank as a metaphor for the accompanying divine presence. Cf. 'rock' as a key title for God: Dt. 32.4, 15, 18, 30f.; cf. Gen. 49.24; 1 Sam. 2.2; 2 Sam. 22.2; 23.3; Pss. 18.2; 62.2; 78.35; Isa. 17.10; 26.4; 30.29; 44.8; Hab. 1.12. Many of these are explicit statements of classic Jewish monotheism, of the unique identity and power of Israel's God; cf. the helpful discussion in Waaler 2008.

clear and unambiguous permission to 'eat whatever is sold in the market without making any judgments on the basis of conscience' (10.25).

But there is more to this quotation than meets the eye. As often, Paul may well have more than the individual verse in mind, and when we look at the whole psalm other perspectives emerge.[158]

First, the psalm is not just a statement about the fact that 'the lord', having made all things, now owns all things, so that his people can expect to enjoy them. It is a strong appeal for monotheistic worship and holiness of life, focused on access to the Temple:

> Who shall ascend the hill of YHWH? And who shall stand in his holy place?
> Those who have clean hands and pure hearts, who do not lift up their souls to what is false, and do not swear deceitfully.[159]

'Lifting up their souls to what is false': in other words, to idols, false divinities. Yes, we hear as Paul quotes the first verse: monotheism means that the lord owns all things and gives them freely to you. But this also means that you must worship him alone, and that you must abjure the behaviour that idolatry awakens. That is exactly the message of 1 Corinthians 10, as we see in another biblical allusion in verse 22 ('Surely you don't want to provoke the lord to jealousy? We aren't stronger than him, are we?'), which echoes one of Paul's favourite passages, Deuteronomy 32.[160]

But there is still more. Those who follow the Psalmist's call to monotheistic holiness

> will receive blessing from YHWH, and vindication from the God of their salvation.[161]

Paul has already spoken of the key motivation for avoiding idolatry: we are the people who eat and drink at the table of the Messiah, and we must not also share the table of demons (10.16–22). The way he makes this point provides another echo of the psalm:

> [16]The cup of blessing which we bless is a sharing in the Messiah's blood, isn't it? The bread we break is a sharing in the Messiah's body, isn't it? [17]There is one loaf; well, then, there may be several of us, but we are one body, because we all share the one loaf.[162]

[158] Perhaps surprisingly, Hays does not develop this point, either in Hays 1989a or in Hays 1997, 175f.; it might have been grist to his mill both in the exegesis of the passage and in his larger thesis about Paul's use of scripture. Witherington 1995, 227 sees the irony in quoting a regular Jewish grace now to be said over potentially non-kosher food, but does not see how the whole psalm contributes to other layers of meaning.

[159] Ps. 24.3f.

[160] 32.21: 'They made me jealous with what is no god, provoked me with their idols'; on Paul's ref. here and its significance see Hays 1997, 169f. See too, later in 1 Cor. 10, the strong monotheism of Dt. 32.39, anticipating some of the more striking statements of Isa. 40—55: 'See now that I, even I, am he; there is no god besides me. I kill and I make alive; I wound and I heal; and no one can deliver from my hand.' See too Rom. 10.19, which quotes the next half-verse; see below, 1180. Other refs. to Dt. 32 are found later in Rom.: Rom. 12.19=Dt. 32.35; Rom. 15.10=Dt. 32.43.

[161] Ps. 24.5.

[162] 1 Cor. 10.16f.

The *blessing* is the thing, and one must not trample upon it. The cultic setting of the psalm, with the cleansing of hands and heart in order to share in the worship, is matched exactly by Paul's appeal. He has not abandoned the Jewish call for holiness; merely redefined it. Nor need we be in doubt as to how – at least in 1 Corinthians – Paul would have understood the closing verses of the psalm:

> Lift up your heads, O gates! and be lifted up, O ancient doors! that the king of glory may come in.
> Who is the king of glory?
> YHWH, strong and mighty, YHWH, mighty in battle.
> Lift up your heads, O gates! and be lifted up, O ancient doors!
> that the king of glory may come in.
> Who is this king of glory?
> YHWH of hosts, he is the king of glory.[163]

The king of glory who, mighty in battle, has now entered into the place where earth and heaven meet, and who is celebrated as such by his followers – this king, Paul would have said, is Jesus the Messiah. He is the one, mighty in battle, who has won the initial victory and will go on to win the final one (1 Corinthians 15.20–8). And this, finally, increases the probability that when Paul quotes Psalm 24.1 in 1 Corinthians 10.26 he understands *kyrios*, as in 8.6, to refer to Jesus himself.[164] Paul's entire argument in 1 Corinthians 8—10 is rooted in a second-Temple monotheism reworked around Jesus the crucified and risen Messiah, and reapplied, in the new eschatological situation that has thereby come about (10.11), to the life of the community that invokes him, that eats at his table, shares his blessing and celebrates his victory. The fresh theology provides the stable basis for the united, holy community, even though that community has none of the regular Jewish worldview-symbols on which to rely for support. And that fresh theology – creational, eschatological and cultic monotheism, brought into three dimensions through having the crucified Jesus at its heart – finds its richest and densest expression in Paul's radical revision of the *Shema*. 'For us there is one *theos*, one *kyrios*.'

(d) Creation, Exodus and Wisdom: Colossians 1

We have already studied the theme of 'wisdom' in the second-Temple period from various angles, and found it almost ubiquitous, closely linked to the themes of king and Temple, expressive of that great flow of narrative and symbol in which the world's creator is revealed as Israel's God, the giver of Torah, the one who dwells in the Temple, the one who acts through the chosen king, the one who renews the covenant ... 'Wisdom', in other

[163] Ps. 24.7–10.

[164] So Hays 1997, 175f.; see Capes 1992; 2004; and esp. the full recent discussion in Bauckham 2008/9, 186–219; and the exposition of the topic below, 701–6.

words, is not so much (as one might think from some studies) a kind of added extra in second-Temple theology, an interesting metaphor or personification to be dropped into an argument to add extra flavour. To speak of 'wisdom' is to draw together several themes into a rich and coherent picture.

To speak of this 'wisdom' is, after all, to speak of the creator God as good, wise, fruitful, utterly and beautifully creative and inventive, unveiling creation as the theatre of his spectacular and harmonious work, revealing Israel (the recipients of Torah, itself conceived as a wisdom-vehicle) as the true humanity reflecting God's image, disclosing the Temple as the place of God's 'dwelling', and, not least, revealing God's plan for the future, the secret wisdom made known in glimpses and mysteries to sages and seers, to (what we call) apocalyptists and mystics. 'Wisdom' is to be found in all of this and more.

Granted all this, and granted all that we have said so far about Paul's vision of Jesus himself, it would be a reasonable hypothesis that he would apply this 'wisdom' teaching, in some way or other, to Jesus. As we have already hinted, some of the passages we have been studying do just this. God 'sends' the son, according to Romans 8.3 and Galatians 4.4, just as the creator 'sends' Wisdom into the world, into the Temple, into Israel, in and as Torah:

> Wisdom praises herself, and tells of her glory in the midst of her people . . .
> 'I came forth from the mouth of the Most High, and covered the earth like a mist . . .
> Over waves of the sea, over all the earth, and over every people and nation I have held sway.[165]
> Among all these I sought a resting-place; in whose territory should I abide?
> Then the Creator of all things gave me a command, and my Creator chose the place for my tent.
> He said, 'Make your dwelling in Jacob, and in Israel receive your inheritance.'
> Before the ages, in the beginning, he created me, and for all the ages I shall not cease to be.
> In the holy tent I ministered before him, and so I was established in Zion . . .
> All this is the book of the covenant of the Most High God,
> the law that Moses commanded us as an inheritance for the congregations of Jacob.[166]

This famous 'wisdom' poem is matched by the one quoted above in connection with Romans 8, namely the 'prayer of Solomon' from Wisdom of Solomon 9. These poems are rich and dense in motif and allusion. They draw together almost every important aspect of the Jewish monotheism of the period: the good creation; humans made to rule God's world; the revelation to Israel through Torah; God's powerful rescuing action in the exodus and his tabernacling presence in the Temple; the sending forth both of Wisdom and of the 'holy spirit' to guide and direct humans in general, Israel in particular, and above all the Davidic king. Sirach is claiming that Israel's one God has really returned to dwell in the Temple, under the form of the 'wisdom' which one acquires through the study and teaching of Torah, the

[165] Other LXX MSS read 'I have acquired a possession', *ektēsamēn* instead of *hēgēsamēn*.

[166] Sir. 24.1, 3, 6–10, 23.

'book of the covenant'. (Since the book climaxes with the portrait of the high priest, the central figure both in the Temple-liturgy and in the teaching of Torah, this is hardly surprising.) Wisdom is claiming that the divine breath by which the world was made was available, on request, to the kings of the earth (and to Israel's king in particular) to enable them to fulfil their awesome responsibilities.

This is the combination of traditional belief which Paul has taken and poured through the funnel of his breathtaking christology into the passages we have already studied. This is the set of themes latent within 1 Corinthians 8.6, with its sense of creation and redemption being accomplished *through* Jesus the Messiah; within Romans 8.3 and Galatians 4.4, with the 'sending of the son'; within the passages we shall study in the next section, where the Messiah constitutes the renewed Temple, the dwelling place of the living God. And this is the set of themes which emerge in the poem which ranks with Sirach 24, Wisdom 9 and Baruch 3 as among the greatest monotheistic poems of the period.[167]

This one, though, is different from those three predecessors in the same way that 1 Corinthians 8.6 is different from the *Shema*. Here, just as with Philippians 2.6–11, we find Jesus himself at the heart of the freshly inscribed monotheistic celebration:

> 15He is the image of God, the invisible one,
> the firstborn of all creation.
> 16For in him all things were created,
> in the heavens and here on the earth.
> Things we can see and things we cannot,
> – thrones and lordships and rulers and powers –
> all things were created both through him and for him.
>
> 17And he is ahead, prior to all else
> and in him all things hold together;
> 18and he himself is supreme, the head
> over the body, the church.
>
> He is the start of it all,
> firstborn from realms of the dead;
> so in all things he might be the chief.
> 19For in him all the Fullness was glad to dwell
> 20and through him to reconcile all to himself,
> making peace through the blood of his cross,
> through him – yes, things on the earth,
> and also the things in the heavens.[168]

This translation of the well-known poem attempts to bring out the balance between the different elements, and also, crucially, the structural divisions which are more obvious in Greek than in English (though I have tried to make it obvious in the way the poem has been here translated and printed),

[167] We should also include Jn. 1.1–18. On Bar. 3 see above, 151–3.

[168] Col. 1.15–20.

especially the way in which verse 17 and the first two lines of 18 form a closely balanced middle section in between the outer sections of verses 15 and 16 on the one hand and 18b, 19 and 20 on the other.[169]

This is not the place for a complete exegesis of this stunning passage.[170] Nor is it the moment to justify, over against the doubters, the satisfying rightness of C. F. Burney's brilliant hypothesis about the way in which the writer[171] has exploited (a) the link of Proverbs 8.22 ('YHWH created me the beginning of his way', *reshith darcō, archē hodōn autou*) with Genesis 1.1 ('in the beginning', *bereshith, en archē*) and (b) the three possible meanings of the preposition *be* and the four possible meanings of *reshith* in that first word of scripture.[172] Who knows what distant ears may hear, of echoes far, allusions near, of rhythms strange and unexpected, patterns earlier undetected? My point here is that, whatever subtleties of poetic composition and biblical (quasi-rabbinic?) allusion we may discern, the poem taken at face value displays exactly that blend of second-Temple monotheism and early, high christology which we have seen to be characteristic of Paul all through. It is a classic statement of the one creator God, Israel's God, and of the one 'through whom' or 'in whom' this God accomplishes every stage of his work. And the 'work' in question, we note, is once again the exodus (see below on 1.13–14). We have, in other words, the same combination of themes that we have observed, in very different contexts, in the other passages studied so far.

What, then, needs to be said about this passage in relation to the christological redefinition of second-Temple monotheism? How does this poem express what Bauckham calls a 'christology of divine identity' while adding the particular dimension of the long-awaited return of Israel's God to his people and to the world?

First, as to the monotheism. The balance of the two main sections displays just that balance of creation and redemption which is so characteristic of the Psalms and other ancient Israelite poetry, not least in Isaiah 40—55: the creator is also the redeemer, and vice versa, and when redemption hap-

169 Full details in *Climax* ch. 5.

170 The commentaries all naturally devote lavish attention to the passage. Among key monographs see e.g. Stettler 2000.

171 I refer to him as 'Paul' because I think he wrote it; and I note that if, as in some hypotheses, Colossians is post-Pauline but the poem is pre-Colossians, then Paul himself turns up again as a candidate for authorship of the poem.

172 Burney 1925. A further echo, somewhere between Gen. 1.1 and Prov. 8.22, is Prov. 3.19, where YHWH founded the earth 'by wisdom' (*behokmah, tē sophia*). Those who doubt Burney's thesis can be represented by Barclay 1997, 67 (followed by e.g. Wilson 2005, 149); in favour, e.g. Bird 2009b, 49f. Barclay's objection, that Paul's readers would not have understood this subtle exegesis of an underlying Hebrew text, is not I think to the point. This would not be the only passage where Paul said more than his first audience would detect (cf. e.g. Rom. 2.29, where his point turns on the fact that 'Judah' in Hebrew means 'praise'). The late lamented historian Thomas Braun, a frequent dining companion of mine in the mid-1970s, was capable of spontaneous multilingual puns and indeed limericks, much enjoyed even by those of us who did not know all the languages involved. Most poets, and indeed writers of prose, regularly allude to things which many readers might miss. Just because some do not heed the summons, that does not mean that wisdom and spirit are not present and at work; we trace but the outskirts of their ways. See the essay on Paul's use of scripture in *Perspectives* ch. 32.

pens it will be as a result of the long-awaited return of the creator in person. This has the effect of ruling out, before it can even begin, any suggestion of dualism, of a God who might be invoked to rescue people *from* an evil creation. (The suggestion which used to be made, that the poem had a gnostic origin, always was absurd.[173]) No: creation is good and God-given, and the work of redemption in verses 18b–20 has nothing to do with abandoning creation and beginning again in some different mode. It is aimed precisely at *new creation*. The poem does not downplay the problems which have arisen within the good creation. That is why there was a task (here unexplained) of 'reconciliation' to be undertaken, as in verse 20. But the problems have not stretched the competence of the creator God. Through the one spoken of here in the third person, the one through whom all things were made in the first place, the creator has accomplished that work of redemption, drawing a line straight down through the world, declaring 'you are here' to the surprised Colossians and to anyone else listening in. Heaven and earth and all that is in them, including all the power structures of the world, were created 'in him, through him and for him' and are now reconciled 'to him and through him'.

So who is this 'he'? Clearly, it is Jesus the Messiah; but, interestingly, the immediately prior description of him is in terms both of 'sonship' and of his 'kingdom'. The poem flows out of Paul's prayer for the young church, with its echoes of the rescue and 'redemption' which found their historical anchor in the exodus, the time when the one God revealed himself in action and then came to dwell in the midst of his people:

> I pray that you will learn to give thanks to the father, who has made you fit to share the inheritance of God's holy ones in the light. [13]He has delivered us from the power of darkness, and transferred us into the kingdom of his beloved son [literally, 'the son of his love', *tou huiou tēs agapēs autou*]. [14]He is the one in whom we have redemption, the forgiveness of sins.[174]

The poem is thus linked closely to the themes we have already studied. What has been accomplished through Jesus is the rescuing kingdom-act of Israel's one God. But its particular christological contribution lies, clearly, in the far more explicit unfolding of the way in which both creation and redemption are accomplished 'through' the Messiah, God's son; in other words, in the large expansion of the *dia*, 'through', which we observed in the terse prayer of 1 Corinthians 8.6. Paul thus both draws on and relativizes the Jewish wisdom-tradition represented for us in Sirach and the Wisdom of Solomon.[175] If it's 'wisdom' you want, he is saying, you have it all in the Messiah (he draws out exactly this point in 2.3): you can find it in and

[173] Käsemann 1964 [1960], 155: apart from what he calls 'Christian interpolations', the poem contains 'the supra-historical and metaphysical drama of the gnostic Redeemer'. This is firmly rejected by e.g. Fossum 1989; see too e.g. Wilson 2005, 125.

[174] Col. 1.12–14.

[175] On 'wisdom-christology' and its problems see further Gathercole 2006b, ch. 8; Macaskill 2007, 144–52.

through the one we now know as Jesus, the 'son of the father's love', in whom all things were created, and through whom all things have been reconciled. The appropriateness of the Messiah, David's heir, Solomon's true successor, as the living embodiment of Wisdom would not be lost on anyone who knew Wisdom 9 or 1 Kings 3, just as the appropriateness of this figure coming to embody the newly built Temple (see below) would be clear to anyone who knew those passages and Sirach 24, and was aware that Solomon's building of the Temple was the major achievement that followed the gift of divine wisdom.

Whether or not Burney was right (though I think he was) to suggest a more subtle exegesis of Genesis 1.1, the mention of the Messiah as both 'image' (verse 15) and 'beginning' (verse 18b) would assuredly send the first-century Jewish ear back to the opening of the Bible. And if, as we considered possible in our earlier discussion, that same first-century ear would discern in the six-day pattern of Genesis 1 a reference to the building of a temple – the whole creation, heaven and earth, as the dwelling place for the creator – then we would not be surprised to discover temple-language, and the language of the divine indwelling within the completed building, within the poem itself. What is more surprising is that, whereas we might expect the poem to speak of the Messiah now dwelling in the new creation, we find instead 'the fullness of deity' dwelling in the Messiah (verse 19). He is now the true temple, the place where heaven and earth meet (appropriately, since he was God's agent in their creation), the means by which, through his shed blood on the cross, heaven and earth are reconciled to God and, it seems, to one another. Within the strongly implicit wisdom-christology of the poem, then, itself building on the notion of the kingdom of God's son in verse 13, we have a temple-christology, which, granted the larger context indicated by Sirach 24 and Wisdom 9, is just what we should have expected. *This is another Pauline statement about the return of Israel's God.* In case we missed the point first time round, Paul says it again in the next chapter:

> In him, you see, all the full measure of divinity has taken up bodily residence. [10]What's more, you are fulfilled in him, since he's the head of all rule and authority.[176]

Granted the multiple resonances between this passage and 2 Corinthians 5 (new creation through the Messiah, as a result of God's reconciling love), I suggest we should take the key christological statement there in the same way, as an expression of the full indwelling of divinity in the Messiah for the accomplishment of reconciliation and new creation:

> [16]From this moment on, therefore, we don't regard anybody from a merely human point of view. Even if we once regarded the Messiah that way, we don't do so any longer. [17]Thus, if anyone is in the Messiah, there is a new creation! Old things have gone, and look – everything has become new! [18]It all comes from God. He reconciled us to himself through the Messiah, and he gave us the ministry of reconciliation. [19]This is how it came about:

[176] Col. 2.9f.

> *God was reconciling the world to himself in the Messiah*, not counting their transgressions against them, and entrusting us with the message of reconciliation.[177]

Or, in the words of the King James Version: *God was in Christ reconciling the world to himself.* This is not to be watered down to *through* Christ, as though the Messiah was a mere agent (as in 'God was punishing Israel *through Assyria*'). By now we have a sufficiently broad-based picture of Paul's christological monotheism to insist that he was saying something much more than this, in line with the earlier statement in 2 Corinthians 4 which is likewise close to the present passage in Colossians, and which we shall study in the next sub-section.

Returning to Colossians, we find this christological monotheism, or monotheistic christology, filled out by the short middle section, verses 17 and 18a, with its two parts each marked with the opening *kai autos*, 'and he'. He – again, the Messiah/Wisdom – is 'ahead, prior to all else', both in the temporal sense and in the sense of ontological priority: he is chief, part of a different order of being, superior not only to ordinary mortal humans but also to angels. 'In him all things hold together': the monotheistic providence with which second-Temple Jews believed the one God governed the world is exercised through the Messiah/Wisdom. Then, in verse 18a, he is the head: not just in relation to 'the body, the church', as though the metaphor of 'head' depended entirely on 'body' at this point, but 'head' in the sense of 'the senior, the supreme one'. He is the place where 'the church' finds its identity, as itself the new creation (once again, we note the obvious resonances with 2 Corinthians 5.17), or at least as the beginning of that much larger project.

This is, then, a christological monotheism which is most obviously *creational*, affirming the goodness of the original creation and announcing the dawn of its renewal. It is also *eschatological* monotheism, in the inaugurated sense that Jesus, as the divine Wisdom, is in himself the God of Israel who has returned to dwell among his people, and in the future sense that looks ahead to the final accomplishment of what has been launched in the Messiah's resurrection. What is more, it is all in the service of worship, of thanksgiving: it is, in other words, also *cultic* monotheism. The aim of it all is that the Colossians will learn how to *give thanks* to God the father for all he has done (1.12). Thanksgiving is, in fact, a major theme of the whole letter.[178] And this thanksgiving is the exact correlate of creational and covenantal monotheism, the appropriate response of God's people to their creator, rescuer and lord. It is what the Psalms are all about. It is the glad celebration of the goodness of God the creator, and the special and particu-

[177] 2 Cor. 5.16–19. See the discussion of the key point in e.g. Furnish 1984, 318 (though he rejects an 'incarnational' reading as extraneous to the context, a view which might be challenged in the light of 4.1–6); see too Bieringer 1987, esp. 304–7. I suspect that scholars have resisted discerning 'incarnational' theology in the passage (another example is Thrall 1994, 432–4) partly at least because they have assumed that such ideas only developed in the later patristic period, whereas my argument is that they are part of Paul's reworked Jewish monotheism.

[178] 1.3; 1.12; 2.6; 3.15, 17; 4.2.

lar goodness which has now rescued people in and through the Messiah. Colossians as a whole, and especially in the poem which encapsulates its main theme, is one of the finest expressions of second-Temple monotheism, and all redefined and reworked around Jesus the Messiah.

(e) 2 Corinthians 3 and 4

We alluded just now to the start of 2 Corinthians 4, which bears a close relationship to the themes we have seen in Colossians 1. The similarity is more than skin deep. This is a passage where the echoes of exodus are profound, speaking directly to the question of a christology of divine identity reworked around the notion that, in Jesus, Israel's God has finally returned.

The point is often missed because of the complexity of the exposition at the end of 2 Corinthians 3, where Paul compares his own hearers with those of Moses. The hearts of Moses' hearers were hard, so that the glory on Moses' face had to be veiled. The hearts of Paul's hearers, however, had been transformed by the new-covenant work of the spirit through which the one God had accomplished what the Mosaic Torah could not (3.1–6), so that they could now gaze at the glory of the Lord without a veil. This passage comes up for fuller treatment elsewhere in the present volume.[179]

Many commentators simply assume that the biblical context of the passage Paul is using is irrelevant. Indeed, many have declared that Paul would not, left to himself, have wanted to drag Moses into his argument, and that he only did so because his opponents forced him into it. Whatever the likelihood of opponents in Corinth quoting Moses against him, what we have in the present passage, from at least 3.7 through to 4.6, is a sustained reflection on one of the most important and profound incidents in the Pentateuch, one with continuing relevance for the second-Temple Jewish expectation of the return of YHWH, that aspect of eschatological monotheism which formed such a vital part of the question (Bauckham's question) of *who* God was (as opposed to *what* God was). He was *the God who had promised to come back*. And that return, to dwell in the restored Temple as in Ezekiel 43, looked back to the scriptural precedent in Exodus 32—40. After the sin of the golden calf, YHWH had declared to Moses that he would no longer accompany the Israelites on their journey.[180] He would absent himself. The tabernacle (whose building-plan Moses had already received) would not be constructed, since it would have no inhabitant. But then Moses intercedes for the people. It is a moving account, which forms the turning-point for the whole book, and thus in a measure for the whole Pentateuch: will YHWH go up in the midst of his people to the promised inheritance, or will he not? Will the tabernacle, the little cosmos, be built in Israel's midst, like a little Eden, or will it not?

[179] See below, 980–4.

[180] Paul refers to the same incident in 1 Cor. 10.7, and arguably elsewhere too, e.g. Rom. 1.23 (cf. Ps. 106.20).

Part of the complexity of the passage lies in the repeated use of the Hebrew *panim*, 'face'. (The Septuagint gives up at this point, treating 'face' simply as a synonym for 'God himself'.) Despite having said that YHWH and Moses were accustomed to speak with one another 'face to face', *panim el-panim*,[181] YHWH now solemnly declares that even Moses will not see his face, because nobody can do that and live. Thus the 'face' of Israel's God will go with the people, in answer to Moses' earnest prayer; but Moses himself, though granted a vision of the divine glory (consisting, it seems, of a recital of the divine characteristics, 'who God is' once more), will not see his face:

> Moses said to YHWH, 'See, you have said to me, "Bring up this people"; but you have not let me know whom you will send with me. Yet you have said, "I know you by name, and you have also found favour in my sight." Now if I have found favour in your sight, show me your ways, so that I may know you and find favour in your sight. Consider too that this nation is your people.' He said, 'My presence [*panai*] will go with you, and I will give you rest.' And he said to him, 'If your presence [*paneika*] will not go, do not carry us up from here. For how shall it be known that I have found favour in your sight, I and your people, unless you go with us? In this way, we shall be distinct, I and your people, from every people on the face of the earth.'
>
> YHWH said to Moses, 'I will do the very thing that you have asked; for you have found favour in my sight, and I know you by name.' Moses said, 'Show me your glory, I pray.' And he said, 'I will make all my goodness pass before you, and will proclaim before you the name, "YHWH"; and I will be gracious to whom I will be gracious, and will show mercy on whom I will show mercy. But', he said, 'you cannot see my face [*panai*]; for no one shall see me and live.' And YHWH continued, 'See, there is a place by me where you shall stand on the rock; and while my glory passes by I will put you in a cleft of the rock, and I will cover you with my hand until I have passed by; then I will take away my hand, and you shall see my back; but my face [*panai*] shall not be seen.'[182]

And so it happens. The divine glory is displayed before Moses, but he does not see the divine face. More commands and injunctions are issued, and then finally Moses comes back down the mountain to the frightened, waiting people. That is the point at which Moses' face shines, because he has been talking with God. The people are afraid, so he puts on a veil when speaking to them, taking it off again when he goes back into the tent of meeting to speak with God.

Only after this is the tabernacle finally constructed, with all its furniture, the priestly vestments and so forth. Then, at last,

> the cloud covered the tent of meeting, and the glory of YHWH filled the tabernacle. Moses was not able to enter the tent of meeting because the cloud settled upon it, and the glory of YHWH filled the tabernacle.[183]

Divine presence, despite Israel's sin; divine glory, despite Israel's shame. This closing scene provides both the huge sigh of relief at the end of the dramatic, long-drawn-out story of Israel's rebellion at the giving of Torah,

181 LXX *enōpios enōpiō*.

182 Ex. 33.12–23.

183 Ex. 40.34f.

and also the closure of the longer narrative that began in the garden of Eden. Despite idolatry, rebellion and sin, Israel has been constituted as the new humanity, the people in whose midst the glory of the one God had deigned to dwell, leading them on their journey to the promised inheritance. The tabernacle is indeed the sign of new creation: the glory that fills it now will one day fill the whole world.[184]

There are no doubt mysteries in plenty to be pondered in all this. But it seems clear where Paul was taking the story.[185] Any second-Temple Jew, reading the exodus narrative and knowing the present Temple to be frustratingly incomplete, would pick up the sense of closure in the text, the fresh act of grace through which YHWH came, despite everything, to dwell with his people, and would long for the same thing to happen once more, for the prophecies of Isaiah 40.5 to come true ('Then the glory of YHWH shall be revealed, and all people shall see it together'), for the prayer of Isaiah 64.1 to be answered ('O that you would tear open the heavens and come down, so that the mountains would quake at your presence'). The exodus-narrative, in other words, would point forwards to the moment when Israel's eschatological monotheism would be fulfilled, and YHWH would return to his people at last.

This is the context in which we can see the full import of the statement about Jesus in 2 Corinthians 4.3–6:

> However, if our gospel still remains 'veiled', it is veiled for people who are perishing. What's happening there is that the god of this world has blinded the minds of unbelievers, so that they won't see the light of the gospel of the glory of the Messiah, who is God's image. 5We don't proclaim ourselves, you see, but Jesus the Messiah as lord, and ourselves as your servants because of Jesus; 6because the God who said 'let light shine out of darkness' has shone in our hearts, to produce the light of the knowledge of the glory of God in the face of Jesus the Messiah.

The Messiah as God's image; as the *kyrios* of the world; as the one through whom new creation has come about, the one in whose very face we recognize, in our hearts, 'the light of the knowledge of God's glory': all this is very similar to Colossians 1, and likewise expressive of wisdom-christology, temple-christology and 'glory'-christology. It is, in other words, classic second-Temple monotheism, redesigned around Jesus.[186] It is, in particular, the transposition into the new key of the twin themes of 'face' and 'glory'. The God who would not show his face to Moses has shown his face to his people in and as Jesus. To speak of seeing 'the glory of God in the face of Jesus the Messiah', in the context of a long discussion of Exodus 33—4, can only mean one thing. *The God who abandoned Israel at the exile, because of idolatry and sin, but who promised to return one day, as he had done in Exodus after the threat of withdrawing his 'presence', has returned at last in and as Jesus the Messiah.* When we read 2 Corinthians 4 in the light of the

[184] See Num. 14.21, and the various statements of this theme listed above, 190–3.

[185] To which he alludes in Rom. 9.15, quoting Ex. 33.19.

[186] See esp. Newman 1992; I hope to have strengthened his overall argument.

expectation of YHWH's return, the high christology, as the expression of creational, cultic and above all eschatological monotheism, rings out clearly. Like all Paul's high christology, it is of course focused remarkably on Jesus as the *crucified* one; he has redefined Messiahship around his cross. And, as we shall now see in Philippians 2, he has thereby dramatically redefined the very meaning of the word 'God' itself.

(f) Philippians 2.6–11

There can be no question about Paul's awareness of what he was doing. By the time he was writing the letters, he was, like Shakespeare, doing nothing by accident.[187] An intelligent second-Temple Jew could not use the language he used about Jesus, and about Israel's one God, without intending the meanings we are discerning. His redrawing of the monotheism of divine identity around Jesus was not arbitrary, a flight of theological fancy. Nor was it simply stuck on to the outside of his view of God, the world, idolatry and the coming judgment. On the contrary, it was right at the heart of it all:

> 9And so God has greatly exalted him,
> And to him in his favour has given
> The name which is over all names:
>
> 10That now at the name of Jesus
> Every knee within heaven shall bow –
> On earth, too, and under the earth;
>
> 11And every tongue shall confess
> That Jesus, Messiah, is lord,
> To the glory of God, the father.[188]

This is of course the second half of the famous poem of Philippians 2. Entire monographs have been written on this passage, and we have no space here to offer the full exegesis for which it cries out.[189] I leave aside, too, the question of original authorship. Paul might have written it himself; it is not unknown for authors to quote their own previous work; or he might have incorporated the work of another, which again is not unknown; but one does not do such a thing without considering quite carefully the way in which the incorporated work contributes to one's intended theme. One does not invite extra birds to nest in one's tree for decorative purposes alone. I therefore treat the poem as, at least in its present context, a deliberate statement of exactly what Paul wanted to say at this point.[190]

[187] Levin 1983, 152, quoting the director Peter Brook speaking about *A Midsummer Night's Dream.*

[188] Phil. 2.9–11.

[189] See recently Bauckham 2008/9, 41–5, 197–210. The collection of essays in Martin and Dodd 1998 is important (not least for the background to contemporary exegetical debates) but uneven.

[190] See further *Climax* ch. 4; though several of the angles I here explore were not then visible to me.

For our present purpose seven points must be made, and made with full and due emphasis.

First, and most important, the whole poem is itself a glorious reaffirmation of second-Temple eschatological monotheism. The key scriptural allusion comes in verse 10, and the passage evoked, Isaiah 45, is by common consent one of the most important texts from one of the most important monotheistic affirmations in the whole of Israel's scripture:

> Assemble yourselves and come together, draw near, you survivors of the nations!
> They have no knowledge – those who carry about their wooden idols, and keep on praying to a god that cannot save.
> Declare and present your case; let them take counsel together!
> Who told this long ago? Who declared it of old?
> Was it not I, YHWH? There is no other god besides me,
> A righteous God and a Saviour; there is no one besides me.
> Turn to me and be saved, all the ends of the earth! For I am God, and there is no other.
> By myself I have sworn, from my mouth has gone forth in righteousness a word that shall not return:
> '*To me every knee shall bow, every tongue shall swear.*'
> Only in YHWH, it shall be said of me, are righteousness and strength;
> All who were incensed against him shall come to him and be ashamed.
> In YHWH all the offspring of Israel shall triumph and glory.[191]

And on goes the prophet in a scathing denunciation of Bel, Nebo and the Babylonians who worship them.[192] YHWH will not share his glory with another; he will not allow carved images to steal the praise that is his alone.[193] The Isaiah text, which conveys this sense of majestic monotheism, is not added on to Paul's poem as a kind of closing flourish, a surface adornment on a poem which has been about something else. Isaiah's extended poem (chapters 40—55) is a statement of that same monotheism, celebrating the strange but victorious work of Israel's God, triumphing over all evil, and his enthronement as the world's true lord. It is a central statement of kingdom-of-God theology in the face of the powers and rulers of the world.

It is, in particular, a central statement, perhaps *the* central statement, of *the return of YHWH to Zion*. The glory will come back (40.5); the watchmen will see and declare it as 'the good news' (40.9); he will come with power, and his 'arm' will rule for him (40.10). He will come as the creator, reducing idols to the worthless rubbish they are, and princes of the earth to irrelevance (40.12–26). He will be with his people on their journey home (43.2). He will act because of his own righteousness; the promise that to him alone every knee shall bow and every tongue shall swear is itself 'a word in righteousness that shall not return' (45.23).[194] He will place salvation in Zion 'for Israel my glory' (46.13).[195] He will bring his righteousness near; his arm

[191] Isa. 45.20–5; the italicized portion, echoed in Phil. 2.10, is v. 23b.

[192] 46.1—47.15.

[193] Isa. 42.8; 48.11.

[194] cf. too 55.11.

[195] The last phrase, *leisraēl tiph'ārthi*, rendered in LXX *tō Israēl eis doxasma*, seems to be a way of expressing the promise that YHWH, in his return to Zion, will glorify Israel with his own 'beauty'.

will rule the peoples (51.5). The messengers who announce the good news will see the great, central event for which Israel had longed:

> How beautiful upon the mountains
> are the feet of the messenger who announces peace,
> who brings good news,
> who announces salvation,
> who says to Zion, 'Your God reigns.'
> Listen! Your sentinels lift up their voices,
> together they sing for joy;
> for in plain sight they see
> the return of YHWH to Zion.
> Break forth together into singing,
> you ruins of Jerusalem;
> for YHWH has comforted his people,
> he has redeemed Jerusalem.
> YHWH has bared his holy arm
> before the eyes of all the nations;
> and all the ends of the earth shall see
> the salvation of our God.[196]

Israel's one God will do all this, comforting and restoring his people (chapter 54) and issuing an invitation to the whole world to come and join in the blessing (chapter 55). And all will be done through the powerful divine 'word' which will not fail to accomplish its purpose (40.8; 45.23; 55.11).

All this might be enough to keep one occupied. But of course the mysterious power of this prophetic tapestry is found in the strange, dark strand which is woven in at four key moments. These are the poems which speak of the vocation and accomplishment of the 'servant', who at one level is 'Israel' and at another level stands over against 'Israel', doing for the people what they cannot do for themselves.[197] And the 'servant', in the final climactic poem, is finally identified as 'the arm of YHWH', albeit unrecognizable in his shameful and disfigured state (53.1). The prophet never resolves this puzzle. Somehow the work of the 'servant', and specifically the redemptive achievement of his suffering and death, are the manifestation in action of the divine 'righteousness', the accomplishment of the divine 'salvation', and above all the full expression of what it means that YHWH, Israel's one God, has at last returned in glory to Zion. He has come back to be enthroned, not only as Israel's true king but as king of the world.

This is, of course, a 'Pauline' exegesis of Isaiah 40—55. So far as I know, the passage was not being read in this way before the public career of Jesus.[198] But when we draw out its central themes in this way and place

[196] Isa. 52.7–10.

[197] The 'servant' poems have often been identified as 42.1–4 (or 1–9?); 49.1–6 (or 1–13?); 50.4–9; 52.13—53.12. But they do not 'come away clean' from the rest of the text; they are stitched closely into the larger whole (cf. e.g. 41.8; 42.19; 43.10; 44.26; 50.10). A Davidic or messianic 'servant' is spoken of in Ezek. 34.23f. and Zech. 3.8. Full discussion in e.g. Balzer 2001, esp. 124–8; Childs 2001, esp. 323–5; Goldingay and Payne 2006, 40, and ad loc.; briefly, e.g. Collins 2009.

[198] For a proposal about Jesus' own understanding of his vocation in the light of Isaiah 40—55, cf. *JVG* 588–91, 601–4.

them as it were on a facing page to Philippians 2.6–11 we discover that not only can a highly plausible case be made for saying that the entire Pauline poem is a fresh meditation on the original Isaianic passage, but that once again Paul's christological revision of Israel's monotheism of divine identity has taken place at its key eschatological moment. *This is what it looked like when YHWH returned to Zion.* The God who refused to share his glory with another has shared it with Jesus; because Jesus has accomplished the task which Israel's God had declared that, at the heart of his 'return', he would accomplish himself. I thus reaffirm the case made recently by Richard Bauckham, that we should almost certainly see here a reference to the Isaianic 'suffering servant'.[199] The idea of the one who is humble and obedient to the divine saving plan, all the way to death, and is then vindicated, is so clearly an echo of the fourth 'song' in particular, and it is so clear that Paul has Isaiah 45 in mind in the climax to the present poem, that it is more reasonable to allow the allusion, and with it the rich scriptural theology of the whole of Isaiah 40—66, than to disallow it out of caution (or, as it may be, out of fear of the theological consequences). Where I go beyond Bauckham is in drawing the implication: Paul, here as elsewhere, is drawing out the christological focus of the ancient Isaianic hope for YHWH's return.

The first thing to note about the present passage, then, is that when read within the context of ancient Jewish hope as expressed classically in scripture it offers itself as a statement of fulfilment. This is how Israel's God came back to do what he had promised.

Second, therefore, this majestic, exultant scriptural declaration of the absolute uniqueness of Israel's God, and his victory over all idols, is the passage chosen as the vehicle through which now to say: the God who will not share his glory with another *has shared it with Jesus.* At the name of *Jesus* 'every knee shall bow, and every tongue confess' (the Septuagint of Isaiah 45.23 has 'shall confess God', *exomologēsetai tō theō*). But what they will now confess is not simply 'God', as in Isaiah, but 'that Jesus, Messiah, is *kyrios*': the last word in that sentence is the first in the Greek, *kyrios Iēsous Christos.* And there can be neither doubt nor cavil, here as in many other cases in Paul, that when Paul writes *kyrios* in relation to Jesus he means his readers to understand, as anyone familiar with the Septuagint would understand, the word YHWH.

The best word for this might be 'explosive'. Paul must have known exactly what he was doing. At the centre of his Jewish-style monotheism is a human being who lived, died and rose in very recent memory. Jesus is not a new God added to a pantheon. He is the human being in whom YHWH,

[199] See in particular Isa. 52.13 (my servant *hypsōthēsetai*, 'shall be exalted') with Phil. 2.9 (therefore God *auton hyperypsōsen*, 'highly exalted him'); Bauckham 2008/9, 205f. shows how Paul appears to have the entire larger picture of Isa. 40—66 in mind, with the 'servant' seen as the means by which YHWH rescues his people and reveals his unique creative and rescuing power. The point does not depend on exact verbal echoes (against the objections of e.g. Hooker 1959, 120f.); notoriously, the LXX for 'servant' here is *pais*, which because of its wider meaning of 'child' would have sent Paul's readers in the wrong direction. What counts is the entire flow of thought, with the explicit verbal and thematic echoes functioning as an anchor.

Israel's one and only God, has acted within cosmic history, human history and Israel's history to do for Israel, humanity and the world what they could not do for themselves. Jesus is to be seen as *part of the identity of Israel's God*, and vice versa. Israel had longed for its God to return after his extended absence. Paul, like the writers of the gospels, saw that longing fulfilled in Jesus.

Third, there should likewise be no doubt that when Paul says that Jesus has received 'the name which is over all names', that name is the holy, divine name, YHWH itself.[200] This theme must then be joined up with Paul's multiple references elsewhere to the 'name' either of God or of Jesus. Now, when people hear the name 'Jesus', they are to bow down, because with that name there is given 'the name above all names'. Jesus, Messiah, is *kyrios*, is YHWH. That is why Paul can speak of things being done 'for the sake of his name', or things happening through Jesus for the sake of God's name. This is a rich seam of thought which we here simply mention.[201] This too is a major monotheistic motif – the 'name' of the one true God over against all the other 'names' that might be named around the world[202] – which Paul has transferred to Jesus himself.

Fourth, the use of such a clear 'YHWH-text' in reference to Jesus opens up the possibility, which has in recent years been extensively studied, of reading several other similar texts the same way. We shall study some of the other central texts in this category in due course.[203]

The fifth point to be noted clearly in Philippians 2.9–11 is the striking differentiation, within this emphatically monotheistic construction, between Jesus the *kyrios* and 'the father'. Confessing Jesus as *kyrios* brings glory to God the father, just as in 1 Corinthians 15.26–8 all things are put in subjection under the Messiah's feet, and then the Messiah himself hands over the sovereignty to the father, so that God is 'all in all'. How are we to explain this remarkable phenomenon (which we shall presently see repeated in other passages)?

One way of explaining this differentiation within a monotheistic statement might be to appeal to pre-Christian Jewish notions of apparently similar phenomena: Philo's *deuteros theos*, for example, or the hypothetical 'great angel' postulated by some as a 'second divinity' within ancient Israel.[204] The work of Richard Bauckham has more or less barred the way to

[200] See now e.g. Bauckham 2008/9, 199f. As Bauckham points out (199 n. 38), however, it may be that Paul was hinting at the fact that the name 'Jesus' itself *contains* the name YHWH, being a contraction of *YHWH yesha*', 'YHWH saves', so that the name 'Jesus' could be 'regarded as a new kind of substitute for or even form of the divine name'.

[201] Jesus' name: Rom. 1.5; 10.13 (see below); 1 Cor. 1.2, 10; 5.4; 6.11; Eph. 1.21; 5.20; Col. 3.17; 2 Thess. 1.12; 3.6. God's name: Rom. 9.17; 15.9; 1 Tim. 3.1; 2 Tim. 2.19; cf. Rom. 2.24. Hence the significance of the early Christian praxis of baptism, prayer, exorcism etc. 'in the name of Jesus'; or indeed suffering 'for his name'.

[202] cf. Eph. 1.21.

[203] Below, 701–7.

[204] See e.g. Barker 1992 and related works. On the idea of 'another god', explaining biblical passages like the revelation to Abraham in Gen. 18, see also Justin Martyr *Dial.* 50, 56. The phrase *deuteros theos* is found in Philo *Quaest. Gen.* 2.62.

this kind of explanation.[205] There were various ways of speaking in a differentiated fashion about the one God of second-Temple Judaism, some of which ways may function in retrospect as signposts to what we find here in Paul. But in no case do they have any sense of referring to an actual human being in recent memory. The one counter-example which might prove the rule is the high-flown language about the Messiah, drawn most likely from Daniel 7 and elsewhere, which as we saw was apparently used by Akiba himself, whose orthodoxy, though not unimpeachable (a clever later rabbi could pick holes in almost anyone), was certainly hard to question at the time.[206] This cautious and apparently risky exploration of the meaning of Messiahship in some strands of Judaism may have provided raw material for the early Christian innovation, but that is rather like saying that the compositor in the music publishing house had a stack of crochets, quavers and minims all ready for the first chord of Beethoven's first symphony. Raw material may be a necessary condition of the music's appearance, but it hardly explains the new thing that then happened. The clear, sharp and unambiguous statements by Paul stand out in a different category from anything we find among his second-Temple near-contemporaries. The only explanation is the obvious one: what drove him to this remarkable fresh use of existing categories, and then to his own coinages out beyond that, was the fact of Jesus – his messianic life and death, and particularly his resurrection and exaltation, without which, of course, his life and death would not have been seen as messianic in the first place.[207]

The sixth point about Philippians 2.9–11 is the way the first half of the poem contributes to the meaning. I have written about this extensively elsewhere and can here briefly summarize. Here are the three stanzas, with Paul's introduction:

> 5This is how you should think among yourselves – with the mind that you have because you belong to the Messiah, Jesus:
>
> 6Who, though in God's form, did not
> Regard his equality with God
> As something he ought to exploit.
>
> 7Instead, he emptied himself,
> And received the form of a slave,
> Being born in the likeness of humans.
>
> And then, having human appearance,
> 8He humbled himself, and became
> Obedient even to death,
> Yes, even the death of the cross.[208]

[205] Bauckham 2008/9, 191 etc.

[206] See Segal 1977.

[207] The question of how several impulses combined to produce 'early christology' is explored further below.

[208] Phil. 2.5–8.

Six sub-points now, apocalypse-like, within this sixth point. First, there is no reasonable doubt that the poem refers to Jesus as the human being who is to be identified with one who, prior to his human conception and birth, was 'in God's form', and who, being already 'equal with God', neither snatched at such a status (he did not need to, since he already possessed it), nor abandoned it, as has often been thought, but rather *gave it its proper interpretation*: not the self-aggrandizement one might have imagined, but a life and a death of self-emptying, humble service.[209]

Second, I persist in thinking that among the many resonances of this poem we are right to discern an echo of Adam in Genesis 1—3. Adam is made to be God's vicegerent over creation, the role which Jesus himself attains in 2.9–11. Adam covets 'equality with God', and thereby incurs the penalty of death; Jesus, already possessing that equality, dies Adam's death as the supreme act of 'obedience', which at once resonates with that most famous Adam/Messiah passage, Romans 5.12–21.[210] The fact that the poem is about much more than this does not mean that we must rule Adam out. On the contrary, the apparent echo of Genesis 1.26 in 2.7, and of Psalm 8.5–6 in the poem as a whole,[211] should alert us to the fact that, though not the main theme, the Adamic reference must not be ignored.[212] Part of Paul's overall narrative world, as we saw, is that God's eventual solution to Israel's plight will thereby solve Adam's plight, and through that in turn re-establish God's kingdom over the whole creation.

[209] See esp. *Climax* ch. 4. My proposals for the reading of v. 6, especially the controverted *harpagmos*, have been widely accepted in recent commentaries and monographs, though not without demur (e.g. Martin 1997 [1967], lxv–lxxiv; this is not the place to attempt a reply to Martin's counter-critique of my earlier criticisms of his proposals).

[210] The 'obedience' of the Messiah comes climactically, as here in 2.8, in Rom. 5.19; it is the category to which Paul has been working up through 'the gift of grace' in 5.15f. and the *dikaiōma* in 5.18.

[211] MT/LXX 8.6–7.

[212] Gen. 1.26: let us make *anthrōpos* according to our image and likeness (*kath' homoiōsin*), to have dominion over all creatures on earth; Phil. 2.7, the Messiah coming to be *en homoiōmati anthrōpōn*, ending up having dominion over everything in heaven, on earth and under the earth. The formulation of 2.6b/c, the Messiah's 'not regarding his equality with God as something to exploit', is not an exact echo of Gen. 3.5, 22 ('you shall be like God' ... 'Adam has become like one of us'), but in the light of the 'obedience' theme of 2.8, resonating with Rom. 5.19, I regard this allusion as probable. In addition, cf. the ref. to Ps. 8.7 in 1 Cor. 15.27, within an 'Adam/Messiah' passage which ends up in a very similar position to Phil. 2.10f. (15.24, 28: the Messiah being subject to God the father, so that God may be all in all; Phil. 2.11: every tongue confessing Jesus the Messiah as *kyrios* to the glory of God the father). The human 'glory', in Ps. 8.5 (MT/LXX 8.6) is explained by the God-given 'dominion' humans are supposed to exercise over the rest of creation, which is 'subjected' to them (*panta hypetaxas hypokatō tōn podōn autou*, 8.7 LXX); cf. the train of thought that runs from Rom. 3.23 (humans lost 'the glory of God') to 8.20f. (creation, having been subjected to humans, waiting for them to be glorified so that it can enjoy its consequent freedom from corruption). Discerning something that might be called an 'Adam-christology' in Phil. 2 does not mean either embracing the idea that pre-Christian Jews could think in terms of 'worshipping' a human being as God's image (against e.g. Fletcher-Louis 1999, esp. 115–17), or using it as a way of ruling out 'pre-existence' (against e.g. Dunn 1980; Murphy-O'Connor 1978). Bauckham (2008/9, 41, repeated at 205) seems to accept Dunn's either/or (*either* 'pre-existence' *or* 'Adam'); it is that antithesis that I am challenging. I share Bauckham's concern, to rule out an interpretation which would say that 2.9–11 expresses 'no more than an Adam Christology', but not his antithesis between 'restoring human dominion over other creatures' and 'establishing YHWH's own unique rule over all of creation'. In line with ch. 7 above I suggest that the latter is accomplished through the former – and that Paul would have seen this as the intention behind Gen. 1.26–8 itself.

Third, we should also see, as I did not see twenty-five years ago in my earlier work on this passage, a clear allusion, relevant not least to the Philippians, to the imperial ideology which, having already been clear enough from the time of Alexander onwards, was now flooding the world in a new form through Augustus and his successors. Jesus is lord, so Caesar is not; his are among the knees that will bow at Jesus' name. The Philippians need to know this if they are to figure out what their own version of 'salvation' means, as opposed to the version which Caesar was enthusiastically proclaiming.[213]

Fourth, this robustly monotheistic poem is introduced primarily in the service of the unity of the church. Verse 5 indicates, not a new topic to verses 1–4, but the way in which their impassioned and detailed appeal for unity is to be accomplished. The Philippians are to think in the same way, to be in full accord, of one mind, having the same love, to renounce ambition and vanity, and to look out for one another's best interests. This apparently impossible ideal is theirs because, being 'in the Messiah', they have 'the mind of the Messiah', as Paul says in 1 Corinthians 2.16; and the Messiah's mind is as we find it in 2.6–8. Learning that mind, and following that path, is the only way to the unity which, as we saw earlier, is so vital as the central feature of Paul's worldview. Here we see, indeed, the development of our key point, the fulcrum of our entire book: for this worldview-symbol to stand, granted that it has been shorn of the symbolic praxis of second-Temple Judaism (circumcision, food laws, sabbath, Temple and so forth), what is required is the robust monotheism that will enable the community to hold firm around its centre. That robust monotheism has been, for Paul, fully rethought around Jesus the Messiah. Messiah-shaped monotheism, focused on self-emptying and crucifixion, is the only thing which will enable the community to hold on to unity and holiness.

Fifth, the poem as it stands thus points onwards to the ecclesiology of 3.2–11. As we shall see in the next chapter, the pattern of christological monotheism turns naturally and properly into the pattern of christological election.

Sixth (the last sub-point): the fulcrum of the poem – the extra line around which everything else balances – is of course the last line of verse 8, *thanatou de staurou*, 'even the death of the cross'. It is indeed possible, as some have suggested, that Paul has added this line in between the carefully balanced three-times-three stanzas of an earlier poem. But it is equally possible that either the poem's original author, or Paul himself if he was that author, saw the Messiah's shameful crucifixion as the paradoxical but utterly appropriate focal point of the whole picture, the moment when the divine purpose was finally unveiled, confronting empires of every sort with the news of God's kingdom, and so placed that line deliberately at the midpoint of the narrative. At the centre of the poem, at the climax of the purpose, at the beating heart of all things, stands the sign of shame and glory:

[213] See below, 1292–9; Oakes 2001; Hellerman 2005; against e.g. Cohick 2011.

all else east or west of Jesus. Exaltation through obedience of God's equal, of the bearer of the name: at this mere mention kings and princes own allegiance.

To return, then, to 2.9–11, after that sixfold digression within the sixth main point, we come at last to the seventh and last one. The flow of thought across the whole poem is remarkably redolent of those ancient stories of Israelite and Jewish heroes, from Joseph to Daniel, who faced shame, humiliation and suffering, and were then exalted to become senior rulers (in Joseph's case, second ruler) in their respective kingdoms.[214] These stories are, again and again, a way of speaking of Israel's God as the one who confronts the pagans with his own kingdom and glory, and whose faithful agents, though suffering in various ways, come to instantiate his rule even in foreign nations. The narratival echoes, resonating back through Israel's scriptures, are thus themselves echoes of specifically Jewish-monotheistic stories. It is not just that Paul has made Isaiah 45.23, that most sternly monotheistic of texts, the key with which to unlock the mysteries of the Messiah's identity and achievement. The door which swings open when that key is turned in the lock is the door to the entire scriptural vision of Israel's one God working out his sovereign purpose through his obedient, and as often as not suffering, servant, and then exalting that servant to power and glory. The radically new note – that the one thus obedient, suffering and glorified is somehow identified as Israel's God himself in person – is of course dramatic and startling, but it does not distort or subvert the larger picture. Indeed, that larger picture always included the promise that Israel's God would come back in person to rescue his people and establish his kingdom, even though nobody imagined that this event would look like the story we find in Matthew, Mark, Luke and John. Paul's picture of Jesus the Messiah, exalted as *kyrios*, does not destroy Jewish monotheism. It fulfils it.

One fascinating verse from another letter may be added here as a tailpiece. Writing to the recalcitrant Corinthians, and teasing them somewhat about the collection money which he was hoping they would have ready in time for his arrival, Paul drops in, almost as a casual aside, a remark about Jesus which, without the other passages we are examining, might be taken in various different ways but which, in the light of Philippians 2 in particular, must be taken as a further indication of the divine status of the one who became human in order to rescue the world:

> You know the grace of our lord, King Jesus: he was rich, but because of you he became poor, so that by his poverty you might become rich.[215]

It is of course open to anyone to point out that the specific means by which Jesus 'made people rich' is the cross, and that since Paul is here asking for

[214] Gen. 37—50, focused here on 41.37–43; Dan. 2.48; 3.30; 5.29. Levenson 1993 observes this theme in relation to Joseph, but Daniel and his companions, not being 'beloved sons', are outside his view.

[215] 2 Cor. 8.9, on which see e.g. Furnish 1984, 417: 'Paul is not speaking about the manner of Jesus' earthly life, but about his incarnation and death as an act of *grace*' (italics original); similarly Thrall 2000, 532–4, against e.g. Dunn 1980, 121–3.

self-sacrificial giving that itself makes good sense in the context. But Jesus' descent from 'rich' to 'poor' does not seem a good description of, say, a supposed contrast between the early and 'successful' days of his Galilean ministry and the later, sorrowful march to the cross. Much more appropriate, with most commentators, is a reading which lines up the verse alongside Philippians 2.6–8. The cross is at the end of the road, to be sure; but the path to the cross begins with the becoming human of the one who from all eternity was 'equal with God'. And, once again, part of the shock of this verse is that Paul can drop such a remark into a different context without any further explanation. He and the Corinthians had many controversial things to sort out, but he could take this point for granted. What he is saying and implying here must be something which was common coin across all his churches, indeed across the whole early church. Without that, he could not so naturally have appealed to it.

(g) Jesus and the Return of YHWH: Conclusion

My argument so far is that the Jewish-style monotheism of 'divine identity' which Paul so emphatically reaffirmed had also emphatically been redrawn around Jesus. In particular, I have argued that in several key passages we can detect the overtones of that exodus-based narrative which formed the basis for the hope that YHWH, having long since abandoned Jerusalem to its fate, would one day return to save his people and to establish his glorious presence in the Temple. As we have seen, there is excellent evidence that this was what Paul intended to convey, in one way and another, in one kind of argument or another. For him, Jesus was to be identified within the second-Temple Jewish belief in who the one God was – *and would be*. This is the full expression of the eschatological dimension of monotheism, carrying within itself also the creational and cultic dimensions. In him, that is to say, Israel's God had indeed returned, and to him therefore could be transferred all that had been said about 'wisdom' as the mode of his presence, the 'wisdom' through which the worlds were made. He was therefore to be discovered in biblical texts which spoke of the *kyrios*, translating the *adonai* which devout Jews said in preference for the sacred name YHWH; and, as such, was to be worshipped, and invoked in prayer.[216] The relationship his followers enjoyed with him was to be understood, and could be spoken of, in the way that devout Israelites from ancient times had spoken of their relationship with YHWH himself. So far, so good.

But is this enough to enable us to understand *why* not only Paul, but apparently all his Christian predecessors and contemporaries, came to this belief? I think not. We have demonstrated *that* Paul (and presumably his predecessors and contemporaries) thought of Jesus in categories belonging to Israel's God, and particularly within the narrative which spoke of the

[216] See below, 701–6.

long-awaited return of this God to Zion. We have not quite explained *why* they would think this way. This brings us to the second major hypothesis of the present chapter.

(iii) Jesus as Risen and Enthroned Messiah

(a) Messiah and 'Son of God'

There are, I suggest, two reasons why Jesus' first followers came to think of him as the embodiment of the returning YHWH. The first has to do with his Messiahship, and we shall examine that now. The second has to do with their sense of his presence through what they understood to be the work of the holy spirit in their hearts and in their midst. We shall examine that in the next section of the chapter.

None of these three lines of approach (the return of YHWH; Jesus' Messiahship; the sense of his continuing presence) constitutes by itself a *sufficient* condition for the rise of the earliest christology such as we find already taken for granted in Paul. Nor would any two of them taken together have been sufficient, I think, without the third. Only the full set of three will do to sustain the historical hypothesis of how this dramatic and extraordinary belief took such a firm hold so early on. Each of these three lines of approach thus constitutes a *necessary* but in itself *insufficient* part of the ultimately sufficient threefold total.

That may seem somewhat abstract; let me put the point more concretely. First, there were plenty of Jews who cherished the hope that YHWH would return one day. None of them came up with anything remotely like early christology. Second, many believed that this or that leader might well be Israel's Messiah. But even Akiba, if rightly reported, did not develop more than a hint of his possible candidate being 'son of the star' in any 'divine' sense. (It is impossible to say what if anything the great sage had in mind by imagining the Messiah sitting on the second of the 'thrones' in Daniel 7.9.) Third, the early Christians did undoubtedly enjoy many vivid 'experiences' of the presence and power of Jesus, but these by themselves would not, I think, have generated the focused and clear set of scriptural echoes and theological articulations which we find in the earliest christology. None of these three lines of approach, then, would by itself generate the kind of evidence we are finding in Paul, our earliest source.

But if, (a) granted the expectation of YHWH's return, (b) a would-be Messiah were to be raised from the dead and thereby vindicated as Messiah, 'son of God'; if such a person were believed to have been exalted to heaven and enthroned as 'lord'; and (c) if his followers were thereafter convinced that he was personally and powerfully present to and with them in a new mode – then the almost instantaneous rise of the christology we find already firmly established by the time of Paul is fully explained. The three elements converge to produce and provide something which none of them, by itself, would have been able to do.

This point places in a larger context the important proposals of Carey Newman and Larry Hurtado. Newman, perhaps twenty years ahead of his time, proposed that the origin of Paul's christology could be found in the motif of 'glory': Paul's experiences of the 'glory' of the exalted Christ convinced him that in Jesus was to be found the divine 'glory' spoken of in scripture.[217] Newman did not explicitly investigate the theme of YHWH's return, or the specific temple-christology which it generates. But even when we place his conception of Paul's (and others') 'experiences' of the glorious Christ within that context, it remains, I suggest, insufficient to explain the christology we actually find. In particular, such experiences do not explain that same most striking title, 'son of God'. That belongs with Messiahship (and with the sense that the Messiah represents Israel, the corporate 'son of God' as in the exodus-narrative). And belief in Jesus' Messiahship depends not on 'exaltation' alone but more specifically on resurrection. Only when we join up the themes of the divine 'return', Messiahship itself (as demonstrated by the resurrection), and the sense of Jesus' continuing presence by the spirit can we explain the phenomena before us.

By the same token, Hurtado's proposal, though vital as a demonstration of just how wrong-headed Bousset's influential construct in fact was, does not in my view go far enough, and places too much weight on the supposed parallels, however partial, between the early Christian view of Jesus and pre-Christian Jewish views of various mediator-figures. Hurtado's emphasis on the context of early Christian worship as the matrix within which christology took shape is I think exactly right as far as it goes, but it fails to take account both of the Jewish hope of YHWH's return and, not least, of the belief in Jesus' Messiahship which had been dramatically confirmed by his resurrection. Indeed Hurtado, like Newman, seems to me to make far too little of the resurrection itself, collapsing it in effect into the concept of 'glorification', and supposing that the early Christian awareness of the latter came through visions and revelations. Such visions and revelations there certainly were, but my point is that without the theme of YHWH's return on the one hand, and the Messiahship of Jesus on the other, demonstrated by the resurrection, they would not have generated that early christology which we find already in Paul.[218] We need a convergence of all three elements to explain the 'why', as well as the 'what', of the earliest christology.

We turn, then, to my hypothesis about the contribution of Jesus' Messiahship to the earliest christology as we see it reflected in Paul.

The starting-point is the meaning of the resurrection itself. When Jesus was found to be bodily alive again three days after his crucifixion, in a transformed physicality for which there was no precedent or expectation, this

[217] Newman 1992.

[218] This comes to a head, for me, in Hurtado 2003, 71–4, though the same questions emerge at several other points too.

convinced his first followers that he really was Israel's Messiah. I have argued this case elsewhere and do not need to repeat the point.[219]

It is of course important to note that resurrection by itself would not mean Messiahship. The Maccabaean martyrs are reported to have predicted their own coming resurrection, and that would not make them Messiahs. If one of the brigands crucified alongside Jesus had been found to be alive again three days later, people would have said the world was a very odd place, but they would not have said he was Messiah. The resurrection, as has often been argued, was taken by the early Christians to demonstrate the truth of the claim which Jesus himself had actually made. He was known to have been crucified as a messianic pretender (the 'title' over his head, 'King of the Jews', must be regarded as historically certain); the resurrection was understood to have reversed the verdict of the court, and thus to have constituted an unambiguous divine declaration that he really was Messiah.

But if Jesus was Messiah, then in some sense or other the central scriptural passages about such a figure must, his followers knew, have come true. Among these, with echoes in Qumran and elsewhere, were of course 2 Samuel 7.12–14 and Psalm 2.7, with their indication that the Messiah would be, in some sense, 'son of God'. This, coupled with the memory of Jesus' own usage of 'father', and indeed 'Abba', in addressing Israel's God, already made it natural for the first disciples to think of him as 'son of God' in this primarily messianic sense. In 2 Samuel 7.12, the early Christians undoubtedly seized on the phrase, 'I will raise up your seed after you,' which appears in the Septuagint as *kai anastēsō to sperma sou meta se*, 'I will *resurrect* your seed after you.' We need look no further for the scripturally generated origins of the statement in Romans 1.3–4: Jesus, from the seed of David according to the flesh, was marked out as 'son of God' through the resurrection from among the dead.[220]

We must note carefully how this argument actually works. I am *not* saying that there was a pre-Christian Jewish belief that the Messiah, if and when he turned up, would be in any sense 'divine'. There are indeed texts which, with hindsight, could be taken to point that way, but despite the best efforts of scholars such as Horbury and Boyarin I remain unconvinced that anyone before Jesus' first followers read them in this sense. Nor am I saying that anyone prior to Jesus' first followers had read 2 Samuel 7.12 as predicting a resurrected Messiah (this is hardly surprising since there is no pre-Christian evidence for a dying Messiah[221]). What I am suggesting is that *the resurrection, demonstrating the truth of Jesus's pre-crucifixion messianic claim, joined up with the expectation of* YHWH*'s return on the one hand and the presence of the spirit of Jesus on the other to generate a fresh reading of 'messianic' texts which enabled a full christological awareness to dawn on the*

[219] cf. *RSG* ch. 19.

[220] See e.g. below, 818f.

[221] The one suggestion of a dying Messiah is in the post-70 *4 Ezra* (7.29); this may itself be dependent on a reading of Dan. 9.26, but again there is no evidence that any pre-Christian writer took that passage in this way.

disciples. I do not think that pre-Christian Jews had read 2 Samuel 7, or Psalm 110 ('YHWH says to my lord, "Sit at my right hand until I make your enemies your footstool"'), or Daniel 7 ('one like a son of man' being exalted to sit on a throne beside that of the 'ancient of days') in ways that anticipated, or could be said to be an antecedent cause of, the very early christology. What I propose is that the combination of (a) the widely held expectation of the divine return to defeat Israel's enemies and rescue his people and (b) Jesus' resurrection, compelling the conclusion that he really was Messiah, created exactly the conditions within which, in a context of (c) worship and an awareness of the presence and power of the same Jesus, texts which had been there all along but never seen in this way (except, perhaps, in sayings of Jesus himself!) sprang into life.[222] The earliest christology was thus firmly anchored in scripture, but the reading of scripture in question was highly innovatory, and did not itself generate the belief.

In particular, the texts I just mentioned quickly attained a prominence within early Christianity which they do not seem to have had before. 2 Samuel 7 is indeed used 'messianically' in the pre-Christian period,[223] but not, as I said, as a prediction of a resurrected Messiah, and not with any sense that the messianic 'son of God' will be identified with the returning YHWH. Psalm 110 crops up all over the early Christian movement, even though we do not find it as a 'messianic' text before then.[224] Daniel 7 was certainly important in pre-Christian Jewish circles, but among the most prominent first-century re-readings of it we find Josephus's implication that it predicts a 'world ruler' and *4 Ezra*'s translation of it into the lion who triumphs over the eagle. In neither case is the 'son of man' figure transformed into the embodiment of Israel's God himself.[225]

What is most striking, I suggest, is that the messianic title 'son of God' came to be used, not least by Paul himself, as the apparently ideal vehicle to express just that combination of ideas I am suggesting. At its ancient heart was the messianic meaning, as in the Psalms and 2 Samuel. But when the early Christians wanted to join this up with their sense that in Jesus Israel's God had returned in person, that very phrase was found to be ideal as a way of expressing differentiation within the identity of the one God, a differentiation with 'wisdom' as its partial explanation: 'when the time had fully come, God sent forth his son ...' The idea of 'wisdom', indeed, helped forge exactly this link, since according to Wisdom of Solomon 7—9 it was simultaneously the self-expression of the one God and the necessary equipment for David's true heir. And, as we saw already in Galatians 4 and Romans 8, the category of 'sonship' at once allowed for expansion to include, as in scripture itself, the whole people of God. This is only comprehensible when we add the spirit into the equation; but, once that is done, the 'sonship' of

[222] For the relevant sayings of Jesus see *JVG*, esp. chs. 11, 12 and 13.

[223] 4Q174 10–14.

[224] Early Christian citations listed in Nestle-Aland: Mt. 22.44; 26.64; Mk. 12.36; 14.62; 16.19; Lk. 20.42f.; 22.69; Ac. 2.34f.; Rom. 8.34; 1 Cor. 15.25; Eph. 1.20; Col. 3.1; Heb. 1.3, 13; 8.1; 10.12.

[225] On Daniel in second-Temple understandings see the frequent discussions in ch. 2 above.

Jesus is shared with all his people. 'Because you are sons, God sent the spirit of his son into our hearts, calling out "Abba, father!".' 'All who are led by the spirit of God are God's sons ... you received the spirit of sonship, in whom we call out "Abba, father".' ... 'Those he foreknew, you see, he also marked out in advance to be shaped according to the model of the image of his son, so that he might be the firstborn of a large family.'[226] And so on.

It is important, therefore, to explore further this category of 'son of God'. People used to appeal to this phrase as though one could thereby 'prove' a high christology in Paul. Older commentaries on Romans 1.3–4 sometimes suggested that Paul was affirming Jesus' 'humanity' and 'divinity' when he declared that Jesus was descended from David's seed 'according to the flesh' and then designated 'son of God in power' through the resurrection.[227] It used to be accepted without question that when Paul referred to Jesus as 'son of God' he was expressing, more or less, a high, virtually Nicene, christology – which he had very likely obtained by drawing on non-Jewish sources for the phrase.[228] That (the non-Jewish origin of the phrase, and the attendant ideas) is the view of Bousset which Hurtado rightly rejects, though without seeing the way in which Paul allows the messianic meaning of 'son of God' then to become the vehicle through which he can appropriately express the simultaneous sense that in this Messiah Israel's one God has at last returned to his people.[229] That older way of reading 'son of God' was called into question when it was pointed out (for instance by Martin Hengel) that the phrase had three possible meanings at the time, all rooted in Israel's scriptures and re-expressed variously in second-Temple literature: first, angels or angelic beings, as in Genesis and Job;[230] second, Israel as a whole, especially at the time of the exodus;[231] third, the son of David, sometimes seen as the coming Messiah.[232] The first of these seems not to be in Paul's mind (nobody has seriously suggested that his view of Jesus as 'son of God' has anything to do with the kind of angelic beings mentioned in Genesis and Job), but the second and particularly the third – which are themselves after all closely linked, since part of the role of the king, it may be suggested, is to sum up the national life of Israel in himself – are extremely relevant. We shall explore this further in the next chapter. But our present task is to look at the ways in which the 'messianic' meaning of the phrase comes to take on fresh meaning, in Paul at least and arguably earlier, through its association with the 'sending' of the son as *the mode of divine return*. Paul has not left the messianic sense behind. As we see at various points in his

226 Gal. 4.6; Rom. 8.14f., 29.

227 e.g. Lightfoot 1904, 245.

228 As still, for instance, in A. Y. Collins 1999.

229 Hurtado 2003, 22f.

230 Gen. 6.2; cf. Job. 1.6; 2.1; 38.7.

231 Ex. 4.22f. (Israel as God's firstborn son); Jer. 31[LXX 38].9 ('I have become a father to Israel, and Ephraim is my firstborn'); Hos. 11.1 ('when Israel was a child I loved him, and out of Egypt I called my son'). Cf. too e.g. *Pss. Sol.* 18.4.

232 2 Sam. 7.14; 1 Chr. 17.13; Pss. 2.7, 12; 89.26f. The refs. from 2 Sam. and Ps. 2 are both included in 4Q174 10–13; cf. 4Q246 2.1. Hengel 1976 remains a classic statement of the evidence.

writings, it remains presupposed, and loadbearing. But he has, as it were, discovered a further sense hidden within it. One might say that Messiahship turns out to have been a category designed for the personal use of Israel's God himself.

This is where something that was already part of Paul's mental furniture seems to have opened up to disclose a deeper truth than had previously been suspected. People have tried from time to time to discern incarnational hints within pre-Christian messianic speculation, but as we have seen these remain uncertain and imprecise.[233] What we have in Paul is firm and clear:

> This is how God demonstrates his own love for us: the Messiah died for us while we were still sinners. [9]How much more, in that case – since we have been declared to be in the right by his blood – are we going to be saved by him from God's coming anger! [10]When we were enemies, you see, we were reconciled to God through the death of his son; if that's so, how much more, having already been reconciled, shall we be saved by his life.[234]

> [3]For God has done what the law (being weak because of human flesh) was incapable of doing. God sent his own son in the likeness of sinful flesh, and as a sin-offering; and, right there in the flesh, he condemned sin. [4]This was in order that the right and proper verdict of the law could be fulfilled in us, as we live not according to the flesh but according to the spirit.[235]

> [29]Those he foreknew, you see, he also marked out in advance to be shaped according to the model of the image of his son, so that he might be the firstborn of a large family.[236]

> [31]What then shall we say to all this? If God is for us, who is against us? [32]God, after all, did not spare his own son; he gave him up for us all! How then will he not, with him, freely give all things to us? [33]Who will bring a charge against God's chosen ones? It is God who declares them in the right. [34]Who is going to condemn? It is the Messiah, Jesus, who has died, or rather has been raised; who is at God's right hand, and who also prays on our behalf! [35]Who shall separate us from the Messiah's love? . . . [38]I am persuaded, you see, that neither death nor life, nor angels nor rulers, nor the present, nor the future, nor powers, [39]nor height nor depth nor any other creature will be able to separate us from the love of God in the Messiah, Jesus our lord.[237]

> [19]I have been crucified with the Messiah. [20]I am, however, alive – but it isn't me any longer, it's the Messiah who lives in me. And the life I do still live in the flesh, I live within the faithfulness of the son of God, who loved me and gave himself for me.[238]

> [4]But when the fullness of time arrived, God sent out his son, born of a woman, born under the law, [5]so that he might redeem those under the law, so that we might receive adoption as sons.

[233] See particularly e.g. O'Neill 1980; Horbury 1998; and now Boyarin 2012. It is safe to say that most scholars have yet to be convinced by this proposal. Certainly we do not need to presuppose any such thing for the development of early high christology to be comprehensible.

[234] Rom. 5.8–10.

[235] Rom. 8.3f.

[236] Rom. 8.29.

[237] Rom. 8.31–5, 38f. Clearly, Rom. 8 as a whole is structured as (among many other things) a major treatment of Jesus as Messiah/son of God, fulfilling the divine purpose through his death and the sending of the spirit into the hearts of those who now share his 'sonship' as younger siblings (nb. the close parallels between 8.15–17 and Gal. 3.28f.; 4.4–7).

[238] Gal. 2.19b–20.

> [6]And, because you are sons, God sent out the spirit of his son into our hearts, calling out 'Abba, father!' [7]So you are no longer a slave, but a son! And, if you're a son, you are an heir, through God.[239]

These dense, rich passages, in each case gathering to a greatness a whole flowing argument, express the two traditional senses ('son of God' as (a) Messiah and (b) Israel-in-person). Indeed, it is partly the obvious linkage of those two, in passages like Romans 8 and Galatians 4, which presses the case that Paul saw Israel's king as summing up his people in himself, to which we shall return. But the point of God *sending* the 'son' introduces a new element. One could say, as Isaiah did, that God had 'sent' the 'servant', or a prophet, or the Messiah. This 'sending', though not directly linked to any 'son of God' reference, does seem to echo Paul's language in these passages:

> Draw near to me, hear this!
> From the beginning I have not spoken in secret, from the time it came to be I have been there.
> And now the Sovereign YHWH has sent me (*apestalken me*) and his spirit.[240]

> The spirit of the Sovereign YHWH is upon me, because YHWH has anointed me;
> he has sent me (*apestalken me*) to bring good news to the oppressed . . .[241]

The sending of a figure equipped with (or accompanied by) the spirit, to do YHWH's work of salvation, fits well within the larger framework of Isaiah 40—66 which was, arguably, one of Paul's two or three favourite scriptural passages. We cannot demonstrate that he had these passages in mind, but we do not need to. The key point is that the 'sending' here implies someone going with a commission from Israel's God to do the work of rescue which will require this figure to be equipped with the spirit of this God. That by itself would not be enough (were we constructing a christology from scratch around this point rather than filling in significant details within a pattern already established) to make us say, 'Ah: so the Messiah is "sent from God", and is therefore in some sense "divine".' But two further considerations point strongly in this direction – in the direction, that is, of understanding 'the sending of the son' in Romans 8 and Galatians 4, and the other 'son of God' passages just noted, to be further signs that, for Paul, Jesus is seen as the second self (so to speak) of Israel's God.

First, there is the notion, which we have already explored, of the figure of Wisdom being 'sent' from God, sent into the world which was made 'through' Wisdom in the first place. Second, there is the remarkable picture in Romans 5 and 8 of the son's death as revealing the father's *love*. This makes no sense unless in some sense father and son are identified, much more closely even than Abraham and Isaac (the obvious biblical paradigm for a father giving up a son to death). In Abraham's case, this was a test of

239 Gal. 4.4–7.

240 Isa. 48.16.

241 Isa. 61.1.

obedience, a challenge to see whether his love for God would override his love for his son. But in God's case, the giving up of the son is seen as God's own love for the world, not only for his people Israel but for the whole creation.

This, perhaps, is why reference to the Aqedah (the 'Binding' of Isaac, as in Genesis 22) is always muted in Paul. He cannot, I think, have been ignorant of the semi-parallel, and seems to allude to it in Romans 8.31–2.[242] But the differences between the two pictures are as important as the similarities, and it is never simply a matter of 'God displacing Abraham' in a traditional picture, still less of 'Jesus displacing Isaac' in a plot-line which otherwise continues as before, only now with a different cast.[243] It is actually a significantly *different* narrative, and we might even say that Paul is *correcting* the already dominant understanding of the story of Abraham and Isaac, relativizing it (and its very ethno-specific application) in favour of the larger story which, he might say, has been supplanted by the growth of the Aqedah-tradition: the equally biblical story of Israel's God sending the servant, or sending 'Wisdom', to accomplish his saving purpose.[244]

So why does Paul stress the sending of the *son*? Quite possibly because he has already developed, or has even inherited from earlier tradition, ways of speaking and praying which belong with a christological monotheism (and, as Bauckham rightly suggests, an eschatological and cultic, as well as creational and covenantal, christological monotheism). These ways of speaking, as we have already seen, identify 'God' as the source and goal of all things by designating him 'father', even while Jesus is designated 'lord', *kyrios*. We might then hypothesize a development in several stages, though as always with such things there is no way we can plot these chronologically. One might imagine the very early Christians, under the impact of the resurrection of Jesus and the fresh scriptural study which it precipitated, doing a variety of interlocking things very early on:

1. using *theos* for God the source and goal of all things, and *kyrios* for Jesus, as in 1 Corinthians 8.6, aware that these corresponded to the Hebrew *elohim* and YHWH, and intending to stress both the unity and the differentiation between the two of them;
2. using the biblical term 'father' to denote God/*theos*/*elohim*;
3. drawing in the originally messianic title 'son of God', already in use for Jesus because of its Davidic overtones and because of Jesus' own way of speaking, as the natural corollary of this 'father'. The one denoted as *theos* is thus seen as 'father' specifically of this 'son', and

[242] Jewett 2007, 536f., reviews the debate and, pointing out that actually the language of 'sparing' and 'handing over' is used quite widely in the LXX and the ancient world in general, agrees with the many who deny that the Aqedah is in Paul's mind here. Hurtado 1999b, 231f. disagrees: the allusion is intended, probably 'to bring a powerful emotive force to the statement'. This does not, however, amount to a transfer of theological capital from the Abraham story to the death of Jesus.

[243] See the wider discussion in e.g. Levenson 1993.

[244] Further details on the debate about possible Pauline use of the Aqedah motif can be found in Jewett, loc. cit.

the one denoted as *kyrios* is seen as 'son' specifically of this 'father', even when that connection is not made explicitly;
4. speaking of 'father and son' in parallel to speaking of 'God and lord';
5. drawing on the 'wisdom' traditions, which were already in use in terms of both the return of YHWH to Zion (Sirach 24) and the equipping of David's son for his royal task (Wisdom 7—9), to speak of the father 'sending' the son (Romans 8.3; Galatians 4.4), and of the father transferring people into 'the kingdom of the son of his love' (Colossians 1.12–13, with the great 'wisdom'-poem of 1.15–20 to follow), and of the *kyrios* as the one through whom all things were made (1 Corinthians 8.6; Colossians 1.16);
6. understanding the whole sequence in terms of the climactic and decisive rescuing act of the one God, the new exodus in which this God had revealed himself fully and finally precisely in fulfilling his ancient promises, saving his people and coming to dwell in their midst.

All this, I stress, is necessarily hypothetical. Unless fresh evidence from the first twenty years of the Jesus-movement were to turn up (the age-old dream of a Christian archaeologist!) it remains impossible to demonstrate that any such sequence of thought actually took place. And 'a sequence of thought' has nothing to do with chronological extension. A mind well stocked with scripture, allied to a heart understanding itself to be transformed by the spirit and attuned to the worship of Jesus, could grasp in an instant what we are forced to reconstruct slowly and carefully. But I submit that this does seem to reflect some aspects of the data we actually possess. Interestingly, though move (4) seems somewhat obvious, Paul seldom uses the word 'father' in direct connection to a designation of Jesus as 'son'. The closest we come in the passages already discussed is where believers cry 'Abba, father', because the spirit of the son has been sent into their hearts, and in Colossians 1.12–14, where 'the father' has 'transferred us into the kingdom of the son of his love'.

All this indicates that, if Paul had been aware of any quasi-divine status accorded to a coming Messiah in the pre-Christian Jewish world, he does not appear to build on such a notion. Rather, he *works up to this conclusion*. He regarded the Messiah as 'divine', in the senses so far explored, not because 'everyone knew' (or some people supposed) that the Messiah would be 'divine', but because of Jesus himself. The person of Jesus himself, and the events of his death, resurrection and exaltation, indicated so firmly that he was to be discerned as the personal presence of Israel's returning God that it was natural to look back at the messianic categories, particularly the striking phrase 'son of God', and to discern within such phraseology hints both of a previously unsuspected identity and of a richly appropriate way of expressing it. In particular, Paul saw in Jesus the shocking and explosive vision of *Israel's God returning at last, as he had always promised*. The 'glory' of Israel's God, which had departed from the Temple so long before, just as had been threatened at the time of the golden calf incident, had returned at last: not, as in Exodus, with God hiding his face so that Moses could only see his back, but rather with his glory shining in full strength 'in the face of Jesus the Messiah', so that those indwelt by the spirit could themselves behold that glory 'with unveiled face'.[245]

All this then plays back into a fresh consideration both of the underlying christology of Romans 1.3–4 and of its essentially monotheistic framework and claim:

> [1]Paul, a slave of Messiah Jesus, called to be an apostle, set apart for God's good news, [2]which he promised beforehand through his prophets in the sacred writings – [3]the good news about his son, who was descended from David's seed in terms of flesh, [4]and who was marked out powerfully as God's son in terms of the spirit of holiness by the resurrection of the dead: Jesus, the Messiah, our lord!
>
> [5]Through him we have received grace and apostleship to bring about believing obedience among all the nations for the sake of his name.[246]

Look first at the classic signs of second-Temple monotheism in this, the grand and solemn opening to Paul's greatest letter.[247] The 'good news' of the one true God, looking back to the Isaianic proclamation on the one hand and out to the imperial announcements on the other, already speaks of the creator God who claims the whole world, and who therefore confronts idols and rulers who try to claim that world for themselves. This is further highlighted in verse 5: Paul's apostleship itself is grounded in the revised monotheism which addresses 'all the nations'. As is now more frequently noted than it used to be, this introduction forms a circle with the dramatic conclusion of the theological exposition of the letter in 15.7–13, where, quoting Isaiah 11.10, Paul speaks of the Davidic Messiah who 'rises to rule the nations, and in [whom] the nations shall hope' (15.12). Again, it is the resurrection that unveils the messianic identity, and with it the summons to worship, to 'hope in him'. This is deeply monotheistic language, of the second-Temple creational, covenantal, cultic and especially eschatological variety. And it joins up exactly with second-Temple messianic expectations, though until Jesus nobody, so far as we know, had thought of making that link.

Further, in Romans 1.4 the resurrection of Jesus had now 'marked him out' as what he already was: God's son, the Messiah. Many others of David's line had come and gone. Some from that extended family, for all we know, might even have been crucified (thousands of young Jews suffered that fate in the suppression of earlier rebellions). What marked Jesus out, what made the early Christians say 'he really was God's son', was not his death, but the

[245] 2 Cor. 3.12—4.6. See above, 677–80, and below, 1091f.

[246] Rom. 1.1–5.

[247] Which has often been marginalized in the haste to get on to 'the righteousness of God' in 1.16–17 – and in the eagerness to protect Paul from any stress on Jesus' Davidic Messiahship; as though Paul would introduce so splendid a letter with irrelevant throwaway remarks incorporating formulae he did not even fully agree with (so rightly e.g. Fee 2007, 243). For this point, and for the exegesis, see Wright, *Romans*, 416–9.

resurrection which vindicated the claims, both explicit and implicit, he had made during his public career, and which therefore unveiled the identity he had possessed all along – and which therefore also unveiled a new and hitherto unsuspected meaning for his death: a decisive, redemptive meaning.[248]

It is important to stress here, as I have done elsewhere, that though the resurrection thus *unveils* what was there before, it does not *confer or create* a new status or identity for Jesus.[249] The key word *horisthentos*, with its root meaning to do with 'marking a boundary', and hence 'defining' or 'determining', has to do with the public clarification, validation or vindication of a previously made claim, not with a claim or status newly introduced. That is quite clear for three reasons. First, in the passages we studied earlier it is the death of God's son that reveals God's love in Romans 5 and 8, and for that to make any sense Jesus must obviously have been 'God's son' when he was crucified. Second, in Romans 1.3–4 itself, the messianic status of 'son of David' already, according to Psalm 2 and 2 Samuel 7, implied that this person was 'son of God', so that the logical order of verses 3 and 4 has the force of a Davidic messianic claim to divine sonship being then validated in the resurrection. Third, and also in this passage, the whole double clause is introduced by the phrase 'the gospel of God ... concerning his son': in other words, the 'son' is the subject of the whole sequence. If there is anything new about Jesus' post-resurrection sonship in this verse, it is simply that his sonship, possessed all along, is now 'in power'.[250]

Indeed, when Paul elsewhere speaks of God 'sending his son', he clearly refers in Galatians 4.4 to his human conception and birth ('born of a woman'), and we may assume that meaning for Romans 8.3 as well, echoing across to Philippians 2.6–8:

> God sent his own son in the likeness of sinful flesh (*en homoiōmati sarkos hamartias*), and as a sin-offering; and, right there in the flesh, he condemned sin.[251]

> Instead, he emptied himself, and received the form of a slave, being born in the likeness of humans (*en homoiōmati anthrōpōn genomenos*). And then, having human appearance, he humbled himself, and became obedient even to death, yes, even the death of the cross.[252]

[248] I say 'hitherto unsuspected', because though the gospels portray Jesus trying to explain this in advance to his followers they also insist that the disciples did not understand it: see e.g. Mk. 10.35–45.

[249] One still meets the suggestion that *horizein* here indicates the conferring of a new status previously unpossessed: e.g. Skarsaune 2002, 307 n. 12. Jewett 2007, 104 claims that Allen 1970 'has shown that *horisthentos* ... in 1:4 is derived from the royal decree language of Ps 2:7 with close analogues in the Aramaic section of Daniel', and deduces from this that the word here means 'installed' in the messianic office. But Allen's argument, which in any case touches only very briefly on Rom. 1.4, is thin, admitting from the start that the 'decree' in LXX Ps. 2.7 is *prostagma*, and speaking of the putative link with Daniel as merely 'conceivable'.

[250] So e.g. Cranfield 1975, 62. Cf. Fitzmyer 1993, 234f., who translates 'established', and comments, 'Before the resurrection Jesus Christ was the Son of God in the weakness of his human existence; as of the resurrection he is the Son of God established in power ...'

[251] Rom. 8.3.

[252] Phil. 2.7f.

Thus, just as in Philippians 2 we saw solid evidence that Paul was identifying the human Jesus as the one who from the beginning was 'equal with God', so in Romans 8.3 and Galatians 4.4 we should be clear that the 'sending of the son', while retaining the messianic overtones of Psalm 2, 2 Samuel 7 and Psalm 89,[253] now clearly also incorporates the theme of what came to be called 'incarnation'. By that I refer to the conception and birth, as a human being, of one who in retrospect is discerned as 'God's son', not just in the messianic or 'Israel' sense but in a sense which passages such as Philippians 2, 1 Corinthians 8 and Colossians 1 attempted to express in the mode of doxology, poetry and prayer.

The joining together of God the father and Jesus the lord is of course regularly made explicit in the opening greetings formulae, or general introductory remarks, of several of the letters. Paul's standard greetings convey 'grace and peace from God the father and the lord Jesus the Messiah': all the letters except Colossians and 1 Thessalonians follow this pattern more or less word for word.[254] While it is noticeable that Paul's habitual phraseology does not include the immediate coupling of 'father' and 'son', preferring 'father' and 'lord', he can with no difficulty speak of the 'son' in the same breath.

All this points to a further element of messianic identification. Not only is the Messiah 'son of God'; he is also *kyrios*, 'lord'. And, in case there were any doubt about his meaning, it has repeatedly been demonstrated in recent times that Paul used this term as a further way of identifying Jesus within the 'divine identity' of YHWH himself.

(b) Jesus as *Kyrios*, Especially in Biblical Quotations

It is now a commonplace to point out that Paul regularly referred to Jesus using scriptural quotations where the Septuagintal word *kyrios* stands for the Tetragrammaton, YHWH.[255] We have seen that in 1 Corinthians 8.6 and

[253] Note the important echoes of Ps. 2 in Rom. 8.17: the 'inheritance' of the messianic 'son' is now the whole world; cp. too 1 Cor. 15.20–8.

[254] Rom. 1.7 (and see the opening flourishes of 1.1, 3f., 6 and 9, with their various linkings of God and Jesus); 1 Cor. 1.3; 2 Cor. 1.2; Gal. 1.3 (see too 1.1: Paul's apostleship is 'through Jesus the Messiah and God the father who raised him from the dead'); Eph. 1.2; Phil. 1.2; 2 Thess. 1.2; Philem. 3. Col. 1.2 simply has 'grace to you and peace from God the father'; several MSS, including very good ones, have naturally added 'and the lord Jesus the Messiah', but the absence of the phrase from many others provides very strong evidence for the shorter reading, being obviously *lectio difficilior*. 1 Thess. 1.1 speaks of 'the church of the Thessalonians in God the father and the lord Jesus the Messiah', so does not repeat that phrase after the following 'grace to you and peace'. 1 Tim. 1.2 and 2 Tim. 1.2 follow the standard pattern, but add 'mercy' to 'grace and peace'; Tit. 1.4 has 'grace and peace from God the father and the Messiah Jesus, our saviour', in line with the emphasis on 'saviour' and its cognates later in the letter (1.3, 4; 2.10, 11, 13; 3.4, 5, 6).

[255] As is well known, in many MSS the LXX does not translate the Hebrew YHWH, but sometimes instead writes either the Hebrew consonants, or Greek letters that are visually similar, or a Greek transliteration (*IAO* or near equivalent). Where, as often, the MSS have *kyrios*, this is a translation, not of YHWH, but of *adon*, 'lord', which was already, in the second-Temple period, the regularly used reverent periphrasis. Bauckham 2008/9, 190 n. 27 is correct to say that *kyrios* is a substitute, not a translation, for YHWH, but it is surely a *translation* precisely of the Hebrew *substitute*.

Philippians 2.11 Paul quotes two of the most obvious 'monotheistic' passages in the whole of Israel's scripture (the *Shema* in the first case, Isaiah 45 in the second). He clearly intends in these passages that the *kyrios*, which in the original stands for YHWH, should now be understood to refer to Jesus himself. Paul is of course quite capable of using *kyrios* in a Septuagint quotation simply to refer to Israel's God, not necessarily to Jesus at all. He is neither wooden nor formal in his usage. But in many passages the reference is clear, and these need to be logged as part of Paul's major and revolutionary redefinition of second-Temple monotheism around Jesus himself.[256]

An obvious place to pick up the thread is Romans 14.11. We have already looked at the passage in another connection, and it is another occasion when, as in Philippians 2, Paul quotes Isaiah 45.23. This is one of the cases when it is not immediately apparent whether the reference is to God himself or to Jesus:

> 7None of us lives to ourselves; none of us dies to ourselves. 8If we live, we live to the lord, and if we die, we die to the lord. So, then, whether we live or whether we die, we belong to the lord. 9That is why the Messiah died and came back to life, so that he might be lord both of the dead and of the living. 10You, then: why do you condemn your fellow Christian? Or you: why do you despise a fellow Christian? We must all appear before the judgment seat of God, 11as the Bible says:
>
> As I live, says the Lord, to me every knee shall bow,
> and every tongue shall give praise to God.
>
> 12So then, we must each give an account of ourselves to God.[257]

One natural way of reading this passage is to take the reference to the 'judgment seat of God' in verse 10, the 'praise to God' in the Isaiah quotation, and the 'giving account to God' in verse 12, as together indicating that 'the Lord' in the Isaiah quotation is likewise a straightforward reference to God the creator, the father, the judge. However, a case can nevertheless be made for reading 'the Lord' here as referring to Jesus, as in Philippians 2.

The case for the reference to Jesus depends on the earlier part of the passage, where verse 9 stresses that the Messiah who 'died and came back to life' (*apethanen kai ezēsen*) now rules as lord over both dead and living, a theme which is then picked up in the phrase 'As I live, says the Lord' (*zō egō, legei kyrios*) at the start of the quotation.[258] I am inclined to follow those scholars who have argued that this is the determinative context, and that therefore the first line in the Isaiah couplet refers to Jesus and the second to God, very much as in the double reference in Philippians 2.10–11.[259] We have here, then, a probable further coupling of Jesus' messianic identity (as the coming judge[260]) with his embodiment of the returning YHWH himself.

256 See esp. Capes 1992; 2004; Bauckham 2008/9, 191–94.

257 Rom. 14.7–12.

258 It is not clear why else Paul has borrowed *zō egō* from Isa. 49.18 as the preface for his quotation of 45.23; see the discussion in Wagner 2002, 336–8.

259 Capes 2004, 129, following Black 1973, 167, against e.g. Cranfield 1975, 1979, 710.

260 From Ps. 2.7–9 etc., as well as obvious passages such as Isa. 11.1–10. In the NT cf. e.g. Ac. 10.42; 17.31; Rom. 2.16; 2 Cor. 5.10.

A less controversial and equally important reference to Jesus as *kyrios* within a scriptural quotation where *kyrios* stands for the divine name is found earlier in Romans, in 10.13:

> [12]For there is no distinction between Jew and Greek, since the same lord is lord of all, and is rich towards all who call upon him. [13]'All who call upon the name of the lord', you see, 'will be saved.'[261]

This is the climax of what is arguably the central passage of Romans 9—11, the point around which the rest of the argument revolves.[262] Paul has told the great story of Israel, from Abraham to the Messiah (9.6—10.4), arguing that in the *Christos*, however paradoxically, God's single purpose and promise from the beginning has found its *telos*, its goal. The result is that the covenant renewal spoken of in Deuteronomy 30 has been inaugurated, and the way to participate in that renewal is precisely to confess Jesus as *kyrios* and to believe that God raised him from the dead (10.9). Paul then amplifies and supports this with two scriptural quotations, first from Isaiah 28.16 ('all who believe in him will not be put to shame'), and then, decisively, from LXX Joel 3.5: 'All who call upon the name of the Lord will be saved'.[263] The context makes it clear both that this refers to Jesus himself, the one who is confessed as *kyrios*, and that Paul intends the full meaning of *kyrios*/YHWH to resonate across from Joel's statement to his own. Once again an essentially *messianic* narrative (with the *Christos* as the goal of Israel's long story) opens up to indicate that this *Christos* is to be identified with the *kyrios* of the Septuagint.

This is not simply a happy linguistic accident in which 'those who call on YHWH's name' happens to have a double referent through being (a) a regular scriptural way of denoting God's people and connoting their faithful allegiance to him over other gods and (b) a regular early Christian way of demarcating the followers of Jesus (though both of these are true as well).[264] The point is more organic than that. Joel's statement coheres with the Deuteronomy passage in pointing to the renewal of the covenant, following the repentance of Israel and the confession that YHWH is indeed her God, 'and there is no other'.[265] Deuteronomy 30 envisaged the transformation of the people's hearts; Joel indicates that God will pour out his spirit upon all flesh, which for Paul elsewhere in Romans is the means by which that heart-transformation will come about.[266] The two naturally go together in Paul's mind. Both passages envisage the coming eschatological moment. In the case of Deuteronomy, this moment will be the ultimate 'return from exile',

[261] Rom. 10.12f.

[262] See Rowe 2000; Wright 2002 [*Romans*], 665f.; and below, 1161–4.

[263] EVV Joel 2.32. The passage (2.28–32 = MT 3.1–5) was popular in early eschatological Christian discourse: cf. e.g. Mt. 24.29; Mk. 13.24; Ac. 2.17–21, 39; Rev. 6.12, 17; 8.7; 14.1.

[264] e.g. 1 Cor. 1.2 and e.g. Ac. 2.21; 9.14, 21; 22.16; 2 Tim. 2.22; for the scriptural background cf. Gen. 4.26; 1 Chr. 16.8; Pss. 99.6; 105.1; 116.4, 13, 17; Isa. 12.4.

[265] Joel 2.27.

[266] Rom. 2.25–9; 7.4–6; 8.5–8.

while for Joel there will be signs in the heavens and on the earth, anticipating 'the great and terrible day of YHWH'.[267] At that time, says the prophet, 'everyone who calls on the name of YHWH will be saved'. Romans 10 thus joins up closely with Philippians 2 and the other texts we have studied. It strengthens and broadens the picture we have been drawing of Paul's christologically revised Jewish monotheism, especially in its eschatological form, and it does so from within an explicitly messianic context.[268]

If this is right, it opens up a possible 'incarnational' reading of Romans 10.6 as well which joins up with the theme explored earlier, that of Jesus as the embodiment of the return of YHWH.[269] I have argued elsewhere that Paul's exegesis of Deuteronomy 30 in Romans 10.6–8 belongs exactly with his understanding of the entire story of Israel from Abraham to the present, with the climax of the story being the arrival of the Messiah, the *telos nomou*, in 10.4.[270] Now, Paul declares, the long-range prophecy of Deuteronomy 30 has been fulfilled: there is a new kind of 'doing of Torah' available through the Messiah and the spirit, and all who 'do Torah' in this way will be saved. But Paul appears to find a further level of meaning within the text. One does not need to go up to heaven, 'to bring the Messiah down' (10.6), or to go down to the depths, 'to bring the Messiah up from the dead' (10.7). The meaning of the second is obvious, but what about the first? Commentators are divided. Some see the incarnation here; others, the second coming.[271] But the way Paul develops the thought strongly favours the former. In 10.9 he explains: 'if you profess with your mouth that Jesus is lord, and believe in your heart that God raised him from the dead, you will be saved.' If the latter half corresponds, as it does, to 10.7, we should assume that the former half is intended to correspond to 10.6:

If you profess with your mouth that Jesus is lord (10.9a) ... to bring the Messiah down (10.6)

[267] Joel 2.31 (LXX 3.4).

[268] On all this see Capes 2004, 127f.; and nb. esp. Davis 1996. These Pauline passages are in my judgment the clearest OT YHWH-texts he applies to Jesus; Capes makes a case also for 1 Cor. 1.31; 2.16 (see Bauckham 2008/9, 182); 2 Cor. 10.17. The texts he applies to God are Rom. 4.7f.; 9.27, 29; 11.34; 15.9, 11; 1 Cor. 3.20; 2 Cor. 6.18. One might also suggest that *kyrios* in Rom. 11.11 refers to Jesus, but that is not necessary for the basic point to stand. Bauckham 2008/9, 191–3, has something of a maximal list of scriptural *kyrios*-references to Jesus: in addition to Rom. 10.13 (Joel 2.32); Rom. 14.11; Phil. 2.10f. (Isa. 45.23), already discussed, he lists 1 Cor. 2.15 (*sic*: sc.=2.16) (Isa. 40.13); 1 Cor. 1.31; 2 Cor. 10.17 (Jer. 9.24) (the 1 Cor. ref. seems to me more secure); 1 Cor. 10.22 (Dt. 32.21a); 1 Thess. 3.13 cf. 2 Thess. 1.7 (Zech. 14.5b) (see below); 2 Thess. 1.9 (Isa. 2.10, 19, 21); 2 Thess. 1.7, 12 (Isa. 66.5, 15). The refs. in 2 Thess. 1, where 'the lord' in v. 9 is flanked by 'the lord Jesus' in v. 7 and 'the lord Jesus the Messiah' in v. 12, resonating with their various LXX echoes, seem clear in their application of *kyrios* to Jesus.

[269] On this see too Capes 2007, 139–48, against e.g. Dunn 1980, 184–7. Capes also suggests (136–9) that the 'stone' in Rom. 9.32f., while echoing a prophecy (Isa. 8.14; 28.16) in which YHWH himself is the 'stumbling stone', reapplies that to the Messiah, so that 'he associates Christ with YHWH and posits him in an eschatological role that scripture reserves for God' (139). Capes does not, however, explore the theme of YHWH's return or its relevance here and elsewhere.

[270] See Wright 2002 [*Romans*], 655–8; and below, 1035, 1172.

[271] See Wright 2002 [*Romans*], 663, citing Cranfield, Fitzmyer and Moo for the former and Käsemann and Dunn for the latter. My present argument significantly strengthens and amplifies the case for the former. Jewett 2007, 625–7, ignores this question and focuses instead on a possible Pauline polemic against zealous Jewish attempts to hasten the coming of the Messiah.

> and believe that God raised him from the dead (10.9b) ... to bring the Messiah up from the dead (10.7)

But the confession 'Jesus is lord' (10.9a) is at once spelled out, as we have just seen, in the strong affirmation, replete with Septuagintal YHWH-echoes, that 'the same lord is lord of all' and that 'all who call upon the name of the lord will be saved' (10.12–13). This implies that in 10.6, as well, Paul is thinking not simply of the 'coming of the Messiah' in a purely human sense, nor yet of his second coming, but of *YHWH himself arriving in the person of the Messiah*, at the climax of the story of Israel.

Paul was after all working, all through, with the larger second-Temple narrative in which, as the crucial element in the renewal of the covenant, YHWH himself would appear from heaven, would return to his people to judge and to rescue. The echoes of 'wisdom' which many have detected in this passage are there, but as elsewhere they are pointers to the larger reality, since 'wisdom' itself was, as we have seen, a way of speaking about a kind of 'return' of YHWH, perhaps in the form of Torah. What we are looking at in this dense and decisive passage, at the heart of the paragraph which stands at the heart of one of Paul's most carefully constructed arguments, is a retelling of the story of Israel in which the YHWH-christology which is often recognized in 10.12–13, and perhaps also in 10.9, is rooted in a *return-of-YHWH* christology in 10.6. Once again, Israel's God has done, in person, what Torah could not do. And this, as we shall see presently, carries strong implications for the proper reading of the advance summary of Paul's argument at the start of chapter 9.

Before we get there, however, there is one further *kyrios*-text which stands out from the much longer possible list. We have referred to Isaiah 40—55 and Deuteronomy 6 as prime candidates for the clearest and sharpest monotheistic statements in Israel's scriptures. Alongside these we must place Zechariah 14.5–9:

> Then YHWH my God will come, and all the holy ones with him. On that day there shall not be either cold or frost. And there shall be continuous day (it is known to YHWH), not day and not night, for at evening time there shall be light. On that day living waters shall flow out from Jerusalem, half of them to the eastern sea and half of them to the western sea; it shall continue in summer as in winter. And YHWH will become king over all the earth; on that day YHWH will be one and his name one.

This prophecy of new creation, with the rivers flowing out of the restored Jerusalem, echoes the end of Ezekiel and thereby also Genesis 2. It also picks up the older vision of Deuteronomy 33.2, where YHWH comes from Sinai with myriads of his holy ones. The combination is instructive: the final 'coming' of YHWH will be both a reprise of the Sinai theophany and a restoration of Genesis 2. The Pentateuch completes its circle, with the prophets pointing to the same fulfilment. The coming kingship of YHWH over all the earth will be his final claiming of sovereignty, as in several psalms, in Daniel and elsewhere; and this will mean the renewal of all creation. And, strikingly, this universal reign of YHWH will mean a kind of eschatological fulfilment of the *Shema* itself: YHWH will be one, and his name one. What began as Israel's prayer of dedication and loyalty will end as the universal, global reality.[272]

Paul alludes to the opening verse of this sequence in 1 Thessalonians 3.13:

> [11]Now may God himself, our father, and our lord Jesus, steer us on our way to you. [12]And may the lord make your love for one another, and for everybody, abound and overflow, just as ours does for you. [13]That way, your hearts will be strengthened and kept blameless in holiness before God our father when our lord Jesus is present again with all his holy ones (*en tē parousia tou kuriou Iēsou meta pantōn tōn hagiōn autou*). Amen.[273]

But the echoes resonate out more widely again. We shall return to this passage when looking at Paul's revised eschatology in chapter 11;[274] but the Zechariah allusion indicates a vision of the oneness of Israel's God that grounds the eschatological reality in which, as in Philippians 2.9–11, all creation joins together in confessing Jesus as *kyrios*, the sovereign one who bears the Name of Israel's God.

This eschatological vision, according to Paul, *has already become a reality in Jesus the Messiah, and in his people*. Here we see the point of the revised monotheism in relation to the central worldview-symbol, the people of God 'in the Messiah'. We shall explore this more fully in chapter 10 below, but it is important to note even at this stage what is going on. Paul's vision of Jesus as 'the human face of God', as the instantiation of YHWH himself, related to 'God the father' as the unique son (see below), is the ground of his vision of the single community, the one people of God who must be guarded as such and defended against all divisions of whatever sort, and must be taught to worship the one God, the father of the lord Jesus the Messiah, 'with one heart and voice'.[275] That which Zechariah envisaged as the final reality, and that to which Paul himself still looked forward in 1 Thessalonians 3.13 and in great passages such as 1 Corinthians 15.20–8, had already been inaugurated through the Messiah's death and resurrection. As in Romans 10.12–13, the fact that there is now 'no distinction' between Jew and gentile who confess Jesus as *kyrios* and believe in their hearts that God raised him from the dead is grounded foursquare on this vision: *ho gar autos kyrios pantōn*, 'the same "lord" is lord of all'.

This fusion of messianic and 'divine' categories in Romans 10 points back to one of the most controversial of Paul's references to Jesus, that in Romans 9.5.

[272] See e.g. Smith 1984, 289; Petersen 1995, 148.

[273] 1 Thess. 3.11–13. The allusion in v. 13 is the more striking in that LXX Zech. 14.5 reads *kai hēxei kurios* <u>*ho theos mou*</u> *kai pantes hoi hagioi met'autou*, 'YHWH <u>my God</u> shall come and all his holy ones with him.'

[274] See below, 1083f.

[275] Rom. 15.6.

(c) Romans 9.5: Does Paul Call Jesus 'God'?

Two quite different lines of thought might indicate, *a priori*, that Paul did not call Jesus *theos*. On the one hand, those in the mainstream line of modern interpretation have doubted whether Paul ever considered Jesus to be in any sense 'divine' (sometimes because of the assumption that no Jew could entertain such an idea), so that the ascription of the word *theos* to Jesus would already be deeply problematical.[276] The reference in Titus 2.13 ('the blessed hope and royal appearing of the glory of our great God and saviour, Jesus the Messiah') could either be translated differently, so as to distinguish between 'our great God' and 'our saviour Jesus', or it could in any case be dismissed as non-Pauline, leaving only the controversial Romans 9.5.

On the other hand, those who have followed the kind of argument I have advanced so far will have noted that again and again Paul refers to Jesus as *kyrios* in contexts (such as 1 Corinthians 8.6 and 15.28, and Philippians 2.11) where he is thereby precisely distinguished from 'God the father'. Anyone following this line will have realized that Paul does indeed believe that Jesus bears as of right the holy Name of God, but it might still appear peculiar for him to muddy the waters by using the word *theos*, uniquely, for the divine son rather than for the father. Why not stick with *kyrios*?

There are, however, strong grounds for supposing that Paul does indeed call Jesus *theos* in Romans 9.5. I have argued this elsewhere and here need only recapitulate.[277] The key point to note is that Paul again fuses two categories: (a) Jesus as Messiah and (b) the final coming of the one true God.

Romans 9.5 concludes Paul's brief catalogue of Israel's privileges. The whole list, translated literally and without punctuation, reads:

> ... they are Israelites of whom the sonship and the glory and the covenants and the lawgiving and the worship and the promises of whom the fathers and from whom the Messiah the one according to the flesh who is over all God blessed for ever Amen.

The view has gradually gained ground among translators and commentators that the 'traditional' interpretation is right after all: the final clause really does say 'who is over all God', and really does ascribe that to the Messiah.[278] Grammatically this seems clearly preferable. But the strongest argument in this direction is that this verse constitutes a programmatic summary statement, comparable to 1.3–4 in relation to the first eight chapters of Romans, which is then cashed out in 10.1–13 particularly, and more especially in 10.12–13 where 'lord of all', with *kyrios* (as we saw) evoking the Name of YHWH, stands at the very heart of the three-chapter section. It is the rejection of this *kyrios* by his fellow Israelites that causes Paul such grief and anguish, but his double formulation here shows how he will proceed to wrestle with the problem: the Messiah belongs to Israel 'according to the

[276] So e.g. Dunn 1988b, 528f.

[277] Wright 2002, 629–31, with ref. to some earlier literature. See now also Jewett 2007, 567f.

[278] Metzger 1973; cf. NIV; NRSV; also UBS (3) and Nestle-Aland (27). See Wright 2002, 630 n. 327; Kammler 2003; and recently Jewett 2007, 567f.

flesh', but he is also God *over all*, Jew and gentile alike. That represents and summarizes both the tragedy of Israel's unbelief and the prospect of God's greater plan, the dialogue between which constitutes the primary argument of chapters 9–11.

I suggest, then, that though Romans 9.5 stands alone in Paul (apart from Titus 2.13) in terms of a direct ascription of *theos* to Jesus, we should not for that reason deny this most natural reading. Theologically it adds nothing to the very high, monotheistically grounded christology we have already seen. Dramatically it adds a great deal; and the start of Romans 9, of all turning-points in Paul's writings, is exactly where we might expect such a gesture. The idea, after all, that Romans 9—11 was somehow soft-pedalling any talk of Jesus, in order to find a non-Jesus-based way forward for Paul's Jewish contemporaries, was always a somewhat desperate move.[279] Rather, we should see a line from this verse through to 10.1–13, and from there to the emphatically monotheistic celebration of 11.33–6 (not that the latter passage is short of christological reference, rather the reverse, as its echoes of christological passages in 1 Corinthians indicate[280]). But for further exploration of that we must wait until the next chapter.

More to the point, we should ask: what then does a reference to the Messiah as *theos* in this verse have to do with a revised monotheism? Simply this: that the whole of Romans 9—11 is in fact one great second-Temple monotheistic argument, telling the story of the covenant God and Israel and insisting that the one God who called Abraham in the first place has been *dikaios*, 'just', true to his promises and his covenant, and that in and through the Messiah he has now renewed the covenant so that there can be *dikaiosynē* for all who believe (10.4). The central section, 10.1–13, which itself climaxes (10.12) in the statement of christological monotheism we have already studied, *ho gar autos kyrios pantōn*, 'for the same lord is lord of all', draws the whole thing together. It insists, once again, that the glorious and classic celebration of monotheism at the end of chapter 11 should not be understood apart from the Messiah, in whose life, death and resurrection, Paul believed, YHWH himself was personally embodied. We might even suggest that, just as the Messiah comes at the end of the list of privileges (as he comes at the *telos* of the narrative in 10.4), so that is the place where the one God is mentioned at last, not merely as the greatest privilege of all for Israel (to be the people of the God who is 'over all'), but as an indication that, in Jewish eschatology, the final 'coming of God' was the centre of it all. Once more, the facts concerning Jesus have enabled Paul to draw together

[279] Krister Stendahl suggested in his last work (Stendahl 1995, 7, 38) that there was significance in the absence of reference to Jesus in Rom. 9—11 after 10.17 – in other words, that Paul was somehow turning away from Jesus and concentrating only on God. This seems to me very strange. Hultgren 2010, 433 goes further: commenting on the doxology at Rom. 11.33–6, he says that 'the last time Christ was mentioned in chapters 9 through 11 is at 9:1–5'. This, breathtakingly, ignores 10.4, 6, 7 and 17 (*Christos*), 10.9 ('lord Jesus') and 10.12–13 ('the lord') – not to mention 10.14, where Paul speaks of 'calling on him' and 'believing in him'. Jesus as the crucified and risen Messiah and lord stands explicitly at the very centre of the whole carefully structured argument (10.1–13). See below, 1161–4, 1175.

[280] cf. e.g. 1 Cor. 2.16; 8.6.

what had previously been kept apart: messianic beliefs on the one hand, the hope for the coming of YHWH on the other.

This brings us back to a point we have made already and which can now be reiterated with renewed force. *None of this seems to have been a matter of controversy within the earliest church.* This indicates, against the drift of studies of early christology for most of the twentieth century, that what we think of as a 'high' christology was thoroughly established within, at the most, twenty years of Jesus' resurrection. In fact, to employ the kind of argument that used to be popular when it ran in the opposite direction, we might suggest that this christology must have been well established even sooner, since if it had only been accepted, say, in the late 40s we might have expected to catch some trace of anxiety or controversy on this point in Paul's early letters at least. And we do not. The identification of Jesus with YHWH seems to have been part of (what later came to be called) Christianity from more or less the very beginning. Paul can refer to it, and weave it into arguments, poems, prayers and throwaway remarks, as common coin. Recognizing Jesus within the identity of Israel's one God, and following through that recognition in worship (where monotheism really counts), seems to have been part of 'the way' from the start.

4. Monotheism Freshly Revealed (2): the Spirit

(i) Introduction

So far we have seen substantial evidence that Paul consciously and deliberately spoke of Jesus within the framework of second-Temple Jewish monotheism, intending thereby not to add Jesus to an incipient pantheon, smuggling in a second God under cover of rhetoric, but to declare that in the gospel events the inner character, being and identity of the one God of Jewish monotheism had been made known in person. A striking enough claim, indeed. But Paul goes further: the God who sent the son also sends 'the spirit of the son'. This is not nearly so prominent as the christological redefinition, but it is there none the less, and it is striking.

The lack of prominence (as also in the 'binitarian' formulae we see so often, for instance, in the picture of 'God and the Lamb' in the book of Revelation[281]) might be taken to indicate a kind of slow development, in which, so to speak, christology was sorted out first while the church took its time to think about whether or not the spirit was equally divine. That is of course how things proceeded as dogma developed in the later councils of the church, with the fourth-century Cappadocian Fathers finally getting around to defining the 'divinity' of the spirit. But I want in this section to challenge strongly any sense that we should project that process back into the earliest period. What we find in the patristic period, not least in the great

[281] Rev. 5.13 etc.

pneumatological works of Basil and the two Gregorys, seems to me more a question of the attempt to appropriate, in language that would then be comprehensible, what was already fully present, in the language of second-Temple Judaism reworked around Jesus and indeed around the spirit, in the very earliest period.[282]

Indeed, with both christology and pneumatology it seems that the normal assumption of many writers is radically mistaken. It is not the case that the New Testament is unclear or fuzzy on these subjects, and that the early Fathers invented a high view of Jesus and the spirit which was then wrongly read back into the early period. Rather, it seems as though the earliest Christians, precisely from within their second-Temple Jewish monotheism, leapt without difficulty straight to an identification of both Jesus and the spirit within the divine identity, which the early Fathers then struggled to recapture in the very different categories of hellenistic philosophy. As with christology, so with pneumatology. The idea of a 'low' Jewish beginning, from which a gradual 'ascent' was made on the dictates of Greek philosophy, is exactly wrong. The Jewish context provided the framework for a thoroughly 'high' christology and pneumatology, and it was the attempt to restate that within the language of hellenistic philosophy, and without the help of the key Jewish categories, that gave the impression of a difficult doctrine gradually attained.

It is of course true that for the early followers of Jesus the spirit was not first and foremost a topic one talked *about*. There was no question of turning the spirit into an object outside oneself, towards which one might point, about which one might hold 'objective' discussions. The spirit was the one who enabled the community as a whole to worship, to live the holy lives required of God's people, to pray, to believe, to worship with a sense of the living presence of God in the midst, to abound in hope, to love, to be transformed by the renewal of the mind, to experience the power of God in healing of bodies and lives, to be united in heart and soul. The early Christians might have said of the spirit what we have said often enough of a worldview: it isn't what you look *at*, it's what you look *through*. The spirit was not, for Paul and his contemporaries, a 'doctrine' or 'dogma' to be discussed, but the breath of life which put them in a position to discuss everything else – and, more to the point, to worship, pray, love and work. We should not, then, be surprised at the relative absence of discourse, including monotheistic discourse, *about* the spirit.

But when it comes, it is clear. In particular, exactly as with christology, what strikes me as most important is what has normally been omitted from discussions. Paul uses, of the spirit, (a) language associated with the long-awaited return of YHWH to Zion, with Israel's God coming back at last to dwell within his Temple and (b) the closely related biblical language associa-

282 For a recent brief treatment of historical pneumatology see Kärkkäinen 2012. The Pauline material on the spirit is magisterially covered by Fee 1994; the powerful recent treatment of Levison 2009 is more relevant to the role(s) of the spirit in Christian experience than to the understanding of the spirit in relation to monotheism.

ted with YHWH being present with his people in the exodus, leading them in their wilderness wanderings. These features indicate that, for Paul at least, the spirit was not simply a generalized or sub-personal divine force that later theology would turn into a third 'person of the Trinity'. As far as Paul was concerned, the spirit, just like Jesus, was doing what YHWH himself had said he would do. The spirit was the further, and ongoing, manifestation of the personal presence of the one God.

(ii) The Spirit as the New Shekinah

It is of course well known that Paul can describe both the church as a whole and the individual Christian as the place where the living God dwells through his spirit. But because the centrality of the Temple in Jewish theology, not least eschatology, has not been brought out, and particularly because the theme of YHWH's return to Zion has not been factored in to discussions of Jewish eschatological monotheism, the full significance of this well-known theme has not been realized. Nor, as a result, have some passages which in fact deserve to be treated within this context received the attention they deserve. My point can be simply stated. When Paul speaks of the individual Christian, or the whole church, as the 'temple' in which the spirit 'dwells', such language from a second-Temple Jew can only mean (a) that YHWH has returned to his Temple as he had promised and (b) that the mode of this long-awaited, glorious, tabernacling presence is the spirit. If we can speak, as we have done, of a christology of divine identity, drawing on the eschatological side of second-Temple monotheism, the evidence compels us to do exactly the same with pneumatology.[283]

The obvious 'temple' passages are quickly listed: three of them in the Corinthian correspondence and one in Ephesians. These passages are, strikingly, associated with Paul's appeal for the two characteristics which we saw to be central to his vision of the church, namely unity and holiness.

First, 1 Corinthians 3. Faced with the problem of personality cults in the church, Paul describes the way in which different tasks have been allotted to different workers. 'I planted,' he says, 'and Apollos watered, but it was God who gave the growth' (3.7). He then changes the image from a farmer's field to an architect's building. He, Paul, has laid the foundation, and other people are building on it. What matters is the quality of material used in the building. Will it be 'gold, silver, precious stones', or will it be 'wood, grass or straw' (3.12)? Sooner or later the truth will out: the coming Day will be revealed in fire, and the work will either shine out the more brightly or be burned up. One might have guessed, through the development of the building metaphor, where all this was going, and as often in Paul the climax of the passage makes the underlying metaphor at last explicit:

[283] It would in principle be good to explore further the second-Temple Jewish context of this theme: cf. e.g. 1QS 9.3–6, where the arrival of the 'spirit of holiness' constitutes the community as the true 'house' in which atonement is made.

> Don't you see? You are God's Temple! God's spirit lives in you (*oikei en hymin*)! If anyone destroys God's Temple, God will destroy them. God's Temple is holy, you see, and that is precisely what you are.[284]

There is no mistaking the point. This is no mere metaphor, a random image culled from Paul's fertile imagination. No ex-Pharisee could write this without intending to say that the founding and building up of the church through the gospel constituted the long-awaited rebuilding of the Temple, and that *the indwelling of the spirit constituted the long-awaited return of YHWH to Zion.* To speak of some force or power 'dwelling' in a 'temple' is one thing; in the ancient pagan world it would already be taken as an indication of the presence of some divinity. To do so in a first-century Jewish context can only mean – must only mean – some kind of identification of the divine spirit with the long-awaited returning Shekinah. For the divine spirit to take up residence in the church is for Exodus 40 and Ezekiel 43 to find a radical, unexpected and even shocking new fulfilment.[285] But there can be no doubt that this is what Paul meant to say.

Granted, for Paul to say this of the Corinthian church, muddled and rebellious as they were, sounds heavily ironic. But he means it. This new Temple is vulnerable. Factional fighting could destroy it. But there is no 'as if' about verses 16 and 17. Unless Paul is totally deceived, the divine spirit has taken up residence in the fellowship of Corinthian believers. The church, as it stands, is thus already the new Temple, and the spirit that dwells within is the new Shekinah. It is hard to see how a second-Temple Jew could give the spirit a higher value than this.

The same is obviously true in the second passage, this time applied perhaps even more strikingly to the individual Christian. Here the challenge is to holiness, particularly sexual holiness:

> Run away from immorality. Every sin that it's possible for someone to commit happens outside the body; but immorality involves sinning against your own body. Or don't you know that your body is a temple of the holy spirit within you, the spirit God gave you, so that you don't belong to yourselves? You were quite an expensive purchase! So glorify God in your body.[286]

It is one thing for 'the church' as a whole to be designated as the new Temple, and for the indwelling spirit to take the role of the Shekinah within it. But it is always possible (and we see this possibility at various points in 1 Corinthians) for particular Christians within the church to be happy with the general truth but not to apply it to themselves. Paul will have none of it.

[284] 1 Cor. 3.16f. It is true, as many commentators point out, that Paul here uses *naos*, the innermost shrine of a temple, rather than *hieron*, the larger temple precinct as a whole (see e.g. Thiselton 2000, 315f.). But since the English word 'temple' suggests in any case a building, rather than a compound containing various buildings including a central shrine as well as some open space, the translation 'temple' here is not inappropriate.

[285] Fee (1994, 114f.) sees this point, predictably, but perhaps surprisingly does not develop it very far in terms of its implications for an early, high and decidedly Jewish pneumatology. He still speaks as though this were, at least at one level, merely another image which Paul seized upon.

[286] 1 Cor. 6.18–20.

What is true of the church as a whole is true of every single Christian. To sin against the body is to deface the divine Temple, to ignore the Shekinah who, in shocking fulfilment of ancient promises, has returned to dwell in that Temple at last.[287] The ethical force of this is obvious; the implications for a theology of the cross ('You were quite an expensive purchase!') are strong; but for our present purposes it is the revised monotheism that is most striking. Once again we must conclude that Paul, thoroughly soaked in the language and hopes of second-Temple Judaism, could only write such a thing if he were fully convinced that the promises of YHWH's return had been fulfilled, not only in Jesus but also in the spirit.

The third passage, 2 Corinthians 6.14—7.1, has sometimes been regarded as an intrusion into the flow of thought of 2 Corinthians.[288] The letter at that point is indeed jerky, switching quickly from the long apologia for Paul's apostleship (2.14—6.13) to the account of his journey through Macedonia which appeared to have been broken off earlier (7.5–16 with 1.15—2.13). That account itself, however, indicates that Paul may well have been writing while on the move, and while in turmoil of spirit. I am inclined to agree with those recent commentators who have regarded it as more plausible to think that 2 Corinthians always was a bits-and-pieces letter, in more or less this order, than to suppose that some later editor has stitched together a number of fragments into the present patchwork quilt. That said, there is no good reason to regard as non-Pauline the very striking 'temple' passage which, once again, comes as part of an appeal for holiness:

> Don't be drawn into partnership with unbelievers. What kind of sharing can there be, after all, between justice and lawlessness? What partnership can there be between light and darkness? What kind of harmony can the Messiah have with Beliar? What has a believer in common with an unbeliever? What kind of agreement can there be between God's temple and idols? We are the temple of the living God, you see, just as God said:
>
> I will live among them (*enoikēsō en autois*) and walk about with them;
> I will be their God, and they will be my people.
> So come out from the midst of them,
> and separate yourselves, says YHWH;
> no unclean thing must you touch.
> Then I will receive you gladly,
> and I will be to you as a father,
> and you will be to me as sons and daughters,
> says YHWH, the Almighty.
>
> So, my beloved people, with promises like these, let's make ourselves clean from everything that defiles us, outside and inside, and let's become completely holy in the fear of God.[289]

[287] See again Fee (1994, 136), but again without developing the point I am stressing.

[288] Full discussion in e.g. Furnish 1984, 371–85; Thrall 1994, 25–36.

[289] 2 Cor. 6.14—7.1. Fee 1994, 336f. rightly sees that this passage is, by strong implication, all about the spirit, even though *pneuma* does not occur until the final verse (and there its apparently more natural meaning is the human spirit).

The remarkable web of biblical allusions amplifies what we might have deduced already from the straightforward statement that 'we are the temple of the living God'. First, there is the promise in the Torah that God will place his tabernacle in the midst of the people; he will dwell with them and 'walk among them'. This promise, rooted in the events of the exodus, and applied to the need for holiness, is reiterated in Exodus, Leviticus and elsewhere.[290] The same promise is linked directly, in Ezekiel 37 (the chapter, of course, which predicts the 'resurrection' of exiled Israel), to the regular covenantal promise 'I will be their God and they shall be my people.'[291]

This would already be enough to tell us that the idea of the church as Temple in this passage was being linked explicitly to the theme of the new exodus in which Israel's God would once again dwell in the midst of his people. But there is more. The appeal to 'come out and separate yourselves' is a direct quotation from Isaiah 52.11:

> Depart, depart, go out from there!
>   Touch no unclean thing;
> go out from the midst of it, purify yourselves,
>   you who carry the vessels of YHWH.[292]

But this passage is of course part of the climax of the great reiterated promise, the major theme of the whole prophetic poem: Israel's God reigns; he has comforted his people; the watchmen sing for joy because in plain sight they see YHWH returning to Zion. And the warning about coming out from Babylon, so as not to be polluted by its idolatry or harmed by its imminent destruction, leads directly to a further statement about the personal presence of Israel's God, leading the people through the wilderness as at the time of the exodus: 'YHWH will go before you, and the God of Israel will be your rearguard'.[293] Indeed, the whole passage is framed as a new exodus: Israel's God is determined to rescue his people from their present slavery as he did when they were in Egypt, and then again when they were oppressed by Assyria.[294] The appeal to 'come out and be separate' flows directly from the promise of the new exodus in which Israel's God will once again come to dwell in the midst of his people. This is the foundation of Paul's belief that the church is 'the temple of the living God'.

And still he is not finished. Those who are thus escaping Babylon are the renewed family of David, the promised messianic people. 'I will be to you as a father, and you will be to me as sons and daughters' is an evocation, and a democratization, of the promise to David concerning his coming 'son', the one who will be 'raised up' – and who will build the Temple:

[290] Ex. 29.45f.; Lev. 26.11–13; Num. 5.3; 35.34; Dt. 6.15; 7.21.

[291] Ezek. 37.27; cf. 34.24, 30; 36.28; 37.23; etc.

[292] cf. too Jer. 51.45.

[293] Isa. 52.12; cf. Ex. 13.21f.; 14.19.

[294] Isa. 52.4f.

> I will raise up your offspring after you, who shall come forth from your body, and I will establish his kingdom. He shall build a house for my name, and I will establish the throne of his kingdom for ever. I will be a father to him, and he shall be a son to me.[295]

Even the final flourish, 'says YHWH, the Almighty', turns out to be a reference to the same passage.[296] And the concluding appeal for a cleansing from all defilement, for a complete holiness, goes of course very closely with the entire theme of the church as the place where the living God has come to dwell as he had always promised.

It is of course true that the spirit is not mentioned at any point in this remarkable passage (unless 'spirit' in the phrase 'flesh and spirit' in 7.1 should be taken that way). But with 2 Corinthians 3 as part of the wider context we can surely take it for granted that this detailed exposition of the church as Temple must presuppose the spirit as the new form of the Shekinah, the tabernacling presence of the God who has accomplished the new exodus. And once more we are aware that it is this theology – a thought-out, scripturally grounded reflection on the one true God in the light of the realities of Jesus and the spirit – that enables the church to be the church, to be both united and holy.

Both of those characteristics are again in strong evidence in the final explicit 'temple' passage. Ephesians began by stating, within the context of an exodus-based paean of praise, that the divine purpose was to sum up all things in heaven and on earth in the Messiah (1.10). The letter then argues in chapter 2 that the powerful redeeming action of divine grace which rescues sinner by grace through faith (2.1–10) results in the coming together into a single family of Jew and gentile alike. As in 1 Corinthians 3, there are advance hints that this is going to turn into a 'temple'-image: the dividing wall that kept Jews and gentiles apart, and which is abolished in the Messiah, may well be a reference to the wall that divided the 'court of the gentiles' in the Jerusalem Temple from the inner area where only Jews could go.[297] Once again Isaiah 52 is not far away: the 'good news' of 'peace' was announced to those both near and far.[298]

With all this in place, the temple-theme finally becomes explicit:

> You are no longer foreigners or strangers. No: you are fellow-citizens with God's holy people. You are members of God's household. You are built on the foundation of the apostles and prophets, with King Jesus himself as the cornerstone. In him the whole building is fitted together, and grows into a holy temple in the lord. You, too, are being built up together, in him, into a place where God will live (*eis katoikētērion tou theou*) by the spirit.[299]

[295] 2 Sam. 7.12–14.

[296] 2 Sam. 7.8.

[297] Eph. 2.14; cf. the theme of 'access' in Rom. 5.1–2. Fee 1994, 682, 686 suggests that the temple-theme only emerges because Paul shifts from a political image to that of a household, which then 'evolves' into that of the Temple, so that the images 'fall all over themselves'. Granted that Paul can and does mix several metaphors together at once, I nevertheless see the temple-theme as more organic to the whole letter than this would indicate.

[298] Isa. 52.7, reflected in Eph. 2.17.

[299] Eph. 2.19–22.

In context, both of Ephesians and of second-Temple expectations, this too can only mean one thing. The hope that one day YHWH would return to Zion, to dwell in the renewed Temple for ever, has now been fulfilled – but in a radical, shocking and unexpected fashion. The role of God's living presence, the glorious Shekinah, is taken by the spirit. Once again, in second-Temple Jewish terms there cannot be a higher pneumatology than this. The spirit is incorporated within the divine identity, the identity which is shaped particularly by the eschatology of YHWH's 'return'.[300]

Once this theme of the spirit as the long-promised indwelling Shekinah is recognized, other passages emerge from the shadows to suggest that they, too, should be included in the reckoning. Among these perhaps the most striking is Romans 8, where the theme of the spirit's 'indwelling' strongly echoes the use of the same word in the 1 Corinthians passages above:

> You're not people of flesh; you're people of the spirit (if indeed God's spirit lives within you [*oikei en hymin*]; note that anyone who doesn't have the spirit of the Messiah doesn't belong to him). But if the Messiah is in you, the body is indeed dead because of sin, but the spirit is life because of covenant justice. So, then, if the spirit of the one who raised Jesus from the dead lives within you (*oikei en hymin*), the one who raised the Messiah from the dead will give life to your mortal bodies, too, through his spirit who lives within you (*dia tou enoikountos autou pneumatos en hymin*).[301]

We notice here, of course, what we might have expected from the fact which we have now clarified, that *both* the Messiah *and* the spirit can be spoken of in terms of the returning and indwelling Shekinah: that Paul can shuttle to and fro between them, not making them straightforwardly identical or interchangeable but nevertheless aligning them closely. This corresponds to Ephesians 3.17, where Paul prays that 'the Messiah may make his home (*katoikēsai*) in your hearts, through faith'. We shall consider this further in the next chapter where we shall observe that Paul's occasional use of 'Messiah in you' (as opposed to the much more frequent 'you in Messiah') is functionally the same as 'spirit in you'. But the main point stands: this is once again temple-language.[302]

That, after all, is more or less what we should have expected both from the dense themes of 8.1–4 and from the larger exodus-narrative which stands under the whole section of Romans. This is the point where, once the problem caused by Torah has been dealt with, the Shekinah can and will come to dwell in the newly built tabernacle, as in Exodus 33—40. And, as we shall shortly see in the second part of our treatment of the spirit within

[300] So Fee 1994, 689f.: 'Here is the ultimate fulfilment of the imagery of God's presence, begun but lost in the Garden, restored in the tabernacle in Exodus 40 and in the temple in 1 Kings 8.' Fee does not, however, trace this same theme forwards explicitly in relation to the long post-exilic hope of YHWH's return; and that is what gives Paul's formulation its particular force in relation to second-Temple eschatological monotheism.

[301] Rom. 8.9–11.

[302] Jewett 2007, 490 mentions the link with the Shekinah, and various promises both biblical (Ex. 29.45f.) and post-biblical (*T. Lev.* 5.2; *T. Zeb.* 8.2) concerning YHWH's 'dwelling' among, or even 'in', his people. But he does not develop this in relation to the promise of YHWH's return.

Paul's revised monotheism, this gives rise at once to a theme we might naturally expect. If YHWH has returned to dwell in the newly built Temple or tabernacle, the exodus-narrative would then require that this divine presence would lead the people through the wilderness to their promised inheritance. For the moment, though, we note the conclusion – which ought, I submit, to be as weighty for systematic theologians as it certainly is within the exegesis of Paul: that the spirit has taken the role of the returning Shekinah. We must say it one more time: in terms of Paul's Jewish world, one cannot conceive of a higher pneumatology than this.

The one remaining passage that might be considered relevant is in Colossians. In that letter, too, there is a reference to the divine 'word' 'dwelling richly among you', and granted the uses of 'word' in second-Temple Judaism and the New Testament it is not impossible that we should see there, too, a sense of the personal presence of the one God, active through the ministries of teaching, exhortation, wisdom and (not least) song.[303] But the passage I have in mind comes at the point where Paul is applying to the Colossians what he said about Jesus himself in the wisdom-poem of 1.15–20, particularly the apparent temple-image of 1.19 ('for in him all the Fullness was glad to dwell [*eudokēsen katoikēsai*]'). He repeats this christological point in 2.9: 'in him all the full measure of divinity has taken up bodily residence (*en autō katoikei pan to plērōma tēs theotētos sōmatikōs*)', and then draws his audience into the same reality: 'you are fulfilled in him (*este en autō peplērōmenoi*), since he's the head of all rule and authority.' There is of course much more going on here than simply this theme, but we should not ignore this passage in considering Paul's vision of the church as the place where the living presence of the one God has come to dwell.

All of this points us forward to the closely correlated theme in which, once more, Paul's second-Temple monotheism of divine identity, especially in its eschatological form, has been reworked. If the spirit is the one who comes to 'dwell' in the 'new Temple' which is the people of God in the Messiah, the spirit is also the one who, like the fiery presence of Israel's God in the wilderness, leads them home to their promised land.

(iii) The Spirit and the New Exodus

Three passages in particular stand out as expressing this view of the spirit. In each case the equivalent features are prominent. First, the spirit is spoken of as the divine spirit, God's own spirit, and also at the same time as the spirit of Jesus or the spirit of the Messiah. There seems at this point to be an interchangeability, which itself tells us quite a lot about how Jesus himself was being perceived; if Jesus' spirit and God's spirit are basically the same, then he, Jesus, has already been placed solidly and inalienably within the meaning of the word 'God'. Second, the passages in question are once more

[303] Col. 3.16; cf. e.g. Wis. 18.14–16; Jn. 1.1–18.

characteristic statements of Jewish-style monotheism (creational, covenantal, eschatological, cultic). This is once more the same pattern that we have observed in the case of Jesus himself.

The first piece of evidence is all the more remarkable if, as I think, it is very early, perhaps in the late 40s. We have already glanced at it in another connection. Paul is speaking about the birth of the renewed people of God, the single family promised to Abraham. In good Jewish style, he does this by retelling the story of the exodus: God rescues his people from their slavery, and then, addressing them as his 'sons', he comes with his own strange presence to accompany them on the journey to their 'inheritance' (though they do their best to rebel, wanting at various stages to go back to Egypt). In doing all this God reveals his own Name: now at last the people discover who he really is (which may mean, in Exodus as we have it, that now at last they discover the meaning of the Name that their ancestors had already used without knowing its full import).[304]

So Paul puts it like this, at the climax of the letter to the Galatians:

> When we were children, we were kept in 'slavery' under the 'elements of the world'. [4]But when the fullness of time arrived, God sent out his son, born of a woman, born under the law, [5]so that he might redeem those under the law, so that we might receive adoption as sons. [6]And, because you are sons, God sent out the spirit of his son into our hearts, calling out 'Abba, father!' [7]So you are no longer a slave, but a son! And, if you're a son, you are an heir, through God.
>
> [8]However, at that stage you didn't know God, and so you were enslaved to beings that, in their proper nature, are not gods. [9]But now that you've come to know God – or, better, to be known *by* God – how can you turn back again to that weak and poverty-stricken line-up of elements that you want to serve all over again? [10]You are observing days, and months, and seasons, and years! [11]I am afraid for you; perhaps my hard work with you is all going to be wasted.[305]

They are, in other words, trying to sneak off back to Egypt, trying to return to the slavery from which they had been rescued.[306] That forms the polemical thrust of the letter all through: to embrace Torah is to embrace a slavery no different in essence from that of the paganism from which the gospel of Jesus the Messiah has rescued you.[307] Here, of course, lies the greatest irony in Paul's use of the exodus narrative for this purpose. In the original story, the gift of Torah was itself the high point, the moment of vision and revelation, the culmination of the rescue from Egypt, the disclosure of God himself and his will for his people. For Paul, however, *the role both of Torah and of the tabernacling presence of God with his people has been taken, jointly, by the Messiah and the spirit.* God sent the son; God sent the spirit of the son, making 'you' no longer slaves but sons, just as in the exodus story. And the point, not to be missed in the middle of all this dense exposition, is that with

[304] Zimmerli 1978, 17–21.

[305] Gal. 4.3–11.

[306] For this whole theme, and its similar statement in Rom. 8, I owe a great deal to Sylvia Keesmaat: see Keesmaat 1999, esp. ch. 5.

[307] cf. 1.4.

this sending of son and spirit *we now know the name of God*. We have discovered, fully and truly, who YHWH is. To go back from this revelation is to go back to Egypt. This is the classic narrative of Jewish monotheism in action: Abraham's God fulfils the covenant by rescuing his people from slavery and leading them home to their inheritance. The God who is revealed in this new-exodus story is the son-sending, spirit-sending God.[308]

The second passage includes a section closely cognate with this short and sharp pneumatological monotheism. In Romans 8 (where almost all Paul's key themes can be found somewhere or other) we find a bewildering flurry of spirit-reference, with the same cumulative impact. The spirit is the personal, powerful manifestation of the one God of Jewish monotheism, the God who, having given Torah, has at last enabled his people to fulfil it and so come into the blessings of covenant renewal; the God who will raise his people from the dead; the God who leads his people home to their true inheritance; the God who, 'searching the hearts', groans within his groaning people within the groaning of all creation; the God from whose love nothing can separate his people. This is, of course, one of the greatest passages in one of the greatest letters ever written. Highlighting one single theme does it scant justice. But to understand the theme, here picked out in bold, we must at least glance at the whole context:

> [1]So, therefore, there is no condemnation for those in the Messiah, Jesus! [2]Why not? Because **the law of the spirit of life** in the Messiah, Jesus, released you from the law of sin and death. [3]For God has done what the law (being weak because of human flesh) was incapable of doing. God sent his own son in the likeness of sinful flesh, and as a sin-offering; and, right there in the flesh, he condemned sin. [4]This was in order that the right and proper verdict of the law could be fulfilled in us, as we live **not according to the flesh but according to the spirit**.
>
> [5]Look at it like this. People whose lives are determined by human flesh focus their minds on matters to do with the flesh, but **people whose lives are determined by the spirit focus their minds on matters to do with the spirit.** [6]Focus the mind on the flesh, and you'll die; but **focus it on the spirit, and you'll have life, and peace**. [7]The mind focused on the flesh, you see, is hostile to God. It doesn't submit to God's law; in fact, it can't. [8]Those who are determined by the flesh can't please God.
>
> [9]But you're not people of flesh; **you're people of the spirit (if indeed God's spirit lives within you; note that anyone who doesn't have the spirit of the Messiah doesn't belong to him). [10]But if the Messiah is in you, the body is indeed dead because of sin, but the spirit is life because of covenant justice. [11]So, then, if the spirit of the one who raised Jesus from the dead lives within you, the one who raised the Messiah from the dead will give life to your mortal bodies, too, through his spirit who lives within you.**
>
> [12]So then, my dear family, we are in debt – but not to human flesh, to live our life in that way. [13]If you live in accordance with the flesh, you will die; but **if, by the spirit, you put to death the deeds of the body, you will live.**
>
> **[14]All who are led by the spirit of God, you see, are God's children. [15]You didn't receive a spirit of slavery, did you, to go back again into a state of fear? But you received the spirit of sonship, in whom we call out 'Abba, father!' [16]When that happens, it is the spirit itself giving supporting witness to what our own spirit is saying, that we are God's children.** [17]And if we're children, we are also heirs: heirs of God, and fellow heirs

[308] Just as in John, where 'the father who sent me' is one of the regular ways of speaking about, and more or less defining, Israel's God.

with the Messiah, as long as we suffer with him so that we may also be glorified with him.[309]

And then, after the climactic promise of the renewal of all creation in verses 19–21, we return to the present reality:

> [22]Let me explain. We know that the entire creation is groaning together, and going through labour pains together, up until the present time. [23]Not only so: we too, **we who have the first fruits of the spirit's life within us**, are groaning within ourselves, as we eagerly await our adoption, the redemption of our body. [24]We were saved, you see, in hope. But hope isn't hope if you can see it! Who hopes for what they can see? [25]But if we hope for what we don't see, we wait for it eagerly – but also patiently.
>
> [26]In the same way, too, **the spirit comes alongside and helps us in our weakness**. We don't know what to pray for as we ought to; but **that same spirit pleads on our behalf**, with groanings too deep for words. [27]And the Searcher of Hearts knows **what the spirit is thinking, because the spirit pleads for God's people according to God's will.**[310]

Resisting the temptation to offer a lengthy exposition of this extraordinary piece of writing, I restrict myself to the three barest points for our present purpose.[311]

First, the entire passage breathes the very air of second-Temple monotheism. The underlying narrative is that of the creator whose good creation has been spoiled and corrupted but who is determined none the less to carry out the plans laid down long ago, plans to rescue and restore it. These covenantal plans, expressed through Torah, had apparently come to nothing because of 'the weakness of the flesh', in other words, the incapacity of the people to whom Torah had been given. (That is what Romans 7.7–25 is all about.) But God has done what Torah could not, accomplishing in the Messiah and by the spirit not only the rescue of humans but the restoration of creation, breathing his own life-giving spirit into human nostrils to give life where there was none. The echoes of Ezekiel 37 in Romans 8.9–11 (the passage we studied a moment ago in another connection) make clear what this is about: resurrection indicates covenant restoration and renewal. And the echoes of Exodus in 8.12–17[312] indicate that, as in Galatians 4, we should understand that the presence of the spirit in 8.12–17, assuring God's people that they are indeed his children (and enabling them to call him 'Abba, father'), is accomplishing what was accomplished in the original story through the tabernacling presence of YHWH during the wilderness wanderings.[313] All this is classic Jewish monotheism, picking up multiple resonances of creation and exodus, of covenant renewal and fulfilment, and

[309] Rom. 8.1–17.

[310] Rom. 8.22–7.

[311] Many of the details are explored elsewhere in the present volume, and of course in Wright 2002 [*Romans*], 596f.

[312] Note, also, the echoes of Ps. 2 in the mention of the 'inheritance' which is the Messiah's and is now shared with his people.

[313] Keesmaat 1999, chs. 2–4.

expressing the presence of Israel's God in terms of the spirit, the spirit of the Messiah, the spirit of the-one-who-raised-Jesus-from-the-dead.[314]

Second, therefore, as with christology, the spirit is not an extra divine force added on to 'God' at the outside, or (worse) a new God added to an incipient pantheon. It was of course a little easier for Paul to say this about the spirit than it was for him to say similar things about Jesus, since readers of Israel's scriptures knew about God's spirit at work in the life of Israel, speaking through the prophets, and so on.[315] But it is striking none the less. *What the one God of Israel had done in the exodus narrative, and had promised to do himself at the eschaton, Paul sees being accomplished by the spirit.*

Third, therefore, we see in this passage, as already in Galatians 4, what even with cautious hindsight we are bound to describe as a nascent trinitarian monotheism. It has none of the hallmarks of the later trinitarian controversies: no mention of 'persons', 'substance', 'natures', of any such analytic or philosophical trappings. But here, at the heart of first-generation Christianity, we have a theology which compelled the later theologians to engage in that kind of discussion: a portrayal of Israel's God in action, fulfilling his ancient promises in utterly characteristic fashion, and doing so not only through, but *as*, 'son' and 'spirit'. There is at least a major question here to which the later trinitarian theologians were giving the best answers they could, granted that they seem to have left behind or bracketed out the more helpful categories of second-Temple Judaism and done their best to express the same ideas in the language of Greek philosophy.

A tailpiece on Romans 8, connecting up with Romans 5. When we began our exploration of Paul's revised second-Temple monotheism, we noticed, in the course of exploring some of his statements about suffering, that in Romans 8.28 he hinted at a connection with the praying of the *Shema*. That passage comes immediately after the passage we were discussing. Here it is, with verse 27 as its lead-in:

> [27]And the Searcher of Hearts knows what the spirit is thinking, because the spirit pleads for God's people according to God's will. [28]We know, in fact, that God works all things together for good **to those who love him**, who are called according to his purpose. [29]Those he foreknew, you see, he also marked out in advance to be shaped according to the model of the image of his son, so that he might be the firstborn of a large family. [30]And those he marked out in advance, he also called; those he called, he also justified; those he justified, he also glorified.[316]

The connection between 8.27 and 8.28 is important: Paul is not plucking 'those who love God' as a new category out of the air, but is indicating that 'loving God' is the proper way to describe what is going on at the heart of the experience he is describing. The inarticulate groaning of the spirit deep

[314] Note this periphrasis for God, paralleled in 4.24f.

[315] cf. e.g. Gen. 41.38; Ex. 31.1–3; 35.31; Num. 11.17, 25; 27.18; Dt. 34.9; Jdg. 3.10; 6.34; 11.29; 13.25; 14.6, 19; 15.14; 1 Sam. 11.5–11; 16.13; Mic. 3.7f.; Isa. 11.2; 42.1; 48.16; 61.1; 63.11; Hag. 2.4f.; Zech. 4.6; 7.12.

[316] Rom. 8.28–30.

within God's people is heard and understood by the listening 'heart-searcher'. God works all things together for good, he says, 'to those who love him': in other words, to those who keep the great command that belongs with 'Hear, O Israel', to love YHWH with all the heart, life and strength, that is the 'obedience' that Jewish monotheism requires. *The spirit enables God's people to keep the Shema.*

The very word *Shema*, in fact, means not merely 'hear', as in 'allow your ears to take in the sound', but 'hear' as in 'hear *and obey*'.[317] A case can be made, in this light, for allowing Paul's remarkable phrase 'the obedience of faith', *hypakoē pisteōs*, to resonate closely with the *Shema*: this is the 'obedience' in which the 'hearing' takes place, namely *pistis*. That link, already at least an echo in Romans 3.30 where, as we saw, the *Shema* is invoked in order to insist that all those who have *pistis* in Paul's sense are part of God's people, points us back to Romans 5, to the passage where the reference to 'loving God' in Romans 8.28 is, I believe, anticipated. I refer to 5.5:

> We also celebrate in our sufferings, because we know that suffering produces patience, [4]patience produces a well-formed character, and a character like that produces hope. [5]Hope, in its turn, does not make us ashamed, because **the love of God has been poured out in our hearts through the holy spirit who has been given to us**.[318]

Most commentators, reacting against Augustine's exegesis which was theologically significant for him in a way it is not for me, have read *agapē theou*, 'the love of God', in Romans 5.5 as denoting God's love for his people, anticipating that theme in 5.8–10 and 8.31–9. But, just as Paul can switch from a clear reference to 'our love for God' in 8.28 to 'God's love for us' in the passage immediately following, and just as 'our love for God' in 8.28 consists in the fact that the inarticulate groaning which comes from the depth of the believer's own personality is nevertheless searched for, heard and known by the 'heart-searcher' himself, so I suggest that in 5.5 'the love of God' refers once more, not to God's love for his people, but to their love for God. This is consonant with the emphasis of the previous passage, which has been not on God's action towards his people but on the development of a spirit-transformed life: suffering, patience, character, hope and, at the bottom of it all, love, the love that is itself enabled, just as in 8.27–8, by the spirit.

It is not clear, in any case, what sense it would make to see God's love for his people located in their *hearts*.[319] On the contrary: the hearts of believers are the places where, and the means by which, they are to love God, according to the *Shema* and in accordance with the restatement of the same theme in 8.27–8. Here again, therefore, we see what we might appropriately call pneumatological monotheism: the spirit, understood as the outpouring of the personal presence and energy of the one true God, enables his people to

[317] cf. Rüterswörden 2006 [1994–5], 255–259, 262, 275f., 278.

[318] Rom. 5.3–5.

[319] This was a point that the late G. B. Caird stressed to me more than once in conversation.

do what the *Shema* required, to love God with the heart, with the strength (6.12–23; 8.12–17)), with the mind (8.5–11; 12.1–2) and if need be, as with Akiba himself, with the life (8.31–9).

The third and final passage that stands out as an example of pneumatological monotheism has a very different character. Here Paul is addressing his beloved and infuriating Corinthians, who need to learn that even though they have all sorts of different gifts, which are genuine gifts from the one true God, they are precisely gifts *of* that one and the same God, and are therefore to be used, not as a means of pulling apart from one another, but rather in order to build one another up in a united 'body'. Yet, at the very moment when he wants so much to speak of the singularity of giftedness and the unity of the *ekklēsia* that results, he says it in three different but interlocking ways:

> [4]There are different types of spiritual gifts, but the same spirit; [5]there are different types of service, but the same lord; [6]and there are different types of activity, but it is the same God who operates all of them in everyone.[320]

Just as in 1 Corinthians 8.6 Paul expanded the *Shema* so as to include Jesus within it, so now he expands the simple statement we might expect him to have made ('all gifts come from the one God') so that it now explicitly includes both the spirit and Jesus.

Whatever else this is, it is certainly not the sudden construction of a tritheistic structure. That would have made entirely the wrong point within the present argument for unity, and would in any case have straightforwardly undermined the theological substructure of the whole letter so far, as well as of Paul's whole theology. The passage appears to be, again, an early and unphilosophical statement of what later writers would refer to as the doctrine of the Trinity. Paul seems to have thought of it as simply the irreducible threefoldness of the divine work in and among his people, even at the point where he is stressing so strongly that in fact it is all one:

> [11]It is the one spirit, the same one, whose work produces all these things, and the spirit gives different gifts to each one in accordance with the spirit's own wishes.
>
> [12]Let me explain. Just as the body is one, and has many members, and all the members of the body, though they are many, are one body, so also is the Messiah. [13]For we all were baptized into one body, by one spirit – whether Jews or Greeks, whether slaves or free – and we were all given one spirit to drink.[321]

Once this point is grasped there is a further passage which, though not so obviously an affirmation of Jewish-style monotheism, nevertheless resonates with the material we have just studied. It also allows us to see the way in which what Paul said about Jesus in relation to the one God of Israel

[320] 1 Cor. 12.4–6. The question of 'trinitarian' language here has been debated (details in Thiselton 2000, 933–5), but many exegetes agree that something like this must be said (e.g. Barrett 1971a, 284; Whiteley 1964, 129 refers to a 'Trinitarian ground plan' at this point).

[321] 1 Cor. 12.11–13. Richardson 1994, 218f. points out how thoroughly theocentric the whole passage is; Martin 1995, 87 stresses that Paul's emphasis throughout the passage is on unity.

could then as it were spill over into what he said about the spirit. We move forward to the very different second letter to Corinth, where a chastened and embattled Paul appears to be facing a much more hostile audience than before. We are at this point revisiting a passage which was important in our earlier discussion of monotheistic christology; here we invoke it in terms of a similarly monotheistic pneumatology.

Second Corinthians 2.14—6.13 is all about the strange character of Paul's apostleship. At least, it has seemed strange to the Corinthians, to the point where they have been taught by other leaders that Paul hardly counts as an apostle at all, and that if he wants to return to Corinth he will have to provide fresh letters of recommendation (3.1). In response to this somewhat brazen challenge, Paul composes, not without considerable irony, a defence of the Messiah-shaped character of his apostleship, and in particular of the way in which his constant trouble and suffering does not undermine his apostolic status but actually constitutes and supports it. Much of this writing, though, is not about the Messiah as such, but about the way in which, by the spirit, Paul's own ministry exemplifies, encapsulates and actually embodies God's faithfulness – that faithfulness which, seen in the Messiah and specifically in his death and resurrection, is then lived out in the true apostolic ministry.[322]

It is the work of the spirit which is highlighted in the spectacular 'new covenant' passage in chapter 3.[323] Paul comes out of his corner fighting:

> [1]So: we're starting to 'recommend ourselves' again, are we? Or perhaps we need – as some do – official references to give to you? Or perhaps even to get from you? [2]*You* are our official reference! It's written on our hearts! Everybody can know it and read it! [3]It's quite plain that you are a letter from the Messiah, with us as the messengers – a letter not written with ink but with the spirit of the living God, not on tablets of stone but on the tablets of beating hearts.

The reference is of course to the promise of Jeremiah and Ezekiel: Israel's God will renew the covenant by writing his law on the hearts of his people, by taking out of their flesh the heart of stone and giving them a heart of flesh instead.[324] In the light of what we have said so far in the present chapter it should be clear that this mention of the heart as the location of law-observance takes us straight back to Deuteronomy, to the *Shema* on the one hand with its following emphasis that the words spoken are to be kept 'in your heart' (Deuteronomy 6.6), and to the promise of covenant renewal on the other, when God's people, after their shameful exile, will seek him with all their heart and soul:

[322] On 2 Cor. 5.21 see Wright 2009 [*Justification*], 135–44 (UK edn.), 158–67 (US edn.) and the essay in *Perspectives* (ch. 5); and see, interestingly, the offhand remarks of Meeks 1983, 186: 2 Cor. 5.21 'stands at the climax of Paul's apology for his missionary career'. See below, 879–85.

[323] On this, see Wright 1991 [*Climax*], ch. 9. The passage has of course been extensively studied: see e.g. Hafemann 1995.

[324] Jer. 31.33; Ezek. 36.26 (cf. 11.19).

> From there you will seek YHWH your God, and you will find him if you search after him with all your heart and soul . . .
>
> [If you] return to YHWH your God, and you and your children obey him with all your heart and with all your soul, just as I am commanding you today, then YHWH your God will restore your fortunes and have compassion on you . . . Moreover, YHWH will circumcise your heart and the heart of your descendants, so that you will love YHWH your God with all your heart and with all your soul, in order that you may live . . . The word is very near to you; it is in your mouth and in your heart for you to observe.[325]

Paul is claiming, in other words, that by the spirit his own apostolic ministry, and indeed the life of the Corinthian Christians, is a fulfilment of that complex of new-covenant promises which are prominent in the Deuteronomic and prophetic tradition, linked directly to the worship of YHWH as the one true God and the forswearing of other gods. The spirit, in other words, enables the Messiah's people to fulfil Torah in the new-covenantal fashion. 'God has qualified us,' Paul continues, 'to be stewards of a new covenant, not of the letter but of the spirit; for the letter kills, but the spirit gives life'.[326]

But this opens up a further possibility which Paul now exploits dramatically in support of his basic contention, that his style of apostolic ministry, in which he uses great 'boldness' and 'freedom', so offensive to the cultural snobs at Corinth, is in fact validated by the inner nature of the gospel itself. Alongside Torah, as the flagship symbol of the life of Israel, stands the Temple; and in the Temple dwells the Shekinah, the 'glory', the radiance of the one true God (as opposed to the shame of the golden calf) which Moses was allowed not only to behold, though not face to face, but actually to reflect. Very well, says Paul, that same glory is what is now bestowed through the work of the spirit: yes, even through the strange, shabby, uncouth, uncultured, and apparently humiliating life and work of the apostle. The key to this passage is to realize that the contrast Paul is drawing is not between Moses and the Messiah, or indeed between Moses and himself, Paul, but rather between (a) the people who heard Moses and (b) the people who hear and receive the apostolic testimony. As in Romans 8.3, the inability of the law to do what it promised was not because of any inherent weakness in itself but because 'it was weak through the flesh' – in other words, because the flawed human beings to whom it was given were incapable of responding appropriately. But now, by the spirit, Paul claims, we are capable, and we do respond:

> [7]But just think about it: when death was being distributed, carved in letters of stone, it was a glorious thing, so glorious in fact that the children of Israel couldn't look at Moses's face because of the glory of his face – a glory that was to be abolished. [8]But in that case, when the spirit is being distributed, won't that be glorious too? [9]If distributing condemnation is glorious, you see, how much more glorious is it to distribute vindication! [10]In fact, what used to be glorious has come in this respect to have no glory at all, because of the new glory which goes so far beyond it. [11]For if the thing which was to be abolished came with

[325] Dt. 4.29; 30.2f., 6, 14.

[326] 3.6; the closest (and highly revealing) parallels are Rom. 2.27–9; 7.4–6.

> glory, how much more glory will there be for the thing that lasts. [12]So, because that's the kind of hope we have, we speak with great freedom.[327]

There is of course a paradox here, as so often in Paul. If there really is 'glory' to be had in the gospel, we can imagine the Corinthians responding, then why can't we see it? That's the point, Paul will respond: we walk by faith, not by sight (5.7). But it is true none the less: if this is really the ministry of the new covenant (and Paul's belief in that depends, ultimately, on his belief in Jesus' resurrection and the gift of the spirit itself), then 'the glory' is in fact being unveiled for all God's people to gaze at. And where do they go in order to do this? Not to the Temple in Jerusalem; not, of course, back to the wilderness tabernacle where Moses met with Israel's God while all Israel waited in fear and trembling outside. For Paul, the place where 'the glory' is now revealed – in other words, the new temple – is in the fellowship of the Messiah's people, where the spirit is at work:

> [15]Yes, even to this day, whenever Moses is read, the veil lies upon their hearts; [16]but 'whenever he turns back to the lord, the veil is removed'. [17]Now 'the lord' here means the spirit; and where the spirit of the lord is, there is freedom. [18]And all of us, without any veil on our faces, gaze at the glory of the lord as in a mirror, and so are being changed into the same image, from glory to glory, just as you'd expect from the lord, the spirit.[328]

This is, of course, the pneumatological correlate of the underlying christology which then emerges in 4.5–6.[329] The quotation in 3.16 is from Exodus 34.34, referring to Moses going back into the tabernacle and so removing the veil which he had put over his face to prevent the Israelites looking at his glory-reflecting face. Paul, uniquely, takes *ho kyrios* here as a reference to the spirit (though instantly glossing this with 'the spirit of the lord', in case anyone should suppose there to be a gulf opening up between the spirit and the lord himself). But the point is that 'freedom', the liberty which the apostle uses as his characteristic style, is validated and vindicated by the inner nature of God's work through the spirit. Where and how, after all, do 'all of us ... gaze at the glory of the lord as in a mirror'? Clearly, I believe, when 'we' are looking at one another: the Corinthians at the apostle, *and the apostle at the Corinthians*, and indeed *the Corinthians at one another*. The lord, the spirit, is at work in their midst, and they are being transformed, whether they know it or not, whether they like its effects or not, whether it is culturally offensive or not, into 'the same image', since each is 'reflecting' in his or her own way the same lord, who is himself 'the image of God', as Paul will say a few verses later (4.4).

With that, we have joined up the present discussion to our earlier one, where it was the Messiah himself who, as God's image, shone with his own face (Paul has not forgotten where he was a few moments earlier) 'the light of the knowledge of the glory of God'. And the place where this light has

[327] 2 Cor. 3.7–12. 'Freedom' here is *parrhesia*, 'boldness', 'frankness of speech'.

[328] 2 Cor. 3.15–18.

[329] See above, 677–80.

shone is 'in our hearts'. In other words (since the division between chapters 3 and 4 is of course irrelevant), this is what happens when the spirit does what Paul says it does in 3.3 and 3.6.

Putting all this together, we reach the following conclusion from these major passages about the spirit. At precisely those points where Paul most strongly highlights the special work of the spirit, he does so within a narrative framework which reinforces the second-Temple Jewish monotheistic structure of thought. The spirit is the one through whom the new exodus comes about, and with it the Deuteronomic fulfilment/renewal of the covenant, the keeping of the *Shema*, the loving of God from the heart and (not least) the establishment of the community as the true temple. Interestingly, as we have seen, the minute the apologia for apostleship is finished, in chapter 6, Paul launches into an exposition of just that, the community as the true/new temple.[330]

(iv) Monotheism and Spirit: Conclusion

All of this indicates that Paul regularly spoke of the spirit, in a variety of contexts, in ways which indicate, granted his own theological context, that he regarded the spirit, as he regarded the Messiah, as the personal presence of YHWH himself. This conclusion is not dependent on one or two verbal echoes, though these are important too. It is dependent on the regular and repeated invocation of the various elements of the foundational exodus-narrative, and on the way in which Paul clearly saw the events concerning Jesus as constituting the new exodus and hence saw the life of the church, indwelt and led by the spirit, as constituting the new version of the time of wilderness wandering. The christology of 'divine identity' is thus matched by the pneumatology of 'divine identity', in both cases focused in particular on the Jewish eschatology of the return of YHWH.

It is perhaps appropriate that it is at the end of 2 Corinthians, where some of the richest christological and pneumatological material is found, that we find one of Paul's most explicitly 'trinitarian' blessings:

> [3]The grace of the lord Jesus the Messiah, the love of God, and the fellowship of the holy spirit be with you all.[331]

That blessing trips unreflectively off the tongue of many a practising Christian in our own day. But for Paul it was a hard-won statement. Paul remained a robust second-Temple Jewish monotheist. That monotheism, ranged against both the dualism that would see the created order as the shabby mistake of a lesser God and the paganism that would cheerfully add yet more 'gods' and 'lords' to an ever-widening pantheon, was now irreducibly threefold. One God, one lord, Paul prays in his radical revision of the

[330] 6.14—7.1 (see above, 369).

[331] 2 Cor. 13.13.

Shema. But, precisely as he prays that prayer, and invokes grace and peace from 'God the father and the lord Jesus the Messiah', he believes that the spirit is at work to enable that prayer and that invocation. Hence: one God, one lord, one spirit.

That, of course, points us on to Ephesians.

5. Monotheism and the Single United Family: Ephesians

It is hard to imagine a more emphatic declaration of 'oneness' than the statement which opens the second half of Ephesians:

> 4There is one body and one spirit; you were, after all, called to one hope which goes with your call. 5There is one lord, one faith, one baptism; 6one God and father of all, who is over all, through all and in all.[332]

The occasion for this remarkable statement is the need to ground the appeal for unity which forms the preceding three verses, echoing passages such as Philippians 2.1–4: love, humility, meekness, patience, making every effort 'to guard the unity that the spirit gives', being bound together in peace.[333] It is, after all, the *unity* of the Messiah's followers that will demonstrate that they are indeed the new humanity, the true people of the one God of Israel. The multiple gifts which the Messiah gives them by the spirit are to be the means, as in 1 Corinthians 12, not of a fissiparous corporate life in which everyone's gifts are used for selfish and separatist ends, but of a common life in which

> we should all reach unity in our belief and loyalty, and in knowing God's son. Then we shall reach the stature of the mature Man measured by the standards of the Messiah's fullness. 14As a result, we won't be babies any longer! We won't be thrown this way and that on a stormy sea, blown about by every gust of teaching, by human tricksters, by their cunning and deceitful scheming. 15Instead, we must speak the truth in love, and so grow up in everything into him – that is, into the Messiah, who is the head. 16He supplies the growth that the whole body needs, linked as it is and held together by every joint which supports it, with each member doing its own proper work. Then the body builds itself up in love.[334]

This is the point at which we can see the point towards which the whole present chapter, and in a measure this entire book, has been building up. We saw in chapter 6 that the symbolic praxis of Paul's worldview – the place where the worldview became visible and tangible – was the concrete reality of the united community, for which Paul works in letter after letter, against one danger after another, from one angle after another. But that worldview, bereft of the community-strengthening symbolic praxis of second-Temple Judaism which Paul has declared redundant on the basis of nothing less than the Messiah's crucifixion (Galatians 2.19–21), has needed the support which

[332] Eph. 4.4–6.

[333] 4.1–3.

[334] 4.13–16.

only a robust and redefined monotheism can give it. That is what we have found right across the letters. Ephesians 4 is either Paul's own exposition of where this all leads, or the work of someone thoroughly in tune with his worldview and theology.

This remarkable statement of monotheistically grounded ecclesial unity is itself firmly anchored in the structured and measured exposition of Ephesians 1, 2 and 3. At the heart of this we find, once again, the new Temple which is also the new humanity; and once more, when Paul speaks of this emphatic unity, he does so in reference to the one God, to the lord Jesus as Messiah and to the spirit. You, he says to the ex-pagans of western Asia Minor, are no longer foreigners or strangers, separated from God's people: you are being built into the new Temple.[335] The central symbol of Israel's life, of second-Temple Jewish aspirations, is being reconstructed – in bits and pieces, scattered all over the pagan world. It is no longer a temple of stone, timber and fine decorations. It is a temple consisting of human beings, a structure 'in the lord', the Messiah being its cornerstone and the living God dwelling within it in the person and power of the spirit. This is Jewish monotheism all right, but thoroughly and controversially revised and reframed. This is a theology developed precisely in order to enable the community of Messiah-believers to stand firm within their worldview, without the symbolic praxis either of Judaism or of paganism (though Jews, seeing the loss of their symbolic praxis, will accuse this community of quasi-paganism, and pagans, seeing its essentially Jewish character, will accuse it of atheism). This is indeed the quintessence of Paulinism, whether it was Paul or someone else who boiled it down into this form.[336]

Once that point is grasped, the threefold monotheism of the letter's majestic opening can be glimpsed as well. Using yet again the narrative framework of Israel's scriptures, with election and redemption signalling an Exodus-and-Deuteronomy context, we find a prayer of blessing, a *berakah*, which is every bit as Jewish in style and content as the *Shema* itself, and again, as with the densely brief 1 Corinthians 8.6, expanded so as to highlight Jesus himself at its heart:

> [3]Let us bless God, the father of our lord Jesus, the Messiah! He has blessed us in the Messiah with every spirit-inspired blessing in the heavenly realm. [4]He chose us in him before the world was made, so as to be holy and irreproachable before him in love. [5]He foreordained us for himself, to be adopted as sons and daughters through Jesus the Messiah. That's how he wanted it, and that's what gave him delight, [6]so that the glory of his grace, the grace he poured on us in his beloved one, might receive its due praise.
>
> [7]In the Messiah, and through his blood, we have deliverance – that is, our sins have been forgiven – through the wealth of his grace [8]which he lavished on us. Yes, with all wisdom and insight [9]he has made known to us the secret of his purpose, just as he wanted it to be and set it forward in him [10]as a blueprint for when the time was ripe. His plan was to sum up the whole cosmos in the Messiah – yes, everything in heaven and on earth, in him.

[335] 2.19–22. For the 'new humanity' see 2.15f.: 'The point of doing all this was to create, in him, one new human being [*hena kainon anthrōpon*] out of the two, so making peace. God was reconciling both of us to himself in a single body, through the cross, by killing the enmity in him.'

[336] So Bruce 1977, ch. 36.

> [11]In him we have received the inheritance! We were foreordained to this, according to the intention of the one who does all things in accordance with the counsel of his purpose. [12]This was so that we, we who first hoped in the Messiah, might live for the praise of his glory. [13]In him you too, who heard the word of truth, the gospel of your salvation, and believed it – in him you were marked out with the spirit of promise, the holy one. [14]The spirit is the guarantee of our inheritance, until the time when the people who are God's special possession are finally reclaimed and freed. This, too, is for the praise of his glory.[337]

This passage rivals Romans 8 in its multiple themes and rich depths, but again we confine ourselves to a few brief observations. As I said, the prayer, deeply Jewish in character, is built around the single purpose of the creator and covenant God, a plan 'for when the time was ripe', to join up the whole cosmos, things in heaven and on earth, in the Messiah.[338] This, in Bauckham's language, is 'eschatological monotheism', comparable to 1 Corinthians 15.20–8 and achieved by the same means, namely the saving work of the Messiah. There the stress was on his victory over the powers of evil and death; here it is on his redemptive death, with echoes of the Passover (deliverance through his blood). The theme of 'inheritance', as in Galatians 3—4 and Romans 8, reminds us once again of Israel's 'inheritance' (the land of Canaan) in Exodus and Deuteronomy, of the Messiah's 'inheritance' (the nations of the world) in Psalm 2, and of the reflection of the latter point in some Jewish texts about Abraham's promised 'inheritance', which would be not simply the land of Canaan but the whole world.[339] All this, in structure and in detail, is deeply rooted in the life and prayer of second-Temple Judaism. And all this, in structure and in detail, has been rethought, reworked and is now (one might say) to be reprayed in terms of the Messiah and the spirit. This is creational and covenantal monotheism recast, without losing its creational and covenantal character, as christological and pneumatological monotheism, and expressed – if we can bear those two further adjectives once again! – as eschatological and cultic monotheism. This framework, and this content, are what the very earliest Christians needed if they were to stand firm, if they were to survive with a worldview that had no symbolic praxis except that which was generated from within the gospel itself. This theology, a lived theology of worship of and prayer to the one creator God, was the vitally necessary adjunct to the nascent worldview.

It was necessary not least because, as with second-Temple Judaism in general, so with this remarkable mutation from within it, such a community, living by such a worldview, was bound to come into confrontation, and sooner or later conflict, with the principalities and powers that claimed to run the world. Judaism, in the Diaspora, had done its best to make and maintain its peace with its pagan neighbours and particularly with Rome, gaining permission to practise the ancestral faith without needing to take part in the local cults, particularly, in the first century, the burgeoning cult

[337] Eph. 1.3–14.

[338] 1.10; see above, 552.

[339] As in Rom. 4.13; for the other Jewish texts see below, 1005, and Wright 2002 [*Romans*], 495f.

of Rome and the emperor.[340] Paul is well aware of the challenges that will be faced by a people claiming to belong to the family of the Messiah, the Jewish 'royal family' as it were, and claiming to tell the Jewish story and so to claim the inheritance of the world: all history had been waiting for *this* moment, not the birth or accession of Caesar; all space, time and matter was summed up in *this* King, not the putative world ruler in Rome! This Messiah, raised from the dead, is the one who has been exalted

> above all rule and authority and power and lordship, and above every name that is invoked, both in the present age and also in the age to come.[341]

The creation of the single family, the new humanity and new Temple, is thus a major *political* act, with resonances out into the world of power. This worldview is not adopted without full awareness of the challenge and the risk. Paul is already suffering the consequences, but that only makes him the more determined. My task, he says,

> is to make clear to everyone just what the secret plan is, the purpose that's been hidden from the very beginning of the world in God who created all things. [10]This is it: that God's wisdom, in all its rich variety, was to be made known to the rulers and authorities in the heavenly places – through the church! [11]This was God's eternal purpose, and he's accomplished it in Jesus the Messiah, our lord. [12]We have confidence, and access to God, in him, in full assurance, through his faithfulness. [13]So, I beg you: don't lose heart because of my sufferings on your behalf! That's your glory![342]

The key line here is verse 10, which draws together the sense of a single great overarching purpose with the sense of the unveiling of God's previously hidden wisdom ('salvation history' *and* 'apocalyptic', if you like), and enables both to ground the richly varied unity of God's people in the Messiah and thereby to confront the powers of the world (which like to think that *they* can bring unity to the human race) with the news that Jesus is lord, and that they are not. 'God's wisdom in all its rich variety': *hē polypoikilos sophia tou theou*, the many-coloured and many-splendoured wisdom of God; that is what is revealed when the church is being what it was meant to be. This would be Paul's answer to those who charge him, in our low-grade postmodern pseudo-morality, with introducing 'sameness' rather than celebrating 'difference'.[343] Not at all, he would reply. It is Caesar who introduces 'sameness'. In the Messiah, God's richly varied creation is enhanced and celebrated. That, indeed, is why Caesar, and all other secular rulers whether official or not, are afraid of it.

And that is why we are not surprised when, at the close of the letter, we discover not a triumphalist, tub-thumping affirmation that everything is basically all right, but a clear-eyed, sober assessment of the battle that still lies ahead. Once again, our modern categories fail to come anywhere near to

[340] See ch. 5 above, and ch. 12 below.

[341] 1.21.

[342] 3.9–13.

[343] cf. e.g. Boyarin 1994.

what Paul is saying. The theology and ecclesiology of the first four chapters of Ephesians sound to western (and particularly protestant) ears as though they proclaim an over-realized eschatology: God has established the church, and all it has to do is to go on celebrating its own existence! That is scarcely even a parody of what Paul is trying to convey. Writing from prison, he knows only too well that the wonderful vision he has laid out, grounded on the resurrection of Jesus, can only be seen if one looks through the lens of suffering, can only be affirmed in the teeth of the apparent evidence of continuing sorrow, wickedness and corruption, and also of powers and authorities both political and 'spiritual':

> [10]Be strong in the lord, and in the strength of his power. [11]Put on God's complete armour. Then you'll be able to stand firm against the devil's trickery. [12]The warfare we're engaged in, you see, isn't against flesh and blood. It's against the leaders, against the authorities, against the powers that rule the world in this dark age, against the wicked spiritual elements in the heavenly places.
>
> [13]For this reason, you must take up God's complete armour. Then, when wickedness grabs its moment, you'll be able to withstand, to do what needs to be done, and still to be on your feet when it's all over. [14]So stand firm! Put the belt of truth round your waist; put on justice as your breastplate; [15]for shoes on your feet, ready for battle, take the good news of peace. [16]With it all, take the shield of faith; if you've got that, you'll be able to quench all the flaming arrows of the evil one. [17]Take the helmet of salvation, and the sword of the spirit, which is God's word.
>
> [18]Pray on every occasion in the spirit, with every type of prayer and intercession. You'll need to keep awake and alert for this, with all perseverance and intercession for all God's holy ones – [19]and also for me! Please pray that God will give me his words to speak when I open my mouth, so that I can make known, loud and clear, the secret truth of the gospel. [20]That, after all, is why I'm a chained-up ambassador! Pray that I may announce it boldly; that's what I'm duty-bound to do.[344]

A chained-up ambassador! There is the shame and the glory of the gospel, cutting across the ways of the world with the powerful and practical revised monotheism which, as one would expect in the second-Temple Jewish world, finds itself pitted against spiritual wickedness of various kinds. Just as the idols in Corinth, though dismissed as 'non-existent' in 1 Corinthians 8.4, are nevertheless the shelter for demonic powers in 10.20, so the official authorities, from Caesar downwards (the 'names that are invoked' in Ephesians 1.21), are put out of business by the exaltation of Jesus, but they still provide flesh-and-blood shelter for the real enemy, the demonic horde and their satanic master, who will act through them given half a chance. One might say that the revised monotheism of Paul's theology is never more truly itself than at this moment, when because of his gospel he is facing, and knows that his communities will face, the kind of struggle which loyal Jews had faced for hundreds of years. The story of Daniel and his friends, of the Maccabees, of heroes and heroines known and unknown, who had invoked the one true God and remained loyal to him under terrible attack – these stories are now claimed by Paul the apostle as part of his own monotheism. Creational, covenantal; christological, pneumatological; eschatological,

[344] Eph. 6.10–20.

cultic; and now, counter-imperial. A new line had been drawn through the world. All this is part of the picture we need to hold in our minds if we are to understand the monotheism which Paul thought through, prayed through, taught through, lived through. And, in the end, died for.

6. Revised Monotheism and the Kingdom of God: 1 Corinthians 15.20–8

This brings us at last to what one might call the real *point* of monotheism, whether in the pre-Christian form by which Saul of Tarsus lived or the Christian form he developed with such astonishing effect. It is possible, alas, that some reading this chapter will suppose that the real point is to 'prove that Paul believed Jesus (or the spirit) was "divine"'. That is cognate with a problem about which I have written elsewhere, that in reading the gospels many generations of Christians have supposed that the real question they were addressing was whether Jesus was, or wasn't, in some sense 'God incarnate'.[345] But with Paul, as with the gospels, that question can all too easily represent a step back from what is actually at issue. When a Pharisee prayed the *Shema*, he was, as we saw, 'taking upon himself the yoke of God's kingdom'. Yes: and when Paul wrote of Jesus (and the spirit) in the ways we have observed, he was doing so, not in order to affirm their 'divinity' for its own sake (indeed, he was presupposing it), but in order to affirm that in and through Jesus and the spirit *the one God had established his kingdom in a totally new and unexpected way*. The point of declaring 'Jesus is lord', with the full sense of *kyrios* we saw earlier, was not, then, that one might feel happy about having made a crucial dogmatic confession. The point was to sign up under the banner of this *kyrios*, implicitly at least against all other claimants to that title, for the kingdom-work in which Paul and his colleagues saw themselves engaged.[346] As I have said elsewhere, incarnational belief is the key in which the music is set, but the tune is the great, swelling theme of the inaugurated kingdom of the one God.

Thus Philippians 2, one of the key texts we studied earlier in the present chapter, *presupposes* the divinity of Jesus but *establishes* his universal sovereignty, both its truth and, equally important, its mode (that it was reached by humiliation and death). Paul at once stresses the need for those who hail this Jesus as *kyrios* to 'work out their own salvation', which I have suggested envisages an opposition to the 'salvation' on offer under the *kyrios* well known to all residents of Philippi. Thus 1 Corinthians 8.6, the small nugget of atomic power which drives the whole discussion of chapters 8—10, states in microcosmic form Paul's belief that Jesus belongs at the heart of the *Shema*, not in order to make that dogmatic point for its own sake (as many today may be inclined to read it, and indeed as some today may be inclined to avoid reading it) but in order to stress that the community founded by

[345] See esp. Wright 2012a [*HGBK*].

[346] e.g. Col. 4.11.

the work of this 'one God, one lord' must learn what it means to live under the *rule* of the crucified one, and not to engage in a trial of strength with him by flirting with the *daimonia* who are only too ready to catch them out.[347]

Once we realize, in fact, where the deep roots of Paul's monotheism (and its revision) are to be found, we should not be surprised that, for him, monotheism (in whatever form) is not a bare belief but an *agenda*. Those roots are found in the Psalms, especially favourites such as 2, 8 and 110; in Isaiah, especially chapters 11 and 40—55; in Deuteronomy. All these speak of Israel's God as the one and only lord of the world, establishing his rule over the nations. They are not about individual human beings believing a dogma and so joining a religion, still less about people assenting to a proposition and so being saved. They are about the fact of God's kingdom – or rather, the hope for God to become king by sweeping aside the pagan idols and the regimes that worship them, by establishing his chosen king, by returning in personal triumph and glory to Jerusalem, to the Temple, to his people.

This, not some abstract doctrinal scheme, is the monotheistic vision of which Paul's redefinitions constitute a fresh and unexpected version. When he speaks of Jesus as God's son, Psalm 2 is never far away. When he speaks of him as the last Adam, we have suggested that Daniel, though perhaps hidden, is not far from the surface of his mind, and Daniel of course shares massively in the kingdom-vision which inspired psalms and prophets alike. And, despite those who have tried to dismiss Colossians and Ephesians as showing signs of a bourgeois second-generation Christianity, settling down in the world, both those letters bear witness to a vision of Jesus, rooted in Israel's scriptures and confronting the powers of the world, which shows every sign of the same counter-cultural, counter-imperial kingdom-theme. For the zealous Pharisee, monotheism could never be a comfortable intellectual affirmation, the considered and judicious opinion of the thoughtful theoretician. It was always something to be invoked in prayer and implemented in kingdom-work and kingdom-living. For the zealous apostle it was exactly the same, with the crucial addition that the kingdom was accomplished through the *death* of the king, and was therefore to be implemented through the suffering, and perhaps also the death, of his witnesses. 'Don't lose heart because of my sufferings on your behalf,' he writes in Ephesians 3.13. 'They are your glory!'

That is why, as we shall see in the next chapter, Paul's hailing of Jesus precisely as *Messiah* is so important – and why, we may suppose, that category has for so long been thoroughly out of fashion in New Testament scholarship. Without pre-empting our later discussion, we may just say this: where theologians concentrated their efforts on the task either of demonstrating Jesus' 'divinity' or of questioning it (or, at least, of questioning whether it was present in the earliest Christian sources), the category of

[347] 1 Cor. 10.20–2.

Messiahship seemed irrelevant. It was Jewish; it was political; what role could it play in Paul's 'Christian' theology? How could it be fitted in with the obviously central theme, that of the crucifixion? But such a way of thinking (which has now in any case run into the sand) comes nowhere near the rich integration of themes in Paul's actual letters. This, in fact, is where the present chapter and the next two are tied tightly together. It is because the redefinition of monotheism we find in Paul focuses on Jesus *in order to highlight the inauguration of God's kingdom in and through him, particularly through his crucifixion* that we are forced to put the category of Messiahship back where it belongs, right at the centre of Paul's thought.[348] The kingdom has been inaugurated through the work of Jesus, who, both as the embodiment of Israel's God and as the single bearer of Israel's destiny, has defeated the old enemy, has accomplished the new exodus, and is now, by his spirit, leading his people to their inheritance – not, of course, 'heaven', but the reclaiming of all creation.

All this comes to classic expression in a passage we have studied elsewhere, but may simply refer to as one last powerful expression of revised monotheism. This is Paul's vision of 'the kingdom of God':

> But in fact the Messiah has been raised from the dead, as the first fruits of those who have fallen asleep. For since it was through a human that death arrived, it's through a human that the resurrection from the dead has arrived. All die in Adam, you see, and all will be made alive in the Messiah.
>
> Each, however, in proper order. The Messiah rises as the first fruits; then those who belong to the Messiah will rise at the time of his royal arrival. Then comes the end, the goal, when he hands over the kingly rule to God the father, when he has destroyed all rule and all authority and power. He has to go on ruling, you see, until 'he has put all his enemies under his feet'. Death is the last enemy to be destroyed, because 'he has put all things in order under his feet'. But when it says that everything is put in order under him, it's obvious that this doesn't include the one who put everything in order under him. No: when everything is put in order under him, then the son himself will be placed in proper order under the one who places everything in order under him, so that God may be all in all.[349]

Of course, those thinkers ancient and modern who have been eager to wish on Paul a thoroughly 'subordinationist' christology have seized upon the last sentences of this passage: here, they say, we see that Jesus is not, for Paul, truly identical with the one God.[350] Not only, however, would this conflict

[348] See also the essay on 'Messiahship in Galatians' in *Perspectives* ch. 31.

[349] 1 Cor. 15.20–8.

[350] This question goes back at least to the time of Origen: see e.g. *De Princ.* 3.5.6f., and dominated both the Arian and the Pneumatomachian controversies (cf. *ODCC* s.vv.), with Subordinationism being eventually condemned at the council of Constantinople in 381. That, of course, has functioned as a challenge to many who have suspected that the earliest Christians, including perhaps Paul, were not as 'orthodox' as the later Fathers might have wished. Even Hays (1997, 266) suggests that 'it is impossible to avoid the impression that Paul is operating with what would later come to be called a subordinationist christology,' granted that 'the doctrine of the Trinity was not yet formulated in Paul's day.' Contrast this with Fitzmyer 2008, 575, who points out that this is the only place where Paul uses the absolute expression 'the son' of Jesus, and that this is therefore 'as close as Paul ever comes to an assertion of the intrinsic relationship of the Son to the Father', providing 'one of the NT springboards for the relation of two persons of the Trinity in later Christian theology'. Cf. too Thiselton 2000, 1238: 'an overreaction to an earlier

sharply with Paul's christological monotheism elsewhere, not least in 1 Corinthians itself. The point is this. The passage clearly belongs with second-Temple monotheism, in declaring that the kingdom of the creator God is to be established in all the world, making no concessions to paganism on the one hand and ruling out dualism ('all in all'!) by insisting that death itself, the corruption and decay of the present physical cosmos, is itself to be defeated and destroyed. But within this monotheism *Jesus is allotted a role which in ancient Israel was spoken of as that of* YHWH *himself.* He is the one who, as in the Psalms and Isaiah, wins the victory over all enemies. The theme of YHWH's triumph over all enemies goes back to Exodus 15, and comes again and again in the Psalms, and in Isaiah 40—66, where it is clear that the victory belongs to Israel's God and to nobody else.

In particular, the defeat and destruction of death itself, here attributed to the Messiah, is spoken of as part of the work of Israel's one God:

> On this mountain YHWH of hosts will make for all peoples
> a feast of rich food, a feast of well-matured wines,
> of rich food filled with marrow, of well-matured wines strained clear.
> And he will destroy on his mountain
> the shroud that is cast over all peoples,
> the sheet that is spread over all nations;
> he will swallow up death for ever.
> Then the Sovereign YHWH[351] will wipe away the tears from all faces . . . [352]

The task which Isaiah declared would be accomplished by YHWH is thus accomplished by Jesus, the Messiah. This passage, then, so far from undermining our earlier christological conclusions, strengthens them, and points beyond them to the larger vision of the kingdom which remained so important for Paul even though it has often been ousted from consideration in post-Enlightenment exegesis.

The point, once more, is that the new state of affairs has been brought about through *the resurrection of the Messiah*. Here again we see the convergence of the two strands which, in the context of early Christian worship and a sense of the abiding presence of the lord, join forces to establish Paul's monotheistic christology. First, Israel's one God has promised to return and accomplish in person the work of salvation. Second, the messianic claimant Jesus of Nazareth has been raised from the dead. These lines of thought, as we saw earlier, enabled the early church to draw on favourite texts, not least Psalm 110.1 and Psalm 8.6, to ground the vision of the Jesus who accomplishes the work of YHWH in the reality of his messianic status and enthronement. That is exactly what we find here. The overlap between the two psalms, both speaking of things being 'put under his feet', points to the enthronement of the Messiah as the truly human being (Psalm 8) and the

naïve dogmatics has made us too timid in what we claim for Paul's respective understandings of Christ, the Holy Spirit, and God.'

[351] In the Heb. 'sovereign' (NRSV 'LORD') is *adonai*, and 'YHWH' has the vowels of *elohim*. The LXX simply has *ho theos*.

[352] Isa. 25.6–8. Paul cites the start of v. 8 (about death being swallowed up) at 1 Cor. 15.54.

Messiah (Psalm 110), sitting at the right hand of the father. It would be a shallow reading of this passage to insist, on the basis of verses 27 and 28, on the separation of Jesus from any sharing of divine status.[353] The whole passage is about the eschatological dimension of a differentiated monotheism, exactly in line with what we have seen in, for instance, 1 Corinthians 8.6, Philippians 2.6–11 and Colossians 1.15–20. And here it is quite explicit that this redefined monotheism does not exist for its own sake as a kind of strange, arbitrary dogma requiring mental assent. To adapt my previous illustration, the redefined monotheism is the grammar and syntax of what Paul is saying. But the sentence he writes is about the one God becoming king.

All this, however, raised in the first century, and raises for Paul's interpreters today, a further and in some ways quite different question. How then did Paul regard the forces over which Jesus had now won the decisive victory? If the notion of the kingdom itself, so often seen as the new exodus, had been transformed by the events concerning Jesus, what about the notions of evil itself, of the powerful slave-master that had kept humans in general, and even Israel in particular, in chains for so long? Or, to put it another way, granted that Paul, like most other second-Temple Jews, expresses a hope for 'salvation', what did he think people needed to be saved *from*?

7. The Dark Side of Revised Monotheism: the New Vision of Evil

(i) Introduction: Jewish Monotheism and the 'Problem of Evil'

The stronger your monotheism, the sharper your problem of evil. That is inevitable: if there is one God, why are things in such a mess? The paradox that then results – God, and yet evil! – has driven monotheistic theorists to a range of solutions. And by 'solutions' here I mean two things: first, the analytic 'solution' of understanding what is going on; second, the practical 'solution' of lessening or alleviating the actual evil and its effects, or rescuing people from it. In various forms of the Jewish tradition, the second has loomed much larger. As Marx said, the philosophers have only interpreted the world, but the point is to change it.[354]

There are, of course, two easy ways out. The first is to say that what seems 'evil' to us is only an outward appearance. The second is to say that 'God' or 'the gods' are detached from this world: bad stuff happens, but they have nothing to do with it.[355]

[353] Of course, the fact that Paul says that 'the son himself will be placed in proper order under the one who placed everything in order under him' can be summarized with the *word* 'subordination' without implying the overtones which that word later came to carry. Whether one can support a phrase like 'ultimate subordination' (Kreitzer 1987, 158–60) is another question.

[354] This is the eleventh 'Thesis on Feuerbach' in Marx 1932 [1845]. I have written on the various 'problems of evil' in Wright 2006a [*Evil*].

[355] For what follows, cf. ch. 3 above.

The first position is that of the Stoic. 'God' and the world are more or less the same. The world is the embodiment of the divine: the way things are is the way things are, and if you don't like it, you are free to leave. The only remaining puzzle for the Stoic, as for Aristotle, was that however wise and virtuous human beings became, they still faced the problem of weakness of will, the failure to live in true harmony with *physis*, 'nature'. They never quite succeeded in becoming the fully virtuous, completely formed, human beings they should have been.[356]

The second position is that of the Epicureans. If the Stoic effectively denies the reality of evil, the Epicurean denies the relevance of the god(s). They (or it) are detached, upstairs, out of sight, uninvolved. The world is developing in its own way and under its own steam, with earthquakes and cancers and all the other interesting phenomena thrown up by the natural processes of the present order; but the god(s) is, or are, safely out of the picture, taking no responsibility for what happens as a result of the random movements of atoms. That is, more or less, how the Enlightenment 'solved' the problem of 'natural evil', ever since the Lisbon earthquake of 1755. The western world has been living with the consequences.[357] This is, as it were, the extreme way of dealing with the 'problem', the polar opposite of the Jewish way. The Jew complains to the creator God and demands that he do something about the problem; the Epicurean denies that any 'god' has ever been, or could ever be, involved. Not for nothing did later Jewish teachers use the word *apikoros*, a version of 'Epicurean', as a term of sharp abuse.

Both of the two great ancient schools, the Stoic and the Epicurean, thus held a kind of theism (in the Stoic case, a kind of monotheism) which generated answers to the worldview questions 'What's wrong?' and 'What's the solution?' The analytic 'solutions' differed, but the practical 'solutions' were simply variations on the shoulder-shrugging suggestion, 'Learn to cope.' The Stoic coped by persuading himself that things outside his own control ought not to be the subject of regret. The Epicurean coped by retreating from the painful world and enjoying such quiet pleasures as might be available.

Some ancient thinkers resisted both of these options and pushed the boundaries towards various types of dualism. It is not easy to reconstruct the history of ancient Zoroastrianism or its later cousin Manicheism, but it seems that, in both systems, there might be one god but there was also an equal and opposite evil force. The good and the bad, the light and the dark, were locked in a long, perhaps interminable, struggle.[358] Meanwhile the 'Academic' philosophers, unsure whether there was enough evidence to

[356] See Arist. *Nic. Eth.* Book 7; for the larger tradition and discussions see e.g. Gosling 1990. Socrates, famously, denied the problem (Plato *Protag.*).

[357] See Wright 2006a [*Evil*], ch. 1, and especially Neiman 2002. The revival of ancient Epicureanism has been one of the major features of western modernity: see e.g. Wilson 2008; Greenblatt 2011.

[358] On Zoroastrianism (whose putative founder, Zoroaster, is a figure of widely varying legends), see Boyce 1991 [1975]; Choksy 1999. Manicheism, the teaching of the third-century AD Persian teacher Mani, was a form of dualism almost certainly distinct from gnosticism proper: see e.g. Jonas 1963 [1958], 40f. and elsewhere; Fowden 1999, 95; Lieu 1999.

make up one's mind, simply held on to a vision of public life and the 'civic religion' which encapsulated it. There was not much 'problem of evil' there; only the random puzzles and sorrows of the world's changes and chances, in which the gods might or might not be involved.

For ordinary, unphilosophically minded ancient pagans, the 'problem of evil' was what happened when, for whatever reason, the gods were angry, or had been bribed by one's enemies, so that bad things happened to the family or the city. Such people, then as now, shrugged their shoulders, grieved over things that brought sorrow whether or not it was logical to do so, experienced the usual human range of guilt and gladness, moral striving and moral failure, and they ran through the range of hopes and fears that, in almost all worldviews, accompany these things. They did their best to bring the gods round to their side (and to enlist their support against enemies) by sacrifices and prayers, by votive offerings, by spells and charms and the thousand small strategies for which the more sophisticated, in the ancient world as in the modern, used terms like 'superstition'. Polytheism has an easier job than monotheism when it comes to guessing why evil happens, but arguably a harder task, certainly a more complicated one, when it comes to doing something about it.

It is important to begin here, if only to get some critical distance on the problems of analysis which have clustered around Paul's account of evil, sin and death, not least (in the primary sources) in the early chapters of Romans and (in contemporary writing) in the approach of Ed Sanders and Douglas Campbell, among others, on the question of 'plight and solution'. What was Paul's analysis of the 'problem of evil'? What was he really saying in the long account of universal sinfulness in Romans 1.18—3.20? How does that fit with what he says about evil and sin elsewhere? Did he start with a view of evil and sin and then discover that Jesus was the answer, or did he start with the fact of Jesus and then, as it were scratching his head in puzzlement, deduce that if God had acted to save people through Jesus there must have been a problem of some sort? Or what?

This question belongs emphatically in the present chapter. Any serious philosophy or religion must give an account of the problems of the world, and that account will be closely correlated with a larger understanding of God (or gods) and the world, and of humans in particular. The monotheism held by most second-Temple Jews was no exception. My argument here is that Paul's account of evil demonstrably belongs within that second-Temple Jewish monotheistic family of 'solutions', that is, analyses on the one hand and practical 'solutions' on the other. What we see in Paul at this point consists, one more time, both of a fundamental reaffirmation of Jewish-style monotheism and of a radical revision of it in the light of Jesus and the spirit. If we are to understand both of these it is important to grasp a bit more fully the ways in which ancient Jewish monotheism thought about evil.

The monotheism of second-Temple Jews generated a more sharply etched idea of evil than we see in the surrounding pagan worldviews, including those of 'monotheists' such as the Stoics. Once you offer, and celebrate, an account of creational and covenantal monotheism such as we find in Israel's scriptures, you are going to run into major problems. If there is one God, if he is the creator of a good world and still basically in charge of it, and if he is in covenant with Israel in particular, then neither the Stoic nor the Epicurean solution will do. Nor is serious dualism an option, though there are times when it will look attractive. If the book of Job had not existed, it would have been necessary to invent it.

Ancient Israel did not, however, attempt a 'solution' in terms of a coherent analysis of why evil existed within the good creation. Job did not 'solve' the problem, but, like some of the Psalms, simply and strikingly reaffirmed the basic monotheistic creed – and complained sharply about the way things were. In the Torah, evil might be traced back to Adam and Eve in the garden, though interestingly there is no sign of this being offered as an ultimate analysis prior to the late first century AD.[359] Or evil might have entered the world through the invasion of strange angelic powers, as in Genesis 6. One might also look back to the arrogance of empire, as in the story of the Tower of Babel in Genesis 11. Or, in relation more specifically to evil within Israel, one could lay the blame on the primal sin of Aaron in making the golden calf (Exodus 32).

These 'solutions' were not, of course, mutually exclusive. That was not how ancient Jews read their scriptures. The various accounts of evil functioned, not as scientific 'explanations', but as signposts to dark and puzzling realities. Human rebellion, idolatry and arrogance, mingled with shadowy forces from beyond the present world, had infected the world, humans and Israel itself. The narratives drew attention to different apparent elements within the problem, and left it at that. No solution was offered to the question of what modern philosophers have called 'natural evil' (earthquakes, sickness and the like). Prophets might highlight particular events as warning signs from the one God – a line of thought echoed at one point by Paul[360] – but nobody, not even Job, seems to have asked why such things existed at all within a good creation. The occasional prophetic promise of a transformed creation bore witness to the fact that some at least had an inkling that the trouble ran right through the cosmos itself; but the offer of an eschatological solution was not matched by an analysis of why a problem existed in the first place.[361]

But if scripture offered no 'solution' in terms of a coherent account of why 'evil' existed in the good creation, it offered instead a 'solution' in terms of what was to be done – specifically, what was to be done by the creator God. The major proposal was first *covenantal* and then *eschatological*: not 'Where did evil come from?' but 'What will the creator God do about it?' Faced with the creational project apparently in ruins, the creator God,

[359] Though we may suppose that the redactor of Genesis may have seen it in those terms, offering Abraham as the 'answer' to Adam: see below, 783–95.

[360] 1 Cor. 11.30.

[361] e.g. Isa. 65.17–25 (cp. 11.1–10).

according to the ancient narrative, called Abram, promised that all the nations would be blessed through him, and renamed him *Abraham*, father of many nations. This is how things would be put right, sooner or later. It turned out to be later. Much later. Abraham's family held within itself the tension not only of weakness of will, as with Aristotle and the Stoics; not only of a sometimes apparently absent god, as with the Epicureans; not only of regular perplexity when all the signs of divine favour or presence seemed to be missing, as with the Academics; not only of a seemingly invincible force of evil, which historically has turned many into dualists; but of a historical combination of all four. Israel went through a repeating cycle, held within the larger implicit narrative of the Deuteronomic tradition: idolatry, divine displeasure, and covenantal punishment (ultimately, exile), followed by at least the promise of an undeserved restoration. The hints of renewed creation which had lurked within the covenantal promise of the holy land seemed to be quashed for ever when the chosen people were taken by force to Babylon. The godless triumphed. Jeremiah's warning about everything reverting to *tohu wa-bohu* seemed to be coming true.

All this emerges powerfully in the Psalms. The promise and prophetic vision are there in Psalm 2, with the nations in uproar and the covenant God settling the matter by enthroning his adopted son as king in Zion; or in the glorious Psalms 96 and 98, which celebrate the coming enthronement of Israel's God as king of the world, returning at last to judge the entire creation, to sort it out once and for all. But the cry of pain is there, too, in Psalms 73 and 74 with their varied pattern of lament, complaint and prayer; in Psalm 88 which leaves the whole sorry matter unresolved in the presence of the covenant God; and in psalms such as 89, which celebrate the great covenant promises and then, in parallel, lament the present distress. The answer provided by the Psalms and the prophets to the larger problems of the whole creation ('God has chosen Israel as the means of the world's redemption; God will one day act to judge and save' – in other words, covenant and eschatology) simply increased the problem. The covenant appeared to fail. Hope seemed endlessly deferred. I described this in chapter 2 above in terms of a harmonic sequence that fails to reach the expected final chord, leaving an increasing, unresolved tension. Or we might describe it as being like a journey whose end seems constantly just around the corner, only for yet another mile of tortuous road to unfold instead. The sense that *we should have arrived by now* became shrill and unbearable.

The more devout one was, the more the problem might seem pressing: 'Why have we fasted, and you haven't taken any notice?'[362] The pagans still ran the world. In Israel itself, wickedness, including collusion with paganism, seemed to earn not divine retribution but political and economic advantage. Some made their peace with the new situation; the book of Ben-Sirach, written perhaps two hundred and fifty years before Paul's letter-writing

[362] Isa. 58.3. The prophet provides an answer: you were doing it for the wrong reasons. But even if people were doing it for the right reasons, the problem remained: YHWH still delayed his coming to save and judge.

period, seems not to regard the problems of the world, or of Israel, in a particularly serious light. Follow Torah, celebrate the Temple cult, and all will be well. The Qumran Scrolls, emerging from the shadows later in the second century, took a very different view, labelling everyone but those of their own sect as 'sons of darkness'. Faced with the destruction of the Temple in AD 70, two writers did what nobody (so far as we know) had done before: they traced the problem back, not simply to pagan idolatry, not simply to the calves which led Israel into sin (that made by Aaron, and those made by Jeroboam son of Nebat), not simply to the mysterious but wicked angels of Genesis 6, but to the primal sin of Adam.[363] Paul's Jewish world, in other words, already supplies us with a spectrum within a spectrum (varieties of ancient Jewish belief, to be located among the varieties of ancient non-Jewish belief) on the subject of evil, including human evil; and by implication, of what might be done about it, by whatever means.[364]

To repeat, none of these approaches attempts to explain why there is 'evil' in the first place within the good creation of the wise creator. They are all ways of articulating the tension, not of resolving it. They are ways, in fact, of saying that there is something absurd about evil, something out of joint, something that doesn't fit. *The fact that one cannot really understand evil is itself an element of creational monotheism*, a demonstration that evil is an intruder, a force not only bent on distorting and destroying the good creation but also on resisting comprehension. If one could understand it, if one could glimpse a framework within which it 'made sense', it would no longer be the radical, anti-creation, anti-God force it actually is.[365]

We note, importantly as part of Paul's context, that for most people in the ancient world the question of 'what might be done about evil' was not a matter of 'salvation'. Most ancients did not suppose that there was anything that one could be 'rescued' from, except perhaps short-term dangers, illnesses or other irritants. Angry gods might be bought off, for a while. The mystery religions, and gnosticism when eventually it developed, did indeed offer a 'salvation' of sorts, but they were the exceptions. And the 'salvation' they offered was very different from that spoken of in most Jewish literature. The gnostic, from within a basically Platonic worldview, wanted to be saved *from* the world. Many later Christians have taken this line, producing considerable confusion which persists to this day. When ancient Jews spoke of salvation, however, they were usually referring to the salvation *of* the world, or of Israel: of a world, or at least a people, over which evil no longer had any power. Neither the average ancient pagan, nor the average ancient Jew, was walking around worrying about how their soul might get to a disembodied heaven after they had died.

[363] *4 Ez.* 6; *2 Bar.* On the rabbinic suggestion that all Israel's subsequent sins were derived first from Aaron's calf and later from those made by Jeroboam, see e.g. bSanh. 102a.

[364] Compare the spectrum of Jewish belief about life beyond the grave, which sits alongside the much wider spectrum of pagan views on the subject: cf. *RSG* chs. 2, 3 and 4.

[365] See the powerful discussion of Sacks 2011, ch. 12.

This emerges clearly if we take the polarized positions of, on the one hand, an extreme Epicureanism, in which all that happens in the present world is a matter of random, blind and godless chance, and on the other hand a solid second-Temple Jewish monotheism, creational, covenantal, cultic and eschatological.

Today's western world is familiar enough with extreme Epicureanism. If the world is a random cosmic accident, why should anything be thought 'evil' or 'wrong' in the first place? Would not all such categories collapse into the projection of our emotions ('theft is wrong' would simply mean 'I don't like theft')? And is not that reduction to emotivism, in fact, what has happened in the post Epicurean world of modern western morality? Get rid of 'god', and you no longer have a 'problem of evil'. All you have is unwelcome 'attitudes' or 'prejudices'. Not that people can easily live like that. They quickly invent new 'moralities' around the one or two fixed points that appear to transcend that subjective, emotive analysis: the badness of Adolf Hitler, the goodness of ecological activism, the importance of 'embracing the Other', and so on. Better than nothing, perhaps; but people who try to sail the moral seas with that equipment look suspiciously like a handful of survivors clinging to a broken spar as the ship goes down and the sharks close in.

But if you are a monotheist – if you are a *creational monotheist of the second-Temple Jewish variety* – then things look very different. You may not have a grand theory as to why evil exists as a whole. There was, after all, no pre-Christian equivalent to the later doctrine of the 'Fall'. But you as a devout Jew will know, well enough, how evil goes about its daily business. You observe that most of the world, being non-Jewish, worships idols. As a Jew, you know that idols are seriously bad for you. They cramp your style, luring you into subhuman or dehumanized behaviour. What's more, they are bad for the world. You, as a human being, are supposed to worship the God whose image you bear, and thus to learn the wisdom you need if you are to look after the world on his behalf. But if you worship idols you merely become like them, dehumanized, unable to exercise your God-given human responsibilities. That much one can learn from the Psalmists, and also from first-century works like the Wisdom of Solomon.[366]

In addition, as we have seen, from the Jewish perspective idols and their temples can be the means by which demons can get their barbed claws into the life of a human, a family or a nation. Demons, within this analysis, are nasty, tricky little things; they are not the actual 'divinities' that the statues in the temples claim to represent (Zeus and his badly behaved tribe, who don't actually exist), but they can still do a lot of damage. Idolatry, in other words, isn't just something you choose to do from time to time. It gives away the responsibility which humans should be exercising over the world to unpleasant and destructive forces. Within human life itself, idolatry becomes habit-forming, character-shaping, progressively more destructive.

[366] cf. e.g. Pss. 115.3–8; 135.15–18; Wis. 15.14–17. On idolatry see now Barton 2007; Beale 2008.

It *enslaves* people. Ultimately, it *kills* people. And it allows creation itself to collapse into chaos. Thus we arrive at 'the problem of human sin', seen from a second-Temple Jewish perspective such as that of Saul of Tarsus. *There are idolaters out there*, and we Jews must not be drawn into their ways. If we allow that to happen, we are back in a new slavery. A new Egypt.

Of course, ever since the regrettable incident of the golden calf, and its sequel at Baal-Peor, it had become clear that the tendency to idolatry was also firmly rooted in Israel itself.[367] Moses' great Song in Deuteronomy 32 had said as much. The Wisdom tradition constantly warned about the dangerous allure of Folly. The prophets routinely rubbed the point home, with the northern Israelite prophet Amos playing the standard rhetorical trick of pointing the finger first at the surrounding nations, then at Judah (well, that was all right, thought his audience, we never liked those southerners anyway), and then, finally, at his native northern Israel as well. Paul pulls off a similar trick in Romans 2.1, to which we shall return.

No doubt there were a thousand different ways in which 'ordinary' Jews – the ones who left no writings, belonged to no parties, joined no revolutions – thought, and presumably prayed, about what was wrong in their world, in their nation, in their own lives. Scripture taught them as clear a moral code as anyone in the ancient or modern world might wish for, and gave them a framework for what to do when they broke it: repentance and sacrifice. That doesn't mean there were no troubled consciences in ancient Judaism. Psalm 51 shows that the idea of a broken and contrite heart was not (as some have oddly suggested) invented by Augustine. What it means, though, is that the Jewish frame of reference, insofar as we understand it, gave people little reason to continue in their anguished or guilty frame of mind. They could say sorry. They could make the appropriate offering. Unless, of course, they were determined to go on sinning (i.e. 'with a high hand'); in which case the problem might be, at least in theory, not so much the troubled conscience as the threat of punitive action.[368] But for most second-Temple writers it seems that 'the problem' could be pushed out into the wider, non-Jewish world. Granted that Israel had sinned grievously and been well and truly punished for it, landing up in exile as Deuteronomy had always warned, the problem now was that the Babylonian pagans were in charge, or maybe the Greeks, or the Syrians. Or, ultimately, the Romans.

And that, of course, was where the problem was intensified beyond bearability. When the Romans took the Temple in AD 70 there was no quick reversal as with the Maccabaean revolt, no sudden lightning-bolt to strike them down, no glorious angels to rescue Israel at the last moment. Some, to be sure, declared that the Temple was unnecessary because Israel's God had provided alternative means of dealing with sin.[369] That looks in retrospect like the most desperate of rationalizations. The best guess is that most of

[367] For the golden calf, cf. Ex. 32.1–35; for Baal-Peor, Num. 25.1–18.

[368] On 'sinning with a high hand' cf. e.g. Num. 15.30f.; Dt. 17.12 (cp. Heb. 10.26). The Mishnah tractate *Kerithoth* deals with sins of that order, and cases of exceptions; cf. mKer. 1.2; 3.2.

[369] On Johanan ben Zakkai see *NTPG* 162f., with refs.

those lucky enough – or unlucky enough! – to survive the fall of Jerusalem and its attendant horrors saw the event in the way that *4 Ezra* and *2 Baruch* describe it: as a deep and unmitigated disaster. The only possible explanation they could offer – not, to be sure, worked out in systematic detail, but indicated clearly enough – was that the sickness of evil in the world was a deeper disease than anyone had supposed, and that Israel was just as badly affected by it as everybody else. The disease went all the way back to Adam himself. That was why it was no use Israel expecting somehow to be exempt from catastrophic divine judgment. Israel was just as much subject to Adam's iniquity as the rest of the world. That notion, so far as we can tell, was not taken up by the rabbis, who as we saw did not have an explicit doctrine of the 'Fall' corresponding to anything like the later Christian formulation. Tracing the world's problems back to Adam was one thing. That was built into the structure of Genesis itself, and recognized as such by some much later rabbis. Understanding that problem to be so deep and dangerous as to make subsequent sin inevitable, even for Israel, was an innovation in those post-70 apocalypses. It was a new idea for Jewish thinkers. With one exception.

Before we explore the way in which Paul provides that one exception, we note the most important point. The idea that for Saul of Tarsus there was no 'problem' in the world, nothing 'wrong' to which the one God was supposed to be providing a solution, is to shrink the second-Temple worldview to a myopic, head-in-the-sand perspective. Just because the soul-searchings of a Martin Luther are not readily paralleled in the Jewish literature of the time, that doesn't mean there is no 'problem' to be seen in such writings. Of course there is: generations have trod, have trod, have trod, and the toil and trade of human folly, the smudge and smell of human idolatry and immorality, have spread their poison around the world, across the holy land, even into the hearts and minds of Israel's rulers ... That was the kind of 'problem' a devout first-century Pharisee would have known: a problem that nagged like a bad tooth, infecting all other joys and sorrows, evoking prayers and scripture-searchings and a constant attempt to make sure that he, at least, was part of the solution, not part of that same problem, an Israelite indeed in whom was no guile, no guilt, a light to those in darkness (as Isaiah had said), one who in the God-given Torah had the key to what human life should be, how the world should be.

A devout Pharisee, faced with this second-Temple problem, would therefore hope and pray, as Daniel did in chapter 9, that Israel's God would do again what he did in Egypt: that he would take pity on his people, remember his covenant with Abraham, Isaac and Jacob, unveil his long-awaited rescue operation, be faithful to his promises. Perhaps, even, that he would send a Messiah, to do what Isaiah had promised in chapter 11. When that great Pharisaic rabbi, Akiba, hailed bar-Kochba as 'son of the star', people disagreed with his timing, or his candidate, or his back-up exegesis and theology, but not with the idea of a Messiah coming to liberate Israel from the pagans, to rebuild the Temple, to establish God's kingdom at last.[370] That was how first-century Jewish monotheism saw 'the problem'; that was the kind of 'solution' for which many longed.

My point thus far can be summarized like this:

1. All views about 'evil' are the correlate of a basic, and often theistic, worldview;
2. All worldviews, except those of the most shallow and unreflective optimist, have some idea that something is seriously wrong with the world, and indeed with human beings, often including one's own self;
3. Monotheists in particular run into a problem which polytheists do not have, and there have been various ways, historically, of addressing that problem;
4. Monotheists of the second-Temple Jewish variety, that is, creational and covenantal monotheists, were bound to have a particularly sharp version of the wider monotheistic problem:
   (a) the world is God's creation, and yet there is evil in it;
   (b) humans are in God's image, and yet they rebel;
   (c) Israel is called to be God's covenant people, and yet is trodden down by the nations.
5. This was addressed
   (a) by varied use of the ancient narratives of Genesis and Exodus;
   (b) by cultic monotheism (especially the sacrificial system); and
   (c) by eschatological monotheism (the hope and promise that one day YHWH would return, would unveil his covenant faithfulness in rescuing his people and renewing all things, and would set up his sovereign rule over the whole world).

The monotheism of Saul of Tarsus generated the problems summarized in (4), and invited the solutions offered in (5). The problem generated by creational monotheism would be addressed by Israel's election; the second-order problem generated by covenantal monotheism would be addressed by eschatology. And my proposal now, in what remains of this chapter, is that Paul the apostle retained these 'solutions' – in other words, that he was still thinking firmly like a second-Temple monotheist – and that he radically modified them in the light of the equally radical modifications he had made within monotheism itself, based on the Messiah and the spirit. His fresh vision of monotheism, in other words, generated a fresh vision of 'what was wrong', but it was not generated from scratch. As he adapted and re-articulated his second-Temple monotheism in the light of Jesus and the spirit, so he adapted and re-articulated, in the same light, his second-Temple monotheistic understanding of what evil was, and what solution might be offered to it, in the same light. The gospel of Jesus the crucified and risen Messiah, and the perceived fact of the divine spirit let loose in the world,

[370] For the prevalence of messianic ideas in second-Temple Judaism see Horbury 1998; 2003, against many doubters.

transforming lives and communities, enabled him to bring into much sharper focus the understanding of evil, and of the divine solution to it, which was characteristic of mainline second-Temple monotheism.

My proposal, then, is that *Paul's radical rethinking of creational and covenantal monotheism contained within itself both an intensification of the problem and an equally radical solution.* As the fall of Jerusalem sent the apocalyptists back to the scriptures, and ultimately back to Adam, so the events concerning Jesus did the same for Paul. The unresolved chord reached screaming point with the stretched sinews of the Messiah on the wood of the cross, and the resolution of Easter bade Paul rise to join in an unexpected song. Monotheism, election and eschatology had come together in a new way: the three parts vied, multiplied, and generated a new harmony which, once Paul had heard it, would not let him go. To be sure, this in turn generated a second-order problem, which emerges in one form in Romans 8 (the 'not yet' of Christian life in between the resurrection of Jesus and the ultimate renewal of all things) and in another form in Romans 9—11 (the question of unbelieving Israel). Paul addressed both of these unflinchingly in terms of the same theology, that of creational and covenantal monotheism (and hence cultic and eschatological monotheism), which he found in Israel's scriptures and never for a moment doubted. He trusted that the God-given resolution to the original problem – in other words, Messiah and spirit – was well capable of handling those that remained.

(ii) 'Plight and Solution' in Paul's Theology

(a) Introduction

If a second-Temple view of the 'plight' of the world, of humans and of Israel is the reflex of a basic second-Temple monotheism, as I have argued, we ought to be able to understand Paul's revised understanding of the 'plight' in terms of his revision of that monotheism. This proposal can be expressed in terms of a contribution to the current debate about 'plight and solution' in his theology.

The debate in question, like many others, was initiated by Ed Sanders in 1977.[371] Did Paul come with a 'problem' or 'plight' to which he discovered that Jesus was the 'solution'? Or was part of the shock of the revelation on the road to Damascus the fact that, since Israel's God had apparently provided him with a 'solution', there must have been some kind of hitherto unsuspected 'plight'? Or what? The standard assumption, since Augustine at least, and especially since Luther, was that Paul had been labouring under the problem of a guilty conscience, aware of his own inability to meet the inexorable demands of the law, and unable to find peace with his maker –

[371] Sanders 1977, 442f. ('the solution as preceding the problem'); 474f. Sanders is explicitly reacting against Bultmann and others like him (e.g. Bultmann 1951–5, 1.190, 227), noting that Bornkamm 1971 [1969], 120 registers a similar protest while retaining the normal 'sin–salvation' expository outline.

and that he discovered the crucified Jesus as the answer to all this. Sanders proposed an alternative view: that Paul had actually, by his own account, been a good, blameless and successful Jew (Philippians 3.4–6), that he had seen nothing wrong with Torah, and that the fresh revelation of Jesus on the Damascus Road forced him to conclude that there must after all have been some kind of a 'problem' to which Jesus was the 'solution'. Sanders then uses this as a way of explaining Paul's apparently bizarre and contradictory statements about the Torah: they were not thought out or logically arranged, but were simply the result of Paul waving his arms around, believing that something must have been wrong with his native Judaism and its law but not having the time or inclination to work out exactly what, and so resorting to a string of odd, disjointed polemical remarks on the subject.

The standard Augustinian approach, in one form or another, is still the 'default mode' for many writers on Paul, not least many commentators on Romans, where these issues are sharply focused. Romans has long been read, particularly at a popular level, in terms of 'sin and salvation' – understood in line not only with the protestant systems against which Sanders was reacting, but also with more or less the entire swathe of western theology since the middle ages. This tradition continues.[372]

Many, however, have followed Sanders in taking the latter approach.[373] Here as elsewhere Sanders is in fact echoing the position of some Reformed theology; in this case, the account given by Karl Barth and some of his followers.[374] Barth reacted sharply against any form of 'natural theology', partly because of his rejection of the liberalism of his teachers, and partly because of his opposition to Nazi ideology. He insisted that all knowledge, including knowledge of evil and sin, is given only in the light of the gospel of Jesus Christ. Sanders represents a less theologically robust version of this account: Paul discovers 'salvation' in Jesus, and as a result rejects all other systems, without really working out why.

Both the 'normal' western view and the view of Sanders and others must, however, be challenged on the basis of the larger account of 'the problem of evil' I have sketched above – and on the basis of the Pauline texts themselves. The question of 'plight and solution' demands to be reframed within the perspective of second-Temple Jewish monotheism and of Paul's christological and pneumatological revisions of it. We must, in other words,

[372] See e.g. Hultgren 2010, and many others within mainstream protestant exegesis. A short but shrewd early assessment of the various debates was provided by Thielman 1989.

[373] See now Sanders 2007; 2008b, 327–9, with refs. to his earlier work; cf. too Räisänen 1986 [1983]; 2008, 326f., with modifications and questions. Watson 2004, 426 joins Sanders in seeing a christologically generated 'contradiction' in Paul's presentation of the law. The main challenge to a 'plight-to-solution' sequence in Paul has now come from Campbell 2009, who has reacted strongly against the same kind of thing, in the wider protestant tradition, that Sanders is rejecting in Bultmann: in Campbell's case, against a 'foundationalist' attempt first to establish 'human sin' and then to offer a remedy. See below for the exegetical outworkings.

[374] Compare Sanders's 'positive' account of the role of Torah within Judaism with the Calvinist view of the Torah as the way of life for a people already redeemed. For Barth cf. Barth 1936—1969, 2.2.92f.: 'it is only by grace that the lack of grace can be recognized as such'. This is picked up and emphasized by Martyn 1997a, 95, 266, and made thematic within his whole scheme.

carry through Sanders's revolution much further than he did himself. The ideas of personal sin and salvation, and the role of Israel's Torah in relation to those questions, remain important, indeed obviously vital, in Paul. But instead of approaching them through the framework of medieval and Reformational theories, we must relocate them within the much larger Jewish framework: monotheism versus idolatry, Torah-keeping versus immorality, the social, cultural and political meanings which went with those antitheses, and not least the larger global and even 'cosmic' perspective which was glimpsed from time to time within Israel's scriptures and later traditions and which Paul brought more fully into the open. We must not, in other words, collude with the relatively modern break-up of 'the problem of evil' into 'natural evil' on the one hand and 'human sin' on the other. Nor, in particular, must we go along with the classic western assumption (still evident in the continuing mainstream tradition and in Sanders's revisionist proposals) that 'salvation' will mean the rescue of humans away from the present world. Insofar as second-Temple Jews reflected on such things, they saw evil of all sorts as an unhappy jumble of disasters at all these levels, and 'salvation' as rescue from *evil* (whether personal, political or cosmic) rather than as rescue from the created *world*. Their monotheism was expressed in the cry for justice and the plea for rescue, two of the great themes of Isaiah 40—55: in other words, for a radical change of affairs *within* the created world. Paul's revised monotheism declared that justice had been done, and rescue provided, in the Messiah and by the spirit. This gave him a much sharper vision of 'the problem', but it did not create it from scratch.

The basic point can be put quite starkly. Paul already had 'a problem'; all devout Jews did, as we have seen. The fact that it was not the same as the 'problem' of the conscience-stricken medieval moralist does not mean it was non-existent. It was the problem generated by creational and covenantal monotheism: why is the world in such a mess, and why is Israel still unredeemed? The revelation of Jesus as the crucified and risen Messiah meant, for Paul, that the covenant God had offered the solution to these problems – but, in offering the solution, Israel's God had redefined the problems, had revealed that they had all along been far worse than anyone had imagined. Just as the normal Jewish monotheism generated a particular analysis of 'the plight', so Paul's revision of that monotheism generated a revised analysis. There is therefore a strong sense in which his understanding of the problem of the world, of humans, and of Israel was newly revealed through the gospel, even though there is another sense in which that understanding remained at its heart that of second-Temple Judaism. The regular problem of continuity and discontinuity is found here, just as at so many other points of Pauline, and indeed early Christian, theology. This already-existing 'plight', it should be noted, is quite different from, and much larger than, the alternative 'plights' envisaged, in dialogue with Sanders, by Sandmel and others.[375]

Paul moved, in other words, from his original understanding of 'the plight' to a 'solution' which revealed the full dimensions of the original 'plight':

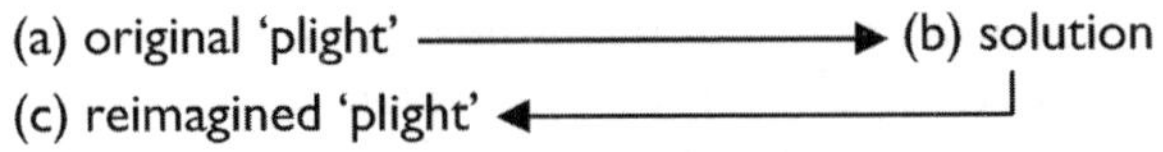

Obviously, (a) and (c) are not the same; but nor are they entirely different. The reimagined plight at (c) is the radical version of (a), forced upon Paul by the solution (b). Sanders is absolutely correct to point out that what Paul says about the 'plight' as he now sees it is a reflex of his grasp of the solution. But he is wrong, I shall argue, *both* to suggest that this reimagined plight (c) was a quite new thing (in other words, denying the existence of (a) at all), *and* to suggest that Paul's expressions of (c), particularly his sharp words about the Jewish law, are simply random and scattered polemical outbursts.

What then was the reimagined plight? How did Paul's grasp of 'the solution' enable him – or, indeed, compel him – to radicalize the original 'plight' which we have set out in the previous section? We can sketch this in three quick moves which we will then substantiate exegetically. The cross, the resurrection and the holy spirit together brought the 'plight' suddenly and sharply into focus.

1. The most obvious element of Paul's revised version of the 'plight' follows directly from the fact of a *crucified* Messiah. 'If "righteousness" comes through the law, then the Messiah died for nothing.'[376] That is basic to everything else.
2. Not so obvious, but equally important, was the fact of the *risen* Messiah. Paul's understanding of the resurrection gave him a much more focused understanding of the creator's purposes for the whole cosmos – and hence of the problem, the 'plight', in which that whole creation had languished.
3. The revelation of the personal presence of Israel's God in the transforming work of the spirit compelled Paul to a recognition of the depth of the human plight. All humans, Jews included, were hard-hearted, in need of renewal in the innermost human depths.

[375] Sanders 1977, 443 n. 5 quotes Sandmel as suggesting that Paul may have had an 'underground' plight which he does not describe: 'a difficulty with the law as adequate to human need'. I agree with Sanders that Phil. 3 and 2 Cor. 3 seem directly to deny such a thing; but Sandmel's formulation does not begin to reach the kind of 'plight' I am envisaging, the whole state of the world and of Israel in particular. The debate has languished for too long in the area of a detached 'religion'.

[376] Gal. 2.21.

Each of these will be explored in separate sub-sections below. But it will be helpful, even at this stage, to point to the larger shape of what had happened on the road to Damascus. Saul of Tarsus was there confronted with the fact of the risen Jesus, and with the immediate conclusion that *he* was therefore the Messiah, that *he* had been exalted to the place of glory and authority at God's right hand – and that monotheism itself had therefore to be reconfigured around a man of recent memory who had not delivered Israel from the pagans, had not intensified Israel's own law-observance, had not cleansed and rebuilt the Temple, and had not brought justice and peace to the world after the manner of Isaiah's dream. This was, in its way, as cataclysmic a reversal of expectations for Saul of Tarsus as the fall of Jerusalem would be for the next generation. It compelled, as did that shocking event, a radical rethink, all the way back to Adam. What happened to Saul of Tarsus on the road to Damascus can be put, from one angle, like this: there was revealed to him an 'answer' to a question which was like the questions he had had but much, much more complex. He was provided with a 'solution' to a problem far deeper and darker than the problem he had been addressing. It was like someone trying to figure out how to draw an accurate circle and then, suddenly, being shown how to construct a perfect sphere. Following his Damascus Road vision, Saul of Tarsus was not thinking, 'Well, I've had this problem for a long time, and now I have the solution to it.' Nor was he thinking, as Sanders and others have suggested, 'Well, I didn't know I had a "problem", but if this is a "solution" there must have been a problem of some sort.' He was asking himself (scrolling through his well-remembered scriptures as he did so): what does *this* 'solution' (the resurrection of the crucified Jesus) have to say to *these* 'problems'? Paul was like a man who, on the way to collect a prescribed medication, studies the doctor's note and concludes from the recommended remedy that his illness must be far more serious than he had supposed.

The answers Paul came up with were neither random nor inconsistent. In his statements about the problem of human sin, and especially of the Jewish law, he was not (against Sanders and others) flailing around like someone who suspects there is a wasp in the room but isn't quite sure where it is.[377] Nor was he offering an account of human sin to which all might give unaided mental assent.[378] He came to the conclusion that *the fact of the crucified and risen Messiah, and of his place at the heart of Jewish monotheism, went hand in hand with an equally radical revision of 'the plight' both of the world and of Israel.*[379] His radical revisions of the second-Temple

[377] Sanders 2008b, 329–33 points out that his view is that Paul was 'coherent' but 'unsystematic'. But the point of his own 'solution-to-plight' model was at least in part to explain the apparent 'contradictions' in what Paul says about the law; and he himself has argued, on the one hand that Rom. 2.1–16 does not appear to fit with the rest of Paul's thought (Sanders 1983, 123–35), and on the other that Rom. 7.7–25 gives 'inconsistent' and 'tortured' explanations (1983, 79–81), and 'does not express existentially a view which Paul consistently maintains elsewhere' (1983, 78).

[378] See Campbell 2009: Campbell does not think Paul himself was guilty of this, either, but he does think it is what Rom. 1.18—3.20, as it stands, now offers.

[379] Keck 1984, as often, has his finger on the point: Paul radicalized the apocalyptists' problem.

monotheism of divine identity thus played straight back into his radical revisions of the second-Temple understanding of the 'plight' of the world and of Israel. Paul did not retain an original 'plight' and merely discover that Jesus was the 'solution' to it. Nor was he, plightless, confronted with a 'solution' for which he felt compelled to cobble together a somewhat random 'plight'. He already had a 'plight'. All Jews did, especially those who were zealously devoted to the one God. But the one God had now offered a 'solution' which, at first sight, did not seem to address the 'plight' at all. Paul therefore rethought the 'plight', exactly as he had rethought the 'monotheism' which framed it: around Jesus and the spirit.

We can therefore spell out the three categories of 'revised plight' as follows.

(b) The 'Plight' Revised (1): in the Light of the Cross

The crucified Messiah meant that the 'problem' must have been far worse than had previously been imagined. Why would the Messiah need to be crucified if the solution to the world's problems lay in Israel's vocation to shine the light of the law into the darkness of paganism? Something more had been provided, and must therefore have been needed. This is what underlies not only Paul's insistence that believing Jews and believing gentiles belong together in a single new family, but also his parallel insistence that all Jews join all gentiles in the dock, charged with the basic fact of sin. And this, I suggest, is why he does what no Jew before him had done (though the point was arguably there in the narrative logic of Genesis 1—12), and traces the problem right back to Adam and Eve. In this respect, the cross functions in relation to Paul's reconsideration of 'the plight' as the fall of Jerusalem functioned in relation to the similar reconsideration we find in *4 Ezra* and *2 Baruch*. If Jerusalem has fallen, they concluded, the Jewish people themselves must be caught up in the primal human sin along with everyone else. If the Messiah has been crucified, Paul reasoned, it can only be because Israel as a whole shared in the plight of all human beings. The innovatory idea of a primal sin infecting all people, Jews included, was something Paul found in scripture. But he went looking for it because of the revelation of the crucified Messiah.

Another way of approaching the same point is to look at what has happened to Paul's notion of the coming final judgment. Saul of Tarsus undoubtedly believed, on the basis of many scriptural warrants, that Israel's God would one day return in power and glory to judge the world. He may have believed, on the basis of texts like Isaiah 11, that he would perform this action of judging the world in and through the coming Messiah. Paul the apostle, believing that Jesus had been demonstrated to be Messiah through his resurrection, believed that the coming judgment would be 'through the

Messiah, Jesus'.[380] But there is more to the messianic revision of 'the plight' than simply knowing the name of the coming judge. Because the Messiah was and is the crucified Jesus, the 'problem of evil' goes much deeper than Paul had previously imagined. Specifically, it runs right through Israel itself. If Israel, God's chosen people, could somehow be affirmed as they stood – if, in other words, 'righteousness' could come by means of Torah – then the Messiah would not have needed to die. The problem appears to be Sin: both Sin as a cosmic power which holds all humans captive, and 'sin' as the deadly disease within all human hearts.

This is the force, particularly, of Galatians 2.15–21. The reason why Paul there argues that it will not do to have separate tables for Jewish Messiah-followers and gentile Messiah-followers is that the cross of the Messiah has revealed a problem – and the solution to that problem – which goes deeper than the Jew–gentile division would indicate.

The cross, he explains in 2.17–18, puts the Jew in a terrible dilemma. Either (a) you must leave behind the Torah's distinction of Jew and gentile, by sharing in table-fellowship with *all* your fellow believers, including the gentiles, or (b) you must rebuild the wall you had torn down, the legal barrier between yourself and the world of 'Gentile sinners' – even if these 'gentile sinners' are now also 'in the Messiah'. In the first case, you will find yourself technically labelled a 'sinner', for sharing fellowship with uncircumcised gentiles. In the second, you will find Torah accusing you of being a 'lawbreaker', because of course you, like all other Jews, have broken the law (including in your earlier sharing table-fellowship with gentiles). Here is the choice: either a 'sinner' or a 'lawbreaker'. Israel's scriptures themselves, as Paul explains in the next chapter, 'shut up everything together under the power of sin' (3.22). There is 'the problem', revealed for the first time, in all its depth, *through the gospel*. That is why the divinely granted solution is itself drastic: death and new life. Nothing else will do. The cross of the Messiah says so:

> Through the law I died to the law, so that I might live to God. I have been crucified with the Messiah. 20I am, however, alive – but it isn't me any longer, it's the Messiah who lives in me. And the life I do still live in the flesh, I live within the faithfulness of the son of God, who loved me and gave himself for me. 21I don't set aside God's grace. If 'righteousness' comes through the law, then the Messiah died for nothing.[381]

This is as explicit as it gets. The death of the Messiah has revealed something previously unimagined (except perhaps by the prophets, and Deuteronomy!): that the 'problem' went deeper than the pre-Christian Pharisee had ever imagined. Simply reinscribing ethnic divisions among the community of Messiah-believers will not do. The only solution to this far

[380] Rom. 2.16. This is one of the rare occurrences of 'through Messiah'; normally when Paul says 'through' in relation to Jesus he says 'through Jesus'. This almost certainly indicates that he is thinking specifically of the coming messianic judgment. (The variant reading 'through Jesus Messiah' is well supported but is clearly 'easier'; see e.g. Fitzmyer 1993, 312; Jewett 2007, 193.)

[381] Gal. 2.19–21.

deeper problem is to die with the Messiah, to put to death the old identity, and to find, in rising with him, a new identity in which those distinctions are no longer relevant.

'Salvation' would therefore now mean, for Paul, not simply 'the age to come', with the promise of resurrection ('rescue from death') for all those who have died as righteous Jews ahead of that very this-worldly 'salvation'. Nor would it simply mean deliverance from pagan oppression as part of that package. That vision of the age to come was the hope articulated in the Maccabaean literature, and we may be sure it was the vision also which sustained Saul of Tarsus. But in the light of the Messiah's cross and resurrection a deeper analysis of the problem could be seen, and with it a deeper meaning for 'salvation'. 'Salvation' must now mean 'rescue from the disease of which pagan idolatry-and-immorality are an obvious symptom', in other words, 'rescue from sin'; where 'sin', *hamartia*, is the deadly infection of the whole human race, Israel included. And once that radicalization is glimpsed, it will become clear – as Paul sees, and as we shall explore presently and then particularly in the next chapter – that Torah, though it is God's good and holy law, not only exacerbates the problem, but was actually given in order that, through exacerbating the problem, it would bring it to the place where it could be dealt with once and for all.

The problem with highlighting 'sin' in this way is that it might appear to offer a sigh of relief to the 'old perspective' on Paul. There we are (one can hear certain readers thinking): we were right all along! The problem is sin; the solution is salvation; it's taken a long time to get round the block and back to where we started, but since we're safely home let's not worry any more about these funny 'new perspectives'. But to think like that would be to collude precisely with a diminished, individualized and often essentially Platonic vision of 'salvation', according to which all that has to happen is for 'souls' to be 'saved' out of this wicked world of space, time and matter, rescued from anything (including 'human works') which looks as though they might emphasize that physical world rather than the 'purely spiritual' one. Over against that shrunken, often Marcionite (sometimes indeed dangerously Manichean) worldview stands the whole argument of Romans 3.21—8.39, with its insistence that humans are made for 'glory', and that 'glory' means inheriting the whole creation as the human sphere of responsibility. Paul's redefinition of 'salvation' does indeed radicalize the (from his point of view) somewhat shallow notion of 'sin' we find among many pre-Christian Jewish writings. The effect of this, however, is not to reinscribe a Platonic soteriology of 'saved souls', but to offer the diagnosis of the problem which has lain all along at the heart of the problem of the creator and the creation: that humans, designed to reflect God's glory and wise sovereignty into the world, have 'worshipped and served the creature rather than the creator, who is blessed for ever'.[382] When humans are 'saved', rescued from sin and its effects and restored to their image-bearing, heart-

[382] Rom. 1.25.

circumcised, mind-transformed vocation, then, according to Paul, *creation itself can and will be rescued* from the bondage to decay which has come about through the human derogation of duty. As for the humans themselves, they will be raised to new life as part of this larger scene, rescued from the death which was the natural entail of that sin.[383] This is a much bigger picture than traditional western soteriology, whether catholic or protestant, liberal or conservative, has usually imagined. It is the picture which, in Israel's scriptures, has to do with the faithfulness of the creator to his whole world, the faithfulness of the covenant God to the promises he had made not only *to* his people but also *through* his people: in your family, all the families of the earth will be blessed.

Within this larger picture we can understand at last what Paul says about the law. We have already sketched this in chapter 7 above, and will return to it at the heart of our treatment of 'election' in chapter 10 below. But for the moment we can highlight the point like this. Within the traditional reading of Paul, the problem of 'the law' was that it condemned sin, and indeed sinners; and the answer of 'the gospel' was to declare that the Messiah had taken that condemnation upon himself. That, to be sure, is part of what Paul says, but Sanders and others were right to observe that much of what Paul says about the law does not fit that over-simple summary. Sanders, for his part, followed by Räisänen and others, proposed that Paul had not thought out his reasons for rejecting the law, so that his polemic was both random and, in a sense, inconsistent. Against both accounts, Paul's new vision of 'the plight', on the basis of the cross, revealed to him not only that the law could not provide 'righteousness' for those under the law (otherwise a crucified Messiah would not have been needed), not only that the law could not equip 'the Jew' to be the light of the world (because it could not effect the personal transformation that 'the Jew' required just as much as 'the gentile'), but also that the law, precisely in its work of condemnation, had a strange but important role to play within the newly revealed divine elective purpose for Israel. This points us to the mysteries of Romans 7 and Romans 9—11, to which we shall return. But it is appropriate to stress at this point that whereas Saul of Tarsus seems to have had no 'problem of the law', Paul the apostle saw the law as playing a crucial role *both* in the freshly perceived 'problem' of Israel *and* in the solution to that problem. At this point the cross has indeed generated a quite new point of view, though this cannot be stated in terms either of the traditional reading (in which 'the law' simply changes from being 'a good thing to be obeyed' to being 'a bad thing now to be abolished') or of the revisionist readings of Sanders and particularly Räisänen (in which Paul hurls miscellaneous but muddled remarks in the general direction of the law). The new point of view will emerge more clearly in the next chapter.

[383] Rom. 1.32.

(c) The 'Plight' Revised (2): in the Light of the Resurrection

The second way in which Paul's existing 'plight' was brought into a larger context and a sharper focus was through the resurrection of Jesus. Not only did this demonstrate that Jesus was indeed Israel's Messiah, despite his shameful execution. Not only did it constitute him as the universal judge at the coming day of judgment. It also pointed to the ultimate nature of the divinely intended future for the whole world, and as such pointed back as well to the deepest level of 'the plight' under which not only Israel, not only humans in general, but the whole creation had been suffering.

The 'new creation' passage towards the end of Isaiah could still envisage death within that new world.[384] A leap beyond that was taken, however, in Isaiah 25.6–9, and Paul homed in on that as a promise which had now come into focus: what the covenant God had done for Jesus he would do not only for all his people but for the whole creation. He would 'swallow up death for ever'.[385] Paul's vision of the ultimate rescue of the entire created order (rather than a rescue of humans *from* creation), a vision which flowed directly from what he believed about the Messiah, impelled him to an understanding of 'evil' as a whole which was more than the sum total of human sins or human deaths. 'Sin' and 'Death' were themselves suprahuman forces bent on corrupting and destroying the creator's good world. Only in the light of the stunning and unexpected nature of the Messiah's victory could the beaten foes be recognized for what they were.

This perspective on 'the problem' as Paul perceived it enables us to integrate, rather than to marginalize, Paul's language about 'the powers'.[386] The problem is *both* personal (the heart infected by sin, corrupting the mind into idolatry and the person into dehumanized behaviour: see below) *and* cosmic, since the worship of idols allows the demons who masquerade behind them to gain power not rightly theirs. Thus both 'Sin' with a capital S and 'the powers', variously described, and also Death itself, have replaced, in Paul's mind, the wicked, idolatrous pagans as seen from within his pre-Christian Pharisaism. 'Sin' and 'Death' are now 'the enemy', to be defeated in the final battle; indeed, they have already been defeated on the cross, and will be defeated fully and finally at the *parousia*.[387] This both/and position will, in our next chapter, enable us to avoid the unfortunate either/or into which certain parts of Pauline studies have recently fallen. For Paul, in the light of cross and resurrection together, the problem of actual human sin, which could be traced back to Adam and Eve, nested within the larger problem of 'Sin' as a suprahuman power, and 'Death' as its equally powerful consequence, and hence within the larger problem of the cosmos as a whole.

[384] Isa. 65.17–25.

[385] Isa. 25.8, quoted in 1 Cor. 15.54.

[386] Among the many works on this theme those of Wink stand out (Wink 1984; 1986; 1992). Cf. too e.g. Caird 1956; Reid 1993.

[387] cf. 1 Cor. 2.6–8; 15.20–8; Col. 2.15.

This redrawing of the traditional picture has brought us back by a different route to the point we reached at the end of our treatment of Paul's revised monotheism – though it was in fact the inner truth in our starting-point as well. As we saw, for a Jew to pray the *Shema* was to 'take on oneself the yoke of the kingdom'. The victory of the one God over the 'powers', through the Messiah, is as we saw earlier one central element in what is meant by that 'kingdom-theology', as we find it (for instance) in 1 Corinthians 15.20–8. Just as what counts with second-Temple monotheism is not an abstract dogmatic analysis and a corresponding mental assent, but signing on as a loyal worshipper and follower of the one God, so what counts with the revised monotheism is not simply adherence to a creedal formula but a commitment to be part of the new humanity, part of those already 'raised with the Messiah'.

This throws the alternative into stark relief. If the one God has already inaugurated his kingdom in and through the Messiah, then the powers of the world are called to account. This applies to any and every power, starting with Sin and Death themselves and working through to all power structures that, as in Romans 8.37–9, might range themselves against the rule of the one God. The revised-monotheistic account of the inauguration of the kingdom of the one God thus insists upon a deeper and broader analysis of 'the problem' than even the earlier so-called 'apocalyptic' visions had offered. The plight to which the gospel offers the divine solution was the plight of the whole created order, with the specifically human predicament as a vital element within that larger picture but by no means comprising the whole picture in itself.

All this means, at a stroke, that the problem Douglas Campbell has identified in the 'normal' readings of Romans 1—3 is a problem for one particular tradition of reading rather than for Romans itself.[388] It also means that we can take fully on board the point made by J. L. Martyn and others, providing as it were the apocalyptic and theological depth to the somewhat pragmatic proposal of E. P. Sanders: the 'apocalypse', the 'revelation' which takes place in the gospel events concerning Jesus, and the gospel proclamation concerning Jesus, includes the unveiling of the 'problem' to which the gospel is the 'solution'.[389] But this can be done *without denying for a moment* that this new 'problem' is the radicalization of the existing one which a first-century Pharisee would have recognized and agonized over. And it can be done while still affirming the rightness, when appropriately radicalized through the gospel, of the 'solution' envisaged by such a first-century Pharisee – in other words, the revelation of the covenant justice of Israel's God, his faithfulness to the promises to Abraham. It is not a matter (as Douglas Campbell has suggested) of Romans 1.18–25 and the following

[388] See Campbell 2009, Parts I, II and III.

[389] We may, however, permit ourselves gentle amusement at the suggestion (Martyn 1997a, 266) that Karl Barth is to be congratulated for having reached this conclusion *on exegetical grounds*. If ever it was clear that a quasi-exegetical proposal was put forward because of a theological *a priori*, it was precisely there. For Barth, *everything* had to be revealed in and only in Jesus Christ, otherwise a dangerous loophole of potential 'natural theology' might be left for the *Deutsche Christen* to exploit.

passage appealing to a 'foundationalist' position, an account of 'the human problem' to which anybody might come by observation and reason alone, and which could then serve as a platform to persuade people first to admit that they were sinners and then to see the Christian message as the answer to their problem. That is the thing to which Campbell is fundamentally objecting, though we may question how much an argument of this type was ever a problem in the pre-rationalist world of the first century.

To this extent, the message about Jesus is indeed logically prior to the full exposition of the human plight. To put it in preacher's language, we learn 'what's wrong' at the foot of the cross. But it would be foolish to suggest that that plight, when fully revealed, had nothing to do with the 'plight' as previously envisaged, or that the 'solution', also now fully revealed, had nothing to do with the 'solution' envisaged by a second-Temple Jew, not least a devout Pharisee.[390] The whole point is that Jesus, the Messiah, has done what the Messiah had to do – only he has done it in such a way as to make one realize that the half had not been told. Or at least, *heard*: Paul would say that it *had* been told, had been there all along in Moses, the prophets and the Psalms, but that he and his contemporaries had been deaf to what the scriptures had been saying.[391]

(d) The 'Plight' Revised (3): in the Light of the Spirit

If Paul's previous understanding of 'the plight' had been radicalized by his understanding of Jesus, specifically his death and resurrection, it also seems to have been radicalized in the light of his understanding of the spirit – particularly the spirit's work in renewing the hearts of God's people. This, of course, was a regular biblical theme. But we may guess that Saul of Tarsus would have been happy to say that the way to the renewal of the heart was the study and practice of Torah. Paul the apostle had discovered otherwise, not least, we may suppose, through watching the work of the spirit among gentiles who had not submitted to Torah, but whose hearts and minds had been renewed so that they were enabled to confess Jesus as lord and believe that the creator God had raised him from the dead, and to love one another across previously insuperable boundaries.[392] And, indeed, to behave in ways previously unimaginable. And, indeed, *not* to behave in ways previously taken for granted.[393]

Like the other early Christians, Paul believed that God's holy spirit had been poured out upon those who believed the gospel, transforming their lives from within both with spiritual gifts and with the more slow-growing

[390] It would also be pastorally foolish to assume that there is no overlap between 'the plight' as seen in the light of the gospel and the multifarious felt 'plights' of human beings in general; but that takes us beyond our present task.

[391] cf. Rom. 10.19–21.

[392] Rom. 10.9–11; Col. 1.8.

[393] cf. e.g. 1 Cor. 6.9–11; Gal. 5.16–26; etc.

but long-lasting 'fruit' of which he speaks in Galatians 5.[394] In several passages Paul makes it clear that this spirit-given character is in fact the kind of human life to which Israel's law had been pointing all along, but which it had been powerless to bring about. The giving of the spirit was seen by Paul, after all, as one of the central *eschatological* gifts: it was another sign, correlated exactly with Jesus' resurrection, that the new age had dawned at last, and that with it a new transforming power had been unleashed into the world.[395] That, then, helped to generate a new glimpse of 'the problem', of which Saul of Tarsus had previously been unaware: Torah, left to itself, *and working on the Adamic human nature of its adherents, i.e. on Israel according to the flesh*, could not give the 'life' that it promised. That life appeared to the devout Jew as a shimmering mirage which retreated as one approached. From this angle, too – also worked out in Romans 7 and 8 – the revelation Paul received on the road to Damascus unfolded to reveal the true plight of Israel. The one God had revealed this 'life' both in the resurrection of Jesus, in the promise of resurrection for all Jesus' people, and in the new moral shaping of their present lives. This was 'what the Torah could not do', because by itself it could not in fact deal with either sin or death.

The presence and power of the spirit thus point back to the same ultimate problem that Paul had glimpsed through the revelation of Jesus himself. Deuteronomy, Jeremiah and others had spoken of the renewal of the heart. When Paul, like the other early Christians, experienced that renewal, and saw others experiencing it, they must have realized how badly it had been needed. Here, too, Paul found the clues in scripture, where Israel had been warned about its own hard-heartedness. But he went looking for those clues, we may surmise, because of the revised monotheism in which the spirit of the one God, the spirit of Jesus, had produced previously unimagined effects on hearts and minds, not only his own but those of converts from every kind of background. The fact of the outpoured spirit, transforming people's inner thoughts and motivations and enabling them to 'love God' as the *Shema* had commanded – and thus locating this work once more within Jewish-style monotheism – gave Paul an all-important clue as to the nature of the 'disease' to which the gospel of Jesus was, he believed, the 'cure'. The theme of the renewal of the heart is found in Qumran. Clearly anyone who knew Deuteronomy 30, and who believed that the covenant had now been renewed, might be expected to claim heart-renewal, or perhaps heart-circumcision, as a sign of that.[396] But the heart-renewal that Paul knew for himself, and saw in some unlikely characters in his congregations ('some of you were like that', he says sharply to the Corinthians after listing several unsavoury lifestyles), moved the question of the heart and its

[394] Other Jewish communities, of course, claimed similar things, the obvious example being the community of the Scrolls: cf. e.g. 1QS 3.6; 1QH 8.20; 20.11f.; CD 5.11–13; 7.4). See esp. Levison 1997.

[395] cf. Rom. 1.4; Gal. 3.1–5, and many other places.

[396] e.g. 1QS 5.5, an echo of e.g. Dt. 30.6 (cf. Rom. 2.29). On the spirit in Qumran cf. e.g. CD 2.12.

condition from being one of a number of issues to a position of prominence it had not had in second-Temple Judaism.[397]

All this helps us to see one key aspect of Paul's freshly envisaged 'plight', and how he got there. This has to do particularly with the significance of Paul's perception that the hope of Israel, the 'eschatology', had been inaugurated but not yet fully completed.

One can put it like this. If Death itself is the real enemy, one might have supposed that YHWH would have dealt with it all at once. 'The resurrection' should have happened, not just to the Messiah all by himself, but to all people, and to the whole world. But that would not have allowed for the fulfilment of the divine purpose, which was the new creation of people whose inner transformation would reflect the divine image as always intended, a people through whom the original intention for creation would then be fulfilled. Paul's vision of an *inaugurated* eschatology, in which the chosen people were reshaped through Messiah and spirit, enabled him to see one key dimension of the problem. The creator always intended to accomplish his purpose *through* human beings. But only through 'the end' somehow being brought forward into the present could that aim be fulfilled, could this renewed humanity be generated.

If, then, Paul had come to see the radical need for a renewed 'people of God' through whom the divine purpose would be accomplished, this represented a significant modification of his earlier views. In his pre-Christian belief, Israel's God was indeed going to act one day to restore all things and to rescue his people, and the people who would inherit that 'age to come' would be marked out in the present by their possession of, and keeping of, Torah. That, as I have argued elsewhere, is substantially what Paul the apostle looks back on as 'justification by works': the marking out in the present, by Torah, of those who would be vindicated in the future. But the cross and resurrection of the Messiah, and the transforming gift of the spirit, launching the creator's new world and new humanity in advance of the final 'end', indicated to Paul that there was a radical problem with this way of looking at things – the same radical problem, indeed, that we have seen all along, namely sin and death. If the Messiah's death and resurrection really did unveil the age-old plan of the covenant God, revealing in action his world-restoring faithfulness and justice, that 'justification by works' was ruled out. For the divine purpose to make sense, the creator God would have to remodel the covenant people itself, though this, too, turned out to be what had always been promised and envisaged in Genesis, Deuteronomy and elsewhere. The problem of 'sin', in other words, was not simply that individuals faced the divine wrath. The problem was that Israel, being infected with sin like everybody else, could not carry forward the divine purpose. This is where the heart of Paul's radically revised view of election, which we shall examine in the next chapter, dovetails with his radically

[397] cf. 1 Cor. 6.11. The theme, arguably, had had this significance for Jesus: see e.g. Mk. 7.1–23; 10.5–9; cf. *JVG* 282–7. The 'sermon on the mount' in Mt. 5—7 is of course centrally concerned with the transformation of the heart: see *JVG* 287–92.

revised view of a monotheistically framed 'problem of evil'. What is required, and what has been provided in Messiah and spirit, is the 'justification' of a new people, in advance of the final day: a transformed covenant people, a remodelled Abraham-family. When the cross reveals to Paul that Israel shares the sin-and-death problem of the whole world, this does not mean that the category of 'Israel', of the covenant family, is abolished. The creator, who has fulfilled his promises in the Messiah, now intends by the spirit to take forward his purposes through this renewed family, a family who, in advance of the final day, have already been declared to be his people, to be 'in the right'.

When we map this solution-driven reworking of the 'plight' on to the picture of second-Temple Judaism we sketched in chapter 2 above, one thing becomes clear. What is now being offered is the 'solution' to the problem of *Israel's 'exile'*, the ongoing condition from the time of the geographical Babylonian exile to the present. In the classic texts like Isaiah 40—55 and Daniel 9, Israel's 'exile' was the result of Israel's idolatry and sin: exile was the covenantal punishment envisaged in Deuteronomy 28 and 29. Thus, near the heart of the complex of elements involved in 'the original plight', then radicalized and reframed in 'the reimagined plight', we find the need for fresh divine action, in faithfulness to the covenant and the 'justice' which that involved, to deal with sin and to regenerate the chosen people as a new kind of family altogether. When Paul speaks of 'justification', it is this complex problem to which he is offering what he sees as the new solution, shaped by Messiah and spirit. The creator God is accomplishing his age-old purpose in a way previously unimagined: by dealing with sin, not only Israel's sin but also that of the whole world, and by thus creating a renewed, faithful and now worldwide family.

What happens, then, when we put together these three elements, cross, resurrection and spirit? Paul has revised his previous understanding of the plight of the world, of humans and of Israel in line with his revision of monotheism itself. Standing behind it all was the strong early Christian belief that in Jesus and the holy spirit the covenant God had returned at last, and had acted decisively to judge and save. The sudden brightness of this light cast dark shadows: if *this* was what it looked like when YHWH returned, all sorts of things were called into question. The resurrection of Jesus constituted him as Messiah, but he remained the *crucified* Messiah, and if in the strange purposes of the one God the Messiah, his one and only true 'son', had had to die, it could only mean that the plight of Israel was far worse than had been thought. The resurrection itself demonstrated that the real enemy was not 'the gentiles', not even the horrible spectre of pagan empire. The real enemy was Death itself, the ultimate anti-creation force, with Sin – the personified power of evil, doing duty apparently at some points for 'the satan' itself – as its henchman. Finally, the experience of the spirit revealed the extent to which hardness of heart and blindness of mind had been endemic up to that point across the whole human race. All these were there in Israel's scriptures, but so far as we know nobody else in second-Temple Judaism had brought them together in anything like the form we find them in Paul. It looks very much as though it was the gospel itself, both in proclamation and experience, which was the driver in bringing Paul to this fresh understanding of 'the plight' from which all humans, and the whole creation, needed to be rescued.

Paul thus came to believe that in and through the death, resurrection and enthronement of Jesus and the outpouring of the spirit *the true nature of the enemy, of 'the problem', had itself finally been revealed.* Just as Isaiah, in a moment of sharp clarity, saw that Assyria was not the real and ultimate problem facing Israel, but that Babylon would be, so Saul of Tarsus, as part of what was 'revealed' on the road to Damascus in the unveiling of the risen Jesus as Messiah and lord, realized that Rome itself, and paganism in general, was not the real problem.[398] The real problem was Sin and Death – enemies which could be tracked, in a way that so far as we know had not been done before then, all the way back to Adam. If Sin and Death had been defeated in the unexpected messianic victory, then they had been the real problem all along. Like *4 Ezra* and *2 Baruch*, Paul was compelled by the pressure of new events to go back more deeply than before.[399]

Like them, this meant discerning the sin of Adam, and the death that it brought in its train, behind all other human sin, including the now evidently chronic state of Israel itself.[400] For *4 Ezra* and *2 Baruch*, the Temple had fallen but the Messiah had not yet come; for Paul, the Messiah had come, and had been crucified and raised, but the Temple was still standing. The parallels are as important as the differences. In both cases the events that had happened pointed to a radicalization of 'the plight'.[401]

With that, inevitably and crucially, Paul gained a new vision of 'salvation' itself. It was not enough that Israel be rescued from pagan attack. 'Salvation' was now revealed as God's rescue from the ultimate enemies themselves. The death and resurrection of Jesus transformed Paul's Pharisaic belief in the bodily resurrection of righteous Jews, to share in the coming kingdom of the one God, into a radicalized version of the same hope: the hope for a totally renewed cosmos and for the people of this one God to be given an immortal physicality to live in it.[402] That is why Romans 8, as the long outworking of 5.12–21, is such a crucial, as well as a climactic, moment in Paul's writing. 'Neither death nor life, nor angels nor rulers, nor the present,

[398] For Assyria and Babylon cf. Isa. 23.13, on which see Seitz 1993, 168f. See too Isa. 39.1–7, where Hezekiah, relieved to be free from the Assyrian threat, agrees all too readily to an alliance with Babylon, only to have the prophet inform him that Babylon would succeed where Assyria had failed.

[399] On Adam in *2 Bar.* see Murphy 2005, 35f.

[400] 'Sin' and 'death' are clearly linked in Gen. 3, but it is not clear that anyone prior to Paul had elevated them into cosmic powers and made their link thematic within a worked-out theology; see Jewett 2007, 374: 'In contrast to intertestamental discussions of Adam, both death and sin appear to function here as cosmic forces under which all humans are in bondage.'

[401] Perriman 2010 proposes that the imminent fall of Jerusalem preoccupied Paul as well. I am not as averse to this proposal as most exegetes would be (see below, ch. 11), but it must remain largely a matter of speculation.

[402] 1 Cor. 15.50–7.

nor the future, nor powers, nor height, nor depth, nor any other creature': this is Paul's equivalent of Isaiah's taunt song against Babylon. He lists, exuberantly, all the forces in the universe that might be ranged against the one God, his people, and his purposes of redemptive new creation. And he declares them all to be impotent against the love of the creator and covenant God, now revealed in the Messiah.

Earlier Jewish writers had seen quite a bit of this, of course. But for Paul the nature and extent of 'the enemy' and 'the problem' were revealed precisely in the act of their overthrow. The full horror of the threatening dragon became apparent only as it lay dead on the floor. The hints had been there already, including the biblical warnings about the corrosive and destructive principalities and powers standing behind outward political enemies and operating through the local and personal 'sin' of individuals. Neither Saul of Tarsus nor Paul the apostle would have supposed one had to choose between the partial analyses offered by Genesis 3, Genesis 6 and Genesis 11: human rebellion, dark cosmic forces and the arrogance of empire all belonged together. A thoughtful and scripturally educated Pharisee could have figured that out already. But for Paul all of these were seen afresh in the light of the gospel. The fungus that had been growing on the visible side of the wall could now be seen as evidence of the damp that had been seeping in from behind. The worrying persistent and ingrained sin of Israel, not merely of the nations, was the tell-tale sign that the principalities and powers of Sin and Death had been at work all along in the covenant people, as well as in the idolatrous wider world.

This is how, as we shall see in a moment, Paul can declare in Romans that the gospel unveils not only God's covenant faithfulness, but also God's wrath. Paul already believed in God's covenant faithfulness, but had not known what it would look like in practice. Now he did. He had also believed in God's coming wrath, but had not realized its full extent. Now, with the gospel message about Jesus, crucified, raised and enthroned, and with the knowledge of what the newly poured-out spirit was capable of doing, he could see that clearly as well.

This meant, in particular, that Paul now had a clear-eyed vision of how 'the problem' affected Israel, too. With this we can see that his discussions of (what we call) 'the problem of the law' were not, after all, a collection of inconsistent, arm-waving generalities.[403] His new vision of 'the problem' was indeed shaped by the gospel. It was not simply a given from his earlier belief. It was certainly not a matter of 'discovering salvation in Christ' and so 'deducing that he must have had a problem', and associating the Jewish law with that problem. Nor, in particular, was it a matter of seeing that the Torah had cursed Jesus (Galatians 3.13 is regularly cited in this connection) and deducing that the one God, in raising Jesus from the dead, had declared the Torah to be at fault – perhaps even demonic – in pronouncing

[403] On the question of 'inconsistency', see esp. *Climax* 4–7.

that curse, and that it was therefore to be set aside.[404] No: Paul saw very clearly that *Israel too was in Adam*, so that the chosenness of God's people, and their commission to bring God's light to the world, had not released them from the grim entail of sin and death. The law, therefore, God's holy, just and good Torah, had come with a purpose: not to attempt to rescue Israel from its Adamic state, *but to draw out the force of sin all the more precisely in Israel*, in order that sin might finally be condemned. That, as I have argued elsewhere, is the whole point of Romans 7.1—8.4.[405] As we saw in chapter 7, the law plays different roles at different stages of (Paul's vision of) the divine purpose. Once we understand that purpose in the nuanced way Paul actually articulates, there is of course plenty of necessary complexity, but no inconsistency.

This brings us at last to Paul's most thorough statement of 'the problem' to which 'the gospel' is the solution.

(iii) The Problem of Romans 1.18—2.16

The problem posed by the opening main section of Romans, which I take to be 1.18—2.16, can be sharpened to an extremely fine point.[406] Why does Paul say *gar* at the start of 1.18 (*apokalyptetai* ***gar*** *orgē theou*)? Why not *de*? Why (in English) is there an apparent causal connection, '*For* God's wrath is revealed'? Should it not be 'but'? How does the 'revelation of wrath' in 1.18 relate to the 'revelation of righteousness' in 1.17?

We can discount two standard but trivial answers to this. The first merely cuts the knot, suggesting that Paul used his connectives in a loose or sloppy way, so that *gar* could mean, more or less, *de* ('but').[407] This ignores the fact that again and again when Paul says *gar* ('for') he means exactly that, not least when it occurs in a tight sequence as here:

> I am eager to preach the gospel in Rome, *for* I am not ashamed of the gospel, *for* it is God's power for salvation to all who believe . . . , *for* God's righteousness is revealed in it . . . , *for*

[404] That imaginative but utterly wrong-headed line of thought has been proposed by many. It stands near the heart of the older protestant analysis of the origins of Paul's gospel: the law cursed Christ, but God raised him, therefore the law was wrong, therefore 'Christ is the end of the law': so, apparently, Stuhlmacher 1986 [1981], 139f., 157f. See too e.g. Burton 1921, 168–72, denying that the 'curse' was anything other than the curse pronounced by a 'legalism' which Paul then rejected; Esler 1998, 184–94, heading his section 'Paul's case against the law'. In fact, Paul's argument hinges on the belief that the 'curse' was proper and God-given (cf. 3.21 and Rom. 7.13, on which see below, 894–7); so, rightly, e.g. Räisänen 1986 [1983], 249.

[405] Wright 2002 [*Romans*], 549–81; and e.g. 1991 [*Climax*], ch. 10.

[406] I take Rom. 1.18—2.16 as the first section within the first main part of the letter, 1.18—4.25. On divisions of Rom. see e.g. Wright 2002 [*Romans*], 396–406.

[407] So e.g. Fitzmyer 1993, 277, citing others who see the particle as 'expressing contrast', and some who regard it 'as a mere transitional particle'. He gives no parallel examples for either of these uses, as indeed, especially in Paul, it would be hard to do. Contrast e.g. Jewett 2007, 151f., who insists that the *gar* be taken 'with full seriousness', since 1.18—2.16 explains the reason why 'salvation' (1.16) is needed. This does not, however, get to the heart of the link between 1.17 and 1.18.

> God's wrath is revealed from heaven, *because* what can be known about God is plain to them, *for* the invisible things of God have been seen . . .[408]

The fact that a paragraph marker is normally inserted between verses 17 and 18 should not be allowed to obscure this sequence of thought. Until it is definitively proved otherwise, we should assume that Paul sees a causal connection at each point in this sequence, which one could state by reading the passage in reverse and substituting 'therefore' for each 'for'. The invisible things have been seen, *therefore* what can be known about God is plain, *therefore* God's wrath is revealed, *therefore* God's righteousness is revealed, *therefore* the gospel is God's power for salvation, *therefore* I am not ashamed of the gospel.

That works all right up to a point, but still leaves the same puzzle in the middle. And the puzzle then relocates slightly, within our western tradition of exegesis at least: what exactly is 'God's wrath', anyway, and how is it 'revealed'? We are not at liberty, though, to say that Paul did not mean what he said, or that he was quoting somebody else with whom he was then going to disagree (see below). That is the exegetical equivalent of the marathon runner who jumps on a bus in the middle of the race to get out of the hard slog and go straight to the finish.

The second standard but trivial answer is that the 'for' in verse 18 is a compressed way of saying, 'and you need this revelation of divine righteousness *because* . . .' In other words, verse 18 is explaining, not how the divine righteousness is revealed, but why that revelation was necessary: 'the gospel is God's power for salvation, revealing God's righteousness from faith to faith; [and you all need this] *because* you are all sinners, under God's wrath, so that there is no other way for you to be saved.' This has been more or less the standard reading in western exegesis from at least Luther onwards. It appears to preserve the sense of the *gar*, but does so at the cost of *apokalyptetai*: nothing new is now 'revealed', since anyone with half an eye open can see that the human race is in a mess. This reading merely reinscribes the standard 'plight–solution' model: 'Here is the mass of sinful humanity, as we always knew (and as anyone can recognize); nobody can be justified by their own efforts; so here is the gospel which tells you that you don't have to be, but that you can be justified by faith instead.' That, I take it, is the reading which Campbell most recently has laboured to overthrow; but it is not one that I have offered myself.[409] Such a reading fails, as I have argued elsewhere and shall demonstrate in the next chapter, first and foremost at the level of exegesis: this is simply not what Paul actually says. He seems to think that something has been *unveiled*, disclosed, made known in a new, dramatic and unexpected fashion. For the standard western understanding of 1.18–32, there is nothing much new about the sinful state of humankind and the divine response. Paul seems to think there is.

[408] 1.15–20. The word 'for', especially when repeated, sounds very stilted in today's spoken English, which is why I have frequently paraphrased it in my own published translation.

[409] Campbell 2009, Part III (313–466).

A third, to my mind still unsatisfying, solution was proposed by C. K. Barrett. He suggested that there was indeed a new revelation of God's wrath, in that in Paul's day one could observe an increase in human corruption, in the outworking of God's anger as humans more obviously reaped the rewards of their own ill-doing. This seems to me an improvement at the level of exegesis, but no better in terms of content. For a start, Paul's polemic against idolatry and its dehumanizing effects was hardly new within second-Temple Judaism.[410] For another thing, I do not think we should accept Dodd's proposal (as Barrett seemed inclined to do) that Paul intended the phrase 'God's wrath' to denote the ongoing and immanent process of moral degeneration described in Romans 1.18–32. For Paul, 'wrath' is the execution of divine punishment on sinners, indicated in 1.32 itself ('they know that God has rightly decreed that people who do things like that deserve death'). There may indeed be a sense in which the essentially future verdict casts its shadow ahead of itself, a kind of grisly dark side of the inaugurated eschatology of justification (the verdict of the *end* already announced in the *present*). But, apart from anything else, when Paul says 'the divine wrath is revealed', and connects that quite tightly with the revelation of the gospel in 1.16–17, we should resist, unless forced to do otherwise, the suggestion that this 'revelation' is something which was taking place simply in the world around.

A fourth, differently unsatisfying, proposal has been put on the table by Ed Sanders himself: that here Paul simply repeats a standard Jewish critique of humankind, and then throws into the mix what amounts to a kind of synagogue sermon (2.1–16) which does not really cohere with what he says elsewhere.[411] This is a counsel of despair. Even more so is the dramatic recent proposal of Douglas Campbell: 1.18—3.20 is not Paul's view at all, but consists in large part of a 'speech in character', putting into the mouth of a hypothetical opponent a kind of Jewish, conceivably even a Jewish-Christian point of view *which Paul is then going to refute*. Campbell advances this with something approaching genius: he makes the best case one can imagine, based on rhetorical styles and ploys that (he says) were adopted and discussed in the pagan world of the day.[412] He is, of course, making a larger theological point, cognate with a position we have seen to be associated with Karl Barth (and picked up by commentators like J. L. Martyn): we must beware of anything remotely approaching 'natural theology', lest we construct an entire system 'from below' and so fall into Arianism or worse.[413] According to this principle, the fresh revelation offered in Jesus must be allowed not only to restate the terms of older discussions but to sweep them away entirely and set up something quite new in their place. But when the sweeping away includes significant sections of Paul's own text, we may be entitled to demur. One should, of course, always

[410] See e.g. Wis. 13.1–19; 15.1–19.

[411] Sanders 1983, 123–35 (see above).

[412] Campbell 2009, 519–41.

[413] See the discussion in *Interpreters*.

be prepared for novelty, to imagine that nobody has seen the point of a particular Pauline passage until our own day (there is no evidence that anyone in the ancient world read Romans as Campbell suggests Paul intended it to be read). But we should only adopt such a drastic solution, which Campbell clearly wants to do for reasons larger than immediate exegetical satisfaction, if exegesis itself cannot come up with anything better.

In fact, it can. The first key point is to note that 'the wrath' is indeed a *future* event (not, as C. H. Dodd and A. T. Hanson tried to argue, the process of moral decay within an ordered world, as described in 1.24–31).[414] Everywhere else, where Paul speaks about 'the wrath of God', this 'wrath' is something that is going to come upon the world, particularly upon idolaters and the like, in the future, in a climactic and decisive moment, not as an ongoing process. It is 'the wrath to come' in 1 Thessalonians 1.10, and this essentially future meaning is reflected in the other related texts.[415] The future 'day' is itself described in 2.5 as one of 'revelation', of 'apocalypse', of the *apokalypseōs dikaiokrisias tou theou*, the 'revelation of God's righteous judgment', an echo of both 1.17 and 1.18. It looks at first glance as if 2.5 is meant as a further explanation of the *apokalyptetai* in 1.18, with 2.16 coming in to back it up.

But how does this help? After all, this idea of the future 'wrath' of the one God against idolaters was not new in Paul's day. It was what the Maccabaean martyrs called down upon the head of Antiochus Epiphanes. It was what the Wisdom of Solomon envisaged coming upon the cynical and brutal wicked ones. So how can Paul say that it is 'revealed from heaven' in some fresh way?

The answer is that for Paul the 'revelation', as with the 'revelation' or 'apocalypse' of God's righteousness in the previous verse, is part of what has happened with the 'revelation' of Jesus the Messiah himself. Just as second-Temple monotheism has been rethought with Jesus in the middle of it, so Paul has also rethought that most immediate corollary of second-Temple monotheism, the promise that the one God will condemn idolatry and evil once and for all and so set the world right at last. And this rethinking, too, has happened around what Paul believes about the Messiah. Once we see 1.18—2.16 as a whole, we note that the whole passage is framed by the 'revelation' which consists of the news, itself part of 'the gospel', that God's judgment will be executed through the Messiah, Jesus (2.16). The coming 'day' of 2.5 is *the 'day' when God judges human secrets through the Messiah.*[416]

At one level this, too, was hardly 'news'. Ever since Psalm 2 at least, the coming Davidic king had been seen as the one who would execute God's judgment on the wicked pagans, and perhaps on wicked Israelites or Jews as

[414] Dodd 1959 [1932], esp. 47–50; Hanson 1957.

[415] The clearest: Rom. 2.5 (twice), 8; 3.5; 5.9; Eph. 5.6/Col. 3.6.

[416] *dia Christou* nb.: unusual, but precise for this very point. The coming day for messianic judgment is, significantly, the climax of the Areopagus speech as well (Ac. 17.31). This will be unwelcome news to those who see that passage as an example of Luke's distortion of Paul, but perhaps the argument should work the other way round.

well. But what Paul says in 1.18—2.16 goes further than this. The fact that it is *the crucified and risen Jesus* who is revealed as the Messiah, the one who embodies and unveils God's righteousness and the one who will enact God's wrath against idolaters, necessarily entails a *drastic revision* in the way 'the wrath' is now seen, a radical deepening of 'the problem' so that it can no longer be seen in terms of 'the wicked pagans and those Jews who collude with them', but rather in terms of a deeper, darker human sickness at a level previously imagined only by . . . well, people like Jeremiah with his sad words about the deceitfulness of the human heart.[417] And writers like the Deuteronomist who insisted that only drastic divine surgery could cure the disease deep within Israelites themselves.[418] And, of course, people like Jesus of Nazareth, who seems to have thought that uncleanness bubbles up from inside a person rather than merely getting into them via 'unclean' food.[419]

This is where, as I argued earlier, Paul's revision of Jewish monotheism in the light of the spirit makes its own contribution to the correlated revision of the 'problem' of which that monotheism had been aware. If Israel's God has sent his Messiah, and if the Messiah has been crucified and raised from the dead, this itself implies a major hermeneutical shift in the way one might now read the ancient promises and warnings. What is 'revealed' in the gospel of Jesus, son of David and son of God (1.3–4), is not only the name of the coming judge. It is the depth, and impartial universality, of the judgment. What is 'revealed' when the spirit goes to work to transform hearts and minds, including the hearts and minds of surprised non-Jews (2.25–9), is not only the possibility of a new kind of life. It is the depth, and impartial universality, of the previous disease. All this is implied when Paul declares that the one God will judge the secrets of the hearts through the Messiah.

The rhetorical 'sting' which Paul effects in 2.1 thus goes deeper than would otherwise have been the case. Having enticed both serious-minded Jews (think of the author of the Wisdom of Solomon, a near-contemporary of Paul) and serious-minded pagans (think of Seneca, another near-contemporary) into broadly agreeing with him in his devastating critique of pagan behaviour in 1.18–32, he turns the tables: you, too, are behaving in the same way. And in the light of what has been 'revealed' in the gospel, he can insist that, in the coming judgment, Jews and gentiles will be on exactly the same footing. The advantages and disadvantages they have had will be taken fully into account (2.12–15). God will show no partiality: there will be no 'favoured nation clause'.[420]

[417] Jer. 17.9.

[418] On the resonances of Rom. 2 with Dt., see e.g. Lincicum 2010, 149f.

[419] Mk. 7.1–23, etc. The insistence on the judgment of the secrets of the heart indicates, I think, that though Paul undoubtedly shared the normal biblical vision of divine wrath being meted out in (what we would call) 'this-worldly' events (see above, 163–75), he was here speaking of something which would go beyond any single such event (against Perriman 2010).

[420] On divine impartiality see esp. Bassler 1982, and e.g. Jewett 2007, 209f.

This too was not entirely new within second-Temple Judaism, though it may well be true to say that Saul of Tarsus would have been shocked to hear it put like this. 'They are Israelites, and theirs is the glory, the sonship, the giving of the law ...' and so on. If he sensed such pain about Israel's failure when he was already a follower of the crucified Messiah, what would he have said before?[421] The notion of divine justice was essential within Judaism, but that justice was balanced by the commitment made to Israel by the covenant God. The problem of holding those two together remains to this day.[422]

That is why Paul's developed picture of what we sometimes call 'the human plight' goes deeper than anything we find in pre-Christian Judaism. This should not be a surprise. It is part of the 'newness' of the gospel that Paul should probe back into the scriptural story of human origins for clues as to what has gone so badly wrong, far more wrong than he had previously thought. Paul, so far as we can tell, was now out on his own, developing an apparently unprecedented theological account of human sinfulness traced back to Adam himself, providing the platform from which he could explain how it was that *Israel, too, was in Adam*, with Torah merely intensifying that plight. It was not enough to say, with many Jewish thinkers before and after Paul's day, that all humans had an 'evil inclination', a *yetzer hara'*, which must be kept in check by the 'good inclination', the *yetzer hatob*.[423] That was just the surface noise, but underneath there lay a much deeper problem, the disease of sin itself. And that disease had to be traced back to its source. Despite some suggestions to the contrary, the line of thought in 1.18–25 has 'Adam' written all over it, even while it also alludes clearly to the primal sin of Israel (the golden calf).[424]

This theme emerges again and again in the spiral argument of Romans.[425] What Paul says in 1.18—2.16 is picked up in 5.12–21 (focused here on 5.20, where the law merely intensifies the plight of the Adamic humanity to whom it is given (i.e. Israel)). The same point is then developed in 7.1–25; it is picked up once more in 9.6–29. Adam and Israel, Adam and Israel ... but in each case the 'revelation' of the deep plight of humankind in general and Israel in particular is answered, just as 1.17 balances 1.18, by a further statement of divine justice and saving purposes.[426] Paul does not often elsewhere mention this Adamic radicalization of 'the plight', but when he does it is clear that its exposition in Romans reflects a position he had thought out very carefully.[427]

[421] Rom. 9.4.

[422] See e.g. Kaminsky 2007; and e.g. Thiessen 2011, 142–8.

[423] See Marcus 1986a, 17f.

[424] cf. e.g. Hooker 1959–60; and cf. too Adams 1997a; further discussion in Jewett 2007, 160–2.

[425] The word *hamartia*, sin, together with its various cognates, occur far more in Rom. alone than in all Paul's other letters put together; and *thanatos*, 'death', together with its cognate *thanatoō*, 'put to death' and *apothnēskō*, 'die', occur as often in Rom. as in all the other letters put together. Clearly 'sin' and 'death' are focal points in this letter in a way they are not, or not to the same extent, elsewhere.

[426] See 5.20b–21; 7.4–6 and 8.1–11; 9.30—10.13.

[427] e.g. 1 Cor. 15.21f.; 2 Cor. 11.3.

The need for 'salvation' (1.16) is thus intensified and radicalized. (Paul, unlike many modern writers, is careful not to say 'salvation' when he means 'justification', and vice versa.) The 'problem' from which one needs to be 'saved' is not simply the problem of pagan idolaters and their wicked ways. Nor is it simply the problem of foreign invasion or oppression, from which one would need to be 'saved'. In Isaiah 40—55, arguably one of Paul's favourite texts, the problem undoubtedly includes, and indeed is focused on, the Babylonian captivity; but the constant reference to the helpless moral and spiritual state of Israel itself, and the nature of the remedy provided (especially in the 'servant' passages) indicates that the ultimate 'plight' lies far deeper. It is the problem which goes down into the depths of the human heart, and in this respect Jews are no different from anyone else. That is why Paul's emphasis on the 'heart' (its wickedness and hardness; the secrets it contains which will come to light) comes out so strongly in precisely these passages.[428] At the level of the 'heart', 'the Jew' is no different from anybody else.

The problem of 'sin', as an infection from which all humans suffer, thus looms larger in Paul (particularly Romans) than in any of his second-Temple contemporaries, for the simple reason that the revelation of Jesus of Nazareth as the crucified Messiah compelled him to this conclusion. The 'solution' which the one God had presented, in raising Jesus from the dead, did not correspond to the 'problem' of which he was aware. It forced him to radicalize that 'problem'. Idolatry-and-immorality was not simply a pagan problem to which Jewish Torah-possession and Torah-keeping would provide the answer, either in terms of protecting Jews from catching the infection or, more positively, enabling them to bring the world back to its senses.[429] Idolatry-and-immorality, rather, was the gentile symptom of the disease *from which all humans, including Jews, were suffering*. That is what Paul learnt from the fact of the crucified Messiah, now exalted and recognized as the inner identity of the one God.

Romans goes on, of course, into the discussion of the particular question of 'the Jew', in 2.17–29. I have discussed that passage in detail elsewhere, and here only need say this.[430] For Saul of Tarsus, it was axiomatic that the creator God would address the problem of the world's sin through Israel. That is what 'election' was all about. But Paul the apostle realized, on the basis of the cross and resurrection of the Messiah and the gift of the spirit – which alerted him to scriptural teachings which had all along said the same thing – that Israel itself was in a hopeless condition. What was now needed was the creation of a new people in and through whom the creator God would take forward his purposes. That line of thought, already outlined in 2.17–29, explains why in Romans 3.21—4.25 Paul's exposition of the 'solu-

[428] Rom. 1.21, 24; 2.5, 15, 29; cf. 5.5; 6.17; 8.27; 10.6–10; see, differently, 16.18. This appears to be a theme more or less peculiar to Romans, with a single exception: 1 Cor. 4.5 corresponds closely to the various uses in Rom. 2.

[429] 2.17–20, on which see article in *Perspectives* ch. 30.

[430] See *Perspectives* ch. 30.

tion' has a vital double focus. The creator God has dealt with the problem of 'sin' as outlined in 1.18—2.16. But he has also dealt with the problem of the covenant people, as outlined in 2.17–29 and re-emphasized through the dense statements of 3.1–9 and then 3.10–20. For Paul, these two problems come together through the 'solution' which the creator God, in his faithfulness to the covenant, has now unveiled: the faithfulness of the Messiah. That is the underlying logic which takes Paul from the freshly envisaged 'plight' of 1.18—3.20 to the freshly unveiled 'solution' of 3.21—4.25.

(iv) Monotheism and the Problem of Evil: Conclusion

I conclude, therefore, that Paul has both rethought his second-Temple Jewish-style monotheism around Jesus and the spirit, and that from within that viewpoint we can see clearly why and how he revised his previous assessment of the 'plight', not only of humans in general but of Israel in particular, and also of the whole cosmos. The gospel events concerning Jesus had constituted an 'apocalypse', not only of the 'good news of salvation', but of the 'problem' from which all people, and the whole created order itself, needed to be rescued.

Paul's robust monotheism allowed fully for the fact of rebellious non-human 'powers' luring humans into idolatry and hence into collusion with their anti-creational and anti-human purposes. Sin in the human heart, darkness in the human mind, dehumanized behaviour in the human life: all went together with the rule of dark forces that operated through idols, including empires and their rulers, to thwart the purposes of the one creator God.[431] And Israel, called to be the light of the world, had itself partaken of the darkness.[432] Israel, too, was 'in Adam'. Once again Ephesians says quite clearly something to which we had been driven by our exegesis of Romans: 'you gentiles' were sinful, and subject to the rule of the 'powers', *and 'we Jews' were in the same condition as well*:

> ... you were dead because of your offences and sins! [2]That was the road you used to travel, keeping in step with this world's 'present age'; in step, too, with the ruler of the power of the air, the spirit that is, even now, at work among people whose whole lives consist of disobeying God. [3]Actually, that's how all of us used to behave, conditioned by physical desires. We used to do what our flesh and our minds were urging us to do. What was the result? We too were subject to wrath in our natural state, just like everyone else.[433]

All this, of course, merely highlights 'the problem'. Even saying that the Messiah is the 'solution', and that this 'solution' identifies, clarifies and radicalizes 'the problem' as it had been seen before, merely bounces the question

[431] These are not to be played off against one another. As we see in Qumran and elsewhere, Jewish thinkers were perfectly capable of speaking almost in the same breath both of human wickedness and of suprahuman evil powers at work: cf. e.g. CD 2.14—3.12; 4.13—5.19.

[432] This is why Israel, despite its vocation, cannot provide the solution to the problem. That is the point of Rom. 2.17–29 (cf. again *Perspectives* ch. 30).

[433] Eph. 2.1–3.

back again. *How precisely does the Messiah provide the 'solution'?* And, not least, how does this newly provided 'solution' relate to 'the solution' as it had been envisaged within the world of Judaism, particularly Pharisaic Judaism?

This raises, at last, the question of *election*, to which we turn in the next chapter, at the heart of Paul's freshly constructed but still deeply Jewish theology. In the traditional schema to which Paul was heir, the one God called Israel as his one people, the bearers of the 'solution' to the problems of the rest of the world. But if the one God has now been revealed as the one God/one lord, and even as God, lord and spirit; and if, with that tumultuous apocalypse focused on the crucified Messiah, 'the problem' of which Jews had long been aware had been redefined, unveiled in all its horrible depth, so that the chosen people themselves were just as much part of that problem as anyone else; what now should be said about 'election'? What should be said about the way in which, ever since Abraham, the chosen people had supposed that the one God would deal with the problems of the cosmos, of the rebellion of the human race, of the exile from the garden? What would happen to the promises to 'Abraham and his seed'? What would become of the gift of Torah, and with it the vocation of Israel to be 'the nation of priests'? What would happen to the great Isaianic vocation, that Israel would be the light of the world?

By now, the answer will not be a surprise. At the heart of Paul's theology, holding together its many varied features in a single, supple, harmonious whole, we find his passionate conviction that the ancient divine solution to the world's problems had not been changed. The creator God would indeed save the world through Abraham's seed. Israel would indeed be the light of the world. But all this, Paul believed, had been fulfilled, *and thereby redefined*, in and around Israel's Messiah and the holy spirit. What Israel and Torah between them could not do, Israel's God had now done. He had been faithful to his promises. He had displayed his *tsedaqah*, his *dikaiosynē*, as Isaiah 40—55 and Daniel 9 had always said he would. And in doing so he had dealt with the 'plight' of Israel, all humankind, and the world at every level, right up to the ultimate problems of Sin and Death themselves.

8. Conclusion

We return to where we began in our examination of Paul's monotheism. If we know anything about Saul of Tarsus, we know that he prayed the *Shema* several times a day. In doing so, he believed he was 'taking upon himself the yoke of the kingdom', committing himself to the sovereignty of the one God not only over Israel but also over the whole world. We have seen that, at the heart of Paul's fresh thinking about this one God, he reworked the *Shema* by discerning, at its heart, Jesus as lord – and with 'lord' deliberately echoing the *kyrios* which in the Septuagint stood for the divine personal name,

YHWH, itself. This reworked *Shema* was not a detached 'theologoumenon', a miscellaneous quasi-philosophical reflection on the one God. It was the beating heart which energized some of Paul's most central reflections on what it meant, in the 'now' of the gospel, to serve this one God and work for his kingdom. We should therefore assume that this reworking, with Jesus in the middle of it, had become central to the continuing monotheistic prayer life of Paul the apostle.

On this basis we may imagine, admittedly as a guess but one well grounded in things we actually know, that the prayer we find in 1 Corinthians 8.6 was the prayer Paul would have prayed as he waited in a Roman prison for the approach of the executioner. Like Akiba, he would be taking upon himself the yoke of the kingdom, though for him this kingdom had now been made known in and through the crucified and risen Messiah. That would make the praying of this great prayer, in its revised form, all the more appropriate. For Akiba, facing torture and death, the prayer would function as a great 'nevertheless'. For Paul, it would be a 'because'. Discerning the crucified Jesus at the heart of the *Shema* meant that Paul had signed on in the service of a lord who had won his kingdom through his own death at the hands of Rome, and who had promised that his followers would inherit their own glory through similar suffering. 'No: in all these things we are completely victorious through the one who loved us.' I imagine him, day by day, praying in the spirit, using the revolutionary new form of the *Shema* in which so much of his ancient tradition of devotion had been woven together with so much of his freshly understood theology:

all' hēmin heis theos, ho patēr, ex hou ta panta kai hēmeis eis auton,
kai heis kyrios Iēsous Christos, di' hou ta panta kai hēmeis di'autou.

For us there is one God, the father, from whom are all things and we to him;
and one lord, Jesus the Messiah, through whom are all things and we through him.

This is the quintessence of Paul's revised monotheism. For him to pray this as the soldier approached with the sword (Paul, the citizen, could expect a kinder death than Akiba's) would be to locate that monotheism exactly where it belonged: bearing witness to the kingship of God and the lordship of the crucified Jesus with his heart, mind, and strength. And, at last, with his life.

Chapter Ten

THE PEOPLE OF GOD, FRESHLY REWORKED

1. Introduction

We come now to the central chapter of this part of the book, and in a measure to the very heart of our entire topic. As we do so, an initial word about an important word.

The word 'election', which we shall use fairly consistently in what follows, has two regular meanings which must be put to one side. First, 'election' means 'choice'; but, apart from that, the sense in which I am using the word has nothing to do with voting systems. There is nothing 'democratic' about 'election' in the sense I intend; which may be one reason why the doctrine of 'election', whether the Jewish doctrine or the Christian one, has been under suspicion in the modern western world. What mattered was not Israel's choice of the one God, but God's choice of Israel. As Jesus said to his followers, 'You did not choose me; I chose you.'[1]

Second, 'election' in this sense has not very much to do with the technical sense of 'election' in the elaborate theological schemes of the sixteenth and seventeenth centuries. Notably in Calvin's theology, but actually also in Luther and most other Reformers, and then particularly in classic formulations such as the Westminster Confession, 'election', coupled with 'predestination', came to signify God's eternal choice of some people to salvation, sometimes with and sometimes without the explicit corollary that God has 'chosen' all the others for the purpose, which they cannot escape, of damnation.[2] I think I understand how that theology came to be so expressed, and what those who worked it out and taught it were anxious to avoid (any suggestion that salvation was somehow, in the last analysis, dependent on human will, effort or achievement). But that is not how I, in common with most other writers today on first-century Judaism, and that strange muta-

[1] Jn. 15.16.

[2] For a classic statement of the C16 and C17 doctrine, cf. e.g. chapter 3 of the Westminster Confession: clause 3 reads, 'By the decree of God, for the manifestation of His glory, some men and angels are predestinated unto everlasting life; and others foreordained to everlasting death' (Free Presbyterian Church of Scotland 1970, 29). For Calvin's mature position see Calvin 1961 [1552], and *Institutes* (Calvin 1960 [1559]), 3.21. The Reformers were picking up similar themes in Augustine (e.g. *De Praedestinatione Sanctorum*) and Aquinas (*ST* 1a, qu. 23). The treatment of election in Barth 1936–69, 2.2 ch. 7 (including an important summary of the history of the doctrine, ib. 12–24) is a majestic but in my view flawed attempt to unite this doctrine from Christian tradition with the first-century Jewish and Pauline meaning of 'election'.

tion within it that came to be called 'Christianity', shall be using the term 'election' itself.[3]

I use the term 'election', rather, to highlight the choice, by the one God, of Abraham's family, the people historically known as 'Israel' and, in Paul's day, in their smaller post-exilic form, as *hoi Ioudaioi*, 'the Jews' or 'the Judaeans'.[4] The word 'election', as applied to Israel, usually carries a further connotation: not simply the divine choice *of* this people, but more specifically the divine choice of this people *for a particular purpose.*

A great deal hangs on this point. It is inevitably controversial, and we must advance it step by step. But, to show the intimate coherence between this chapter and its predecessor, let me say this by way of introduction. As we saw, a creational monotheist has a particular kind of 'problem'; actually, a creational monotheist might well say that it is *the creator God* who has a 'problem', namely that the world seems not to be in the condition that its creator might be supposed to have wanted. Here, as we saw, the types of monotheism divide. Unlike Epicureans, Stoics and others, the creational monotheist, believing that the one God made the world and remains intimately and responsibly connected to it, does indeed have a problem: why are things in such bad shape? And for the creational monotheist who believes that the one God chose Israel, and made great, world-changing promises to Israel – well, there the problem is compounded. Why are things as they are *for Israel*? And how are the promises *through Israel for the world* now going to be accomplished?

The analysis of how this strange state of affairs came to be (the philosophical 'problem of evil') seems not, for the most part, to have worried the ancient Israelites, though theories were advanced about it from time to time. As Marx saw, the point was not to analyze the world but to change it; and that, it seems, was the purpose of Israel's 'election' in the first place. Asking the question, 'What would the creator God have done if humans had not sinned?' is futile; but we can put it the other way round, and say that, in Israel's scriptures at least, the call of Abraham and the choice of Israel as God's special people takes place not just *in the context of* universal human sin and wickedness, but somehow *in relation to* that universal human failure. Israel is called to be *different*; but, in and through that difference, to *make a difference.* Israel is called to a task (in the words of a learned Jewish correspondent, echoing centuries of tradition) of 'repairing the world in God's name'.

[3] For a brief summary of how 'election' is used in discussion of second-Temple Jewish ideas, see e.g. Gathercole 2010. I note that Roetzel 2003, ch. 6 is entitled 'The Grammar of Election'; Roetzel and I disagree about many things in the subject-matter, but not on the appropriateness of the word in relation to Paul's theological understanding of God's people.

[4] That word in Greek seems to carry geographical connotations (the inhabitants of 'Judaea') as well as ethnic (members of the tribe of Judah – though 'the Jews' of this period included Benjaminites, such as Saul of Tarsus himself, and Levites, as well as members of the tribe of Judah), and there were of course substantial Jewish communities in a Diaspora stretching from Babylon in the east to Italy, France and even Spain in the west. Among recent discussion see e.g. Mason 2007; Schwartz 2007; Barclay 2011, e.g. 9f. n. 19; Thiessen 2011, 149 n. 2.

That is why, in case anyone might be wondering, what we are calling 'election' has to do with the rescue of the world, of creation, of humankind: in short, with *salvation*. The choice of Abraham is a *rescuing* choice, the apparent divine answer to the failure of humankind from Adam and Eve through to the Tower of Babel. What sort of 'rescue' that might be, and how it might be worked out, is the problem at the heart of this chapter. But it is important to notice that in highlighting monotheism, election and eschatology we are not therefore side-lining, or marginalizing, 'salvation' and all that goes with it. Nor are we 'subsuming soteriology under ecclesiology', as some have charged me and others with doing. We are, rather, seeking to locate a biblical theology of 'salvation' where it seems to belong: as the aim and goal of the divine purpose of election. And part of the point, part of the problem – the problem with our description of 'election' itself, but also the problem over which Paul agonized day and night – was the relationship between election as the rescuing choice *for* Israel and election as the rescuing choice *through* Israel. For Paul, that question was finally resolved, as was everything else, in the death and resurrection of the Messiah, to which the present line of thought will lead us at the proper time.

I shall presently argue, in line with chapter 2 above, that Paul assumed a particular version of this view of election, and that whether or not the view he held was widely shared in his day, or was representative of earlier Israelite belief (or is indeed representative of widespread Jewish belief in our own day), it is the one he held, and it is the context in which what he said makes the sense he thought it made. And I shall argue throughout this chapter that, as with monotheism, so with election: Paul radically revised this Jewish belief in the light of Jesus and the spirit. As we watch him doing this we see his best-known (and sometimes most controversial) doctrines unfold in new ways: the meaning of the cross, of 'justification' and the law, of 'Christian ethics'. And as we expound these doctrines within this context we begin to realize why, in the letters that deal most centrally with these topics, the question of Israel – of Abraham, Moses, the Torah, the covenant promises – looms so large. In much western reading of Paul, the 'Jewish background' (how Paul would have snorted at that phrase, as though two millennia of divine call and purpose could be mere 'background') has been pushed into, well, the background, doing violence to the letters themselves. Think of the fate of Romans 9—11. Over against that tradition, we dare, by placing soteriological concerns back within their Jewish context, to allow Paul to address them in his own way. His own very Jewish way. And his own radically revised very Jewish way:

> For Paul and his circle, however, the unexpected, almost unthinkable claim that the Messiah had died a death cursed by the Law entailed a sharp break in terms of the way in which the people of God would henceforth be constituted and bounded.[5]

[5] Meeks 1983, 168.

Quite so. The redefinition of election around the Messiah. There is more to be said than that, but not less. It is a signpost on the way. That is where we shall be going.

This means that the present chapter is the place where we shall address, and hope to gain fresh clarity on, what are usually seen as the central topics of Pauline theology, particularly the complex of issues which centre upon salvation itself. I have elsewhere given an account of the current debates on these topics, and can here simply summarize to set this chapter in its scholarly context.[6]

We may distinguish seven broad emphases. My own view is that all seven have proper roles to play, and that – though they may now seem to us to be quite different, and even antithetical! – each needs the others if it is to be understood in the way Paul understood it. This sort of thing is common enough when we try to grasp the meaning of words and concepts within the relatively recent past; how much more when we go back to the very different world of a first-century Jew.[7]

Pride of place presumably still belongs to *justification*, if only because for so many years that doctrine, expounded in Romans, Galatians and Philippians 3, has been assumed by many to be the quintessential heart of Paul. Questions remain, of course, as to what precisely Paul meant by it, how it relates to the larger picture of salvation itself, and how it relates, both theologically and exegetically, to the other six. I hope my treatment here will offer help on all of these.[8] Since the language of 'justification', in itself (arguably) and certainly in the way Paul speaks of it in Romans 2 and 3, brings with it the idea of a law court in which all humans first stand guilty in the dock (Romans 3.19–20) and then, to their astonishment, hear the announcement that they are pronounced 'in the right' (Romans 3.21–6), the emphasis on justification is frequently spoken of as *forensic*. We should note, however, that the explicitly 'forensic' nature of justification is unique to Romans. If we only had Galatians and Philippians, the only reason for supposing that the language of 'righteousness' and 'justification' was 'forensic' would have to lie in the meaning of the words themselves, which would be problematic.[9]

[6] See *Interpreters*.

[7] cf. the remarks of Lewis 1960 [1942], 16, on the difficulty of understanding Milton's concept of 'solemnity': 'It has been split up, or dissociated, by recent developments, so that we now have to represent it by piecing together what seem to us quite unconnected ideas, but are really fragments of that old unity.'

[8] See my own exposition of Paul's doctrine in Wright 2009 [*Justification*], as well as the treatments of key passages in Wright 2002 [*Romans*].

[9] As is well known, the Greek root *dikaios* can go two ways in English: either into 'just, justice, justify, justification' or into 'righteous, righteousness'. Neither of these English clusters carries the same range of overtones as the Greek, particularly when we recognize that Paul's Greek is itself carrying overtones from the LXX and hence from underlying Hebrew expressions. The attempt of Sanders to use only the latter ('to righteous') and of Westerholm to coin barbarisms from the Greek ('dikaiosify', 'dikaiosness', etc.) have, understandably, not caught on. Martyn's use of 'rectify', perhaps closer to the German *Recht* and *Rechtfertigung*, carries its own multiple overtones, and is itself part of Martyn's attempt to get rid of 'forensic' meanings in favour of (so-called) 'apocalyptic' or 'cosmic' ones. See below.

Discussions of justification are often dovetailed with the second category, frequently called *anthropology*. This is in my view an unfortunate label, since the word regularly refers to a secular academic discipline (the study of human beings, with particular reference to origins, classifications and cultures), whereas its use as a shorthand in the study of Paul has a different focus and flavour. 'Anthropology' as a way of getting at the heart of Paul's soteriology is associated particularly with Rudolf Bultmann, who famously declared that

> Every assertion about God is simultaneously an assertion about man and vice versa.

This led at once to the conclusion that

> For this reason and in this sense Paul's theology is, at the same time, anthropology.

Bultmann's development of the point shows what he means, and introduces his entire scheme:

> Every assertion about God speaks of what He does with man and what He demands of him ... The christology of Paul likewise is governed by this point of view. In it, Paul does not speculatively discuss the metaphysical essence of Christ, or his relation to God, or his 'natures,' but speaks of him as the one through whom God is working for the salvation of the world and man. Thus, every assertion about Christ is also an assertion about man and vice versa; and Paul's christology is simultaneously soteriology.
>
> Therefore, Paul's theology can best be treated as his doctrine of man: first, of man prior to the revelation of faith, and second, of man under faith, for in this way the anthropological and soteriological orientation of Paul's theology is brought out.[10]

Bultmann thus subsumed the whole of Paul's theology under these two headings: 'Man Prior to Faith' and 'Man Under Faith'. This is not the place to discuss the proposal, except to note how it relates to the other six overall theories. It is frequently combined with justification, so that the latter term denotes the event in which 'a new understanding of one's self takes the place of the old'.[11] It is frequently taken in a very individualistic sense: that is, Paul's picture of salvation is about what happens to *this* human being who, convicted of sin, hears the word of grace in the gospel and decides to believe. As such it is often played off against 'incorporative' ideas, and particularly 'salvation-historical' ideas, in which the larger whole of the church on the one hand, or of a continuous history of Israel on the other, is seen as a threat to, or a diminution of, the proper stress on the personal faith of each individual. Bultmann himself was indeed able to speak both of 'the history of salvation' and its being 'oriented toward mankind, and not the individual'.[12] But subsequent exegesis of key passages has found it difficult to

[10] Bultmann 1951–5, 1.191. Refs. in the notes immediately following are to this work.

[11] Bultmann 1.269. The whole passage is interesting in terms of Bultmann's anticipation, through his theories of gnostic myths and his rejection of a 'Greek-idealistic' picture, of first Käsemann's and then Martyn's embrace of 'apocalyptic' over against a supposed 'salvation history'.

[12] Bultmann 1.269.

hold these things together. 'Apocalyptic' itself, in any meaningful first-century sense, has no place in Bultmann's construction, though the word has been used to denote the in-breaking revelation of the gospel, producing a fairly similar 'before' and 'after' to Bultmann's. 'Transformation' is explicitly ruled out:

> No break takes place; no magical or mysterious transformation of man in regard to his substance, the basis of his nature, takes place.[13]

What is being ruled out here, clearly, is any notion of an *inner* transformation; we catch the echoes of the sixteenth-century Reformation, rejecting any idea that 'grace' is tied to, or dependent upon, something which has happened or is happening in 'nature'. As for 'covenant', my final category and my own proposal, Bultmann applies to it the strictures we find in Ephesians about sexual impurity: it is not even to be named among you.[14] Since the Lutheran existentialist knows that all things Jewish are, for Paul, part of the problem rather than part of the solution, any idea of the covenant belongs, along with the Jewish law, under 'man prior to faith'.

After justification and anthropology comes the notion of '*being in Christ*'. This is sometimes referred to as 'incorporation' or 'participation', and Albert Schweitzer, perhaps misleadingly, called it 'mysticism'. Ever since Schweitzer and Wrede the stand-off between 'incorporation' and 'justification' (or, if you prefer, 'participatory' and 'forensic' accounts) has formed the main battle-line in debates over Paul.[15] This has echoes of earlier debates between Lutheran and Reformed theologies, with the Lutherans stressing justification, and seeing 'being in Christ' as a secondary or subsidiary theme, and the Reformed reversing the sequence, or at least insisting that 'justification' only really means what it means when it is seen within the larger 'in Christ' picture. (Those who privilege 'justification' at this point regularly suspect that to make 'in Christ' the major focus is to place ecclesiology over soteriology, or the church over the individual; at this point 'anthropology' often comes in as well.) Exegetically, this battle-line has often settled on Romans 1—8, with those who favour 'justification' as the Pauline centre highlighting chapters 1—4, and seeing the rest as 'implications' or 'applications' of the doctrine there expounded, and those who favour 'being in Christ' highlighting instead chapters 5—8. In terms of scholarly debates, E. P. Sanders has given fresh impetus to the privileging of 'incorporative' ideas in Paul, while leaving the door wide open for fresh research by admitting that the notion itself remains difficult to understand.[16]

[13] Bultmann, 1.268f. This is a revealing passage in terms of Bultmann's need to affirm some kind of continuity in order to avoid the idea of transformation while ruling out 'a continuity of development as understood within the Greek-idealistic picture of man'. The protestant nervousness about 'mysticism' peeps out in contemporary writings, too: see e.g. Schreiner 2010, 172 n. 86, commenting that Longenecker uses the word 'mystical' 'but does not mean by it the removal of one's personality'.

[14] Eph. 5.3.

[15] See Neill and Wright 1988 [1964] 403–5.

[16] Sanders 1977, 549; see the discussion below, 825–35.

The fourth obvious category has perhaps the most misleading label of all. Romans does not of course stop at chapter 8; it goes on to chapters 9—11. There, some have declared, is the real heart of what Paul is about. To describe this, they have sometimes used the phrase '*salvation history*', indicating that what matters is, so to speak, 'what Israel's God was up to in the story of the chosen people from Abraham to the present'. The now well-known difficulty with this is that the very phrase 'salvation history' has been associated, at least by its detractors, with the idea of a steady, progressive, immanent process or development. This is the kind of thing which classic Protestantism has always rejected (because it sounded too much like the normal picture of the medieval church, an institution simply rumbling on under its own steam and needing to hear the radically new word of God); which Karl Barth and his followers rejected in the 1920s (because they saw how a Hegelian liberalism had allowed German theology to assume that the world was developing in the right way, leading to the disaster of the First World War, and again needing a fresh word); and which the Confessing Church rejected in the 1930s (because the 'German Christians' were proposing a 'salvation history' in which the German people had been raised up to a position of global pre-eminence, which for Barth and others simply needed the word 'No!').[17] But not only does Romans 9—11 belong where it is in Paul's great letter, linked to the first eight and the last five chapters by a thousand golden threads; the same theme, of the fulfilment of the promises to Abraham, of (to put it at its most general) a positive and not merely negative relation between the divine word and work in Israel's scriptures and the fresh divine word and work in the Messiah, is closely intertwined with the other regular themes in such passages as Galatians 2, 3 and 4, and manifests itself in many other places as well. However much we resist any suggestion that Paul had in mind an immanent process, a smooth crescendo or development, from Abraham all the way to the Messiah and beyond – however much, in fact, we take fully into account the fact that he, like many other second-Temple Jewish writers, seems to have thought as much in terms of a 'damnation history' as of a 'salvation history'! – we cannot conclude a discussion of Paul's soteriology without fully factoring in Paul's clear sense, reaffirmed throughout our own previous chapter, that the God now revealed in Messiah and spirit was indeed the one God of Israel, and that the word of God had not failed (Romans 9.6). It is for this reason, and in this sense, that I and others have sometimes used the word 'covenant', though since this is often confused with 'salvation history', and rejected on grounds similar to those which have caused people to react against such an idea, I prefer here to list it as a separate item (the seventh category, below).

[17] A classic recent statement of the 'No!' is given in Käsemann's rejection of Stendahl's reading of Paul (Käsemann 1971 [1969], ch. 3 (cf. too e.g. Käsemann 1980 [1973], 264). See my discussion in *Perspectives*, ch. 1 (= Wright 1978). It remains an open question whether Käsemann really understood what Stendahl was saying; whether, indeed, he even grasped the quite subtle position of Cullmann 1967 [1965], which was in some ways the more obvious target.

The apparently polar opposite position to 'salvation history', defining itself regularly in antithesis to it, is the recent proposal which, following the lead of Käsemann, has used the word *'apocalyptic'*. I have discussed this elsewhere.[18] The proper emphasis here is on the freshness of the divine action in the gospel events, the new unveiling of things previously unimagined, the opening of previously blind eyes to truths otherwise invisible. The flagship of this neo-'apocalyptic' reading is the commentary on Galatians by J. Louis Martyn, in which certain elements of Galatians 3 and 4 which many exegetes see as Paul's own beliefs – particularly the positive account of the covenant with Abraham – are ascribed instead to the 'teachers' who have infiltrated the Galatian churches and whom Paul is fiercely resisting.[19] Martyn's proposal still has plenty of questions to answer, not least whether it can give a good account of Romans, and whether indeed the word 'apocalyptic' can appropriately be used to describe a standpoint which seems not to be that of any actual second-Temple 'apocalyptic' texts. But his strong point stands. Any overall account of Paul must certainly factor in the sense of radical newness which features so regularly in his writings.

The sixth element, which has received more attention in recent years, is that of *transformation* or even *deification*. This obviously coheres with a major theme in eastern orthodox theology, and equally obviously flies in the face of much western, particularly protestant, thought. Some recent writers have nevertheless pointed out that Paul's language in itself, and in its probable resonances in wider greco-roman culture, must be taken at least to include, and perhaps to foreground, the idea that the divine life itself is transforming believers, shaping them from the inside out according to the pattern of the Messiah.[20] This certainly picks up something Paul says from time to time. 'The Messiah lives in me,' he declares at the climax of one of his most characteristic paragraphs. But how this then coheres, again both exegetically and theologically, with any of the five emphases listed above has not been so clear.

The seventh and last element, for which I and others have argued, not as an alternative to the rest but as a potentially unifying perspective, is that of the *covenant*. It is surprising, in fact, that E. P. Sanders did not move in this direction, since he argued strenuously for a 'covenantal' reading of rabbinic and other forms of Palestinian Judaism, making the point as he did so that the reason the rabbis do not often use the word 'covenant' itself is because it is everywhere presupposed.[21] The same point could, and in my view should, be made about Paul, and the present book constitutes, among other things, an argument for that. However, to remain with exposition: the point

[18] See index, s.v. 'apocalyptic'; e.g. 40f., 61; and the discussion in *Interpreters*.

[19] Martyn 1997a; see too de Boer 2011. Martyn himself depended heavily on de Boer 1988 (written under Martyn's supervision); see too e.g. de Boer 1989 and other works listed in de Boer 2011, xxiii.

[20] So e.g. Gorman 2009; Blackwell 2011; Litwa 2012.

[21] Sanders 1977, 236f., 420f. A major recent work on 'covenant' is that of Hahn 2009: at 19–21 Hahn summarizes recent work on 'covenant' themes in Paul, which reveal how confused the present discussion has been.

of invoking 'covenant' as a controlling theme in Pauline soteriology is to highlight the way in which, in key passages in Galatians and Romans in particular, Paul stresses that what has happened in the gospel events has happened in fulfilment of the promises to Abraham, and has resulted in the formation (or the re-formation) of a people who are bound in a common life as a kind of extension or radical development of the covenantal life of Israel. The word 'covenant' is intended, in this way of looking at things, precisely to avoid any kind of simplistic developmental scheme, and to highlight instead, for instance, Paul's retrieval of the exile-and-restoration theme in Deuteronomy, which is about as far from a smooth or immanent historical progression as it could possibly be. I therefore use the word 'covenant' as a shorthand, a convenient label, to propose a way of reading Paul's key texts through which the other apparently disparate emphases can be brought together. All disciplines, and all accounts of Paul, employ shorthands. It is about as useful to object to 'covenant' on the grounds that Paul does not often use *diathēkē* as it would be to object to 'anthropology' on the grounds that Paul seldom, in the relevant passages, uses *anthrōpos*.[22] Or, indeed, about as useful as to argue for a modern construct called 'apocalyptic' on the grounds that Paul sometimes uses the Greek word *apokalypteō*.

Part of the question before us has to do with *balance* between different elements and with the *precise meanings* of Paul's own key terms. Most exegetes, faced with the question of justification, would agree that Paul taught that believers enjoy (a) a present state of *dikaiosynē*, (b) a future vindication in the final judgment and (c) a gospel-driven and/or spirit-enabled transformation of character. The question is how these relate to each other, which of them (or which combination of them or elements in them) is properly denoted by the language of 'justification' itself, and how some or all of this relates to, and affects one's view of, the biblical promises and history. Similarly, many exegetes would agree that Paul regarded believers as being *en Christō*; as (in some sense) belonging to the family of Abraham; as enjoying a new moment brought about by the fresh, dramatic act of the events concerning Jesus; as nevertheless standing in some sort of continuity with divine actions and promises from long ago. The question again is how all these relate to one another. Once again we notice that in passages like Galatians 2.19–21 or Philippians 3.2–11 more or less all of these ideas come rushing together. But such passages, precisely because they are so dense, may not necessarily be the best places in which to explore the precise meanings which Paul assigns to the various different concepts involved.

In what follows there will not, of course, be space to engage in much explicit debate with the proponents of these seven positions (and their many sub-variants). I intend, rather, to expound a line of thought from within Paul's letters themselves and let the themes sort themselves out as I do so. Nevertheless, I hope that the proposal I am making in this chapter, as well as in the closely related section on Israel and its future in chapter 11, will offer

[22] e.g. in Gal. the only potentially significant use is at 2.16.

a way of drawing together the proper emphases of all seven, while allowing them the space to make their own distinctive contributions.

The seven, after all, do not stand in exact parallel with one another. They are not seven different answers to exactly the same question. That is part of the problem: each of them assumes, in offering an account of Paul's central soteriological themes, a somewhat different account of the 'plight' to be solved and/or of the context Paul was addressing.[23] That is a further reason why (in addition to the internal logic of exploring Paul's revised monotheism) it was appropriate to offer an account of the 'plight' at the end of the previous chapter.

It might seem that by framing my account of Paul's soteriology in terms of the reworking of the second-Temple doctrine of election I am already tipping the scales in favour of some kind of 'salvation history'. Some kind, perhaps, but not the sort of thing Käsemann or Martyn were reacting against. Rather, the hypothesis at the heart of this book is that Paul's thought is best understood in terms of the revision, around Messiah and spirit, of the fundamental categories and structures of second-Temple Jewish understanding; and that this 'revision', precisely because of the drastic nature of the Messiah's death and resurrection, and the freshly given power of the spirit, is no mere minor adjustment, but a radically new state of affairs, albeit one which had always been promised in Torah, Prophets and Psalms. The radical newness, then, does not alter the fact that Paul's theology is still a 'revision' of Jewish theology, rather than a scheme drawn from elsewhere, as advocates of a non-Jewish Paul have regularly supposed. So, as the framework for my hypothesis, I have taken from the Jewish sources themselves the basic beliefs of monotheism and election, which together generate some form of eschatology. We have already examined Paul's reworked monotheism. We now turn to 'election', in the hope that by doing so we will be able to understand and articulate each of Paul's emphases in itself, in its exegetical contexts, and in its proper relation to all the others.

2. Israel and Its Purpose

(i) Adam and Abraham

We need to begin by recapitulating the fundamental shape of a second-Temple understanding of election: that is, of the divine calling of Israel, and the purpose for which that call was made. We have written about all this before, in the first volume and elsewhere.[24] But we must summarize again,

[23] Each of them also assumes a 'placing' of Paul in terms of what is still thought of as the 'history of religion': those who think of Paul as a very Jewish thinker tend to go for 'participation' and/or 'salvation history', or some variation on them, while those who suppose that his gospel effected a break with his native Judaism tend to go for 'justification', 'anthropology' and/or 'apocalyptic', or some variation on them. This has been very misleading. See again Neill and Wright 1988 [1964], 403–30; above, e.g. 140–2; and the treatment in *Interpreters*.

[24] Not least Wright 1991 [*Climax*] 21–6 and *NTPG* 262–8.

to sharpen up the point against those who would blunt it or turn it aside altogether. *As far as Paul was concerned, the reason the creator God called Abraham in the first place was to undo the sin of Adam and its effects.* Paul's basic contention, in the area of election, was that, through the Messiah and the spirit, this God had done what he promised Abraham he would do. It's as simple as that.

Well, perhaps not quite. For a start, there is the question as to whether that understanding of the divine purpose in calling Abraham will really do. For another thing, there is the question of the 'covenant': is that an appropriate term to use to describe something that Paul affirms, or is it something against which he sets his face? And, for another, we shall be pushing a boulder uphill into a strong wind, since one of the presently prevailing moods of scholarship is all in favour of a supposedly 'apocalyptic' reading of Paul in which there is no sense of 'continuity' with Abraham at all, but rather instead a radical inbreaking, an 'invasion' of the world, an entire overthrowing of existing categories, not least the long narrative of Abraham and his family.[25]

Yet another problem is as it were the mirror-image of that one. We have to contend with what one can only call a revived anti-Christian polemic in which anything, absolutely anything, that is said by way of a 'fulfilment' of Abrahamic promises in and through Jesus of Nazareth is said to constitute, or contribute to, that wicked thing called 'supersessionism', the merest mention of which sends shivers through the narrow and brittle spine of postmodern moralism. How can we say what has to be said, by way of proper historical exegesis, in such a climate?

In and through all of this we shall have to explore, in the present chapter, the scriptural frame of reference for some of the key terms Paul uses in this connection, particularly the blessed word *dikaiosynē*, traditionally rendered 'righteousness'. This alone would make a substantial book.

We begin, then, with the promises to Abraham.[26] I make no apology for repeating things I have said before, since even where one would expect a ready awareness of these points they do not seem to be widely known or understood. Indeed, almost every part of the story we must now briefly rehearse is of profound relevance for the understanding of Paul. Readers familiar with Genesis and Exodus may indeed be tempted to skip the next page or two, but I would ask them to slow down and ponder how the story works. It is within this narrative, re-read in the light of Jesus the Messiah, that Paul finds some of his most profound theology.

The first point is a comparatively simple observation with the deepest consequences. Within Genesis itself, there are strong signs that the narrator of the book as we now have it intends both a *parallel*, and a linked *sequence*, between Adam and Abraham. The call of Abraham is joined both to the creation of Adam and to the fall of Adam: to his creation, as recapitulation; to

[25] See above, in connection with 'apocalyptic'; and see *Interpreters*.

[26] I refer to the patriarch as 'Abraham' throughout rather than swapping to and fro between 'Abram' (his name prior to Gen. 17.5) and the fuller form. On Paul and Abraham see *Perspectives* ch. 33.

his fall, as rescue.[27] My point here is not only that this is clear in Genesis itself, but that this awareness of Abraham's call, together with elements of his story, was recognized in second-Temple Judaism and on into the rabbinic world; and that if we are to interpret Paul within his own world this implicit narrative must be taken with the uttermost seriousness.

We begin with Genesis, where *the promises to Abraham* directly echo *the commands to Adam*. First, the command to the original humans:

> God blessed them, and God said to them, 'Be fruitful and multiply, and fill the earth and subdue it; and have dominion over the fish of the sea and over the birds of the air and over every living thing that moves upon the earth.'[28]

Then the promise to Abraham:

> I will make of you a great nation, and I will bless you, and make your name great, so that you will be a blessing. I will bless those who bless you . . .
>
> I will make my covenant between me and you, and will multiply you exceedingly . . . I will make you exceedingly fruitful . . . and I will give to you, and to your seed after you . . . all the land of Canaan . . .
>
> Because you have done this . . . I will indeed bless you, and I will multiply your descendants as the stars of heaven and as the sand which is on the seashore . . . and by you shall all the nations of the earth bless themselves, because you have obeyed my voice.[29]

Then the promise to Isaac:

> I will be with you, and will bless you; for to you and to your seed I will give all these lands, and I will fulfil the oath which I swore to Abraham your father. I will multiply your seed as the stars of heaven, and will give to your seed all these lands; and by your seed all the nations of the earth shall bless themselves.
>
> Fear not, for I am with you and will bless you and multiply your descendants for my servant Abraham's sake.[30]

Then the promise to Jacob; first, through the blessing of his father Isaac:

> God Almighty bless you and make you fruitful and multiply you, that you may become a company of peoples. May he give you the blessing of Abraham, to you and to your seed with you, that you may take possession of the land of your sojournings which God gave to Abraham.[31]

Then the blessing of God himself upon Jacob:

[27] It is remarkable that Levenson 1993, who has the sharpest eye for verbal and thematic links elsewhere in Gen., only comments on one part of this. The only commentator I know who highlights the key links is Cassuto 1961–4, 2.124f.; 1961, 39f.

[28] Gen. 1.28.

[29] Gen. 12.2f.; 17.2, 6, 8; 22.16–18.

[30] Gen. 26.3f.; 26.24.

[31] Gen. 28.3f.

> I am God Almighty: be fruitful and multiply; a nation and a company of nations shall come from you ... the land which I gave to Abraham and Isaac I will give to you, and I will give the land to your descendants after you.[32]

Then Jacob's words to Joseph:

> God Almighty appeared to me ... and said to me, 'Behold, I will make you fruitful, and multiply you ... and I will give you this land, to your seed after you.'[33]

Then the narrator's comment, towards the end of Genesis and at the start of Exodus:

> Thus Israel dwelt in the land of Egypt ... and they gained possessions in it, and were fruitful and multiplied exceedingly ...
>
> But the Israelites were fruitful and prolific; they multiplied and grew exceedingly strong, so that the land was filled with them.[34]

The same theme recurs as Moses is interceding for the Israelites after the golden calf incident, in the renewed promises in the 'covenantal' passage in Leviticus, and then again in Deuteronomy.[35]

Two points need to be drawn out of this material. First, the fact that the *commands* to Adam turn up as *promises* thereafter (with the exception of Jacob in Genesis 35.11, where a new command is issued) say something about the shift of perspective. From now on 'being fruitful and multiplying' will be a gift. Something has happened which means that Adam's descendants cannot simply be told to do this; the creator God will do it himself, and will (according to Genesis 17) do it 'exceedingly'. This promise is highlighted, of course, as again and again 'being fruitful and multiplying' looks like being thwarted by barrenness (Sarah, Rebecca, Rachel), by fratricide (Cain and Abel; Esau and Jacob; Joseph and his brothers) and by sheer blundering (Abraham and Sarah in Egypt; Sarah and Hagar; Isaac and Rebecca in Egypt).[36] The great climax of this apparent threat to the promises is of course the near-sacrifice of Isaac in Genesis 22, a scene at once horrible and majestic, full of dark meaning and mystery, a source of terrible fascination and yet hope for readers from the earliest times to our own.[37] The point remains: Abraham's fruitfulness, the multiplication of his family, the recapitulation of the Adamic blessing, remains a strange gift, not something that can be presumed upon, always under threat from every angle, yet winning through.[38]

[32] Gen. 35.11f.

[33] Gen. 48.3f.

[34] Gen. 47.27; Ex. 1.7.

[35] Ex. 32.13; Lev. 26.9; Dt. 1.10f.; 7.13f.; 8.1; and cf. the echoes in 28.4, 63; 30.5, 16.

[36] Levenson 1993, 91 suggests a parallel between the sin in the garden (Eve 'took the fruit and gave it to her husband', Gen. 3.6) and Sarah's giving of Hagar to Abraham ('she took her maid and gave her to her husband', Gen. 16.3).

[37] On all this, see esp. Levenson 1993; Moberly 2009.

[38] Levenson 1993, 93f. draws out further resonances: as Eve's birth-pangs are 'greatly increased' (Gen. 3.16), so paradoxically God will 'greatly increase' Hagar's descendants (16.10); and both passages look on to the explosive scene of Gen. 22.

Second, there is of course the closest correlation between the placing of Adam and Eve in the garden of Eden and the promise to Abraham and his family about the land of Canaan. To any Israelite or Jewish reader, the connection would be obvious, not least after the exile (when many suppose the book attained its present shape). Adam, given the garden to look after, disobeyed and was expelled. Israel, given the land to look after, disobeyed and was exiled. The return from exile ought thus to be like a return to Eden, a reclaiming of the original promises to Abraham and, behind that, the commands to the human race. That is indeed the overtone of passages such as the following:

> And when you have multiplied and increased in the land, in those days, says YHWH . . .
>
> Then I myself will gather the remnant of my flock out of all the lands where I have driven them, and I will bring them back to their fold, and they shall be fruitful and multiply.
>
> They shall increase and be fruitful; and I will cause you to be inhabited as in your former times, and will do more good to you than ever before. Then you shall know that I am YHWH.
>
> I will signal for them and gather them in, for I have redeemed them, and they shall be as numerous as they were before.[39]

If Abraham and his family thus *recapitulate* the role of Adam, they are also the ones in whom the creator God determines to *rescue* the human race from its plight. This has been well brought out in Michael Fishbane's remarks about Adam, Noah and Abraham.[40] Noah, he writes, is portrayed in Genesis 9.1–9 as 'a new Adam', who 'presides over a restored world, a renewal of creation depicted in the terms and imagery of Gen. 1:26–31'.[41] He points out that the promise given at Noah's birth, that this child will bring comfort because of the curse on the earth, echoes the words of Genesis 3 where God had cursed the ground because of human sin.[42] There is then a careful balance in the narrative: as there have been ten generations from Adam to Noah, so there are ten generations from Noah to Abraham, and it is to Abraham that God now makes the promise of 'land, seed and earthly blessing'. 'In this typological context,' comments Fishbane,

> it cannot fail to strike one that these three blessings are, in fact, a typological reversal of the primordial curses in Eden: directed against the earth, human generativity, and human labour.[43]

[39] Jer. 3.16; 23.3; Ezek. 36.11; Zech. 10.8. For other resonances of 'Eden restored' in the prophets see *NTPG* 264.

[40] Fishbane 1988, 372; though Fishbane simply offers this, ahistorically as it were, as an example of 'typologies of a biographical nature', not as the launching of a major theme which will resonate through subsequent biblical theology.

[41] Fishbane 1988, 372.

[42] Gen. 5.29 with 3.17.

[43] Fishbane 1988, 372f. One must sadly comment that this point has, actually, failed to strike a great many modern western readers of Genesis, but one is grateful for those whose ears have been open to such echoes.

As Jon Levenson expands the point:

> The man without a country will inherit a whole land; the man with a barren wife will have plenteous offspring; and the man who has cut himself off from kith and kin will be pronounced blessed by all the families of the earth.[44]

The link between Adam and Abraham is thus not only *resumptive*, getting the human project back on track after the fall, the curse and the exile from the garden. It is also *redemptive*. God acts to undo the fateful sin in the garden, and he does so not least through the offering of Abraham's beloved son Isaac. Though the multiple resonances of that story echo in many directions through later Jewish as well as Christian thought, there is something about the angel's words to Abraham after his willingness to sacrifice Isaac which implies that a barrier has been broken, that the promise can flow not only to Abraham's family but out into the wider world:

> By myself I have sworn, says YHWH: Because you have done this, and have not withheld your son, your only son, I will indeed bless you, and I will make your seed as numerous as the stars of heaven and as the sand that is on the seashore. And your seed shall possess the gate of their enemies, and by your seed shall all the nations of the earth gain blessing for themselves, because you have obeyed my voice.[45]

This appears to be, in other words, not simply a narrowing of focus, a 'redemption' which consists in Abraham and his family being rescued from the ruin of the world. It is about the rest of the world being blessed as well, because of Abraham – though it is not clear, as we shall see, that this focus was maintained in the subsequent tradition. How, in any case, will it all work out? This introduces a further major theme within Genesis itself: there is the closest of links *between Abraham and the exodus*. First, Abraham and Sarah themselves go down into Egypt, almost immediately after receiving the initial promises. They go because of a famine, but Pharaoh, discovering how beautiful Sarah is, takes her into his house, only to then give her back to Abraham, and send them both away, when YHWH afflicts his house with great plagues.[46] Anyone who knows the later story of the exodus itself, and gives the matter a moment's thought, is bound to conclude that Abraham and Sarah are enacting in advance what their descendants three generations later will do: the famine, the sojourn, the plagues, the exodus. This is the context in which we should place the promise, in the all-important covenant chapter (Genesis 15), that Abraham's seed will live as aliens in a foreign land and then, in the fourth generation, come out and inherit the land of Canaan:

> As the sun was going down, a deep sleep fell upon Abram, and a deep and terrifying darkness descended upon him. Then YHWH said to Abram, 'Know this for certain, that your

[44] Levenson 1993, 84.

[45] Gen. 22.16–18; see Levenson 1993, 140f.

[46] Gen. 12.10–20.

> seed shall be aliens in a land that is not theirs, and shall be slaves there, and they shall be oppressed for four hundred years; but I will bring judgment on the nation that they serve, and afterwards they shall come out with great possessions. As for yourself, you shall go to your ancestors in peace; you shall be buried in a good old age. And they shall come back here in the fourth generation; for the iniquity of the Amorites is not yet complete.[47]

As Levenson comments, in this oracle 'YHWH provides Abram with the interpretation of his own life.' Not only has he been living, to this point, in the hope of apparently unlikely descendants,

> he has also been proleptically living their life in his. In the prophecy that interrupts the covenant-making ceremony, Abram's experience is shown to have been itself akin to a prophetic sign-act. It is a biographical pre-enactment for the providential design for the whole people of Israel.[48]

That is then the setting for the making of the covenant itself:

> When the sun had gone down and it was dark, a smoking fire-pot and a flaming torch passed between these pieces. On that day YHWH made a covenant with Abram, saying, 'To your seed I give this land, from the river of Egypt to the great river, the river Euphrates, the land of the Kenites, the Kenizzites, the Kadmonites, the Hittites, the Perizzites, the Rephaim, the Amorites, the Canaanites, the Girgashites, and the Jebusites.'[49]

And this provides the full meaning of the opening of the chapter, which likewise resonates into much later tradition:

> After these things the word of YHWH came to Abram in a vision, 'Do not be afraid, Abram, I am your shield; your reward shall be very great.' But Abram said, 'O Sovereign YHWH, what will you give me, for I continue childless, and the heir of my house is Eliezer of Damascus?' And Abram said, 'You have given me no seed, and so a slave born in my house is to be my heir.' But the word of YHWH came to him, 'This man shall not be your heir; no one but your very own issue shall be your heir.' He brought him outside and said, 'Look towards heaven and count the stars, if you are able to count them.' Then he said to him, 'So shall your seed be.' And he believed YHWH; and he reckoned it to him as righteousness.[50]

The promise of 'reward'; the promise of numberless 'seed'; the promise backed up by the uncountability of the created heavenly host. That is what Abram 'believed'; and whatever different generations of readers heard and hear in the unprecedented comment that YHWH 'reckoned it to him as righteousness', the rest of the chapter, whose end we have already noted, provides the first and most obvious meaning. The word of promise is confirmed by the making of the *covenant*:

> Then he said to him, 'I am YHWH who brought you from Ur of the Chaldeans, to give you this land to possess.' But he said, 'O Sovereign YHWH, how am I to know that I shall possess it?' He said to him, 'Bring me a heifer three years old, a female goat three years old, a

[47] Gen. 15.12–16.

[48] Levenson 1993, 88.

[49] Gen. 15.17–21.

[50] Gen. 15.1–6.

> ram three years old, a turtle-dove, and a young pigeon.' He brought him all these and cut them in two, laying each half over against the other; but he did not cut the birds in two. And when birds of prey came down on the carcasses, Abram drove them away.[51]

The making of the covenant then comes in two parts: first, this preparation, then, the smoking fire-pot and flaming torch passing between the pieces of the animals. And, in between, the promise of the exodus. Every part of this chapter belongs intimately with every other part. When later generations speak of the promise to Abraham's seed, the promise of the land, the covenant, or the exodus, any one of these four elements can and does evoke all the others.

The covenant is then confirmed, and a fresh sign of it given, two chapters later:

> YHWH appeared to Abram, and said to him, 'I am God Almighty; walk before me, and be blameless. And I will make my covenant between me and you, and will make you exceedingly numerous.' Then Abram fell on his face; and God said to him, 'As for me, this is my covenant with you: You shall be the ancestor of a multitude of nations. No longer shall your name be Abram, but your name shall be Abraham; for I have made you the ancestor of a multitude of nations. I will make you exceedingly fruitful; and I will make nations of you, and kings shall come from you. I will establish my covenant between me and you, and your seed after you throughout their generations, for an everlasting covenant, to be God to you and to your seed after you. And I will give to you, and to your seed after you, the land where you are now an alien, all the land of Canaan, for a perpetual holding; and I will be their God.'[52]

The sign that is then given is of course the sign of circumcision; 'So', says this God, 'my covenant shall be in your flesh an everlasting covenant.'[53] And, though Ishmael, born to Hagar in chapter 16, will also be blessed and promised great fruitfulness, it is the child yet to be born to the barren Sarah with whom the covenant purposes are to be taken forward:

> Your wife Sarah shall bear you a son, and you shall name him Isaac. I will establish my covenant with him as an everlasting covenant for his seed after him . . . My covenant I will establish with Isaac, whom Sarah shall bear to you at this season next year.[54]

Whatever the historians may say about the actual origins of the Israelite sense of being the covenant people of the God they knew as YHWH, this great narrative, with all its human interest and suspense, was seen by the Jewish people long before the days of Saul of Tarsus as the foundation charter for the people of Israel, giving them an anchor for their own faith and a spur to their own hope. The covenant with Abraham, the promise of innumerable 'seed', the gift of the land and the promise of rescue from slavery – and now the covenant sign of circumcision.

[51] Gen. 15.7–11.

[52] Gen. 17.1–8.

[53] 17.11, 13. The word 'covenant' occurs no fewer than eight times in 17.1–14.

[54] Gen. 17.19, 21.

It should be no surprise, then, that the establishment of the covenant with Abraham is recalled when, at the appointed time, the enslaved Israelites cry to their God for help:

> Out of the slavery their cry for help rose up to God. God heard their groaning, and God remembered his covenant with Abraham, Isaac and Jacob. God looked upon the Israelites, and God took notice of them.[55]

The promise, with some of the details about the present inhabitants of the land, is then rehearsed in more detail:

> He said, 'I am the God of your father, the God of Abraham, the God of Isaac, and the God of Jacob ... I have observed the misery of my people who are in Egypt; I have heard their cry on account of their taskmasters. Indeed, I know their sufferings, and I have come down to deliver them from the Egyptians, and to bring them up out of that land to a good and broad land, a land flowing with milk and honey, to the country of the Canaanites, the Hittites, the Amorites, the Perizzites, the Hivites, and the Jebusites.'[56]

Moses then, convinced of his commission despite misgivings and initial setbacks, is sent with a strong word of YHWH's covenant loyalty:

> God also spoke to Moses and said to him: 'I am YHWH. I appeared to Abraham, Isaac and Jacob as God Almighty, but by my name YHWH I did not make myself known to them. I also established my covenant with them, to give them the land of Canaan, the land in which they resided as aliens. I have also heard the groaning of the Israelites, whom the Egyptians are holding as slaves, and I have remembered my covenant. Say therefore to the Israelites, "I am YHWH, and I will free you from the burdens of the Egyptians and deliver you from slavery to them. I will redeem you with an outstretched arm and with mighty acts of judgment. I will take you as my people, and I will be your God. You shall know that I am YHWH your God, who has freed you from the burdens of the Egyptians. I will bring you into the land that I swore to give to Abraham, Isaac, and Jacob; I will give it to you for a possession. I am YHWH."'[57]

And the story then rolls out, exactly as in the miniature version at the end of Genesis 12: the confrontation with Pharaoh, the plagues, the exodus. Only this time the firstborn son who is to be killed is not Isaac, as in Genesis 22, but the firstborn of all Egypt; and Israel is redeemed, spared from the death of the firstborn, by the Passover lamb. The blood of the lamb was to be the sign by which 'redemption' (a metaphor from the world of slavery, but here rooted in the actual slavery of Israel in Egypt) was to be effected.[58] The children of Israel are thus liberated, and begin the long march to their 'inheritance', the land promised to Abraham.

On the way, of course, they are given the Torah, and that is another story. And, in particular, they are given the tabernacle, seen later of course as the forerunner of the Jerusalem Temple. But the purpose of rehearsing all this in such detail is to lay the foundation for the further reflection that this story,

[55] Ex. 2.23–5.

[56] Ex. 3.6–8; cf. too 3.16f.

[57] Ex. 6.2–8.

[58] Ex. 12.12f., 23–7.

with these resonances, remained powerfully present within the generations of Judaism leading up to the first century. Each element is important. Abraham and his 'seed' are the true humanity, the ones in whom Adam is recapitulated and rescued, the ones to whom the land had been promised, the ones who would cry to YHWH from slavery and exile and for whom the memory of the ancient covenant would remain valid and salvific. Indeed, just as Genesis and Exodus, taken together, come round in a circle, with the divine presence dwelling in the midst of the people at the end as it had with Adam and Eve in Eden, so the whole Pentateuch as it now stands comes round in a greater circle, as the closing chapters of Deuteronomy, which we looked at in more detail in chapter 2, speak of a final great exile and a final great redemption from that exile. The story of Adam and Eve expelled from Eden, of Abraham going to Egypt and coming back, of Abraham's descendants going to Egypt and coming back, will be acted out once more in the much later generation that will go into exile and then be brought back – precisely as the great act of covenant renewal which follows the awful act of covenant punishment. As we saw in chapter 2, there is evidence in plenty that these texts were being read in just this way by people in the second-Temple period: no doubt not by all, but by plenty. Not least in the circles with which Saul of Tarsus was associated.

Examples, too, abound in the second-Temple period of the link between Adam and Abraham, though here we find, particularly and understandably when the pagan world has been persecuting and trampling on the Jews, a focus on Abraham not as the means of blessing for the world but as the reason why his physical family constitute the true humanity. The following must suffice.[59] In Ben-Sirach, the high priest in the Temple is like Adam ruling over all creation.[60] *Jubilees* makes the link not with Abraham but with Jacob, but to the same effect: Jacob and his descendants are the true heirs of Adam.[61] The covering of Adam's nakedness is reflected in Israel's refusal of the gentile habit of naked athletics.[62] Abraham blesses the creator God because he has made him 'like the one who made everything', and from him there will come 'a righteous planting for eternal generations' and 'a holy seed'.[63] The elderly Abraham blesses Jacob with the blessings of his own ancestors, right back to Adam himself, declaring that through this blessing creation itself will be renewed, and invoking over him 'the blessings with which God blessed Noah and Adam'.[64] The *Testament of Levi* speaks of a coming great priest through whose work creation will be renewed and Israel inherit its blessing:

[59] Here the work of Scroggs 1966 is still important; though Scroggs consistently screens out the links with Abraham, jumping straight from Adam to Sinai. For subsequent studies see e.g. Levison 1988; 2010, the latter with recent bibliography.

[60] On Sir. see Hayward 1991.

[61] *Jub.* 2.23; presumably this is to avoid the problems raised by Ishmael and Esau.

[62] *Jub.* 3.30f.

[63] *Jub.* 16.26.

[64] *Jub.* 19.24f.; 22.13.

> he shall open the gates of paradise; he shall remove the sword that has threatened since Adam, and he will grant to the saints to eat of the tree of life ... Then Abraham, Isaac, and Jacob will rejoice.[65]

In *1 Enoch*, Adam appears in a dream as a white bull; the patriarchs, too, are white bulls, and after the long and complex story of their descendants there is finally another white bull born: some suppose this to be the Messiah.[66] In *4 Ezra* we find at last, a generation after Paul was writing, the Jewish tradition reflecting on the long-term effects of Adam's sin; and there the story is told with the key individuals standing out: Adam, Noah, Abraham, David.[67] The key moment in this narrative of 'Adam to the present' is the point at which, as 'Ezra' complains to the covenant God,

> You made an everlasting covenant with him, and promised him that you would never forsake his descendants; and you gave him Isaac, and to Isaac you gave Jacob and Esau ... yet you did not take away their evil heart from them, so that your law might produce fruit in them.[68]

Then the connection is made explicitly: Israel is the true seed of Adam himself:

> On the sixth day you commanded the earth to bring forth before you cattle, wild animals, and creeping things; and over these you placed Adam, as ruler over all the works that you had made; and from him we have all come, the people whom you have chosen.[69]

This then merely increases the problem of monotheism plus election: how has it all gone so horribly wrong?

> All this I have spoken before you, O Lord, because you have said that it was for us that you created this world. As for the other nations that have descended from Adam, you have said that they are nothing, and that they are like spittle, and you have compared their abundance to a drop from a bucket. And now, O Lord, these nations, which are reputed to be as nothing, domineer over us and devour us. But we your people, whom you have called your firstborn, only-begotten, zealous for you, and most dear, have been given into their hands. If the world has indeed been created for us, why do we not possess our world as an inheritance? How long will this be so?[70]

The divine response to the seer's complaint once again makes explicit the *salvific* purpose of the divine call to Abraham, though the salvation in question is now for Abraham's family only:

> So I considered my world, and saw that it was lost. I saw that my earth was in peril because of the devices of those who had come into it. And I saw and spared some with great difficulty, and saved for myself one grape out of a cluster, and one plant out of a

[65] *T. Lev.* 18.10–14.

[66] *1 En.* 90.37; see discussion in ch. 2 (above, 122f.).

[67] *4 Ez.* 3.5, 10f., 13–15, 23, 26.

[68] 3.15, 20.

[69] 6.53f.

[70] *4 Ez.* 6.55–9. For the idea of the world being made for Israel see too 7.11; 8.44; 9.13.

> great forest. So let the multitude perish that has been born in vain, but let my grape and my plant be saved, because with much labour I have perfected them.[71]

This vision of the world being made for Israel, of (in other words) Israel as the true humanity, the genuine heirs of Adam, is then narrowed again, to focus more specifically on groups that see themselves as the true heirs of Israel. We should therefore expect to find this theme in works like the Qumran Scrolls, and sure enough, there it is:

> For God has chosen them for an everlasting covenant and all the glory of Adam shall be theirs.
>
> God, in his wonderful mysteries, forgave them their sin and pardoned their wickedness; and he built them a sure house in Israel whose like has never existed from former times till now. Those who hold fast to it are destined to live for ever and all the glory of Adam shall be theirs.
>
> Thou wilt cause them to inherit all the glory of Adam, and abundance of days.[72]

This whole strand of thought – Israel as the true heirs of Adam, Abraham as the one who comes to set things straight – finds its way straight into the thought of the rabbis. It was, they say, on account of Abraham that the world was created in the first place.[73] More particularly, Abraham was the one through whom God planned from the outset to put the world right if and when it went wrong. Here we glimpse again the wider perspective which we saw at least hinted at in Genesis itself:

> Why is Abraham called a great man? Because he was worthy of being created before the first man. But the Holy One, blessed be he, thought, 'Perhaps something may go wrong, and there will be no one to repair matters. Lo, to begin with I shall create the first Adam, so that if something should go wrong with him, Abraham will be able to come and remedy matters in his stead.'[74]

That remains, to my mind, one of the clearest statements of the link between Adam and Abraham, which was standard in the multiple readings of Genesis across this period. The question of how this link played out – whether, as we said before, the Abrahamic purpose was designed to rescue the whole of the human race, or rather to rescue Abraham's family *from* the rest of the human race – receives a variety of answers, but the underlying point remains: the promises to Abraham were understood in relation to the

[71] *4 Ez.* 9.20–2; a similar complaint is found in *2 Bar.* 14.17–19. It appears that the original 'some' who are spared are Noah and his family, but the 'grape' and the 'plant' are clearly Abraham and his family: for the image, see e.g. Ps. 80.8–19; Isa. 5.1–7, etc. Further discussion of these passages can be found in Hooker 1967, 49–56.

[72] 1QS 4.23; CD 3.20; 1QH 4 (formerly 17).15 (tr. Vermes). See, similarly, 1QLit. Pr. 2.3–6; 4QpPs37 3.1f.; on these, see the note in *Climax* 24 n. 30.

[73] *Gen. Rabb.* 12.9; Neusner 1985, 129 comments that this is a 'familiar point'.

[74] *Gen. Rabb.* 14.6. The discourse goes on to liken Abraham to the midpoint of a roof, supporting the weight of the sloping beams either side; and to a virtuous woman who has been brought into a house in disarray in order to teach the occupants proper conduct.

problems caused by Adam. Their intention was to get the human project back on track after the disasters of the fall, the flood and the idolatrous Tower. The covenant that YHWH made with Abraham was the way of sealing this intent, binding this God to his promise and Abraham's family to this God, assuring Abraham of the 'seed' that would inherit the promises, the promises which were focused on the land as the new Eden, promises which would be fulfilled by the exodus from Egypt as the great act of redemption. This dense confluence of themes – promise, family, land, exodus – resonated across the centuries and the several varieties of Jewish life and thought, albeit with the question always pressing as to where it would all end up. The covenant, as we shall see, forms the essential and non-negotiable context within which the writings of Paul (especially Romans and Galatians, where Abraham plays such a central role, and Romans and 1 Corinthians 15, where Adam plays such a central role) demand to be read.

(ii) Covenant, Law Court and 'Righteousness'

Before we can get to that point, though, we need to draw some firm conclusions about key terms and themes. When, from now on, I refer to the 'covenant', and describe Paul's theology in those terms, I refer to the theme which, so strongly emphasized in Genesis 15 and 17 and Exodus 2, 3 and 6, draws together Abraham as the divine answer to the problem of Adam, the promises about the 'seed' and the land, and the exodus as the way by which Abraham's family would journey to that inheritance. When, in this context, we see Paul addressing the question of human sin, and, like *4 Ezra*, tracing this problem back all the way to Adam, we should not be surprised if he draws on this same tradition of the divine covenant. I cannot stress too strongly, in view of persistent misunderstandings in some quarters, that, within this confluence of themes, 'covenant' and 'salvation' belong tightly together, the latter as the goal of the former, the former as the means of the latter. To play them off against one another is to indicate that one has not paid attention to the entire train of thought we have been exploring. And – a related but different point – there is no longer any reason for New Testament scholars to resist, as they often have done over the last century, reading Paul in the light of second-Temple covenant theology. There is no need to flatten out covenantal language into something else, or to take obvious covenantal references as an indication that Paul is here quoting and perhaps neutralizing a formula from an earlier 'Jewish Christianity' which (of course!) he himself opposes. These are the flailings of the tail of an older history-of-religions project that has now, to be honest, reached the end of its natural life.[75]

To get back on track, we need to glance at the cluster of words and phrases which, in many biblical contexts, help to hold in place the notion of

[75] See *Interpreters*. I have in mind, for instance, the anguished attempts to protect Paul from 'covenantal' thinking in e.g. Rom. 3.24–6 (see e.g. Käsemann 1980 [1973] ad loc.).

'righteousness', particularly 'God's righteousness'. The biblical terms for various attributes of the divine character and activity overlap considerably, and we would be wrong to play them off against one another. We have mentioned the divine 'righteousness' (*tsedaqah/dikaiosynē*); but we often find, in the same passages, 'judgment' or 'justice' (*mishpat/krisis*); truth/truthfulness (*emunah/alētheia*); steadfast love (*raham* or *hesed/eleos*); and, in slightly different mode, 'salvation' (*teshu'ah/sōtēria*). Both in the Hebrew and in the LXX these seem to intertwine; all together are ways of speaking of the character and even identity of the one God, but with the different attributes called up for the particular nuances required. Thus, we can say that this God's 'salvation' is his rescue-operation; his 'steadfast love' is that because of which he will woo his people back again, forgiving their previous wrongs; his 'truth' (which can also be expressed as 'trustworthiness', *pistis*) is that because of which he will say what he means and do what he says; his 'justice' is the characteristic because of which Israel will know that they can rely on him to do what is right; and, above all, his 'righteousness' is his *faithfulness to his previous commitments*, particularly of course the covenant. This last, however, needs a more detailed exposition and explanation.

We may therefore attempt, one more time, to set out the way in which the language of 'righteousness' – of, that is, Hebrew *tsedaqah* and the LXX *dikaiosynē* – functions in the key texts which Paul's quotes, allusions and echoes indicate as his natural mental habitat. We can assume Genesis and Deuteronomy, of course, and here add the Psalms and Isaiah 40—55 in particular. How did these complex and tricky words function?[76] It is clearly impossible in the present context to explore and explain the large number of biblical references even to 'righteousness', let alone all the terms that are correlated with it in the Hebrew Bible or Septuagint. But something at least must be said, if only in summary.[77] There are four layers of meaning to be noted, which for first-century Jews would almost certainly not be felt as separate: the general meaning, the law court meaning, the covenantal meaning, and the eschatological meaning.

1. The word *tsedaqah/dikaiosynē* and its cognates in the Israelite scriptures seem to have the primary meaning of 'right behaviour'. But the emphasis is not merely on implicit conformity to a law or abstract standard, though that may be involved as well, but to the question of being in right *relation* with others. This raises problems, because in the discourse of modern Christian piety people have often spoken, not unnaturally, of 'a relationship with God', a phrase which can then slide to and fro between (a) the sense of personal intimacy between the believer and God (or Jesus) on the one hand and (b) the *status* which, in traditional presentations of 'justification by faith', the believer has in the (implicit) divine law court. One might of course speak carefully about the first as an actual 'relationship', such as

[76] Older studies such as those of Schrenk 1964 [1935] and Seebass and Brown 1978 [1971] are helpful as an initial survey, but still oriented more towards previous, more dogmatic debates than to Paul's second-Temple context. Onesti and Brauch 1993 bring matters a bit more up to date.

[77] See too Wright 2002 [*Romans*], 398–401.

that between friends, or between parent and child, and about the second in terms of a quasi-legal 'relation', where one stands *in relation to God* or to God's law court; but this kind of careful distinction, not surprisingly, is hard to maintain in practice. The combination of (a) western individualism and (b) a residual sense that 'justification by faith' was unknown before the death of Jesus has meant both that the words and meanings have slid to and fro between these two options and also, more particularly, that the context which Paul so frequently evokes, that of the covenant 'relationship' between YHWH and Israel, has simply been ignored.

2. The word-group does in fact have specific, though potentially confusing, reference to the *law court.* (I stress, for the avoidance of doubt, that we are talking here about an ancient Israelite law court, in which all cases were what we would call 'civil' cases, there being no 'director of public prosecutions'.) The judge would be faced with, and would decide between, the plaintiff and the defendant, and the judge's obligation would be to try the case fairly (i.e. not accept bribes or exercise favouritism), to uphold the law, to punish wrongdoing and to vindicate the innocent, with a special eye on the weak and vulnerable, those who have nobody to plead for them. The action of the judge in thus deciding the case properly is *mishpat/krisis,* 'judgment'; but when the judge does all these things properly he is *tsaddiq/dikaios,* 'in the right'. Or, to put it another way, his *tsedaqah/dikaiosynē,* 'righteousness', has been displayed in his proper discharge of his duties. He must 'do *tsedaqah* and *mishpat, dikaiosynē* and *krisis*'; in other words, he must first decide the case properly and then take the appropriate action.

Meanwhile, when the word 'righteous' is applied to one of the parties in front of the judge, either the plaintiff or the defendant, it seems capable of two different though subtly related meanings. On the one hand, it can refer to the *moral character* of either plaintiff or defendant; are they 'righteous', of good character, having behaved appropriately (in relation to the present lawsuit in particular)? On the other hand, it can refer to the *status* which one or the other will have when the judge has made up his mind and pronounced his verdict: one of the parties will be 'in the right' *in terms of the court's decision*, and the other one will be 'in the wrong'. The relationship between these two senses of 'righteous' and 'righteousness' is complex, and nothing much is gained by trying to privilege one over the other, whether by making the 'moral character' meaning primary and seeing the 'status after the verdict' as reflecting it, or by insisting on the priority of the legal status and understanding the 'moral character' reference as indicating the actual character which ought to reflect the court's decision.

Two famous biblical passages show how this can work. When Judah hears that his daughter-in-law Tamar is pregnant out of wedlock, he assumes the role of judge, commanding her to be burnt. But when Tamar reveals that he is himself the father of her as yet unborn child, he declares, 'She is more in the right than I,' *tsodqah mimeni,* literally 'She [is] righteous other than me,' which the LXX translates as *dedikaiōtai ē egō*, 'She has been justified rather than me.'[78] Though the Hebrew could be taken in various ways, the Greek version makes it clear: Judah is treating this sharp little scene within the long-running soap opera of Jacob's dysfunctional family as if it were a lawsuit between Tamar and himself, and he is declaring that the imaginary court has found in her favour. She has, in other words, been 'justified'. No doubt her playing the whore was in itself morally reprehensible after a fashion, though not nearly as much as his in not providing for her in the first place, then using her as a whore and not caring whether he had fathered a child. But that is not the point. He is not saying that Tamar has behaved less badly than he has, or (to put it positively) that she possesses a bit more 'righteousness', in terms of 'morally upright character', than he does. Nor, I think, is he saying that Tamar has managed to take a step towards repairing the family relationship.[79] He is saying that she is in the right and he is in the wrong. It is a quasi-legal judgment. The case has been decided.[80]

The second example is, I think, clearer again. David is on the run from Saul. He and his men are hiding in a deep cave, and Saul goes into the front part of the same cave to relieve himself. David, egged on by his men, creeps up from behind as though to kill Saul, but only cuts off the edge of his cloak. After Saul has left, David calls after him and explains what he has done. This time the implicit lawsuit between the two parties becomes explicit:

> May YHWH judge between me and you! May YHWH avenge me on you; but my hand shall not be against you ... May YHWH therefore be judge [*dayin/kritēs*], and give sentence [*shaphat/diakstēs*] between me and you. May he see to it, and plead my cause, and vindicate me against you.[81]

Saul responds, accepting the scenario of a lawsuit in which he and David are appearing before the divine tribunal, and acknowledges that David has won the case:

> You are more righteous than I; for you have repaid me good, whereas I have repaid you evil.[82]

Here I think the NRSV lets us down, by implying, despite the explicit law court context, that what is at stake is a comparison between two moral char-

[78] Gen. 38.26.

[79] So e.g. Grieb 2006, 60.

[80] Seifrid 2001, is thus correct to challenge NIV 'She is more righteous than I,' and to conclude that 'the narrative depicts justice in a concrete form, as a matter of competing claims between two parties,' though Seifrid's linkage of this to community norms (according to which Tamar was actually legitimated) seems to me to blur the essential point. See Skinner 1910, 454f.: 'lead her out' (38.24) is 'a forensic term', meaning that the scene is to be understood as an informal law court, so that the key sentence is 'she is in the right as against me.' Skinner refers to Kautzsch 1910, para. 133b (430 n. 2): '*tsādaq min* expresses not a comparison, but only a relation existing between one person and another,' citing Job 4.17; 32.2.

[81] 1 Sam. 24.12–15 [MT/LXX 24.13–16].

[82] 1 Sam. 24.17 [MT/LXX 24.18].

acters ('*more* righteous than I'). The Hebrew is very similar to that of Genesis 38: *tsaddiq athah mimeni*, 'You are *tsaddiq*, rather than me': in other words, in any suit at law only one party can be 'in the right', and on this occasion it will be David, not Saul.[83] Of course, the moral character corresponds to the verdict; but here, as with Judah and Tamar, the primary meaning is the *verdict*, and the *status* which results from it.

My point here is that this is how the language of *tsedaqah/dikaiosynē* works within a law court setting. First, the judge's own *dikaiosynē* is a matter of the way in which he tries and decides the case. Second, the *dikaiosynē* of the two parties at law *is a matter of which way the verdict goes* – which, if the judge is doing his job properly, ought of course to correspond to their earlier behaviour, measured against the appropriate norms. It is, of course, quite possible for someone who in other respects is a bad character to be innocent of a particular charge, just as it is possible for someone who is actually guilty nevertheless to be acquitted by the court. In both these instances the person in question is still declared *dikaios*, demonstrating clearly that the verdict 'righteous', 'in the right', is a matter of *the status conferred by the court's verdict*, rather than overall moral character.

3. The plot thickens when this language is used in relation to how matters stand between YHWH and Israel, because they are bound together by covenant (the face-to-face reality to which the often-used term 'relation' or 'relationship' refers as through a glass darkly). The general plea of the Psalmist, that the covenant God will hear his case and vindicate him against his wicked enemy,[84] then becomes the very specific plea of Israel as a nation: that YHWH will sit in judgment over the pagan nations that are oppressing Israel, and will vindicate his covenant people.[85] This is the scene we find, famously, in Daniel 9. Of course, the situation is complicated, because (as various biblical writers freely acknowledge) the trouble that has come upon Israel is itself the result of the covenant: this is what YHWH always said he would do when his people were unfaithful (especially, of course, in the closing chapters of Deuteronomy). Nevertheless, it is YHWH's *tsedaqah*, his *dikaiosynē*, that is then appealed to as the reason why he will surely act afresh to save, to liberate, to *vindicate* Israel at last. The classic passage, two chapters on from Daniel 7, is the great prayer which as we saw earlier gave many second-Temple Jews a clue as to what was happening to them and when it would all end.

The prayer begins precisely by invoking God as the covenant God, and admitting (like Jacob with Tamar) that he is in the right and Israel is in the wrong:

> Ah, Lord, great and awesome God, keeping covenant and steadfast love with those who love you and keep your commandments, we have sinned and done wrong, acted wickedly and rebelled ... Righteousness is on your side, O Lord [*leka adonai hatsedaqah/soi, kyrie,*

[83] The LXX, however, seems this time to have taken it the other way: *dikaios su hyper eme*.

[84] e.g. Ps. 26.1.

[85] e.g. Ps. 74.1–11, 18–23.

hē dikaiosynē], but open shame, as at this day, falls on us ... All Israel has transgressed your law and turned aside, refusing to obey your voice. So the curse and the oath written in the law of Moses, the servant of God, have been poured out upon us, because we have sinned against you ... Indeed, YHWH our God is right [*tsaddiq/dikaios*] in all that he has done; for we have disobeyed his voice.[86]

With that clear, Daniel turns to invoke the combination of the divine mercy and 'righteousness' as the reason why, despite it all, he must now rescue his people from their exile:

And now, O Lord our God, who brought your people out of the land of Egypt with a mighty hand and made your name renowned even to this day – we have sinned, we have done wickedly. O Lord, *in view of all your righteous acts* [*cecol tsidqotheka/kata tēn dikaiosynēn sou*], let your anger and wrath, we pray, turn away from your city Jerusalem ... We do not present our supplication before you on the ground of our righteousness, but on the ground of your great mercies.[87]

The italicized phrase seems, in the Hebrew, to refer to YHWH's 'righteous acts', as in the NRSV translation. But the LXX has rendered it with *dikaiosynē*, and interestingly the Theodotion version, rendering it with *en pase eleēmosynē sou*, 'in all your mercy', keeps the reference to a divine attribute rather than to earlier divine actions.

It is this sense of God's *dikaiosynē*, I suggest – as an attribute revealed in action – that then comes to dominate in those passages in the Psalms and Isaiah where, above all, we naturally look to find the context of Paul's thought in this area. Modern English translations, seeing the connection between 'God's righteousness' as an attribute of his character (specifically now his faithfulness to his covenant with Israel) and as something which is revealed in particular actions (in Daniel 9, as often, his rescue of his people from Israel), frequently translate *tsedaqah/dikaiosynē* as 'salvation' or near equivalent; but this fails to bring out the point to which Isaiah regularly appeals, which is that these are acts done because of YHWH's prior commitment to Israel. As Onesti and Brauch put it:

The concept of righteousness in the Hebrew Bible emphasizes the relational aspect of God and humanity in the context of a covenant ... The Hebrew meaning of justice means more than the classical Greek idea of giving to every one their due. Usually the word suggests Yahweh's saving acts as evidence of God's faithfulness to the covenant. For this meaning of righteousness of God, *dikaiosynē* is not as flexible as the Hebrew word ... An essential component of Israel's religious experience was that Yahweh was not only Lord of Law but also the one who was faithful to it. God was faithful to the covenant. God's righteousness was shown by saving actions in accordance with this covenant relationship ... Righteousness is not primarily an ethical quality; rather it characterizes the character or action of God who deals rightly within a covenant relationship ... The covenant faithfulness of God, the righteousness of God, is shown by Yahweh's saving acts.[88]

[86] Dan. 9.4–5, 7, 11, 14. The same basic point is made in e.g. *4 Macc.* 4.21: the Syrian persecution is to be understood as God's 'righteous' chastising of his faithless people.

[87] Dan. 9.15–16, 18.

[88] Onesti and Brauch 1993, 828f.

The 'covenantal' meaning, especially as applied to YHWH himself and to his people's loyalty to him, thus resonates across many strands of biblical and later Jewish thinking. The righteousness of the covenant God, seen in his everlasting covenant with Abraham, will find expression in his rescue of his people, as part of his universal sovereignty.[89] Different groups, as we would expect, say things differently from one another. At Qumran the divine faithfulness is naturally interpreted in terms of the sect's own belief that the covenant has been renewed with them while the rest of Israel remains in unrecognized and unconfessed sin.[90]

4. But the covenant is not the last layer of meaning. Here we echo in part the sense of interlocking narratives which we studied in chapter 7. Precisely because Israel's God is the creator of the whole world, he is as we saw responsible for putting that world to rights in the end. He must act as judge, not only for Israel, but for the whole of creation. There is thus a global, or even a cosmic, level to the notion of the divine 'righteousness': the creator will judge the whole world and set things right once and for all, like a judge finally holding the great Assize in which all the unresolved troubles of a community are sorted out at last. This belief, celebrated frequently in the Psalms and informing the great prophets, is repeated in many later Jewish texts.[91] But this is not to be played off against the 'covenantal' meaning. The powerful link of creation and covenant in Genesis itself tells a different story. It is this link that fostered the hope, through to Paul's day and beyond, that when YHWH did finally judge the whole world Israel would at last be vindicated against her enemies. This eschatological vision, variously expressed both in writings we think of as 'apocalyptic' and in quite different works such as the Wisdom of Solomon, thus draws together all four strands of meaning (right behaviour; law court; covenant; cosmic rectification). God's eschatological judgment will be the ultimate cosmic law court, but it will also be the moment of ultimate covenant vindication.

That explains, at least in part, why the word *dikaiosynē* is so difficult to translate. We simply do not have, in contemporary English (or, I think, German or French), a word or even a single phrase that can sum up the broad ethical and 'relational' sense, add to it the overtones of the law court, give it the extra dimensions of the divine covenant with Israel and set it within a worldview-narrative that looked ahead to a final judgment in which the creator would set all things right at last. If we imagine the notion of 'God's restorative justice' on the one hand, and 'God's covenant faithfulness' on the other, as two points in a triangle, the *tsedaqah elohim* or *dikaiosynē theou* might be found as the third point which links them in a fresh, combined sense. It is because our own phrase 'the righteousness of God', with its background in the medieval notion of the *iustitia dei*, has long since struggled to carry any of those three meanings, and indeed in many quarters

[89] e.g. *Jub.* 22.15; Bar. 5.9; *Pss. Sol.* 8.32; *T. Naph.* 8.3; 2 Macc. 1.24–9.

[90] cf. e.g. 1QS 1.21–5: Israel as a whole has sinned, ignoring God's righteous deeds, but the community will confess its own sins as part of claiming the covenant blessing for themselves.

[91] e.g. *1 En.* 62.3; *4 Ez.* 7.33–5; 9.13. Josephus reflects this belief: e.g. *War* 7.323; *Ant.* 2.108; 11.55.

has long since given up that struggle altogether, that the western traditions of Pauline exegesis have found his usage so difficult to understand.[92]

Once we get our heads back into Paul's world of second-Temple Jewish reading of scripture, however, we can not only make sense of this key concept, but also of the related concept of the *tsedaqah* or *dikaiosynē* of God's people. This too is polymorphous, but coherently so. Clearly at one level the word denotes what we rather flatly think of as ethical behaviour. But when we speak of the behaviour of Israel as YHWH's people, 'ethics' is not enough. We are talking about covenant behaviour. Because of Israel's strong belief in an ordered society, ultimately responsible to God as the judge, this moves to and fro, in and out of an implicit law court situation, as we saw with Judah and Tamar and with David and Saul, so that 'righteous' can sometimes mean 'morally upright' and sometimes 'in the right' in a legal sense. If the judge has been doing his job properly, the latter would be taken to imply the former. And because many Israelites in the biblical period, and many Jews thereafter, believed in the responsibility of their God to call the whole world to account in the end, all of this was held within an eschatological framework. Different aspects of this complex set of words, and the world of thought which they evoked, naturally come to the fore in different contexts, but the whole web of meaning retains a basic coherence in which law court, covenant and global or cosmic eschatology do not cancel one another out but rather reinforce one another.

We conclude from all this that the appeal to the divine *dikaiosynē* functioned, in Paul's world, both in terms of *theodicy* – explaining, in a measure, why strange and sad things had happened – and in terms of *soteriology* – appealing for ultimate rescue none the less. 'God's covenant faithfulness' is the attribute of YHWH which provided the grounds for believing that he would do again what he did in Exodus 2, 3 and 6, namely, remember his promises to Abraham, Isaac and Jacob and act to liberate his people in whatever 'new exodus' they might need. I have written elsewhere about the way in which 'the righteousness of God' in key texts from the second-Temple period highlights both (a) the covenant justice because of which God's people are punished by being sent into exile *and* (b) the covenant faithfulness which can be appealed to as the reason for God's forgiving them and bringing them back again.[93]

When we come to Paul's own favourite texts (such as Isaiah 40—66) with this in mind, we see one passage after another in which the same theme

[92] It is this that calls into question Carson's polemic (Carson 2004, 50–2) against some contemporary interpretations. To suggest that linking the *dik-* words with 'covenant' means 'leaving out' 'justice/righteousness' is puzzling nonsense; his implication, that this is what 'Käsemann's heritage' is trying to do, is very strange, since (a) Käsemann was relentlessly opposed to 'covenantal' ideas in Paul, and (b) Käsemann was certainly not a 'new perspective' proponent. Carson's 'stinger in the tail', that 'covenantal' ideas mean that *dikaiosynē* 'is one big step removed from the cross' – a suggestion he seems to attach to me, though without any supporting evidence – shows that he simply has not listened to what is being said. The cross is at the very heart of Paul's covenantal and forensic theology.

[93] For Dan. 9; Ezra 9 etc. see Wright 2009 (*Justification*) ch. 3; and also ch. 2 above, 142–51. Perhaps the most important modern treatment is that of Williams 1980. For intertestamental texts cf. e.g. *T. Dan.* 5.7–13; *1 En.* 95.7; 1QS 11.12; 1QH 4.37; 1QM 18.8.

makes arguably the best sense. Here, for a start, is part of the first 'servant song':

> I am YHWH, I have called you in righteousness; I have taken you by the hand and kept you;
> I have given you as a covenant to the people, a light to the nations,
> to open the eyes that are blind, to bring out the prisoners from the dungeon,
> from the prison those who sit in darkness.
> I am YHWH; that is my name; my glory I give to no other, nor my praise to idols.
> See, the former things have come to pass, and new things I now declare;
> before they spring forth, I tell you of them.[94]

God's 'righteousness' is the reason why he has emphasized his 'teaching', despite Israel's failure;[95] and in the confrontation between himself and the pagan idols, there can be only one victor:

> Declare and present your case; let them take counsel together!
> Who told this long ago? Who declared it of old? Was it not I, YHWH?
> There is no other God besides me, a righteous God and a Saviour; there is no one besides me.
> Turn to me and be saved, all the ends of the earth! For I am God, and there is no other.
> By myself I have sworn, from my mouth has gone forth in righteousness a word that shall not return:
> 'To me every knee shall bow, every tongue shall swear.'
> Only in YHWH, it shall be said of me, are righteousness and strength;
> all who were incensed against him shall come to him and be ashamed.
> In YHWH all the offspring of Israel shall triumph and glory.[96]
>
> Listen to me, you stubborn of heart, you who are far from righteousness;
> I bring near my righteousness, it is not far off, and my salvation will not tarry;
> I will put salvation in Zion, for Israel my glory.[97]

As a result, the invitation can go out: YHWH's 'righteousness', his faithfulness to what he had promised to Abraham, will now bring worldwide salvation in the form of the promised new creation, the restored Eden:

> Listen to me, you that pursue righteousness, you that seek YHWH.
> Look to the rock from which you were hewn, and to the quarry from which you were dug.
> Look to Abraham your father and to Sarah who bore you;
> for he was but one when I called him, but I blessed him and made him many.
> For YHWH will comfort Zion; he will comfort all her waste places,
> and will make her wilderness like Eden, her desert like the garden of YHWH;
> joy and gladness will be found in her, thanksgiving and the voice of song.
> Listen to me, my people, and give heed to me, my nation;
> for a teaching will go out from me, and my justice (*mishpat*) for a light to the peoples.
> I will bring near my righteousness swiftly, my salvation has gone out and my arms will rule the peoples;
> the coastlands wait for me, and for my arm they hope.

[94] Isa. 42.6–9.

[95] 42.21.

[96] 45.21–5.

[97] 46.12–13. NRSV has misleadingly translated *tsedaqah* as 'deliverance' rather than 'righteousness' in these instances.

> Lift up your eyes to the heavens, and look at the earth beneath;
> for the heavens will vanish like smoke, the earth will wear out like a garment, and those who live on it will die like gnats;
> but my salvation will be for ever, and my righteousness will never be ended.[98]

When YHWH acts to rescue his people, this will be the manifestation of his own 'righteousness', the faithfulness through which he will establish his covenant with his people:

> YHWH saw it, and it displeased him that there was no justice.
> He saw that there was no one, and was appalled that there was no one to intervene;
> so his own arm brought him victory, and his righteousness upheld him.
> He put on righteousness like a breastplate, and a helmet of salvation on his head;
> he put on garments of vengeance for clothing, and wrapped himself in fury as in a mantle . . .
> And he will come to Zion as Redeemer, to those in Jacob who turn from transgression, says YHWH.
> And as for me, this is my covenant with them, says YHWH: my spirit that is upon you, and my words that I have put in your mouth, shall not depart out of your mouth . . . from now on and for ever.[99]

There are of course plenty of places in the same book where the prophet speaks of the 'righteousness' of the people. But these passages, coupled with the many similar references in the Psalms and elsewhere, are the scriptural basis for the claim that when a first-century writer, speaking of God providing salvation in line with his covenant with Abraham, refers to God's *dikaiosynē*, he is speaking (a) of an attribute of God himself and (b) more specifically of the attribute of *covenant faithfulness*. Not just the divine mercy (which would act even on behalf of the undeserving); not just the divine 'salvation' (which would consist simply of YHWH's rescuing of his people, without explanation); not even his 'steadfast love', though that would be closer. The divine *covenant faithfulness* brings all these and more together.

(iii) The Covenant Purpose: Through Israel to the World

It is in these passages from Isaiah that we find restated the theme which, as we saw, seems to have been one likely interpretation of Genesis. Paul at least seems to have taken this theme for granted, though it has remained controversial: that the covenant, YHWH's choice of Israel as his people, was aimed not simply at Israel itself, but at the wider and larger purposes which this God intended to fulfil *through* Israel. Israel is God's *servant*; and the point of having a servant is not that the servant becomes one's best friend, though that may happen too, but in order that, through the work of the servant, one may *get things done*. And what YHWH wants done, it seems, is for his glory

[98] 51.1–6; again, NRSV renders *tsedaqah* in vv. 5 and 6 as 'deliverance'. See too, similarly, 56.1.
[99] 59.15–21.

to extend throughout the earth, for all nations to see and hear who he is and what he has done. Hence the famous passages, one of which we have already quoted:

> I am YHWH, I have called you in righteousness, I have taken you by the hand and kept you;
> I have given you as a covenant to the people, a light to the nations,
> to open the eyes that are blind . . .[100]

The same theme is stated slightly more expansively in the next 'servant song':

> And now YHWH says, who formed me in the womb to be his servant,
> to bring Jacob back to him, and that Israel might be gathered to him,
> for I am honoured in the sight of YHWH, and my God has become my strength –
> he says, 'It is too light a thing that you should be my servant to raise up the tribes of Jacob and to restore the survivors of Israel;
> I will give you as a light to the nations, that my salvation may reach to the end of the earth.'[101]

It has been commonplace in many discussions of biblical theology to see these passages as expressing the same vocation that appears, on the face of it, to be contained in the Abrahamic promises: through you all nations will bless themselves, or perhaps will pray to be blessed as you are blessed. With these promises, again, it has been common to link the remarkable statement in Exodus, after the escape from Egypt and immediately before the revelation of the Torah on Mount Sinai:

> You have seen what I did to the Egyptians, and how I bore you on eagles' wings and brought you to myself. Now therefore, if you obey my voice and keep my covenant, you shall be my treasured possession out of all the peoples. Indeed, the whole earth is mine, but you shall be for me a priestly kingdom and a holy nation.[102]

The particular calling of Israel, according to these passages, would seem to be that *through* Israel the creator God will bring his sovereign rule to bear on the world. Israel's specialness would consist of this nation being 'holy', separate from the others, but not merely for its own sake; rather, for the sake of the larger entity, the rest of the world.

It has recently been claimed that to read these texts in this light is to impose on them an essentially 'Christian' scheme, forcing them to serve a purpose which is apparently 'supersessionist' – since the claim is then made that this vocation, of Israel being a 'light to the nations', has been fulfilled in

[100] Isa. 42.6f. NRSV mg. comments on the phrase 'a covenant to the people': 'Meaning of Heb uncertain'. That may be because of the singular 'people' where we might have expected 'peoples', but the text is scarcely unclear, and the following clause 'a light to the nations' gives the most natural sense, as in the next passage below.

[101] Isa. 49.5f.

[102] Ex. 19.4–6.

Jesus the Messiah. Since I think that is exactly what Paul is talking about, it may be worth saying something briefly about this counter-claim.[103]

First, it will not do to accuse H. H. Rowley of 'supersessionism' because of his careful study, two generations ago, of 'The Biblical Doctrine of Election'.[104] Rowley, after all, was writing for an English theological public for whom 'election' had long been a bad word, evoking images of a hard-line ideological Calvinism, which had produced by reaction a kind of Marcionism. We have to remind ourselves that in many protestant theological circles in the middle of the twentieth century the Old Testament was given scarcely a glance, with a few 'proof texts' thrown in to stiffen an argument but with scant attention paid to the full sweep of the biblical narrative and its inner theological dynamics. Against that background, where Rowley was substantially rehabilitating a way of understanding theology that allowed Israel's scriptures to be heard in what was then an unusually full and clear way, it seems harsh to accuse him of some kind of anti-Jewish prejudice.

Second, it has to be said that Joel Kaminsky's own reconstruction of a doctrine of Israel's 'election' from which all thought of wider purpose has been removed remains unconvincing, both as an account of the texts we have just mentioned and in its own terms. When he borrows from Michael Wyschogrod the idea of a God who, like a parent playing favourites, simply and blatantly prefers one nation above the others, and suggests that this is a sign of just how vivid and believable this God (God?) is, he will I imagine find rather few, including among his fellow Jews, who are prepared to go along with him.[105]

Third – a point that could be amplified considerably further – it has to be said that the charge of 'supersessionism', so readily flung around these days at anyone who has the temerity to say anything like what Paul was actually saying, needs (to say the least) to be clarified. Let us suggest three versions at least: a 'hard' supersessionism, a 'sweeping' supersessionism and a 'Jewish' supersessionism – which last, I shall suggest, does not deserve the name.

First, a 'hard' supersessionism. This is what we find in some early Christian writers who, ignoring Paul's warnings in Romans 11 against gentile arrogance, did appear to teach that Jews were now cast off for ever and that

[103] See particularly Kaminsky 2007.

[104] Rowley 1964 [1950].

[105] See Kaminsky 17, 67f., citing Wyschogrod 1983, 64f.: 'Because a father is not an impartial judge but a loving parent and because a human father is a human being with his own personality, it is inevitable that he will find himself more compatible with some of his children than others and, to speak very plainly, love some more than others.' Kaminsky, summarizing this (67), states that 'If God's love is like human love in any way whatsoever, then it is unlikely that God has an identical love for all nations and all individuals.' He uses the Joseph story to suggest that the non-chosen brothers are required to 'mature enough to accept life's unfairness', whereupon they may receive some benefit handed on from those who, unlike them, have been chosen. There is much one could say about this, as indeed about Kaminsky's whole thesis. For the moment we simply note that, as Bassler 1982 has made clear, the ancient Jewish idea that the one God in fact has 'no favourites', though clearly emphasized by Paul (Rom. 2.11; 3.29f.), was certainly not a Christian innovation. Compare e.g. *Jub.* 5.16; 33.18; *2 Bar.* 44.4; the idea goes back, among other places, to Dt. 10.17; 2 Chr. 19.7. In all of these it is strongly affirmed precisely that Israel's God *is* an 'impartial judge' as well as many other things.

gentile believers had replaced them as the people of God.[106] This could be drawn in the following way:

According to that scheme, Jewish people have no place in the church, so that one has to say that Paul and the others were lucky to make it in before the door slammed shut. I am not aware that anyone in recent times has argued that Paul thought like that, and it seems unlikely that anyone in the western church has dared to suggest anything of this order since the 1950s. But if there really is such a thing as real, no-nonsense 'supersessionism', this, I suggest, is what it might look like. My own hunch is that such a view gained ground enormously in the fourth and fifth centuries. Though I would not wish to join in the fashionable cheap-and-cheerful Constantine-bashing, it has to be said that when Christianity became the religion of the empire it faced new challenges and temptations, and did not always rise to the challenges or refuse the temptations. As so often in other areas, however, what has now happened is that the neo-moralism of the late twentieth century, seeing the horrible anti-semitism of Nazi ideology (which was of course essentially pagan, though sometimes borrowing some clothes designed to look 'Christian'), and noting its apparent continuity with some earlier manifestations of the same poison, has projected the whole thing back to the earliest days. This serves neither historical research nor contemporary ethics. 'Hard supersessionism' deserved the severe advance warnings that Paul issued in Romans 11, but it is not normally to be found in contemporary biblical scholarship.

There is, however, a phenomenon which is alive and well today, including in some prestigious places, which we might call 'sweeping supersessionism'. This is the sweeping claim, in line with a certain style of post-Barthian (and perhaps 'postliberal') theology, that what happened in Jesus Christ constituted such a radical inbreaking or 'invasion' into the world that it rendered redundant anything and everything that had gone before – particularly anything that looked like 'religion', not least 'covenantal religion'. This view is unlike 'hard supersessionism' because it denies that there is any historical continuity at all: it isn't that 'Israel' has 'turned into the church', but rather that Israel, and everything else prior to the apocalyptic announcement of the gospel, has been swept aside by the fresh revelation. This approach was associated with some of the great names of a former generation such as Ernst Käsemann, for whom the target of Paul's polemic was 'homo religiosus', by which he meant 'the hidden Jew in all of us', instantiated in anything that approached any kind of continuity (let alone 'covenant'). We may detect here a continuing protestant concern with any kind of 'catholic' attempt to turn the church into a *Heilsanstalt*, an

[106] This is regularly taken to be the implication of e.g. *Barn.* 4.7; 9.4; 14.1–5.

institute for dispensing salvation.[107] This post-Käsemann 'sweeping supersessionism' (though obviously it has not been called that) has been enthusiastically revived in J. L. Martyn's commentary on Galatians, and welcomed with open arms by many in the broadly Barthian tradition.[108] This way of looking at things could be drawn in the following manner:

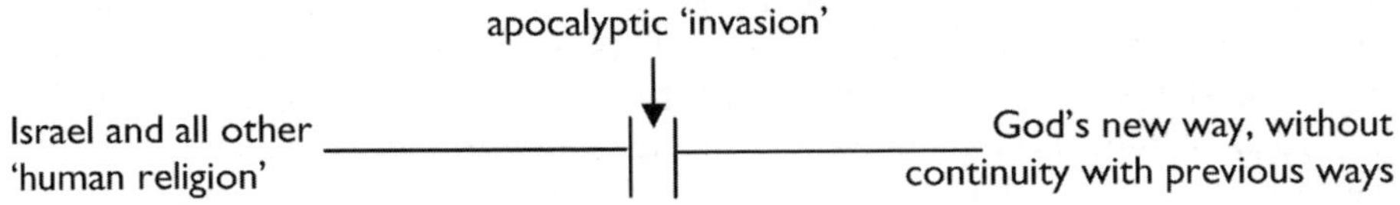

Even drawing it this way could give the wrong impression, as though there were after all some left-to-right continuity in the picture, whereas according to the enthusiastic proponents of the apocalyptic 'invasion' the gospel events have swept away the 'old age' entirely, so that the 'new age' they have ushered in simply operates in a different mode. This carries, so it seems, none of the old propensity of the 'hard supersessionism' to say that Jewish persons are not welcome within the new way. It is just that being Jewish, and adhering to the Jewish hope that God would fulfil his long-awaited promises to Abraham, appears to be exactly the wrong kind of thing. It is what, according to Martyn, Paul's opponents in Galatia had been teaching. And Paul insisted that any such thing – any continuity with Abraham, let alone Moses – had been swept away in the 'apocalypse' of Jesus and his death. The new reality thus 'supersedes' the old. Attempts by Martyn and his followers to resist this conclusion from their teaching simply fail.[109]

[107] For Käsemann's discussion of Israel as *homo religiosus* see e.g. Käsemann 1969 [1965], 183–7 (186: 'Israel has exemplary significance for [Paul]; in and with Israel he strikes at the hidden Jew in all of us, at the man who validates rights and demands over against God on the basis of God's past dealings with him and to this extent is serving not God but an illusion.' See too e.g. Käsemann 1980 [1973], 302.

[108] At least, in the tradition of Barth's great Romans commentary. Whether the later Barth, e.g. the Barth of *CD* 4.1, would have approved is another question. There is an oddity here: among the roll-call of those eager to sign up to Martyn's version of Käsemann's 'apocalyptic' theory is Harink 2003, whose fourth chapter accuses the present writer, at length, of 'supersessionism', and thereby opens the door for other similarly misguided charges (e.g. W. S. Campbell 2008). This is not the moment for refutation; merely for noting the irony.

[109] Martyn recognizes a problem here and tries to ward it off (e.g. Martyn 1997b, 204–8). But his basic 'polarity' between 'religion' and 'apocalyptic' (1997b, 78f., in an essay partly repeated in his 1997a, 35–41) inevitably drives him in this direction, since for him (in good Barth/Käsemann fashion) 'religion is the human being's superstitious effort to come to know and to influence God, rather than the faith that is elicited by God's invasive grace' (1997b, 79) – and this, for Martyn, is what is at stake in Paul's opposition to the Galatian 'teachers', who are of course offering a form of Judaism. Saying that this is not an attack on Judaism because the issue at stake is internal to the church (80), or because there were no Jews in the Galatian cities (82), is mere prevarication: Martyn admits 'that the letter does contain an *implication* with regard to Judaism' (80, his italics), and if Judaism remains a 'religion' then the critique remains. Anyway, the case for a South Galatian destination is now overwhelming (see e.g. Mitchell 1993b, 3f.), and there were plenty of Jews there.

The third variety ('Jewish supersessionism') is what we find in Qumran.[110] This is the claim that the creator God has acted at last, in surprising but prophecy-fulfilling ways, to launch his renewed covenant, to call a new people who are emphatically in continuity with Abraham, Isaac and Jacob, to pour out his spirit afresh upon them, to enable them to keep Torah in the new way he had always envisaged and to assure them that he and his angels were present with them in their worship (even though they were not in the Jerusalem Temple) and that their united community was to be seen as the real focal point of 'Israel'. Members of the Qumran community were of course all Jews, but most Jews were not members of the community. Other Jews were at liberty to join, by means of (as with most monastic communities) a process of testing and probationary periods. They would have to take upon themselves the special responsibilities of this new community, and live up to them. Members of this community saw the rest of the Jewish world as dangerously compromised, with even the zealous Pharisees being 'speakers of smooth things', and (depending on your theory) some at least of the priestly class totally compromised and corrupt. This picture therefore looks like this:

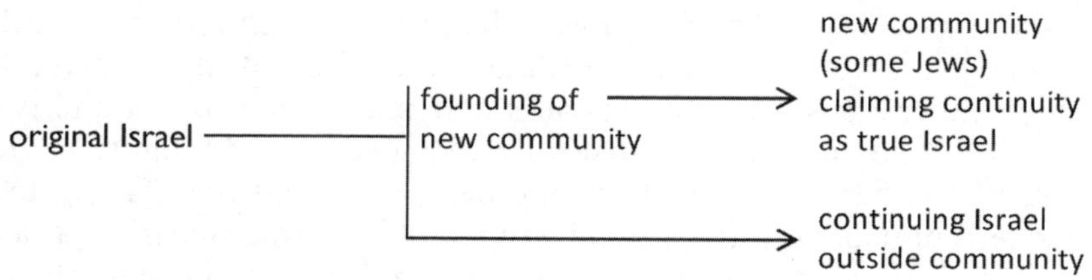

It is of course not only in Qumran that we find this kind of pattern. We may surmise that many of the smaller Jewish groups and parties at the time of the war of AD 66–70 might have seen themselves in much this way ('Look! Here is the Messiah! Those who follow him are the true Israel, and all others are renegades!'). That, in sociological jargon, is the classic position of any and every 'sect'.[111]

Is this position 'supersessionism' in any meaningful sense? A case could be made for using that word. But, unlike the two previous models, in both

[110] See Levenson 1993, x: 'Nowhere does Christianity betray its indebtedness to Judaism more than in its supersessionism.' In other words, Judaism has always contained a narrative pattern in which a late-born son supplants older brothers, or a new movement (such as Qumran) claims to represent or embody the true people of God. One could even regard the Mishnah as 'supersessionist', since it sketches a way of being Jewish which many Jews of earlier generations would neither have recognized nor approved.

[111] Studies of 'sectarianism' have proliferated in recent years, in relation to the ancient world in general and Judaism and early Christianity in particular. A helpful study is that of Elliott 1995, who lists (81–4) no fewer than twenty-one characteristics of the 'sect'. The word 'sect' is of course almost always etic, and frequently polemically so; those in such groups regard themselves, almost by definition, as the true inheritors of the original parent body. See, more broadly, the work of Philip Esler: e.g. Esler 1994, esp. chs. 1, 4 and 5.

of which there is a definite sense of *replacement* of Israel and everything it stood for with something quite new, there is here a characteristically Jewish note of *fulfilment*. It would be extremely odd if, in a group whose whole existence depended on being the people of a promise-making God, nobody was ever allowed to claim that the promises had been fulfilled, for fear of being called 'supersessionist'. Was John the Baptist a 'supersessionist'? Was Jesus? The claim could of course be challenged: *your* idea of 'fulfilment' doesn't fit with *ours*, or the events that *you* claim constitute 'fulfilment' don't look like what *we* expected to see under that heading, and therefore your claim is falsified. But the idea that such a claim could never be made looks as if it is cutting off the branch on which its entire worldview had been sitting. I submit that the oddity of calling Qumran theology 'supersessionist', granted the sense which that somewhat sneering term has come to bear, is so great that we should probably think of a different way of describing such a worldview.

My proposal has of course been (in chapter 6 of the present work and elsewhere) that Paul's revision of the Jewish view of election was more or less of the same type as what we find in Qumran. Call it 'Jewish supersessionism' if you like, but recognize the oxymoronic nature of such a phrase. The scandal of Paul's gospel, after all, was that the events in which he claimed that Israel's God had been true to what he promised centred on a crucified Messiah. That is the real problem with any and all use of the 'supersession' language: either Jesus was and is Israel's Messiah, or he was not and is not. That question in turn is of course directly linked to the question of the resurrection: either Jesus rose from the dead or he did not. Trying to use postmodern moralism, with its usual weapon of linguistic smearing, as a way to force Christians today to stop saying that Jesus was Israel's Messiah is bad enough, though that is not our current problem. Trying to use that moralism as a way of forcing first-century historians to deny that Paul thought Jesus was the Messiah, and that the divine promises to Israel had been fulfilled in him, simply will not do.[112]

Are we saying, then, that in Paul's view God chose Israel for a purpose he intended to accomplish *through* Israel? Yes. Does this 'instrumentalize' Israel, and the notion of election, as has been suggested? Yes and no. It is a well-known phenomenon in Israel's scriptures that God can use people or nations as 'instruments' in his purpose: Assyria in Isaiah 10, Cyrus in Isaiah 45. But those 'instruments' were ignorant of YHWH and his purposes.[113] Israel was supposed to be aware of them, to be the faithful, obedient servant through whose glad self-offering the purposes of the covenant God might be set forward. That, at least, is one way of reading both the scriptural tradition and such post-biblical reflections as we find on similar themes. And that, I

[112] It is noticeable that Harink 2003, ch. 4, never even mentions, let alone discusses, the passages in which Paul says exactly this (e.g. Rom. 2.25–9; 2 Cor. 1.20; Gal. 2.19f.; Phil. 3.2–11).

[113] At least, that is what YHWH says in Isa. 45.4; but in 45.3 the purpose is stated as 'so that you may know that it is I, YHWH, the God of Israel, who call you by your name'. Presumably the point is that when YHWH calls Cyrus he is ignorant, but ought not to remain so.

suggest, is the right way to read the crucial passage (often misunderstood) in Paul himself:

> [17]But supposing you call yourself 'a Jew'. Supposing you rest your hope in the law. Supposing you celebrate the fact that God is your God, [18]and that you know what he wants, and that by the law's instruction you can make appropriate moral distinctions. [19]Supposing you believe yourself to be a guide to the blind, a light to people in darkness, [20]a teacher of the foolish, an instructor for children – all because, in the law, you possess the outline of knowledge and truth.[114]

We commented on this passage already in chapter 6, and here summarize briefly in the light of our fuller exposition elsewhere.[115] This passage is not talking about 'the boast of "the Jew"' in the sense that 'the Jew' is supposing him- or herself to be morally superior to the rest of the world and therefore not to be in need of 'salvation'. The passage is talking about 'the boast of "the Jew"' – of, we remind ourselves, Paul himself before his conversion – to be the Isaiah 42 people, the Isaiah 49 people, the light to the gentiles, the one who would open blind eyes, the teacher of babes. Torah gives 'the Jew' the outline of knowledge and truth; it is then the responsibility of 'the Jew' to pass this on to the world, to obey the vocation to bring a balance to the world, to mend the world.[116]

It is vital to realize that Paul does not deny any of this. This really was and is, he believes, Israel's vocation. Many first-century Jews might, for all we know, have disagreed. They might have said, 'Oh, you Pharisees! You're always supposing you can fulfil those Isaiah-prophecies!' We have no means of knowing.[117] But we can know that Paul really did believe this – and we can guess, accurately I suspect, that this really was how Saul of Tarsus had seen the Jewish vocation. *Abraham's family are supposed to be the ones through whom Adam's sin is undone*: that, as we have seen, was woven tightly not only into the fabric of Genesis and Exodus, but also into several strands of Jewish thought in Paul's period and on to the rabbis beyond. Paul is here facing this claim. Granted the universality of human sin, as highlighted by the 'apocalypse of the wrath of God' in the gospel (Romans 1.18—2.16), what is to be done? Step forward the faithful Jew: this is the task of Abraham's family, to be the people through whom all this would be put right.

[114] Rom. 2.17–20.

[115] See *Perspectives*, ch. 30.

[116] Kaminsky 2007, 147–57 seems to me to make very heavy weather of denying that texts like Isa. 40—55 speak of a divine vocation to Israel to be the light of the world. Isa. 49.6 could hardly be clearer. This has nothing to do with 'imperialism' (151) or with an 'instrumentalising' of Israel that would undermine the relationship of love between YHWH and his people (156). Nor does this then 'dissolve [Israel's] uniqueness by extending their elect status to everyone in the world' (154); it is exactly the thrust of Paul's thinking, not least in Romans, that the single divine plan remains 'to the Jew first and also, equally, to the Greek' (Rom. 1.16). Kaminsky pleads that we should 'understand the Hebrew Bible's theological language in its own terms' (158). I agree.

[117] On the question of whether any, or many, Jews of Paul's day did undertake missionary work, see e.g. McKnight 1991; Bird 2010.

And Paul warns that the boast cannot be made good. Romans 2.21–4 has often caused exegetes to puzzle: surely Paul doesn't think all Jews are adulterers, or all rob temples? No. That would only be the point (if at all) if he was trying to prove that all Jews need to be saved from their sin. He is not. He is demonstrating that the national 'boast' of 'the Jew', namely that Israel as a whole is charged with putting the world to rights, cannot be made good, because of the glaring errors of some which have resulted, as every Jew knew, in the prophetic denunciations which indicated that the vocation had been stood on its head. Instead of the gentiles looking at Israel and praising Israel's God, it was working the other way: they were looking at Israel *and blaspheming Israel's God*.[118] That is a severe and serious thing to say, but Paul is not saying it on his own authority. He is quoting Isaiah 52.5, and thereby echoing also Ezekiel 36.20. This does not merely have the effect of saying, 'There you are; your own prophets have said that your vaunted boast has been turned upside down'. It does something more interesting still. Both passages come in the middle of sequences of thought in which Israel's God is not only charging Israel with this fault *but also announcing the remedy*; and the proof that this is how Paul's mind is working at this point is that he at once follows the same line of thought in his extremely important passage 2.25–9.

Take, first, Ezekiel 36. The prophet has already denounced God's people up and down. Now he turns, not for Israel's sake but for the sake of God's own name, to the vision of how YHWH will reveal his salvation and thereby gain glory from the nations. This prophecy stands exactly in the tradition we have described in this chapter so far:

> But when they came to the nations, wherever they came, they profaned my holy name, in that it was said of them, 'These are the people of YHWH, and yet they had to go out of his land.' But I had concern for my holy name, which the house of Israel had profaned among the nations to which they came.
>
> Therefore say to the house of Israel … I will sanctify my great name, which has been profaned among the nations, and which you have profaned among them; and the nations shall know that I am YHWH, says the Sovereign YHWH, when through you I display my holiness before their eyes. I will take you from the nations, and gather you from all the countries, and bring you into your own land. I will sprinkle clean water upon you, and you shall be clean from all your uncleannesses, and from all your idols I will cleanse you. A new heart I will give you, and a new spirit I will put within you; and I will remove from your body the heart of stone and give you a heart of flesh. I will put my spirit within you, and make you follow my statutes (*en tois dikaiōmasin mou poreuēsthe*) and be careful to observe my ordinances (*kai ta krimata mou phylaxēsthe kai poiēsesthe*). Then you shall live in the land that I gave to your ancestors; and you shall be my people, and I will be your God.[119]

Did Paul have this passage in mind? Most certainly. Observe what follows immediately in Romans 2:

[118] Rom. 2.24.

[119] Ezek. 36.20–8.

[25]Circumcision, you see, has real value for people who keep the law (*ean nomon prassēs*). If, however, you break the law, your circumcision becomes uncircumcision. [26]Meanwhile, if uncircumcised people keep the law's requirements (*ta dikaiōmata tou nomou phylassē*), their uncircumcision will be regarded as circumcision, won't it? [27]So people who are by nature uncircumcised, but who fulfil the law (*ton nomon telousa*), will pass judgment on people like you who possess the letter of the law and circumcision but who break the law.

[28]The 'Jew' isn't the person who appears to be one, you see. Nor is 'circumcision' what it appears to be, a matter of physical flesh. [29]The 'Jew' is the one in secret; and 'circumcision' is a matter of the heart, in the spirit rather than the letter. Such a person gets 'praise', not from humans, but from God.[120]

Here are people, in other words, in whom Ezekiel's prophecy of restoration has been coming true! The echoes are clear and produce excellent sense, though that sense was not, we may suppose, welcome to Paul's 'kinsfolk according to the flesh', any more than it would have been to Paul himself before his conversion.[121]

So what about the other passage, the actual quotation from Isaiah? Here too the scriptural basis, when explored, yields rich results, this time into the wider flow of thought which continues on into Romans 3:

Now therefore, what am I doing here, says YHWH, seeing that my people are taken away without cause? Their rulers howl, says YHWH, and continually, all day long, my name is despised. Therefore my people shall know my name; therefore on that day they shall know that it is I who speak; here am I.

How beautiful upon the mountains are the feet of the messenger who announces peace,
who brings good news (*hōs euaggelizomenos agatha*), who announces salvation,
who says to Zion, 'Your God reigns.'
Listen! Your sentinels lift up their voices, together ... in plain sight they see
the return of YHWH to Zion.[122]

And the passage goes on, of course, into the fourth servant song, portraying the one who was exalted and lifted up, startling nations and kings, wounded for our transgressions and bruised for our iniquities, the righteous one whose faithful obedience would make many righteous, who bore the sin of many and made intercession for the transgressors. This is the passage, in other words, towards which Paul is working now quite rapidly, as he aims very shortly to announce the 'good news' that God's righteousness has been unveiled in the events concerning Jesus the Messiah, and particularly his obedient sacrificial death, all the way through to the closing statement of Romans 4, where Jesus is 'handed over because of our trespasses and raised because of our justification'.[123]

[120] Rom. 2.25–9: see below, e.g. 814, 836f., 921–3, 958, 1432, 1642. As we saw at n. 112 above, this passage, one of the most important for Paul's redefinition of election, is never mentioned by Harink 2003 in his over-eager attack on what he sees as 'supersessionism'.

[121] W. S. Campbell 2008, 104 suggests that 'the Jew' in vv. 28 and 29 is 'a real Jew in the sense of being both circumcised and living in the faith of Abraham'. The fact that these people seem to be the same as those described as 'uncircumcised' in vv. 26f. does seem to cause problems for such a proposal.

[122] Isa. 52.5–8.

[123] Rom. 4.25; for the echoes of Isa. 53 see Wright 2002 [*Romans*], 503f.

Three things stand out for our present purposes about this remarkable double 'echo'. First, Paul's apparent charge against his fellow Jews, picking up the prophetic charge of Isaiah and Ezekiel, is real and fully meant, but it occurs in contexts which are already pregnant with hope. Yes, Israel has got it badly wrong; but this is not the end of the matter. YHWH is even now at work to sort everything out in a great act of redemption. Second, in the Ezekiel passage we see adumbrated just that 'new covenant' language – the spirit, the law in the heart, the fresh keeping of Torah's requirements – which we find again and again in Paul, not only in this passage.[124] This is a very strong indication that Ezekiel does indeed stand behind Paul's words in Romans 2.25–9, even though Paul is there speaking paradoxically of non-Jews who find themselves doing what Ezekiel saw God's renewed people doing.[125] Third, the Isaiah passage points dramatically forward to the revelation of God's ultimate plan of salvation, the personal obedience of the servant through which that worldwide light-to-the-nations plan would after all be put into operation. The failure of God's people as a whole has not thwarted the divine plan *to save the world through Abraham's family*, to lighten the nations through Israel. That is exactly what Paul will now proceed to argue.

But before we can get to that point in our own argument we must pause, take stock and summarize some further aspects of this Israel-shaped vocation. Each element now could be developed at length, but it is important to state these very briefly for the moment.

1. Within the framework of the covenant outlined so far, in which Israel was called to be the people through whom the one God would rescue the world, Israel was called to be the *Shema* people, confessing the one God and loving him with heart, mind and life itself.
2. Israel was called to be the people shaped by the creator God's 'wisdom'. Again, we looked at this earlier. For many in Paul's day, this 'wisdom' was contained, more or less, in Torah.
3. Israel was called to be the people in whom, therefore, the life held out by Torah would become a reality – both in the sense of the 'life' of glad, loving obedience and the 'life' promised to Torah-keepers (much as the 'tree of life' remained, tantalizingly, in Eden).
4. Israel was the people in whose midst the living God had deigned to dwell, first in the pillar of cloud and fire, then in the wilderness tabernacle, and finally in the Temple in Jerusalem.
5. Israel was to be the people who inherited YHWH's sovereign rule over the world. The promised land was a sign of this, but already by the first century many Jews had glimpsed the possibility, already implicit

[124] cf. e.g. Rom. 8.5–8; 10.5–13; 2 Cor. 3.1–6; Gal. 5.16–26.

[125] cf. Rom. 9.30: gentiles, who were not pursuing 'righteousness', have received 'righteousness'.

within the Adam–Abraham nexus, that the land was simply an advance signpost to YHWH's claim over the whole of creation.[126]

6. Israel was to be (according to the Pentateuchal origins and the second-Temple writings already noted) the people who would discover YHWH's faithfulness to the covenant through the pattern of slavery and exodus, of exile and restoration.

God; God's wisdom; God's life; God's presence; God's universal rule; God's faithfulness. At every point the self-aware self-identification of Israel meant that many of Paul's contemporaries were looking for that new day to dawn in which, at last, God's covenant faithfulness would be unveiled in a great act of redemption, of new exodus, of return from exile. According to Deuteronomy 30, that would happen when Israel, much as in Ezekiel 36, was keeping Torah from the heart as a result of God's new act of covenant grace, for the sake of his own name. And, granted the pressures of the first century, pressures both social and political on the one hand and exegetical and theological on the other, we can see that the question faced by Saul of Tarsus and his contemporaries could have been put like this: granted God's covenant with Abraham, and granted the widespread failure of most within Israel to be true to the covenant, to keep Torah properly, and granted the continuing ambiguity of a Temple with a corrupt priesthood and a land ruled over by pagans – granted all this, when is YHWH going to do what he has promised, what will it look like, *and how can we tell in the present time who are the genuine Israel*, the ones who are showing the signs of that new, dawning day? This, as I argued at the end of the previous chapter, was at the heart of the 'plight' of which we might expect an early first-century Pharisee to be aware.

And this, as I suggested there and will now explore, was radically revised around the new, unexpected and indeed shocking revelation which Saul of Tarsus received on the road to Damascus. God's righteousness had been revealed *in the faithful death of Israel's Messiah*. This is the very heart of his redefinition of 'election', and also the very heart of his 'gospel'.

3. Israel's Messiah as the Focus of Election

(i) Introduction: Jesus as the Messiah of Israel

(a) Introduction

This is the point at which one of the major moves in my whole argument takes place. *The purpose for which the covenant God had called Israel had been accomplished, Paul believed, through Jesus.* The entire 'theology of election' we have examined in the preceding pages is not set aside. It is brought

[126] This emerges in Paul at Rom. 4.13, but the idea is much older, being rooted in passages like Ps. 72.8–11, as developed in e.g. Sir. 44.21; *Jub.* 19.21; *2 Bar.* 14.13.

into fresh focus, rethought, reimagined and reworked around Jesus himself, and particularly around his death, resurrection and enthronement. Christology, in the several senses that word must bear, is the first major lens through which Paul envisages the ancient doctrine of Israel's election.

It is hard to express just how dramatic Paul's view of Jesus actually was. We saw in the previous chapter that he believed that in him Israel's God had returned in person to liberate his people. We are now going to see that he also believed that the divine purpose for Israel itself had been accomplished through him. He was, in other words, the place where the God of Abraham and the people of Abraham met: monotheism and election in person. When we understand Jesus in this double Pauline perspective – and when, subsequently, we also understand the spirit in a similar way – the elements of Pauline soteriology that previously appeared disparate come together in a whole new coherence. With this, we have arrived at the central section of the central chapter of Part III. This is the very heart of Paul's theology. This is where all the birds come in to land.

The fact that Jesus, in Paul's understanding, had fulfilled and accomplished the divine purpose for Israel is encapsulated, I propose, in the notion of *Messiahship*. Paul's theology turns, at its centre, on the belief that Jesus of Nazareth was and is Israel's Messiah, the long-promised one from the line of David, the one through whom Israel's final battle was to be fought, the Temple was to be cleansed and rebuilt, God's justice and peace were to be established in the world and the ancient promises to Abraham were to be fulfilled. This double claim – that Paul believed Jesus to be the Messiah, and that this was the central hinge of his theology – was massively counter-intuitive to his unbelieving contemporaries, and it has been massively counter-intuitive, for almost exactly the opposite reasons, to the majority of western scholars in the last century or so. Paul's Jewish contemporaries could not believe that Israel's Messiah would be crucified; most modern scholars have not been able to understand why it should matter that the crucified saviour should be Israel's Messiah. Since we cannot get much further in our argument without this point being established, we shall have to explain and justify it before we can proceed.

If this first task – explaining and justifying Paul's messianic belief and its meaning – is a tall order, it diminishes before the second task which this section must address, which is to explain how, according to Paul, the death of Jesus precisely as Israel's Messiah had the effect that I shall argue it did, namely of bringing to its appointed goal the whole purpose of election. This will involve, naturally, a detailed blend of exegesis and thematic exposition, but both the passages and the themes will be approached from what is, in terms of the recent history of Pauline studies, unusual angles. My hope is that this will carry conviction through the sense that it makes of the passages in their larger contexts, and through the coherence of the themes in themselves and with one another.

(b) Jesus as Israel's Messiah

Jesus, then, as Messiah.[127] The 'minimalist' approach of much modern exegesis has allowed, grudgingly, that Paul may make one or two references to Jesus as Messiah: Romans 9.5 comes to mind, but since the same exegetes do not make that verse in any way loadbearing within Paul's larger structure it appears a meaningless concession.[128] One might have thought that certain other passages would force their way into even such a short list: Romans 1.3, for instance, and 15.12, in both of which there is clear reference to Jesus as the Davidic king. (Ah, but, say the detractors, the former is a pre-Pauline formula which Paul quotes in order to move beyond it, and the latter simply a rhetorical flourish. We have ways of making texts silent.) Some have highlighted the scandal of *Christos estaurōmenos* ('Christ crucified') in 1 Corinthians 1.23 as an obvious example, since the scandal for Jews is precisely that of a crucified *Messiah*. Those who remain unwilling to countenance the messianic possibility will declare that the scandal is of hailing a crucified man as one's saviour, not that of suggesting him as Messiah. And so on.

I have suggested elsewhere that the widespread and continuing messianic belief in the early church (all four canonical gospels; Revelation; Ignatius of Antioch; the 'brothers of Jesus' who are brought before Domitian on a charge of belonging to a royal family; and so on) indicates clearly enough that the Messiahship of Jesus remained a powerful and important notion

[127] See the preliminary statements in e.g. Wright 1991 [*Climax*] 41–9, and *Perspectives* ch. 31. It is noticeable that some scholars who have studied Paul's communities with a less heavy-handed theological agenda have had no difficulty in seeing Jesus as 'Messiah' in Paul: e.g. Meeks 1983. The whole topic has now been revitalized and set on a new footing by the work of Novenson 2012. Among earlier statements pointing in the right direction: Dahl 1992, 391f. (referring also to his earlier essays now in the overlapping volumes Dahl 1974 and 1991). Charlesworth 1992b shows how much Paul has been ignored when it comes to Messiahship: the massive volume, entitled *The Messiah: Developments in Earliest Judaism and Christianity*, devotes only a few pages, and no main article, to Paul. This view is reflected, too, in Chester 2007; though Chester agrees that Paul does believe Jesus to be Messiah, and links this with some elements of his teaching, he finds that Paul's 'main focus is not on Jesus as messiah; nor do messianic categories play a prominent part in his theology' (109). See further below.

[128] See e.g. Hengel 1992, 444: 'It is disputed whether "Christos" here [i.e. 1 Cor. 15.3f.] is still a messianic title, or – as otherwise almost always in Paul – used as a proper name' (citing Hengel 1983, 65–77, 179–88). The fact that Hengel goes on to affirm the messianic significance of the early confession in 1 Cor. 15 scarcely diminishes his overall dismissal of the term; he uses the long-familiar *religionsgeschichtlich* argument that people outside Judaism would not have understood the meaning of Messiahship. Despite Chester's rebuke (2007, 118) I stick to my view (*RSG* 555) that Hengel regards as an illusion the messianic significance that I have discerned in Paul. To be sure, Hengel does see some messianic significance, but he dismisses at the root all the possibilities I was exploring. See e.g. Hengel 1983, 65–77; 1995, 1–7; e.g. 1983, 67: 'in his letters [Paul] has no occasion to give reasons for this obvious insight [that *Christos* means "Messiah"] or to develop it'; 68, citing Kramer 1966 to the effect that 'all the statements in the letters make good sense even to those who only know that Christ is a surname for Jesus'; and 69, again citing Kramer to the effect that even when 'Christ' with the article is found, 'in no case can we discover an appropriate reason for the determination' (one might suggest that this was because Kramer was looking hard in the wrong direction); 72, 'that it is precisely as a "proper name" that "Christos" expresses the uniqueness of Jesus as "eschatological bringer of salvation"'; 76, 'It makes little sense to seek to discover in Paul the use of the name as a title'; 1995, 4 n. 5: in Rom. 9.5 it 'almost improves the sense' to suppose that the article indicates a titular usage, but 'since Paul nowhere else uses the word as a title it is better to render it here as the name'.

right across the first century or so of the new movement.[129] From this perspective alone it would be very surprising if Paul, soaked in scripture, telling and retelling the story of Israel, and using the word *Christos* extremely frequently to refer to Jesus, had allowed the notion of Messiahship to sink below the level of consciousness.[130] But that argument, though I believe it does generate an *a priori* case for assuming a messianic reference in his writings, does not take us very far into the detail. The fact of widespread early Christian belief in Jesus' Messiahship is well known among scholars, and it has not resulted in a recognition of the same belief in Paul, except perhaps as an assumption which is then left behind in the fuller development of his theology.[131] Three larger arguments suggest themselves – though, as often, the ultimate demonstration of the case is the sense that it then makes of an enormous amount that will otherwise remain unclear.

First, look at the way Paul deploys 'royal' passages from the Psalms and Isaiah. We see this first in Romans 1.3–4, already cited; if anyone is inclined to respond that this is a mere opening gambit, soon to be abandoned, we should note that the passage demonstrably functions as the major thematic statement at the start of this great and carefully composed letter.[132] The echoes here are, uncontroversially, of Psalm 2.7 and 2 Samuel 7.12–14. This is the Davidic 'Son of God'. He is declared to be so through his resurrection from the dead, echoing the Septuagint in particular of 2 Samuel 7.12: *kai anastēsō to sperma sou*, 'and I will raise up/resurrect your seed' is followed in verse 14 by *egō esomai autō eis patera, kai autos estai moi eis huion*, 'I will be to him a father, and he shall be to me a son.' This promise is then celebrated in another psalm, 89.26–7, where the Davidic king will cry 'My Father' to YHWH, and YHWH declares, 'I will make him my firstborn.'

But it is Psalm 2 that resonates particularly in Romans 1.3–4. The nations are in uproar, the kings and rulers of the earth are in rebellion 'against

[129] Wright 1991 [*Climax*], 42, with refs. This is contrary to the widespread assumption (e.g. Schnelle 2005 [2003], 438f.) that the title *Christos* 'soon became simply a name for Jesus', and that insofar as gentile churches gave it any meaning it would be the general one of 'anointed' and hence 'nearness to God'. Though he does say that, even as a name, it 'always has the overtones of its original titular significance', he neither spells out what that might be nor allows it any active role in Paul's theology.

[130] *Christos* occurs around 270 times in the seven 'main' letters, over 70 times in Eph., Col., and 2 Thess., and over 30 in the Pastorals. It is this that causes John Collins, one of today's leading experts in second-Temple Judaism, to declare that 'if this is not ample testimony that Paul regarded Jesus as messiah, then words have no meaning' (Collins 2010 [1995], 2). He also cites Rom. 1.3f. in support, and refers to Collins and Collins 2008, 101–22. Compare the measured scorn of Agamben 2006, 14–18 (quoted below at 835) for those who treat *christos* as a proper name – including the practice, in the Nestle-Aland Greek Testament, of printing *Christos* when deemed a proper name (e.g. Gal. 3.24–9) and *christos* when deemed a title (e.g. Mt. 16.16). (The explanation of this, given e.g. in NA 25, 63*, has been dropped in later edns., but the practice continues.)

[131] e.g. Chester 2007, 120f. As will appear from the previous chapter, I agree with Chester that Paul speaks of Jesus as 'extraordinarily exalted, indeed divine'; but this proper emphasis, which I have located within an understanding of Paul's revised monotheism, does not relativize or eliminate the full and vital messianic significance which I am here locating within an understanding of Paul's revised election-theology.

[132] See Wright 2002 [*Romans*], 418; and *RSG* 242–5 and elsewhere (*pace* Chester 2007, 111 who finds the point 'unconvincing', perhaps because he would not grant the larger exegetical framework within which it does in fact make convincing sense). See now e.g. Kirk 2008, 37–9.

YHWH and his anointed', *kata tou kyriou kai kata tou christou autou* (2.2). God's response is to laugh at them, and declare that he has established his king on Zion, his holy hill (2.6). The psalm then shifts into the first person, with the king himself declaring: 'I will tell of YHWH's decree: YHWH said to me, "You are my son, I have begotten you this day"' (*huios mou ei su, egō sēmeron gegennēka se*). And the anointed king continues, explaining that YHWH has given him, as his 'inheritance', not just the land of Israel (the 'inheritance' promised to Abraham, Isaac and Jacob) but the whole world, all the nations: 'Ask of me,' said YHWH, 'and I will give you the nations as your inheritance' (*dōsō soi ethnē tēn klēronomian sou*), 'and the uttermost parts of the earth (*ta perata tēs gēs*) as your possession.' The king is to subdue them firmly, and warn them about the danger of his wrath (2.9–12). All this coheres with the immediate context in Romans, in which, after showing that Jesus has been declared as 'God's son', Paul emphasizes that his own apostleship has the aim of bringing about 'the obedience of faith, for the sake of his name, among all the nations' (*en pasin tois ethnesin*). At one of the key points in the letter when Paul returns to the theme of his own apostleship, he quotes a psalm which again resonates with Psalm 2 at just this point: 'their sound has gone out into the whole earth (*eis pasan tēn gēn*), and their words to the ends of the world (*eis ta perata tēs oikoumenēs*).'[133] And, as the letter-opening develops, he explains that he is not ashamed to bring this 'good news' to Rome itself (he hardly needs to add, to the home of the current World Ruler, the imperial 'son of God'), going on to explain that, with the revelation of Jesus as Messiah, the divine wrath has been newly revealed against all human ungodliness and wickedness.[134]

The further context in Romans is also important. The theme of 'inheritance' plays a significant part, initially in the development of the promise to Abraham (from 'the land' to 'the world' in 4.13[135]), and then in the climactic statement in chapter 8: 'If we're children, we are also heirs (*klēronomoi*): heirs of God, and *fellow heirs with the Messiah* (*synklēronomoi de Christou*), as long as we suffer with him so that we may also be glorified with him.'[136] And the 'inheritance' in question is unquestionably the whole world, as in Psalm 2 and as in the explosive promise about creation's renewal in Romans 8.18–24. Interestingly, several of Paul's uses of the *klēronomos* root occur when he is talking about 'inheriting God's kingdom', which goes closely with the 'messianic' theme at least in the basic text of Psalm 2.[137]

Still in Romans, we move to 15.1–13, which is increasingly being seen, not as a rhetorical flourish falling off the back of the letter, but as the carefully designed goal of the entire theological argument. The passage begins

[133] Rom. 10.18, qu. Ps. 19 [LXX 18].5.

[134] Rom. 1.18; 2.16. All this, together with Rom. 8.17f., makes it bizarre for Chester to claim (2007, 114) that Ps. 2, Isa. 11, etc. are 'precisely the texts that Paul does *not* use' (ital. orig.), and that they are 'conspicuous by their absence'.

[135] See above, 622, 730.

[136] 8.17.

[137] 1 Cor. 6.9, 10; 15.50; Gal. 5.21; Eph. 5.5.

with a reference to *ho Christos* as the one who, according to Psalm 68, did not please himself, but took on himself the reproaches of the people.[138] It continues with *Christos* becoming 'a servant to the circumcised on behalf of God's truthfulness, to confirm the promises of the patriarchs, and that the gentiles would glorify God for his mercy'; we shall comment further on this summary narrative presently. There follows the string of four scriptural quotations, the reverse as it were of the *catena* of 3.10–18: Psalms, Torah and finally Prophets declare that gentiles will join in the praises of God's people. The last quotation – hardly chosen at random – is from Isaiah 11:

> There shall be the root of Jesse,
> the one who rises up to rule the nations (*ho anistamenos archein ethnōn*);
> the nations shall hope in him.[139]

Again, just as in 1.3–4, the resurrection of the Davidic king is the sign that he is to rule the nations. The whole Isaiah passage (11.1–10, with this as its climax) is one of the great messianic oracles, highlighting the shoot from Jesse's stock as the one equipped with YHWH's spirit in order to bring justice to the nations and peace to the natural world, filling the earth with the quality of 'knowing-YHWH' as the waters cover the sea. We could put the conclusion negatively: if Paul had wanted to turn people's minds away from the idea of a Davidic Messiah whose resurrection established him as the true world ruler, accomplishing the creator's purpose for the whole creation, he went about it in a very strange way indeed.[140]

The other obvious passage in which Paul uses clear scriptural 'messianic' texts to speak about Jesus is our old friend 1 Corinthians 15.20–8.[141] Here, at the heart of the claim about God's kingdom coming through the intermediate state of the rule of Jesus himself – the notion of *basileia*, 'kingly rule', ought to be enough on its own to say 'Messiah' at this point! – Paul quotes from Psalm 110, which might have a claim to be the best-known 'messianic' text among first-century readers:

> 24Then comes the end, the goal, when he hands over the kingly rule to God the father, when he has destroyed all rule and all authority and power. 25He has to go on ruling, you see, until 'he has put all his enemies under his feet'.[142]

[138] Rom. 15.3, qu. Ps. 69.9 [LXX 68.8].

[139] Rom. 15.12, qu. Isa. 11.10.

[140] The passage which follows (15.14–21), describing Paul's missionary work to date, is likewise replete with messianic reference, indicating that the *Christos* has been named and proclaimed around the world to bring the nations into obedience to him, in fulfilment of the fourth 'servant song' (Isa. 52.15: 'that which had not been told them they shall see, and that which they had not heard they shall contemplate': see Wagner 2002, 329–36). Jewett 2007, 916 points out that this offers 'an effective reprise of 1:1–15 and the earlier use of Isa 52 in 10:15–17.'

[141] Chester 2007, 111 agrees that this is 'messianic' (though he says at 112 that this passage, and others like it, 'can be read without an understanding of *Christos* as messiah, yet still make complete sense'). But he shows how completely he misses the point when he adds (111) that in 1 Cor. 15 Paul is 'moving the messianic expectation to a transcendent level, away from any specific realization on earth', citing the (to my mind very unconvincing) comments of MacRae 1987, 171f.

[142] 1 Cor. 15.24f., qu. Ps. 110.1.

Paul's whole sequence of thought goes perfectly with the psalm. God instructs 'my lord', the Messiah, to 'sit at my right hand, until I have put all your enemies under your feet'. The Messiah, in other words, is ruling the world while God himself acts, through him, to defeat all his enemies. Paul clearly has the whole psalm in mind, with the king going off to destroy all opposition to his rule (110.5–7), reminiscent of Psalm 2.9–11. The 'enemies' that Paul envisages are not, however, human enemies on a battlefield, but, as we have already seen, the 'last enemies', finally Death itself. Paul then switches back to the echoes of Psalm 2, speaking of the king as 'the son', who will be placed in his proper order under the rule of 'the one who placed everything in order under him'. The goal of the narrative sequence, matching quite closely that in Philippians 2.6–11, is that 'God may be all in all,' with Jesus, the Messiah, as the sovereign one *through* whom that divine reign is established. There should be no doubt whatever that the *narrative role* which Paul assigns to Jesus in this passage is that of Israel's Messiah. There can be no doubt that the biblical quotations and allusions are to passages commonly used as messianic in early Christianity. When, in that context, Paul refers to Jesus as *Christos* four times in the four opening verses (15.20–3), it takes a peculiar sense of stubbornness to resist the conclusion that he meant, without strain or difficulty, to designate him as 'Messiah'.

The other biblical passage alluded to in this paragraph from 1 Corinthians 15 is Psalm 8.6 (LXX 8.7): 'he has put all things in order under his feet', *panta hypetaxa hypo tous podas autou.*[143] This obviously echoes the reference, in Psalm 110.1, to things being put 'under his feet', but this is no mere surface allusion. Psalm 8 is the point at which the Psalmist picks up the story of Adam and Eve and celebrates the fact that, in creating human beings, God has given them dominion over all the works of his hands, 'putting all things in subjection under their feet'. Paul's larger argument, begun in 1 Corinthians 15.21–2 and concluded in verses 45–9 (but an important theme through the whole carefully constructed chapter), is that in Jesus God has *addressed and solved the problem of the sin of Adam and its effects*. This, as we have seen, was the purpose of Israel's election, according to a strong strain of thought running from the Pentateuch itself right through to rabbinic Judaism. In other words, the driving force of the whole chapter is that *in Jesus* the creator God has done that for which he called *Israel*. It is now Israel's representative, rather than Israel as a whole, who constitutes the 'true humanity', under whose feet all things are placed in subjection. The role of the Messiah and the role of the Human dovetail perfectly.

That then sends us across to Paul's other well-known use of Psalm 8, which is again in the context of the exaltation of Jesus and his winning the final triumphant victory. Philippians 3.20–1 is rooted in the earlier statement of 2.9–11, as its many verbal echoes indicate.[144] The power which enables Jesus to 'transform our present body' to be 'like his glorious body' is

[143] LXX *panta hypetaxas hypokatō tōn podōn autou*.

[144] cf. e.g. Fee 1995, 381–4; Bockmuehl 1998, 236; among older literature, see esp. Hooker 1971.

the power 'which makes him able to bring everything into line under his authority', *tou dynasthai auton kai hypotaxai autō ta panta.* Again, we note the allusion to Psalm 8, echoing the Adam-christology which is one element (not the only one, but not unimportant) in 2.6–11: Jesus is the one exalted as the truly image-bearing human being, ruling the whole world on behalf of the father. As the previous verse emphasizes, he is *sōtēr* and *kyrios* (both of course Caesar-titles); and he is *Christos.* Though not so clear as Romans or 1 Corinthians, this passage too speaks in scriptural language about the one through whom the creator God has won the victory, and will implement that victory, over all the powers of the world. If we meet such a person in Jewish expectation, we know who he is. He is the Messiah.

All these themes cluster together in Ephesians 1.20–3:[145] resurrection, sitting 'at the right hand', sovereignty over all powers and authority, and everything being placed 'under his feet':

> 20This was the power at work in the Messiah when God raised him from the dead and sat him at his right hand in the heavenly places, 21above all rule and authority and power and lordship, and above every name that is invoked, both in the present age and also in the age to come. 22Yes: God has 'put all things under his feet', and has given him to the church as the head over all. 23The church is his body; it is the fullness of the one who fills all in all.

The point should now be clear. This combination of themes, read within their scriptural context, are sufficient to push us in the direction of saying, 'The one of whom all this is said is Israel's Messiah.'

This use of scriptural texts to describe the accomplishment of Jesus, then, constitutes a first strong argument for saying that Paul really does intend 'Messiah' when he writes *Christos.* A second theme, subordinate but very interesting, comes in strongly in support. In the Jewish wisdom tradition, 'wisdom' was associated especially with the royal house, notably with Solomon, David's son and successor. When we find Jesus referred to in Colossians 2.3 as 'the place where you'll find all the hidden treasures of wisdom and knowledge', one *prima facie* explanation is that he was and is the Messiah. This reference, introduced by a rather emphatic use of *Christos* at the end of 2.2, should send us back to the 'wisdom'-poem in chapter 1 to read it again as also a messianic meditation. A further point, linked to this one (but everything is linked once one begins to see the scriptural basis), is that in Jewish tradition the Messiah is among other things the Temple-builder, and in Paul's view Jesus is the one through whom the new 'Temple' has come about. But of all that, more anon.

More substantially, and developing the sub-argument from the previous point, we should pay close attention to the *narrative line* of several passages in Paul, notably in Galatians but by no means only there, in which Jesus, designated as *ho Christos*, plays the narrative role which in second-Temple Judaism would be taken by the Messiah.[146] Here is the great story of Israel, from Abraham to the present: promises made, thwarted, derailed, brought

[145] On Eph. see above, 56–61.

[146] See *Perspectives* ch. 31.

back on track, searching for fulfilment. Here, at last, is that fulfilment, the moment when, and the one through whom, all has been brought to its appointed destiny, the destiny which means *klēronomia*, the 'inheritance' promised to Abraham and now shared with a worldwide people (3.18, 29; 4.1). And how has this happened? Through the coming of the 'seed' of Abraham, *hos estin Christos*, 'who is Christ' (3.16); through the promise being given to believers 'on the basis of the faith of Jesus Christ', *pistis Iēsou Christou* (leaving aside for the moment the question of how exactly to translate that phrase). All has been fulfilled because as many as were baptized into *Christos* have put on *Christos*; they are all one in *Christos*, and those who belong to *Christos* are Abraham's seed. Who is this *Christos*? In the explanatory passage which follows, he is 'God's son' (4.4), who then shares his sonship with all those who believe, who through the spirit's gift call God 'Abba, father'. They are then not only adopted children: they are 'heirs' once more. Again, I submit that it takes a peculiar kind of resistance to the text (and to its close resonances with the similar passages in Romans), first to deny that here we have a constant reference to the story of Israel from Abraham to the fulfilment of promise, and second to deny that the one who brings Israel's story to that fulfilment, and who is spoken of as *Christos*, is the Messiah. Recognizing this, on the other hand, resolves several of the major exegetical difficulties in the passage, as we shall see.[147]

The other obvious passage where the same argument applies is Romans 9.6—10.13. Despite the ongoing controversy over the meaning of this whole passage (on which, see the next chapter), it seems to me that a very strong *prima facie* case can be made for seeing Paul's intention as being to present a narrative outline of the history of Israel from Abraham to the present time, working through the other patriarchs to Moses and then to the prophets, the exile and ... the Messiah. *Telos gar nomou Christos* in 10.4 (regularly translated 'Christ is the end of the law') is not an abstract statement about 'Christ' and 'the law', but a climactic statement about where the whole line of thought had been going, rooted of course in the organically important 9.5. Torah tells a great narrative, and its goal and conclusion is the Messsiah. What follows ought to make this even clearer. In Deuteronomy 30, Moses had written of the strange new way in which the law would be fulfilled when, with the curse of exile at last over, Israel would be renewed. Paul interprets this passage with reference to what has happened in *Christos*, and the response to him that comes in confessing him as lord and believing that the one God raised him from the dead. Here, in other words, we have a long, careful retelling of Israel's story brought to a deliberate conclusion, with the central character at that conclusion designated with the Greek word for 'Messiah'. It is very hard to resist the conclusion, not only that Paul really did believe that Jesus was Israel's Messiah, but that this belief

[147] Contrast Sanders 2008b, 328 n. 8: 'God sent Christ to save the whole world without regard to the prior election of Israel.' That is truly extraordinary – especially from one so attuned to themes in second-Temple Judaism; if I am right, Paul sees the mission of God-in-Christ precisely as the *fulfilment* of the prior election of Israel.

played a massively important role in his entire theological understanding. Any resistance which is still offered must face the challenge that it may appear to have prejudged the issue.

Of course, all this will be as nothing to those who are determined on the one hand to regard Paul's use of scripture as ad hoc and informal, a snatching of texts from thin air to lend apparent authority to conclusions reached on other grounds, and those who are equally determined on the other hand to insist that Paul has no narrative theology, in particular no sense of the flow and sweep of Israel's history and its urgent need to find resolution, to see promises fulfilled, hopes at last accomplished.[148] To such persons one might simply say, 'Well, look and see the sense that this makes of everything else.' But there are one or two other arguments which come in here as well.

For a start, there is the linguistic evidence, set out recently by Matthew Novenson, that *Christos* is in fact neither a proper name (with denotation but no necessary connotation) nor a 'title' as such (with connotation but flexible denotation, as when 'the King of Spain' goes on meaning the same thing when one king dies and another succeeds him). It is, rather, an *honorific*, which shares some features of a 'title' but works differently.[149] It is quite extraordinary (to speak very frankly) that the work of W. G. Kramer, published in English in 1966, should have continued to be the reference point for discussions of 'christological titles'.[150] It was always deeply flawed, insensitive to the actual way Paul used the words in question, trying to analyze them as though they were mathematical symbols rather than real words being used in real sentences and arguments. Novenson's work now sets a new standard for discussion of *Christos* in particular, demonstrating that the way it functions linguistically, within the larger world of Greek usage in late antiquity, fits extremely well with royal 'honorifics' and not at all with proper names.

'The Messiah', then, *ho Christos*, is for Paul not simply an individual, Jesus of Nazareth, who happens to have acquired a second proper name through the flattening out of the royal title that other early Christians were eager still to affirm. The royal meaning of *Christos* does not disappear in Paul's writings. It is present, central and foundational. Though sometimes the word *seems* to function more or less as a proper name (any word, repeated often enough, can appear to have its surface indentations worn smooth), its connotations are never far beneath the surface and often show clearly through. Obvious examples of the same phenomenon are easy to find: the phrase 'Archbishop of Canterbury' is often used without any thought of Canterbury as a place, but only with the intention of denoting the present holder of the office; but at a moment's notice the geographical and cultural reference to Canterbury itself can be retrieved. The obvious first-century example is 'Augustus'. Octavian, the adopted heir of Julius Caesar, took the *name* 'Caesar', was granted the *title* 'Imperator', and from

148 See the essay on Paul's use of scripture in *Perspectives* ch. 32.

149 Novenson 2012.

150 It is still the first ref. in e.g. Hengel 1992, 445 n. 66.

27 BC assumed the *honorific* 'Augustus', meaning 'venerable' in the sense of 'holy', 'worshipful'. This word, properly speaking, was neither name nor title; hence, 'honorific'. The word 'Augustus' could often be used simply to denote the man; but the echoes and connotations of the *divi filius* were never far away, and regularly evoked.[151] Thus, even when *Christos* clearly denotes the man Jesus, invoked as *kyrios* by his first followers, I propose that throughout the first century of the movement at least the word carried echoes and connotations which were always within easy reach. And there is one connotation in particular which I believe offers the solution to one of the most long-standing puzzles in modern Pauline research.

(c) Jesus as Israel's *Incorporative* Messiah

The particular point is this (and this is where this exposition of *Christos* as 'Messiah' in Paul joins up with the previous exposition of second-Temple views of Israel's election). In passage after passage in Paul the point being made is that *Jesus, as Messiah, has drawn together the identity and vocation of Israel upon himself.* This, like 'Messiahship' itself, remains a controversial and contested point, and we need to be clear what is being said and on what grounds. The question of 'corporate christology', encapsulated in phrases like *en Christō* and images like 'the Messiah's body', has been a puzzle for many years, and even those who have made it central have not given accounts of it which have carried conviction among other researchers.[152] The same is true for the many proposals that have been made in articles and monographs.[153] My own proposal, which like much else could be spelled out more fully, is that the two 'unknowns' are mutually explanatory: the 'unknown' solution to the question of *en Christō* goes with the normally 'unknown' Pauline feature of Jesus' Messiahship. To put it plainly: the 'incorporative' thought and language which so pervades Paul is best explained in terms of his belief that Jesus was Israel's Messiah.

[151] See Novenson 2012, 93–7. In the Church of England the word 'venerable' is officially attached to archdeacons, which makes its use as the translation of *augustus* (or its Greek equivalent *sebastos*) complicated, not to say comic. We might come closer with the papal phrase 'his Holiness', or even the splendid phrase used for the (Orthodox) Ecumenical Patriarch: 'his All-Holiness'.

[152] e.g. Schweitzer; Sanders. Dunn 1998, 393 suggests reasons for the decline in popularity of Schweitzer's 'mysticism' (the psychological critique and the rise of existentialism after the First World War). Dunn seems to assume, wrongly in my view, that what Schweitzer meant by 'mysticism' was the same as what e.g. Catholic theologians and spiritual directors meant by it; and one could comment that totalitarianism, with the individual subject to a collectivist State, was equally a product of the First World War. The real reason for Schweitzer's unpopularity was his implicit high, sacramental ecclesiology, conflicting with the liberal protestant paradigm which still carries weight among scholars.

[153] Moule 1977, ch. 2, provides quite a full summary to that point: on Paul cf. esp. 54–63; on 'body of Christ', 69–89. Moule offers no major new hypothesis as to why Paul wrote in this way, and ultimately regards the material as evidence that Paul thought of Jesus as more than an individual human figure (62, 65) – in other words, that the 'incorporative' language is ultimately evidence for, and to be seen as part of, at least an implicitly 'divine' view of Jesus. From the previous chapter it will be clear that I have no problem with this conclusion, but I do not think that the *en Christō* and 'body of Christ' language is best explained in that way. An important subsequent survey is that of Wedderburn 1985: see below.

Paul, I propose, exploited the notion of 'Messiahship' in such a way as to say two things in particular. First, the vocation and destiny of ancient Israel, the people of Abraham, had been brought to its fulfilment in the Messiah, particularly in his death and resurrection. Second, those who believed the gospel, whether Jew or Greek, were likewise to be seen as incorporated into him and thus defined by him, specifically again by his death and resurrection. The full range of Paul's 'incorporative' language can be thoroughly and satisfactorily explained on this hypothesis: that he regarded the people of God and the Messiah of God as so bound up together that what was true of the one was true of the other. And this becomes in turn the vital key to understanding the close and intimate link between 'incorporation' and 'justification', between 'participatory' and 'forensic' accounts of Paul's soteriology – not to mention the themes of salvation history, 'apocalyptic' and transformation. That is why it is important to be as clear as possible at this point.

This proposal about incorporative Messiahship is not, of course, new.[154] It has, though, escaped notice, for two obvious reasons, and one perhaps less obvious. First, 'Messiah' has been outlawed as a category in Paul; second, scholarly discussion of 'Christology' has naturally focused on the question of Jesus' 'divinity' (so much so, in fact, that the word 'Christ' has often been taken as a 'divine' title, which even in early Christianity it never was). Third, we might suggest, the notion of Israel's vocation on the one hand, and the notion of a christologically grounded view of 'the church' on the other, have not been welcome guests in the liberal protestant houses where much biblical study has taken place. But at this point objections will arise: the real reason for ignoring this kind of proposal, some may say, is the absence of evidence. Where do we find this supposedly Jewish notion of the unity between the Messiah and his people? And if the answer is 'Why, in Paul himself', does this not become dangerously circular?

Not necessarily. It is true that we look in vain, in the messianic or quasi-messianic movements of the last two centuries BC and the first two centuries AD, for anything like the 'incorporative' language we find in Paul. Those who wrote the Scrolls believed in a coming Messiah – perhaps even in two of them – but they do not speak of themselves as 'entering' this person or of then being found 'in him'. Those who followed bar-Kochba, including

[154] See Dahl 1941, 227, insisting that the messianic reference lies at the heart of the concept of the 'body of Christ': it is 'in and with Christ that the messianic community appears'. The presupposition for this incorporative language is thus found 'in dem jüdischen Gedanken von der Einheit zwischen Messias und messianischer Gemeinde', 'in the Jewish conception of the unity between the Messiah and the messianic community' (my tr.). Dahl cites Schmidt 1919, 217–23; Rawlinson 1931, 275ff. (*sic*: actually, Rawlinson 1930, 225ff.). The key passage in Rawlinson is 232: Jesus 'stands absolutely alone as the true seed of Abraham . . . it is only by being gathered to Him, in the new Israel, that anyone else can inherit the promises.' The phrase 'new Israel' is, as I shall argue, going too far; at most, Paul might have said 'renewed Israel'. Rawlinson goes on (235): 'To be "in Christ" and to belong to the New Israel are from henceforth the same thing. The New Israel, according to the New Testament thought, is "in Christ" as the Jews were in Abraham, or as mankind was in Adam. The Messiah, the Christ, is at once an individual person – Jesus of Nazareth – and He is more: He is, as the representative and (as it were) the constitutive Person of the New Israel, potentially inclusive.' This seems to me on target, but as yet insufficiently grounded.

Akiba himself, believed he was the Messiah, but we have no reason to think that they spoke of themselves as being 'incorporated' into him. The biblical texts regularly cited in second-Temple messianic speculation (the 'sceptre' of Genesis 49, the 'star' of Numbers 24 and the obvious passages in the Psalms and Prophets) give shape and colour to that royal hope, and certainly indicate that the coming king will act powerfully on behalf of his people, but they do not include the idea, in whatever form, that the coming Messiah will sum up or incorporate his people in himself.

Looking more widely, we note the older view that ancient peoples in general, and Jews in particular, held a concept of 'corporate personality', according to which a fluidity existed between some individuals and groups, and specifically between a ruler and his people. Earlier sweeping proposals on this subject have retreated in the face of sharp critique, though that may simply mean that the theories were unworkable, not that there was no data to be explained.[155] Attention has often been drawn, in Paul himself, to the incorporative phrases 'in Adam' and indeed 'in Abraham', the former in close parallel to 'in Christ' and the latter in fairly close proximity.[156] But even there we seem to be dealing with analogies, not with sources or origins of Paul's remarkable way of speaking.[157]

In order, then, to propose an account of Paul's 'incorporative' phrases in which the key explanatory element is the hypothetical binding together of the Messiah and his people, I am not suggesting that such an idea was already well known or widespread in Paul's day. Nor am I suggesting that there was a ready-made and widely understood concept of incorporation into which Paul simply had to slot the word 'Christ'. What I am suggesting – on analogy with my hypothesis about the origin of 'high' christology' in the previous chapter – is that *the events of Jesus' death and resurrection compelled Paul in this direction, and caused him to read old texts in new ways.*

It is particularly the resurrection that matters here. A Pharisee like Saul of Tarsus undoubtedly believed passionately in resurrection; but it would be the resurrection of all Israel at the end of time. No Pharisee imagined that

[155] Wedderburn 1985, 97 n. 52 cites Porter 1965 and Rogerson 1970, and cautiously suggests that, once exaggerated claims are scaled back, there remain certain phenomena which the phrase 'corporate personality' was trying, perhaps unhelpfully, to explain. Among older works those of Hooke 1958 (esp. 204–35) and Johnson 1967 remain significant.

[156] 'In Adam': 1 Cor. 15.22; 'in Abraham', or at least 'in you' as applied to Abraham: Gal. 3.8 (quoting Gen. 12.3 and/or 18.18), followed by a statement of people of faith being blessed 'with faithful Abraham', echoing Paul's combined use of 'in Christ' and 'with Christ' (e.g. Rom. 6.4–8, 11; Gal. 2.19f.). It is not, however, strictly true, as Wedderburn 1985, 88 suggests, that Gal. 3.8, 14 supplies 'a use of *en* with a person's name'; it is *en* with a pronoun. See too, however, 'in Isaac' in Gen. 21.12, quoted in Rom. 9.7 (noted by Wedderburn 94 n. 26).

[157] So Wedderburn 1985, 91.

one person would be raised from the dead ahead of everyone else.[158] When, therefore, it happened to one person, as Paul believed it had – and when, in particular, it happened to someone who had been executed as a would-be Messiah – it meant at once that *Israel's God had done for Jesus what it had been supposed he would do for Israel.* Not only therefore did the resurrection demonstrate that Jesus was after all Israel's Messiah, despite the verdict of the court. The resurrection also declared, for Paul, that the divine purpose for Israel had been fulfilled, uniquely and decisively, in this Messiah, this Jesus. He was, in effect, Israel in person.[159] And it was precisely *as Messiah* that he therefore represented his people.

The origin of 'incorporative christology' is therefore close to, and parallel with, the origin of 'incarnational christology' which we explored in the previous chapter. Paul's fresh understanding of Jesus as YHWH in person, returned in glory, drove him back to the scriptures to ferret out texts he knew but had not read that way before. In the same way, his fresh understanding of Jesus as the summing-up of the divine purpose for Israel drove him back to the scriptures, not least to the story of Abraham and, behind that, the story of Adam, and to glimpse in both of them the notion, and in the Abraham story a linguistic way of expressing this notion, that the vocation and/or destiny of people could be bundled up within the vocation and/or destiny of that one person. It is, I think, much easier to believe that Paul came to this view as a result of his belief in Jesus' resurrection, and then discovered resonances of it in the scriptures, than to suppose that he had always thought in terms of people being 'in Adam' or 'in Abraham' and then transferred that notion to the Messiah.

Among other biblical contexts for this notion, I have previously explored one which is both more explicit than the 'Abraham' passages and also more obviously 'royal'. It is not, so far as I know, picked up by second-Temple writers (though we must regularly remind ourselves what a small and random sample of work we have from that period, always liable to be pleasantly disrupted by a shepherd boy looking for a goat and finding a scroll). It does, however, offer a clearly 'incorporative' idea in which the people of Israel as a whole are somehow 'in' the king, 'in' David – even when David is dead and gone and the reference is to his grandson.[160] The suggestive background to this is found in the narrative about David and Goliath: why has Saul, head

[158] The possible exception – Herod's reported remark about Jesus being a resurrected John the Baptist (Mk. 6.14–16) – is discussed in Wright 2003 (*RSG*), 412 and elsewhere. The more normal view is displayed in Mk. 9.10, where the disciples are puzzled at Jesus' suggestion of one resurrection ahead of all others (cf. *RSG* 414f.). When the Pharisees in Ac. 23.9 are trying to exonerate Paul, they suggest that his experience of meeting the living Jesus might be a case of a 'spirit' or 'angel' appearing to him: in other words, of an apparition of a recently dead, and still dead, person, such as the praying church assumed Peter to be in Ac. 12.15. They did not imagine for a moment that someone might actually have been bodily raised from the dead. See *RSG* 133f.

[159] A parallel to this line of thought was offered by Robinson 1952, 58: when Saul of Tarsus heard the risen Jesus saying, 'Why are you persecuting me?' (Ac. 9.4; 21.7; 26.14), he concluded that there was some sort of identity between Jesus and the persecuted church. This is no doubt relevant, but I do not think it can function as a complete explanation for Paul's incorporative belief and expressions.

[160] cf. *Climax* 46f.

and shoulders above all other Israelites, not himself gone out to fight the Philistine giant? In his place, *representing* the whole nation and fighting its battle all by himself, we find the young David; and his victory is a major step towards his own becoming king, as Saul readily perceives.[161] It is within that setting, of David's kingship, that we find the sudden incorporative usage of being 'in David' or 'in the king', when, after Absalom's rebellion, the people of the northern tribes complain to those of the south:

> We have ten shares in the king (*bamelek/en tō basilei*), and in David (*bedawid/en tō Dauid*) also we have more than you.[162]

This then leads at once to the rebellion of Sheba son of Bichri, a Benjaminite. Benjamin was of course one of the southern tribes; a rebellion there would be even more disastrous for David's kingdom than a northern revolt. The slogan used by Sheba again speaks 'incorporatively':

> We have no portion in David,
> no inheritance (*nahlah, klēronomia*) in the son of Jesse!
> Everyone to your tents, O Israel![163]

That rebellion was crushed, and the full kingdom established again under David and then under Solomon. But almost the same phrase was picked up by the northern tribes after Solomon's son Rehoboam refused to listen to their complaints:

> What portion do we have in David?
> We have no inheritance in the son of Jesse.
> To your tents, O Israel!
> Look now to your own house, O David.[164]

The idea of 'inheritance' is, as we have seen, important for Paul in connection with the Messiah: those who belong to him share the 'inheritance' which YHWH promised him in Psalm 2, namely the whole (renewed) creation. So, as I proposed earlier, while these texts cannot be cited as evidence of ideas prominent in the first century, they do at least suggest a matrix of biblical thought to which Paul might go back in his mind as he struggled to understand the significance of one person, a messianic pretender, being raised from the dead, as he had imagined would happen to the whole people of the one God. In these passages – the Goliath incident, and the rebellions with their slogans – there is a sense that the king represents his people, or alternatively (as with the young David) that the one who successfully fights

161 1 Sam. 17; for the enmity, 1 Sam. 18.6–9. The whole incident follows closely upon Samuel's secret anointing of David (16.13).

162 2 Sam. 19.43 [MT 19.44]; the LXX (2 Kgds. 19.44) adds, in between these two clauses, *kai prōtotokos egō ē sou*, 'and I, not you, am the firstborn'. For the idea of 'shares' in the kingdom cp. 1 Kgs. 11.30f.

163 2 Sam. 20.1. I have altered NRSV to reflect the Heb. and LXX more closely in this and the following citation.

164 1 Kgs. 12.16.

the nation's battle all by himself is thereby qualifying himself as king. His fate becomes theirs, his inheritance becomes theirs, his life becomes theirs. To be 'in the king', or now, for Paul, 'in the anointed one', the Messiah, is to be part of the people over which he rules, but also part of the people who are defined by him, by what has happened to him, by what the one God has promised him. That is how Paul uses the incorporative language of *en Christō* and similar phrases, as we shall now see.

I do not now think (as I once did) that these interesting biblical passages themselves constitute the explanation for his usage. But once the resurrection has raised the question as to why the creator God has done for one person what he was supposed to do for all Israel, and once Paul has recognized, as he surely did very quickly, that this means (a) that Jesus is Israel's Messiah and (b) that the national destiny has been fulfilled in him, then texts like this may indicate a context, a climate of thought which western individualism finds it hard immediately to grasp, within which Paul's regular incorporative language would make the sense to him that it manifestly did.

I propose, therefore, that Paul understands Jesus of Nazareth to be, indeed, Israel's Messiah, the king from the house of David, the 'son of God' in this sense (and in other senses, as we have seen, but not to the exclusion of this one). Paul sees Jesus as the one who has been established as Messiah through his resurrection, drawing Israel's history to its strange but long-awaited resolution, fulfilling the promises made to Abraham, inheriting the nations of the world, winning the battle against all the powers of evil and constituting in himself the promise-receiving people, so that all 'in him' might receive those promises, precisely not in themselves but insofar as, being 'in him', they are incorporated into the True Jew, the one in whom Israel's vocation has been fulfilled.

The principal argument in favour of this entire hypothesis is the way in which the elements of Pauline soteriology, normally regarded as disparate and to be played off against one another, come together in a fresh, and remarkably coherent, way when viewed from this angle. It will take the rest of the present chapter to explore this. For the moment, I cite briefly, in advance of detailed discussion later on, the three passages in which it seems to me most obvious; I then offer equally brief reflections on the way in which the key incorporative phrases actually function.

The most obvious passage, to my mind, is Romans 3.1–26. As we shall see, the problem which Paul faces is not simply universal sin, but the failure of Israel to be 'faithful' to the divine vocation (3.2–3). This is resolved dramatically, in the unveiling of the divine righteousness (3.21), through the 'faithfulness' of the Messiah, Jesus. Anticipating the summary of the whole picture in 5.12–21, where the action of the Messiah is described as 'obedience', what we see in 3.22 is the Israel-faithfulness through which the divine purpose of 'redemption' is accomplished: hence, in the telling phrase, *dia tēs apolytrōsis tēs en Christō Iēsou*, 'through the redemption which is in Messiah Jesus'. This single phrase anticipates the entire later exposition of the divine rescuing action that is set out in Romans 5—8, scooping it all up as it were and compressing it into this little ball so that it can play its crucial role in the exposition of justification (3.21—4.25). 'In Messiah', in other words, and by means of the redeeming action accomplished through his 'faithfulness' to the divine Israel-purpose, all those who believe are now declared to be 'in the right'.

This emerges in several interlocking ways in the entire argument of Galatians 2.15—4.11. I have expounded this elsewhere and can be brief.[165] The argument turns on the distinction between the promises to Abraham, which Paul declares are fulfilled in the Messiah, and the giving of the Torah, which Paul declares has done its God-given job and is now no longer relevant for the definition of God's people. The single family which had been promised to Abraham can be spoken of simply as *Christos*, as (controversially) in 3.16 but (rather obviously) in 3.26–9. This *Christos* is the 'son of God' who shares that sonship with all who, by the spirit, can call God 'father' (4.6–7). This has nothing to do (as is sometimes suggested) with the replacement of the old Israel with a new one, and everything to do (as is less frequently noted) with Paul's belief that Israel as a whole is summed up and redefined in and by *Christos*. That, indeed, is the whole point of the decisive summary in 2.19–20, which again we shall consider later on. Once again, being 'in the Messiah' and being 'justified by faith' are tightly combined in this passage.

The third obvious passage is Philippians 3.2–11. Paul begins by contrasting the kind of Jew he himself had been with the kind of Jew he considers himself now to be: 'We', he declares, 'are the "circumcision"' – we who worship God by the spirit, and boast in King Jesus, and refuse to trust in the flesh.' If you want to know where Israel is, in other words, look to Israel's Messiah. If you want to see 'the circumcision', look to those who belong to Israel's Messiah. 'Whatever I had written in on the profit side, I calculated it instead as a loss – because of the Messiah' (3.7). Paul had been seeking to secure and solidify his place within the Israel that would be vindicated on the last day, but now has discovered that the Messiah himself, having already been vindicated by Israel's God, is the one and only place where that secure identity is to be found. We miss the force of the passage unless we see that here, just as in Romans 3 or Galatians 3, the Messiah is the place where, and the means by which, Israel's destiny is realized and membership in Israel, in 'the circumcision', is assured. Thus, again just as in Romans and Galatians, the statement of 'justification' (underlined below) nests within the larger statement of 'being in the Messiah' (in bold below):

> In fact, because of the Messiah I've suffered the loss of everything, and I now calculate it as trash, so that my profit may be the Messiah ...
> **and that I may be discovered in him**,
>   not having my own covenant status (*dikaiosynē*) defined by Torah
>   but the status (*dikaiosynē*) which comes through the Messiah's faithfulness:
>   the covenant status from God (*tēn ek theou dikaiosynēn*) which is given to faith.

[165] See *Perspectives* ch. 31.

> **This means knowing him, knowing the power of his resurrection, and knowing the partnership of his sufferings. It means sharing the form and pattern of his death, so that somehow I may arrive at the final resurrection from the dead.**[166]

It is, in other words, 'in the Messiah', in the Israel-in-person, that Paul finds the identity and hope he had formerly sought through his intense observance of Israel's Torah. The *status* of being 'justified', declared to be 'in the right' and a member of the people of the one God, is given on the basis of *pistis*, the 'faith' of the believer which identifies him or her as part of the family of the 'faithful' Messiah (see below). This, though dense, is as clear a summary as anything in Paul of the way in which the divine purpose in election has been fulfilled in Israel's Messiah.

Within that picture, we may briefly glance at the incorporative phrases which have given so much trouble to exegetes and yet which, once the central principle of Messiah/Israel is grasped, make good and clear sense.[167]

Paul, as is well known, sometimes writes *en Christō*, sometimes *eis Christon* and sometimes *syn Christō*; sometimes, also, *dia Christon* or *dia Christou*: 'in Messiah', 'into Messiah', 'with Messiah', 'through Messiah'.[168] These phrases can go quite closely with the use of the genitive, 'belonging to the Messiah', which already gives a strong hint as to how the incorporative language is meant to function. We notice, too, that Paul does not normally write *en Iēsou*, but frequently says *dia Iēsou* ('in Jesus'; 'through Jesus').[169] He does, however, sometimes write *dia Christon* or *dia Christou*, but there too one can regularly see a messianic meaning at work.[170]

This is of course a simplified picture, since the phrases in question are frequently longer (*en Christō Iēsou*, for example, or *dia Iēsou Christou*). One might also factor in phrases focused on *kyrios* (*en kyriō*, and the like) and the various uses with pronouns (*en hō*; *en autō*: 'in whom'; 'in him'). The suggestion that the variations in case and word order (*Christos Iēsous* as against *Iēsous Christos*, and so on) occur purely for the sake of euphony, or through unthinking variation, is both improbable in itself and unwarranted exegetically.[171] Paul in fact is very precise: he never says *eis Christon* ('into the Messiah') when he means *en Christō* ('in the Messiah'), or vice versa. (Nor, by the way, does he confuse 'being in the Messiah' with 'the Messiah being in us', to which we return later on.) Once we grasp the meaning of Messiahship in his writings, there is no need to flatten out his very precise

[166] Phil. 3.8b–11.

[167] I here amplify and develop the short treatment in *Climax* 44–6. The topic remains ripe for more detailed investigation.

[168] 'Through Messiah' can, of course, go either way: when translating *dia* with the genitive it would mean 'through' as in 'by means of', and with the accusative it would mean 'through' as in 'because of'.

[169] The one occurrence of *en tō Iēsou*, 'in Jesus', is explained by its special context (Eph. 4.21). In Gal. 3.14 Vaticanus has *en Iēsou Christō* where almost all other MSS have *en Christō Iēsou*.

[170] cf. e.g. Rom. 2.16, where the divine judgment will be exercised *dia Christou Iēsou*, 'through Messiah Jesus', reflecting the standard Jewish belief in the Messiah as the agent of eventual judgment, stemming from passages like Pss. 2.9–11; 110.1–2, 5–6 and Isa. 11.3–5, and articulated in e.g. *Pss. Sol.* 17.21–32; 18.7f. (cf. too e.g. Ac. 17.31).

[171] e.g. Kramer 1966, 84–90, 133–50 and elsewhere.

language, or to chop it or stretch it on the Procrustean bed of our own de-messianized (and often de-Judaized) theological understandings.

Notice how Paul's key 'messianic' phrases function in a fairly literal rendering of Galatians 3.24, 26–9:

> The law was our guardian *into Messiah*, so that we might be justified by faith ... For you are all children of God, through faith, *in Messiah*, for as many as were baptized *into the Messiah* have put on the Messiah. There is neither Jew nor Greek, there is neither slave nor free, there is no 'male and female', for you are all one *in Messiah Jesus*. But if you *belong to Messiah* (*ei de hymeis Christou*), you are Abraham's seed, heirs in accordance with promise.

And then, in 4.7:

> So you are no longer a slave, but a son.

You come (in other words) 'into Messiah' in baptism, and as a result you are, you stand, you exist, 'in Messiah'. That is a basic statement of Christian identity, and it clearly sustains Paul's statements about justification earlier in the chapter and the passage.

But Paul also speaks, it seems, of a further journey 'into Messiah', where 'Messiah' clearly denotes not simply the individual person, but the people who find their identity, and crucially their unity, in him. (We saw this in our first chapter, in the curious but important verse Philemon 6.[172]) To come 'into Messiah' in this way is not simply 'eschatological' in the sense of the *eventual* goal, as proposed by some.[173] Rather, it is 'eschatological' in the sense that the eschatology has already been inaugurated, and 'Messiah' is already a corporate as well as a personal reality. In the Messiah Jesus, God has launched his project of bringing the human race together into a new unity, and those who believe in him are summoned into that *koinōnia tēs pisteōs*, that fellowship of faith, in which their previous differences are transcended.

Thus 2 Corinthians 1.21, in a dense manner of speaking familiar throughout that letter and echoed elsewhere, but sadly obscured by the translations:

> The one who establishes us with you *into Messiah*, and has anointed us, is God.

Most translations render *eis Christon* here as 'in Christ', but Paul's point here is precisely that the fissures that have opened up between him and the Corinthian community need repair, and that it is God who will do this, bringing them together 'into the Messiah', that is, into the unity which they

[172] Above, 16–18.

[173] e.g. Stuhlmacher 1975, 33. That, no doubt, stands in the background, though I am not sure that Paul ever actually uses *Christos* in that way.

properly possess 'in him' but which is now seen as the goal of a journey.[174] Here, as in Galatians 3.16 and elsewhere,[175] *Christos* denotes 'the Messiah and his people', or perhaps better 'the Messiah as the representative of his people', the one *in whom* that people are summed up and drawn together, with the main point being the *unity* of that company, and in particular their unity across traditional boundary-lines.[176] In the fascinating verse which condenses the whole thought of Philemon, the *koinōnia* of faith is designed *to generate that actual unity*, across traditional boundaries such as those mentioned in Galatians 3.28, which will find particular focus in the new, unexpected and indeed shocking unity between the master and the runaway slave. In Galatia, the issue was believing gentiles belonging as equal members in Christ's family alongside believing Jews; in Philemon, the issue is the slave and the free. But the underlying theology is the same. Whoever wrote Ephesians certainly saw things in this light: the aim of God's gift of varied ministries is so that, leaving immaturity behind, 'we may all attain to the unity of the faith and of the knowledge of the son of God, to mature manhood, to the measure of the stature of the fullness of *Christos* … to grow up in every way into the one who is the head, *Christos*'.[177] In other words, those who through baptism and faith have made the initial journey *eis Christon* are now summoned to work on the further, and very challenging, task of a full unity with all other Messiah-members, a task which Paul can characterize as itself a move *eis Christon.*

All this can be seen on a large scale in Romans, taken as a whole. The 'bookends' of the letter, as we noted, are the twin statements about Jesus'

[174] Among recent commentators, Thrall 1994, 2000, 151–9 sees the problem of the unexpected *eis Christon* clearly, and suggests that rather than the normal baptismal meaning of entry 'into Christ' it may here have an eschatological reference, picking up and condensing 1 Cor. 1.8f., where the same verb (*bebaioō*) is used of the present security of God's people against the coming Day, and God's faithfulness is immediately spoken of as calling his people into the *koinōnia* of Jesus the Messiah (Thrall, 159). See too Furnish 1984, 137: all of them together are being incorporated 'into the body of Christ', which can scarcely mean baptism, that having already happened, but rather the building up of that body to be what it should be. If I am right, Paul's meaning both in 2 Cor. 1.21 and here in Philem. 6 is situated as it were half way between the more normal baptismal reference of *eis Christon* and this eschatological one: God's purpose in the present is the unity, in Christ, of all his people, and the journey to that unity is properly described as a journey *eis Christon*, 'into Messiah'. If, of course, we add Ephesians 4.12, 13 and 15 into the argument (see below), this all becomes much clearer, but that raises further questions – and indeed some may see it as a weakness to offer an account of 2 Cor. and Philem. which coheres so well with Eph! 2 Cor. 11.3, the other obvious non-baptismal use of the phrase, is different again, denoting the single-minded devotion 'to the Messiah' which ought to characterize his people.

[175] On Gal. 3.16 cf. *Climax* ch. 8.

[176] Wall 1993, 200 sees that proper weight must be given to the *eis* in Philem. 6, but does not see how this relates to the question of unity, limiting it rather to Philemon's own spiritual maturity. Ryan 2005, 224 is typical of many: Paul's writing *eis Christon* when he appears to us to mean *en Christō* is purely 'stylistic variation' (see too Harris 1991, 252f.). Dunn 1996, 320 describes the phrase in Philem. 6 as 'awkward' and, after listing one or two unsatisfactory options, says that nevertheless 'its basic force is clear: all that is spoken of in the rest of the verse has its validity and effectiveness because of their relation to Christ, or perhaps more specifically, by "bringing us into (closer) relation to Christ"', citing Harris 1991, 253 for the first and Moule 1957, 142 and others for the second. This, I believe, is *not* the 'basic force' of *eis Christon*, here or elsewhere: *Christos* designates, as in Galatians 3, the single 'messianic family' in which radical differences are overcome. See further above, 16–19.

[177] Eph. 4.13–15.

messianic resurrection and worldwide rule (1.3–5; 15.12). And the letter that is framed in this way contains at its heart, in chapters 6—8, the exposition of what it means to come 'into the Messiah' at baptism, and so to be 'in the Messiah' with all the benefits that thereby accrue. All of this we shall explore further in due course.

(d) Conclusion: Paul and Messiahship

We have now made the case that Paul regarded Jesus as Israel's Messiah, and that he saw and expressed that belief in terms of the Messiah's summing up of Israel in himself, thereby launching a new solidarity in which all those 'in him' would be characterized by his 'faithfulness', expressed in terms of his death and resurrection. This, I shall now suggest, is the key to, and the foundation for, the way in which Paul reworked the Jewish belief in Israel's election. Within that, it is the key to, and the foundation for, his famous doctrine of justification. The combination of Messiah and Israel provides a way into the very heart of Paul's soteriological beliefs which draws together the regularly dismembered elements of his thinking and writing into a full and coherent whole.

As a tailpiece to this argument, I return to the sharp statement of the Italian philosopher Giorgio Agamben, who comes to the question as a linguist and a philosopher rather than as a theologian or 'New Testament specialist'. In his fascinating comparative study of the letter to the Romans and the philosophical writings of Walter Benjamin, Agamben launches a stern attack on those who have supposed that the word *Christos* could ever, in a writer like Paul, function as a mere proper name:

> Each reading and each new translation of the Pauline text must begin by keeping in mind the fact that *christos* is not a proper name, but is, already in the Septuagint, the Greek translation of the Hebrew term *mashiah*, 'the anointed', that is, the Messiah. Paul has no familiarity with Jesus Christ, only with Jesus Messiah ... A millenary tradition that left the word *christos* untranslated ends by making the term *Messiah* disappear from Paul's text ... That the term *Christ* consequently never appears in our text [i.e. Agamben's own book] is not meant to signal any polemic intention nor a Judaizing reading of the Pauline text; rather, it entails an elementary philological scruple that all translators should follow, whether or not they be equipped with an *imprimatur*... One should never forget that it is beyond an author's power to take a term that is in current use into the linguistic context of his life and make it into a proper name, especially with regard to a fundamental concept, such as that of the Messiah for a Jew.[178]

It is a pity that these words had not been pinned on the notice-boards of university faculties and seminaries a long time ago. But let us at least make up for lost time. What does it mean if, in the context of Paul's view of

[178] Agamben 2006, 15–17 (see also above, 559). He cites Huby 1957 [1940] as an example of the mistake he has in mind, but he could have chosen perhaps two-thirds of present-day western NT scholars, and at least three-quarters of those writing in most of the C20.

Israel's election as God's people, we suppose that he really did see Jesus, not just as the 'lord', as we saw in the previous chapter, but as Israel's Messiah?

(ii) Jesus as the *Faithful* Messiah of Israel: Romans 3 and 4

With the changing fashions of theological and exegetical argument, it has been extraordinary to see the energy with which the question of *pistis Christou* ('the faith[fulness] of Christ'? or 'faith in Christ'?) has been addressed over the last thirty years. What began as a question, then an initial proposal, has become a substantial industry, generating more debate than one would have believed possible. The debate has now been pressed down and sprinkled together, and is threatening to nest in every tree.[179] As with most topics in the present book, this discussion could easily be a book in itself, and most of that might be footnotes to those who have discussed, in great detail, every argument, every passage, every verse.

Every verse, that is, except one – which I believe to be vital, normally ignored, and actually decisive for what is arguably the most central statement of this particular theme anywhere in Paul.[180] One can often tell whether a particular Pauline line of thought is being followed by the attention that is given, or not given, to crucial turns in the argument, and it is fascinating to see that in some of the central discussions of *pistis Christou* in recent days Romans 3.2 has played virtually no role whatever.[181] But it is this verse that sets up both the dense and intricate argument of 3.1–9, which (despite frequent assertions from those who project their own puzzlements onto Paul!) is not at all muddled or confused.[182] In particular, it throws the weight of the larger discussion forward to the crucial statement of 3.22. So as not to keep the reader in suspense, the argument goes like this: the 'faithfulness' which was required of Israel, but not provided, has now been provided by Israel's representative, the Messiah.

We have to begin with that key paragraph, Romans 2.25–9. Once we grasp how that paragraph actually works – that Paul here really does envisage people of any and every background being regarded as 'circumcision'

[179] See now the introduction to the second edition of Hays's groundbreaking work (Hays 2002 [1983], xxi–lii); and the full and highly annotated collection of essays in Bird and Sprinkle 2009. The debate between Hays and Dunn (in Hays 2002 [1983], 249–97) is now a classic statement of two main opposing positions. An important older discussion, referring to previous treatments, is that of Hanson 1974, 39–51.

[180] On what follows see more fully (in addition to Wright 2002 [*Romans*], 452f.) the relevant article in *Perspectives* (ch. 30).

[181] It hardly features in the index to Bird and Sprinkle 2009. Even Hays 2002 [1983] seems not to discuss it. Dunn 1998, 384f. claims that the 'flow of argument' in the key passages supports the 'objective' reading of *pistis Christou*, but it is precisely the flow of argument in Rom. 3 that provides the strongest case for the 'subjective' reading, at least in 3.22.

[182] See the classic statement of Dodd 1959 [1932], 71: 'The argument of the epistle would go much better if this whole section were omitted.' Schreiner 2001, 215 suggests that the 'objective genitive' interpretation – which he supports across the board – 'makes the best sense of the flow of thought in Romans 3:21—4:12 and Galatians 2:16—3:9'. That remains to be seen. The foundation of my case is that the 'subjective genitive' makes far and away the best sense of Rom. 3.1–31, with the focus on 3.2 and 3.22.

and as 'Jew' – it is obvious that he then needs to ask the question of 3.1: what is the point of being a Jew? Is there any 'advantage' to it? What does one gain by being circumcised? He has stated in 1.16 that the gospel is 'for the Jew *first* and also, equally, for the Greek'.[183] He has declared that the divine wrath is revealed, through the gospel which unveils the Messiah as the impartial judge of all, against all humans, again 'the Jew first and also the Greek' (2.9, 10). But then – and this is where things start to unravel in traditional readings of the letter – he has agreed that 'the Jew' might well say that Israel has been called to be the light of the world (2.17–20). Is not this the answer to the problem?

And we must insist that Paul's answer is: Yes. Paul does not back off from agreeing with the 'Jewish' boast, because it is inscribed into his Bible and his own second-Temple worldview on the basis of nothing less than the unshakable promises of God. As in John's gospel ('salvation is of the Jews'[184]) so here: God has promised to bless the world, to undo the sin of Adam and its effects, through the call of Abraham, and God will be true to that promise even if Israel as a whole lets him down. That, more or less, was what Isaiah 52 and Ezekiel 36 were about. Now this is how it appears in Paul:

> [1]What advantage, then, does the Jew possess? What, indeed, is the point of circumcision? [2]A great deal, in every way. To begin with, the Jews were entrusted with God's oracles. [3]What follows from that? If some of them were unfaithful [to their commission], does their unfaithfulness nullify God's faithfulness? [4]Certainly not! Let God be true, and every human being false! As the Bible says,
>
> So that you may be found in the right in what you say,
> and may win the victory when you come to court.[185]

The key here, as I have stressed, is verse 2, which is usually ignored or misunderstood. They were *entrusted*, says Paul, with the oracles of the one God. Some commentators have walked right up to the point, glanced in its direction and then passed by on the other side. Others have never come near it in the first place.[186] The word 'entrusted' is always used by Paul in the same sense that it bears in secular Greek: to entrust someone with something is to give them something which they must take care of *and pass on to the appropriate person.* Paul was 'entrusted' with a commission, according to 1 Corinthians 9.17; with the gospel to the uncircumcised, in Galatians 2.7; with the gospel, according to 1 Thessalonians 2.4.[187] In no case did this commission or this gospel relate ultimately to Paul himself; it was given *to* Paul in order that it be given *through* Paul to the people for whom it was intended. This, indeed, may be why Paul speaks, uniquely for him, of 'the oracles'. God's

[183] See Cranfield 1975, 1979, 91: the phrase *te prōton kai* in 1.16 indicates a 'basic equality' but an 'undeniable priority'.

[184] Jn. 4.22. This of course depends on what we mean by 'salvation': see Loewe 1981.

[185] Rom. 3.1–4.

[186] Some (e.g. Dunn 1988a, 131) see the close connection of the various *pist-* roots here, but not the point: Dunn sees this as 'a play on the concept of *pistis*' but says that 'its scope is not clear' – even though he then goes on to say that the 'oracles' are 'given to the Jews to hold in trust for others'.

[187] See too 1 Tim. 1.11.

purpose, he believed, was that through Israel the gentile world might hear what, to them, would appear to be 'divine oracles', even though Israel would have known they were more than that.[188] The whole sentence, and the whole drift of the passage ever since 2.17, is not primarily about 'Israel's guilt', but about *God's purpose, through Israel, for the world.*

That is why I have added the words 'to their commission' in verse 3. Paul is not accusing them of 'unbelief', of failure to believe in Jesus as Messiah and lord or in his resurrection. And when he speaks of 'their unfaithfulness' in the second half of verse 3, this sense is still required: does *their failure to do what their Abrahamic and Isaianic vocation demanded* mean that somehow God himself is now going to prove unfaithful?

This, it should now be apparent, is a kind of second-order version of the well-known problem of divine justice. The normal mode of the problem goes like this: the creator makes promises to Abraham's family; Abraham's family misbehave; how is this God then going to save them without being accused of favouritism? That remains important at another level of the argument, but Paul has for the moment left it behind in favour of a significantly different problem: the creator makes promises *through* Abraham to the world; Abraham's family fail to pass on the 'oracles', in other words, to be the 'light to the nations, the guide to the blind' and so on that they were supposed to be (2.17–20); how is this God then going to keep his promises *through Israel* to the world? If the person responsible for delivering the mail has proved untrustworthy, how can I keep my promises to send you a letter by that same mail system?

The faithfulness of God at the end of verse 3 is then, still, the determination of the covenant God to do what he has promised, even if the people through whom the promised blessings were to be delivered seem to have let him down through their own 'faithlessness'. This becomes clear at the start of the next verse, where *alētheia*, 'truth' or better 'truthfulness', substitutes for *pistis*, 'faithfulness'.[189] This then generates what appears to be a third-order dispute: if Israel's God is going to do what he promised despite the failure of Israel, why should Israel be blamed? – as it will be, according to

[188] See particularly Williams 1980, 267f., building on Manson 1962a, 1962b; see too Stowers 1994, 166f. Another commentator who comes close to this sense is Cranfield (1.179). But even he seems to draw back from the clear statement to which he had seemed to be building up: 'The Jews have been given God's authentic self-revelation in trust to treasure it and to attest and declare it to all mankind . . . They alone have been the recipients on behalf of mankind of God's message to mankind.' In the note (179 n. 3) he stresses the difference between 'entrust' and 'give', but then seems not to know how to apply it: 'They have been given [the oracles] not to do what they like with them but to conduct themselves towards them according to the will of Him who has entrusted them to them, and to Him they will have to give account.' It looks as though Cranfield has his finger on the right point but is then determined to make this fit, somehow, with an overview of the passage which implies that it is still really all about 'the guilt of the Jews' rather than 'God's project *through* the Jews'. Jewett 2007, 243 says that 'Paul has not lost track of his argument about the failure of all humans despite the impression made on many commentators'; but it is Jewett, like most others, who has lost the track, since the argument here is about the failure of Israel to be faithful to its commission, to be the light of the world, not (at this point) the failure of all humans.

[189] In English, 'truth' and 'trust' are verbally cognate as well as overlapping in meaning. For Paul, the words *pistis*, 'faithfulness' or 'trustworthiness', and *alētheia*, 'truth' or 'truthfulness', possess a considerable overlap of meaning even though they are not etymologically related.

2.27, where 'the uncircumcision that fulfils the Torah' will 'judge' circumcised lawbreakers. With this, we are fully into the list of questions to which Paul will return in 9.6–29, though in the present passage they end in a *reductio ad absurdum* in verse 8 (if people think that Paul's argument leads them to say, 'Let's do evil so that good may come,' there is only one thing to say: that people like that, at least, deserve the judgment they get!).

With that, Paul has dealt in a preliminary way with the problem of 2.17–20: yes, Israel really was chosen in order to be the means of blessing for the world, and yes, despite Israel's failure to be faithful to that commission, the covenant God will be faithful to that promise, *to bless the world through Israel*. But what he has not yet done is to say *how* this God will do that. Paul has, however, set up the problem in such a way that we can see, in principle, what is now required: if the covenant God is going to bless the world through Israel, he needs *a faithful Israelite*. In 3.21–6 Paul argues that this is exactly what has now been provided.

Once we understand *Christos* as the Messiah, Israel's representative, Israel-in-person if you will, the logic works out immaculately. (a) The covenant God promises to rescue and bless the world through Israel. (b) Israel as it stands is faithless to this commission. (c) The covenant God, however, is faithful, and will provide a faithful Israelite, *the* 'faithful Israelite', the Messiah. It is the tight coherence of this train of thought, rather than any verbal arguments about subjects and objects, prepositions and case-endings on the one hand, or preferential theological positions on the other, that persuaded me many years ago that Romans 3.22 speaks of the Messiah's faithfulness. It persuades me still.

To be sure, a vote for a so-called subjective genitive reading of *pistis Christou* in Romans 3.22 does not give carte blanche to any and every possible interpretation of such a reading. Thus, for instance, I do not think Paul is here speaking of Jesus being 'justified by faith'; it is neither his faith nor his belief that is here spoken of, but his faith*fulness* to the divine plan for Israel.[190] Nor does it mean, in any way, that the human faith by which 'the believer' responds to the gospel of Jesus the Messiah is downplayed or undervalued. Far from it: Romans 3.22, which otherwise would be a tautology, speaks of the divine action being *through* the faithfulness of the Messiah *for the benefit of* all who have faith. The former does not cancel out the latter; it puts it in its proper context. Rather, as we shall see, the point is that the faithfulness (*pistis*) of the Messiah is that which marks him out as the true Israelite, the promise-bearer, the one who accomplishes at last the purpose for which the creator called Israel in the first place. Those who believe the gospel, 'who believe in the one who raised from the dead Jesus our lord' (4.24), are thus appropriately marked out by that badge of *pistis*, their own *pistis*, not as an arbitrary sign, not because it means that they have had some kind of religious experience and so must have been converted, not because 'faith' is a special, meritorious form of interiority which this God

[190] Against e.g. Hanson 1974, 45–51, who argues that 'Christ lived by faith', and indeed was justified by faith, refusing to live by the law.

decides to reward, but because *pistis*, faithfulness, (a) always was supposed to be the badge of Israel, (b) now has been the badge of Jesus, and so (c) is the appropriate badge – the only badge! – by which Jesus' followers are to be marked out. To this, too, we shall return.

Before we can reach the pay-off of this argument, we must remind ourselves that as well as dealing with this second-order (though absolutely vital) question about Israel's vocation, Paul has also yet to address the massive problem of good old-fashioned human sin (to be more precise, idolatry and immorality) spelled out in 1.18—2.16. There are therefore (at least) two questions on the table, and it is confusion between these two that has, in my view, bedevilled the reading of Romans 3.21—4.25.

First, the creator God has made promises to bless the world, and in 2.1–11 Paul has indicated that there is to be a final judgment at which people will be judged impartially on the basis of what they have actually done.[191] But as things stand, in the summing up of 3.19–20, it is clear that all humans, Jew and gentile alike, stand in the dock, guilty as charged. Invoking Torah itself ('we have Torah; that sets us apart'[192]) only seems to makes matters worse: through Torah comes the knowledge of sin.[193]

But then, second, the creator God has said nevertheless that he will save the world *through Israel.* That was the force of the covenant, and the God who made it will not set it aside. However, the Jewish boast of thus being 'the light of the world' (2.17–24) will not work, because of Israel's unfaithfulness. The creator faces a double problem: how to save anyone at all, let alone (as promised) people of all sorts; and how to save them *through Israel.* If he cannot do these things, the divine quality which is regularly invoked in the Psalms, in Isaiah and in those great passages such as Daniel 9 – the quality which we call the divine *tsedaqah*, *dikaiosynē*, the 'faithfulness' or 'righteousness' of Israel's God – is radically called into question.

How, then, should we read Romans 3.21–2? Clearly, in relation to both of these two questions, which are indeed in the last analysis not two but one. In relation to the first, the creator must somehow deal with the problem of universal idolatry and immorality, here scrunched together under the general word *hamartia*, missing-the-mark, the failure to be genuinely human. But, in relation to the second, God must somehow deal with that problem *through faithful Israel.* If he does not do the first, then the whole project of creation is a terrible blunder. If he does not do the second, then the call of Israel as the means of rescuing and restoring humankind and the world is itself an equal blunder. How then can he do the latter (fulfilling his promises to Israel), and so do the former (rescuing the world from *hamartia*), without

191 It is a desperate exegetical expedient to suggest that Paul does not really mean what he has said here, or that the possibility of some 'doing good', as in 2.7, 10 is a 'hypothetical category' which he will then declare to be null and void. A list of those who take this view is given in Schreiner 1998, 114f.; he himself considers this position, but eventually rejects it.

192 Ps. 147.20.

193 3.20; this is of course spelled out in far more detail in 7.7–25.

appearing to be guilty of *prosōpolēmpsia*, 'respect of persons', which Paul has ruled out in 2.11?

The reason Romans 3.21–31 is so dense is that Paul is, quite properly, answering these two questions together. And the answer to both is the same: *the Messiah, the faithful Israelite, has been faithful to death, and through him the faithful justice of the covenant God is now displayed for all, Jew and gentile alike.*

It is clearly necessary, before reading 3.21–31, to reach a preliminary conclusion about the meaning of *dikaiosynē theou*, often translated 'the righteousness of God'.[194] I suggest that we are bound, in the light of all that has gone before, in the light of all the biblical texts which Paul is implicitly evoking (which I explored in chapter 2 above), and in the light of the climax and conclusion of Paul's present argument (4.1–25), to understand *dikaiosynē theou* (a) as God's own 'righteousness' (rather than a status of 'righteousness' granted, imputed or otherwise given to humans); (b) as God's own 'righteousness' with the focus, very specifically, on his *covenant faithfulness* in the sense of 'doing what he promised to Abraham, in Deuteronomy, in the Psalms, and through Isaiah, Jeremiah and Ezekiel'; (c) as God's own 'righteousness' in the sense of his faithfulness *to the covenant promise to bless the nations through Israel.* Out beyond this again – though without skipping stages, still less cancelling them out! – there is the sense (d) that the divine faithfulness to the *covenant* is the appointed means of the divine faithfulness to the *creation*. The creational dimension of *dikaiosynē theou* has been made famous in our generation by Ernst Käsemann, and properly so, in reaction against views which would limit the phrase to individual justification and salvation. But Paul's own faithfulness to the biblical tradition, and more importantly to the notion of the one God and his own faithfulness, means that he cannot and will not bypass, on the way to the eventual rescue of all creation (Romans 8), the divine faithfulness to the covenant with Abraham – as Käsemann had him bypass it.[195]

There are various ways of paraphrasing to bring all this out. I here employ the long version: 'the faithful justice of the covenant God'.

This, then, is how I suggest we are bound to read Romans 3.21–2, if we have truly understood Romans 2.17–20 and 3.1–4:

> [21]But now, quite apart from the law (though the law and the prophets bore witness to it), God's faithful covenant justice has been displayed. [22]God's faithful covenant justice comes into operation *through the faithfulness of Jesus the Messiah*, for the benefit of all who have faith.

[194] This is clearly not the place to enter into lengthy discussions of the debate. Jewett 2007, 141f. has a helpful summary, though omitting the covenantal resonance which is arguably one of the primary senses. Other helpful (though by no means unanimous) summaries include Stowers 1994, 195–203; Moo 1996, 70–5; Witherington 2004, 52–4; Keener 2009, 27–9. The older summary of German debate by Brauch 1977 remains useful to understand the presuppositions and background story behind some more recent interpretations.

[195] See Käsemann 1969 [1965], ch. 7; and of course 1980 [1973], 24–30.

This, to repeat, has nothing to do with Jesus' own 'faith' in the sense of his 'religious awareness', his belief in God, his refusal to trust in his own good works, or anything like that. That is to pull the meaning of *pistis* away from where it was in 3.2–4 and off into the realm of normal Christian dogmatics, thus failing to pay attention to what Paul is actually talking about. Just as in other key passages where *God's* saving action is worked out through *the Messiah's* saving action, so here. The point in the present argument is that God's faithful-*to*-the-covenant action ('the covenant' being, we remind ourselves, the means of dealing with human sin) is also God's faithful-*through*-the-covenant action, and the 'through-the-covenant' bit refers to the role of Israel, Abraham's people: the role now taken by the Messiah, alone. In this opening summary (densely packed, as often in Paul) of what is about to follow, Paul signals that something has been accomplished, as an action of the creator God through Jesus the Messiah; in other words, an action of the creator God through Israel-in-the-person-of-Jesus-the-Messiah. Through this action, through this Messiah, the blessings always promised to and through Abraham and Israel are now available, as always intended, for the whole world.[196]

But why does Paul refer to the act of the Messiah, or rather the act-of-God-through-the-Messiah, as his 'faithfulness'? Why not his 'giving of himself to death' (since it seems clear that he intends to *denote* the crucifixion of Jesus) or some equivalent phrase? What is being *connoted* by referring to Jesus' death under the rubric of 'faithfulness'? Does this even make sense?

First, by speaking of the Messiah's 'faithfulness', Paul clearly intends to relate the action (or passion) of the Messiah to the purpose of God to which Israel had been *un*faithful.[197] This has been our argument all along.

But this points to a second feature: by speaking of the Messiah's death as an act of 'faithfulness' Paul makes it clear that what is accomplished through the Messiah (through the-Messiah-as-Israel-in-person) is the fulfilment of the active will and purpose of the covenant God. It is not, in other words, something done by a human being over against the creator, or to persuade the creator to do something he had not previously had in mind, or any such notion. Rather, the word 'faithfulness' denotes a movement *from* the creator God, *through* Israel-in-the-person-of-the-Messiah, *towards* the world.

Third, in other words, this notion of 'faithfulness' allows Paul to speak, at the point where in chapter 5 he is summing up where he has got to so far, of the divine *love* seen in the death of the son. For that to make any sense, there has to be a flow from the creator, through the death of Jesus, out towards the sinful world (as well as an intimate connection between the one God and the son, as we saw in the previous chapter).

[196] To the argument sometimes advanced, that the Greek Fathers, who after all spoke Paul's language as natives, did not pick up this meaning, I would want to ask the counter-question: were they aware of the Jewish and covenantal argument Paul is mounting? If not, it is not surprising that this outflowing of that theme escaped them as well. In fact, as Ian Wallis has convincingly shown (Wallis 1995), many of the early Fathers did indeed see 'Jesus' faith' as in some sense both paradigmatic and causative for Christian faith: see Hays 2002 [1983], xlvii–lii.

[197] See Hays 2002 [1983], xxx–xxxi.

Fourth, the notion of 'faithfulness' connects very closely with that of the Messiah's 'obedience', and here we note the further summary of the argument in 5.12–21. To be sure, at that point (as in Philippians 2.8) Paul chooses the notion of 'obedience' not least because of the contrast, explicit in Romans 5 and implicit in Philippians 2, with Adam. But, as has often been remarked, the two are not far apart. The same action is denoted. But in the first case ('faithfulness') the focus is on the substance of the commission and the direction of its movement, from the sender of the blessing to the eventual recipients, via the 'faithful' intermediary; while in the second case ('obedience') the focus is simply on the relationship between the initiating sender and the obedient intermediary. But the two are, obviously, joined in the famous phrase 'the obedience of faith', *hypakoē pisteōs*, which Paul uses in 1.5 and 16.26 as the summary of what the gospel will effect in its hearers.[198] In other words, it makes sense, not only because of the turn in the argument at 3.2–3 but also because of the wider resonances, that Paul should refer to the saving action (i.e. the saving death) of Jesus the Messiah as an act of *faithfulness*.

So how does what Paul actually says about the death of Jesus in 3.23–6 reflect this emphasis on that death as Jesus' act of messianic, Israel-representing faithfulness? To begin with, of course, there is the summary statement of human sinfulness in 3.23: all sinned (the aorist tense presumably refers to the sin of Adam, as in 5.12–21) and came short of the divine glory. That is, they failed to be the people through whom, as his image-bearers, the creator would exercise his dominion in the world.[199] But this statement draws down the focus of the chapter no longer onto the *means by which* the saving covenant plan was to be taken forward (i.e. through Israel, and now through the faithful Messiah), but onto *the specific problem* which meant that rescue was required. Sin, *hamartia*, has hardly been mentioned up to this point; 2.12 uses the verb to summarize the general problem already outlined, and 3.9 and 20 draw that to a point. It looks, then, as though the word here is a summary of the larger problem of idolatry and immorality, sketched in 1.18–32, extended to include the supercilious moralist in 2.1–11.[200] But this summary mention of the human problem is matched by the summary mention of the divine solution: the word *charis*, 'grace', occurs here for the first time in the letter, indicating that the 'revelation of God's faithful covenant justice' in 3.21 is a free gift, not occasioned or caused by anything within humans.[201]

How then does Romans 3.21–6 articulate the meaning of Jesus' death in the context of this argument? The passage is, of course, notorious in its

[198] On the textual problems of 16.25–7 see recently Jewett 2007, 997–1011, arguing strongly for interpolation. Among many who argue for its originality cf. e.g. Moo 1996, 936–41; Marshall 1999.

[199] On the idea of the 'image' as reflecting the divine stewardship and rule over the world see e.g. Middleton 2005.

[200] The further question, of 'sin' as a *power*, emerges – not as an alternative analysis but as a probing of extra depths within the present one – in chs. 5—8.

[201] On 'gift' in Paul and his wider context see Barclay and Gathercole 2006, and a forthcoming volume from Barclay.

dense and complex detail, and we must be sure to highlight its main features if we are not to lose sight of the beach while studying the grains of sand.[202] There is a hard truth to be learned here as well: those who have read Romans as embodying one particular and shrunken form of 'the gospel' (humans sinned, God sent Jesus, faithful humans are forgiven) have often treated this passage as though it offers Paul's central statement of 'the meaning of the cross', and have done their best to make it conform to the required theological patterns. It looks, however, as though this is a highly compressed statement of the meaning of Jesus' death, meant to serve the larger argument, which is about the divine covenant faithfulness.

First, then, we note the massive emphasis, throughout the passage, on exactly that theme. So strong is this stress that, in the mid-twentieth-century tradition that wanted to avoid covenantal notions at all costs, parts of this dense passage were dismissed as a pre-Pauline tradition that Paul was quoting and (not always clearly) modifying. This desperate expedient, which would never have been advanced unless the material were deeply unwelcome (in this case for the obvious reasons that existentialist Lutheran theology wanted to have nothing to do with Jewish covenantal theology), ought now to be set aside as an historical curiosity.[203] Paul has said at the start of the paragraph that the events to be related constitute the disclosure of the divine covenant-justice-faithfulness, and this is what we find. As usual in Paul, if we want to understand a dense paragraph, we should look to the end, to see where he at least thinks it all comes out; and in 3.26 we find him saying that all this has taken place 'to demonstrate [God's] faithful covenant justice in the present time: that is, that he himself is in the right, and that he declares to be in the right everyone who trusts in the faithfulness of Jesus'.[204] That should be clear enough. God made covenant promises, promises to do with the setting-to-rights of the whole world; in Jesus he has been faithful to those promises, so that the creator God is himself 'justified',[205] that is, shown to be in the right, specifically in that he is 'justifying' the one who is described here in terms of Jesus' own faithfulness. Perhaps the point of the final dense clause, *ton ek pisteōs Iēsou*, literally 'the one

[202] See further the complementary account below, 995–1007, as part of the discussion of justification.

[203] Though it in fact continues unabated: see Jewett 2007, 269–71, referring to several predecessors and theories, especially in the schools represented by Bultmann and Käsemann. It is of course perfectly possible that Paul is here quoting traditional material, as one might do in a sermon or a lecture – or even a footnote! – when wanting to produce an easy commerce of the old and the new, to add dignity and resonance to a paragraph. This is scarcely proved by unique vocabulary; Rom. is Paul's longest letter, and it would be surprising if he did not say some things here which he has not elsewhere (there are in any case unique words in most of the letters). The underlying point is the attempt (as with the dismissal of Rom. 1.3–4 as a mere traditional introduction without relevance for the rest of the letter) to distance Paul from supposedly 'Jewish Christian' concerns such as covenant, Messiahship and so on. This belongs, ultimately, with the ideologically driven and now historically discredited programme of F. C. Baur.

[204] The translation of v. 26 remains tricky. Should the 'and' be read as additional (so that there are two statements being made, one about the divine justice in and of itself and one about the justification of Jesus-faith people), or epexegetic (so that there is one statement being made, explaining the divine justice *in terms of* the justification of believers), or what? For the options, see Jewett 2007, 292f.; the latter seems preferable, though the sense still requires further explanation.

[205] As in 3.5, quoting Ps. 51.4 [LXX 50.6].

out of the faith[fulness] of/in Jesus', is precisely to run together the two elements of 3.22, namely Jesus' own faithfulness as the act whereby redemption is achieved and the faith of the believer which becomes the badge of membership in the Messiah's people. If this is correct, we could perhaps paraphrase as 'everyone who shares in the faithfulness of Jesus'.[206] We shall return to 'justification' in the next part of the chapter; for the moment, suffice it to note that the faithful act of the Messiah means that God has been faithful to his promises.

Working from the beginning (3.21–3) and the end (3.26) of this short paragraph into the dense statement in 3.24–5, we discover that the faithful death of Jesus (which Paul sees in 5.6–10 as an act of divine *agapē* and in 5.15–19 as the act of the Messiah's *hypakoē*, 'obedience') is more specifically an act of *exodus*. It is a 'redemption' (3.24); *apolytrōsis* is used directly in Jewish texts in reference to that great moment when God fulfilled the promises to the patriarchs by his Passover act of rescuing Israel from Egypt.[207] And this 'redemption', as we saw, is 'in Messiah Jesus'. This phrase has the effect of fusing together the covenantal and forensic argument of the present paragraph with the 'incorporative' exposition of chapters 5—8, rooting them both in the idea that the divine purpose for Israel and through Israel has now been accomplished in the Messiah.

All this goes some way towards contextualizing, if not fully explaining, the sacrificial meaning of verse 25: the *hilastērion* is the place in the tabernacle or Temple where atonement is made through the outpoured sacrificial blood of the victim. Paul seems to be drawing together three things: first, the exodus itself, as the great covenant-fulfilling act of rescue and 'redemption'; second, more specifically, the Passover lamb, whose blood averted the death of the firstborn; third, the sacrifice offered as a 'propitiatory' in the tabernacle or Temple. He stresses the divine *forbearance* in the phrase at the start of verse 26 (*en tē anochē tou theou*): in times past God had overlooked, or 'passed over', the sins that had been committed, but now, through this redemptive sacrificial act, he has dealt with them.[208]

So, to put the question again: how does this complex of exodus motifs and sacrificial ideas stack up as a statement of the Messiah's Israel-representing *faithfulness*? The answer seems to lie in Paul's retrieval of certain themes available at the time in which the sacrificial overtones already there in the fourth servant song were being reused in connection with martyrs whose deaths were thought to be in some sense redemptive.[209] Paul's language does not directly echo any of those sources at this point, but his thought seems to run like this: (a) the saving plan for the world which the prophets had seen as Israel's vocation would always involve Israel (or righteous martyrs within Israel) becoming a kind of sacrifice through which not

[206] Jewett 2007, 293 opts for 'faith in Jesus'.

[207] The noun *apolytrōsis* is not used in this sense in the LXX, but the cognate verb *lytroō* frequently is: cf. e.g. Ex. 6.6; 15.13; Dt. 7.8; 13.5 [6]; 15.15; 21.8; 24.18.

[208] For the details, and for fuller argument, see Wright 2002 [*Romans*], 472–7.

[209] See again *Romans* 474–7.

only Israel itself but also the whole world would be rescued from its sinful, rebellious state; (b) this was the sacrifice offered by Jesus, precisely in his capacity as Israel's representative Messiah. This was what it meant, in other words, for him to be 'faithful' to the gracious divine plan, the single plan that lay behind, and was expressed in, the promises to Abraham.

All this depends on the assumption that Paul held in his mind a holistic vision and understanding of the great scriptural books, especially Genesis, Exodus, Deuteronomy and Isaiah, which stand behind, and come to fresh expression within, so much of his thinking. We can only begin to understand the finer points of what he says if we hold them in our minds, as great interlocking wholes, while we are reading him. Many ideas from these books were being expressed in new ways as loyal Jews faced new and dangerous situations in the centuries leading up to Paul's day. But when we put them together we can see at least the outline of a picture which appears to be the one he has in mind: a picture of what Israel's faithfulness, as the means of the 'redemption' in which the covenant faithfulness of the one God would be enacted, might look like. As I put it some years ago:

> In Isaiah 40—55 we have a sustained exposition of the righteousness of God, focused more and more tightly on a suffering figure who represents Israel and fulfills YHWH's purpose of being a light to the nations and whose sufferings and death are finally seen in explicitly sacrificial terms. We have, that is, exactly that combination of elements that we have observed, and that are otherwise puzzling in exactly that combination, in Rom 3:21–26. In other words, the sacrificial language of 3:25, used in connection with the violent death of a righteous Jew at the hands of pagans, makes sense within the context of the current martyr stories; but those martyr stories themselves send us back, by various routes, to Isaiah 40—55; and when we get there we find just those themes that we find in Romans 3.[210]

The perspective which all this opens up is the central viewpoint of the present book: *the redefinition, in and around Jesus the Messiah, of the Jewish doctrine of election, rooted in the covenant theology of Genesis and Deuteronomy and worked out through Jesus' saving death and resurrection.*

This perspective is elaborated by Paul in Romans 3.27—4.25, which for the sake of completeness we must presently summarize. But this is the moment to make clear one of the central claims of this book, perhaps one of the most important in current debate. *The covenantal perspective on election, and its redefinition through Jesus the Messiah, provides the larger category within which 'juridical' and 'participationist' categories can be held together in proper Pauline relation.* The debate (in other words) which has rumbled on ever since the nineteenth century as to whether Paul was 'really' an 'incorporative' thinker who sometimes used 'juridical' language for particular purposes, or vice versa – or whether, as with some extreme proposals, one must choose one set of language and arguments and rule the other out

[210] Wright 2002 [*Romans*] 475. The idea of the divine covenant faithfulness is central to Isa. 40—55 as a whole, both when the idea is explicitly mentioned (e.g. 46.13; 51.5f., 8) and when it is not, since the entire section, like Dan. 9, has to do with the divine faithfulness because of which Israel will be released from the exile which is the result of its sin.

altogether – can be, and must be, resolved by the introduction and exposition of a third, larger, more biblically rooted category. This category, like a massive mountain a mile away from the front door, dominates the view so entirely that many people, glancing out, never even notice it, focusing instead on one or other of the more obvious hills in the foreground. These turn out, in fact, to be spurs of the major mountain, perhaps even consisting of cooled lava left behind when the volcano erupted two thousand years ago.

My central proposal can then be seen to good effect in the way the argument of Romans 3 and 4 plays out. The 'boasting' which is eliminated by the gospel revelation of God's righteousness (3.27) is the 'boasting', not just of the Jewish claim to be morally upright and so not to need 'saving' (or at least not in the same way as gentiles), but rather of the Jewish claim to be the means through which God would rescue the world from its plight. Here again we see a solution-to-plight answer, though rooted as before in Paul's earlier perception of the 'plight', then radicalized through Jesus. Boasting is excluded, declares Paul, not by the *nomos ergōn*, 'the law of works', but *dia nomou pisteōs*, 'through the law of faith[fulness]'.

Paul is not saying, then, that the Jewish claim is ruled out by the Torah through which one might demarcate Israel as the people of God and so remain for ever as God's servant people. He is saying that it is ruled out because the Messiah's faithfulness, in accomplishing the purpose for which this God called Israel in the first place, has established for all time the central category by which this people are to be marked out, and that category, that badge, is *pistis*. This is 'the Torah of faith': the 'Torah' (i.e. the 'covenant charter', the divinely given means of drawing the boundary around the people) which consists, not of those 'boundary markers' that separate Jews from gentiles (that is the early 'new perspective' insight of James Dunn, and though it has required some modification its basic point still stands[211]) but rather of that 'boundary marker' which, because it was the Messiah's own category, says, 'Here are the Messiah's people.' 'For we reckon that a person is justified by *pistis* apart from works of Torah' (3.28): in other words, one is reckoned to be within the justified people, those whom this God has declared 'righteous', 'forgiven', 'members of the covenant', on the basis of *pistis* and that alone. That – the Messiah's faithfulness, in which his people share through their own *pistis* as in (my reading of) 3.26, and also in 4.24–5 – is the basic sign of membership.

If this were not so (3.29 has long been a key point within a broadly 'new perspective' reading) then the one God would appear to be the God of the Jews only, rather than of the gentiles as well. If keeping 'works of Torah' was what counted for ultimate covenant membership, only Jews, the people who possessed Torah, would have been able to belong. But how could that be? By Paul's own account, let alone that of Genesis or Isaiah, the point of an elect people in the first place was so that through them the one God

[211] See esp. Dunn 2008 [2005], chs. 3, 8, 17, 19 (originally published in 1985, 1992, 1998 and 2002 respectively).

would bless the whole world. Here Paul returns to the most foundational confession of Jewish faith, the *Shema*: since God is one, he is God of gentiles as well as Jews. Monotheism undergirds not only election, but also the christologically redefined election: this God will justify circumcision on the basis of *pistis*, and uncircumcision through *pistis*. Same badge, different route: Jews, already covenant members, need to be freshly ratified, while gentiles, coming in from outside, need to make their entrance.[212]

This, Paul proposes, is what Torah was about all along. Of course, from the perspective of Saul of Tarsus, and of those who were still in the position he had once been in, it would have looked as if this whole line of thought overthrew Torah. The claim in Romans 3.31 ('Do we then abolish the law through faith? Certainly not! Rather, we establish the law') is therefore much more than a way of saying, 'I will now proceed to prove my point by some exposition of Genesis.'[213] It is a way of saying, as Paul will say again much more fully in chapters 8 and 10, that the faithful death of the Messiah, unveiling as it does the faithful covenant justice of the one God, picks up and fulfils the major themes of the Pentateuch itself, and more. It reads the Pentateuch as unfulfilled prophecy (see chapter 2 above, and chapter 11 below), and says: this is where the story was going all along.

And so back to Abraham.[214] More than an example of faith, more than an example of justification by faith, Abraham was the one to whom had been made those world-resonating promises, back in Genesis 12, 15, 17 and 22. Paul quotes from Genesis 12 in Galatians 3, and Genesis 22 in Romans 8; here he concentrates on Genesis 15 and 17, which not insignificantly are the main *covenant* chapters. Not to see this is to miss the whole line of thought. Paul has announced that God has in the Messiah unveiled his covenant faithfulness; now he goes back to the covenant itself to prove the point.

Romans 4, in fact, contains one of the key verses that gives the lie to those who say that the *dikaiosynē* language ought not to be interpreted in 'covenantal' terms. In Genesis 17.11, Abraham received circumcision 'as a sign of the covenant', *en sēmiō diathēkēs*. Paul, referring to this passage, speaks of Abraham receiving circumcision 'as a sign and seal *of the righteousness of faith*', *tēs dikaiosynēs tēs pisteōs*, which he had while still uncircumcised. The covenant had already been established in chapter 15; that was when God had made the promise of countless 'seed', Abraham had believed this promise and God had 'reckoned it to him as righteousness' (Genesis 15.6). Now we see that Paul understands that word 'righteousness' as a way of referring to the status Abraham had in the covenant which God had made with him: in other words, Paul is understanding Genesis 15.6 as a

[212] So *Romans* 483.

[213] This has been a regular 'minimalist' reading of 3.31 – and indeed of ch. 4: see e.g. Käsemann 1980 [1973], 105: 'The statement makes sense only as a transition to ch. 4,' and ch. 4 is then headed 'Scriptural Proof from the Story of Abraham'.

[214] See *Perspectives* ch. 33.

way of introducing the rest of Genesis 15, which describes the making of the covenant and the promise about the Exodus.[215]

That then helps us to see what is going on in the opening paragraph of Romans 4. I still hold firmly to the (revised version of) Richard Hays's brilliant suggestion for the translation of verse 1: 'Have we found Abraham to be our ancestor in a human, fleshly sense?'[216] The question faced here is: granted the covenant, who then are Abraham's children? The question of Romans 4 is not, 'How can we be justified by faith and have our sins forgiven?' (though forgiveness of sins is an important sub-theme, as in verses 7 and 8). The main question is, 'Who are the children of Abraham? If we have become covenant members, might that mean we have to join Abraham's physical family?' – the question, in other words, of Galatians. Paul demonstrates, point by point, that Abraham's family was always intended to be a worldwide, jew-plus-gentile family, and that this worldwide family is what the covenant God has accomplished through the death and resurrection of the Messiah, giving them the same badge that Abraham himself had, namely *pistis*, and 'faith' of a particular sort: faith in the creator God, the life-giving God (4.17–25).

This reading of the chapter integrates the otherwise difficult verse 4.16–17:

> [16]That's why it's 'by faith': so that it can be in accordance with grace, and so that the promise can thereby be validated for the entire family – not simply those who are from the law, but those who share the faith of Abraham. He is the father of us all, [17]just as the Bible says, 'I have made you the father of many nations.' This happened in the presence of the God in whom he believed, the God who gives life to the dead and calls into existence things that do not exist.

This is pretty much the heart of Paul's answer to the opening question (not a parenthesis, as in some translations and commentaries).[217] The promise must be valid 'for all the family', *panti tō spermati*, literally 'all the seed'.

What then about the very specific, and often-repeated, promise about the land? It has been universalized. 'The promise to Abraham and his seed *that he would inherit the world*', says Paul in verse 13. Inherit the world? That evokes the royal promise of Psalm 2; but other Jewish texts had already applied it to Abraham, had already seen that the Abrahamic promise, because it concerned the reversal of Genesis 3 and 11, must envisage not

[215] See too Ps. 106.31, where Phinehas's zealous action was 'reckoned to him as righteousness from generation to generation for ever', the Psalmist's summary of Num. 25.12f. (cp. Sir. 45.24; 1 Macc. 2.54): 'I hereby grant him my covenant of peace. It shall be for him and for his descendants after him a covenant of perpetual priesthood, because he was zealous for his God, and made atonement for the Israelites.' This clearly indicates an ongoing covenantal relationship: so, rightly, e.g. Watson 2004, 177. On the idea of 'covenant of peace' cf. Isa. 54.10; Mal. 2.4f.

[216] nb. this represents a significant modification to Hays's original proposal (Hays 1985; reprinted in Hays 2005, 61–84; see Wright 2002 [*Romans*] 489f.); Hays has accepted my modification, which avoids most of the problems subsequent writers have seen in his suggestion (more details *Perspectives*, 579–84). Most commentators have, I think, not understood why Hays's proposal was on the right lines, and have not noticed this modification in it: see the puzzled dismissal in e.g. Jewett 2007, 307f.

[217] Details, again, in *Perspectives*, 579–84.

simply one small strip of territory but actually the entire world, of which Abraham's God was after all the creator.[218]

The combination of limitless 'seed' on the one hand and limitless land on the other – that is the 'reward' which God promised Abraham. As an aside, but an interesting one: the mention of 'reward' in 4.4, and the consequent brief discussion about earning or not earning 'rewards' in verse 5, has sometimes been taken as a sign that the chapter is, after all, 'really' about the question of 'justification by faith' in the old sense of 'Do I have to earn my salvation, or is it a free gift?' This misses the point. In Genesis 15, the chapter which Paul is discussing throughout Romans 4, God begins by declaring to Abraham that 'his reward (*misthos*) will be very great.' Abraham, puzzled, asks God what this can mean, since he has no heir. God, in reply, promises him 'seed' as numerous as the stars in the sky, and the whole land of Canaan. That is the 'reward'. Paul, picking up this language from the chapter which is solidly in his head, allows a side-metaphor to develop out of it, which by coincidence happens to overlap with one way of expounding an 'old perspective' view of justification. But that 'old perspective' reading can safely be set aside in favour of Paul's Genesis-based covenantal reading – which, to repeat, includes 'forgiveness' within it, precisely because the covenant was always there in the first place to deal with the sin of Adam, but which does not need to go very far into the fine points of 'earning' as against 'receiving gifts' because, though those questions were indeed of interest to some Jews in the period (and to far more Europeans in the late middle ages), they were certainly not Paul's primary concern.[219]

The redefinition of election around Jesus the Messiah, then, comes to one of its primary focal points in Romans 3.21—4.25, and never more so than when Paul draws the whole of Romans 1—4 into a single closing statement:

> [23]But it wasn't written for him alone that 'it was calculated to him'. [24]It was written for us as well! It will be calculated to us, too, since we believe in the one who raised from the dead Jesus our lord, [25]who was handed over because of our trespasses and raised because of our justification.[220]

The echoes of Isaiah 53 in this last formulaic statement give us a clue as to what Paul has in mind. The faith of Jesus' followers is always at least, for him, the faith that God raised Jesus from the dead (10.9), here expressed as faith *in* 'the one who raised from the dead Jesus our lord'. Abraham's faith in God the creator, the life-giver, is thus well re-expressed in terms of Christian faith in the raising-Jesus God. Same God, same faith, same justification. But this is no mere parallel, no mere wearing of the same badge. This is about the fulfilment of a two-millennia-old promise, the unveiling of the faithful covenant justice of the God who told Abraham he would give him an Adam-rescuing family, and who has now done exactly that. This is

[218] See below, 1005 n. 661 for other second-Temple references to this theme.

[219] See *Perspectives*, 558f., 584–8, 591f.

[220] 4.23–5.

the point at which we finally see, after the dense statement of 3.24–6, how the *dikaiosynē theou* is revealed in the death and resurrection of the Jewish Messiah. This is the theme that draws together the normally divided strands of Paul's soteriology. This is how Paul has reworked, around Jesus the Messiah of Israel, the ancient doctrine of Israel's election. This, he was saying, is how the Messiah's faithfulness revealed, in action, the faithfulness of God.

(iii) Jesus the Faithful Messiah and the Problem of Torah: Galatians 2—4

(a) Introduction

It would be possible, and indeed exciting, to go straight on from the point we have now reached and look at least at Romans 5—8. Part of the overall argument of this book, as I hinted a few pages ago, is that this covenantal perspective, the redefinition of 'election' through the Messiah and the spirit, provides a viewpoint from which the now traditional standoff between 'juridical' categories (Romans 1—4, supposedly) and 'participationist' categories (Romans 5—8, supposedly) can be resolved in a deeply satisfying way, taking full account of the theme which so much exegesis on those lines has ignored, namely the Jewish *covenantal* theme which Paul, like so many of his contemporaries, traced back to Abraham, and interpreted through the lens of Exodus, Deuteronomy, the Psalms and not least Isaiah. But a little delayed gratification will not go amiss at this point. We must turn aside to see another smouldering bush: in this case, the one called Galatians 2—4.

Here, in fact, all the 'categories' of modern analysis are cheerfully jumbled up. If all we had was Galatians rather than Romans, it is unlikely that anyone would have thought to separate out 'juridical' images from 'participationist' or 'anthropological', or for that matter 'salvation historical', or 'apocalyptic', or 'covenantal', or 'transformative' in the way they are now routinely handled.[221] Here these elements all belong together, not in a muddle (as though seven blindfolded cooks were all trying to add their favourite ingredients to a stew), but in a co-ordinated and coherent line of thought. The same is in fact true in Romans, though the point there is more subtle and will need to be set out later on.

Another advantage in moving to Galatians at this point is that it will enable us to discuss more directly the question of Torah in relation to Paul's soteriology. This is bound to be central to any account of his redefined view of election, since Torah is of course one of the central elements in the original belief, so that any redefinition must show what has happened to it; and the question of 'Paul and the law' has of course been one of the most contentious in the multiple debates for which I hope this chapter, and this

[221] True, Martyn 1997a manages to do this for 'apocalyptic'; but only by dint, as I shall show, of ascribing to Paul's opponents some key elements of Paul's own beliefs. For one kind of 'covenantal' reading of Gal. 3 cf. Hahn 2009, 238–73. I broadly agree with much of Hahn's reading, though I am not yet convinced that the Aqedah lies behind 3.13f. and 3.15–18.

book, will provide a fresh angle of vision.[222] As I made clear in chapter 7, I believe that most attempts to address the question of Paul's view of the Jewish law have failed to connect with the reality of his thought (often, then, accusing him of muddle or worse) because they have failed to see the various interlocking narratives which comprise the structure of his worldview, and the way in which the narrative of Torah belongs within them.

As we turn to Galatians 2—4, we meet the familiar dilemma. It would be possible, and enticing, to write a full commentary on these wonderful, challenging chapters. Those who have studied them intensively will be frustrated by the necessary brevity of what follows. I shall concentrate on the points necessary for the argument, advancing my present case about the way in which Israel's theology of election is redefined around the Messiah, and the way in which, within that, Paul deals with the problem of the Jewish law.

(b) Galatians 2.15–21

If I were going to pick one passage to make my present point about the Torah, it might well be Galatians 2.15–21. This is all about redefinition, the radical redefinition that can only be captured in the dramatic picture of someone dying and coming up a new person:

> Through the law I died to the law, so that I might live to God. I have been crucified with the Messiah. [20]I am, however, alive – but it isn't me any longer, it's the Messiah who lives in me. And the life I do still live in the flesh, I live within the faithfulness of the son of God, who loved me and gave himself for me.[223]

Paul is not here recounting his own 'religious experience' for the sake of it. He is telling the story of what has happened to Israel, the elect people of God – and he is using the rhetorical form of quasi-autobiography, because he will not tell this story in the third person, as though it were someone else's story, as though he could look on from a distance (or from a height!) and merely describe it with a detached objectivity. It matters of course that this was indeed his own story. No doubt the experience Paul had on the Damascus Road and in the few days immediately afterwards may well have *felt* as though he was dying and being reborn. But what we have here is not the transcript of 'experience', as though he was appealing to that (curiously modern) category for some kind of validation. Peter had 'experience' as well; so did Barnabas; so, not least, did James and the people who had come from him in Jerusalem. So, of course, did the Galatians. By itself, 'experience' proves nothing. 'Yes, Paul', they could have said; 'That's what happened to you, but for us it was different.' No: what mattered, for Paul, was

[222] See e.g. Sanders's account of the Jewish belief in election (Sanders 1977, 87–101).
[223] Gal. 2.19–20.

the Messiah, and the meaning of his death and resurrection in relation to the category of the elect people of God.[224]

In case anyone who has read thus far happens not to know what Galatians 2 is all about, we had better provide a brief explanation. Paul, writing to churches in what is now central Turkey (the precise location is not our present concern), is alarmed because word has reached him that his ex-pagan converts have been told, by people scholars have variously called 'agitators', 'teachers', 'missionaries' or even 'circumcisers', but whom almost all assume to be Jewish, that the gospel Paul had preached was deficient. Paul's gospel message had got the Galatians to believe in Jesus, but had not brought them properly and fully into the covenant family.[225] They needed to belong to Abraham's people, which meant, in accordance with Genesis 17 and the massive weight of subsequent scripture and tradition, that the males among them should be circumcised, and (it seems, though this is not so central) that they should accept other Jewish customs as well. Paul's authority and credibility have been impugned. His Galatian converts are, it seems, on the point of following the advice they are now getting and becoming full members of the Jewish community, by the males being circumcised.[226]

Paul's strategy in response opens with the scene-setting in the first two chapters, where Paul for various reasons describes his own life and ministry, especially in relation to the Jerusalem apostles. A kind of transition then occurs in 2.11–21, since this account of his meeting with Peter, and his summary of what was said on that occasion, are laid out in such a way as to raise very sharply the central issues which are then discussed in chapters 3 and 4, and applied in chapters 5 and 6. All this can be said irrespective of any analyses of the letter in formal rhetorical terms, helpful though that has been as well.[227]

In setting the scene, Paul emphatically declares both his independence from the Jerusalem apostles and the fact that, when they did meet, they agreed on the substance of the gospel and divided their areas of work.[228] But then comes the key point: something happened at Antioch, Paul's base, which focused attention on what he sees as basically the same issue that is now facing the Galatians. By giving a brief description of what happened, of the line he took in the sharp disagreement with Peter and of the theological rationale behind his position, he hopes both to set the record straight about the Antioch incident itself and to set the stage for the full-dress argument he

[224] See e.g. Schreiner 2010, 170: '"I" is used representatively.' I disagree with Schreiner, however, in his suggestion that 'dying to the law' applies by implication to all believers, i.e. to gentiles as well as Jews. Gentiles were not 'under the law' in the way that Jews were: see below, 1034.

[225] We note a well-known but still often ignored point: the word 'judaizers' is inappropriate to denote these rival teachers, because it properly refers to gentiles who are trying to become Jewish. As Paul says to Peter in Gal. 2.14, 'How can you compel gentiles to judaize?' See Mason 2007.

[226] On the various reconstructions of the situation in Galatia, see the very different accounts in e.g. Schreiner 2010, 31–52; de Boer 2011, 50–61; Hardin 2008 (who is different again); and the salutary remarks of Barclay 1987.

[227] Betz 1979 started the ball rolling in this direction, though by no means all have adopted his conclusions. See further esp. Witherington 1998, 25–36.

[228] Independence: 1.11–24; agreement: 2.1–10.

is about to present. The strategy is as effective today as it was then. By paying close attention to Galatians 2.11–21 we see the challenge he is facing in the whole letter, and the theology with which he is addressing it. (The further question, as to whether Paul lost the argument with Peter and if so what happened next, would take us too far afield.[229])

The issue at stake in Antioch consisted, quite simply, in the question: were Jewish Messiah-believers allowed to sit and eat at the same table as non-Jewish Messiah-believers?[230] Paul's reconstruction of what happened goes in four stages.

First, the church in Antioch had been used to eating all together. They had made no distinction among Messiah-believers on the basis of their ethnic origin. We may assume, from the sequel, that this was a fairly radical move for Jews who had previously held to some form of the taboo which required them to eat separately from gentiles.[231]

Second, Peter comes to Antioch and is happy to join in with the practice that has thus become established. Paul appears to regard this as in line with their earlier agreement.

Third, 'certain people come from James', in other words, from Jerusalem. Paul is careful not to say 'James sent certain people', leaving open the question of whether they represented James's actual views. When they arrive, Peter changes his policy – whether because of something they say, or simply because Peter knows what they may think, or imagines what James might well say – and 'separates himself, being afraid of the circumcision people' (2.12).

Fourth, the rest of the Judaeans present (except Paul himself, we understand!), go along with Peter: Paul's word for this is 'co-hypocrites', fellow play-actors (2.13). A note of sorrow enters: 'even Barnabas', who had shared Paul's early missionary work and (according to Acts) had been of great help to him at a difficult time, went along with Peter and the others.[232]

It is important to be fully clear on what the issues were. This was not a matter, as some have absurdly suggested, of people 'learning table manners'.[233] The question was as central as anything could be: is the community of Messiah-believers one body or two? Which is the more important division: that between Jews and non-Jews (because Messiah-believing Jews would still be able to eat with non-Messiah-believing Jews), or that between those who believed and those who did not? Was Messiah-faith simply a sub-

[229] See e.g. Dunn 1990, 129–82; Dunn 1993, 129–31, concluding that Paul lost the argument at Antioch (i.e. that Peter did not give way), and that this view is now 'common'. Nothing in my present argument depends on this one way or another.

[230] Paul says 'eating with gentiles' in 2.12, but the rest of the argument makes it clear that he means gentile *believers*, not ordinary pagans. In 1 Cor. 10.27 he cheerfully allows believers to accept meal invitations from unbelievers. This may mean that the meals in question in Gal. 2 were specifically Christian fellowship-gatherings, presumably including eucharistic meals.

[231] On the vexed question of *amixia* ('not mixing [with gentiles]') see above, 93f.

[232] cf. Ac. 9.27; 13.1–3, 42–52; 14.1–20.

[233] To view such suggestions, one might google 'new perspective' and 'table manners'.

set of Judaism, leaving the basic structure untouched, or did it change everything?

One thing was clear to Paul: if the community of Messiah-believers was a two-tier body, this meant that pressure was being put on the gentile believers to convert to Judaism. Whether or not anyone was actually saying this, the fact of table-separation made it clear: there is an inner group and an outer group. Again, we do not know if people were telling the gentile believers that they needed to belong to the inner group (the fully-Jewish group) in order to be 'saved'; the word 'salvation' and its cognates does not occur in Galatians, remarkably enough, and we should be wary of importing it.[234] (Far too many discussions of 'justification', which *is* a central and vital topic in Galatians, assume that 'salvation' is more or less the same thing, which for Paul it certainly is not.) More likely, I think, they were left to understand that there was indeed an inner circle of membership in this body, and that it would be very desirable for them to join it; and that this meant becoming fully fledged Jews in the manner of proselytes. The first thing Paul tells us he said to Peter implied this: by doing what he was doing, he was 'forcing the gentiles to judaize', in other words, to become Jews. Peter might have responded that he was doing no such thing, but Paul's point was that Peter was putting the gentile believers in a position where they effectively had no choice.

Paul's initial counter-argument to Peter's action is to point up its inconsistency. Peter has been acting in one way, and what he is doing now is going in the opposite direction. (Hence the charge of 'hypocrisy'.) Up to now, Peter, a Jew, has been 'living like a gentile' rather than a Jew (2.14). What does that mean? That Peter had been worshipping idols, attending pagan temples, engaging in drunken orgies? Presumably not. It meant that, up to that point, Peter had been ignoring the normal Jewish taboo according to which Jews and gentiles would not eat together. He was therefore cutting clean through one major boundary marker in the Jewish way of life. But now he is turning the tables. He is putting apparent moral pressure on the gentile Messiah-believers to 'live like Jews', in other words, to join the company of Torah-keeping Abraham-children, the elect people of God.

And Paul's response to that is: *election has been redefined around the Messiah*. Here is the paradox: the Messiah means what he means precisely within the world of Judaism and its categories, not least its scriptural traditions. Paul is not talking (as some have tried to suggest) about a 'Christian Messiah' as opposed to the 'Jewish Messiah'.[235] No such distinction existed: the point is that he believes Jesus to be Israel's Messiah, and believes in consequence that 'Israel', the elect people, consists of those who (in some sense or other; that is the problem) belong to him. But when it comes to the scriptural traditions within which 'Messiah' means what it means, we meet the irony: one of the greatest scriptural traditions, seen not least in the Prophets,

[234] But cf. Ac. 15.1, where in a similar situation the hard-liners in Jerusalem were saying that unless gentile converts were circumcised they could not be 'saved'.

[235] See Novenson 2014 (forthcoming), ch. 2.

was the tradition of radical *critique from within*, a critique that from Deuteronomy onwards was quite prepared to say that God would remould his elect people, would fulfil his purposes for them, and through them, in surprising and disturbing ways.

Paul was fully aware of those traditions, as well as of the shocking nature of what he was saying. He had, after all, been a more hardline Pharisaic Jew than Peter, Barnabas or even, we assume, James. And he now declares that the prophetic witness has come true. God has indeed redefined his elect people; and he has done so around Israel's Messiah. The 'elect', in other words, consist primarily of the Messiah himself, and secondarily of all those who belong to him. *All*: there is the rub. If you were a first-century Jew, and had come to believe that Jesus was indeed Israel's Messiah, it would be hard to quarrel with the statement that Israel had been redefined around him. But if your worldview was still anchored to the symbols that kept Israel apart from the nations, you would want to quarrel about what 'all' might mean, and how this new body would be marked out.

Paul would be up for the quarrel. He knew the moves. The opening statement says it all:

> [15]We are Jews by birth, not 'gentile sinners'. [16]But we know that a person is not declared 'righteous' by works of the Jewish law, but through the faithfulness of Jesus the Messiah.[236]

At a stroke, Paul has told us what it means to be 'declared righteous'. It means to have God himself acknowledge that you are a member of 'Israel', a 'Jew', one of the 'covenant family': the 'righteous' in that sense. Yes, 'righteous' means all sorts of other things as well. But unless it means at least that, and centrally, then verse 16 is a massive non sequitur. 'We are Jews by birth, not "gentile sinners"'; to say that, in the setting of a dispute about who you can eat with, and in the context of a statement about people 'living as Jews' and 'living as gentiles' where what they have been doing is eating together (or not), leaves no elbow room for the phrase 'declared righteous' to mean anything else at its primary level. *The whole sentence, in its context, indicates that the question about two ways of 'being declared righteous' must be a question about which community, which table-fellowship, you belong to.* Do you, along with your allegiance to Jesus as Messiah, belong to a table-fellowship that is based on the Jewish Torah? If you do, says Paul, you are forgetting your basic identity. What matters is not now Torah, but Messiah. *Justification is all about being declared to be a member of God's people*; and this people is defined in relation to the Messiah himself.

In particular, what matters is the saving death by which the Messiah fulfilled God's covenant purpose for his elect people. The terms are set: either Torah, or the Messiah and his faithfulness: and his 'faithfulness' here, as becomes clear in 2.20, denotes his faithful, loving, self-giving to death (see below). The Messiah is not, as it were, simply a fixed point around which the people must regroup. The manner of the Messiah's fulfilment of his

[236] Gal. 2.15f.

task, i.e. his death and resurrection, must form the central characteristic of his people. The cross and resurrection thus provide the fresh shaping of election. If Jesus is indeed Israel's Messiah, then 'Israel' will now be formed according to the pattern of his death and resurrection. That is the point towards which this whole paragraph is working.

The phrase about 'the faithfulness of Jesus the Messiah' in verse 16a could of course be translated 'faith in Jesus the Messiah'. I regard the line of thought in Romans 2.17–20, 3.1–4 and 3.22, discussed above, as constituting a strong *prima facie* case for taking it as 'the Messiah's faithfulness', but it is true that the phrase as it stands in its present context could go either way. Some will say that the next line (2.16b) ought to push the interpretation in the direction of 'our faith in Jesus the Messiah', since Paul goes on to say, 'That is why we too believed in the Messiah, Jesus.'[237] But that does not seem to me to end the argument. If I am right about 'the Messiah's faithfulness' in Romans 3, the phrase does not indicate the personal religious affective state of Jesus, but *his faithfulness unto death*. It was a way of *denoting* his saving death and *connoting* the fact that in giving himself up to death he did so as the supreme act of Israel's covenant faithfulness. This was how the age-old divine saving plan had to be carried out.[238]

The emphasis at the end of Galatians 2 on the death of Jesus and its meaning can then be seen as making a loop with this earlier statement. The crucifixion of the Messiah (2.19); his loving self-giving on behalf of his people (2.20); his death, which cannot have been 'for nothing' (2.21) – all these connect up with his 'faithfulness', stated twice in 2.16 as the means of his people's 'justification'. In 2.19 we see what 'the Messiah's faithfulness' actually means: when Paul says 'I live within the faithfulness of the son of God,' he explains this at once by adding 'who loved me and gave himself for me'. This triple statement in verses 19–21 is explicitly set over against 'the law', providing exactly the same antithesis which we find in verse 16 ('a person is not declared "righteous" by works of the Jewish law, but through the faithfulness of Jesus the Messiah').[239]

Here is the antithesis, stated twice in verses 19–20 and 21:

I died to the law	I live within 'the faithfulness of the Messiah' who loved me and gave himself for me
if 'righteousness' is through the law	then the Messiah died for nothing

[237] We should note the different phraseology: 'We too believed,' he says literally, '*into* Messiah Jesus.' This strongly implies the 'entry' into the solidarity of the Messiah which is spelled out in 3.25–9 (see esp. 3.26).

[238] In here adopting 'the faithfulness of the Messiah' as the correct understanding, I do not wish, as with de Boer 2011, to read all subsequent references to 'faith' as denoting Jesus' death (de Boer does allow for a reference to human faith at e.g. 192, 239). It would be unfortunate if that (extreme?) position were to push exegetes back towards the 'objective genitive' interpretation (faith *in* Jesus) in 2.16, 3.22 and other key passages.

[239] As Michael Gorman has expressed it to me: the relationship Saul of Tarsus had with Torah was one of possession; the relation Paul the apostle has with the Messiah is one of participation.

in parallel with, and completing the thought of, verse 16:

one is not 'righteous' by works of the law	but through the Messiah's faithfulness
not on the basis of works of the law	we might be declared 'righteous' on the basis of the Messiah's faithfulness

I conclude, in other words, that there are six things are going on here.

First, Paul understands the saving death of the Messiah in terms of his loving self-giving, construed as his great act of covenant faithfulness to Israel's God.[240]

Second, he understands this action as drawing to its divinely ordained focal point the entire story of the election of Israel (that is why he can say 'the grace of God' in verse 21, as a further way of referring to what has happened on the cross), and *redefining* it around the Messiah, who has at last offered to the covenant God the 'faithfulness' of Israel.

Third, Paul understands that redefinition as the outworking of the Messiah's death and resurrection. The boundaries of Israel are not merely slackened or tightened, a few key adjustments here and there; they are radically redrawn. *The boundaries of God's people now consist of the Messiah and his death and resurrection*, and as a result Israel itself – here referred to by Paul with this deeply poignant autobiographical 'I' – has been put to death and raised to new life. This, we should note in relation to wider debates, has nothing whatever to do with the replacement of Israel by something else (as in the so-called 'apocalyptic' interpretation) but everything to do with the fulfilment of the divine purpose for Israel in and through Israel's own representative Messiah.

Fourth, Paul refers here movingly to his own journey of death and new life, not for its own sake but in order to explain that this is true of all who belong to the Messiah. He now shares, participates, finds himself caught up in, the Messiah's death and resurrection: he is 'crucified with the Messiah', and he now 'lives within the faithfulness of the son of God, who loved me and gave himself for me'. This 'participation' in the Messiah is the heart of the passage. It is, I suggest, the *basis for* the status of 'righteousness', and for the act of 'justifying' by which God creates that status.[241] I do not think, however, that 'being in Messiah' and 'being justified' are the same thing, as we shall see later.

Fifth, in 2.20a Paul adds a subtly different note. I am, he says, alive, 'but it isn't me any longer, it's the Messiah who lives in me'. This indwelling of the Messiah himself in the believer is reflected in other passages such as Romans 8.9–11, where there is a fluidity between the indwelling Messiah and the spirit (also called 'the spirit of the Messiah' and 'the spirit of the one

[240] Gorman 2009, ch. 2 argues that this is to be seen as the Messiah's quintessential act of covenant faithfulness, in which the ideas of loyalty to God, obedience to God and love of God are merged into one. These are indeed all present, though whether this supports Gorman's analysis of how Paul's soteriology works here remains to be seen.

[241] As in Phil. 3.9 (see above): 'to be found in him, not having a righteousness of my own, but that which is through the faithfulness of the Messiah'.

who raised the Messiah from the dead'). It also anticipates the notion of 'the Messiah being formed in you' in 4.19. This, again, is not the same thing as Paul being 'in the Messiah'; nor, I think, is it the same as 'being justified'. It is part of the total complex of soteriology, the separate but interwoven strands of which we shall lay out more fully in due course.

Sixth, to the question of 'How can you tell who belongs to this family?' Paul has the appropriate answer: if the family is redefined by the Messiah's *pistis*, then those who themselves have *pistis* are clearly the members of this family. The declaration that this is so, and that the community is defined in this way and no other, is what Paul means by 'justification'. The basis of that new reality – to repeat – is the Messiah's death and resurrection as the strange fulfilment of Israel's vocation and destiny, and the believer's participation in that death and resurrection.

The two verses in between the opening (2.16) and dramatic closing (2.19–21) of this sequence spell out the consequences in terms of the debate both in Antioch and, by implication, in Galatia.

First (2.17), it might appear that Paul is saying that the Messiah, in forcing loyal Jews to sit and eat with 'gentile sinners', is compelling them to become 'sinners' themselves. This is similar (not identical) to the charge we met in Romans 3.7–8, and receives similarly short shrift. The Messiah is not an agent of 'sin'. There must be some other explanation for what is going on.

Second, crucially (2.18), what Peter was doing in Antioch was 'to build up again the things he tore down', in other words, to reconstruct the wall of separation between Jewish Christians and gentile Christians. (It is clear, in other words, that Paul is still thinking of the very specific situation in Antioch and its theological meaning.[242]) But if Peter rebuilds the wall that consists, more or less, of Torah and its rules about *amixia*, not associating with gentiles, then the Torah itself will accuse him – of breaking it. 'I demonstrate that I am a transgressor', *parabatēn emauton synistanō*: a 'transgressor', that is, a breaker of the law, not merely a 'sinner' which would be true of pagans as well. The choice Peter faces is clear: either become a 'sinner' by eating with gentile Christians, or become a 'transgressor' by rebuilding the accusing Torah![243] But once you grasp the reality of the Messiah's achievement, then you realize that the community, the elect people, have been redefined by their own Messiah, and by his death and resurrection. The wider fellowship of all those who belong to the Messiah is then not

[242] It is striking that in v. 18 Paul shifts from 'we' to 'I'. I do not think this means that v. 18 no longer refers to Peter; the 'I' is for rhetorical effect, and v. 18 is offered as an explanation (*gar*) of v. 17. See Schreiner 2010, 169: 'Paul continues to address Peter, but he refers to himself as a representative of the Jewish people.'

[243] For the distinction between 'sin' and 'transgression', see Rom. 5.12–14. What would the 'transgression' be in this case? Hays 2000, 242 suggests two options: (a) rebuilding the Jew/gentile wall would transgress the gospel imperative; (b) rebuilding the wall would imply that his single-community work to date had in fact been a transgression. Hays cautiously prefers the latter; I suggest it is more likely that Paul means, in line with 2.16c ('by works of the law shall no flesh be justified') and 3.10f., 22, that for Peter to return to the divided world of Torah would be to return to a world where all were in fact condemned (see also, of course, Rom. 3.19f.; 4.15; 5.20; 7.7–25).

simply a company of 'sinners', but of 'forgiven sinners'. 'He loved me and gave himself for me', constituting his people as a people that had died to sin and risen into a new life, his own new life.

That is how the doctrine of election is reconfigured around the Messiah. In a single paragraph, in what was quite possibly his earliest letter, Paul has sketched in outline one of the most dramatic and wide-ranging doctrinal reformulations in the history of Christian thought. It ranks with the redefinition of monotheism in 1 Corinthians 8.6, and has proved equally hard for modern thought to take in. But we should note that this reformulation, like that one, has nothing of dry, abstract dogma about it. Monotheism was about *loving* the creator God, and Paul's redefinition focused on that as well. Election is about the people *loved by* this God, and specifically by his 'son'. For Paul that is central to the redefinition too: 'the son of God loved me and gave himself for me'. Indeed, that mention of 'love' ought to have told us, with its echoes of Deuteronomy and elsewhere, that this was all about the divine purpose in election.[244] The ancient Jewish doctrine (the covenant God loving and choosing his people) is being dramatically reaffirmed even as it is being dramatically transformed. Because Jesus is Israel's Messiah, his fate must be seen as the realization and fulfilment of Israel's destiny and hope. Because he is the *crucified* Messiah, that realization and fulfilment must involve a transformation for which the only image that will do is dying and rising again. The death of the old identity and the birth of the new one: no wonder Paul knew that 'the crucified Messiah' was a 'scandal' to his fellow Jews.[245] It remains so. Unless we grasp this point, however, we have failed to see the very heart of his thought.

(c) Galatians 3.1—4.11

(α) Introduction

The central argument of the letter to the Galatians (3.1—4.11) is all about the redefinition of 'election' around Jesus the Messiah, the topic of our present chapter. We must therefore now examine this section of Galatians as a whole and in some of its parts in particular. Once again, I take as axiomatic (what most commentators have decided to ignore) that when Paul writes *Christos* he intends to *denote* Jesus and to *connote* his status as Israel's Messiah, the one in whom the destiny and purpose of Israel is fulfilled.[246]

When we try to gain a perspective on the section as a whole, one of the most noticeable things is the way in which Abraham frames the argument of chapter 3. After the opening challenge (3.1–5), Abraham is introduced, with

[244] Dt. 4.37; 7.8; 10.15; Isa. 43.4; 63.9; Jer. 31.3; Hos. 11.1; Mal. 1.2. This theme is explicitly linked with the exodus in the Dt. refs. and also in Hos.

[245] 1 Cor. 1.23; Gal. 5.11. On the historical and sociological context of this 'scandal', see Barclay 2011, esp. chs. 6 and 7.

[246] See *Perspectives* ch. 31.

quotations from Genesis chapters 15, 12 and 18 in quick succession.[247] As with Romans 4, Paul seems intent on expounding the meaning of the Abraham story, and on doing so with three things particularly in mind. First, he knows that Genesis 15 is the *covenant* chapter: this is where God establishes his covenant, including the promise about the redeeming event of the exodus. Second, he insists that Abraham was promised a worldwide family: God said that he would bless all the nations 'in Abraham'.[248] Third, he draws particular attention to the fact that the characteristic of this worldwide family, if its members are to be true to their founding charter, is *pistis*: Abraham believed God ... so 'the people of faith are blessed along with faithful Abraham.'[249]

That is the opening of the argument, and the closing is similar. Ten verses pass in the latter half of the chapter (3.19–28) without mention of the patriarch, but when we get to the end (3.29) it is clear that he – or rather, his family – has been the subject all along:

> [27]You see, every one of you who has been baptized into the Messiah has put on the Messiah. [28]There is no longer Jew or Greek; there is no longer slave or free; there is no 'male and female'; you are all one in the Messiah, Jesus. [29]And, if you belong to the Messiah, you are Abraham's family (*sperma*, 'seed'). You stand to inherit the promise (*kat' epangelian klēronomoi*, 'heirs according to promise').[250]

The question of the whole chapter, then, must be understood as follows: who exactly constitutes the children, the 'seed' (*sperma*), of Abraham? The opening of the main argument (3.6–9) declares that the 'family' is the *covenant* family, the *worldwide* family of many nations and the family of faith. The closing declares that the 'family', the *sperma*, consists of those who belong to the Messiah, who constitute the single family ('all one') in him, with no distinctions of ethnic origin, social status or even gender. If that were all that the chapter consisted of, it would be fairly easy to see the point, and to grasp the way in which this statement of election-redefined-around-the-Messiah functioned in relation to 2.15–21, with reference both to the Antioch incident and to the situation in Galatia.

But Paul of course needs to say more. Specifically, within this framework, he needs to say more about the Torah, because it is Torah, the Jewish law, which the ex-pagan converts in Galatia are being encouraged to embrace. This is where our own exposition of the redefinition of election around the Messiah needs to get its teeth into this most chewy of Pauline problems, which has given generations of exegetes indigestion as they have tried to swallow it whole as part of the wrong sort of theological diet.

[247] It may be that we should see Abraham in 3.1–5 as well, since the reception of the spirit (3.2, 3, 5) is connected closely with the Abrahamic promise in 3.14 and with the (Abrahamic) notion of 'inheritance' in 4.6f. See the important work of Morales 2010. On Abraham in Galatians see *Perspectives* ch. 33.

[248] 3.8, quoting Gen. 12.3 and 18.8.

[249] 3.9.

[250] 3.27–9.

Paul needs to warn the Galatians of what would be involved were they to embrace Torah. That is what they would be doing if they got circumcised. They may not realize all that such an action would mean, and Paul urgently needs to explain it to them.[251] His argument takes four stages.

First, he shows that the Torah initially threatened to block the promises to Abraham altogether. The Messiah's death, however, has taken care of that problem (3.10–14).

Second, he insists that the promise to Abraham continues to take precedence over Torah. Just as a will, once made, takes precedence over subsequent alterations, so the initial Abrahamic covenant cannot be affected by the much later addition of the Torah (3.15–18). It is significant that the word for 'will' is *diathēkē*, 'covenant': since Paul is referring to Genesis 15 in this chapter, it is natural to hear that overtone as well.[252]

Third, Paul needs to explain the *purpose* of Torah. This purpose was important, God-given, *but essentially negative*. Torah was never, in fact, intended by God to be the means through which the Abrahamic promise would be accomplished (3.19–22). It had a different, equally God-given purpose.

Fourth, and leading up to the final statement about Abraham's single family, Paul must explain how the Torah then relates to what the covenant God has done in the Messiah (3.23–9).

This then opens the way for a different approach to the same questions in 4.1–11, to which we shall come presently.

Paul's overall point, throughout Galatians 3 and 4, is *narratival*, as we saw in chapter 6. Once you understand how the story works, the great covenant story from Abraham to the Messiah, you can see (a) that the Torah was a necessary, God-given thing, with its own proper role within that story, and (b) that the God-given role of Torah has now come to a proper and honourable end – not that there was anything 'wrong' with it, but that it was never designed to be permanent. The latter is what Paul specially needs to stress, but the former point is vital (despite the long and loud chorus of dualistic readers) to avoid any slide towards Marcionism. Granted (b), any attempt to go back to Torah would be an attempt to turn back the divine clock, to sneak back to an earlier act in the play – and thereby to deny that the Messiah had come, that he had completed the divine purpose, that in him the Abrahamic promises had now been fulfilled. It is the same choice that faced Peter: either belong to the redefined elect family, the people of Abraham, or rebuild the walls of Torah around an essentially Jewish ethnic family – which would imply that the Messiah would not have needed to die (2.21).

[251] de Boer 2011, 154, 164, refers to my previous work as though I were somehow claiming that Paul was seeing continuity between the Mosaic Torah and the newly created community in the Messiah. I am not sure how this misunderstanding has occurred. My argument has always been that Paul sees the gospel as fulfilling, not the Mosaic covenant, but the Abrahamic one, which always (so Paul argues) envisaged a single family characterized by faith, both elements of which would be impossible under an absolutized Mosaic Torah.

[252] So, rightly, e.g. Schreiner 2010, 226f.: see further below, 868 and esp. n. 266.

Galatians 3 is not, then, an argument hinging on the theological contrast between 'grace' and 'law', or even the psychological contrast between the struggle to please a legalistic God and the delight of basking in the undeserved pleasure of a gracious one. Those contrasts are indeed present as resonances, and later theologians were not wrong to draw out such implications. But the point at which those extra meanings took over and became central, displacing the actual argument Paul was mounting, was the point at which the exegetes ceased to listen to him and began to listen instead to the echo of their own voices bouncing off parts of his text. What is lost thereby is not inconsequential: the sense of Paul's concern for the *single family*, in radical, Messiah-based continuity with the people of ancient Abraham and also in radical, crucified-Messiah-based discontinuity with the people formed by Torah. That loss has infected much of the Christian world over many centuries, with dark effects of various kinds, particularly as a concern to stress the appropriate discontinuity has been transformed into an eagerness to deny the appropriate continuity. As historical exegetes, of course, it is not up to us to dictate to Paul what he ought to have said, or indeed to worry about the long-term effects either of understanding him or misunderstanding him, but to track as best we can what he said in fact. And here, in Galatians 3, the point about Torah is not that it engenders or fosters 'legalism', as the 'wrong' sort of religion (pulling yourself up by your moral bootstraps), but that Torah belongs in a period of history which the Messiah's faithful death and resurrection have now brought to its appointed goal. To go back to Torah, as the Galatians would do were they to get circumcised, would be like someone who is driving freely down a road going back deliberately to the place where there was a blockage and a consequent traffic jam (3.10–14); like someone refusing a rightful inheritance because a third party had tampered with the will (3.15–18); like an adult going back into the care of a babysitter (3.23–8). We take each in turn.

(β) Galatians 3.10–14

First, the traffic jam. Verses 10–14 are notoriously difficult, but as with the chapter as a whole, so with the parts: look at the opening and closing, discern what Paul at least seems to think he is saying, and see how the middle bit works out.[253] Paul has just said that Abraham is to have a worldwide covenant family, characterized by *pistis* (3.6–9). That is what he says the covenant God has achieved through the Messiah's death: the statement of that event in verse 13 is followed by what appears to be the triumphant conclusion, that 'the blessing of Abraham' (which presumably means 'the blessing God promised to and through Abraham') might come upon the gentiles in the Messiah, Jesus, and that 'we' – which in context must mean 'we Jews', not included in the previous clause – might receive the promise of

[253] On this passage, see Wright 1991 [*Climax*], ch. 7. See now, among the plethora of commentaries and articles, Wilson 2007.

the spirit, through faith. As in some other passages, this differentiation between gentile believers and Jewish believers is not a differentiation between two different families. Nor is it saying that gentile believers and they alone receive the blessing of Abraham, or that Jewish believers, and they alone, receive the promised spirit. Paul is differentiating between the two different routes by which these two groups came *into* the one, single family: gentiles were brought in from the outside; Jews, already in a sense within the covenant, were renewed as such by the gift of the spirit, whose first evidence is faith. And he is thereby highlighting the things each group particularly needed: gentiles, to inherit the Abrahamic blessing; Jews, to be renewed in covenant membership.[254]

So the Messiah's death enables the promise to Abraham to be fulfilled: gentiles brought in, Jews renewed. Why was this necessary? Because Torah had stood in the way, causing the traffic jam which prevented 'the blessing of Abraham' flowing smoothly forward from him to this promised worldwide family.[255] When the covenant God gave Torah to Abraham's descendants on Mount Sinai, Paul is saying, it did indeed promise life, but it also warned of the divine curse on all who did not obey. Abraham's descendants were the ones through whom the divine promises were supposed to be flowing to the nations; but now they themselves were under the curse.

Here we are at more or less the same point as in Romans 3.2, only with the difference that Paul has brought Torah into the equation as well. The curses of Deuteronomy, as we saw in chapter 2, were widely regarded in second-Temple Judaism not as a vague warning that from time to time people might disobey and be 'cursed', but as a linear, historical prophecy of what was going to happen to Israel, and hence – because it *had* happened, and everybody knew it – as a prophecy whose results were still all around. Israel was under the Deuteronomic curse; yes, some might suppose that the curse had now been lifted through the rebuilt Temple (Ben-Sirach might have said that), or through the work of the Maccabees (many thought that to begin with, but enthusiasm waned), or through the covenant renewal of the 'Teacher of Righteousness' (though Qumran understood eschatology as being at most inaugurated, not yet fully realized). Most would have accepted that the curses threatened in the later chapters of Deuteronomy were not yet lifted. Both Philo and Josephus see those closing chapters as constituting a prophecy still looking for fulfilment. To put it more positively, the era of new-covenant blessing promised in Deuteronomy 30 had not yet arrived.[256]

Paul then looks back at the full sweep of the history of Israel, and hears within it a second voice, declaring that God's final purpose of constituting a covenant people would never be accomplished through Torah in any case.

[254] See more fully below. On covenant renewal and the spirit see e.g. Rom. 2.25–9; 3.28–30; 7.4–6; 10.6–13; 2 Cor. 3.1–6; Eph. 2.11–22.

[255] There is perhaps an echo here of the attempts by zealous Judaeans – including his own former self, which would show that this is not a random or wild accusation – to 'prevent us speaking to the gentiles so that they may be saved' (1 Thess. 2.16a). On this, see Barclay 2011, 170–7.

[256] See above ch. 2, and esp. 124–6, 143–63.

The prophet Habakkuk announces, in line with what God said to and of Abraham, that covenant membership would be demarcated by faith.[257] Some have suggested that already here Paul is detecting echoes of the Messiah's own faithfulness, and his consequent life (as in 2.20).[258] This is possible but not, I think, necessary for his argument to work. Rather, he points out that Torah always envisaged a way of life which was bounded by its own regulations and decrees: the 'life' that it promised was a life given to those who would 'do them', as Leviticus made clear.[259] But the effect of this was to leave Israel, the bearers of the promise, stationary in the traffic jam, unable to move forward with the promise and convey it to the rest of the world. Torah, by requiring full obedience and by placing the curse on anything less, left no way forward, either for Israel itself or for the promises they were bearing for the nations.

Paul's point in verse 13 is thus not a generalized statement about the effects of the Messiah's death, as has often been imagined. No doubt there are ways in which these profound and resonant words can be reapplied, but our task is to discern Paul's original meaning. The Messiah, he says, has borne the curse *hyper hēmōn*, 'on our behalf': the 'we' here is again *the people of Israel*. The gentiles were not 'under the curse of the law'; the law of Moses did not apply to them, nor was their being cursed by it ever suggested in Deuteronomy, nor was any such curse on non-Israelites ever a problem blocking the way for the Abrahamic promises to flow through to the world. Verse 13 only makes sense if the Messiah somehow *represents* Israel, so that he can appropriately *act on their behalf* and in their place. Exegetes and theologians have often postulated an unnatural and unnecessary either/or between Jesus as 'representative' and Jesus as 'substitute'. Here the matter is quite clear: *because* he is Israel's representative, he can be the appropriate substitute, can take on himself the curse of others, so they do not bear it any more. And the point, once more, is not simply that those who were 'under the curse' are now under it no longer. That is not what verse 14 says. The point is that the promise to Abraham, which had got stuck in the traffic jam of Torah-curse, can now resume its journey down the road towards its destination. The Messiah has dealt with the roadblock, and the promise can reach out to the nations.

The 'curse', then, was not a bad thing foisted on people in general, or Israel in particular, or Jesus above all, by a bad law which was going against the will of the one God. That strange idea has had a long run for its money

[257] Hab. 2.4 in 3.11; and cf. Rom. 1.17c. Paul's interpretation of the Hab. verse has generated a good deal of discussion: see e.g. Watts 1999; Yeung 2002, 196–25; Watson 2004, 112–63.

[258] See Hays 2000, 259; Hays 2005, 119–42.

[259] Lev. 18.5, also quoted at Rom. 10.5, on which see below, 1171–3 (and cp. the interesting discussion of Barth *CD* 2.2.245). Gal. 3.11 remains difficult, but three points stand out. (a) Paul is echoing 2.16 (cf. Rom. 3.19f.) and 2.21: Torah, and works of Torah, cannot justify. (b) From this he draws the conclusion: *because* nobody is justified in Torah, *it is obvious that* the just will live by faith (reading *dēlon hoti* as a single phrase, with a comma after *theō* (see Wright 1991 [*Climax*], 149; and now Schreiner 2010, 211f., with other refs.). (c) Torah cannot be aligned with this *pistis* because it necessarily and rightly (see 3.22) insists on performed obedience, herding Israel as it were into the prison of disobedience (Rom. 11.32) which is the place of the curse. This is admittedly dense, but nobody expects Gal. 3 to be simple.

in Pauline scholarship, frequently indeed being held out as the explanation for the origin of his distinctive theology: (a) as a Pharisee he believed that Torah had cursed the crucified Jesus; (b) on the Damascus Road he discovered that God had vindicated Jesus; (c) he deduced that Torah had been wrong to curse him; (d) he deduced that Torah could not be the good and life-giving thing he had always imagined; (e) he therefore developed his 'Torah-free' gospel.[260] But this is not what Paul says, here or anywhere else. Of course, we need the fuller multifocal vision of the other relevant texts as well, not least Romans 7.7—8.4, to make the point; but already here in Galatians 3 it should be clear enough, especially in the light of our earlier analysis of Paul's narrative world, that such a negative view of Torah is utterly mistaken. Torah, in Paul's vision, had a specific job to perform within the deeply and necessarily ambiguous vocation of Israel. Israel was called to bear the solution to the larger human problem, but was itself part of, enmeshed within, that same problem. Only when Torah is flattened out into a generalized moral standard, a kind of early version of the Kantian categorical imperative, given as a first attempt to make human beings 'righteous' – a picture so far from Paul's mind as scarcely even to represent a caricature – could any such idea gain currency. The whole point of Galatians 3 is that Torah belongs at the key intermediate stage in the divine purpose. It was shaped to perform the task that was necessary if Abraham's children, carrying the worldwide promise, were themselves to be narrowed down to a single point, that of their representative Messiah. That in turn was necessary, as Paul makes clear in 3.22, because otherwise it would look as though Israel was somehow – perhaps even through the mere possession of Torah! – automatically rescued from the plight of all humankind.

This is where we should hear, loud and clear, the echoes of 2.19–21: through Torah I died to Torah, so that I might live to God ... because 'if "righteousness" comes through Torah, then the Messiah died for nothing.' Paul is claiming that his own story embodies what has in fact happened, through the Messiah's death and resurrection, to Israel as a whole. Torah's proper role, he now sees, was not to bring the 'righteousness' and life of which it spoke, but to demonstrate that, up to the coming of the Messiah, Israel could not attain that goal, and to 'shut up everything together under the power of sin' in order that the promise could be given equally to all believers.[261] The answer to the problem, in 2.19–21 just as here in 3.10–14, is the death and resurrection of the Messiah, and the death and resurrection, with him, of Israel according to the flesh:

> I have been crucified with the Messiah; I am, however, alive – but it isn't me any longer, it's the Messiah who lives in me. And the life I do still live in the flesh, I live within the faithfulness of the son of God, who loved me and gave himself for me.

[260] A good example is de Boer 2011, 213f., who suggests that the curse is pronounced '*by the law*', not '*by God*' (his italics), and that 'Christ has triumphed over the law's curse, putting an end to its malevolent effects on human life.' Hays 2000, 260f. describes such a line of thought as 'highly speculative', but this is too generous: it is plain wrong.

[261] 3.22; again, cf. Rom. 11.32.

The force of all this for the Galatians should be obvious. You Galatians, he is saying: you gentile Messiah-believers – you have only had the chance to belong to the Messiah's family because the Torah, which necessarily and rightly imposed a curse on Abraham's family, standing in the way of the Abrahamic promise ever reaching you, has been dealt with by the Messiah's own death! The thought therefore of you gentile Christians going back and solemnly taking Torah upon yourselves, by becoming circumcised, is ridiculous. Why carefully wend your way back to the traffic jam, in order to sit there, stalled and stationary, with unredeemed Israel?

In my earlier work on this passage I stressed, as I still would, the role of the 'curse' within Israel's Deuteronomic narrative.[262] In line with many other second-Temple Jews, Paul seems to have read the closing chapters of Deuteronomy not as a generalized warning about an ahistorical and repeated 'pattern' of (a) obedience leading to blessing, (b) disobedience leading to curse and (c) fresh obedience leading to fresh blessing, but as a linear prophecy of events that would unfold slowly, as a single great narrative, leading to the ultimate 'curse' of exile itself and then to the final redemption indicated in Deuteronomy 30. Paul, like the author of Baruch, like the writer of 4QMMT, like many other Jews of his day, believed that the 'curse' of exile still rested on unredeemed Israel. But he believed that, through the Messiah, Israel's God had broken through to covenant renewal at last, as in Deuteronomy 30. The ultimate demonstration of this is in Romans 10.6–8, which we will study later on. But it makes excellent sense of the present complex paragraph. The Messiah has come to the place and the point of the curse, of exile, bearing that curse on behalf of his people and so making the way through for the God-given worldwide plan, entrusted to Abraham's family, to be put into operation at last.

This points, in my view, to a particular view of verse 14b, already sketched a moment ago. The first half of the verse is unproblematic: getting rid of the 'curse' enables the Abrahamic blessing to flow to the gentiles as always intended (3.8). But does this leave Jews themselves still under the 'curse'? No. The Messiah opens the way for them to come into the moment of covenant renewal, the moment which Paul can evoke with a mention of Deuteronomy 30, or of Jeremiah 31, or of Ezekiel 36 or indeed of Joel 2.32.[263] I think it probable, therefore, that the 'we' of 3.14b ('that *we* might receive the promise of the spirit, through faith') refers at least primarily to Jews who, by faith, come into the same new-covenant membership into which gentiles are being welcomed. As elsewhere, two different starting-points and two different doorways lead to a single destination.[264]

[262] See again ch. 2 above, and Wright 1991 [*Climax*], ch. 7.

[263] e.g. Rom. 2.25–9 (Dt. 30.6; Jer. 31.33; cf. Rom. 10.6–8 with Dt. 30.12f.); Rom. 10.13 (Joel 2.32 [LXX 3.5]); 2 Cor. 3.3 (Jer. 31.33; Ezek. 36.26); the list could be considerably extended.

[264] For the view that 3.14b refers to Jews and gentiles equally see e.g. Hays 2000, 262. For the two different starting-points leading to the same destination compare Rom. 3.30.

(γ) Galatians 3.15–18

This brings us to the middle section of the chapter, verses 15–18, which goes very closely with the short section that follows, verses 19–22.[265] Here the image shifts: Paul picks up the language of 'covenant' from Genesis 15 and 17, and indeed from Exodus and Deuteronomy,[266] and exploits the fact that the same word can denote the 'will' or 'testament' of someone who has died. (Actually, even to speak of two different 'meanings' of the word is misleading. As far as Paul is concerned, there is one word, *diathēkē*, and one meaning: the covenanted will of the one who laid it down.)

The argument turns on another tricky word, *sperma*, 'seed'. *Sperma*, as we have seen, regularly functions as a collective noun, 'family', as does its Hebrew original, *zera'*.[267] It is often, perhaps misleadingly, translated 'descendants'. The point of verses 15–18 can be expressed quite simply: (a) God promised Abraham a single family, not two families; (b) the law threatens to create two families (as was already visible in Antioch when Peter and the others withdrew from table-fellowship with uncircumcised believers); but (c) the law cannot be allowed to overthrow the original promise and intention. To spell this out: God intended to give Abraham a single family, and, as Paul insists in 3.27–9, where he draws together the threads of the whole chapter, that is what he has done in the Messiah. The Torah must therefore not be absolutized in such a way as would create two families, a Jewish one and a gentile one – and perhaps more, because once ethnicity becomes a factor in the family identity there would be nothing to prevent further ethnic or geographical division.

Exploiting the different shades of meaning within *diathēkē* enables Paul to introduce in verse 18 the notion of 'inheritance', *klēronomia*, to which he will return in the triumphant summary of 3.29 ('if you belong to the Messiah, you are Abraham's family; you stand to *inherit* the promise'). This is one of the many links between the present passage and Romans, where in chapters 4 and 8 the 'inheritance' is not simply 'the land', one piece of territory out of the whole world, but the 'inheritance' which will consist of 'all nations', the inheritance which all Abraham's family will share.[268]

Once again the framework of the short argument of 3.15–18 seems secure, but the details in the middle are normally regarded as problematic.

[265] See Wright 1991 [*Climax*], ch. 8.

[266] Most of the Gen. refs. are in ch. 17; the word *diathēkē* is sprinkled through Ex., with occasional refs. in Lev. and Num., and then is strongly emphasized in Dt., particularly in Dt. 29. I regard it as not just improbable but impossible that Paul, in a chapter framed by Genesis and focused on Deuteronomy in vv. 10–14, would in vv. 15–18 use the word *diathēkē* without intending reference to 'the covenant'.

[267] I intend 'family' here in a diachronic, not merely synchronic, sense, i.e. corresponding at least as much to 'family tree' as to 'family gathering'. For the interpretation here see, in addition to *Climax* ch. 8, the essay on 'Messiahship in Galatians' in *Perspectives* ch. 31.

[268] See also 4.1–7. In Rom. 8.17–26 it is clear that Paul hears, in the language of 'inheritance', a strong echo of the foundational messianic Ps. 2, whose v. 8 promises that God will give the Messiah 'the nations for your inheritance' (*dōsō soi ethnē tēn klēronomian sou*) and the ends of the earth as his possession.

In particular, the singularity of the 'seed' has apparently been narrowed down in verse 16 to one person:

> It doesn't say 'his seeds', as though referring to several families, but indicates a single family by saying 'and to your seed', meaning the Messiah (*hos estin Christos*).

This verse has regularly been invoked as an example of Paul's extraordinary (and, some have said, 'rabbinic') methods of exegesis: he deduces the singularity of person from the singularity of the word *sperma*! How strange is that? (Indeed, the passage has become something of a favourite with people who want to be able to say, 'Look how strangely the early Christians – and particularly Paul – read the Bible!'[269]) But in fact it is not at all strange. Paul has not forgotten, as many exegetes have, the *incorporative meaning* of the honorific *Christos*.

Galatians 3, indeed, is perhaps the most obvious passage to make the point (a) that Paul really does mean 'Messiah' when he writes *Christos* and (b) that (as we saw earlier in this chapter) the role of the Messiah throughout the passage is precisely incorporative. The argument of Galatians is that the divine purpose in election has found its goal (and hence its redefinition) in the Messiah, so that one cannot go back to Torah in order to confirm or solidify one's membership in the family. As in Antioch, Torah would once more divide the family into two.

In fact, 3.16 can perhaps best be read as precisely an echo of the Antioch incident, seen in the light of Genesis 13, 17 and 24.[270] Peter, lurching back towards James and the others, is re-erecting the barrier of Torah and thus creating a plurality of families. Paul, emphasizing the Messiah and his faithful death, and the identity of the elect people in him, insists on the single family, all eating together. It is only when that context is forgotten (in the rush to have Paul speak about the difference between law-piety and faith-piety, between different sixteenth-century models of justification and assurance) that the focus of what he is actually saying is ignored. Then his key move, the representative and incorporative nature of Messiahship, is lost to view altogether. (It is, after all, still unwelcome to many Protestants, afraid of anything 'corporate' lest it drive them towards Rome, or anything 'political' lest it reunite their 'two kingdoms'.)

Put Paul's argument back together again in its own terms, however, and it works perfectly: (a) the creator and covenant God intended a single family, and promised it to Abraham; (b) he has now created it in the Messiah; (c) Torah would create a plurality; therefore (d) to go back to Torah would be to go against the original intention, now accomplished in the Messiah. Torah, in other words, cannot annul the promise made to Abraham nearly half a millennium earlier (3.17).

The ultimate reason offered in 3.18 stands in close parallel to 2.21:

[269] A gentle version of this can be found in Dunn 2009 [1987], 109f., 173. Barton 2011 [1988], 29 regards Gal. 3.16 as a 'stock example' of the way the NT mistreats the OT.

[270] 'And to your seed': Gen. 13.15; 17.8; 24.7.

2.21 If *dikaiosynē* came through Torah the Messiah died for nothing	3.18 If *klēronomia* came through Torah it would nullify the promise to Abraham

– which shows, among other things, the extent to which *dikaiosynē* and *klēronomia* themselves stand in parallel for Paul, the former as the covenant *status* and the latter as the covenant *promised inheritance*; and also the parallel between the promise to Abraham and the Messiah's faithful death, which is after all the double theme of so much of the rest of the chapter.

But if the covenant God always wanted to produce this single family for Abraham, and if Torah got in the way of that intention, why did he give Torah in the first place? That is the natural question Paul now faces.

(δ) Galatians 3.19–22

Anyone following Paul's argument is bound to wonder, at this point, why the Torah was necessary. It seemed, after all, to be blocking the Abrahamic promise, first in its journey to its destination (verses 10–14), and second in its creation of the single 'seed' (verses 15–18). Here, in a passage more or less unrivalled for its density anywhere in his writings, Paul alludes to a point we have already noted in passing, and which emerges more fully in Romans: Abraham's family, the Israelite people, were themselves part of the problem. The fact that he does not say that clearly and explicitly has constituted the real problem of understanding these four verses.[271] Once we supply that key, the door will open.

As usual, the outer verses of the passage give us the clue. The law, Paul begins (3.19a), was 'added' (in other words, like the codicil to the covenant, as in verse 17) 'because of transgressions'. Some have said that here, as in Romans 5.20, Paul saw the law as being given in order to *increase* transgression, or at least to turn 'sin' in the abstract into the concrete 'transgression', the breaking of a commandment. That is not impossible.[272] But he does at least seem to mean this: God intended to produce 'the single seed', but in the meantime Israel, the promise-bearer, the family from whom 'the seed' would come, was itself sinful, and could not be affirmed in that condition. The end of the paragraph (3.22) links up with this beginning: 'scripture shut up everything together under the power of sin, so that the promise ... might be given to those who believe.' Somehow, what Paul says about Torah in 3.19–22 has to do with the fact of Israel's sinfulness. God could not simply proceed to work his larger purposes through Abraham's family as though there was nothing wrong with them. This ties in with the discussion of

[271] Just as in many rabbinic discussions, the key point today's reader needs is omitted; one of the joys of Danby's edition of the Mishnah (Danby 1933) are the footnotes supplying the missing punch-lines. Pauline commentary sometimes needs to do the same, and this is a classic example.

[272] Hays 2000, 266f. discusses no fewer than five alternatives, homing in on Paul's seeing the law being given either to *identify* sin or to *restrain* it. Martyn's conclusion that the law was given to produce transgressions (1997, 354) may be closer to the truth than Hays supposes, and closer to the divine intention than Martyn supposes. Cf. Rom. 5.20; 7.13–20; 9.30–3 (see below, e.g. 894–900; 1176–81).

Habakkuk and Leviticus in 3.11–12. The fact that Torah informed the Israelites, in no uncertain terms, that they were sinful, and were breaking the law itself, *was itself part of the divine purpose*: receiving the promise, and belonging to 'the seed', would never be defined that way, but only on the basis of *pistis*. There may be more to Paul's thought here than this, but there is not less.

Once again Paul adds a reference to the faithfulness of the Messiah, this time anticipating the statement, in 3.24–9, of the Messiah's achievement and the way in which this constitutes the Abrahamic family. Verses 19a and 22 thus establish a framework for our present short paragraph: Torah was necessary because of Israel's sin. This brings into more specific focus the divinely appointed remedy, namely (a) the coming of the *sperma* (3.19), that is, the *family* to whom the promises had been made, the family already defined in 3.16 as the Messiah and his people and (b) 'the faithfulness of Jesus the Messiah' (3.22). These, if not exactly two different ways of saying the same thing, are two pathways which are already converging and which will do so completely by the close of the chapter. The Messiah's faithfulness both *accomplishes* and *defines* the united and renewed family of Abraham.

The middle verses (3.19b–21) of this little paragraph have frequently led exegetes astray, particularly into thinking that Paul is here denying the divine origin of the law, blaming it instead on angels, perhaps even hinting that these might be wicked or malevolent angels.[273] No such idea is present. The Jewish tradition of angels assisting in the giving of the law never has that intent. Paul is not saying that the law is against the promises. He sees, of course, that some might draw that false conclusion, and he wards it off in his usual fashion (*mē genoito*, verse 21). The problem he has identified, and here summarizes in this ultra-dense fashion, is that although Torah offered life, *it could not give it* – not through its own fault, but through the sinful human nature of the Israel to which it had been given. For Paul, of course, the Messiah has done what the law could not do, though that is not his explicit point in this short paragraph.[274]

The fact that this brings us right into the centre of a theme which Paul repeats from different angles in two other key passages (Romans 7.7—8.11 and 2 Corinthians 3) should encourage us to think we are on the right lines in this analysis. In Romans he insists that though Torah condemned and killed 'me', the fault was not in Torah, nor even in 'me' (the Israelite qua Israelite), but in 'sin' itself, the Adamic power that was at work within even

[273] The suggestion that the Torah came from anywhere other than Israel's God (e.g. Martyn 1997a, 354, 364–70) is firmly resisted by Hays 2000, 267. De Boer 2011, 226, however, says that the question [of 3.19a] 'already presupposes that God did *not* give the law' (his italics), though he then modifies this radically: 'certainly not as a life-giving instrument of justification'. He rejects any suggestion that, at least for Paul in Galatians, the covenant God might have had other reasons for giving the law. The idea of a non-divine origin of the law is sometimes linked to the mention of angels in 3.19c, lining these up with malevolent heavenly beings in Gen. 6, via traditions in the Enoch literature and elsewhere (despite the tradition of good angels being involved in the divine giving of Torah: e.g. Dt. 33.2 (LXX); Ps. 68.17 [LXX 67.18]; *Jub.* 1.27–9; Ac. 7.38, 53; Heb. 2.2; other texts in Martyn 1997a, 357 n. 208).

[274] cf. the sequence of thought that runs from Rom. 7.10 ('the commandment which was unto life') to 8.2, 6, 10 and 11: Messiah and spirit together bring about the 'life' which the law could not. See below.

the chosen people. Torah, therefore, promising life (7.7), could not provide it, 'being weak through human flesh' (8.3); in other words, it was unable to offer the remedy for the sinful condition of 'the flesh'. That is why, he says, God condemned sin 'in the flesh' – in other words, in the flesh, and the death, of the Messiah. That whole argument, coherent within its own context, maps well onto the present passage, with 2.15–21 in the recent background and 4.1–7 coming up shortly. In 2 Corinthians 3 Paul appears to contrast his own ministry with that of Moses, but the real contrast is neither between himself and Moses, nor between gospel and law, but between *the people whom Paul is addressing*, who are 'new covenant' people with Torah now written on their hearts, and *the people Moses was addressing*, whose hearts, he says, were hard. In both cases, Romans and 2 Corinthians, the problem is *the puzzling and continuing sin of the promise-bearing chosen people*. Thus again, as in Galatians 3.22, the (deliberate and intended) effect of giving Torah to sinful Israel was to shut up the nation, along with the rest of humanity, in the prison-house called 'sin'.[275]

The point of verses 19b–20 is then as follows.[276] Paul is still thinking of the single 'seed' as promised to Abraham according to 3.16. But the law, as we saw, would not produce that single 'seed'. Left to itself, it would insist on separating Israel from the gentiles, and so would produce at least a duality, probably a plurality, of 'families'. (Any such 'families' would then have to face the further problem, that Israel would be 'transgressors' while all others would be 'sinners', as in 2.17–18.) But what Paul is primarily concerned with, both in his description of the Antioch incident and in the entire train of thought from 3.16 to 3.29, is the *singularity of the promised family*; and that is what is in view here. The law was given through angels 'at the hand of a mediator', in other words, Moses.[277] Moses, however, cannot be the mediator of the single family.[278] He is the mediator of a law which separates Jews from gentiles, as James and those who came from him to Antioch were insisting, and as Peter agreed. No, insists Paul: the God of Abraham desires a single family, and that family cannot therefore be constituted by Torah. How do we know that this God desires that single family? *Because God is one*. Just as in Romans 3.30, the singleness of the one God himself undergirds the singleness, the unitary Jew-plus-gentileness of the family. Monotheism, freshly understood through Messiah and spirit, provides the ground and source for the fresh christological understanding of election.

Paul, of course, has expressed all this very compactly: *ho de mesitēs henos ouk estin, ho de theos heis estin*. Whichever way we read this, Paul's point to the Galatians, and retrospectively to Peter at Antioch, is this: go with Torah,

[275] 3.22; cf. Rom. 11.32.

[276] For the details, see Wright 1991 [*Climax*], ch. 8.

[277] Rightly e.g. Schreiner 2010, 242, against many other speculations.

[278] Reading *ho de* in 3.20 as the subject, resumptive of *mesitou* at the end of v. 19, and *mesitēs* in 3.20 as the complement: 'he, however, is not the mediator of "the one".' The thought is not very different if we read *ho de mesitēs* as the subject and leave the complement to be assumed: 'the mediator, however, is not [the mediator] of "the one".' See *Climax*, 169f.

and you are joining a divided family, which is not God's final intention, not what he promised Abraham. Stick with the final, single family – into which you Galatian gentiles have been happily incorporated! – and not only will you not *need* Torah; you *must* not embrace it. To do so would be, at best, to turn back the clock on the divine eschatological purposes, and at worst to spurn and snub the creation of the single family through 'the Messiah's faithfulness'. If covenant membership, or inheriting the Abrahamic promise, could have come through Torah, the Messiah's faithful death would have been unnecessary and pointless. The long, dark, strange divine plan, as set out in Israel's scriptures, involved 'all things' being 'shut up together' under 'sin'. This echoes, not by distant analogy but because this is precisely part of Paul's point, the long, dark strange plan announced to Abraham in Genesis 15 which involved his descendants being enslaved in Egypt until the time appointed, in order that, when the right time finally arrived (see 4.4), the long-awaited promise of 'inheritance' might be given to 'those of faith' (*tois pisteuousin*) on the basis of 'the faithfulness of Jesus the Messiah' (*ek pisteōs Iēsou Christou*). That is how Paul lands firmly with both feet at 3.22. And with that he has laid the foundation for the last paragraph of chapter 3, where all the threads of the argument are tied together in a flurry of christological redefinitions of the people of the one God.

(ε) Galatians 3.23–9

Paul tells the story one more time. It is of course a double story. First, something has *happened* in which the divinely promised and providentially ordered narrative has reached its goal. You cannot jump back to an earlier stage in that narrative without committing folly and worse. That is to tell the story from the standpoint of the perceived continuity between the Abrahamic promises and the messianic fulfilment. But, second, he also tells the story the other way round, from the standpoint of the perceived *dis*continuity between Moses and Torah on the one hand and the Messiah on the other: something *new* has happened: a fresh divine act has broken into the divinely appointed cul-de-sac into which Israel had been forced by Torah. The long years when things seemed only to be getting worse are now over; a new age has overtaken a surprised and unready world. Though I distrust and largely reject these labels, Paul here balances the story of 'salvation history reaching its climax' with 'the announcement of the apocalyptic gospel', and vice versa.

Look back first, he says, at how things were: before the coming of *pistis*, which he has hypostatized so that it stands for the messianic moment, the great transformation, we (that is, Israelites/Jews) were under lock and key, guarded securely against the day when the eschatological plan would finally be revealed. The Torah was keeping the Jewish people under strict supervision, stopping them drifting away from the divine purposes altogether (as their own history, and its accompanying prophecies, insisted they were prone to do, and as the great prophetic song of Deuteronomy 32 had said they would do). The Torah was in fact like a babysitter, a *paidagōgos*, a role somewhat outside the repertoire of today's western world, but which we can safely say was not a 'tutor' in the sense of a 'teacher' or 'schoolmaster', as in older translations, but more of a hired hand, who kept his eye on the youngsters, made sure they didn't get up to mischief and took them to and from school.[279] And the point of all this is to say that with the coming of 'faithfulness', *pistis*, 'we' have grown up: we are no longer under the *paidagōgos*.

Even in that implicit narrative we can see the double nature of what has happened. (a) There is a sense in which a period of time has now at last reached fulfilment. (b) There is also a sense of a long, tedious and frustrating period suddenly being ended by a new event. The family has come of age, and with that coming-of-age it has also acquired its much wider circle of members: 'we' Jews were once under the *paidagōgos* and are now no more, 'for you are all children of God, through faith, in the Messiah, Jesus' (3.26).[280] Your faith, Paul declares, is the badge which demonstrates that you are 'in the Messiah': that is what the succeeding verses will then amplify and undergird.

The point is then becoming clear, and Paul now spells it out and amplifies it up to the decisive final verse 29. *You are all God's children*: that is the basic point, the point Peter needed to hear, and the point the Galatians particularly need to hear – remembering that 'sons of God', the literal translation here, carries a strong echo of Israel, especially at the time of the exodus.[281] You are *already* God's children, Abraham's family: you need no boost to your status. And you are God's children *in the Messiah*. How do you know this? Because (verse 27) you have *put on the Messiah*, clothed yourselves with him; that is the meaning of baptism, quite possibly with reference to the actual ceremony involving fresh clothes for those who come up out of the 'death' in the water to the 'new life'.[282] This then generates a particular practical conclusion, directly relevant both to the Antioch situation and the Galatian challenge: there is no longer Jew or Greek, no longer slave or free; there is no 'male and female';[283] for 'all of you are one in the Messiah, Jesus.'

[279] On *paidagōgos* see the helpful excursus in Witherington 1998, 262–7. Other refs. in Hays 2000, 269.

[280] There is more or less a consensus among commentators that 'through faith' and 'in Messiah' are separate phrases, each of which qualify 'you are all children of God' (in other words, that Paul is not saying 'through faith in the Messiah'): see e.g. Hays 2000, 271; Schreiner 2010, 256. De Boer 2011, 245 suggests that this is an 'awkward juxtaposition' leading to a 'redundancy', but this seems overly harsh, and his suggestion that Paul is here quoting a baptismal formula, though quite possible, remains uncertain.

[281] See Wright 1991 [*Climax*], 43f.; cf. e.g. Ex. 4.22f.; Dt. 14.1f.; Hos. 11.1; Sir. 36.17; *3 Macc.* 6.28; *4 Ez.* 6.58.

[282] For the 'through death to life' motif, cf. of course 2.19–20. On early Christian baptismal practices, cf. e.g. Taylor 2006.

[283] As Witherington 1998, 27f. points out, one of the effects of the Galatian Christians adopting Jewish identity-badges would be to make women second-class citizens, since only males would bear the covenant sign of circumcision.

One! That was the point of the chapter, from 3.15 right through to 3.29; that was the key element on which so much turned, as it was the key point which Paul was most anxious to convey to Peter at Antioch and to the Galatians in writing this letter. Paul does not, of course, mean that all ethnic, social and gender distinctions cease to have any meaning at all. In many places in his writing he is clear that one must still learn how to behave wisely within these as within other structures.[284] But these differences no longer count in terms of being part of Abraham's family. That is the thrust of what he is saying. And, though he has used plenty of 'righteousness' language in the chapter so far, which might have made some think he was expounding a 'juristic' frame of thought, the reference in the last few verses of the chapter is solidly 'participationist': in the Messiah, baptized into the Messiah, putting on the Messiah, all one in the Messiah, belonging to the Messiah and therefore Abraham's single 'seed'. At this point what has been meant by 'participationist' theology joins up at once with the 'salvation-historical' perspective, both finding their meaning within a 'covenantal' frame of thought. In Galatians 3, therefore, the various categories into which Paul's thought has been split up come back together in a rich unity – which is pleasing, since rich unity is itself the theme of the chapter.

This does not mean, though, a Galatians-based victory for those who insist that Paul's thought is basically 'participationist' *rather than* 'juristic' – or, for that matter, a victory of 'covenantal' or 'salvation-historical' ideas, in the sense of a smooth 'fulfilment', a steady crescendo from promise to fulfilment, over 'apocalyptic' ideas in the (modern) sense of a radical, unprecedented, unexpected divine irruption into the normal order of things. On the contrary. Taking the 'juristic' and 'participationist' debate first: the juristic categories employed earlier in the chapter still count. They have not been displaced or squeezed out. But the 'participationist' categories themselves are here deployed precisely, if ironically, for the situational and polemical purpose which Wrede and Schweitzer saw as belonging to Paul's 'juristic' terminology, namely the incorporation of gentiles into the single family. In fact, *both 'juristic' and 'participationist' categories have this function, because both are themselves functions of Paul's larger category, which is the covenant between the creator God and Abraham and the single family that has now been created in fulfilment of that covenant.* Turning to the 'covenantal' and 'apocalyptic' debate: the whole point of the chapter is that the one God has done what he promised Abraham he would do, in the original covenant chapters in Genesis. But in order to do that this God has had to smash open the shell of Torah, and with it the 'present evil age' in which those under Torah were trapped, in order to bring about the radical new result we see in the Messiah. The Messiah, after all, is equally at home in covenantal as in apocalyptic Judaism – perhaps for the very good reason that the distinction between those two modern categories is just that, a modern distinction of which first-century Jews were innocent.

[284] e.g. 1 Cor. 7; 11.2–16; Eph. 5.21–33; Col. 3.18f. To charge him with inconsistency at this point is to muddle up different kinds of questions.

Galatians 3, then, is one key expression of Paul's redefinition of election through the Messiah. The opening passage of chapter 4, which in one sense continues the argument and in another sense extends it in a new direction, provides a further angle on the same point.

(ζ) Galatians 4.1–11

'Let me put it like this': the opening *legō de* of 4.1 indicates that Paul is taking a deep breath and coming back through the same narrative in a way which sharpens up some points and thereby takes his overall argument forward. As we saw earlier, Paul is now talking about the exodus, which of course belongs closely with the previous argument about Abraham and his family; part of the divine promise in Genesis 15 was precisely concerning Abraham's family becoming slaves and then being rescued.[285] Here, the 'heir' to the family is enslaved – or as good as: the young son may be on his way to 'inherit' the whole estate. Paul picks up the motif of 'inheritance' in the last verse of chapter 3 and makes it a key term in 4.1, using it then to frame 4.1–7 since it recurs in 4.7 as the decisive conclusion to the present passage. For the moment the young 'heir' is kept under guardians and stewards until the time the father has set for the coming-of-age ceremony; but now the 'heir' turns out to be the entire family of 'sons' who, as in 3.26, consist of all those who belong to the Messiah, here further characterized as those in whom the spirit has come to dwell (4.6–7).

Paul has in mind here *a chronological sequence* in which the coming of the Messiah and the spirit occur at a late stage in a long process. This seems so obvious to me that I find it hard to credit that people would deny it, but deny it they have, on the basis of a supposed 'apocalyptic' viewpoint, which Paul is supposed to have shared, in which there is no preparation, no build-up, but simply a sudden 'invasion' into the present world from outside altogether.[286] If this was what Paul had in mind, he has expressed it in a singularly misleading fashion. This is a story which awakens echoes of the exodus, and though of course that great event did involve the sudden irruption of divine judgment and rescue into the ongoing life of Egypt, the whole story is predicated on the belief that this was what God promised Abraham hundreds of years earlier, and that this promise had now at last come to pass.[287] So here: the story involves a young son growing to maturity, and though the moment of coming-of-age arrives as a sudden and new thing,

[285] See esp. Keesmaat 1999, with the discussion above, 656f.

[286] See esp. Martyn 1997a, 388, changing 'when the time had fully come' to 'at a time selected by [God]', and unravelling the controlling metaphor of the chapter, in which the 'father' has long ago set a time for the young 'heir' to reach maturity, by suggesting that 'God *invaded* the partially foreign territory of the cosmos' (italics original). In order to sustain this strange reading, Martyn sets up a straw man: 'Paul does not think of a gradual maturation, but rather of a punctiliar liberation' (389). I know of no exegete advocating the idea of a 'gradual maturation'.

[287] Ex. 2.23–5 with Gen. 15.13–16.

effecting instant and important change, it can hardly be said to be a bolt from the blue.

For Paul, it was in fact a matter of *chronological* fulfilment: 'when the fullness of time arrived', *hote de ēlthen to plērōma tou chronou*. Not even *tou kairou*, the particular moment, but *chronou*, the sequence of time which has now gathered to a *plērōma*, a fullness.[288] As in *4 Ezra*,

> He has weighed the age in the balance, and measured the times by measure, and numbered the times by number; and he will not move or arouse them until that measure is fulfilled.
>
> the Most High has looked at his times; now they have ended, and his ages have reached completion.[289]

If anything in Jewish literature is 'apocalyptic', it is surely *4 Ezra*.[290] This is how one of its greatest expositors explains the idea involved:

> The idea of the fixed times is to be found in many apocalypses and in other contexts in Judaism of the age. Thus one can point to all the predictive visions that divide history into a given number of segments ... This idea too makes possible the revelation of the end, which, when it became combined with intense eschatological expectation, had great implications for apocalyptic revelatory understanding ... There is the idea that God controls and determines the length of the world age. This is fixed and can be known or revealed. These times and this age will reach an end; indeed, that end is approaching.[291]

We cannot, then, invoke something called 'apocalyptic' to rule out the idea of a continuous flow of history, looking back to Abraham and trusting in the promises God made to him, and eventually reaching a point of 'fullness' which, precisely in Jewish apocalyptic, and as evidenced by the lion-vision towards the end of *4 Ezra* 11, would be the moment when the Messiah would appear. The radical newness of this moment does not constitute a denial of all that has gone before. Thus we arrive at Galatians 4.4–5:

288 de Boer 2011, who does not discern any reference to the exodus in this passage, first suggests that 'fullness' really means, in a sense, 'end', and then makes 'the fullness of time' mean its opposite, namely 'a clean break with the past' (262). The obvious fact that Paul is indeed talking about a new period of time is not, as de Boer assumes, antithetical to the idea of a long previous period under divine control. So far from being an 'optional feature' of apocalyptic eschatology, the idea of a protracted time of suffering and waiting (not, to be sure, of 'gradual maturation') is built into most second-Temple thinking (see the frequent discussions in ch. 2 above, and immediately below).

289 *4 Ez.* 4.36f.; 11.44.

290 Nor can this point be escaped by the (to my mind) dubious move (de Boer 1989) of suggesting that *4 Ezra* is a different type of apocalyptic from what we find in Paul, corresponding more to the views of his opponents.

291 Stone 1990, 98, 352. In his commentary at 3.9 (1990, 69) he lists the other passages which indicate a view of fixed times: 4.27, 33–4; 5.49; 6.5f.; 7.74; 13.58; 14.9; *2 Ap. Bar.* 21.8. The expression 'in its time', referring in 3.9 to the Flood, is paralleled at 8.41, 43; 10.16; 11.20; 14.32. We could cite, from a work which is not usually thought of as 'apocalyptic', the same notion in Tob. 14.5, 'when the times of fulfilment shall come', which in LXX BA reads *heōs plērōthōsin kairoi tou aiōnos*, and in S reads *hou an plērōthē ho chronos tōn kairōn*. There should be no doubt that Paul, writing Gal. 4.4, belongs in the widely known world represented by both these second-Temple texts.

[4]But when the fullness of time arrived, God sent out his son, born of a woman, born under the law, [5]so that he might redeem those under the law, so that we might receive adoption as sons.

This is both an *exodus*-event, with God remembering the promises and delivering his people ('redeeming slaves' being the classic exodus-motif, resulting in Israel as 'God's son'), and a clear *apocalyptic* event, the sudden unveiling of the long-awaited solution to Israel's problem; and also a clear *messianic* event, with the 'sending' of the 'son'. From all these points of view, this packed little sentence contains all the elements of election-redefinition we have already seen, contained within a narrative which awakens echoes of the first exodus, which as we saw was accomplished by God specifically in fulfilment of the covenant promises to Abraham. QED.

But of course there is more. In the original exodus-event, the Torah, to begin with, played a fairly positive role. Israel journeyed to Mount Sinai and Moses was there given the law. Granted, the first word that the law spoke was one of judgment, since while Moses was up the mountain Aaron was making the golden calf; but Torah was seen thereafter as a good thing in the sense of the positive way of life for the rescued people. Here in Paul, however, the law is part of the enslavement from which the new exodus frees God's people.[292] That is at the heart of what Paul wants the Galatians to understand, as he had wanted Peter to understand it in Antioch. For gentile Messiah-believers to take Torah upon themselves would be to embrace the life of slavery, to go back to Egypt.

The irony of this situation (sharply reflected in 4.3, where 'we', the Jewish people, had been 'under the *stoicheia*', the 'elements of the world') comes about because of the strange situation described in 3.19 and 3.22. There was nothing wrong with Torah, nothing inherently enslaving about it. But when the good Torah was given to the Israelites, it was bound to enslave them, because they were sinful. That was all it could do, and it was a good thing that it did it. This irony will not be explained until Romans 7 and 9, to be considered later. For the moment we note the sharp edge of Paul's messianic redefinition of the Jewish doctrine of election: those who belong to the Messiah are not under Torah. Jewish Messiah-believers have been redeemed from that state; gentile Messiah-believers must not enter it.

The passage continues with the further redefinition in terms of the spirit, to which we shall return (4.6–7). For the moment we simply notice how 4.8–11 then functions.[293] This revelation of the true God in his redemptive work, through Messiah and spirit, tells the Galatians that through these means they have come 'to know God, or rather to be known by God'. That is where they already are. It would be absurd for them to step back from that glorious position into a world governed once again by the *stoicheia*.

[292] This is, of course, the point which Martyn and others are trying to bring out by their denial of any continuity, though that denial effectively throws the Abrahamic baby out with the Mosaic bathwater. See e.g. Martyn 1997a, 306 ('Paul marches clean off the Abrahamic map'), 343–5.

[293] See above, 656–8.

All this brings us at last to the heart of Paul's life and thought. For Paul, Jesus is Israel's Messiah; he is the *faithful* Messiah, whose death has accomplished God's saving plan. We have seen how this work relates to Torah. This prepares us now to examine the central point: that, by his death, Jesus is the Messiah through whom Israel's God has reconciled the world to himself. There are of course other passages in which this comes to expression, including vital statements such as Galatians 2.19–21 and the shorthand summaries in 1 Corinthians 15.3 and elsewhere.[294] But the sustained expositions of the theme in 2 Corinthians and Romans are, on any account, at the centre of it all.

(iv) Jesus as the Messiah through Whom God Has Reconciled the World

(a) 2 Corinthians 5.11—6.2

We turn now to a rather different passage, in which the question of God's faithfulness to the Abrahamic covenant initially appears to play no role. But when we read this passage in the light of Romans and Galatians (as we are surely justified in doing) we can clearly see the larger picture Paul is painting.[295] Basically, he is arguing that the one God has accomplished, through Jesus the Messiah, the work of universal reconciliation which had been promised in the prophets, and particularly in Isaiah.[296] This link with Isaiah, when studied carefully, indicates that here, too, the divine covenant faithfulness emerges as the central theme. Once again, election – God's covenantal purpose to bless the world through Israel – has been accomplished through the Messiah. Paul here develops this in terms of that work now being implemented through his own apostolic work, but it is the Messiah's underlying achievement, and the consequent redefinition of the Isaianic theme of election, that we must draw out.

As throughout 2 Corinthians 3—6, Paul is explaining the nature of his apostleship over against those who have scoffed at him as a poor public performer, an altogether inferior specimen to the new teachers who arrived in Corinth after he left.[297] We pick up the passage where he has just explained the strange nature of his apostleship within the framework of a revised eschatology (5.1–10: see chapter 11 below). All his work is to be seen against the backcloth of God's shining of the new-creation light in Jesus, the one

[294] e.g. Rom. 14.8f.; Col. 2.14f.; 1 Thess. 4.14; 5.10; and the profound meditations on the cross in e.g. Phil. 2.6–8; Col. 1.19f.

[295] As I hinted in the Preface, though we must of course treat each letter on its own terms, it is normal in the study of any writer or indeed artist to allow chronologically adjacent works to illuminate one another.

[296] A full study of Paul's use of Isa. in this passage is now provided by Gignilliat 2007.

[297] Almost all now agree that Paul's apostleship is the main topic of this whole section. Hafemann 2000a, 235, 241 gives headings of 'Paul's Motivation for Ministry' and 'The Consequences of Paul's Ministry' for 5.11–15 and 5.16—6.2 respectively; Keener 2005, 181 heads 5.11—6.10 'Persevering Ambassadors of Reconciliation'.

who was crucified and raised, and the one who, as Messiah, will execute the coming judgment.[298] This explains, he says, why it is that his ministry takes the shape and pattern it does. It is all because of the thing he mentioned in Galatians 2: the love of the Messiah:

> [13]If we are beside ourselves, you see, it's for God; and if we are in our right mind, it's for you. [14]For the Messiah's love makes us press on. We have come to the conviction that one died for all, and therefore all died. [15]And he died for all in order that those who live should live no longer for themselves, but for him who died and was raised on their behalf.[299]

'One died for all, and therefore all died': that is about as central a Pauline statement of the meaning of Jesus' death that we could wish for. And Paul's point is that this is at the centre, too, of his apostolic ministry: this death, the manner of it, and the love that brought it about, have transformed Paul's vision of how the one God was going to act in relation to the whole world – have transformed, in other words, his vision of 'election', of God's covenant purposes and his faithfulness to them. Indeed, through the Messiah God has effected the greatest purpose of all: the renewal of creation itself, adumbrated in each person who is now 'in the Messiah' (5.17). This is what the Messiah's 'love' has accomplished.

This has happened in a twofold pattern: first, the Messiah's work; second, the apostolic ministry through which that work is put into operation. Here, as so often in the New Testament, we have the to-and-fro between the unique *achievement* of the Messiah and its *implementation* in the work of the gospel. (This is the answer to those who puzzle about the differences between Jesus' 'teaching' and Paul's, as though they were two professors teaching similar courses! If the present passage had been read in the way I am expounding it now, the problem would never have arisen.) The two are obviously closely linked, and this double reality lies at the heart of Paul's exposition of his own personal commission. God has acted in the Messiah, uniquely and decisively; Paul's apostolic work derives from this and implements it, and even embodies it. He has already stated this double point once, in verse 15:

(a) He died for all	(b) in order that those who live should live no longer for themselves but for him who died and was raised on their behalf.

He then sets this preliminary statement within the context of 'new creation' (verses 16–17) and the utterly fresh perspective which that provides on everything and everyone. (We note that Paul is still basically talking about 'how we should view people', in order to further his argument about the nature of his own apostolic ministry.) He then restates the double point again and again. Here are the first two, in 5.18 and 5.19 respectively:

[298] 4.5f.; 5.10.

[299] 2 Cor. 5.13–15.

(a) [God] reconciled us to himself through the Messiah
(b) and he gave us the ministry of reconciliation.

(a) God was in the Messiah reconciling the world to himself,
not counting their transgressions against them
(b) and entrusting us with the
message of reconciliation.

Paul here inserts an extra verse (20), explaining in more detail how it is that his own ministry is characterized by the fact that God, and the Messiah, are speaking through him. He is an ambassador, who speaks not on his own authority but as the mouthpiece of the monarch he represents. The whole emphasis of the passage thus falls, not so much on the Messiah's death as such, but on *the way in which this reconciling death is then conveyed through the apostolic ministry*. The antithesis, already moving in a crescendo from verse 18 to verse 19, reaches its climax in verse 21, where the redefinition of election – election in action! – as a result of the Messiah's death is worked out in apostolic ministry:

(a) The Messiah did not know sin, but
God made him to be sin on our behalf,
(b) so that in him we might embody
God's faithfulness to the covenant.

This reading of 2 Corinthians 5.21 has inevitably proved controversial.[300] The verse, after all, has had a venerable history as the main statement of 'imputed righteousness', in which, while the believer's sin is reckoned to the Messiah, 'his righteousness' is reckoned to the believer.[301] But the more the passage is studied in relation to the whole line of thought from 5.11—6.2 (not to mention 2.17—7.1), and the more the reference to Isaiah 49.8 in 6.2 is factored in, the more that traditional meaning seems quite beside the point, and the more the idea of the apostle *embodying* the divine covenant faithfulness emerges as the natural and right meaning. This is in any case strongly implied once one (a) makes the switch from the regular reading of 'God's righteousness' as 'a righteous status from God' to the more plausible

[300] For my original exposition, see the essay in *Perspectives* (ch. 5; original: 1993); cp. Wright 2009 [*Justification*], 135–44 (US edn., 158–67). See the reaction in e.g. Schreiner 2001, 201 ('a strange and completely implausible interpretation'; cf. too Bird 2007, 84, 'simply bizarre'): but Schreiner and Bird appear only to have seen the very brief summary in Wright 1997 [*What St Paul*], 104f., not the fuller statements. See too Keener 2005, 187: 'they [ministers of the new covenant] are "God's righteousness" not as "the justified" but as agents of the message of God being reconciled with the world'; Hays 2005, 148: 'our vocation is to embody the message of reconciliation by *becoming* the righteousness of God . . . a visible manifestation of God's reconciling covenant love in the world' (italics original). The idea is developed in a radical and political direction by Grieb 2006, who (though seeing the difficulties of doing so) wants to extend the 'we' of 5.21 to the whole church (65); see too Gorman 2009, 87f. My sense that the 'we' is specifically apostolic comes from the entire context and argument. A similar case to mine, but avoiding explicit 'covenantal' reference, has been argued independently by Hooker 2008.

[301] That reading depends, of course, on a slide from 'God's righteousness' to 'the Messiah's righteousness', for which, notwithstanding 1 Cor. 1.30, there is no justification here. To make this point is hardly 'pedantic' (Bird 2007, 83, against Gundry).

reading of it as 'God's own righteousness',[302] and then (b) adds the point that this divine righteousness, specifically in Isaiah 40—55 from which Paul is about to quote, is not simply to do with the creator's faithfulness to the creation, but more specifically with the divine *covenant faithfulness*.[303]

This strong initial possibility is strengthened by other considerations. In terms of our present argument, we need only say this.

First, one of the most powerful confirmations of this way of reading the text comes in the immediately following verses, 6.1–2. Here Paul quotes Isaiah 49.8, which flows right out of the second 'servant song':

> I listened to you when the time was right,
> I came to your aid on the day of salvation.

As usual, we should pay attention to the larger context of Paul's scriptural quotations, and when we do so here the effect is dramatic. The very next lines speak of the servant as the agent of God's 'covenant to the people':

> I have kept you and given you as a covenant to the people,
> [LXX has *diathēkēn ethnōn*, 'a covenant of the nations']
> to establish the land, to apportion the desolate heritages . . .
> Lo, these shall come from far away, and lo, these from the north and from the west,
> and these from the land of Syene.[304]

The two verses preceding Paul's quotation comprise the famous passage in which the servant's mission is extended to include the gentiles:

> It is too light a thing that you should be my servant to raise up the tribes of Jacob
> and to restore the survivors of Israel;
> I will give you as a light to the nations [LXX adds: *eis diathēkēn genous*, 'for a covenant of the people'], that my salvation may reach to the end of the earth.
> Thus says YHWH, the Redeemer of Israel and his Holy One, to one deeply despised, abhorred by the nations, the slave of rulers,
> 'Kings shall see and stand up, princes, and they shall prostrate themselves,
> because of YHWH, who is faithful, the Holy One of Israel, who has chosen you.'
> [LXX *hoti pistos estin ho hagios Israel, kai exelexamēn se.*][305]

[302] This is the argument of Käsemann against Bultmann: see e.g. Käsemann 1969 [1965], ch. 7, based not least on Stuhlmacher 1966. Barrett 1973, 180f. recognizes that Käsemann's view of *dikaiosynē theou* might point to a fresh interpretation of the present verse (as indeed it does: see Käsemann 1969, 181, and see further Hooker 2008, 370f.), but resists it.

[303] Furnish 1984, 340, says that within 'apocalyptic Judaism' the phrase 'is to be associated primarily with the power by which God establishes the covenant and maintains his faithfulness to it'; this is more or less right as a summary of the second-Temple meaning, but not as a summary of the position of Käsemann and Stuhlmacher, whom he cites, and who are in fact anxious precisely to bypass 'covenantal' meanings. Even though Furnish 338–59 treats 5.20f. as part of a new section running on to 6.1–10, he does not see that the Isa. quote in 6.2 lends strong support to a 'covenantal' reading of 5.21b.

[304] Isa. 49.8b, 12. The servant as a 'covenant of the nations' is also found in 42.6. For the *diathēkē* theme in Isa. 40—66 cf. also 54.10; 55.3; 56.4, 6; 59.21; 61.8. The specific 'servant' and 'covenant' references occur within the larger context of the Isaianic promise of 'new creation', as here in 2 Cor. 5.17: see esp. e.g. Beale 1989; Kim 1997.

[305] Isa. 49.6f. Despite his careful probing of the Isa. text, Wilk 1998, 96–101, never sees its implication for 5.21b, remaining content to see *dikaiosynē* there as 'abstract for concrete', i.e. meaning 'justification' (98). That ignores both the echoes of Isaiah and the precision of Paul's language, here as elsewhere.

This is 'election theology': the divine choice of Israel, in order that *through* Israel the covenant God may work his saving purposes for the whole world. Paul's whole point is that this covenant faithfulness of the one God, having been *enacted* in the death of the Messiah, is now being *embodied* in his own representative, ambassadorial, apostolic ministry. 'God is making his appeal through us', as he says in verse 20. In the light of 2 Corinthians 4.7—5.10, this clearly cannot mean only 'through what we say out loud'. It means, 'through our suffering and perplexing apostolic life'.[306] The point that Paul wants to get across to the Corinthians is that the strange, apparently inglorious apostolic life he leads is in fact the place where, and the means by which, the divine glory, his reconciling faithfulness, is to be seen. That is why the careful build-up of double statements concludes: 'so that in him *we might come to embody God's faithfulness to the covenant*'. God's covenant faithfulness is what was revealed in the Messiah's faithful death.[307] Now it is freshly embodied precisely in the faithful suffering of the apostle.[308]

Even if there were not already a strong case for translating *dikaiosynē theou* in its other occurrences (all in Romans) as 'God's faithfulness to his covenant', this contextual and biblical argument would push us hard in the direction of that meaning in 5.21. To put it negatively: the normal reading of the verse, in which, while the believers' sin is 'imputed' to the Messiah, the Messiah's righteousness is 'imputed' to the believer, cannot explain (a) why it is *God's* righteousness that is spoken of, not the Messiah's; (b) why the verb is *genōmetha*, 'become', rather than something to do with 'reckoning', as in Romans 4.3–6; and (c) why Paul would have said something like this as the climax of his long and carefully structured argument about his own ministry and regular 'appeal for reconciliation', rather than, as I am suggesting, something about the theological depth of that apostolic vocation. Even if there were a good argument for reading the idea of 'imputed righteousness' in other passages, there are none, except a (much) later tradition, in the case of this one.[309] To the contrary: all the signs are that here, finally picking up the idea of covenant renewal from 2 Corinthians 3.1–6, we have a solid statement of God's fulfilling of his covenant promises

[306] This is why 5.20b ('We implore people on the Messiah's behalf to be reconciled to God') is to be taken as a general statement, not, as with most translations, a sudden appeal to the Corinthians themselves to be reconciled, either to God or to Paul; that makes no sense in the context, and anyway depends on unwarrantedly adding 'you' as the object of 'implore' (against e.g. Furnish 1984, 339; Keener 2005, 186f., who thinks that Paul here and elsewhere is in fact urging the Corinthians to be reconciled, citing 6.1 and 13.5; but these do not make the same point as 5.20).

[307] Rom. 3.21–6.

[308] 2 Cor. 4.7–15; note the emphasis on faithfulness in 4.13. Gignilliat 2007, 104f. notes the possibility of this reading, but, like Hafemann 2000a, 248, is content to reaffirm the traditional reading, suggesting (as does Grieb 2006, 65) that my account does not do justice to the antithesis in 5.21. My problem is that the traditional reading itself does not do justice to the way in which that antithesis picks up and amplifies the two previous antitheses of 5.18 and 5.19; nor does it do justice either to Paul's own theme throughout the passage (his own apostolic ministry as the carrying forward of the accomplishment of the Messiah) or to his careful rooting of this in the specifically 'covenantal' and 'servant' passage from Isaiah.

[309] None of this has any bearing on my reading of 2 Cor. 5.21a, in which the Messiah was 'made to be sin for us', and where something like the traditional 'imputation' ('our' sins being 'imputed' to the Messiah) is still appropriate; see below, 897–902, 963.

through the Messiah. The result is the bringing of 'reconciliation' to the world through his death. This means that the divine purpose in the 'choice', i.e. 'election', of Israel (Isaiah 49.7) has been accomplished through the Messiah and his saving death. Now, in and through the apostolic ministry, the one God is being faithful to his covenant. The apostles not only talk about this faithfulness: they embody it, sharing the messianic sufferings through which it was accomplished in the first place (4.7–18; 6.3–10). That is what it means to say that Paul and his apostolic colleagues actually 'become' God's 'righteousness'. They embody his faithfulness to the covenant. The focus in the passage is the specific question Paul is discussing, namely the nature of his apostleship. But his underlying theological and exegetical point is that *this is what 'election' looks like when it is reworked around the Messiah.*

We should not miss, of course, at this stage in the overall argument of the present chapter, what Paul is saying about the meaning and effect of Jesus' death. His main point – the exposition and explanation of his Messiah-shaped apostolic ministry – only means what it means because underneath it at every point there stands the reconciling death of Jesus:

> The Messiah's love makes us press on. We have come to the conviction that one died for all, and therefore all died. And he died for all in order that those who live should live no longer for themselves, but for him who died and was raised on their behalf.
>
> [God] reconciled us to himself through the Messiah ...
>
> God was reconciling the world to himself in the Messiah, not counting their transgressions against them ...
>
> The Messiah did not know sin, but God made him to be sin on our behalf ...[310]

It is all about the action of God in the death of the Messiah; or, as in Romans 8.35 or Galatians 2.20, about the *love* of the Messiah as the embodiment of the saving, reconciling action of the one God. Paul can say this several different ways, or indeed several times over in pretty much the same way, as in verses 14 and 15; but it all comes back in the end to the climactic statement to which, as so often, Paul builds up step by step. He is alluding, of course, to basic Christian teaching which the Corinthians knew well, as the repeated 'for us' demonstrates with its echoes of his summary of the gospel in the earlier letter.[311] He is not expounding it afresh, but showing that the teaching they already know is what gives the shape and surprising character to his own vocation. As for the substance, particularly of 5.21a, Craig Keener has put it well:

> Presumably the Corinthians were familiar with Paul's teaching that Christ's death appeased God's wrath, hence reconciled humanity to God (Rom 5:9–11). In the becoming sin of one who 'knew no sin' (5:21; cf. Rom. 3:20; 7:7), Paul may combine the notion of

[310] 2 Cor. 5.14f., 18, 19, 21.

[311] Note the sequence: 'for all', 'for all', 'for them' and finally 'for us' (vv. 14, 15a, 15b, 21); cf. 'he died for our sins' in 1 Cor. 15.3.

unblemished sacrifices with the scapegoat that came to represent or embody Israel's sin (Lev 1:3; 16:21–22). Because Paul is about to quote a servant passage from Isaiah in 6:2, he may also think of the servant whose death would bring Israel 'peace' (Is 53:5–6).[312]

We note, finally, the characteristically Pauline combinations: the worldwide scope of the gospel with the sharply personal focus; the substitution of saviour for sinner with the insistence that the whole thing is the action of God (rather than a ploy to pacify an otherwise uncaring god); a reconciliation already achieved (verse 19) with a reconciliation which needs to be accepted (verse 20). To highlight either pole of any of these three is to purchase an apparently straightforward 'Pauline theology' at the cost of true Pauline depth. At the cost, Paul would have said, of the gospel itself.

(b) Romans 5.6–21

This exposition of the reconciling work of the Messiah in 2 Corinthians 5 sends us back to Romans, to pick up part of the argument where we left off earlier and to explore his other great statement of 'reconciliation'. Paul's exposition in Romans 3.21–6 of the death of Jesus as the 'faithfulness' through which God's own covenant faithfulness was revealed, leading to the exposition of the reworked covenant in 3.21—4.25, has brought him in chapter 5 to the point where he can sketch the larger picture and draw preliminary conclusions. The death of the Messiah reveals not only God's justifying purposes but also, in particular, God's *love*. This is such a familiar theme in the New Testament that it is easy for expositors to skip over it with a glad recognition of its personal meaning, without reflecting on the way in which the notion of divine love is tied so closely in Israel's scriptures with the notion of election and covenant.[313] For Paul, however, this is arguably central.

Romans 5.6–11 has as good a claim as most passages to express the heart of Paul's theology. The paragraph is built up step by step, drawing together things already said in chapters 1—4, preparing the way for the compressed summary of the whole plan of salvation in 5.12–21, and pointing forward to the final celebration in 8.31–9. Thus:

> [6]This is all based on what the Messiah did: while we were still weak, at that very moment he died on behalf of the ungodly. [7]It's a rare thing to find someone who will die on behalf of an upright person – though I suppose someone might be brave enough to die for a good person. [8]But this is how God demonstrates his own love for us: the Messiah died for us while we were still sinners.
>
> [9]How much more, in that case – since we have been declared to be in the right by his blood – are we going to be saved by him from God's coming anger! [10]When we were enemies, you see, we were reconciled to God through the death of his son; if that's so, how much more, having already been reconciled, shall we be saved by his life. [11]And that's not

[312] Keener 2005, 187. For the sacrificial notions Keener refers also to Dunn 1998, 217–9.

[313] See above, 860 n. 244.

> all. We even celebrate [or: 'boast': the verb is the same as in 2.17; 3.27] in God, through our lord Jesus the Messiah, through whom we have now received this reconciliation.[314]

In context, this is explaining (*gar*, verse 6) the previous summary (5.1–5) of where the argument of the letter has now come: being justified by faith, we have peace with God (5.1), and the result is 'the hope of the glory of God' (5.2). With so much going on in verses 1–11, it is easy to lose track of Paul's main emphasis, but that verse provides the clue: 'hope' is where the paragraph is going, and it finally gets there in verses 9 and 10.

But the point is to *ground* this hope utterly and completely in something that has *happened*. The death of the Messiah, understood as the climax of the scriptural narrative of the covenant love of the creator God, is the moment when and the means by which this God has, as Paul said in 2 Corinthians 5.19, reconciled the world to himself. Here Paul focuses once more on the deeply personal meaning: 'for the weak', 'for the ungodly', 'for us sinners', 'for enemies'. No possible category is omitted. Nobody can say, reading this paragraph, that they are automatically excluded.

The opening paragraph of the chapter ends with 5.5: 'hope does not make us ashamed, because the love of God has been poured out in our hearts through the holy spirit who has been given to us.' Paul does not mention the spirit again until 7.6, and then only as a foretaste of what is to come in chapter 8. Instead, in 5.6–11 he explains the basis of hope, not yet in terms of what God has done and is doing 'in us', as in chapter 8, but in terms of what we might call the objective basis for this, what God has done 'for us'. The repeated *hyper*, 'on behalf of', in verses 6, 7 and 8, insists on looking back to what the Messiah has done, or rather, as in verses 8 and 10, what God has done in and through the Messiah. Clearly, Paul is here saying in other terms what he had said in 3.21–6, where God 'put Jesus forth' (3.24) to reveal his 'righteousness'. Here God 'demonstrates his own love' 'through the death of his son' (5.8, 10, anticipating 8.32). The same reality is viewed through two adjacent windows; or perhaps the same window, once at sunrise and once at sunset.

These verses do not offer a 'theory about the atonement' as such. Their *literary* function is to draw a preliminary conclusion from the letter so far, in order then to sketch in 5.12–21 the larger picture which forms the groundwork for 'the redemption in the Messiah' in chapters 6—8. Their *rhetorical* function is to invite the hearers to gratitude, celebration and worship. Their *theological* function is to explore various interlocking levels of meaning within the death of Jesus: its character as a gift of sheer undeserved grace and love; its embodiment of the long-promised rescuing love of Israel's God; its specific focus on the needs of the 'weak' to be given God's power,[315] of the 'sinners' to be forgiven, and above all of the 'enemies' to be reconciled (verses 6, 8 and 10); its justifying function, through the Messiah's

314 Rom. 5.6–11.

315 This is not said here, but 1.16 speaks of the gospel's 'power to salvation' in the context of ideas very similar to those in this paragraph.

sacrificial death; and thus its role as the ground of hope itself. There is much more that Paul could say, and does say elsewhere, about the meaning of Jesus' death. What he has said here belongs to his overall argument rather than to any abstract theory. But the overall argument is itself pointing to some of the deepest meanings about the Messiah's death. Grasp this, Paul is saying, and you will have *hope*.

This latter point, expressed in verses 9 and 10, is where the *gar* in verse 6 was looking. Why does hope not make us ashamed? Verse 5b, as we saw, looks ahead to the work of the spirit to answer this question, but that presupposes the different answer given in verses 6–11, or rather in verses 9 and 10, which stand on the ground that has been established in verses 6–8. The 'therefore' of verse 9 (*oun*) draws the conclusion from verses 6–8, showing that the phrase 'justified by his blood' is another way, for Paul, of saying or summarizing what he has said in those verses ('the Messiah died for the ungodly, for the sinners'). As in 2 Corinthians 5, Paul is speaking of an objective historical accomplishment – not of course in order to obviate the need for people to believe (5.1), to 'be reconciled to God' (2 Corinthians 5.20), but to ground that response in something outside themselves.

This enables him to state, for the first time since the introductory 1.16–17, that all this is leading to *salvation*. The theme appears at last, like the royal flag eventually being run up the flagpole in a city formerly under hostile occupation. Within the whole of Romans there are only three passages which join together 'justification' and 'salvation' (often used as near-synonyms in later Christian discourse, but not usually by Paul). 1.16–17 is the first: the gospel is God's saving power because in it God's righteousness is revealed from faith to faith. 5.9–10, our present passage, is the second, building on the 'revelation of God's righteousness' in the death of Jesus in 3.21–6: we are *justified* by his blood, and will therefore be *saved* from the coming wrath. 10.9–11 is the third, and is every bit as important thematically and structurally as these first two:

> If you profess with your mouth that Jesus is lord, and believe in your heart that God raised him from the dead, you will be saved. Why? Because the way to covenant membership [*dikaiosynē*] is by believing with the heart, and the way to salvation is by professing with the mouth. The Bible says, you see, 'Everyone who believes in him will not be put to shame.'

We note another close link between the three: 'I am not ashamed of the gospel' in 1.16, 'hope does not make us ashamed' in 5.5, and now 'everyone who believes will not be put to shame' in 10.11. It looks as though we are at one of the mountain-tops in the letter from which the other great summits can be viewed, along with the pathways which lead between them. And, though the word 'salvation' and its cognates do not occur in 8.31–9, that paragraph must surely be counted as another place where these themes meet and merge (see below).

The point of it all, here in chapter 5, is then *salvation*. The word 'salvation' stresses as it were the negative pole ('salvation *from*') of the future hope: in this case, 'from God's coming anger'.[316] In 5.2 Paul balances this, as in 8.18–30, with the positive pole (saved *for*): in this case, for 'the glory of God', which according to 3.23 had been lost through sin. And, having spoken so far of the Messiah's death 'on our behalf', he changes at the end of verse 10: we are saved '*in* his life', *en tē zōē autou*.[317]

The emphasis of the paragraph thus falls on the summary in verse 9, the deeper explanation in verse 10 and the celebration in verse 11. And it is in the deeper explanation that we find, too, the explanation of 'peace with God' in 5.1: the 'enemies' have now been 'reconciled', as in 2 Corinthians 5.18, 19 and 20.[318] Every way you analyze the plight of the human race, the love of God and the death of the Messiah have proved more than adequate to meet it. The theme of 'reconciliation', though verbally rare (and hardly featuring at all in the Hebrew Bible), nevertheless seems to sum up so much of what the prophets had foretold: 'You will be my people and I will be your God.'[319] This theme is closely joined in scripture with two others, both very germane to Romans. First, the dwelling of YHWH with his people; second, the transformation of the heart. Both are here in Romans 5: the 'access to grace' in 5.2 is a temple-image, while the 'love poured out in the hearts' in 5.5 indicates the transformation promised by the prophets. Both come together in the idea of 'celebrating in God' in 5.11. Much of Paul's ministry is about 'reconciliation' between different people and groups. That was what he was doing with Philemon and Onesimus. But all of that is rooted in the ultimate 'reconciliation' which God himself has effected in the death of his son. The paragraph thus brings us back to the main theme of our own present chapter. Israel's doctrine of election, seen now through the prophetic lens of the promises of restoration and renewal, has been reworked by Paul from top to bottom around the Messiah (particularly his death) and the spirit.

The 'boast' of 5.11 (the word I have translated as 'celebrate' here is cognate with the 'boast' of 2.17 and 3.27) might appear, in current western thinking at any rate, to be subject to the same critique that Paul had offered in those earlier passages. The sting of the 'boast' here, however, is drawn by two things. First, there is the overall context in which Jew and gentile alike have been reduced to the status of guilty sinners, standing in the dock with nothing to say in their defence (3.19–20). All is therefore of grace; the 'boast', as he says elsewhere, is not in oneself but in the lord.[320] Second,

[316] cf. 1 Thess. 1.10. Within the structure of Romans this is the real answer to the problem of 1.18—2.16.

[317] The word *en* can also be translated 'by', as in *KNT*; but it could also be looking ahead to the incorporative meanings in chs. 6—8.

[318] This is in fact the only other passage where this root occurs in the whole NT, with the trivial exception of 1 Cor. 7.11 and the highly significant exception of Rom. 11.15, on which see below, 1198–1200.

[319] e.g. Ex. 29.45; Jer. 24.7; Ezek. 36.28; and frequently.

[320] 1 Cor. 1.31.

there is the suffering which is the necessary badge, indeed the Messiah-shaped badge, of membership in his people (5.3; 8.17–25).

That is not to say that there is not still here a 'scandal of particularity'. Of course there is. That comes with the territory of monotheism and election.[321] The redrawing of both doctrines around Jesus (and the spirit, as we already glimpse in 5.5) retains the shocking character of the original, if anything more so. But here the Pauline vision of the love of God likewise retains its character as the *electing* love, in Paul's (and, he would have said, Isaiah's) vision of that election: the love that chooses to act in a particular way through a particular people, and ultimately through that people's representative, in order that, through this means, the world as a whole might be rescued. This (as we might expect after Romans 4) has all the hallmarks of the ancient Israelite sense that the creator God called Abraham and his people in order that through them he might rescue all the tribes of Adam.

It is no surprise, then, that the very next sentence goes on to introduce the larger picture. This is where we see at last the full sweep of the narrative from Adam to the Messiah, gazing as though from a great height where all detail has shrunk to a blur (including, sometimes, such trivial syntactical features as subjects, verbs and objects) and only the great, broad lines stand out:

> [12]Therefore, just as sin came into the world through one human being, and death through sin, and in that way death spread to all humans, in that all sinned ... [13]Sin was in the world, you see, even in the absence of the law, though sin is not calculated when there is no law. [14]But death reigned from Adam to Moses, even over the people who did not sin by breaking a command, as Adam had done – Adam, who was the original prototype of the one who would come.[322]

The reason it looks as though Paul was sidetracked at the end of verse 12 is that he was. He does not finish the sentence he began until he finally returns to the point in verse 18. But (with Paul there is always a 'but') the intrusion in verse 13 of the question of the law, bursting in upon the picture of Adam and the Messiah which Paul is constructing, embodies in its *rhetorical* invasiveness the *theological* point Paul is making about the law 'coming in alongside' (as he puts it in 5.20).[323] The puzzle created by the Torah is held within the larger narrative.

Here, in fact, we are back in the same territory as in Galatians 3. The Mosaic law has intruded into the Adam–Messiah picture, just as it did into the Abraham–Messiah picture. There is a reason for this. The Torah, too, is part of the strange doctrine of election which is then being reworked around Jesus the Messiah. Paul's point, throughout this chapter, is that *the one God has accomplished, through the obedience of the one man Jesus the Messiah,*

[321] See Levenson 2012, 27f.

[322] Rom. 5.12–14.

[323] Ironically, the notion of 'invasion', so important in Martyn's account of the divine action in Christ, appears in Paul in terms of the divine giving of Torah, bursting in upon the larger sequence from Adam to the Messiah. This is only resolved in Rom. 7—8 and 9—10 (see below).

that which he purposed when he called Abraham and made the covenant with him, namely the rescue of the Adam-project. Romans 5.12–21 is a summary statement of the reworking of election.

Indeed, this God has now done a greater thing even than he promised to Abraham. No longer are the restored people simply going to become numerous, and occupy their own land. The people who benefit from the Messiah's work will share his rule over the cosmos (5.17). This is how election is reworked around the Messiah:

> [15]But it isn't 'as the trespass, so also the gift'. For if many died by one person's trespass, how much more has God's grace, and the gift in grace through the one person Jesus the Messiah, abounded to the many. [16]And nor is it 'as through the sin of the one, so also the gift'. For the judgment which followed the one trespass resulted in a negative verdict, but the free gift which followed many trespasses resulted in a positive verdict. [17]For if, by the trespass of the one, death reigned through that one, how much more will those who receive the abundance of grace, and of the gift of covenant membership, of 'being in the right', reign in life through the one man Jesus the Messiah.[324]

Thus *the obedience of the Messiah* is the means by which the purpose of election, the rescuing and restoration of the human race, is accomplished. As we saw, the notion of the Messiah's 'obedience' is Paul's way, here and in Philippians 2.8, of *denoting* Jesus' death and *connoting* the way in which that death was (a) the opposite of Adam's disobedience and (b) more particularly the obedience to the Israel-shaped, election-driven saving plan of the covenant God:

> [18]So, then, just as, through the trespass of one person, the result was condemnation for all people, even so, through the upright act of one person, the result is justification – life for all people. [19]For just as through the disobedience of one person many received the status of 'sinner', so through the obedience of one person many will receive the status of 'in the right'.
>
> [20]The law came in alongside, so that the trespass might be filled out to its full extent. But where sin increased, grace increased all the more; [21]so that, just as sin reigned in death, even so, through God's faithful covenant justice, grace might reign to the life of the age to come, through Jesus the Messiah, our lord.[325]

Here might we stay and speak of a story divine and human, all-encompassing and many-sided, full of love and grief and purpose. That is for another occasion. For the moment we simply note the point: as the 'faithfulness' of the Messiah was a way of referring to his death, making it clear that he was therein offering God the 'faithfulness' to which Israel was called but in which Israel failed, so the 'obedience' of the Messiah in this passage, also obviously referring to his death, is the way of making it clear both that he is being the 'obedient servant' and that he is thereby reversing and undoing the effects of Adam's 'disobedience'.[326] And the divinely

[324] Rom. 5.15–17.

[325] Rom. 5.18–21.

[326] The word *hypakoē* is more or less absent from the LXX. However, the notion of 'obedience' is regularly expressed in Israel's scriptures through the root *shema'*, regularly translated with *akouō* or, as an abstract noun, *akoē*. See Rüterswörden 2006 [1994–5].

appointed purpose for achieving that end always was the election of, and the covenant with, Abraham and his 'seed'. God has done, through the Messiah, what he had said he would do in 'election'.

The role of Torah within this purpose will become apparent in Romans 7. For the moment it is expressed in the dense and cryptic 5.20: 'the law came in alongside *so that* (*hina*) the trespass might be filled out to its full extent'! Paul said *hina*, and he meant *hina*: this was the divine purpose. We are here, as we anticipated, not far from the strange statements of Galatians 3.19 and 22. Something seems to have happened in relation to the particular Israel-stage of the divine purpose, something which will give yet more depth to Paul's view of the obedient death of the Messiah. But again we note: this is simply part of the reworking of 'election'. The law defined Israel, and filled out Adam's trespass precisely within Israel. The Messiah has come to that very point, so that 'grace might increase all the more' right there.

One final but vital note. Many of Paul's expositors have supposed that he gave up talking about 'righteousness' and so forth in chapter 4, and that in chapters 5—8 he was no longer dealing in 'juristic' or 'forensic' categories, but now in 'incorporative' or 'participatory' ones. Here, however, at the climax of chapter 5, we find that Paul's way of speaking about the work of the one God in the Messiah is not twofold, but single: neither merely 'juristic' nor merely 'participationist', but essentially *covenantal*, including within that 'apocalyptic' and 'messianic'. The occurrence of *dikaiosynē*, here and (as we shall see) elsewhere in Romans 5—8, particularly in the climax of 8.31–9, is not a strange, unnatural hang-over from chapters 1—4. As in Galatians 3 and Philippians 3, the language of the law court belongs intimately, in Paul's mind, with the language of incorporation into the Messiah and his people. Romans 1—4 and 5—8 are not alternative patterns of redemption. They are a sequential argument, and when Paul wants to show how the sequence works he refers back, in summary form, to the longer arguments already made – just as, in 2.25–9 in particular, but also in a dense phrase like 3.24 ('through the redemption in Messiah Jesus'), he has anticipated in 1—4 arguments which he will now make more fully. I suggested above that in 3.24 he was as it were scooping up the whole of Romans 5—8 and placing it, as a small nugget, within his argument about the revelation of the divine covenant faithfulness. Here it happens, as it were, the other way around. 'Grace reigned through righteousness to eternal life', or, as I have translated it myself, 'through God's faithful covenant justice, grace might reign to the life of the age to come'. The revelation of the divine righteousness, as in 3.21—4.21, is now placed within the overall statement of the divine purpose from creation to the new age, as in 5.12–21. And all happens 'through Jesus, the Messiah, our lord'. Here once more we see election reworked around the Messiah.

(c) Romans 7.1—8.11

Within the particular argument of Romans, Paul must then develop his central picture of what 'being in the Messiah' actually means. He expounds that in Romans 6, to which we shall return; but our own argument demands that we jump to Romans 7 and 8. After all the things Paul has said, cryptically and curiously, about the Torah, it is time to explain just where the law fitted in to God's purposes.[327]

It is not only unfinished business within Romans, of course, that gets picked up and addressed here. Galatians, too, left several stones unturned on this path, to say the least, and there are puzzles elsewhere as well.[328] They, too, are in principle discussed here. In terms of the multiple narratives which form Paul's worldview (chapter 7 above), we are now close to the heart of the 'Israel' narrative, so that we begin to glimpse the way in which the 'Messiah' narrative, in dealing with Israel's particular problem, deals thereby with the problem of Adam which Israel was supposed to solve but which Israel had instead deepened. Before we get lost among the individual trees of Romans 7, then, we remind ourselves which bit of the forest we are investigating. We are looking, not so much for the full analysis of what Paul here says about the Torah, still less for what Paul here says about the always-contentious 'I', but for what he says about the Messiah, and about the way that the divine purpose in election came to fruition, and hence to radical redefinition, through him.

This is already set out, briefly, in 7.4–6, which we could summarize by saying: the purpose which the covenant God had spoken of to Israel in terms of the 'new covenant' (Deuteronomy 30; Jeremiah 31; Ezekiel 36) has now been fulfilled through the Messiah's death and the gift of the spirit. With that, we find ourselves on the map of other related passages in Romans, particularly 2.25–9 and 10.5–13, which are both needed for the full picture to emerge. But for the moment we look at what Paul says in 7.4 about the transition that has occurred: 'You died to the law through the body of the Messiah, so that you could belong to someone else.' This is a further statement of election redefined around the Messiah.

Paul is here developing the image he has sketched in 7.1–3: a married couple, with the husband dying and the wife being free to marry again. But things are somewhat more complex. In Paul's use of the image, both the death and the remarriage happen to the same person: '*you* died to the law ... so that *you* could belong to someone else.' This is obviously close to what he says in Galatians 2.19–20, where 'I am crucified with the Messiah ... nevertheless I live'), but it is not at once apparent how that makes Romans 7 more comprehensible. Some have given up, accusing Paul of

[327] This was a point well made by Robinson 1979, 79f., citing 3.20, 31; 4.15; 5.13, 20; 6.14; and then 7.5f. He might have added 3.21 ('apart from the law').

[328] e.g. 1 Cor. 15.56 ('The "sting" of death is sin, and the power of sin is the law') – which, without Rom. 7, would be completely incomprehensible. Cf. the negative statements about the law in e.g. Eph. 2.15; Phil. 3.9; Col. 2.14f.; and, in a measure, the argument of 2 Cor. 3.

'confusion worse confounded'.[329] But the charge is unwarranted when we read the chapter in the light of what has gone before.

The clue is found in Romans 6, where the 'old human' refers back to Adam, the head of a humanity characterized by sin and death.[330] There, in 6.6, the 'old human' has died in baptism, 'so that the bodily solidarity of sin might be abolished, and that we should no longer be enslaved to sin'. That is the picture which Paul has in mind. The 'marriage' illustration develops the point of 6.3–14: the death that occurs (the Messiah's death, shared by the believer through baptism) sets a person free from the 'old human', the 'old Adam', *to whom one was bound by the law*. Without that death, the law still binds one to Adam, but with the death of the old Adam in baptism the law no longer has a claim. The law is not the first husband, but the thing which binds 'you' to that first husband (Adam).

But the 'you' who is bound by the law to Adam is not just anybody. It is, once again, 'the Jew'. Here we are, for a moment, back in 2.17–20. 'The Jew' claims to possess, in Torah, 'the form of knowledge and truth'. But Torah and prophets themselves, while agreeing with the statement in theory, turn round and accuse 'the Jew' of not having kept Torah itself (2.21–27). Thus, too, in 3.20, 'through the law comes the knowledge of sin.' Here again we meet the problem which Paul finds at the heart of the doctrine of election. Israel is called by God for a purpose. Israel is given Torah in order to keep that purpose, and the nation, on the right track. Yet all that Torah seems able to do is to declare that Israel has broken it. However true that is – and Paul, as we have seen, has discerned in the gospel of Jesus the Messiah that it is more true than he had previously imagined – it appears to leave the whole divine purpose in election, in the call and commissioning of Israel, in abeyance. We are once again back where we were at the start of chapter 3. What can be done? How can the covenant God be faithful to the promises he has made, promises to work not just *for* Israel but *through* Israel for the world? Those questions have not gone away. We have now dug deep down underneath them, and are arriving at Paul's understanding of the very heart of the divine purpose in reworking election around Jesus the Messiah. This passage is regularly admitted to be dense and difficult, but it is within these thickets, I submit, that the most important quarry in Pauline theology has been hiding all along.

Paul's analysis of what has happened comes in three stages, set out in Romans 7.7–12, 7.13–20 and then, in conclusion, 7.21–5. This is not the place for a full commentary. I highlight only the features that seem to me

[329] Dodd 1959 [1932], 120. See the proper correction to this in e.g. Keck 2005, 175–7.

[330] Dunn 1988a, 360f., says 'the imagery of 6:18–22 is still strongly in Paul's mind', which is true; but the theology of 6.3–14 is underneath that again, and also underneath the present passage.

important within the present argument. No doubt there is plenty of room for further exploration at many other levels.[331]

First, in 7.7–12, Paul tells the story of Israel at Sinai in such a way as to echo the story of Adam in the garden.[332] He explains, in other words, that what happened to Israel when Torah arrived on Mount Sinai was a recapitulation of the primal sin of Adam. The echoes of both events resonate together here, but the main topic of the passage is the Torah, and the point here is that Torah, though promising life, brought death, because as soon as there was a commandment there was a temptation, which proved irresistible.

The resonances between Eden and Sinai are profound. It is almost as though Torah drew together the two trees: the tree of life, which held out a promise that was not taken up, and the tree of knowledge of good and evil, which held out a warning that was not heeded. 'Sin', which serves here as a way of talking both about 'the satan' in the garden and the presence of the sinful tendency (more than the evil *yetzer* but not less) within every human being, deceived 'me' and so killed 'me'.[333] 'The commandment which pointed to life turned out, in my case, to bring death.'

Paul insists, as in Galatians 3.19 and 22, that this was not the fault of the Torah itself, of the 'commandment'. The commandment really did 'promise life' (7.10 – the start of a key sequence of thought which comes to an exhilarating climax in 8.11). The law and the 'commandment' are 'holy, upright and good' (7.12). This is not just a knee-jerk reaction, the old Pharisee unwilling to think of Torah as other than utterly good. It remained the apostle's settled conviction.

So where did the problem lie? The problem was with what we may call the Adamic nature of Israel: the problem, in other words, within 'me'. That is the answer Paul gives to the next question, in verse 13: 'Was it that good thing, then, that brought death to me?' Was Torah, however good it appears to be, really responsible for 'my' death? The answer, in 7.14–20, is that the person who lives under Torah is, as a matter of objective theological reality

[331] See the fuller discussion in Wright 2002 [*Romans*], 562–72, and behind that in *Climax* ch. 10. I assume the division of the chapter (7.7–12; 7.13–20; 7.21–5), according to the very careful structuring of the argument (with e.g. Jewett 2007; against e.g. Fitzmyer 1993 and Byrne 1996, who like many, including the NA text, suggest a paragraph break after v. 13). I also assume (see *Romans* 551–4) that the 'I' of Rom. 7 is not a form of psychological autobiography (which would in any case, though no doubt interesting, offer little help in a theological argument, since others might respond that their 'experience' was different), but rather a rhetorical device to enable Paul, as in Gal. 2.17–21, to speak of Israel without speaking in the apparently distancing third person. I assume that he is thereby speaking of Israel in terms of the kind of Jew he once was, offering in retrospect a theological, rather than a psychological, analysis of the situation of those who are given the law (7.7–12) and who delight in it (7.13–20) but who, with the benefit of hindsight, he believes to have been clinging the more tightly to their own death-warrant. Perhaps one could say that he uses the *language* of psychology, after a fashion, to express what he now believes to have been *theologically* true of all those, himself included, who lived 'under Torah'.

[332] See e.g. Käsemann 1980 [1973], 197: 'vv. 7–13 look primarily to people under the Torah … and Adam is portrayed as their prototype.'

[333] On the *yetzer ha-ra'*, the 'evil inclination', seen by some rabbis in balance with the 'good inclination', the *yetzer ha-tob*, see e.g. Strack and Billerbeck 1926–61, 4.466–83; Marcus 1986a. The proposal of Davies 1980 [1948], 27 that in Rom. 7 'Paul reflects and possibly actually has in mind the rabbinic doctrine of the Two Impulses' has not met with subsequent favour: see e.g. Dunn 1988a, 391.

(by no means necessarily of psychological self-awareness) constantly in two minds. The vocation of the devout Jew is to delight in Torah: Psalm 19 and Psalm 119 sum up this delight, even excitement, and Paul will not say a word against it. But the very Torah in which Israel rightly, properly and vocationally delights also bears witness that Israel is part of the problem as well as part of the solution. *Israel, too, is in Adam.*[334] That is the problem to which Paul will allude in 8.3: the Torah was 'weak because of human flesh', in other words, because of Israel's 'flesh', that identity with the whole human race which Israel inevitably shared but which would inevitably mean that Israel, as it stood, could not become the people Torah would otherwise have made them. It is not a matter, in Käsemann's unfortunate expression, of 'the hidden Jew in all of us'. The problem is the hidden 'Adam' in the Jew.[335]

At the head of the dense analysis of the plight of Israel under Torah, however, there stands the all-important verse 7.13.[336] Here, notably, there are two *hina*-clauses, two indications of the divine purpose in giving the law:

> Was it that good thing, then, that brought death to me? Certainly not! On the contrary; it was sin, *in order that* it might appear as sin, working through the good thing and producing death in me. This was *in order that* sin might become very sinful indeed, through the commandment.

The problem under which Israel suffers (in Pauline retrospect) is not, then, simply a difficulty to be got over. It is not that Torah is frustratingly difficult to keep. It is, rather, that Torah was given as *part of the divine purpose in election*; but the purpose, it seems, included a necessarily negative element. This is what was anticipated in Galatians 3.19, where he says that the law was given 'because of transgressions', and 3.22, where he says that scripture 'shut up everything under the power of sin', which Paul echoes in the present letter in 11.32. It was, in particular, what Paul had hinted in the cryptic line in Romans 5.20: Torah intruded into the Adam–Messiah sequence *in order to* 'increase the trespass'. The double *hina* in 7.13 is, in other words, not out on its own. With Christian hindsight, Paul is offering a consistent account of Torah which indicates that it had a particular *and negative* role to play within the overall purpose of election.[337] And, to insist on the point, which will come to full expression in Romans 9—11, this particular and negative role was itself divinely intended.

The divine purpose was, it seems, *to allow sin to do its worst in Israel itself, precisely through the Torah.* This is not (in case there should be any

[334] I argued in *Climax* ch. 12 that there were also echoes of Cain (Gen. 4.1–16) in Rom. 7.13–20.

[335] See above, 807f.

[336] Part of Paul's reason for casting this argument in the form of anguished autobiographical analysis, I believe, is his intention to parody the similar statements in pagan moralists from Aristotle onwards, and thereby *both* to address that felt plight *and*, more specifically, to indicate to the devout Jew – to his former self! – that all Torah could actually do was to raise one to the level of the puzzled pagan moralist. See *Romans*, 553f.

[337] One should at this point compare Rom. 2.17–20 and 9.30—10.13, but to do so here would take us too far off course. See below, 1165–81.

doubt) a matter of the creator 'causing' sin. It is a matter of his responding to the fact of sin in the world by deciding to lure it on to one place, to cause it to be focused on one point, *in order that* (there it is again) it can be dealt with right there. This, in fact, is where 5.20–1 already pointed, though with such dense brevity that the point might be missed. As often, we have to appeal to a fuller statement to understand a compressed formulation.

How does this, so to speak, 'work'? And what has this to do with the messianically redefined election?

'Sin' here, as is often remarked, is far more than the sum total of all human wrongdoing, of idolatry and immorality. Sin is the dark power which has corrupted humankind and God's good creation, the power which is actually the same as 'the satan' but which Paul, by speaking of it as a subpersonal force, can portray as something that can grow and swell, become more fully its true self, show itself up in its rightful colours. Why would God want to allow such a thing? Here we are in fact near the heart of the doctrine of election, seen with Paul's christological hindsight which has made him rethink both 'plight' and 'solution' in what appears a dizzying spiral of reflection on the Messiah's death. The double *hina*, 'in order that', in 7.13 picks up the *hina* of 5.20 and spells it out: the divine purpose is that, through Torah, 'sin' might swell to its full size, *in order then to be dealt with once and for all.* And the place where that swelling was to happen, to Paul's horror in retrospect, was precisely the elect people, Israel: the Israel that clung to Torah because it was after all the God-given law, holy and just and good. It is as though Paul is envisaging the covenant God playing a trick on 'sin' (and also, as a secondary result, playing a trick on Israel itself, as Jeremiah almost said): by giving Israel the Torah, 'sin' seizes its opportunity, and displays – in the people of God, no less! – just what havoc it can wreak. Without realizing that it is being led into a trap, 'sin' has a field day, 'producing in "me" all kinds of covetousness' (7.8). But the trap has been set. This is the divine plan for dealing with 'sin'; this is what, for Paul, 'election' really meant. The intention was to bring 'sin' to one spot, where it could be judged and condemned.[338]

The precise ways in which 'sin' grew to its full height in Israel Paul does not here spell out. We might hazard a guess that it might have something to do with his own sense of the enormity of opposing and persecuting the *ekklēsia tou theou*, the Messiah in and among his people.[339] It may simply

[338] This, by the way, is the Pauline truth at the heart of all those agonized existentialist analyses which, seeing that Rom. 7 was more than autobiography but not seeing its 'Israel'-dimension and its restatement of election, had unwittingly locked away the theological tools they needed to probe to the heart of the present passage. See, classically, Kümmel 1974 [1929], followed particularly and influentially by Bultmann's famous essay of 1932 (= Bultmann 1960, 173–85 or Bultmann 1967, 53–62; cf. too the sharp summary in Bultmann 1951–5, 1.266f.). The problem with these analyses, seen purely as exegesis, was the proposal that the 'I' of the passage could in fact keep the law, but was wrong to try – the very opposite of what Paul says (see rightly e.g. Schreiner 1998, 373). For the possible if distant prophetic echo, cf. Jer. 20.7.

[339] cf. 1 Cor. 15.9; cp. 1 Tim. 1.15; and cf. 1 Thess. 2.16 again. Jewett 2007, 440–5, 449, who in Jewett 1971 had followed a line similar to Kümmel and Bultmann, has now explored the possibility that Paul refers both to Jewish zealotry (of his own pre-conversion sort) and pagan competition for honour.

have something to do with the particular inappropriateness of the people to whom so much had been given nevertheless behaving in the way the rest of the world was doing, as in Romans 2. But the point, in any case, seems to be more one of theological reality than any particular sin ('sin' here is anyway a power that takes over human life rather than particular wrong action); and again in any case Paul is clear that 'it is no longer I that do it, but sin that dwells within me.' That makes little sense in terms of personal responsibility. Hippolytus's famous escape clause, that it was the tongue that swore while the mind remained unsworn, is not what Paul is trying to say.[340] Rather, Paul's point is that Israel's vocation in election was never to be the automatically 'good' chosen people, always obedient and consciously and deliberately faithful. Strangely, since the creator God both called Israel to be the means of rescuing humankind (knowing, with the golden calf incident, with Deuteronomy 32, and with the great prophetic denunciations, that Israel was a nation of rebels) and since this God gave Israel the holy, just and good Torah (that affirmation of Torah's goodness is itself a striking affirmation both of Jewish-style monotheism and of Jewish-style election), it must be the case that the one God intended this Torah for a purpose, beyond that of merely stopping Israel going to the bad in the time between Sinai and the coming of the Messiah. Now, at one of the most profound moments anywhere in his writing, Paul sketches what that purpose was. Israel was called in order to be the place where sin would grow to full height, so that it might at last be fully and properly condemned. If sin was to be defeated, this was how it had to happen.

So how was sin to be condemned? Answer, once again: in Israel's representative Messiah. This is where election-including-Torah is redefined dramatically around the crucifixion. The line of thought that runs from 3.20 ('what you get through the law is the knowledge of sin') to 5.20 ('the law came in alongside, so that the trespass might be filled out to its full extent') and then on to 7.13 ('It was sin . . . in order that it might appear as sin . . . in order that sin might become very sinful indeed, through the commandment') finds its proper conclusion in Romans 8.3:

> 3For God has done what the law (being weak because of human flesh) was incapable of doing. God sent his own son in the likeness of sinful flesh, and as a sin-offering; and, right there in the flesh, he condemned sin.

This is near the heart of Paul's 'atonement-theology' – which is another way of saying that it is near the heart of his redefinition of election. Certainly this brief statement contains more elements of that abstract entity, 'atonement', than any other passage in Paul. Strangely, it does not look exactly like any of the things currently on the open market under the title of 'Paul's atonement-theology'. What exactly is he saying? Six things at least, I reckon, each of which could be expanded considerably but must be stated briefly here for the sake of clarity.

[340] Eurip. *Hippol.* 612.

This is a theology of *representation*, but in a more subtle way than that notion is often expressed. 'The son of God' denotes Jesus, of course, and connotes, simultaneously, his messianic status and his 'divinity' in the sense we studied in the previous chapter. As Messiah, he represents Israel, which in turn represents the whole human race. That is how 'election' works in Paul's redefinition.

It is also a theology of *substitution*, but not quite of the usual kind. The Messiah's death is the means by which sin is condemned, and this explains why, two verses earlier, Paul can say that there is 'no condemnation for those in the Messiah'. Paul does not, however, say what many preachers do, that 'God condemned Jesus.' He says, rather, that 'God condemned sin *in the flesh* of his son.' That makes a considerable difference.

It is also a theology of *sacrifice*, but again not of the usual kind. The sacrifice in question is the sin-offering, which in Leviticus and Numbers was designed precisely to deal with sins that were unwitting (I didn't know it was wrong and/or I didn't realize I was doing it) or, more importantly, unwilling (I knew I shouldn't do it and I meant not to do it but I somehow did it anyway). The opposite of those is 'sinning with a high hand', i.e. knowingly and deliberately; no sacrifice can be offered for that, and the only result is condemnation. But, as I argued a long time ago, the point of the sin-offering in the present context is that it is the specific sacrifice to deal with precisely the problem that Paul has analyzed in Romans 7: 'I don't do the good thing I want to do, but I end up doing the evil thing I don't want to do.'[341]

It is also, particularly and obviously, a theology of *judicial punishment* or *condemnation*. As I said a moment ago, the fact that 'sin' is 'condemned' in the flesh of God's son means that 'there is now no condemnation for those who are in the Messiah.' The condemnation has clearly been transferred: no *katakrima* for those in the Messiah, because the one God *katekrinen* sin in the Messiah's flesh.[342] But the punishment, here at least, is not so much the punishment that 'I' deserved, but the punishment that 'sin' deserved. Part of the whole point of chapter 7 was to distance the 'I' from 'sin', and to make it clear that it was the latter that was at fault and needed to be condemned.

It is a theology of *Israel's purpose*, of 'election' in other words, but not in the way one might imagine. Here we are near the heart of Paul's revision of election in and around the Messiah. This is not a way of taking 'election' away from Israel – far from it: it is the horrifying realization, in the light of the fact of the crucified Messiah, that Israel was called to be the place where 'sin' would be 'condemned in the flesh' – and that the Messiah has taken that role on to himself, individually. It is only when theologies of election

[341] On all this, see *Climax* ch. 11; on 'sinning with a high hand' see e.g. Num. 15.30; cf. Dt. 17.12, and e.g. mKer. 1.2; 2.6; 3.2. Bryan 2000, 142 suggests that from Sinai onwards Israel knew what the law said, so that all subsequent sin was 'sinning with a high hand'. Had this been so it is strange to find the distinction in Torah itself, as Bryan himself (100–2) indicates.

[342] Jewett 2007, 484 is right to say that *katekrinen* is 'the point of emphasis' in the sentence, but it is strange that he does not then draw out the link with 8.1, and indeed the tight line of thought that looks back to 2.1–11 and on to 8.31–9: see below. Contrast e.g. Moo 1996, 477.

miss out this central point that they go bad and accuse one another of take-over bids. This fulfilment is of a different order.

It is also, finally, a theology of *divine victory*. The force and power of 'sin' have been ruining the good creation, and this moment is the moment of triumph, corresponding to the crossing of the Red Sea or, indeed, to Judith's cutting off Holofernes's head. This, again, both is and isn't quite like the normal *Christus Victor* atonement-theologies. Paul comes close to that kind of thing in a couple of other passages,[343] but here the note of victory is as it were hidden behind, but only just behind, the fact of sin's condemnation. We should not, because it is hidden, downplay this element in Romans 8. In chapters 5, 6 and 7, 'sin' has been increasingly present and troubling, and the fact that it is now judicially condemned has the force of the victory we know from the book of Revelation: 'The accuser of our comrades has been thrown down!'[344] When Paul speaks of being 'more than conquerors' at the end of the chapter (8.37), he is not making a new point. He is drawing out the significance of what he had said in the opening verses of the chapter.[345]

I stress: all this is precisely election-theology, reworked and rethought around the Messiah. It is about the covenant purpose which the one God had for Israel, as Paul now saw it, and the way in which this had been fulfilled, and thereby reshaped, in and through Jesus as Israel's representative. This is how, in Paul's mind and heart, the strange vocation of Israel, shaped by the one God not least through the giving of Torah, has worked out. Israel itself was to be the place where 'sin', the great deceit, the great infection of the human race, was to be overthrown, condemned, defeated. This purpose, Paul declares, has now been accomplished in the Messiah.

This means that we must hold firmly in our minds a conviction which remained central for Paul: that this divine purpose, though he (Paul) had rethought it around the Messiah, was the purpose the one God had had in mind all along, from the beginning, in calling Israel, and particularly in giving the Torah. Torah had, all along, been the divinely appointed means of tricking 'sin', luring it to come and do its worst so that it might be condemned at that point, much as 'the rulers of this age' had been tricked into crucifying the lord of glory and so signing their own death-warrants.[346] Here we see again the plight–solution–plight spiral which we studied towards the close of the previous chapter. The revelation of a crucified Messiah has caused Paul to reflect, from all that he knew of Israel's traditions, on how Israel's God had done all things in such a way as to lead up to this point, but in a way which nobody before had imagined. When, therefore, we speak of 'election reworked', we must not imagine that Paul was merely playing games with the original doctrine, using it as a convenient peg on which to hang his own quite different ideas. He believed that, with Jesus

[343] 1 Cor. 2.8; Col. 2.13–15.

[344] Rev. 12.10.

[345] See the echoes of 8.1–4 in 8.32–4.

[346] 1 Cor. 2.8.

being revealed as Israel's Messiah, the true, original 'doctrine of election', the great Fact at the heart of Israel's national life, had at last been unveiled.

Consider once more. Paul knew that there was a 'problem of evil' before Jesus ever emerged into the public eye. But Paul had perhaps hoped that strenuous Torah-keeping, resulting maybe in more suffering of the kind undergone by the Maccabees, would see off the problem. He knew that the gentiles were wicked idolaters, and that their idolatry let loose forces of evil in the world that could do terrible damage. But he had perhaps hoped that one day the Messiah would come and smash them all with a rod of iron, dashing them into pieces like a potter's vessel. He had been aware that Israel itself (and he himself) was prone to sin. But he had presumably believed that the sacrificial system, not least the sin-offering, would deal with that problem.

What he had not envisaged, what so far as we can tell nobody had ever imagined, was that all these dreams and hopes would come true not just *through* the Messiah himself, as the agent of divine judgment and redemption, as the bringer of the new exodus, but *in the flesh of* the Messiah himself, the 'son of God' in the three senses we have seen (Messiah; Israel's representative; the one who shares the inner being of the one God). Paul had certainly not envisaged that the shameful death of 'God's son' would be the reason why he, Paul, would write a letter to Rome, the home of a different 'son of God' and a different 'good news', to say that he, Paul, was not ashamed of the 'good news' of the son of David whose resurrection had marked him out as son of God in power. There is indeed a line that runs straight from Romans 1.3–4 to Romans 8.3–4, taking in at a gulp on the way the huge argument of 3.21—4.25. It is the line which declares that here, in the apocalyptic gospel events, the God-given covenant purpose for Israel has come true at last. Paul's argument is this – and it stands here at the heart of his greatest letter: that the one God, in his supreme act of faithfulness, and through the faithfulness of the Messiah, had unveiled the inner meaning that had been present in the election of Israel from the beginning.

Once again we must take note of what has happened through our approaching Paul's soteriology in this way. The decisive statement in Romans 8.1–4 is nothing if not *forensic*. In 8.1 and 8.3 the cognate words *katakrima* and *katekrinen* send us back at once to the great Assize of 2.1–16, and that is quite deliberate. And yet Romans 8 is supposed to be the very heart of Paul's 'incorporative' christology and soteriology – as indeed it is. Likewise, we should not be surprised – as we would be if we listened to the siren call of those who want to split Romans 1—8 into two incompatible sections! – at the fact that Paul very carefully uses *dikaiosynē* and one of its key cognates in 8.1–11, despite the fact that in the normal divisions of the letter he had stopped using that language by the end of chapter 4, or at most the start of chapter 5. But this, too, is quite deliberate. To say it once more: *the division between 'juristic' and 'participationist' analyses of Paul's soteriology is based on a failure to understand his underlying 'covenantal' thought*. When he says that the 'right and proper verdict' of the law is now fulfilled 'in us, as we live not according to the flesh but according to the spirit' (8.4), we should hear the *dikaiōma* in question as the mirror-image of the *dikaiōma* spoken of in 1.32, the 'decree' that 'those who do such things deserve to die.'[347] After all, Romans is at one level about death and life; and here in 8.1–11 'life' is one of the main themes, the 'life' that the law promised (7.10) but could not give (8.3). Instead, 'the law of the spirit of life' (8.2) results in 'life and peace' (8.6), and will 'give life' to the mortal bodies of those who are 'in the Messiah' and indwelt by the spirit.[348]

And the key verse in all this, which has puzzled generations of commentators, is 8.10: the body is dead because of sin, but the spirit is life 'because of *dikaiosynē*'.[349] 'Because of righteousness', say older translations, as well they might; but what does this mean? It means, I suggest, that once again Paul has scooped up an entire train of thought from elsewhere in the letter and has placed it, in this highly condensed form, at the heart of the present argument. Here there should be no doubt: *dikaiosynē* refers to the verdict 'righteous' issued in the present over all those who believe, issued because of the Messiah's faithfulness, his self-giving to death. In this single line Paul has taken the whole argument of 3.21—4.25, as indeed he already did in 5.6–11, and is drawing the consequences, as he already promised in 1.16–17.[350] Just as Romans 3.24 indicated that 'being in Christ' belonged at the heart of the exposition of justification, so Romans 8.10 indicates that 'righteousness' – the status which results from the verdict of the divine court, the polar opposite of 'condemnation' as in 8.1, the status which carries with it the notion of 'covenant membership' as in Romans 4[351] – belongs at the heart of the exposition of 'being in Christ'.

There is therefore now no contradiction between 'justification' and 'being in Christ', between law court language and incorporative language; for the law of the covenant, the election reworked around the Messiah, has rescued Paul's theology from the sterile antitheses of later inappropriate categories. What the older schemes could not solve, because the place of Torah in Paul

[347] I therefore do not think that the *dikaiōma* in 8.4 refers to a kind of inner law keeping, as described in 8.5–8 (as most commentators: see e.g. Jewett 2007, 485), but rather to the 'just decree' which, on the analogy of 1.32, and with 2.7, 10, 13b in mind, might be expressed by saying, 'Those who do such things deserve to live.' When the actual commands of Torah are referred to, it is normally in the plural, *dikaiōmata*, as in e.g. Dt. 30.16, echoed in Rom. 2.26.

[348] On the significance of 'life' here, see e.g. Kirk 2008, esp. 125–31.

[349] Jewett 2007, 492 cites Lietzmann 1971, to the effect that the word-parallelism here is stricter than the thought itself ('as often in Paul', adds Lietzmann). Moo 1996, 492 sees the link with e.g. 5.21 but does not develop it.

[350] I earlier suggested (2002 [*Romans*], 584) that *dikaiosynē* here referred to the divine righteousness, but this seems to me now far less likely. Cranfield 1975, 390 assimilates *dikaiosynē* here, as do some translations, to 'justification', but this, though undoubtedly expressing a truth (against e.g. Käsemann 1980 [1973], 224, who insists that the word here must refer to spirit-led Christian behaviour; see too Keck 2005, 204), is not what Paul says. On the vexed question of 'spirit' (human, or divine?) I still think (against Wright 1991 [*Climax*], 202) that Paul is here speaking of the divine spirit, making the close link with 8.2 in particular (so, powerfully, e.g. Schreiner 1998, 414f., following e.g. Fee 1994, 550f.).

[351] Compare the antitheses in 2.12f.: some will be 'condemned', others 'justified'. For 'covenant membership' here see again *Climax*, 202.

seemed so opaque, has been resolved by paying attention both to the multi-layered narrative structure of his thought in general and to the covenantal narrative of Israel in particular. Once we place at the centre Jesus as Israel's Messiah, and then as Israel's *representative* Messiah, and see in him both the *katakrima* and the *dikaiōma*, mercy and truth will meet together, and even 'apocalyptic' and 'salvation history' may kiss each other. And, as we shall see, the notion of the spirit's indwelling will then give life and coherence to the whole mortal body of Pauline soteriology.

(v) Jesus the Messiah through Whom God's Love Holds His People Secure: Romans 8.31–9

All this comes to a fresh expression, not simply a restatement of what has gone before (though it contains that too), in the last great paragraph of Romans 8. Here it is clear that when Paul speaks of God's 'love' he really is thinking in the Deuteronomic categories of 'election'. 'Who shall bring a charge against God's elect (*kata eklektōn theou*)?', he asks, rhetorically; and he answers his own question with a messianic interpretation of three passages: Genesis 22, Isaiah 50 and Psalm 44. But it isn't only a 'messianic' interpretation. It is also a people-of-God-in-the-Messiah interpretation. It is about 'us', who, as in 8.17–21, share in the 'sufferings of the Messiah' so that 'we' can also share his glory.[352]

The interpretation of these three primary biblical passages (Law, Prophets and Writings) goes again to the very heart of Paul's reworking of election *around Jesus the Messiah*. We cannot stress too strongly that this is not a 'transfer' of 'election' from the community of ethnic Israel to someone else (e.g. a gentile 'church'). It is the focus of election on Jesus precisely as Israel's Messiah. If people (obviously, in Paul's day, Jews who did not believe that Jesus was Israel's Messiah) wanted to object to what Paul was doing, it was with his identification of Jesus as Messiah that they would have to quarrel, and did in fact quarrel. In our own day, a similar objection has hidden behind an apparently political complaint: 'the church' has supplanted 'Israel'. No doubt 'the church' has often been guilty of thinking just like that, and one contemporary trend in 'New Testament scholarship', namely the fad for a so-called 'apocalyptic' which has taken leave of its Jewish roots, decided that God has ignored the historical back-story of Israel and spoken of a completely new thing arriving in Jesus, is the most obvious current candidate. But Paul will have none of that. As far as he is concerned, the resurrection of Jesus (here at 8.34) is the anchor. Jesus is the Messiah; therefore all the Jewish traditions of 'election' must be refocused on him, reworked through him. This raises enormous problems – precisely the ones Paul himself raises in the next chapter, and part of what is going on in

[352] See Hays 1989a, 57–63.

Romans 8, paradoxically, is setting up those problems – but it also provides a different answer to those usually supposed.[353]

Here again, just as in 8.1–11, we find no contradiction between 'being in Christ' ('incorporative' or 'participatory' language) and the ideas of 'condemnation' and 'justification' ('forensic'). Romans 8.31–9 is the dramatic and appropriate conclusion as much to Romans 1—4 as to Romans 5—8. Paul's reference to Israel's God 'giving up' his son in 8.32 reminds us of 4.24–5 (and as we shall presently see Paul may be thinking of Abraham here, as well as there). His claim that the one God is the 'justifier', challenging anyone now to 'condemn', looks back through 8.1–4 all the way to 2.1–16 and to 3.21–6 in that light. His focus on the incarnate love which sustains those 'in Christ' through all sufferings echoes 5.1–11. The whole paragraph is about what it means to be 'in Christ'; but the whole paragraph only makes the sense it does because justification lies at its heart.

The Jewish traditions of election had their basis, of course, deep in scripture. Among those traditions, one that loomed large, giving historical root and validation to all subsequent ones, was Abraham's 'offering' of his 'only son' Isaac – or rather, his readiness to offer him, with a ram being killed at the last minute instead.[354] Many writers have traced the powerful and moving way in which this ancient story, full of psychological terror but also pregnant with covenantal meaning – loyalty pledged, obedience offered, promises reaffirmed – continued to resonate through the later 'moments' in Israel's story. Passover, the death of the lamb in place of the firstborn, was the most obvious.[355]

The story is dense enough for a three-hour opera, but is told in a mere nineteen verses. Here is the main narrative:

> After these things God tested Abraham. He said to him, 'Abraham!' And he said, 'Here I am.' He said, 'Take your son, your only son Isaac, whom you love (LXX *ton huion sou agapēton, hon ēgapēsas*; the LXX thus uses *agapētos* to represent *yehideka*, "your one and only"), and go to the land of Moriah, and offer him there as a burnt-offering on one of the mountains that I shall show you.' So Abraham rose early in the morning ...
>
> Isaac said to his father Abraham, 'Father!' And he said, 'Here I am, my son.' He said, 'The fire and the wood are here, but where is the lamb for a burnt-offering?' Abraham said, 'God himself will provide the lamb for a burnt-offering, my son.' So the two of them walked on together.
>
> When they came to the place that God had shown him, Abraham built an altar there and laid the wood in order. He bound his son Isaac, and laid him on the altar, on top of the wood. Then Abraham reached out his hand and took the knife to kill his son. But the angel of YHWH called to him from heaven, and said, 'Abraham, Abraham!' And he said, 'Here I am.' He said 'Do not lay your hand on the boy or do anything to him, for now I know that you fear God, since you have not withheld your son, your only son, from me'

353 Hays 1989a, 61: 'What Paul has done, in a word, is to interpret the fate of Israel christologically.' This I believe to be spot on in terms of Rom. 11.21, which Hays is there expounding; and the point here is that this interpretation grows directly out of Rom. 8 and elsewhere, where the *election* of Israel is interpreted christologically.

354 Isaac was of course Abraham's second son, but Sarah's only one; part of the strange darkness in the story is caused by the problem of Ishmael in the preceding chapters.

355 Levenson 1993 is now a classic treatment; see now Ripley 2010, with bibliog.

(*ouk epheisō tou huiou sou tou agapētou di'eme*; again the LXX *agapētos* translates *yehideka*, 'your one and only'). And Abraham looked up and saw a ram, caught in a thicket by its horns. Abraham went and took the ram and offered it up as a burnt-offering instead of his son. So Abraham called that place, 'YHWH will provide'; as it is said to this day, 'On the mount of YHWH it shall be provided.'

The angel of YHWH called to Abraham a second time from heaven, and said, 'By myself I have sworn, says YHWH: Because you have done this, and have not withheld your son, your only son (*tou huiou sou tou agapētou*, again translating *yehideka*), I will indeed bless you, and I will make your seed as numerous as the stars of heaven and as the sand that is on the seashore. And your seed shall possess the gate of their enemies, and by your seed shall all the nations of the earth gain blessing for themselves, because you have obeyed my voice.'[356]

Out of the thousand things one might say about this narrative, we confine ourselves to two. First, we are inevitably struck, and can only conclude that the narrator intends us to be struck, by the internal repetitions: Abraham's threefold 'Here I am', for sure, but particularly 'your son, your only son, the one you love', with the Hebrew word *yahad* repeated: 'the one', the singular son, the special and beloved one. This, of course, provided endlessly fertile soil for later Jewish elaboration and exploration of various kinds.[357] Such exploration returned again and again to the question of Abraham's 'seed', the people descended from Isaac and Jacob, and the way in which this family was sustained by the apparent validity of Abraham's 'sacrifice', and Isaac's willingness to be 'bound' (which took on more prominence in the tradition; granted that the sacrifice was in fact aborted at the last minute, the willingness of both father and son to go through with it became the key theological element). *This story became, in fact, both the narratival fountainhead and the theological substructure of Israel's election*, and guaranteed that at the heart of that notion of the people's chosenness there would be the strange and challenging notion of divine provision, a provision that went beyond and indeed counter to human expectation. God would bless the world through Abraham's 'seed', but from the beginning this seed, and this blessing, were to be seen as a gift of grace, an unexpected 'provision', not something that could be clung to or taken for granted. That, it need hardly be said, is a point which has resonated with multiple meanings in the history of the Jewish people through many centuries.

Second, it is precisely this story to which Paul goes back, through the clear allusion of Romans 8.32. He gives it the meaning one might almost have expected to emerge in chapter 4 and which, we might conclude, has been deliberately held back for this climactic moment. It is striking that in

[356] Gen. 22.1–3, 7–18.

[357] See, for a start, Ginzberg 1937 [1909], 1.279–86; and the developments outlined in Ripley 2010. The rich rabbinic developments of the theme, including some kind of 'atoning' significance, are evidently post-Christian (so e.g. Davies and Chilton 1978; Segal 1984), but fresh retellings of the story feature frequently in the second-Temple period (e.g. *Jub.* 17, 18; 4Q225; and various passages in Philo, Josephus, Ps.-Philo and *4 Macc.* noted in Ripley). Though Paul was probably not replying to a nascent Aqedah-based 'atonement' theology, then, there is no need to deny that he may have had the passage, and perhaps some contemporary Jewish interpretations, in mind (Fitzmyer 1993, 531f. is right to question a reference to the developed rabbinic tradition).

his exposition of Abraham's faith in Romans 4 Paul neither mentions nor alludes to Genesis 22 (unless the mention of Jesus and his death and resurrection in 4.24–5 be reckoned such an allusion; but if it is, it is already subversive). In the same way, it is striking that here in chapter 8 it is of course the covenant God himself who 'does not spare his only son'. Instead of Abraham, God; instead of Isaac, Jesus; *and, instead of a death averted, a death embraced.* There is here, quite obviously, a major *relativization* as well as a major recalling of that most crucial moment in Jewish election-theology. The 'offering of the beloved son' that stands at the narratival fountainhead for the newly revealed doctrine of election, giving it its particular theological shape, is not, after all, Abraham's offering of Isaac, but that immeasurably greater offering, towards which the Aqedah of Genesis 22 was simply the most striking and moving of long-range signposts.[358]

We can hardly stress too strongly a point already made but in need of repetition. The reason Paul could make this major move, still *within* second-Temple Judaism, was not in order to legitimate 'the church'; not because he saw Jesus as 'the church's Messiah' or 'the Messiah of Christian belief'; but precisely because he believed that Jesus was *Israel's* Messiah, the Messiah of Jewish expectation. Nor can we emphasize too strongly that the reason Paul regarded Jesus as Messiah was not because of polemical intentions in relation to his own idiosyncratic plan to include gentiles without them being circumcised (include them in what? we might ask), but because, and only because, he believed that Israel's God had raised this crucified would-be Messiah from the dead and that therefore (as in Romans 1.3–4) his messianic claim had been demonstrated beyond question.[359] The insistence upon gentile inclusion without circumcision, and on the view that all those 'in the Messiah' now constituted 'God's elect' (8.33), followed from that belief. 'If righteousness came through the law, the Messiah died for nothing.' It did not generate it.

If Paul has here provided a fresh reading of Genesis 22, he has done the same, in verses 33 and 34, with Isaiah 50.[360] His re-reading of this crucial prophetic passage represents a huge step, but one that is fully comprehensible once the basic structure of his belief is grasped. We recall that Paul frequently refers to his own ministry in terms of Isaiah 49. He seems not to have thought of the prophetic texts atomistically, as isolated fragments, but to have seen them – certainly these central chapters in Isaiah – as a seamless whole, more or less a continuous narrative.[361]

[358] For other ways of reading the Aqedah as echoed in the present passage (or, indeed, ways of denying such echoes), see the discussion in Jewett 2007, 536–8.

[359] Against Levenson 1993, ch. 15, esp. 209–13.

[360] See Wilk 1998, 280–4; against e.g. Jewett 2007, 541, who thinks the Isaianic echo is 'rather distant' and 'quite faint'.

[361] Paul seems to cling particularly to the sense that, whereas the servant might say that his work was 'in vain' (Isa. 49.4), the fresh commission would come, to restore the tribes of Israel and to be the light to the nations (49.6). See e.g. Gal 2.2; 4.11; 1 Cor. 15.58; 2 Cor. 6.2; Phil. 2.16; 1 Thess. 3.5; cp. too Isa. 65.23. On Isa. in Gal. see Ciampa 1998; in 2 Cor. 6, see Gignilliat 2007.

As far as we can tell, there were two main ways of reading the 'servant songs' in the Judaism of Paul's day. There was a 'messianic' reading; but, in this reading, the Messiah did not suffer, but rather inflicted suffering on the enemies of the covenant God (i.e. the gentiles), much as in Psalm 2 and the lines of thought that derive from it. There was a 'suffering' reading, for which the best early evidence is the martyr-theology in the book of Daniel; but this 'suffering' was not that of the Messiah. These two, I have argued elsewhere, had already been combined.[362] Paul here picks up the second reading in particular, where the 'servant' is construed as the people who, though suffering, are trusting Israel's God for deliverance in a great forensic judgment scene. But he does so because, first and foremost, this people has been constituted as the Messiah's people, who share his sufferings in order to share his glory and inheritance (8.17–18).

The echo of Isaiah 50 in Romans 8 not only locates the suffering community on the map of the divine promise to Israel. It enables Paul to tie this promise closely to the story of Abraham to which he has just alluded: 'Listen to me, you that pursue righteousness,' declares the prophet in the section immediately following:

> Look to the rock from which you were hewn, and to the quarry from which you were dug.
> Look to Abraham your father and to Sarah who bore you;
> for he was but one when I called him, but I blessed him and made him many.[363]

This in turn points forward, as does the echo of Genesis 22, not only to the massive question which Paul must address in Romans 9, but to the means by which he will answer it. 'Those who pursue righteousness', or not as the case may be, are the subject all through (as in 9.30). The way by which they are to understand the strange divine purposes in their history is through a fresh understanding of Abraham and Sarah (9.6–9). Isaiah 51 emphasizes again, in line with chapters 42 and 49, that the saving work for which the servant is called, and in which he is vindicated, extends to the nations far away (51.4–6).

This brings us back to Psalm 44 (LXX 43), quoted in verse 36. We have discussed this before in connection with monotheism itself.[364] Once again Paul is claiming that texts which speak about the people of God, about their allegiance to the God of the covenant and about their consequent suffering are properly to be understood in relation to those who belong to Jesus the Messiah.[365] This time, as in Galatians 2.20, he uses the language of 'love' in

[362] See *JVG* ch. 12, esp. 588–91.

[363] Isa. 51.1f.

[364] See above, 634–6.

[365] Jewett 2007, 548 suggests that the citation only makes sense if some in Rome had been questioning whether the sufferings of Paul and other Jewish Christians indicated that they were not true disciples. That is not impossible, but I suggest that the larger context of the psalm as a whole, and its earlier echo in 8.28 (see again above, 634–6), indicates that Paul, in addition to providing a citation from the 'writings' to go with Torah and prophets (vv. 32 and 34), was placing the whole early Christian movement on the map of the true people of the one God, praying this psalm of suffering and hope. See too the suggestive comments of Hays 1989a, 57–63, linking this psalm to Gen. 22 and noting its slightly fainter echoes of Isa. 53 (which, though far off from Ps. 44, is brought near by the reference to the 'servant' in 8.34).

relation to the Messiah himself, modifying or contextualizing that in the final verse (8.39) so that it becomes 'the love of God in the Messiah, Jesus our lord'. This notion of 'love' does not just, as it were, indicate a strong emotion on the part of the covenant God, an emotion which leads him both to generous self-giving and to unbreakable commitment no matter what may come in the way. It has to do with the divine covenant with Israel, sustained by the divine *hesed*, as celebrated again and again in scripture. Paul's reference here to God's love in the Messiah thus marks the Messiah and his people as the *covenant* people, the *elect*, as explicitly in verse 33.[366] This in turn links verses 35–9 closely to the Aqedah allusion in verse 32, because, as we saw, in the original Hebrew, and even more in the Septuagint, the stress there lies on Isaac as the 'beloved' son. Paul does not use that word here for the Messiah in relation to God, choosing instead to refer to him as *ho idios huios*, 'God's *own* son', his only and special son. The 'love' in the story now extends to all the Messiah's people: what has passed between father and son in the terrible self-giving of the cross now forms a unit from which covenant love reaches out to embrace that larger company. 'Who shall separate us from the Messiah's love? ... Nothing in all creation will be able to separate us from the love of God in the Messiah, Jesus our lord.'

The electing love of God in the Messiah is thus a *victorious* love, overcoming every force or power that might stand in its way, and enabling the objects of that love themselves to be 'completely victorious' (*hypernikōmen*, 8.37). As in 1 Corinthians 15.20–8, with which Romans 8 already has so much in common, Paul sees the present time as one in which the Messiah is winning the victory which will be complete when death itself is defeated, and God is 'all in all'. At every point in this celebratory conclusion to the argument of chapters 5—8, itself perhaps the most carefully constructed of any passage in his writings, he has made it clear that *the Jewish category of 'God's elect' has been redefined: first and foremost, in and as the Messiah himself, and second, and derivatively, to refer to the Messiah's people.* Election is reworked, at every point, around the Messiah, and specifically around his death and resurrection.

We may sum up where we have got to so far. It should be clear that Paul has consciously redrawn his picture of God's elect around Jesus of Nazareth, and that he has done so on the basis of his resurrection from the dead, which marked him out as Messiah. This in turn has enabled him to understand the crucifixion of Jesus as the event which, however paradoxically or unexpectedly, has actually accomplished the goal for which Israel had been chosen in the first place, namely that of dealing with the large-scale problem of evil. From this perspective we can see a flurry of other themes coming together, in all of which it appears that Paul was exploring, and expressing in fresh ways, the notion that in Jesus the Messiah the divine plan for Israel

366 *kata eklektōn theou*; one of the rare occurrences of the term in Paul, but the reality is everywhere. Here it is quite clear that 'God's elect', which in Judaism would unambiguously have meant ethnic Israel or some purified subset thereof, refers, equally unambiguously, to those who are 'in the Messiah'.

was coming to a fulfilment which was both the original divine intention and also far beyond anything Israel had previously imagined.

(vi) The Messiah, the Hope of Israel, and the Torah: Conclusion

We have already seen that for Paul Jesus embodied and expressed the faithful love of the covenant God for his people. We have seen that he thought *both* of Jesus *and* of himself in terms of the 'servant'-vocation highlighted in the central section of Isaiah.[367] We also saw, in the previous chapter, that Paul drew heavily on the Jewish 'wisdom' traditions to understand the truth about Jesus. This, though at one level an expression of rethought monotheism, is also an expression of reworked election, since it was precisely in Israel that 'wisdom', through the medium of Torah, was supposed to have come to dwell.[368] As in some of the same traditions, this meant that Jesus had to be seen as the place where the creator God had come to make his abode: Jesus was, in other words, the true Temple, the heart of the life of Israel:

> 19For in him all the Fullness was glad to dwell
> 20and through him to reconcile all to himself,
> making peace through the blood of his cross,
> through him – yes, things on the earth, and also the things in the heavens.[369]

> 9In him, you see, all the full measure of divinity has taken up bodily residence.[370]

This is what stands behind and underneath the notion explored at more length above, that Jesus somehow was able to *embody* the faithful love of the creator God, so that his death could be an *expression* of that love, indeed, its classic and defining expression (Romans 5.8–9). And this in turn means that Jesus, completely in line with the hope of Israel, was to be seen as the genuine human being, the 'true Adam', the ultimate image-bearer, doing for Adam what Adam could not do for himself, reversing the 'fall' and reinscribing the notion that image-bearing humans were to be set in authority over God's creation.[371] When he receives the 'inheritance' which is his as Messiah, in the parallel passages of Romans 8.17 and Galatians 3.29 and 4.1, 7, this is also *both* the 'inheritance' which was promised to Abraham *and* (since Abraham's task was to reverse the problem of Adam and so to get the 'true humanity' project back on track) the 'inheritance' of Adam himself. Jesus as Messiah thus inherits all that God had promised to Israel in the person of the king, that is, sovereignty over the world. With that, Jesus stands, for Paul, where Adam stood in Genesis 1.26–8.

[367] See Hays 1989a, 63.
[368] Sir. 24 etc. See above, 654–90.
[369] Col. 1.19f.
[370] Col. 2.9.
[371] Rom. 5.14–21; 8.29; 1 Cor. 15.20–8; Phil. 3.20f.

But it was, for Paul, the death of Jesus which ultimately accomplished that bringing together of the whole world. This is seen in passages we have studied such as Galatians 2.15–21, where Jesus' death is the principal reason why Jewish believers and gentile believers belong at the same table; 3.10–14, where Jesus' death opens the way for the Abrahamic blessing to flow to the nations; and Romans 3.21–31, where the faithful, redeeming, sacrificial death of Jesus is the means whereby Jew and gentile come together in faith. But the same thing is also clear in passages we have not studied, such as Ephesians 2.14–18, where the death of Jesus has broken down the dividing wall between the two great divisions of humanity, reconciling both to the one God in a single body and announcing peace.

All this means, in particular, that Jesus was, for Paul, the place where the highly paradoxical Torah itself came to full expression. One cannot think of Israel's election without thinking of Torah. One should not think of Paul's reworking of election around the Messiah without seeing that in this move the Torah is not set aside as an early, second-rate and now irrelevant attempt at solving the human problem, but is rather reaffirmed, with great paradox, and within a radically new context. Yes: the Torah was not the means of the 'revelation of God's righteousness' which came in the gospel; but nevertheless 'the law and the prophets bear witness to it' (Romans 3.21), and 'the law of faith' does not abolish the law, but rather establishes it (3.31). This does not merely mean that Paul can find scriptural proof-texts for the gospel. That is not the way he thought. Rather, it seems to mean that the Torah itself, seen precisely as Israel's charter of election, as the narrative of the divine purpose, came to definitive and conclusive fresh expression in Israel's representative Messiah – *both* in his death *and* in his resurrection. His whole life, with those moments as its defining climax, constituted for Paul his 'obedience', his 'faithfulness'. And, though Torah could not be the means of unveiling the divine righteousness, Torah nevertheless bore witness to the obedient faithfulness through which that unveiling took place.

What exactly does this mean? One might point to the striking formulae, in Paul and elsewhere, which highlight the sinlessness of Jesus.[372] That remains a remarkable enough thing to say about any human being who had lived a public life in very recent memory. But the idea of Torah coming to fresh expression in Jesus is considerably deeper than simply the early Christian belief that Jesus had lived without sin.

First, there is the *Shema* itself, a classic summary of Torah. We have seen that, for Paul, this came to full expression in Jesus; in him, according to 1 Corinthians 8.6, the *Shema* was fulfilled in a new and definitive way.

Second, in Romans 7.1—8.11, focused on the climactic 8.3–4, we have seen that *what the Torah could not do* the covenant God did by the sending of the son and the sending of the spirit. In particular, the death of the son brought to its head that condemnation of 'sin' which was necessary for its power to be broken. Torah had led 'sin' into the trap, the Israel-shaped trap

[372] 2 Cor. 5.21a; cf. Jn. 7.18; 8.46; Heb. 4.15; 7.26; 1 Pet. 2.22.

(Romans 5.20), getting it to do its worst right there, in Israel ... so that in Israel, or rather in Israel *in the person of the representative Messiah*, it could be condemned. That, as we shall see, is one of the vital moves which will help us understand Romans 9—11. But the point for the moment is that in the Messiah we see Israel's Torah coming to full, if again unexpected, expression. When he accomplishes his strange task, his bearing in the flesh of the divine condemnation of sin, Torah looks on with gladness. He has dealt with the sin-in-the-flesh which prevented its life-giving intention from coming to fruition.

This then plays out dramatically in Paul's fresh reading of Deuteronomy 30 in Romans 10. There, as we shall see, confessing Jesus as lord, and believing that he is raised from the dead, is counted as the equivalent of that Torah-observance to which Israel was called as the new covenant sign. And there Jesus as 'lord' is lord *of all*, Jew and gentile alike. This too, Paul would claim, is part of the significance of his representation of Israel, his summing up in himself of Israel's vocation as the elect people of the covenant God. Of course, this means at the same time that the Torah's role of keeping Jews separate from gentiles has been abolished, set aside.[373] But even there the note of fulfilment must not be missed, because even at that point Torah was (according to Paul) serving the *divine* purpose, working as a *paidagōgos* to keep Israel safe until the time of maturity. The very abolition of that particular role is itself part of the fulfilment.

Within Paul's mature thought, then, Jesus appears unambiguously as the man who served the creator and covenant God with utter, faithful obedience, obedience unto death; the faithful obedience which Israel should have offered but did not. Jesus appears as the man who then receives, on the third day, the resurrection as the sign that he was indeed 'God's son', the anointed king, Israel's representative, the world's true lord: in other words, the Messiah. And if Jesus is the place where Torah is strangely fulfilled, where Israel is strangely embodied, this is because, overshadowing even that great claim, he was the place where the faithfulness of the covenant God had been ultimately embodied as well. Monotheism freshly understood is the hidden secret behind election freshly reworked. And if the divine faithfulness has been embodied in the Israel-faithfulness of the Messiah, we should not be surprised if, ever after, the people who belong to the Messiah are thus to be defined in turn as Messiah-faithful people: *hoi ek pisteōs Christou*, 'those of the faithfulness of the Messiah'. That, in turn, is the key to one of Paul's most famous, and misunderstood, doctrines.

At the centre of it all, with the sharpest paradox, there stands the cross. The cross is, for Paul, the sign of the centre: the centre for Israel, the centre for humankind. It is the middle of everywhere, the definite line which refocuses edge-lured minds, the axis of everything. This could, of course, be seen, and has often been seen, as a mere human claim, one empire drawing its line *here* while another draws its line *there*. But we should be in no doubt

[373] Gal. 2.15–21; 3.10–14, 15–22; Eph. 2.14–18; Col. 2.13–15.

as to why Paul believed that the creator God had drawn it here, in the sign of a crossbar bisected by a vertical. The cross was, after all, the 'death of choice' for Romans to inflict on rebel subjects, for the greatest empire the world had ever known to stamp its authority on anyone who got in the way, particularly on anyone who spoke of, or seemed to be embodying, an alternative empire, a different *kind* of empire. For Paul, that was exactly Jesus' crime. He represented and embodied the kingdom which was Israel's dream: the kingdom of the creator God, through whose victory death itself would be defeated, so that with that defeat all the powers of the world might be called to account. Thus

> None of the rulers of this present age knew about this wisdom. If they had, you see, they wouldn't have crucified the lord of glory.[374]

> He stripped the rulers and authorities of their armour, and displayed them contemptuously to public view, celebrating his triumph over them in him.[375]

> God's wisdom, in all its rich variety, was to be made known to the rulers and authorities in the heavenly places – through the church! This was God's eternal purpose, and he's accomplished it in the Messiah, Jesus our lord.[376]

The cross stands, for Paul, as the arrow which marks the central point of 'the faithfulness of God'. It is the point from which the enthroned Messiah can look to east and west, to north and south, and like Abraham gaze upon all the lands of his inheritance. Their rulers have now been defeated through his death, and they and their people can be summoned to 'faithful obedience, for the sake of his name'.[377] It is through his 'giving himself for our sins' that he has 'delivered us from the present evil age': every syllable of that double statement must be given full weight if we are to understand how it is that the Messiah has accomplished the purpose for which the covenant God called Israel in the first place.[378]

Here, then, is Paul's vision of how the Messiah, particularly in his death and resurrection, had redefined around himself the very grammar of election, looking all the way back to Abraham. The patriarch believed, and was declared for ever 'in the right'. His seed would be enslaved within a land not theirs; God's faithfulness would guarantee both Passover and promise: inheritance, and blessing for the world. They waited. Psalms and prophets sang of peace, a covenant of justice. And, instead: exile; hope lost; the rise of bestial empires. Then, when the times and tears had overflowed, God sent his only son, the strangest king, to be for Israel what they could not be: obedient; faithful; Passover in person. He was the seed, the servant and the son; the chosen; the beloved; the victory won.

[374] 1 Cor. 2.8.

[375] Col. 2.15.

[376] Eph. 3.10–11.

[377] Gen. 13.14; cf. 28.14; Ps. 2.8; Rom. 8.17; 1.5.

[378] Gal. 1.4 (against Martyn 1997a, 88–91, who divides the verse into two and has Paul only really approving the first half).

4. Election Reworked around the Spirit: the Messiah's Justified People

(i) Introduction

I shall now approach what is arguably Paul's most famous doctrine, and for many theologians the centre of his thought. I shall come at it from an angle that most will find unfamiliar. I believe that this way in, despite its apparent novelty, offers a direct route to its very heart. I propose that we envisage Paul's soteriology, including but going wider than his 'doctrine of justification', in terms once more of his reworking of the Jewish doctrine of election, dependent on the christological understanding we have just studied, but this time particularly in the light of the spirit. If the election of Israel was the solemn and unbreakable divine promise to save the world through Abraham's seed, Paul sees that promise as *accomplished* in the Messiah and *applied* through the spirit. And 'justification' is something that happens, as it were, right in the middle of that work. Those who have just read the previous chapter will perhaps realize that the fresh vision of 'justification' which I am proposing stands squarely on the foundations of Paul's fresh vision of 'monotheism'.

In terms of the history of Pauline interpretation, this proposal aims to accomplish four important things. First, it enables us to show, in terms of the structure of the argument as well as its detailed content, that the stand-off between 'juridical' and 'participationist' themes in Paul can be resolved once and for all by the appeal to the more basic Jewish category of God's plan *for* Israel and *through* Israel: that is, through a fresh appreciation and appropriation of the language of 'election' and particularly 'covenant', the larger category within which the language of the law court and the language of incorporation nest comfortably side by side. Second, and consequent upon this, it locates 'justification' solidly within Paul's vision of the Messiah as Israel's representative; that is, in traditional dogmatic language, it places 'justification' within the 'in Christ' complex – but *without* thereby relativizing it or implying that it plays only a minor function, as in the tradition which has followed Wrede and Schweitzer all the way to Sanders and now Campbell. Third, it will enable us to differentiate between the many different aspects of Paul's thought about how the people-of-God-in-the-Messiah are rescued from sin and death, and about who and what they now really are, without dividing these different aspects or playing them off against one another. Fourth, in and through all of this we can insist both (a) that Paul's vision of justification and salvation remains rooted in the promises given to Abraham and his 'seed' (in other words, he does not sweep these to one side in favour of mere novelty; he remains a deeply and utterly Jewish theologian) and (b) that this vision does not supplant ethnic Israel in favour of 'the church', but rather sees ethnic Israel and its election summed up gloriously in Israel's own Messiah and his death and resurrection, generating an 'Israel' which is then defined, once more, through and in relation to him precisely as Israel's Messiah. This will satisfy neither the ardent 'sweeping supersessionist', for whom nothing short of a new act without historical antecedent will do, nor the ardent 'anti-supersessionist' for whom nothing will do short of a denial that Jesus was Israel's Messiah. Paul will not please either party, and neither shall we. We shall aim merely to satisfy the criteria of historical and theological investigation by demonstrating the deep structural and exegetical coherence of his thought at this, one of its most contested points.

It is important to note, before going any further, that the word 'justification' has itself had a chequered career over the course of many centuries of debate. As the major historian of the doctrine has noted, the word has long since ceased to mean, in ecclesial debates, what it meant for Paul himself – which is confusing, since the debates have gone on referring to Paul as though he was in fact talking about what they want to talk about. It is as though the greengrocer treated you to a long discussion of how onions are grown, and how best to cook with them, when what you had asked was how much he would charge for three of them.[379]

The range of the word 'justification' has sometimes been expanded to the point where it has been used to denote the whole of soteriology, starting with the mysterious grace of the creator God and going all the way through to final salvation. 'Justification' has then regularly been confused with 'salvation' (a problem exacerbated by many translations that have muddled up the words for 'righteousness' and 'salvation', not least in Isaiah 40—55).[380]

This has had a dangerous double effect. On the one hand, when people have seen how the different elements of Paul's soteriology are all interconnected they have sometimes used the word 'justification' as though it covered all of them. They have then highlighted one or other of those elements as if it were itself the heart of 'justification' rather than a vital part of 'salvation', irrespective of the actual meaning of the word itself and its very specific job in its contexts. On the other hand, it has been possible for people who see the sharp and focused job the word actually performs to suppose that this precise meaning can then be isolated, put on a pedestal and used to relativize, or even to warn against, all the other interconnected elements of what Paul actually says. The first expands the word to cover too much data. The second shrinks the data to fit the actual word.

Thus, in the first category, we have the famous discussion of Hans Küng, in which, by expanding 'justification' to mean more or less 'how people get saved', he discovers that, at that level of generality, he agrees with Karl Barth.[381] More recently, we have had proposals that the actual *meaning* of 'justification' itself can be focused on the inner transforming work of the

[379] See McGrath 1986, 1.2f., discussed in Wright 2009 [*Justification*], 59f. (US edn., 79f.). Cf. my earlier treatments in e.g. Wright 1980 ('Justification', reprinted in *Perspectives* ch. 2).

[380] It is startling to find so careful an exegete as Schreiner (1998, 68 n. 12) saying that he does not distinguish as sharply as some between 'righteousness' and 'salvation'.

[381] Küng 1964 [1957].

spirit.[382] In the second category, we have the fierce reaffirmation of a strict protestant emphasis, in which 'justification' denotes simply the divine declaration pronounced over faith, through which 'the righteousness of Christ' is imputed to the believer, and in which any attempt to add anything else – 'transformation', 'being in Christ', 'ecclesiology', 'ethics', whatever – is deemed to be a dangerous dilution of divine prerogative, leading people to rely, for their sense of identity and assurance, on something about themselves rather than solely on the sovereign grace of the one God.[383]

Over against both of these positions, and mindful of the impossibility in a book of this size of debating with more than a limited selection of conversation partners, I wish to argue for a third option. I agree with the first viewpoint that Paul's language of 'justification' is closely, carefully and consistently integrated with all other aspects of his soteriology. But I agree with the second that the word 'justification' itself retains a very particular and clear-cut meaning which cannot be expanded to cover those other aspects. Is it possible to hold these two things together?

Only if we include all three of Paul's basic elements. Too often discussion has been confined to two: (a) the grace of the one God and (b) the work of the Messiah. These are obviously vital, but for Paul they are intimately connected with (c): the work of the spirit. As we have seen, this forms a key part of his redefinition of monotheism itself, and what he says about justification, as with the larger category of election itself, grows directly out of that. The holy spirit is, in fact, the usually forgotten element in justification, and I am convinced that only when we come at the doctrine from this angle (taking as read all that has already been said about the one God and the Messiah) can we gain the full Pauline picture.[384]

(ii) Election Redefined: Gospel and Spirit

The obvious place to begin is with 'the gospel'. Paul defines himself as a gospel-person: his chosen self-designation, at the start of his most carefully thought-out letter, is that of someone 'set apart for God's gospel'. He can state the content of his 'gospel' in a variety of ways, always focused on something the creator God has done, in fulfilment of promise, in and through Jesus of Nazareth, Israel's Messiah:

[382] e.g. Gorman 2009, ch. 2; e.g. 55, speaking of 'justification' and 'reconciliation' as being 'synonymous'. See below. Gorman brings together 'co-crucifixion', 'transformation' and much more, which does indeed reflect the complex Pauline interplay of ideas; but I question whether Paul uses the word 'justification' and its cognates to *denote* this larger complex.

[383] See particularly e.g. Piper 2002; 2007 (to which I respond in *Justification*); among many others, e.g. Waters 2004. Two symposia setting out a variety of views are Husbands and Trier 2004 and McCormack 2006b; my own essay in the latter vol. is reprinted in *Perspectives* ch. 18. A massive work bent upon reaffirming a traditional protestant viewpoint over against the so-called 'new perspective' is Carson, O'Brien and Seifrid 2001–4.

[384] On all this, see the helpful and provocative work of Vanhoozer 2011, and my response in the same vol.

> [1]Let me remind you, brothers and sisters, about the good news which I announced to you. You received this good news, and you're standing firm on it, [2]and you are saved through it, if you hold fast the message I announced to you – unless it was for nothing that you believed! [3]What I handed on to you at the beginning, you see, was what I received, namely this: 'The Messiah died for our sins in accordance with the Bible; [4]he was buried; he was raised on the third day in accordance with the Bible; [5]he was seen by Cephas, then by the Twelve; [6]then he was seen by over five hundred brothers and sisters at once, most of whom are still with us, though some fell asleep; [7]then he was seen by James, then by all the apostles; [8]and, last of all, as to one ripped from the womb, he appeared even to me.'[385]

> [1]Paul, a slave of King Jesus, called to be an apostle, set apart for God's good news, [2]which he promised beforehand through his prophets in the sacred writings – [3]the good news about his son, who was descended from David's seed in terms of flesh, [4]and who was marked out powerfully as God's son in terms of the spirit of holiness by the resurrection of the dead: Jesus, the Messiah, our lord! [5]Through him we have received grace and apostleship to bring about believing obedience among all the nations for the sake of his name. [6]That includes you, too, who are called by Jesus the Messiah.[386]

Two significantly different definitions, but with a single ultimate content: prophetic promise, God's action in the Messiah and his death and resurrection, and the resulting summons to believing obedience.

We can track each element of this a little further. The prophetic promise is what we should expect from the word 'gospel' itself, since its obvious biblical background is found in one of Paul's favourite texts, the central section of Isaiah. There, the 'good news' is that the covenant God has fulfilled his ancient promises and is now rescuing his people from the slavery caused by their own sin, defeating the pagan empire that has held them captive and sending them home to their promised land – and, in so doing, is *revealing himself*, his sovereign kingship, his righteousness, his salvation and above all his glory. And all this happens through the work of the 'servant'. The second time we meet 'the one who tells good news' is immediately before the final poem in which the suffering and death of the 'servant' effects forgiveness and liberation for God's people.[387]

The other obvious context for 'gospel' in Paul was the world where Caesar reigned supreme. In that world, Caesar's birth, his accession and his rule itself were spoken of as 'good news' – as indeed they were, in a fairly limited sense, for those who had suffered the chaos of civil war and all that went with it. By Paul's day that threat had receded for the moment; the notion of 'good news' was no doubt received with the usual measure of detachment and cynicism which accompanies the self-glorying of empires.[388]

But when Paul spoke of 'gospel' he thereby denoted a message which, in fulfilment of the scriptural prophecies and in implicit confrontation with

[385] 1 Cor. 15.1–8.

[386] Rom. 1.1–6. Bird 2007, 69 rightly notes that neither of these 'gospel summaries' mentions justification, and quotes Luther in support: 'The gospel is a story about Christ, God's and David's Son, who died and was raised and is established as lord. This is the gospel in a nutshell' (*LW* 35.118). Would that all Luther's would-be followers had paid attention.

[387] Isa. 52.7, pointing to 52.13—53.12; cf. 40.9; 41.27; 61.1; see too 60.6.

[388] Details in ch. 5 above. For the question of different modes of written resistance to empires, see e.g. Scott 1990, with Portier-Young 2011, Part I.

the newer imperial realities, declared the 'good news' of God's kingdom in and through the life, messianic achievement and supremely the death and resurrection of Jesus. This gospel message far transcended the individualistic message of 'how to be saved' which the word 'gospel' has come to denote in much contemporary western Christian expression. It remained intensely personal in its radical application, but only because it was first cosmic and global in scope: the world had a new lord, the Jewish Messiah, raised from the dead. That is why, as we saw, for Paul 'the gospel' even included the news of the just divine judgment against all human wickedness. In a world of moral and social chaos, 'judgment' is good news, as the Psalms insisted repeatedly.[389] Now, for Paul, the 'good news' of Jesus told a story which (a) stretched backwards to Abraham and the prophets, (b) looked on to an eschaton in which the creator God would be all in all, (c) focused on the crucial events to do with Jesus as Messiah and (d) challenged its hearers to respond with *hypakoē pisteōs*, 'faithful obedience'.[390]

This brief discussion of Paul's gospel thus indicates that, for him, 'the gospel', also translatable as 'the good news', was the *power* of the creator God. It is tempting to say, 'the gospel *carried* this divine power,' or 'the gospel *conveyed* this power.' Paul simply says it *is* this power:

> [14]I am under obligation to barbarians as well as to Greeks, you see; both to the wise and to the foolish. [16]I'm not ashamed of the good news; it is God's power, bringing salvation to everyone who believes – to the Jew first, and also, equally, to the Greek. [17]This is because God's covenant justice is unveiled in it, from faithfulness to faithfulness. As it says in the Bible, 'the just shall live by faith'.[391]

It is important to note that 'the gospel' here in Romans 1.16 does not mean 'how to be saved'. Nor does it mean 'how to be justified', as in some popular readings of verse 17. The logic of the sentences indicates without any doubt that 'the gospel' here *must refer back* to what he has already said in 1.3–4: that, the statement about Jesus, is the *content* of the gospel, and what is described here in 1.16–17 is its *effect*. In the original there is a clear sequence marked out by the repeated *gar*, 'for': 'I am eager to preach the gospel to you in Rome, *for* I am not ashamed of the gospel, *for* it is God's power to salvation, *for* God's *dikaiosynē* is revealed in it.' Turning these 'for' clauses the other way around, into 'therefore's, we read: God's *dikaiosynē* is revealed in the gospel, *therefore* it is God's power to salvation, *therefore* I am not ashamed of it, *therefore* I am eager to preach it to you in Rome. Either way the result is the same. 'The gospel' is not itself 'how to be saved' or 'how to be justified'. 'The gospel' is God's good news, promised long ago, about his dying and rising son, the Messiah, the lord of the world. *When this message is announced, things happen*: (a) the creator God is shown to be 'in the right' in that he has kept his promises, (b) people of all sorts, Jew and Greek

[389] e.g. Pss. 67.4; 96.10–13; 98.7–9.

[390] e.g. Rom. 1.5; 16.26.

[391] Rom. 1.14, 16–17.

alike, receive 'salvation' as a result of the divine power, (c) Paul is not ashamed (as he might have been, announcing a message which he knew to be folly to Greeks and a scandal to Jews) and (d) he is the more eager to preach the same message anywhere and everywhere, not least right under Caesar's nose in Rome.

But how then does this 'power' function? Paul is in no doubt: when he tells the story of Jesus as the long-promised crucified and risen Messiah of Israel, and announces that he is now the world's true lord, *God's spirit is at work*. Gospel and spirit go tightly together in his theology. Paul does not envisage a sequence of events in which first he tells people about Jesus, then they decide whether or not they are going to believe his message, and only then does the spirit descend upon those who have already believed. For Paul, belief itself is something which is effected on the one hand through the spirit and on the other through the word of the gospel – which he can also summarize as 'the word of the cross', especially when he wants to rub his hearers' noses in the shocking reality of that shameful event.[392]

This ought not to be controversial, because some of the central passages where Paul says more or less exactly this are straightforward and clear. The faith which believes the gospel is the faith which believes that Jesus rose from the dead, and that he is now the world's true lord: that is what Paul says in Romans 10.6–13, which is full of resonances with 1.15–17. But 'nobody can say "Jesus is lord" except by the holy spirit': that is a basic criterion which he sets out for the muddled Corinthians at the beginning of his discussion of spiritual gifts.[393] This should alert us to the fact that, although he does not mention the spirit expressly in Romans 10, at the crucial point in his argument he quotes from Joel 2.32 ('all who call on the lord's name will be rescued'), which is the continuation of the great promise that in the last days the covenant God promises to 'pour out his spirit upon all flesh'.[394] I and others have argued elsewhere that we must understand the same work of the spirit here as Paul alludes to elsewhere.[395]

In particular, we might notice the 'new covenant' passages such as Romans 2.25–9, 2 Corinthians 3 and Romans 7.4–6. It should be clear from these, and especially from Romans 8.9–11 where Paul insists that anyone who does not possess the spirit of the Messiah does not belong to him, that the gift of the spirit is not a *further* gift, out beyond initial Christian experience or even initial Christian faith, but is rather the life-giving energy by which someone is enabled, in the first place, to believe that the one God raised Jesus and to confess that Jesus is lord.

This is the import of one of the most striking Pauline affirmations of God's reworking of 'election' through powerful word and spirit:

[392] 1 Cor. 1.18—2.5.

[393] 1 Cor. 12.3.

[394] Joel 2.28.

[395] See Wright 2002 [*Romans*], 666; and e.g. Schreiner 1998, 562. It is surprising to find that Fee 1994 has no mention of Rom. 10.13.

> [4]Dear family, beloved by God, we know that God has chosen you; [5]because our gospel didn't come to you in word only, but in power, and in the holy spirit, and in great assurance.[396]

'We know that God has chosen you': this, in Greek, is *eidotes tēn eklogēn hymōn*, 'knowing your election'. We could have deduced as much from the title 'beloved by God', but this confirms it. Here we have an explicit statement of 'election reworked': the notion of 'election' is of course rooted in the scriptures, but Paul is cheerfully restating it in relation to those who have heard and received the gospel. And the sign of that *eklogē*, that 'election' – of a small bunch of pagans in a busy seaport in northern Greece! – is that 'the gospel' has not simply come to them in an empty 'word', but in power, in the spirit and with 'great assurance', *plērophoria pollē*. The word *plērophoria* already means 'full conviction'; adding *pollē* might seem over-egging the pudding, but the result is as much conviction as a sentence can possibly carry, 'full and complete conviction', 'total assurance'. Whatever it was that the spirit was doing, it worked.

Paul describes his 'gospel' a few verses later in a different but related way. The Thessalonians, he says,

> turned to God from idols, to serve a living and true God, and to wait for his son from heaven, whom he raised from the dead – Jesus, who delivers us from the coming fury.[397]

That is a thumbnail sketch, from another angle, of the same message we find in Romans 1 and 1 Corinthians 15. The elements are the same: the God of creation and covenant; the son of God whom he raised from the dead; the coming day of judgment; the assurance of deliverance.

The second Thessalonian letter offers a similar compact expression of what Paul thought happened when people believed the gospel. Here, after having sketched the terrible fate awaiting those who refuse to love and believe the truth, Paul refers once more to what happened to the Thessalonians when he preached the gospel to them:

> [13]But we always owe God a debt of gratitude for you, my family beloved by the lord, because God chose you as the first fruits of his work of salvation, through sanctification by the spirit and belief of the truth. [14]To this he called you through our gospel, so that you might obtain the glory of our lord Jesus the Messiah.[398]

'The gospel', then, is the instrument through which the covenant God 'calls'; and when Paul says 'call' he means an effective, powerful summons.[399] The spirit is the driving force behind this; belief of the truth is the first consequence, as one key element in being 'set apart' by the spirit for the divine purposes. Ultimate glory is the goal; redefined election is the overall picture.

[396] 1 Thess. 1.4f.

[397] 1 Thess. 1.9f.

[398] 2 Thess. 2.13f.

[399] For the sense of 'call' here see the summary statement in Kruse 1993, with earlier bibliog.

This short statement actually anticipates the great summary in Romans 8.28–30 (chosen, called, glorified).

Paul, clearly, does not have a single formula for speaking of how the gospel does its work. He says something slightly different each time he mentions the point, giving us the sense that this is something he has observed again and again and which he can describe in a variety of ways. Returning to 1 Thessalonians, we find him putting it like this:

> [13]So, therefore, we thank God constantly that when you received the word of God which you heard from us, you accepted it, not as the word of a mere human being but – as it really is! – the word of God which is at work in you believers.[400]

God's word *at work*: the Greek is *energeō*, something of a favourite with Paul. God 'works' through Peter's gospel ministry to the circumcised, and through Paul's to the uncircumcised.[401] God 'worked' in the Messiah in raising him from the dead, and that same power is at work in his people.[402] God is 'at work' in your midst, he says to the Philippians, to will and to work for his good pleasure.[403] Whatever variety of Christian gift is being exercised, whatever ministry is going ahead, it is the same God who 'works' all of them in everyone.[404] And, in a particularly telling passage for our present theme, this God 'works' powerful deeds in the midst of the Galatians, as he did in the initial arrival of the gospel itself:

> [2]There's just one thing I want to know from you. Did you receive the spirit by doing the works of Torah, or by the message which produced faith (*ex akoēs pisteōs*)? [3]You are so witless: you began with the spirit, and now you're ending with the flesh? [4]Did you really suffer so much for nothing – if indeed it is going to be for nothing? [5]The one who gives you the spirit and performs powerful deeds among you – does he do this through your performance of Torah, or through the message which produced faith (*ex akoēs pisteōs*)?[405]

This can be read (and translated) in such a way as to make it sound as though one *first* hears and believes and only *then*, as a kind of reward, is granted the spirit. But this, I am convinced, is wrong. The key repeated phrase, *ex akoēs pisteōs*, could certainly mean, by itself, 'through the hearing of faith', that is, through the 'hearing' which is a hearing-and-believing.[406] One might even translate it 'through hearing and believing' – which could (though not necessarily) be taken to mean that the sequence is: first, hearing; second, believing; third, receiving the spirit. But the word *akoē* in Greek, while it can mean 'hearing', either the faculty of hearing or the act of

[400] 1 Thess. 2.13.

[401] Gal. 2.8; cf. Col. 1.29.

[402] Eph. 1.20; cf. 3.20.

[403] Phil. 2.13.

[404] 1 Cor. 12.6.

[405] Gal. 3.2–5.

[406] See the helpful outline of options in Hays 2000, 251f. (and see more fully Hays 2002 [1983], 124–32); de Boer 2011, 174f.; both emphasize the objectivity of the proclamation rather than the human act of hearing and believing. On the other side, see e.g. Williams 1989; Dunn 1993, 154.

hearing, or even the organ of hearing, i.e. the ear, can also mean 'the thing which is heard', in the sense of a report, a rumour, a message, an account. This is the sense in which *ex akoēs pisteōs* is more regularly, and I believe rightly, taken.[407] The message itself is the thing which does the work – and the work here is the work precisely of the spirit.

The second key word here, *pisteōs*, 'of faith', could then have at least two meanings and be taken in at least two senses, depending on how the genitive is read. *Pistis* can mean 'faith' or 'faithfulness', and the genitive by itself is sufficiently flexible to mean either 'which concerns' or 'which produces'. We thus have:

1. The message which concerns faith: i.e. a message about faith itself. This is unlikely: Paul announces the Messiah. Faith is what results from that announcement, not the content of the announcement itself.
2. The message which *produces* faith. This is quite likely. Certainly Romans 1.15–17 and the passages above from the Thessalonian letters assume that the gospel message evokes faith.
3. The message which concerns *faithfulness*. This is quite possible: as we have seen, one way of Paul's telling the story of Jesus was precisely to do with his death as the great act of faithfulness. It is quite likely, as we saw, that Paul was referring to the Messiah's faithful death in Galatians 2.16–21.
4. The message *which produces* faithfulness. This is possible, but less likely. Paul does believe that gospel-believers are called to be 'faithful'. That is probably the meaning of *pistis* in Galatians 5.22. But the main thing here seems to be that the Galatians, like Abraham, *believed* the good news when it was spoken to them.

The likely options, then are (2) and (3), and for our present purposes it does not much matter which we choose. The point, either way, is that the agency through which the spirit has worked in their lives is the *message* through which the covenant God has worked – the message which, indeed, may well have been couched in terms of the Messiah's faithfulness, and certainly resulted in the production of 'faith' in the hearers. As we shall see, that nexus, across what seems to us a quite substantial gap between two different meanings of *pistis* – a gap which may have seemed much smaller to Paul! – is part of the point: when the gospel is announced, the spirit works *through* the message that is proclaimed. The result, one way or another, is 'faith'. That is what Paul is talking about for at least half of Galatians. At the start of the vital chapter (Galatians 3) in which the whole point is precisely the fulfilment of the promises to Abraham concerning his family, and the reshaping of that family not around Moses but around the Messiah, Paul sees the work of the spirit, through the gospel, as foundational. This is, for him, what the reworked election looks like in practice.

[407] So BDAG 36.

If the work of the spirit, producing the reshaped family, is thus one of the immediate and necessary correlates of Paul's gospel, we should expect to see in his writings statements about that family which reflect this view. One of the most dense and powerful, and decisive for understanding several other debates and especially for framing his doctrine of justification itself, is Romans 2.25–9, especially the final verse. Here, in the middle of what is normally but misleadingly thought of simply as a demonstration of universal sinfulness, Paul sketches the spirit-shaped version of 'election' which continues to resonate throughout much of the letter:

> Circumcision, you see, has real value for people who keep the law. If, however, you break the law, your circumcision becomes uncircumcision. Meanwhile, if uncircumcised people keep the law's requirements, their uncircumcision will be regarded as circumcision, won't it? So people who are by nature uncircumcised, but who fulfil the law, will pass judgment on people like you who possess the letter of the law and circumcision but who break the law.
>
> The 'Jew' isn't the person who appears to be one, you see. Nor is 'circumcision' what it appears to be, a matter of physical flesh. The 'Jew' is the one in secret; and 'circumcision' is a matter of the heart, in the spirit rather than the letter. Such a person gets 'praise', not from humans, but from God.

This is as clear a statement of election-reworked-by-the-spirit as any we find in Paul. Following on from the dismissal of the 'boast' of 'the Jew' in 2.17–24,[408] Paul is here anticipating his later arguments in order to show, at the present moment in the letter, that the covenant God is not going to be restricted in his purposes by the failure of 'the Jew'. The covenant God has not given up on the category of 'circumcision', on the idea of there being an elect people; he has merely redefined it, as in Philippians 3.3. Nor is the idea of such a redefined circumcision a hypothetical category which Paul will later declare to be null and void.[409] The 'poetic sequence' of Romans, that is, the way things are laid out in the letter itself, by no means corresponds, as generations have misleadingly supposed, to the implicit 'referential sequence', the *ordo salutis* beloved of dogmaticians, in which Romans 1.18—3.20 is *only* about 'demonstrating that all are sinful', 3.21—4.25 *only* about 'justification by faith' and 5—8 *only* about 'being in Christ' (or whatever). That is not how Paul writes.[410] He is once again 'borrowing' from his

[408] See the article in *Perspectives* ch. 30.

[409] cf. e.g. Watson 2004, 352f.; though Watson rightly sees that 'the distinctively Christian terminology in 2.27–9 is a difficulty' for this view. A fatal difficulty, in my opinion. Bell 2005, 190–6 argues unconvincingly that 2.27–9 describes non-Christians; the fact that 1.18—3.20 as a whole is arguing that 'all have sinned' does not mean that Paul cannot include within that argument hints of other themes.

[410] For the distinction between 'poetic' and 'referential' sequences, see Petersen 1985, 47–9, discussed in *NTPG* 403f. Confusion here has generated perplexity among interpreters who have supposed that Paul should not have spoken so soon in the letter about people actually fulfilling the law; but that is to treat the *poetic* sequence as if it were *referential* (see discussion in Moo 1996, 176). The fact that Paul is using clever rhetoric here, as throughout Rom. 2 and 3, does not however mean that 'we should not . . . drag "gospel" into all this' (Bryan 2000, 96). The parallels in Phil. 3, 2 Cor. 3 and Rom. 7.6 indicate that the present passage belongs tightly within his central and gospel-based theology. This is not to 'christianize' his argument 'too early' (Byrne 1996, 104); that, too, confuses 'poetic' and 'referential'. The present passage is *both* an 'inner-Jewish' discussion (the implied dialogue of 2.17–29) *and* a key move within the larger, developing argument of the letter.

fuller expositions – in this case, Romans 8 and Romans 10 – in order, briefly but powerfully, to show what, in his view, 'circumcision', and even 'Jew' itself, now mean. Other Jewish writers, notably Philo, had discussed the question of circumcision and its meaning, but Paul, though not here shifting from strictly Jewish and indeed biblical arguments (in other words, not moving into a Platonic mode of thought), is nevertheless far more radical than Philo or any other contemporary Jew had been.[411]

We note four things in particular about this revised election. First, these people who are now to be called 'circumcision' actually 'keep the law's requirements' (2.26); they 'fulfil the law' (2.27). Paul has not yet, of course, explained in Romans how such a thing can be.[412] For the moment the idea of uncircumcised people keeping the commandments sounds like an oxymoron, much as 1 Corinthians 7.19.[413] He clearly has in mind a different sort of law-fulfilment, to which he will refer again obliquely in 3.27 and 8.5–8, and again, still more obliquely, in 9.31–2, before suddenly explaining what he means in 10.5–13, and then going on to a wider application in 13.8–10. How this works out we shall see in due course. But for the moment we can say that the proposal that there might be a category of people to be called 'circumcision', who in some sense keep the law, and yet who are not themselves circumcised Jews, is indeed a drastic reworking of election. And, though Paul does not mention Jesus in this short section (of course, Paul would say Jesus was presupposed), he does mention the spirit as the agent by which election has been reworked.

Second, remarkably, Paul claims that these 'uncircumcised lawkeepers' will *judge* the 'circumcised lawbreakers'. The idea of the elect people sitting in judgment, which we find again in 1 Corinthians 6.2, goes back to Daniel 7.22.[414] It is, very specifically, part of the idea of the chosen people. Now this, too, is reworked, and in a shocking way: instead of the Jews judging the nations of the world, Paul envisages these uncircumcised lawkeepers as judging those Jewish lawbreakers. (We should I think assume that 'lawbreakers' here is also a redefined category.) It is hard to overstate just how powerful this point of redefined election actually is.

Third, Paul draws a contrast between 'Jew' and 'Jew': the outward one and the 'secret' one. This anticipates, among other things, his distinction of 'Israel' and 'Israel' in 9.6. To show exactly what he means, he takes the word 'Jew' itself, which in its Hebrew form means 'praise', and declares that the 'Jew in secret' gets 'praise' – in other words, receives this noble appellation –

[411] So, rightly, Barclay 2011, ch. 3 (orig. 1998), against e.g. Boyarin 1994. It is quite possible that Paul is aware of 'circumcision' and 'uncircumcision' as terms which would be heard polemically in Rome (so e.g. Marcus 1989), but this has not, I think, shaped his actual argument.

[412] That is presumably why Käsemann (1980 [1973], 73) resists the idea that v. 26 already refers to gentile Christians, only allowing this in v. 29 (75) (note Käsemann's antipathy towards any kind of 'law-fulfilment', as at 76f.); but this is unnecessarily restrained. Paul regularly introduces a topic obliquely, bringing it step by step towards full clarity. Moo 1996, 171 points cautiously in the right direction.

[413] See above, 361, 513; and below, 1036, 1434–43.

[414] cf. too e.g. Wis. 3.8; 4.16; *Jub.* 24.29; 1QS 8.6; and, in the NT, Mt. 11.20–4; 19.28; Rev. 20.4.

from the covenant God rather than from humans.[415] The emphasis on the 'secret' echoes 2.16, which speaks of the coming judgment of the secrets of the heart; and the echo is confirmed by the reference here to the 'circumcision of the heart'. This finally tells us what the passage is all about. Heart-circumcision is what the Torah itself had declared would be necessary if Israel was to be brought back from exile, released from the covenantal curse and enabled to be the true people of the covenant God. This reference to Deuteronomy 30.6, and to prophetic texts most likely dependent on it,[416] goes with a string of texts which speak of the restored covenant in terms of the renewed heart.[417] We should be in no doubt that this is what Paul has in mind here.[418] This is 'election reworked', but exactly in line with what the prophets had promised.

Finally, he makes the contrast which occurs again in an explicit 'new covenant' context in 2 Corinthians 3.6, again right after speaking of the work of the spirit in the heart. The 'Jew', the 'circumcised person', of whom he speaks – despite some translations, he does not add the adjectives 'renewed', or 'true', with either of these – has this status 'in the spirit not the letter' (*en pneumati ou grammati*). This contrast has passed into such frequent proverbial use in contemporary English ('the spirit of the law' versus 'the letter of the law') that it is important to step back from that meaning, and its regular use as a kind of liberalizing excuse for ignoring what the law actually says, and examine Paul's point afresh. He has already spoken of the circumcised person as having the *gramma*, the 'letter', of the law (2.27). This in context must refer to ancestral possession of the Mosaic code (as in 2.19–20). Here in 2.29, as in 2 Corinthians 3.6, the same meaning forces itself upon us.[419] Nor is the contrast of 'letter and spirit' simply a question of hermeneutical method, as some have suggested with reference to 2 Corinthians 3; or, if it is, it is a 'hermeneutical method' of a drastic sort, namely the principle that the people who not only understand Torah but also 'keep' and 'fulfil' it (Romans 2.26, 27) are people who have undergone a radical transformation

[415] So e.g. Dunn 1988a, 123; Fitzmyer 1993, 323, and many others. Käsemann 1980 [1973], 77 dismisses this idea, which he says comes from an 'initially English tradition', on the grounds that a Roman audience would not have understood it. That is unproveable, and anyway beside the point. Even 'purposeful communicators' (Barclay 2011, 71, agreeing with Käsemann) may use word-play that not all hearers will understand. The attempt of Käsemann (77) to suggest that this passage resonates, not with a Jewish context, but with the Stoicism of Marcus Aurelius 4.19.2; 12.11 is a fine example of Schweitzer's point about people getting water from far away in leaky buckets when there was a flowing stream right beside them.

[416] cf. too Dt. 10.16; Lev. 26.41; Jer. 4.4; 9.25f.; Ezek. 44.7, 9. The theme of heart-circumcision (or lack thereof) is echoed in the NT (Ac. 7.51) and in other second-Temple writings, e.g. 1QS 5.5; 1QH 2.18; 1QpHab 11.13; 4Q177 185; *Jub.* 1.23; *Od. Sol.* 11.1–3; Philo *Spec.* 1.305. *Migr. Abr.* 92, sometimes cited here, makes a different point.

[417] Jer. 31.33; 32.39f.; Ezek. 11.19; 36.26–8; the Ezek. refs. also speak of the transforming gift of the spirit.

[418] His implicit antithesis not only between 'spirit' and 'letter' (see below) but between 'spirit' in v. 29 and 'flesh' in v. 28 likewise belongs closely with his regular antithesis, stated already in relation to Jesus himself in 1.3–4 and developed in e.g. 8.5–8. For a full line-up of regular antithesis, cf. Gal. 4.21–31.

[419] cf. BDAG 205f., with classical parallels both for the sense of *gramma* as a book and for the contrast between (a) a 'living' law and (b) a 'dead' one which becomes a mere *gramma*.

of the heart.[420] Paul would no doubt have said that the obedience which flows from the renewed heart does indeed constitute a fresh hermeneutical activity. He is here referring to the Mosaic law, and saying that in the renewed election, the new covenant, the spirit will accomplish 'what the law could not do'. He is, of course, referring to the divine spirit, promised by the prophets, and now, he believes, poured out upon a people consisting not only of believing gentiles (as we might have imagined from this passage alone) but also, of course, of believing Jews.[421]

One cannot stress too strongly that none of this implies a 'critique of Judaism'. As in 2.17–20, Paul is not saying there is anything wrong with being Jewish, or that Jewish religion is inherently bad (or, with Martyn and others, that all 'religion' is bad, with Judaism forming the immediate example![422]). Rather, as Keck stresses, 'Paul's argument is actually an expression of Judaism's conviction about God's impartiality'.[423] One could go further: Romans 2.25–9 is a careful thinking through of what precisely is meant by the warnings and promises stated clearly in Judaism's own scriptures. It is a following through of the eschatological narrative of scripture itself, as Romans 10.1–13 will make clear.[424]

These five verses at the end of Romans 2, then, form a dense but classic statement of reworked election. As I have indicated, Paul will return to this theme again and again. Its statement here, in advance of any explanation of justification itself, indicates well enough that within at least the rhetorical strategy of Romans he has no intention of allowing the build-up of forensic metaphors in chapter 3 to stand by itself. What he has to say about (a) the unveiling of the divine righteousness and (b) the pronouncement of a righteous status for all who believe (with (a) being the *ground* of (b), not the same thing), takes place, as 3.24 itself declares, as one key moment *within* the creation of the family of the renewed covenant.

The paragraph at the close of chapter 2 continues to resonate throughout the letter. Those with ears to hear will continue to detect echoes in passages such as 3.27–31; 4.11–12; 4.16–17; 7.4–6 (where, in verse 6, the spirit/letter antithesis is repeated, as though to remind readers to have 2.25–9 in mind throughout what follows, all the way into chapter 8); 8.1–11; 8.27; and indeed 8.31–9 itself. Then, in chapters 9—11, we find the same only more so. The discussion of 'Israel and Israel' in 9.6; the shocking inclusion of

420 See Fitzmyer 1993, 323 on patristic understandings of the phrase.

421 Fitzmyer 1993, 323 strangely suggests that 'the real Jew' in mind here is 'an Israelite with a circumcised heart'. Unless Fitzmyer is using 'Israelite' itself in an extended sense, this seems an unwarranted restriction: the rhetorical strategy of the whole paragraph depends on the subject being gentiles throughout. Cp. e.g. Rom. 4.11f.

422 Or, with Jewett, that 2.17–24 is addressing 'the bigot'.

423 Keck 2005, 88.

424 This note of eschatology is what is missing from Barclay's account (2011, ch. 3). His suggestion (79) that Paul has stretched biblical language here in a way that 'threatens to subvert the historical continuity of the Jewish tradition' seems to me to miss Paul's point, which is that scripture itself points forward to a radical transformation *within* that historical continuity. Israel's God always promised in scripture that he would act in a radical new way; Paul is saying that this has now happened. Apocalypse and salvation history (to use the jargon) are here mutually defined.

gentiles in 9.24–6; the gentiles 'obtaining *dikaiosynē*' while Israel does not 'attain to the law' in 9.30–3; and, above all, the strange spirit-driven fulfilment of the law in terms of the covenant renewal promised in Deuteronomy 30 (10.4–13); all these speak of the reworked election in ways which echo 2.25–9. Some of them explicitly speak of justification; others do not. But the way in which these themes resonate across the letter indicates beyond any doubt that in this letter at least Paul explicitly locates his exposition of justification within his understanding of the way in which, by the spirit, the ancient biblical notion of election itself has been definitively reworked.

(iii) Faith, Justification and the People of God

(a) The Shape of Justification

My case, here and elsewhere, is that the language of 'justification' – the various Pauline uses of the *dikaios* root – have their Pauline home within the redefinition of election, the subject of the present chapter. That is, they take for granted the belief (a) that Israel was chosen, with a purpose, by the creator God; (b) that this purpose had to do with the creator's ultimate plan to set the whole creation to rights; and (c) that this purpose was to be taken forward through the setting to rights of human beings. That complex of thought, which I have explained in some detail already in chapter 7, then comes to birth in what for us may appear a complex framework of thought, though for Paul it will all have fitted together so well that it appeared simple and could be encapsulated in short, pithy summaries.

How is one to display an argument like this to best advantage? As with all major Pauline topics, we face the choice of either working through all the relevant passages and then drawing conclusions, or setting out a working hypothesis and then showing how the key passages reflect it. For present purposes I choose the latter course.[425] There is also a choice (to say the least) of conversation partners, where the demands of space impose their own rather severe limitations.[426]

[425] Of course, either method takes its place on the larger hermeneutical spiral of many years of reflection, recorded in part in *Perspectives* and in commentaries etc.; the move from historical exegesis to thematic analysis and back again is never-ending. I am naturally aware of the major ongoing discussions of 'justification' as a topic in historical and systematic theology, and what follows will inevitably have considerable relevance to those debates (since most of the debaters hold a high view of scripture in which what Paul actually says is supposed to be decisive and determinative!). However, it will of course not be possible to engage with details. For an important recent symposium see McCormack 2006b.

[426] For much of my career I have been in implicit and sometimes explicit debate with Jimmy Dunn, and in the present section we may refer esp. to Dunn 1998, 335–89. Since we are often lumped together under the broad and now unhelpful label of 'new perspective', it is worth noting that despite much two-way traffic of thought our disagreements loom at least as large, in my mind at least, as our agreements. Among recent German treatments I take Schnelle 2005 [2003], 454–72 as representative. Since we have mentioned the 'new perspective', it is worth recalling, as people often do not, that an early advocate of some relevant lines of thought was George Howard: see e.g. Howard 1967 and 1969; and perhaps especially Howard 1970 and 1979.

Here then is my proposal. Paul's redefinition of election on the basis of the work of the Messiah and around the work of the spirit can be seen in relation to a complex but clear sequence of ideas. In other words, one can only understand Paul's 'justification by faith' as the leading edge of *this* narrative, *this* sequence of thought. The doctrine itself – properly, justification by grace through faith in the present time on the basis of the work of the Messiah – comes as the crucial seventh and final element in this sequence. The first six, which are necessary for the full impact of that final move to be felt, are presented here in brief, having been discussed earlier in the present book. This admittedly rather dense summary looks back to the summary of 'righteousness' language in Judaism (section 2 (ii) above), and shows how Paul now transforms it in the light of Messiah and spirit. It offers (a) an explanatory narrative for the many things Paul says about justification and (b) a range of technical terms which, though somewhat clunky, may be useful shorthands for discussion.

So to the detail. I include in **bold type** some technical terms that will be useful in subsequent discussions.

1. *God the creator intends at the last to remake the creation*, righting all wrongs and filling the world with his own presence. This is the 'end' or 'goal', the 'eschaton', towards which God is working. This is 'eschatology': perhaps specifically '**creational eschatology**', distinct from (say) a 'gnostic' eschatology which would look for a future in which the created order was abandoned rather than rectified.[427] We shall study this further in the next chapter. Paul's overarching statement of hope is seen most fully in Romans 8 and 1 Corinthians 15. Once that larger picture is grasped it can be glimpsed in many other passages, such as Philippians 3.20–1. The creator's intention to do this, and his 'justice' in putting things right, is what stands behind the medieval idea of a 'iustitia distributiva' by which the one God rewards the good and punishes evil.

2. *For this to happen, humans themselves have to be 'put right'*. The main problem standing in the way both of the original purpose of creation and (now) of its renewal and restoration is the failure of humankind to act as God's image-bearers in the world. God must therefore put humans to rights in order to put the world to rights. (One might call this focus '**anthropological eschatology**'.) This problem is due to human idolatry, and to the consequent fracturing of human behaviour, which means that humans have failed to bring the creator's

[427] I use the word 'rectified', which has featured in some recent accounts of justification, in its normal English sense of 'put to rights', 'sorted out', 'repaired', 'set back as it should be'. It carries an implicit judicial overtone, which is why the final divine act is seen as 'judgment' (Ps. 96.10–13, etc.); but the emphasis in the word falls on the eventual state of restoration, with the implication of affirming the goodness of the original thing, not so much on the judicial decision by which that end is achieved. I do not, however, find that 'rectify' and 'rectification' are sufficient to cover all the elements in Paul's larger picture – unlike e.g. Martyn 1997a; Harink 2003 (on which see McCormack 2006a).

fruitful ordering to bear on the world. (This complex of idolatry and dehumanizing behaviour is what Paul calls 'Sin', which can refer to (a) the specific acts which embody such behaviour, (b) the state in which those who behave that way are living, and/or (c) the dark power that appears to drive them in that direction.[428]) Paul's statement of the problem of sin and evil is classically found, of course, in Romans 1.18—2.16, and summarized again in 3.9–20.[429] It is drawn on in the statements about Adamic humanity in Romans 5, and in many other passages such as Ephesians 2.1–3 and the various descriptions of pagan humanity scattered throughout the letters.[430] I argued in chapter 9 that Paul had grasped a wider and deeper vision of this problem through his redefinition of monotheism by means of Messiah and spirit. It was this problem which generated the specifically Pauline, and then Christian, view of 'salvation'. It is important to note, as I have done on many occasions before, that despite popular Christian parlance 'justification' and 'salvation' are emphatically not the same thing, and to confuse them is to make careful exegesis, not to mention theology, ultimately impossible.[431] It would be easy to skip straight from here to the 'forensic eschatology' of point 4 below, but to do that would short-circuit the underlying biblical narrative to which Paul, at least, pays close attention. The next move, therefore, has to do with the covenant people.

3. *God's way of accomplishing this is through the covenant.* God's purpose of rectifying the world, setting it to rights, following the failure of humans and the corruption of the world, was focused on the call to Abraham and his 'seed'.[432] As we have seen already, from Paul's perspective the covenant which the creator God established with Abraham was the chosen means of dealing with 'sin' in order to implement 'creational eschatology': hence the promise to Abraham that he

[428] The problem of evil non-human forces ('powers'), which Paul sees as defeated in the Messiah's death (Col. 2.15), is to be understood within this larger picture: see above, e.g. 632, 740, 752–71.

[429] I have argued above, and at more length in *Perspectives* ch. 30, that 2.17—3.8 have a different purpose, relating not to the sinfulness of Israel in itself but to Israel's failure to be 'faithful' to the vocation to be the light of the world.

[430] e.g. 1 Cor. 5, 6; Gal. 5; Eph. 4.17—5.20; Phil. 3.18f.; Col. 3.5–11; 1 Thess. 4.4–6.

[431] Even Sanders sometimes lapses at this point: e.g. Sanders 1977, 451f., 545. I am at a loss to know why so careful a scholar as O'Brien should suppose I have confused the two (O'Brien 2004, 288). Clearly the final event when the one God creates a new world and raises the dead will constitute *both* the ultimate 'rescue' of his people from death, i.e. 'salvation', *and* the ultimate verdict in their favour ('justification', as in Rom. 2.13; Gal. 5.5). Clearly, too, Paul can speak of present 'salvation' just as he can of present 'justification' (e.g. Rom. 8.24). Both terms, then, can *denote* the same event or fact. But they *connote* quite different things: the one, rescue, as from a danger or plight; the other, vindication, as in a law court. I note, as I have elsewhere, that both 'justification' and 'salvation' are major themes of Rom., but that 'salvation' is absent from Gal.: food for thought.

[432] For this whole section see esp. ch. 2 above, and also section 2 of the present chapter. It is noteworthy that Schreiner 2010, 390–2, summarizing 'justification' as it relates to Galatians, manages not to mention Abraham. Contrast e.g. Gathercole 2006a, stressing the importance of understanding righteousness in covenantal terms.

would have a worldwide family, which is where Paul picks matters up in Galatians 3 and Romans 4.[433] This was the necessary move in setting the whole creation to rights. Once Israel's God had made those promises, the scriptures insisted that he would be faithful to them, doing what he had promised not only *for* Israel but *through* Israel. This, in other words, is '**covenantal eschatology**'. To add 'covenant' to 'setting right' is specifically not, as it has often been portrayed, a matter of adding a 'horizontal' dimension to a 'vertical' one. This is to miss the point entirely, which is that the creator God *called* Abraham to be the means of *rescuing* humans and the world: a doubly 'vertical' theme, if you like.[434]

This divine faithfulness to the covenant, spelled out in Deuteronomy and elsewhere in terms of both punishing the covenant people for sin and subsequent merciful restoration, is spoken of in several key passages in terms of the *righteousness* of the one God (*tsedaqah elohim, dikaiosynē theou*). This was seen as the divine characteristic because of which the creator would do what he had promised.[435] The theme of 'covenant' and 'covenant faithfulness' is the full biblical setting for what has often been spoken of as the 'relational' aspect of the notion of *tsedaqah/dikaiosynē*. By itself, the word 'relational' is vague, suggesting that 'justification' is about 'someone's relationship with God'. That, in a very general sense, is not untrue, but to substitute 'relation' for 'covenant' is to take a large step away from historical moorings.[436]

Paul's own covenantal eschatology is the radical development of a basic second-Temple Jewish line of thought which Pharisees and some others might be expected to hold.[437] Most Jews of the period were not, it seems, asking themselves how they might escape from a post-mortem judgment and arrive safely in some kind of otherworldly bliss. They were not, that is, concerned about the questions with which the word 'justification' has come to be associated in today's

[433] On these passages, and on the confluence there of 'righteousness' and 'covenant membership' (which is not a 'problem', as suggested by e.g. Bird 2007, 74), see 'Paul and the Patriarch' in *Perspectives* ch. 33. One writer who has offered suggestive ways of holding together Pauline strands that others separate is Bruce Longenecker: see e.g. Longenecker 1998.

[434] e.g., surprisingly, Bird 2007, 1, 19, 113, 153. The covenant is not simply about 'ecclesiology' (O'Brien 2004, 289f.). See too Moo 2004, 187, 216. I am not at all saying, as some have supposed, that 'the whole world is in Israel'; rather, Israel is the creator's means of rescuing and blessing the whole world (see Vanhoozer 2011, 244, quoting Horton).

[435] The obvious examples are in Isa. 40—55 and Dan. 9; see ch. 2 above. The basis for it all – the 'covenant' with its warnings and promises, to which YHWH will be 'faithful' – is found in passages like Lev. 26.1–45; Dt. 7.12—8.20; 11.26–8; 26.16—28.68. The attempt to split up 'covenant' and 'righteousness' (e.g. Schreiner 2001, 199, relying on Seifrid 2000) fails not least because of Paul's central use of Gen. 15 where the two are inextricably intertwined.

[436] See Dunn 1993, 134. Many studies of the relevant words look back to Ziesler 1972 which, though flawed in some ways, sets out the material helpfully.

[437] See ch. 2 above.

western world.[438] Many first-century Jews were, however, principally concerned about the question of how and when the one God would come in power to rule the world, rescuing his people and establishing his 'kingdom', the long-awaited 'age to come'. Within that, many were concerned about their own membership in that coming 'age'. Many of them, as we saw in chapter 2, were living out of some version of the narrative which combined Deuteronomy 27—32 and Daniel 9: they had a sense, in other words, that after long years of 'curse' and 'exile' there would come a great new moment of 'covenant renewal', of rescue and redemption. Many of them, then, might have put the question like this: (a) Israel's God will bring about his new world, raising his people from the dead to share in it; (b) clearly, not all Jews will have a share in this new world;[439] so (c) how can we tell, *in the present time*, who will be among that newly constituted, resurrected and reigning eschatological people? That is the precise context in which questions about 'works' might arise – though, since 'justification' is not a major topic in second-Temple Judaism, this is rare, with Qumran providing (in 4QMMT) the only solid example (see below).

Saul of Tarsus would probably have answered that question by speaking of the law-based covenant status outlined in Philippians 3.5–6 and hinted at in Romans 9.31 and 10.2–3. Serious, 'zealous' Torah-keeping in the present time would mark out in advance those who, in the age to come, would be raised from the dead and have a share in judging and ruling within the reign of the one God. 'Marked out' would of course be literally true in the case of circumcision. This, together with the other ethnic badges such as food-laws and sabbath-keeping, and behind these the entire way of life focused on Torah and Temple, formed a nexus of 'works of Torah' through which one might tell in advance who would be declared to be *tsaddiqim/dikaioi*, 'righteous', 'covenant members', in the future.

There is, however, not much evidence that pre-Christian Jews spoke of that kind of 'advance marking out' in terms of 'justification'. This already presents us with an apparent oddity: might it be the case that not only Paul's particular view of justification, but also the idea of *any* 'doctrine of justification', let alone its apparent central importance, is itself a Christian innovation, like some of the others we have seen? Did Paul introduce the category out of nothing? Why then would he speak, looking back at his former self, of 'justification by

[438] This is of course the source of many confusions: when people say, 'What did Paul say about "justification"?', they usually mean, 'What did he say on the topic of how people are converted, "saved" and assured of a safe passage to "heaven"?' These questions, when properly reframed, are of course important, but they are not exactly what Paul means by the word 'justification' itself. All this means that much of Carson, O'Brien and Seifrid 2001 is simply beside the point, despite the high quality of many of the essays.

[439] See mSanh. 10.1–4, where the opening statement that 'all Israel has a share in the age to come' is at once qualified with substantial lists of those excluded.

works of the law'? Was that whole idea a Christian back-projection? Here we are once more, clearly, faced with the question of 'plight and solution'. And, again, the answer is more subtle than a simple either/or will allow.

The clearest pre-Christian statement of something like 'justification' is in Column C of 4QMMT.[440] There, those who keep particular 'works of Torah' in the present time will have 'righteousness' reckoned to them. Such people, in other words, *will be reckoned to be part of the covenant family now, in the present*, against the day when the new age arrives and all will be revealed. That question, of the *advance* signs of *future* vindication, was thus already on the table in second-Temple Judaism. I see no sign that it was central, but it was present and thinkable – especially among sectarian groups who wanted to assure themselves that, despite their present marginal status, they would in fact be seen as the true covenant people once the new age arrived. One might even suggest that, with Qumran at least, some kind of inaugurated eschatology was present: now that the Teacher of Righteousness had led the way, the new covenant had been secretly launched. Belong to *this* group *now*, marked out by *these* signs and symbols, they might have said, and you will be among those to be vindicated when the moment comes. We have no reason to suppose that hard-line Pharisees like Saul of Tarsus held a similar secretly inaugurated eschatology, but the same line of thought would still be relevant. If you clarify and intensify Torah-keeping in *this* way ('zeal'), you will certainly inherit the age to come. You may even help to bring it about.

That model (the signs in the present which tell, already, who will inherit the coming age) remains in Paul. His doctrine of 'justification' has a similar *shape*. But the *content* has shifted dramatically in four ways, each as a result of Messiah and spirit.

First, eschatology has been inaugurated in a new and dramatic way. Paul believed that *the new age had already arrived* with the death and resurrection of the Messiah and the gift of the spirit. The moment for which Pharisees and Essenes were hoping had already come about. The question of who would be vindicated, and who would be ruling and judging, in the future, had been answered: it was the Messiah himself. He was the king; he would rule; he would judge. He was, that is, the vindicated-Israel-in-person. We should be clear that Paul's Jesus-shaped 'but now' represents a radical novelty. Other groups (notably the Essenes) may have held some kind of inaugurated eschatology. But nobody else claimed that a representative Israel-in-person figure had been raised from the dead.

Second, the Messiah's death was not incidental (a mere step on the way, as it were, to vindication). The fact, and especially the manner,

[440] See *Perspectives* ch. 21. Gathercole 2004, 238 n. 38 shares my reservations about Dunn's handling of this topic (Dunn 2008 [2005], ch. 14 (orig. 1997)).

of his death indicated that the covenant God would not affirm Israel as it stood. The strange covenantal story of judgment, curse and ultimately exile had reached its height. With the hindsight of the resurrection, the cross meant (as we saw in chapter 9) that the 'problem' had been far worse than anyone had imagined. Israel as a whole shared fully in the plight of the world. No longer, therefore, could one look ahead to the age to come and envisage some zealous Jews already being well qualified to share in its life, in the coming divine reign. The only way into the age to come would be by dying and rising again.

Third, the outpouring of the spirit indicated to Paul that the promises of Deuteronomy 30, and the echoing promises of Jeremiah and Ezekiel, had been fulfilled. The Messiah had been vindicated; but he was not alone. Somehow, he would share his status and role with his people.[441] There was now already a circumcised-heart people, in whose common life and individual transformation a strange new form of 'lawkeeping', both related and unrelated to the Pharisaic keeping of Torah, had now appeared. This offered a kind of parallel to the Pharisaic hope of a present zealous keeping of Torah through which one might be marked out in the present with a 'righteousness', a covenant status, that would be vindicated in the future. But the new kind of life was of an utterly different kind, not least in that it was a fresh and free gift from the covenant God himself.[442] In particular, the first and most characteristic sign of this people, which became its badge, had nothing to do with the 'works of Torah' which marked out the Jew from the pagan (or with the sectarian 'works of Torah' which marked out one sect from another, as in 4QMMT). Its badge was the Messiah-badge, namely *pistis*. This is the explanation (which the structure of the present chapter is designed to set forward) of why *pistis* is the single badge by which the single Abraham-family, 'justified sinners', are recognized. *Pistis* is, in other words, the Israel-characteristic which, according to Romans 3.2 and 3.22, was lacking in Israel itself and provided by the Messiah. *Pistis* is therefore the appropriate sign that a human being is a Messiah-person, 'in the Messiah', 'belonging to the Messiah': part of the covenant people, one of those about whom the covenant God himself declares, in advance of the final declaration which will consist in resurrection itself, that this person is *dikaios*, part of Abraham's single, sin-forgiven covenant family. Within this *pistis* we must therefore include all that Paul includes: cross-and-resurrection-shaped belief, trust and faithfulness.

Fourth, therefore, and most radically, the circumcised-heart people, marked out by *pistis*, was a company that included Jews and gentiles alike. Nor was this simply a generous if surprising extension. It

[441] This is the only explanation for passages like Rom. 5.17; 1 Cor. 6.2.

[442] Phil. 3.7–11.

was the whole point all along. The Messiah would be lord of the whole world, and Paul has glimpsed how that broad vision and hope is put into detailed practice by the actual working of gospel and spirit.

This actual working involved the application of the Messiah's death and resurrection to the whole people. If the Messiah had died and been raised, this was to be the paradigm for the people as a whole. Israel (and any and all Jews) would have to die in order to be raised; and in that death they would bid farewell to the God-given markers of ethnic identity which had rightly sustained them up to that point. For the same reason they would therefore welcome, as equals within the Messiah's strange new family, all those gentiles who had made the same death-and-life journey and who, like them, were marked out by the badge of *pistis* itself. This is more or less exactly what Paul means when he speaks of the gospel bringing salvation 'to the Jew first, and also, equally, to the Greek'.[443]

These four points compel a further important reflection. Much as with the idea of 'resurrection' in second-Temple Judaism and early Christianity, *something that was previously peripheral has now become central.*[444] This parallel is not accidental. 'Justification' was not a hot topic in first-century Judaism. It became so in Paul's work and thought for the reasons set out a moment ago (1: inaugurated eschatology through Messiah and spirit; 2: radical redefinition of the 'plight'; 3: the new work of the spirit; 4: redrawing of the symbolic world to include believing Jews and gentiles on equal terms). All this means that attempts to address the question of what pre-Christian Jews thought about 'justification' are regularly flawed. First, to ask what pre-Christian Jews thought about 'how to be saved' is not quite the same question. Second, when such Jews *did* talk about something like what Paul was talking about their discussions were not loadbearing in the same way that his became.

This fourfold revision and radicalization of what we may somewhat anachronistically refer to as a second-Temple view of 'justification' means that we can now propose, as a possible new theory within the history of that doctrine, a hypothesis about how Paul came to develop it in the way he did.[445] He began, as a Pharisee, in the line of zealous Jews indicated in passages such as 1 Maccabees 2. He believed that those who were zealous for Torah would, like Phinehas, have 'righteousness reckoned to them', that is, that they would be marked out in the present as true covenant members in advance of the coming new age. But the fact of the crucified and risen Messiah, and the gift of the spirit, indicated that the new age had already been inaugurated in the present, and with an unexpected character. And part of that character was the recognition that the new age could be brought

[443] Rom. 1.16.

[444] cf. *RSG* 477, 681.

[445] For a survey of theories on this subject see Schnelle 2005 [2003], 465–7.

about only if the creator God dealt, more radically than had been imagined, with what now appeared as the full and awful plight of the human race, Israel itself included.

How could that be done? Ancient Israelite culture indicated an obvious answer: the divine law court. The one God would sit in judgment. That was how human judges restored and 'rectified' human communities. The divine judge would do that as well. But this raises another obvious question: supposing all are guilty? What will the judge do then? Ancient Israel and second-Temple Judaism would answer: this God is in covenant with Abraham, and Abraham's seed will be spared. Did not the Psalms regularly cry out to the covenant God for vindication against oppressive enemies, casting Israel in the role of plaintiff in the divine law court and the pagans in the role of guilty defendants? The covenant would be the answer to the forensic problem. But Paul has apparently ruled out that option. All are guilty, and the divine judge is impartial.[446]

Then comes the radically new answer. If the Messiah's death has indicated that the problem was deeper than previously imagined, the Messiah's death will unveil the deeper solution as well. The divine covenant faithfulness is revealed in the gospel. The covenant is indeed the answer to the forensic problem – but it is the covenant as fulfilled in the faithful obedience of the Messiah and the outpouring of the spirit. The radicalization of the 'plight' which we studied earlier, itself the result of Paul's reflection on the Messiah's death, went hand in hand with the radicalization of the 'solution'. *In the language of 'righteousness' and 'justification', already implicit in the covenantal train of thought, Paul found the perfect vehicle to explain how the covenant God, through the Messiah and the spirit, had dealt with the deeper problem of human sin, including Jewish sin.*

Here, exactly as with his revision of monotheism, Paul the apostle was compelled by the gospel events to search the scriptures afresh, to ferret out passages and themes which might not have been central in second-Temple reflection but which now pressed themselves upon him. To expound this theme *he did not need to add a different kind of discourse to that of the 'covenant'*. The covenant had already been expressed in the language of the law court. And, as he radicalized the 'covenantal' meaning of the righteousness of both the one God and his people, that meaning opened up to reveal its 'forensic' depths. This third point (covenantal eschatology), routinely omitted from discussions of the fourth one (forensic eschatology), is in fact its proper explanatory framework. I shall suggest presently that, though both of them are regularly implied in Paul's mentions of justification, the covenantal meaning is far more prominent in Galatians and Philippians, while, following an interesting and often unremarked

[446] Rom. 3.19f.; 2.9–11.

anticipation of forensic language in 1 Corinthians, the two come together in a complex but coherent unity in Romans.[447]

4. *This is how the creator God will put humans to rights.* The covenant will be the means of sorting out the problem of universal human idolatry and sin. Because of the failure of humans and the corruption of creation, when the creator puts things to rights, 'rectifies' the situation, he will be acting in the way a human judge acts when re-establishing 'justice' in a community. The case will be tried. The verdict will be reached, announced and implemented. In human courts in ancient Israel, this means declaring one party 'in the wrong' and the other party 'in the right'.[448] Already we note an important point: the idea of the one God as 'judge' grows directly out of the ancient Israelite perception of this God as 'creator'. This particular God has a *responsibility* to sort out the mess in his creation, to call it to account, to set everything right. He also has the *power* and authority to do so in a way that no other being has. Thus the 'law court' or 'forensic' imagery, in Israel's scriptures and on through to Paul, is not simply one miscellaneous metaphor among others. Nor is it a particularly 'legalistic' way of thinking as opposed to some other (e.g. 'relational').[449] It does not mean that one can *only* think of this God acting in 'legal' or 'law court' (i.e. 'forensic') terms – just as the fact that other ways of thinking (such as 'reconciliation', or 'love' itself) are equally appropriate does not mean that one can then dispense with the 'legal' idea of everything being 'put right' or 'rectified' at last. Such language expresses one important and non-negotiable facet of the whole, even while dovetailing comfortably with other aspects of the wider purpose already mentioned. 'Law court' language expresses, in a non-transferable way, something vital and central about the determination of the creator God to put all things right at last. One cannot, of course, make the law court the only matrix of understanding, even for 'justification'. We need covenant, eschatology, participation and much besides. Equally, though, one cannot marginalize 'forensic' language and hope to escape scot-free.

[447] Bird 2007, 153 suggests that Gal. is more accommodating for a 'new perspective' reading, and Rom. for a 'reformed' reading. I find this more than a little bizarre; the *only* thing that might be said for it is that Gal. does indeed concentrate on the question of 'who belongs to Abraham's family', and, unlike Rom., never mentions 'salvation', while Rom. puts the whole picture together in a fresh way.

[448] In ancient Israel there was no 'director of public prosecutions', so all cases were a matter of one person (the plaintiff) against the other (the defendant). Clearly, either might be found 'in the right': if this was the defendant, the declaration would be an 'acquittal', but if the decision went in favour of the plaintiff it would simply mean that his case had been upheld.

[449] One must not confuse 'law court' ideas with 'relational' ones. As we have seen, the notion of 'relational' is a fuzzy way of talking about the covenant. Law court and covenant belong together but not in the sense that the 'relational' language of the latter intrudes upon the 'law court' metaphor. As soon as we think of the 'relationship' between the defendant and the judge it is clear that the 'forensic' image no longer works.

It is therefore proper and natural, within ancient Judaism, to speak of the creator's rectifying work in metaphors drawn from the 'forensic' or 'law court' setting. God, as the righteous judge, will set all things right, and will thereby display his own 'righteousness' in that (forensic) sense. We might call this '**forensic eschatology**'. As we have already stressed, the 'righteousness' of a judge, seen from the biblical point of view, consists in trying the case fairly and impartially, being true to the law, punishing wickedness, and vindicating those in the right, with special reference to the helpless (orphans, widows and the poor). Paul's forensic eschatology, envisaging the creator as a judge acting justly ('the righteousness of God') to set creation to rights and to do so impartially, is again seen most fully in Romans, this time in 2.1–16. This God will judge the secrets of human hearts 'through Jesus the Messiah, according to my gospel' (2.16).[450] But it is not only in Romans. The theme of the final judgment at which God will judge righteously recurs again and again. We shall develop this, too, in the sixth point below, and more fully in the next chapter.[451]

We thus find, in Paul, '**covenantal *and forensic* eschatology**', and, with that, a further depth in the phrase 'the righteousness of God'.[452] This God will not only act in fidelity to the covenant; when he does so, that will be the means by which he will *put all things right, like a judge finally settling a case.* The *forensic* meaning of the divine righteousness thus originated in the *covenantal* context in the first place (Israel's belief in the ultimate justice of the one God; Israel's appeal to that ultimate justice as the source of rescue and vindication), and belongs closely with it. If, of course, the covenantal narrative is confronted with the problem that the covenant people, like everyone else, are sinful and guilty before the divine tribunal, the forensic setting will not only make that clear but also offer the appropriate model for displaying the divine solution. Part of the reason why Romans 1.18—4.25, and especially 3.21–31, are as dense and complex as they are is because *both* of these things, covenant and law court, are being discussed together.[453]

[450] It is the combination of covenant faithfulness with forensic righteousness (especially impartiality) that makes the thesis of Kaminsky 2007 (that the creator God simply does have a 'favourite nation clause') so implausible in terms of Israel's scriptures themselves.

[451] e.g. Rom. 14.10–12; 2 Cor. 5.10; etc.

[452] McCormack 2004, 113–7 stresses the importance of the covenant as the context for justification; but my sense is that 'covenant' here has a different meaning from that which I am proposing. The result is that he wants to include 'transformation' within justification itself, which as I argue below is not true to Paul (see also e.g. 117, where McCormack summarizes Calvin: 'God's declaration in justification is revelation, and revelation transforms the whole person'). Vanhoozer 2011, 251 is I think closer to the mark. Fee 1995, 322 n. 35 emphasizes 'God's covenant loyalty to his people, and thus his and their relationship based on the new covenant', which seems to me exactly right, but he then gently plays this off against 'forensic' meanings. I think they are mutually interpenetrating and mutually interpretative.

[453] The caricature of my and other views offered by Carson 2004, 50–2 – with, as usual, minimal reference to my actual writings – is simply a way of not attending to what is being said.

5. *All these themes point forward to the decisive divine judgment on the last day*, in other words, to '**final eschatology**'.[454] Paul in many passages reaffirms the basic Jewish belief, summing up all the previous four points: (1) there will come a day when the creator will finally call the whole world to account and 'rectify' it at last; (2) this will include the final 'rectification' of human beings, in other words, their reconstitution *as* fully human beings, through the resurrection, so that they will share the creator's rule in the new world; (3) this will be the ultimate fulfilment of the Abrahamic covenant, the moment when the creator and covenant God blesses the whole world through Abraham's 'seed', fully, finally and for ever; (4) the resurrection, i.e. the rescue from death itself and the ultimate reconstitution of image-bearing humans, is to be seen as their ultimate *vindication* in the legal, forensic sense. All this will come about because the creator God, who is also the covenant God, will at the last demonstrate his *faithfulness* to the covenant *and hence also* to the creation. To pull these apart – and with them some key passages in Paul's letters – is to place dogma ahead of historical exegesis.

Within the larger picture which Paul offers in Romans, this *forensic verdict* which is also the ultimate *covenantal declaration* is the verdict that will be issued publicly, finally, impartially and righteously, on the last day.[455] Paul sees this as part of the renewal of all things, the establishment of the new heavens and new earth. The future verdict will consist, according to Paul, of the gift of 'life': the *dikaiōma* that meant 'death' is matched by the *dikaiōma* that meant 'life'.[456] That is why Romans 8 then develops exactly this theme: these people will be raised bodily from the dead to share in the glory of the Messiah (Romans 8.17–30). Once again we note the dovetailing of forensic and covenantal ideas. The 'verdict' here, and in 8.33–4, is certainly 'forensic', but the idea of the two verdicts of 'life' and 'death' is certainly 'covenantal', as in Deuteronomy 30.15–20 and elsewhere. And once again the whole thing is 'incorporative'. The place where the verdict 'no condemnation' is issued is precisely 'in Messiah Jesus'.[457]

This *final justification* is referred to decisively much earlier in the letter, in Romans 2.12–13, which itself summarizes the larger statement in 2.5–11. These clear and sharp statements are by no means to be set aside, as is the habit of some, on the grounds either that they set up categories which Paul will then show to be empty (an odd way of laying the foundation for so carefully crafted a letter) or that Paul

[454] On all this see esp. Yinger 1999; and, behind that, the important article of Snodgrass 1986.

[455] Often forgotten in this connection is 1 Cor. 4.1–5 (see below); 4.5 in particular is very close to Rom. 2.16 and 2.29. An Anglican theologian is wryly amused to see a polemic against this Pauline emphasis, in its expression by a C17 archbishop, in Collins 2004, 180.

[456] cf. Rom. 1.32; 5.18 (*dikaiōsis zōēs*); 7.10; 8.4, 9–11. See above, e.g. 900f.

[457] Rom. 8.1, 2.

is here simply quoting a Jewish perspective which he does not himself share. Here is the full statement in 2.4–11:

> Don't you know that God's kindness is meant to bring you to repentance? [5]But by your hard, unrepentant heart you are building up a store of anger for yourself on the day of anger, the day when God's just judgment will be unveiled – [6]the God who will 'repay everyone according to their works'. [7]When people patiently do what is good, and so pursue the quest for glory and honour and immortality, God will give them the life of the age to come. [8]But when people act out of selfish desire, and do not obey the truth, but instead obey injustice, there will be anger and fury. [9]There will be trouble and distress for every single person who does what is wicked, the Jew first and also, equally, the Greek – [10]and there will be glory, honour and peace for everyone who does what is good, the Jew first and also, equally, the Greek. [11]God, you see, shows no partiality.

The impartiality and 'just judgment' of God: these are essential elements in God's own *dikaiosynē*, his 'righteousness', in the classic biblical terms of judiciary responsibility.[458] This careful statement of a 'forensic' eschatology then contextualizes the following statement (2.12–13) of God's final 'justification':

> [12]Everyone who sinned outside the law, you see, will be judged outside the law – and those who sinned from within the law will be judged by means of the law. [13]After all, it isn't those who *hear* the law who are in the right before God. It's those who *do* the law who will be declared to be in the right!

Hoi poiētai nomou dikaiōthēsetai – 'those who do the law will be justified': those words have struck terror into the hearts of unsuspecting Protestants. Some have expressed surprise that such words should be found in the New Testament, let alone in a letter by Paul.[459] That, of course, is why some theories have done their best to muzzle or neutralize them.[460] But there are plenty of signs elsewhere in the letters that Paul means exactly what he says. The question then is: what does he mean by 'doing the law', and what, in this instance, does he mean by 'will be justified'?

Paul will come back again and again to the question of 'doing the law' throughout Romans, with the particular climax to that build-up of thought coming in 10.6–11. To this we shall return. But we must stress here, because it is vital for the logic of this fifth point and the ultimate seventh one, that Paul is here talking about a *future* and *final* 'justification', which the context makes clear will take place on the

[458] cf. e.g. Ex. 23.2f., 6–9; Lev. 19.15; Dt. 16.18–20; 24.17; 27.19; Ps. 82.2; Prov. 18.5; Eccl. 5.8; Isa. 10.2; Am. 5.12. For the judge 'declaring one in the right and the other in the wrong' cf. e.g. Dt. 25.1; for God doing this, 1 Kgs. 8.32.

[459] Eisenbaum 2009, 237 reports that on one occasion 'the student reader thought she had a typo in her Bible because she did not believe that Paul could say that the doers of the law would be justified'.

[460] cf. e.g. O'Brien 2004, 268, quoting Avemarie 2000, 274 to the effect that the promise of life in Rom. 2 'is never fulfilled because "all are under sin"' as in 3.9. Avemarie insists (ib.) that the whole of 1.18—3.20 is to be seen as '*remota gratia*': a classic case of allowing the big picture to trump the tell-tale details. The whole question is helpfully laid out in Bird 2007, ch. 7.

last day, the day of final judgment. Paul here envisages the final scene of present world history as a great law court setting in which God the creator, the just and impartial judge, will sum up the complete lives of all human beings and declare that some are 'in the right' and others not.

This just judgment (*dikaiokrisia*, 2.5) will be on the basis of the totality of the life that has been led. God will 'repay to each according to their works'. Paul never for a moment undermines this biblical and traditional saying, widespread across the thought of ancient Israel.[461] It is itself part of the 'righteousness of God', the 'just judgment' in which the creator will be seen to have acted 'impartially' (Romans 2.11).[462] This is the same picture that we find in the other briefer references such as 2 Corinthians 5.10, to which we shall return in reviewing Paul's eschatology in the next chapter.

The point which must then be noticed is the all-important difference between the *future* verdict and the *present* one – and the reason why this difference occurs, and the consequences which follow from it. To get at this we need a brief digression into the overall logic of Romans 1—8.

Many factors have contributed to obscuring the link between future and present justification in Romans. First, there has been a tendency (already mentioned) to set chapter 2 aside altogether, or otherwise neutralise its force, perhaps by insisting that the *only* thing Paul is doing there is working towards the conclusion of 3.19–20, that all humans are guilty, and that he must not be allowed to hint at anything else on the way to that point. Second, more specifically, there has been a tendency, which has become thematic in the whole scholarly discipline of reading Paul, to treat the language of 'justification' as though it belonged in a quite different seam of thought from Paul's language about being 'in Christ', so that, as we have seen, 'forensic' and 'participationist' strands of thought have been deemed incompatible and so played off against one another, perhaps in the interest of, or at least picking up rhetorical energy from, an implicit and essentially modern privileging of 'individual salvation' over 'ecclesiology'. This has meant that when Paul speaks of 'judgment' or 'condemnation', or indeed 'justification' and 'righteousness', in passages that have been deemed to be 'participatory', he is not taken seriously.[463] Third, as a result, there has been a tendency to split off Romans 1—4 from 5—8, and both from chapters 9—11, not to mention 12—16: to allow the undoubted transitions in the *argument* of the letter to be translated into differences of *theology*. But only when the contribution of each section to the overall whole is taken into account can we

[461] Job 34.11; Ps. 62.12 [LXX13]; Prov. 24.12; cf. too Isa. 59.18; Jer. 17.10; 21.14; 32.19; Ezek. 18.30; 33.20; Sir. 11.26; 16.12–14; 35.24; 51.30; *4 Ez.* 7.35.

[462] See the discussion in e.g. Bassler 1982.

[463] e.g. at Rom. 6.13, 16, 18, 19, 20; 8.10 (all *dikaiosynē*); 8.30 (twice), 33 (*dikaioō*); 8.4 (*dikaiōma*).

understand the particular place of each within the letter, never mind within Paul's wider theology.

All this has meant that when Paul returns to the language of condemnation and justification in Romans 8 the connection with chapter 2 is often ignored. Yet there it is: Paul's argument obviously goes through different phases, but it is nevertheless a single argument running seamlessly from chapter 1 all the way to chapter 8 (never mind the further seamless thought that runs into 9—11 and indeed right through to 16). The famous opening of chapter 8, *ouden ara nyn katakrima tois en Christō Iēsou* (there is therefore now no *katakrima*, no 'condemnation', for those in the Messiah Jesus), ought to send the reader's mind straight back to the *krima* of 2.2, which was then picked up in 5.16 and 5.18 (the *katakrima* which came on all humanity following Adam's transgression). The declaration in chapter 8 that this condemnation has been taken away, since it has been borne, exhausted, in the 'condemnation' of sin itself in the Messiah's flesh (8.3), ought to evoke the sense that a problem introduced several chapters earlier has finally been resolved. God 'condemned' sin in the flesh (8.3): the *katekrinen* here is linked closely to the *katakrima* in 8.1, and thence to 5.16, 18 and back to 2.1–11.[464]

That is why the answer in 8.34 to *tis ho katakrinōn*, 'Who is there who will condemn?', is (by obvious implication), 'Nobody'. That is the rhetorical equivalent of the formal, logical conclusion in 8.1. This whole train of thought, coming out finally in chapter 8, answers closely to the set of questions in chapter 2. Only when the two are split off from one another, through the spurious and shallow division of Romans on the basis of two supposedly different types of thought or systems of soteriology, can this point be missed. *In Romans 8 we return to the future verdict, and discover that, because of the Messiah* (point 6 below), *it corresponds to the present one issued on the basis of faith* (point 7 below).

By the same token, the future verdict (which will consist, in concrete terms, of the resurrection of all the Messiah's people, and hence the divine 'declaration' about them, as about the Messiah himself in 1.4, 'this really is my son') will be in accordance with the *dikaiōma tou nomou*, the 'just requirement of the law'.[465] The two terms *katakrima* and *dikaiōma* are opposites, corresponding to *krithēsontai* and *dikaiōthēsontai* in 2.12–13: on the one hand, the negative verdict and the consequent punishment (corresponding to the warnings in 2.8–9), and on the other the positive verdict and the consequent resurrection life (corresponding to the promises in 2.7 and 10). This *dikaiōma* will be 'fulfilled in us who walk not according to the flesh

[464] cf. *krinō*, (2.1 (twice), 3); *katakrinō* (2.1); *krima* (2.2, 3); *dikaiokrisia* (2.5); the double *krithēsontai* and *dikaiōthēsontai* (2.13), and the final *krinei* of 2.16. Cf. too the warning of 2.27. It is this entire train of thought to which Paul is referring back in 8.1, 34.

[465] I take *nomos* here, as normally in Paul, to refer to the Torah itself: see below.

but according to the spirit'; this in turn corresponds closely with what is said in 2.25–9 about 'the uncircumcision that keeps the just requirements of the law' (*hē akrobustia ta dikaiōmata tou nomou phylassē*), which can also be spoken of as the 'naturally uncircumcised that completes the law' (*hē ek physeōs akrobustia ton nomon telousa*).

When looking ahead with Pauline eyes at this final verdict it is impossible – though many have tried – to omit the work of the spirit. This whole section of our present chapter, in fact, is designed to highlight the fact that Paul's doctrine of justification depends strongly upon the spirit just as much as on the Messiah: here, at the heart of the redefinition of election, it is essential. Paul has already hinted at this in 2.25–9, and it comes out into the open first in 5.5 and 7.4–6 and then, at length, in chapter 8. The tendency in some quarters to downplay the role of the spirit, as though one could understand any part of Christian theology without it, has been disastrous. It is the spirit, after all, whose work indicates that Christian living is not a zero-sum game, so that *either* 'God does it all' *or* 'we do it all'. That false notion is always raised whenever anyone draws attention to Paul's strong words about a *final* justification on the basis of the whole life, with the constant implication that unless one simply says 'God does it all' we are forfeiting assurance, or even salvation itself. We shall come back to this in point 7 below.

The particular thing to notice here is that, at the final judgment, the 'work of the law' which will not only cause certain people to be vindicated (2.13) but actually to take part in the 'judging' of others (2.27) is the result of the work of the spirit (2.29). This, as we shall see, forms the crucial link with the initial work of the gospel. As Paul says in Philippians, in a passage not sufficiently pondered by those who try to reconstruct his justification-theology: the one who began a good work in you will thoroughly complete it by the day of Messiah Jesus.[466] That is why, in Romans 8.10, he can declare that, though the body is dead because of sin, 'the spirit is life *because of righteousness*.' This leads directly to the spirit-driven resurrection of all those whom the spirit indwells. In other words, those who are 'in the Messiah', who are the same people as 'those in whom the Messiah's spirit dwells' (though the two phrases do not mean the same thing), already possess the status of *dikaiosynē*, 'righteousness'; and the resurrection will reaffirm that status. Thus, as the language of 'condemnation' comes back at last in chapter 8, so too does the language of 'righteousness' and 'justification': 'It is God who justifies (*theos ho dikaiōn*); who will condemn?'[467] The whole of Romans 8 is every bit

[466] Phil. 1.6.

[467] Rom. 8.33.

as much about 'justification' as it is about 'incorporation' or the work of the spirit.

This explains the point of 8.12–17, echoing (as I suggested) the declaration of 1.4. As Easter declared that Jesus had all along been 'God's son', so even now the spirit bears witness with the believers' spirits that they are 'God's children'. The resurrection itself will say the same thing, in the language of event rather than word. That is why Paul speaks of believers 'awaiting our *adoption*, the redemption of our bodies' (8.23). That is why, too, the Messiah is seen as the 'firstborn among many siblings' (8.29). Indeed, though the theme of 'adoption' is comparatively rare in Paul, when we find it, here and in Galatians 4, it emerges as central. One might see it as a key, Messiah-shaped focal point of covenantal theology – which would be why Paul mentions the notion again in listing the privileges of Israel in Romans 9.4–5.[468]

All this only makes sense if we allow the striking vision of final judgment in Romans 2 to have its full effect. Take that away, and one of the greatest chapters in Paul (Romans 8) becomes a scatter of general reflections about the spirit, Christian behaviour and cosmic eschatology. These are, in fact, vital and carefully integrated features within a much larger, but still theologically coherent, overall discourse.

Paul's vision in Romans 1—8, then, has as its framework the all-important narrative about *a future judgment according to the fullness of the life that has been led*, emphasizing the fact that those 'in Christ' will face 'no condemnation' on that final day (2.1–16; 8.1–11, 31–9). The reason Paul gives for this is, as so often, the cross and the spirit (8.3–4): in the Messiah, and by the spirit, the life in question will have been the life of spirit-led obedience, adoption, suffering, prayer and ultimately glory (8.5–8, 12–17, 18–27, 28–30). *This is not something other than 'Paul's doctrine of justification'*. It is its outer, eschatological framework. We know bits of this larger, final-eschatology story from other letters – Philippians, already quoted; 1 Corinthians 4.1–5 and 15.20–8, of course; hardly at all in Galatians, though there is one tell-tale reference to a future 'justification'.[469] But here in Romans it is spelled out most fully, and most tightly integrated. And, to repeat a vital point about the character of Paul's theology, that integration makes nonsense of all schemes that depend on regarding Romans 1—4 and 5—8 as representing two different types of thought or systems of soteriology. That division results from failing to notice Paul's larger controlling category, namely, the covenant

[468] The only instances of *hyiothesia* in Paul are Rom. 8.15, 23; 9.4; Gal. 4.5; Eph. 1.5. The study of Byrne 1979 is still valuable.

[469] 5.5: we are waiting eagerly, by the spirit and by faith, for the hope of righteousness (*hēmeis pneumati ek pisteōs elpida dikaiosynēs apekdechometha*). Here 'righteousness' is a *future* reality, and the role of the spirit in the patient waiting for it echoes Rom. 8 exactly, even verbally (cf. Rom. 8.19, 23, 25).

promises made by God to Abraham to deal with the problem of the world's sin and its consequences. Those, Paul insists, are the promises to which the covenant God has been true in the Messiah. The *faithfulness* of this God is the underlying theme of Romans 1—8 . . . as it is also the problem, and then the solution, throughout Romans 9—11.

This digression into the inner logic of Romans, particularly the close ties between the much-loved chapter 8 and the usually ignored chapter 2, has brought us to the point where we can at last appreciate what comes, logically and theologically, in between the two. The point about Christian eschatology is that in the Messiah the hoped-for 'end' has already appeared 'in the present time'. Eschatology has been *inaugurated.* It is because of the Messiah's unexpected death and resurrection, bursting in upon the present time from the promised future, that the verdict to be announced on the last day can itself be anticipated in the present. Once we have grasped the first five points in this sequence, in other words, we are ready first for the sixth (the Messiah), and then at last for the seventh (the 'justification in the present').

6. *The events concerning Jesus the Messiah are the revelation, in unique and decisive action, of the divine righteousness.* Everything depends – literally, logically, personally and above all theologically – upon this. The long-awaited *future* event has come forward into the *present* in the Messiah (as expounded, in relation to the Messiah himself, in chapter 9 above). This means that the one God has displayed his *dikaiosynē* in both senses (covenant faithfulness and forensic justice, tightly interwoven, and together working for the rectification of the whole creation) in the events concerning Jesus. He has condemned sin in his flesh, and has vindicated Jesus himself in his resurrection, marking him out as Israel's Messiah and hence as the bearer of the Israel-shaped covenant purpose. This God has thereby fulfilled his Israel-plan in the Messiah, whose death and resurrection are the *instruments* of this purpose and the first *instantiation* of it (in the sense that Jesus' death *is* the condemnation of sin and that his resurrection *is* the beginning of the new creation). He has decisively launched the creator's project of putting the world itself to rights.

The critical move here is to affirm, with Paul in Romans 3.22, that the Messiah has been 'faithful' to that covenant plan, the plan through which Abraham's seed would bless the world. His 'faithfulness', also expressed as his 'obedience', is the sign that Israel's role in the divine purpose has devolved onto him. And of course, for Paul, what this means in concrete terms is his death on the cross. The Messiah himself, in some versions of this narrative, is referred to as *ho dikaios*, 'the righteous one'.[470] Whether or not we press that point, we see here the main thrust of Romans 1.3–4, and we understand more fully why Paul has used *that* opening precisely for *that* letter. The resurrection is the divine declaration that Jesus really was, all along, 'son of God', in all the senses we explored in the previous chapter. To that extent, the resurrection of Jesus was itself a *judicial* declaration: over against the verdict of the courts of Caiaphas and Pilate, condemning Jesus as a blasphemous pseudo-Messiah, the resurrection declared that he was 'in the right'.[471] And if he was in the right, he really was Messiah; the resurrection was a *covenantal* declaration. *He really was Israel's representative.* The 'end', the 'goal', the 'eschaton', has thus already arrived proleptically in the present, and with it the announcement of *where the new covenant people of the one God, the forgiven-humans, are to be found and recognized.*

These events concerning Jesus, and the announcement of them as 'good news', therefore provide a sudden, bright glimpse of the fact that this God is 'in the right' in relation both to the covenant with Israel and to the problem of human sin and cosmic corruption. This vision is what Paul refers to in Romans 1.17 and 3.21 as the unveiling of the divine righteousness.[472] One might refer to all this in terms of '**inaugurated forensic and covenantal eschatology**'.

This inauguration, then, has taken place in the Messiah. Just as the wilderness tabernacle was as it were a micro-Eden, a miniature new world, so the resurrection of Jesus is to be seen as the sharply focused rectification, putting-right, of the whole created order. The divine verdict *against* the power of sin on the cross (Romans 8.3) results in the divine verdict *in favour of* creation in the resurrection. As we saw earlier, the Messiah is thus the revelation-in-action of the divine faithfulness in the full, combined sense. In him the intended 'goal' has come forward into the present. In his physical body he is the living presence of the creator and covenant God (Colossians 1.19–20; 2.9). His dying flesh has borne the weight of sin's condemnation (Romans 8.3); his resurrection embodies the start, and the means, of

[470] See the various positions represented by e.g. Hays 2005 [1989b], 119–42; Schreiner 1998, 74; Watts 1999.

[471] This presumably stands behind the otherwise surprising 1 Tim. 3.16, *edikaiōthē en pneumati.*

[472] It may be asked whether there is a distinction between *apokalyptetai* in 1.17 and *pephanerōtai* in 3.21. The present tense of the first seems to focus on what happens, and goes on happening, whenever Paul announces the gospel and someone comes to faith, while the perfect tense of the latter focuses on what *has* happened, a past event with continuing meaning and effect, in the events concerning Jesus (so e.g. Cranfield 1975, 202). Whether there is also a subtle shading of the verbal meaning ('revealed', with the emphasis on something not previously seen now being disclosed, and 'made manifest', with the emphasis on something previously only faintly glimpsed being now spread out for all to see) is more debatable: Cranfield suggests that *apokalypteo* and *phaneroō* are at this period more or less synonymous. I venture the possibility that *apokalypteō* highlights the sudden dawning of faith when a person is grasped by the truth of the gospel, while here at least *phaneroō* may indicate the visible spreading out of the truth of the divine righteousness before all peoples (cf. 3.27–30).

the whole new creation (1 Corinthians 15.23). He is therefore the true 'seed' of Abraham (Galatians 3.16, 19, 29).

The entire Jew-plus-gentile family, now designated as 'Abraham's seed', has that title because they are 'in him' and 'belong to him' (Galatians 3.26–9); and the badge of that belonging is of course *pistis*, the 'faith' which believes that the one God raised Jesus from the dead (Romans 4.24–5; 10.9). That 'faith' itself is not, as some might suppose, either an arbitrary standard or a kind of religious characteristic which the creator happens to approve. The *cognitive content* of the faith (believing that Jesus was raised) corresponds to the *character* of the faith as the first sign of new life (see 7 below), and grasps above all, in the light of the resurrection through which the cross is seen not as a shameful defeat but as a glorious victory, that the *faithful death* of the Messiah was the ultimate act of divine judgment on sin, in other words, the covenantal act through which humans are rescued from sin and death and Abraham's blessing flows out to the world.

This is why Paul can describe the divine action of 'justifying' as being 'through the redemption which is *in Messiah Jesus*' (Romans 3.24). Once we join up the *forensic* eschatology with the theme of the *covenant*, there is no longer a problem about integrating any of it with Paul's regular *incorporative* theme. Were it not such an ugly tongue-twister, one might be tempted to refer to Paul's 'inaugurated/incorporative forensic/covenantal eschatology', or his 'inaugurated-eschatological forensic-covenantal incorporation'. Perhaps it would be easier in German. Or perhaps we should just say, as Paul himself does, 'justified in the Messiah' – remembering all that is now built into that dense phrase.

Because, and only because, the Messiah has died and been raised, fulfilling the creator's covenantal purpose and thereby revealing his 'righteousness', in all senses, before the world, the bursting of the creator's future purpose into the present time is matched exactly by the declaration, in the present and in advance, of the verdict of the last day (point 5 above). Now at last we can understand Paul's great theme of justification by grace, through faith, *in the present time.*

7. When Paul speaks about people being 'justified' in the present, he is *drawing on the framework of eschatological, forensic, participatory and covenantal thought* I have sketched above. He does so in order to insist, from a variety of angles because of the different arguments he is mounting, that ***in the present time*** *the covenant God declares 'in the right', 'within the covenant', all those who hear, believe and obey 'the gospel' of Jesus the Messiah.*[473] The *future* verdict (point 5) is thus brought forward into the *present*, because of the utter grace of the one

[473] For 'obeying the gospel' see Rom. 10.16; 2 Thess. 1.8. This is cognate of course with *hypakoē pisteōs* in Rom. 1.5 and elsewhere. A similarly comprehensive description of the different aspects of justification, but importantly without the covenantal dimension, is provided by Schnelle 2005 [2003], 470.

God seen in the 'faithful' death of the Messiah (point 6) and then at work, as we shall now see, through the spirit in the gospel.

Several things need explaining here: seven of them, in fact, nested within this seventh point itself.

(i) First, as we indicated above, the verb *dikaioō* is *declarative*. When the judge in an ordinary Hebrew law court finds in favour of a person, that person is thereby deemed to be 'in the right' (Hebrew *tsaddiq*; Greek *dikaios*). Though this word can also (confusingly to us) denote the person's character or behaviour, in virtue of which the decision has been made, the meaning of *dikaios* within the law court setting is not 'righteous' in the sense of 'this person is well-behaved and so deserves to win the case,' but rather 'this person has received the court's favourable verdict.'[474] The declaration, in other words, is not a 'recognition' of 'what is already the case', nor the creation of a new character, but rather the *creation of a new status*. Up to that point, within the courtroom metaphor, prisoners in the dock have the status, in terms of the court (and thus of the wider society which the court represents), of being under accusation. Now, after the declaration, they have a new standing in the community. The court has found in their favour; they are 'in the clear', 'in the right'. They can walk away with head held high. Their *status* has, in that sense, been 'rectified', though to speak thus might easily cause confusion here, suggesting that after all the notion of 'personal transformation' might be smuggled in to the very precise meaning of 'justification'. What has happened, rather, is that the social standing of the person within the community has been 'put right', sorted out, re-established.

The Greek word for this new status is *dikaiosynē*. This is what it means for 'righteousness' to be either 'reckoned' or 'accounted' to someone. They possess 'righteousness' as a result of the judge's *declaration*.[475] Up to the moment when the judge says, 'I find this person *dikaios*,' it makes no difference how upright and innocent the person in question may be; until the declaration at the end of the case, they do not possess that status *in the forensic context and sense*. Here Vanhoozer is particularly helpful: 'Never mind imputed righteousness,' he says; 'the first thing to clarify is what, for lack of a better term, we may call *locuted* righteousness.'[476] He quotes Thiselton, probably the sharpest mind on such matters in biblical studies for a century or more: 'It is not a descriptive locution, but an illocutionary speech-act of declaration and verdict.' The judge's declaration works on the analogy of other speech-acts which *create* a new status or situation: 'You're fired'; 'I pronounce that they are husband and wife';

[474] This is clearly expressed by e.g. Caird 1976, 138.

[475] See the earlier discussion of Gen. 38.26; 1 Sam. 24.17.

[476] Vanhoozer 2011, 248 (italics original).

'I declare the meeting adjourned.'[477] The declaration creates and constitutes a new situation, a new status.[478]

We stress again: this is a *declaration*, not a *description*. It does not *denote or describe a character*; it *confers a status*. In that sense, it *creates* the status it confers. Up to that point, the person concerned cannot be spoken of as 'righteous', but now they can be and indeed must be.[479] Thus the *status* of being 'in the right', reckoned 'righteous', is actually *created by*, and is *the result of*, the judge's declaration. That is what it means to say that the status of 'now being in the right', *dikaiosynē*, has been *reckoned* to the person concerned.

At this point it ought to be clear beyond any further cavil that this 'status', which the person has as a result of the declaration of the judge, cannot be the same as the 'righteousness' of the judge himself.[480] The judge's own 'righteousness' consists in hearing the case fairly according to the law, remaining impartial, supporting widows and orphans, punishing evil and upholding the good. To say that *this* 'righteousness' is somehow accounted to, or accredited to, the

[477] Thiselton 2000, 455f.; his 455–8 constitute an extremely important statement on how the whole language-system of justification works, a statement which deserves to be brought out of its hiding one-third of the way through a book even larger than the present one. He builds on the work of Searle 1969 and Austin 1975, and here cites and discusses Wolterstorff 1995, 75–94 and others. Vanhoozer also cites, helpfully, Searle 1979, 26.

[478] I am not clear that this *declarative* sense is fully grasped in Käsemann's statement (1980 [1973], 112f.) that God 'makes the ungodly person a new creature' and in that sense 'really makes him righteous'. The word 'righteous' is too slippery in English at least, and I suspect *gerecht* in German may be too: this is bound to appear as though 'righteous' means 'in principle a morally upright person', which corresponds to the Tridentine view that one might have expected Käsemann to reject. See too, rightly, Schreiner 2001, 205 (correcting his earlier position in Schreiner 1998); and see the discussion in Bird 2007, 12–14. This highlights the danger with using 'rectify' for 'justify': it can easily imply that something has happened in justification which will not actually happen until final 'justification', i.e. until the resurrection.

[479] Schreiner 2010, 155 seems to me to misunderstand this, suggesting that judges do not, themselves, 'make' anyone 'righteous'. If 'righteousness' here is *the status conferred by the judge's decision* then, in that sense only, 'making someone righteous' is precisely what the judge does at the end of the trial. McCormack 2004, 107 likewise thinks that 'the human judge can only *describe* what he hopes to be the real state of affairs' (italics original) so that 'the human judge's judgment is in no sense effective; it does not create the reality it depicts. It seeks only to conform to an already given reality.' But he then, unlike Schreiner, contrasts this with the divine verdict: 'God's verdict differs in that it creates the reality it declares ... so a judicial act for God is never merely judicial; it is itself transformative.' This is (a) a false antithesis: both the human judge and the divine judge do indeed *create* the new *status*; (b) a false inference: McCormack (much like Gorman 2009, 101) is confusing the transformation of *status* with the transformation of *character*, which, though inseparable in fact, is not what is denoted by the language of 'justification' itself. The danger with making a word do something outside its job-description is that the job it was supposed to do gets neglected.

[480] Contra e.g. Schreiner 2001, 201, who, though seeing the importance of the divine judge, then slides into vague and essentially unbiblical formulations. Vanhoozer 2011, 258 tries to resist the point by saying that 'the Reformers were talking about the *status* of *Christ's* covenant faithfulness' (italics original). To this I reply (a) that the Reformers were not usually talking about the covenant at all, at least not in the sense that I have been using that term; (b) that many of their successors have been allergic to covenantal ideas; (c) more importantly, both the Reformers and their successors regularly elided the idea of 'Christ's righteousness' with that of 'God's righteousness', wrongly interpreting the latter as 'the righteous status' of God's people, and taking references to the divine righteousness (e.g. Rom. 3.21), read in that sense, as references to the former, thus missing the point Paul was actually making and elevating something he was not saying to the status of a central doctrine.

vindicated defendant makes no sense: it would mean saying that such a person is deemed to have tried the case fairly, and so forth, which is obviously not the point. Likewise, the meaning of 'righteousness' as applied to the vindicated defendant (or, indeed, a vindicated plaintiff) is that the person has been declared to be in the right – which is not what is being said when one speaks of the 'righteousness' of the judge. This confusion goes back to the medieval ontologizing of *iustitia* as a kind of quality, or even a substance, which one person might possess in sufficient quantity for it to be shared, or passed to and fro, among others. This mistake has been perpetuated, in more recent times, by the proper and understandable desire to affirm the security of the believer's status by speaking of 'the righteousness of God', or even, as Paul never does, 'the righteousness of Christ', as being like a capacious cloak which the believer can put on.[481] Paul, however, has other ways of achieving the latter aim, as we shall see.

The fact that being thus 'accounted righteous' has to do with a *forensic status* rather than with any kind of recognition of an earlier-formed character, or promise of subsequent character-transformation (such as might be implied here by the language of 'rectification'), can be seen if we consider the case of a miscarriage of justice. In a court case it is of course to be hoped that the judge's declaration will correspond to earlier reality: that the person now given the *new* status of 'righteous' in this *forensic* sense will in fact have been 'righteous' in the sense of 'having good character', and specifically in terms of being innocent of the charges in the particular case. But in the case of a miscarriage of justice, where a guilty person may have been acquitted, the verdict 'in the right' still means that the person concerned has the status of *dikaiosynē*. The person concerned might actually be a notorious and wicked character, not well-behaved at all. They might in fact be guilty of the crime in question, and might have obtained the verdict by luck, bribery or juridical incompetence. The fact remains: when the court finds in their favour, they are 'declared to be in the right'.

This kind of miscarriage of justice is, of course, what Paul at first seems to be indicating when he says that all those who believe the gospel are *dikaios* – despite the fact that a moment before they had been standing guilty in the dock with nothing to say in their defence.[482] This is where it looks as if the one God is doing precisely what scripture says a judge must never do – indeed, what this God

[481] The much-loved Isa. 61.10, often cited in this connection (cf. Job 29.14; Bar. 5.2), does not refer to the righteousness of the covenant God himself, but, as with Phil. 3.9 (see below), to the righteous status (i.e. here that of covenant membership) which is the gift *of* the covenant God.

[482] Rom. 3.19f.: the law court metaphor is apparent throughout.

himself says he will not do! – namely, acquit the guilty.[483] This paradox is of course what centuries of protestant thought in particular have gloried in above all, namely the 'justification of the ungodly', the free and gracious divine act which overrides all questions of desert, merit, qualification or lack thereof, and which gratuitously confers the status 'righteous' on those who have done nothing to deserve it.[484]

The first thing to get clear, then, is that the word 'justification', within its forensic sense, refers very precisely to *the declaration of the righteous God that certain people are now 'in the right', despite everything that might appear to the contrary.*

It is all too easy, when thinking through this whole initial line of thought, to suppose that Paul is *only* talking about human sin and justification. But, as we have seen at length already, he employs the same language, at the same time, to address the issue of Abraham's eschatological family, and the question of whether Jews are automatically in it, and whether gentiles, coming in, need to take on full Torah-observance, particularly circumcision. Having discovered more precisely how the 'forensic' language works, then, how does it apply to these 'covenantal' questions? The question of the divine 'righteousness' was, after all, raised most acutely in the first century not as an abstract question about how the creator would deal with sin, but as a covenantal question about how and when the covenant God would fulfil his promises and rescue his people.[485]

When we think of the 'declaration' of the covenant God, in the light of all that has been said so far, it should be clear that for Paul this declaration was made, foundationally, when Jesus was raised from the dead. This event was to be interpreted as the declaration that Jesus really was Israel's Messiah, and that Israel was being reconstituted in and around him. The divine covenantal declaration about the Messiah is then brought forward, through the preaching of the gospel and the work of the spirit, and repeated in the case of believers. What the one God said of Jesus at Easter – the covenantal declaration as well as the announcement of Jesus' 'vindication' in a forensic sense – is now said 'upon faith', *epi tē pistei*. We must explore this further below.

In Paul's theology all this means two tightly interconnected realities, both of which he urgently wants to stress. First, all those over whom that declaration is made are *permanently* 'in the right'. The status of *dikaiosynē* is not temporary. It truly anticipates the verdict which will be issued on the final day. This is why 'justification' is the

[483] cf. e.g. Ex. 23.2, 6, 7 [*ou dikaiōseis ton asebē heneken dōrōn*]; Lev. 19.15; Dt. 1.17; 10.17; 16.18–20; 24.17; 27.19; 2 Chr. 19.6f.; Ps. 82.2; Prov. 17.15; 18.5; 24.23f.; 28.21; Eccl. 5.8; Isa. 5.23 [*hoi dikaiountes ton asebē heneken dōrōn*]; 10.2; Jer. 5.28; Am. 5.12; Mal. 2.9. Passages which include a reference to the judgment of the one God himself include Ex. 23.7; Dt. 1.17; 10.17; 2 Chr. 19.6f.

[484] See particularly Käsemann 1980 [1973], 112f.; Jewett 2007, 314f. Jewett stresses, against various commentators, that 'faith' is not itself a surreptitious form of 'religious qualification'.

[485] See B. W. Longenecker 1990.

heart of what later generations would rightly see as Christian *assurance*. Properly speaking, 'justification' is not 'how someone becomes a Christian', but 'how someone who becomes a Christian through believing the gospel and being baptized can be sure they will receive the verdict "righteous" on the last day'. The judge has already pronounced it, and his word will stand. Second, this declaration, and this status of *dikaiosynē*, applies equally and on the same basis to *all* who believe the gospel, Jew and gentile alike, fulfilling the covenant promise of Abraham's worldwide family. It is in other words the basis, the only basis, for full church membership – because, by their very character, the declaration and the *pistis* over which it is made both look back to the Messiah himself who constitutes in himself the renewed people of the creator and covenant God. The second point is the main theme of Galatians, though with echoes of the first; both together, fully interwoven and interlocking, provide the main theme of Romans. Paul would, I think, have said that the second point reinforces the first: it is by being accepted as a member of the single family that people are strengthened in their assurance. This is part of the meaning of *agapē*.

This leads us directly to the second sub-point.

(ii) The second thing that needs explaining is that this present verdict is utterly dependent, for Paul, on the *past work* of the Messiah (point 6 above). His faithfulness to death (also spoken of as his 'obedience') is the moment when Israel's appointed task, of rescuing humankind and the world, is at last accomplished. The promised future burst into the present in the cross and resurrection, revealing the ultimate judgment and covenant faithfulness of the one God, precisely *through* his 'faithfulness', for the benefit of all believers (Romans 3.21–2). Paul has a dozen or more ways of talking about the cross as a single, past achievement. All that he says about present status, forgiveness, covenant membership and everything else depends on this. *The present declaration 'in the right', 'covenant member', depends on the past achievement of the Messiah's saving death.*

We have already stressed this point earlier both in the present section and in the whole chapter. It remains to note, however, that in many discussions words like 'ground' and 'basis' appear (as in 'the cross is the ground of justification' or 'on the basis of faith').[486] These words, with their implicit building metaphor, should not be absolutized and then made the subject of inquisition. What counts is the *historical narrative* in which the actual work of the Messiah opens up the new world over which the word 'forgiveness' is written, the new multi-ethnic family promised in the Abrahamic covenant. A firm grasp of biblical eschatology means that a nervous grasp on non-eschatological terminology can be relaxed. In particular, as we saw

[486] See O'Brien 2004, 292f.

above, this second point should not be ontologized into any idea of the Messiah's own 'righteousness', or his 'obedience to the law'.[487]

(iii) The people declared to be 'in the right' are the people who are *incorporated into the Messiah.* Present justification is utterly dependent on the past achievement of the cross, but the Messiah is not merely a figure of history whose achievement has created a new possibility. The Messiah is the one 'in whom' his people are what they are. The verdict, then, is announced '*in* the Messiah'.[488] One can see the link, perhaps, by saying that the verdict which the living God announced when he raised Jesus from the dead ('he really is my son', as in Romans 1.4) becomes the verdict the same God announces over all who are incorporated into the Messiah. What is said of the Messiah is rightly said of those who are 'in him'. That is why 'adoption' in Romans 8 or Galatians 4 is simply a way of exploring the meaning of 'justification', rather than a separate category.[489]

It is striking that in each of his major expositions of justification Paul says, almost in one case as an aside, that justification is something that happens 'in the Messiah':

> They are justified freely by his grace through the redemption which is *in the Messiah*, Jesus.
>
> If, in seeking to be declared 'righteous' *in the Messiah*, we ourselves are found to be 'sinners' . . .
>
> . . . that I may gain the Messiah, and be found *in him*, not having a 'righteousness' of my own which is out of the law but that which is through the faith[fulness] of the Messiah, the righteousness from God which is upon faith.[490]

[487] I understand the reasons for the drift in this direction (the 'active obedience of Christ', as in some strains of Calvinist and indeed Anglican theology). Even Vanhoozer's gracious advocacy (2011, 250f.) cannot overturn the fact that Paul never puts it like this, and that he arrives by quite other means at the goal towards which this formulation is aiming. Yes: the faithful are accounted righteous 'in the Messiah'; but this is not because the Messiah possesses something called 'righteousness', earned by his own personal covenantal lawkeeping, which he can share with or 'impute' to his people, but because the Messiah *is* the covenant-people-in-person, demonstrated as such by his being raised from the dead. Since I regard the word 'righteousness' as having 'covenant membership/faithfulness' as one of its Pauline meanings, one could then say that, since those who are 'in the Messiah' have his 'covenant membership/faithfulness' reckoned to them, this counts as a form of 'imputed righteousness'; but again Paul never says that, and this is not at all what the advocates of 'imputation' are thinking of.

[488] So, rightly, e.g. Hays 2002 [1983], xxix–xxiii. This point goes back to Calvin, and is one of the most important in the present debate (joining together 'incorporative' and 'forensic' languages, as Paul himself does). McCormack 2004, 110 seems to me wrong to make the idea merely functional, speaking of a 'conformity of my life to [Christ's] life of obedience . . . a union of wills'. He is anxious to avoid a 'Greek ontology of pure being' according to which the idea of 'union with Christ' would mean 'a substantial participation in the being of Christ' (112); but might there not be – as Schweitzer thought – precisely a *Hebrew* concept of such participation?

[489] This is the point which, going back within the protestant tradition at least to Calvin, is rightly stressed by Vanhoozer 2011. I had thought I had emphasized it in earlier writings, but in case I had not made it sufficiently clear I am glad to do so now. On 'adoption' see now the important study of Burke 2006.

[490] Rom. 3.24; Gal. 2.17; Phil. 3.8f.; all translated fairly literally.

In other words, the Messiah's death constitutes the past event which enables justification to take place, and the Messiah's present incorporative life is the context within which it makes sense for the one God to make the same declaration over people *now* that he made over the Messiah himself in the resurrection. The verdict pronounced over the Messiah's *pistis* is now pronounced over the *pistis* of those who are 'in him'. The Messiah died to sin, once for all; this person is 'in the Messiah'; therefore this person is deemed, reckoned, accounted to have 'died to sin'. That is exactly what Paul says in Romans 6, but it is not a new point; it is simply a restatement in other terms of what he had said in chapter 3. Indeed, if we see 3.24 ('redemption in the Messiah') as an advance shorthand summary, chapter 6 is not even really 'in other terms'. It is drawing out what was already hinted at. Thus *the present declaration 'in the right', rooted in the Messiah's death, is pronounced over all who are 'in the Messiah'.*

This is *not*, however, a matter of the Messiah possessing in himself the status of 'righteous', and this 'righteousness of the Messiah' somehow being 'imputed' to the believer.[491] I understand the almost inevitable pressure towards some such reading, granted the medieval context to which the Reformers were responding, and the pastoral needs which such an idea of 'imputed righteousness' is believed to address. But it is not Pauline. (a) Paul never speaks of the Messiah having 'righteousness'. In the one place (1 Corinthians 1.30) where he comes closest, he also speaks of him having 'become for us God's wisdom – and righteousness, sanctification and redemption as well'. So if we were to speak of an 'imputed righteousness' we should add those others in as well, which would create a whole new set of doctrinal puzzles. (b) The second half of the apparent 'exchange' of 2 Corinthians 5.21 is not about 'the Messiah's righteousness', but about 'God's righteousness'; and it is not about 'imputation', but about Paul and those who share his apostolic ministry 'becoming', that is, 'coming to embody', that divine 'righteousness' as ministers of the new covenant.[492] (c) When Paul does speak of things that are true of the Messiah being 'reckoned' to those who are 'in him', the focus is not on 'righteousness', but on death and resurrection (Romans 6.11). That is actually a much stronger basis for the pastoral application which those who teach 'imputed righteousness' are rightly anxious to safeguard. Those who belong to the Messiah stand on resurrection ground.[493]

[491] Among the voluminous recent discussions see the helpful historical note in McGowan 2006, 153f.; and see Bird 2007, ch. 4. Gundry 2004 is in my view correct to contest the classic notion of 'imputation', though his own way of putting things creates to my mind almost as many problems again.

[492] See above, 874–85.

[493] For a more extended discussion, see Wright 2002 [*Romans*], 533–41. Rom. 5—8 is Paul's 'argument for assurance'; and at its heart we find crucial passages such as 8.5–8, 12–17.

As we have seen, the sign that one is 'in the Messiah' is twofold: baptism and faith. The former we shall come to presently; the latter needs attention at this point. We can set aside the older views that 'faith' is an 'easier' kind of 'work', something people will be able to do having failed the harder test of keeping the law; or that 'faith', as opposed to 'legalism', is the kind of religious attitude that the creator had wanted all along, the kind he therefore rewarded when he found it in Abraham. Faith, in Paul's sense, is the Messiah-badge, because it was his *faithfulness* in the sense of his *faithfulness to the covenant*, his *obedience unto death*, that accomplished the divine purpose; and also because it is the belief that the one God raised him from the dead.[494] The word 'faith' functions like the word 'view' in the sentence 'Do you have a view from your room?': it is defined in relation to its object. The 'view' from the room is not something you possess. It consists precisely in being able to see the distant scene. The 'faith' in Paul's sense is not valued for a 'quality' it possesses in itself. It is defined entirely by, and in terms of, its object. It is what it is because it looks away from itself, and looks towards, and leans all its weight upon, the single act of the one God in the Messiah. It then becomes, as with Abraham, the sign of truly human life, giving glory to the powerful creator and believing that he does what he promises.[495] And it becomes, in particular, the sign of the new covenant, the true 'doing of the law'.[496]

(iv) All this comes true in personal reality *because of the work of the spirit*.[497] This point alone justifies the placing of this entire discussion under the head of 'election redefined through the spirit'. The place of the spirit in all this is often either misunderstood or not even grasped, but it is fundamental for Paul. The spirit works, through the proclamation of the good news of the Messiah, to generate faith in humans and to constitute all those who believe as the single forgiven family promised to Abraham.[498] Nobody, says Paul, can say 'Jesus is lord' except by the spirit; and, as he elsewhere explains, 'Jesus is lord'

[494] Rom. 4.24f.; 10.9.

[495] Rom. 4.18–22, reversing 1.18–26.

[496] Rom. 10.5–11.

[497] Bird 2007, 173 says that this effectively shifts the material cause of future justification from christology to pneumatology. I deny the disjunction: the spirit is in any case the Messiah's own spirit, and everything the spirit does is done by applying the work of the Messiah, which remains foundational.

[498] Jewett 2007, 315: 'The Spirit was understood to evoke positive responses to the gospel, making persons know in the depth of their despair and dishonor that together they could call God "Abba" and live as honored "children of God".' One might want to integrate Jewett's sociological 'despair and dishonor' back into the more usual theological analysis, but his point about the sovereign faith-evoking work of the spirit is well taken. So too e.g. McCormack 2004, 108: 'Paul understands faith to be a gift of God wrought by his grace in the human heart.' Quite so (against e.g. Schreiner 2001, 194, 208 who suggests that the gift of the spirit is consequent upon justification). Historically, this brings us to the questions often considered under the Latin tag of *ordo salutis*, the attempt to line up chronologically the various elements which take someone from the unregenerate state of sin to the ultimate state of salvation (see e.g. McGowan 2006). Paul does not discuss these questions, though some have seen Rom. 8.29f. as a hint in that direction.

is the most basic Christian confession, the outward and verbal sign of the inward belief in Jesus' resurrection.[499] 'The gospel came to you in power, in the holy spirit, and with full conviction,' he says to the Thessalonians; 'it was, after all, not a human word, but the divine word which was at work in you believers.'[500] In explaining to the Philippians that their suffering is itself a gift of God, he brackets this along with the earlier gift of faith, and this resonates with the statement a few paragraphs earlier that 'the one who began a good work in you will thoroughly complete it.'[501] Faith, it seems, is the beginning of the 'good work' begun as a sheer gift. 'You have been saved by grace, through faith,' he explains in the circular we call 'Ephesians'; and 'this doesn't happen on your own initiative; it's God's gift.'[502] This raises other questions for us, and indeed for Paul himself: why, for instance, do some believe and others not?[503] That has pushed some towards Jacobus Arminius, saying that 'faith' as it were comes from the human side, with justification and the gift of the spirit consequent upon it. It has pushed others towards a kind of Barthian position (whether or not Barth would have held such a thing), saying that 'justification' itself happens before all time, or at least in the one-off events of Jesus' death and resurrection, and certainly prior to anything 'happening' in the believer. The former delays divine action until the human initiative has taken place; the latter insists on divine initiative to the point where human response is hardly necessary. But if we stick with Paul there can be no doubt that he saw the work of the spirit, through the proclamation of the crucified and risen Jesus as lord, as the effective and immediate cause of people coming to believe that the one God had indeed raised Jesus from the dead. And that was, of course, the *pistis* which Paul described as relating directly to the divine verdict in the present.[504] Election, redefined around the Messiah through the resurrection, is then opened up by the spirit to include all those who are 'in the Messiah'. *The faith because of which the one God declares those in the Messiah to be 'in the right' is itself the work of the spirit through the proclamation of the gospel.*

We should note, in the light of what we have said earlier, that when Paul speaks of the work of the gospel he is saying things which he might just as well have said of the spirit. That which God has done once for all in the Messiah is put into effect in the lives of communities and persons through the spirit-energized announcement of the messianic achievement. Thus, though the spirit is not mentioned as

[499] 1 Cor. 12.3; Rom. 10.9f. Here too the spirit is present just behind the argument, through the quotation from Joel 2.32 in Rom. 10.13: see below, e.g. 1077, 1164–6, 1249.

[500] 1 Thess. 1.5; 2.13.

[501] Phil. 1.29; 1.6.

[502] Eph. 2.8.

[503] cf. e.g. Rom. 10.14–21.

[504] cf. again Rom. 10.9; cf. 4.24f.

such in Romans 3 and 4, Galatians 2, or Philippians 3, the other places where the spirit is brought into the picture make it clear that Paul is presupposing it elsewhere also. One cannot, in writing dense theology, say everything one might in principle have said on every occasion – though the pressure to do so, lest someone accuse you of missing something out, can become acute.

Does this mean that 'justification' is dependent upon, or subsequent to, 'regeneration'? I am sometimes accused of saying this, though since 'regeneration' is not a term that occurs in any of Paul's discussions of justification it is not a way of speaking I would favour.[505] 'Regeneration' is primarily a Johannine concept, and we should be wary of superimposing it on Paul's careful language and categories. The fear, of course, is that 'justification' would after all depend on 'something in me' – the beginnings, some might say, of 'subsequent ethical transformation', taking us back to the earliest Reformation debates.[506] Well: if the alternative is to say that 'justification' is the divine declaration made in the death and resurrection of Jesus, which is then simply enjoyed in faith, we would be on the way to a universalism which, however popular in some circles, would not be favoured by my ultra-Reformed critics. Nor, more to the point, would it make sense in the light of Romans 2.1–11.[507] We need, rather, to make a distinction.

It is true that the spirit who, through the gospel, inspires the first whisper of faith is the same spirit who then goes to work so that the person who has believed 'does the work of the law' in the way spoken of in Romans 2, 3, 8 and 10.[508] To that extent, as Paul insists in Philippians 1.6, 'the one who began a good work in you will thoroughly complete it by the day of Messiah Jesus.' There is continuity; and the spirit, Paul would insist, remains sovereign throughout. But the point is that the first sign of the spirit's work through the gospel is different in *character* from all that subsequent development. The first sign, the bare confession that Jesus is lord, the first sense in the heart that the creator God raised him from the dead, is precisely as we have seen a looking *away* from oneself and an utter trusting in the divine action in the Messiah. To turn that utter self-abandoning trust into a possession – like someone trying to 'possess' the view from their room – would be instantly to falsify it. The faith because of which one is declared 'righteous' consists simply of the helpless trust in what the one God has done in Jesus. Everything that comes later, the hard moral work of producing 'the fruit of the spirit', the putting to death of the deeds of the body and so forth – all that has a very different

[505] See e.g. Bird 2007, 103f., 184.

[506] cf. e.g. O'Brien 2004, 292.

[507] This kind of universalism is implicit in the theology of 'rectification' offered by Martyn and de Boer: if God has 'rectified' the world, the presence or absence of explicit faith becomes irrelevant.

[508] See below, 746 and elsewhere.

character from this initial utterly astonished and utterly humble spirit-inspired, gospel-driven confession that the crucified and risen Jesus is lord.

The later moral work matters. But the verdict *dikaios*, 'righteous', 'forgiven', 'covenant member', which is issued, as Paul says, 'upon that faith' (Philippians 3.9) – this verdict is not dependent upon that subsequent work. This is where we must sharply distinguish the *meaning* of 'justification' from the *concomitant fact* not only of personal renewal but even of *theōsis* (see below). 'Justification' does not denote those things. It is the initial verdict of God. Indeed, it is only the person who has heard that initial verdict, and understood what it really means, who can then go to work, still of course entirely in the power of the spirit, to do the things which Paul describes in Romans 8, Galatians 5 and elsewhere.[509]

The character of this initial faith, inspired by the work of the spirit, because of which the verdict *dikaios* is issued in the present time, means that 'assurance' – of membership in the single family, of the favourable verdict at the final assize – really does depend on something 'outside oneself', namely the unique and unrepeatable death and resurrection of Jesus the Messiah. Christian faith is precisely the glad and grateful grasping of that death as 'for me'. The proposal in some theology to ontologize this by speaking of a 'iustitia aliena', an 'alien righteousness', that is, a 'righteousness' which is and remains 'someone else's' as opposed to 'my own', is a valiant attempt to say again what Paul says in Philippians 3.9: 'not having my own *dikaiosynē* defined by Torah, but the *dikaiosynē* from God which is given to faith'. But the crucial mistake here – which a focus on the reshaping of election through the spirit helps us to avoid – is to separate what Paul explicitly joins in Philippians 1.6 and elsewhere. The confusion comes, I think, not least through the talk of 'regeneration' which has intruded into the conversation at the point where Paul speaks of the 'call' (what some theologians call the 'effectual call').[510] The point about the 'call' is that it is not 'an invitation to enjoy a new kind of religious experience'. It is a sovereign summons to acknowledge the risen Jesus as lord. It, like the 'faith' which it inspires, is all about Jesus, not about oneself. And what Paul elsewhere says even about all subsequent Christian life and work applies to the ultimate degree to the faith which responds to the call: 'yet not I, but the Messiah who lives in me'; 'it wasn't me, but God's grace which was with me'; 'struggling with all the energy which is powerfully at work in me'.[511] To speak in this way is not to court, as people sometimes

[509] That answers O'Brien 2004, 292, who suggests that the 'net effect' of seeing faith as the result of the spirit's work would be 'to undermine the basis of assurance'. The Paul of Phil. 1.6 would disagree.

[510] Rom. 8.29; Gal. 1.15; etc.

[511] Gal. 2.20; 1 Cor. 15.10; Col. 1.29. Cf. again Eph. 2.8: 'This doesn't happen on your own initiative; it's God's gift.'

sneeringly say, 'synergism' within a zero-sum understanding of Christian living (God does this bit, I do that bit, so we co-operate).[512] Leaving aside the fact that Paul himself uses the very word in a positive sense in 2 Corinthians 6.1 ('as we work together [with God]', *synergountes*), we must stress that a confluence between the divine life and the human life is precisely what the gospel brings about. But for that we need to move to our next category.

(v) The fifth basic point requires care and caution. What about *transformation*? The old protestant–catholic debates about justification often focused on the question of whether justification preceded or followed any change or transformation in the individual. Protestants regularly insisted that it preceded any such change, making it clear that justification was an act of utter, unmerited grace, not simply responding to a prior act of the individual. Catholics regularly saw 'justification' as being an *infusion* of 'grace' as a character-transforming power.[513] Debates aside, however, it is clear, as we have seen, that for Paul (a) 'justification', the declaration of 'righteous' over a person, is made *epi tē pistei*, 'upon faith', as in Philippians 3.9; (b) the 'faith' in question is, specifically, the belief that the one God raised Jesus from the dead, and that he is therefore Messiah and lord, as in Romans 10.9–10; (c) this faith itself arises from the work of the spirit through the gospel, as in Romans 10.13–15; (d) the work of the spirit can also be spoken of as having the initial result of the believer crying 'Abba, father', signalling adoption (Romans 8.15; Galatians 4.6). Clearly any attempt at an oversimplification, omitting the work of the spirit from the picture, will not do – however 'normal' such an omission has been in western theology.

But it is this same spirit which then, according to Paul, brings about the *final* resurrection (Romans 8.9–11); and the spirit is spoken of in that same passage as 'the spirit of the Messiah', or even just 'the Messiah' himself.[514] The same passage also emphasizes that the gift of this indwelling Messiah-spirit is basic to all Christian existence: 'anyone who doesn't have the spirit of the Messiah doesn't belong to him' (8.9b). This is closely cognate with the famous statement in Galatians 2.20: 'It isn't me any longer, it's the Messiah who lives in me.' When we put all this together, it is clear that, for Paul, the work of the spirit is basic to all Christian existence; that the spirit effects both the Abba-

[512] Bird 2007, 174 stresses that the statements of assurance in Rom. 5.1 and 8.1 look back to the work of Jesus. So they do; but they are both explained, in the latter case at length, by the work of the spirit.

[513] For an updated and eirenic – but to my mind inconclusive – continuation of this conversation see Reumann, Fitzmyer and Quinn 1982; and see the suggestive article of Lane 2006. Part of the trouble here, to be sure, is that the word 'grace' is easily misunderstood: for Paul it is a shorthand way of speaking of the gracious and utterly merciful act of the one God, but one can easily (but wrongly) suppose that it refers to a kind of spiritual or supernatural substance. Bird 2007, 67 n. 33 helpfully skewers the false antithesis between the 'imputation' and 'infusion' of 'righteousness'.

[514] Gorman 2009, 4 is perhaps misleading to speak of an 'easy interchange' here; the passage is complex, and Paul's language is precise throughout.

response of the adopted child to the one God and the *pistis* whose content is the resurrection of the crucified Messiah; and that the declaration *dikaios*, 'in the right', is therefore bestowed on those who are both 'in the Messiah' *and indwelt by the Messiah's spirit, by the Messiah himself.* Everything else Paul says about the spirit, not least in the adjacent passages in Romans 8, leaves us in no doubt that it is the same spirit that produces the radically transformed life which Paul insists must characterize the Messiah's people. And all this is well explained, of course, by what we saw in chapter 9: that Messiah and spirit together have provided, for Paul, the fresh meaning of Israel's one God himself. The complex simplicity of nascent trinitarian monotheism undergirds the simple complexity of Pauline soteriology.

This is where some have said that therefore the word 'justification' actually *denotes* the inner transformation which is effected by this indwelling.[515] My negative response to this is not driven by any knee-jerk desire to maintain my protestant credentials. Those have long since been taken from me, whether rightly or wrongly; perhaps that, too, will be sorted out on the last day.[516] No: my response to the proposal to identify 'justification' with the spirit's transformation is that this is not what the word means, either in itself or in its contexts. 'Justification' denotes the divine *declaration*. This word, 'in the right', is pronounced as an act of utter grace on the basis of the Messiah's death.[517] The people over whom this declaration is pronounced are those who believe the gospel message about Jesus; and this faith is the first sign of the work of the spirit. That is why Paul declares, as though to sum up the entire argument of Romans 5—8, that 'the one who began a good work in you will thoroughly complete it by the day of Messiah Jesus' (Philippians 1.6). That provides the key distinction. 'Justification' does not take place on the basis of any developed character-change. Nor does the word even *denote* the first beginnings of that, the work of the spirit by which someone calls the one God 'Abba' and believes in the risen Jesus. The word *denotes* the sovereign declaration of the covenant God.

Nor do the adjective 'righteous' and the abstract noun 'righteousness' *denote* anything about the change of heart whose first flutterings produce that faith. They *denote* the 'standing' which the believer has from that moment on, on the basis of the divine declaration, as a full, forgiven member of the single people of the covenant God. And it is

[515] Gorman 2009, 2, 40, 44. Oddly, at the same time Gorman seems to omit other key dimensions of justification, such as the place of Abraham or the Pauline emphasis on the coming together of Jew and gentile (e.g. 53).

[516] I may perhaps invoke, on my own account, 1 Cor. 4.5.

[517] Seifrid 2004, 149, misunderstanding this point, accuses me of saying that justification 'is construed as a pronouncement upon a human quality'. In the same passage he accuses John Piper of 'standing outside a Reformational framework' (149) and of advocating something 'nearly Tridentine' (150). Let the reader judge – or perhaps, in view of 1 Cor. 4, refrain from doing so.

because of the spirit, working in this way, that Paul can argue throughout Romans 5—8 that the future verdict announced over the entire life (Romans 2.1–16; 8.1, 31–9) will correspond to the present verdict that has been issued over nothing but *pistis* (3.21—4.25). That is the point of the advance summary of 5—8 in 5.1–5. Thus the spirit's work is vital; the inner transformation by the indwelling of the Messiah himself is vital; but *neither of those is what the word 'justification' means, or what the word 'righteousness' refers to.*[518]

This tricky and somewhat tortuous discussion might not have been necessary if more attention had been paid to Romans 2.25–9. That is where, within the actual argument of Romans, Paul has already sketched out (before we get anywhere near 3.21–31, the formal exposition of justification in the present) what is involved in belonging to the people of the renewed covenant. There is such a thing as heart-circumcision, as Deuteronomy had said. And this results in a new form of 'keeping the law' – whether or not the person concerned is a circumcised Jew.

As it stands this is teasing and provocative: what can this 'law-keeping' consist of? Only in Romans 10 does it finally become clear: it consists of confessing Jesus as lord, and believing that the one God raised him from the dead. But we should allow Paul to state his own terms, not least the ones he formulates in, it seems, a deliberately paradoxical way. When he speaks of people being justified by grace in the Messiah (3.24) and through *pistis* (3.25), and then goes on to speak of the *nomos pisteōs*, the 'law of faith' (3.27), those who have read 2.25–9 ought already to catch on to what he is saying. When they reach 10.1–13 they should nod in recognition: this was what it was all about. Once the multiple misunderstandings of various ecclesial traditions have been put to one side, Paul is after all not so unclear. What he says in one place cryptically, he regularly explains more fully later on.[519]

'Transformation', then, is emphatically part of the Pauline vision, the full picture both of 'covenant membership' and of 'salvation'. The indwelling of the Messiah-spirit is a basic, not a secondary or subsequent, element in all Christian existence. But the powerful work of the spirit, in and through the proclamation of the gospel, is not the same thing as 'justification'. 'Justification' is the declaration of the one God, on the basis of the death of Jesus: *this really is my adopted*

[518] Schreiner 2001, 192 explains how he had previously supposed that 'righteousness' could be both forensic and transformational and how he was persuaded out of that view. Unfortunately the change did not lead him to embrace a covenantal meaning, which would not have undermined the 'forensic' one but rather enhanced it. Gorman 2009, 54f. is right to say that 'the judicial image must be understood within a wider covenantal, relational, participatory and transformative framework' (and, we might add, 'apocalyptic' and 'salvation-historical' as well, to make the party more or less complete); but to understand something within a framework is not the same as understanding the meaning of the word itself. The hands on my clock must be understood within the framework of the whole mechanism, and of my need to know the time; but the hands are not the same thing as the pendulum, or indeed as my daily schedule.

[519] On Paul's view of the law see further below, 1032–8.

child, a member of Abraham's covenant family, whose sins are forgiven. And that declaration, in the present, anticipates exactly the final verdict which can also be described as 'adoption' (all this language, of course, reflects Israel's 'adoption' as 'God's son' at the exodus[520]): 'we who have the first fruits of the spirit's life within us are groaning within ourselves, as we eagerly await our adoption, the redemption of our body' (Romans 8.23). Whichever way you look at justification, whichever Pauline context you line up beside it, it always retains this character: the ultimate future brought forward into the present, and the two joined by the link of the spirit.

What then has happened to the *ordo salutis*, the hypothetical 'order of events in the process of salvation'? This is not, as we have said, something which Paul addresses head on, though the partial summary in Romans 8.28–30 points in that direction. It is the fruit of later attempts to construct a single scheme out of his various statements. But his answer would, I think, be fairly clear. We must remember, of course, that what to the theologian may appear as separate and consecutive 'moments' are likely to appear, to the new convert or indeed to the evangelist who is preaching the gospel, as a confusing jumble, just as the moment of falling in love, which a psychiatrist or even physiologist might explain in terms of minutely analyzed separate stages, most likely is not experienced in that way at the time. But we may at least try, even though the stages do not sound as exciting as the reality.

First, the spirit works through the proclamation of the gospel.[521] This powerful work of the spirit upon the human heart is what Paul labels the 'call'. Second – though as I say it may not feel like a subsequent event – the person answers the 'call' by 'confessing with the lips that Jesus is lord and believing in the heart that God raised him from the dead'. This is the faith like Abraham's, because of which, third, the one God declares, covenantally, that this person is a member of the family, and forensically, that this person is 'in the right', that their sins are forgiven. The word for *both* of these 'declarations' – which are of course not two but one – is 'justification'; the present and inalienable status resulting from both of them is 'righteousness'. That status is the basis both for assurance of final salvation and for assurance of membership in the single family; and the single family is the company of those with whom, according to Romans 5.17, the sovereign God will share his rule over the world. 'Those he called, he also justified; those he justified, he also glorified' (Romans 8.30).

Turning this sequential model round and looking at it from another angle, we discern that all of this happens through, in and for the Messiah: 'Those he foreknew, he also marked out in advance to be

[520] Ex. 4.22.

[521] Paul, of course, reaches back behind this 'first', to the ancient Hebrew notion of the divine foreknowledge and plan (Rom. 8.28f.), but he never spells out how he understands these.

shaped according to the model of the image of his son, so that he might be the firstborn of a large family' (8.29). That is why, among other things, the intermediate state between initial justification and the final verdict is to be marked, again as in Romans 8, by the Messiah-shaped cruciform life of holiness and suffering, by the spirit's transforming work, including the famous 'groaning' in prayer (8.26–7). None of these larger issues, even though they contextualize what Paul means by 'present justification', are the same thing. Justification is the divine declaration, creating the new status of 'righteous', 'adopted child', because of which the believer can move forward in the Christian pilgrimage. At every stage it utterly presupposes the one-off decisive work of the Messiah; at every stage it utterly requires the work of the spirit. This is the beating heart of redefined election.

(vi) The divine declaration issued over faith – 'in the right' in terms of the law court, 'adoption as sons and daughters' in terms of the covenant family – is the basis of unity 'in the Messiah' across traditional barriers. In other words, the declaration 'righteous' made by the one God is also, inescapably and centrally, the declaration that all those so designated constitute the Messiah's people, 'the Jew' of Romans 2.29, 'the circumcision' of Philippians 3.3.

This is further clarified, importantly for present debates, by recalling that 'the Jew', 'the circumcision', is basically, for Paul, the Messiah himself, and only secondarily those who belong to him. But the point of justification on the basis of Messiah-faith rather than on works of the law is now clear: this justification, precisely by 'justifying the ungodly', brings into this single Messiah-family a great company from every nation. The verdict *dikaios* issued in justification declares that the Messiah's people form *the single worldwide family*. One could put it even more strongly. The reason the divine declaration 'righteous' is issued, on the basis of the Messiah's death and 'for the benefit of all believers', is to constitute that single family, whatever its moral or ethnic background, as the worldwide company which the covenant God had always promised to Abraham. This is how Jew and gentile are joined together 'in the Messiah'. This is how the Messiah's people are to share his work, indeed his rule (5.17), in all the world. They are 'saved' for a purpose; and they are 'justified' in the present so that they may be assured that they are already a full part of that saved-for-a-purpose family.

This is where the 'covenantal' meaning of justification reasserts itself within the 'forensic' framework in which the future verdict is anticipated in the present. This is where, in other words, the third point above (the covenantal meaning) is revealed as the other side of the coin of the fourth point (the forensic meaning). In terms of 'how people get saved from sin and final judgment', one might say that the fulfilment of the Abrahamic covenant in the Messiah is the way by which the forensic verdict, future and present, is reached. In terms, however, of Paul's actual arguments, first in Galatians and then also in Romans, we will shortly suggest that it works the other way round. The underlying point of Paul's arguments in both letters is covenantal: this is how Jews and gentiles belong, in the Messiah, in the single family. And for that to happen the verdict 'condemnation' must have been replaced by the verdict 'righteous'. In other words, to oversimplify just a little: if we ask the sixteenth-century 'forensic' question, 'How can I find a gracious God?', the answer is 'through the covenantal work of Messiah and spirit'. But if we ask Paul's question, 'How can believing Jews and gentiles form one body in the Messiah?', the answer is 'through the announcement, in the present, that all who believe in the gospel are *dikaioi*, that the future verdict "no condemnation" has been brought forward, through the faithfulness of the Messiah, for the benefit of all who have faith'. This is Paul's inaugurated eschatology in full covenantal and forensic balance.

The creation of the single family in place of the divided peoples of the world – with the Jew/gentile split being the most obvious division for a Pharisee! – was in fact the central message that Paul wanted to get across to the muddled Galatians. It was the starting-point for what he wanted to say to the church in Rome. Paul could use it as the springboard for what he wanted to say in Philippians 3. And it is 'justification' – the divine declaration on the basis of Messiah-faith – that alone can constitute such a family. Once we have worked through the first five preliminary points, we ought to realize that this sixth one is where it has all been going. *Those who are declared or accounted 'righteous' on the basis of Messiah-faith constitute the single covenant family which the one God has faithfully given to Abraham.* The vocation of 'the Jew' in Romans 2.17 has devolved onto the Messiah himself.

But the community of the Messiah's people cannot be defined by Israel's law and the 'works' which it requires. The two reasons for this join together, as we see in Galatians 2.16–18. On the one hand, everyone 'in the law' has in fact broken the law. On the other hand, the effect of Israel's law is to divide the human race into two. The justification of the ungodly, by the fresh act of divine grace, is not only the divine means of forgiving sinners. It is also, for the same reason and as part of the same act, the divine means of creating the single Abraham-family. Indeed, it is *because* of the forensic verdict that the covenantal declaration can take place: the one God 'justifies the ungodly', bringing them into the one family. The fact that the one God has done this is the main reason why Paul sees the gospel of Jesus as the announcement that this one God has been 'faithful'. At this point we realize precisely that 'the righteousness of God' itself is not just *forensic* but *covenantal*, and that these are not two but one. And here we understand at last the full and urgent significance, within his historical and ecclesial context, of Paul's doctrine of justification. It is central, not marginal; polemical, yes, but not *merely* polemical.[522]

This sixth point, then, shares with the whole scheme a stress on *inaugurated eschatology*. Paul holds before the Roman church (15.7–13) the vision of a single community united in worship of the one God. That is the ultimate goal, which is properly anticipated in the present by the declaration that all who believe the gospel share equal membership in Abraham's family. Just as the life of the age to come is to be seen in advance in the personal and bodily behaviour of believers,[523] so the church as a whole, in its present life, must *anticipate* the ultimate unity on the basis of what has *already* been announced in the present verdict '*dikaioi*'. Believing Jews and believing gentiles already have *dikaiosynē* reckoned to them, and their present *koinōnia* must reflect that fact. That is the point of the whole letter to Galatia, and within Romans the specific point of 14.1—15.13. The verdict of the future has been brought forward into the present, redefining election around Messiah and spirit. Those caught up in this work of the gospel must live already as the single family for whom Messiah-faith, generated by the spirit, is the only badge of membership.

(vii) There remains the seventh point, and it will come as a surprise to some – but not to those who know Romans, 1 Corinthians, Galatians and Colossians. The actual event *in the present* which corresponds in advance to the actual event (resurrection) on the last day is *baptism*.[524]

Baptism *does*, outwardly and visibly (as the sacramental textbooks say), what justification *says*. Justification is the declaration made by the one God himself; baptism makes that divine word tangible and visible. Baptism, like justification, points back firmly to the death and resurrection of Jesus as the ground and means of the single divine saving action. Baptism, like justification, is inextricably linked with the work of the spirit through whom the whole church, now incorporating new believers, confess that Jesus is lord, affirm that the one God raised him from the dead and commit themselves to living under that lordship and trusting themselves entirely to his saving accomplishment.[525] Baptism, like justification, brings people from every background into the single family whose incorporative name is *Christos*, providing the basis for their common life.[526] In justification,

[522] Bird 2007, 30 is wrong, then, to lump my view along with those of Wrede, Schweitzer and others; see too Schreiner 2001, 192–4.

[523] As, for instance, in Rom. 6.1–14; 12.1–2; 13.11–14; 1 Thess. 5.1–11.

[524] See Schnelle 2005 [2003], 465. On baptism see above, 417–27; and e.g. Wright 2002 [*Romans*], 533–6.

[525] 1 Cor. 12.1–3, 12–13.

[526] Gal. 3.27, in the context of 3.26–9.

the covenant God 'reckons' that all who believe are 'righteous'; in baptism, Paul tells the Romans to 'reckon' that what is true of the Messiah is true of them – specifically, his death to sin and his coming alive to the one God.[527] Justification provides the solid platform, the new status of 'righteousness' as a pure gift, on which the entire edifice of Christian living is constructed; baptism reminds the whole church, and tells the new candidates, that they stand on resurrection ground. Justification brings the future *verdict* into the present; baptism brings the future *resurrection* into the present – and the future 'verdict' is of course the 'forensic' dimension precisely of that future resurrection.[528] Both ensure, when properly understood, that the entire Christian life is known to be 'in the Messiah', planted and rooted in his death and resurrection, and enabled by the spirit. Both are subject to the same problems: an over-concentration on the 'objectivity' and the '*extra nos*' of justification can lead to a carelessness about actual faith, never mind actual moral life, and an over-concentration on the 'objectivity' of baptism can lead to a similar casual or careless approach to actual Christian obligations. Paul addresses the first of these in Romans 6 itself, and the second in 1 Corinthians 10.

In exegetical terms, Romans 6 belongs intimately with Romans 3 and 4, as the combination of the same themes in Galatians 3 indicates. Once again, the argument of Romans 6—8 does not offer a different kind of soteriological thought to that of chapters 1—4; they are part of a single, though complex, train of thought. Baptism is as it were the *public celebration of justification by faith*, the active and visible summoning up of the exodus-events which were themselves freshly encoded in the death and resurrection of Jesus and the constitution of the believing community as the exodus-people who have firmly and decisively left Egypt behind and are being led by the spirit to their inheritance. It emphasizes, as does justification, the emphatic 'now' of Christian faith and life and the equally emphatic 'not yet', and holds them in proper balance. Here, in Romans 6, is the true Pauline 'imputation': 'calculate yourselves as being dead to sin, and alive to God in the Messiah, Jesus.'[529] Though Paul does not mention baptism in Galatians 2, those who know Romans 6 will have no difficulty detecting the baptismal resonances of 2.19–20. We have quoted it more than once before, but it bears repetition:

[527] Rom. 6.11 with 4.3–5, 10f., 23f.; cf. Gal. 2.19f.

[528] Despite an older view which insisted that 'present resurrection' was found only in Eph. and Col., it is in fact quite clear in Rom. 6: 'you' must 'reckon yourselves' to be 'alive to God' (6.11). This is not an invitation to imagine something which is not true. Rather, it is (a) the direct meaning of 6.5, 8 and (b) the necessary prelude to 6.12–14: the baptized are to yield themselves to God *hōsei ek nekrōn zōntas*, 'as those alive from the dead'. Unless there is a sense in which they are already raised, this is mere fantasy. See further e.g. Catchpole 2004; Gorman 2009, 74–6; and Wright 2002 [*Romans*], 538; 2003 [*RSG*], 251–4.

[529] Rom. 6.11.

> Through the law I died to the law, so that I might live to God. I have been crucified with the Messiah. I am, however, alive – but it isn't me any longer, it's the Messiah who lives in me. And the life I do still live in the flesh, I live within the faithfulness of the son of God, who loved me and gave himself for me.

That is the statement of the larger reality within which 'justification' nests. All these things have to happen, and do happen, when someone 'becomes a Christian'. 'Justification' is the declaration *that* those to whom they happen, those who now find themselves 'in the Messiah', with his death and resurrection 'reckoned' to them, are the single, sin-forgiven family promised by the covenant God to Abraham. And baptism is the action which turns that declaration into visible, concrete, symbolic praxis. Those who are baptized, in the ceremony that confesses Jesus as the crucified and risen lord, are therefore as it were in themselves small working models of inaugurated eschatology. They are also, in Paul's mind, designed to be agents of that same inaugurated eschatology in the world; but that is a further point to be explored later.

And, talking of small working models, we have now completed this sevenfold working model of what I take Paul's teaching on 'justification' to be all about. It is therefore almost time to turn to the relevant texts to see how it all works out in specific contexts.

Before we plunge into these passages more fully, though, a couple of reflections suggest themselves about where we have now arrived.

The notion of justification was at best marginal to the second-Temple belief in election. It was not needed, except (as in Qumran, and perhaps the *Psalms of Solomon*) when different groups began to think of themselves as in some sense the true remnant, the real 'Israel'.[530] With Paul, as we have seen, justification comes right into the centre, not despite but because of the fact that it is necessarily polemical. This observation enables us to see the ways in which this redefinition of election stands in very close parallel to the redefinition of monotheism we observed in the previous chapter. As we saw, in Paul the creational and covenantal monotheism characteristic of a devout first-century Pharisee is reconfigured around Messiah and spirit. Within that, we can trace the origin of christology through the themes of YHWH's return to Zion; through the resurrection and enthronement of the Messiah; and through the evidentiary work of the spirit. Now it appears that justification itself is built on more or less identical foundations. Justification depends on the fresh revelation in action ('apocalypse!') of the covenant God. Justification is unveiled through the resurrection of the Messiah, indicating that he and his people are the new covenant people, and that his death has defeated the ultimate enemy. Justification is effected through the work of the spirit, active in the preaching of the gospel to bring about the

[530] It is noteworthy that the *Eerdmans Dictionary of Early Judaism* (Collins and Harlow 2010), while naturally having an article on 'election', has none on 'justification'.

faith which joins up with the first two points, calling the one God 'father' and hailing the Messiah as the risen lord. We should not be surprised that in Paul monotheism and election join up. The faith that says 'Jesus is lord' and 'the covenant God raised him from the dead' is simultaneously (a) acclaiming this revised monotheism in the power of the spirit and (b) displaying the badge which says, 'Justified'.

This redefinition of 'election', initially around the Messiah (as earlier in this chapter) and now through the work of the gospel and the spirit, is the main theme of Romans 3 and 4, Galatians 2, 3 and 4 and Philippians 3.2–11.[531] Without pretending to offer the complete millimetre-by-millimetre exegesis that one might ideally want, we may suggest that the following reading of these key passages will provide a coherent and satisfying account, not least of the verses and phrases which are sometimes thought to point in other directions. Despite some of my critics, I persist in the claim that the best argument is always the sense that is made of whole passages in Paul rather than isolated sayings.[532]

As already in this chapter, I defer a consideration of Romans 9—11. Though it obviously has to do with the redefinition of election, its tight argument makes it difficult to extract individual themes. Its eschatological orientation makes it natural to tackle it in chapter 11 below.

So, though I am now inevitably going over ground already traversed elsewhere, I do so with one or two fresh aims in mind.

In particular, I am intending now to test my tentative hypothesis about the origin and development of Paul's view of justification. In Galatians and Philippians one can read the 'justification' language almost entirely in terms of 'covenant' and its redefinition, whereas in Romans that meaning is interwoven with the 'law court' imagery. My developmental proposal, then, is that since the only sort of 'justification' of which we are aware in second-Temple Judaism had to do with the redefinition of covenant membership, there is a possibility that Paul, having used the language in that primary sense in Galatians, went on from there to explore and develop its potential forensic meanings as a second layer. This then ties in with our exposition of 'plight and solution': Paul did not, we suppose, begin with the question of 'How can I be justified?' in a modern western sense, but came to his mature view, with all the varied elements fully integrated, initially through the sharp controversy in Galatia and then through various other pressures. At the same time, it is clear that already by the time he writes 1 Corinthians 4 he has firmly in mind, and running off the tip of his tongue, ideas and phrases which he will incorporate into Romans 2, which as we have seen is a key passage, a lynch-pin of much of this thought.

But we must proceed in order. The main aim now is to show, through brief consecutive exposition, how the sevenfold doctrine of justification is

531 I have recently tried to set this out afresh (see Wright 2009 [*Justification*] chs. 5, 6 and 7). What follows now reflects both continuity with, and development beyond, what was said there.

532 It is noticeable that throughout Bultmann's account of Paul in his *Theology*, the actual arguments of whole passages are very rarely mentioned.

presented in these passages and how the seven themes of Paul's soteriology, by which we mean 'forensic', 'participatory' and above all 'covenantal' eschatology, with their apocalyptic, anthropological, salvation-historical and transformational meanings all resonating, cohere and nest within one another throughout. And if all these sevens make the present exposition sound like something out of Revelation, that may after all not be inappropriate. Paul does after all announce the doctrine in terms of the *apokalypsis* of the divine righteousness.

(b) Galatians 2.15—4.11

We must now explore the way in which, in the central argument of Galatians, the election of Israel is redefined not only around the Messiah but also around the spirit. The gospel, as we saw, works through the spirit to produce 'faith'. That 'faith' becomes *the* boundary marker of Abraham's family, trumping all other contenders, particularly the traditions of table-fellowship and circumcision that would keep Jews and gentiles apart even within the Messiah's baptized and believing people.

The reason Paul was talking about 'faith' in Galatians is because it was, for him, the key answer to the question raised by the Antioch incident on the one hand and the Galatian problem on the other. The question at Antioch (2.10–14) concerned table-fellowship: were believing Jews to eat with believing gentiles or not? Peter, by his behaviour, was turning this round, in a way which anticipated the problem in Galatia: were (male) gentile believers to be required to join the inner circle of God's people, of Abraham's family? In other words, were they to 'judaize', to get circumcised? In both cases, Paul's answer was expressed in terms of *justification*, of *faith* and particularly of *Jesus* himself and his death – and with, as we noted, baptism either explicitly or implicitly part of the mix. But the context indicates well enough that these themes are to do with *membership in the people of Israel's God*; in other words, they were 'covenantal'.[533]

In Antioch, 'those who came from James' believed that the answer to the question about table-fellowship had to do with the basic Jewish identity-marker of circumcision. To Paul's horror, Peter and Barnabas, who had previously been happy to eat with gentiles, went along with the new arrivals. For those from Jerusalem, circumcision was the badge of the covenant, the key marker of the elect people. Paul, however, regarded circumcision as irrelevant for Jesus' followers and their identity, because election itself had been redrawn around Jesus himself. In its place there was another marker,

[533] It is remarkable that Schreiner 2010, 150–76, manages to expound Gal. 2.15–21 without discussing the question Paul and Peter were actually facing, treating the entire passage instead as being only about how sinners come to be 'in the right'. This is clearly vital, but not to the exclusion of the question of the status of believing gentiles, which continues to be the subject of ch. 3.

which equally well drew a line in the sand, but drew it at quite a different place: Messiah-faith.[534]

'We are Jews by birth, not "gentile sinners". But we know that a person is not declared "righteous" by works of the Jewish law, but through the faithfulness of Jesus the Messiah.'[535] With these words (2.16a), Paul states the working principle to which he held, fiercely, in Antioch, in the controversy in Galatia, in the Jerusalem Conference (whenever it was held) and, so far as we can tell, throughout his ministry.[536] We saw in the earlier part of this chapter that this principle was rooted, not in a piece of missiological pragmatism (we must somehow get gentiles to join in, but we'll have to make it easy for them), nor in a sense of laxity towards Jewish traditions (as though Paul was typical of Diaspora assimilation[537]), but in the fact of the crucified Messiah, the one upon whom Israel's destiny and identity had devolved and who, through his crucifixion, had put to death all human 'identities' in order to bring them through into a new existence corresponding to his own risen life. What we now notice is that it is the *pistis Iēsou Christou*, the faithfulness (i.e. the faithfulness-unto-death) of Jesus the Messiah, which then constitutes the appropriate badge of the community that finds itself redefined around him in turn. In response to 'the faithfulness of Jesus the Messiah', Paul declares (2.16b) that 'this is why we too believed in the Messiah, Jesus; so that we might be declared "righteous" on the basis of the Messiah's faithfulness, and not on the basis of works of the Jewish law.'

It is of course possible to translate this occurrence of *ek pisteōs Christou* as 'on the basis of faith in the Messiah'. Actually (to the chagrin, no doubt, of the hard-liners either way) I do not see that much hinges on this here. The point still stands, that it is the *faithful death* of Jesus that reconstitutes the people of God, and it is *the faith of believers* which therefore appropriately marks them out as members of that people. And, though I do think that *pistis Christou* really does mean 'the Messiah's own faithfulness' here in 2.16 and elsewhere (in 3.22, for instance), the point of *pistis* for much of

[534] This scarcely means that Paul, faced with the rival 'missionaries', was being 'equally cliquish and coercive' (so Eastman 2006, 313). This assumes, first, that Paul is objecting to his opponents because they were teaching the wrong sort of religion while he was teaching the right sort, whereas in fact he was announcing eschatological fulfilment. (Eastman 2010, 370, following Martyn 1997a, 41, tries to get off the hook of making Paul anti-Jewish by suggesting, despite the whole argument of Gal. including such passages as 1.13, 2.15 and the whole Abraham-argument, that 'there is no Jewish horizon in Galatians'; but this is absurd.) Second, it assumes that his criterion for the right sort of religion was some kind of modern 'inclusive' relativism, whereas his criterion for eschatological fulfilment was the crucified Messiah himself. His objection to the missionaries in 4.17 was not that they were being 'exclusive' or 'cliquish' or even 'coercive' per se, but that they were defining the people of God in terms of Torah rather than in terms of the (crucified) Messiah, as in 2.15–21. Paul's ways of dealing with threats to that identity, in the Corinthian correspondence as well as Gal., would scarcely meet the stern and inflexible demands of today's liberal relativism. On Eastman see also Dunne 2013.

[535] On the 'but' here, as a translation of *ean mē*, see Hays 2000, 237 in dialogue with e.g. R. N. Longenecker 1990, 83f.; Dunn 1993, 137f. Hays has recently pointed out to me that *ei mē* in Rev. 21.27 strongly supports the reading 'not . . . but . . .', as opposed to the reading 'not . . . except in the case of . . .'. We might also compare e.g. 1 Cor. 14.6.

[536] Though cf. Campbell 2011.

[537] Watson 1986 argued for pragmatism, but in the second edn. (Watson 2007 [1986]) has modified this considerably. Barclay 1996, ch. 13 sees Paul as an anomalous Diaspora Jew; cf. above, 400, 445.

Galatians is that this is the badge worn by the Messiah's community. Such people are thus *defined as people of 'faith'* – not in the modern sense of 'faith' as 'religious belief' (most people in the ancient world, like most today, had some kind of 'religious belief'!), but very specifically the 'faith' that confesses Jesus as lord and believes that the one God raised him from the dead.[538] Once again, this 'faith' is for Paul much closer to 'the Messiah's "faithfulness" to the divine Israel-purpose' than the split between 'faith' and 'faithfulness' in western theology (and modern English usage) would indicate. The actual content of both is, after all, the death (and resurrection) of the Messiah himself.

For Paul, the community is defined by the Jesus-shaped Messiah-faith which has been produced by the spirit, at work through the gospel. This is the primary thing Paul wants to say in Galatians: that *all those who have this 'faith' belong in the same, single community, eating at the same, single table*. We recall our earlier expositions of Galatians 2, 3 and 4: this is the heart of it. *And this is, more or less, what Paul means by 'justification by faith'*. 'We are', he says to Peter, 'Jews by birth, not "gentile sinners", but we know that one is justified ...' (2.15–16). In other words, 'We belong by birth to *this* community, not *that* one, but we know that *the question of belonging to the people whom the covenant God is declaring to be his own ...*'

The phrase 'we know that one is justified' (16a) is thus to be understood in close correlation to the 'Jews or gentiles' which immediately precedes it (15b), rather than being thought of as a different or new point. As we have seen, it is still possible to do what earlier generations did: to ignore the context of the Antioch-incident, where the contentious issue of table-fellowship is front and centre, and to insist that from verse 16 onwards Paul is talking, in the abstract, about 'how people get justified' (or even, though as we have seen Galatians never mentions this topic, 'how people get saved').[539] But the case for reading the whole paragraph, through to the end of the chapter, as precisely Paul's commentary on the Antioch table-fellowship controversy, closely cognate as it was with the problem in Galatia, is overwhelming. In other words, 'so that we might be justified' in Galatians 2.16 does not simply mean 'so that we might attain a righteous standing before God', though that is obviously part of the core meaning of the term. Rather, it *must* mean, in order for the sentence to work in its context, 'so that we might be declared to be *members of God's single family*'. Words mean what they mean within their sentences and contexts, and *dikaiōthōmen* here must refer to God's declaration that all believers are part of his family. Without this, the passage makes no sense. The sentence-structure in the Greek of verses 15 and 16 emphasizes this, since the main verb is right at the end, so that these two clauses stand close together and provide the joint subject. Taken literally it reads: 'We Jews by birth and not gentile sinners but knowing that one is not

[538] Nor, by the way, does this 'faith' consist in 'believing true doctrine' – in believing, for instance, the 'right' things about 'justification by faith' itself. That is, I think, a problem within some neo-Reformed writers. I have addressed this question elsewhere (e.g. Wright 1997 [*What St Paul*, UK edn.] 159).

[539] See n. 533 above, referring to Schreiner as one example among several.

justified ... even we believed into Messiah Jesus ...'[540] In other words, to repeat, 'even we believed' goes with 'Jews and not gentiles', and the 'but' indicates that the 'knowing that one is not justified ...' introduces a modification of the Jew/gentile question rather than a new point.

The negative proof of this, as in Romans 3.20, is the echo of Psalm 143.2: 'by works of the law no creature will be declared "righteous".' The Psalm reference is indeed an echo, not an exact quotation, and is slightly more distant than the similar echo in Romans: 'in your sight', says the psalm, 'shall no living creature (*pas zōn*) be justified.'[541] In Romans Paul backs this up by pointing out that 'through the law comes the knowledge of sin.' Though he does not say this explicitly here, the following passage seems to bear it out, all the way to Galatians 3.22 (where 'scripture', i.e. Torah and the rest, 'shuts up everything under sin'). In fact, the reference to gentile *hamartōloi* (sinners) in 2.15, and the way in which that is picked up in verse 17, indicates that the question of 'sin', particularly the 'sin' of which gentiles are assumed to be automatically guilty and in which Jews might be in danger of sharing, is very present to his mind. But the point is not 'So there you are: you're all sinners'; but 'Because of sin, you face more of a problem than you realize about your own covenant membership.' Certainly in Galatians, where the 'sin' root (*hamartia*) occurs only in this passage and two other places, one of them the letter's opening formula, it is clear that *Paul's whole argument is about membership in the single family, sharing the same table-fellowship, not primarily about the way in which sins are dealt with and the sinner rescued from them.*[542] He *presupposes* the 'anthropological' point (that all, Jews included, are sinners), but his point is not 'This is how sinners get saved' but 'This is how people are marked out as members of the covenant family.' The 'forensic' and 'anthropological' hints are held within the 'covenantal' meaning.

The point of 2.16, then, is this. If the Messiah's faithful death and resurrection have redefined the people of God, that definition is worked out, marked out, among that people in terms of *pistis*: '... a person is not declared "righteous" by works of the Jewish law, *but through the faithfulness* (*dia pisteōs*) of Jesus the Messiah ... That is why we too *believed in the Messiah* (*eis Christon Iēsoun episteusamen*): so that we might be declared "righteous" *on the basis of the Messiah's faithfulness* (*ek pisteōs Christou*), and not on the basis of works of the Jewish law.' Neither the noun (*pistis*) nor the verb (*pisteuein*) occurs again in Galatians 2 after these three references in verse 16, but that solid statement hangs over, and interprets, the rest of the

[540] See Hays 2000, 236f.

[541] Paul, adding 'by works of the law' (as in Romans), has omitted 'in your sight', and (again as in Romans) has substituted 'all flesh' (*pasa sarx*) for 'all that lives'. The complexities this introduces are not our present concern: cf. Hays 2000, 240f.

[542] The other uses are 1.4; 3.22 (see below). To the argument that e.g. Gal. 3.10–14 is about how people are delivered from sin, I answer that yes, there is an implicit deliverance there, but the point of the passage is still about how 'the blessing of Abraham' comes upon the gentiles and the promised spirit is outpoured. Dealing with sin is the means whereby the larger divine purpose is accomplished; Paul presupposes (and occasionally refers to) the former in order here to expound the latter.

chapter. If 'I' have thus been redefined through 'my' sharing in the Messiah's faithful death and resurrection, the correlative badge which demonstrates this sharing, and hence this new identity, is clearly *pistis*. That was the point to be made in Antioch, and is the point to be made to the Galatians: all those *who believe*, who show thereby that they are remade according to the Messiah's *faithful* death and resurrection, belong together at the same table. The unity of the Messiah's people, especially in their table-fellowship, thus flows as a non-negotiable imperative from the gospel itself.

Before the sharp intake of breath from certain quarters has subsided, let me repeat at once: the question of eating at the same table, or not, has nothing to do with 'table manners' in some genteel but theologically trivial sense, as is sometimes sneeringly suggested. It has everything to do with the formation and maintenance of a people who know themselves precisely to be, in Paul's introductory words, the people who have been 'rescued from the present evil age' by the Messiah's 'giving himself for their sins'.[543] Paul echoes that formula at the heart of his powerful appeal at the end of chapter 2: the son of God 'loved me and gave himself for me'.[544] But that cannot be taken as reinscribing the false distinction according to which Paul can only be referring to one of the two: *either* membership in the single family with the single table, *or* forgiveness of sins; *either* 'ecclesiology' *or* 'anthropology'. The point of Paul's whole theology – of, we might say, the theology of Genesis and the Psalms, of Exodus and Deuteronomy and Isaiah, and his retrieval of them through the lens of the gospel – was that *through* God's people the one God would provide the solution to the larger human plight. And that would be also the solution for God's people themselves, since they too shared in the plight.

There is very little reference to this plight in Galatians: almost no mention of 'sin', no mention at all of 'death'.[545] That, no doubt, is why there is no mention either of 'salvation' – a salutary warning to those who regularly confuse 'salvation' with 'justification', or indeed Romans (where 'salvation' is a main theme) with Galatians.[546] Paul no doubt believes that the Galatian Messiah-people have been 'saved'. That is after all the meaning of 1.4, where he uses the comparatively rare word *exaireō*, 'to deliver' or 'rescue'.[547] It is

[543] 1.4.

[544] 2.20.

[545] Sin: 1.4 (the formula already quoted); 2.17 (in the context of the discussion about 'gentile sinners'); 3.22 ('scripture shut up everything under sin' – with 'sin' here being a power that enslaves rather than a deed of wrongdoing). Contrast the literally dozens of references to 'sin' in Romans, especially chs. 6 and 7.

[546] de Boer 2011, 28 n. 38, notes that Gal. does not use the language of 'salvation', but says he is using it as a 'convenient shorthand', despite his own warning (2) against importing ideas from one letter to another.

[547] The fact that this phrase is unique in Paul does not necessarily mean he is quoting a formula (see de Boer 2011, 29f.). Even if he is, that certainly does not mean that he is quoting it in order to disagree with it. He is talking about being snatched out of 'the present evil age', for which this verb is appropriate, rather than being 'saved', rescued, from sin and death. The former alludes to a situation out of which one is rescued; the latter, to the enemies from whose threat one is delivered. The two are obviously close, denoting the same event but giving it a different shade or nuance.

just that this is not the subject of the letter. The letter is about *the definition of the community* as the people who are already declared to be in the right, declared to be part of God's single family, the true children of Abraham. That definition assumes that the sins of such people have been dealt with, but that is not Paul's theme. His theme is the fact that this people has been demarcated by *pistis*. And the way he speaks of this demarcation is through the language of 'justification'. Here, in what may be Paul's earliest letter, and certainly his earliest extant exposition of 'justification', there should be no doubt: the primary meaning is 'covenantal', containing with it hints of 'anthropology' and of 'forensic' meanings but not reducible to those terms. As we have already seen, Paul effortlessly integrates this with the 'incorporative' theme ('seeking to be justified in the Messiah', verse 17) and also that of 'transformation' ('I am, however, alive – but it isn't me any longer, it's the Messiah who lives in me', verse 20). But these do not tell us the meaning of 'justification' itself. They tell us how the other members of the cluster of soteriological themes relate to the one which is here central: the definition of all who share this *pistis* as members of the same covenantal family, on the basis of the death of the now risen Messiah.

This then leads naturally into the great central argument of Galatians 3.1—4.11. Here the redefinition of God's people around the Messiah, which we have already established, is played out explicitly in terms of the demarcation of those who belong to the Messiah, and who are therefore to be regarded as the redefined 'elect', in two closely correlated ways. They are marked out by the spirit, and by faith.

The explicit place of the spirit at various points in the argument of chapters 3 and 4 brings to light what, I suggested earlier, is implicit also in Galatians 2: it is the spirit's work, through the preaching of the gospel, which generates the 'faith' which is then the sign of the redefined election. That is the underlying theme of this whole section of my argument.

The opening flourish in 3.1–5 focuses on the Galatians' receiving of the spirit.[548] At first sight, to modern eyes – including those of most commentators – this is basically 'an appeal to experience'. They 'received the spirit', presumably with powerful manifestations (verse 5), without any need for circumcision, so why would they need it now? This presupposes a somewhat modern view of 'religious experience', which may or may not have been so relevant to Paul and his converts; more importantly, it ignores the strong link between the spirit, as received initially in Galatia, and the promise to Abraham. This becomes explicit in 3.14. The spirit is the foretaste and guarantee of the 'inheritance', one of the main themes of Genesis 15, the chapter Paul expounds through the rest of Galatians 3. It looks as though he is not simply saying, 'You had an initial and exciting spiritual experience

[548] de Boer 2011, 166f. proposes that receiving the spirit is the major theme of the whole section, though he has to assume its presence behind Paul's references to 'the promise'. Since he does not want to attach this too closely to a positive reading of Abraham, this seems to me to cause various problems, though there is no space to take this further here.

without getting circumcised, so why not carry on in that way?',[549] but more particularly, 'You already received the guarantee of your Abrahamic inheritance without getting circumcised, so why would you need a different kind of guarantee now?' This proposal is underscored by the link between 3.1–5 and what follows, indicated by the *kathōs* in 3.6.[550] But how does this link actually work?

The original promise concerned the *land.* In Romans, though not in Galatians, Paul explains how he now sees this: the promise, he says, concerned not one country but the whole world.[551] He places considerable emphasis on the theme of 'inheritance' at the end of chapter 3 (3.29), and returns to it after explaining the same points from a different angle in 4.1–7. This time he is more explicit about the link between spirit and inheritance: it is because of the spirit's work, enabling believers to call the one God 'Abba, father', that they know they are 'heirs'. It looks as though, despite the dense and allusive style, Paul at least supposes that by speaking of receiving the spirit in 3.1–5 he is not simply 'appealing to religious experience' but is already saying, 'So – you really *are* already Abraham's heirs, through the faith-inducing message!'[552] Galatians 3.1–5 is therefore plausibly to be read as a further redefinition of the Abrahamic covenant, and hence of the whole notion of election, by means of the spirit.

The redefinition of election is indeed the message he wants to get across in 3.6–9, where the conclusion is drawn at once from the quotation of Genesis 15.6:

> Abraham 'believed God, and it was counted to him for righteousness.' So you know that it's people of faith who are children of Abraham.[553]

This, in regular Pauline fashion, is then at once expanded and explained:

[549] Witherington 1998, 199 speaks of an 'appeal to the supernatural work of God' as a familiar greco-roman argument. This may be so but the link with the Abrahamic promise is in my view at least equally strong. R. N. Longenecker 1990, 101f. criticizes Barrett 1947, 2 for speaking of this as a 'pragmatic argument', and says that this comes from not seeing any continuity of argument between this passage and the rest of the letter. This is undoubtedly a frequent problem, but Longenecker himself does not appear to note the specific link with Abraham.

[550] The *kathōs* should not be reduced to a shorthand for *kathōs gegraptai*, 'as it is written', as though it is merely a formula introducing a quotation (with e.g. Witherington 1998, 213; against e.g. R. N. Longenecker 1990, 112 who takes Abraham simply as an 'example' here; cf. too Martyn 1997a, 296f.; de Boer 2011, 189). Dunn 1993, 160 takes it as a quotation-formula, but stresses the 'implicit equation of "receiving the Spirit" and "being reckoned righteous"', seeing the two as 'different ways of describing the opening up of a positive relationship with God'. Once one translates that back into covenantal language it makes what seems to me the right point.

[551] Rom. 4.13; see above, 849; and Wright 2002 [*Romans*], 495f.

[552] This conclusion is strengthened by passages like 2 Cor. 1.22; 5.5; Eph. 1.14 in which the spirit is the *arrabōn*, the 'down-payment', of what is to come (in Eph. this is explicitly the 'inheritance', coming at the end of the prayer which is itself a quasi-exodus narrative). Dunn 1993, 153 emphasizes both the vital and personal nature of the spirit-experience (i.e. this is not just a 'logical deduction'!) and also the fact that Paul saw receiving the spirit as a fulfilment of OT prophecy of the 'eschatological hope of Israel' (Isa. 32.15; Ezek. 37.4–14; Joel 2.28f., picked up in second-Temple writings e.g. 1QS 4.18–21). See too Williams 1997, 85: the spirit was the sign of incorporation 'into the deity's end-time people'.

[553] 3.6f.

> [8]The Bible foresaw that God would justify the nations by faith, so it announced the gospel to Abraham in advance, when it declared that 'the nations will be blessed in you'. [9]So you see: the people of faith are blessed along with faithful Abraham.[554]

This is, in a sense, the main point of the chapter, but Paul knows that he has a lot of work to do to back up this preliminary conclusion against those who insist that the Torah is the way to inherit the Abrahamic promises. We have already examined the next paragraphs from the point of view of the Messiah's achievement; we now revisit them from the point of view of the spirit.

Galatians 3.10–14 once more sets Torah over against this faith-family, showing that Torah effectively shuts up the Abrahamic promises and (as in Romans 4.14–15) prevents them getting out to the wider world.[555] Verse 11 echoes 2.16: nobody is justified in the law. This now points forward to the answer cryptically revealed in Habakkuk 2.4; there *is* an opening for people to be 'justified', but it is a different one, corresponding to the point already made from Genesis 15. At this time of crisis, the true people of God will be recognized by their *pistis*. Paul backs this up with Leviticus 18: Torah insists on obedience as the way to 'life' (as it was bound to do, for paradoxical reasons which Paul, and we, will explore later). But where this obedience has not been forthcoming the Abrahamic promises are blocked. It looks as though Jews will not inherit the promises, because of their failure to keep Torah, and gentiles, because Torah excludes them anyway. The Messiah's curse-bearing death then releases 'us' from the law's curse, so that the blessing of Abraham might after all flow out to the nations, and – this is the point for our present purposes – 'so that we might receive the promise of the spirit, through faith'. Here is the redefinition of election, writ clear, cognate both with Romans 2.25–9 and with Romans 4.9–17: the covenant is renewed through the divine spirit, and Jews who want now to belong to Abraham's renewed family must be spirit-people and faith-people. Once more, as in 2.15–21, what Paul says *presupposes* that there was a problem (the curse of the Torah) which has now been dealt with. But the *main line of thought* is the question of how the worldwide-family promises made to Abraham are to reach their destination. Paul himself refers to this in the next verse in terms of a *diathēkē*. Granted our whole exposition so far we should not be shy about calling his present line of thought 'covenantal', though a case for 'salvation-historical' might be made as well (as long as we issue the now routine health warning against supposing that this means steady development or 'progress'). The balance of the two clauses in 3.14 may reflect a sense of two different things required by two different groups: the gentiles need 'the blessing of Abraham' to flow outward to them, while the Jews need to be renewed in their covenant membership by receiving the spirit. Alternatively, the 'we' in the second half may mean 'we all, believing

[554] 3.8f.

[555] More details above, 863–7.

Jews and believing gentiles alike'.[556] Either way, the two are closely linked. God *promised* to *bless* the nations through Abraham, which Paul elsewhere interprets in terms of his 'inheriting the world': now, with the 'blessing' flowing out at last, the 'promise' is being proleptically fulfilled in the gift of the spirit to believers of all nationalities. This is how (Paul is implying) any Jew who wants to inherit the Abrahamic promises must do so.[557]

The next two paragraphs have been studied in other connections, but we note here that the section ends in verse 22 with another evocation of the same point: scripture concluded everything under sin, 'so that the promise ... should be given to those who believe'. The promise itself comes through the 'single seed', the Messiah, and his faithfulness. 'Those who believe' are therefore those who wear the badge which marks them out as Messiah-people, as *faithful*-Messiah-people. And the whole context, with 3.14b at its centre, strongly suggests that Paul would cheerfully have unpacked this in terms of the work of the spirit, as in 3.1–5 and 4.4–7.

The two paragraphs that follow (3.23–9 and 4.1–7) are then, I suggest, to be read in close parallel. The *legō de* in 4.1 ('This is what I mean' or 'Let me put it like this') suggests that Paul is coming back over the same territory from another angle, not making a substantially different theological point. This emerges in the link between (a) the emphatic 'you are all sons of God' in 3.26, which explains why believers are no longer 'under the *paidagōgos*', and (b) the maturity of the 'son', after a period of subservience, in 4.1–7. We should, then, allow the two paragraphs to interpret one another; and we should note particularly that throughout these two paragraphs Paul is using material, and forms of theological expression, which correspond *both* to what we find in Romans 1—4 *and* to what we find in Romans 5—8. We have here, in other words, a fusion of the so-called 'juridical' and the so-called 'participationist' modes of thought. They come together precisely in the classic Pauline redefinition of election; in other words, within the framework of *covenant*, of the *apocalyptic unveiling* of the long-awaited arrival of the saving purpose which Israel's God had always promised and intended, and particularly here the *incorporative* significance of people coming to be 'in the Messiah'. Again, the fact that Paul does not mention the spirit in 3.23–9 should not blind us to its implicit presence, which becomes explicit in the climax of 4.6–7.

Thus in 3.23–9 we have, beyond any doubt, the redefinition of Abraham's family – in other words, of election; and this is effected, as we have already

[556] See the different positions in e.g. Hays 2000, 262 (the second clause refers to all believers) and Witherington 1998, 240 (only to Jewish believers, though of course not denying that gentiles too receive the spirit). Hays says that 'the experience of the Spirit is interpreted as the fulfilment of what Scripture has promised: the blessing of all nations.' Martyn 1997a, 322–4, predictably tries to keep plenty of clear blue water between Abraham and the fulfilment of promise.

[557] The link of the promised spirit with the promise to Abraham is denied by e.g. Kwon 2004, 108–11. Schreiner 2010, 218 n. 100 argues, against this, that the Abrahamic promise can have more than one aspect; I am suggesting that Paul sees the spirit as the foretaste of 'inheriting the world'. De Boer more or less identifies the two clauses in 3.14 (2011, 195), and states (197 n. 283) that Paul 'ignores the promises made to Abraham concerning a multitude of physical descendants who would inherit the land'. I do not think it is Paul who is ignoring these promises.

seen, around Israel's Messiah himself. The way the family is redefined around the Messiah is clearly through *pistis*, which Paul hypostatizes, giving it a character and a history – hardly a 'salvation history' in any normal sense, since most of the time is spent in slavery:

> Before this faithfulness (*pistis*) arrived, we were kept under guard by the law, in close confinement until the coming faithfulness should be revealed. Thus the law was like a babysitter for us, looking after us until the coming of the Messiah, so that we might be given covenant membership (*hina dikaiōthōmen*) on the basis of faithfulness (*ek pisteōs*). But now that faithfulness has come, we are no longer under the rule of the babysitter. For you are all children of God, through faith, in the Messiah, Jesus.[558]

This is obviously a tendentious translation – but then all translations of a passage like this must make some fairly sharp assumptions. I offer it partly because I think Paul intends the closest possible link between (a) the Messiah and his achievement and (b) the notion of 'faithfulness', and partly because it is important to jolt ourselves out of familiar, but now it seems misleading, assumptions. The final phrase in particular is by no means easy: you are all God's children *dia tēs pisteōs en Christō Iēsou* could mean 'through faith in the Messiah, Jesus', or 'through the faithfulness which is in the Messiah Jesus'; or, taking the two elements in parallel rather than in sequence, 'you are all God's children (a) through faith and (b) in the Messiah, Jesus.' Nothing much for our present argument hinges on settling this exactly, though the more I have lived with this text the more I think the third solution is the right one.[559] Whichever way we look at it, the point is that 'in the Messiah' the badge of the community is clearly *pistis*.

To stress the point once more: it is noticeable that here Paul moves seamlessly between what are sometimes regarded, particularly in expositions of Romans, as different modes of thought or types of soteriology. The mention of people being 'in the Messiah', correlated exactly with faith, law and justification in verses 23–5, is then explained with reference to the baptismal 'entry into Messiah' and 'putting on the Messiah', resulting in the common life in which 'you are all one in the Messiah' (3.27, 28). This leads into the conclusion of the chapter: those who are thus the Messiah's people (note the way the genitive *Christou* has the same function as the 'in' references) are Abraham's *sperma*, the single promised 'seed', and share his inheritance. This incorporative (one might almost say 'ecclesiological', and certainly 'covenantal') conclusion all stands under the rubric of 'through faith' in 3.26: all that is said about baptism and the single family presupposes *pistis*. For a further explanation of what this 'faith' is and how it comes about, we turn to 4.1–7. This is where we see the full sequence, and discover that it is indeed the spirit that has been the operating principle all along, the one through whom – or perhaps we should say through whose implementation of the messianic achievement – 'election' is redefined.

[558] 3.23–6.

[559] Hays 2000, 271. Dunn 1993, 202 states that 'Christ Jesus' has 'replaced ethnic Israel as the social context of this sonship'.

As we have seen, 4.1–7 is a retold exodus-narrative. The 'son', presently enslaved, is 'redeemed' by the act of the covenant God, and given the presence of this God as the guide for the journey to the 'inheritance'. It is the spirit that functions as the divine presence on that journey, enabling the 'heirs' of 3.29 to attain their 'inheritance' in 4.7. The spirit, as in Romans 8.15, enables this redeemed people to say 'Abba, father', thus confirming with this 'faith' the redefinition of the exodus-family, the ones who know themselves to be 'God's children'.[560] It is perhaps unusual for this 'confession' of the divine fatherhood, with the Aramaic word 'Abba', to be seen by Pauline scholars as the expression of 'faith', but I think this is again because of the unwarranted disjunction that has been made between 'juristic' and 'participationist' terminology, backed up by an unwillingness on the part of some who favour 'juristic' models to allow any mention of the spirit, let alone of a theme like 'adoption', into the tight definition of 'justification by faith'. It seems to me however that here, and in the equivalent passage in Romans 8, we have precisely an expression of 'faith'.

If, after all, Paul's redefined monotheism consists of the 'one God, the father, and one lord Jesus the Messiah' of 1 Corinthians 8.6, it would be strange to say that 'faith' consisted of confessing Jesus as the risen Messiah and lord and not at all confessing this God as father. In fact, as 4.8–11 indicates, Paul is thinking very much of this redefined monotheism, and of the way in which it stands robustly over against all forms of paganism – including, disturbingly, what Paul seems to be indicating is a Jewish version of paganism, the concentration on 'days, months, seasons and years' which would put gentile converts back under the rule of the *stoicheia* from which they had so recently escaped. Thus it seems to me that in 4.1–7 (a) Paul is indicating what precisely the 'faith' is of which he has been speaking up to this point; (b) he is stressing that it is brought about (as in 3.14) by the work of the spirit; and (c) he is insisting that this is the sign of membership, the Jew-and-gentile-alike membership, in the new-exodus people of the one God, the covenant family promised to Abraham. Here we have, once more, election redefined through the spirit. And here we have, once more, a rich combination of covenantal, participatory, transformative and salvation-historical motifs, held within a larger argument in which the anthropological and forensic notes, though not strongly present, may be lurking in the background.

(c) 1 Corinthians

At the start of Paul's exposition of his own apostolic calling, the positive side of his negative warnings about the dangers of personality cults, we find him speaking in terms of a final, eschatological law court. This is the first

[560] Ex. 4.22 (cf. Hos. 1.10; 11.1; Sir. 36.17; *3 Macc.* 6.28; *Jub.* 1.23–5; *4 Ez.* 6.55–9; *Pss. Sol.* 17.26f.).

time he has been explicit about this kind of thing, and the passage strongly anticipates some key features of Romans:

> This is how we should be thought of: as servants of the Messiah, and household managers for God's mysteries. And this is what follows: the main requirement for a manager is to be trustworthy (*pistos*). Having said that, I regard it as a matter of minimal concern to think that I should be interrogated (*anakrithō*) by you, or indeed by any human court. I don't even interrogate (*anakrinō*) myself. I don't actually know of anything that stands against me, but that isn't what vindicates me (*oude en toutō dedikaiōmai*); it's the lord who interrogates me (*ho anakrinōn me*).[561]

Paul seems to envisage the possibility of being tried by some kind of assembly. The repeated word *anakrinō* can, but need not, have hostile intent, and 'interrogate' seems to catch that ambiguity. Though he will later say that 'the saints', who will one day be judging angels, ought to be able to try ordinary human cases here and now (a fascinating point to which we shall return presently), he does not envisage that they will actually be the ones holding him to account; and in any case he is here balancing the 'now' of 6.1–5 with a firm 'not yet'. Apostles, as household managers, are answerable to their *kyrios*, and his judgment will be reserved for the last day. But then he goes on:

> So don't pass judgment on anything (*mē pro kairou ti krinete*) before the time when the lord comes! He will bring to light the secrets of darkness, and will lay bare the intentions of the heart. Then everyone will receive praise – from God.[562]

This is the same picture of final judgment that we find in Romans 2.16 and 2.29. The secrets of all hearts will be exposed, and 'praise' will come, not from humans but from the one God.[563]

This close similarity between 1 Corinthians 4 and Romans 2, both in theme and in language, reminds us of something we should in any case guess: that Paul, like all travelling speakers (and many writers), often says very similar things on different occasions, sometimes several years apart. But my point in flagging up this passage, which is not of course dealing directly with 'justification' in any of the senses we have been studying, is that it shows two things which are very relevant to the sevenfold sketch we drew of how Paul's doctrine of justification 'works'.

First, it demonstrates how comfortable Paul is with this regular picture of a *future* law court, in which Jesus the 'lord' will be the judge and the one God will be giving the 'praise' that will then be due. Second, it shows that he is used (as it were) to thinking back from that point, to envisaging a possible anticipation, in the present time, of the verdict that will be issued in the future. Here Paul is telling the Corinthians that when it comes to assessing

[561] 1 Cor. 4.1–4. The Corinthians seem to have been 'assessing' Paul for his rhetorical skills (so Witherington 1995, 137f.; Hays 1997, 66).

[562] 1 Cor. 4.5.

[563] Thiselton 2000, 341f. defends this link with Rom. and Gal. against e.g. R. F. Collins 1999, 173 who considers it a different point. See too Fitzmyer, cited below.

the performance of apostles, the final judgment will be the thing; they should not try to pre-empt it or bring the verdict forwards. He uses for 'interrogation' a verb which is cognate with the various 'judging' verbs in Romans 2, and speaks more explicitly of 'judging' in verse 5. When he speaks of being 'vindicated' he uses the *dikaioō* root which we now know so well. And the criterion according to which he will be judged is his *pistis* (verse 2), in the sense of his 'faithfulness to his commission', much as with Israel in Romans 3.2.[564] And the whole discussion, all the more considering that Paul is not here talking about soteriology at all, demonstrates solidly that we are right to take Romans 2 as referring to a *final* judgment whose verdict might indeed be anticipated in the present time. This way of thinking is clearly one with which Paul is very comfortable.

This is not the first time in the letter Paul has spoken about a coming final judgment. In the previous chapter he writes of the judgment that awaits all who work to build up the church. There is coming a 'day' in which 'the fire will test what sort of work everyone has done.'[565] We shall look at this further in the next chapter. But in the two following chapters he speaks of ways in which that future judgment can and should be brought forward into the present time within the life of the church. Faced with flagrant scandal, the church must do *in the present* among its own membership what the one God will do *in the future* in relation to the rest of the world:

> Why should I worry about judging people outside? It's the people *inside* you should judge, isn't it? God judges the people outside. 'Drive out the wicked person from your company.'[566]

Paul, indeed, has already passed sentence on the offender, from the other side of the Aegean Sea:

> Let me tell you what I've already done. I may be away from you physically, but I'm present in the spirit; and I've already passed judgment, as though I was there with you, on the person who has behaved in this way.[567]

The internal discipline of the church is therefore a kind of anticipated eschatology, lodged between the verdict that has *already* been pronounced by Paul and the verdict that will come on the last day. All this has a very familiar shape to those who have grasped how Paul's doctrine of justification actually works. Just as the verdict 'righteous' comes forward into the present from the last day, being pronounced within history in the Messiah's death and resurrection and in the divine pronouncement over faith, so the discipline Paul envisages is a way of bringing final condemnation forward into the present, implementing the verdict he has already pronounced himself

[564] Fitzmyer 2008, 213 says this is not about 'justification' in the usual sense, 'because it is not a matter of *pistis*'. But that, according to Paul in v. 2, is exactly what it is. Paul's 'doctrines' do not live in a world detached from all his other concerns.

[565] 1 Cor. 3.13.

[566] 1 Cor. 5.12f.

[567] 5.3.

from a distance, *so that the person concerned, having been 'judged' here, may be 'saved' later*:

> You must hand over such a person to the satan for the destruction of the flesh, so that his spirit may be saved on the day of the lord Jesus.[568]

Whatever precisely Paul means by this – and commentators are, not surprisingly, divided on the matter – our present point has to do with the inaugurated eschatology of judgment: the verdict of the future is enacted in the present.

A very similar idea, again not always noticed in discussions of Paul's idea of eschatological judgment and vindication, is found in the discussion of behaviour at the eucharist in chapter 11:

> You see, if you eat and drink without recognizing the body, you eat and drink judgment on yourself. That's why several of you are weak and sick, and some have died. But if we learned how to judge ourselves, we would not incur judgment. But when we are judged by the lord, we are punished, so that we won't be condemned along with the world.[569]

Again, our present purpose is not to comment on Paul's views about what actually happened in such cases. The point is that for the Messiah's people the *future* verdict, in this case 'judgment', is brought forward into the present, in order that it may be finished.[570] We are given to understand that when the future condemnation arrives in the present in the form of discipline, whether imposed by the church itself, as Paul envisages in chapter 5, or in the form of divine punishment as here, this does not affect the basic status of believers, who have already been assured of their justification (6.11). Indeed, this is the way in which any future condemnation that might have seemed appropriate is dealt with here and now precisely in order to maintain that future verdict intact.[571]

The other passage in which the idea of future judgment is brought forward into the present is 1 Corinthians 6.1–6. Paul assumes – and suggests that the Corinthians ought to know this as well – that in the judgment on the last day, which he elsewhere speaks of as exercised by God himself, or by Jesus as lord, the Messiah's people will share in that work. Faced with the prospect of lawsuits between believers, Paul reacts in horror:

> Don't you know that God's people will judge the world? And if the world is to be judged by you, are you really incompetent to try smaller matters? Don't you know that we shall be judging angels? Why not then also matters to do with ordinary life?[572]

568 1 Cor. 5.5. See the discussion in e.g. Witherington 1995, 158; Thiselton 2000, 397–400.

569 1 Cor. 11.29–32. The older article of Moule 1964 is still valuable. The 'punishment' is clearly intended to have a positive role: see Thiselton 2000, 898 and e.g. Hays 1997, 202: 'Where the church exercises such disciplinary discernment, God's judgment is averted; where the church fails to exercise discernment, God's judgment intervenes to prevent them falling under final condemnation.'

570 Or, with Sampley 2002, 936, it might be seen simply as a 'wake-up call'.

571 For a similar train of thought cf. e.g. Ps. 94.12f.; Heb. 12.3–11.

572 1 Cor. 6.2f.

Both halves of this – Christians sharing in a future judgment even of angels, and the conclusion that they ought therefore to be able to 'judge' ordinary cases in the present as well – may seem extraordinary to us. The first, however, is well established in Jewish tradition, going back at least to Daniel 7, and is picked up elsewhere in early Christianity.[573] The second is the direct, if startling, corollary of Paul's sense that the 'end', specifically the 'judgment', has already broken into the present in the Messiah and the spirit. That is my sole point at this stage: to show that, even when he is not discussing 'justification' as such, his mind regularly and easily works on the basis that the coming day of judgment has already arrived in the present in the Messiah, and is to be implemented and applied in the community in the power of the spirit. That is the basis on which he declares that what will be true about the future must become true in the present life of the church. The behaviours whose practitioners 'will not inherit the kingdom' in the future must not be allowed within the church; conversely, the coming resurrection means one's body must be a place where God is glorified in the present.[574]

There are two other passages in the Corinthians correspondence which are of particular significance for the redefinition of election. We have already looked at 2 Corinthians 5.21. We must now turn our attention to one of the most remarkable expositions of the role of the spirit in this redefinition: 2 Corinthians 3.

(d) 2 Corinthians 3

Paul's purpose in 2 Corinthians 3 is to explain that his style of apostleship is the real thing, not a shabby and second-best alternative. His argument hinges on his explanation that the scriptural promises of the 'new covenant' have come true in them by the spirit in whose power he, Paul, has been ministering as an apostle. *Election redefined*, in other words, *by and around the spirit*: the Messiah's people constitute the community of God's long-promised covenant renewal.

This is hardly controversial – though scholars who have wanted to segregate Paul from 'covenantal' ideas have had to suggest that he was, as it were, playing away from home at this point, responding to opponents rather than taking a line he would have chosen left to himself.[575] That suggestion hardly fits with the fact that he uses similar imagery in a couple of other places (Romans 2.25–9; 7.4–6) where such a possibility seems much less likely. This whole seam of thought appears to be part of his central thought, not bolted on from the outside for an occasional polemical flourish.

[573] Dan. 7.22, 27; cf. Wis. 3.8; Sir. 4.15; 1 QpHab 5.4; *1 En.* 1.9; 95.3; 104.2; *Test. Abr.* 1—4; cf. Mt. 19.28; Lk. 22.30; Rev. 2.26; 20.4, etc. Rosner 1990 suggests that this theme may echo Moses' appointment of assistant judges in Ex. 18.13–27.

[574] 5.12f.; 6.1–4, 9f., 13f.

[575] See the discussion in Thrall 1994, 2000, 236–9.

The first clear sign that Paul is expounding the biblical idea of the 'new covenant' in 2 Corinthians 3 comes in verse 3, where he echoes Ezekiel's repeated prophecy of a change of heart for God's people, removing the heart of stone from their flesh and giving them a heart of flesh:[576]

> It's quite plain that you are a letter from the Messiah, with us as the messengers – a letter not written with ink but with the spirit of the living God, not on tablets of stone but on the tablets of beating hearts.

In the two relevant passages Ezekiel also speaks of giving the people 'a new heart and a new spirit'.[577] He contrasts the previous stony-hearted condition of God's people and the new condition in which, equipped with a new heart and a new spirit, they will be able to keep the Torah from the heart.

Paul develops this picture in an implicit dialogue with the description of the original giving of the law on Mount Sinai, telescoping together the 'tables of stone' in Exodus[578] with the 'stony hearts' of Ezekiel. The ministry he has exercised in Corinth, he suggests, has fulfilled the prophetic promises by producing this new kind of 'letter', written with the spirit of the living God on the 'tablets' of fleshly, beating hearts.[579] And they, the Corinthians, are the living proof of this fulfilment: You are a letter from the Messiah, with us as the messengers.

The echoes of Ezekiel enable us to see what Paul is saying underneath the compressed double reference. Paul's hearers – the muddled and recalcitrant Corinthians! – have had their hearts transformed in accordance with the prophecy. The living God has, by his spirit, taken the 'heart of stone' out of their flesh, and given them a heart of flesh; and, as part of the same operation, he has written the 'letter from the Messiah' on those hearts. At this point other echoes, more distant but still clearly audible, emerge: those of Jeremiah 31. Before we get to verse 6, where the reference is clear, we can discern in verse 3 that Paul is already thinking of the relevant passage:

> The days are surely coming, says YHWH, when I will make a new covenant with the house of Israel and the house of Judah . . . this is the covenant that I will make with the house of Israel after those days, says YHWH: I will put my law within them, and I will write it on their hearts; and I will be their God, and they shall be my people. No longer shall they teach one another, or say to each other, 'Know YHWH', for they shall all know me, from the least of them to the greatest, says YHWH; for I will forgive their iniquity, and remember their sin no more.[580]

The echo in 2 Corinthians 3.3 is made through the idea of 'writing on the heart'. For Jeremiah what is written is the Torah; for Paul it is the 'letter

[576] Ezek. 11.19; 36.26. On the complex interweaving of biblical passages throughout this chapter see Hays 1989a, ch. 4.

[577] In 11.19 the MT has *leb echad*, 'one heart', but some MSS read *hdsh*, 'new', as in 18.31; 36.26.

[578] Ex. 31.18; 32.15; Dt. 9.10f.

[579] In my own translation I have rendered *sarkinais* at the end of the verse as 'beating' rather than 'fleshly', to make it clear that, unlike *sarkikos*, the word *sarkinos* carries no pejorative overtones: the point is the conformity between 'the living God' and the living (as opposed to stony) hearts.

[580] Jer. 31.31–4.

from the Messiah'; but the point is the same. The living God, by his spirit, has done the new thing that has transformed this community into being a people who know him. This is then the ground of Paul's confidence in verses 4 and 5: this God has 'qualified' him for this work, so that he does not need 'qualifications' of any other sort from any other source. (That, it seems, was the question that had been raised by the Corinthians themselves.) Thus Paul can come out and say it. He and his apostolic colleagues (Timothy is named as co-sender of the letter in 1.1) are 'stewards of a new covenant', *diakonoi kainēs diathēkēs*, 'not of the letter but of the spirit'. Their gospel ministry has had the effect, through the spirit, of bringing about the 'new covenant' spoken of by Jeremiah: in other words, of redefining election.

The phrase 'letter and spirit' has of course sent all kinds of hares bounding across the landscape of scholarship in modern times. A particular impetus was given to this when the Romantic movement made a superficially similar distinction between 'letter and spirit' in terms of outward form and inward feeling:

> Mentally the Romantic prefers feeling to thought, more specifically, emotion to calculation, imagination to literal common sense, intuition to intellect ... Non-philosophical Romanticism disdains ordinary rationality as a practical makeshift for the earth-bound, yielding only a truncated, superficial, and distorted picture of the world as it really is. The directly intuitive, even mystical, apprehension of the world which we owe to poets and other such creative geniuses does not stand in need of any reasoned support or articulation.[581]

Many have read Paul in that light, and have therefore inevitably misread him, since Paul, being born some time before Schelling or Coleridge, had not had the benefit of Romantic philosophy. Paul's distinction is quite different, as also from today's colloquial phrases 'the letter of the law' and 'the spirit of the law', where 'the spirit of the law' means, basically, that one can disobey what the law actually says because one is in tune with a different and higher principle.[582] Even though Paul's phrase is at least partially responsible for that common way of speaking, it is not what he is talking about.

He is talking about the difference between *the Mosaic law*, which, being engraved on stone tablets, is unable to change the hearts of the hearers, and *the holy spirit*, unleashed through the preaching of the good news about Jesus the Messiah, transforming the hearts of the hearers so that they are now different people. The result is threefold. First, according to the echo of Ezekiel, their hearts are *cleansed* as well as renewed. Second, according to the Jeremiah echo, they have a new *knowledge* of the covenant God. Third, according to the multiple echoes of Exodus, Ezekiel and Jeremiah, taken together, they have a new possibility of *obedience*. Paul's reference here to

[581] Quinton 1995.

[582] Paul is not, then, referring simply to a 'hermeneutical principle', that by the spirit one can now interpret Torah differently; see below.

the 'spirit' is not, as in Romanticism, an appeal to a higher principle to get one off the hook of actual boring obedience. It is his way of explaining the new, integrated humanness, reflecting the divine image (3.18), which he believes is created through the gospel and the spirit and which results in a new type of community.

It is ironic that Paul should be saying these things to the very people who have cast doubt upon his apostolic legitimacy. His point is precisely that those who are indwelt by the spirit find themselves gazing at 'the same reflection' when they are looking at one another with unveiled face.[583] But this is an all-or-nothing appeal, and he does not shrink from it.

His basic claim could not be clearer. The spirit has redefined 'election', the covenant status of the people of God. The covenant is not now a matter of possessing or hearing the Mosaic law. It is a matter of the transformation of the heart, wrought by the spirit.

We should not miss (though many have) the background context in Exodus in particular.[584] We have explored this in the previous chapter and need only refer to it briefly here. Paul is appealing to the story of what happened after the making of the golden calf. Moses had been up the mountain, receiving not only the tablets of Torah but the instructions for making the tabernacle in which Israel's God was to dwell in the midst of his people. Their high-handed idolatry led to the threat that the divine presence would not, after all, go with them; they would have to make do with an angel. Moses then engages in serious, bargaining prayer: Israel is after all God's people, and it is his reputation that is at stake in all this. God relents: 'My presence shall go with you.'[585] That is the point at which the covenant God reveals his glory (though not his face) to Moses, after which two things (in particular) happen: Moses' face shines and has to be veiled so as not to frighten the people,[586] and the tabernacle is after all constructed, with the divine presence in cloud and glory coming to dwell there to lead the people to their inheritance.[587] There is of course an ambiguity at this point: the divine presence comes to dwell in the tabernacle, to lead the people on their journey, but the tabernacle remains outside the camp. Paul's echo implies a considerable contrast. The Shekinah dwelt in the tabernacle, separated from the people. Now, the divine spirit has come to dwell within the renewed people themselves.

Paul, reflecting on this narrative, is saying just as much about the fulfilment of the tabernacle promise as he is about the fulfilment of Torah. As we saw in the previous chapter, those who gaze with unveiled face at the glory of the lord (2 Corinthians 3.18) are those who find in their hearts 'the light of the knowledge of the glory of God in the face of Jesus the Messiah' (4.6).

[583] See Wright 1991 [*Climax*], ch. 9.

[584] On this, as on much else, I am indebted to Scott Hafemann (though without endorsing all his conclusions): see, on this point, Hafemann 1995, 225–31.

[585] Exod. 33.14.

[586] Exod. 34.29–35.

[587] Exod. 40.34–8.

They themselves are the new tabernacle or Temple, as Paul indicates in 6.16–18. The promise that Israel's God would accompany his people to their inheritance, renewed after Moses' prayer, has become the reality that he will dwell *within* them. That is the effect of joining together Exodus, Ezekiel and Jeremiah, rethinking that combination in the light of the spirit. This is a central moment in Paul's spirit-focused redefinition of election.[588]

We should note that though 2 Corinthians 3 is clearly *covenantal* and *transformational*, it is not for that reason any less *juridical*. Paul describes his new-covenant ministry as the *diakonia* of *dikaiosynē*, contrasting this with the *diakonia* of *katakrisis*, judgment (3.9). This has the regular *anthropological* result, the movement from death to life (3.6). There is little explicit sign of *participationist* language here (though there is plenty in the surrounding chapters), but we may also trace the presence of a *salvation-historical* perspective from the puzzling hard-heartedness of ancient Israel, through the prophecies of renewal, to the work of the Messiah and Paul's consequent ministry; and also of an *apocalyptic* element in the fresh unveiling of the divine glory both in the face of Jesus (4.6) and in the opening of eyes and ears through the gospel (3.16–18). Once more the elements that are sometimes played off against one another in analyzing Paul are found together here in a seamless whole.

(e) Philippians 3.2–11

1 Corinthians 4 has provided an interlude, away from discussions of salvation or of covenant membership. With Philippians we are back on more familiar territory. Here, however, it is easier than in Galatians to see that Paul's argument is *solely* about 'covenant membership' and its redefinition through *pistis*. There is nothing here explicitly about 'salvation': no mention of sin, of the curse of the Torah, of the effect of the Messiah's death (except in relation to sharing his sufferings).[589] Clearly the same ultimate end is in view, since the goal of the pilgrimage Paul here describes is resurrection, which is of course the 'deliverance' from the 'last enemy'. But the emphasis of the passage is precisely not 'so that is how I shall be "saved"', but 'so that is how I will be demonstrated to be truly within the covenant people'. Resurrection here functions to round off the argument which begins with the claim in 3.2: 'We are the "circumcision".'[590] This is not a claim about 'how I earned my salvation' or 'how I realized I did not have to earn my salvation'. It is a claim about *membership in God's people*. And the claim is then

[588] On 2 Cor. cf. also above, 874–85, esp. on the controversial 5.21.

[589] Against e.g. Cook 2011, 358, who supposes that Paul is attacking opponents who contend that 'observing the law will bring salvation from the bondage to sin.' Cook says, dramatically, that Phil. 3.2 'essentially summarizes the core of Paul's epistle to the Galatians'.

[590] The claim is obviously cognate with Rom. 2.29, which as we saw goes with passages like 2 Cor. 3.3–6, and implicitly invokes the entire biblical and Jewish picture of 'heart-circumcision', as in e.g. Dt. 10.16; 30.6; Jer. 4.4; 9.25f.; Ezek. 44.7, 9; *Jub*. 1.23; 1QpHab 11.13; 1QS 5.5; 1QH 10 (=2).18; 23 (=18).20; Philo, *Spec. Leg*. 1.305: so e.g. Cousar 2009, 69.

advanced in two ways: first, by reference to the Messiah, and his crucifixion and resurrection; second, by the personal link to the Messiah, summed up in the *pistis* which we know from elsewhere he saw as the work of the spirit.[591] On the passage as a whole, Dunn seems to me correct: this passage has been neglected, and could be 'a major resource for moving the debate [on Paul and the law] beyond the impasse in which it was in danger of becoming stuck'.[592]

There are, of course, some scholars who would prefer it if Paul had never said what we find in Philippians 3.2–11.[593] This is where the apostle offers a sharp contrast between the privileges and status he enjoyed in his former life and the status he now possesses in the Messiah. Attempts are regularly made to say that any accurate summary of this passage is necessarily 'supersessionist'. Dunn makes the point which should hardly have been necessary:

> The coming of Jesus Messiah, and of the Spirit into the hearts of those who believe in this Jesus, had fulfilled Israel's hope for the age to come. *It is fulfilled hope* that he had in mind, *not superseded hope*.[594]

This is exactly right, though I fear it will not satisfy all the doubters and critics. If Paul really did believe that Jesus was Israel's Messiah – and the paragraph, not to mention the rest of Paul's writing, makes no sense unless we see that belief at its heart – then it is impossible to imagine him, or any second-Temple Jew in a comparable position, supposing that this Messiah could have his followers while 'Israel' could carry on as though nothing had happened. That, indeed, would be the route to the true 'supersessionism': the idea that Jesus had started a new movement discontinuous with Israel's history from Abraham to the present.[595] To claim, instead, that this history is affirmed, validated *and now fulfilled*, however surprisingly, by the arrival of Israel's Messiah – to call this 'supersessionism' is a cynical misuse of words. Was Akiba 'supersessionist' when he hailed bar-Kochba as Messiah and summoned Israel to rally to the flag? Paul is indicating a messianic identity and way of life which he sees as genuine worship of the God of

[591] As we see in 3.2: 'we worship by the spirit of God' (which I now believe to be the right reading, despite my own translation: see e.g. Caird 1976, 134; Metzger 1994 [1971], 547).

[592] Dunn 2008 [2005], 469 n. 2. Dunn's own chapter (ib., 469–90) is I think substantially on target, though at certain points I think he could have gone further (see below). Refs. to Dunn in what follows are to this chapter.

[593] Harink 2003, though strongly critical of my reading of this passage (157f.), offers no alternative. The brief account in W. S. Campbell 2008, 149f. repeats Harink's bizarre charges against the present writer (it is at least a refreshing novelty to be accused of holding 'a modern liberal form of individualism', the very opposite of what some of my critics think I believe). This marginalizing of Phil. 3.2–11 is cognate with the fact that, as mentioned above, neither writer discusses Rom. 2.25–9, apart from a couple of sentences in Campbell 2008, 104 which do not address the heart of the matter.

[594] Dunn 2008 [2005], 473 (my italics). I am not sure, though, that O'Brien 1991, 358, cited by Dunn, provides an example of 'supersessionism' in pointing out that the definite article in 'the circumcision' makes an exclusive claim. He is actually saying, I think, much the same thing as Dunn.

[595] Which is, of course, what we find by implication in the work of Martyn 1997a; 1997b, and others: see *Interpreters*.

Israel – only without circumcision and other Torah-badges.[596] That is the paradox which characterizes Paul at every point.

But the main point for our purpose is to show *how* election has thus been redefined in relation to Paul (as a chief exemplar, as in Galatians 2.16–21): in other words, how he describes what constitutes membership in this messianically redefined covenant people. Here we find, as in Galatians 3.23—4.7, a close integration of the various strands of thought which are sometimes thought to belong to different theological or soteriological 'systems' or categories: the 'covenantal' categories of 'circumcision' and 'righteousness in the law'; the 'incorporative' categories of being 'in the Messiah'; the 'forensic' language of 'righteousness' itself; the 'anthropological' language of leaving behind an identity 'according to the flesh'; the 'transformational' language of sharing the Messiah's sufferings in the hope of sharing his resurrection.[597] And all is set within the implicit narrative that what Israel had hoped for had now been, and was now being, accomplished: in other words, some kind of salvation history; and this, as usual, is balanced by the strong sense that something has happened to break open any kind of mere continuous historical development or evolution and reveal a quite new divine gift which rendered worthless all that had gone before ('apocalyptic', perhaps). All of these and more have their part to play, together with another note which is not struck so clearly elsewhere: the personal *knowledge* of the Messiah, expressing an intimacy of relationship which belongs with passages like 1.21–3 earlier in the letter.[598] One might align that with 'transformation', and it undoubtedly includes that, but seems if anything to go further again.

All these come together in a tight-packed statement of who Paul now is, and who by implication all the Messiah's people now are. Paul uses the singular 'I' in verses 4–11, but he does so to give sharp focus to the larger claim advanced by the plural 'we' in verse 3. (As in Galatians 2 and Romans 7, we may suppose that Paul uses the 'I' not least because he does not wish, in describing his kinsfolk according to the flesh, to say 'they'.)

We saw in an earlier chapter how sharp Paul's redefinition of election really was:

> [2]Watch out for the dogs! Watch out for the 'bad works' people! Watch out for the 'incision' party, that is, the mutilators! [3]We are the 'circumcision', you see – we who worship God by the spirit, and boast in the Messiah, Jesus, and refuse to trust in the flesh.[599]

'We are 'the circumcision'': not 'the true circumcision', but simply 'the circumcision', much like 'the Jew' (not 'the true Jew') in Romans 2.29. And those who insist on physical circumcision, thereby 'trusting in the flesh' – well, they are 'the "incision" party', the people who like to make cuts and

[596] See Bockmuehl 1998, 192.

[597] cp. Rom. 8.17. The present passage joins together the themes which Gorman 2009 explores, though he does not use it particularly to develop his theory of transformational justification.

[598] Note also the unique '*my* lord' in 3.8: see e.g. O'Brien 1991, 388.

[599] Phil. 3.2f. See above, 362f.

mutilations in their flesh. Along with Galatians 5.12, this is perhaps the fiercest thing Paul ever says about people who stand where he himself once stood. But the explanation, though couched in more measured terms, carries the same stark contrast:

> [4]Mind you, I've got good reason to trust in the flesh. If anyone else thinks they have reason to trust in the flesh, I've got more. [5]Circumcised? On the eighth day. Race? Israelite. Tribe? Benjamin. Descent? Hebrew through and through. Torah-observance? A Pharisee. [6]Zealous? I persecuted the church! Official status (*dikaiosynē*) under the law? Blameless.
>
> [7]Does that sound as though my account was well in credit? Well, maybe; but whatever I had written in on the profit side, I calculated it instead as a loss – because of the Messiah. [8]Yes, I know that's weird, but there's more: I calculate everything as a loss, because knowing Jesus the Messiah as my lord is worth far more than everything else put together! In fact, because of the Messiah I've suffered the loss of everything, and I now calculate it as trash, so that my profit may be the Messiah, [9]and that I may be discovered in him, not having my own covenant status defined by Torah (*mē echōn emēn dikaiosynēn tēn ek nomou*), but the status which comes through the Messiah's faithfulness (*alla tēn dia pisteōs Christou*): the covenant status from God (*tēn ek theou dikaiosynēn*) which is given to faith (*epi tē pistei*). [10]This means knowing him, knowing the power of his resurrection, and knowing the partnership of his sufferings. It means sharing the form and pattern of his death, [11]so that somehow I may arrive at the final resurrection from the dead.[600]

Throughout this whole passage, the question at issue is not 'How might I earn God's favour?', but 'What are the signs that I am a member of God's people?'[601] And, as in Galatians 2, the answer is twofold, negative and positive. First, the signs in question are not the signs that mark out Israel according to the flesh. Second, the signs in question are the signs that show that one is a Messiah-person, a spirit-and-faith person.

Begin at the end (3.11). The hope of Israel, at least as seen by a zealous Pharisee, was the resurrection of the dead. That hope has now been reaffirmed in the Messiah. But the means to this final, and typically zealous-Jewish, goal is not the observance of Torah, as he might once have said, but rather the sharing in the Messiah's death and resurrection. Here, just as in Galatians 2.19–20, it is those central, 'faithful' events which set the pattern for membership in the covenant family. There, Paul looked *back* to a death he had *already* died and a new life he *already* lived; here, he looks at a death he *continues to die* through the sufferings which he understands as the messianic sufferings in which he is privileged to share, and a future life to which he looks *forward* (though 'knowing the power of his resurrection' in verse 10 is the present anticipation of that life). This pattern of present suffering and future resurrection is, of course, typical of one strand in second-Temple Judaism, not least that represented by the Maccabaean martyr-stories.[602]

The line of thought that ends with resurrection begins with a 'reckoning' which follows the pattern of some of the dominical parables. Like the treasure in the field, or the great pearl, 'knowing Jesus the Messiah as my lord is

[600] Phil. 3.4–11.

[601] Rightly, Dunn 2008 [2005], 473.

[602] cf. *RSG* 150–3.

worth far more than everything else put together' (3.8). This 'knowing', a noun not used in this sense in Romans, corresponds to the 'knowing' of 1 Corinthians 8.1–7 and also Galatians 4.9. In both cases the 'knowing' which humans do is quickly turned around: what matters is God's 'knowing' of you![603] But there is none the less a 'knowing' which the follower of the Messiah has, a 'knowing of God' as the one who is now both 'father' and 'lord' (1 Corinthians 8.6) and as the one who sent the son and sent the spirit of the son (Galatians 4.4–7). This 'knowledge of God' seems to derive, not indeed as some used to think from 'gnosticism', but from the ancient Israelite sense of 'knowing God' or 'knowing YHWH'.[604] Paul here picks up this language 'and fills it with a specifically Christian content and with a peculiarly personal intensity'.[605] In Galatians this 'knowing' is correlated with 'faith' in the way that 3.23–9 is balanced by 4.1–11. In 1 Corinthians 8 the discussion hinges on 'knowing' rather than 'faith' (*pistis* and its cognates are rare throughout 1 Corinthians), though 'faith' is the key term in the parallel discussion in Romans 14. But here in Philippians the close link of 'faith' and 'knowing' seems clear from the join between verses 9 and 10. The genitive construction (*tou gnōnai auton*) at the start of verse 10 serves actually to *define* the 'faith' which receives the divine gift of the status of 'righteous' at the end of verse 9.

The central point, then, is in the main emphasis of 3.9: 'that I may be discovered in him', in other words, 'that I may prove to be in him' (*[hina] heurethō en autō*).[606] As in Romans 3.24 (the redemption which is '*in* the Messiah, Jesus') and as in Galatians 2.17 (seeking to be justified *in the Messiah*) and 3.26 (you are all sons of God '*in* the Messiah, Jesus'), so here the *location* logically precedes the *status*. Those who are in this 'place', namely 'in the Messiah', are credited with the status which, as in Galatians 2.15–21, refers to membership in the covenant people. This is of course the subject of the whole paragraph, as introduced by 3.4–6: the attempt to get round the emphasis on national or ethnic status in the first six of Paul's categories, and to allow the seventh, interpreted in a 'reformational' sense, to trump them all, simply will not do.[607] The listing of circumcision, race, tribe, descent, sect (i.e. Pharisee) and zeal are none of them about 'moral achievement'.[608] Together they strongly suggest that his claim to have been 'blameless' in relation to 'righteousness under the law' was not about 'amassing merits

603 1 Cor. 8.1–3; Gal. 4.9.

604 Isa. 11.9; Jer. 9.24. On 'knowing God' in Paul cf. e.g. Rom. 11.33; 2 Cor. 2.14; 4.6; 10.5; and cf. esp. 1 Cor. 13.12.

605 Caird 1976, 137, comparing Gal. 2.20; 6.14.

606 Fowl 2005, 154 points out that Paul here shifts from being the subject of the narrative to being part of a story in which the Messiah is the subject.

607 As e.g. Seifrid 1992, 173f.

608 Against e.g. O'Brien 1991, 384, 394. O'Brien is responding to Sanders 1983, 43–5, but as he notes Sanders may not have made the best case that could be made for a 'non-legalistic' reading. Hooker 2000, 526 points out that NIV's 'legalistic righteousness' is unwarranted. See too Dunn 2008 [2005], 476 n. 28.

and achievements', either.[609] It was a matter of *demonstrating*, through Torah-practice, one's covenant membership as per the previous six categories. Nor was Paul here claiming a lifetime of sinless perfection, but rather a status kept 'without blame' by the usual Jewish method of repentance and sacrifice.[610] All this was a matter of *covenant status*, possessed already in virtue of birth and exemplified in terms of Torah-keeping. That is the meaning of the *dikaiosynē*, 'righteousness', of which he speaks in verse 6. The whole point is to highlight Paul's supreme status as a member of the covenant people in excellent standing.

The point he then makes – the turning-point of the passage, corresponding to and based upon the christological turning-point indicated in Philippians 2.6–7, is that the covenant people has been redefined in, through and around the Messiah himself. His 'obedient' death (2.8), which Paul elsewhere describes as his 'faithfulness' to the divine plan, now indicates where covenant membership is to be found and the means by which one may be assured of it.[611] To belong to God's freshly defined people, one must be 'in him', wearing the badge of *pistis* which was the sign of his own solo accomplishment of Israel's vocation ('faithfulness'). Being 'in the Messiah', as clearly here as anywhere in Paul, is the new way of saying 'in Israel'. Not to draw that conclusion would be to deny that he really was the Messiah, which for Paul would mean denying that he had been raised from the dead.

Once again the wider context determines the meaning of the key terms. The *dikaiosynē ek nomou* (3.9) which Paul had once possessed was 'the covenant status defined by Torah', which he set out in 3.4–6. In that passage Paul was not, as I just said, describing the often-imagined Jewish quest for moral achievement, but the much-evidenced Pharisaic quest for secure covenant status. That solidifies the meaning of 'righteousness', *dikaiosynē*, here as elsewhere. The language is indeed 'relational'; but the 'relation' in question is that of the *covenant*, and that, as we have seen, always dovetailed, as

[609] Against Bockmuehl 1998, 201–5. I do not think Bockmuehl has explained in his commentary, even at 188 where he seems to approach the question, how this repeated emphasis fits together with his fine exposition of Jewish nationalist 'zeal' (194–201). Despite what he says at 201, it is not clear from vv. 5–6 that we are dealing with 'a human quality of uprightness in relation to the requirements of the Torah'. 4QMMT, which he cites, does not help his case, as I have shown in my essay on the text (now in *Perspectives* ch. 21). In my view Dunn 2008 [2005], 480 concedes too much at this point. Philippians 3.4–6 seems to me a classic statement of the Pharisaic position which I set out in chapter 2 above (179–93) and which forms the backdrop for so much Pauline thinking.

[610] See, rightly, Seifrid 1992, 174; Dunn 2008 [2005], 479f.

[611] On the Messiah's 'faithfulness', see above, esp. 836–51. On the present passage, see e.g. O'Brien 1991, 398f. (in favour of the reading here adopted); Fee 1995, 325f. (against it). Reumann 2008, 495f. comes down heavily in favour of the traditional objective genitive reading (once one has deciphered his telegraphic style); but then he has always tended to play safe and adopt traditional Lutheran readings. Hooker 2000, 528 appears to suggest that the Messiah's faithfulness actually constitutes the 'righteousness' promised by Israel's God to one who would be faithful. This might produce a new version of 'imputed righteousness', though she does not develop that idea.

far as Paul was concerned, with the 'forensic' context.[612] The 'righteousness' is the status of the *tsaddiq*, the 'righteous' person who, like Abraham or Phinehas, is a true covenant member. Paul is clear that he still needs to have this 'covenant status'. He has not swept away the 'Israel'-categories, like those who, clinging to the word 'apocalyptic', want him to have nothing to do with Abraham, with the covenant or with the whole story of Israel. His fresh vision of the one God, and the people of this one God, has not in the least abolished the category of 'Israel', as some would like to suppose (and as some have accused me of saying). But the point is that *election has been redefined in the Messiah*; and the covenant status Paul knows he still needs is found 'in him' and only in him, through his 'faithfulness', his 'obedience unto death' as in 2.8. Not for the only time, the present passage echoes 2.6–11 quite closely.[613] That, indeed, is part of the point: the 'him' in 3.9, 'in whom' Paul desires to be 'found', is of course the 'lord Jesus Messiah' of 2.6–11, which is why those who are 'in him' are to share the fellowship of his sufferings in the hope of resurrection. Once again the compressed 'doctrine of justification' here, which is in the present context explicitly about covenant membership rather than 'salvation from sin', is focused on the Messiah himself. He *is* the 'covenant location'; and 'righteousness' is the 'covenant status' declared by Israel's God over everyone who is 'in' that location – because of course, if they are 'there', his death and resurrection are 'reckoned' to them, as in Romans 6.2–11. 'Participation in the Messiah' and 'the forensic declaration "in the right"' are both part of a single whole. And that single whole is covenant membership, and its redefinition through Messiah and spirit.[614]

The status Paul therefore possesses is 'the righteous status which is from God', *hē ek theou dikaiosynē*. This is now given to, or bestowed upon, faith.[615] Despite older attempts to make this phrase equivalent to the *dikaiosynē theou* itself ('God's righteousness'), as though the latter phrase referred to the righteous status of the covenant member rather than the righteousness of the covenant God himself, the unique *ek*, 'from', gives the

[612] This slices through the muddling debates, going back in recent times to e.g. Ziesler 1972 (cf. e.g. O'Brien 1991, 396), as to the meaning of *dikaiosynē* in 3.9. There is no need to suggest that the first use is 'moral' and the second 'forensic'. Both are 'covenantal' – which is interpreted forensically (on the analogy of the 'status' in the law court) and is closely connected to (though not identified with) a clutch of connected concepts including participation and transformation. Dunn 2008 [2005], 483f. speaks in terms of 'relationship with God', and of the law being a less 'immediate' means of this than faith. This threatens to collapse the discussion back into a comparison of different 'types of religion', from which a covenantal eschatology would free it completely. Käsemann 1980 [1973], 24, 27 shows how slippery the category of 'relationship' can be.

[613] I was first alerted to this by Hooker 1971, 355–7, but the point is now regularly made in many commentaries, e.g. the very helpful Bockmuehl 1998, 206; Dunn 2008 [2005], 487 n. 69, with other refs.; and Hooker herself again, half a lifetime later (2000, 527).

[614] Dunn 2008 [2005], 487f. stresses the coming together of 'forensic' and 'participationist' categories, but not the underlying and unifying covenantal theme.

[615] There is no verb for 'given to' or 'bestowed upon'; these are my attempts to flesh out *epi tē pistei*.

game away.[616] The *dikaiosynē* here is precisely not God's own righteousness, as in Romans 3.21 and elsewhere. It is the status which is *from* God *to* those who 'believe', and who thereby wear the Messiah-badge on the basis of the Messiah's own faithfulness.[617] As for the *pistis* upon which this status of *dikaiosynē* is declared, we should assume that here as elsewhere in Paul it is the work of the spirit through the gospel. That is certainly implied in 1.6 ('the one who began a good work in you will thoroughly complete it by the day of the Messiah Jesus'), and is expressed more explicitly in 3.3 when Paul gives, as one of the signs of new-covenant membership, 'we who worship by the spirit of God'. That spirit-led worship, as in Galatians 4.7, is part of what Paul means by *pistis*. And all this contributes to Paul's stark claim, echoing the redefinition in Romans 2.29: 'we are the circumcision.' This belongs, as we have seen, with Paul's regular notion of covenant renewal, of the spirit-driven transformation of the heart.

Philippians 3 thus coheres completely with Galatians and with Romans in its theological understanding and the language in which it expresses it. As Caird saw a generation ago, Paul has neatly expressed the past, present and future tenses of what it means to be a Messiah-person: the righteous status already given 'in the Messiah'; the present sharing of his sufferings; the future resurrection.[618] Like Galatians 3 in particular, this passage draws together into a single line of thought (covenantal and ecclesial) the elements of 'juridical' and 'participationist' theology which are sometimes wrongly played off against one another. It assumes, ultimately, a soteriology which climaxes in resurrection. But the point here is not to say, 'This is how one is saved,' but 'This is how one is known as a covenant member.' The central category which holds everything together is neither 'juridical' nor 'participationist', though both are emphatically central. It is not 'salvation-historical' or 'apocalyptic' as such, though again both are implied. It is not 'anthropological' or 'transformational', though we can see both of those standing behind and beneath Paul's actual argument. The argument itself is about the ancient Jewish doctrine of election: in other words, of the covenant status of the people of God. This, Paul believes, has now been redefined in terms of the Messiah himself, and then in terms of the *pistis* which, along with the 'fellowship of his sufferings', is the badge Paul elsewhere, and here in 3.3, associates with the gospel-work of the spirit. This is what 'justification by faith' is all about.

[616] With e.g. O'Brien 1991, 397f., against a line from at least Bultmann onwards. It is curious to find Schreiner (2001, 200) among the Bultmannites on this question; curiouser still for one of his theological position to accuse those who differ of 'reading Paul far too technically' (see his own proper warnings [206] about the danger when a word 'bleeds into other terms'). To be sure, Phil. 3 is covering very similar ground to Rom. 3.21–31 or 10.2–4, but Paul, here as ever, is sure-footed and says very precisely what he means. Tyndale's maxim, of never altering a syllable of God's word, comes to mind. Nor is it clear that saying the divine righteousness is a 'gift' actually belongs within the 'forensic' category where Schreiner tries to put it: what is 'forensic' about a 'gift'?

[617] Fowl 2005, 154 seems to me uncharacteristically confused at this point.

[618] Caird 1976, 138f.

It is almost time to turn to Romans itself. But before we get there we have one more short visit to pay. Though Colossians does not speak about 'justification' in so many words, it does warn about a particular danger which, as I have argued elsewhere, may well be in effect the same danger against which Paul is warning in Philippians 3.

(f) Colossians 2

Was there a 'heresy' in Colosse, and if so what was it? Most scholars have thought there was, though it has proved curiously elusive.[619] I have in the past taken the view, following Morna Hooker, that there was in fact no particular present and pressing threat, and that Paul's warnings in Colossians 2 were more generalized, warding off potential threats rather than addressing specific local difficulties. And the potential threat I think he had in mind, here as in Philippians 3, was related to the actual threat posed in Galatia: that those who had come into the Messiah's family would be attracted by the synagogue.[620] I do not think the Colossian church was facing a crisis of Galatian proportions, but Paul would be well aware that throughout Asia Minor the same problems might well occur. If I am even half right, this means that, even though Colossians 2 mentions neither justification nor the spirit, it must nevertheless be included within an overall discussion of Paul's messianic redefinition of election.

The main emphases of Colossians 2, I suggest, belong with, and only with, a coded description of the world of the synagogue. After the initial warning in verse 8, to which we shall return, Paul has three basic points to make.

First, those who belong to the king, the Messiah, are fulfilled in him, that is, in the one in whom 'all the full measure of divinity has taken up bodily residence' (verse 9). That, as we saw in the previous chapter, is temple-language. Jesus is the true Temple, and those who belong to him somehow share in that identity. Second, the Colossian Christians have already been 'circumcised' – but it is a new sort of 'circumcision', which involves not cutting off the foreskin but putting off 'the body of flesh', the old solidarity of 'fleshly' identity. This has happened in baptism, in which they have died and been raised with the Messiah (verses 11–12). Third, the Torah, which had formerly stood against them because of their being 'gentiles', has nothing more to say against them, since God has dealt with that whole problem through the Messiah's cross (verses 14–15). Once we cut through the complex language, these are the three things he wants to get across, and they are

[619] Among recent discussions cf. Arnold 1995; Dunn 1996, 23–35 (and see Dunn 1995); Sumney 1999, 192–208; Wilson 2005, 35–58; Witherington 2007, 107–11; Moo 2008, 46–60; Bird 2009b, 15–26.

[620] Hooker 1973; my own view was first published in Wright 1986b, 23–30, 100–28, now followed and developed by Dunn in particular (see previous note). I drew attention to this again in Wright 2005a [*Fresh Perspectives*], 117 (despite the warning in e.g. Aletti 1993, 18). There is no space here to engage in a large and lively debate; sufficient to note the possibility that Col. 2 should be considered in connection with our present theme.

striking indeed: Temple, circumcision, Torah. This can only be a veiled warning against the attractions of the Jewish way of life.

The specific warnings which follow have the same basic DNA. Questions of food and drink, or specific holy days including sabbaths, are much more likely to be part of a Jewish system than anything else (verses 16–19). Specific regulations about what may and may not be touched, tasted or even handled occur in many religious and social cultures and customs, but verses 20–3 go well with the general tenor of Diaspora Judaism, as many of the commentators already referred to have explored. And the echoes of Galatians and Romans at many points (e.g. the lining up in verse 8 of the *stoicheia* with the 'traditions' that might be enticing them, and the dying and rising in baptism) indicate further that we are in the right area.

How then would the warning work? Why does Paul identify his target as 'philosophy and hollow trickery?' As is often noted, both Philo and Josephus use the word 'philosophy' to identify the Jewish way of life, and as we saw in chapters 3 and 4 above it was if anything a more natural word to use than 'religion', since Jews, like Paul's communities, did few of the things that 'religions' normally did.[621] The case I have made before, and repeat here, is that Paul is doing again what he began to do in Galatians. He is describing the life of the synagogue as if it were, in effect, a form of paganism, enslaved to the *stoicheia* and to the kind of dietary and calendrical observances that went with that, and describing the Messiah's people by contrast as those who had escaped that slavery through their sharing in his death and resurrection. There is, to be sure, a good deal of technical detail, particularly in verses 16–19, which may relate to particular phenomena and teaching prevalent in the Jewish circles of Asia Minor at the time. Certainly there is no way back to the eager 'gnostic' hypotheses of earlier days.[622] If Paul had been warning against more specifically pagan influences, there are several things in the world of Asia Minor which we might expect him to mention, but which he does not. A general warning against the lure of the synagogue, with sidelong glances at some kinds of devotional and ascetic practices now somewhat opaque to us, is the best guess. This then would constitute a further example of 'election redefined around the Messiah'.

The key point here, apart from the focus of the basic argument on Temple, circumcision and Torah, is buried in verse 8. We have seen elsewhere that Paul, as part of his redefinition of election, is capable of using or even coining puns to make his point. Thus he speaks of the *Ioudaios* whose 'praise' (for which the Hebrew is 'Judah') is from God rather than humans (Romans 2.29); of the *katatomē* whose claim to be the *peritomē* is upstaged by the Messiah and his people (Philippians 3.2–3). It is not therefore farfetched to

[621] cf. Philo *De Somn.* 2.127; *Leg.* 156, 245; *De Mut. Nom.* 223; *Omn. Prob. Lib.* 88; Jos. *Ap.* 2.47; *War* 2.119; *Ant.* 18.11. Cf. too *4 Macc.* 1.1; 5.10, 22; 7.7–9.

[622] See esp. Wilson 2005, 49, 57: 'the Colossian "heresy" is beyond question not yet a developed Gnosticism . . . On the other hand it is significant that the most recent proposals [about the "heresy"] all in some way look back to Judaism . . .'

suggest that he does something similar here.[623] My proposal is that he has here used a very rare word for a very precise purpose. 'Watch out,' he says, 'that nobody uses philosophy ... *to take you captive*.' The word he uses for 'take captive' is *sylagōgein*, here in the present participle *sylagōgōn*; it is the only occurrence of the word in all early Christian literature, and indeed one of only three surviving occurrences of the word from across the many centuries of ancient Greek.[624] Paul had other words available to him if he wanted to say 'take prisoner' or 'enslave'.[625] Why would he choose such an unusual term here?

My proposal is to treat the word as an ironic pun on the Greek word *synagōgē*, 'synagogue'. There is no verbal form of this word, but it would not be difficult to imagine one. Nor would it be difficult to see how the two words would resemble one another. 'Watch out,' he might be saying, 'that there isn't anybody there who might "en-synagogue" you': *blepete mē tis hymas estai ho* ***synagōgōn***, as opposed to *blepete mē tis hymas estai ho* ***sylagōgōn***. Paul's letters were of course designed to be read out loud, and phonetically the two are extremely close. So close, in fact, are the liquid 'l' sound and the nasal 'n' sound that grammarians regularly lump liquids and nasals together. They share elements of morphological behaviour, and under certain circumstances can easily be swapped.[626]

That is perhaps the most important thing to remember. But visually something similar happens as well. Written in small Greek letters, you only have to turn a lambda upside down to create a nu with a tail: from λ to ν. Written in block capitals, as are all our early manuscripts of the Greek New Testament, the 'n' and the 'l' are even closer: ΣΥΝΑΓΩΓΩΝ as against ΣΥΛΑΓΩΓΩΝ, the capital N adding the final vertical stroke to the capital Λ. But, granted the setting and the intention of oral performance, it is the phonetic proximity that counts first.

It is of course impossible to prove that this was in Paul's mind. That is how it is with this kind of hypothesis. The proposal has the merit, though, that it fits tightly with a tight reading of Colossians 2; that it resonates with Paul's verbal trickery at two closely cognate moments in other letters; and that it gives to the whole passage a sense of allusive irony which seems to me to belong at this point. Serious scholars who would never dream of wordplay in theological discourse may of course object, but I think it cannot be lightly dismissed.[627] Paul is consciously remoulding the entire notion of election around the Messiah, and he is well aware of the extraordinary theological task he is undertaking. We should not be surprised if in the process

[623] Against e.g. Witherington 2007, 154. The passage in Phil. 3.2 also begins with *blepete*, 'watch out'.

[624] BDAG 955 and LSJ 1671 give only two other uses: the AD C3 novelist Heliodorus (10.35) and the obscure C5 public speaker Aristaenetus (2.22).

[625] He uses *doulagōgeō* in 1 Cor. 9.27; *aichmalōtizō* in Rom. 7.23; 2 Cor. 10.5; cf. 2 Tim. 3.6.

[626] cf. Moulton and Turner 1906–63, 2.103, para. 42. I am grateful to Jamie Davies for his linguistic expertise on this point.

[627] e.g. Moo 2008, 185; contrast the more positive note in Bird 2009b, 75. Dunn 1996, 147 simply records the proposal without comment, though it would cohere well with his own position.

he attempts also some mildly extraordinary verbal tasks, in order to embody, as well as to express, the revolution he sees taking place.

With all this, we turn at last to Romans.

(g) Romans 3.21—4.25

Romans 3.21—4.25, one of the great passages in this, the greatest of all letters, is founded on the same belief that Paul announced proleptically in 1.16–17: that in 'the gospel', that is, the message about Jesus the Messiah and his death and resurrection as the fulfilment of God's scriptural promises, 'God's righteousness' is revealed.[628] Though the spirit is not mentioned in this passage, Paul draws on several themes which he elsewhere, both in this letter and in Galatians, associates closely with the spirit's work. This is the beginning of the single argument which, reaching its height in chapter 8, provides Paul's most thorough exposition of the spirit-driven reworked election.

However Irish it may seem, the proper place to begin a discussion of Romans 3.21 and onwards is with Romans 3.20. Here Paul refers to Psalm 143.2 [LXX 142.2]. Though not a direct quotation, it is close enough for a strong echo: 'in your sight shall no living creature be justified,' *ou dikaiōthēsetai enōpion sou pas zōn*. At the front of this, Paul has added *ex ergōn nomou*, 'by works of the law'; he has substituted *sarx*, 'flesh', for *zōn*, 'living creature'; and, because he is speaking in the third person rather than the second, has substituted *autou* for *sou*: 'by works of the law shall no flesh be justified in *his* sight.' He has rubbed in the point of his addition about the law by adding, at the end, 'through the law, you see, comes the knowledge of sin' – an idea to which he will return, particularly in chapter 7. (That ought to function as an advance sign – one of many – that Romans 1—8 is not the stitching together of two different types of theology, but a single coherent flowing argument. Once we grasp that, we see that it is true also of Romans 1—11 . . . but of that more anon.)

As has often been pointed out, this echo of Psalm 143.2 massively undergirds the assumption that the underlying subject is God's own 'righteousness'.[629] The psalm opens with an invocation:

> Hear my prayer, YHWH;
> give ear to my supplications in your faithfulness (*en tē alētheia sou*);
> answer me in your righteousness (*en tē dikaiosynē sou*).[630]

This fits closely with Romans 3.3–7, where God's faithfulness (*pistis*), his truthfulness (*alētheia*), his righteousness (*dikaiosynē*), his judgment (*epei pōs krinei ho theos ton kosmon*), his truthfulness (*alētheia*) again and his

[628] See above on the difference between 1.17 (*apokalyptetai*) and 3.21 (*pephanerōtai*). On the divine righteousness see above, 480, 801–4, 841, 928, 991; and below, 1003, 1054–6, etc.

[629] See Williams 1980; Hays 2005, 50–60, and elsewhere.

[630] Ps. 143.1 [LXX 142.1]. *Alētheia* here corresponds to *emunah*, and *dikaiosynē* as usual to *tsedaqah*.

glory (*doxa*) are all introduced in quick succession. The subject of the passage is the one God himself, and the way in which these various divine attributes or characteristics, apparently called in question, will in fact be vindicated. By invoking the opening of Psalm 143, Paul is continuing this train of thought: the Psalmist is appealing from this position of helplessness ('in your sight shall no one living be justified') to God's truthfulness and righteousness as the divine characteristics because of which the one God will nevertheless come to his aid. He is thereby standing on exactly the same ground as the great prayers of Daniel 9, Ezra 9 and Nehemiah 9.[631] The helplessness of God's people causes them to cast themselves on the truth and righteousness of God. That is the underlying logic of Romans 3.20, solidly supported in the passage that now follows.

It is important to see 3.21—4.25 as a whole. What we call chapter 4 is not merely a 'proof from scripture' of 3.21–31. It consists of a sustained and quite detailed exposition of Genesis 15, the chapter in which God makes the covenant to which, Paul is arguing, he has now been faithful.[632] When we remind ourselves what, in second-Temple Jewish thought, was seen as the *purpose* of the Abrahamic covenant, namely the undoing of the sin of Adam and the reversal of its effects, we realize that this is precisely what, here and in chapters 5—8, Paul says has been achieved through Jesus the Messiah. All this builds up intense pressure for us to accept the normal biblical and post-biblical reading of the phrase 'God's righteousness'. The phrase does not denote a human status which Israel's God gives, grants, imparts or imputes ('a righteousness *from* God' as in Philippians 3.9), or a human characteristic which 'counts' with God ('a righteousness which avails before God').[633] Nor does it denote the saving *power* of the one God, as Käsemann and others argued in a last-ditch attempt to prevent Paul from affirming Israel's covenant theology.[634] It retains its primary scriptural meaning, which is that of God's *covenant faithfulness*. This includes, and indeed focuses on, God's *faithful justice*, his determination to put the world to rights through putting humans to rights, and within that his faithfulness to the promises made in the Torah, promises to Abraham in Genesis about a worldwide family and promises to Israel in Deuteronomy about the curse of exile that would follow rebellion and the restoration which, consequent upon the circumcised

[631] See above, 119f.

[632] See more fully 'Paul and the Patriarch': *Perspectives* ch. 33.

[633] The first is properly a 'genitive of origin', the second an 'objective genitive' (which requires that *dikaiosynē* is seen as implying an active verb, a quality which 'does something', 'which prevails with God'). These are often muddled in discussion. See the diagram in Wright 1997 [*What St Paul*], 101.

[634] Käsemann 1980 [1973], *passim* (esp. 23–30), and Käsemann 1969 [1965], ch. 7. The presupposition is expressed in Jewett 2007, 319: to mention the covenant 'would retain the premise of Israel's preeminent position as Yahweh's sole covenant partner'. Paul's exposition, in Romans and elsewhere, of covenant *renewal* shows how misleading this is; and the balance of 1.16 ('to the Jew *first*, and also equally to the Greek') indicates well enough how Paul understood the matter.

heart, would reverse the disaster.[635] That, Paul declares throughout this section and indeed in the whole letter, is what Israel's God has done in the Messiah and what he is now doing, through the gospel and through faith, for the benefit of all who believe – an operation (gospel and faith) which elsewhere he describes as being the powerful work of the spirit.

This results in the dramatic reworking of 'election', in this case of the standard 'election' categories (a) *hoi dikaioi* and (b) 'seed of Abraham', in terms of *pistis*. As with the Messiah himself, so with his people: this revelation of God's faithful covenant justice is 'for the benefit of all believers' (3.22), because the Messiah's redemptive sacrifice unveils God's *dikaiosynē* as being the quality because of which he justifies *ton ek pisteōs Iēsou* (3.26). That latter phrase is a kind of portmanteau expression which echoes, and conveys in miniature, the two meanings expressed more fully in 3.22: (a) Jesus' messianic faithfulness (the Israel-faithfulness which, according to 3.2, Israel had not offered),[636] and (b) the faith of believers. Paul envisages a new corporate reality, a new social community, coming into being through the gospel, a reality in which all previous systems of privilege, boasting, honour and shame are done away with.[637] And all this happens precisely *in the present time*: it is 'now' (3.21), as in the emphatic declaration of 2 Corinthians 6.2; it is *en tō nyn kairō*, right here in the present moment of opportunity (3.26). It is not (that is to say) away in the future, on the last day. The verdict of the last day stands in the background of Romans 3, having been articulated quite fully in chapter 2. But, as in a different context in 1 Corinthians 4, Paul envisages this verdict being heard here and now, because it has been brought forward into the present. The Messiah has embodied and instantiated God's promised eschatological condemnation of sin and launching of the new creation, and all those who 'have faith' of this sort (further defined in 4.24–5) share, in the present, in the divine verdict which was announced in his resurrection (as in 1.4).

Thus – a point of considerable importance in the larger debates about the shape and nature of Paul's theology – the nexus between the Messiah's faithfulness and the *pistis* of believers indicates that, just as in Galatians 3 and Philippians 3 (see above), what we loosely think of as 'justification' is very closely joined in Paul's mind with the incorporation of believers into the messianic reality of Jesus' death and resurrection.[638] Knowing how Paul

[635] For the older German debates, see Brauch 1977. See further the major review in Williams 1980. Jewett 2007, 272–5 offers a curious mixture: in Rom. 3.21 he reads *dikaiosynē theou* as a subjective genitive, referring to 'God's saving activity', rooting this in the OT but without reference to the covenant (272f.); then on 3.22 he says one should assume 'that an objective genitive is employed here *as in the preceding verse*' (my italics), referring to a 'righteousness deriving from God' which is 'imparted to all' who have faith. When he goes on to speak of people having 'access to the righteousness of God' (278) we seem to have left the biblical and Jewish base behind altogether.

[636] On *pistis Christou* here see Jewett 2007, 277.

[637] This is the proper emphasis of Jewett 2007; though Jewett then plays this off against the 'forensic' meaning of justification, to 'avoid a legalistic theory of salvation' (298) – a somewhat bizarre way of saying he wants to avoid the normal theories in which 'legalism' is seen as the problem, not the solution.

[638] This also explains, in reverse as it were, the continuance of 'justification' language in the more obviously 'incorporative' section of the letter, chs. 6—8. See also e.g. 891, 900–3, 1011–13, 1024f.

writes, we might anticipate that he will express all this in a tight, dense phrase; and here it is. 'Through the redemption which is in Messiah Jesus' (3.24). It will take all of chapters 5—8 to unpack what that actually means, but Paul here brings the whole of that subsequent section into play within the specific argument about the manifestation of the divine faithfulness in the present time.

For the moment, however, we must focus on what he says here, in verses 25 and 26, about the effect of Jesus' death.[639] Actually, the words 'death', 'die' and so on do not occur here, and nor do 'cross' or 'crucify'. The one word which specifically refers to the events of Jesus' execution is 'blood', indicating already that Paul is thinking in sacrificial terms. But we should be in no doubt: the central way in which Paul sees 'the righteousness of God' unveiled is in Jesus' death, as described in this dense and crowded little passage.[640] And it is Jesus' sacrificial death, of course, which accomplishes justification, as Paul says in the summary statement at 5.9.

The present passage is dense because Paul is saying (at least) three things at once, and combining as he does so allusions to, and echoes of, several different though related biblical and post-biblical themes. The framework, emphasized in the remarkable repetition of 'righteousness' in verses 25 and 26, is the unveiling of God's covenant faithfulness, whose meaning becomes more fully apparent in chapter 4: this is how God has accomplished what he promised to Abraham, namely, that the world described in 1.18—2.16 would be put right at last, would be rescued – through the call of Israel (as in 2.17–20) to be the light that would shine in the darkness. The complexity comes not least from this point: that whereas in most biblical and post-biblical thought the divine covenant faithfulness was appealed to in favour of what God might do *for* Israel, here the point is what God always planned to do *through* Israel, and has now done *through the faithfulness of the Messiah*, the 'faithfulness' which led to and climaxed in his self-giving to death. Paul is thus taking themes to do with the establishment and renewal of the covenant *with* Israel and using them, completely consistently with his vision of the covenant purpose *through* Israel, to explain what the covenant God, who is also the creator God, has now done for all people, Jew and gentile alike. This is all part of his redefinition of election.

When we find a concentration of language such as we do here, with the unveiling of God's righteousness mentioned no fewer than five times in five verses (and two uses of the cognate verb), the obvious thing to do is to look for a biblical passage with a similar concentration of the same theme; and the obvious candidate is Isaiah 40—55. Nothing there approaches this average of once per verse, but the words *tsedeq* and its cognates occur thirty times in these sixteen chapters, thus possessing a good claim to be one of

[639] See above, 843–6. The present account, as part of the theme of *justification*, is closely complementary to the earlier one, as part of the theme of the Messiah's *faithfulness*.

[640] I take it for granted that whether or not Paul was quoting, or even adapting, a formula, he used these words because they expressed exactly what he wanted to say.

the section's major themes.[641] And of course the figure which appears within that whole section, like a tune emerging in the middle of a complex tone poem, only to be paused, reprised, developed and at last brought to a triumphant climax, is the servant. He is both Israel and one who stands over against Israel; he will not only restore the people of Israel from their exile but will be a light to the nations.[642] His obedience leads to a shameful and shocking death, shocking partly because of its shamefulness, partly because of its vicarious character[643] and partly because, uniquely in Israel's scriptures, it constitutes a human sacrifice.[644] What almost happened to Isaac actually happened to the servant. He is 'the righteous one' who will 'make the many righteous' and will 'bear their iniquities'.[645] Within the larger flow of the section, the servant's successful mission accomplishes the renewal of the covenant (chapter 54) and of creation itself (chapter 55), with the open invitation going out to 'everyone who thirsts' to share in the covenant originally made with David.[646]

All this resonates with Paul's thought at many points, but perhaps nowhere so powerfully as in this section of Romans. There is much more that could be said, but this is enough, I think, to warrant the firm conclusion that when Paul describes the death of Jesus in sacrificial language, emphasizing in every line that this is how the divine righteousness has been revealed, he is deliberately setting up a complex chain of allusion and echo in which Isaiah 40—55 in general, the figure of the servant in particular and the fourth servant song climactically, are central and loadbearing. Whatever else Paul thinks 'justification' is about, it is certainly about the fulfilment of the divine covenant plan for, and through, Israel. Attempts to avoid this conclusion are simply missing the point.

This highlights once more the theme we saw earlier: the *faithfulness* of the Servant-Messiah as the quality through which all this has been accomplished. It is because of this faithful act that the Abrahamic covenant is fulfilled, bringing the 'ungodly' into the single covenant family, as in chapter 4 and as is summed up in 5.6–11.[647]

This essentially *covenantal* reading of Isaiah 40—55 and Romans 3.21–6 contains within itself the *forensic* or *law court* imagery we have already seen to be prominent in the passage. Paul has built up in the earlier sections a great barrage of accusation, resulting in all humankind standing defenceless in the dock, a situation summed up in Adamic terms in 3.23: all sinned, and

641 cf. *tsaddiq*, adjective: 41.26; 45.21; 49.24; 53.11; *tsdq*, verb: 43.9, 26; 45.25; 50.8; 53.11; *tsedeq*, noun: 41.2, 10; 42.6, 21; 45.8, 13, 19; 51.1, 5, 7; *tsedaqah*, noun: 45.8, 23, 24; 46.12, 13; 48.1, 18; 51.6, 8; 54.14, 17: thirty occurrences of the root, several of them clustered here and there.

642 49.5–7; note the link between 49.7 and 52.15.

643 'Wounded for our transgressions, crushed for our iniquities; upon him was the punishment that made us whole, and by his bruises we are healed . . . YHWH has laid on him the iniquity of us all.'

644 Isa. 53.10: 'when you make his life an offering for sin', an *'asham* in Heb., LXX *peri hamartias*, the regular translation of 'sin offering'.

645 Isa. 53.11

646 Isa. 55.3.

647 See above, 960f.

fell short of God's glory. This is a greater 'exile' even than that addressed by Isaiah, but because of the wider vocation already envisaged in Isaiah 49 Paul finds himself justified in extending the effect of the servant's death as the means of dealing with this entire load of human sin. The 'righteousness' of God which was called into question by the failure of Israel to be 'faithful' to the divine commission (3.2–3) has been put into effect through the faithfulness of the Messiah. Up to that point, God's 'kindness and forbearance' (2.4) meant that sin had not been punished as it deserved. Now God is seen to be simultaneously 'in the right' himself, principally in terms of his faithfulness to the covenant and secondarily, within that, in terms of the implicit lawcourt scene, and 'putting right', that is, 'justifying', *ton ek pisteōs Iēsou*, 'the one from the faithfulness of Jesus', the 'Jesus-faith' people. The divine act of dealing with sin through the sacrificial death of the faithful sin-bearing servant is central to the passage; which means that the *forensic* account of sin, punishment and atonement is to be located within, and only understood in relation to, the wider *covenantal* theme.

The same is true in relation to the 'faith' which is the badge of membership in Abraham's single family, as chapter 4 will make clear. Jesus' *pistis* evokes the *pistis* of all those who believe the gospel, and this *pistis* thereby becomes the appropriate badge both of their membership in the covenant family and of their sharing in the results of his 'faithful' sin-bearing vocation. 'Justification by faith' is not *only* 'forensic' or *only* 'covenantal'. It is the one because it is the other; and Paul might well have been frustrated at the thought that we, like someone whose spectacles are out of focus, persisted in talking about two things when he, thinking biblically, could only see one.

Paul seems thus to have taken what up to then might have been read as a statement of how YHWH's election of Israel itself would be confirmed, and has transformed it, in line with what he perceived as its true intention, into a statement of how YHWH's election of Abraham's whole family would be accomplished. That is characteristic of his whole hermeneutic, as well as his whole theology.

The Messiah's redemptive death, thus applied to believers, then unveils the redefinition of election:

> [27]So what happens to boasting? It is ruled out! Through what sort of law? The law of works? No: through the law of faith! [28]We calculate, you see, that a person is declared to be in the right on the basis of faith, apart from works of the law.

The 'boasting' of 'the Jew' (as in 2.17; that is the obvious reference which explains this sudden question) is ruled out. This 'boasting', as we saw, was not simply the boast which said, 'We are automatically morally superior, because we are God's chosen people and we possess the law.' It was, more specifically, the 'boasting' which said, 'We are *the solution to the problem of humankind* because, as God's chosen and law-possessing people, we are the guide to the blind, the light to those in darkness, and so forth.'[648] This boast

[648] See *Perspectives* ch. 30.

has been ruled out, in Paul's argument so far, because, while Israel was in fact unfaithful to that commission, the Messiah has been faithful to it. He has accomplished that 'solution' which shimmered like a mirage in the aspirations of Israel but melted away as one came closer. All of this Paul has telescoped together in another typically terse phrase. What has ruled out 'boasting' is not 'the law of works' – it is not simply, in other words, that Israel has failed to keep up to the standard Torah demanded. Rather, the faithfulness of the Messiah, and the faith of his people, *is what the law required all along as the means of taking forward the divine purposes.* Hence the almost impossibly dense (though characteristically Pauline) phrase: 'through the law of faith', *dia nomou pisteōs*. Paul will not explain how this apparent oxymoron works until 9.30—10.13. But we do well not to dissolve its oddity ahead of that time by supposing that *nomos* here does not mean Torah.[649] The boasting of Israel ('we are the solution to the problem') is excluded because Israel's God has done, through the Messiah, what Israel could not do.[650]

This is then explained (*gar*, 3.28) as follows: We reckon (the word is mathematical: we calculate) that a person is 'justified by faith' apart from works of the law. In other words, granted the whole argument so far: the covenant God now declares, in the present time, that the presence of *pistis* is the (messianic) sign of covenant membership; is the sign that someone is part of Abraham's family; is the sign that their sins are dealt with by the sacrificial redemption effected through the Messiah (3.24–6). All this must happen 'without works of the law', for the reason stated in verses 29 and 30 (whose opening *ē*, 'or', indicates the intimacy of the logical connection): if it were not so, this God would be God of the Jews only, whereas *Shema*-based monotheism itself declares, in the teeth of so much second-Temple election-theology (not to mention some Jewish writing in our own day!), that this God is actually the God of gentiles also.[651] Election is therefore redefined, not just around the Messiah and his faithful death, but around the Messiah's faithful people.

This new people is composed, not only of gentiles, of course,[652] but of Jews and gentiles alike who display this *pistis*, the badge of membership. This is the same badge, whether one's covenant status is thereby renewed (the circumcised being justified *ek pisteōs*) or initiated (the uncircumcised being justified *dia tēs pisteōs*). Paul's claim, which is to be made good as the argument progresses, and particularly in 7.1—8.11 and 9.30—10.13, is that

[649] Jewett 2007, 297 suggests that 'the Jewish concept of law is thus rendered ambivalent,' and points to the development, in chs. 4, 7 and 8, of 'an interpretation of the law that excludes boasting'. He might have included 2.25–9 and 10.1–13, too. Jewett is in my view wrong then to suggest (303) that at least in 3.31 Paul is thinking of 'law in general' rather than the Jewish law.

[650] cf. 8.3: the one God has done what Torah could not do, by sending the Messiah and the spirit.

[651] On Kaminsky 2007 see above, 806.

[652] That would be the proposal of a hard-edged 'supersessionism' (see above, 806f.), of which some are still accused. Jewett 2007, 330 is wrong to say that Moo 1996, 278f. and Schreiner 1998, 231 'believe that Paul eliminates Jews from Abraham's promise': they say what Jewett himself says, that Paul 'includes Jewish as well as Gentile believers'.

this radical reworking of election is not the abolition of Torah, but what Torah intended all along (3.31).

The whole of Romans 4 then follows, not as a 'proof from scripture' of a 'doctrine', nor as an early example of an 'experience' of a person of faith, nor as a mere polemical aside against hypothetical opponents who have brought Abraham into the argument even though Paul himself would not have done so.[653] Romans 4, rather, is Paul's exposition, in line with Galatians 3 but going further, of the covenant made in Genesis 15.[654]

More specifically, Romans 4 spells out the way in which this covenant with Abraham is now being fulfilled. The Messiah's faithful death and resurrection is basic (4.24–5), and its result is the calling into being, as a kind of resurrection from the dead on the one hand and a creation out of nothing on the other (4.17), of a single Jew-plus-gentile family marked out by the *pistis* which reflects Abraham's own. The language of 'justification' in 4.25, summing up the whole chapter and indeed the various sections of the letter (from 3.21, from 1.18, and indeed from the very beginning) that here reach a preliminary climax, is emphatically both *forensic* and *covenantal*. Jewett sees this point well, albeit through the lens of the 'honour/shame' question which dominates his commentary:

> When converts accept the gospel in faith, they are 'reckoned' to be right before God and are placed in a community in which honor is dispensed according to a new principle of equality ... This 'our' [as in 'our justification' in 4.25] encompasses both the Jewish and the Gentile believers for whom the gospel's power is effective for righteousness ... They are all heirs of Abraham's promise, sharing his faith that God is the one who 'who (*sic*) gives life to the dead and calls that which does not exist into existence'.[655]

In other words – in the categories which Jewett does not use, but to which his exposition points throughout – election has been redefined. Abraham's family has been redrawn not only around the Messiah but to include all those who, through the spirit-driven work of the gospel (compare 1.16), believe in this life-giving God.

Romans 4, then, is through and through *covenantal*; hardly at all *soteriological*, though of course the whole point of Abraham's calling was to be the means of rescuing the world from its plight. That summary sentence, in good Pauline fashion, reduces a much longer argument to shorthand.[656] To spell it out just a bit more: Paul takes us back to Genesis 15, where we read that God promised Abraham a 'reward' (15.1). Abraham questioned

[653] I refer to the patriarch as 'Abraham' throughout to avoid confusion, although of course he is 'Abram' until Gen. 17.

[654] Carson 2004, 51 n. 15 cites Seifrid 2001, 424 to the effect that in the Hebrew Bible the terms *berith* and *tsedeq* (*sic*: sc. *tsedaqah*) 'almost never occur in close proximity'. He does not see that Gen. 15, one of Paul's favourite texts, is precisely one of the places where they come together; or that in Rom. 4.11 Paul substitutes *dikaiosynē* for the LXX's *diathēkē*. For fuller refutation of Seifrid on this point see e.g. Bird 2007, 36–9. Jewett 2007 manages to make it right through the chapter with only one mention of 'covenant', and that a negative one (see above).

[655] Jewett 2007, 343.

[656] See *Perspectives* ch. 33.

how he could inherit this 'reward', since he had no child; the 'reward', we are given to understand, would consist of a family, and a land for them to live in. God then promised him 'seed' like the stars in heaven (15.5); Abraham believed God, 'and it was reckoned to him as righteousness' (15.6). This faith was not, then, simply about believing that this God could do the impossible. Nor was it simply (though this is closer to the mark) a matter of believing that this God would give life to the dead and call into existence that which did not exist. It was a matter of Abraham's 'reward', which I take (in Genesis 15.1 and here in Romans 4.4) to be a reference to his 'inheritance', on the one hand, and his limitless 'seed' on the other. This is what was promised, and this is what, through the creation of the family characterized by *pistis*, Abraham has now received on the basis of the work of the Messiah. That is, after all, what Romans 4 is all about, as we shall see in a moment.

This way of reading the chapter resolves the problem about the apparently difficult opening question.[657] The chapter is about *Abraham's family*, about the question of the 'inheritance' which the covenant God had promised him – in other words, about the subject-matter of Genesis 15, and particularly about the promise which Abraham believed and to which, Paul is arguing in this continuation of his exposition of the *dikaiosynē theou*, his God has been faithful.

Here, then, is verse 1: 'What shall we say? Have we found Abraham to be our forefather according to the flesh?' In other words, if we have come to be part of the family of God, as in the radical revision of election in 3.27–31, does this mean (as the Galatian converts had supposed) that one had to become part of the *physical*, 'fleshly' family of Abraham? This question is then backed up by a counterfactual statement (4.2): If Abraham had been 'justified by works', he would have *kauchēma*, a 'boast' – but (Paul quickly adds) 'not before God'. (That 'before God' is going to be important all the way through, coming back at last in the conclusion of the main argument in verse 17.) The point here is that even though 'the Jew' in 2.17 has had that 'boast' removed, perhaps Abraham might be able to 'boast' that he was, in himself, the one through whom God's answer to Adam's problem had been provided.[658] No, says Paul: it was just that Abraham believed the promise God made to him. Hence the reference to the 'reward': this has nothing to do with 'a reward for meritorious action', in some abstract system of 'making yourself good enough for God', but is a clear reference to Genesis 15.1: 'Do not be afraid, Abram, I am your shield; your reward shall be very great.'[659] The point of verse 4 ('Now when someone "works", the "reward" they get is not calculated on the basis of generosity, but on the basis of what

[657] See the discussion in *Perspectives* 579–84.

[658] Note, again: this 'boast' is not about 'Look how morally virtuous I am; I don't need saving,' but about 'I can be the one through whom God rescues the world.'

[659] Against e.g. Gathercole (and cf. Seifrid, who notices the reference but not the point). For the notion of 'shield', *magēn*, see Dt. 33.29, where Israel is 'a people saved by YHWH, the shield of your help', resulting in victory over enemies.

they are owed') is not to highlight the position of the putative Pelagian, but to stress that Abraham's 'reward', the inheritance he was promised and the seed who would inherit it, was not something God was forced to give him because Abraham had deserved it. Rather, as in verse 5, Abraham simply believed God; and, says Paul, when someone 'believes in the one who declares the ungodly to be in the right', then they have done nothing to earn the status of being 'world-inheritor' (4.13). Rather, 'that person's faith is calculated in their favour, putting them in the right.'

It has been normal, in the exegetical tradition, to say that by referring here to God 'justifying the ungodly', Paul is referring to God's justifying of Abraham himself. He was (it is said) a convert from paganism, who had come to believe in the one God (though that in itself hardly makes him 'ungodly'). He was not even circumcised at that point. But this is not what Paul is talking about. Paul is saying that, when God promised Abraham this massive family, that he would be 'the father of many nations' (Genesis 17.5, quoted in 4.17), this required of Abraham the faith that God would indeed 'justify the ungodly' – not himself and his physical family, who were in that sense 'godly', but the nations outside, who were by definition not 'godly'. That then refocuses the question, not on 'how Abraham got justified', as though by an inner analysis of his moral condition or lack thereof, but on 'how Abraham believed that God would give him this extraordinary family', which is after all what the chapter is about.

Look at it this way. God told Abraham what his 'reward' would be: he would inherit the world, and be the father of many nations (4.13, 17). If he was to believe this, Abraham would have to believe that God would 'justify the ungodly': that he would, in other words, bring into his family gentiles who at present seemed totally outside it. That reading of 4.5 coheres exactly with the reading just given of 4.1, looking back also to 3.27–30. It also looks on to the quote from the psalm which follows: David declares the divine blessing on people whose transgressions are forgiven, on the one to whom the true God does not reckon sin. (It also goes closely with Galatians 3.8, where the promise that all nations would be blessed in Abraham is interpreted by Paul as 'scripture foreseeing that God would justify the gentiles by faith'.)

This 'blessing', according to verses 9–12, comes on the uncircumcised. Paul is not here talking about Abraham needing to be forgiven for his sins, but about the fact that, in order to fulfil his promise to Abraham, the covenant God was going to forgive the 'sins' of the 'gentile sinners' (see Galatians 2.15) who would be brought into the family if the promise to Abraham was going to hold. That then keeps the focus of 4.9–11 firmly on the fact that, even at the moment of receiving the covenant sign of circumcision, Abraham was becoming the model for others who would come into the family through their uncircumcision, having 'righteousness' reckoned to them as well. Verse 12 then completes the picture, just in case anyone should suppose that covenant membership was now going to be for gentiles only: the circumcised, too, are Abraham's children, *provided that they copy what Abraham did* (i.e. believe God's promise) when uncircumcised.[660]

This radical redefinition of election – which Paul does not intend as a redefinition of Genesis 15 itself, but as a true and proper reading, however much against his own earlier tradition – comes back at last to the 'reward', that is, the 'inheritance' which God promised Abraham. In Genesis, of course, the 'inheritance' is the promised land. Here, as in some earlier Jewish tradition and indeed arguably in the line of thought indicated by Genesis itself (in the Abraham/Adam nexus), it is the whole world, the *kosmos*.[661] And it is Abraham's worldwide 'seed', the *sperma*, who will inherit it: 'the promise to Abraham and his *sperma* that they should inherit the *kosmos*'. That is how Paul is reading Genesis 15. Here, picking up the point of 3.21 ('apart from Torah') and 3.28 ('apart from works of Torah') and echoing the longer argument of Galatians 3, he declares that this world-inheriting promise *cannot come about through the mediation of Torah*. The all-important distinction is not between 'people who make a moral effort and achieve moral standing' and 'people who do not', but between Jews (*hoi ek nomou*, 'those of the law') and *pan to sperma* (4.16), 'the whole seed'.[662]

Exactly as in Galatians 3, then, the *single seed* and the *worldwide inheritance* dominate the picture. If Torah were to take over, the promise would be snuffed out, and Abraham's 'faith' itself would be emptied of significance: not just in that he would appear to have believed in vain, but in that the *specific* faith he had – belief that the covenant God would call gentiles to be part of his family, i.e. belief that this God would 'justify the ungodly', and belief that this enormous 'family' would 'inherit the world' – would be unfounded. If his God were to decree, instead, that inheritance and membership in his 'seed' would be through the medium of Torah, this could not happen. As in Galatians 3.22, Torah shut everything up under sin; here Paul says that it 'works wrath'. Left to itself, Torah would then mean the end of the promise, the end of the multi-ethnic seed, the end of the worldwide inheritance. But – tantalizingly anticipating 6.14 and 7.4–6 – 'where there is no law, there is no transgression.' And that in turn points on to 8.12–25, where the 'worldwide inheritance' is the redeemed cosmos which the Messiah will share with his people.[663] Once again the 'normal' lines of division between Romans 1—4 and Romans 5—8 prove illusory. It is the same argument all through. The covenant with Abraham, here expounded at length,

[660] This corresponds, therefore, to 11.23: *ean mē epimenōsin tē apistia*. See below, 1161, 1213, 1215, 1221f., 1230f., 1238, 1245 and 1253.

[661] On 'inheriting the world' in Judaism cf. e.g. *Jub.* 17.3; 22.14; 32.19; Sir. 44.21; *1 En.* 5.7; *4 Ez.* 7.59. See esp. above, ch. 2, and esp. Wright 2002 [*Romans*], 495f. This promise has not been 'spiritualized', and to describe it as 'a-territorial' (Dunn 1988a, 213, following Davies 1974, 179), while correct in ruling out 'a more nationalistic understanding', could undermine Dunn's proper emphasis (ib.) on 'the restoration of God's created order, of man to his Adamic status as steward of the rest of God's creation'. See further Hester 1968.

[662] It is remarkable that Jewett 2007, 312 reverts here to the question of 'whether righteousness can be earned by pious works'.

[663] As Jewett rightly sees (2007, 325f.).

provides the best vantage point from which to see all the varieties of forensic, incorporative, anthropological, salvation-historical, apocalyptic and transformational categories of Paul's soteriology in their proper light and perspective.

Verses 16 and 17 can now come into their own. 'Normal' readings of Romans 4 leave them somewhat stranded, a convoluted ramble about Abraham's seed and God's promise.[664] They are instead, as they stand, the quintessence of the whole thing, even though as often with Paul's quintessences they are boiled quite dry: *dia touto ek pisteos hina kata charin eis to einai bebaian tēn epaggelian panti tō spermati ...*, literally 'therefore by faith so that according to grace so that the promise might be valid for the whole seed'. It was not, in other words, Abraham who put everything right for the world, reversing Adam's sin; it was the one God. Otherwise, if it had been by anything other than 'faith', it would no longer have been by God's grace, and gentiles could not have come in to take up their promised membership as part of 'the whole seed'. And, by contrast to what would have happened if 4.13–15 had gone the other way – if, in other words, the Torah had indeed been the medium by which the Abrahamic promises had had to be carried forwards – the 'whole seed' would now consist not only of the 'seed' who were 'from the law', in other words, the Jewish element in Abraham's family, but also (the 'seed', understood) who were 'out of the faith of Abraham'.

Abraham is thus 'the father of us all': the stone that some exegetical builders have refused is in fact the climax, the head of the corner, the answer to the question of 4.1. We do not have to regard Abraham as 'our forefather according to the flesh', Paul is concluding, because he is the father of us *all*, Jew and gentile alike, in accordance with the promise of Genesis 17.5 which made him 'the father of many nations'.[665] This is so important that Paul, unusually, repeats it in the next verse: he hoped against hope that he would become 'the father of many nations'. That repetition says it all: this is what the chapter is all about, the way by which election is redefined. This is the way the one God always intended to work (and this is what Abraham always believed that he would do) in order to include gentiles in his 'seed'. What this always meant, and still means for Paul, is something about the character of the one God himself. That, indeed, is what the whole discussion is about. The character of 'faith' alters depending on what sort of God one believes in. In 4.5 it was 'the God who justifies the ungodly'; here it is also 'the God who

[664] e.g. NRSV, which places parentheses around 'for he is the father of all of us, as it is written, "I have made you the father of many nations"', and then links to the remainder of v. 17 with a dash. This drastic punctuation, typical of many, is a way of admitting that the line of thought has not been understood. See further *Perspectives* 579.

[665] Sir. 44.19–21 is an important part of the context here, both positively and negatively: Abraham was the 'great father of many nations', who kept the law of the Most High and entered into covenant with him, and proved faithful when tested (the Aqedah, in other words). God then promised him a countless family, to whom he would give 'an inheritance from sea to sea, and from the Euphrates to the ends of the earth' – in other words, the Davidic promise of Ps. 72.8 (cf. 89.25) (see too the echo of Gen. 12.3 LXX in Ps. 72.13). Paul sets aside Abraham's lawkeeping, and (as we have seen) transfers the Aqedah from Abraham and Isaac to God and Jesus; but he retains the covenant (though for Paul this was made on God's initiative, not Abraham's), and the worldwide scope of the promise.

gives life to the dead and calls the non-existent into existence'. In 4.24–5 it will be 'the one who raised from the dead Jesus our lord, who was handed over because of our trespasses and raised because of our justification'. The same God, of course, viewed from three complementary angles.

This shows that the *all'ou pros theon* of 4.2 has had its full effect. Did Abraham have a 'boast'? Not before the one God! Abraham was not, in himself, the means by which the problem of the world was to be resolved, because the character of the God in whom he believed was the character of 'ungodly-justifying', of grace, of raising the dead. And this in turn answers, fully and finally, the opening question: have we found Abraham to be our forefather according to the flesh? No: he is 'the father of many nations'. Membership in the family the covenant God had promised him was always 'by faith, so that it might be by grace'. That is the outworking of Paul's radical revision of the second-Temple Jewish doctrine of election, based on the fact of Israel's Messiah and now worked out through consideration of the people who, by faith in the God who raised Jesus from the dead, have come to belong to Abraham's family.

With that, the main argument of the chapter is done, and Paul can move into the exposition, which is more regularly understood, of how all those who believe 'in him who raised from the dead Jesus our lord' share the faith of Abraham (4.18–25). This passage also includes, as again is commonly noted, the explicit reversal of the description of human degeneration in 1.18–25, and the consequent fruitfulness (despite earlier barrenness) of the primal couple in God's family.[666] The strands of Genesis 15 are thus tied together. The whole seed; the whole inheritance; guaranteed through the Messiah, as himself the gift of the one God,[667] to all those who share (by the spirit, Paul might have said) the faith of Abraham. Election redefined.

This brings us at last to one of the most celebrated passages – but also one of the most misunderstood – anywhere in Paul's writings.

(h) Romans 5—8

As we shall do with Romans 9—11 in the next chapter, I want to begin this brief discussion of Romans 5—8 in the middle. Often swamped by the major debates going on to left and right, Romans 7.4–6 connects closely with the themes of spirit-driven redefinition of election which we have seen elsewhere, not least in Romans 2.25–9 and 2 Corinthians 3. In both of those, especially the former, we discovered a breathtaking redefinition of election, parallel to Philippians 3.2–11 and in direct intentional continuity with the promises of Deuteronomy and Jeremiah:

> The 'Jew' isn't the person who appears to be one, you see. Nor is 'circumcision' what it appears to be, a matter of physical flesh. [29]The 'Jew' is the one in secret; and 'circumcision'

[666] See Wright 2002 [*Romans*], 500; and e.g. Adams 1997a.

[667] nb. the 'divine passive' *paredothē*, 'he was given up,' at 4.25.

> is a matter of the heart, in the Spirit rather than the letter. Such a person gets 'praise', not from humans, but from God.[668]

We note again: not 'the true Jew', or 'the real Jew': simply 'the Jew'. Paul's warrant for this remarkable claim is found in Israel's scriptures themselves. The promise of the circumcision of the heart is part of the vital 'new covenant' and 'return from exile' passage in Deuteronomy 30, and was drawn on elsewhere, particularly by Jeremiah. This was not, then, a new idea thought up by Paul as a way of distancing himself from his Jewish context. It was the belief expounded by the Jewish sacred texts themselves, picked up by Paul to explain what he believed had happened, on the basis of the Messiah's work, through the spirit of the Messiah. As with the Israel's Messiah himself, the spirit is not some alien force, but rather the fresh (though long-promised) manifestation of the one God of Jewish monotheism.

This notion of covenant renewal through the spirit, adumbrated in Romans 2 and picked up here in Romans 7 (and developed in Romans 8) gives us a clear hint of the main point to be made in this sub-section (which cannot, of course, provide anything like a full commentary on this major section). By the end of Romans 4 Paul has developed his argument that all who believe the gospel are the true, forgiven family of Abraham, no matter whether they are Jews or gentiles. This is the manifestation, in the present time, of the 'righteousness', the covenant faithfulness and justice, of Israel's God, the creator. But Paul had set up this discussion of justification by sketching quite an elaborate and detailed scenario of the *final* judgment in chapter 2. How will the verdict issued in the present correspond to the verdict on the last day? What are the assurances that the present verdict will not be overturned, leading to false hope? And, since the promise to which the one God has now been faithful in Jesus the Messiah involved not only Abraham's Jew-plus-gentile family but also their inheritance of the *world*, how – how on earth, we might say – will this be accomplished? Perhaps the most vital thing to grasp here is that Romans 5—8 is not expounding a different set of questions and answers, or using a different type of theology ('participationist' or 'mystical', say, as opposed to 'forensic') from what we found in chapters 1—4. As we saw in our earlier brief account of the 'doctrine' itself, there are hints all the way through 5—8 that Paul is still thinking of 'righteousness' and its cognates. The dramatic concluding statement in 8.1, and its outworking in 8.31–9, confirms that he has been moving slowly but surely towards answering the questions left open at the end of chapter 4. (He has also, of course, set up the questions which must then be addressed in chapters 9—11, but we shall come to that later.) And, as should by now be expected, my argument here is that in Romans 5—8 as well the underlying framework of his thought is *covenantal*, in the senses already explained, holding together not only 'forensic' and 'incorporative' ideas but also our other old friends, 'anthropological', 'salvation-historical', 'apocalyptic' and 'transformational'. Indeed, it is the tumbling together of all these

[668] Rom. 2.28f. See above, e.g. 362, 539, 812–4, 836f., 921–3, 958; and below, 1432, 1642.

strands in these spectacular chapters that gives them their particular vibrant energy.

I begin, then, with the opening of Romans 7, where the 'new covenant' theme already noted in 2.25–9 comes to the fore. In 7.1–6, following the 'marriage illustration' which has given commentators so much unnecessary trouble,[669] Paul offers a compressed summary of what has happened to those who, formerly having been 'in the law' (in other words, Jews or proselytes), have now had their lives transformed through the death and resurrection of the Messiah. To that extent, this passage is quite a close parallel to Galatians 2.19–20, and should be interpreted in that light.

We need to begin by clarifying one or two things about 7.1–3:

> Surely you know, my dear family – I am, after all, talking to people who know the law! – that the law rules a person as long as that person is alive? The law binds a married woman to her husband during his lifetime; but if he dies, she is free from the law as regards her husband. So, then, she will be called an adulteress if she goes with another man while her husband is alive; but if the husband dies, she is free from the law, so that she is not an adulteress if she goes with another man.

The first point to get clear is that 'the law' is not the 'first husband'. It is the legality that binds husband and wife together. Second, Paul is still expounding the line of thought that has come out of chapters 5 (particularly 5.12–21) and 6 (particularly 6.6), which means that 'the first husband' is best taken as 'Adam', or as the 'old human' (6.6). Third, therefore, it is natural for Paul to switch to and fro, when talking about the person who has 'died', between a third party ('the old human' in 6.6; the 'former husband' in 7.2–3) and the first person ('we') or second person ('you'). The shift between 'we' and 'you' is equally visible in chapter 6, where 'we' died with the Messiah (6.2), 'we' were baptized into his death (6.3), 'we' were buried with him (6.4) and where 'you' must reckon yourselves dead to sin (6.11). So here in chapter 7 'you, too, died to the law through the body of the Messiah' (7.4a) so that 'we' could bear fruit for God (7.4b and similarly in 7.5–6). In other words, the 'old husband' is indeed the 'old human', the 'old Adam' – but, exactly as in chapter 6, this is not some character other than 'you'. The 'you' personalizes and gives rhetorical force and direction to the earlier more general exposition. And from all that has been said so far, both in chapter 2 and in the opening sections of the present chapter, it ought to be clear: if the Adam-problem is being addressed, this will be *through the covenant*. Only, as we now know from Romans 2, 3 and 4, the covenant family 'according to the flesh' is incapable of providing the solution. Has Paul then abandoned the covenant? No: his whole thesis is that the covenant God has been faithful by *renewing* it, just as he promised he would.

Now that that little matter is cleared up – if we follow Paul's train of thought through the previous chapters it becomes relatively straightforward – we can focus on the spirit-driven redefinition of election that is contained in a nutshell in 7.4–6. 'In the same way', says Paul,

[669] See Wright 2002 [*Romans*], 558f.

you too died to the law through the body of the Messiah, so that you could belong to someone else – to the one who was raised from the dead, in fact – so that we could bear fruit for God. [5]For when we were living a mortal human life, the passions of sins which were through the law were at work in our limbs and organs, causing us to bear fruit for death. [6]But now we have been cut loose from the law; we have died to the thing in which we were held tightly. The aim is that we should now be enslaved in the new life of the spirit, not in the old life of the letter.

The 'you' consists now, it seems, of two people: one who died and the other who now has a new life. This 'you' has come to this new state through the Messiah, who died and was raised from the dead. The first half of this is very close to Galatians 2.19 ('through the law I died to the law, so that I might live to God. I have been crucified with the Messiah'), but the second half is developed further. In Galatians 2.20 Paul says, 'I am, however, alive – but it isn't me any longer, it's the Messiah who lives in me.' In the present passage this is expanded: he speaks both of the spirit and of the renewed humanity. 'Bearing fruit', as in 7.4b, may be an allusion to Genesis 1.28 (in the light of the still-echoing story of Adam from chapter 5 and on into 7.7–12).[670] Whereas previously the Adamic humanity was producing fruit for death, with Torah being used by sin as its base of operations (7.8), the death of the Messiah has set 'us' free from the old humanity and from the Torah which enslaved 'us' to it, and the aim is now that 'the new life of the spirit' should replace 'the old life of the letter'. To all this, with its many analogies to other passages, Paul adds another theme, which in his Jewish context could only mean one thing. Those who belong to the Messiah are now, he suggests, *married* to him, in a fruitbearing relationship. The obvious echoes are of the relationship of YHWH with his people, a theme which comes into prominence precisely in the context of the 'divorce' of exile and the 'remarriage' of return.[671] Unless we are to say that Paul did not intend such resonances, we should assume that the whole passage is about the renewal of the covenant – through the Messiah, the 'new husband', the last Adam.

This passage, closely cognate with 2 Corinthians 3 and Romans 2.25–9, is thus a further example of Paul's reworking of election in the light of the spirit. It does not in itself give voice to 'juristic' or 'apocalyptic' themes, but as we shall see the surrounding passages supply them in good measure. It is emphatically *covenantal*, and obviously *participationist* and *transformational*. It has a salvation-historical dimension (the move from old covenant to new), and obvious anthropological content (from the passions of the flesh to the new life in the spirit). It has the same character of inaugurated eschatology that we have seen in the doctrine of justification itself, which is hardly surprising considering that Paul has not, after all, stopped talking about it when he reached the end of chapter 4. It sums up a great deal that has already been said in Romans 5 and 6, and it points on towards what is to

[670] Though Paul's word, *karpophoreō*, is almost unknown in the LXX and certainly does not occur in Gen. 1. On the possible resonances of the word see Jewett 2007, 435.

[671] cf. e.g. Isa. 50.1 with 54.5–8; Hos. 1—2, esp. e.g. 2.16–19. Hos. 2.1, 23 is quoted by Paul in a similar context in Rom. 9.25f.

come in Romans 8 in particular. It functions, then, as an appropriate gateway into the larger unit at whose centre it falls.

Romans 5—8 is structured with tight rhetorical skill. It is far and away the most formally presented and carefully elaborated of any such sustained passage in Paul; it is impossible to think of it as a random train of thought, dictated off the top of the apostolic head, pausing here and there on a whim to change direction or answer detached 'objections'. This tight structural control is evident not least in the way in which the opening and closing (5.1–11; 8.18–30 and 31–9) highlight the same themes. It looks as though Paul has deliberately stated them up front, as is often his way, and then argued through to them at a deeper level.

Equally, it is important to stress that this section belongs exactly where it is in the argument of the letter as a whole. Like the second movement in a symphony, it has its own complete and careful integrity, but it also picks up themes and energy from the opening movement and carries them forward towards the third and fourth. From the opening 'therefore' in 5.1 to the concluding flourish with all its resonances with Romans 2, the section offers itself as a *further development of*, not an *alternative theological structure to*, chapters 1—4. Equally, in its retelling of the exodus-story in a new mode, the section highlights themes which point forward (see below). Romans 5—8 describes what Israel's God has done in and through Israel's Messiah, and this necessarily sets up both the question of 9—11 and the further, though organically related, question of 12—16, particularly its heart, 14.1—15.13.

Romans 5—8, in other words, means what it means in relation both to 1—4 and 9—11 and, indeed, 12—16. It is not possible here, of course, to trace or comment on all the dozens of links, but it is vital to recognize that they are there. Without this, it would be easy to imagine that one could lift chapters 5—8 out of Romans whole and entire, using the passage to construct a 'Pauline soteriology' or some such thing which would be free from the 'juristic' language of chapters 1—4 and the 'Israel'-dimension of chapters 9—11, and free instead to exhibit an unsullied version of 'participationist' thought. But this, though often attempted by implication and sometimes by bold direct frontal assault, is disastrous both exegetically and theologically.[672]

Consider, for a start, how most if not all of the elements of *both* 1—4 *and* 5—8 *and* 9—11 are found, not separated out, but stitched tightly together, in both Galatians 2, 3 and 4 and Philippians 3. (We have made the same point above from the other side of the fence, as it were, but it is important to remind ourselves of it here as well.) Granted, there are many elements of Romans 5—8 which are not echoed in those passages. That is inevitable. But we have the supposedly separate main themes (justification, being-in-Christ, baptism, the question of Abraham's family) as part of the same discourse, supporting and interacting with one another, not as disparate elements floating uneasily on top of one another like oil and water. Unless

[672] For a discussion of the recent proposal of Campbell 2009, see *Interpreters*.

we are to say that between writing Galatians and Philippians on the one hand and Romans on the other Paul had a sudden realization that he was combining different schemes of thought, which he then proceeded to separate out, we will naturally conclude that the rhetorical demands of his presentation in Romans have caused him to highlight certain features at certain times but without having now come to regard them as radically different or even incompatible.[673] All through all these passages he is concerned with the radical redrawing, around the Messiah and the spirit, of Israel's scripture-based covenant theology. Within that project, these various themes can be presented in several different ways, but always in full compatibility with one another.

In particular, when we come to Romans 5—8 with the question in mind, How did Paul rethink the election of Israel around the Messiah and the spirit?, we cannot but notice that many of the themes he explores in these chapters are precisely the themes which he then lists as a summary of the privileges of Israel in 9.4–5:

> [4]They are Israelites; the sonship, the glory, the covenants, the giving of the law, the worship and the promises all belong to them. [5]The patriarchs are their ancestors; and it is from them, according to the flesh, that the Messiah has come – who is God over all, blessed for ever, Amen!

'Sonship' is obviously a major theme of 8.12–17; 'glory', of 8.17–30. 'The covenants' are more controversial, but I am inclined to say that this is seen in Romans 4 on the one hand (Abraham) and Romans 7 on the other (Sinai). The giving of the law likewise looks back to Romans 7 and various earlier references. 'Worship' is what the human race refused to give to the creator in 1.18–23 and what Abraham gave instead in 4.18–21, but the word more naturally refers to temple-worship, and I believe that reference is more subtle, hinting both at the life of prayer of God's people (as in the 'Abba'-prayer of 8.15) and, not least, at the temple-theme in chapter 8.[674] 'The promises' takes us back to Romans 4, as does the reference to 'the patriarchs', at least to one of them. The Messiah himself is one of the main themes of 5—8 as a whole, whose every section ends with a refrain, like a great bell: *through our lord Jesus the Messiah*; *in the Messiah Jesus*. The achievement of Jesus, who is the Messiah, and the incorporative life of the Messiah, who is Jesus, are central to both form and content.[675] When Paul writes Romans 9.4–5 he cannot be unaware that he is listing privileges which he has just set out with great care as now being ascribed to the Messiah himself and, in and through him, to all those who belong to him. That is why the agony of 9.1–5 is what it is. But that means that he is aware that

[673] This means that I am precisely not forfeiting the combination, within a larger view of Paul's soteriology, of 'participation' and 'justification' in Romans, as Gorman suggests (2009, 102f.); merely indicating how they make their particular points in particular passages.

[674] cf. too Phil. 3.3 ('we worship by the spirit of God'): see above, 985 n. 591.

[675] 5.11, 21; 6.11, 23; 7.25a (and cf. 7.4–6); 8.11, 17, 29 and supremely 39. The Messiah is also, of course, discussed at length in several of these paragraphs.

'election', in the way he would have thought of it as Saul of Tarsus, is not just redefined around the Messiah. It is also redefined by the spirit, in, for and around all those who belong to the Messiah.

These, however, are just pointers to the deeper material in chapters 5—8. Our quest here is first to see how justification itself 'works', particularly in relation to the spirit (and these chapters are vital for understanding that), and second to see how the regularly separated elements of Paul's thought, especially 'juridical' and 'participationist' on the one hand, 'apocalyptic' and 'salvation history' on the other, and also 'transformation' and 'anthropology', are held together within an essentially *covenantal* framework.

First, we note the distinct marks of covenant renewal. In this section Paul develops, little by little at first and then dramatically, his view that the spirit enables all those who are justified by faith to live as the biblical people of God. For a start, they are enabled to *love* the one God from the heart. This is controversial in terms of 5.5,[676] but not in terms of 8.28. As we saw in the previous chapter, the latter passage resonates with the *Shema* which, already hinted at in 3.30, may be thought to stand behind even such notions as 'the obedience of faith'. In the faith and love which the spirit generates, this worldwide people of the creator God offer to him the worship which was most centrally characteristic of Israel. Paul may even be hinting in 8.26–7 at the 'prayer of the heart', the habitual and eventually subconscious praying of a prayer such as the *Shema* which forms the innermost life of the one who thus prays. When, in the next breath, he refers to 'those who love God', we should take this as a sign that the prayer inspired by the spirit, and heard by 'the one who searches the hearts', may well be the *Shema* itself, perhaps in its messianic reworking.[677]

But loving the one true God, though central, is by no means the only sign in these chapters of Paul's spirit-centred redefinition of election. The hint of new covenant theology in 7.6 (a hint confirmed, as we saw above, by the parallel in 2 Corinthians 3) explodes into life in chapter 8, where the 'law of the spirit of life in the Messiah Jesus' liberates those 'in the Messiah' from sin and death and enables them to have the 'mind' which is 'life and peace' – a pairing of abstracts which is interestingly reminiscent of biblical covenant language.[678] Here, in particular, we find themes familiar from second-Temple Judaism: new exodus, suffering, inheritance, the fulfilled law, the rebuilt Temple, the call to holiness, the new creation. In fact, 'new exodus' is such an all-embracing theme that the best way of expounding Paul's redefinition of election in the present chapters is to let that narrative take us through, and to note the other themes as they occur.

The 'new exodus' theme, like so much else in Romans and Galatians, is rooted in the divine promise made to Abraham. The covenant promises in Genesis 15 were focused on the *seed* and the *inheritance*; the patriarch was

[676] See Wright 2002 [*Romans*], 517.

[677] Above, 661–70.

[678] e.g. Mal. 2.5; cf. too the 'covenant of peace' in Num. 25.12; Isa. 54.10; Ezek. 34.25; 37.26; Sir. 45.24. Many of these passages from the prophets are in contexts which are echoed strongly in Rom. 8.

told that the seed would obtain the inheritance by first being enslaved and then being rescued and brought home to their promised land. This Passover-sequence – liberation from slavery by coming through the Red Sea, arriving on Sinai and being given the Torah (with all the resulting problems) and finally being led by the presence of YHWH himself in the pillar of cloud and fire until they arrived in the land – this sequence is now recapitulated, majestically (but to most commentators invisibly) in chapters 6—8.[679] Once the stage is set – the promises to Abraham now fulfilled in Jesus the Messiah (chapter 4) and the whole Adam-to-Messiah sequence revealed (5.12–21) – then the story can begin.

First, the crossing of the Red Sea. In chapter 6, the old-Adam people who were enslaved to sin are liberated through the water of baptism, in which the Messiah's 'death to sin' and 'coming alive to God' is 'reckoned' to them. As the Messiah's people they are therefore the new-exodus people, the freed former slaves, who have to learn new habits of heart and body commensurate with their freedom (6.12–23). The old ways are 'unfruitful' (6.21); the new ways have their *telos*, their 'goal', in 'eternal life', the life of the age to come, which Paul will eventually describe more fully in chapter 8. With this, we are very close, though in different ways, both to Galatians 3.23–9 and to Galatians 4.1–7.

The freed slaves then arrive at Mount Sinai, and that is the next stop in Paul's narrative. Here in Romans 7, with such considerable and sophisticated artistry that it has remained opaque to most modern commentators, he weaves together the story of Israel at Sinai with the story of Adam in the garden – a classic rabbinic-style move, allowing two great scriptural narratives to interpret one another and to generate a third. In 7.7–12 the 'commandment which was unto life', that is, the Torah itself (which really did promise 'life'[680]), stands in parallel with the forbidden tree in the garden and, mysteriously, with the tree of life that remained untouched. Israel is lured by sin into breaking the commandment, just as Adam and Eve were lured by the serpent into eating from the tree of the knowledge of good and evil:

> Apart from the law, sin is dead. [9]I was once alive apart from the law; but when the commandment came, sin sprang to life [10]and I died. The commandment which pointed to life turned out, in my case, to bring death. [11]For sin grabbed its opportunity through the commandment. It deceived me, and, through it, killed me.[681]

This is the story of Israel under Torah, exactly as in 5.20: 'the law came in alongside, so that the trespass might be filled out to its full extent.' The arrival of Torah precipitates Israel into recapitulating the sin of Adam. Grasping this, and its range of implications, is at the heart of grasping Romans in general and the question of redefined election in particular.

[679] For this theme see 'New Exodus' in *Perspectives* ch. 11.

[680] cp. Gal. 3.21; cf. Lev. 18.5 etc.

[681] Rom. 7.8b–11.

The story of Israel's 'fall' might, after all, seem remote and scarcely interesting to gentile Christians in Rome. I sometimes wonder whether such imagined uncomprehending listeners are really the coded presence of modern western scholars and preachers who are hoping that Paul will, in his every sentence, say something readily accessible to the deeply non-Jewish concerns of our own day. But what is of most concern to Paul, speaking as he says 'to those who know the law' (7.1), is to tell the story of Israel *because it is the story of the world's redemption.* 'Those who know the law' might mean Jewish Christians, but might well mean gentile Christians who had been proselytes or God-fearers; Paul, in any case, is articulating a narrative which far outstrips any small-scale concerns of this or that group. To tell the story of Israel is not to focus attention back on a matter that interested another group at another time. Paul might have put it like this: if you want to know how you will arrive at 'eternal life', the promised inheritance, you have to learn that 'salvation is of the Jews', and you have to understand how the story of Israel actually works, even though to begin with it may appear (to gentiles!) remote or irrelevant. One cannot, in other words, appreciate the fruit which grows in Romans 8 unless one has understood the roots – the very Jewish roots – in Romans 7.

The chapter focuses on verse 13, which as we saw has the all-important double *hina*, reflecting the *hina* in 5.20.[682] This is the divine purpose: that sin be drawn onto this one place, onto Israel, so that it can be dealt with conclusively by the covenant God himself in the person, in the flesh, of Israel's Messiah, the son of this very God (8.3). Here is the significance of the story of Israel, which will be at once picked up in chapter 9: Israel's vocation is to be the bearer of this terrible destiny, a destiny meant not for Israel as a nation but for Israel's Messiah, in other words, for Israel's God himself in the person of his son. The potential tragedy, though, is never far away, and will come if Israel, so keen on being the bearer of this destiny, insists on keeping it for itself rather than allowing the son to take it instead ... and then if those who claim to follow that son decide to make that position of Israel permanent. That is what chapters 9—11 are all about, and without this understanding of chapter 7 they will be incomprehensible, as indeed they have often appeared. The point of Israel's election was not 'for the creator God to have a favourite people' but *for the sin of Adam to be dealt with.* Election itself, and Torah as the gift which sealed election, was designed – this is Paul's point – to draw sin onto that one place so that it could be successfully condemned right there. Paul has, as we saw, redefined election around Israel's crucified Messiah. Now he redefines it around the people who, in the spirit, discover themselves to be the Messiah's people.

But the story which arrives at that point in Romans 8 has one more twist in its tail. Adam's descendants began with the murderer Cain, regarded by the rabbis as the classic example of a man with a 'double heart', *leb wa-leb*, the man who was told that sin was crouching at the door, desiring him, but

[682] Above, 890f., 895–7.

that he must master it.[683] The double heart of Cain is reflected closely in Paul's account of the 'divided self' – if that is what it is – in 7.14–20. This passage is not primarily a description of general human moral incompetence, though it has plenty of resonances at that level. It is certainly not an account of Paul's own pre-conversion unsuccessful struggles with moral obedience: what use would a one-dimensional autobiography be in such a sustained piece of theological writing? One counter-example, one person who could say that they had not experienced such a struggle, would undermine the whole argument. Nor is it at all an attempt to discuss, and perhaps to upstage, the Stoic question of 'self-mastery', though no doubt those familiar with that discourse would hear echoes as well. Nor is it (the favoured interpretation of the older existentialist theology) an account of the 'meta-sin' of supposed Jewish 'legalism', where the gift of the law lured Israel into trying to keep it and thereby to establish a works-righteousness before the one God.[684] Had that been the case, Paul should not have written, 'I can will what is right, but I cannot do it,' but rather, 'I can do what is right, but I ought not to will it.' Nor, despite many advocates, is Romans 7.13–20 a description of the normal life of the Christian, wanting to be holy and failing.[685] Even though I once read the passage in this way, I read it thus no longer.[686]

That is not to say that echoes of all these other discourses cannot be heard here. That, indeed, is part of Paul's skill in writing as he does. But his much deeper purpose is to describe, from the inside (through the rhetorical 'I', rather than by way of pointing the finger from a safe distance), *the plight of Israel under Torah*, seen indeed with Christian hindsight but looking back upon a journey which was the necessary journey of the people of God, the deep, dark roots of the tree which has now borne the fruit of life.

The point is that Israel, given Torah, genuinely and rightly delights in that Torah. 'The Jew' – and here we are safe in saying that Paul knows first hand what he is talking about, even though 'autobiography' is not the point

683 On this see Wright 1991 [*Climax*], ch. 12.

684 This was, famously, the line taken by Kümmel, Bultmann and others: see Wright 2002 [*Romans*] 554. Jewett 2007, 468 takes a similar view: 'the frustration consisted not in the ability to perform the zealous deeds he felt were justified, but in the inability of such deeds, motivated by a sinful system of competition for honor, to achieve the good.' In other words, where Rom. 7 appears to be saying that the 'I' cannot do the 'good thing' it wants to do, Jewett (updating the existentialist line in a socio-cultural direction) suggests that the 'I' can do the zealous Torah-deeds it wants but that they do not achieve the ultimate resultant 'good'. This interpretation remains ingenious but unwarranted. The idea of a meta-sin, connected with Israel's abuse of the law, is however found in Rom. 9.30—10.3, and the net result is not too far from Jewett's proposal: zealous Jews abusing Torah as a charter of national privilege. See below, 1161–95.

685 The best known exponents of this viewpoint are Cranfield 1975, 340–70 and Dunn 1988a, 374–412. The Achilles heel of all such proposals is the direct contradiction between 7.14, where the 'I' is 'carnal, sold under sin', and the strong statements of chapter 6 which indicate that this is precisely not the Christian's status.

686 The first version of my paper on *peri hamartias* in Rom. 8.3 (in *Studia Biblica 1978*, vol. 3, ed. E. A. Livingstone; Sheffield: JSOT Press, 453–9) included a final note agreeing with Cranfield (and also Dunn 1975b). By the time the publication appeared I had already changed my mind to the position now expounded in Wright 1991 [*Climax*], ch. 10 and Wright 2002 [*Romans*], 561–72. When the original paper was revised for *Climax* (ch. 11) the ending, like the 'old Adam' in 6.6 or the 'former husband' in 7.1–4, was done away with.

– really does love Torah: two of the greatest poems in scripture, perhaps in all the world, are the psalms we call 19 and 119, the latter celebrating Torah from every possible angle, the former balancing it with the power and glory of the sun itself. That is what Torah is like. Not to recognize that is to take a large step towards Marcion, or indeed towards the gnosticism that would scorn the created order as well. But the people of the creator God, though rightly delighting in Torah, find that there is a radical mismatch between Torah and the 'fleshly' existence of Israel itself. *The problem, once again, is that Israel too is 'in Adam'*. The life of Israel under Torah thus becomes like the life of Adam's descendants, only more sharply focused – *but with salvific intent*: Israel's plight, clinging to Torah for dear life but thereby finding it to be the means of condemnation, has one end only in view. The end in question is condemnation, but the condemnation in question is *the condemnation of 'sin' itself.*

This is why Paul cannot and will not describe this plight in terms of 'they', but only of 'I'. The 'plight' does not mean that it was a bad thing to be a Jew, or a stupid thing to love and cherish Torah. (Notice how we are here in similar territory to the start of chapter 3.) It means that this was a good and God-given vocation which was cognate with, and the absolutely necessary prelude for, the good and God-given sending of the son, Israel's representative, to fulfil all righteousness, to complete the unfinished agenda, to be the embodied self-revelation of the covenant God, appearing 'in the likeness of sinful flesh and as a sin-offering', to take upon himself, in his flesh, the condemnation which was waiting to fall, not indeed upon Israel, certainly not upon Torah (which was only doing its God-appointed job), but upon sin itself. The force of 7.13–20 comes in the statement which Paul repeats in verses 17 and 20: it is no longer 'I' that do it, but 'sin'. There is nothing wrong with being Israel; nothing wrong with Torah. What is wrong is 'sin'. And that is what is to be dealt with. The struggles described in 7.13–25 are the necessary vocation of the people who bear the Abrahamic promise forward, through the strange, dark time of Torah (just as in Galatians 3), to the point where 'the obedience of the one man' will establish 'the many' as 'righteous', so that where sin abounded through the strange gift of Torah, grace might also super-abound (5.20–1). This is not a 'salvation history' of a smooth development, an evolutionary process. This is a long and difficult story filled with agony and puzzlement, and yet being seen *as* the single story of the chosen people – in the light of the fresh, shocking revelation of the son and his crucifixion and resurrection.

The summary conclusion of chapter 7 (note the language of verse 21, which is that of drawing the conclusion of a calculation) is then all about the law, the Torah. The attempt to turn *nomos* into a general 'principle' at this point constitutes a failure to read the text, a folly which results in futility.[687] The whole chapter has been a close and careful account of what happens when Torah arrives in Israel and when Israel then lives with it. To say that

[687] See the discussion in Jewett 2007, 469.

the conclusion has nothing to do with the main subject of the previous discussion is like rearranging the final movement of Mozart's 'Jupiter' symphony for a rock band.

The problem is, of course, that at this point it is not simply the 'I' that appears to be divided (though, as we have seen, the 'I' is not actually divided, but ends up in verses 17 and 20 on the right side of the equation, with 'sin' on the wrong side). It is Torah itself:

> This, then, is what I find about the Torah: when I want to do what is right, evil lies close at hand! [22]I delight in God's Torah, you see, according to my inmost self; [23]but I see another 'Torah' in my limbs and organs, fighting a battle against the Torah of my mind, and taking me as a prisoner in the Torah of sin which is in my limbs and organs.[688]

There is no point trying to soften this. Paul knows what he is doing and fully intends the dramatic effect. Torah woos 'me' into the love of God; Torah imprisons 'me' in my sin. Is this not what he said already in Galatians 3.22? Torah shut up all things under sin, even while holding out, in the *Shema* and elsewhere, the most wonderful promise of life and love. That is the calling of Israel prior to the coming of the Messiah: to be the people in whom this agony, which is also the agony of Adam, created in the divine image but now dead because of sin, is experienced and clung to against the day when, in the Messiah, it will be resolved once and for all.

The final word of chapter 7 sets up the scene for just such a resolution:

> [24]What a miserable person I am! Who is going to rescue me from the body of this death? [25]Thank God – through Jesus our Messiah and lord! So then, left to my own self I am enslaved to God's law with my mind, but to sin's law with my human flesh.[689]

'Left to myself': *autos egō*, the phrase Paul will use at the start of chapter 9 when he is describing his own agony precisely over his 'kinsfolk according to the flesh' (9.3). Indeed, chapter 9 is incomprehensible without chapter 7, just as chapter 7 is incomprehensible without 2.17—3.9 and such previous hints as 5.20 – and just as chapter 7 itself has raised massive questions to which only a discussion such as that in chapters 9—11 can serve as at least a preliminary answer. The carefully co-ordinated complexity of Romans has to be followed through in depth for it to yield its secrets. Here we have the conclusion of chapter 7, which rightly finds expression in the form of a lament. The problem is not Torah; the problem is not the vocation to be Torah-people; the problem is the Adamic humanity, 'the body of this death', corresponding to the 'body of sin' in 6.6. What is required is what Paul has already hinted at in 7.4–6, which indeed sums up the whole of 7.7—8.11 in advance. *Here is the story of the covenant people, redefined around the Messiah and now around the spirit*: election redefined. Through Jesus, the Messiah and lord, the problem of Adamic humanity has been dealt with. Israel, the unwilling and uncomprehending captive within this Adamic humanity,

[688] 7.21–3.

[689] 7.24f.

can now discover that its beloved Torah was itself acting as jailor and judge – a task for which the covenant God had given it in the first place![690] But Israel can then, through Messiah and spirit, find release, and discover that the life promised by Torah is available at last.

At that moment, exactly consonant with the whole thrust of 3.21—4.25, the Israel that has lived under Torah and found it bringing only condemnation (3.19–20; 4.15; 5.20) is transformed into the people promised to Abraham by the covenant God. The natural branches of the tree have been joined by a great company from outside, together forming a plant which grows out of the pain borne for so long by Israel and now concentrated on, and exhausted in, the Messiah himself. Thus, by the spirit, the creation of the new-covenant people has taken place in a great act of Torah-fulfilment and election-redefinition:

> [1]So, therefore, there is no condemnation for those in the Messiah, Jesus! [2]Why not? Because the law of the spirit of life in the Messiah, Jesus, released you from the law of sin and death.
>
> [3]For God has done what the law (being weak because of human flesh) was incapable of doing. God sent his own son in the likeness of sinful flesh, and as a sin-offering; and, right there in the flesh, he condemned sin. [4]This was in order that the right and proper verdict of the law could be fulfilled in us, as we live not according to the flesh but according to the spirit.[691]

We have already spoken of the Messiah's role in this explosive moment. The point now is the redefinition of election in and through the spirit, for the whole renewed people of God, both those who spent long generations in the theological *thlipsis* of 7.13–25 and those who, coming in from outside, look on with awe and gratitude at the Israel that bore the 'messianic woes' all the way up to the Messiah's own coming. Now at last the law's God-given intention, translated into the work of the spirit, is going to be fulfilled: the *dikaiōma tou nomou* in 8.4, the 'right and proper verdict of the Torah', will be accomplished when the 'dead body' of 7.24 is raised to life by the spirit, because the indwelling spirit has replaced the indwelling 'sin' of 7.17, 18, 20:

> [10]But if the Messiah is in you, the body is indeed dead because of sin, but the spirit is life because of covenant justice. [11]So, then, if the spirit of the one who raised Jesus from the dead lives within you, the one who raised the Messiah from the dead will give life to your mortal bodies, too, through his spirit who lives within you.[692]

[690] This is the force of Gal. 3.22; Rom. 9.30–3; and in the present sequence Rom. 5.20; 7.13. The line of thought reaches its own climax in Rom. 11.32. See below (on Paul and the law).

[691] 8.1–4.

[692] 8.10f. The parallel and hence contrast between the two 'indwellings' of chs. 7 and 8 has not been sufficiently remarked. On the questions of whether the 'spirit' here is the divine or human spirit, and the relation of 'covenant justice' (*dikaiosynē*) to the earlier uses of the word in the letter, see Wright 2002 [*Romans*], 584. I have, in the intervening decade, changed my mind on *dikaiosynē* here: I now think it refers to the believer's status, though of course the divine covenant faithfulness is always to be seen standing behind that again. 'The spirit is life because of righteousness' could be seen as a summary of 5.1–5.

It is just as Paul said in Philippians 3.7–11. The resurrection from the dead, the ultimate hope of Israel, the gateway to the 'life of the coming age', is the prospect for those who through the spirit constitute the renewed (though still suffering) 'elect', the transformed and now worldwide people of the one God. The spirit is doing 'what the Torah could not do, because it was weak through the flesh'; that is, giving the life it promised (7.10) but could not deliver because of the Adamic humanity of its original recipients. This is exactly the same point as we find, within the different epistolary contexts, in Galatians 3 and 2 Corinthians 3. The point is that the death of the son of God has dealt with that Adamic humanity, so that now, by the spirit, all who are part of the Messiah's people (all this still depends upon the incorporative vision of baptism-into-Messiah in Romans 6) will share the bodily resurrection for which the earlier 'resurrection' which takes place in baptism itself is the advance signpost.

The tell-tale sign that the spirit is at work is found in verses 5–9. The mind that is focused on the flesh will die, but the mind that is focused on the spirit will have life and peace. All this depends once more on *status*: flesh or spirit? Paul is clear: those who are in the Messiah, indwelt by the spirit, are not defined in terms of *sarx*: 'you are not in the flesh, you are in the spirit, if indeed God's spirit lives within you.'[693] This does not mean, of course, that they have ceased to live a normal human 'bodily' life; merely that the *sarx*, which for Paul is always a negative term, always pulling down towards decay and death, towards the old creation which is subject to futility, is no longer the defining factor. Instead, the 'life' that the law had held out is given at last: there is a direct line from 7.10 ('the commandment which pointed to life') to 8.1 ('the law of the spirit of life in the Messiah, Jesus') and on to 8.6 ('focus [the mind] on the spirit, and you'll have life and peace') and thence, via 8.10 ('the spirit is life because of covenant justice') to the climactic 8.11 ('the one who raised the Messiah from the dead will give life to your mortal bodies, too, through his spirit who lives within you').

Here, then, is the Sinai-element in the story of the 'new exodus'. Telling this story at all, in relation to the whole people of God in the Messiah, is itself, for Paul, a massive act of redefining election: *we*, the Messiah's people, are the ones in whom Israel's greatest narrative has come true in the new way we always hoped for. We are, in ourselves, the new tabernacle (see below), and even Torah itself is now coming alongside to cheer us on the homeward road. This is the very centre of Paul's redefinition of election around the spirit. The multiple echoes of Romans 2.25–9 in 8.1–11 make the point graphically: where the spirit has done and is doing all this, we are to recognize 'the Jew', 'the circumcision'. The lament of 9.1–5 strongly confirms this analysis. Had the redefinition been less clear, the lament would have been less necessary.

But before we proceed we need to notice one other factor which has sneaked up on us almost unawares. If this renewed people, the Messiah's

[693] Rom. 8.9; cf. Gal. 2.19f.

people, are the people in whom Torah is at last able to do what it always intended, this people is also *the new tabernacle*. We noticed this theme in chapter 6, when discussing the worldview-symbols of Paul's *ekklēsia*. We developed it in chapter 9, to argue for an early, high, Jewish pneumatology. We return to it now once more in relation to the transfer, to the whole people of God in the Messiah and by the spirit, of the idea that the living God has determined to dwell among and within his people.

At this point a whole new theme opens up, which until recently would have been thought impossible for Paul, but which, in the light of the redefined election by the spirit, is not only possible but vital. If the spirit of the living God dwells within his people, constituting them as the renewed tabernacle (or the new Temple; but at this point Paul is still clearly working with the exodus narrative, where it is the wilderness tabernacle that matters), then the work of this transforming spirit can and must be spoken of in terms, ultimately, of *theōsis*, 'divinization'.[694]

Again, the shock waves. Protestants are not supposed to talk about *theōsis*; they leave that to Catholics, and especially to the Orthodox. But what if Paul himself was pushing in that direction? Is that not what is at stake in 2 Corinthians 3 and 4 – that the light of the knowledge of the glory of the Messiah has shone 'in our hearts', so that we recognize in one another the living presence of the living God, by the spirit? Did that not constitute God's people not merely as those in whose midst the living God had deigned to dwell, but those in whose *hearts* this had happened? And, if so, what has this done to 'justification'?

But is not *theōsis* what we find now, in Romans 8? Consider:

> you're people of the spirit (if indeed God's spirit lives within you [*oikei en hymin*]; note that anyone who doesn't have the spirit of the Messiah doesn't belong to him). [10]But if the Messiah is in you, the body is indeed dead because of sin, but the spirit is life because of covenant justice. [11]So, then, if the spirit of the one who raised Jesus from the dead lives within you [*oikei en hymin*], the one who raised the Messiah from the dead will give life to your mortal bodies, too, through his spirit who lives within you [*dia tou enoikountos autou pneumatos en hymin*].

We are here at a very similar point to 1 Corinthians 3.16, where the indwelling of the spirit of God (*oikei en hymin*) constitutes God's people as the Temple; and also close to 2 Corinthians 6.16, where God's people, as the Temple, fulfil the promise of the Torah itself, that this God would 'dwell within' his people (*enoikēsō en autois*) and go about among them.[695] The mention of the Messiah's dwelling in them by the spirit brings in the obvious allusion to Colossians 1.27, 'The Messiah in you, the hope of glory', to which we shall return in the next chapter, and, with it, to Ephesians 3.17,

[694] Or indeed 'Christosis', as in the title of Blackwell 2011.

[695] 2 Cor. 6.16, quoting a conflation of Ezek. 37.27 (*estai hē kataskēnōsis mou en autois*) and Lev. 26.11 *kei emperipatēsō en hymin*). Thrall 1994, 477 suggests that Paul's opening word *enoikēsō* 'is the equivalent of Ezekiel's *kataskēnōsis*' and perhaps also an echo of 1 Cor. 3.16. She points out that the whole of 2 Cor. 6.16 is redolent with 'covenant' language: 'Paul sees these scriptural promises fulfilled in the community he has founded as the messenger of the new covenant.'

where the Messiah will 'dwell (*katoikēsai*) in your hearts through faith'. In Colossians, of course, the Messiah is himself the one in whom all the divine fullness was pleased to dwell (*katoikēsai*). And with that we are tapping into a large biblical frame of reference, focused more or less equally on the wilderness tabernacle, constructed after the debacle with the golden calf but nevertheless providing the movable home for Israel's God for the next few hundred years, and on the Temple in Jerusalem, where according to the Psalms and the Deuteronomic narrative the one God had deigned to 'dwell'.[696]

It might be thought that the hints about the spirit, or the Messiah, 'indwelling' God's people in Romans 8.9–11 was quite a slender basis on which to propose a Pauline theology of 'new Temple' and, thereby, of the *theōsis* of God's people. But Paul himself builds on this foundation in verses 14–17, which explain the moral challenge of living by the spirit, not the flesh, in terms of the journey of the people of God, the journey that will lead to the 'inheritance':

> [12]So then, my dear family, we are in debt – but not to human flesh, to live our life in that way. [13]If you live in accordance with the flesh, you will die; but if, by the spirit, you put to death the deeds of the body, you will live.
>
> [14]All who are led by the spirit of God, you see, are God's children. [15]You didn't receive a spirit of slavery, did you, to go back again into a state of fear? But you received the spirit of sonship, in whom we call out 'Abba, father!' [16]When that happens, it is the spirit itself giving supporting witness to what our own spirit is saying, that we are God's children. [17]And if we're children, we are also heirs (*klēronomos*, cognate with *klēronomia*, 'inheritance'): heirs of God, and fellow heirs with the Messiah, as long as we suffer with him so that we may also be glorified with him.

The challenge here is cast in terms of the continuing exodus-narrative: you are on the road to your 'inheritance', your promised land, the fulfilment of God's promise to Abraham (4.13); so don't even think of going back to Egypt! 'You didn't receive a spirit of slavery to go back into a state of fear': as in 1 Corinthians 10, Paul is echoing the story of the wilderness wanderings in order to urge the Messiah's people to learn from the mistakes of that generation. In particular, they must recognize that the one they call 'father', in the spirit-inspired expression of faith by which they call out 'Abba',[697] has adopted them as his 'children', fulfilling the exodus-story in this respect also: Israel is my son, my firstborn.[698]

That statement should be gently modified; the adoption is at one remove. As always, Paul is clear that election is redefined *first* in Israel's Messiah. He is the 'firstborn among many siblings' (8.29). But here the status of 'God's children', derived from his, is reaffirmed and the consequences drawn: if children, then inheritors, inheritors of God and co-inheritors with the Messiah. The 'inheritance' is now clear, from its first hint in Romans 4.13 to its

[696] e.g. 1 Kgs. 8.27 (one of many); and e.g. Pss. 132.8, 13f.; 135.21, etc.

[697] See above, on Gal. 4.6.

[698] Ex. 4.22.

full expression in 8.18–25: it is the whole world. That is what God promised Abraham, according to Paul. It is what God promised the Messiah, in the foundational messianic Psalm 2. It is now what God intends to share with all his people: that is what it means to be 'heirs of God, and fellow-heirs with the Messiah'. We are here very close to Galatians 3.21—4.7, and with the same import: election redefined, first around the Messiah, now around the work of the spirit.

But the idea of being 'led' by the spirit, on this journey through the wilderness to the 'promised land', indicates that the implicit temple-theme of 8.9–11 is being followed through in terms of *the guiding presence of God himself* in the wilderness tabernacle, in the pillar of cloud by day and fire by night. 'All who are led by the spirit are the children of God': the 'leading' of God in the wilderness is now fulfilled in the 'leading' of the indwelling spirit.[699] And this means that, for Paul, the indwelling spirit is taking the place, within the church as a whole and within each of the Messiah's people, of that fiery, cloudy pillar, the living and dangerous presence of God himself. We might have deduced all this already from 2 Corinthians 3, but here we have it at the heart of the great story, the exodus-narrative itself replayed through Messiah and spirit all the way to new creation.

The natural consequence, of course, is once again *theōsis*, divinization. But it is, as has recently been stressed, a *cruciform* 'divinization', involving the constant life of putting to death the flesh and coming alive to the spirit.[700] That has been the point ever since chapter 6, and it is reaffirmed here and in the other cognate passages. In particular, we think of Philippians 3.9–11, where the sufferings of the Messiah are the means of 'sharing', or 'being conformed to', his death, and are thus also the pathway to the resurrection; and 2 Corinthians 3, leading as it does straight into the description of cruciform apostleship in chapters 4—6.[701] The similar train of thought in the present passage indicates that we are in the same territory: if we suffer with him, we shall be glorified with him (8.17). This then opens up the 'new creation' passage in 8.18–25, where the present sufferings and groanings of God's people are mapped onto the larger picture of the groanings of the whole creation, waiting for God's new world to be born. All this recalls so many aspects of second-Temple Jewish identity and aspiration that there should be no doubt what is going on. Paul is retelling Israel's narrative (including the theme of being the true humanity through whom the world is to be brought back into the creator's design) around Jesus and the spirit.

That, after the further brief mention of the spirit's work in the heart, producing the true *Shema*, the love of God, leads Paul into the hammer-blow conclusion of 8.29, in which everything that might be said about Israel is now said about the people of the one God in the Messiah and the spirit:

[699] See Keesmaat 1999, 66–74 and frequently.

[700] So e.g. Gorman 2001, 2009.

[701] See Fee 1994, 869; Renwick 1991; and, on Eph 2.30, Fee 686–90; on 4.30, Fee 712–4.

> [28]We know, in fact, that God works all things together for good to those who love him, who are called according to his purpose. [29]Those he foreknew, you see, he also marked out in advance to be shaped according to the model of the image of his son, so that he might be the firstborn of a large family. [30]And those he marked out in advance, he also called; those he called, he also justified; those he justified, he also glorified.[702]

It will be obvious to anyone who knows Genesis, Deuteronomy, Isaiah and the Psalms (to look no further!) that these great affirmations are drawn directly from the larger and longer narrative of the covenant people. They constitute, in the first instance, a massive claim about the Messiah: upon him has now devolved the identity of the covenant people of the one God. They then constitute, following from this, an equally massive claim about those who are indwelt by the spirit: they are 'in the Messiah', and as such they are to be seen as the single family promised by the one God to Abraham, however much they may at present look like a somewhat strange and motley crew, having come in from gentiles as well as Jews.

Election is redefined. Around the Messiah; through the spirit.

And all this means that Romans 5—8 has indeed developed the earlier theme of 'justification' to its proper conclusion. The verdict issued in the present over *pistis* will indeed correspond to the verdict of the last day. The same inaugurated eschatology undergirds the whole scheme. Indeed, without Romans 5—8 the inaugurated eschatology of 1—4 has not been fully explained. (That is why an exposition that fails to treat chapters 5—8 as part of 'justification' ends up also marginalizing chapter 2.) The *katakrima* of which Paul warns in 2.1–11 has disappeared for those 'in the Messiah', because the 'condemnation' which 'sin' required has been meted out in the Messiah's death (8.3). This demands, of course, that we read the dense statements about the cross in 3.24–6, 4.25, 5.6–11, 7.4–6 and 8.3 as all interrelated, drawing on an implicit fuller understanding although only saying, on each occasion, what is required by that specific argument.

It is justification, indeed, that occupies Paul almost to the end of the section. When the question is raised in 8.34, 'Who is to condemn?', the answer is, by implication, 'Nobody', because 'it is God who justifies,' by means of the Messiah's death, resurrection and now heavenly intercession (8.33–4). When we allow Paul to develop the 'forensic' language in his own way and at his own pace, we see that he himself dovetails it completely – just as in Galatians 3 or Philippians 3, but at far greater length! – with his 'incorporative' language, as indeed he indicated in 3.24 ('justified . . . through the redemption which is in the Messiah'). Both are held within the overall exposition of an essentially covenantal theology.

The two statements 'We are justified by *pistis*' and 'There is no condemnation for those who are in the Messiah' are thus functionally equivalent. Each means what it means in close relation to the other. To attempt to separate them, and to treat Romans 1—4 and 5—8 as though they were

[702] 8.28–30.

expositions of different kinds of soteriology, is to transform the rhetorical strategy of this particular letter into a theological dichotomy.

Within this, the other elements make themselves at home. Anthropology, transformation, and our old friends 'apocalyptic' and 'salvation history': there is plenty of each in Romans 5—8. Once again, when we hold them within the covenantal theme, they lose the angular character that has made some play them off against one another.

The covenantal theme that undergirds all of these, and which finally re-emerges into the open, bringing the music back into the major key, is the language of love. The obvious background for this is the relationship of YHWH to his people as described in Israel's scriptures.[703] Paul states the theme in advance in 5.1–11, and then, after exploring it from all the angles of the intervening material, returns to it as he draws the whole section to its rhetorical climax. This passage itself picks up the long biblical tradition of trusting the covenant God through thick and thin and combines it with the messianic theme expounded throughout the chapter so far:

> Who shall separate us from the Messiah's love? Suffering, or hardship or persecution, or famine, or nakedness, or danger, or sword? As the Bible says, 'Because of you we are being killed all day long; we are regarded as sheep destined for slaughter.' No: in all these things we are completely victorious through the one who loved us. I am persuaded, you see, that neither death nor life, nor angels nor rulers, nor the present, nor the future, nor powers, nor height, nor depth, nor any other creature will be able to separate us from the love of God in the Messiah, Jesus our lord.[704]

The unbreakable covenant love of YHWH for his people, arguably the most central expression of Israel's election, has been focused on, and revealed in, the son. And this unbreakable love is the secure resting-place of all those who, by the spirit, are 'in the Messiah'.

This is not something other than 'justification by faith'. This is what justification looks like in solid reality: battered, but believing; suffering, yet sustained by the spirit; dying, but knowing that death itself has been defeated. The *pistis Christou* of 3.22 is the *agapē Christou* of 8.35, and the answering *pistis* of the believer has become, as in 8.28, the answering *agapē* which, by the spirit, keeps the *Shema*. At this point Paul's reworking of both monotheism and election come together in typical Jewish expression: a celebration of divine love, a trust in divine victory. God himself, and his covenantal faithfulness, are unveiled in the Messiah and unleashed through the spirit, within the eschatological horizon of the whole new creation.

There is of course one more section of Romans which has a direct bearing on 'justification', namely 9.30—10.13. Since we shall deal with this section more fully in the next chapter we here put it to one side, though in several important senses it completes the picture, being the clearest exposition to be

[703] 'Through him who loved us' (8.37), being in the aorist, refers back to the crucifixion itself, as in e.g. Gal. 2.19f.: see e.g. Cranfield 1975, 1979, 441; Jewett 2007, 549. The theme which re-emerges here is of course that stated already in 5.6–11. On the love of YHWH for his people, as a model for the relationship between Messiah and believers, see Tilling 2012.

[704] 8.35–9.

found anywhere in Paul of his belief that Messiah-faith was the sure sign of covenant renewal, and that both justification and salvation were to be seen in those terms and no others.[705]

(i) Conclusion: Justification in Christ, by Grace, through Faith, in the Present Time

We have now studied the large-scale themes of Paul's redefinition of election, and shown that those themes, drawn together in and around the Messiah, are then replayed in and through the Messiah's people, who, through the work of the spirit, bear the primary and distinguishing badge of *pistis*. Once this larger picture is in place, we notice other smaller-scale but tell-tale markers of the same phenomenon, markers which by themselves might only raise an eyebrow, but which when located on the main map serve as genuine signposts to what Paul has in mind. We may simply note these as we move towards the summing-up of this chapter.

Two obvious verbal clues come in Paul's regular address to his churches. First, they are 'called'. We have seen this in its full setting in Romans 8.28; but Paul also refers to Messiah-people as 'the called' in various passages – not to mention the cognate 'called out', in other words, *ekklēsia*. There is the opening greeting of Romans itself, where he addresses the church as 'you also, called of Jesus the Messiah (*klētoi Iēsou Christou*)'. This is repeated in the next verse with a different connotation which we shall address in a moment.[706] A similar greeting in 1 Corinthians is followed later in the first chapter by the use of 'the called' as a way of referring to the Messiah's people, deputizing as it were for the more normal 'believers': 'to those who are called, both Jews and Greeks'.[707] The cognate noun, 'call', is used in the same sense in various passages.[708] The verb itself, in this sense, is more frequent again.[709] The resonances with the ancient 'call' of Israel, particularly in Isaiah 40—55, make this both powerful and poignant,[710] and set up in particular the discussion of Romans 9—11, where the divine 'call' is one of the central themes.[711]

The natural twin theme here is that God's people are called to be *holy*. Paul can of course draw this out in his various passages of ethical exhortation. But what is quite telling is the way he can refer to the Messiah-people

[705] See below, 1165–81.

[706] Rom. 1.6f.

[707] 1 Cor. 1.2, 24.

[708] 1 Cor. 1.26; 7.20; Eph. 1.18; 4.1, 4; perhaps also Phil. 3.14 (though in a somewhat different sense); 2 Thess. 1.11; 2 Tim. 1.9.

[709] 1 Cor. 1.9; nine times in 1 Cor. 7.15–24, where 'to be called' is Paul's shorthand for 'hearing and believing the gospel and becoming a member of the Messiah's people'; Gal. 1.6, 15; 5.8, 13; Eph. 4.1, 4; Col. 1.12; 3.15; 1 Thess. 2.12; 4.7; 5.24; 2 Thess. 2.14. Cf. too 1 Tim. 6.12; 2 Tim. 1.9.

[710] e.g. Isa. 42.6; 43.22; 48.12; 49.1; 51.2 (the 'call' of Abraham). Most uses of *kaleō* in the LXX are of the actual naming of people, which may also be significant particularly in Rom. 9—11.

[711] 9.7, 12, 24, 25, 26; 11.29.

as *hagioi*, 'holy ones' or 'saints', as a kind of title. In the greeting in Romans this is coupled with another Israel-title, 'God's beloved, called to be saints',[712] and in various later references in the letter it is simply a way of saying 'God's people'.[713] The Corinthians, too, are 'called as saints', *klētoi hagioi*, not (I think) in the sense that they are, as it were, called to be saints eventually but have a long way to go before that word can truly be used of them, but rather that, having been 'called', they *are* 'saints', set-apart-for-God people, whether or not they behave like it.[714] The same pattern is repeated in other greetings,[715] as well as in other casual references to the Messiah-people.[716]

These small signposts, I repeat, point to the larger reality which we have studied. It is time now to sum this up, and to make some necessary distinctions between the different aspects of this redefined election. In particular, we must clarify as sharply as we can the central point: how does Paul's doctrine of 'justification by faith in the present time' relate to this larger whole of election redefined?

I have argued throughout this chapter that the ancient Israelite, and second-Temple Jewish, sense of what it meant to be the chosen people of the creator God was transformed in Paul's understanding. He saw it as having been reworked around Jesus, Israel's Messiah, and particularly by his crucifixion and resurrection; and, in consequence, it was further reshaped around the Messiah's spirit, who through the powerful gospel message 'called' people of every background and type to belong to the single family which the one God had promised to Abraham. I have argued, in particular, that to understand 'justification by faith' it is necessary to see that the 'faith' in question is not a particular way of being religious (a 'trusting' way, say, as opposed to a 'hard-working' way), but is rather the way of being 'faithful' to the divine call and gospel which echoes, and re-encapsulates, the 'faithfulness' of the Messiah himself, which was in turn the representative 'faithfulness' of Israel (Romans 3.22 with 3.2). All this shows, I believe, that for Paul the whole business of 'justification' was tied tightly together with his larger theology, though playing a particular role of its own. Now that we have surveyed nearly the whole of the Pauline evidence on the subject of redefined election, it is time to look at the role of 'justification' more precisely.

712 Rom. 1.7.

713 Rom. 8.27; 12.13; 15.25, 26, 31; 16.15.

714 1 Cor. 1.2; cf. 6.1, 2, where 'the saints' is a clear ref. to Dan. 7.18, 22 and 27, and ascribes to the Christian community in Corinth the eschatological role ascribed in [first-century readings of] Dan. to the righteous within Israel; cf. 1 Cor. 14.33; 16.1, 15.

715 2 Cor. 1.1; Eph. 1.1; Phil. 1.1; Col. 1.2.

716 2 Cor. 8.4; 9.1, 12; 13.12; Eph. 1.15, 18; 2.19 (where the *hagioi* are specifically the people of Israel to whom gentile believers are now joined in fellowship; but, despite the refs. in Rom. 15 and 2 Cor. 8 and 9 to the 'saints' in Jerusalem, it is certainly not the case that Paul reserves this title either for Jewish believers or for believers in Jerusalem); Eph. 3.5, 8, 18; 4.12; 5.3; 6.18; Phil. 4.21, 22; Col. 1.4, 12, 26; 3.12 (a remarkable cluster of redrawn-election motifs: 'as God's chosen, holy and beloved', *hōs eklektoi tou theou, hagioi kai ēgapēmenoi*); 1 Thess. 3.13 (though there the 'saints' are those that have died; cf. 2 Thess. 1.10); 5.27; 1 Tim. 5.10.

As we saw, Paul makes a clear distinction between the future 'justification', the verdict which will be issued on the last day on the basis of the totality of the life led (which in the case of the Messiah's people will be a life generated and sustained by the spirit), and the present justification which is the verdict announced on the basis of nothing but Messiah-faith. Once we locate both of these events, as Paul does again and again, within the larger picture of the work of gospel and spirit, and once we see as clearly as Paul did that all that is said of the Messiah's people is said precisely because they *are* 'the Messiah's people', and can be spoken of as being 'in him', it ought to be clear that there is a threefold sequence, each part of which is importantly related to the others though playing significantly different roles. This threefold summary is an attempt, in the light of the intervening exegesis, to say again in even shorter form what was set out above in seven somewhat longer points. We note again, for the avoidance of doubt, that Paul sees all these three points as utterly dependent on the basic gospel events of the Messiah's death and resurrection, the events in which Israel's God dealt with sin and launched his new creation. As Paul puts it in Galatians 2.17, the basic position which the Messiah's followers trust they occupy is 'to be justified in the Messiah', *dikaiōthēnai in Christō*.

1. There is the powerful work of the spirit through the gospel, which 'calls' people to faith. It is on this basis alone that people are declared to be 'in the right', the correlate of which is that they are, again on that basis alone, full members of the family, the people of Abraham, the people of the Messiah. *This is justification by grace through faith in the present.* Because of the Messiah's death and resurrection, the ancient people of God has been transformed and its doors thrown wide open to people of all sorts and conditions, and the gospel message of Jesus' scripture-fulfilling death and resurrection does its work of summoning people to the 'obedience of faith'. The two events which Paul sees as tightly joined together, baptism 'into the Messiah' on the one hand and the emergence of faith on the other (calling God 'Abba'; believing that he raised Jesus from the dead; confessing Jesus as lord), are the necessary *and sufficient* evidence that the spirit has been at work through the gospel, that this person has died and risen with the Messiah, that this person has the Messiah's death and resurrection 'reckoned' or 'imputed' to them (Romans 6.11) and that this person has passed beyond the sphere where 'sin reigns in death' (Romans 5.21) and so is quit of any obligation to 'sin' as a power or a sphere. In terms of the argument of Galatians 2, 3 and 4, such a person is every bit as much a full member of the family, every bit as qualified to share table-fellowship with every other member, as the most senior apostle. (Paul has some wry words about seniority among apostles, but that is another story.[717]) In terms of the

[717] Gal. 2.6, 9.

argument of Romans 3 and 4, such a person is a full and proper part of the family *which the one God promised to Abraham in the first place*, though of course nobody had seen it like this until after the coming of the Messiah. In the case of such a person, the entail of sin which had run from Adam through the whole human race, bringing with it the threat of wrath and ultimate death, has been turned away. The logic of justification by grace through faith thus comes full circle: from (a) the faithful death and resurrection of the Messiah, as the rescuing act in which the one God fulfilled his ancient promises by sheer grace, through (b) the declaration that those who (through gospel and spirit) come to believe are the Messiah-people, the faith-people, the forgiven people, the Abraham-people and back again (c) to the Messiah himself as the one 'through whom are all things'. That is the initial, present, dramatically new divine gift in the gospel of Jesus the Messiah.

2. There is the unbreakable promise that, by the same spirit, all the people thus described will in the end be raised from the dead to share the 'inheritance' of the Messiah, the worldwide inheritance promised to Abraham. 'The one who began a good work in you will thoroughly complete it by the day of the Messiah Jesus.'[718] It is the spirit who will raise these people from the dead, the spirit who indwells all those who belong to the Messiah (Romans 8.9). So, among the advance signs that this will happen, we note that the same spirit enables these people to put to death the deeds of the body, to walk 'not according to the flesh but according to the spirit'.[719] This is how Paul has finally explained the otherwise unusual description of the people in Romans 2.7 who 'patiently do what is good, and so pursue the quest for glory and honour and immortality', and who will be given 'the life of the age to come', *zōē aiōnios*.[720] These are the people who 'do what is good' and so receive 'glory, honour and peace' (2.10); they are the people who 'do the law' and so 'will be declared to be in the right'. As we saw earlier, the anxious protestant principle of never allowing anyone to 'do' anything which appears to contribute to any sort of justification has pushed exegetes into declaring that these solemn statements are either strange irrelevancies or, at most, the setting up of categories which Paul will then declare to be empty. But the close correlation of these statements in 2.7–10 with the similar ones in 2.25–9 (coupled with the fact that Romans 1.18—2.16 is a rather different sort of passage from what that older exegesis had imagined) means that we should read them as referring in advance to Messiah-believing people, Jews and gentiles alike (2.10). They are then more fully described in the 'new covenant' language of 2.25–9 (where the

[718] Phil. 1.6.

[719] Rom. 8.4–8, 12–14.

[720] Normally (but confusingly, because of its Platonic resonances) translated 'eternal life'. See above, 163f., and below, 1060.

focus is on Messiah-believing *gentiles*, but the point is the same), and more fully again in chapters 5—8 and especially 8.4–17. There is after all no reason, except exegetical tradition, why the rhetorical flow of Paul's argument in Romans should follow the chronological flow of an *ordo salutis*, though the assumption that this is the case has been so firmly planted in the exegetical and theological traditions that it may be hard to uproot it.

3. Between (1) the beginning of the work of the spirit and (2) its triumphant conclusion, Paul envisages a spirit-led life which does not in any way contribute to initial justification, *or to the consequent assurance of final justification which that initial justification brings*, but transforms the life of the person who has already come to faith. This transformation enables such a person to 'live by the spirit and not fulfil the desires of the flesh' (Galatians 5.16); or, in the language of Romans 8, to have the 'mind of the spirit', the *phronēma tou pneumatos*, rather than the 'mind of the flesh', the *phronēma tēs sarkos*. Such people will then 'put to death the deeds of the body'; from a study of Paul's own congregations we may conclude that he knew as well as we do that this does not happen automatically or easily.[721] It is too shallow to call this 'ethics', since it goes way beyond either a deontological framework (discovering the 'rules' and trying to keep them) or a utilitarian/consequentialist framework (figuring out and implementing the greatest happiness of the greatest number) which the word 'ethics' regularly refers to. It obviously works quite differently from existentialism, which reduces ethics to 'authenticity'; and to emotivism, which reduces ethics to personal predilection or prejudice.[722] It is better to speak, at this point, of the transformation of character which is such a regular Pauline theme:

> We also celebrate in our sufferings, because we know that suffering produces patience, [4]patience produces a well-formed character, and a character like that produces hope. [5]Hope, in its turn, does not make us ashamed, because the love of God has been poured out in our hearts through the holy spirit who has been given to us.[723]

> [1]So, my dear family, this is my appeal to you by the mercies of God: offer your bodies as a living sacrifice, holy and pleasing to God. Worship like this brings your mind into line with God's. [2]What's more, don't let yourselves be squeezed into the shape dictated by the present age. Instead, be transformed by the renewing of your minds, so that you can work out what God's will is, what is good, acceptable and complete.[724]

[721] Rom. 8.13; Col. 3.5, 9.

[722] On the superficial similarity between an emotivism that stresses 'doing what comes naturally' and a Pauline emphasis on acting out of the transformed heart and mind, see Wright 2010 [*Virtue Reborn* (UK); *After You Believe* (US)], chs. 5, 6.

[723] Rom. 5.3–5.

[724] Rom. 12.1–2.

I have written about all this elsewhere.[725] For the present purpose, the point is made sufficiently that, when we factor the spirit into the reworking of the Jewish doctrine of election, we can see *both* the centrality and uniqueness of present justification by faith *and* its relation to the two other 'moments', the ultimate future justification and the life of transformed character.

This is important in relation to current debates. Some have tried to insist that 'justification by grace through faith' is so all-encompassing that it must have nothing to do with the final judgment according to works.[726] Paul's statements about the latter must then be set aside or at least neutralized. Others have tried to suggest that Paul's whole soteriology is contained in Romans 5—8, where a 'participatory' framework *rather than a 'juristic' one* is offered, and that we must therefore exclude the 'juristic' from consideration.[727] Others again have tried to subsume the specifically 'juristic' note – justification as the verdict in the divine law court, ahead of the production of any 'works' of any sort whatever – within the larger context of the transformation of character, whether conceived in terms of virtue-ethics or of '*theōsis*', or, in a measure, both.[728] I agree that transformation is important, and I have tried to show how I think it is *related to* justification by grace through faith. But it is not the same thing. One cannot suddenly expand Paul's very precise *dikaiosynē* terminology to cover a much larger range of soteriological material, however much the church, forgetting its roots in Jewish covenantal theology, moved in that direction. A child, knowing that a Disneyworld vacation was in the offing, might wrongly imagine that the entire trip, including a coast-to-coast drive, was all in a sense taking place in 'Disneyworld', mistaking the part for the whole. That, I think, is what has happened here, though of course one would not want to suggest that the resulting theories had a certain Mickey-Mouse flavour to them. Thus, even though Romans 3.21–31 is part of the same flow of argument as Romans 5—8, and Galatians 2.15–21 is part of the same flow of argument as Galatians 4—6, and even though these two larger arguments do develop a view of the spirit's work in the transformation of character which can properly be seen both as virtue and as *theōsis*, this does not take away from the fact that when Paul speaks of *initial justification by faith* he means it as a very particular, specific claim. What then does this initial justification mean? It means that, ahead of any transformation of character other than the bare, initial *pistis* which by definition looks helplessly away from itself and gratefully towards the saving work of the Messiah, this person is welcomed into the sin-forgiven family, with the badge of membership being that confession of faith and nothing else. The inaugurated-eschatological assurance which this welcome provides is thus both *forensic* (the verdict of

[725] Wright 2010 (as n. 722 above).

[726] The main charge against me on the part of e.g. Piper 2007 is that, by insisting on the *final* 'justification' in the language of Rom. 2, I am bringing back 'human works' into the equation and so making 'assurance' depend on 'performance', rather than on the supposed 'imputed righteousness of Christ'.

[727] So Campbell 2009.

[728] See Gorman 2009.

'not guilty' in the present will be repeated in the future) and *covenantal* (full membership in Abraham's family is granted at once and will be reaffirmed in the resurrection). The two dimensions join up in practical ecclesiology: the mutual welcome which Paul urges in Romans 14 and 15 is the concrete, bodily form which 'forgiveness' is supposed to take in the present time.

Once we take into account the overall covenantal framework, then, we see why initial justification is so important. It is not just because of the need for 'assurance', in the terms of classic protestant theology, though that remains important. It is because of the need to be clear that *all* such believers belong to Abraham's single family. Paul never forgot the battles in Antioch and Galatia.

This argument has brought us, step by slow step, to more or less the same point that Paul reached at the end of Romans 8, or indeed the middle of Galatians 4. This naturally projects us forward into the question of 'Israel according to the flesh', which might be thought to be the heart of his reworking of 'election'. However, quite apart from the already cumbersome length of the present chapter, what Paul says about Israel, particularly in Romans 9—11, belongs properly with his eschatology. We must therefore defer the question to the next chapter. For the moment there is one more pressing matter to address, albeit briefly.

(j) What Then about Torah?

Kindling the flames of an old debate may be a risky thing to do, but it cannot be helped. We spoke about Paul's view of Israel's law in chapter 7, in discussing the complex and interlocking narratives in which his worldview came to expression. Now, in the light of this discussion of election, we must revisit the question. I have suggested at several points that what Paul believed about the Torah was a function of what he believed Israel's God had purposed to do in and through his people, and had now accomplished in the Messiah and the spirit. We are now in a position to draw these threads together. Fortunately, we do not have to retrace our exegetical steps: enough has been said about the key passages. Likewise, to annotate these points in relation to the thousands of debates about 'Paul and the law' which have raged this way and that over generations would be cumbersome and in any case unnecessary.[729] Unlike most expositors, I have chosen to locate this

[729] In recent decades, one may cite the notable discussions of Dunn 1998, 128–59, 625–9 (while questioning whether the placement of the initial section, within the overall category of 'Humankind under Indictment', was likely to do it full justice); Schnelle 2005 [2003], 506–21 (within the section headed 'Anthropology: The Struggle for the Self'). The main treatment in Schreiner 2001 is a chapter headed 'Dishonoring God: the Violation of God's Law' (103–25), though references to the law are scattered throughout the book. Major treatments in the 1980s include Sanders 1983 and Räisänen 1986 [1983], both arguing for serious Pauline inconsistency (on which see Wright 1991 [*Climax*], ch. 1; and, on key exegetical questions, chs. 7–12). Further back again, Ridderbos 1975 [1966] offers a main treatment of the law as part of 'The Life in Sin' (91–158), though he has a later section on the 'third use of the law' (278–88); Cranfield 1979, 845–62 remains a masterpiece of Reformed exegesis, though still in my view insufficient to explain the full contours of the Pauline landscape. Thielman 1994 offers a mediating

discussion within the wider question of 'election', which means attempting to understand the *narrative roles* of Torah within the complex stories Paul is telling (above, chapter 7). The main question in recent debate has been, Is what Paul says about the Jewish law consistent and coherent, and if so, how do we explain its various parts? To suppose the only real question to be whether Paul thought the law was a good thing or a bad thing is to guarantee that one will not understand half of the relevant passages. At this stage, the best thing to do will be simply to set out, in a series of propositions, the ways in which Torah functions within Paul's view of the divine covenantal purpose. The supporting exegetical arguments for these propositions are all contained in either the present chapter or chapter 7.

1. Easily the most important place to start is with Paul's ringing affirmation that Torah was and remained *the God-given law, holy and just and good*. Nothing he says about those functions of Torah which some have labelled 'negative' detract from this. The mention of angels assisting in the giving of Torah, or of its being given through a 'mediator', in no way suggest that Torah is less than fully God-given and God-intended.[730] What is more, Paul saw Torah not simply as a set of commands, but as a *narrative*: the story of creation and covenant, of Adam and Abraham, focused particularly on Exodus and finally articulated in the covenantal warnings and promises at the end of Deuteronomy. All this Paul fully affirmed as divine in origin, positive in intent, and fulfilled (albeit in unexpected ways) through the gospel.
2. Inside this affirmation, however, not undermining it but explaining it, is Paul's sense of *the specific purpose for which Torah was given to Israel*. Of course, if one starts (as many do) with the assumption that the obvious reason for giving Israel the law must have been to enable the people to keep it perfectly and so be 'saved' by their moral efforts, then the purpose that Paul articulates will indeed appear 'negative'. However, for Paul this was a *necessary* 'negativity'; indeed, a *God-given* negativity. 'It was added because of transgressions,' he says; 'scripture concluded all things under sin'; 'the law came in alongside, so that the trespass might be filled out'; the law was given *so that* sin might appear as sin, and *so that* it might become 'exceedingly sinful' through the commandment.[731] This appears, too, in his comment that the people to whom Torah was given were themselves hard-hearted.[732] The problem Moses faced was not that Torah was a bad thing, but that it necessarily and rightly pronounced condemnation on its hearers. Neither Torah nor Israel's God himself could collude with hard-hearted stubbornness and its consequent behaviour. There

position. The key section in Wolter 2011 (351–8), though short, explores the question from a variety of angles.

730 Gal. 3.19f.

731 Gal. 3.21, 22; Rom. 5.20; 7.13.

732 2 Cor. 3.14.

may be some systems in which lawgivers tone down the ideal standards to fit people's capabilities, but Israel's Torah was not like that. That is why it already contained provision for sin in terms of repentance and the sacrificial system; which is why, as we saw, someone like Paul could say of his former self what Luke says of Zechariah and Elizabeth: 'blameless'.[733] But this did not mean that the law would then cease to condemn Israel as a whole; or that, when it did so, it was acting outside the will of the God who had given it.

3. This 'negative' purpose had a double function, related directly to what Paul saw as *the divinely intended purpose of there being a covenant people, and hence a law*, in the first place. The plan was never simply to create and perfect a pure people. It was that, through Abraham's family, the creator would *rescue* the rest of the world. This would be accomplished, specifically, by the work of Torah in drawing 'sin' onto one place, in order that it might be condemned there. This train of thought, expounded in Romans 7 and 8 and reaching its peak at Romans 8.3, is what Paul is hinting at in those other 'negative' remarks. Second, however, it was necessary to keep Israel as it were under lock and key – or, to use Paul's own metaphor, under the rule of the *paidagōgos* – until the Messiah's arrival. But from Paul's perspective there was no chance that anyone, however devout, would in fact keep Torah perfectly: 'through the law comes the knowledge of sin.'[734] From one point of view this might be taken as a further demarcation of Israel: through the law comes the knowledge of *the sin which those pagans out there are committing*. To that extent, the law did indeed function as a fence around Israel. But for Paul 'through the law comes the knowledge of sin' meant, more particularly, that those who embraced Torah for themselves – i.e. the Jewish people – were themselves under the covenantal curse which Torah pronounced on those who broke it. Moses himself, at the climax of Torah in Deuteronomy, had warned that this curse would unfailingly fall on Israel itself.[735] 'Whatever Torah says, it speaks to those who are under Torah' – in other words, to Israel.[736]
4. However, these different overlapping and interlocking functions meant that devout Jews like Saul of Tarsus were bound to treat Torah not as a puzzling vocation but *as a badge of privilege*. Torah set Israel apart from the world: very well, Israel was to be for ever the set-apart people. The signs of this set-apartness were well known both to Jews and to non-Jews in the first century: the specific 'works of Torah'

[733] Phil. 3.6; Lk. 1.6.

[734] Rom. 3.20.

[735] Dt. 28.45–68; 29.19–29; 32.4–42.

[736] Rom. 3.19. Attempts to make *nomos* in passages like this refer to a 'general' law applying to all humankind must be seen as a failure in the light of Paul's many specific discussions of Israel's law itself, not least in Rom. 7 (cf. e.g. Jewett 2007, 303). The question of whether or not *nomos* has the definite article is not to the point: Greek articles do not work the same way that English ones do.

which consisted of circumcision, sabbath and the food laws, together with a geographical focus on Jerusalem and its Temple and a widely assumed (though no doubt often flouted) endogamy. It was assumed that Torah as a whole was to be kept, and would maintain the separation between Israel and the nations; but these were the 'works' which would stand out in particular as having that function.[737] Paul the apostle put these different functions of the law together, and concluded that Torah declared that the devout Jew (his own former self) had in fact broken it – at the very moment when he was rightly clinging to it. Or, to put it another way, the law functioned as the marriage-document to bind Israel, not after all to YHWH as one might suppose, but to Adam. Saul of Tarsus would have said that zealous Torah-keeping in the present would indicate who from among the covenant people would be vindicated in the future by being raised from the dead. No, says Paul the apostle: that is 'a covenant status of my own [i.e. of ethnic Israel], based on Torah'.[738] However much one 'pursues Torah', or a 'righteousness' based on it, one will never in fact 'fulfil Torah'. Anyone who makes such an attempt will therefore 'stumble'.[739] However, because of (2) above, even this stumble will turn out in retrospect to have been part of Torah's purpose. Paul expresses these paradoxes by speaking of a 'double Torah': the one in which the loyal Jew delights, and the one which is at work in his or her Adamic humanity to breed sin and death.[740]

5. Within these paradoxes and puzzles, Paul discerned *the strange vocation of Israel*: Torah was a narrative – and he believed that it had devolved onto Israel's single representative, the Messiah. That is why Paul declares both that the Messiah died under the law's curse, and that the Messiah was the *telos*, the goal, of the law.[741] The former was not, as many have supposed, a way of saying that the law had overreached itself, and had then been proved wrong when Jesus was vindicated in the resurrection. It was, rather, a way of saying that the necessary and appropriate curse of the covenant had fallen on the Messiah as Israel's representative. He had borne in himself the result of Israel's failure, so that the blessing promised not just *to* Abraham but *through* Abraham could now flow to the gentiles. The God-given law had to do what it did, but once that had been done, and the curse exhausted in Jesus' representative death, the entire Mosaic dispensation would be seen as a long bracket within the story of Abraham's people. The law, it seems, had a God-given but time-limited purpose. Once that purpose had been fulfilled it was no longer relevant as the

[737] As we saw, in 4QMMT the 'works of Torah' that were advocated were designed to mark out one group *within* second-Temple Judaism from other Jews who did things differently.

[738] Phil. 3.9.

[739] Rom. 9.30–3.

[740] Rom. 7.13–25.

[741] Gal. 3.13; Rom. 10.4.

marker of the covenant people. One of the basic mistakes of modern scholarship has been to flatten this eschatological *narrative* into an abstract scheme in which the law must be either a bad thing now happily pushed out of the way (as many within an older Lutheranism supposed) or a good thing now fulfilled and vindicated (the basic 'Reformed' view). The only way to understand Paul is to transpose these questions into the more many-sided Israel-and-Messiah narrative that he tells and retells. Within that, all the apparent 'negativity' about the law in Galatians is fully taken care of, without moving, as many have done, towards the basically Marcionite position of suggesting that not only the law but the Abraham story itself was something Paul would happily get rid of. To understand the 'curse of the law' one must understand the Deuteronomic framework within which it made the sense it did.

6. *Exile would be replaced by restoration.* Torah said it would happen, and despite its earlier negative role Torah would still have a part to play when the great day came. Exile was where the Israel-narrative had got to, Paul believed; but in Deuteronomy (and Isaiah, and Daniel, and many others) exile would be followed by restoration. Paul believed that this restoration had now happened in the Messiah. When Jews and gentiles alike found themselves called by the gospel to believe in Jesus as the risen lord, Paul was clear that *this very belief was the true fulfilment of Torah itself.* As we shall see in the next chapter, he draws in Romans 10 on Deuteronomy 30 to make the claim that when someone confesses Jesus as lord and believes that the one God raised him from the dead they are in fact doing what Torah itself, looking forward to the return from exile and the renewal of the covenant, had always promised would happen. This is what Paul is referring to when, cryptically, he speaks of Torah in terms of 'the law of faith'.[742]
7. Social, indeed ecclesial, consequences follow at once. *All those who believe are now demarcated as the true Torah-keeping people,* in other words, the people of the renewed covenant. Torah, as now redefined around Messiah and spirit, retains its community-shaping and community-defining function. This then produces new paradoxes: neither circumcision nor uncircumcision matters, since what matters is 'keeping God's commandments'![743] But, with this new-covenant redefinition, we find the characteristically Pauline rejection of any attempt to go on defining the covenant community by 'works of Torah' in the earlier sense (4 above). Once again, there are two reasons. First, if Torah-works such as circumcision and food laws defined the new-covenant people, that would perpetuate the Jew/gentile division which has now been overcome in the Messiah

[742] Rom. 3.27.

[743] 1 Cor. 7.19; cf. Rom. 2.27: 'the uncircumcision that fulfils the law'.

and spirit. 'The law of commandments and ordinances' functioned like a wall to keep the pagans out, but it is now demolished.[744] Second, even within the apparent safety of an Israel living within the 'fence' of Torah, there was no way through to the new covenant. Torah merely brought wrath, by revealing the Adamic sin which had not been dealt with.[745]

8. This leads to Paul's remarkable developed statements about the way in which *Messiah-people do in fact keep Torah*. They 'fulfil its decrees'.[746] Torah is actually upheld through Messiah-faith.[747] Again and again Paul speaks of the work of the spirit as enabling people to fulfil Torah in a way previously impossible.[748] This appears to go beyond the 'faith' spoken of in point (6) above, and into the transformation not only of the heart but of the entire life.
9. Once this is grasped, and within this context, we can understand how Paul can develop the point to include *a fuller range of ethical behaviour as a new form of Torah-keeping*. The spirit produces *agapē*, and this *agapē* is the fulfilling of Torah – though we note with interest that certain aspects which would have maintained Jew/gentile separation, such as the sabbath, are never mentioned in this connection.[749]
10. Now at last it becomes apparent what Paul means by the fulfilment of the *dikaiōma* of the law in Romans 8.1–11: *Torah's aim, to give life, is fulfilled in the resurrection*. Paul had already spoken of the Torah being 'unto life'.[750] Now, by the spirit, not only is the principle of life implanted in the hearts of believers; the ultimate fulfilment is assured. And that is not just a miscellaneous, however glorious, future hope. It is specifically and uniquely *the hope of Israel*. That is exactly the point both of Philippians 3.2–11 and Romans 8.1–11. When Paul speaks of the spirit indwelling believers and giving them new bodily life, he is saying that what Torah had promised is now at last to be accomplished. 'Do this,' says Torah, 'and you will live'; Paul, radically redefining 'Do this' around Messiah and spirit, looks ahead and sees that what Torah could not do, through no fault of its own, Israel's God has done in the Messiah and will do for all his people. The promise of Torah, the hope of Israel, was 'life'. It was, in fact, nothing other than resurrection.

[744] Eph. 2.14f.

[745] Rom. 4.15 with 7.7–25; cp. Gal. 2.17f. Holding these two things together (Torah as separating Jew and gentile; Torah as condemning its possessors for failure to keep it) is vital to avoid reducing 'works of Torah' simply to the outward symbols, however important they are. I would like to think that this move would reduce the gap between myself and e.g. Gathercole 2006a, 237–40.

[746] Rom. 2.26f., looking back to 2.7, 13, etc.

[747] Rom. 3.31.

[748] Rom. 8.5–8. On the way all this works out see further e.g. below, 1433f.

[749] Rom. 13.8–10; Gal. 5.14; cf. 5.23.

[750] Rom. 7.10; cf. Gal. 3.21.

5. Conclusion: Election Redefined

There is no need for a lengthy conclusion. All that remains is to point outwards, from the detailed discussions we have had, to the larger world of Pauline questions to which this chapter contributes.

First, and perhaps most important, there should be no question that Paul remained a deeply *Jewish* thinker. However much his 'kinsfolk according to the flesh' might have gnashed their teeth at his conclusions, his entire argument was that Israel's one God had been faithful to his word. He had done what he said he would do – even though this had only become clear with the dramatic and unexpected unveiling-in-action of his covenant purposes in the Messiah and the spirit. At every point Paul was at pains, not merely to 'illustrate' his argument with scriptural quotations (as though he were a mere proof-texter), but to argue precisely that the covenant God had done what scripture had all along predicted.

What we have seen, in fact, is a redefined Jewish perspective, which is neither that of a simplistic 'salvation history' nor that of a simplistic 'apocalyptic'. As we shall see more fully in the next chapter, the narrative of Israel was anything but a smooth and evolving 'history of God's mighty acts'. If anything, it was a history of divine judgment, of Israel being cut down to a remnant, of the covenant people apparently being led up a blind alley. That, of course, has been the strength of the anti-'salvation history' movement in recent times. The labels 'salvation history' and 'apocalyptic' are in reality two inadequate, half-broken signposts to a larger, richer reality than either had imagined. That is the reality which, I have suggested, is better described with (mutually defining) words such as 'messianic' and 'covenantal' – provided those are seen as heuristic devices to signal what Paul is saying, not Trojan horses in which other types of thought might be smuggled in.

If we manage to get beyond the false stand-off between 'salvation history' and 'apocalyptic', and also between 'participatory' and 'juristic', we should also manage, with this analysis, to transcend the low-grade either/or that has been taking place between 'old' and 'new' perspectives. I have no interest in perpetuating such a squabble. I trust that the present chapter, and indeed the whole book thus far, has presented an analysis of Paul in which a thick historical description of his social and cultural context, and the positioning of his communities within that context, can be fully and richly integrated with a thick theological description of what he had to say on the key contested topics, not least salvation, justification and the law. The attempt by some 'old perspective' writers to suggest that some of us who have been labelled as 'new perspective' thinkers have given up on ideas such as sin, salvation, atonement and so on ought now to be seen for what it is. Equally, the attempt by some to use elements of a 'new perspective' analysis to avoid theology ought likewise to be renounced. *Of course* Paul was dealing with actual communities in which the pressure to decide questions of table-fellowship, of *adiaphora* in food and drink, of the necessity or otherwise of circumcision, was intense; and of course it is trivial to think of such things as irrelevant 'works-righteousness' in an older protestant sense. But *of course* Paul was dealing with the biggest issues in the world: the question of creator and cosmos, of humans and their idols, of sin and death and of ultimate rescue from both of them, of Israel and the nations and, at the centre, of Jesus and his cross and resurrection, and of the gift of the spirit. And *of course* all these things joined up, since the theology itself pointed again and again to the intention of the creator God to live in and among his people, so that their common life was no mere accident, an incidental function of their pragmatic desire to meet up for worship from time to time, but the rich redefinition of nothing less than Israel's central symbol, the Temple. Part II of the present book thus integrates fully with Part III, the worldview-analysis with the redefined theology. Not only do they belong closely together in the sense simply of sitting side by side and keeping one another company. By this stage of the argument we see more clearly, I think, that *this* worldview needs something like *this* theology to sustain it. The combination of the two presents a sketch of Paul's world of practice and belief in which the false antitheses regularly found in analyses of Paul may perhaps be eliminated.

In particular, we have shown in this chapter the rich integration of 'juridical' with 'participationist' language and thought. As with the other great divides that have bedevilled the discipline, we have argued that the two coexist perfectly coherently in Paul and, once more, should not be played off against one another. The 'juridical' language – the running law-court metaphor of Romans 3, the language of 'justice', 'justification' and so on – is not just 'one metaphor among many', because in Israel's scriptures, certainly the way Paul read them, the obligation of the one God to 'judge' the world was absolute. The alternative would be chaos come again. The creator must, in the end, put all things right. 'Juridical' language is not a mere pragmatic offshoot of something more fundamental, introduced solely (as Wrede thought, with Schweitzer at this point largely agreeing) for the sake of pressing the point about gentile inclusion. It is basic and non-negotiable. Nor can the language of the law court be reduced to the rationalistic parody in which unbelievers are bludgeoned into accepting a strange pseudo-intellectual logic which leads them to some kind of conversion.[751] Paul's juridical language is simply not like that. Equally, Paul again and again makes it clear that 'justification' is something that happens because of the messianic events of Jesus' death and resurrection, and through the spirit-driven means of gospel, faith and baptism by which people come to be 'in the Messiah'. Schweitzer's basic instinct was right – he was, after all, heir to the Calvinist tradition as well as several others – when he said that the language of 'justification' belonged ultimately within the language of 'being in Christ'. Where he was misleading was first in labelling the latter reality 'mysticism', and second in using his true insight about (a) the nesting of

[751] As Campbell 2009 suggests.

'juridical' language within 'participationist', and (b) the function of justification within Paul's arguments for gentile inclusion, to suggest that 'justification' was a mere polemical tool for use in key debates. Once again, we need better categories. I hope the present chapter has helped to provide them. We shall revisit this discussion towards the conclusion of this book.

For the moment, however, we may say this on one of the most important topics of all. I hope to have laid to rest the extraordinary and persistent notion both that Paul used the word *Christos* as a mere proper name and that the notion of Jesus' Messiahship plays no particular role within the apostle's theology. I would actually put it the other way round: the failure of many generations of scholars even to glimpse the rich messianic meaning which pervades so much of Paul's writing is a measure of how inadequate such readings have been, and helps to explain why so many other issues have remained puzzling and unresolved. There are big questions waiting in the wings at this point, of course, not least the question of politics: if Jesus is Messiah, does this mean that Paul is committed to some version of the Jewish political dream? Paul's answer comes in passages like Philippians 2.6–11, 1 Corinthians 15.20–8 and Romans 8. For Paul, Jesus as Messiah is the world's true lord. That is what ancient Israel's expectation of the coming king always stated. Paul celebrates that belief unreservedly: it has been fulfilled, he believes, in Jesus. Jesus' shameful death on the cross has radically redefined the very notions of power, empire, kingdom and lordship; but his resurrection has radically reaffirmed them all, albeit in this radically redefined form. Perhaps, after all, that is at the root of the rejection of resurrection in so much liberal protestant theology: Easter would blow the lid off the Enlightenment settlement in which the church looked after 'spirituality' while allowing the politicians and imperialists to run the world.[752] That position will be implicitly undermined in chapter 12 below.

But the question of christology, seen in this chapter as part of the redefinition of the ancient Jewish doctrine of *election*, must ultimately join up with the question of christology in the previous chapter, where it is part of the redefinition of ancient Jewish *monotheism*. Confusion has often reigned in Pauline scholarship when these two have been squashed together, for instance in the attempts to demonstrate the historical derivation of early Christian worship of Jesus in terms of exalted (pre-Christian) ideas about a Messiah, or in the proposal that Paul's incorporative christology is itself a sign of a belief in Jesus' 'divinity'. As I suggested in chapter 9, I do not believe that the earliest Christians had started with ideas about exalted human (or angelic) figures, or even abstractions like 'wisdom', and, attaching them to Jesus under the impulse of remarkable 'experiences', had built up to a picture of his 'divinity'. They were starting, I argued, with promises that Israel's God had made concerning the things he was intending to come and do in person, and they were telling those stories once more in the shocked belief that Israel's God had done what he promised – in and as

[752] cf. *RSG* chs. 18f.

Jesus of Nazareth. They were not telling stories about humans and discovering that they could reach up to the one God. They were telling stories about the one God in the dazed, awed belief that they were now telling these same stories about a human being.

That remains true even if any sense of an 'incorporative Messiah' were to be bracketed out of the picture. But once we add that element into the mix, as we have done in the present chapter, we find ourselves returning to the theme which played a central role in chapter 9. The Temple in Jerusalem, and behind that the tabernacle in the wilderness, drew together monotheism and election: the God who deigned to dwell with his people, and to be known in terms of that dwelling, provided, in himself and his presence, the ultimate definition of his people. If he was 'the God who dwells in Jerusalem', Israel was the people who structured their life around the call to worship him there. In Israel's scriptures, these elements were joined in the person and work of the king, who would build or cleanse the Temple and lead the people in worship. We have no clear evidence that any pre-Christian Jews had tied all these strands together in such a way, though some features of this picture are visible at Qumran. But for Paul, as he drew out the significance of what all the earliest Christians believed about Jesus' messianic life, death and resurrection, the categories of monotheism and election themselves came together and generated a new combined picture in which the Temple itself came into fresh prominence. The promise that one day YHWH would return to the Temple, rescuing his people and bringing justice to the world, turned into the announcement that he had indeed returned, *in and as his people's representative.* He was himself, in some sense, the one who built the Temple and the one who would dwell in it. And the Temple he built was not made of timber and stone, but of flesh and blood. Here the major themes of Paul's thought meet and merge: Israel's God, coming back to rescue his people and the world and to dwell with them for ever; Israel itself, God's people, redefined around the Messiah and spirit who were themselves the means and mode of that dwelling.

Perhaps the closest Paul comes to saying all this is that remarkable catena of quotations which suddenly bursts out as he reflects on the church's vocation to be God's Temple:

> We are the temple of the living God, you see, just as God said:
>
> I will live among them and walk about with them;
> I will be their God, and they will be my people.
> So come out from the midst of them,
> and separate yourselves, says the Lord;
> no unclean thing must you touch.
> Then I will receive you gladly,
> and I will be to you as a father,
> and you will be to me as sons and daughters,
> says the Lord, the Almighty.[753]

[753] 2 Cor. 6.16–18, quoting or echoing Lev. 26.11f.; Ezek. 37.27; Isa. 52.11; Ezek. 20.34, 41; 2 Sam. 7.14.

The final promise takes what the covenant God said to David about his royal son, in connection with David's plan to build the Temple, and turns it into a promise for, and about, all his people. The living presence of the one God is promised to the Messiah's people, as part of the kaleidoscopic array of promises which, in context, speak not only of Temple-building but of resurrection, of divine victory and divine kingdom.

But, since all of these are precisely elements of the future hope both of ancient Israel and of second-Temple Judaism, we must now turn to the final chapter of Part III. Monotheism has been rethought around Messiah and spirit. Election has been similarly reworked. There remains eschatology.

Chapter Eleven

GOD'S FUTURE FOR THE WORLD, FRESHLY IMAGINED

1. Introduction

Many ancient Jews clung on to a hope which had specific content and shape. Rooted in scripture, this was a hope not just for an individual future after death, but for a restoration and renewal of the whole nation, and perhaps even for the entire created order.[1] Such Jews were distinguished from their pagan neighbours, however, not simply by the precise content of this hope, but by the fact that they had any large-scale hope at all. To be sure, some elements of Jewish hope for a life beyond the grave have antecedents, and then parallels, not least among the peoples further east, though our evidence for ancient Babylonian and Persian eschatology is by no means as full as we would like, and certainly not sufficient to mount a detailed comparative study. Egypt, too, had a particular tradition of future hope, though this seems to have been simply for a significant life in the world of the dead, not for the renewal of present national fortunes, let alone of the world.[2] But the peoples of Greece and Rome, and the lands into which the culture of the former and the empire of the latter had made such powerful inroads, were, by comparison with the Jewish people, 'without hope'. That is Paul's blunt verdict.[3] If there was a 'golden age', it was in the distant past, not in the future. It would be very odd for a Dictionary of Judaism not to have a substantial entry on 'Hope', even if, after the scholarly custom for preferring five syllables to one, such an entry might be called 'Eschatology'. There is no such entry in the *Oxford Classical Dictionary*.[4]

The verdict 'without hope' might at first seem harsh. Did not many hope for a blissful life beyond the grave, whether in the Elysian fields, conversing with fellow-philosophers, or at least for a reincarnation in which a better fate might await them than they had previously enjoyed? Well, yes, they did.[5] But the judgment remains. There is nothing in the literature of Greece

[1] On C1 Jewish hope see *NTPG* ch. 10; and above, ch. 2, esp. 108–75.

[2] On all this see *RSG* 124f., pointing out that the older attempts to 'derive' developed Jewish beliefs from e.g. ancient Persia now seem considerably less secure. See too Collins 2000b, distinguishing 'political eschatology', 'cosmic eschatology' and 'personal eschatology' and tracking the varied beliefs of many cultures.

[3] Eph. 2.12.

[4] On the apparent exception of Virgil *Ec.* 4, see below. For the idea of rotating historical periods, with the golden age eventually reappearing, see *JVG* 451 n. 32. On these see Collins 2000b.

[5] See *RSG* 47–51, 77–80.

or Rome that remotely corresponds to what we find – to look only at the most obvious of passages – in Isaiah and the Psalms:

> A shoot shall come out from the stock of Jesse, and a branch shall grow out of his roots. The spirit of YHWH shall rest on him ... He shall not judge by what his eyes see, or decide by what his ears hear; but with righteousness he shall judge the poor, and decide with equity for the meek of the earth ... The wolf shall live with the lamb, the leopard shall lie down with the kid, the calf and the lion and the fatling together, and a little child shall lead them ... They will not hurt or destroy on all my holy mountain; for the earth will be full of the knowledge of YHWH as the waters cover the sea.[6]

> Let the sea roar, and all that fills it; the world and those who live in it.
> Let the floods clap their hands; let the hills sing together for joy
> at the presence of YHWH, for he is coming to judge the earth.
> He will judge the world with righteousness, and the peoples with equity.[7]

A world set free both from human injustice and from 'natural' violence; a world in which oceans and mountains themselves will rejoice at a new fulfilment; a world in which all peoples will celebrate the fact that everything has been set right at last. That is the ancient Israelite vision, variously re-expressed in Jewish texts across the second-Temple period.[8] This is not simply a hope *beyond* the world. It is a hope *for* the world. The difference is all-important, and is rooted, as those two extracts and many others indicate, in the ancient Israelite and Jewish belief that the true God, Israel's God, was the *creator* of earth as well as heaven. Sooner or later he would put all things right, and there would be – you can feel it in those texts – a cosmic sigh of relief. That, we hear from lambs and wolves alike, is what we've been waiting for. About these things we have already spoken in detail, in the present volume and elsewhere.[9]

There is one element within this Jewish hope which I did not even mention when writing *The New Testament and the People of God* twenty years ago. This element then made an appearance, to my own surprise and the alarm of some of my friends, when I struggled in *Jesus and the Victory of God* to express Jesus' own self-understanding, and found my way to a theme which I, and most others, had more or less ignored in our probing of first-century eschatology: the return of YHWH to Zion.[10] Since then this theme, set in its proper ancient context of the Jewish hope for a 'new exodus', has been explored by various writers, and has now made its way back to where it belongs, as a central element in the understanding not only of first-century Jews but also the early Christians.[11] When Mark introduces John the Baptist with two verses, one from Malachi and the other from Isaiah, it

[6] Isa. 11.1–4, 6–9.

[7] Ps. 98.7–9.

[8] See e.g. Collins 2010a.

[9] Above, e.g. 163–75; and see esp. *NTPG* ch. 10; *RSG* chs. 3 & 4; and Wright 2008 [*Surprised by Hope*].

[10] *JVG* ch. 13. See above, 157, 633, 653–6, 663f., 673–5, 681–90; and below.

[11] cf. e.g. Watts 2000 [1997].

was easy until recently to ignore the fact that both were speaking, not of the arrival of a 'Messiah' (and of a 'forerunner' to prepare the way for such a figure) but of the arrival of YHWH himself.[12] This is quite rightly having a revolutionary effect on gospel christology, where, in place of the older view that the synoptics had a 'low' christology and John a 'high' one, the truth is dawning that Mark, Matthew and Luke have just as 'high' a christology as John, only expressed in a way for which earlier generations of scholars were unprepared.[13] The dynamic vision of God in ancient Jewish traditions – the idea of a God who had abandoned the Temple at one point but had promised to return to it later – does not seem to have impinged much on scholarship until recently. This, too, is another way in which the ancient Jewish vision stands out sharply from the greco-roman world. The gods and goddesses there, no doubt, often seemed to behave in puzzling ways. But the idea of a larger *narrative* in which a particular god would do something so drastic as first abandoning his chosen earthly residence and then promising to return to it at last was unknown. Even in the darkest days of Athens' humiliation at the end of the fifth century, one does not hear that Athene had abandoned the city but would return in triumph at some future date.

As we have seen before, however, it is at this point – the idea of a larger narrative – that Israel in any case stood out as distinct from the rest of the world.[14] Israel's ancient scriptures told a story which stretched out its arms to encompass the distant past and the ultimate future. Telling that story, and finding appropriate ways of living within it, were the natural outflowing of Israel's creational monotheism: the world which the one God has made, though puzzling and often tragic, still belongs to this God, and part of the task of the people who give their allegiance to this God is precisely to tell and retell the story, whether as prayer or lament, as history or prophecy.[15] Telling that story, and living in it, was therefore a central and inalienable part of what it meant for Israel to be the covenant people of this one creator God.

Israel's eschatology thus grew from within the very heart of monotheism and election.[16] If there is one God, responsible for the world; and if this God has called Israel to be his people; then there must be a future for the world in which this God will set everything right, restoring and renewing creation – and this future must fulfil the promises made to Israel in particular. Since we have seen in the two previous chapters that Paul had rethought his own

[12] Mk. 1.2f., quoting Mal. 3.1; Isa. 40.3.

[13] See the forthcoming work on the gospels by Richard B. Hays. See too the brief statement in Wright 2012a [*HGBK*], ch. 5.

[14] Ch. 7 above. On the Roman imperial narrative, the sole apparent exception, see above, 299–312.

[15] One need only think of psalms such as 89, or 104–7, to see the point.

[16] It is noticeable that in Schechter 1961 [1909] there is no separate chapter on 'eschatology', but the future hope is expounded in various places precisely in relation to the election of Israel and the coming divine kingdom. In Montefiore and Loewe 1974 [1938] there is a chapter on 'The Life to Come: Resurrection and Judgment', in which are highlighted the themes we take up here. Schreiner 2001, 453f. rightly insists that though 'eschatology' can be treated as a separate topic it actually characterizes the whole of Paul.

Jewish monotheism, and the doctrine of election, around Jesus the Messiah on the one hand and the spirit on the other, we should expect that he will have done the same with ancient Jewish eschatology. And this is exactly what we find. The present chapter will thus do in relation to 'hope' what the previous two did in relation to Paul's vision of the one God and the people of that one God.[17]

Discussions of Paul's eschatology have traditionally concentrated on three topics in particular. What exactly did Paul hope for? What were the sources for this hope, and how did Paul modify or depart from them? Did his eschatology develop during the course of his brief letter-writing career?[18] The first question subdivides, raising once more the question of 'apocalyptic' and 'eschatology': what sort of eschatology did Paul hold, and to what extent was that in continuity and discontinuity with what had gone before? In particular, did he believe that the world of space, time and matter was shortly going to come to an end, or did he, like many writers in the tradition of Jewish apocalyptic, use that kind of imagery to describe a dramatic transformation that would happen (presumably by a fresh divine action) *within* the present order? And, to bring things to a particular focus, how did the 'now' and the 'not yet' relate to one another in his thought?[19]

When this kind of question has been raised in relation to Jesus and the gospels, it has been possible for scholars to simplify matters by insisting either that Jesus only spoke about a kingdom which was about to appear (but had not yet done so) or that he only spoke about a kingdom which was already present.[20] With Paul that option is closed. Both are found even in the seven letters now generally agreed to be from his pen. We do not have the option to excise either his 'now' or his 'not yet' passages.

All these questions, I have come to think, are best addressed from within the matrix of first-century Jewish hope. As with monotheism and election, so with eschatology: Paul's complete vision of what lay in the future, and of how that hope had already been 'inaugurated' in the present, can be comprehended in terms of the modification of Jewish eschatological beliefs by means of (a) Jesus as the crucified and risen Messiah and (b) the gift of the spirit. Of course, there is a sense in which Paul's theology is 'eschatological' through and through – not that he spent all his time talking about the future, but that all his thinking, on all key topics, was shaped by his belief that in Jesus, and especially in his death and resurrection, the expected 'end' had come forward into the middle of history, and that by the work of the spirit, implementing the achievement of Jesus, the long-awaited renewal was

[17] A previous, much shorter, version of this argument was sketched in ch. 7 of Wright 2005a [*Fresh Perspectives*]. In the present treatment I am highlighting things somewhat differently and addressing two major issues for which the earlier treatment had no space.

[18] The regular Pauline theologies, naturally, treat eschatology; though the question of whether it forms a separate topic at the end of a list (as for instance in Ridderbos 1975 [1966], ch. 12; Dunn 1998, §12, 18, 19; Schreiner 2001, ch. 16; Schnelle 2005 [2003], ch. 22; Wolter 2011, ch. 9), or a fundamental category, remains open. In the present book I am treating it, in a sense, as both.

[19] On Paul's eschatology see the helpful summaries and analyses in Kreitzer 1987; 1993.

[20] See *JVG* ch. 6.

already starting to take place. This has been clear throughout the previous two chapters. In both monotheism and election, something promised in Israel's scriptures, and hoped for in the second-Temple period, had now, already, come true – albeit in a new and shocking form.

But (to lapse into the normal technical language) though this eschatological hope had been well and truly *inaugurated*, it was not yet *consummated*.[21] I have sometimes been strangely accused of holding an over-realized eschatology, but I hope the present chapter will put paid to such rumours.[22] The 'not yet' is as important, and in its way just as interesting, as the 'now'. And when we look at the 'not yet' areas of Paul's thought, we find that they fall into two categories, of which the second then subdivides.

First, there are those aspects of ancient Israel's hope which were clearly *not* fulfilled at once in Jesus and the spirit. Sin and death were still present realities in Paul's world, as his own suffering reminded him day by day. Wolves and lambs, literal and metaphorical, had yet to make up their ancient quarrel. The creation had been flooded neither with justice nor with peace. But the vision that these things *would* happen had not gone away. Rather, a new road to it had been opened up – by the achievement of the Messiah and the work of the spirit.

That is why, to take the obvious example to which we shall shortly return, 'the day of YHWH' in the Hebrew scriptures has become 'the day of the lord Jesus' in Paul. Several aspects of the older hope are thus 'translated' into a new, Pauline form. Studying these phenomena will enable us to answer the three standard questions we mentioned a moment ago. First, Paul shared the detailed and complex eschatological expectations of much second-Temple Judaism, which cannot be reduced to the scholarly oversimplifications sometimes misleadingly associated with the word 'apocalyptic'. Second, he mostly drew on his biblical and Jewish traditions for this, not on non-Jewish sources (though some of his eschatological language had strong echoes in the pagan world). Third, to suggest a straightforward 'development' of his eschatology is in fact a further oversimplification which acknowledges neither the subtle complexity of all his thought nor the situational dynamics which called forth (for instance) a good deal of eschatological teaching in 1 Thessalonians and hardly any in Galatians.[23] The rich, dense coherence which we have seen in his vision of monotheism and election is once again on view as we contemplate his eschatology.

Second, there are two areas of eschatology which, though not strange from the scriptural viewpoint, are opened up in a new way. These two areas are what we might call *ethics* and *ethnics*: the question of what to do and how to do it, and the question of Israel.

One can see the first to good advantage by asking: if 'the end' has come, if all the promises really do find their 'Yes' in the Messiah as Paul says in 2 Corinthians 1.20, why are even the Messiah's followers not themselves

[21] The distinction goes back a long way, for instance to the seminal work of Ladd 1974a, 1974b.

[22] e.g. Allison 1999.

[23] On the question of development between 1 Cor. and 2 Cor. cf. esp. *RSG* chs. 6 and 7.

perfect? Why do they still sin, and what should be done about it? That places Paul's entire *ethical* thought within the category of inaugurated eschatology. In one sense, the question is familiar: many second-Temple writers reflected on what it would mean for the chosen people to be holy. For Paul, however, there was a new framework. He addressed the new situation with a Messiah-shaped and spirit-driven exposition of the call to holiness by means of a transformation of mind, heart and will, and hence of action. As we saw in chapter 6, the unity and holiness of the Messiah's people stood at the heart of Paul's symbolic worldview: the outward markers of Jewish life (circumcision, the food laws, the sabbath) were no longer required, but the moral standards which were supposed to distinguish Israel from the nations were if anything intensified.

Likewise, if Israel's God has been faithful to his promises, then why has Israel as a whole – most of Paul's Jewish contemporaries, that is – rejected the message? And what will Israel's God do about it? That places Paul's entire reflection on *ethnic Israel* within the same framework of inaugurated eschatology. In one sense, again, the question is familiar: many second-Temple writers reflected on the obvious failures of the Jewish people, and on the question of what their God would do next. But for Paul there was a new framework: he analyzed the failure of Israel to believe the gospel in terms of the messianic fulfilment of scriptural promises and warnings, setting the stage for a subtle and powerful exposition of how 'all Israel shall be saved'.

Both of these questions – ethics, and the future of Israel – belong in one sense just as much in chapter 10, with 'election', as they do here. But only when we address them within the context of Paul's freshly reworked eschatology, I believe, will they reveal their full dimensions.

The source from which all these streams flow is Paul's belief that with the resurrection of Jesus the hope of Israel had been split into two. Jesus had been raised first, demonstrating him to be Israel's Messiah; all his people would be raised later, at the moment Paul calls 'the end'.[24] The future had burst into the present, close up and personal; at the same time, the future remained future, glimpsed as in a darkened mirror. This sudden irruption of future into present, Paul concluded, was not simply a strange accident, as though a cog had slipped in the providential clock, leading it to strike the hour too soon. Paul was not just freewheeling pragmatically into an unexpected situation, making up inaugurated eschatology on the hoof. When he reflected on what was *already* the case and how that related to what was *not yet* the case, but would become so through Messiah and spirit, he advanced arguments which *sought to explain that this interval, however unexpected, had itself a specific purpose within the divine economy*. To repeat and amplify what was said above: within eschatological ethics, this purpose has to do with the present development of *character*. The present time is the time of the formation of truly human beings; this cannot be achieved at a stroke, precisely because of what a human being is. Within the eschatology

[24] 1 Cor. 15.24.

of Israel's election, it is the need to bring all, Jew and gentile alike, 'under sin', in order that all who are saved may be saved by mercy alone. The inaugurated eschatology caused Paul 'great sorrow and endless pain in [his] heart' (Romans 9.2), but he discerned a clear though startling divine purpose in the time-lag. This was how God had planned it all along, to ensure that his entire plan of salvation would depend, not on privilege, but on mercy (Romans 11.32). The present time is the time when, after the long years in which Israel was called to be the light of the world, the mission to the gentiles was to be the means of rescuing Israel itself.

Three areas, then: features of the ancient Jewish hope redrawn around Jesus and the spirit; eschatological ethics; and the future of Israel. In order to see all this clearly we shall need to begin by recapitulating enough of the previously sketched picture of Jewish hope to set the discussion in context. Then we shall remind ourselves, again briefly, of the ways in which Paul saw the hope of Israel *already realized* in the Messiah and the spirit, as set out in chapters 9 and 10. That will lead naturally to the question of the 'not yet', and the way in which the *still-future* hope is likewise to be understood in terms of that Messiah-and-spirit reshaping of Israel's expectation, in the three larger categories outlined a moment ago.

2. Israel's God and the Story of Hope

Much second-Temple Jewish eschatology was focused, as I have argued already, on the scripturally highlighted expectation that YHWH would return to Zion.[25] This became the matrix from which there grew a good deal of first-century Christian theology. Israel's hope *had* already come to pass through Jesus and the spirit; Israel's hope *would still* come to pass, again through Jesus and the spirit.

Central to all this was Paul's belief, which we studied in chapter 9, that the creator God had made himself known in person in and as Jesus the Messiah. Biblical motifs originally related to YHWH could thus be re-expressed in relation to Jesus. This prepares the way for specifically eschatological motifs in which the same thing happens.

Likewise, Paul's understanding of the spirit as the personal presence of the same God informed his eschatology, both in its 'now' and in its 'not yet'. Some of the biblical promises of future divine presence and action were seen to be fulfilled in the present gift of the spirit. This, too, we studied in chapters 9 and 10. Others, yet to be fulfilled, would come about through the future work of the same spirit.

The present chapter thus not only builds on the two previous ones but contributes as it were in reverse to the arguments of both, consolidating and filling out further the picture we have already drawn. Monotheism, election and eschatology are not, for Paul, three detached loci. We separate them out,

[25] cf. Adams 2006.

as the doctor separates in her mind the physics, chemistry and biology of the patient, not in order to keep them apart but in order to understand more fully the complex interworkings of the whole.

The post-exilic hope that YHWH would return at last to dwell in the Jerusalem Temple and to put all things to rights is rooted in the much older expectation of 'the day of YHWH'. This idea was already well enough established by the eighth century BC for the prophet Amos to reinterpret it, taking what seems originally to have been a promise of YHWH's victory over Israel's enemies and turning it into a warning that when YHWH arrived in judgment Israel itself would face the most severe inquisition.[26] The theme of YHWH's 'day' is widespread among prophets on either side of the Babylonian exile, with most of the references carrying the same thrust. The idea that Israel, the people of God, was itself under the judgment which was often invoked on the nations was scarcely a first-century or Christian innovation.[27]

The coming judgment on that 'day' was seen in various ways, but among the most obvious was that of military action. So-called 'natural' disasters or unexpected events might also figure in the mix. YHWH, being the creator God, could act as he pleased within creation. The greatest model of all, the exodus, had after all been accomplished without any human assistance. But, insofar as there was a 'normal' way for the judgment to operate, it was through kings, armies, battles and conquests. YHWH will use the king of Assyria as a stick with which to beat his people, though the pagan monarch himself will then be judged for his arrogance. The king of Babylon will take Jerusalem; a new king of Persia will order its restoration.[28] At the same time, however, the hope also grew that the positive side of YHWH's future action, the final restoration of Israel and the overthrow of all enslaving powers, would be accomplished through the true Israelite monarch, the anointed son of David.[29] That scenario, already sketched in Psalm 2, underlies and shapes numerous expressions of biblical and Jewish hope right across the period.[30] All of this is rooted, as one can see again and again in Israel's scriptures, in the vision of YHWH as the creator who made human beings as his image-bearers, the ones through whom he would exercise his stewardship over his world as it were from within. As with later (including early Christian) readings of Psalm 8, the biblical vision of *human* sovereignty over the world is brought into sharp focus in the vision of *messianic* sovereignty.[31]

[26] Am. 5.18–20.

[27] e.g. Isa. 2.12; 22.5; Jer. 46.10; Ezek. 7.7; 13.5; 30.3; Joel 1.15; 2.11, 31; 3.14; Obad. 15; Zeph. 1.7, 14; Zech. 14.1; Mal. 4.5; cf. 'the day' or 'the days', with similar effect, in Isa. 13.6; Ezek. 7.10; 12.23; 21.25; 22.4. See the brief summaries and bibliographies in e.g. Hiers 1992; Allison 2007a.

[28] Assyria: Isa. 10.5–19; Babylon: Jer. 27.6–11; Persia: Ezra 1.1–4 (cf. Isa. 45.1–6).

[29] Details in *NTPG* 307–20; and cf. *JVG* 481–9.

[30] Dan. 7; *Ps. Sol.* 17, 18; etc.

[31] Obvious examples include Rom. 8.17–20; 1 Cor. 15.27; Eph. 1.22; Heb. 2.6–9.

The transformation of the pre-exilic 'day of YHWH' motif into its post-exilic successor is shaped above all by the widespread belief that YHWH had abandoned the Temple to its fate at the hand of the Babylonians and, despite its rebuilding, had never returned. The promise of that return is stated most fully at the end of Ezekiel, balancing the dramatic story, near the beginning of the book, in which the divine presence takes its leave.[32] But the aching sense of absence, coupled with further promises – and warnings! – that this absence will not last for ever, continue to echo through the post-exilic period, summed up vividly in Malachi. The priests, ministering in the renewed Temple, are bored and careless. But Israel's God is not finished. There will come a final messenger of warning, and then 'the Lord whom you seek will suddenly come to his temple'.[33] But, as with Amos several centuries earlier, so now: 'who can endure the day of his coming, and who can stand when he appears?'[34]

This hope for YHWH's return continued unabated throughout the period.[35] Among the most obvious passages are those which link the divine return directly to YHWH's royal victory over the pagan nations and to the long-awaited 'return from exile'. This is what it means when the prophets speak of Israel's God being, or becoming, 'king'. Isaiah 52 says it all:

> How beautiful upon the mountains are the feet of the messenger who announces peace, who brings good news, who announces salvation, who says to Zion, 'Your God reigns.' Listen! Your sentinels lift up their voices, together they sing for joy; for in plain sight they see the return of YHWH to Zion. Break forth together into singing, you ruins of Jerusalem; for YHWH has comforted his people, he has redeemed Jerusalem. YHWH has bared his holy arm before the eyes of all the nations; and all the ends of the earth shall see the salvation of our God. Depart, depart, go out from there! Touch no unclean thing; go out from the midst of it, purify yourselves, you who carry the vessels of YHWH. For you shall not go out in haste, and you shall not go in flight; for YHWH will go before you, and the God of Israel will be your rearguard.[36]

This hope for YHWH's return, picking up elements of 'the day of the lord', belongs (like a great deal of second-Temple writing) within the expectation of a 'new exodus'.[37] It is in the book of Exodus, after all, that we find not only the great liberating act, freeing the Israelites from foreign rule, not only the majestic moment when the Torah is given on Mount Sinai, but also, as the climax of the book and hence of the entire biblical narrative to that point, the construction of the tabernacle and the glorious presence of the covenant God taking up residence in it – despite the awful moment when it seemed as though his presence would be withdrawn for ever because of Israel's sin with the golden calf. (A compromise was reached, as

[32] Ezek. 40—8, focused on 43.1–9, and the closing promise (48.35) that the city will be called *YHWH shamah*, 'YHWH is there'. For the Shekinah abandoning the Temple: Ezek. 10.1–22; 11.22–3.

[33] 1.5, 11; 3.1 (cf. too 4.5–6).

[34] Mal. 3.2; cf. Am. 5.18.

[35] Full survey of relevant texts in *JVG* 615–24; cf. too *HGBK* ch. 5.

[36] Isa. 52.7–12.

[37] cf. e.g. Wis. 10—18.

we saw in chapter 9: YHWH agreed to accompany the people, but his tabernacle remained outside the camp.) The presence of the creator God with the first humans in the garden, as in the opening of Genesis, looks forward to this moment at the end of Exodus, as Abraham's family, the new form of the human race, journey to their 'garden', their promised land. Moses puts the finishing touches to the tabernacle and its furniture, and then:

> the cloud covered the tent of meeting, and the glory of YHWH filled the tabernacle. Moses was not able to enter the tent of meeting because the cloud settled upon it, and the glory of YHWH filled the tabernacle ... The cloud of YHWH was on the tabernacle by day, and fire was in the cloud by night, before the eyes of all the house of Israel at each stage of their journey.[38]

As we find later, at key moments in Israel's subsequent story, the Israelites and the later Jewish people came to regard it as the norm, the desired state, that the strange, dangerous presence of Israel's God would dwell in their midst, first in the tabernacle and then in the Temple in Jerusalem.[39] This, they believed, was how things should be. And if, for comprehensible reasons, that immediate presence had been withdrawn, as it was at the time of the exile and afterwards, resulting in the people's renewed captivity, then to hope for YHWH's return was to hope as well for national restoration, for escape from slavery, for peace and prosperity, for the new exodus. 'The return of YHWH to Zion' was thus closely integrated with all other aspects of the ancient Jewish hope. To put it more strongly still, pointing forward to a key moment in Paul's greatest letter: if someone from this context were to speak of 'the hope of the glory of God', this is the vision they would be invoking. One day the glory, the tabernacling presence of YHWH, would return, and all flesh would see it together.

The theme of YHWH's 'filling' the tabernacle, and later the Temple, was seen by some ancient writers as pointing forward to a greater 'filling' yet, pointing back once more to the story of creation. This already appears in a surprising 'aside' in Numbers, when YHWH is assuring Moses of his forgiveness after the people's rebellion against the idea of going into the promised land:

> Then YHWH said, 'I do forgive; just as you have asked; nevertheless – as I live, and *as all the earth shall be filled with the glory of YHWH* – none of the people who have seen my glory and the signs that I did in Egypt and in the wilderness, and yet have tested me these ten times, and have not obeyed my voice, shall see the land that I swore to give to their ancestors; none of those who despised me shall see it.'[40]

This idea is repeated variously in later texts, often in settings which indicate that this is the implicit larger hope, out beyond the immediate horizon. What YHWH does in the tabernacle or Temple is a sign and foretaste of what

[38] Ex. 40.34–5, 38–9.

[39] Isa. 6; 1 Kgs. 8; etc.

[40] Num. 14.20–3.

he intends to do in and for the whole creation.[41] Sometimes, to be sure, the same idea is expressed with a centripetal rather than a centrifugal motif, with the nations of the world converging upon Jerusalem to worship the God who has taken up residence there once more.[42] Israel's central symbol thus spoke both of the powerful presence of the creator God, returning to live in the midst of his people, and of the promise, as in the Psalms and Isaiah, to renew the whole creation.[43] The complex of 'new-exodus' themes fits together in different patterns, but with the same regular overall content: Israel's God will act to rescue his people, to overthrow their pagan oppressors, to enable them to keep his Torah at last, to fill the whole earth with his glory and to set up his kingdom of justice, peace and prosperity. Not all these themes are found in all texts, of course. No doubt many first-century Jews lived out their lives without much clear sense of what seems to us, their later long-range readers, quite explicit. But there is a family likeness right across the large and diverse range of later biblical texts, second-Temple sources and some at least of the rabbis, which completely justifies the presentation of this overall, if generalized, picture.[44]

Four further themes fill out the picture.

(1) First, in some texts but not all, and in some political movements of the time though not all, the key agent of this whole programme is the coming king, the Messiah.[45] As long as the Jewish people sang the Psalms, they could hardly avoid the classic vision of Psalm 2:

> Why do the nations conspire, and the peoples plot in vain?
> The kings of the earth set themselves, and the rulers take counsel together, against YHWH and his anointed [*meshiho*, 'his messiah'], saying,
> 'Let us burst their bonds asunder, and cast their cords from us.'
> He who sits in the heavens laughs; YHWH has them in derision.
> Then he will speak to them in his wrath, and terrify them in his fury, saying, 'I have set my king on Zion, my holy hill.'
> I will tell of the decree of YHWH: he said to me, 'You are my son; today I have begotten you.
> Ask of me, and I will make the nations your heritage, and the ends of the earth your possession.
> You shall break them with a rod of iron, and dash them in pieces like a potter's vessel.'

[41] 1 Kgs. 8.11; 2 Chr. 5.14; 7.1; Ps. 72.19; Isa. 6.3; Ezek. 10.4; Hab. 2.14; cf. the promise in 2 Macc. 2.8. On the link of Temple and creation see esp. Beale 2004.

[42] Zech. 14.16–19, though the passage also contains elements of warning. On the pilgrimage of the nations (e.g. Isa. 2.2–4 (= Mic. 4.1–4); Isa. 25.6–10; 56.6–8; 66.18–23; Zech. 8.20–3) see esp. Donaldson 1997, 187–97. Note also the symbolic role of the story of the Queen of Sheba coming to Solomon (1 Kgs. 10; 2 Chr. 9: in the latter, 9.23 adds to 1 Kgs. 10.24 the note that 'all the kings of the earth' came to Solomon). A verbal echo of Zech. 8.23 (and Isa. 45.14) may be heard at 1 Cor. 14.25.

[43] cf again Pss. 96; 98; Isa. 55.

[44] One theme, important in the second-Temple period, appears absent in the NT, namely the reassembly of the ten lost tribes: see e.g. Ezek. 37.15–28; Hos. 1.10f.; Zech. 10.6–12. Starling 2011 has explored the possibility that Paul does in fact work with this notion in e.g. Rom. 9.25f. where Hos. 1.10 and 2.23 are cited.

[45] On messianic expectations see *NTPG* 307–20; *JVG* 477–89; and above, 815–36.

> Now therefore, O kings, be wise; be warned, O rulers of the earth.
> Serve YHWH with fear, with trembling kiss his feet, or he will be angry and you will perish in the way; for his wrath is quickly kindled.
> Happy are all who take refuge in him.[46]

The same vision, of YHWH's anointed king ruling the nations of the earth and calling them to account after their arrogant folly, reappears elsewhere. It functions, obviously, as one way of bringing to expression the larger Jewish hope for the creator God to exalt his people, to liberate them from their enemies and to bring his sovereign rule to bear on all the world. Thus, while it seems to be true that by no means all Jews were 'expecting a Messiah', and that those who did hold such a hope conceived and expressed it in different ways, when such expectations existed they formed a sharp point of the national hope, not a separate or detached phenomenon.[47]

(2) When this great liberation came about, with or without a 'Messiah' to lead the way and fight the key battle, this would be the moment when the covenant was renewed. We have studied this in detail in chapter 2 above. Here we simply note that the idea of covenant renewal itself goes back to the Pentateuch, specifically to the closing chapters of Deuteronomy, seen in the first century (at least by Josephus and Philo) as a kind of long-range prophecy both of the devastation of the nation and perhaps of its eventual restoration after judgment.[48] The later prophets who drew on this same theme of covenant renewal, particularly Jeremiah and Ezekiel, did so explicitly in terms of the prophecies of restoration after exile and of the return of YHWH to his people. They stressed, again in line with Deuteronomy, the renewal (or 'circumcision') of the heart which would transform Israel at last into a people who would be able to keep Torah properly. The idea of covenant renewal, we note, is an affirmation both of the goodness of the covenant in the first place and of its inability (not through its own fault but through the hard-heartedness of the people) to make them the people they were called to be.

The covenant, too, supplies the inner meaning, in relation to Israel, of the character of Israel's God. Israel would finally be rescued *because this God kept his promises*: the promises to Abraham, the promises of Exodus and Deuteronomy, the promises of the Psalms, Isaiah and the rest. One of the most obvious ways in which this vision of God as the faithful, covenant-keeping God was expressed was through the repeated, though today often misunderstood, notion of the *tsedaqah elohim*, or in the Septuagint the *dikaiosyne theou*, phrases which are regularly translated into English as 'the

[46] Ps. 2.1–11.

[47] e.g. Ps. 72; Isa. 9.2–7; 11.1–16; 42.1–9; 61.1–11; 63.1–9.

[48] cf. Dt. 30.1–20; 32.36, 43 (in the context of a lengthy and scathing denunciation of the people in their present state). See above, e.g. 117–31.

righteousness of God'.[49] This 'righteousness' formed the backbone of the great prayer in Daniel 9 which both explains why the exile happens and appeals for it to come to an end at last:

> Righteousness is on your side, O YHWH, but open shame, as at this day, falls on us ... To YHWH our God belong mercy and forgiveness, for we have rebelled against him ... So the curse and the oath written in the law of Moses, the servant of God, have been poured out upon us, because we have sinned against you. He has confirmed his words, which he spoke against us and against our rulers, by bringing upon us a calamity so great that what has been done against Jerusalem has never before been done under the whole heaven ... Indeed YHWH our God is right in all that he has done; for we have disobeyed his voice.
>
> And now, O YHWH our God, who brought your people out of the land of Egypt with a mighty hand and made your name renowned even to this day – we have sinned, we have done wickedly. O YHWH, in view of all your righteous acts, let your anger and wrath, we pray, turn away from your city Jerusalem ... We do not present our supplication before you on the ground of our righteousness, but on the ground of your great mercies.[50]

YHWH is 'in the right': *hatsedaqah, hē dikaiosynē,* is on his side, expressing itself equally appropriately in the curse which Deuteronomy foretold[51] and in the mercy and forgiveness which was also promised and which his previous 'righteous acts' (*tsidqotheka, ten dikaiosynēn sou*) had foreshadowed.[52] This points towards the full meaning of the phrase, or its near equivalents, in sundry second-Temple texts, such as the Scrolls or *4 Ezra*. God's *dikaiosynē* is that which is called into question when Israel suffers major disasters (since, as Israel's covenant God, he should have been preventing such things from happening), but the same characteristic can then be evoked as the explanation of the disaster (since the covenant always envisaged penalties for disobedience) as well as the reason why he will in fact be merciful in the end (since the covenant always envisaged mercy on the other side of judgment), even though this mercy may take different forms from those which many Jews had been expecting or wanting.[53] Within situations of great stress and grave disaster, it is precisely the *dikaiosynē theou* that is

[49] Out of the massive secondary discussion of this phrase three points emerge. First, since Paul in his discussion of *dikaiosynē theou* regularly engages with biblical passages (esp. the Psalms and Isaiah) in which it occurs, it makes sense to begin from the meaning of the phrase in those contexts (over against those who argue that Paul is giving it a new meaning without reference to earlier usage). Second, the attempt by Käsemann and his followers to suggest that the phrase denotes 'God's salvation-creating power' as a 'technical term' in ancient Judaism, without reference to the covenant with Israel, fails in its exegesis both of the second-Temple texts to which they appeal and of Paul – though Käsemann is undoubtedly correct to understand the phrase as denoting the righteousness of the creator God himself (and the 'cosmic' dimensions of his responsibility and action) rather than a 'righteousness' which is given, reckoned, imputed or whatever to those who have faith. Third, more positively, the context of books like *4 Ezra*, and the exegesis of passages like Rom. 3.1–9 as well as chs. 4 and especially 9—11, show that Paul's meaning is very closely tied to the idea of the divine faithfulness to the Abrahamic covenant (called in question when disasters happen), even though the events of Messiah and spirit have caused Paul to rethink what that covenant actually meant. For more on this see Käsemann 1969 [1965], ch. 7; Brauch 1977; Williams 1980; Soards 1987; and above, e.g. 480, 801–4, 841, 928, 991, 1003.

[50] Dan. 9.7, 8, 11–12, 14, 15–16, 18.

[51] Dan. 9.11–13 clearly refers to Dt. 27—8.

[52] 9.16. The reading *dikaiosynēn* is that of the LXX; Theodotion has *en pasē eleēmosynē sou.*

[53] On God's righteousness in *4 Ezra* and Rom., see B. W. Longenecker 1990; 1991.

both questioned and evoked. This is a central element in second-Temple Jewish eschatology, perfectly dovetailing with all the other themes we are noting.[54] Though the 'righteous acts' of Israel's God are, in effect, great deeds of saving power, that denotation does not obliterate or ignore the connotation, that these are saving acts *done precisely in fulfilment of the covenant promises*.[55] Had they been miscellaneous 'saving acts' without reference to any long-term promises or commitments, there would have been other ways of referring to them. The mention of *dikaiosynē* indicates that such actions reveal the fact that Israel's God has been faithful to the covenant. Even if we were to flatten out the meaning of the Hebrew and Greek words so that they simply meant that such actions were the 'right' thing for YHWH to do, the reason why rescuing Israel was the 'right' thing for him to do was precisely because he was bound in a special relationship to his people.

(3) When that happens, several strands of expectation envisaged that the nations of the world would perceive it not simply as bad news (being defeated and smashed to pieces) but also as good news. YHWH will be glorified beyond the borders of Israel.[56] Though many texts in the scriptures and subsequent Jewish writings continued to speak of a coming judgment on the nations, some saw a different though parallel vision (parallel in that the fate of the nations still depends upon God's final great act for Israel): when the one God restored the fortunes of his people, the nations would come flocking in pilgrimage towards Zion:

> In days to come the mountain of YHWH's house
> shall be established as the highest of the mountains,
> and shall be raised above the hills;
> all the nations shall stream to it.
> Many peoples shall come and say,
> 'Come, let us go up to the mountain of YHWH,
> to the house of the God of Jacob;
> that he may teach us his ways
> and that we may walk in his paths.'
> For out of Zion shall go forth instruction,
> and the word of YHWH from Jerusalem.
> He shall judge between the nations,
> and shall arbitrate for many peoples;
> they shall beat their swords into ploughshares,
> and their spears into pruning-hooks;
> nation shall not lift up sword against nation,
> neither shall they learn war any more.[57]

[54] e.g. the idea of a 'new exodus': in the original exodus, YHWH remembers his covenant with Abraham, Isaac and Jacob (Ex. 2.24; 6.5), and acts accordingly.

[55] cf. e.g. Pss. 7.9f.; 35.24; 40.10–12; 50.6; 97.6; Isa. 41.10; 51.1, 5f., 7f.; 54.17. This is not infrequently obscured by translations which render *tsedaqah/dikaiosynē* and their cognates with words like 'deliverance' or 'salvation'. The mighty deeds of Israel's God have the *effect* of 'rescuing' his people, but they have the *character* of things done because of covenantal commitment; and it is this character that is connoted by the *tsedaqah/dikaiosynē* root.

[56] Mal. 1.5; 1.14.

[57] Isa. 2.2–4, more or less identical to Mic. 4.1–3; cf. too Jer. 3.17.

This hope is another way of putting the vision of cosmic renewal in Isaiah 11.1–10, and finds further expression in the famous passage in Isaiah 49:

> And now YHWH says . . .
> It is too light a thing that you should be my servant
> to raise up the tribes of Jacob
> and to restore the survivors of Israel;
> I will give you as a light to the nations,
> that my salvation may reach to the ends of the earth.[58]

The same vision, expressed in a variety of ways, continues to haunt the whole book of Isaiah. The 'servant', like the coming Davidic king in chapter 11, will establish justice to the ends of the earth. Foreigners will join themselves to YHWH, so that his house will be a house of prayer for all peoples.[59] When Israel is restored, the nations will come to its light, and kings to the brightness of its dawn.[60] They will bring their treasures to Jerusalem, so that YHWH's house may be filled with splendour.[61]

The theme emerges again in the book of Zechariah:

> Sing and rejoice, O daughter Zion!
> For lo, I will come and dwell in your midst, says YHWH.
> Many nations shall join themselves to YHWH on that day, and shall be my people;
> and I will dwell in your midst.
> And you shall know that YHWH of hosts has sent me to you.[62]

> Thus says YHWH of hosts:
> Peoples shall yet come, the inhabitants of many cities;
> the inhabitants of one city shall go to another, saying,
> 'Come, let us go to entreat the favour of YHWH, and to seek YHWH of hosts;
> I myself am going.'
> Many peoples and strong nations shall come to seek YHWH of hosts in Jerusalem,
> and to entreat the favour of YHWH.
> Thus says YHWH of hosts: In those days ten men from nations of every language
> shall take hold of a Jew, grasping his garment and saying,
> 'Let us go with you,
> for we have heard that God is with you.'[63]

> Then all who survive of the nations that have come against Jerusalem shall go up year by year to worship the King, YHWH of hosts, and to keep the festival of booths. And if any of the families of the earth do not go up to Jerusalem to worship the King, YHWH of hosts, there will be no rain upon them.[64]

These oracles are surrounded by others which envisage a great triumph *over* the nations, and that apparent tension continues across the second-Temple

[58] Isa. 49.5–6. The 'light to the nations' theme flickers briefly in Wis. 18.4b; *T. Lev.* 14.4.

[59] Isa. 56.6–8.

[60] Isa. 42.3–6; 60.3–7; cf. 25.6–10a; 66.18–21.

[61] Hag. 2.7.

[62] Zech. 2.10f.

[63] Zech. 8.20–3.

[64] Zech. 14.16f.

period, just as the Psalms could speak in one breath of the nations of the world being smashed in pieces like a potter's vessel and in the next of all the ends of the earth remembering and returning to YHWH.[65] Thus the great thanksgiving prayer in the book of Tobit branches out from considering how YHWH has treated his own people in their exile and restoration to a vision of the nations streaming in to worship:

> A bright light will shine to all the ends of the earth;
> many nations will come to you from far away,
> the inhabitants of the remotest parts of the earth to your holy name,
> bearing gifts in their hands for the King of heaven.
> Generation after generation will give joyful praise in you;
> the name of the chosen city will endure for ever.[66]

And this is backed up by a solemn promise:

> After this they all will return from their exile and will rebuild Jerusalem in splendour; and in it the temple of God will be rebuilt, just as the prophets of Israel have said concerning it. Then the nations in the whole world will all be converted (*epistrepsousin*) and worship God in truth. They will all abandon their idols, which deceitfully have led them into their error; and in righteousness they will praise the eternal God.[67]

Other texts from roughly the same period show signs of a similar point of view: not necessarily an actual pilgrimage to Zion, but certainly the nations coming to salvation as a by-product of the end-time restoration of Israel.[68] If it is fair to say that this theme is not especially prominent in the literature of Qumran, or the Pseudepigrapha,[69] it is also important to remember that books like Isaiah continued to be treasured and studied, and the Psalms continued to be sung. How Israel's God was going to accomplish all these varied things in relation to the rest of the world was never made clear. That he would eventually do so could not be doubted without doubting monotheism itself. YHWH was the one creator God and it was his eventual responsibility to sort out the whole creation. Since he had promised to come back and live in Jerusalem for ever, it was clear that the nations would have to come there to worship him, whether or not they would have to be dealt with severely first in order to learn the lesson. In one way or another, this

[65] Pss. 2.9; 22.27f.; cf. 66.4; 67.3f.; 68.32; 72.8–11; 86.9; 102.22; 117.1.

[66] Tob. 13.11. There are hints of the same thing in e.g. *1 En.* 10.21; 57.3; 90.33; 91.14; cf. too *4 Ezra* 13.13.

[67] Tob. 14.5–7.

[68] So e.g. Donaldson 1990, 8.

[69] cf. *T. Zeb.* 9.8; *T. Benj.* 9.2; *Sib. Or.* 3.767–95. The vision of *Pss. Sol.* 17.26–46, cited by Moo 1996, 684 as the clearest example of the tradition, seems to me dubious: the nations will indeed 'come from the ends of the earth to see his glory' (17.31), but this is in the context of aliens and foreigners being driven far away (17.28) and of the gentile nations serving under the yoke (17.30), which hardly sounds like the vision of Isa. 2 or Zech. 8; the passage is actually cited by Schweitzer 1968 [1930], 178 as a rejection of 'universalism' and consequently a contradiction of Isaiah and Zechariah. See further Donaldson 1990, 9.

'pilgrimage of the nations to Zion' was a significant, though not highly developed, part of the vision of the future.[70]

(4) One way of speaking about the great coming future was to divide world history into two chronological periods: the 'present age' and the 'age to come', the 'new age'. By the time of the rabbis, the notion of 'two ages' had become well established, and the distinction between 'the present age' and 'the age to come' – the present time when evil seemed to be triumphing, and the future time when it would have been overthrown – was well known.[71] But the distinction goes back well into the second-Temple period, with its roots in the scriptures themselves.[72] It is by no means indicative, as is sometimes said, of a 'dualism', one of the characteristics ascribed to the movement loosely and unhelpfully called 'apocalyptic' or 'apocalypticism'.[73] Indeed the idea of 'two ages', a 'present (evil) age' and the 'age to come', is not at all the prerogative of a single movement within the second-Temple Jewish world. It is simply part of that world as a whole – embraced, no doubt, by some more enthusiastically than others, but expressive of a Jewish way of looking at things, a Jewish way of telling the world's great story, which continued and flourished unabated long after people had stopped writing 'apocalypses'. The distinction of the two ages was almost inevitable, granted the parlous state of Israel on the one hand and the spectacular biblical promises on the other. The only alternative (which was of course embraced by some in due course) was some kind of gnosticism: if there was no future within the present world of space, time and matter, perhaps the answer was to escape into a different sphere altogether. It is important to note, then, that the distinction between the 'present age' and the 'age to come' was a way of *not* capitulating to that ontological 'dualism'. It was a way of affirming the goodness of the created world and the belief that its creator would eventually liberate it from its present condition. Somehow, the present time could not be 'all there was'. Israel's God was committed to doing something new. And this new 'age', *aiōn* in Greek, would mean new

[70] On this tradition see esp. Donaldson 1990, and older works referred to there; e.g. Schoeps 1961 [1959], 219–29.

[71] Classic expression of this point is found in *4 Ezra* 7.50: 'The Most High has made not one age but two'; cf. too e.g. *1 En.* 71.15; *2 Bar.* 14.13; mAb. 4.1; mSanh. 10.1; bBer. 9.5. Copious other refs. are listed in e.g. de Boer 2011, 30f. For discussion cf. *NTPG* 252–4; 299f.; with Moore 1927, 1.270f.; Schürer 1973—1987, 2.495. Sanders 1992, ch. 14 offers a good overall picture though with occasional strange lacunae.

[72] See *NTPG* 299f. We might cite passages such as Isa. 2.2–5.

[73] cf. *NTPG* 252–5, where I distinguish ten different things sometimes called 'dualism'. As I say at 253, 'virtually all second-Temple Jews, with the possible exception only of the aristocracy, believed that they were living in a "present age" which was a time of sorrow and exile, and which would be succeeded by an "age to come" in which wrongs would be righted and Israel's god would set up his kingdom'.

life: hence the phrase *zōē aiōnios*, 'the life of the age [to come]', frequently and unhelpfully translated 'eternal life'.[74]

(4) The fourth and final element – which caused considerable surprise and alarm in some Jewish circles – was resurrection. Here too I have set out the material elsewhere.[75] The point to note for our present purposes is that 'resurrection' was not an isolated or speculative promise, bolted on to the outside of other second-Temple Jewish expectations. Like the rest, it was rooted deep within the ancient scriptures, in their twin notions of YHWH as creator and as judge. If he was to set the world right at last, it would not do for him, as creator, to obliterate it, or to decide after all that the created order of space, time and matter was a bad thing, rather than (as in Genesis 1) a good thing. There were earlier hints and guesses which could be taken, and were sometimes taken later on, to point to a renewed bodily life the other side of a period of being bodily dead. These hints and guesses came to life particularly in the book of Daniel and then, spectacularly, in 2 Maccabees, which grew out of and helped to sustain the vision of most Jews, certainly all Pharisaic Jews, in the time of Saul of Tarsus.

These four themes thus flesh out the vision of YHWH's return and the establishment of his kingdom, the vision (that is) which we may securely suppose to have been held by a devout and zealous Pharisee such as Saul of Tarsus. The Jewish hope was not a collection of miscellaneous motifs strung together with the string of political expediency – though of course political hope, or even ambition, regularly fuelled its expression. It formed a more or less coherent whole, expressing and embodying the two basic beliefs (monotheism and election) that we have already studied. It highlighted the notion of victory: YHWH's victory over all enemies, from Egypt to Babylon and beyond; the Messiah's victory over the nations and their rulers; the creator's victory over chaos and injustice within the whole creation. It was energized by the notion of faithfulness: YHWH had promised to do this, and do it he would. But it foregrounded particularly the notion of *presence*: YHWH would return to live in the midst of his people. This would be the ultimate vindication of Israel as YHWH's people, but behind that it would be the vindication of monotheism itself:

> They will call on my name, and I will answer them. I will say, 'They are my people'; and they will say, 'YHWH is our God.' . . .

[74] This phrase first makes its appearance in Dan. 12.2, i.e. in a context of a two-age scheme with resurrection hope as the content of the 'age to come'. Within second-Temple Judaism cf. e.g. *Ps. Sol.* 3.12; 13.1; Wis. 5.15 (in the context of the future 'kingdom of God'); 2 Macc. 7.9, where the first of the martyrs claims that his God will raise him up to 'an everlasting renewal of life' (*eis aiōnion anabiōsin zōēs*), which in context clearly means resurrection (cf. 7.14, 23, 29, on which see *RSG* 150–3); *4 Macc.* 15.3; cf. 1QS 4.7. On 'eternal life' in the Johannine writings cf. *RSG* 441, 463f. Cranfield 1975, 147 is remarkably vague, calling *zōē aiōnios* simply 'a comprehensive term for final blessedness'. Dunn 1988a, 85 is in my view misleading, translating the phrase 'life without end' and saying that this 'would be readily comprehensible to Greeks', implying that it was playing into a Platonic vision of life after death rather than the very specifically Jewish two-age doctrine.

[75] *RSG*, esp. chs. 3, 4. It is remarkable that Sanders (1992, 298–303) does not integrate 'resurrection' into his very this-worldly picture of Jewish eschatology.

And YHWH will become king over all the earth; on that day YHWH will be one and his name one.[76]

This hope was *expressed* in a wide variety of ways: in psalms, in visions, in political movements which promised to create the conditions for it to happen, and in narrative which, like the Pentateuch itself, was read both as history and as prophecy. It was *expected* both as the long-awaited fulfilment of promises and as a new thing: one of the most regular prophetic promises is that when YHWH acts to do what he had always intended to do this will take everyone, Israel included, by surprise. It was *experienced* in fits and starts: some at least of those who lived through the Maccabaean revolt really did believe the ancient prophecies were at last being fulfilled, and the Qumran sect would not have existed were it not for the belief that the promises had been fulfilled in advance, albeit secretly, in their community, and would be fulfilled more completely in the coming days.[77] Expressed, expected and experienced (you can take the scholar out of the pulpit but you can't take the pulpit out of the scholar): the ancient hope of Israel came to fresh and coherent life not only in texts but also in movements, in prayer, in faithfulness, in zeal. This is the hope which fired Saul of Tarsus in his own life of Torah-devotion. And in his zealous persecution of the early church.

Our task now is relatively straightforward. I shall argue that Paul, with this complete and striking Jewish hope in his head and his heart, believed both that it *had already* been fulfilled in Jesus and the spirit, and that it *was yet to be* more completely fulfilled. The 'now and not yet' shape of all this is obvious, and often pointed out.[78] What is not so often noticed is that both the 'now' and the 'not yet' embody very closely the christological and pneumatological revision of the central and enlivening hope of second-Temple Judaism, and indeed of the ancient scriptures of Israel themselves.

3. Hope Realized and Redefined

(i) Through Jesus

The obvious and easy starting-point for understanding Paul's reimagining of Jewish eschatology is the place we reached a moment ago. Nobody had been expecting 'the resurrection' to happen to one person in the middle of ongoing history. Those who expected 'resurrection' expected it to happen to everybody, or at least to all the faithful, at the end of history when the new age dawned and the divine justice and mercy flooded Israel and the world.

[76] Zech. 13.9; 14.9.

[77] See e.g. 1 Macc. 14.4–15. On Qumran's eschatology cf. *NTPG* 203–9; *RSG* 181–9.

[78] cf. e.g. Aune 1992, 602f. Aune is right to say that a major difference between Paul and his Jewish context is that for him the age to come has already in some sense arrived in the present, but I do not think this results in the distinction being 'softened or blurred', as he suggests. The distinction between the two ages remains clear.

The point has often been made, but needs to be stated again, because it is the foundation of everything that Paul the apostle came to believe: if Jesus of Nazareth had been raised from the dead, then it meant either that the whole cosmos had gone completely mad or that 'the resurrection' had come forward into the present, in just this one case, with Jesus leading the way and everyone else following in due course.

Again, by itself this might not have made much sense. Why Jesus? one might ask; and why would his resurrection mean that others would follow? Here we encounter one of the other key implications of Easter: if Jesus had been crucified as a messianic pretender, but had been vindicated by being raised from the dead (which could only be the work of the creator God), then he was, after all, Israel's Messiah.[79] And that, as we have already seen, compelled a fresh evaluation of more or less everything else. *Israel's hope had been realized; Israel's hope had been redefined.* 'Look! The right time is now! Look! The day of salvation is here!' Paul casts himself as the latter-day prophet, announcing that Isaiah's ancient vision has come true at last.[80]

That Paul was thinking in exactly these ways – resurrection dividing into two, resurrection meaning that Jesus really was the Messiah – is clear from two seminal passages. We have already studied these in connection with our earlier discussion of Jesus' Messiahship itself, but it is important to look at them again from this angle. Taking the latter point first:

> ... God's good news, which he promised beforehand through his prophets in the sacred writings – the good news about his son, who was descended from David's seed in terms of flesh, and who was marked out powerfully as God's son in terms of the spirit of holiness by the resurrection of the dead: Jesus, the king, our lord![81]

Here, introducing his greatest letter, Paul highlights right at the start the universal early Christian conviction: the resurrection was the public divine declaration that Jesus was indeed Israel's Messiah, and hence the world's true lord. We note, too, the mention of the spirit, seen by Paul as the active agent in giving life both to Jesus' dead body and, at the end, to the bodies of believers.[82] And, as the letter unwinds, the notion of the messianic 'son', the one who (in line with Psalm 2) will have the nations for his 'inheritance',

[79] See *RSG* 554–63. Perhaps, indeed, it was this – God doing for Jesus what Paul had expected him to do for Israel – which compelled Paul towards that tight nexus of Messiah-and-Israel which was such a feature of his theology (see above, 815–36).

[80] 2 Cor. 6.2, referring back to Isa. 49.8; see the discussion above, 874–85. On Paul's strongly eschatological use of 'now', see above, 550–62. The 'now' is not the 'now' simply of a smooth chronological progression, steadily reaching its climax as a clock hand reaches midnight. It is the surprising 'now' when the phone rings at three in the morning with news of a new grandchild. We knew she was coming at some point, but were not expecting her just then.

[81] Rom. 1.1–4. 'God's son' is of course messianic, alluding to Ps. 2.7 and similar passages such as 2 Sam. 7.12–14, where a hint of resurrection ('I will raise up your seed') goes with the promise of sonship. Attempts to marginalize this passage on stylistic or linguistic grounds, or to suggest that it embodied a traditional formula which Paul was quoting merely to fit in with expectations rather than to express his own conviction, fails because of the tight thematic links between these verses and several key elements in the letter, not least its theological conclusion, 15.12. See above, 815–36.

[82] Rom. 8.11.

sharing his status with all his people, comes to full expression in the central climax of 8.18–30.

Jesus' Messiahship is also central to the classic passage in which Paul explains the other foundational point, that the notion of 'resurrection' has itself now split into two:

> But in fact the Messiah has been raised from the dead, as the first fruits of those who have fallen asleep. For since it was through a human that death arrived, it's through a human that the resurrection from the dead has arrived. All die in Adam, you see, and all will be made alive in the Messiah.
>
> Each, however, in proper order. The Messiah rises as the first fruits; then those who belong to the Messiah will rise at the time of his royal arrival. Then comes the end, the goal, when he hands over the kingly rule to God the father, when he has destroyed all rule and all authority and power. He has to go on ruling, you see, until 'he has put all his enemies under his feet'. Death is the last enemy to be destroyed, because 'he has put all things in order under his feet'. But when it says that everything is put in order under him, it's obvious that this doesn't include the one who put everything in order under him. No: when everything is put in order under him, then the son himself will be placed in proper order under the one who placed everything in order under him, so that God may be all in all.[83]

This passage displays a great deal of Paul's reimagined Jewish eschatology, not simply these opening points about the temporal division of 'resurrection' and about the link between the Messiah and his people through the harvesting metaphor of the 'first fruits'. It is also the classic passage for Paul's vision of 'the kingdom of God', which, like resurrection, has itself split into two. The Messiah's own temporary kingdom is already inaugurated, while the final 'kingdom of God', when God is 'all in all', is still to come. It is, however, guaranteed by the victory which the Messiah has already won.[84]

Within that context, we find two further important themes: the scripture-based victorious rule of the Messiah in the present time, and his 'royal arrival' (*parousia*) in the future. We shall say more about the *parousia* in a moment. But the fact that Paul sees Jesus *as already ruling the world*, after the manner of a king who is now consolidating an initial victory over rebel subjects, indicates clearly what has happened. This is the ancient Jewish vision of world sovereignty, such as we find in Daniel 7.[85] It is focused, as in the Psalms, on the Messiah himself:

> To him was given dominion and glory and kingship, that all people, nations and languages should serve him. His dominion is an everlasting dominion that shall not pass away, and his kingship is one that shall never be destroyed ... The holy ones of the Most High shall receive the kingdom and possess the kingdom for ever ... Then judgment was given for

[83] 1 Cor. 15.20–8. The theme of a *messianic* kingdom which expresses and anticipates the ultimate *divine* kingdom has deep Jewish roots, as we can see in e.g. Schechter 1961 [1909], ch. 7, esp. 103.

[84] 'Kingdom of God' is comparatively rare in Paul; but when the phrase occurs it is clearly a concept he can take for granted. See Rom. 14.17; 1 Cor. 4.20; 6.9f.; 15.24, 50; Gal. 5.21; Eph. 5.5 (where he speaks of 'the kingdom of the Messiah and of God'); Col. 1.13; 4.11; 2 Thess. 1.5. Cp. the 'royal' language at e.g. Rom. 5.17, 21; 6.12–23; 1 Cor. 4.8; 15.23–8. In the Pastorals cf. 1 Tim. 1.17; 6.15; 2 Tim. 4.1, 18.

[85] See above, 114–21.

> the holy ones of the Most High, and the time arrived when the holy ones gained possession of the kingdom ... The kingship and dominion and the greatness of the kingdoms under the whole heaven shall be given to the people of the holy ones of the Most High; their kingdom shall be an everlasting kingdom, and all dominions shall serve and obey them.[86]

> I will tell of the decree of YHWH: he said to me, 'You are my son; today I have begotten you. Ask of me, and I will make the nations your heritage, and the ends of the earth your possession. You shall break them with a rod of iron, and dash them in pieces like a potter's vessel.'[87]

> May he have dominion from sea to sea, and from the River to the ends of the earth. May his foes bow down before him, and his enemies lick the dust.[88]

These are the themes in the background of 1 Corinthians 15.20–8, joining the dots to complete Paul's scripture-based picture. In the foreground are two more quotations from the Psalms, the one linked to the rule of the 'son of man' and the other to the victory of the Messiah:

> YHWH says to my Lord, 'Sit at my right hand until I make your enemies your footstool ... YHWH is at your right hand; he will shatter kings on the day of his wrath. He will execute judgment among the nations, filling them with corpses; he will shatter heads over the wide earth.

> What is a human being, that you are mindful of him? The son of man that you care for him? You have made him a little lower than God, and crowned him with glory and honour. You have given him dominion over the works of your hands; you have put all things under his feet.[89]

The passage in 1 Corinthians thus gives every indication that Paul had combined these great biblical themes: Adam, creation and the dominion of humans over the animals; the Messiah, his victory over the nations and his continuing rule until all are subject to him; the hope of resurrection set before all the people of God. We can already see that Paul is lining up Jesus, as Messiah, with Adam (verses 22, 45–9), and it is abundantly clear here and elsewhere, as we said before, that Paul sees the resurrection as constituting Jesus as Messiah. What this passage reveals further, albeit densely, is the intimate connection between those two (Adam and Messiah) in Paul's mind. Whether or not we can conclude that he read Daniel 7 itself messianically, and was deliberately echoing it in this passage, is another

[86] Dan. 7.14, 18, 22, 27. This is of course the famous 'son of man' vision, drawing on the ancient theme of the human one set in authority over the animals. Through the fresh readings of Dan. 7 which we find in the second-Temple period we can watch the way in which the symbolism of the original vision (where 'one like a son of man' functions as the literary symbol for 'the holy ones of the Most High') turns into the belief (as e.g. in *4 Ezra* 11—12) that the coming Messiah will represent Israel as a whole.

[87] Ps. 2.7–9.

[88] Ps. 72.8–9.

[89] Ps. 110.1, 5–6 (v. 1 quoted in 1 Cor. 15.25); 8.4–6 (quoted in 15.27). In the NRSV the latter passage is made inclusive by being put in the plural; in the Heb. and Gk., and for Paul, it is in the singular as here, and since Paul clearly took the masculine singular in this case as a reference to Jesus it is best to leave that explicit. Note the combination of echoes of Pss. 2 and 8 at Rom. 8.17–21.

matter, but in the light of this convergence of themes I think it highly probable.[90] Josephus gives clear evidence that many Jews in the middle of the first century looked to Daniel as predicting that 'at that time a world ruler would arise from Judaea'. Josephus says, with what sincerity may be debated, that this was in fact a prophecy about Vespasian.[91] Paul, beyond any doubt, fully and thoroughly believes that it was a prophecy about Jesus, a prophecy now already fulfilled. This vision of Jesus, already ruling the world, is near the heart of Paul's inaugurated eschatology, his drastic revision of the Jewish hope.[92]

It was not, of course, the kind of 'rule' that many had imagined. The bracketing out of political readings of Paul (resulting, for instance, in people insisting that Paul avoided the idea of Jesus' Messiahship, despite regularly calling him *Christos* and evoking scriptural promises about the Messiah to expound the significance of his achievements) has sidelined the question which ought to arise at this point.[93] The newer 'political' readings of Paul, in their eagerness to have the apostle speak to the present day, do not always get the answer right, either. Here and in several other passages Paul declares loud and clear that Jesus is already the world's true lord and king; that he is already reigning. What did he mean?

Paul knew as well as we do that this claim seemed absurd. Not only did he believe that a once thoroughly dead man was now thoroughly and bodily alive again, but he believed that this same man was already in charge of the world, despite the fact that murder and mayhem continued and that he, Paul, a key representative of this dead-but-now-alive man, was suffering imprisonment and persecution! The claims for Jesus' sovereignty are made, though, right across the Pauline letters, and we cannot wish them away as a slip of the pen. The only possible conclusion is that for Paul the 'rule' of Jesus was something very different from the picture in either Psalm 2 (bruising people with a rod of iron) or Psalm 110 (shattering kings and breaking heads). But here, as often, the difference between prophecy and fulfilment is not to be located where much western exposition has imagined, namely at the axis between 'politics' and 'piety', with the 'rule' taking place, safely and conveniently, only in the hearts of believers and/or in a distant 'heaven'. That is the highway to gnosticism, and was indeed one reason why many would later take that road. Politically speaking, it was convenient and quite safe.[94] When Paul said that Jesus was now in charge, he meant something much more dangerous and subversive. He meant, in some sense or other, that Caesar was not the world's ultimate ruler. That qualification, 'in

[90] The same probability emerges through Paul's use of the 'stone' imagery in relation to Jesus and his installation as Messiah/world ruler. This draws obviously on Ps. 118.22 (cf. too Mk. 12.10 par.; Ac. 4.11; 1 Pet. 2.7) and Isa. 8.14; 28.16 (quoted in Rom. 9.33); but it also resonates closely with Dan. 2.34–5, 44–5, which itself anticipates the climax of Dan. 7. See *NTPG* 291–7.

[91] Jos. *War* 6.312–14 (and cf. 3.399–408); cf. *NTPG* 304, 312–4; and above, 116f., 130f., 142f.

[92] cf. above, 142–8 for discussion of the close links in the second-Temple period between a Daniel-based hope and the understanding of covenant renewal as in Dt. 30.

[93] See above, e.g. 817–25.

[94] See Wright 2006b [*Judas*], ch. 5.

some sense or other', should not be allowed to blunt the edge of Paul's belief.

The same point emerges in Acts. Luke does not attempt to rebut the charge levelled against the apostle in Thessalonica: Paul was saying that there was 'another king, Jesus!'.[95] When Paul goes on to Athens and defends himself against serious accusations, he navigates the choppy and dangerous waters of rival theologies, but comes back to the same message of an inaugurated kingdom:

> Now, instead, [God] commands all people everywhere to repent, because he has established a day on which he intends to call the world to account with full and proper justice by a man whom he has appointed. God has given all people his pledge of this by raising this man from the dead.[96]

A strong case can be made for saying that whenever Paul refers to Jesus as *kyrios* – from Romans 1.5 onwards! – it is this that he has in mind: the sovereign rule of the Messiah, inaugurated already, fulfilling the prophecies in which the world would at last be brought to book by the true human in charge of the 'animals', by the Messiah in charge of the nations. Certainly the concept of the messianic 'inheritance', in the sense of Jesus' sovereignty over the whole world, is assumed by Paul to be central, as in Romans 8.17–25, in which the 'now and not yet' consists of Jesus already ruling the world and his people promised their share in that saving, liberating regime – even though at the moment their participation in it seems to consist mostly of mysterious groanings and inarticulate prayers.[97] The kingship of Jesus is already, for Paul, a present reality. He is 'at the right hand of God', as in Psalm 110.[98]

The biblical resonances of this language ought to indicate well enough that Paul has in mind the ancient Jewish overlap of heaven and earth, so that when he speaks of the exaltation or ascension of Jesus he is not talking about primitive space travel but about Jesus now being installed at the place of executive power in the cosmos. Thus, in Ephesians, we find the same combination of themes as in 1 Corinthians 15:

> This was the power at work in the king when God raised him from the dead and sat him at his right hand in the heavenly places, above all rule and authority and power and lordship, and above every name that is invoked, both in the present age and also in the age to come. Yes: God has 'put all things under his feet', and has given him to the church as the head over all.[99]

And in Philippians the point is equally clear:

[95] Ac. 17.7.

[96] Ac. 17.30–1. For a fresh interpretation of the whole speech, opening new possibilities for reading it as a genuine summary of Paul's message, see Rowe 2011.

[97] 8.23, 26–7.

[98] Rom. 8.34.

[99] Eph. 1.20–2.

> That now at the name of Jesus
> every knee within heaven shall bow –
> on earth, too, and under the earth;
>
> And every tongue shall confess
> that Jesus, Messiah, is lord,
> to the glory of God, the father.
>
> ... We are citizens of heaven, you see, and we're eagerly waiting for the saviour, the lord, King Jesus, who is going to come from there. Our present body is a shabby old thing, but he's going to transform it so that it's just like his glorious body. And he's going to do this by the power which makes him able to bring everything into line under his authority.[100]

This in turn points to the full statement, in Colossians, of Jesus' world sovereignty:

> ... For in him all things were created,
> in the heavens and here on the earth.
> Things we can see and things we cannot,
> – thrones and lordships and rulers and powers –
> all things were created both through him and for him.
>
> And he is ahead, prior to all else
> and in him all things hold together;
> and he himself is supreme, the head
> over the body, the church.
>
> He is the start of it all,
> firstborn from realms of the dead;
> so that in all things he might be the chief ...[101]

As I have argued elsewhere, the spectacular poem of which this forms a part represents a subtle and dense reworking of Jewish wisdom-themes. These are themselves closely linked in the tradition with royal expectations, based on the memory of Solomon as (a) the ultimately wise man, (b) the peaceful ruler of David's extensive kingdom and (c) the one to whom the kings of the earth would bring gifts. They are also linked with the promise of the vindication of the righteous and the overthrow of tyrannical and enslaving rulers, and with the theme of creation itself and the place of humans within it. The Wisdom of Solomon is of course another place where these themes all come together. Whether or not Paul was consciously echoing that book, he certainly shares the same heritage.

It is in Colossians, too, that we find one of the clearest statements of the victory which has already been won, bringing to inauguration that crucial element of Jewish eschatology. In a breathtaking shift of perspective, Paul declares that God

[100] Phil. 2.10–11; 3.20–1.

[101] Col. 1.16–18. On the poem see Wright 1991 [*Climax*], ch. 5.

> stripped the rulers and authorities of their armour, and displayed them contemptuously to public view, celebrating his triumph over them in him.[102]

This seems to be cognate with the cryptic line in 1 Corinthians, where Paul says that 'the rulers of the present age' didn't know about God's secret, hidden wisdom. 'If they had, you see', he writes, 'they wouldn't have crucified the lord of glory.'[103] Assuming that by 'the rulers of the present age' Paul means Caiaphas, Pilate and the power-systems which they represented, what this seems to indicate is that when these 'rulers' crucified Jesus they were, in fact, signing their own death warrant. Here, in line once more with Jewish eschatological expectations, we find Paul alluding to the distinction between 'the present age' and 'the age to come'. The 'present age' is ruled over precisely by people like Caiaphas and Pilate, while the age to come is ruled over by ... Jesus. The two 'empires' stand, for the moment, side by side: just as in Galatians 1.4 (see below), so in Colossians 1.13 he declares that God 'has delivered us from the power of darkness, and transferred us into the kingdom of his beloved son'.[104]

How has this happened? Paul is under no doubt. It is through the cross, always remembering that it is the cross of the one who was then raised; without the resurrection, the cross would simply be a defeat, and the powers of the world would still be in charge. The cross is the victory through which the powers of the old age are brought low, enabling the new age to be ushered in at last. Here, once again, we see what was foundational for Paul: *that which Jewish eschatology looked for in the future*, the overthrow of the enslaving evil powers and the establishment of YHWH's reign instead, *had truly been inaugurated in and through the messianic events of Jesus' death and resurrection.* As a result, the 'rulers of the present age' are now 'being done away with'.[105] Their power is at an end, and they unwittingly brought that result upon themselves by crucifying the one who always was 'the lord of glory' and who is now revealed as such through his resurrection. The fact that Paul can drop this reference into an argument which is basically about something else (though of course in the end all these things join up) indicates well enough how solidly established it was in his mind.

Referring to the cross, even implicitly, as God's victory over the rulers of the present age, and hence as inaugurating the 'age to come', takes us across to another key mention of this same inaugurated-eschatological version of the 'two ages' theme: Galatians 1.4. Here, in the highly significant introduction to his most polemical letter, Paul announces that when Jesus died on the cross he

> gave himself for our sins, to rescue us from the present evil age, according to the will of God our father, to whom be glory to the ages of ages, Amen.

[102] Col. 2.15.

[103] 1 Cor. 2.8.

[104] Col. 1.13; the next verse amplifies that in terms of 'redemption, the forgiveness of sins', exactly as in Gal. 1.4 ('who gave himself for our sins, to rescue us from the present evil age').

[105] 1 Cor. 2.6.

Here, again in line with the Jewish notion we mentioned above, Paul designates 'the present age' as basically 'evil'. We should not make the mistake of supposing he was a dualist at heart. The 'evil' of the present age, in Jewish thought, consists not in the present world being a dark, wicked place from which we should try to escape, but in the intrusion into, and infection of, God's good creation with the power of evil.[106] The idea of the Messiah 'giving himself for our sins' is every bit as central for Paul himself as the 'rescue from the present evil age', as is clear from the repetition of the idea of the Messiah 'giving himself for me' in the climactic and decisive 2.20.[107] The two go together, as always in Paul, with the first enabling the second: it is because, on the cross, sins have been dealt with that the power of the 'present evil age' is broken. But once again the point is clear. *The 'age to come' has now been inaugurated*, with Jesus as its agent and leader.[108] This means that 'the life of the age [to come]', *zōē aiōnios*, is now the ultimate future state, that is, resurrection within the renewed creation – but one which is *already assured* for those who are 'in the Messiah'.[109] With this language, too, Paul is locating himself firmly within second-Temple apocalyptic eschatology, and declaring that 'the age to come' has already arrived in Jesus and is therefore secured for all his people.

If all this is so, we should expect to find that the new exodus *has taken* place and *is taking* place. This, too, is right there in the middle of Paul's thought. Exodus language comes naturally to him as he reflects on what God has done through the Messiah, in the passage we glanced at a moment ago:

> He has delivered us from the power of darkness, and transferred us into the kingdom of his beloved son. He is the one in whom we have redemption, the forgiveness of sins.[110]

[106] On 'dualism' see *NTPG* 252–6. Gal. 1.4 is a key text in the construction of Martyn 1997a, on which see below.

[107] Against Martyn 1997a, 95–7, who sees 'gave himself for our sins' in Gal. 1.4a as a concession to the traditions which the Galatian 'teachers' propounded and which Paul himself wished, if not to deny, then at least to place in a different light.

[108] Elsewhere in Paul: Rom. 12.2 ('don't let yourselves be squeezed into the shape dictated by the present age'); 1 Cor. 1.20 ('where is the debater of this present age?'); 3.18 ('if anyone . . . supposes they are wise in the present age, let them become foolish . . .'); 2 Cor. 4.4 ('the god of this world has blinded the minds of unbelievers'). The other passages where Paul seems to call the present age 'evil' is Eph. 6.13 ('this dark age'); cf. 'these are wicked times we live in' (literally 'the days are evil') in 5.16. The contrast of 'the present time' and that which is to come is also evident in Rom. 8.18; 1 Cor. 2.6, 8; 7.26; Eph. 2.2. This is clearly among Paul's fundamental beliefs. It is remarkable to find Schnelle 2005 [2003], 580 suggesting that Paul takes over this Jewish idea 'only partially and in a broken form'. I would say that he takes it over completely and in a christologically fulfilled form.

[109] cf. Rom. 2.7; 5.21; 6.22, 23; Gal. 6.8. The wider context in Rom. leaves no doubt that Paul, like Dan. or 2 Macc. (see *RSG* 109–15, 150–3), is thinking of resurrection within the new creation as the content of this 'life'. The difference between Paul and John at this point is that in John (e.g. 3.15f., 36, etc.) 'the life of the age [to come]' is emphatically an 'already'; Paul obviously agrees with an 'already' status but uses *zōē aiōnios* primarily to look forward. Closer to Paul are e.g. Mk. 10.17, 30; Ac. 13.46, 48.

[110] Col. 1.13f. 'Redemption' (*apolytrōsis*) regularly refers to what God accomplished in the slave-freeing act of the exodus (above, 845).

More particularly, the exodus forms the main backdrop for one of Paul's most decisive statements of God's action in the Messiah:

> When we were children, we were kept in 'slavery' under the 'elements of the world'. But when the fullness of time arrived, God sent out his son, born of a woman, born under the law, so that he might redeem those under the law, so that we might receive adoption as sons.
>
> And, because you are sons, God sent out the spirit of his son into our hearts, calling out 'Abba, father!' So you are no longer a slave, but a son! And, if you're a son, you are an heir, through God.[111]

The 'new-exodus' language is clear: from slavery to sonship, by means of God's 'redemption', resulting in this people being the 'heir' of the 'inheritance'.[112] Paul develops this more fully in Romans 6—8, where the narrative of the exodus stands, arguably, behind the entire exposition. In Romans 6, those who are 'in the Messiah' are brought from slavery to freedom; in Romans 7, the story takes us to Mount Sinai; then in Romans 8, with echoes of the Galatians passage, the Messiah's people are 'led', not by the cloud and fire, but by the spirit, and, assured of that 'sonship' which is itself an exodus-blessing, they are on the way to the 'inheritance'.[113]

This is the larger context which enables us to understand Paul's more incidental references to the same point, such as his exhortation in 1 Corinthians 10. The original exodus events happened as 'patterns' for us, Paul declares, to warn us in our own pilgrimage in case we make the same mistakes as they did. They were 'baptized into Moses', and they all 'ate the same spiritual food and drank the same spiritual drink'.[114] In other words, the baptism and eucharist which mark out the church are exodus derivatives, as one might expect granted Paul's other language about them.[115] They have launched the Messiah's people on their own exodus journey, and

> these things happened to them as a pattern, and they were written for our instruction, since it's upon us that the ends of the ages have now come.[116]

In other words, being the people of the new exodus goes very closely with being the people of the 'age to come' which has already been inaugurated in the Messiah.[117] At every point the conclusion is the same: that which the Jews had expected has been fulfilled, though in a highly surprising way, by the God whose purpose was implemented in the Messiah.

As with everything else in Paul's thought, all this leads by one route or another to the achievement of Israel's God in and through the Messiah's cross. This, too, is a vital and central element in Paul's inaugurated

[111] Gal. 4.3–7.

[112] For 'sonship' in this context cf. Ex. 4.22. On the 'exodus' motif here see above, 656–8.

[113] See *Perspectives* ch. 11; and Wright 2002 [*Romans*], 510–12.

[114] 1 Cor. 10.2f.

[115] The Messiah is seen as the Passover lamb in 1 Cor. 5.7; and see above.

[116] 1 Cor. 10.11.

[117] On 'ends of ages' see above, 552.

eschatology. Not all his statements of the achievement of the cross fit snugly within a 'new-exodus' theme, but some (including those just mentioned) clearly do, and the others draw on related biblical passages such as Isaiah 40—55. The danger, in western theology at least, has been that what is usually called 'atonement' is seen in a dehistoricized fashion, as though the cross functioned simply as the peculiar historical outworking of an essentially abstract or 'spiritual' transaction. But if we keep second-Temple Judaism in mind, the reality of what Paul means by 'redemption' was that Israel's God had acted decisively within history to deal with evil in general and the sin of his people in particular, meaning that with this blockage out of the way the new creation could be set in motion, starting with the resurrection of Jesus and continuing to its completion in the renewal of all things. In the end, the one God would be 'all in all'. The cross, then, is not simply part of the definition of God (chapter 9, above) or the key fulcrum around which the purpose of God in election is accomplished (chapter 10, above). It is also at the heart of Paul's inaugurated eschatology.

All this meant, for Paul, that the one God had now acted out his faithfulness to the covenant. He had kept his promises, specifically the promise to Abraham and the many other promises which flowed from that. In the light of our exposition of Paul's narrative world in chapter 7, we do not need to labour the point that to speak of the divine covenant faithfulness is not to suggest that, for Paul, the covenant with *Moses* is as it were to be ratified as it stands. As we saw in the previous chapter, the relationship of gospel to law – specifically, the Mosaic law – is far more complex. We concentrate here, rather, on the *inaugurated eschatology* in which what Israel expected – that the one God would act out of faithfulness to the covenant, passing judgment on the wickedness of the world, rescuing his people from that wickedness and its consequences, and establishing his justice and mercy in the whole world – had been fulfilled in and through the Messiah. The questions that rang through Jewish minds from Daniel to *4 Ezra* and beyond – questions about how the covenant God would fulfil his promises, how he would make the new exodus happen, how he would bring the exile to an end at last and (in the case of *4 Ezra* and *2 Baruch*) what on earth he was doing in the recent shocking events – these were all questions about the *tsedaqah elohim*, the *dikaiosynē theou*, the 'righteousness of God'.

The fact that this English phrase does not instantly suggest those meanings to most readers today leaves us in a quandary to which there is no obvious right answer, and we must do the best we can. I have suggested 'God's covenant justice' in some passages, and 'God's covenant faithfulness' in others. The point, as the whole of Romans 4 and then Romans 9—11 insists, is that God has done, in the events concerning Jesus the Messiah, what he always *intended* to do, and what he always *promised* to do, even though nobody prior to Jesus, certainly not Saul of Tarsus, had thought it would work out like this. That is the dialectic between those uncomfortable categories, 'salvation history' and 'apocalyptic': God always said he would act shockingly and unexpectedly, and that is precisely what he has done. The gospel of Jesus the Messiah, and his faithful obedience to death, was the unveiling in action of God's faithful covenant justice – but it was 'to the Jew first and also, equally, to the Greek', with Jews equally under judgment.[118] When the gospel was announced, Paul believed, it unveiled this covenant justice again and again.[119] Paul can refer to the whole Messiah-event as 'God's covenant faithfulness', precisely because in Jesus and the spirit the promises God made, not only to Abraham but also in Deuteronomy 30, have been and are being fulfilled.[120]

Ultimately, as we have insisted throughout, the reason the covenant was there in the first place was to address and solve the problem which the creator had faced from the time of Genesis 3. How was his purpose for the whole creation now to be fulfilled? The call of Abraham, and the promises that were made to him, were specifically designed not just *for* Abraham and his family but for the larger purposes that the creator God intended to accomplish *through* Abraham and his family. Clearly, the redemption of human beings – their rescue from the guilt and grip of evil, and their fresh embodiment in the ultimate resurrection – is at the centre of this. But, as those redemptive passages themselves make clear, the point of rescuing human beings, like the point of calling Abraham in the first place, was not for their own sake, but in order, through them, to rescue the world. Inaugurated eschatology ought therefore to result in *new creation*, not yet of course complete, but at least decisively launched.

That, too, is what we find. 'If anyone is in the Messiah, there is a new creation!'[121] Most now read this line, rightly in my view, as pointing not just to what is true of the 'anyone' in question (though it surely does that as well), but beyond that to the larger reality of 'new creation' that the gospel has opened up. The Greek is simply *ei tis en Christō kainē ktisis*: 'if anyone in Messiah, new creation!'. The single newly created human being functions as a small window on the new, large, eschatological reality. God is renewing the world, and is calling human beings both to be renewed in themselves ('be transformed', says Paul, 'by the renewing of your minds'[122]) and then, it seems, to be agents of that renewal. And in that new creation the divisions of the human race that marked, and marred, the 'present age' are to be done away. 'Circumcision, you see, is nothing; neither is uncircumcision! What matters is new creation.'[123] The whole argument of Galatians depends on the assumption that in the Messiah and by the spirit this 'new creation' has decisively begun. After all, 'the Messiah gave himself for our sins to rescue us from the present evil age' (1.4)! If the 'new creation' had still been in the future, Paul's opponents would have been right to insist on the ethnic

[118] Rom. 1.16; 2.1–11.

[119] For the first: Rom. 3.21–6 (and in fact 3.21—4.25 as a whole); for the second, Rom. 1.16f.

[120] Rom. 10.3 with 9.7f. (Abraham) and 10.6–9 (Deut. 30). See below, 1165–76.

[121] 2 Cor. 5.17.

[122] Rom. 12.2.

[123] Gal. 6.15.

boundary-markers that kept the chosen people safe and sound (but also 'under Torah', with all the tensions of Romans 7) while awaiting the new day. Here as elsewhere, Paul's real objection to those who would perpetuate such things was that they were *past their use-by date*. The divisions of humanity belonged to the old age, and the new had already arrived. Not, of course, that it was complete. That, as always, constituted the tension in Paul's thought. We wait with patience, he says, for the time when 'creation itself [will] be freed from its slavery to decay, to enjoy the freedom that comes when God's children are glorified'.[124] If we are to understand the *not yet* in Pauline theology, we must do so in the light of the *now* on which he insists again and again. God *has already* delivered us from the present evil age, he says, and *has already* made us part of his new creation. The future still matters enormously. But we must not imagine, because of the *not yet*, that Paul had forgotten the *now*.

All this massive inauguration of eschatology, accomplished by Israel's God through the Messiah, draws the eye up to one final point. If it has all happened in such a rich combination of scriptural fulfilment, practical Christian living and everything in between, what has happened to the central theme itself, the return of Israel's God to Zion? What is the Pauline equivalent, if there is one (and, granted all that we have said, it would be very surprising if there were not such a thing), to the Johannine 'the word became flesh, and lived among us', where the English verb 'lived' inadequately translates *eskēnōsen*, 'pitched his tent' – in other words, picking up the overtones John intends us to hear, 'tabernacled' in our midst?[125] Where is the christological 'new temple' in Paul's theology?

We have already answered this question in chapter 9. Despite earlier generations in which doubt was cast on any suggestions of a high christology in Paul, we can firmly say that he believed that Israel's God was fully and personally present in and as Jesus the Messiah. There are two places in particular in his writings where we detect that Johannine theme of the divine glory returning as promised to live within the temple – but with the temple in question being, not the building in Jerusalem, but the person of Jesus himself. Both 2 Corinthians 4.5–6 and Colossians 1.15–20 make this clear. The tabernacling presence of God in 2 Corinthians 4 is part of the theme of new covenant and new creation that pervades Paul's account of his Messiah-shaped ministry throughout chapters 3, 4, 5 and 6. And the 'indwelling' language of Colossians 1 and 2 picks up the language of the Shekinah dwelling in the Temple. This, Paul is saying, is the reality for which post-exilic Judaism had longed. The covenant God had returned in person, in the person of Jesus. Redefined monotheism and redefined eschatology dovetail together exactly.

[124] Rom. 8.21.

[125] Jn. 1.14.

(ii) Through the Spirit

Perhaps the clearest sign that Paul is thinking in terms of a surprising fulfilment of the Jewish hope of YHWH's return to his people is his further use of 'temple'-imagery in relation to the indwelling of the divine spirit within the Messiah's people. This too we have studied already. Three times he says this, twice in relation to the church as a whole and once in relation to individual Christians.[126]

This imagery is anything but an incidental metaphor (which is how many commentators have treated it in the past). An erstwhile Pharisee would be unlikely to toss around the idea of the Temple, so central to the Judaism of the period, as one image among many. The stress on the Temple's holiness in all three passages, and on the building of the Temple in the first of them,[127] indicates that it is indeed Israel's Temple that Paul is thinking of, and we are therefore not merely encouraged but compelled to take these passages as an indication of the strange fulfilment of the ancient Jewish hope. YHWH has returned at last, but not as the pillar of cloud and fire, and not to dwell in Herod's Temple in Jerusalem. His powerful, personal presence has come to inhabit his people, turning them individually into walking temples and corporately into a single body designed for praise, holiness and sacrifice.[128] This is the long-awaited new temple, inhabited personally by the long-awaited God of Israel.

This theme of the new temple thus belongs, in Paul, equally to the Messiah and to his spirit-filled people, and it is not surprising that we find him oscillating easily between the two. One such passage is Romans 8.9–11, where the notion of the spirit's 'indwelling' is a strong indication of the implicit 'temple'-theme, though the absence of this theme from much Pauline scholarship (and the presence in the passage of several other important ideas) has meant that most exegetes have missed the point altogether.[129] God's spirit, he says, 'lives within you', *oikei en hymin*. He repeats this in verse 11: the spirit of the one who raised Jesus from the dead 'lives within you', *oikei en hymin*. When the divine spirit takes up residence in a place, that place becomes a temple, whether it realizes it or not; when a second-Temple Jew speaks of this happening, with the result that the Temple itself is reconstructed (presumably as a still more fitting residence for the divine spirit), this cannot simply be an isolated prediction of a strange future event. It is another instance of Paul's inaugurated eschatology. Israel's God had long promised that the Temple would be rebuilt and that he would come and dwell in it. Paul has combined these elements in a new way – first the

[126] Church as temple: 1 Cor. 3.16f.; 2 Cor. 6.16–18; Christians as temples: 1 Cor. 6.19f.

[127] 1 Cor. 3.10–15 uses building imagery in a way which suggests that Paul has had the Temple in mind for some verses before he mentions it explicitly in 3.16f. See above, 391f.

[128] cf. e.g. Rom. 12.1f.; and again 1 Cor. 3.16f.; 6.19f.; 2 Cor. 6.16–18, insisting on a new sort of endogamy (see above, 369, 444).

[129] See above, 716f.

indwelling, then the rebuilding – but it is these same elements of the Jewish hope that he has reworked.

This points across to another somewhat surprising passage in Colossians, which again is not normally read in this way but perhaps ought to be. The Messiah, living within his people, is 'the hope of glory'.[130] The 'glory' here is not, I think, simply the 'glory' that each individual Christian awaits. As we saw, it is the 'glory' of Israel's God which, as promised, will flood and drench the whole world. This 'glory' – the personal and sovereign presence of Israel's God – will come back not simply to the Temple in Jerusalem, not simply to be within Israel, but to fill all creation. As a sign and foretaste of that still-future 'filling', the Messiah is dwelling within his people in the present time, even within the little group of new-minted Christians in the small town of Colosse. The present possession of 'the Messiah' as the one who, by his spirit, indwells his people, is the inauguration of the promise of YHWH's return. This is part of what Paul means, to be sure, when he writes that all God's promises find their 'yes' in the Messiah, one of the clearest statements of the principle that our whole present chapter is expounding.[131]

The mention of 2 Corinthians takes us back once more to one of the central chapters for Paul's view of the spirit. Chapter 3 has long been controversial: why would Paul want to spend so much time talking about Moses? One regular answer, of course, is that he didn't want to do so, but that his opponents forced him into it by speaking of Moses and his glorious ministry in contrast to Paul and his apparently less than glorious one.[132] That might indeed be part of the explanation in this case. One can never rule out such a possibility. But it is hardly a sufficient reason for Paul's development of the theme. Like a good chess player, Paul was well capable of taking something his opponent had done and responding with a fresh and brilliant move that was much more than a mere tit-for-tat response. The moment a public speaker longs for is when a heckler, thinking to have scored a clever point, succeeds in raising, in just the right way, the topic one wished to address anyway.

What is often missed here is that Paul is expounding, more fully than elsewhere (though he alludes to the theme in various places), the passage in Exodus in which Moses wrestles with Israel's God over the promise to live within his people, in their midst. For this we may simply refer to our previous treatment of the same theme in chapter 9. For our present purposes we note, in particular, that Paul brings together the dramatic 'now' of the present indwelling spirit with the equally dramatic 'not yet' of 2 Corinthians 4.7–12: we have this treasure in earthenware pots. But Paul's description of the present painful state of affairs is not simply a way of balancing out the glorious truth he has just unveiled. The inner renewal (4.16), in the midst of

130 Col. 1.27. See *Perspectives* ch. 23.

131 2 Cor. 1.20.

132 Paul's opponents are of course shadowy characters, seen darkly in a mirror, regularly invoked by scholars as convenient explanations for various phenomena, in particular for why Paul spoke of things which the same scholars think irrelevant to his central thought. On the problem, see e.g. Barclay 1987.

that suffering, is the *present* reality which functions as the signpost to the *future* reality.

Galatians and Romans pick up the same theme: the presence of the spirit is the sign, for Paul, that YHWH has returned as he had always promised. In Galatians 4.1–7 Paul is evoking the theme of the exodus, the redemption of the slaves so that they now become 'sons'. But it is precisely in the exodus that we have not only the fresh revelation of the divine name (Exodus 3.13–15) and of the divine nature as the covenant-keeping God (6.2–8; 34.6–7), but also the fulfilment of the promise that this God would, despite his people's rebellion and idolatry, come and live in their midst. Here in Galatians this picture is developed in relation both to the Messiah and to the spirit, here described as 'the spirit of his son'. The living God has come in the person of his son to rescue his people, and in the work of the spirit to dwell within them. As we saw in chapter 9, Paul can then refer to this whole complex of thought by saying, 'now that you've come to know God – or, better, to be known *by* God'.[133] What drives the appeal of 4.8–11, at the root, is not some odd scheme or strange new prejudice on Paul's part, but his conviction that with the son and the spirit Israel's hope has been fulfilled. The covenant God has returned to dwell in and with his people.

This is spelled out, as we have seen several times, in relation to the work of the spirit transforming the *heart*. That vital little passage, Romans 2.28–9, which stands behind so much of the rest of the letter, insists that the thing for which Israel had hoped had been accomplished by Israel's God through the spirit:

> The 'Jew' isn't the person who appears to be one, you see. Nor is 'circumcision' what it appears to be, a matter of physical flesh. The 'Jew' is the one in secret; and 'circumcision' is a matter of the heart, in the spirit rather than the letter. Such a person gets 'praise', not from humans, but from God.

In other words: the promises (and warnings) of Deuteronomy, Jeremiah and Ezekiel have been fulfilled, and this fulfilment is open to all, Jew and gentile alike.[134]

Paul uses the running theme of these promises and warnings to his advantage in his argument for the inclusion of the uncircumcised. Since what counts for the prophets, when it comes to membership in the renewed covenant, is the circumcision of the heart, this is clearly unrelated to the circumcision of the flesh. Physical circumcision is neither a necessary nor a sufficient condition for the real circumcision (though he does not use the word 'real', here or in the parallel in Philippians 3.3) which is the badge of the new-covenant family. The passage is thus all about inaugurated eschatology. The ancient Israelite hope, and more recently the second-Temple Jewish hope, is fulfilled through the coming into being of a Jew-

[133] Gal. 4.9 (above, 376, 643, 657).

[134] Warnings: Dt. 10.16 (cf. Lev. 26.41); Jer. 4.4; 9.26; cf. Ezek. 44.7; promises: Dt. 30.6; Jer. 31.33; 32.39f.; Ezek. 11.19; 36.26f.

plus-gentile family whose hearts have been transformed through the work of the spirit.

Paul alludes to this heart-transformation in three further passages as Romans continues (5.5; 6.17; 8.27), showing that we are still on track. The theme then comes to the fore dramatically in the passage we shall be studying from a different angle in the final main section of the present chapter, where he describes the way in which Israel's God can and will answer the prayer he, Paul, has been praying for the 'salvation' of presently unbelieving Jews. Paul picks up the strand of 'heart-transformation' in Deuteronomy 30, linking it with Deuteronomy 9.4 ('Do not say in your *heart*') with, presumably, just this desired effect:

> Don't say in your *heart*, Who shall go up to heaven? (in other words, to bring the Messiah down), or, Who shall go down into the depths? (in other words, to bring the Messiah up from the dead). But what does it say? 'The word is near you, in your mouth and in your *heart*' (that is, the word of faith which we proclaim); because if you profess with your mouth that Jesus is lord, and believe in your *heart* that God raised him from the dead, you will be saved. Why? Because the way to covenant membership is by believing with the *heart*, and the way to salvation is by professing with the mouth.[135]

Here too, as in Romans 2, the point is then made: this is for all, since there is no distinction between Jew and Greek (10.12). This passage, which grows out of the spectacular 'new covenant' exposition of 7.1—8.11 and all that goes with it, is near the very centre of Paul's inaugurated eschatology. God has done at last what he had promised, even though it looks nothing like what the people who had been clinging to that promise had been expecting (10.2–4). As Josephus claimed to do, Paul read the closing chapters of Deuteronomy as an eschatological prophecy coming true in his own day. The hope of Israel was being realized.[136]

Here, in particular, the spirit is the active agent, though not explicitly mentioned. As often, Paul's brief reference to one part of a key text brings with it the resonances of the larger section. Immediately after the passage just cited, he explains that the abolition of distinction between Jew and Greek is because 'the same lord is lord of all', rich (i.e. in mercy and grace) towards all who call upon him. Then, in 10.11, he quotes Joel 2.32:[137] 'all who call upon the name of the lord will be saved.' This is part of the longer prophecy of a covenant renewal in which, precisely, all and sundry will be involved:

> Then afterwards I will pour out my spirit on all flesh; your sons and your daughters shall prophesy, your old men shall dream dreams, and your young men shall see visions. Even on the male and female slaves, in those days, I will pour out my spirit. I will show portents in the heavens and on the earth, blood and fire and columns of smoke. The sun shall be

[135] Rom. 10.6–10. For fuller exegesis see below, 1174–6, and Wright 2002 [*Romans*], 658–64.

[136] cf. Dt. 32.21, quoted in Rom. 10.19 (and nb. 32.20, where YHWH says 'I will see what their end will be', which in the LXX is *deixō ti estai ep'autois ep' eschatōn*. It is not surprising that this was read by some, including Josephus, as a long-range prophecy of Israel's ultimate future (on Josephus here see above, 130f.).

[137] 3.5 MT/LXX.

> turned to darkness, and the moon to blood, before the great and terrible day of YHWH comes. Then everyone who calls on the name of YHWH shall be saved; for in Mount Zion and in Jerusalem there shall be those who escape, as YHWH has said, and among the survivors shall be those whom YHWH calls.[138]

Within this spirit-driven inaugurated eschatology all sorts of other new things begin to happen, not least of course the transformation of behaviour upon which Paul insists throughout his writings.[139] Many times, despite his own polemic against those who try to live within Torah (i.e. as though the new day of the gospel had not dawned), he nevertheless speaks of a 'fulfilment' of Torah on the part of those who believe and are led by the spirit. They are not 'under Torah', but they nevertheless do what Torah intended.[140]

There can be no doubt, then, that for Paul the long-awaited expectation of Israel has begun to be realized. Those who believe his gospel are, as it were, starting again not only like the original exodus generation (1 Corinthians 10) but also like the wife in the original primal pair, with the Messiah playing the role of husband (2 Corinthians 11.2–3).[141] New creation in its fullest sense is still, of course, awaited, and that is why the Messiah's people 'groan' in the present.[142] But to deny that it has already begun is to cut off the branch upon which the whole early Christian movement, and Paul's theology within it, is sitting.

Paul, then, sees Israel's hope as *realized* in the present time, albeit in a radically new way, reconceived around the Messiah and the spirit. But this realization is clearly and importantly incomplete. There is a 'not yet'. And this, too, Paul has expressed as a messianic and pneumatological reworking of the same Jewish hope.

4. Hope Still to Come – through Jesus and the Spirit

As with the present, so with the future: the central promise is that YHWH will return in glory to his people, bringing all things to completion, overcoming all enemies, vindicating his people and establishing his kingdom at last. And the central achievement of Paul in relation to this great hope was to transform the ancient Israelite vision of 'the day of YHWH' so that it became 'the day of the Messiah', or – with that characteristic ambiguity we

[138] Joel 2.28–32 (3.1–5 MT/LXX).

[139] e.g. Rom. 6.12–23; Gal. 5.16–26; see below.

[140] e.g. Rom. 2.26, 27 (remarkably explicitly); 3.27, 31 (remarkably cryptically); 8.4 and, by clear implication, 8.7–9 ('the mind focused on the flesh is hostile to God. It doesn't submit to God's law; in fact, it can't ... But you're not people of flesh; you're people of the spirit ...' In other words, there is a sense in which you *do* now 'submit to God's law': the sense, presumably, of 8.4). See too 10.4–13; 13.8–10; 1 Cor. 7.19; Gal. 6.2. On not being 'under the law': Gal. 5.18. On the whole theme see above, 1032–8, esp. 1037f.

[141] For the 'new marriage' to the Messiah rather than Adam see too Rom. 7.1–4, on which see above, 892f.

[142] Rom. 8.23.

studied in chapter 9 – 'the day of "the lord"', where 'the lord' clearly denotes Jesus the Messiah but also, through the Septuagintal echoes of *kyrios*, resonates powerfully with the divine name itself.[143]

Sometimes Paul uses the whole biblical phrase, 'the day of the lord', often modifying it with the name of Jesus:

> [God] will establish you right through to the end, so that you are blameless on the day of our lord, King Jesus.[144]

> ... you must hand over such a person to the satan for the destruction of the flesh, so that his spirit may be saved on the day of the lord Jesus.[145]

> We are your pride and joy, just as you are ours, on the day of our lord Jesus.[146]

> You know very well that the day of the lord will come like a midnight robber.[147]

> Please don't be suddenly blown off course, in your thinking ... through a letter supposedly from us, telling you that the day of the lord has already arrived.[148]

Sometimes, instead, he uses 'the day of the Messiah' or a similar variant:

> The one who began a good work in you will thoroughly complete it by the day of the Messiah Jesus.[149]

> Then you will be ... sincere and faultless on the day of the Messiah.[150]

> That's what I will be proud of on the day of the Messiah.[151]

And sometimes he just speaks of 'the day', clearly referring to the same moment and modifying it in various ways, not least with warnings of judgment:

> You are building up a store of anger for yourself on the day of anger, the day when God's just judgment will be unveiled.[152]

> ... on the day when (according to the gospel I proclaim) God judges all human secrets through King Jesus.[153]

> The night is nearly over, the day is almost here.[154]

[143] Dunn 1998, 308 notes this usage in passing, but avoids the christological implications.
[144] 1 Cor. 1.8.
[145] 1 Cor. 5.5.
[146] 2 Cor. 1.14.
[147] 1 Thess. 5.2.
[148] 2 Thess. 2.2.
[149] Phil. 1.6.
[150] Phil. 1.10.
[151] Phil. 2.16.
[152] Rom. 2.5.
[153] Rom. 2.16.
[154] Rom. 13.12.

> Everyone's work will become visible, because the Day will show it up, since it will be revealed in fire.[155]

> Don't disappoint God's holy spirit – the spirit who put God's mark on you to identify you on the day of freedom.[156]

> May the lord grant him to find mercy from the lord on that day.[157]

> The lord, the righteous judge, will give [the crown of righteousness] to me as my reward on that day.[158]

In order to explain both the idea which Paul is expressing here and the way in which he came to see this as a good way of expressing it, we need to draw on much of the material we have surveyed in earlier chapters. The important point is this. The idea of a coming 'day' when the creator of the world, Israel's covenant God, would act in judgment and mercy was, as we saw, an important theme in the biblical prophets. Paul believed that the accomplishment of Jesus as Messiah, and the gift of the spirit, meant that in one sense the new day had already dawned: 'the day of salvation is here'. But, just as 'resurrection' itself had as it were split into two, so 'the day' itself had divided up into the 'day' – the ongoing 'now' of the gospel – in which promises were truly fulfilled, not just anticipated, and the further 'day' in which the work would be complete and the creator would be 'all in all'. We have already quoted 1 Corinthians 15.20–8, in which the distinction is made, and where 'the end' (*to telos*) in verse 24 ('then comes the end, the goal, when he hands over the kingly rule to God the father, when he has destroyed all rule and all authority and power') clearly refers to the same moment as 'the day' elsewhere in the letter (as cited above). Chapter 15 of course yields further rich material concerning what will happen on that 'day', to which we shall presently return.

It will be, it seems, primarily a day of *judgment*. Not simply 'condemnation', though 'judgment' includes that, as in Romans 2.5, quoted above. It will be 'judgment' in the more ancient biblical sense: the time when everything gets sorted out, when everything that needs putting right is put right. It will be the time when all secrets are disclosed, when the quality of work done by the lord's people will appear, and when in particular those who have borne fruit through their work will receive their proper reward (Paul is not nearly as queasy about the idea of 'reward' as some of his zealous post-Reformation followers). When we put together the various passages cited above it appears that for most of the time the different imagery used to describe the day (such as fire, in 1 Corinthians 3) is just that, imagery. There is also, however, a puzzling sense in one of the references that perhaps, as in

[155] 1 Cor. 3.13.

[156] Eph. 4.30.

[157] 2 Tim. 1.18.

[158] 2 Tim. 4.8.

the Old Testament, this 'day', too, will divide up into different 'moments', some of which may fall *within* the present course of world history:

> Please don't be suddenly blown off course in your thinking, or be unsettled, either through spiritual influence, or through a word, or through a letter supposedly from us, telling you that the day of the lord has already arrived.[159]

The point has been made often enough, but is worth repeating: if the Thessalonians were likely to receive a message or letter telling them that 'the day of the lord has already arrived', then presumably they at least did not suppose that 'the day of the lord' meant the actual dissolution of the space–time universe. But perhaps Paul did not, either. We must probe further in his eschatology to find out.

In particular, we must consider the possibility that Paul, who was most likely more aware than we are of how prophetic traditions worked, not only believed in a 'now' and a 'not yet', as though there were two and only two 'moments' in Christian eschatology, but also in penultimate fulfilments, particular moments which one might interpret in terms of their relation to the one-off fulfilment in the Messiah and the ultimate future 'day'. This, I think, is what is going on in the Thessalonian correspondence. Clearly, he is looking ahead to the ultimate 'last day' when Jesus will return and the dead will be raised.[160] But he is also looking ahead to a very specific moment when something strange and dark will happen. Speaking of the Judaeans who have done their best to prevent the spread of the gospel, as they did their best to get rid of Jesus, he declares that 'the fury has come upon them for good'.[161] We must return to this passage later in the present chapter. Suffice it to say for now that it looks as though Paul here, and in the passage quoted above from 2 Thessalonians, may reflect the widespread early Christian awareness that Jesus had prophesied the imminent destruction of Jerusalem, and that when that terrible event came about it was to be interpreted in the same way that Jeremiah had interpreted the similar disaster six hundred years before.[162]

Before leaving the notion of 'the day of the lord', though, we must re-emphasize the basic theological point. In the second-Temple period, 'the day of YHWH' would have struck the chords of 'the return of YHWH to Zion'. What we find in Paul's new concept of 'the day of the lord *Jesus*' is another manifestation of the same reimagined hope. When Paul spoke about the future day of Jesus, he was speaking of the time when, in the person of his son, Israel's God would come back once and for all, to call the whole world to account and to establish his reign of justice, mercy and peace.

[159] 2 Thess. 2.2.

[160] 1.10; 2.19; 3.13; 4.13—5.11.

[161] 1 Thess. 2.16.

[162] Perriman 2010, 50f. makes perhaps more of this theme than is exegetically warranted, but since most exegetes ignore it altogether there is perhaps a balance to be redressed. See below, 1154. There is also of course the whole theme of the 'man of lawlessness' and the 'restrainer' in 2 Thess. 2.1–12, on which see, in addition to the commentaries, Ridderbos 1975 [1966], 508–28.

The best-known Pauline term to denote this coming moment is of course *parousia*.[163] Unlike most of Paul's technical terms, this word has no biblical overtones. It comes, rather, from the classical world, and its simple and basic meaning is 'presence' as opposed to 'absence', as when a friend is here in the room with me rather than being on the other side of town.[164] However, if the friend, having been far away, then turns up on the doorstep, his or her *presence* will be rightly perceived as the result of *having arrived*, and thus the word *parousia* slides gently from its home base, *presence*, into the meaning *arrival*.

As such, it can be used of all kinds of situations, whether it be a friend making the journey across town or an official state visit from royalty or nobility. The latter is particularly noteworthy when, for instance, *parousia* is used of Caesar or some other high official paying a visit to a city or province or, indeed, returning to Rome or some other centre after such a trip.[165]

In parallel with this particular and well-known usage, *parousia* was also widely used to denote the 'appearance' or 'manifestation' of a divinity. (Since the Caesars were on their way to being regularly divinized in Paul's day, the 'imperial' and 'divine' meanings could already be combined.) A striking example, in relation to Israel's God, is found in Josephus, when he speaks of the thunderbolts on Mount Sinai as signifying the *parousia tou theou*, the 'arrival' of Israel's God to do business with Moses.[166] Equally interesting is his description of what happened once the tabernacle had been constructed in the wilderness:

> He came as their guest and took up His abode in this sanctuary ... While the heaven was serene, over the tabernacle alone darkness descended, enveloping it in a cloud not so profound and dense as might be attributed to winter storm, nor yet so tenuous that the eye could perceive a thing through it; but a delicious dew was distilled therefrom, revealing God's presence [*theou dēlousa parousian*] to those who both desired it and believed in it.[167]

Josephus rather carefully qualifies his statement by adding a romantic touch to the scene, and then implying that the 'presence' was only revealed to those who wanted or believed in it, thereby appearing to distance himself from any strong affirmation of its objective reality. This should not obscure the point, which is obviously relevant to the way we have approached the whole subject of Paul's revised version of second-Temple eschatology. Paul, I have been arguing, saw the future in terms of the ultimate fulfilment of the

[163] For details on the following analysis, cf. LSJ 1343; BDAG 780f., with copious references. For a summary of key issues see e.g. Allison 2007b, 296.

[164] Compare the 'ordinary' uses in e.g. 1 Cor. 16.17; 2 Cor. 7.6, 7; 10.10; of Paul himself, Phil. 1.26; 2.12.

[165] cf. e.g. Polybius 18.48.4; *3 Macc.* 3.17; of the arrival of an army, 2 Macc. 8.12; other refs. in BDAG 781.

[166] *Ant.* 3.80; Thackeray ad loc. tr. 'the advent of God'.

[167] *Ant.* 3.203.

promise that YHWH would return. Here Josephus uses the word *parousia* to denote one of the moments that stood as a paradigm for that hope.[168]

These two meanings (the royal arrival of a monarch or similar official, and the manifestation or powerful presence of a divinity) seem to be combined in a creative way by Paul himself. As far as he is concerned, Jesus is not 'absent' or far away. As the risen sovereign of the whole world, he is always present and powerful. But one day this powerful presence will be revealed in action in a new way, when in the perception of those to whom he is thus revealed it will seem as though he has in fact 'arrived'. Like a king returning from abroad to reclaim his rightful possession, he will 'come' from heaven to earth, not for a brief visit but to combine the two into one:

> We are citizens of heaven, you see, and we're eagerly waiting for the saviour, the lord, King Jesus, who is going to come from there. Our present body is a shabby old thing, but he's going to transform it so that it's just like his glorious body. And he's going to do this by the power which makes him able to bring everything into line under his authority.[169]

But when this happens it will also be like the 'manifestation' of a divinity, for the very good reason that it *will* be the manifestation of the one who, as we saw earlier, Paul regarded as the living human embodiment of Israel's God. For that reason we need to note, at the same time, the term *epiphaneia*, 'appearing' (as in the English 'epiphany'), which could carry the same double meaning as *parousia* (with other shades as well): the 'manifestation' of a divinity[170] or the accession of an emperor.[171] This abstract term is related to the verb *phaneroō*, 'to make manifest',[172] and both the noun and the verb draw our attention to the fact that the early Christians, Paul included, did not think of Jesus as a long way away from them and needing to make a substantial journey to come back, but rather of Jesus as present but hidden and needing to be made manifest.[173]

Despite its non-biblical background, then, the content with which Paul fills the word *parousia* indicates well enough that this future moment will be the time when the long hope of Israel will be realized, as with the expected return of YHWH:

[168] cf. too *Ant.* 9.55, summarizing the effect created in 2 Kgs. 6.15–19: Elisha prays that God will 'reveal ... His power and presence [*emphanisai tēn hautou dynamin kai parousian*] to his servant'. Here *parousia* is simply 'presence' – 'the fact that he was there all along' – rather than 'arrival'.

[169] Phil. 3.20f. Neither *parousia* nor *epiphaneia* (see below) occur here, but nobody will doubt that this passage describes the event for which Paul elsewhere uses those and similar terms.

[170] e.g. Plut. *Them.* 30.

[171] Of Caligula: *Inscr. Cos.* 391. On *epiphaneia* see LSJ 669f.; BDAG 385f.

[172] BDAG 1048.

[173] Thus e.g. Col. 3.4; cf. 1 Pet. 5.4; 1 Jn. 2.28; 3.2 (*phaneroō*); 2 Thess. 2.8, where *epiphaneia* is combined with *parousia* ('with the unveiling of his presence', *tē epiphaneia tēs parousias autou*); BDAG suggest that here *epiphaneia* 'refers to the salvation that goes into effect when the *parousia* takes place', but this hardly fits the sense either of the verse or of the words. *Parousia* here is the 'presence' of the lord, and *epiphaneia* its unveiling – not, in 2 Thess. 2.8, for salvation, but for judgment on 'the lawless one'. *Epiphaneia* is comparatively frequent in the Pastorals: 1 Tim. 6.14; 2. Tim. 1.10; 4.1, 8; was this because of a desire on the part of the writer to contrast Jesus with Caesar, whose *epiphaneia* was celebrated? See esp. the emphatic Tit. 2.13.

> The Messiah rises as the first fruits; then those who belong to the Messiah will rise at the time of his royal arrival [*parousia*].[174]

> When our lord Jesus is present once more [*en tē autou parousia*], what is our hope, our joy, the crown of our boasting before him?[175]

> That way, your hearts will be strengthened and kept blameless in holiness before God our father when our lord Jesus is present again [*en tē parousia tou kyriou hēmōn Iēsou*] with all his holy ones.[176]

> We who are alive, who remain until the lord is present [*hoi perileipomenoi eis tēn parousian tou kyriou*], will not find ourselves ahead of those who fell asleep.[177]

> May your complete spirit, soul and body be kept blameless at the coming [*en tē parousia*] of our lord Jesus the Messiah.[178]

> Now concerning the royal presence [*hyper tēs parousias*] of our lord Jesus the Messiah, and our gathering together around him . . .[179]

> The lord Jesus will destroy [the lawless one] with the breath of his mouth, and will wipe him out with the unveiling of his presence [*tē epiphaneia tēs parousias autou*].[180]

What has happened, it seems, is a combination of five things:[181]

1. There is the older Jewish expectation: YHWH will come back, with all his holy ones,[182] and will sort out the mess of Israel and the nations once and for all.
2. There is the messianic version of this expectation: David's son and heir will destroy the wicked with the sword of his mouth and the breath of his lips.[183]
3. Then there is Paul's reappropriation of these and related traditions, based on his firm belief (itself grounded in Jesus' resurrection) that the hope of Israel had been dramatically inaugurated through Jesus and the spirit: this future scenario had come to birth in the present, but with the all-important eschatological now-and-not-yet division.
4. Then, since Paul identified Jesus as the one in and through whom YHWH had become personally present, it was not difficult to transfer to

[174] 1 Cor. 15.23.

[175] 1 Thess. 2.19.

[176] 1 Thess. 3.13.

[177] 1 Thess. 4.15. Dunn 1998, 299f. is right to stress that the primary action in the whole scenario is that of God himself, but offers little more help. Schreiner 2001, 460f. seems to leave open the traditional literalistic reading of a 'rapture'. For more details on this controversial passage see *RSG* 214–19.

[178] 1 Thess. 5.23.

[179] 2 Thess. 2.1.

[180] 2 Thess. 2.8; see n. 173 above. The 'lawless one' himself also has a *parousia* in v. 9; this usage seems to be formed by analogy with that of Jesus, much as in Revelation the Beast is a parody of the Lamb.

[181] Dunn 1998, 295f. rightly sees the novelty of Paul's *parousia*-teaching, but not the rootedness of this idea in ancient Jewish ideas about YHWH's return.

[182] Zech. 14.5.

[183] Isa. 11.4.

him the still-future expectation of YHWH's 'day' or 'coming' or 'appearing'. This sustained the 'divine manifestation' meaning of both *parousia* and *phaneroō*.
5. Finally, it will not have been lost on Paul that *parousia*, *epiphaneia* and related ideas were familiar as terms for the royal visit, or appearing or return, of Caesar himself.[184]

When, therefore, he speaks of Jesus' triumphant return in power to establish his sovereign rule over the whole world, and when he uses, in relation to Jesus, language which was in fairly common use for the return or appearance of Caesar, the present 'world ruler', we should draw the obvious conclusion. Just as the ancient Israelite expectation of 'the day of YHWH' included the hope that YHWH would be revealed as the true ruler of the world by the overthrow of pagan tyrants, whether of Egypt, Babylon or anywhere else, so Paul's expectation of 'the day of the lord' included the expectation that, on the last day, that which was already true would at last be revealed: Jesus is lord, and Caesar is not.[185]

The immediate result of all this, in terms of final eschatology, is that the creator and covenant God will, at the last, put the whole world to rights.[186] Here I see no reason to doubt that Paul meant what he wrote in Romans 2.1–16, despite the large number in recent years who have proposed either that this is simply a Jewish tradition which he quotes in order to show how superior the gospel is, or a hypothetical case which will be rendered null and void by the fact that (as he goes on to demonstrate) all alike are sinful, or – the most recent, and extreme case – that this is part of a 'speech in character' which Paul cunningly puts into the mouth of an opponent whom he will then outflank.[187] On the contrary: the whole passage is important as part of the foundation for what Paul is going to say in each section of Romans.

The passage's importance lies not least in its final line: the creator God will judge all human secrets 'through King Jesus'. This is not simply a Pauline appendix to a non-Pauline final scenario. Rather, with the resurrection of Jesus and his installation as Messiah, it makes sense – good, first-century Jewish sense – to think that Jesus himself will be the one through whom the

[184] Ridderbos 1975 [1966], 535f. is wrong to imply that one has to choose between seeing Sinai-imagery and Emperor-imagery here. It is precisely part of Paul's genius to combine Jewish sources and gentile targets.

[185] See below, ch. 12.

[186] In American, I understand, people do not use this expression, replacing it with 'put the whole world right' or something similar. Even Australians, I discover, sometimes need to have it explained. The reason I retain the English usage is because 'putting something *to rights*' carries not only the meaning of sorting it out, making it work properly, putting right what was wrong with it, but also the notion of *justice*. Despite the dangers of our late-modern 'rights culture', always threatening to collapse into the mere swapping of thwarted prejudices, the idea of restoring someone's proper 'rights', and doing so on a cosmic scale, is endemic to the biblical notion of justice.

[187] For these three options see e.g. Sanders 1983, 123–35; Käsemann 1980 [1973], 73 ('the possibility here is also fictional, at least in the immediate context'); Campbell 2009, 547–71. Ridderbos 1975 [1966], 553 argues strongly against the 'hypothetical' line, as taken by Lietzmann 1971, 39f., citing the parallel in e.g. Rom. 14.10f.

one God exercises the judgment which many Jews believed was coming upon the world. And the emphasis at the centre of the passage is on that characteristically Pauline (and not so characteristically first-century Jewish) theme, that Jew and gentile stand on absolutely level ground on that final day.

The first six verses set the scene:

> So *you* have no excuse – anyone, whoever you are, who sits in judgment! When you judge someone else, you condemn yourself, because you, who are behaving as a judge, are doing the same things. [2]God's judgment falls, we know, in accordance with the truth, on those who do such things. [3]But if you judge those who do them and yet do them yourself, do you really suppose that you will escape God's judgment?
>
> [4]Or do you despise the riches of God's kindness, forbearance and patience? Don't you know that God's kindness is meant to bring you to repentance? [5]But by your hard, unrepentant heart you are building up a store of anger for yourself on the day of anger, the day when God's just judgment will be unveiled – [6]the God who will 'repay everyone according to their works'.

This opening paragraph (verses 1–3), springing the trap on the self-satisfied moralist, simply assumes a future judgment. The second (verses 4–6), warning against taking the divine kindness and forbearance for granted (these themselves are a familiar second-Temple theme, an explanation for why judgment is delayed), simply assumes that there will be a coming 'day of anger', 'the day when God's just judgment will be unveiled' (verse 5). The Greek is *apokalypseōs dikaiokrisias tou theou*, the day 'of the revelation of the righteous judgment of God'. Paul has already spoken (1.18) of the *apokalypsis* of God's wrath as a present event, though what exactly this means remains controversial.[188] But 2.1–16 is clearly looking to the future as a further 'apocalypse' (if we dare use that muddled modern English term to translate its quite clear Greek homonym). If there is a sense in which the veil has been pulled back, through the messianic events concerning Jesus, on the *present* state of the world as being under the wrath of the creator, there will come a further time when the creator's just and proper determination to draw a line between good and evil, and to rid the world of the latter, will itself be unveiled. (We remind ourselves, in line with various writers, that if the creator does not, at the end, rid the world of evil, then – to put it no more strongly – his credentials both as the creator and as the God of justice are severely called into question.[189]) And part of this future unveiling of the creator's right and proper decision[190] will be, as in verse 6, the classic principle: 'he will repay everyone according to their works.' This uncontroversial

[188] See above, 764–71.

[189] On this, see e.g. Cranfield 1975, 1979, 108f.: if God 'did not react to our evil with wrath' it would raise the question 'whether God could be the good and loving God', since 'indignation against injustice, cruelty and corruption' is 'an essential element of goodness and love in a world in which moral evil is present'.

[190] A *krisis* is basically a decision between two or more things. The word then quickly passes into the making of judgments; then, more specifically, legal judgments, deciding officially between right and wrong.

maxim goes back at least to the Psalms and Proverbs,[191] and is echoed in many strands of later Jewish thought.[192] It can hardly be thought un- or sub-Christian, since it reappears in one form or another not only in Paul but in several other strands of the New Testament.[193] One could only deny its validity if, with some late-modern trends, one were to convert the quite proper doctrine of 'justification by faith' into its modernist parody, that of a God who shrugs his shoulders over human behaviour and 'tolerates' anything and everything.

These preliminaries over, Paul then states more fully how he conceives the final future judgment working out:

> 7When people patiently do what is good, and so pursue the quest for glory and honour and immortality, God will give them the life of the age to come. 8But when people act out of selfish desire, and do not obey the truth, but instead obey injustice, there will be anger and fury. 9There will be trouble and distress for every single person who does what is wicked, the Jew first and also, equally, the Greek – 10and there will be glory, honour and peace for everyone who does what is good, the Jew first and also, equally, the Greek. 11God, you see, shows no partiality.

Verses 7 and 8 state the general principle, in terms not of individual, one-off actions but of the whole tenor of a person's habitual life. We note that Paul here sees 'the life of the age to come' (*zōē aiōnios*), in good Jewish style, as the ultimate destination, while 'wrath and fury' will be the lot of those who do not attain that 'life'.[194] We also note that the description of the first category includes patience in doing good, and the *pursuit* of the goals of glory, honour and immortality. Paul does not imply that people necessarily attain them fully, still less that they 'earn' them as a right. All this, I think, is Pauline innovation, carefully designed to eliminate in advance any suggestion that he might after all be telling people that, in principle, they were supposed to be earning their membership in the 'age to come'. Then comes the second, more obvious, Pauline innovation. Repeating the double statement, this time the other way round (in verses 7 and 8 he mentions the good first, and the wicked afterwards; now, in verses 9 and 10, he mentions the wicked first and the good afterwards), he twice emphasizes 'the Jew first and also, equally, the Greek'. And then, just to rub home the point, he states another biblical maxim which, though well known, was not normally applied like this: 'God shows no partiality.'[195] So far this is very Jewish and also very Pauline: Paul is gently modifying a standard Jewish theme in the light of his larger theology, rooted as it is in the Messiah and the spirit.

The point about gentiles and Jews is then expanded further in 2.12–16:

[191] Pss. 28.4; 62.12 [LXX 13]; Prov. 24.12.

[192] e.g. Jer. 17.10; 32.19; 50.15, 29; Job 34.11; Eccl. 12.14; Sir. 35.19 [LXX 35.22]; *T. Lev.* 3.2; *Pss. Sol.* 9.5.

[193] 2 Cor. 5.10; 11.15; Mt. 16.27; 2 Tim. 4.14; 1 Pet. 1.17; Rev. 2.23; 18.6; 20.12f.; 22.12.

[194] On *zōē aiōnios* see above, 163f., 1029, 1060.

[195] 2 Chr. 19.7; Sir. 35.14f. [LXX 12f.]. These look back to e.g. Dt. 10.17; Job 34.19. The point is repeated frequently in the NT: Ac. 10.34; Gal. 2.6; Eph. 6.9; Col. 3.25; 1 Pet. 1.17. On the whole theme see Bassler 1982.

> [12]Everyone who sinned outside the law, you see, will be judged outside the law – and those who sinned from within the law will be judged by means of the law. [13]After all, it isn't those who *hear* the law who are in the right before God. It's those who *do* the law who will be declared to be in the right!
>
> [14]This is how it works out. Gentiles don't possess the law as their birthright; but whenever they do what the law says, they are a law for themselves, despite not possessing the law. [15]They show that the work of the law is written on their hearts. Their conscience bears witness as well, and their thoughts will run this way and that, sometimes accusing them and sometimes excusing, [16]on the day when (according to the gospel I proclaim) God judges all human secrets through King Jesus.

The passage has, understandably, provoked controversy, particularly between those who conclude that the gentiles who have 'the work of the law written on their hearts' are, so to speak, 'good pagans', and those who conclude (not least but not only on the grounds that Paul declares in due course that there are no 'good pagans' as such) that these are actually Christians, an anticipation of the category we meet, much less controversially, in 2.26–9.[196] I have in the past argued the latter case, and I stick to it, though I do think that Paul has quite deliberately left the matter apparently open for the moment and has, again quite deliberately, used language that might be recognized by a Stoic moralist.[197]

The point I want to draw out here, in line with what was said in chapter 10 above, is that in these five verses it is abundantly clear that when Paul speaks of 'justification' he is referring to something that will happen on 'the day', the *future* day when the creator God will judge the secrets of the hearts. We cannot deduce, from the placement of this point within the argument of Romans, that this final judgment is therefore in some sense 'primary' over the inaugurated-eschatological verdict of which Paul speaks in Romans 3.21—4.25. (The rhetorical needs of the letter could well trump the theological order that Paul might employ in the abstract. Paul is not committed to laying out his thoughts to correspond to a post-Reformation *ordo salutis*.) However, in this case it does appear that when we meet the *present* verdict in 3.21—4.25 it is indeed logically, as well as rhetorically, related to 2.1–16. In other words, the 'but now' of 3.21 indicates the *bringing into the present* of a moment – the final divine judgment – which Paul is also happy to think of as future. And the criterion for this future judgment is 'doing the law' (2.13, 14).

This, of course, is the point which has caused so many to deny that Paul really meant what he says here.[198] It is always possible to cut the knot of his dense and complex arguments, and so to reduce his thought to a shallow 'coherence' which does not, however, plumb its true depths. Far better, in my judgment, to stick with what he actually says, and then see how he

[196] I originally wrote 'uncontroversially'; but that was before I had read Hultgren 2010, 131.

[197] On all this, see below, 1379–82; and see 'The Law in Romans 2' in *Perspectives* ch. 9.

[198] See the passages in Sanders and Käsemann referred to above, n. 187; and Eisenbaum's comment (above, 937 n. 459). Schreiner 2001, 279–82 says that although the 'hypothetical' reading is attractive it is to be resisted; at 469–71 he offers a cautious balance.

explains himself as the letter goes forward. In this case, he has more to say about gentiles 'doing the law' in 2.26, 27, and he explains it in 2.28–9 in a way which looks reasonably similar to the present passage. There is a hint, too, that Paul sees faith itself as a fulfilment of the law in 3.27; a further hint about a different kind of lawkeeping in 8.4–7; and then, in his spectacular exegesis of Deuteronomy 30, Paul finally reveals what he means by 'doing the law' (10.6–10). I have written about these in the previous chapter, except for the last, which comes later in the present one. My purpose here is simply to draw attention to the fact that a reading of 2.1–16 is available which makes good sense of the passage both in its context and in the wider context of Paul's theology, not in tension with 'justification by faith' but precisely as its eschatological horizon. There will come a day when God will put the whole world to rights, including judging the secrets of all human hearts and lives. And this judgment will be exercised, perfectly consistently with Jewish messianic expectation, through the judge himself, Jesus the Messiah.[199] Romans 2.1–16 does indeed embody traditional Jewish eschatology, but it has been rethought around the Messiah and around the principle of 'no respect of persons' which, while itself rooted in the ancient scriptures, had attained a new focus through Paul's understanding of the gospel and the gentile mission.

This, in other words, is a further aspect of our thesis throughout this chapter: Paul has reworked Jewish eschatology around Jesus. (The spirit is in hiding in the section just quoted, but if we allow 2.25–9 to stand as an interpretative elaboration of 2.12–16 then the spirit is there too.) This is the *final justification* of which we spoke in chapter 10. Only in the light of Paul's carefully and thoroughly developed eschatology can we understand key doctrines such as justification by faith.[200]

There ought in any case to be no question about Paul holding firmly to a Jewish-style notion of a coming day of judgment. He repeats the point later in Romans:

> We must all appear before the judgment seat of God [several manuscripts read 'of the Messiah'], as the Bible says:
>
> > As I live, says the Lord, to me every knee shall bow,
> > and every tongue shall give praise to God.
>
> So then, we must each give an account of ourselves to God.[201]

And he says substantially the same thing in 2 Corinthians:

> For we must all appear before the judgment seat of the Messiah, so that each may receive what has been done through the body, whether good or bad.[202]

[199] Nb. the striking similarity to the conclusion of the Areopagus speech (Ac. 17.31); cp. Ac. 10.42.

[200] See above, e.g. 925–66.

[201] Rom. 14.10–12.

[202] 2 Cor. 5.10; cp. Ac. 10.41.

A remarkable passage in 1 Corinthians confirms the same theme, fitting very closely both with Romans 2.12–16 and with 2.29:

> So don't pass judgment on anything before the time when the lord comes! He will bring to light the secrets of darkness, and will lay bare the intentions of the heart. Then everyone will receive praise – from God.[203]

In context, this is almost a throwaway line, simply brought in to underline a point about how the Corinthians should think about Paul and Apollos. The Corinthians are in danger of sitting in judgment on their own apostles and teachers. Don't even go there, says Paul. Judgment and vindication are God's business, delegated to Jesus, and he will carry out this duty at the appointed time.[204]

This makes it all the more striking when we find passages in which believers are encouraged to think of themselves as *sharing* that future role of judgment – and even, on occasion, anticipating it in the present:

> Can it really be the case that one of you dares to go to law against a neighbour, to be tried before unjust people, and not before God's people? Don't you know that God's people will judge the world? And if the world is to be judged by you, are you really incompetent to try smaller matters? Don't you know that we shall be judging angels? Why not then also matters to do with ordinary life? Is it really true that there is no wise person among you who is able to decide between one Christian and another?[205]

This is an extraordinary passage for more than one reason. One suspects that the Corinthians might well have answered Paul's repeated 'Don't you know', with 'No, actually, we didn't know that'. Certainly it is not something that Paul troubles to mention elsewhere; though the occasional comments about the renewed people of God 'reigning' (Romans 5.17) may indicate that the other hints about this 'reign' may not be entirely sarcastic.[206] The most likely explanation is that Paul, like some other early Christians, firmly believed that the future rule of the Messiah would be shared with his people.[207] The most likely explanation of this, in turn, is that passages such as Daniel 7 were woven deeply into Paul's belief-structure, so that though he clearly saw Jesus as the unique Messiah and 'son of God', he saw the 'kingdom' which Jesus had inherited – the sovereign rule over the world, bringing the divine order into the chaos of the 'monsters' – as given to 'the holy ones'.[208]

[203] 1 Cor. 4.5.

[204] See too the substantial account in 2 Thess. 1.5–10, with the developed picture of coming judgment on the AntiChrist in 2.8–12.

[205] 1 Cor. 6.1–3, 5.

[206] 1 Cor. 4.8. See above, 481, 544.

[207] cf. e.g. Rom. 5.17; 2 Tim. 2.12; Rev. 5.10; 20.4; 22.5 (cf. 3.21). Cf. too Mt. 19.28; Lk. 22.28–30; *Pss. Sol.* 17.26, 29.

[208] Even if the 'holy ones' of Dan. 7.18, 22, 27 were originally angels (see e.g. Collins 1993, 304–19), it seems clear that by the first century the passage was being read in terms of the faithful Jewish people as a whole. This is the best explanation, too, for passages like Wis. 3.8; Sir. 4.15.

This, I think, is the best explanation too for the subtle meaning, often missed, at the heart of the great eschatological climax of Romans 8. It is not so much that the non-human creation is going to *share* 'the glorious liberty of the children of God', as several translations imply.[209] Indeed, in the earlier hint of the same point in Romans 5.2, most translations seem to balk at the idea that would, as I argued before, be suggested to a second-Temple Jew by the phrase 'the hope of the glory of God'. To a Jew who knew Isaiah, Ezekiel and the rest, 'the hope of the glory of God' would imply the hope that the divine glory would return to the Temple at last, and would deliver Israel from bondage to the nations. When, therefore, in Romans 5 and 8, Paul speaks of a coming glory through which *creation itself* is going to be released from its 'bondage to decay', we are not only invited but I suggest compelled to hear two closely related strands of thought coming to new expression. First, the whole created order has been in its own 'Egypt', from which it will now have its own 'exodus'. Second, as with the first exodus, and as with the repeated prophecies of the 'new exodus' upon which the early Christians drew, the means by which this will come about is the personal, glorious presence of Israel's God, coming back at last, as he came to dwell in the wilderness tabernacle in Exodus 40, and as in Isaiah 40 and 52 he promised to do once more.

This double theme of exodus and glory is exactly what Paul is exploring at this point. But the 'glory' in question is not now something apart from the humans involved, something at which they might (or might not) be allowed to gaze. This is where the vision we studied in 2 Corinthians 3, with the glory already present by means of the spirit, gives shape also to the future hope. The ultimate 'return of YHWH to Zion', as translated by Paul into the future hope redefined around Messiah and spirit, is that those who suffer with the Messiah will be glorified with him (Romans 8.17). 'Rejoicing in the hope of the glory of God' (5.2) can, then, be seen in terms of 'sharing' the divine glory, but for a full understanding it is important not to short-circuit the Jewish hope and jump straight into the (usually rather vague) modern expression of Christian hope in terms of 'glory' as an inexact synonym, or at least metonym, for 'heaven'. Paul is not here talking about 'heaven'. He is talking about the renewal and restoration of creation, and about the role within that purpose, under the creator God, of human beings in whom the spirit has been at work. The Messiah will 'inherit' the whole world, as Psalm 2 promised. He is, after all, the true seed of Abraham, to whom that promise had already been made (Romans 4.13). And the Messiah's people, the full seed of Abraham, will share that inheritance, because the divine spirit has taken up residence in them to enable them to fulfil the intention which the creator had purposed, from the beginning, for his image-bearing human creatures.

If, then, humans are supposed to be running the world under the rule of God (not worshipping it as idolators, as in 1.25, or exploiting it out of greed,

[209] NRSV: 'obtain the freedom of the glory of the children of God'; NJB: 'brought into the same glorious freedom as the children of God'; NEB 'enter upon the liberty and splendour of the children of God'.

as in Ephesians 5.3–5), the hope of creation is for these humans to take up their ancient charge once more. That is why creation is waiting on tiptoe for God's children to be raised from the dead, to become at last the wise stewards of God's world (8.19). The 'glory' of God's children is precisely that which creation will *not* share, since the 'glory' is the glorious *rule* through which creation itself will be set free from corruption, 'to enjoy the freedom that comes when God's children are glorified'.[210] That is what it means, I think, for the Messiah's people to be 'co-glorified' with him (8.17). This, then, is yet another part of Paul's 'not yet', the future eschatological scenario which has been rethought around Messiah and spirit. 'Those he justified, he also glorified': this does not mean, as it has so often been taken to mean, that 'those he justified *in the present time* will be "glorified", that is, assured of "heaven", in the *future*'. The aorist tense of 'glorified' is not simply 'prophetic', as is often claimed, stating as a past event something which can be utterly relied upon. 'Justification' is both present and future, which is part of the point of Romans 8 in any case; and so is 'glorification'. The point is that Israel's God justifies humans, puts them right, so that they can be people through whom the world is put right. That rule over the world, in both present and future, is what in Romans 8 Paul denotes by the language of 'glory'. The echoes of Psalm 8.6–7 in Romans 8.20–1 are all-important here:

> You have made them [human beings] a little lower than God,

wrote the Psalmist,

> and crowned them with glory and honour.

This 'glory and honour' is not something other than what immediately follows: the next verse, rather, explains what this 'glory and honour' are all about:

> You have given them dominion over the works of your hands;
> you have put all things under their feet (*panta hypetaxas hypo tōn podōn autōn*).

Paul is contrasting the creator's intention, to 'subject' the creation to humans, with the post-fall reality that it has been 'subjected' instead to 'futility' (*mataiotēs*) (8.20). When human beings are raised from the dead, however, having been delivered from death itself and from the sin which brings it about (8.10), then creation will itself be set free to be truly itself at last under the rule of the redeemed 'children of God' (8.21).

Romans 8, of course, stands alongside 1 Corinthians 15: the two great expositions of Paul's vision of new creation.[211] In Romans 8, the picture is of

[210] NTE.

[211] It is remarkable that Schreiner 2001, a book whose title heralds Paul as 'apostle of God's glory in Christ', appears to offer no treatment of 8.18–30. At 328 he speaks of the 'heavenly inheritance', which

the birth-pangs through which the new world will be born. In 1 Corinthians, it is the great victory over all the forces of evil, up to and including death itself. But the result is the same. God will be 'all in all' (1 Corinthians 15.28). This is not pantheism, in which the divine is everything and everything is divine. It is, to coin an ugly term, the eschatological goal of 'the-en-panism'. The prophet glimpsed the world already full of divine glory; one day it will be filled in a new way, as the waters cover the sea.[212] This, we might suggest, is a clue to the old question as to why a good God would create a world that was other than himself: would that not necessarily mean something less than perfect, and would that not compromise the supposed divine goodness? No: the creator has made a world that is other than himself, but with the capacity to respond to his creative power and love in worship and praise, and with the capacity in particular to be filled with his breath, his life, his spirit. And when that happens, it will not constitute something other than 'the hope of the glory of God', the ancient hope of Israel. It will be that hope, translated and transformed, through the Messiah and the spirit. This will be the ultimate messianic victory: the divine love, poured out in the death of the divine son, will overcome all obstacles and enemies. Indeed, it will enable his people to overcome them, and more than overcome them (Romans 8.37).

These pictures fill out the incidental (and otherwise tantalizing) references to 'new creation' we find in 2 Corinthians 5.17 and Galatians 6.15. Paul would have endorsed the vision at the close of the book of Revelation: the creator will, at the last, remake the entire cosmos, eliminating decay and death and all that causes them. That will be the triumphant reaffirmation of the original creation, achieved through the long and dark story of the covenant which was shockingly fulfilled in the Messiah.

The outworking of that achievement will be through the spirit. Romans 8 makes clear that the spirit is the one through whom those 'in the Messiah' will be raised from the dead (8.10–11). This is of course a major and central theme of Paul's 'not yet' eschatology, worked out in great detail, from its Jewish roots, in terms of Messiah and spirit. I have offered quite a full account of it elsewhere, together with its corollary, an 'intermediate state' between present death and future resurrection – again, a Jewish idea reworked around Messiah and spirit.[213] It is the spirit's work in the present, leading them to their 'inheritance' (not, now, the 'promised land', but the entire creation), and groaning within them in their life of prayer, that anticipates in the present that saving rule over creation which they will exercise in the future. Here again Paul has taken a strand from ancient Jewish expectation[214] – a strand which, though infrequent in the literature, expresses perhaps the deepest level of expectation that a creational monotheist can hold – and has imagined it afresh in the light of the Messiah and the spirit. His

implies that he has not seen the point of the 'inheritance' in Rom. 8, where the whole cosmos, liberated from corruption, is the 'inheritance'.

212 Isa. 6.3; 11.9; Hab. 2.14. (Other similar refs. above, 190–3.)

213 On all this see *RSG* Part II. On the 'intermediate state' see too Ridderbos 1975 [1966], 497–508.

214 e.g. Isa. 65.17–25, itself a reworking of 11.1–10; 66.22; cf. 2 Pet. 3.13; *4 Ezra* 7.75.

hope for the bodily resurrection of all the Messiah's people, repeatedly emphasized, constitutes the dramatic and decisive claim that Israel's hope, already fulfilled in the Messiah, will be fulfilled, by the spirit, in and for all his people.[215] This is why, more than once, Paul can speak of the present gift of the spirit as the *arrabōn*, the 'down-payment', the foretaste of what is to come, the signpost towards the final goal.[216]

It should now be clear that Paul's vision of the future is, once again, the radical redrawing of the Jewish expectation. The hope which has been fulfilled has also thereby been reshaped. The present judgment passed on sin in the Messiah's crucifixion points on to the future, ultimate judgment that will be passed on the last day, when 'the day of YHWH' in the Old Testament has been transformed into 'the day of the lord (Jesus)' in the new. This transformation has generated a new category. Changing the hope for the return of YHWH into the hope for the return of the Messiah opened up the possibility of a more direct confrontation between that *parousia* and the 'arrival' or 'presence' of a pagan emperor of deity. Paul was not slow to take up such possibilities. And in the resurrection death itself would be defeated, as the 'last enemy'.[217] This is the negative way of saying what Paul says positively in Romans 8 and 1 Corinthians 15: the whole creation will be set free from its present slavery to corruption, and the one God will be 'all in all'. Though Paul seldom says so explicitly, this is the ancient Jewish hope for 'the kingdom of God', brought into sharp focus through the gospel. This, the ultimate vision of Jewish hope, *has been* fulfilled in Messiah and spirit, and *will be* fulfilled in the same way.

We can then, by way of summary, fill out our earlier answers to the three main questions about Paul's eschatology. Paul's hope was nothing less than the redemption and renewal of all creation, and of humans within that. This would be the result of the divine 'judgment', exercised through the Messiah himself on his 'day', whose verdict is already known for those 'in the Messiah'. Paul did not shift an inch from the ancient Jewish hope, claiming rather in one passage after another that it was fulfilled in the Messiah and the spirit. He could draw on other ideas, such as that of *parousia*, but all the actual elements of his future expectation are fully explicable in terms of scripture on the one hand and the gospel on the other. As for whether his eschatology developed, it is hard to say.[218] I have argued elsewhere that we would be wrong to postulate such a development between 1 Corinthians and 2 Corinthians. There is clearly considerable difference of emphasis between the various letters: the Thessalonian correspondence has a good deal to say about the coming day, Galatians virtually nothing and the other

[215] On Paul's hope of resurrection see the full discussion of all relevant passages in *RSG* Part II (207–398).

[216] Rom. 8.23; 2 Cor. 1.22; 5.5. Eph. 1.14.

[217] 1 Cor. 15.26.

[218] See the discussions in e.g. Ridderbos 1975 [1966], 491f., 500 n. 33; Dunn 1998, 310–13; Schnelle 2005 [2003], 581–7.

letters somewhere in between.[219] As usual, Paul seldom says the same thing twice, though he can come back through familiar territory from a new angle.

It is within Paul's freshly reworked eschatology that we can now approach two of the most tricky topics in his whole thought: the questions of *ethics* and the questions of *ethnics*. How does Paul's eschatology shape his vision of Christian living, behaviour and action? And how does his vision of the divine action in Messiah and spirit enable him to tackle the question of 'all Israel'?

5. Eschatology and Christian Living

(i) Introduction

The two outstanding questions raised by Paul's inaugurated eschatology, (1) questions of Christian behaviour and action and (2) the future of 'Israel', are, for Paul, substantially new questions. Yes, of course: Jews and gentiles alike had endlessly discussed questions of what we call 'morality', of human behaviour and action, just as Jews had endlessly puzzled over the question of how the covenant God would save his people in the end. But, just as no Jewish thinker before Paul had faced the question we must study in the next section (the question of what would happen if the Messiah came and most of his people rejected him), so it is fair to say that no Jewish thinker before Paul faced the question of what would happen in an interim time, a time when the Messiah had come, when the spirit had been given, and yet humans were not yet perfect and a final end had still not appeared. And of course no non-Jewish thinker had framed the question of human behaviour in that way, either.

One might propose exceptions. The Qumran scrolls provide evidence of a community which believed that the new covenant had been inaugurated, the spirit had been given and a new fulfilment was now happening in which new codes were appropriate. In a different key, Ben-Sirach believed that the divine wisdom had come to dwell in the Temple in the form of Torah, so that the combination of proper Temple-cult and proper Torah-teaching would exemplify and/or bring about a new Eden, a freshly watered garden. The ancient prophetic dream of a time when all the covenant people would keep Torah properly was being glimpsed, grasped at, imagined and even attempted.[220] Granted. But with Paul the question was posed quite differently. For both Qumran and Sirach it could be assumed that the ultimate goal

[219] The only mention of the future hope in Gal., apart from warnings about 'not inheriting the kingdom of God' (5.21), is in 5.5: 'we are waiting eagerly, by the spirit and by faith, for the hope of righteousness.'

[220] e.g. Jer. 31.31–7; Ezek. 36.16–38. One might also add the efforts of Philo to translate Moses into terms of hellenistic philosophy and thus to enable his contemporaries to appropriate Torah in a new way.

was to keep Torah, and that the people doing the Torah-keeping would be Jews: loyal Jews; perhaps a minority, a remnant; but Jews for sure. Paul approaches the question quite differently, as will be obvious to anyone who grasps his Messiah-and-spirit-based redefinition of election. For Paul, the Messiah has come, and has been crucified and raised from the dead; and with that a previously unimagined door has opened in a previously impenetrable stone wall, revealing a new world beyond, enticing and troubling in equal measure. It is a world in which non-Jews will, in some sense, 'do the Torah', while Jews themselves will come by faith to belong to a family in which Torah is no longer either the boundary or the ultimate goal. Theologically this is like an eighteenth-century artist walking into a room full of Picassos. All the perspectives are wrong, jarring, frightening. But the new world beckons, because the Messiah has led the way into it. That is how Paul saw what we call ethics. Nobody, so far as we know, not even Jesus himself, had faced the challenge of figuring out how it would work from that point on.[221]

The word 'ethics' is itself, of course, a problem. It comes to contemporary discourse carrying baggage from the philosophical debates of the last few centuries, which have often been framed in ways that meet Paul only at a tangent. That is why some recent writers have preferred phrases like 'moral vision', and why I have spoken here of 'behaviour' and 'action'.[222] This is not the place to explore such matters. Our task is to understand Paul. But, closer to home, there is another problem. Though all students of Paul can see at a glance that he is very concerned with appropriate Christian living, the western protestant tradition has been cautious, perhaps too cautious, in how it has approached the subject. If Paul's theology of redemption provides the main structure of his thought, and if his redemptive theology finds its centre in 'justification by faith', and if 'justification by faith' means that one must place no reliance on 'works' in the sense of moral performance, then it is hardly surprising that 'ethics' as a subject has been pushed towards the back of the book. The subject is then hidden in a sanitized compartment to stop its dangerous germs of potential 'works-righteousness' from leaking out to infect the main body of doctrine. This protestant impulse has regularly tended to cut the connecting cables between faith and obedience.[223] But if, as I have been arguing, this whole way of looking at Paul is subtly but deeply mistaken, and if his thought is better understood in terms of his Messiah-

[221] See Bockmuehl 2000, 162: Jesus, so far as we know, did not even begin to address the question of how gentiles should behave within the company of his followers. This is among many reasons why it is wrong to suppose that the traditions found in the gospels are primarily a reflection of the life of the early church: see e.g. *NTPG* 421f.

[222] 'Moral vision': e.g. Hays 1996b; cf. too Meeks 1996, 3. Ridderbos 1975 [1966], 274 comments wisely on the way in which the Enlightenment in general, and Kant in particular, have skewed the relevant debates. The word 'ethics' goes back in the tradition, of course, to Aristotle (see above, 201f., 234f.); for the ancient philosophical schools, this was closely linked with 'physics', a description of 'what there is' (see below, 1098f., on 'indicative' and 'imperative').

[223] It is to the credit of e.g. Ridderbos 1975 [1966] and Schreiner 2001 that this is not the case, but that Christian behaviour finds a more Pauline place near the centre of their works. See too Bockmuehl 2000, 147.

and-spirit-driven reformulations of the ancient Jewish doctrines of monotheism, election and eschatology, then all sorts of things begin to look quite different.[224] Fear not: this is not a prelude to smuggling in 'works', to building up again a life of proud (or perhaps anxious) moralism. That is simply anachronistic. Once we understand how Paul's eschatology works, and how moral behaviour and indeed moral *effort* (a major theme in Paul, screened out altogether within some interpretative traditions) is reconceived within that world, any such imagined danger disappears.[225]

A similar problem, stemming from both the Reformation and the Enlightenment, is that 'ethics' is often conceived individualistically, whereas everything Paul says about behaviour he says in relation to the whole community, that is, the Messiah's people as a whole and sometimes the wider society as well.[226] (This links the present discussion to my analysis of the centre of Paul's worldview in Part II above.) As I have argued elsewhere, one of the major differences between virtue ethics in the ancient non-Jewish world and their equivalent in Paul is that for the tradition from Plato and Aristotle onwards 'virtue' was basically a solo occupation, whereas for Paul it was, and could only be, a team sport.[227] Most of Paul's imperatives are plural, and this is not accidental. Likewise, we should in fact follow Paul's own train of thought on 'justification' itself into the wider notion of 'justice', that is, of a community that embodies in its own life the wise ordering which is the creator's will. When he talks about 'love', and seeks to put that into practice in the churches to which he writes, he is talking specifically about something that happens within, and something that transforms, whole communities.[228]

If everything Paul said about Christian behaviour he said within a carefully thought out theological and ecclesial framework, it is more specifically the case that everything he said about Christian behaviour he said within an (often explicit) framework of revised eschatology.[229] A gap had opened up

[224] An obvious point: any kind of Jewish-style monotheism carries with it a primary 'ethical' obligation, namely, not to worship idols.

[225] Schnelle 2005 [2003], 546 rightly states that when someone is 'accepted' through the gospel, that acceptance is 'unconditional but not inconsequential'.

[226] 'Community' is one of the three focal points in the sweeping analysis of Hays 1996b. The relation of Paul's churches to wider society is especially in view in Rom. 12.14—13.10 (see Wright 2002 [*Romans*], 712–27), which is the principal location of Paul's important teaching on non-retaliation and learning the art of peace, a theme elsewhere associated more with the church's own life but here looking outwards (12.17–21; cf. Rom. 14.17, 19; 15.13; 1 Cor. 14.33; 2 Cor. 13.11; Eph. 2.14–17; Phil. 4.7, 9; Col. 3.15; 1 Thess. 5.13, all contrasting with the 'imperial peace' of 1 Thess. 5.3). On this see recently e.g. Swartley 2006.

[227] cf. Wright 2010 [*Virtue Reborn/After You Believe*], 187f./216–18.

[228] cf. e.g. Dunn 1992; Gorman 2011.

[229] On the tight integration of theology and ethics in Paul see e.g. Hays 1996b, 18, 20, 46, 56 n. 1 (against those who suppose that his 'ethics' is simply a random mélange of unsorted bits and pieces); behind this, cf. the whole work of Furnish 1968: as he says (13), 'the apostle's ethical concerns are not secondary but radically integral to his basic theological convictions', making any separate analysis of a 'Pauline ethic', apart from theology, problematic. Bockmuehl 2000, 149 points out that in the ancient world all 'ethics' were deeply 'religious', with hellenistic moral teachings nested within a larger assumed world of pagan divinities.

in his previously assumed chronology, with 'the resurrection' already happening in the case of Jesus but not yet happening for anybody else. Locating the Christian pilgrimage within this chronological gap not only enabled Paul to give fresh shape to the moral arguments familiar to Jews and non-Jews of his day; it also enabled him to glimpse an answer to the question of *why*, in the providence of the creator God, such a gap should have been necessary. Why not act all at once, to produce the long-awaited perfection? Paul's answer was deeply humanizing: the one God did it this way in order to enable the humans who would share in the running of his new creation to develop the character they would need for that ultimate task. A moment's thought will reveal a gulf between this vision of 'Christian ethics' and the popular notion that Paul, and other early teachers, were providing apparently arbitrary 'rules', cobbled together in a mixture of tradition and prejudice. Once we understand not only the inaugurated-eschatological *shaping* of Paul's moral world, but also what he seems to have conceived as the *purpose* of that inaugurated eschatology, all sorts of issues appear in a new light.

This way of handling Paul's 'eschatological ethics' is radically different from those in which such a phrase would have to do with the 'imminent *parousia*'. I have argued elsewhere against that basic idea as a historical construct in its own right, let alone as a shaping force for theology or ethics.[230] For Paul what mattered was primarily something that *had* happened, namely, the resurrection of Jesus and the gift of the spirit: eschatology still involved a solidly future dimension, as we have just seen, but when I speak of 'eschatological ethics' I refer not to an ethic determined by a sense that the world was about to end but to a sense of human vocation shaped equally by what *had* recently happened and what *would* one day happen.[231]

This helps particularly with the frequently repeated proposal that Paul's ethics are a matter of 'indicative' and 'imperative': what you already *are* 'in the Messiah', over against how you *must now behave*. There is of course a well-established linguistic point here, made two generations ago by Rudolf Bultmann and endlessly repeated.[232] It is, however, oversimple to suppose that 'theology' is located with the 'indicative' and 'ethics' with the 'imperative'. Life is more complicated than that, as the integration just noted bears

[230] See *NTPG* 342f., 459–64; cf. too *JVG* 360–8. See further, on the critical passage in 1 Cor. 7.29–31 (from whose slender beam great weights have been suspended), Thiselton 2000, 580–3.

[231] This 'now and not yet' was how Paul thought on a cosmic scale, but it was also true at a local level: '[Paul] envisioned a corporate narrative in which his communities began as slaves of various vices and then pursued the goal of their transformed existence. He writes in the middle of that narrative . . .' (Thompson 2011, 207).

[232] Bultmann 1995 [1924]. See the discussions in e.g. Ridderbos 1975 [1966], 255–8; Furnish 1968, 242–79; Dunn 1998, 628–31; Burridge 2007, 105f. Perhaps the most positive thing one can say about the 'indicative/imperative' question is the comment of Wolter 2011, 315: this corresponds to the relation between election and Torah.

witness.[233] In fact, the modern splitting of 'indicative' and 'imperative' seems to bear witness, not to a division of thought in Paul himself, but to a desire to render his thought into the categories of post-Enlightenment theory on the one hand, and the ancient non-Jewish ethics on the other. To highlight the linguistic forms is a kind of demythologization, or even potential paganization, of the underlying reality, which is the eschatological tension caused by the gap between the arrival of 'the end' in the middle of history with Jesus' resurrection and the still-to-be-awaited further 'arrival' of 'the end' in the sense of 1 Corinthians 15.24 ('then comes the end (*telos*)').[234]

Locating Paul's 'ethics' in this newly opened up eschatological gap helps, as well, in discerning the origins of his thought about Christian behaviour and action. Gone are the days when it could be assumed that Paul, having set out his primary theological proposals, simply shovelled in a miscellany of hellenistic *paraenesis* to give his churches something to be going on with.[235] Indeed, despite the widespread use of that word in this connection, Udo Schnelle is undoubtedly correct to raise the question as to whether one should not rather speak, as Paul does, of *paraklēsis*, 'encouragement'.[236] The question of the origin of Paul's ethical thought has wobbled to and fro for some time now on the old lines of a history-of-religions debate: was Paul basically a Jewish thinker or a Greek one? Did he get his ideas from the scriptures (particularly from the Torah itself) or from his surrounding culture?[237] This discussion, however, needs to be relocated within the larger

[233] It is, in particular, wrong to suggest that Paul divided his letters into 'doctrinal' and 'ethical' sections (so, rightly, e.g. Dunn 1998, 626f.; Burridge 2007, 106). Romans, sometimes astonishingly cited as an example, at once gives the game away, with a tight integration of theology and ethics being obvious in e.g. 2.12–16, 25–9; 4.20–5; 6.2–23; 8.5–16 and indeed 12.1–2; 14.1—15.13. The best actual example might be Eph., with an almost formal bipartite structure (1—3; 4—6); but, quite apart from questions of authenticity, there is plenty of 'ethics' in the first half and plenty of 'doctrine' in the second.

[234] Schnelle 2005 [2003], 547f. launches a detailed attack on the 'indicative/imperative' analysis, demonstrating its inadequacy and proposing instead a paradigm of 'transformation and participation' (as in his earlier article, Schnelle 2001). This seems to me substantially on the right lines. See too now Zimmerman 2007. The much-vaunted split between 'is' and 'ought' is commonly thought to go back to Hume and Kant; but, while they did indeed envisage an epistemological separation between empirical truths and moral values, they both believed that moral value could be stated *as a kind of reality*. Almost all Hume's own moral judgments are formed with the verb 'is'. I owe this point, as indeed much else, to Prof. Oliver O'Donovan.

[235] Hays 1996b, 17, rightly rejects such theories (as expounded by M. Dibelius and others). The word *paraenesis*, which means 'exhortation', is not found in the NT, and its cognate verb, occurring twice in Ac. (27.9, 22), is not used by Paul.

[236] Schnelle 2005 [2003], 556; see too Thompson 2011, 59f.; but cf. e.g. Wolter 2011, 311f., advocating what seems basically a heuristic use of *paraenesis*. Paul uses both *paraklēsis* and its cognate *parakaleō* frequently: cf. BDAG 764–6.

[237] On Paul's scripturally rooted ethics see esp. Rosner 1994; Bockmuehl 2000, 145–73; Tomson 1990; and esp. Thompson 2011. On the greco-roman world of moral exhortation see the important work of Malherbe 1986; Meeks 1986b; 1993; 1996. Posing some difficult questions of detail to the question of 'Paul and scripture' in ethical contexts is Tuckett 2000, though we may suspect that Tuckett has not fully grasped the larger point that Hays and others are making. Dunn 1998, 662 suggests that the denial of Paul's use of scripture in his ethics is 'one of the curiosities of twentieth-century exegesis'. The curiosity is, of course, explicable by the implicit dominance of a quasi-Marcionite reading. This has survived the transition from an older Lutheranism, in which 'the law' was rejected in favour of 'justification by faith', to a newer liberal or even postmodern theology in which scriptural reference as a whole is relativized in favour of the 'inclusion' of a wide range of cultural norms and practices. See the description in

picture of election and Torah which we have sketched in chapter 10 above. From that viewpoint it will become clear that Paul was indeed a deeply biblical thinker, in his 'ethics' as in everything else; that he believed in a strange new sort of transformed Torah-fulfilment which was open to gentiles as well as Jews; and that he believed that such Torah-fulfilment would form the Messiah's followers into a kind of genuine humanity, the sort of thing which his pagan contemporaries glimpsed from time to time but confessed their own inability to attain. This explains the way in which he frequently alludes to themes and categories from his wider non-Jewish environment, as is now routinely shown.[238]

This opens up a new perspective (so to speak) on the question not only of the origin of Paul's ethics but of what we might call his 'public theology'. In the ancient non-Jewish world of Paul's day 'ethics' related directly to 'physics': behavioural norms were correlated to 'the way things are'. That, actually, might have been an obvious location for the combination of 'indicative and imperative'. But for Paul the whole point was that a *new* world had been launched in and through Jesus. This is the strong point of today's so-called 'apocalyptic' interpretation: Paul sees everything in a new light because the new world has come into existence. 'Ethics' may still be related to 'physics', but only in the sense that 'the way things are' has been radically transformed by the events concerning Jesus, and will be further radically transformed when what was there begun is finally complete. 'Ethics' must relate, then, to a radically redrawn 'physics': new action in a new age. But at the same time Paul believed, on classic Jewish grounds, that this new world was the new *creation*, in continuity with the old, however much radically transformed. That is why his 'ethics' have a close analogy on some points at least to those of his non-Jewish contemporaries (see below). His aim and hope is that the new way of life in his churches will commend itself to the pagan world, not as an odd, bizarre way to be human, but as a way which makes sense of their own deepest aspirations. We shall pursue these matters further in chapter 14 below.[239]

This complex picture of Paul's ethical thought is not, then, reducible to terms of 'Jew or Greek', indeed of 'derivation' as a controlling category. Nor can it be caught in the oversimplifications of a grammatical slogan. It is about the eschatological and behavioural aspect of the redefined election we examined in the previous chapter, itself rooted in Paul's revised monotheism. And this fascinating development of a new kind of 'ethics', dependent on what we might call a new kind of 'physics' – the new creation! – is what provides the shape for the rest of this section. The new creation – both the *new* creation and the new *creation* – has already been launched, and Messiah-people must learn how to live within that new world. They are 'already in the new age'. Equally, the final *new creation* is yet to come, and

Thompson 2011, 12, including G. Strecker's suggestion that 'concrete norms would violate Paul's message of freedom' and R. Scroggs's aligning of Paul with 'situation ethics'.

[238] See e.g. the works of Meeks and Malherbe, as in the previous note.

[239] An important monograph in relation to all this is that of Rabens 2010.

their behaviour must look ahead to, and live in accordance with, something which is 'not yet' a present reality.

(ii) Already in the New Age

Paul leaves his hearers in no doubt that an event has happened in the middle of history through which the long-awaited 'new age', the 'age to come' of Jewish expectation, has dawned. Jesus 'gave himself for our sins', he writes in what may be the earliest paragraph of his that we possess, 'to rescue us from the present evil age, according to the will of God our father'.[240] As a result, they must not let themselves 'be squeezed into the shape dictated by the present age'. Rather, he declares to his Roman audience, you must 'be transformed by the renewing of your minds'.[241] When he speaks of a 'new creation', and of people sharing in that new reality, this is what he has in mind: something has come about through the achievement of Jesus, something in which those who are 'in the Messiah' now share, and that 'something' is a previously unimagined state of affairs: 'the age to come' has arrived, even though 'the present age' is still rumbling on its way. This is the famous 'overlap of the ages', of which we spoke earlier.[242] Those who find themselves in the middle of the picture we drew in the previous chapter – the reconceived election by gospel, spirit, baptism and faith – are to be taught the significance of the final worldview question: What time is it?

One of Paul's favourite images to express this overlap of the times or ages is that of the new day which is dawning. We who are familiar with jet-lag are used to the idea that the sun may already be rising in, say, Hong Kong, while it is still midnight in Johannesburg. I do not know if the ancients, whose fastest method of travel was on horseback, understood what we now think of as time-zones. Did a Roman living in Spain, for instance, know that his friend serving in the army in Syria was enjoying sunrise an hour or two ahead of him? That, in any case, is the kind of image Paul is using: he tells the citizens of the night-bound world that they are to live as though they belonged to the new day. The night is passing, he says, and the day is at hand. This has a trace of theological metonymy as well as metaphor, since it obviously correlates with the 'day of the lord' of which we spoke earlier. Paul develops the image to suggest the contrast between the sort of behaviour that prefers the cover of darkness and the sort that is happy to be under public scrutiny – a hint that his 'ethic' is not simply a matter of private and peculiar 'Christian morality', but in line with what the pagan world around knew in its bones was healthy and wise behaviour.[243] 'The works of darkness' are shameful even to speak of, and need to be exposed by the light. He quotes what appears to be an early hymn to this effect:

[240] Gal. 1.4.

[241] Rom. 12.2.

[242] Above, 477f., 500. On 'new creation' cf. e.g. 2 Cor. 5.17; Gal. 6.15.

[243] Rom. 13.11–14. See above, 614; and below, 1374–6.

> Wake up, you sleeper!
> Rise up from the dead!
> The Messiah will shine upon you![244]

The same image enables him to echo some well-known sayings of Jesus about watching out for burglars in the night, though in characteristic Pauline fashion he develops this metaphor by means of two or three others: the woman will go into labour (echoes, there, of the old biblical theme of the 'birthpangs of the new age'), so one must not get drunk, but must put on armour for the day:

> We daytime people should be self-controlled, clothing ourselves with the breastplate of faith and love, and with the helmet of the hope of salvation.[245]

And of course the image of 'sleeping' and 'waking', picked up in these passages, goes very closely with the event that had generated this new moment. The metaphor of 'sleep', for death, and of 'waking up', for resurrection, was already well established in Jewish thought, looking back to Daniel 12.2. For Paul, the resurrection of Jesus had ushered in the dawn of the 'age to come', and all those who were 'in the Messiah' through baptism were declared to be 'daytime people'. The resurrection functioned, for him, as the platform on which the Messiah's people now stood, on which they could learn to become genuine human beings at last:

> Don't you know that all of us who were baptized into the Messiah, Jesus, were baptized into his death? That means that we were buried with him, through baptism, into death, so that, just as the Messiah was raised from the dead through the father's glory, we too might behave with a new quality of life. For if we have been planted together in the likeness of his death, we shall also be in the likeness of his resurrection ...
>
> But if we died with the Messiah, we believe that we shall live with him. We know that the Messiah, having been raised from the dead, will never die again. Death no longer has any authority over him. The death he died, you see, he died to sin, once and only once. But the life he lives, he lives to God. In the same way you, too, must calculate yourselves as being dead to sin, and alive to God in the Messiah, Jesus.[246]

'Calculate yourselves ... alive to God.' There is no sense here, as one popular view has it, that Paul thinks the baptized have died to sin but that he is postponing their 'resurrection' to the future.[247] Paul's argument would make no sense if that were the case. Clearly there is still a future resurrection, as in Romans 8.9–11. But if they are already 'in the Messiah', and if the Messiah has died and been raised, then they must 'calculate themselves' as being raised 'in him' or 'with him'. The future tenses of verses 5 and 8 are *logical* futures, not chronological: 'if X is the case, Y will also be the case'. Paul's point, in urging his readers to 'calculate' or 'reckon' that they are already raised with the Messiah, is precisely that their behaviour must

[244] Eph. 5.11–14.

[245] 1 Thess. 5.8, within the larger paragraph of 5.1–11.

[246] Rom. 6.2–5, 8–11.

[247] See e.g. Schnelle 2005 [2003], 579, with many commentaries.

undergo a radical change. If they are not in some sense already 'alive from the dead', he is asking for the impossible:

> So don't allow sin to rule in your mortal body ... Rather, present yourselves to God, *as people alive from the dead*, and your limbs and organs to God ... [248]

This is, then, substantially the same point that we find in Colossians 3. After explaining in chapter 2 that there is no help to be found in the spurious moralisms on offer elsewhere, Paul sets out a different way. The new *status* must be the basis for new *behaviour*, which is to be achieved by implementing the death-and-life of the Messiah, and which can be spoken of in terms both of a *new human nature* and of 'putting on the Messiah' like a suit of clothes:

> So if you were raised to life with the Messiah, search for the things that are above, where the Messiah is seated at God's right hand! Think about the things that are above, not the things that belong on the earth. Don't you see: you died, and your life has been hidden with the Messiah, in God! When the Messiah is revealed (and he is your life, remember), then you too will be revealed with him in glory.
>
> So, then, you must kill off the parts of you that belong on the earth: illicit sexual behaviour, uncleanness, passion, evil desire and greed (which is a form of idolatry). It's because of these things that God's wrath comes on the children of disobedience. You too used to behave like that, once, when your life consisted of that sort of thing.
>
> But now you must put away the lot of them: anger, rage, wickedness, blasphemy, dirty talk coming out of your mouth. Don't tell lies to each other! You have stripped off the old human nature, complete with its patterns of behaviour, and you have put on the new one – which is being renewed in the image of the creator, bringing you into possession of new knowledge. In this new humanity there is no question of 'Greek and Jew', or 'circumcised and uncircumcised', of 'barbarian, Scythian', or 'slave and free'. The Messiah is everything and in everything![249]

The Messiah's resurrection, then, has brought about total change. Those who have died and been raised with him have a new identity; patterns of behaviour which belong with the old life must simply be killed off. There is a to-and-fro implied here between what is already true at one level ('you *have* stripped off the old human nature') and what must become true by sheer, new-creational moral effort ('you *must* kill off ...'). The clear implication is that the latter is possible because the former has happened; and here, as in Romans 6, the reason appears to be baptism.[250] Of course, here as in Romans (and Galatians 3.25–9) this is closely correlated with faith. But Paul believed that in baptism one entered a new reality, a new family, a new version of the human race, in which all sorts of things were possible that previously had not been. Paul elsewhere (not least in 1 Corinthians 10) has some sharp reminders for people who presume upon baptism as if it operated by magic; but that is no reason to ignore what he actually says about it. For Paul, the resurrection of Jesus was a truth not just about the Messiah

[248] Rom. 6.12f.

[249] Col. 3.1–11.

[250] Col. 2.11–12, which underlies the entire argument from 2.13 to 3.17.

but about all those who were 'in him', and baptism celebrated that truth about the whole church while incorporating another member into it.[251] Christian behaviour was what it was because of that *past* event through which the 'age to come' had become a reality for the believer.

The incorporation of the believer into the Messiah is the context within which we can understand Paul's exhortation to *imitate* him. More precisely, Paul urges his hearers to imitate *him* as he imitates the Messiah, or perhaps to join him in imitating the Messiah.[252] This is not applied so much in terms of every detail of ordinary life, but in terms of the central events of the gospel and the pattern they create, as we can see in the sequence of thought which joins Philippians 2.5–11 to 3.2–11 and thence to 3.17. Paul imitates the Messiah in giving up his privileges and status, and he urges the Philippian Christians to take him, doing this, as their model. This is a very similar line of thought to what we find in 1 Corinthians 8—10, summed up in 11.1. In particular, this helps us understand the meaning of that much-debated verse Philippians 2.5, which I have translated, 'This is how you should think among yourselves, with the mind that you have because you belong to the Messiah, Jesus.'[253] It is not a matter of a surface-level 'imitation', with people simply attempting to copy Jesus and so make themselves better people. It is a matter of the 'mind of the Messiah' which they already possess (see below), and of them allowing this shared and transformed 'mind' to work out into actual patterns of thought and then behaviour (as in 2.1–4).[254] The outward signs of this can be seen in the various places where Paul seems to be echoing actual sayings of Jesus.[255] But the underlying reality is that the Messiah's people are as it were enfolded within the *narrative* of Jesus' incarnation, crucifixion, resurrection and exaltation. This is where some recent writers have referred to 'cruciformity' or even 'Christosis', and where the line of thought explored by Morna Hooker over many years, that of 'interchange', comes into its own.[256] All this is seen once more, bringing the argument of Romans to its climax, in 15.3, 15.5 and 15.7: the community is to live by the negative rule of not pleasing oneself, and by the positive rule of mutual welcome, both of which are modelled by and 'in accordance with' the Messiah himself as foreshadowed in scripture and as acted out in the gospel events:

[251] See above, 421–4.

[252] So e.g. 1 Cor. 4.6, 16; 11.1; Phil. 3.17; 4.9; Col. 3.15; 1 Thess. 1.6; 2.14; 2 Thess 3.7, 9; and 'imitating God' in Eph. 5.1. See Hays 1996b, 31; Burridge 2007, 144–8, with good discussion of recent literature. See too the suggestive study of Eastman 2008.

[253] Or, as Gorman 2009, 11 suggests: 'Cultivate this mindset in your community, which is in fact a community in Christ Jesus . . .'

[254] See e.g. Bockmuehl 1998, 121–3; behind that, Hurtado 1984; also now Fowl 1998; Dodd 1998. The objections of Käsemann 1968 to an 'ethical' reading of Phil. 2.6–11 are well explained by Morgan 1998, e.g. 59, 67: his target was an 'ethical idealism' which 'would not get us out of the old world'. Most of those advocating an 'ethical' reading today are not, I think, proposing what Käsemann was denying. An important recent study is that of Hood 2013.

[255] On sayings of Jesus in the letters of Paul, see the important study of Kim 1993.

[256] See e.g. the first four chapters of Hooker 1990, and the helpful brief summary now in Hooker 2013; Gorman 2013. On 'transformation', see the discussions above, esp. 952–60.

> We, the 'strong' ones, should bear with the frailty of the 'weak', and not please ourselves. Each one of us should please our neighbour for his or her good, to build them up.
>
> *The Messiah, you see, did not please himself.* Instead, as the Bible says, 'the reproaches of those who reproached you are fallen on me'. Whatever was written ahead of time, you see, was written for us to learn from, so that through patience, and through the encouragement of the Bible, we might have hope. May the God of patience and encouragement grant you to come to a common mind among yourselves, *in accordance with the Messiah, Jesus,* so that, with one mind and one mouth, you may glorify the God and father of our Lord Jesus the Messiah.
>
> Welcome one another, therefore, *as the Messiah has welcomed you,* to God's glory. Let me tell you why: the Messiah became a servant of the circumcised people in order to demonstrate the truthfulness of God – that is, to confirm the promises to the patriarchs, and to bring the nations to praise God for his mercy.[257]

The underlying logic here is very close to that of Philippians 2 (and, indeed, to the appeal for Messiah-shaped generosity in 2 Corinthians 8.9). And the end in view is the same, too: in Philippians, it is the unity of the church at the deepest level (2.1–4); in Romans, it is the mutual welcome which leads to shared worship.[258]

The identity of this new community, which Paul urges so passionately to imitate the Messiah, is bound up with the narrative which dominates so much early Christian thought: that of the new exodus. As we have seen, Romans 6 is all about those who come through the water of baptism, like the Israelites coming through the Red Sea, and who are therefore *freed slaves* on the one hand, and a *holy people* on the other because they are 'sanctified' by the powerful presence and guidance of the spirit.[259] This of course joins up once more with the whole theme of revised 'election', and it carries clear obligations:

> But now that you have been set free from sin and enslaved to God, you have fruit for holiness. Its destination is the life of the age to come. The wages paid by sin, you see, are death; but God's free gift is the life of the age to come, in the Messiah, Jesus our lord.

> So then, my dear family, we are in debt – but not to human flesh, to live our life in that way. If you live in accordance with the flesh, you will die; but if, by the spirit, you put to death the deeds of the body, you will live.

[257] Rom. 15.1–9. On this see esp. Thompson 1991, 208–41.

[258] Burridge 2007, 148 expounds all this well, but at the end seems to me to hint at a somewhat different agenda. He is right to say that Paul highlights Jesus' deeds rather than his words, and to see this focused particularly on the cross. But to slide from that, via 'concern for others, especially the weaker', to Jesus' 'acceptance of others, what we have called his open pastoral practice' needs to be confronted more explicitly with Rom. 6.2–11 (which Burridge expounds at 102–7, but does not seem to relate to the idea of 'open practice'); cf. too 8.12–16, which strangely does not appear in Burridge's index). As Burridge himself notes (176), Jesus' 'open pastoral practice' itself included saying things which made some people go away sorrowfully, unable to meet the stringent moral demands of Jesus' brand of 'inclusivity' (Mk. 10.22).

[259] The word 'sanctify' and its cognates have a long history in Christian moral discourse, but its temple-overtones, which would be obvious to a first-century Jew, are not normally explored (e.g. the minimal reference in Johnson 2009, 100). Paul's use of *hagiasmos* and similar terms reflects his new-temple theology, as in the passage from 1 Cor. 6 just referred to, and as in Rom. 8.9–11. The Christian, indwelt by the spirit, is a 'holy place' in the sense of the biblical sanctuary. That is why for Paul 'sanctification' goes so closely with 'glorification' (since the divine glory comes to dwell in the sanctuary).

> All who are led by the spirit of God, you see, are God's children. You didn't receive a spirit of slavery, did you, to go back again into a state of fear? But you received the spirit of sonship, in whom we call out 'Abba, father!'[260]

In other words: you have come through the Red Sea; you are on the way to your inheritance; so don't even think of going back to Egypt! This is age-to-come ethics, located within Paul's reworked eschatological narrative. Learn where you are in the story, he says, and what time it is, and questions about appropriate behaviour will appear in the proper light. The challenge in Romans 8.12–16, repeating the stark choice faced by the Israelites in the wilderness, is that of the two ways: one path that leads to death, the other that leads to life.[261] It would be possible, reading this out of context, to suppose that he was setting up exactly that kind of merit-based system which his own doctrine of justification should have destroyed several chapters earlier. I have answered this objection in the previous chapter.

This brings us to another feature of Paul's eschatology which bears strongly on the question of present Christian behaviour: the kingdom of God. Though this is normally, in Paul, a future reality (and will therefore be covered in the next sub-section), Paul can also speak of it as a present truth to which behaviour must conform. This is clear in Romans 14.17: 'God's kingdom … isn't about food and drink, but about justice, peace, and joy in the holy spirit.' In addition, we note that in the cryptic mention of 'the kingdom of the Messiah and of God' in Ephesians 5.5 it is probable that Paul understands the Messiah's kingdom to be the present reality, as in 1 Corinthians 15.25, and the divine kingdom the future reality.[262] He is not always strictly 'consistent' in his usage, no doubt precisely because he is always aware of the 'already' and the 'not yet' jangling against one another.

If the Messiah's resurrection is for Paul the crucial factor in determining the Christian's *status* and *goal*, the powerful agent by which, in the meantime, humans are enabled to turn that status into behaviour is of course the *spirit*. Indeed, one may put it the other way round: the spirit is given so that those who are 'in the Messiah' can *anticipate*, in present behaviour, the life of the coming age. The role of the spirit has already emerged in some of the passages quoted, and it becomes a major theme in Galatians 5 and 6 in particular. I have written about this at length elsewhere and do not need to repeat the point here.[263] One thing we should note, however: when Paul speaks of the 'fruit of the spirit', in contradistinction to the 'works of the flesh', he is not talking of things that happen 'automatically', as some contemporary romantic or existentialist thinkers would suppose.[264] Part of the mystery of the spirit's work, at least as Paul understands its work, is that that work does not cancel out human moral effort, including thought, will,

[260] Rom. 6.22f.; 8.12–15.

[261] cf. Dt. 3.15–20.

[262] On the temporary messianic kingdom cf. e.g. Aune 1992, 603.

[263] Wright 2010 [*Virtue Reborn*/*After You Believe*].

[264] Gal. 5.19–23.

decision and action. Rather, it makes them all possible. It opens up a new kind of freedom and offers help, encouragement and companionship in discerning and putting into practice the fresh actions to which different believers may be called (see below). That is why Paul can speak of his own hard work and then, in the same breath, declare that it was actually the divine power at work within him. It felt like hard work at the time – which is why he regularly encourages his hearers not to give up when faced with the same challenge – but in retrospect he knows that the energy came from elsewhere.[265]

One or two important final notes about what it means that those in the Messiah are already part of the God-given new age. First, as we have seen often enough, those in the Messiah and indwelt by the spirit form the people to whom Paul gives the word 'the Jew', 'the circumcision' and even – if that reading is correct – 'the Israel of God'.[266] He speaks to the Corinthians about the time 'when you were pagans (*ethnē*)', and assumes that despite that background they can be included in the 'we' that speaks of the ancient Israelites as 'our ancestors'.[267] He appeals to the Thessalonians, in a strongly worded section which is rightly to be seen as a summary of his main ethical stance, that they should no longer behave 'like gentiles who don't know God'.[268] He sees the church standing out from the world around, living by a kind of fulfilled-Jewish standard through which all others – including Jews themselves! – are now to be judged:

> So people who are by nature uncircumcised, but who fulfil the law, will pass judgment on people like you who possess the letter of the law and circumcision but who break the law.
>
> There must be no grumbling and disputing in anything you do. That way, nobody will be able to fault you, and you'll be pure and spotless children of God in the middle of a twisted and depraved generation. You are to shine among them like lights in the world, clinging on to the word of life.[269]

Or, more bluntly:

> So this is what I want to say; I am bearing witness to it in the lord. You must no longer behave like the gentiles, foolish-minded as they are. Their understanding is darkened; they are cut off from God's life because of their deep-seated ignorance, which springs from the fact that their hearts are hard. They have lost all moral sensitivity, and have given

[265] So e.g. 1 Cor. 15.10, 58; Col. 1.29; on hard work and not giving up: Gal. 6.9; 1 Thess. 5.14; 2 Thess. 3.6–13.

[266] cf. Rom. 2.29; Phil. 3.3; Gal. 6.16. On the relevant debates, and particularly on Rom. 9—11, see below.

[267] 1 Cor. 12.2; 10.1.

[268] 1 Thess. 4.5. On the role of 1 Thess. in general and 1 Thess. 4 in particular as effective summaries of Paul's ethics see Thompson 2011, ch. 3. Actually the definite article in the Greek of 4.5 might suggest 'like *the* Gentiles, who don't know God': not that there are some gentiles who do know this God and some who don't, but that gentiles, by definition, do not know the true God. The close implied link between wild lust and idolatry is reinforced by the explanatory note in Eph. 5.5 and Col. 3.5, where sexual greed is said to be (a form of) idolatry.

[269] Rom. 2.27; Phil. 2.14–16.

> themselves over to whatever takes their fancy. They go off greedily after every kind of uncleanness.
>
> But that's not how you learned the king! – if indeed you did hear about him, and were taught in him, in accordance with the truth about Jesus himself. That teaching stressed that you should take off your former lifestyle, the old humanity. That way of life is decaying, as a result of deceitful lusts. Instead, you must be renewed in the spirit of your mind, and you must put on the new humanity, which is being created the way God intended it, displaying justice and genuine holiness.[270]

Here, of course, we meet the familiar paradox once more.[271] Paul is urging his converts to maintain what is in all sorts of ways a thoroughly and strictly Jewish lifestyle, over against the swirling currents of pagan amorality. But he wants them to do this *without becoming ethnically Jewish*, without circumcision, the food taboos and the sabbath. He instructs them to live a life which, for the Jew, focused on Temple and Torah and on the family home in which, with Jew marrying Jew, the life and the lifestyle would be maintained. Paul takes it for granted that the Messiah, the ultimate representative Jew, has created in himself a new people, a new home, a new temple, a new way of life in which all the moral distinctives between Jew and pagan would be maintained.[272]

We might even suggest that this is the real reason for the inclusion of those much-debated 'household codes'.[273] It is not simply that Paul wants Messiah-people to live a socially respectable family life, though he does to be sure want Christians to be known by their neighbours for their adherence to basic moral norms.[274] It is, rather, that just as Jews in the Diaspora were sustained in their distinctive life not only by the synagogues but just as much by their home life, so Paul sees the home life of the new people to be a vital context within which the practice of following and imitating the Messiah is to be inculcated and sustained. Such codes would not, therefore, simply be an accommodation to prevailing social mores – as is already indicated by the various specifically Christian modifications and startling innovations, such as crediting children and slaves with serious responsibility, and giving strict and counter-cultural instructions to husbands and slaveowners. They offer evidence of a fundamentally Jewish, and indeed renewed-Jewish, perception of the dispersed messianic people.[275]

270 Eph. 4.17–24. The idea of 'putting on the Messiah' itself partakes in the 'now and not yet' of Paul's ethics: it has in principle already happened (Gal. 3.27) and it is something which the baptized must be sure to do (Rom. 13.14; Col. 3.10).

271 See esp. above, ch. 6; and below, ch. 15.

272 Sanders 1983, 201f. helpfully summarizes Newton 1985: 'Paul was concerned with the church's *unity* (and thus denied the parts of the law which separate Jew from Gentile), and also with its *purity* (and thus insisted on keeping aspects of the law which kept the church pure from the contagion brought by idolatry and sexual immorality)' (italics original). This is the major exception to Paul's normal rule (Sanders 1983, 178) that 'the factors which separated Jews from Greeks must be given up by the Jews'.

273 Eph. 5.21—6.9; Col. 3.18—4.1; 1 Pet. 2.18—3.7. Cf. Towner 1993; Boring 2007; and below, 1375.

274 e.g. Rom. 12.9–15.

275 One might contrast, e.g., Paul's advice to slaves and masters with the rather different advice in Sir. 33.25–30 (though cf. the change of tone in 33.31–3).

At the heart of Paul's 'fulfilled-Jewish' vision of the moral life we find a point which should not be controversial but often is: those in the Messiah, indwelt by the spirit, are assumed to fulfil the real intention of Torah.[276] Paul never spells out as precisely as we would like him to the difference between the 'works of Torah' which cannot bring justification and the 'work of Torah' which, written on the heart, produces even among gentiles the lifestyle which Torah wanted to produce but, because of unredeemed Adamic 'flesh', could not. (This is the distinction which older theology tried to capture in the imprecise, and potentially misleading, distinction of the 'moral' and 'ceremonial' law.) Generations of quasi-Marcionite post-Reformation readings, eager to label the Jewish law as a 'bad' thing now happily 'abolished' in the gospel, have produced a climate of thought where Paul's key sayings on this point have not been taken seriously, but he means them all right. This is where the so-called 'new perspective', and the contribution of James Dunn in particular, have been especially helpful.[277] Some Jewish teachers said that if only all Israel were to keep Torah for a single day, then the Messiah would come. Paul reverses the point: now that the Messiah has come, his true people will truly 'keep Torah', even though this Torah-keeping will not look like what those teachers had imagined:

> If uncircumcised people keep the law's requirements (*ta dikaiōmata tou nomou phylassē*), their uncircumcision will be regarded (*logisthēsetai*) as circumcision, won't it? So people who are by nature uncircumcised, but who fulfil the law (*ton nomon telousa*), will pass judgment on people like you . . .
>
> Circumcision is nothing; uncircumcision is nothing; what matters is keeping God's commandments!
>
> So what happens to boasting? It is ruled out! Through what sort of law? The law of works? No: through the law of faith.
>
> God sent his own son . . . in order that the right and proper verdict of the law (*to dikaiōma tou nomou*) could be fulfilled in us, as we live not according to the flesh but according to the spirit.
>
> Look at it like this. People whose lives are determined by human flesh focus their minds on matters to do with the flesh, but people whose lives are determined by the spirit focus their minds on matters to do with the spirit. Focus the mind on the flesh, and you'll die; but focus it on the spirit, and you'll have life, and peace. The mind focused on the flesh, you see, is hostile to God. It doesn't submit to God's law, in fact, it can't. Those who are determined by the flesh can't please God.[278]

The point is often missed in the flurry of other ideas in Romans 8, but it is clear: *the 'mind of the spirit' submits to Torah.* Those who are 'in the flesh', by which Paul obviously means those outside the Messiah's community of

[276] On this see e.g. Ridderbos 1975 [1966], 278–88, against A. Nygren in particular (who wants to rule out any positive sense of Torah) and also H. Lietzmann (who wants to insist that the Christian must simply act spontaneously, without legal instruction); Dunn 1998, 631–42; Schreiner 2001, 321–9. See esp. the helpful summary in Rosner 2003, 214–16.

[277] See e.g. Dunn 2008 [2005], chs. 17, 19; and cf. e.g. Wolter 2011, 322f.

[278] Rom. 2.26f.; 1 Cor. 7.19; Rom. 3.27; 8.3–8; cf. Hays 2005, 149–51.

faithful and baptized people who have died and been raised with him (7.4–6), have 'the mind of the flesh', which summarizes the description he had given in 1.18–32. This 'mind' does not, and cannot, submit to the divine law. But from this it should be clear that 'the mind of the spirit' *does* submit, in the senses indicated in 2.25–9 and elsewhere. That is why 'the right and proper verdict of the law' is pronounced over them, namely that they will 'have life', as Paul indicates in the two short paragraphs 8.9–11 and 8.12–16. This is, clearly, not a matter of slavishly looking up texts in Torah and trying to make them fit every question Paul and his communities might face. He clearly does not do that.[279] He is after something deeper, something which will sometimes (as in eating meat offered to idols) cut across what a strict interpretation of Torah itself would have said.[280]

This then points forward to two further 'law-fulfilment' passages in Romans. The first, at the heart of Romans 10.1–13, we shall consider more fully below. The second, less complicated, sums up the ten commandments, and insists that all of them are fulfilled in the law of love:

> Don't owe anything to anyone, except the debt of mutual love. If you love your neighbour, you see, you have fulfilled the law. Commandments like 'don't commit adultery, don't kill, don't steal, don't covet' – and any other commandment – are summed up in this: 'Love your neighbour as yourself.' Love does no wrong to its neighbour; so love is the fulfilment of the law (*plērōma nomou*).[281]

This is itself summed up in Galatians:

> You must become each other's servants, through love. For the whole law is summed up in one word, namely this: 'Love your neighbour as yourself.'[282]

And there is a lot to be said for seeing the same idea under the cryptic phrase in the next chapter:

> Carry each other's burdens; that's the way to fulfil the Messiah's law.[283]

No doubt this has rhetorical, as well as theological, force: 'if it's lawkeeping you want, go for the Messiah's law!' The latter phrase, as is well known, is

[279] So, rightly, Schnelle 2005 [2003], 552f. Schnelle does not, I think, see the deeper sense of 'fulfilment' which lies underneath these surface discrepancies. The argument of Bockmuehl 2000, ch. 7, that what we have in Paul and elsewhere in early Christianity is a taking up of what later came to be seen as the 'Noachide' commands – that is, laws for all humans, not just for Abraham's family – is an ingenious attempt to preserve a sense that Paul was indeed drawing on specific Torah-commands for his ethical instructions.

[280] The question is examined from a modern systematic theological perspective by Meilander 2011, 581–3.

[281] Rom. 13.8–10; cf. Wolter 2011, 338.

[282] Gal. 5.13f. This introduces, of course, the sequence of thought which climaxes in the 'fruit of the spirit', the first of which is 'love'. Witherington 1998, 381 points out that 'summed up' here is *peplērōtai*, 'has been fulfilled', from the same root as *plērōma* in Gal. 4.4, and that this is 'eschatological language', indicating the promised time when the basic intention of Torah, 'to produce a unified people of God, unified on the basis of love toward the one true God and toward each other', is fulfilled.

[283] Gal. 6.2.

controversial: as with many key moments in Paul's writings, he sums things up in a phrase which is a bit too dense for us easily to unpack it. Some have suggested that he here means the Mosaic law as reinterpreted through the lens of the work of Jesus; others, that it is simply the teaching of Jesus himself that is in mind. Many variations on these have been canvassed.[284] I suspect, in view of the rest of my present argument, that he has coined the phrase in a deliberately teasing fashion, but that he is alluding yet again to something he says repeatedly: that the entire incarnation, life, death and resurrection of Jesus form not only a standard to be adhered to as an external 'command', not only the locus of clear and sharp moral teaching, but also the inner life which must now shape and direct all Christian living. The underlying point should not be in doubt. Paul understands the Messiah's people to have been liberated from the 'old evil age', to have entered the 'new age', to be 'daytime people' charged with living by the standards of light even though the world around is still in darkness. As such, he sees them as the people of the renewed covenant, the people in whose hearts and lives the Torah, for all its necessarily negative work, is actually fulfilled.[285] That fulfilment points forward all the way to resurrection itself, the ultimate fulfilment of Torah's promise of life; and within that eschatological framework, based on the Messiah and energized by the spirit, the behaviour which Paul expects of those 'in the Messiah' is precisely *Israel*-behaviour, fulfilled-Torah behaviour. Messiah-people must be 'blameless'.[286] They must be different from the world around, not by the 'works' which separated ethnic Jews from the rest of the world but by the change of heart, mind and life to which Torah pointed and which, through the Messiah and the spirit, the one God has now produced. Messiah-people are already in the new age. Their baptism, justification and spirit-indwelt sanctification give them the platform on which to base this lifestyle. This is the first and major element of Paul's eschatological ethics.

(iii) Not Yet Perfect: Inaugurated but Incomplete

The second major element, following through the logic of inaugurated eschatology, is that in certain respects the 'new age' has *not* yet arrived. At one level this might appear to be a problem, but Paul is clear that it is in principle a good thing. If the creator were to foreclose on the world at once, the result would be widespread condemnation. The reason there is a delay is because of the divine *mercy*. 'Don't you know', writes Paul, 'that God's

[284] An excellent recent brief survey and summary is that of Schreiner 2010, 358–60, though I want to firm up his conclusion a bit more: I agree that for Paul the law is to be interpreted christocentrically, and in relation to love, but in addition to Christ's life and death as 'the paradigm, exemplification, and explanation of love' (Schreiner 2010, 360), something needs to be said about the inner transformation and motivating power, as in Gal. 1.16 ('to reveal his son *in me*') and 2.20 ('the Messiah lives *in me*').

[285] On the negative work of Torah see above, 1033f.

[286] cf. e.g. Phil. 2.15; Col. 1.22; 1 Thess. 3.13; 5.23. On the notion of early Christian perfection cf. e.g. Ridderbos 1975 [1966], 265–72.

kindness is meant to bring you to repentance?' The day of judgment is coming, but it is held back in order to allow a breathing space, time for people to come to their senses, turn from their wickedness and live. But if they fail to make proper use of this interval, this gap, the delay will only make matters worse. They will be hardened, like Pharaoh, so as to be the more fit for the judgment when it eventually comes.[287] Paul is not content, then, simply to accept the idea of a divided eschatology as a new, bizarre fact and work around it. The idea of an interval is not new. It was already well known in ancient Judaism, in which hope deferred had become a way of life, and in which the long interval between scriptural promises and eventual fulfilment was well known and variously interpreted. Even the idea of an interval *between Messiah's coming and the final end* was not entirely new: we catch echoes of such a thing in *4 Ezra*, and in the notion of a messianic task, including cleansing the Temple and fighting the ultimate battle.[288] Paul filled these earlier ideas with the more specific content gained from his belief that in the Messiah the resurrection itself had already happened, producing a different sort of interval, one in which that resurrection power, unleashed through the spirit, was available in the gospel to transform lives.

There is therefore a strong sense of 'not yet' about Paul's eschatology which has a clearly visible effect on his teaching about Christian behaviour; but that which is 'not yet' is not merely postponed to some unidentifiable future date. The fact that the 'not yet' is nevertheless assured means that it must be *anticipated* in the present.

There is a crucial link, for a start, between Christian behaviour and the *future* resurrection. The whole of 1 Corinthians is dominated by the theme of resurrection which Paul eventually states towards the end of the letter, and in chapter 6 we see a striking example of this:[289]

> 'Food for the stomach, and the stomach for food, and God will destroy the one and the other' – but the body is not meant for immorality, but for the lord, and the lord for the body. What's more, God raised the lord; and he will raise us, too, through his power.
>
> ... Or don't you know that your body is a temple of the holy spirit within you, the spirit God gave you, so that you don't belong to yourselves? You were quite an expensive purchase! So glorify God in your body.[290]

The point here is *continuity*. Those who already stand on resurrection ground, and must learn to live in this new world, need to be reminded that what they do with their bodies in the present matters, because the spirit who dwells within them will cause them to be raised as the Messiah was raised.

[287] Rom. 2.4–6; see e.g. Wis. 11.23. For judgment being delayed until the wicked are ready cf. Gen. 15.16.

[288] cf. *4 Ezra* 7.26–36: after the temporary messianic kingdom, and the death of the Messiah himself, there will be an interval, followed by a general resurrection. At that point, 'compassion shall pass away, and patience shall be withdrawn'; 'only judgment shall remain, truth shall stand, and faithfulness shall grow strong' (7.33f.).

[289] On resurrection as the theme of the whole letter, see *RSG* ch. 6. On the present passage see *RSG* 288–90.

[290] 1 Cor. 6.13f., 19f.

Knowing where one is within the essentially Jewish story-line as now further defined by the Messiah's death and resurrection commits one also to a sober assessment that one has not yet arrived at the destination, is not yet perfect:

> I'm not implying that I've already received 'resurrection', or that I've already become complete and mature! No; I'm hurrying on, eager to overtake it, because King Jesus has overtaken me. My dear family, I don't reckon that I have yet overtaken it. But this is my one aim: to forget everything that's behind, and to strain every nerve to go after what's ahead. I mean to chase on towards the finishing post, where the prize waiting for me is the upward call of God in King Jesus.[291]

Chasing towards the line: one of Paul's various athletic metaphors, indicating that the 'not yet' of eschatology does not mean hanging around with nothing to do.[292] And this gives rise at once to a sharp statement of the kinds of behaviour which are not appropriate for people running that as yet unfinished race. They are to maintain the position they have already attained, and shape their behaviour in the light of the still-unrealized goal.[293]

This has a strongly negative as well as positive point. We noted above that Paul believes in some sense in a *present* 'kingdom of the Messiah', and also 'kingdom of God', but normally when he speaks of the latter he is referring to the ultimate future. When he does so, it is sometimes in order to warn that there are certain present lifestyles which are simply incompatible with being part of that future. This is much more than simply providing a kind of 'negative warrant', a stick as opposed to a carrot. It is reminding people of an analytic truth: when the creator finishes his kingdom-project, those who are included within it will be those who have already learned to embody the kind of human life which reflects his own character. That is what is meant by saying that people who do certain things, who embrace certain habits of life, 'will not inherit the kingdom'. As long as we regard 'inheriting the kingdom' in terms of 'going to heaven' – as much of the Christian tradition has done – this, again, is bound to look like a merit-based soteriology (or at least a demerit-based condemnation!). But if, as I have argued throughout, this language reflects Paul's vision of the coming divine rule over the whole creation, and of humans being called to share in this rule, we get a rather different picture: these are the sort of people through whom the one God will establish his sovereign rule, bringing his wise order to his world.[294] Paul is thinking of the formation of a genuine humanity who will reflect the divine image into the world; and the things which mar this image are to be left behind in dying with the Messiah in baptism, in the sanctifying presence of the spirit and in the divine verdict of 'righteous' issued over faith:

[291] Phil. 3.12–14.

[292] See also e.g. 1 Cor. 9.24; 2 Tim. 2.5; 4.7f.; Heb. 12.1f.; and, for the image, *4 Macc.* 6.10; 17.11–16.

[293] Phil. 3.15–16; 17–19.

[294] On 'inheritance' and the renewed cosmos, see Rom. 8.18–26 (above, 488f.).

> Don't you know that the unjust will not inherit God's kingdom? Don't be deceived! Neither immoral people, nor idolaters, nor adulterers, nor practising homosexuals of whichever sort, nor thieves, nor greedy people, nor drunkards, nor abusive talkers, nor robbers will inherit God's kingdom. That, of course, is what some of you were! But you were washed clean; you were made holy; you were put back to rights – in the name of the lord, King Jesus, and in the spirit of our God.[295]

The point is repeated in Galatians, after the list of the 'works of the flesh': 'people who do such things', Paul declares, 'will not inherit God's kingdom'.[296] And it is expanded in Ephesians 5:

> You should know this, you see: no fornicator, nobody who practises uncleanness, no greedy person (in other words, an idolator), has any inheritance in the Messiah's kingdom, or in God's. Don't let anyone fool you with empty words. It's because of these things, you see, that God's wrath is coming on people who are disobedient.
>
> So don't share in their practices. After all, at one time you were darkness, but now, in the lord, you are light! So behave as children of light. Light has its fruit, doesn't it, in everything that's good, and just, and true. Think through what's going to be pleasing to the lord. Work it out.[297]

We should probably take the double 'kingdom', of the Messiah and of God himself, in the same sense as we find in 1 Corinthians 15.20–8. There the Messiah is already ruling, and will hand over the kingdom to his father once he has overcome all his enemies, death itself being the last. Thus here in Ephesians 5 'the Messiah's kingdom' presumably indicates the *present* 'rule of the Messiah' in and through the present church (as I suggested above), and 'God's kingdom' presumably looks ahead, as with 1 Corinthians 6 and Galatians 5, to the time when the one God will be 'all in all'.[298] Once again the warning comes in connection with habits and lifestyles, especially in the area of sexual behaviour, which destroy genuine humanness, and from which faith, baptism and entry into the community of the Messiah's people ought to deliver people.[299] We note once more – and will shortly return to the point – that Paul does not usually produce a list of bad behaviours in order just to say, 'don't do it!'. He explains that there are two things which enable one to escape from the slavery of such a lifestyle. First, remember who you are in the Messiah, where you are in the eschatological narrative: already released from slavery and 'sanctified' by the spirit, declared to be 'in the right' on the basis of faith, promised the 'inheritance'. Second, *work it out*. Think it through. At the centre of Paul's vision of a renewed humanity is the renewed *mind*. To this we shall shortly return.

There are, as we have seen, some ways in which the future can and must be anticipated in the present; but there are also ways in which that future must *not* yet be anticipated. The surprising news that the Messiah's people

[295] 1 Cor. 6.9–11. Elements of this, as of all translations, are of course controversial: see the extensive discussions in the commentaries, esp. Thiselton 2000, 438–55; Fitzmyer 2008, 254–8.

[296] Gal. 5.21.

[297] Eph. 5.5–10.

[298] Though cf. Rom. 14.17 (see above, 663, 668, 1063).

[299] So too 1 Thess. 4.3–5.

will share in the judgment of both recalcitrant humans and rebellious angels means, on the one hand, that Paul can challenge his hearers to produce from among their number people who are already capable of sorting out local disputes.[300] But he is equally clear that there are other matters in which final judgment is deferred, and one must not jump the gun. Among those matters are the assessment of his own apostolic performance. That kind of judgment belongs to the lord alone, and to the future day:

> So don't pass judgment on anything before the time when the lord comes! He will bring to light the secrets of darkness, and will lay bare the intentions of the heart. Then everyone will receive praise – from God.[301]

A similar reticence, holding back from a 'judgment' which is the lord's sole prerogative, is evident in Romans 12 and 14. In Romans 12, vengeance belongs to the lord, so human vengeance is ruled out: one must leave room for the divine anger to do what it has to do in its own time and way.[302] This is closely correlated with the passage that follows immediately, about human rulers and authorities with their God-given but strictly penultimate jurisdiction. This is a matter of disentangling the different layers of 'judgment', and making sure that the judgment which belongs to the creator – including that which he delegates to civic officials, and for which he will hold them responsible – is not usurped in an excited rush of over-anticipated eschatology.[303] This comes out as well in Romans 14, where the tendency for Christians to 'pass judgment' on one another in relation to matters which Paul deems to be 'adiaphora', such as food, drink and special holy days, must be ruled out. 'If you want to exercise your judgment', he says with gentle sarcasm, 'do so on this question: how to avoid placing obstacles or stumbling blocks in front of a fellow family member.'[304] This ruling, which plays a vital part in Paul's larger vision of church unity, is framed entirely in terms of eschatology, reworked as always around Jesus and the spirit.

Paul, then, insists that the Messiah's followers have to learn to live in the 'not yet' as well as the 'now'. This is not, to repeat, a matter of merely marking time. The interval has a Messiah-shaped purpose. This emerges in particular when we consider the centre of Paul's ethics, which I have elsewhere argued to be a kind of Christian transformation of the ancient traditions of virtue, of character-development. This, indeed, is the point at which his ethical teaching is at the same time closest to, and most interestingly distinguished from, that of the world around.[305] As with the tradition from Plato

[300] Rom. 2.27; 1 Cor. 6.1–6.

[301] 1 Cor. 4.5.

[302] Rom. 12.19.

[303] Rom. 13.1–7: see below, ch. 12.

[304] Rom. 14.13; cp. the whole discussion of 'judgment' in 14.1–12, where everything is located in relation to the forthcoming eschatological judgment (14.10–12).

[305] See Wright 2010 [*Virtue Reborn/After You Believe*], esp. chs. 5 and 6, which provide a much fuller discussion of the matters which follow here. See further Harrington and Keenan 2010; Thompson 2011.

and Aristotle onwards, Paul has a goal in view, but his goal is not Aristotle's 'happiness', *eudaimonia*. Nor is the attaining of that goal a matter, as it is in Aristotle, of the 'self-made man' producing the cardinal virtues of courage, justice, temperance and prudence that were required for a soldier or statesman in ancient Greece. Paul's goal, his *telos*, is the mature humanity which reflects the divine image and which will be reaffirmed in the resurrection.[306] The attaining of that goal is as much a matter of self-denial as of self-fulfilment. And the virtues which are to be produced include four which no ancient pagan would have recognized as positive character-traits: patience, humility, chastity and above all *agapē*, 'love'.[307]

At crucial points Paul, like other early Christians, can state all this in terms of character-development:

> Through [Jesus the Messiah] we have been allowed to approach, by faith, into this grace in which we stand; and we celebrate the hope of the glory of God.
>
> That's not all. We also celebrate in our sufferings, because we know that suffering produces patience, patience produces a well-formed character, and a character like that produces hope. Hope, in its turn, does not make us ashamed, because the love of God has been poured out in our hearts through the holy spirit who has been given to us.[308]

Here again we glimpse not only a sense of *what* one is supposed to be doing during the interval between the Messiah's resurrection and the final day, but also *why* this interval is necessary. The interval is enabling the growth to maturity of human beings who are being fitted to be partners, stewards, in the ruling of the creator's new world.[309] Those he justified, he also *glorified*; and that 'glory', as we saw, includes, and perhaps here is focused on, the sharing in the divine *rule* over creation. Because the creator's character has been revealed in the crucified Messiah, the normal modes by which the world is run must be stood on their heads, as Jesus himself had repeatedly insisted. Instead of pride and power, humility and service; instead of military victory, the strange power of suffering – something which Paul never

[306] The 'virtue'-tradition has often been discounted within protestant circles, but it seems to me that it fills precisely the gap which is evident in various accounts of Paul's ethics: for instance, in Dunn 1998, 669 where he tries to balance the 'outward' and 'inward' aspects; or Meilander 2011, 583–6, who expounds the mainstream 'virtue'-tradition but finds it hard to see how Paul might fit into it.

[307] See Blackburn 2008 [1994], 381: these four would have been 'unintelligible as ethical virtues to ancient Greeks'. See e.g. Dunn 1998, 665; Thompson 2011, 106 on humility. Paul of course speaks warmly of the virtuous pagan life in e.g. Phil. 4.8 (see e.g. Schnelle 2005 [2003], 556f.). But Schnelle does not see the radical discontinuity. When he says (558) that Paul's imperative 'has no really new content', since 'what is essentially human must not be newly created and thought through', I suspect that this comes over as sharper than he really intends (the German original is 'das Humanum musste nicht neu erschaffen und bedacht werden'). The translator, M. E. Boring, comments to me that, for Schnelle, 'Paul's ethic … is not utterly discontinuous with the ethics advocated by Hellenistic Judaism and Greco-Roman ethics in general, but is certainly not reducible to them' (personal communication, 7 March 2013). With that I would agree, but I think the sentence as it stands implies a stronger identification between Paul's ethics and those of his wider context. What is ruled out is the position of e.g. Betz 1979, 282 (lists like Gal. 5.19–25 'sum up the conventional morality of the time'). To look no further, 'sexual offenses (or offenders) appear in all of the vice lists in the Pauline literature, but do not appear in Hellenistic vice catalogs' (Thompson 2011, 94).

[308] Rom. 5.2–5.

[309] Rom. 5.17; 8.17–30.

tires of emphasizing.[310] Suffering was itself a sign, for Paul in his Jewish context, that one was living between the times, caught between promise and fulfilment, between the passing of sentence on the old world and the final disappearance of evil. Hence the Jewish theme of 'tribulation', which Paul recapitulates in a Christian key precisely as part of his 'not yet'.[311] And that is part of the reason why he can speak, however paradoxically, of suffering setting off a train of character-development which leads, not to despair, but precisely to *hope* – which again would not have been one of the Greek or Latin virtues. For Paul, character-development is above all eschatological, because it is derived from the promised future which has already come forward into the present in the person of the Messiah and the work of the spirit.

It is no surprise, then, to discover that for Paul the road to this character-development, this growth in genuine humanness, will involve the messianic way of dying and rising. This is part of his theme of imitating the Messiah, not in a superficial way, but at the level of the transformation of heart, character, mind and life.[312] Those who have already died and been raised with the Messiah, as in Galatians 2.19–20, must learn to 'crucify the flesh with its passions and desires' (5.24), to kill off the things which belong with the pagan way of life to be renounced (Colossians 3.5), to 'put to death the deeds of the body' (Romans 8.13). This is a regular theme of Paul's moral discourse, and it is obvious where it came from. The fact that this 'putting to death' will require moral effort, and that such effort is itself part of the 'fruit of the spirit', is indicated by the fact that in the list of 'fruit' he includes 'self-control', *engkrateia*. The 'fruit' does not, then, appear 'automatically', any more than a fruit tree will continue to blossom and bear fruit if left untended and unprotected against predators.

When it comes to particular things that need to be killed off, Paul focuses attention on two areas in particular: angry speech and behaviour on the one hand, sexual malpractice on the other. We cannot here explore either in detail, since our purpose is simply to indicate how his commands embody his messianic and spirit-led inaugurated eschatology. Paul envisages a renewed humanity in terms of *new creation*, a new world in which the creator's original intention would at last be fulfilled; and this new world is to be seen in advance in the Messiah's people. Angry speech and behaviour destroys that vision within the church, whose unity as we saw in Part II was for Paul the central symbol of the Christian worldview. Sexual immorality destroys the vision of a new creation in which the purpose begun in Genesis 1 and 2 can at last find fulfilment. Genesis 1, 2 and 3 stand, after all, rather obviously behind his great eschatological passages, Romans 8 and 1 Corinthians 15. The new creation is the renewal of creation the way it was meant to be. It is not the scrapping of the present world and the launching of

[310] e.g. Rom. 8.17–27; 1 Cor. 4.9–13; 2 Cor. 4.7–18; 6.3–13; Phil. 1.29f.; 2.17f.; 3.10; Col. 1.24f.; 1 Thess. 3.1–4.

[311] See Allison 2007b, 298.

[312] See Schnelle 2005 [2003], 548f.

something quite different. This is why his sexual ethic focuses so clearly on marriage as the norm for sexual behaviour.[313]

The eschatological dimension to his ethic is also the reason why Paul can advocate the possibility of celibacy. This was counter-intuitive in much of the ancient world, especially in the case of women.[314] Paul's permission is explicitly related to his eschatological perspective. We should avoid the excesses of those who have argued from 1 Corinthians 7 that Paul really did think the space–time universe was about to disappear.[315] But he clearly understands the present time, both the 'present time' of famine and distress across the world of the eastern Mediterranean in the early 50s, and the 'present time' between the Messiah's first coming and his second, to be limited and temporary. One should act in relation to the longer purposes of the creator, not out of short-term goals. That is the way, in the present, to build the character-strengths which will form the true humanity in the creator's future world.

In particular, Paul famously highlights love, the self-giving love for which he, like other early Christians, adopted the previously more general word *agapē*.[316] This character-trait is one of the three which Paul specifies as things which will last into the future world, when activities like tongues and prophecy will be no longer needed: this, of course, is the ultimate meaning of an eschatological ethic, something inaugurated in the present which will last into, and indeed be a central characteristic of, the future new creation.[317] Love also heads the list of qualities which together make up the singular 'fruit of the spirit'.[318] It is the one thing which 'fulfils the law'.[319] It is the means by which the entire 'Messiah's body' holds together: it is no accident that 1 Corinthians 12 is followed immediately by 1 Corinthians 13, and no accident either that the development of the 'Messiah's body' image in Ephesians 4 ends with that body 'building itself up in love'.[320] And this 'love' is very practical. When Paul tells the Thessalonians to love one another more and more, he is most likely referring not to emotional feelings but to practical financial help and support within the church.[321] It is love that drives his complex and evidently somewhat embarrassing programme to raise money from largely gentile churches to give to the struggling Jewish Christian community in Jerusalem.[322] And it is love, in the form of true

[313] See esp. 1 Cor. 5.1–13; 6.9–21; 7.1–40; Gal. 5.13–21; Phil. 3.17–19; Col. 3.1–11; 1 Thess. 4.3–8.

[314] 1 Cor. 7.8, 25–40. See e.g. Witherington 1995, 173–81.

[315] cf. *NTPG* 342f., 459–64.

[316] On *agapē* and its cognates see BDAG 5–7. A glance at the concordance to the LXX indicates that the word's pre-Christian usage by no means had the high sense we find in John or Paul; it is, then, insufficient to say that Paul 'derives the term *agapē* from the Septuagint' (Thompson 2011, 180). Ridderbos 1975 [1966], 293 notes that Paul is here close to the preaching of Jesus.

[317] 1 Cor. 13.8–13.

[318] Gal. 5.22.

[319] Rom. 13.8–10; Gal. 5.14.

[320] Eph. 4.16.

[321] 1 Thess. 4.9–12.

[322] On the Collection, see below, 1202, 1255, 1495–7, 1507.

koinōnia, that he sees evident in the gift which the Philippians have sent him in prison.[323]

Love, then, is obviously and uncontroversially central to Paul's vision of the Christian moral life, in a way which was not true in either Judaism or the greco-roman world. 'Love your neighbour as yourself' is of course a command in Torah.[324] It is reflected in the various rabbinic sayings which expound the Golden Rule.[325] But it is fair to say that one could read through second-Temple Jewish literature for a long time before coming upon any mention of such a notion, let alone any attempt to make it central, the quality 'which ties everything together and makes it complete'.[326] One does not expect to find a poem like 1 Corinthians 13 at Qumran, or within the Wisdom of Solomon, or indeed the *Psalms of Solomon*. Nor can one find anything like it in ancient paganism, where care for others extended only to immediate family and close associates.[327] This promotion of the 'love' command to its position of prominence in early Christianity fits exactly with several other features we have seen in Paul's theology as a whole: something which was there in the ancient scriptures, but which emerges in a new way as a result of the work of the Messiah and the gift of the spirit.

It is of course fair to say that the central position of 'love' within Paul, and indeed John,[328] is not matched in terms of literary structure and thematic emphasis in Mark, or Acts, or Hebrews, or Revelation. That is why it cannot serve by itself as a catch-all concept for the whole early Christian moral vision.[329] But it is also fair to say that Mark's picture of Jesus going to his death, the glimpses in Acts of the community of goods in the early church, and the vision of the conquering Lamb in Revelation, all demonstrate in practice what it was that John and Paul summed up in their use of the word *agapē*. John and Paul are not out on a limb. They are putting into clear language the larger challenge, which is that of the cross itself, the place where both of them see what the word 'love' really means.[330] And Hays is surely

[323] Phil. 1.9–11; 4.10–20.

[324] Lev. 19.18, cited at Rom. 13.9; Gal. 5.14; Mt. 22.39 and pars. Cf. esp. Furnish 1972.

[325] e.g. Hillel (bShabb. 31a); cp. e.g. Tob. 4.15; Sir. 31.15. Cf. R. N. Longenecker 1990, 243f.

[326] Col. 3.14. The major exception is probably Philo *Virt.* 51–174, which expounds the Mosaic law in such a way as to bring out the elements of kindness and mercy throughout, and contrasts them with pride and arrogance. A much shorter version of the same point is found in Jos. *Ap.* 2.209–14. For the idea of *agapē* (in this case love of 'wisdom') as the fulfilling of the laws, cf. Wis. 6.17f. Brotherly or neighbourly love is commanded in e.g. *T. Reub.* 6.8f.; *T. Iss.* 5.2; 7.6; *T. Gad* 4.2; 5.2f.; *T. Zeb.* 5.1; *T. Benj.* 3.3f. Cf. too *T. Gad* 4.7: 'the spirit of love works by the Law of God through forbearance for the salvation of mankind' (tr. H. C. Kee in Charlesworth 1983, 815); cf. too *Aristeas* 227. All these are important, and sometimes show signs of the 'double commandment' of loving God and neighbour, but hardly constitute a major or central theme in second-Temple Judaism comparable to the place of *agapē* in early Christianity (against Thompson 2011, 39f., who seems to me to overstate the case quite considerably; one cannot build much on e.g. Tob. 4.13).

[327] cf. Wolter 2011, 335–7. Wolter holds on to the possibility of 'love' as an 'organizing centre'. On the love-command at Qumran, restricted to fellow members of the community, cf. e.g. 1QS 1.3, 9; 9.16, 21; CD 6.20f. On love in the ancient greco-roman world see the summary in Klassen 1992, 382–4.

[328] cf. Jn. 13.34f.; 1 Jn. 4.7f.

[329] So, rightly, Hays 1996b, 200–3.

[330] Rom. 5.6–11; cf. Jn. 3.16; 1 Jn. 3.1; 4.7–12.

right to say that the English word 'love' has become too generalized, too floppy, to carry this sharp and challenging meaning in today's world. As I said myself in an earlier book, 'The English word "love" is trying to do so many different jobs at the same time that someone really ought to sit down with it and teach it how to delegate.'[331] This does not mean at all that Hays has 'dismissed' or 'abandoned' the notion of love, as has strangely been suggested.[332] On the contrary: two of his three organizing principles for New Testament ethics, namely 'community' and 'cross', are quite simply all about *agapē*. The problem is that our word 'love' is still regularly used, at both scholarly and popular levels, in ways that have little to do with either.[333]

It is love, not least, that is Paul's aim when teaching the churches in Rome and Corinth about things which must not divide the church, the things later called *adiaphora*. It becomes clear, as we read Romans 14.1—15.13 and 1 Corinthians 8—10 (not to mention 1 Corinthians 12—14, where chapter 13 forms the still centre amid a whirligig of charismatic energy[334]) that throughout these discussions he is concerned for the health of the whole body, which includes the educated consciences of every member.[335] Paul, as a pastor, knew that conscience was a sensitive instrument, and if roughly handled might suffer lasting damage. This, too, is part of the 'not yet' of the gospel. Presumably Paul thinks that in the new creation such problems will disappear. Learning how to live wisely within a world, and a church, in which such issues loom large is for him a further impetus towards a Messiah-shaped love in which no party insists on 'rights' and all concentrate on mutual responsibility and service.[336]

For the development of this kind of character, there is one thing above all which Paul sees as an absolute necessity: the formation of a Christian *mind*. Over and over again he urges his hearers to learn to think clearly; not to be deceived by smooth and slippery talk, especially when it concerns matters of

[331] Wright 2010 (*Virtue Reborn*/*After You Believe*], 157f./183.

[332] Burridge 2007, 108f. misses the point: Hays explains that 'love' will not do as an overall theme *for the whole NT*, for reasons just given. Burridge strangely says that Hays's treatment of Paul 'does not include love at all!' (108, exclamation original), which overlooks Hays 1996b, 35. Burridge says, in the same passage, that Campbell 2005, 117 is 'commenting on Hays' abandonment of love'; but what Campbell says, with approval, is that Hays, like Hauerwas and many others, has been prompted 'to abandon "love" *as a central organizing principle for Paul's ethics, and for ethics more broadly*' (my italics).

[333] One might also suggest that Hays's third category, 'new creation', is also all about *agapē*, both in the generous self-giving love of the creator and in the way of life which is the central characteristic of the new world.

[334] Hays 1996b, 35 points out that it is there, in a passage on the unity of the church, that we find the great love-poem, not (say) in the context of the discussion of marriage in ch. 7.

[335] Bockmuehl 2000, 168 suggests that 1 Cor. 8—10 is not after all about *adiaphora*, since Paul still insists that one must 'flee idolatry' (10.14). But that is just the point: Paul is distinguishing between the things which are mandated (no idolatry, which for him means no going on to the premises of idol-temples and their attendant eating-rooms) and the things which are indeed 'indifferent' (permission to eat anything sold in the market (10.23) – which no observant Jew could have granted). The point about 'things indifferent' is that one must tell the difference between the things that make a difference and the things that do not.

[336] See esp. 1 Cor. 8.7–13; 10.25—11.1.

moral behaviour; to gain the wisdom and insight they need to navigate the dangerous waters of the world.[337] This theme reaches one kind of climax in the remarkable claim in 1 Corinthians 2:

> Someone living at the merely human level doesn't accept the things of God's spirit. They are foolishness to such people, you see, and they can't understand them because they need to be discerned spiritually. But spiritual people discern everything, while nobody else can discern the truth about them! For 'Who has known the mind of the Lord, so as to instruct him?' But we have the mind of the Messiah.[338]

As so often in Paul's thought, he holds together the fact that something is a fresh gift, a new revelation which could not have come about through human study and contemplation, and the fact that it must nevertheless be developed and worked at. If the latter were not the case, he would not have needed to write any letters at all: he would just rely on the spirit to produce 'the mind of the Messiah' in his congregations. But that is not how things work – not because Paul is after all a pragmatist who fails to live up to his own theory, but because his theory is precisely that what the one God wants to do in the world, and in people's hearts and lives, he wants to do *through* human agency. The work of pastors and teachers, and of an apostle who combines both and more besides, is therefore needed both to remind those 'in the Messiah' that the Messiah's 'mind' is already given to them as their birthright and that they need to inhabit it, to develop it, to learn to think straight and not to be deceived, to grow up in their thinking and no longer think baby-thoughts. We have already seen how this works in relation to Philippians 2.5, and several have argued that actually Philippians as a whole is focused on the need to develop and maintain specifically Christian patterns of thinking.[339] Paul intends that Christians should grow to maturity, and his pastoral work is constantly aimed at this.[340]

The reason for this, and the fullest sustained exposition of what it means, is found in Romans. One recent writer has seen Romans not only as a *description* of the acquisition of the Christian mind but as a kind of therapy: the hearers, as they listen again and again to the letter, are meant to find themselves brought from the 'darkened mind' of chapter 1 to the 'transformed and renewed' mind of chapter 12.[341] The letter is meant not simply to *instruct* the hearers about this necessary transformation, but actually to accomplish it. Whether or not this attractive thesis is accepted, the vital role of the mind is indeed a central theme of the letter:

> Ever since the world was made, [God's] eternal power and deity have been seen and known in the things he made. As a result, they have no excuse: they knew God, but didn't

[337] See, almost at random: Rom. 16.17–20; 1 Cor. 3.18–23; 6.9; 14.20; 2 Cor. 11.3; Gal. 6.7; Eph. 4.14, 23; 5.6; Col. 2.4, 8; 2 Thess. 2.3. See too the warnings against 'deceit': Eph. 4.22; Col. 2.8; 2 Thess. 2.10.

[338] 1 Cor. 2.14–16.

[339] See also, similarly, Phil. 1.9f.; 1 Thess. 5.21. See Schnelle 2005 [2003], 551; Fowl 1990; 1998; Meeks 1991; and see below, 1124f.

[340] 1 Cor. 14.20; Eph. 4.14–16; Col. 1.28; 4.12.

[341] Griffith-Jones 2012.

honour him as God or thank him. Instead, they learned to think in useless ways, and their unwise heart grew dark. They declared themselves to be wise, but in fact they became foolish. They swapped the glory of the immortal God for the likeness of the image of mortal humans – and of birds, animals and reptiles.

So God gave them up to uncleanness in the desires of their hearts, with the result that they dishonoured their bodies among themselves. They swapped God's truth for a lie, and worshipped and served the creature rather than the creator, who is blessed for ever, Amen . . .

Moreover, just as they did not see fit to hold on to knowledge of God, God gave them up to an unfit mind, so that they would behave inappropriately . . .[342]

Paul here assumes three things. First, the human mind can in principle grasp the truth about the creator God. Second, the *mind* determines the *behaviour*. Third, the *mind* is closely linked to the *heart*: the reasoning faculty is linked to the driving centre of the personality, with its emotions and longings. From these he argues three further things. First, idolatry produces a darkening of the heart and a failure to think straight, an inversion of wisdom and folly. Second, this results in dehumanized and dehumanizing behaviour. Third, the creator allows this process to take its natural course: the 'unfit' decisions lead to an 'unfit' mind, a mind not fit for purpose, for the purpose of grasping the truth and living in the light of it. That is a core part of his diagnosis of the problem of the whole human race.

As we saw earlier, Paul's description of Abraham's faith in chapter 4 provides a significant reversal of Romans 1. The word 'mind' is not mentioned, but the same overall picture is produced, this time in positive mode:

He didn't become weak in faith as he considered his own body (which was already as good as dead, since he was about a hundred years old), and the lifelessness of Sarah's womb. He didn't waver in unbelief when faced with God's promise. Instead, he grew strong in faith and gave glory to God, being fully convinced that God had the power to accomplish what he had promised.[343]

Paul might have summed up those sentences by saying that Abraham had learned to think straight about the creator God; that he had grasped the truth; and that his mind, rather than being 'unfit', was doing its proper job.

The dilemma of the 'mind' is then displayed, and resolved, in the dense and complex passage Romans 7.7—8.11. First, it is held captive, so that even when it wants to do the right thing it cannot:

I delight in God's law, you see, according to my inmost self; but I see another 'law' in my limbs and organs, fighting a battle against the law of my mind, and taking me as a prisoner in the law of sin which is in my limbs and organs.

What a miserable person I am! Who is going to rescue me from the body of this death? Thank God – through Jesus our king and lord! So then, left to my own self I am enslaved to God's law with my mind, but to sin's law with my human flesh.[344]

[342] Rom. 1.20–5, 28.

[343] Rom. 4.19–21.

[344] Rom. 7.22–5.

As I have argued elsewhere, this is Paul's retrospective Christian diagnosis of the problem of Israel under Torah.[345] Unlike those described in chapter 1, this 'mind' is not 'unfit': it really does delight in the God-given law. But Israel too is part of Adamic humanity, here seen in terms of 'the flesh', and until 'the flesh' as the locus of powerful sin has been dealt with there is no hope, but only frustration. Then, however, the gospel provides the remedy for just this condition. As we saw a few moments ago, whereas 'the mind of the flesh' is hostile to the creator and his law, 'the mind of the spirit' is given life and peace, and can at last 'submit to the law' and thus 'please God'.[346] In case that last deduction is challenged, we note that this is exactly what Paul then says in the glorious conclusion to the sequence of thought, where the key elements of the diagnosis of evil in chapter 1 are reversed:

> So, my dear family, this is my appeal to you by the mercies of God: offer your bodies as a living sacrifice, holy and pleasing to God. Worship like this brings your mind into line with God's. What's more, don't let yourselves be squeezed into the shape dictated by the present age. Instead, be transformed by the renewing of your minds, so that you can work out what God's will is, what is good, acceptable and complete.[347]

Once again we note the primacy of worship, the worship of the true God. Once again we note the tight nexus between mind and behaviour. Once again we see the eschatological location of it all: 'the present age' will try to claw believers back into its grip and squeeze them into the old shape, but the believer must be transformed, as a whole person, by the renewing of the *mind*. This is the key to Paul's regular motif about learning to think straight, about not being deceived. And this will be the key, too, to some practical issues yet to be addressed: 'Each person must make up their own *mind*' (14.5).

Paul's whole written work, in fact, could be seen as an extended application of Romans 12.1–2. Here is the true God who is worthy of worship with our whole selves, body and all. Learn to think straight, as members of the age to come which has already been launched. Discover in this way, in thought and practice, what a genuine and God-pleasing human life looks like. And, in particular, *work out what God's will is*. That 'working out', *dokimazein*, lies at the heart of Paul's vision of Christian *freedom*: it is not only freedom *from* the deadly constraints of sin and death, but also freedom *for* the multiple and varied styles of service to which one may be called. We should not be surprised that in Romans 12 the opening general command quickly gives way to a scattering of possible gifts and callings, or that this resonates with the central image of the 'Messiah's body' in 1 Corinthians 12.[348] The different *charismata* in these two passages and elsewhere are one

[345] On all this, see Wright 2002 [*Romans*], 549–72, and above, 892–7.

[346] Rom. 8.5–8.

[347] Rom. 12.1–2. I have paraphrased the notoriously difficult phrase *logikē latreia* as 'worship like this brings your mind into line with God's' to bring out one aspect at least of what I take Paul to be saying: see further e.g. Schnelle 2005 [2003], 555; Jewett 2007, 729–31.

[348] Rom. 12.3–8; cf. 1 Cor. 12.12–31.

aspect of that freedom: different people have different callings, and must think wisely through what that means and where they belong within the larger whole. That is what Paul is getting at in his tight little exposition of Christian *thinking* in Romans 12.3: 'Don't think of yourselves more highly than you ought to think. Rather, think soberly (*phronein eis to sōphronein*), in line with faith . . .'

This comes to the fore again particularly in Philippians, which as we saw can be regarded as a particularly concentrated exposition of how Christians should think.[349] Paul wants his hearers to think out for themselves, and put into practice, wise decisions as to what conformity to the Messiah's pattern looks like in *this* situation or *that* one, not just in obedience to clear moral norms – though there are obviously plenty of those – but in the practical reasoning that, aided by the spirit, learns the 'Messiah's mind' in day-to-day choices whose freedom only emerges once those moral norms are recognized (as one only discovers the 'freedom' to drive around the countryside once the 'norms' of traffic rules are recognized). 'Work at bringing about your own salvation,' he instructs them, not at all in the sense of 'save yourselves by your good works', as some have anxiously imagined, but 'figure out what *your* version of *sōtēria* is going to look like in practice', as opposed to the 'salvation' offered elsewhere.[350] 'Think through what's going to be pleasing to the lord,' he says in Ephesians. 'Work it out.'[351] 'Don't be foolish', he goes on, 'but understand what the lord's will is.'[352] 'Test everything,' he tells the Thessalonians.[353] This is what it will look like to discover, more as an art than a science, what sort of a *poiēma*, a 'work of art', one is supposed to be, and hence what sort of 'good works' may have been prepared, ahead of time, for one to 'walk in'.[354]

This development of a Christian 'mind', not simply in the sense of a calculating-machine that deduces norms from first principles, but in the sense of developing the freedom to think wisely and carefully about particular vocational and innovatory tasks, is at the heart of Paul's vision of Christian character – in the sense of 'character' as formed through the 'strengths', i.e. the 'virtues', that we have discussed. From this there flows an ethic which is not so much about listing rules to keep (though they will be there in case the characters, not yet fully formed, are tempted to go astray again) but rather about teaching people to think as day-dwellers in a still darkened world.[355] Paul would have understood the old maxim about giving someone

[349] cf. *phroneō* in Phil. 1.7; 2.2 (twice), 5; 3.15 (twice), 19; 4.2, 10 (twice). Various different senses are included in these but the concentration is still remarkable: see Meeks 1991; Fowl 2005, 80–92.

[350] Phil. 2.12: cf. below, 1295f.

[351] Eph. 5.10. I have here rendered *dokimazein*, the same verb as in Rom. 12.2, with those two expressions: it is about thinking something through and working out its relevance in particular situations.

[352] Eph. 5.17.

[353] 1 Thess. 5.21: again the verb is *dokimazein*.

[354] Eph. 2.10.

[355] On the continuing if subordinate place of 'rules' within a virtue-based Christian ethic see Wright 2010 [*Virtue Reborn/After You Believe*], 171f. [US edn. 200f.].

a fish and feeding them for a day as opposed to teaching them to fish and feeding them for life. He did from time to time give people blunt and direct instructions, to keep them on the rails for the immediate future. But he was far more concerned to teach them to think through, with a mind renewed by the spirit, what it meant to live in the new age when the two ages were still overlapping. Indeed, he was concerned to teach them to think, reflexively as it were, about the mind itself, and about its role within the total self-sacrificial obedience of the whole person. This, he would have said, is what it means to have the mind of the Messiah.

My case throughout this sub-section has been that Paul's reflections on and teachings about Christian behaviour are best understood as part of his modification, by Messiah and spirit, of the Jewish eschatology in which the age to come was to arrive and transform all things. And for this purpose, with all its constituent parts, right down to every moral decision, every blossom that points to the 'fruit of the spirit', every virtue painfully won, Paul sees the full achievement of the Messiah, and the implementation of that achievement by the spirit, as picking up and bringing into fresh focus *the whole intention of Torah.*[356] Paul is quite capable of simply quoting a passage of Torah as authoritative. His writing is often telegraphic, and he does not usually add the footnotes to explain his hermeneutical theory of precisely how Torah, having been in one sense left behind at the cross, is in another sense projected forward into the present time. We find ourselves filling in those gaps from the hints he gives here and there. It is far too simplistic, and tends to marginalize Paul's own focus on Messiah and spirit, to suggest either that he leaves Torah behind entirely as a moral code or that he simply uses and develops it with little or no break. There are some ways in which it is clearly left behind: the distinctive badges of ethnic identity such as circumcision and food laws on the one hand, the sacrificial cult on the other. There are other ways in which it is emphatically restated: the command to love the neighbour, and the strict rules on sexual behaviour. But we should never forget that Paul, like many of his contemporaries, saw Torah itself as much more than a list of commands. It was a *narrative*, and the commands were embedded within it as pointers to the character of the people of the covenant God. Paul saw that narrative fulfilled in the Messiah and the spirit. It is not surprising that in that fulfilment he should have found, though not yet fully explained, fresh ways of speaking of Torah and the way of life it always intended to generate.

I have argued in particular in this section that Paul understood the new interval that had surprisingly opened up between the resurrection of the Messiah himself and the consummation of all things as being a necessary if unexpected part of the divine plan. He shaped his ethical teaching at every point by the combination of the 'now' (the Messiah has already died and been raised, the spirit has already been given, the day has already dawned, the Messiah's people have been rescued from 'the present evil age') and the

[356] On Torah see above, 1032–8.

'not yet' (we have not yet attained what we are promised, we are not yet made perfect, we must judge nothing before the time). And he has seen that the unexpected interval has a specific purpose: to allow a space in which there can be formed a genuine human character, with renewed minds, spirit-transformed hearts and bodily obedience all in tune with one another and with the creator. This has its own eschatological purpose, summed up in Romans 5—8 with the word 'glory': the creator intends, as in Psalm 8, to put humans in charge of his world, and the present chronological gap between the work of the Messiah and the final new creation is required for such humans to have their character formed, indeed *con*formed 'to the image of his son, so that he might be the firstborn of a large family'.[357]

We shall shortly turn to the other unexpected interval which confronted Paul: the time when, following the widespread Jewish rejection of the Messiah, gentiles were coming in instead. He understands, analyses and resolves this problem in a very similar way to what he has done in relation to moral behaviour. The covenant God is using the present time to 'make my "flesh" jealous, and save some of them'. But before we get there we have the last element of the 'not yet' to consider. The battle is not yet done.

We should not be surprised that Paul sometimes uses the imagery of warfare. He is regularly dealing, after all, with what happens when people try to do what he says in Romans 12, to live according to the age to come rather than the present age from which they have been rescued, and find that they are swimming upstream against a fast-flowing current. To think of this in terms of a great battle has many Jewish precedents, including some where it was meant literally, as in the great revolts of AD 66–70 and 132–5. The myth of a cosmic battle goes a long way back in the tradition.[358] For Paul, of course, the battle has been redefined, like everything else, by the Messiah's death and resurrection. When Paul picks up the image it is not only metaphorical but also largely defensive: as is often pointed out, the only offensive weapon in this set of armour is the sword, which is the divine word:

> Put on God's complete armour. Then you'll be able to stand firm against the devil's trickery. The warfare we're engaged in, you see, isn't against flesh and blood. It's against the leaders, against the authorities, against the powers that rule the world in this dark age, against the wicked spiritual elements in the heavenly places.
>
> For this reason, you must take up God's complete armour. Then, when wickedness grabs its moment, you'll be able to withstand, to do what needs to be done, and still to be on your feet when it's all over. So stand firm! Put the belt of truth round your waist; put on justice as your breastplate; for shoes on your feet, ready for battle, take the good news of peace. With it all, take the shield of faith; if you've got that, you'll be able to quench all the flaming arrows of the evil one. Take the helmet of salvation, and the sword of the spirit, which is God's word.
>
> Pray on every occasion in the spirit, with every type of prayer and intercession. You'll need to keep awake and alert for this, with all perseverance and intercession for all God's holy ones – and also for me![359]

[357] Rom. 8.29.

[358] Aune 1992, 598.

[359] Eph. 6.11–19.

This famous passage is echoed elsewhere in Paul's writings, and requires little extra comment here.[360] The main thing for our purposes is that at no point does Paul allow the 'now' to eclipse the 'not yet'. He is never complacent. Indeed, it is because of the 'now' that the 'not yet' comes into focus; unless the Messiah had fought and won the decisive battle, his followers would not be precipitated into theirs.

The other thing to notice here is that prayer plays a necessary and central role within the whole between-the-times stance. Never was this more powerfully expressed than in that climactic eschatological passage, Romans 8 itself. Here the 'now' of inaugurated eschatology, with the spirit already dwelling in the transformed hearts of believers, is fused with the 'not yet' in which world and church alike are groaning in travail. At that moment, when by the spirit the people concerned are keeping the *Shema*, 'loving God' from the heart, when monotheism and election come together most obviously in their new messianic shape, Paul speaks of a 'groaning', the birth-pangs of the new age coming to inarticulate expression. The lament which arises from Israel's prayer down the centuries is transformed into the groaning which takes place when the one God comes to the heart of the world's pain, producing the messianic shape of a people bearing the sorrows of the world into the presence of the creator:

> The spirit comes alongside and helps us in our weakness. We don't know what to pray for as we ought to; but that same spirit pleads on our behalf, with groanings too deep for words. And the Searcher of Hearts knows what the spirit is thinking, because the spirit pleads for God's people according to God's will.[361]

This, for Paul, is not something other than eschatological ethics. It is at its very heart. The practice of prayer, itself energized by the spirit and formed after the pattern of the Messiah, gives evidence of the same transformation we have observed throughout. The people who are called to stand at the crossroads of time, the strange interval between the 'now' and the 'not yet', the present and the future, are also called to stand at the intersection of heaven and earth, sharing the pains and puzzles of the present creation but sharing also in the newly inaugurated life of the spirit. Romans 8.26–7 is in fact part of the outworking of the temple-theology of 8.9–11. As the Temple was the place where the one God chose to dwell in the midst of his people, so those who belong to the Messiah are the new temple where this one God now dwells in the midst of his world. This, indeed, is part of what is meant by 'glorification'. The glory, the Shekinah, has returned, not in a blaze of fire and light but in the prayer of unknowing, the intercession that cannot yet come into articulate speech, the voice of the voiceless like the cry of a child waiting to be born. This is what inaugurated eschatology not only looks like but feels like. For Paul, the battle image of Ephesians 6 and the inarticulate

[360] cf. 1 Thess. 5.8. The echoes of Isa. 59.17 are important: this suit of armour is, more or less, the one which YHWH himself wears when winning his decisive victory. Cf. too Wis. 5.18.

[361] Rom. 8.26f.

prayer of Romans 8 belong closely together. Those phenomena take, no doubt, many forms. But there is always a recognizable shape: the messianic and spirit-led transformation of the eschatology of a Pharisaic Jew.

The gospel of Jesus raised new questions for Paul, and the question of Christian life and behaviour was one of the most important. He answered it in a way entirely consistent with the way he answered the questions of monotheism and election; indeed, his answers belong in many cases within the realm of 'symbolic praxis', part of the Christian worldview itself. How Jesus' followers behaved was to embody the new covenant and new creation. To be sure, his ethical teaching was framed in such a way as to take on the wider discussions of the world around him. We shall return to that in chapter 14. But its roots were Jewish and messianic.[362] Paul never shifted from that ground. That is why the other major new question which the gospel had raised was, for him, so painful. And so important.

6. The Eschatological Challenge of Redefined Election

(i) Introduction

If the question of Israel was painful and important for Paul, it remains difficult and contentious for us. But it cannot be avoided. Over many years I have observed that several lines of early Christian thought, in the gospels as well as in Paul, converge not only on Romans 8 but also on Romans 9—11. Once you take seriously the Jewish rootedness of the early Messiah-movement, you cannot avoid addressing these issues; and these three chapters, now widely acknowledged as the rhetorical heart and climax of his greatest letter, are where Paul has said most fully, and (we must assume) most carefully, what he thinks on the subject. And alongside Romans 9—11 we find two other passages, one in Galatians and one in 1 Thessalonians, which are often, and rightly, referred to in the same breath.

This is not to say that these passages, particularly Romans 9—11, come to us as neat, packaged, detached theological statements, without specific historical context or rhetorical intention. Far from it. History and rhetoric must be taken fully into account. But we must remind ourselves that a good deal of what we know about the historical context of all the letters is gained by elaborate mirror-reading; in other words, by informed guesswork. We know vastly more about what Paul actually says in Romans (or Galatians, or whatever) than we do, independently of the letters, about the context into which, or the purposes for which, the documents were sent. Granted all this, and granted that I have written elsewhere on the contexts and purposes,

[362] cf. Thompson 2011, 109: 'Paul reflects the influence of the Greco-Roman moralists less than do his predecessors in the Diaspora. He is indebted to the Holiness Code, the summaries of the law, and the Jewish paraenetic tradition. Undoubtedly, the humiliation and self-denying love of Jesus provided Paul's deeper insights into the nature of love, the dominant feature in Paul's lists.'

there is a good deal to be said for providing a fresh *exegetical* account in terms of the letters in question.

As we do so, the rhetorical needs of the present book must also be taken into account. I write into a situation where certain quite different pressure groups are looking over my shoulder. A word about each may help.

First, there is the traditional Protestant for whom 'justification by faith' is more or less what Luther, and/or the Westminster Confession, said it was. From that point of view, the emphasis I have put on Israel, on the covenant with Abraham and the fulfilment of that covenant in Jesus the Messiah, and on the covenant membership which God's people enjoy because they are 'in the Messiah' and wearing his own badge of *pistis* – all this is a strange irrelevance, or even a dangerous 'ecclesial' distraction from 'the gospel'. In many traditional protestant readings of Romans at least, Abraham in chapter 4 is simply an 'example' or a 'proof from scripture' of the 'doctrine of justification by faith' – a reading which I have done my best to argue out of court in this book and elsewhere.

Second, there is the strongly would-be 'pro-Jewish' post-holocaust reading of Paul in general and Romans in particular, which would approve of my placing the question of Israel at the centre of interest but not at all of what I have done and am doing with it. For such writers, who would include the late and gracious Krister Stendahl but also John Gager, Lloyd Gaston and recent apologists such as Pamela Eisenbaum and William Campbell, anything short of a two-covenant solution, in which God is happy for gentiles to be Christians but would prefer Jews to remain Jews – and in which Paul endorses this point of view – is regarded as suspicious and probably (that blessed word again) 'supersessionist'.[363] This kind of writing thrives, particularly in North America, on a half-truth which, when portrayed as the only truth, becomes an untruth: that the position of the church for many generations has been that of a 'replacement theology' in which the church (thinking of itself as a non-Jewish body) has 'replaced' Israel in the divine purposes, a position which has been justified in terms of a negative portrayal of Judaism as a bad or inadequate sort of 'religion'. There have of course been some would-be Christian thinkers who have said that kind of thing. But this is where the trap of treating early Christianity as basically a 'religion' in the eighteenth-century sense, and of then comparing it with other 'religions' as though it were appropriate to line them up and compare their 'good' and 'bad' points, comes home to roost.[364] For the first Christians, the point was not about 'religion', but about coming to terms with the fact that if Jesus really was Israel's Messiah, as they believed the resurrection had demonstrated him to be, then in some sense or other the narrative and identity of Israel had not been 'replaced' but fulfilled – fulfilled by him in person, and therefore fulfilled in and for all his people. When Akiba hailed bar-Kochba as Messiah, and some of his colleagues objected, would

[363] See Stendahl 1995; Gager 1983; Gaston 1987; Eisenbaum 2009; W. S. Campbell 2008; 2012. On the whole question see Hays 1996b, 411–17; 2000, 308f.

[364] See ch. 4 above.

they, or indeed he, have said that Akiba was 'replacing' something called 'Judaism' with something different? Clearly not.[365] We must never forget that in Paul's sharpest writing, as in Galatians, we are witnessing an *inner-Jewish dispute*, not a dispute between 'Jews' on the one hand and somebody else on the other. Indeed, it also seems to be an *inner-Christian* dispute: the 'agitators' in Galatia, like Peter in Antioch, considered themselves followers of Jesus. Whatever has happened to these texts in subsequent re-readings (and perhaps misreadings), any historical investigation must take serious account of these dimensions, and not reduce them to anachronistic over-simplifications.[366]

In between these two extremes there are many other positions, two of which are popular in western circles for very different reasons. First, there is still in North America a remarkable undertow from the now traditional 'dispensationalism' of the nineteenth-century Plymouth Brethren. According to one version at least of this understanding of the scriptural narrative, many of the biblical promises to the Jewish people were never fulfilled when Jesus appeared, and they are still due to be fulfilled in a concrete sense (a geographical 'return from exile' and an actual rebuilding of the Temple) in the 'End Times'. This is not the place to describe these views in full, let alone to critique them. I have done my best to undercut the implicit eschatology of this position in my work on the resurrection, and do not need to repeat the argument here.[367] But the legacy of such views, and their easy assumption in many ecclesial and educational contexts, is still strong. Even among those from that background who have distanced themselves from some of the wilder flights of 'End-Times' fancy the belief still persists (a) that 'the Jews' must still return to 'their land' at some point and (b) that Paul more or less said something to this effect in Romans 11. (The further points (c), that the event of the founding of the State of Israel in the late 1940s was the beginning of the 'fulfilment' in question, and (d) that this must be allowed to have a powerful influence on the western powers' Middle East policy, take us way beyond our present concern, but still exercise a profound influence in some circles where the writings of Paul are discussed.) Thus, even though Romans 11 actually says nothing about a geographical 'return' (saying 'the redeemer will come from Zion' hardly counts), the sense that Paul

365 Sometimes summary remarks give the game away. Mark Nanos, writing a blurb for Bachmann 2008 [1999], says that Bachmann's arguments challenge interpretations 'that continue to be instrumental for expressing negative views of Judaism through Paul's voice, as well as cornerstones of replacement theology'. To set up the question in this way, or to warn against the 'disinheritance' or 'expropriation' of Judaism (Bachmann 2008 [1999], 123; 2012, 104), however justified in terms of positions misguidedly taken over recent centuries, is a sure way to rule out any genuine historical understanding of early Christianity, where the strong note of *fulfilment*, emphasized across the whole early church, presupposed a strong and positive evaluation of Israel's traditions and hopes.

366 See, rightly, Hays 2000, 300, 302. The description of 'supersessionism' in Martyn 1997a, 450 n. 168 is no doubt accurate as an account of how some people have thought, but Martyn does not see (a) that there is indeed a sharp opposition in the text between what Paul might have described as two visions of the people of God – i.e. Paul is taking one side in an inner-Jewish dispute; and (b) that his own view, throughout his commentary, is pressing for opposition to and abandonment of all 'religion', of which the obvious example in Galatians is some form of Judaism, and its 'replacement' with something else.

367 *RSG*; *Surprised by Hope*. On 'dispensationalism' see e.g. Mason 2000; Marsden 2006 [1980].

must somehow in that chapter be talking about a 'final salvation of the Jews' has often, in my view, clouded the judgment even of some otherwise fine exegetes.[368]

Second, there is in many parts of the western world a very different mood, namely that of relativism and universalism. All faiths are basically as good as one another, and all sensible people now realize this and act accordingly.[369] Again, it would help to have Paul on one's side in saying this; and, though there are many passages in his letters where he does not look one tiny bit like a relativist, let alone a universalist, one can (it seems) ignore them and concentrate on the passages where he stresses 'all': one man's stumble led to condemnation for 'all' and one man's act of righteousness led to the justification of life for 'all'; God has shut 'all' in the prison of disobedience so that he may have mercy upon 'all'.[370] Thus, though the exegete may draw back from saying so explicitly, Paul can triumphantly be invoked against – triumphalism; at least, against the triumphalism of saying that one particular 'way of salvation' is the only way. (The 'relativism' in question is itself of course the haughty triumph of a post-Enlightenment progressive modernism.) To this extent, the question of 'the Jews' then becomes, in a way strangely parallel to Ernst Käsemann's very different proposal, all about 'religious humanity' in general; except that for Käsemann *homo religiosus* was a bad thing, 'the hidden Jew in all of us', to be struck down by the anti-religious gospel of Jesus, while in the relativistic or universalistic perspective all 'religions' turn out to be good after all (except, presumably, their conservative or fundamentalist versions, which the relativist would deplore while still insisting that people who held such views would nevertheless be saved, if only through the fires of the modernist thought-police). There are some signs that some of Käsemann's exegetical grandchildren may be taking this sort of route.[371]

It may seem demeaning to the historical and exegetical nature of our present task to allow such questions even the briefest of air time, but I think

[368] I initially wrote these lines in December 2009. In August 2011 the *New Yorker*, which used to employ rigorous fact-checkers, published an account (Lizza 2011) of the then would-be Republican Presidential candidate Michele Bachmann (no relation, I think, of the German scholar cited a few notes back). Bachmann had once lived on a kibbutz in Israel, explained the article, 'a state whose creation, many American evangelicals believe, is prophesied in the Bible'. By way of explanation, the article adds an astonishing parenthesis: 'St. Paul, in the Letter to the Romans, says that Jews will one day gather again in their homeland; modern fundamentalists see this, along with the coming of the Antichrist, as presaging the Rapture.' The truly striking thing is that in the subculture in question it is simply taken for granted that Paul in Romans prophesies the return of the Jews to their homeland, something which is of course never mentioned, or even hinted at, in the actual text of the letter. The author of the article, and the editor of the prestigious magazine, clearly took this fundamentalist assumption for granted.

[369] cf. Esler 2001, 1205: there is 'a modern aversion to the powerful in-group/out-group antipathies of the first-century Mediterranean world which are largely alien to modern North American and northern European culture and which interpreters are often slow to recognize in NT texts'. This is of course true, but anyone who supposes that the modern culture in question has no in-groups and out-groups, and that it does not indulge in 'violent stereotypification and vilification', only needs to turn on the television.

[370] Rom. 5.18; 11.32.

[371] I think, for instance, of those who have gone further than J. L. Martyn did and have basically embraced a would-be Pauline universalism. The obvious example is de Boer 2011; see below for his disagreement with Martyn on Gal. 6.16.

it is necessary because, having been around such discussions most of my life, I have observed these and similar pressures and have often had cause to wonder about their insidious effect on historical exegesis. I hasten to add (since, if I don't, reviewers no doubt will) that I too have all kinds of interests, partisan views, quirky ideas, situational perspectives, hopes and fears about what might turn out to be true, and indeed about what Paul might really have meant, and whether *that* was true. Perhaps, at the risk of allowing autobiography to intrude upon a historical discussion, I should state one or two of these at the outset.

First, for the first twenty years of my life I was not aware of what one might call the 'Jewish question'. I had Jewish friends at school, but their ethnic identity and religion was taken for granted and was never a matter for comment, let alone discussion, let alone prejudice of thought or action. I remember only one moment, in my first twenty years, of hearing anything approaching an anti-semitic remark (it was directed against a Jewish friend whose Jewishness was otherwise taken for granted), and what I mostly remember about that moment was sheer puzzlement at its absurdity and complete irrelevance. On a wider scale, we naturally heard about the holocaust, but it was like a horror movie, way beyond our ability to comprehend. It may be hard for American Christians to believe, but neither the church of my upbringing nor the less formal Christian fellowships of my teenage years ever mentioned 'the question of Israel'.

When, in my twenties, I first became seriously aware of the plight of the Jewish people in the aftermath of the Nazi atrocity, and came upon would-be Christian reflections on the subject, my gut reaction was to hope, with some excitement, that the New Testament might indeed predict a great future for the Jewish people, and that twentieth-century events might perhaps relate to that. Some of my earliest explorations into Romans 9—11 were made in the hope and expectation that this would turn out to be so. Alas: I discovered, try as I might, that the exegesis simply did not work. I abandoned that view for those reasons alone. My emotional sympathies were still with Israel, in the first and the twentieth century, but I could no longer compel Paul's text to predict a large-scale, last-minute 'rescue' of all, or even most, Jews (and, as I say, there was never any question of discovering predictions of a 'return to the land' in Romans 11).

Since then I have looked at the question from every angle open to me, not least through repeated visits to the middle east, including a spell as a visiting Professor at the Hebrew University. These visits (to put it mildly) have added several different and conflicting impressions and points of view.[372] This increasingly dense and contested view of contemporary events has formed a counterpoint to my continuing attempts to understand Romans 9—11. Each time I come back to the passage I ask myself whether I am about to change my mind once more. (That has happened to me in other areas; serious changes of mind are one of the excitements and challenges of

[372] For some reflections on this in a different mode, see Wright 1999 [*The Way of the Lord*].

mature scholarship.) In some ways I would quite like to do so. I take no pride in holding a minority position. But as a historian and exegete I must stick to the text and try to understand what it actually says, not what I might like it to say.

To those who comment, 'But you're a bishop, so presumably you take a "Christian" view,' I reply: Yes; but the 'Christian' view I take, in my tradition at least, is to let the text be the text, rather than make it say what we want. There is after all no one 'Christian' view on these matters. If it turns out that Paul says things I do not want to hear, I shall live with it. If it turns out that I say things which Paul doesn't want to hear, perhaps he will one day put me straight. If it turns out that Paul says things the twenty-first century doesn't want to hear, it's better that we get that out into the open rather than sneakily falsifying the historical evidence to fit our predilections.

With that, to business. Before we reach Romans 9—11 itself, we begin with Galatians and 1 Thessalonians: and, first, with one of the sharpest and most difficult of Paul's polemical passages.

(ii) Galatians 4—6

The passage in question is the final part of the letter to the Galatians. Opinion is divided on how chapters 4, 5 and 6 are related to the earlier parts of the letter; I have myself in the past tended to see the main argument as concluding at 4.11, though I am now moving towards those who see it continuing through as far as 5.1. Nothing much for our purposes hangs on this question, but we simply note that the 'allegory' of Sarah and Hagar, in Galatians 4.21—5.1, can be seen both as the culmination of the long argument from the start of chapter 3 and also as setting up the terms for the concluding (and quite complex) exhortations.

First, then, the allegory itself:

> 21So, you want to live under the law, do you? All right, tell me this: are you prepared to hear what the law says? 22For the Bible says that Abraham had two sons, one by the slave-girl and one by the free woman. 23Now the child of the slave-girl was born according to the flesh, while the child of the free woman was born according to promise.
>
> 24Treat this as picture-language. These two women stand for two covenants: one comes from Mount Sinai, and gives birth to slave-children; that is Hagar. 25(Sinai, you see, is a mountain in Arabia, and it corresponds, in the picture, to the present Jerusalem, since she is in slavery with her children.) 26But the Jerusalem which is above is free – and she is our mother.
>
> 27For the Bible says,
>
> Celebrate, childless one, who never gave birth!
> Go wild and shout, girl that never had pains!
> The barren woman has many more children
> Than the one who has a husband!
>
> 28Now you, my family, are children of promise, in the line of Isaac. 29But things now are like they were then: the one who was born according to the flesh persecuted the one born according to the Spirit. 30But what does the Bible say? 'Throw out the slave-girl and her son! For the son of the slave-girl will not inherit with the son of the free.' 31So, my family, we are not children of the slave-girl, but of the free.

> [5.1]The Messiah set us free so that we could enjoy freedom! So stand firm, and don't get yourselves tied down by the chains of slavery.

Abraham had two sons: yes indeed. If we have guessed rightly what arguments the 'agitators' were putting forward, it is not unreasonable to suppose that they may have used this story to explain to the erstwhile pagan Galatians that they were only second-order citizens in Abraham's family. They were, after a fashion, in the position of Ishmael, and it was time for them to join the true covenant family, the Isaac-children, by getting circumcised.[373] With due regard for the problems of 'mirror-reading', this guess may be better than most, though it would be wrong to conclude that Paul only talks about Abraham, here or elsewhere, because his opponents have forced him to do so.[374] Likewise, it would be wrong to focus too much attention on Paul's comment about his own 'picture-language'. The word he uses, *allēgoroumena*, indicates a broad category of figurative speech, including typology, and should not be taken to indicate that Paul is treating the Torah in the same way as, say, Philo – though making Sarah and Hagar stand for different abstractions, 'slavery' and 'freedom', 'flesh' and 'spirit', does seem to point in that direction as well. Paul's aim, though, is not to draw attention away from the story to focus instead on qualities to be cultivated by the individual. He is continuing to talk about the actual 'inheritance' of Abraham's family, as throughout 3.1—4.7. The point is not the private or individual cultivation of inner dispositions, but the public demarcation of Abraham's family.[375]

Whether or not Paul is here responding directly to a different use of Genesis, his own position soon becomes clear. The genuine children of Abraham, the 'Isaac-like' children as opposed to the 'Ishmael-like' ones, are those who, relying on the divine promise, are thus embracing freedom, rather than those who, relying on the 'flesh', are thus embracing slavery. These two contrasts, slave and free on the one hand and promise and 'flesh' on the other, dominate most of the paragraph, though it is clear that Paul has other contrasts in mind as well which he can correlate with these, the most obvious being that in 4.29 we find 'flesh' contrasted with 'spirit'. The slave/free contrast picks up and develops further the theme of 4.1–7, where Paul was plugging in to a different slave/free moment in the scriptural narrative,

[373] This is not as straightforward as it might sound, since in Gen. 17.25f. Ishmael was circumcised before Isaac was even born.

[374] The seminal essay on this topic is Barrett 1976 (= ch. 9 in Barrett 1982). On 'mirror-reading' see the rightly famous article by Barclay 1987 (reprinted in Nanos 2002b, 367–82, from which I cite). Barclay 381, after applying quite stringent tests, thinks it 'probable' that Paul's opponents made reference to the Sarah–Hagar narratives.

[375] On 'allegory' here see esp. Witherington 1998, 321–3; de Boer 2011, 295f. Hays 2000, 301f. is right to say that all Paul means here is a 'figurative sense', though he also rightly notes (1989, 215) that typology is a sub-species of allegory. Betz 1979, 243 n. 49 quotes Quintilian (9.2.46) to the effect that when a metaphor is pushed far enough it becomes an allegory.

namely the liberation from Egypt.[376] The promise/flesh contrast likewise picks up earlier themes, this time from chapter 3.[377]

Paul's basic strategy, which he has approached through the rhetorically skilful 4.12–20, is to offer a stark choice. We note again that he is *not* talking about 'Judaism' and 'Christianity', but about two very different visions of the essentially Jewish belief that the Messiah has come and that what matters is the formation of Messiah-communities. The 'agitators' are convinced that gentiles entering a Messiah-community must be circumcised; Paul is convinced that they should not be. Thus the 'agitators' want 'to shut you out, so that you will then be eager for them' (4.17): in other words, like Peter refusing to allow gentile Christians to eat with him (2.11–14), they are in effect forcing such people to 'judaize' in order to belong to the innermost circle. That is why, later on, Paul restates the agitators' intention: they 'are trying to force you into getting circumcised' (6.12). Now Paul addresses the problem with a sharp either/or: perhaps after all it is *they* who ought to be shut out!

This conclusion is quite popular in current exegesis.[378] It has not, however, gone unchallenged, since it appears to offer a vision of the Messiah's people which is just as 'exclusive' as that of the 'agitators' themselves.[379] But that is indeed Paul's position. It is difficult to read Galatians 1.6–9, 2.11–21, 5.2–12, or 6.11–17 – to cite only the most obvious passages – and suppose for a moment that Paul was aiming in this letter to bring about a result where, in Galatia, 'everyone has won and all shall have prizes'. That result is not normally achieved by throwing around anathemas and warning about people 'bearing their condemnation' (5.10).[380] We should note, however, that he is writing about *discipline*, not about the eternal salvation of those against whose teaching he is warning. 'Salvation' as such is never mentioned in this letter, though of course it stands just off stage throughout. He is concerned with the health of the community. As we know from his disciplinary methods elsewhere, drastic action may sometimes be necessary precisely in

[376] Hagar was of course Egyptian (Gen. 16.2f.; 21.9), but Paul shows no sign of making that link between her and the later slavery in Egypt.

[377] Rightly, Hays 2000, 301.

[378] See e.g. R. N. Longenecker 1990, 211–17; Witherington 1998, 325–9; Hays 2000, 303–6.

[379] So Eastman 2006, 313, using the language of postmodern moralism: 'rather than creating inclusive, graceful communities, [Paul] exercises his authority to evict those who pose a threat to his leadership and his preaching. If such exclusive power is the tactical purpose of 4.30, then in a sense Paul is no better than the other missionaries ... his use of power to "cast out" those who oppose him is equally cliquish and coercive.' But Paul is not opposing the 'agitators' because they are 'cliquish' or 'coercive'. He is opposing them because they are abolishing the scandal of the cross (5.11), seeking to avoid the persecution which it would bring (6.12) and so misunderstanding the entire nature of the gospel (1.6–9), denying its 'truth' (2.5, 14) and undermining the freedom it brings (5.1, etc.). This has nothing much to do with the postmodern sin of 'deporting' or 'silencing' different or dissenting voices (Eastman, 327), and everything to do with the fact that, as Eastman elsewhere says, 'Paul's Christ-centered gospel is exclusive and unapologetically hegemonic in the claims it makes on ... Christians' (329).

[380] To say nothing of the sharp words in 5.12.

order to safeguard ultimate salvation.[381] That, I suggest, is how we should then read Galatians 4.21—5.1: starting with 'Are you prepared to hear what the law says?' in 4.21, it reaches its climax with 'What does the Bible say? Throw out the slave-woman and her son!'

It is perhaps important not to over-read this command. Paul is quoting from Genesis 21.10, and he does not add a sentence to apply the passage to the Galatian situation.[382] The quotation remains a strong hint rather than a direct command. It is strong, though. Paul has placed it at the rhetorically powerful moment near the end of the paragraph. He clearly intends that it should be applied to the present situation, since he has in the previous verse (4.29) drawn a parallel between the 'persecution' of Isaac by Ishmael and the present circumstances.[383] He has linked that parallel to the quotation by asking, 'But what does the Bible say?' This makes it clear that what Sarah said to Abraham in the original story is now to be heard as a word of *graphē*, 'scripture', by the community – and paid attention to, as indicated in 4.21.

Even if this hint is so strong as to constitute an effective command, however, Paul is not saying that any of the Galatian believers themselves should be 'cast out', even if some have already gone the whole way and got circumcised. The problem is the false teachers – or perhaps one in particular, as 5.10 perhaps indicates.[384] Their teaching constitutes a radical misunderstanding of the nature of the Abraham-family to which they are trying to appeal. Such a misunderstanding cannot be *adiaphora*, like the decision to eat (or not to eat) meat offered to idols, or indeed any meat at all.[385] Indeed, the things which Paul considers 'indifferent' are precisely the things which, if insisted upon, would indeed divide the community along Jew/gentile lines, which is precisely what the 'agitators' (like Peter in Antioch) are effectively doing. And Paul sees this as a denial of the 'truth of the gospel' itself. Nothing less is at stake than the fact of the Messiah's crucifixion: like so much else in the letter, the present passage is held between 2.19–21 on the one hand ('I have been crucified with the Messiah ... if "righteousness" comes through the law, then the Messiah died for nothing') and 6.14 on the other ('God forbid that I should boast – except in the cross of our lord Jesus the Messiah, through whom the world has been crucified to me and I to the world'). The force of the paragraph is not simply, 'You must not listen to

[381] 1 Cor. 5.1–5 (cf. 2 Cor. 2.5–11). Note that Paul uses the image of leaven, as a corrupting presence needing to be purged from a community, in both passages: 1 Cor. 5.6–8; Gal. 5.9. Eastman 2006, 332 sets up a straw man by suggesting that Gal. 4.30, read in the light of Paul's 'angry and dismissive voice', 'seems to pronounce a final judgment that permanently excludes the other missionaries and their followers from the life of the Spirit and the reign of God'. These ideas are not mentioned here.

[382] The fact that the verb remains in the singular, however, is presumably irrelevant (against Eastman 2006, 324; see too Eastman 2007, 133): to do so would have made no sense within the quotation.

[383] On the strange question of what exactly Ishmael was doing in Gen. 21.9 that was so offensive, see the rabbinic traditions discussed helpfully by Meeks 1982, 69f.

[384] So e.g. Perkins 2001, 92f. (cited by Eastman 2006, 319f.), distinguishing between Galatian Christians themselves, i.e. Paul's actual audience, and 'visitors whose views cause agitation in the community' who 'might be sent packing'.

[385] 1 Cor. 8; Rom. 14.

these other views, but must stand firm in your identity as Isaac-children, children of promise, the people of freedom and of the spirit.' It is, more sharply, once the hint has been understood, 'You must *reject* the alternative teaching, and *eject* those who are teaching it.'[386]

All this (to locate the present discussion within our own much larger argument) is a clear redefinition of election, as in our previous chapter. And it is done on the same terms as usual: the 'freedom' of the Isaac-children is that which was acquired for them by the Messiah;[387] they are the people who, as in Romans 2.28–9, are defined in terms not of flesh but of spirit.[388] Those who emphasize the 'flesh', i.e. the necessity for circumcision for gentile converts, do not count as genuine children. (We notice once again that the target of Paul's polemic is not 'Jews' or 'Judaism', but one particular form of *Jewish Christianity*, namely a form that insisted on circumcising believing gentiles.) Election redefined, then, around the Messiah – especially his cross – and the spirit.

We have not yet, however, considered the very centre of this difficult passage, and when we do so we see how important this passage is not only for Paul's redefinition of second-Temple election but also for his reworking of second-Temple eschatology, the subject of the present chapter. As so often, Paul quotes from Torah and prophets side by side, and here the prophetic passage has powerful resonances. Isaiah 54.1, quoted in verse 27, was already connected in post-biblical Jewish thought with the notion not only of restoration after exile (its obvious referent in context) but also with Sarah on the one hand (it echoes the mention of Sarah's childlessness in Genesis 11.30) and the 'new Jerusalem' on the other.[389] So what harmonies are set up by these various echoes?

It has recently been argued that the quotation from Isaiah 54.1 in 4.27 should be understood in relation to a regular and repeated use of the central chapters of Isaiah throughout Galatians, and that this quotation in fact forms a kind of rhetorical and scriptural climax to the entire argument from the start of chapter 3, or even the end of chapter 2.[390] Isaiah 54 speaks of the restored Jerusalem, and had already been understood in Jewish tradition in terms of Sarah, referred to explicitly in Isaiah 51.1–3.[391] But Isaiah 54 also comes, of course, immediately after Isaiah 53, where the servant is finally vindicated and exalted after his suffering and death. And this triumph is itself the long-awaited kingdom of YHWH: the fourth 'servant song' was the vision which explained the 'gospel' announcement in Isaiah 52.7–12. And

[386] Eastman 2006, 324, 327 seems to me to pose a false alternative: Paul is not suggesting expulsion, but rather that the community should stand firm. The text seems to me to suggest that the latter will be a lot easier if the former takes place.

[387] 5.1, summarizing what was spelled out in 2.19–21, 3.13–14 and 4.4–7.

[388] 4.29, summarizing what was said in 3.2–5, 14 and 4.6–7, and looking ahead to 5.16–26.

[389] See Witherington 1998, 334; Hays 2000, 304; and the detailed studies of Willitts 2005; Eastman 2007, 141–55; and Harmon 2010, 173–85. Sarah is referred to in Isa. 51.1–3, her only appearance in the OT outside Genesis itself.

[390] See Harmon 2010, here at 177, 183.

[391] So Hays 2000, 304.

Isaiah 54 goes on to celebrate the fact that YHWH himself is Jerusalem's husband (54.5), who is re-establishing his 'covenant of peace' with her once and for all (54.10). This in turn leads to the universal invitation of the gospel (55.1), through which YHWH promises to establish the Davidic covenant with all who come (55.3).

This rich cluster of themes resonates at so many levels with so much that Paul is talking about throughout Galatians that it is hard to imagine that his quotation of Isaiah 54.1 was a random proof-text thrown in for mere rhetorical effect. The reference constitutes a clear claim: the Messiah's people, the servant's people, are the 'children of the barren woman', that is, of Sarah. They are 'children of promise', because they have believed God's promises as Abraham did, as in 3.6–9. And, not least, these promise-children are the true *returned from exile* people: that was what Isaiah 54 was celebrating. The return from exile has happened at a 'heavenly' level, that is, within the newly enacted purposes of the creator, producing once again the 'now/not yet' contrast, in this case that between the 'present Jerusalem', still enslaved (both theologically and perhaps, in Paul's view, because of Roman domination),[392] and the 'Jerusalem above', already established on earth in the action of the covenant God through the Messiah and the spirit.[393] The eschatology of a restored Jerusalem has finally come to pass in terms of the new messianic community characterized by promise, spirit and freedom. The ecclesiology of the single community, which as we saw in chapter 6 was central to Paul's symbolic world, is itself central to his inaugurated eschatology. And we should not be surprised that when the central symbol is under attack, as it was in Galatia, he reacts with full force. One cannot undermine central worldview-symbols and expect to be 'tolerated'. And the point of locating all this within 'eschatology' should now be clear. *This is not a debate about 'types of religion'. It is a matter of eschatology.* Either the long-awaited 'age to come' has arrived with the Messiah or it has not. Paul announces that it has – precisely through the Messiah's death and resurrection and the work of the spirit. The message of the 'agitators' clearly implies that it has not. When we frame these complex passages and questions within Paul's overarching inaugurated eschatology we see not only that the use to which they have been put in 'Christian/Jewish' polemic was unwarranted in the first place, but also that the reaction to that abuse continues to miss the point. Nor is this about an 'apocalyptic' moment which sweeps away all previous 'religion'. It is about the fulfilment of the ancient covenant plan in the Messiah and the spirit – and about the various strategies used in the first century, as well as in the twenty-first, to avoid the radical implications of that fulfilment.

[392] See Hays 2000, 303f. Schreiner 2010, 302 questions this, but says that perhaps the present Jerusalem was seen by Paul as 'still in the wilderness': this is odd, because the 'wilderness' people were the exodus generation who, though not yet obtaining their inheritance, were by definition free from slavery in Egypt.

[393] For the notion of the 'new' or 'heavenly' Jerusalem cf. e.g. *4 Ezra* 7.26; 10.25–8; 13.36; *1 En.* 90.28f.; *2 Bar.* 4.2–6; Heb. 12.22; 13.14; Rev. 3.12; 21—2; see further R. N. Longenecker 1990, 214.

Mention of the covenant plan brings us back to the last section of the paragraph to be considered here, namely Paul's introduction to the Sarah/Hagar theme in verses 24 and 25. These women, says Paul, are 'two covenants'. It is the only time he ever uses the phrase. Some have suggested that he is referring, as in 2 Corinthians 3, to the 'old covenant' and the 'new covenant' mentioned in Jeremiah 31.[394] But this is highly unlikely. The 'old/new' scheme refers in 2 Corinthians 3 to the renewal of the *Mosaic* dispensation, but here in Galatians the context of chapter 3, where the original Abrahamic covenant is expounded at length, sets up a contrast not between the old (Mosaic) covenant and its renewal but between the Abrahamic covenant, as in Genesis 15 and Galatians 3, and the Sinai covenant made through Moses. That was what was going on in 3.15–29, and it fits the present passage very well. In this context, Sarah is not just an allegorical signifier for the Abrahamic covenant, but part of the means by which it was fulfilled: she is metonymy here, not simply metaphor. How then does Hagar fit in? Simple: Sinai is a mountain in Arabia, and it was well known (at least Paul thought he could assume it) that Hagar, being the mother of Ishmael, was the ancestress of the Arabians.[395] Hagar has metonymic connections with Sinai, as Sarah does with Abraham. Here again we see Paul's revised eschatology, exactly as in 3.23–9: now that the Messiah has come, we are no longer under the Torah. And – a brilliant polemical side-thrust, but fitting exactly into the same revised eschatology – we no longer take orders from 'the present Jerusalem'. We belong to the new Jerusalem, not in the sense of 'going to heaven when we die', but in the sense that the long-awaited return from exile, and indeed rebuilding of the temple, has happened. The heavenly Jerusalem has come to earth in the person of Jesus the Messiah and the power of the spirit. The people who are therefore celebrating the new day of Isaiah 54, the surprising yet long-promised birth of children for Sarah/Jerusalem, on the basis of the work of the servant, must avoid all temptations to go back to Babylon, back into slavery. 'The Messiah has set you free' (5.1): it is substantially the same point as in 3.13–14, where the law's curse of exile has been undone by the Messiah's redemptive death. The Mosaic Torah had kept the Israelites confined, locked up, enslaved, under the rule of the *paidagōgos*, under the care of enslaving powers, under the curse of exile, until the coming of the Messiah.[396] Torah formed a 'yoke', a word sometimes used by the rabbis in a good sense but here, perhaps with

[394] So e.g. Betz 1979, 243–5.

[395] See Betz 1979, 245 n. 70, questioning whether the Galatians could have made the link (suggested already by Lagrange): see Ps. 83 (LXX 82).7; 1 Chr. 5.19. This provides a clear reason for supporting the shorter reading in 4.25 (*to gar Sina horos estin en tē Arabia*), from which the other readings are easily explicable (against e.g. R. N. Longenecker 1990, 211f.; Dunn 1993, 251f.; Witherington 1998, 332f.; Hays 2000, 302). The definite article, much puzzled over and in my view misrepresented e.g. by Martyn 1997a, 436–8; Schreiner 2010, 301f., is no problem: 'Sinai', an indeclinable noun, is the subject; the *to* refers back to the same word in the previous verse; *horos*, 'mountain', is the complement. See further *Perspectives* ch. 10, esp. 155 n. 12.

[396] See 3.10, 19, 22, 23, 24; 4.1–3.

deliberate irony, indicating slavery.[397] But, as in 4.1–7, the slaves have now been freed. The ancient narrative of Exodus has come true again in the newer reality of return from exile. And with that freedom, the returned-from-exile freedom, the blessing of Abraham has come upon the gentiles, the spirit has been poured out on people of faith irrespective of ancestry, and second-Temple Jewish eschatology has been well and truly inaugurated. The Sarah/Hagar 'allegory' says again, with more bells and whistles than one can easily hold in one's head all at once, and with consequently massive rhetorical effect, what Paul had been saying throughout chapter 3. The promise to Abraham has been fulfilled; the 'inheritance' is secure for all his 'seed'; and the law of Sinai is quite simply out of date.

Is Paul saying, then, not just that non-Messiah-believing Jews will not inherit the Abrahamic promises, but also that Messiah-believing Jews *who insist on circumcision for gentile converts* will not inherit them? That brings us back to where we were a few minutes ago. If Paul is continuing to speak, not of salvation, but of discipline and of the nature of the Christian community, the following passage makes sense. Up until 5.1 Paul has been expounding the Abraham/Sinai contrast, and urging the Galatians to reject, and perhaps eject, the teachers who are saying that the only way to Abraham is through Sinai. Now, in 5.2–6, he assumes, not a soteriology primarily, but an ecclesiology, and explains that there is no room within the Messiah's people, here and now, for people who insist on circumcision or who think that being circumcised themselves will solidify their membership. Begin at the end of the short paragraph, where, with the characteristic double *gar*, Paul explains the reason for the previous three verses:

> [5]For we are waiting eagerly, by the spirit and by faith, for the hope of righteousness. [6]For in the Messiah, Jesus, neither circumcision nor uncircumcision has any power. What matters is faith, working through love.[398]

Here is election and eschatology, redefined around Messiah and spirit, folded up and put into a paper bag. When he says '*what matters* is faith, working through love', what he means by 'what matters' is 'what counts as the definition of the community'. Circumcision, or the lack thereof, were being seen as community markers: the circumcised were 'in', the uncircumcised were 'out'. No, says Paul, all that has gone. There is a new set of markers: (a) being in the Messiah, as the controlling category; (b) faith, as in the whole letter to date; (c) working through love – the first mention in Galatians of what suddenly becomes a major theme.[399] It is important to remind ourselves that he is *not* saying that being a gentile is now what matters rather than being a Jew, but rather that ethnic background *of whatever sort* counts for nothing within the community of God's people. The 'neither circumcision nor uncircumcision' point is, obviously, one of the main

[397] cf. e.g. mAb. 3.5.

[398] 5.5f.

[399] The verb of course occurs at 2.20.

thrusts of the whole letter, and he will return to it towards the end in another memorable definition, just as he used the same phrase in a different context in 1 Corinthians.[400]

Working back through the explanations, verse 5 provides the only mention in Galatians of 'hope', of a future 'righteousness' at the last day. This, in shorthand, is eschatology redefined: the ultimate hope of *dikaiosynē*, of vindication on the last day, has nothing to do with producing the 'works of Torah'. It is a matter of the spirit, of faith and of hope. The echoes of Romans 5.1–5 ought to be clear.

Verses 5 and 6 provide the support for the four rapier-thrusts of verses 2, 3 and 4. Once you see what it means to be 'in the Messiah' in verses 5 and 6, it becomes analytically true that this messianic identity is irrelevant, and of no use, to someone who insists on getting circumcised (verse 2). To do that, says the erstwhile hardline Pharisee, is to sign on for a programme of total lawkeeping (verse 3), resulting in someone desperately trying to build the new Jerusalem while still in exile in Babylon – and while the new Jerusalem has already been established! The result, in verse 4, is that such a person is saying, with their actions, that they are not part of the Messiah-family, not part of the spirit-family, not part of the entire new creation launched by 'grace'. Again there are echoes from earlier in the letter, this time 1.6 and 2.21: the one God called them in the first place by the 'grace' of the Messiah, and to turn to the law would be to set that grace aside. He is not saying such a move would be permanent. He is suggesting that, if it became permanent, it would be fatal. There are no promises of 'inheritance', or 'freedom', or ultimate 'righteousness', for those who decide to leave the dwelling-place called 'grace', where 'faith working through love' are the only badges of occupancy, and to move back to the old house called 'law'.

We can move rapidly over the next paragraphs, since they have comparatively little to contribute to our present topic of Paul's view of Israel within his revised eschatology. I note simply, in passing, my disagreement with the normal reading of Galatians 5.17–18, a passage which sounds as though it had escaped from Romans 7:

> [17]For the flesh wants to go against the Spirit, and the Spirit against the flesh. They are opposed to each other, so that you can't do what you want. [18]But if you are led by the Spirit, you are not under the Law.[401]

As in some other passages, Paul has missed out a middle term in his implied syllogism. We might expect him to say, 'if you are led by the spirit, you are not in the flesh', much as he does in Romans 8.9. The fact that instead he says 'you are not under the law' is easily explained, since for Paul, as in Romans 7.5, being 'in the flesh' is directly correlated with being 'under the law' – and those who are in the Messiah, who have died and been raised with him (Romans 7.6 here echoing Galatians 2.19–20), have ceased to be,

[400] Gal. 6.15; 1 Cor. 7.19.

[401] 5.17–18. On this, see Wright 2010 [*Virtue Reborn*/*After You Believe*], 163–71/189–98.

in that technical sense, 'in the flesh', that is, they are no longer defined in terms of that 'fleshly' existence, and have come instead to be defined in terms of Messiah and spirit. Galatians 5.17 and 18, then, function like a miniature version of Romans 7.7–25 and Romans 8.1–11, as indeed we might have expected from 5.16, which declares that those who live by the spirit will not do what the flesh wants them to do. In other words, we have here again a small glimmer of that larger inaugurated eschatology we see in Romans and elsewhere.[402] The covenant has been renewed, and the people of God have been transformed. To live according to the flesh – whether in the sense of a focus on ethnic identity and thus on circumcision, or in the sense of the 'works of the flesh' listed in verses 19 and 20 – is to stay in the old world. Paul's eschatological vision is of those who 'belong to the Messiah' (5.24) having 'crucified the flesh', exactly as in 2.19: indeed, they are to be people for whom, through Jesus, 'the world has been crucified to them, and they to the world'. But that already points us on to the final paragraph of the letter.

When Paul takes the pen in his own hand to sign off (6.11), he cannot resist one final flourish. He returns to the point he made earlier: the 'agitators' are simply wanting to avoid persecution themselves, which means they are trying to avoid the cross (6.12). They do not themselves keep Torah – or not in the way that Saul of Tarsus would have done, as in his self-description in 1.14! – but they simply want 'to boast in your flesh' (6.13). That, however precisely we reconstruct the hypothetical historical situation, is what he means by saying that they are trying to 'force you into getting circumcised'.[403] This leads to a further breathtakingly radical summary redefinition of election around the cross of the Messiah:

> [14]As for me, God forbid that I should boast – except in the cross of our lord Jesus the Messiah, through whom the world has been crucified to me and I to the world. [15]Circumcision, you see, is nothing; neither is uncircumcision! What matters is new creation. [16]Peace and mercy on everyone who lines up by that standard – yes, on God's Israel.[404]

We had better take these three verses slowly. This is a major moment in Paul's understanding. Tired, but satisfied that he has made the case, he is now drawing the threads together. At such a moment a speaker or writer tends to say what comes from the depths of heart and mind.[405]

[402] Against e.g. Barclay 1988, 112; Hays 2000, 326.

[403] 6.12, echoing 2.3 and 2.14. On the historical situation see e.g. Jewett 2002 [1970–1]; Hardin 2008; and, among the commentaries, the thorough if cautious survey of Schreiner 2010, 30–51.

[404] 6.14–16.

[405] Bachmann 2008 [1999], 115 is wrong to suggest that v. 16 has a 'not insignificant independence' – a rather obvious attempt to split the final phrase from the whole thought of the letter which, from every other point of view, looks as though it is being restated in summary form throughout 6.11–17. So too Eastman 2010, 386, suggesting a 'shift of focus' in 6.16b comparable to that between Rom. 8 and Rom. 9. The problem with this is (a) that 6.16b consists of only four words, and (b) that Paul then 'shifts' back again dramatically in 6.17.

For a start, there is no 'boasting'. The obvious parallel is in Romans, where it is particularly the 'boast' of 'the Jew'.[406] The other close parallel is 1 Corinthians 1.31, where Paul quotes Jeremiah 9.22–3: the one who boasts should boast of the lord.[407] Here, as in 1 Corinthians, the 'boasting' is specifically in the *crucified* lord, for the same reason as in Galatians 2.19–20: his death has constituted 'my' death. Only now Paul puts together the 'representative autobiography' of 2.19–20 with the cosmic scope of 1.4, where that same self-giving death of the Messiah was the instrument of God's delivery of his people from 'the present evil age'. This is how it has happened: what occurred on Calvary was the earthly instantiation and outworking of a much larger and darker battle. 'The world has been crucified to me': the old has passed away, as in 2 Corinthians 5.17, and the new has come. What the gospel has unveiled is not a 'new way of being religious', not even a 'new way of being saved'. (As we have seen, 'salvation' is not mentioned in this letter.) Nor is it even 'a new way of being God's people', though that is certainly involved. It is nothing short of 'new creation'. A new world has come into being, and everything appears in a new light within it. To highlight this point has been the strength of the so-called 'apocalyptic' emphasis in recent American writing on Paul.

This 'new creation', furthermore, now becomes the defining mark of the people of God: neither circumcision, nor uncircumcision, is anything; what matters is new creation! This is obviously parallel to 5.6, and elsewhere to 1 Corinthians 7.19, and the point is, in the language we have adopted in this book, that *eschatology defines election*: the 'new creation' determines the identity of the single family, the 'seed' promised to Abraham, and in doing so utterly relativizes the marks of circumcision, on the one hand, or any possible gentile pride in uncircumcision, on the other. (This is not insignificant when it is implied, whether through unthinking anti-Jewish sentiment in the church or in the natural pro-Jewish reaction, that 'the Jews' have been *replaced* by 'gentiles'. Paul would be just as hard on that nonsense as he is on the essentially anti-eschatological position of the 'agitators'.)

But it still matters that God's people are God's people. As in every breath of the letter so far, Paul understands God's people in terms of the Messiah and his death and resurrection, and in terms of the people who, through their *pistis*, are declared to be members of his extended family, the true and single *sperma* of Abraham. Anyone who reads Galatians 1.1—6.15 in anything like this way – and the cumulative case is massive – will find it almost literally unthinkable to suppose that when Paul then says, 'Yes, on God's Israel' at the end of verse 16 he should mean anything other than this: that the noble, evocative word 'Israel' itself now denotes, however polemically,

[406] Rom. 2.17; 3.27; cf. 4.2.

[407] cf. too 2 Cor. 10.17; Phil. 3.3.

the entire faith-family of the Messiah, defined by 'faith working through love' (5.6) and 'new creation' (6.15).[408]

The evidence for this position is many-sided and powerful. First, there is as I say the cumulative weight of the entire letter.[409] Paul's whole argument is that the one God has one family, not two, and that this one 'seed' consists of all those who believe in Jesus the Messiah, with no distinction of Jew and Greek, slave and free, male or female. He has spoken of this single family as 'the church of God', *ekklēsia tou theou*, the people whom he formerly persecuted (1.13).[410] The only other time he uses exactly this phrase it is interestingly distinguished from both 'Jews' and 'Greeks', giving strong support to the possibility that Paul was using it in the same sense here.[411] His struggle in Jerusalem and Antioch for 'the truth of the gospel' was precisely the battle to ensure that Jewish and gentile Messiah-believers belonged without distinction at the same table, as the sign of their membership in the single family, defined by nothing other than Messiah-faith (chapter 2). The argument of chapter 3 was that God always promised Abraham a single family in which gentiles would have an equal share, and that this has been provided through the Messiah and the spirit: all the baptized and believing Messiah-people form the single 'seed' who are the true 'heirs' of the promise. Chapter 4 reinforced that from several different angles, and chapter 5 turned up the

[408] At this point the majority of recent commentators are agreed: e.g. Betz 1979, 322f.; Sanders 1983, 174; R. N. Longenecker 1990, 298f.; Williams 1997, 167; Martyn 1997a, 574–7; Witherington 1998, 453; Hays 2000, 346; Stanton 2001, 1165 (this interpretation 'is now widely accepted'); Bell 2005, 179f. (though Bell misleads by labelling this a 'substitution model'); Schreiner 2010, 381–3 (with copious literature); Cohen 2011, 344 (the latter the more interesting in that it is part of the *Jewish Annotated New Testament*); see too Ridderbos 1975 [1966], 336; Barclay 1988, 98 n. 34; Longenecker 1998, 87f., 176f. (though holding open wider possibilities, which he has now embraced in Longenecker 2012, 16f.); Schreiner 2001, 82f.; Schnelle 2005 [2003], 589f.; Bird 2012, 27. Interestingly, this is the position taken by all those in Nanos 2002b who refer to the question; Nanos himself, in Nanos 2002a, does not discuss the point. Dunn 2008 [2005], 245, 252 (articles orig. pub. 1993, 1994) might be taken to support the majority view, but his fuller account (Dunn 1993, 344–6) suggests a view more like (one reading of) Rom. 11, namely that by 'the Israel of God' Paul is referring to the Jew–gentile believing church *and* the as yet unbelieving Jewish people, making the point that in Gal. Paul is not *excluding* future Jewish converts (whoever thought he was, I wonder?). For the history of the debate see Schreiner, loc. cit., and e.g. Eastman 2010, 369: among the main supporters of the minority view we must esp. mention Burton 1921, 358; Richardson 1969; Mussner 1974; and, most recently and impressively, de Boer 2011, 404–8 (the more interesting in that this is one of the places where de Boer parts company from Martyn). The minority view itself divides, with some (e.g. Richardson 1969, 82–4) seeing 'the Israel of God' as present Jewish Christians, some (e.g. Bachmann) seeing the phrase as denoting all Jews, and some (e.g. Burton) hinting that Paul might even be referring specifically to his opponents and those who shared their views.

[409] Curiously ignored by Eastman 2010. See, rightly, Sanders 1983, 174; Weima 1993, 105; Schreiner 2010, 383: 'The decisive argument for seeing the church as the Israel of God is the argument of Galatians as a whole.'

[410] Remembering that *ekklēsia* was a normal word for 'synagogue'. Hence the redefinition in 1.22: the messianic 'assemblies' in Judaea, as opposed to the non-messianic ones (cf. too 1 Cor. 15.9; 1 Thess. 2.14). De Boer's suggestion (2011, 407f.) that 'the church of God' in 1.13 referred to 'the mother church in Jerusalem' is curious: Paul clearly persecuted more widely, and despite what de Boer says at 2011, 85–8, I see no good evidence that he would have referred to the Jerusalem Christians in that way.

[411] 1 Cor. 10.32: 'Be blameless before Jews and Greeks and the church of God.' Thiselton comments (2000, 795), 'In 10:1–22 Paul has stressed the continuity of the Church with Israel; the phrase **the Church of God** in this context calls attention at the same time to a discontinuity, as if to imply that "the people of God" are partly redefined, although not in exclusivist terms since their roots and basis of divine promise and covenant remain in continuity with Israel's history' (bold type original).

ironic and polemical volume to a level where even those theologically stone-deaf could hardly miss what was being said. The context of the letter as a whole thus all points one way.[412]

So, too, does the context of the final paragraph itself – again, often ignored or downplayed by those who challenge the majority reading.[413] This paragraph actually reflects rather closely the blunt and polemical opening, with its mention of the world-redeeming death of the Messiah, the 'troublers' and the repeated anathemas.[414] If we remove the last six words of verse 16, *kai epi ton Israel tou theou* (literally: 'and upon the Israel of God'), nobody could imagine that these seven verses did anything other than summarize and emphasize the rest of the letter.[415] In particular, we should note verse 17, often ignored in this connection: 'For the rest, let nobody make trouble for me. You see, I carry the marks of Jesus on my body.' That offers a strong and again ironic and polemical reinforcement of 6.15, where neither circumcision nor uncircumcision matters: the marks of persecution which Paul bears, the sign of his sharing of the Messiah's sufferings, are the only physical marks which mean anything, and anyone who tries to say otherwise is 'making trouble' for him.[416] And the earlier parts of the paragraph, 6.11–15, tell the same story, in the same tone. If we are to read the last phrase of verse 16 in any other sense we would be, in effect, treating it as a strange aside, like someone in the middle of a speech turning to say something in quite a different tone of voice.

What about the word 'Israel' itself? It is of course true that Paul uses the word sparingly throughout his letters (except for Romans 9—11), and nowhere else in Galatians at all.[417] But the word was in any case multivalent in the hellenistic-Jewish world of Paul's day.[418] It was by no means equivalent to *hoi Ioudaioi*, 'the Jews': a powerful memory remained of the fact that the original chosen people, the children of 'Israel' i.e. Jacob, had been cut down to a remnant by the disappearance of the ten northern tribes, leaving only the two tribes of Judah and Benjamin and such Levites as lived among them – and they had themselves then been taken to Babylon, whence some

[412] Bachmann's argument (2008 [1999], 101–6, 121–3), that Gal. has an 'orientation toward the history of redemption', and that therefore Paul maintains 'the priority of Judaism', is an argument against a de-Judaized and non-covenantal reading of the letter such as used to be popular in Germany and elsewhere; but it is scarcely an argument against the view expounded throughout the present book.

[413] So, rightly, Sanders 1983, 174: 6.12–13 recalls 2.14; 6.14 recalls 2.20.

[414] 1.4; 1.7; 1.8f.

[415] Bachmann 2008 [1999], 107 is wrong to suggest that 6.11–17 is 'less aggressive' or 'more gentle' than what has gone before. Paul's tone, here as throughout the letter, is a mixture of irony and pastoral concern. But every single verse in the paragraph is sharp and clear, with multiple echoes of the letter in general and not least of its equally important opening. See, more accurately, Weima 1993, 90–2; Beale 1999, 205.

[416] cf. too 4.12–14.

[417] cf. 1 Cor. 10.28; 2 Cor. 3.7, 13; Eph. 2.12; Phil. 3.5. Many writers insist, correctly, that we cannot invoke Rom. 9—11 to help us at this point; Gal. must stand on its own terms. Furthermore, even in Rom. 9—11, despite many claims, the use is not unambiguous or univocal: see, rightly, Davies 1984, 343 n. 20.

[418] On what follows see the still very helpful analysis of K. G. Kuhn and W. Gutbrod in *TDNT* 3.359–91. It is too simple to take the usage of 1 Macc. (Jews refer to 'Israel', non-Jews to 'the Jews') as representative of the period (Stendahl 1995, 4): for a start, 2 Macc. is very different.

but not all had returned. The word *Ioudaios*, 'Jew', thus strictly denoted the tribe of Judah, extended to include returnees from Benjamin and Levi, and was used in various ways in the second-Temple period, sometimes but not always by 'Jews' to refer to themselves, more often by non-Jews to refer, sometimes contemptuously, to the Jewish people whether in the middle east or in the Diaspora. Meanwhile the word 'Israel' was likewise used in a variety of ways, but often in careful distinction from 'Jew' or 'Jews', and usually in the context of evoking the original biblical sense of the covenant people, carrying the claim and/or the hope that the present *Ioudaioi* would turn out at the last to be the 'Israel' of whom it would be said that 'all Israel has a share in the age to come'. The word was subject to constant, and implicitly polemical, redefinition, right across the world of second-Temple Jewish sectarianism: it was, obviously, a word that everyone wanted to claim, from Qumran to the rabbis. It was connected, not least, to the expectation (or the claim) of a Messiah, and/or to the belief that the present group was a kind of Israel-in-waiting, a 'remnant' out of which the ultimate Israel might grow. There is of course no precedent in second-Temple literature for a meaning of 'Israel' which would correspond to the meaning most commentators believe it must bear in Galatians 6; but then there wouldn't be. Until Paul, nobody had imagined what it might mean for the people of God if the Messiah appeared *and was crucified*. Unprecedented situations generate unprecedented results.[419]

Obviously, then, if Paul were to use 'Israel' in this passage to mean 'the whole seed of Abraham, believing Jews and believing gentiles together', this would constitute a seriously polemical redefinition. But that is hardly foreign either to his practice in general or to the present passage in particular. In general, we have already had occasion to notice his breathtaking redefinition of 'Jew' itself in Romans 2.29, and of 'circumcision' in Romans 2.26 and Philippians 3.3. We studied numerous other redefinitions in the previous chapter, such as the striking use of 'temple'-language, and of the covenant promises, in 2 Corinthians 6.16.[420] Within the present context, there are several other sharp, almost gnomic redefinitions of traditional terms, and densely compressed summary phrases: 'the Messiah's law', in 6.2, for instance – an otherwise unexplained coinage, adding a genitive to a major term to indicate a significant if perhaps opaque modification; 'the world crucified to me and I to the world'; 'new creation'. Perhaps we should add *zōē aiōnios*, a phrase not used elsewhere in the letter and itself constituting a redefinition of the Jewish idea of 'the life of the age to come'.[421]

[419] I am reminded of a moment in Worcester College, Oxford, not long after women were first admitted as Fellows, when one such woman became engaged to one of the existing male Fellows. When, that evening, I proposed that the assembled company rise and drink their health, the Senior Fellow, a lawyer, objected that there was no precedent for such a thing. I pointed out that, in the nature of the case, there could not have been. (We compromised: we drank their health, but stayed seated.)

[420] The attempt of Bachmann 2008 [1999], 112 to diminish the force of these parallels must be counted a failure.

[421] See above, 163f., 1060.

Are there any signs that 'Israel of God' might be just such a polemical coinage, like 'the Messiah's law'? Was it, perhaps, a phrase already used by Paul's opponents as a way of denoting what they saw as the genuine people of God, i.e. the circumcised?[422] Whether or not the latter suggestion has merit, there is excellent reason to suppose that Paul regularly employed such polemical redefinitions, not least of Jewish prayers and blessings. For a start, the adjectival genitive 'of God' clearly introduces a *modification* of 'Israel', as the phrase 'of the Messiah' modifies 'law' in 6.2. Paul was capable of simply taking over major community-defining terms such as 'Jew' or 'circumcision', as we saw, without adding any adjectives or genitives, but when such additions occur we may rightly suspect that a similar redefinition is going on.

But why would he say 'of God'? Here there should be no doubt, in the light of Galatians as a whole, of the intended effect. Not only do we have 'the church *of God*' in 1.13. We also have Paul saying in 2.19, 'Through the law I died to the law that I might live *to God*.' The idea of such an antithesis would have made no sense to Saul of Tarsus, but that is the effect of coming to terms with a crucified Messiah. Then there is the clipped but actually clear 3.20: the mediator, that is, Moses, is not mediator of the single family promised to Abraham, *but God is one*, and therefore desires, and has created in the Messiah, exactly such a single family.[423] We might also compare the striking role of 'God' in 4.7, 8 and particularly 9: those 'in the Messiah' are children and heirs of God, have come to know God or rather to be known by him, and must not turn back to the *stoicheia* – which, however puzzling a usage it may be, is obviously closely related in Paul's mind to the Galatians' desire to get circumcised.

All this points us on, from earlier moments in the letter, to the highly probable reading of the additional phrase 'of God' in 6.16b. 'The Israel of God', in the light of the letter so far, *must* mean 'the household of faith' (6.10), 'those who walk according to the rule of new creation as opposed to that of circumcision/uncircumcision' (6.15), and so on.[424] Paul is talking precisely about an 'Israel' not defined by *sarx*, 'flesh', but by the Messiah in whom the grace of God has been embodied (2.19–21). This in turn points to, and is then strengthened by, the implicit antithesis, 'Israel according to the flesh', in 1 Corinthians 10.18, however much commentators resist such a

[422] For this suggestion, cf. Betz 1979, 323, and later discussions e.g. Weima 1993, 105.

[423] See above, 871–3. This point is similar to that made by Martyn 1997a, 576.

[424] de Boer 2011, 406 suggests that it constitutes a 'significant problem' for this view that 'the Israel of God' is 'far removed' from 'all who will follow this standard'. This is clutching at straws: (a) seven words is hardly 'far removed'; plenty of Paul's arguments depend on much more long-range connections; (b) *ep' autous* undoubtedly refers back to 'all who follow' etc., and that effectively closes the gap to a mere two words (*kai eleos*).

possibility.[425] Granted, there is no equivalent 'Israel according to the spirit' in Paul (though we might compare once more Romans 2.25–9 and Philippians 3.3), but that means little: as Galatians 4.21—5.1 demonstrates, Paul has several overlapping contrasts up his sleeve and can draw on them at will. He is after all writing urgent, compressed letters, not a doctoral dissertation in systematic theology. The high probability, therefore, is that with 'Israel of God' in 6.16b we are faced with a Pauline innovation.[426]

How then does verse 16 actually work? The first half is clear: literally, 'as many as walk by that rule, peace upon them ...' The 'rule' in question is obviously that of verse 15: neither circumcision nor uncircumcision, but new creation. The 'as many as' here seems to be in deliberate contrast to the 'as many as' in 6.12 (literally, 'as many as want to make a good showing in the flesh, they are compelling you to be circumcised'): here is the one group, the circumcisers, and here is the other group, the neither-circumcision-nor-uncircumcision people. The whole paragraph is shaped and structured as a contrast between these two groups.

The sentence itself is tricky, because of the two occurrences of *kai* in the middle (in addition, that is, to the one at the start of the verse). 'Peace upon them *kai* mercy *kai* upon the Israel of God.' Greek *kai* can of course mean not only 'and' or 'also', that is, signalling a new entity being added to those already indicated, but also 'even', that is, signalling a further meaning to be found within those already indicated. It can, in other words, be a mark of addition, but also of intensification.[427] Thus there might be three options:

1. peace and mercy (a) upon them ('those who walk by this rule) and (b) upon the Israel of God (a different group from 'them');

2. (a) peace upon 'those who walk by this rule', and (b) mercy even for 'the Israel of God' (a different group from 'those who walk by this rule');

3. peace and mercy upon 'those who walk by this rule', yes, even upon 'the Israel of God' (i.e. the same group).

[425] Eastman 2010, 368 and Bachmann 2012, 87 both cite Schrage 1995, 442f. to the effect that the 'Israel' spoken of in 1 Cor. 10.18 is 'the idol worshipping [Israel] of vv. 6–10'. But Paul's point here, as in 10.1–4, is not to say that the idea of Israel's 'feeding' and 'participating in the altar' represented their subsequent rebellion. He is simply stating what is true of ancient, biblical Israel as a whole. The implicit contrast is evoked by the fact that in 10.1, as negatively in 12.2, Paul is telling Israel's story in such a way as to include the Corinthian Christians within it, while differentiating them precisely from ethnic Israel as such; cf. again 10.32, and e.g. Wolter 2011, 413f., and below, 1231–52.

[426] For the idea of this as a 'Pauline innovation' see e.g. Wolter 2008, 155–8. In view of the use of 'God' in the letter so far, reaching its climax here, I regard it as less probable that 'Israel of God' was a phrase coined by the 'agitators' and taken over by Paul.

[427] i.e. the so-called 'epexegetic' *kai*. This summary is itself a considerable oversimplification, as the entry for *kai* in BDAG 494–6 indicates (nb. 494: 'the vivacious versatility of *kai* ... can easily be depressed by the tr. "and", whose repetition in a brief area of text lacks the support of arresting aspects of Gk. syntax'). See the full note of Beale 1999, 206 n. 7.

The third of these is the one which, I am suggesting, the whole letter would indicate. Is there anything in the grammar to suggest that this is ruled out? No. Indeed, it might be thought that the second *kai* actually makes (b) at least very difficult. If Paul had wanted to say 'peace upon *this* group and mercy upon *that* one', it would have been much clearer had he missed out the second *kai* altogether: *eirēnē ep' autous* on the one hand, and *eleos epi ton Israēl tou theou* on the other. The second *kai*, coming so soon after the obviously 'additional' one between *eirēnē* and *eleos*, is far more likely to be intensive, that is, to be supplying an extra dimension of meaning to something already mentioned, not introducing a new element.

This probability is strengthened by the echo, here, of what was most likely already in Paul's day a well-known Jewish prayer formula, seen to good advantage in the last of the so-called 'Eighteen Benedictions': 'Show mercy and peace upon us, and on thy people Israel.'[428] Similar formulae are found in the *Kaddish d'Rabbanan*: 'May there be abundant peace from heaven, and a happy life for us and for all Israel'; 'He who maketh peace in his high places, may he in his mercy make peace for us and for all Israel'.[429]

One might of course object that such prayers do envisage two different but overlapping groups: (a) the congregation praying this prayer and (b) the larger company of 'all Israel'. One could argue on this basis that perhaps Paul, too, has a pair of groups in mind: (a) 'those who walk by this rule', and (b) 'those Jews who do not at present walk by this rule but may in the future come to do so'.[430] But there are obvious responses to this. First, if Paul is alluding to any such prayer-formulae, he may well be adapting it to new use, changing the order of 'mercy and peace' and employing this otherwise unknown phrase 'Israel of God'. So it is not certain that he must be following the pattern of two overlapping but distinct groups, either. But, second, it is perhaps possible, if he is following some such pattern, that he thinks of 'those who walk by this rule' not in the first instance as a general statement about 'all those in the Messiah', but as a specific description of what he wants to see in Galatia, with 'the Israel of God' then following as the larger category of 'all the Messiah's people, whoever and wherever they are'. Third, however, we must be alert to the fact that Paul can pick up ancient Jewish prayers and make them serve new purposes. Just as he can *narrate* believing

[428] SB 3.579. The dating of the Eighteen Benedictions is not important for our purposes; I assume that such formalized prayers from later generations grew out of long-standing traditions going way back into the second-Temple period.

[429] *ADPB* 16.

[430] This is the solution preferred by De Boer 2011, 407f. Of course, this would not satisfy the hopes of at least Bachmann and similar thinkers, for whom the idea of future Jewish *conversions*, or of presently law-observant Jewish Christians coming round to Paul's point of view, would still mean 'replacement', 'displacement' or whatever. De Boer's proposal, that Paul has in mind 'the churches of the Petrine mission', recognizing its proper mission to Jews (though not its improper invasion of Paul's territory according to the agreement of Gal. 2.7–9), looks like a valiant attempt to avoid (for him) the Scylla of saying that here 'Israel' means 'the church' and the Charybdis of having Paul here invoke a blessing on those anathematized in 1.8f. (de Boer has responded to this, in correspondence, by saying that Paul does indeed invoke the divine 'mercy' on them). It is ironic that de Boer invokes Romans at this point, having attempted from the start (2011, 2) to suggest that such a move would be, if not actually illegitimate, then certainly dangerous.

gentiles into the story of Israel, as in 1 Corinthians 10,[431] so he can *pray* them there as well. We observed two chapters ago how he breathtakingly rewrites the *Shema* itself, the prayer which marks out Israel as the truly monotheistic people.[432] We might observe, closer to home, that in Galatians 3.28 he implies a drastic revision to a well-known synagogue prayer: his claim that 'there is neither Jew nor Greek, slave nor free, no male and female' answers quite directly to the prayers of thanks that the person praying has not been made a heathen, a slave or a woman.[433] (Similar invocations are found within the non-Jewish world as well. It is not only Jewish traditions that Paul is rejecting.[434]) It seems to me highly likely, and in keeping with the tone as well as the content of Galatians, that Paul would at this climactic and summary moment at the end of the letter offer a prayer which echoed, but also subverted, invocations which he knew from childhood and which had earlier served to reinforce the distinction between Jew and gentile, between circumcised and uncircumcised, which he now so emphatically rejected on the basis of the crucified Messiah and the spirit.[435]

If there is no good reason to see 'the Israel of God' as a different group from 'those who walk according to this rule', there is no good reason either to press the word 'mercy' as though, either by its strange placing *after* 'peace', or its meaning in Romans 9—11, it would have to carry the connotation of a further act of divine redemption for a group at present resistant to the Pauline gospel.[436] For Paul, the idea of 'mercy' cannot be separated from the gospel of the Messiah.[437] More importantly, it may well be that 'peace and mercy' is another echo of Isaiah 54. Paul has already quoted 54.1 at 4.27, where as we saw it forms something of a climax to the argument not only of the paragraph but of the central argument of the letter. In 54.10, in the middle of the promise of a new creation from 'the Holy One of Israel' who is also 'the God of the whole earth' (54.5), the prophet declares

> For the mountains may depart and the hills be removed,
> but my steadfast love (*eleos*) shall not depart from you,
> and my covenant of peace (*eirēnē*) shall not be removed,
> says YHWH, who has compassion on you.

It has been argued forcibly that this passage, and similar passages elsewhere in scripture and second-Temple literature, were being echoed by Paul at this

[431] Hays 2000, 346 n. 302.

[432] Above, 661–70.

[433] *ADPB* 6f.; cf. SB 3.557–63: cf. tBer. 7.18; j.Ber. 13b; bMenah. 43b.

[434] e.g. Diog. Laert. *Vit. Philos.* 1.33; Plut. *Marius* 46.1.

[435] Dunn's point (1993, 344) that such prayers were 'strongly Jewish' hardly means that Paul must be hinting, by using them, at a diminution of his christocentric and 'new-creation' position.

[436] Against Eastman 2010: the appeal to how Paul 'surely' must have felt about his kinsfolk (388) tells us nothing about what Paul actually wrote in this letter.

[437] The words *eleos* and *eleeō* are used in Rom. as often in relation to gentiles (Rom. 9.23; 11.30, 31, 32; 15.9) as in relation to Jews (Rom. 9.15, 16, 18; 11.31, 32). One cannot therefore deduce from this word – even supposing one could argue straightforwardly from Rom. to Gal. 6.16! – a supposedly special Pauline emphasis of 'mercy' for presently unbelieving Jews.

point, and that this, granted Paul's other use of the same passages, makes a further strong case for seeing 'the Israel of God' in 6.16b not as a separate entity but precisely as the believing church.[438]

The case for the majority view, then, is overwhelming. It is not unthinkable to challenge it, as we have seen: many, seeing only too well the implications of this position, have, like Peter in Antioch, drawn back, fearing the circumcision party (I speak, of course, in human fashion, because of the weakness of the flesh). But if it were the case that Paul, suddenly at this late stage, meant something else by 'God's Israel' – meant, for instance, to refer either to all Jews, or to all Christian Jews, or to some subset of either of those whether now or in the future – then he would, quite simply, have made nonsense of the whole letter. Why write Galatians 3 and 4, if that was where it was going to end up? Why not settle for two families, two 'inheritances', instead of the single one? Why not allow that people who want to follow Moses can do so, and that those who want to follow Abraham without Moses can do so too? Why not, in short, behave as if the Messiah had not been crucified? That is what such a position would amount to.

Paul will have none of it. He bears in his body the only marks that count: not the knife-mark of circumcision, but the cuts and bruises of physical persecution, of the stones that were thrown at him in one city and the synagogue-beatings received in another, of 'countless floggings', a beating with rods and no doubt much besides.[439] He is himself a living, breathing demonstration of what it means that the world is crucified to him and he to the world. This, he suggests as in 2 Corinthians, is what 'new creation', or at least its emissary, looks like as he walks around the world.[440] 'I have been crucified with the Messiah. I am, however, alive – but it isn't me any longer, it's the Messiah who lives in me.' And it is the *crucified* Messiah that so lives. That is Paul's fresh, eschatologically oriented understanding of election. Controversial then, controversial now.

(iii) 1 Thessalonians 2

From the heights and depths of argument and pathos in Galatians to an altogether different letter, and yet one with considerable challenges for the interpreter. We have noted the various ways in which 1 Thessalonians highlights both the power of the gospel and the change in life that comes from being grasped by it. One of the other things, though, that Paul knew would happen when people came to believe in Jesus the Messiah was persecution. So when he is encouraging the Thessalonians to stick with the word of God that has done its work in them, one of the arguments he uses is that they, by

[438] So Beale 1999, esp. e.g. 208. The other texts he proposes are Pss. (LXX) 84.11; 124.5; 127.6; Ezra 3.11; 1QH 13.5; *Jub.* 22.9.

[439] 6.17; cf. 2 Cor. 11.23–5; we do not know, of course, how much of what Paul there reports had already been suffered before his writing of Galatians.

[440] 2 Cor. 5.17 with 4.7–18 and 6.3–10.

their suffering, have already shown that they know it is God who is at work in them, and that they are firmly located on the map alongside others who have been persecuted, and indeed with Jesus himself. All this provides further evidence of Paul's redefined election and eschatology.

But, in saying this, Paul says something more. This reflects not just a personal frustration with the non-believing Judaeans,[441] but a theological judgment about where they stand within God's newly revealed eschatological purposes:

> [14]For, my dear family, you came to copy God's assemblies in Judaea in the Messiah, Jesus. You suffered the same things from your own people as they did from those of the Judaeans [15]who killed the lord Jesus and the prophets, and who expelled us. They displease God; they oppose all people; [16]they forbid us to speak to the gentiles so that they may be saved. This has had the effect, all along, of completing the full total of their sins. But the fury has come upon them for good.[442]

Certain things stand out in this (to us) remarkable outburst. First, we should not make the trivial but far-reaching mistake of thinking that the outburst is directed against 'the Jews'. Paul was himself of course Jewish; the people he describes as 'assemblies (*ekklēsiai*) of God in Judaea in the Messiah, Jesus' were Jews. The parallel Paul is drawing is between the Thessalonian Messiah-people, who are being persecuted by their pagan neighbours, and the Messiah-people in Judaea, who are being persecuted by non-Messiah-believing Judaeans. There is therefore no particular 'bias against Jews' here, as has sometimes been suggested.[443] As many have seen, the comma often placed between verses 14 and 15 is grammatically unwarranted.[444] The phrase 'who killed the lord Jesus and the prophets' restricts the phrase 'the Judaeans': instead of 'the Judaeans, who killed ...' it is 'the Judaeans who killed ...', which I have paraphrased above 'You suffered the same things from your own people as they did from those of the Judaeans who killed the lord Jesus and the prophets.' In other words, Paul is being quite specific here. He is not lumping all Judaeans together (still less all 'Jews'! – Paul himself being a Jew, like all the first Christians), and declaring that they were all alike guilty of all these crimes, and that 'the fury' or 'the wrath' has come upon all of them indiscriminately. 'He does not speak of all

[441] The term is of course geographical, not ethnic.

[442] I see no need here, by the way, to think in terms of interpolations or later scribal alterations (as proposed by e.g. Pearson 1971 and others since; firmly refuted by e.g. Donfried 1984; Davies 1984, 124–7; Weatherly 1991; Malherbe 2000, 164f.; Sänger 2010, 135). That has too long been the refuge of scholars who should have known better. Yes, no doubt manuscripts get altered; but the burden of proof lies on those who propose such a thing with no textual evidence, not least to explain why someone would have inserted *this* material *here*. Watson 2007 [1986], 81 n. 66 rightly points out that if Paul can cite Ps. 68.23f. 'even in the relatively irenical Romans 11' there is no reason to suppose that 1 Thess. 2.14–16 is inauthentic.

[443] Best 1972, 122 goes so far as to say this comment is 'anti-Semitic'. As Fee (2009, 102f.) points out, that is like accusing someone of anti-Americanism because they criticize the current President. This is an 'inner-familial conflict' (Wolter 2011, 416).

[444] Fee 2009, 95f.; cf. too Gilliard 1989.

Jews, but of those who acted against their fellow Jews.'[445] Rather, he is specifying that strand of current Judaean activity which, having strongly opposed Jesus and sent him to his death, was now continuing in the same vein by opposing the Messiah-people in their taking the gospel to the gentiles.

This is of course heavily ironic, in that Paul himself had been one of the very people involved in such activity. The list of wrongs which Paul lays at the door of this group of Judaeans, then, reaches its climax in their opposition to the gentile mission, which joins up with what has happened to the Thessalonians, who, according to Acts, were the targets of local persecution not least because of Jewish jealousy.[446] Paul's own former persecution of the early church maps exactly on to this movement.[447]

Second, though, Paul places this persecution of the Judaean Messiah-people by their fellow countrymen on the chart of a longer opposition to the movement – specifically, in line with violent Judaean opposition to Jesus himself. It comes as a shock, after a couple of generations in the twentieth century in which we have all bent over backwards to insist (in line with the gospel accounts) that Jesus of Nazareth was crucified by Roman soldiers on the order of the Roman governor, to have Paul say the unmentionable, that the reason all this happened was (again in line with the gospel accounts) that the Judaean leaders handed Jesus over to just that fate.[448]

The addition of 'and the prophets' after 'killed the lord Jesus' looks like the traditional accusation of prophet-killing that we find in Matthew 5.12 and elsewhere.[449] This seems the more likely in view of the echo in 2.16 of Matthew 23.32–3: 'fill up, then, the measure of your ancestors', referring to the ancestors who had themselves persecuted the prophets. The idea of 'filling up' a measure of sin, after which judgment must fall, goes way back to Genesis 15, where the delay in Abraham's children coming back to their inheritance is said to be because 'the iniquity of the Amorite is not yet full'.[450] Paul, in line with this tradition, is envisaging the particular Judaean leaders and activists responsible for these wrongs as the leading edge of a kind of anti-*Heilsgeschichte*, an ongoing rebellion against God's will which ultimately led to the death of Jesus and is now working its way out in opposition to the gentile mission. (One might imagine that Paul could offer a theological account of this movement in terms reminiscent of Romans 7: this fierce, zealous adherence to Torah was actually increasing the grip of

[445] Malherbe 2000, 169.

[446] e.g. Ac. 17.5–14; 18.12–17.

[447] 1 Cor. 15.9; Gal. 1.13f., 23; Phil. 3.6; 1 Tim. 1.13; cf. Ac. 8.3; 9.1f., 21; 22.4f.; 26.9–11. As is now frequently pointed out, an earlier scepticism about Acts' accounts of Paul preaching in synagogues is directly contradicted by Paul's own testimony about his receiving synagogue punishments (2 Cor. 11.24–7); cf. too 1 Cor. 9.20–2, and e.g. Meeks 1983, 26; Sanders 1983, 190–2; Malherbe 2000, 175.

[448] See *JVG* ch. 12.

[449] e.g. Mt. 21.35f.; 22.6; 23.34, 37; Ac. 7.52. It seems to me less likely that it refers to the killing of some early Christian prophets (Fee), and it does of course make his view about the absence of the comma even stronger; but why Paul would single out the killing of early Christian prophets here, when there was an old and strong tradition about the killing of prophets, is a mystery to me at least.

[450] Gen. 15.16.

'sin'.) The point is this: there was already an established tradition in which second-Temple Jews would narrate a historical sequence of wrongdoing through which divine wrath would accumulate towards an ultimate day of reckoning. Paul, invoking that tradition, turns it back on those whose actions reflected his own earlier 'zeal'.[451]

If this is so, it strengthens what already seems to me the likely reading of the sharp conclusion to verse 16: 'the fury has come upon them to the end'. Let us be clear: if we met a statement like this in a document which we knew came from later than AD 70 (say, the *Epistle of Barnabas* or a similar text), we would have no hesitation in saying that it was referring to the fall of Jerusalem. Why should we resist such a conclusion just because we are sure that 1 Thessalonians was written about twenty years before that cataclysmic event? If, as I have argued elsewhere, Jesus himself really did utter solemn oracles against Jerusalem in general and the Temple in particular, warning his contemporaries that to oppose his kingdom-movement would have the consequence of calling down the wrath of Rome upon the city, then it is already highly likely that this was well known in the early Christian movement.[452] If others, like Stephen, had been accused of speaking against the city and the Temple, it looks as though the early Christians had something of a reputation for saying similar things to what they remembered Jesus saying. For Paul to echo that tradition does not seem to me impossible or unlikely. Just because this is the only place where we can detect such a thing (I bracket out 2 Thessalonians here, partly because many are unsure about its Pauline standing and partly because today's scholarship still finds it difficult to interpret), that does not mean that he could not or would not have said anything like this.

The alternative, canvassed by Robert Jewett nearly thirty years ago and still not unattractive, is that Paul was referring to a similar, if smaller-scale, event which had happened in very recent memory.[453] Early on in the procuratorship of Ventidius Cumanus, a stupid soldier made a provocative gesture at the large crowd assembled for Passover, provoking a riot which in turn provoked a backlash. In one account Josephus says that twenty thousand died; in another, more than thirty thousand.[454] It is perfectly possible

[451] cf. e.g. Dan. 8.23; 2 Macc. 6.14; Wis. 19.3–5; *LAB* 26.1–3; and, not least, the instructive parallel in *T. Lev.* 6.3–11. There, 'Levi' describes the punishment of the sons of Hamor for the rape of Dinah (Gen. 34.1–31). Their wickedness, says 'Levi', was the accumulation of previous sins: they persecuted Abraham when he was a nomad, they harassed his flocks when pregnant and they grossly mistreated 'Eblaen' (an otherwise unknown character). So, the text says, 'this is how they treated the nomadic people, seizing their wives and murdering them' (6.10). Then the result of this stored-up wickedness: 'the wrath of God ultimately came upon them' (*ephthasen de hē orgē ep᾽ autous eis telos*). (Tr. H. C. Kee in Charlesworth 1983, 790.) See too Gaventa 1998, 37. The likelihood of dependence between this passage and 1 Thess. 2 is minimal; this seems to be a regular way of second-Temple thinking about how providence deals with accumulated sin. The parallel suggests (against Malherbe 2000, 178f., who sees *eis telos* as 'eschatological') that we are right to look for a specific first-century event as the content of 'the wrath' in 1 Thess. 2.16. Eschatology, for Paul, is frequently inaugurated.

[452] See *JVG* ch. 8.

[453] Jewett 1986, 37f., and Jewett 2002 [1970–1], 340f., referring to earlier articles of Johnson 1941 and others, and canvassing other violent incidents in Judaea as alternative options.

[454] Jos. *Ant.* 20.105–12; *War* 2.223–7; cf. *NTPG* 175 for the larger context.

that Paul would have seen such an event as part of the providential outworking of the Judaeans' earlier refusal to heed the Messiah's message of peace.[455] The 'zealous' revolutionaries of the time, among whom the young Saul of Tarsus would have numbered himself,[456] had seen the divine wrath as continuing against Israel, needing to be appeased and turned away by violent actions which would purge God's people of their treachery and impurity. Paul, familiar with this language, would then in the present passage be declaring that, on the contrary, it was such actions, against both Jesus himself and his followers, that had brought 'the wrath' to such a peak. This was a normal first-century Jewish way of thinking about the strange interplay of politics and providence, and it makes good sense to suppose that Paul, encouraging his churches as they themselves faced persecution, would have invoked in such a way the roughly parallel situation in Judaea. The passage would thus constitute yet another Pauline reworking of Jewish tradition, in line with his taking over words like 'Jew' and 'circumcision'.

This, to repeat, does not make him anti-Jewish, still less anti-semitic – any more than Josephus was anti-Jewish for blaming the disaster of AD 70 on violent Judaean troublemakers. Paul would have snorted at the very suggestion. As with Elijah and Ahab ('Is it you, you Israel-troubler?' 'It isn't me that's troubled Israel, it's you and your father's house!'[457]) he would insist that the charge rebounds. In any case, his point here is that the Judaeans who opposed Jesus and the first Christians were typical, precisely not of 'Jewish' behaviour, but of *local opposition*, which in the Thessalonians' case was obviously non-Jewish.[458] Part of our difficulty here is caused by the extremely low grade of much contemporary moral discourse, in which everything is reduced to being 'pro-' this or 'anti-' that, as though there were no more nuanced positions available, and as though, in particular, all ethical or theological *judgments* could be reduced to 'prejudices' and 'attitudes'. This is not the place to develop a counter-critique. But it is necessary to note the problem, in order to clear the hermeneutical space to say what needs to be said about 1 Thessalonians 2.14–16: (a) it is certainly original to Paul; (b) it does not constitute or express an anti-Jewish attitude, still less anything 'anti-semitic'; (c) it refers to the (perhaps quite small) subset of Judaeans that had been behind the move to get rid of Jesus, and that is now behind the opposition to the gentile mission; (d) Paul perhaps sees this as an acceleration of wickedness towards a judgment which either will fall on them or has already done so, in line with Jesus' words, which were themselves in line with ancient prophecy;[459] (e) this will be *eis telos*, not a 'final eschatological

455 cp. Lk. 19.41–4.

456 cf. Gal. 1.13f.; Phil. 3.6.

457 1 Kgs. 18.17f.

458 cf. 'from your own people', *hypo tōn idiōn symphyletōn* (2.14), indicating 'the same tribe or people group' (BDAG 960). This does not undercut Ac. 17.5–15, where local Jewish groups were involved in the initial opposition to Paul and his message; what is indicated is the local non-Jewish hostility which continued thereafter.

459 See esp. e.g. Lk. 19.42–4, which echoes various scriptural prophecies but cannot be reduced to an 'after the event' post-70 write-up for the good reason that some of the things predicted did not actually happen (see *JVG* 348f.).

judgment' as in Romans 2.1–16, but the completion of the 'wrath' which is the tragic consequence of their own actions.

Nothing is said here about the 'ultimate future' for 'the Jews'. That is a problem we bring to this text from Romans 9—11 on the one hand and from modern concerns on the other, but which is simply not under consideration at this point. The passage is after all directed, not to a 'statement' about 'the Jews', but to an encouragement to the Thessalonians in the face of their own local opposition. The implication is that, sooner or later, the providence of God *will deal with the local Thessalonian opposition, too*. The word of God is at work in their midst;[460] Paul knows that what God begins, he will bring to completion.[461] What we can hear, however, not far behind this text, is an echo of Paul's warning in Romans 12: vengeance belongs to God alone. To say that *divine* wrath has come, or is coming, upon wrongdoers is to say, by clear Pauline implication, that *human* wrath is inappropriate.[462] Those who (like the present writer) have not had to live with violence and the threat of violence, as many in the middle east tragically still do, are ill placed to pass moral, let alone theological, judgments on those like Paul for whom that was a constant reality.

This short passage in an early letter points on, however poignantly, to a long passage in a late one. As most pastors will realize, it is not a long step from sharp words against someone to bitter tears and grief on their behalf. We should thus not be altogether surprised – still less postulate a major change of mind or heart – when we turn from 1 Thessalonians 2 to Romans 9—11. This is where the covenantal challenge of Paul's redefined eschatology comes into full focus at last.

(iv) Romans 9—11

(a) Introduction

It is easy to be overwhelmed by Romans 9—11: its scale and scope, the mass of secondary literature, the controversial theological and also political topics, and the huge and difficult questions of the overall flow of thought on the one hand and the complex details of exegesis and interpretation on the other.[463] For our present purposes I want to keep a clear focus on certain issues to do with Paul's redefinition of the foundational Jewish doctrines.

[460] 2.13; 2.14–16 is introduced with *gar*: Paul at least supposes 2.14–16 is an explanation of why he can give thanks for what is going on in their midst, not a detached statement about events in Judaea (see Malherbe 2000, 167).

[461] Phil. 1.6.

[462] Rom. 12.19–21 (with 13.4!).

[463] Among my previous readings: Wright 1991 [*Climax*], ch. 13; *Romans*, 620–99. Those familiar with these earlier treatments may like to know that the argument of the present section proceeds by a different route. It would have been possible to extend the present section into a long book of its own by engaging in more detail with recent literature, not least Bell 2005 and Wilk and Wagner 2010.

The present section, of course, could almost as well be discussed under his revision of 'election'; the fact that I discuss it here, under 'eschatology', has to do with the fact that the reason he retells the story of Israel's election and the divine covenant purposes in Romans 9—10 is because he then wants to peer into the future, and to say 'what now?'. In other words, as we saw at the start of the previous section of this chapter, we are now faced with the second of two areas where precisely the shape of Paul's revised monotheism and election leave him with two questions: how then shall Christians behave, and what is the future of God's elective purposes for Israel? Nobody before Paul had faced the question of how second-Temple eschatology would be affected if the Messiah arrived and most of his people failed to recognize him. Paul is out on his own at this point, thinking through a fresh model of Jewish eschatology in the light of Messiah and spirit.[464]

We have already seen, throughout this Part of the book, that several lines of thought earlier in the letter point forward sharply and clearly to elements within Romans 9—11, with more subtlety than is usually noted. One good thing about the scholarship of the last fifty years: we hear no more, these days, of the previously common view that these chapters are irrelevant to the rest of the letter, perhaps even an old sermon about 'the Jews' which Paul happened to have with him and decided to insert into the Roman letter at this point.[465] That devastating misreading grew out of, and then further contributed to, a mid-century scholarly mood which is now quite hard even to remember, since so much has happened to alter the landscape. But when we have agreed that these chapters belong where they are, bound into the letter's whole structure by a thousand silken strands, we have not yet made much real progress in exegesis or theology. How are we to find the heart and centre of what Paul is saying here about God's electing and above all eschatological purposes?

Four preliminary points about these chapters are important in shaping our discussion and developing our thesis. Keeping these in mind may help to retain some clarity in the midst of necessary complexity.

1. For a start, if Romans as a whole is a book primarily about God, that is particularly so here, especially in chapters 9 and 11. Here we find, straight off, the question of God's word, God's children, God's promise, God's purpose in election, God's call, God's love (and hatred), God's justice (or injustice), God's mercy, God's power, God's name, God's sovereignty, God's will, God's rights as the potter over the clay, God's wrath and power, God's patience, God's glory and God's people.[466] And that's only chapter 9. Anyone even mildly interested in God might find plenty here to be going on

[464] The spirit is not mentioned as such in chs. 9—11, but as we shall see is visible just underneath the argument in 10.12f.

[465] Dodd 1959 [1932], 161–3. In this, Dodd was representative of a much wider sweep of scholarship. I remember on my first visit to Bonn, in 1976, being introduced to the great Heinrich Schlier. He asked me about my doctoral work; I said I was exploring the links between Rom. 9—11 and the rest of the letter. His only response was, 'Very daring! Very daring!' On the relationship in question see now e.g. Schnelle 2005 [2003], 591f.

[466] 9.6, 8, 8f., 11, 12, 13, 14, 15f., 17, 17, 18, 19, 21, 22, 22, 23, 25.

with, but Paul is not done yet. These questions lead the eye up to the central discussion of God's *dikaiosynē*, his 'righteousness', at the start of chapter 10. This then brings us to the heart of the whole section, which runs through the middle of chapter 10; and that in turn sets the scene for more discussion – of God. Has God forsaken his people, Paul asks; and he gives a clear answer. In developing it he moves at last to statements rather than questions: statements of God's kindness and severity, God's power once more, God's future purposes, God's gifts, God's call once more, and God's present purpose in shutting up all in the prison of 'disobedience' in order to have mercy upon all.[467] This entire structure – questions, questions and yet more questions followed at last by statements, particularly about God's future purposes – shows that we are right to treat this entire section under 'eschatology'. The questions are those raised by the Messiah-and-spirit-shaped inaugurated eschatology we have already seen; the answers are the result of a similar rethinking of the hope of Israel, all in terms of monotheism itself. We are not surprised when the chapter, the section and the whole argument of the letter to this point are summed up and rounded off with a celebration of 'the depth of the riches and wisdom and knowledge of God', unsearchable in his judgments and inscrutable in his ways, and an ascription of glory, in the style of classic Jewish monotheism, to the one 'from whom, through whom and to whom are all things'.[468] This echoes, in the mode of praise, the similar ascription of blessing at the start of the section, where it was offered in the mode of lament.[469] Nor are we surprised, looking back, to remind ourselves that this is indeed the climax of a letter whose stated topic was the 'righteousness of God' revealed in 'the gospel of his son' (1.16–17 with 1.3–5) – a point that should never be forgotten. This whole section, then, is about God.[470] If we came upon it in the desert, smouldering with latent Presence, we might find ourselves impelled to take off our shoes. Removing shoes is not something exegetes often do (we like our footnotes the way they are), but granted that even exegetes may have a life, including a devotional life, outside the exegetical task, we may cautiously take that dimension as read and proceed to reflect on the other introductory aspects of the section.

2. The second point is this: unless one is particularly short-sighted it is clear that Romans 9 belongs smack in the middle of that second-Temple genre which consists of retellings of Israel's story (one thinks of *Jubilees*; of *Pseudo-Philo*; of Josephus, of course; and, in the early Christian writings, of passages like Acts 7 and Hebrews 11).[471] Here is Abraham; then Isaac; then, via Rebecca, Jacob and Esau; then we pass to Moses and his stand-off with Pharaoh; then we move to the period of the prophets, and their vivid denunciations (and also promises) to the people of Israel. The story then

[467] 11.22, 23, 24, 29, 29, 32.

[468] 11.33–6.

[469] 9.4f. Jewett 2007, 556 draws attention to this parallel.

[470] Among recent comments, see e.g. Grieb 2010, 391.

[471] See above, 114–39.

seems, so to speak, to run into the sand: even if Israel's sons are numbered like the sand of the sea, only a remnant will be saved (9.27); but then we come to the Messiah himself (10.4), and with him the long-awaited fulfilment of the promises of Deuteronomy 30 (10.6–10) and of other key prophecies (10.11–13). It ought to be completely uncontroversial to point out that *this is Israel's story*, told of course, like every other retelling, from a particular point of view. There is simply no possibility that Paul was making general theological points and just happened, by a quirk of coincidence or subconscious memory, to frame these general points within something that looks like Israel's story but wasn't really intended that way.[472] This chapter walks like Israel's story, talks like Israel's story ... it *is* Israel's story. From one angle.

But what then happens to the story? That is the question that haunted so many thinkers, mystics, rabbis and others in the period from the Babylonian exile right through to the Mishnaic period and beyond. How do you tell the story when the story seems to have got stuck? Answer: new mysteries may be revealed. Fresh possibilities may emerge. And particularly, as we saw in chapter 2, there might perhaps be a prophetic sequence on which to hang one's apocalyptic hat, or one's chronological calculations based on Daniel 9, or one's hope for fresh 'wisdom'. Some of the prophets had spoken of a coming great reversal, when the story would come back with a bang, the world would be turned the right way up, God would reveal his currently well-hidden faithfulness. Maybe, even, the Messiah would appear. Sometimes those prophecies spoke of covenant renewal, with the heart being softened and Torah at last obeyed in a new way. Sometimes they included the remarkable passages in Isaiah about the servant who would be a light to the nations. Sometimes they offered explanations – often cryptic, often powerful – for why the present Israel was in such dire straits. Sometimes all these lines of thought ran back to the Pentateuch: to the great single (if complex) story of Abraham, of the exodus, of Moses, of Moses' own prophecies at the end of Deuteronomy. Normally, routinely, they clung on for dear life to the one God who, having created the world, and having called Israel, was the one and only sheet-anchor for all the promises, all the possibilities.

When Paul gets to the 'end' of the story in 9.26–9, and to its further, new 'end' in 10.21, he too draws on exactly these resources to take it forward. We

[472] Harink 2003, 175f. suggests that 'the story of Israel seems (to most readers except Wright) not often to come into view ... in Paul's letters'. He accuses me of constructing this narratival worldview 'out of the texts of Judaism of Paul's time', a charge to which I plead guilty – except that it was not the second-Temple Jews who invented the sequence of Abraham, Isaac, Jacob, Moses, the prophets, the remnant, the Messiah and the new covenant. According to Harink (176 n. 31) 'Wright simply drags that story line to the text and superimposes Paul's argument upon it', whereas 'Isaac and Ishmael and Jacob and Esau appear in 9:7–13 not as characters in a history of the "covenant people" but as paradigmatic examples or *types* of God's sovereign, selective, and often surprising act ...' (177, emphasis original); so too with Moses, Pharaoh and so on (178f.). Harink's real target becomes obvious (178): 'Paul traces no story line from Israel in the past, through Israel in the present, to Israel (or Israel's replacement, the church) in the future.' But the idea of 'replacement' has always been alien to my exegesis. Harink, one might say, has dragged that idea to my text and superimposed my argument upon it (much as Bell 2005, 159f. has done with his phrase 'substitution model').

ought not to be surprised at his hints of covenant renewal, based on Isaiah and Deuteronomy, in 9.30—10.21. Granted all we know of Paul's way of thinking, we ought to have expected cryptic but prophetically based explanations for Israel's present plight. We should have anticipated that the Messiah would appear in Paul's argument, as in his previous argument in chapter 3, and indeed as in some (by no means all) retellings of Israel's implicit narrative, as the fulfilment, the manifestation, of God's righteousness. We might have known Paul would go back to Deuteronomy 30 and offer his own creative re-reading of that vital passage. And we should of course have assumed that, with or without shoes on his feet, he would invoke the one God, the one lord. We should, in other words, have been able, granted the narrative frame of chapter 9, to see through a glass darkly the shape, and possibly the content, of chapter 10.

But how might the story go on from there? The truly remarkable thing about Romans 11, not I think sufficiently commented on (including in my own various earlier attempts), is that from here onwards Paul is out on his own. He is, in respect of this larger question, in the same position he was in when telling converts what their life should now be like: how to be the renewed people of God when the boundary of Torah is no longer there, or not in the same way. There are no Jewish texts, in scripture or in the second-Temple period, that address the question of what happens when the Messiah turns up and most of Israel rejects him, when the covenant is renewed and most of Israel opts out. At least, if one reads Psalm 22 or Isaiah 53 messianically, one might assume that some sort of rejection had occurred, but there is no road map for imagining what might come next. So Paul is faced with the task of thinking (and, as he tells us, praying) his way into a new world, a strange, unmapped new land, working out, from first principles, what *ought* to happen next, what ought *not* to happen next, and how one could say all this to a church in Rome in which Israel's story might not have been the topic of conversation on everyone's lips – or, if it was, might have been accompanied by a sneer or a wink.

First principles? For Paul, that meant God, and that meant Jesus. It has been a commonplace of one strand of writing about Paul and Romans to suggest, following the late and much lamented Krister Stendahl, that Paul deliberately soft-pedalled any notion of Jesus in these chapters, in order to make room for those Jews who simply couldn't get their heads or hearts around the idea that he really was the Messiah after all. With the greatest respect (and I well understand why Stendahl and others wanted Paul to sing that song), I believe this is radically mistaken.[473] It isn't just that Paul refers

[473] Stendahl 1995, 38: 'Perhaps [Paul] didn't want Christians to have a "Christ-flag" to wave', and so constructed the closing doxology with reference only to God.' (Stendahl is wrong to say that it is the only such doxology in Paul: cf. Phil. 4.20.) This in any case ignores Paul's revised monotheism (ch. 9 above). See too, breathtakingly in view of 9.30—10.17, Hultgren 2010, 433: 'The doxology makes no mention of Christ ... the last time Christ was mentioned in chapters 9 through 11 is at 9:1–5.' I suspect that when Keck 2005, 282 says that 'apart from 9:5 and 10:17 Christ is not mentioned in chaps. 9—11' this is a misprint for 'apart from 9:5—10:17 ...', though since that section comprises nearly half of 9—11, including its vital centre, the point is less significant.

explicitly to the Messiah, and to his death and resurrection, at the very centre of this discussion. The Messiah is in fact woven tightly into the fabric of the whole argument, especially when Paul is having to think in fresh ways, to move forwards in hope but also in warning. But to see this more clearly we must make the third general introductory point.

3. The third point ought to be obvious, but is sometimes challenged. The entire section comes about in response to the double problem faced by Paul at the end of Romans 8: his fellow Jews, by and large, rejected Jesus himself; and now they are, by and large, rejecting the gospel message about him. Those who have tried to advocate a new approach to Paul at this point have done their best to play this down, but it is inescapable. The basic category to which Paul returns several times is that of *unbelief*: they did not believe Jesus himself, and they have not believed the message about him.[474] They did not pursue 'the law of righteousness' by faith (9.32); they are lacking in the 'faith' described in 10.6–13; if they are to be 'grafted back in again' that can only be on the basis that they 'do not remain in unbelief' (11.23); they have 'disbelieved' (10.21, 11.31). This is at the heart of the other ways in which Paul gets at the same point: they have stumbled over the stumbling-stone (9.32); their zeal is not according to knowledge (10.2); they are 'disbelieving and disagreeable' (10.21, quoting Isaiah 65.2); they have 'tripped up' (11.11); they have committed a 'trespass' (11.11–12), which has resulted in 'impoverishment' (11.12). They have thus been 'cast away' (11.15), like branches broken off from the parent tree (11.19–24). All this constitutes a 'hardening' (11.7, 25), making Paul's unbelieving fellow Jews into 'enemies' (11.28) because of 'disobedience' (11.30–2). All of this means, hardly surprisingly, that Paul experiences constant and terrible grief on their behalf, since he believes that all of this, as it stands, threatens their very salvation (10.1). Everything he has said about faith up to this point in the letter, especially in chapters 3 and 4, indicates that the one thing which marks out Abraham's genuine family is the one thing most of his fellow Jews do not have. Whatever one may say about his resolution of this question in chapter 11, we gain nothing by pretending that his analysis of the plight is other than sharp, unrelenting and dire.

4. The final introductory point has to do with the remarkably careful, almost artistic, structure of the section. The closest thing I know to this elsewhere in Paul might be 1 Corinthians 15; but that was only fifty-eight verses, and this is ninety. Structural analysis (as opposed to structural*ist* analysis, which I would not dream of inflicting on Paul) is tricky but often necessary if we are to see where Paul wanted the emphasis to lie, how the

[474] Rightly, Jewett 2007, 557. Gaston 1987, 92 protests too much: 'How is that people can say that chapter 9 deals with the unbelief of Israel when it is never mentioned . . .?' He assumes, among other things, that one can split 9.1–29 off from the rest of the discussion, and that if Paul was talking about Jewish 'unbelief' this would constitute an attack on 'Judaism' as such. Without this 'problem', why the heartbreak in 9.1–5, why the prayer in 10.1? Gaston once admitted to me that his view of 9—11 would be easier to sustain if Paul had not written 11.23; he is followed by Harink 2003, 169f., who skips over 11.23 in a dense footnote (173 n. 24).

different parts make up a carefully constructed whole.[475] The more I have pondered this section, the more convinced I have become that Paul intended the carefully crafted pattern I shall propose, and that he intended it to carry the theological weight that was vital for his entire argument.

It may be news to some readers of Paul that any writer ever thinks like this. We are so used to being told that Paul's letters are 'occasional', that they were in any case dictated not written;[476] the implication being that he dashed them off without thinking where he was going, making it up as he went along much as Tony Blair's 'New Labour' Party tinkered with the British Constitution in the late 1990s and early 2000s. We are on absolutely safe ground in saying that Romans (and chapters 9—11 in particular) was not like that. The structure is clear; the balance is remarkable; the rhetorical effects are intended; the theology is reflected in the way the parts fit together into the whole. Paul was not thinking this through for the first time as he paced the room while Tertius waited, stylus in hand. He had been through these arguments countless times, in synagogues and lecture halls, in the tent-maker's shop and in the homes of friends. He had long pondered the various ways in which he might make his point, and had long settled in his mind on a particular strategy.[477] That strategy involved a careful structure and balance, a particular shape, a deliberate way of drawing the ear and the mind to focus on what was central and important. I am almost tempted to liken this section to a poem by George Herbert.

The basic analysis of Romans 9—11 is actually not difficult, but when done is striking. The opening and closing choose themselves, as we have already seen: 9.1–5 and 11.33–6, five verses in the one and four in the other, each ending with an invocation of blessing to God himself.[478] The outer flanking sections, the great long arguments of chapters 9 and 11, likewise balance quite well: 9.6–29 and 11.1–32, the latter being a bit longer, but both subdividing, if not sharply, into three 'movements'. By almost universal consent, the middle of the section is then constituted by 9.30—10.21.[479]

Within that central section, the same pattern repeats. 9.30–3, highlighting the paradox of gentile inclusion and Jewish incomprehension, is balanced by 10.18–21, on the same theme only more so: four verses in each

[475] Here we may cite in particular Aletti 2010 [1992], 213–20. I reached my conclusions independently but it is good to see them confirmed by so expert an analyst.

[476] e.g. Stendahl 1995, 6.

[477] See e.g. Wagner 2002, 269f.; contra e.g. Tobin 2004, 319, 380, and esp. Watson 2007 [1986], 322: 'As Paul embarks on his long discussion of Israel's election, he himself does not know exactly where the argument will take him. It is *as he writes* that he receives insight . . .' (Watson's italics). Even if the structural balance were not so careful, I find it incredible to suppose that Paul had not faced these questions, and discussed them and taught about them, over and over during the years preceding Romans. Paul has *shaped* the discourse rhetorically so as to lead the hearer on a journey with deliberate twists and turns (and, no doubt, so as to reflect his own prayerful agonizing: so e.g. Grieb 2010, 396); but when he writes Romans he knows the end from the beginning, and knows how to set out the argument to maximum effect.

[478] See Keck 2005, 226; Jewett 2007, 556; Wilk 2010, 239–41. This balance seems to me to rule out the idiosyncratic suggestion of Tobin 2004, chs. 9–12, that the real section is chs. 8—11 and (302) that 8.31–9 somehow balances 11.25–36.

[479] So, rightly, Aletti 2010 [1992], 217f.; and e.g. Getty 1988.

case (with more words in 10.18–21). Coming closer to the very heart of it all, the opening verses of chapter 10 (10.1–4) are in a sense balanced by the exposition of Paul's gentile mission in 10.14–17 – again, four verses in each case, the earlier ones continuing to expound the 'unknowing' of Israel, the latter ones developing the means of gentile inclusion.[480] That then leaves 10.5–13, structurally the heart of it all: nine verses which begin with the exegesis of Leviticus and then particularly Deuteronomy, and conclude with the invocation of Isaiah and Joel, all pointing to the great theme of covenant renewal. And in the middle of it all, right at the very centre, is the statement which constitutes as clear a vision of Paul's central theological theme as we could wish to find: 'if you confess with your mouth that Jesus is lord, and believe in your heart that God raised him from the dead, you will be saved'.

Thus we detect a careful chiastic structure. There is room for debate about details, but not, I think, about the overall effect:

```
9.1–5                                                              11.33–6
        9.6–29                                           11.1–32
                9.30–3                          10.18–21
                        10.1–4          10.14–17
                                10.5–13
                                  10.9
```

A moment's reflection on the central passage 10.5–13, with its statement about Jesus and about faith and salvation, will reveal that it is straightforwardly impossible to read Romans 9—11 as anything other than a statement firmly and deeply grounded in christology (in the sense of Paul's belief about the Messiah). The middle passage is itself flanked by further references to the Messiah (10.4, 'The Messiah is the goal of the Law', and 10.14, 'How shall they call on him in whom they have not believed?'). But the nine central verses (10.5–13) contain no fewer than seven references to Jesus, ruling out any challenge to the proposal that the Messiah, and the justification and salvation available in him, is central to the whole of chapters 9—11:

> [5]Moses writes, you see, about the covenant membership defined by the law, that 'the person who performs the law's commands shall live in them'. [6]But the *faith*-based covenant membership puts it like this: 'Don't say in your heart, Who shall go up to heaven?' (in other words, to bring **the Messiah** down), [7]or, 'Who shall go down into the depths?' (in other words, to bring **the Messiah** up from the dead). [8]But what does it say? 'The word is near you, in your mouth and in your heart' (that is, the word of faith which we proclaim); [9]because if you profess with your mouth that **Jesus is lord**, and believe in your heart that **God raised him from the dead**, you will be saved. [10]Why? Because the way to covenant membership is by believing with the heart, and the way to salvation is by professing with the mouth.[11]The Bible says, you see, 'Everyone who believes **in him** will not be put to

[480] On this division between 10.17 and 10.18, see the use of *rhēma Christou* in 10.17, picking up the *rhēma* of Dt. 30.14 in 10.8. However, since the quote from Ps. 19 in 10.18 also uses the word, perhaps we should rather divide between 10.18 and 10.19. This would not make much difference. Dahl 1977, 143 n. 24 proposes that a new start is made at 10.1. There is clearly a break at this point, but most rightly see the *ti oun eroumen* of 9.30 as indicating the start of a larger section, admittedly summarizing 9.6–29 but doing so in such a way as to point on to 10.1–21 and indeed beyond.

shame.' [12]For there is no distinction between Jew and Greek, since **the same lord is lord of all**, and is rich towards all **who call upon him**. [13]'All who call **upon the name of the lord**', you see, 'will be saved'.

Not only is there no distinction between Jew and Greek; there is no distinction here between Romans 9—11 and Romans 1—4, or for that matter Romans and Galatians. We are on extremely familiar territory – except, of course, for the remarkable exegesis of Deuteronomy. In fact, Paul says what he says if anything more clearly here than anywhere else. He carefully distinguishes 'justification' and 'salvation', while also closely correlating them; he lines up (a) the personal belief and confession and (b) the coming together of faithful Jew and faithful Greek; he draws together the law and the prophets, reading the Torah prophetically and the prophets as pointing to a different kind of Torah-fulfilment.[481] Though he does not mention the spirit explicitly, the reference to Joel 2.32 (LXX 3.5) in verse 13 is from the passage made famous by Acts 2, where it is the key Pentecost-text, to explain that the manifestations of God's spirit on that occasion were the signs of the covenant being renewed around the Messiah. Paul does not need to spell this out.[482] Anyone who knew the strands of thought in his world of second-Temple Judaism would have picked up the signals already. This is all about the fulfilment of Deuteronomy 30: in other words – though this is almost always missed by commentators! – *covenant renewal and the end of exile*.[483] It is all about God's righteousness revealed in the good news of the Messiah for the benefit of all who believe. That is, after all, what Paul had said the letter was to be about, right back in 1.16–17, itself based on 1.3–5. And that is the theme through which he will finally come back and answer the question of the unbelief of Israel.

If I am correct in suggesting that, in addition to the linear narrative of Israel, we also have in these chapters a carefully structured chiastic whole, we will do well to begin at the heart and work out from there, moving step by step back up the levels of the chiasm. That way we may stand less chance of being overwhelmed with necessary details by the time we get to the passage which stands foursquare at the centre of it all. We begin, therefore, in the middle, with 10.1–17 (whose heart, as I say, is 10.5–13, and within that 10.9), before proceeding to 9.30–3 and then 10.18–21, and from thence outward to 9.6–29 and finally 11.1–32. That will bring us at last to the outer framework with their balancing, and yet so very different, doxologies. Both the lament of 9.1–5 and the praise of 11.33–6 are in evidence all the way through, not least in the passage to which we now turn. Romans 10.1–17 stands, arguably, at the very centre of this section. I believe this was quite deliberate on Paul's part, and it therefore makes sense to begin at this point.

[481] See Watson 2004, 329–41; Watson 2007 [1986], 330 n. 46.

[482] cf. e.g. Rowe 2000, 152–6.

[483] See again above, 117–39.

(b) Exile, Justification, the Righteousness of God and Salvation: 10.1–17

9.1–5 11.33–6
9.6–29 11.1–32
9.30–3 10.18–21
10.1–4 **10.14–17**
10.5–13
10.9

We had better pause for a moment, before plunging in, to make clear what was latent earlier in the present book (in chapter 2) and which now becomes manifest.

We spoke before about the way in which the narrative of Israel in Romans 9 appeared to run into the sand. This is of course because of the 'exile', both the actual geographical exile and the muddle of partial return, which generated new theological and narratival puzzles. As we saw earlier, at least *some* Jews in the period, including significant writers, did not really believe 'the exile' was yet over. Some of those writers, including interestingly both Josephus and Philo, re-read the Mosaic prophecies in Deuteronomy 27—30, and also in Deuteronomy 32 and 33, as large-scale long-range warnings and promises about what would happen to Israel, and what YHWH would do in and for Israel, *beacherith hayamim*, in the latter days. The 'curse' would continue, and then, at last, YHWH would circumcise people's hearts so that they would obey him and keep his Torah from their heart. That was how he would restore their fortunes. And that needed to happen because, as Moses himself had warned, Israel was still after all rebellious and recalcitrant. That sense of an overarching *narrative* is what makes sense of the otherwise apparently disparate uses of the closing chapters of Deuteronomy in texts as disparate as 4QMMT, Baruch, Josephus and Philo.[484]

Granted that context (and granted that, even though not all Jews of Paul's day would have thought like that, some clearly did, and their world of thought appears to form the matrix for Paul's own reading), it should be reasonably obvious what Paul thinks he is doing in his re-reading of Deuteronomy 30 in Romans 10.6–8, as the denouement of the long story

[484] See e.g. Wagner 2002, 254–7 and 166 n. 143. It is puzzling that Lincicum 2010, 153–8, having set up the discussion, does not follow it through to this conclusion. This may be cognate with the surprising absence from his book of Steck 1967. See too, similarly, Waters 2006. Jewett 2007, 626 (following Dunn 1988b, 603–5) notes how the passage is used in second-Temple Judaism but does not perceive the significance of this for Paul's argument. By contrast Ciampa 2007, 109 at least points momentarily in the right direction, albeit almost as an afterthought: 'Moses looks forward to a future day when God's presence and word would be restored to his people ... after they had returned to God and seen the end of their exile.' On Bekken 2007 see below. On the parallels with 4QMMT and Baruch see my essay in *Perspectives* ch. 21; and see Wright 2002 [*Romans*], 658–63. Wagner 2002, 115, 166 points out a further Qumran parallel, namely 4Q504 frgs. 1–2 cols. 5–7, esp. 5.6–14 with its allusions to Lev. 26.44f. and Dt. 30.1f., which 'metaphorically places the community "in exile", petitioning God for deliverance' (Wagner 166 n. 143), 'with its assurance that God will gather repentant Israel from the ends of the earth' (Wagner 115 n. 233). We note that in 5.15 the community claim that God has 'poured his holy spirit upon us', a classic sign of covenant renewal.

that began in 9.7–9 with the Abrahamic promise and family.[485] He is doing, from this angle and within the context of the present argument, exactly what he did in 2.25–9 within that context and argument. That is, he is drawing on scriptural resources to say: this is the new covenant, this is the true Torah-fulfilment, this is the heart-circumcision, this is the work of the spirit not the letter, this is where we find 'the Jew' (Romans 2.29). The curse of exile, as in Deuteronomy 27 and 28, is over; here is the real restoration.[486] When we add to this picture the wider strands of thought that converge at this point, he is also saying: this is where we find 'the circumcision' (Philippians 3.3), the chosen, the called, the 'seed of Abraham' (Galatians 3.29), the ones who love God from the heart (1 Corinthians 8.3; Romans 5.5) – in other words, the *Shema*-people. Here, at the centre of Romans 9—11, is Paul's richest statement of what he thinks has happened to the doctrine of election as he had understood it in his Pharisaic days. It is precisely *eschatological*: that is, it has been transformed around the Messiah who has inaugurated the long-awaited new covenant. And it is now transformed also around the spirit who, promised by Joel, enables people to 'call on the name of the lord', which as we saw earlier is itself a way of invoking the God of Abraham *by invoking Jesus himself.* Freshly understood monotheism gives birth to freshly understood election, and both can only be understood from the standpoint of freshly understood eschatology. This is the deep theological structure of what Paul is doing; attempts to impose an older dogmatic framework such as 'God's sovereignty' in chapter 9 and 'Israel's responsibility' in chapter 10 have little merit, and actually distort the text.[487] That is why I and some others have become convinced that when Paul quotes Joel 2.32 (LXX 3.5) in 10.13 he intends a reference to the whole passage, in which the promise of the spirit is prominent as one of the key features of the coming eschaton.[488] This maintains the narrative of Israel exactly as we would expect on the analogy with other 'new-covenant' movements such as Qumran.

[485] However well one knows the exegetical tradition, one still gasps with astonishment at the list of distinguished writers who have proposed that Paul is not really quoting or using Dt. 30 at all, merely echoing its apparently proverbial sayings: e.g. Sanday and Headlam 1902 [1895], 289; Davies 1980 [1948], 153f.; others in Badenas 1985, 253 n. 297; Tobin 2004, 344 should now be added. Longenecker 1991, 220 n. 2 and Bekken 2007, 4 n. 11 are wrong to include Barrett 1971b [1957], who does indeed say (198) that Paul quotes Dt. 30. A truly distant echo of Dt. 30 can be found at *Thomas* 3 (Elliott 1993, 136).

[486] Bekken 2007, 16 speaks of the 'eschatological aspect' of Paul's thought (and, at 187, of the 'eschatological perspective'), but despite drawing attention to passages in Philo which point in this direction (e.g. *Vit. Mos.* 2.288), he never sees how his other important Philonic parallels make sense within this larger eschatological narrative. It is a measure of this that, astonishingly, the highly important parallel in 4QMMT appears only fleetingly in his work (2f., 118).

[487] So, rightly, Watson 2007 [1986], 322f.

[488] See Joel 2.28f. (LXX 3.1f.): the whole passage (2.28–32; LXX 3.1–5) is quoted in Ac. 2.17–21; cp. Ac. 2.33; 10.45; Rom. 5.5. See Schreiner 1998, 562: 'Paul would certainly have identified the prophecy of Joel with the outpouring of the Spirit on those who confessed Jesus as Messiah and lord.' He points out that the *all* of the quotation relates also to the 'all flesh' in 2.28 (3.1) upon whom the spirit will be poured out, thus emphasizing again the inclusion of gentiles. Moyise 2010, 75 suggests a similar echo at 1 Cor. 1.2; see too Fatehi 2000, 232.

We should not be surprised, then, to find such a clear statement of 'justification by faith' at just this point. Indeed, were it not that western theology did not really know what to do with Romans 9—11 as a whole, still less with Paul's reading of Deuteronomy 30, one might have supposed that it would have been Romans 10.9–13, rather than Romans 3 or Galatians 3, that would have been the parade text for this greatest of Reformation doctrines. Such are the ironies of hermeneutics. It is all here (building on 2.25–9, 3.21—4.25 and also in a measure 8.1–11 and 8.31–9, which as we saw in the previous chapter are extremely important for justification): the faithfulness of God; the work of the Messiah as the ground and basis for it all; belief in God's raising of Jesus as the tell-tale signal that precipitates the divine verdict 'righteous'; and the confession 'Jesus is lord' as the public, outward behaviour (signalling, of course, an entire world of obedience to this Jesus) which is the pathway from the *initial* 'justification', based on nothing other than faith, to the *final* 'salvation' which is based on the whole of life – life lived in the Messiah and in the power of the spirit. Here is 'justification' once more, once more at the heart of Paul's redefined election, once more meaning what it means within the revised eschatology. (What we do *not* have, since it was the key to what Paul was saying in Romans 1—4 but not here, is specific 'lawcourt' imagery.) Here is the strong assertion that there is 'no distinction between Jew and Greek' because of *this* christology and *this* soteriology.

Here, in other words and above all, is the renewal of the covenant; and here we have as clear an indication as we ought to wish for that when Paul uses the language of *dikaiosynē* that is what he is talking about. Scholars have puzzled over the way in which Paul introduces Deuteronomy 30: having ascribed Leviticus 18 to 'Moses', Paul personifies *hē ek pisteōs dikaiosynē*, 'the righteousness of faith', as the 'speaker' in Deuteronomy.[489] But, as the many and diverse second-Temple Jewish thinkers we have already studied all knew, this was the passage in which was prophesied the return from exile and the renewal of the covenant. Thus, as in Romans 4.11, Paul takes a passage which is about the *covenant* and speaks of it in terms of *dikaiosynē*. That is why I have elsewhere translated 10.6a 'But the *faith*-based covenant membership puts it like this'. Once we fully grasp the role of Deuteronomy 30 in second-Temple eschatology, as we tried to do in chapter 2 above, one traditional problem after another in the exegesis of the chapter

[489] See, famously now, Hays 1989a, 1–5, 73–83. Hays describes all this as 'baffling' and as 'an apparently capricious act of interpretation' which 'looks on the face of it like a wild and disingenuous piece of exegesis' (73f.), so that 'the argument ... rests on sheer force of assertion' and on a metaphorical reading which 'seems especially jarring to modern historically sensitive readers', even though the echoes of the wisdom tradition 'suggest hauntingly that Paul's reading is less arbitrary than it sounds' (82). But once we see the wisdom tradition in the parallel Bar. 3 (highlighted by Suggs 1967; made central by e.g. Keck 2005, 253) not as an independent feature but as part of the widespread second-Temple *new-covenant* and *return-from-exile* reading of Dt. 30, the exegesis is neither capricious, wild, nor disingenuous, and the poor historically sensitive readers may be put out of their misery. On the present passage as a 'speech in character' cf. Stowers 1994, 309; Tobin 2004, 343.

and of the whole section is resolved.[490] Romans 10.1–13, in this light, is in fact as central a Pauline passage as one can imagine. And it is indeed exactly and precisely the centre of the carefully constructed whole we know as Romans 9—11.

In particular, it focuses attention on, and fully clarifies, 'the righteousness of God'. Romans 10.3 remains inevitably controversial, not least because of the variant reading caused by one or more scribes who felt that Paul had used the word *dikaiosynē* once too often and that they should give him a little help with his style.[491] I have encountered copy-editors like that, too, but they are usually to be resisted when every word in a dense passage is actually doing its bit for the common cause. And what Paul says here about the 'righteousness of God' is so revealing, so supportive of the case we argued before about Romans 3.21 and 1.17, that it is worth drawing attention to the completion of this argument as well. There should be no question, here or elsewhere, of 'the righteousness of God' being seen as the righteous status which humans receive from God, though that continues to be assumed here and there.[492] When Paul speaks of 'God's righteousness' in 10.3 as something of which Paul's unbelieving Jewish contemporaries were 'ignorant', he is, I suggest, invoking the entire train of thought from 9.6 forward. It was that strange narrative of God's elective purposes which raised the question of God's righteousness in the first place (9.14, *mē adikia para tō theō*, 'is there injustice with God'), and Paul answered the question with more of the same narrative. When we put together the 'ignorance' motif in 10.3 with the material towards the end of the chapter, and ask what Paul supposed these people were ignorant *of*, it is clear: (a) that they were ignorant of what God had all along been doing in their history, in other words, of the way in which the purpose of election had actually been working out not just through the choice of Abraham but also through the narrowing down of his offspring to an exiled remnant; and (b), exactly cognate with that, they were ignorant of the fact that the crucified Jesus was the Messiah. In Romans 1.17 and 3.21–6 it was the crucified and risen Jesus (and the gospel message about him) that revealed God's righteousness.[493] Here we have exactly the same point, shaped exactly to fit the present argument.

Paul believes that the right response to God's righteousness would be to *submit* to it (10.3). This is an unusual way of putting it, but the implication seems to be that God's sovereign will is revealed in the events in which his

[490] This is not to say that the present chapter provides a full or detailed answer to the fascinating study of Watson 2004, esp. ch. 7. I do think, though, that Paul does overcome the 'dichotomies' which appear to be set up. He is saying, just as in Rom. 3.27–30 and 8.5–8, that faith in Jesus as the risen lord is in fact the 'doing of the law'. It is not just 'doing' that is redefined (see the comments on Hays and Wagner in Watson 2004, 331 n. 35) but the law itself.

[491] The MSS, though significantly divided, are overall in favour of the longer reading, which is clearly the harder and to be preferred: see e.g. Jewett 2007, 606, who attributes the omission (in the MSS ABDP etc.) to haplography.

[492] e.g. Bekken 2007, 164; Hultgren 2010, 382.

[493] On the Jewish 'ignorance' cf. Ac. 3.17.; cp. 13.27; 1 Cor. 2.8; 1 Tim. 1.13; and, wider, Lk. 23.34; Jn. 16.3.

'righteousness' is displayed, and that the path of wisdom, never mind loyalty, is to accept that this is how God has willed it. We should not suppose, though, that this 'submission to God's righteousness' *denotes* something other, in Paul's mind, than believing the gospel of Jesus the Messiah and being baptized into him. The *connotation* of submitting to God's righteousness, however, has to do with the results that this would have for the loyal Jew. For that, we cannot do better than reflect on the journey Paul himself had travelled: being 'crucified with the Messiah' (Galatians 2.19), discovering that all previous gain was to be counted as loss for the sake of knowing the Messiah (Philippians 3.7–11), embracing the scandal of the cross (1 Corinthians 1.23; Galatians 5.11) and discovering that Abraham's family was much larger, and more varied, than one had ever dreamed possible (Romans 4.1–25; Galatians 3.23–9) and that it was defined not by the marks of Jewish ethnicity but by 'Messiah-faith'.[494] All of this is of course part of his overall theology of the covenant with Israel and its renewal through the Messiah.

Instead of thus 'submitting to God's righteousness', Paul's unbelieving fellow Jews were, he says, 'seeking to establish their own righteousness'. We remind ourselves that here Paul is talking not least about his own former self; this passage has the strong tinge of autobiography about it, as the reference to 'zeal for God' makes clear.[495] Of course, the phrase about 'their own righteousness', glimpsed out of context in the dark with the light behind it, with a glass of Wittenberg beer in hand and another already on board, could no doubt be read as indicating that these Jews were guilty of proto-Pelagianism, imagining that by doing 'good works' in the sense of making the moral effort to keep Torah they were earning favour, or indeed 'righteousness', with God.[496] But the entire narrative sweep of chapters 9—11, not to mention the absence of any language about 'good works' anywhere in 9.30—10.21, makes this extremely unlikely.[497] The story Paul is telling is about the covenant narrative of Israel, and about the fact that, to his own surprise and shock, this narrative has been turned inside out through the Messiah and the spirit so as to include gentiles within it. The status of *dikaiosynē* which the unbelieving Jews thought to establish for themselves is therefore a status of 'covenant membership' *which would be for Jews and Jews only*. That was the problem. And it was writ large right across second-Temple Judaism, inscribed not least by the earlier Saul of Tarsus and his zealous colleagues. This has been, from the start, one of the key insights of the so-called 'new perspective' on Paul.

[494] Rom. 3.21—4.25; Gal. 2.15—4.11; Phil. 3.2–11.

[495] 10.2, *zēlon theou*; cf. Gal. 1.14; Phil. 3.6; cf. 'Paul and Elijah' in *Perspectives* ch. 10. Ortlund 2012 attempts to reinstate an 'old perspective' reading ('zeal' as 'general obedience to Torah') over against a focus on maintaining Israel's ethnic distinctiveness.

[496] cf. Luther 1971 [1516], 288f.

[497] 'Works' are mentioned in 9.12 and 11.6: see below. A more subtle version of Luther's position is offered by Seifrid 2007, 652f.

It is important to make it clear at this point (since we are not ignorant of certain devices) that to discern a *problem* in the idea of 'seeking to establish their own status of covenant membership' has nothing whatever to do with the supercilious (and, for all I know, supersessionist) tendency to claim the apparent high moral ground of late-modern 'universalism' and to look down one's nose at those benighted Jews with their 'particularism'. It may be that some, not least within the so-called 'new perspective', have surreptitiously smuggled in such false ideas to spy out the freedom which people have to think Jewish thoughts, to relish the Jewish doctrine of election, to affirm the call of Abraham himself as one of the great moments in world history. Let it be said loud and clear that Paul's critique at this point, and my attempt to analyze and re-express it, would be straightforwardly derailed by any such modernistic moralization. Save him from his friends, I cry, as I read the philosopher Alain Badiou congratulating Paul on 'The Foundation of Universalism'.[498] (Of course, when Badiou says, repeatedly, that Paul's own foundation was Jesus' resurrection, which he knows, and assumes his readers know, to be a fantasy and a fable, that does rather let the cat out of the bag ... because Jesus' resurrection is, from a modernist and indeed moralizing standpoint, one of the least 'universal' and most 'particular' things Paul could have affirmed.) On the contrary. Paul has *reimagined*, reconceived, the Jewish doctrine of election. He is just as 'particularist' in his own way, because he believes that Jesus of Nazareth was and is Israel's Messiah. He has tried to say what he has seen in the Messiah, which is that this was the true meaning of the doctrine of election all along, that it is only in the Messiah that the living God has provided and will provide covenant renewal, justification, life, and new creation itself. That particularism is just as unwelcome in modernistic circles as the supposed Jewish particularism out of which it grows and which it claims to fulfil. If that fulfilment remains a scandal to Jews, it also remains folly to Greeks, including the Greeks who define themselves in terms of Voltaire and Rousseau, of Kant and Hegel.[499]

By the same token (continuing this long but perhaps necessary aside), to insist now on the virtue of particularism has nothing whatever to do with the *post*modern moralism (often, pseudo-moralism) which exalts the particular, the little story, the individual speciality, over the bland and hegemonic universal. These fashions in popular culture come and go, and shine their broken lights variously on this or that aspect of religious and other traditions. They do not offer serious fixed points around which to reorganize exegesis and theology. When Paul says that his unbelieving Jewish contemporaries 'were ignorant of God's righteousness, and, seeking to establish a righteous status of their own, did not submit to God's righteousness', he is not subtly privileging a modernistic universalism against a pre-modern Jewish version of postmodern particularism. He does indeed advocate something that can loosely be called 'universalism', namely the coming together

[498] Badiou 2003.

[499] See now particularly Levenson 2012, 18–35. This is not the place to take up the key issues raised by this fascinating book.

of Jew and Greek, slave and free, male and female in the one people of the Messiah. But to advocate this position because it reminds one of modernistic universalism, or indeed to criticize it on the same grounds, is to commit the kind of massive, whole-hog anachronism that we would commit if we congratulated Paul on his ecological sensitivity in taking a sailing boat from Caesarea to Rome while everyone else was getting into their jumbo jets. Or if we criticized him for carrying all that cash on his person from Corinth to Jerusalem when any sensible person would have sent it by American Express credit transfer.

In fact (to come back down to earth, or at least to text, after these flights of fancy) we may note one of the more interesting little echoes that bounce off the biblical walls when Paul writes Romans 10.6. He has just quoted Leviticus 18.5, as indeed he had done in Galatians 3.12, in order to point out, as in Galatians 5.3, that if what you want is 'righteousness under Torah', a covenant status marked out by Torah itself, there is only one way forward: you have to 'do' the whole thing. He has stated often enough, in this letter and elsewhere, the problem with that ambition: it's impossible. That is the plight of the 'I' in Romans 7, and that is why the boast of a covenant status defined by Torah is self-defeating, as Paul pointed out briefly and cryptically in Galatians 2.17–18. But Paul then comes to Deuteronomy. He does not start straight in with chapter 30, as one might expect granted the prominence of that text in some parts of his background. Rather, he begins with what looks like an innocent opening gambit, but which carries a direct challenge to the position he has mentioned in 10.3. The initial warning comes from Deuteronomy 9.4, and this is how it runs:

> Do not say in your heart, 'It is because of my righteousness that YHWH has brought me in to occupy this land': it is rather because of the wickedness of these nations that YHWH is dispossessing them before you. It is not because of your righteousness or the uprightness of your heart that you are going in to occupy their land; but because of the wickedness of those nations that YHWH your God is dispossessing them before you, in order to fulfil the promise that YHWH made on oath to your ancestors, to Abraham, to Isaac, and to Jacob. Know, then, that YHWH your God is not giving you this good land to occupy because of your righteousness; for you are a stubborn people. Remember and do not forget how you provoked YHWH your God to wrath in the wilderness; you have been rebellious against YHWH from the day you came out of the land of Egypt until you came to this place.[500]

There is a great deal compressed into these verses, and it bears a remarkable similarity to several things that Paul is saying throughout Romans 9—11 but especially at this point. For a start, the passage invokes the oath made by YHWH to Abraham, Isaac and Jacob. For another thing, it makes clear that, left to itself, Israel is stubborn and rebellious – the same charge that Moses himself will lay against God's people at the end of the book, in the great

[500] Dt. 9.4–7. Cf. Hays 1989a, 78f.; Lincicum 2010, 155; Ciampa 2007, 107. Watson 2004, 338f. suggests that Paul's additions from there (and Dt. 8.17) are designed to disguise the fact that Dt. 30 is in fact about 'the righteousness of the law'. I have proposed a different way forward, in line with Rom. 2.25–9 and elsewhere: Paul is drawing attention to the fact that, under the new covenant of Dt. 30, a new meaning has opened up for 'doing the law' itself.

'song' of chapter 32 which Paul will quote in 10.19. But, in particular, what we have here is the question of Israel's own 'righteousness' *in relation to the non-Israelite nations*. The status Israel hopes to invoke, against which Moses is warning, is a status of 'righteousness', based it seems on an imagined success in keeping God's law, which will make Israel automatically superior to the other nations. This, we may assume, is more or less what Paul means by 'their own righteousness' in 10.3, corresponding to the 'righteousness of my own' which he renounced in Philippians 3.9. Moses responds to the possibility of such a claim by making it clear that, though the other nations are indeed wicked, Israel too has no particular moral worth to write home about. At the 'end of the law', the close of the Five Books, Israel will inherit the promised land. But this is happening, not because of Israel's special merit but because of God's promise to the patriarchs, another theme to which Paul will return. Deuteronomy 9.4 thus sparks off a resonant set of echoes which, like the notes of an orchestral chord still audible in the concert hall, create just the context within which then to hear Deuteronomy 30.

Paul's basic claim about Deuteronomy 30 is that the great change in Israel's fortunes which that chapter describes – or, as many of his contemporaries would have said, prophesies – is precisely what has come about through Jesus the Messiah. Deuteronomy 30 comes, as we have remarked before, at the turning-point of Israel's prophetic history, the moment for which so many were waiting during much of the second-Temple period, and the moment for which Paul's own narrative in Romans 9.6–29 was implicitly waiting as well. In fact, if we treat the Pentateuch as containing, in both history and prophecy, the full story of the people of God (and there is, as we saw in chapter 2, some evidence that some Jews did see it like that), we could plausibly suggest that what Paul is doing in 9.6—10.13 is *telling the Torah's own story of Israel*, from the call of Abraham through to the ... *telos*, the 'goal', the 'end' in the sense of 'the moment when, with the covenant renewed, Israel would finally be established as God's people'. *Telos gar nomou Christos*, writes Paul (10.4): the Messiah is the end, the goal, the final destination of Torah.[501] This is where the narrative had been heading all along. Through the Messiah the prophecies have come true, the covenant has been re-established, exile is over, God himself has acted to unveil his faithfulness to his promises, and God's people are now able ... to keep Torah from the heart.

[501] The phrase has of course generated enormous discussion, polarized between those who think *telos* here means 'cessation' (e.g. Schnelle 2005 [2003], 346f.; Watson 2004, 332) and those who think (in line with the main linguistic arguments, for which cf. Badenas 1985, 38–80) it means 'goal' or 'destination' (e.g. Keck 2005, 248–50; Jewett 2007, 619f.). Our argument goes much further than Jewett, encompassing also the sense that with the Messiah the narrative of Israel from 9.6 onwards has arrived at the 'goal' marked out by Moses' prophecy. Starling 2011, 153f. approaches this solution without (it seems to me) quite grasping it: '[Christ] comes after the era of the law, with all its blessings and curses, not as a continuation or extension of Moses' ministry, but as the next (and intended) turn of the story, to which Moses himself pointed forward and in which the law of Moses will be "fulfilled" by being written on the heart.' If I am right, Paul is proposing that with the Messiah the era of new blessings, promised by Moses himself, has arrived.

How so? Paul has spoken elsewhere of the heart-circumcision that Deuteronomy predicted, and has said, remarkably enough, that people with that transformed heart 'fulfil the Law' and keep its commandments.[502] Now, reading Deuteronomy 30.12–14, he discerns within it a pattern which he recognizes: it is the pattern of the Messiah, seen as God's revelation of his own 'word', coming from God to Israel and enabling Israel to be God's people in a new way. There is room here for some further pondering, though not in the present book, about the implicit theology of grace at work in this ancient passage:

> This commandment that I am commanding you today is not too hard for you, nor is it too far away. It is not in heaven, that you should say, 'Who will go up to heaven for us, and get it for us so that we may hear it and do it?' Neither is it beyond the sea, that you should say, 'Who will cross to the other side of the sea for us, and get it for us so that we may hear it and do it?' No, the word is very near you; it is in your mouth and in your heart for you to do it.[503]

Note the repeated 'so that we/you may do it'. In the Septuagint, this is expressed with various uses of the common verb *poiein*. And that is the link Paul makes with the passage from Leviticus he has just quoted: the one who *does* them, *ho poiēsas auta*, shall live in them. Paul is not playing off Leviticus against Deuteronomy, a 'legalistic' form of Judaism against a 'non-legalistic' one. He is not reading the Pentateuch as containing two strands, as Dodd thought two generations ago and as some have argued afresh in recent times.[504] Paul is using Deuteronomy 30 to say: Ah, but in the enabling promise of covenant renewal, God himself holds out a new way of 'doing the law', a way which will be 'in your mouth and in your heart', a way which will come from God himself in the form of his 'word', and which will enable you to 'do' it. This is the massive claim which Paul is making through his bold and creative, but covenantally coherent, use of Deuteronomy.

Notice how this coheres, too, with the passage that follows, where the thought is developed. The Greek term for 'word' in this passage of Deuteronomy is *rhēma*. Paul hardly ever uses this term elsewhere.[505] But it comes again and again in Romans 10, and in exactly this sense: the idea of the divine initiative which, in the form of the spoken word, brings new life and new possibilities.[506] This echoes, albeit distantly, the passage about 'new

[502] Rom. 2.26f.

[503] Dt. 30.11–14 (NRSV altered).

[504] Dodd 1959 [1932], 177 congratulates Paul on anticipating 'modern criticism' in seeing Lev. as 'hard and mechanical' and Dt. as having 'more of the prophetic spirit'. On an altogether more sophisticated plane, Watson 2004, 314f., 331–3 and elsewhere nevertheless still insists on a sharp antithesis between Lev. 18.5, quoted in Rom. 10.5, and Dt. 30.12–14, quoted in 10.6–8. At 341 Watson suggests that Paul 'heard two voices in the Deuteronomy passage' itself. Watson later (2004, 415–73), in a remarkable discussion, explores the ways in which the end of Dt. forms part of a long-range prophecy of exile and return. This, I think, actually undermines his earlier position and suggests a much closer and more eschatologically integrated reading of different Pentateuchal emphases.

[505] 2 Cor. 12.4; 13.1 (in an LXX quote); Eph. 5.26; 6.17.

[506] Rom. 10.8 (twice), 9, 17, 18; elsewhere in Paul, 2 Cor. 12.4; 13.1; Eph. 5.26; 6.17.

creation' in Isaiah 55, in which the 'word', the *rhēma* in the Greek, comes down from heaven like the rain and the snow, not returning to YHWH empty, but fulfilling his purpose and making the thorny land sprout fresh shrubs.[507] After the initial quotation of Deuteronomy 30.14 in 10.8, 'the word is near you, in your mouth and in your heart', together with its explanation, 'this is the word of faith which we preach', Paul makes it clear, in going on to describe just that 'preaching', that 'the word' is the powerful thing, the divine initiative, which summons people to hear, believe and obey. 'The word' is what will create them as Deuteronomy-30 people, new-covenant people.

But that is not the end of it. After quoting Isaiah 52 as the explanation of the gentile mission (10.15), and Isaiah 53 as a way of holding on to the question of continuing unbelief (10.16), Paul concludes: 'so faith is from hearing, and hearing is through the word of the Messiah', *dia rhēmatos Christou*. The exegete, having wrestled with Paul's use of Deuteronomy 30 in Romans 10.6–8, may have heaved a sigh of relief and forgotten this key term within a verse or so; but as far as Paul is concerned the train of thought has continued into the following passage, and indeed spills over into verse 18 as well, with another Septuagint quote, this time from the great psalm of creation and Torah: 'their sound went out into the whole land, and their words, *ta rhēmata autōn*, to the ends of the earth'.[508] Clearly the powerful divine *rhēma* is at the front of his mind throughout this whole sequence of thought.

Three things should by now be coming clear. First, 10.1–17 (and, within that, 10.5–13) does indeed make a statement which is fit to stand as the vital centre of Romans 9—11. Second, this passage expresses exactly the same theology of justification and salvation that we find elsewhere in the letter and in Paul's other letters, only if anything more clearly. Third, it offers a very full answer to the prayer which Paul describes himself as praying in 10.1 (as opposed to the prayer he describes himself as *not* praying in 9.4): the prayer that comes from his own heart, in relation to his unbelieving kinsfolk according to the flesh, the prayer 'unto salvation', *eis sōtērian*: in other words, 'that they may be saved'. This last point must now be developed a bit further.

The theme of 'salvation', we recall, is unmentioned in Galatians. But it is stated as a major theme at the beginning of Romans (1.16), it is expounded in the central part of the letter (5.9–10; 8.24) and it now comes to particular fine-tuned expression. The paragraph 10.1–17 looks as though it constitutes Paul's own basic answer to the question raised by his own reported prayer, as to how this 'salvation' might come about for his kinsfolk according to the flesh (and indeed anyone else, since he says more than once that this is equally true for non-Jews). He has explained, quite fully and in terms of central prophetic texts, how it is that Israel's God has provided for Israel's

[507] Isa. 55.11.

[508] Ps. 19.4 [LXX 18.5], qu. in 10.18.

salvation through Israel's Messiah. I have highlighted the texts relating to salvation, and italicized verse 9, which stands at the very centre of 9—11 as a whole:

> [5]Moses writes, you see, about the covenant membership defined by the law, that 'the person who performs the law's commands **shall live in them**'. [6]But the *faith*-based covenant membership puts it like this: 'Don't say in your heart, Who shall go up to heaven?' (in other words, to bring the Messiah down), [7]or, 'Who shall go down into the depths?' (in other words, to bring the Messiah up from the dead). [8]But what does it say? 'The word is near you, in your mouth and in your heart' (that is, the word of faith which we proclaim); [9]*because if you profess with your mouth that Jesus is lord, and believe in your heart that God raised him from the dead,* ***you will be saved****.* [10]Why? Because the way to covenant membership is by believing with the heart, and **the way to salvation** is by professing with the mouth.[11]The Bible says, you see, 'Everyone who believes in him **will not be put to shame**.' [12]For there is no distinction between Jew and Greek, since the same lord is lord of all, and is rich towards all who call upon him. [13]'All who call upon the name of the Lord', you see, '**will be saved**'.

This theology and exegesis generate mission: people need to believe, so they need to hear, so they need to have someone sent to them, someone through whose witness the powerful *rhēma* can do its Deuteronomic work, its spirit-work of circumcising hearts and producing faith and confession (10.14–15), even if the unbelief of which Isaiah spoke remains a continuing sorrow (10.16–17). At this point we simply note this link between the prayer of 10.1 and the exposition of Deuteronomy and Joel in 10.5–13: if the passage is really as central to the whole of 9—11 as I have been suggesting, this will in turn be an important clue to other exegetical and theological issues.

In particular, this means that if Paul had held, or had even thought of holding, the kind of 'two-covenant' theory espoused in some circles, according to which Jews are saved by being good Jews and gentiles are saved by becoming Christians, he would have had no need to pray the prayer of 10.1, let alone 9.1–5, in the first place. What is more, when he speaks in 11.26 of 'all Israel being saved', he has already told us in considerable detail in the present passage what he thinks 'being saved' involves, and how it is effected. In a piece of writing as carefully balanced as Romans 9—11, we do well to pay close attention to what has been put at the very centre.[509] And in a treatment of Paul's eschatology, such as we are offering in the present chapter, we do well to note at the exegetical outset that Paul has placed here at the heart of his discussion a description of the way in which the ancient covenant has been renewed. Faith and confession in the risen lord Jesus is the true 'doing of the law' which characterizes those who belong to the renewed covenant. As we shall see, Paul's emphatic inclusion of *gentiles* within the ranks of those prophesied in Deuteronomy and Joel as people of the renewed covenant (10.12) is a clear signpost to the way his mind is working in the next chapter as well. The *inauguration* of this eschatology in 10.4–17 looks ahead to its *consummation* in chapter 11. The basic question of the

[509] For this whole theme, see Rowe 2000.

whole three-chapter section has been posed in 10.1, and the basic answer given in 10.2–13.

(c) The Surprised gentiles and the Jealous Jews: 9.30–3; 10.18–21

We now pan the camera back from this dense, central passage of 10.1–17, and examine briefly the shorter passages either side of it, which link it to the two longer main sections which comprise most of chapters 9 and 11 respectively.

9.1–5 11.33–6
9.6–29 11.1–32
9.30–3 **10.18–21**
10.1–4 10.14–17
10.5–13
10.9

Chapter 9.30–3 draws together the threads of 9.6–29 in order to move things on to the next stage of the argument. In that earlier passage, for the most part, Paul has been talking about God's strange purpose in narrowing Israel down to a 'remnant' (9.27–30, the end of the line that started with the selection of Isaac rather than Ishmael in 9.6–9). But he has also hinted, out of the blue as it were, that in the same process God is also getting ready to welcome gentiles into the family (9.24). In the four-verse summary at the end of the chapter, he draws this together with three controlling themes: 'righteousness', Torah and the stumbling stone. And the main point, here as in 10.18–21, is that 'Israel' (as a whole; Paul will point out in 11.1–6 that he and others like him constitute the present 'remnant') has strangely failed to arrive where they had hoped, and that gentiles have found themselves arriving there instead.

The place where they have arrived is 'righteousness', *dikaiosynē*. We find once more that the best sense is made of the passage if we take this term as referring to 'membership in God's people', in other words, to 'covenant status'. Gentiles, Paul says, picking up from the sudden and surprising 9.24 (on which see below) and the sustained exposition of 3.21—4.25, have received this 'righteousness', this status as members of God's covenant family. Those who read the text this way, in the light of the strange new form of law-fulfilment Paul has in mind, will arrive at his meaning here, while exegetes who approach in the more normal way will fail to do so. Why? Because they are not thinking in terms of the covenantal narrative of chapter 9, but in terms of an abstract theological system. That approach would expect Paul to say that 'Israel, hunting for righteousness, did not attain righteousness'; but what he says is 'Israel hunting for *the law of righteousness*, did not attain *to the law*.'[510] Paul, unlike many of his interpreters, is already building into his

[510] RSV, unpardonably, translates 'who pursued the righteousness based on law'; so too NRSV, 'Israel, who did strive for the righteousness that is based on the law'. Cf. too Sanders 1983, 42; Zeller 1984, 184; Fitzmyer 1993, 577f.

discussion a positive meaning of the law, anticipating what he will say in 10.6–8, which is that, however surprisingly, faith in Jesus as the risen lord is in fact the true law-fulfilment spoken of in Deuteronomy. Israel was pursuing *the right goal* (the Torah) *by the wrong means* (works!). Paul is already hinting at the reading of Leviticus and Deuteronomy we were discussing a moment ago: the Torah itself can indeed be attained, and gentiles are indeed attaining it (alongside the Jewish remnant), because they are doing so by faith.

If we fail to hear the echoes of Romans 7.1—8.11 at this point, we need to re-tune our hermeneutical hearing aids.[511] Here at the end of chapter 9 we find ourselves at the further unwinding of the spiral of argument which began way back in chapters 2 and 3 and continued with the throwaway remarks of 5.20 and 6.14, generating Paul's head-on discussion of the matter in 7.7–25. There, Israel rightly clung to Torah, because Torah really is God's word, holy and just and good; but Israel found that Torah gave sin its opportunity, and that sin thereby deceived and killed those who were embracing Torah. That, we saw, had an explosively positive purpose: 'sin' was itself lured into doing its worst in one place, so that it could be condemned there, 'in the flesh' of the Messiah. Israel, embracing Torah, did not succeed in fulfilling Torah ... but (8.3–4) God has done, in the Messiah and the spirit, 'what was impossible for Torah'. So here Israel pursued Torah and failed to attain to it; but in 10.1–13 Paul demonstrates that there is a new 'fulfilling of Torah', through the covenant-renewing work of Messiah and, by implication, the spirit. And the 'stumbling stone' in 9.32–3 seems to play a similar role in the present sequence of thought to Paul's earlier exposition of sin being lured on to one place, to be condemned.

A major difference between the two passages is that in 9.30–3 Paul is no longer talking about 'sin'. The word *hamartia* and its cognates, massively present throughout Romans 1—8 and especially chapters 5, 6 and 7, occur precisely once in this section, in 11.27, and that in a biblical citation. Nevertheless, we see clearly a very similar train of thought: Israel is embracing Torah, struggling with it, getting it wrong, stumbling over the stone ... and then come the Messiah and the covenant renewal. Romans 9.30—10.13 thus resonates with the sequence of thought in 7.7—8.11, especially 7.21—8.4.

So what are we talking about this time? What is the same, and what is different? With this question we approach near the heart of the darkest mystery in these chapters.

The idea that the law would have made Israel alive, had it been able to do so, goes back in Paul's thought to Galatians 3.21. Israel was correct, in other words, to look to the law as 'the law of righteousness', the law through whose possession and keeping Abraham's physical children would be assured of the status of being God's people in perpetuity. But they 'did not attain to the law', because, Paul declares, they were pursuing it in the wrong

[511] Barrett 1982, 140 points out that Rom. 7 sheds light on the present passage, though he does not develop the point in the way I am doing.

way. They were pursuing it, hunting for it, 'not by faith but *as though* by works', *hōs ex ergōn*; and the *hōs* says it all. '*As if* by works'; but, from Paul's point of view, it was never supposed to be 'by works', but always 'by faith'. Here we are back with Romans 3.27–31: boasting is excluded, 'by what law? of works? No: through the law of faith.' Because (to telescope together the different segments of Romans for a moment), though Paul does indeed see the law as erecting a solid boulder between the promises God made to Abraham and the fulfilment of those promises in the creation of a single worldwide family, the fault is not in Torah itself but, as Paul has insisted in passage after passage, *in the people to whom Torah was given – or rather in their Adamic condition*. They are 'in Adam' like everyone else. But their use of 'works' (sabbath, food laws, circumcision and so on) as the way of 'hunting for the law of righteousness' was the way of using some of the badges of Torah-keeping as the way of doing what Deuteronomy 9 warned them against, setting themselves up to be inalienably God's people, and keeping everyone else at bay.

But this itself was not outside the divine purpose. That is the point of the 'stumbling stone' image. Israel has misused the Torah, *but God seems to have intended that Israel should do just that.*[512] Here we are again back with Romans 7, this time with that repeated *hina* in 7.13 which echoes the all-important *hina* in 5.20.[513] So what is he saying? That the purpose of Torah was *to increase sin*? To 'magnify the trespass'? Yes, because God's aim – his aim, Paul seems to be saying, in election itself, not as a sub-plot but as the main idea all along, finally now revealed in the Messiah – was so that through Israel, and through Torah's strange work in Israel, God might draw sin on to that one place, on to the Messiah as Israel's representative, on to the Messiah as the embodiment of God himself, God in the person of his 'Son', so that God himself might deal with 'sin' by both enacting and enduring its condemnation in himself. That was the point of 7.7—8.11, especially of 7.13 and 8.3–4. Now, at the next point up the spiral of the argument of Romans, we have in 9.30—10.4 something similar but different. No longer are we talking about the death of the Messiah bearing the condemnation for sins. We are talking about Israel itself, as the elect people, being redefined, reconstituted, around Israel's own Messiah and on the initiative of Abraham's God, so as to include all those non-Israelites who were envisaged (along with Israel itself) in the original Abrahamic promises. And Paul sees *that this too was necessary for the plan to work*. Israel had to 'stumble' so that the world might be saved. That is the clue not only to the 'stone' image in 9.32–3 but to a good deal of chapters 9 and 11. And that is the point at which his revision of election gives birth to his revision of eschatology.

[512] Watson 2007 [1986], 330 is anxious that my earlier treatment of this passage shifted the focus from the sovereign divine agency 'to the dubious category of 'Israel's fault''. Paul *does* speak about a 'fault' in 9.31 and 10.3, but I hope it is clear that I agree with Watson here about Paul's theological priority, and about the apparent scriptural foundation for what 'Israel' did, and about the inappropriateness of 'Israel's fault' or 'Israel's responsibility' as a heading for 9.30—10.21 (see too Watson 323 n. 39).

[513] See above, 894f.

This leads to a vital point. I have suggested that Torah functioned as the 'stumbling stone' in 9.32–3. But we should hear in the Isaiah quotation at the end of verse 33 ('the one who believes in him/it will never be put to shame') a reference also to the Messiah (as in the apparent meaning of 'believing in him' in the final line, echoed in 10.11, and as in some other early Christian uses). (In Isaiah 8.14, we note, the 'stone' appears to be God himself.)[514] This is confirmed in 10.11 by the repetition of the same clause, quoted from Isaiah 8.14, with the addition of *pas*, 'all', 'everyone',[515] where it is clear that the object of faith is the Messiah himself. Here we are near the heart of the strange situation Paul is explaining throughout these chapters. He discerns a close link between God's work through Torah and God's work in the Messiah. To put it another way, the rejection of the Messiah himself, and of the gospel message about him, is seen by Paul as cognate with, and expressive of, the failure to 'pursue' Torah in the way that would lead to covenant membership. Or, to put it yet another way, if anyone, Jew or gentile, is to attain to the *dikaiosynē*, the covenant status, held out in Deuteronomy 30 as the real 'return from exile', they must do so by *pistis*, the 'faith' which some gentiles now have (9.30) while many Jews do not (9.32). Pursuing Torah as a charter of national privilege circumscribed by 'works' would not do; that is the problem which Paul then sums up in 10.2–3. The Messiah – and when Paul says *Christos* at this stage of Romans we should hear, bundled up inside that word, all that has been said about him in chapters 1—8 – is the *telos nomou*, the goal of Torah. The two lines converge. To confess Jesus as lord and to believe that God raised him from the dead is to 'attain the Torah', the *nomos dikaiosynēs*, the 'law of covenant membership', the point towards which the whole Pentateuch was heading. Conversely, to reject the Messiah is to fail to attain Torah, to stumble over the stone. Some gentiles have now done the first; many Jews have now done the second. And the point of 9.32–3 is to say: this too is the deliberate work of God. He has placed in Zion the stone over which they would trip, the Torah, the Messiah. Why? Paul has not yet said, except in the most cryptic hint in 9.22–4, to which we shall return. It is wrong to play off the two possibilities, Torah and Messiah, against one another. Paul allows resonances of both to jangle together before resolving them in chapter 10 into a new and previously unsuspected harmony.[516]

Reading 9.30–3 in this way as an introduction to 10.1–17 can then be balanced by studying the conclusion to the central section of 9—11, in other

[514] See the other relevant NT passages: 1 Pet. 2.8; cf. Mt. 16.23; 18.6f.; Lk. 17.1; Mt. 21.44 (cf. Dan. 2.34f., 44f.). Elsewhere (1 Pet., Mt.) these texts have been combined with Ps. 118.22f. (the rejected stone which becomes the cornerstone) but Paul does not go in that direction here. Full discussion in the commentaries: e.g. Keck 2005, 244f.; and cf. e.g. Oss 1989; Wagner 2002, 126–45.

[515] Holding together the train of thought that runs from the *panti tō pisteuonti* in 10.4 to the *pas* (in the quotation from Joel) at 10.13.

[516] Barrett 1982, 144 argues strongly for Torah as the main referent of the 'stone', without quite seeing how Paul draws Torah and Messiah together – and without reflecting that the problem chs. 9—11 are addressing, which Paul is here summarizing, is that his Jewish contemporaries have failed to believe in the Messiah. See the summary of positions in Keck 2005, 245.

words, 10.18–21. Here Paul draws on a psalm, on Deuteronomy again (chapter 32 this time) and on Isaiah (writings, Torah, prophets). His purpose is to say, first, that despite the unbelief mentioned in 10.16, God's word is indeed going out and doing its work. It may be that the balance within Psalm 19, celebrating creation (especially the sun) in the first half and Torah in the second, had caused Paul to ponder the relationship between God's revelation to the whole world in creation and the revelation to Israel in Torah.[517] The Israel-specific revelation picks up, it seems, the larger message to the whole human race. But in the middle of that, Israel *did* always know *that gentiles were going to be brought in to make Israel jealous*. That is what Deuteronomy itself had claimed, what Moses himself had warned. If there is any mention of 'supersession' anywhere in Paul, it might just be here – in a key passage from Moses himself! Gentiles will come in *and make Israel jealous*. That only makes sense if, as I have been arguing all along, Paul really does hold that the Messiah-family into which gentiles are incorporated is 'the circumcision', and so forth. But the potential charge of 'replacement', which one can hear going on in the background at this point like a dripping tap, is undone in the next chapter by the way in which Paul develops and exploits Moses' word about 'jealousy'. This is not 'replacement'; it is fulfilment. To this we shall shortly return.

The Isaiah passage, on the other hand (it is a single verse, Isaiah 65.1, which Paul has quoted in two parts), simply states the two conclusions and leaves them side by side, repeating exactly the point made in 9.30, only this time in terms not of the *nomos dikaiosynēs*, but of Israel's God himself: gentiles, who were not looking for YHWH, have found him, while Israel, supposedly YHWH's own people, have remained 'disobedient and recalcitrant', *apeithounta kai antilegonta*, 'not-obeying and speaking-against'.[518] Here is the massive paradox with which Paul is wrestling: (a) the one God chose a people; (b) after a long time he did what he had promised and sent them their Messiah – and they rejected him; (c) this God renewed the covenant, and the covenant people for the most part refused to join in.[519] Where can Paul now turn? How can he begin to understand what this strange and apparently unpredictable God has been up to? This is perhaps the biggest question in the whole of Paul's eschatology. It is possible, however, that even in the last devastating quote from Isaiah there is a hint of what is to come. Just as Paul in the next chapter will exploit 'I will make you jealous' from 10.19 (quoting Deuteronomy 32.21), we might see 'All day long I have stretched out my hands' in 10.21 (quoting Isaiah 65.2) not simply as a gesture of divine frustration, but also as a continuing commitment. Israel's God, like the father of the Prodigal Son, will go out to reason with the older

[517] Paul spoke about the revelation in creation in 1.18–23.

[518] Nb. Ac. 13.45, where the *Ioudaioi* in Pisidian Antioch are filled with *zēlos* and 'speak against' what Paul has said (*antelegon*). See Bell 1994, 312–17.

[519] The obvious echoes of Jn. 1.10f., and of parables such as those in Mt. 21.28–32; 22.1–14 indicate that Paul is not out on a limb at this point from wider early Christian perceptions. Those two parables are separated by the 'wicked tenants' (Mt. 21.33–46), including Jesus' warning about the 'stone' (21.42).

brother who, for apparently good reasons, has decided to stay out of the party.[520]

Faced with the ultimate eschatological question, and with the consequent search for fresh wisdom, the Paul we know will always answer that wisdom is to be found *in the Messiah*.[521] The Messiah, somehow, will provide the clues. It is in and through him, after all, that God's righteousness has been unveiled. But what will those clues look like? How will they play out? We go back to the first full passage in the section, Romans 9.6–29, to find the first part of the answer.

(d) Bearers of God's Strange Purpose: Romans 9.6–29

We move back up the chiastic structure to the first main sub-section, 9.6–29, which balances 11.1–32, its final main sub-section:

9.1–5 ... 11.33–6
9.6–29 ... 11.1–32
9.30–3 ... 10.18–21
10.1–4 ... 10.14–17
10.5–13
10.9

Paul sets off in 9.6 on a narrative, instantly recognizable as the narrative of Israel. In chapter 11 he is indubitably pointing to the final end of this same narrative, the time of redemption, the completion of God's purposes, familiar in outline from second-Temple eschatology. This, in fact, is how that eschatology regularly works: first you tell the story of Israel so far, and then you look on to what is still to come. That is why our consideration of chapters 9—11 belongs at this point in the book, within the overall discussion of Paul's revision of second-Temple eschatology.

We have seen that 9.30—10.13 stands in between the two elements of this basic narrative. That is the new thing, the messianic story which has intruded, functioning now as the fulcrum around which everything else moves. There is a rough sense, in fact, in which chapter 9 is about the past, chapter 10 about the present and chapter 11 about the future.[522] But 10.5–13, and indeed the immediately larger section to which it belongs, 9.30—10.13, is not itself part of the great narrative. It stands upright in the middle of that story, the *telos* of all that has gone before – and perhaps, though Paul does not put it like this, the *archē* of all that will now follow. It is the messianic moment, the 'but now', the sudden sabbath which creates a new sort of time, a heaven-and-earth time, a time when the 'word', the *rhēma Christou*, can leap down from heaven and do its work of replacing the thorn with the myrtle, its work of renewing and circumcising hearts so that they can

[520] See Keck 2005, 261f.; and of course Lk. 15.31f.

[521] Col. 2.1–3.

[522] See e.g. Tobin 2004, 321.

believe and confess the gospel. The Messiah is both in time and out of time, transforming time itself and inevitably therefore eschatology too. Romans 9—11 thus exhibits in its very literary form the combination of (what ought to be meant by) 'salvation history' on the one hand and (what ought to be meant by) 'apocalyptic' on the other. God has done, in the middle of Israel's history but disrupting and rearranging that history, the thing he had always promised. And only in the light of that 'vertical' disruption does the 'horizontal' narrative, from Abraham to the 'remnant' in chapter 9 and from the 'remnant' to the fulfilment of the patriarchal promises in chapter 11, make the sense it does.

But this messianic moment, even though it has a different character in relation to time before and time after, nevertheless does belong at the centre of precisely this narrative. To this extent, we might even see Romans 9—11 not simply as a chiasm but as a cruciform structure, with this great vertical providing the definite line, the straight-downward line, that refocuses the edge-lured arguments and holds them together as they spread out into past (9.6–29) and future (11.1–32). All else east or west of Jesus: the arrow that says 'You are here'.[523]

A fanciful notion, no doubt. And yet there is something about the cruciform shape of the argument which infects the details, too, and that is the rubric under which we now turn to 9.6–29. Paul, I propose, is re-reading the story of Abraham's family in the light of the great vertical which he knows is coming up, the messianic event which had forced him to rethink everything, to conclude that this was what it had meant all along. 'It cannot be that God's word has failed': so, if God's word has now been spoken and heard in and through the scandalous crucified Messiah, the one in whom the *dikaiosynē theou* has been revealed (3.21), the one whose rejection embodies the 'stumbling' over the 'stone', we must assume that the story of election had somehow reflected this cruciform necessity all along in a way which only the inaugurated messianic eschatology can reveal.

Once again Romans 7 is an essential part of the background. There, Israel's problem was that, being given Torah and rightly delighting in it, Israel found that Torah became the place where 'sin' gained its opportunity, indeed, grew to its full height. But that, too, was exactly what God had planned (5.20; 7.13). That was the way by which sin could be condemned – not in Israel, but in the representative who was also Israel's substitute, properly acting as Israel-in-person but also properly doing for Israel what Israel could not do (and was not meant to do) for itself (8.3). Now here, in 9.6–29, in the story of election itself, we find the strange principle, which it will take to the end of chapter 11 to work out, that Israel is indeed 'the people of the Messiah' – and that this means, in the massive corporate version of Galatians 2.19, 'I through the Law died to the Law; I am crucified with the

[523] All this is hugely annoying, no doubt, both for the modern universalist and the postmodern particularist; but, as Mr Bingley said to his sister Caroline when she suggested that it might be more rational to have conversation rather than dancing at a ball, it would indeed be much more rational, but it would not be near so much like a ball.

Messiah'. Yes, there is a further word, 'Nevertheless I live'; but that will not come until chapter 11. For the moment, Paul tells the narrative of Israel under the rubric of the crucified Messiah. Just as, in our reader's eye, we can see the cross etched into the structure of Paul's argument, so Paul, in the eye of his heart, could see the *stauros tou Christou* written across the pages of history. When the Messiah died, he was doing, close up and personal, what Israel had, all unknowing, been living through ever since the time of Abraham. No wonder Israel 'was ignorant of God's covenant faithfulness'. Think of Jeremiah. If God's people had known what this would involve, they might have opted out a lot earlier. It was to the same end: as with the Messiah, so with Israel itself. Israel was to be cast away so that the world might be redeemed.

Some theories of election have stopped short of the first hurdle in this sequence, fearful of saying something politically incorrect. They have thereby missed entirely the extraordinary achievement of Paul in these chapters. He is not here offering a 'theology of history' in some grand developmental or Hegelian sense. Nor is this a theory of predestination, or a philosophical discourse about determinism and free will. This is a passage in which we discover that the living God has scratched his name on the hard rock of history. But we only learn to read that name when we have come to know it in the Messiah, whether in the blinding glare of a Damascus Road or the slow, watery light of a December morning.

I have suggested that 9.6–29 is parallel, within Paul's overall design, to 11.1–32. This is not just a matter of loose structure. There are numerous thematic parallels as well, ideas which are absent in 9.30—10.13. Both passages have to do with the patriarchs and the promises God made to them. Both stress the 'call' of God, the 'mercy' of God and the fact that neither are dependent upon 'works'. Both insist upon the 'patience' of God, while emphasizing God's activity in 'hardening' people. Both highlight the 'remnant', albeit in perhaps a slightly different sense. Both, interestingly, use the word 'Israel' in more than one way.[524] These themes are not distributed in the two sections in exactly the same way, but there is nevertheless a sense that in chapter 11 Paul is working his way back to where he started. This can be seen at a glance:

9.6–13 'Israel' and 'Israel'	11.25–32 'Israel' and 'Israel'
9.14–26 Patriarchs Pharaoh 'hardened' (to make God's name known)	11.11–24 Patriarchs non-remnant 'hardened' (so that gentiles are included)
9.27–9 Remnant	11.1–10 Remnant

[524] On all this see Aletti 2010 [1992], 217, comparing 11.25–32 in particular with the various sections that precede it; and Aletti 2012, 138.

This begs questions, of course, as do all chiastic schemes. The single words and phrases I have used here do not represent a full or balanced summary of the subtle arguments Paul makes in each of these passages. There are difficult questions about the subdivision within 9.14–29, which I have not attempted to resolve here (there are slight turns in the argument at verses 19 and 24 as well as 27). In particular, the mere suggestion that the distinction of two 'Israel's in 9.6 might be parallel to a similar phenomenon in 11.25–6 will already produce wailing and gnashing of teeth in certain quarters.[525] There are also themes in common to the larger units (9.6–20 and 11.1–2) which do not fall in the equivalent place: the emphasis on 'not by works', for instance, in 9.12 and 11.6, and the strong note of 'mercy' in 9.15–16 and 11.31–2. The parallels in chapter 11 to the notion of 'hardening' in 9.17–18 come in 11.7 and 25 (and with a different term). But all the same the parallels are remarkable. They suggest that Paul, having worked his way forward from 9.6 to 9.29 in a series of careful steps, is then retracing those steps, not slavishly but still quite thoroughly, as he writes chapter 11. Chapter 11 is, as it were, much harder work. Nobody has told that story before, whereas the narrative outline of 9.6–29 was extremely well known. Anyway, the payoff of this proposal will appear more fully when we ourselves reach Romans 11 presently, but it is important to be aware of the parallels as we study chapter 9.

So what is going on in 9.6–29? It may surprise some to reflect that it would be hard for a devout Jew – Saul of Tarsus, say – to find fault with the overall movement of the passage.[526] There were plenty of other second-Temple retellings of Israel's narrative. They would have gone along with the line of selection from Abraham through Isaac to Jacob, allowing Ishmael and Esau to fall by the wayside. No first-century Jew would have supposed that the 'seed of Abraham' was continued equally by Ishmael as well as

[525] Eastman 2010, 377 n. 34 says that it is confusing at 9.6 to speak of a division *within* Israel. In my view, faced with Paul saying 'not all of Israel are Israel', it is confusing not to. Her suggestion, that 'the distinction is between the line of promise and those descendants of Abraham who became the progenitors of the gentiles', introduces a novel element: since when were Ishmael and Esau the father of all gentiles? At 382 n. 51 she suggests that I draw a distinction 'between ethnic Israel and Israel as "the Messiah and his people"', but that is misleading, implying that ethnic Israel is automatically excluded from the latter category, which is what Paul is denying in 11.11–24.

[526] Jewett 2007, 590 rightly points out that the objections raised in 9.14, 19 would actually be 'unacceptable' from 'the perspective of Jewish orthodoxy'. See too e.g. Johnson 1989, 148. Contrast Wolter 2011, 425, who supposes that here Paul is in dialogue with his own former self. Barclay 2010 draws a sharp contrast between Rom. 9—11 and Wis., which postulates the kind of ordered and symmetrical moral and rational cosmos that Rom. 9—11 appears to subvert with its stress on the apparent unpredictability and incomprehensibility of God's purposes, so that (for instance) the story of Jacob and Esau (Wis. 10.9–12) teaches a moral lesson which Rom. 9.10–13 appears to rule out. Paul's theology, says Barclay (109) has been 'twisted ... into this strange shape' because of the 'gift' which is the Christ-event. I fully agree that Paul has rethought Israel's election, and indeed 'morality, justice [and] reason' themselves (Barclay 108) around the Messiah, but I still see broad convergence at a deeper level: telling *this* story is the key to God's dealings with the world. As far as I can see, the main thing a Pharisee might object to would be the 'calling' of gentiles in 9.24 and their inclusion in the 'returning exiles' prophecy of Hos. 2.1, 25 (9.25f.).

Isaac, or that Esau shared the same 'elect' status as Jacob.[527] They would have agreed, further, that God had the right, faced with the bullying Pharaoh, to reveal his own name and power in all the world through the events of the exodus. They would certainly have agreed that when Israel made and worshipped the golden calf God had the right to do what he pleased, and if he showed mercy to some, that was up to him (9.15, quoting Exodus 33.19). They would have reflected, with Paul, on the strange ways that Israel had come through the failure of the monarchy and the eventual exile, and that YHWH again had the right to remould Israel through such events, as a potter would remould clay. That brings us all the way from 9.6 to 9.23, with any Jewish listeners nodding in sympathy. This is their story.[528]

Then comes the first point where something new happens, something that Saul of Tarsus and his kinsfolk according to the flesh would not have expected or approved. The 'vessels of mercy, prepared in advance for glory', consist, it seems, of 'us whom he called, not only from among the Jews but also from among the gentiles' (9.24). This would indeed be highly controversial, as would Paul's use of Hosea 2 to back up the point (9.25–6).[529] One is reminded of the moment in Acts when the crowd listened attentively to Paul until he mentioned gentiles, at which point chaos broke out once more.[530] But with the last three verses of the section (9.27–9) there could again be no quarrel. The prophets had spoken of a remnant, of Israel being narrowed down to a point, a *hypoleimma* (a 'remainder', like the numbers left over after a division sum), a *sperma*, a seed that remained after the tree had been cut down.[531] Paul was simply rehearsing what devout Jews already knew.

It appears, then, that apart from the mention in 9.24 of gentiles as among the 'called', who have been 'foreordained to glory', *what Paul says in 9.6–29 would not have been controversial, at least to the kind of Jew he was thinking of in 10.3*, those who have 'a zeal for God', albeit not according to knowledge; those, that is, among whose number he would have placed himself until his meeting with Jesus on the road to Damascus. No Jew would have objected to the proposition 'Jacob I loved, but Esau I hated' (it was, after all, in the Bible); no Pharisee would deny that God was right to condemn both Pharaoh and those who worshipped the golden calf. No second-Temple Jew who had studied the prophets would doubt that God-the-potter had the right to remould the clay, and that he had done so in fact. Nobody doubted,

[527] cf. e.g. *Jub.* 15.28–32; 20.11–13. The sharp distinction between the Israelites and their Abrahamic cousins is reinforced in passages like Ps. 83.6–8. For other second-Temple retellings of Israel's story see above, 121–39.

[528] cf. Getty 1988, 457: 'Paul is broadening his understanding of Israel to include the gentiles, not attacking the fundamentals of Israel's theology.'

[529] See esp. Starling 2011.

[530] Ac. 22.22.

[531] cf. Isa. 6.13; not that Paul is explicitly alluding to this, but the point of *sperma* here does not seem to be the positive one of 'Abraham's seed' in the sense of 'the full family' but rather 'what is left . . .'. It goes with the theme that runs from Isa. 1.9 (which is what Paul quotes explicitly) through 4.2 and is picked up in 6.13 but also in e.g. 10.22, which Paul quotes in 9.27.

with ten tribes lost half a millennium earlier and much of the remainder scattered around the world, that God had left 'only a remnant'.

This leaves us with a question which is not sufficiently asked. Who then is Paul really addressing in this whole section? What is he trying to say to them?

Part of the answer must lie in the implicit addressee of the questions in 9.14 and 9.19: is God unjust in his 'love' for Jacob? Is God unfair in blaming those who are 'hardened' by his own will? These questions would more likely be raised, I think, by *gentiles*: gentiles who had found the whole story of Israel challenging in the very idea of there being a chosen people, let alone the Jewish people, and gentiles who, with a bit of moral philosophy in their heads or at least in their popular culture, would hear the story of Israel and at once begin to raise questions about what sort of God would behave in so unprincipled a fashion. Gentiles who might well be disposed to regard the Christian message and experience as something which had now left behind its Jewish roots altogether ...[532]

This is a rather different way of reading the chapter from the way frequently proposed. Many have suggested, as a kind of interim solution to the question of the integration of chapters 9—11 into the letter, that Paul is facing the problem: if people are going to believe the promises set out in chapters 1—8, might they not reasonably ask why, granted the apparent failure of the promises to Israel, they should nevertheless trust this God? I do not think that captures the heart of Paul's argument, or indeed his wider theology. *Israel is not simply an example of a people to whom God made promises in the past.*[533] Israel was and is, for Paul as for Israel's own scriptures, the people through whom God would bless the world. This section is where Paul shows how, in the Messiah, God *has* done that, and *will* do it, and what that strange new fulfilment means for Israel itself.

This is, I believe, the right way to approach 9.6–29. It points forward at once to the thrust of chapter 11, which is warding off precisely the kind of gentile arrogance that would want to turn the tables against ethnic Israel and deny them any part in the divinely planned future. The significance, then, of saying that 'the word of God has not failed' in Romans 9.6 is not merely to do with theodicy, 'justifying' or explaining away what God has done. It is a point, directed at gentile Messiah-believers in Rome, which says, 'Do not imagine that your inheritance of Israel's promises means that you can discount their history, their scriptures, their very election. On the

[532] I thus agree with e.g. Stowers 1994, 287f., though for interestingly different reasons; see too Keck 2005, 241. Nanos 2010a, 349 grasps this point but in my view mistakes its rhetorical force. Paul is not undoing the 'no distinction' of 2.7–11; 3.23, 27–30; 4.13–17 and particularly 10.4–13. He is warding off a dangerous and false corollary of that position. Nanos's attempt to get Paul to say that the 'faithfulness' of Israelites would consist in recognizing that a new day has dawned (though without themselves believing Jesus to be the Messiah) so that now they are to join in the project of being heralds to the nations (350 n. 25, 351, 364–6) must be regarded as a failure: 10.14–17 is completely dependent on 10.1–13, making it clear that the 'heralds' are those who announce Jesus as the risen lord, so that all alike may believe in him. If Nanos were correct, Paul has seriously misstated his own position in 9.30—10.13.

[533] I have in mind here especially Käsemann (e.g. Käsemann 1969 [1965], 187); but he is representative of a much larger tradition of reading.

contrary, their entire story stands firm, makes sense in its own terms and is the foundation of yours as well.' Paul is not trying to make the ancient Israelite theology of election stand on its toes and do tricks. He is allowing it to be itself. This is the point that gentile Christians in Rome need to take on board. They have to learn that they have been, as Hays puts it, narrated into the story of Israel, as in Galatians, 1 Corinthians 10 and elsewhere.[534] This is Israel's story, and they should be so lucky as to find themselves part of it (11.11–24: see below).

My first proposal about 9.6–29, then, is this. The reason Paul is telling the story of Israel in this way is not to make a point 'against' Jewish unbelievers, but to tell their story *from their own point of view* (except for the sudden insertion of gentiles into the story in 9.24) and to defend this way of telling the story, at least preliminarily, against the charge which he knew would come from gentile (including gentile Christian) interlocutors. Paul must after all have had this conversation hundreds of times as he explained things to gentile converts and taught them the scriptures. His point here is *to establish the basic Jewish doctrine of election*, not to undermine it or even, at this stage, to modify it except by that one proleptic hint about gentile inclusion, a hint he could of course have backed up from within the covenantal scriptures themselves, though he does not do that here.[535] He does not want to modify the narrative, but to draw out from it (and to rub gentile noses in the point) the truth that the entire story of God's purposes into which they have come (through inheriting the sonship, the glory, the covenants and so forth, and particularly the Messiah) has been this story and no other: the story of the free electing grace of the God of Abraham. Even the narrowing down of Israel to a 'remnant', a 'seed', in 9.27–9 cannot, as it were, count 'against' Israel or for that matter against God. It is not an 'anti-Jewish' or 'unJewish' way of saying what has happened. Torah, prophets and writings all concur. Granted human sin, and Israel's own recapitulation of Adam's trespass, God had the right and perhaps even the duty to do what he had done. My first main point about this section is therefore that Paul's primary 'target audience' here appears to be the puzzled gentile Christians in Rome.

The argument of 9.6–29 is held together by the mention of the 'seed' in 9.7 and 9.29. Paul begins by affirming that 'not all of Israel are in fact Israel',[536] that 'not all Abraham's children are his "seed", but "in Isaac shall your seed be called"', and he ends with 'unless the Lord of hosts had

[534] Hays 2000, 346 n. 302; cf. Keck 2005, 225: 'When Paul explicitly addresses Christian gentiles (11:13–24), he insists that they are actually *being included in Israel*' (my italics).

[535] Rom. 9.24–6 thus functions, both thematically and in terms of playing an advance role within the argument of 9—11, somewhat as 2.25–9 does within the argument of 1—8.

[536] Jewett 2007, 575 speaks of the 'true Israel', a phrase Paul never uses but which (as with the equally non-existent phrases 'true Jew' in 2.29 and 'true circumcision' in Phil. 3.3) express what he has in mind. See too Gaventa 2010, 259, pointing out that some (e.g. Moo 1996, 573) read 9.6b the other way round ('All those who are of Israel, these are not Israel').

left us seed'.[537] This brings us to the second main point about this section. Paul has built into his unexceptional narrative of Israel's election certain features which we can see to be hints of that larger purpose which will then unfold. Within the story, in a manner to which no well-educated or zealous first-century Jew could object, there was a distinction made between the 'children of Abraham': not all of them count as *sperma*, 'seed', because the 'seed' is the people who are 'called in Isaac'.[538] This re-introduces the distinction between 'children of flesh' and 'children of promise': only the latter are *sperma*. We would not know, on the basis of the present passage alone, that Paul had in mind that the *sperma Abraam* would include Messiah-believing gentiles, as he insists in chapter 4 and indeed in Galatians 3. He has the soft pedal on at the moment, hitting the same notes but keeping the overtones quiet. But they are there, ready to be reawakened when the music changes key, fleetingly in 9.24 and then, spectacularly, in 9.30—10.13.

In the same way, although no well-taught second-Temple Jew could object to the exposition of the Jacob/Esau scenario in 9.10–13, Paul is building into the picture a fresh element which he will exploit in due course. If God was already choosing and calling people without any prior merit, there should be no problem about God then calling gentiles despite them not having, or keeping, Torah. We should again be alert to the echoes of 2.25–9. The principle of election is the necessary basis for the surprising things that God has planned all along. The promise to Abraham always envisaged that God would justify gentiles by faith (Galatians 3.8) and that God would 'justify the ungodly' (Romans 4.5). Now, it seems, the principle of election itself points the same way. Positively, it means that God can do surprising new things, not only on the basis of human 'works' but simply on the basis of his 'call': 9.12 ('not because of the works but because of the one who calls') is thus itself a highly cryptic foretaste of the less cryptic but still surprising 9.24 ('us whom he called not only from among the Jews but also from among the gentiles').

The negative point – a distinction between *tekna* and *sperma*, in other words, a distinction between the 'children of Abraham' (both Isaac and Ishmael) and the 'seed' who are the line of promise, and ultimately the distinction between one 'Israel' and another in 9.6b – is carried forward by Paul to explain the obvious fact that, through successive national disasters, there had been a distinction among the descendants of Jacob (= Israel) as well. Many second-Temple Jewish retellings of the story, naturally happy to go along with the bracketing out of Ishmael and Esau, would have baulked at applying the same principle to the offspring of Jacob.[539] At the moment,

[537] For the *inclusio*, see e.g. Keck 2005, 238. This confirms, to my mind, the meaning of 9.7 (with e.g. Dunn 1988b, 540; Tobin 2004, 327; against e.g. Hafemann 1988, 44; Fitzmyer 1993, 560): the 'children' is the larger category (divided into 'children of promise' and 'children of flesh'), while the 'seed' are identified with the 'children of promise'.

[538] Another 'in' with a patriarch, as in Gal. 3.8.

[539] We might compare the narrative of *Jubilees*, in which the separation of Isaac from Ishmael and Jacob from Esau are well marked but the twelve sons of Jacob are affirmed – even though, by the time the book was written, most of them had disappeared.

though, Paul's point would simply be to follow the narrative through and to demonstrate that, both in the time of Moses and the golden calf and in the days of the prophets, God was bound to whittle down Jacob's family, too, to a much smaller number. But the positive point, too, is being built in meanwhile: the same sovereignty by which God has the right to narrow Abraham's seed down to a 'remnant' is the sovereignty whereby he can and does call surprising new people to be part of the same family.[540]

The negative point is still on display in 9.14–18, where Paul is as ever aware of the narrative context of the passages he cites. Once more he is not expecting any dispute from Jewish hearers, including (if any such were to stumble upon this text) any hard-line Pharisees. When Israel worshipped the golden calf, the question was not whether God had the right to have mercy on whom he had mercy, but whether he was going to have mercy on *any at all*, or was going to blot them all out and begin over again with Moses himself.[541] There is here an echo, in the prayer which Moses prayed at that point, of the prayer Paul said that he might have prayed.[542] Moses proposed to God that he himself should be 'blotted out of the book that you have written'; Paul had contemplated praying that he might be *anathema apo tou Christou*, under a ban and away from the Messiah, on behalf of his kinsfolk.[543] This echo may introduce into the argument a note which would indeed imply a critique of presently unbelieving Jews: they are being aligned with the generation that committed idolatry in the wilderness![544] The echo of Exodus 32, however, is distant in Romans 9.3, only perhaps being amplified when we get to 9.15 with its explicit quotation of Exodus 33. We may suppose that Paul already had this in mind when dictating 9.3, but it does not distract from his main point.

His chief emphasis, again, is that God has the right to do all this. In particular, he chooses to highlight God's address to Pharaoh, explaining that part of the point was to display God's power and make known his name in all the world. Here again Paul is building in elements which will be important for the way his argument goes. The 'hardening' of Pharaoh is explicitly said to be in the service of the worldwide proclamation of God's name, and this too is preparing the way for 9.24 and also for 11.7–10, 11–15, and 25. But at the moment he is saying nothing that would be unacceptable to an eavesdropping Pharisee. He is offering a very specifically Jewish, and biblically rooted, analysis of what has happened to Israel between the promises to the patriarchs and the present small 'remnant'.

540 Keck 2005, 239f. is right to say that in the prophetic literature the idea of the 'remnant' was a sign of hope. But Paul's quotations of Isa. in 9.27–9 refer to this group as simply the small number left after a process of judgment. In 11.1–6 Paul does indeed turn the idea in a positive direction, but this is not evident in 9.27–9.

541 Exod. 32.10. To suppose that Paul did not intend, and his hearers could never have understood, a reference to the golden calf incident (Harink 2003, 170) is to fail to see how second-Temple Jews, their heads full of Torah, constructed discourse.

542 *euchomēn*: 'I could pray'? 'I might have prayed'? 'I used to pray'? See Jewett 2007, 560f.

543 Ex. 32.32; Rom. 9.3.

544 cf. too Rom. 1.23 with its echo of Ps. 106.20 (as well as e.g. Jer. 2.11).

When we move on to the potter and the clay, in response to the moral-philosophical objection of verse 19, Paul once again has in mind the context within which those images were born. He is not talking about 'humans in general', about God treating people in an arbitrary and whimsical fashion. He is talking about Israel, and now at last about the *purpose of election*: that all this 'choosing' is not for its own sake, not (as was supposed in some medieval, Reformation and Puritan theology) in terms of God's arbitrary 'choice' of people for salvation, but in terms of *God's wider purpose which was to be carried forwards through the people he was thus shaping.*

The purpose for which God was shaping this people, however, could not simply be the pleasant one of developing the world into the kind of creation he had always intended. This is the point where the modern idea of 'apocalyptic' must make its point against the equally modern construct of 'salvation history'. There can be no smooth crescendo from the call of Abraham to the new creation. The call of Abraham must be the call of a people through whom God would deal with the evil that had infected the world. At the heart of those modern, and comparatively trivial, debates we find the much deeper and darker point: that for the call of Abraham to be effective in accomplishing God's purpose, Abraham's family would be the ones in whose history would be inscribed, simultaneously, the rebellion of all humanity and the divine solution to that rebellion. That is what Paul will unfold in the explosive centre of chapter 11, where the christological redefinition of eschatology reaches its own climax.

Once again, in 9.22 and 9.23 in particular, we need to recall Romans 7. The choice of Israel, and the giving of Torah to Israel, was not so that Israel could be 'the chosen people' in an easy-going sense, obeying Torah and enjoying for ever the status of being God's special ones.[545] The specialness of Israel consisted precisely, according to Romans 5.20 and 7.7–25, in being the people in whom, even paradoxically through Torah itself, 'sin' could do its worst, increasing and bringing into sharp focus the 'problem of Adam', allowing sin to grow to its full height. And, whether we want to hear this or not, Paul has said in 1 Thessalonians 2 that the full height of that sin was the handing over of Jesus to the Romans and so to his death, and the similar opposition to God's purposes which consisted of trying to stop the gentile mission going ahead – the activity in which he, Paul, had previously taken a leading role. As a result, the tears, grief and prayers of 9.1–5 and 10.1 were on behalf of a people who Paul knew had been the people of Romans 5.20, the people of Romans 7, the people who had a 'zeal for God' but not 'according to knowledge', the people who, being ignorant of what God was up to in his covenant purposes, were merely heightening the problem of Romans 7.24.

The point then is this: 'What if God ...' (9.22) – in other words, Paul is beginning to suggest a new *interpretation* of this narrative, an interpretation in line both with the selection he has made from Israel's whole wide history

[545] This is where the restatements of one kind of traditional Jewish 'election' by e.g. Kaminsky, following Wyschogrod (see above, 806), seem to be more or less exactly what Paul is opposing in 10.3.

and the way he has highlighted that selection, but an interpretation which grows also out of his own perception, that is, out of the gospel itself. Perhaps, after all, it is at this point, in verse 22, not simply in verse 24 with the mention of gentile inclusion, that he begins to say things which our eavesdropping Pharisee might have begun to worry about. 'Supposing', he says, that

> God wanted to demonstrate his anger and make known his power, and for that reason put up very patiently with the vessels of anger created for destruction, [23]in order to make known the riches of his glory on the vessels of mercy, the ones he prepared in advance for glory – [24]including us, whom he called not only from among the Jews but also from among the gentiles?

In other words, supposing that God's larger purposes required that, as with Pharaoh, the evil which had infected the world needed to be gathered together and dealt with, in order that then a new thing might emerge as a fresh gift of creative grace? Supposing, as in Romans 7, that sin needed to be lured on to one spot so that it could be condemned right there? Supposing, now, that Israel's whole history was a kind of large-scale instantiation of this point, with the redemptive purposes of God being etched into history in the story of Israel itself? Supposing, in other words, that the doctrine of election *always envisaged the elect themselves being the people through whom God would perform the negative task essential to rescuing the world, namely the outpouring of his anger and power*? This is such an enormous thing to suggest that we can easily see why Paul casts it in the mode of a tentative proposal, a 'What if', much as in Philemon he inserts a *tacha*, 'perhaps', into the crucial interpretative sentence.[546] It is not, then, that 'election' simply involves a selection of some and a leaving of others, a 'loving' of some and a 'hating' of others. It is that the 'elect' themselves are elect *in order to be the place where and the means by which God's redemptive purposes are worked out*. That will not mean that the 'elect' escape from the plight of the world. On the contrary, it means that they will be led, in the strange providence of God, to the place where the plight of the world goes to its deepest point.[547]

We should be under no doubt as to the shocking nature of this proposal. The idea of 'hardening', carried forward from the discussion of Pharaoh in 9.17–18 to the discussion of Israel at the time of the exile (the pot in the hands of the potter) in 9.20–3, is not about a *temporary* 'hardening'. Pharaoh was not hardened for a time and then as it were unhardened. When Paul speaks elsewhere of God bearing with much patience those who are fitted for destruction (2.3–6), he knows that some will turn from their wickedness, but for the rest the patience of God merely allows them to go on, with a 'hard and impenitent heart', until they are fit for judgment (2.5). That, as we saw, is a frequent second-Temple theme.[548]

[546] Philem. 15.

[547] For the 'Christian' version of this see Rom. 8.18–27.

[548] See above, 1151–6, on 1 Thess. 2. See e.g. Keck 2005, 234.

In the present argument, however, I suggest that Paul saw the 'hardening' of Israel – the entire theme of exile, alluded to in 9.20–9 and again in 11.8 (see below) – as part of *the saving purposes of God.* This, as he explains in chapter 11, is how it had to happen, so that the world might be redeemed, so that 'mercy' might extend to 'all' once they had been shut up in the prison-house of 'unbelief' (11.32).

Where might Paul have got such an idea? Might it not be, exactly, in the train of thought we see in Romans 5.20 and 7—8? Might it not arise because he has seen that *that was what had happened to Israel's representative, the Messiah himself?* According to Romans 8.4, the Messiah himself was the place where, at the climax of Israel's history, sin did its worst – even, with extreme paradox, the sin of his being 'handed over', which was itself the means of the divine 'handing over'![549] – in order that sin itself might then be condemned. I am following Paul's own lead in addressing these issues through a 'what if', because even exegetically, let alone theologically, we would be right to sense here an ocean of possibilities and problems crashing in twenty-foot waves over our heads whichever way we try to swim. But might it not be that Paul, in the years of reflection and debate that have led up to the writing of this extremely careful piece, has determined to approach the new, eschatological question of Israel's election through the question of *the Messiah's own election*, that is, the Messiah's own standing at the point where Israel's history reached its zenith? And might that not be because he saw the Messiah as Israel's representative precisely in terms of the 'servant' figure of Isaiah 52 and 53, as indicated by Romans 10.14–17? This motif of 'hardening', in other words, should not be read as a rejection of Israel, of Israel's specialness, of Israel's call to be the light of the world, the bearer of God's promises to the nations. This is, on the contrary, the way in which that call had to become a reality. That was how it had been with the Messiah himself.

If all this is so (if we at least hold it in our minds as a possibility, before we even look on to 10.4 where Paul says more or less exactly this) then we might glimpse the possibility that the reference to the Messiah being 'from their race according to the flesh' in 9.5 (which echoes the 'of the seed of David according to the flesh' in 1.3, and with the same preliminary, scene-setting intent) would indicate a determination to understand, and to retell, the story of Israel in terms of God's strange plan to work out his worldwide purposes, the long entail of the promises to Abraham. We might glimpse the possibility that God had done this by allowing the people of Israel, not least through Torah, to become the very place where God's condemnation of evil might be seen and known, not for themselves but precisely because they were the 'people of the Messiah'. Might it not be that Paul was determined now to understand the history and purpose of Israel in terms of the Messiah, not only as representative but also as substitute? What if Paul were re-reading the whole history of Israel through the lens of the cross?

[549] cf. the paradox of Ac. 2.23; 3.13; cf. the motif of 'ignorance' in 3.17; and, for Paul's 'handing over' language, Rom. 4.25; 8.32, with their echoes of Isa. 53.12.

If that is so – and what Paul writes next does indeed indicate that we are on the right lines – then we can see a bit more clearly what is going on throughout this whole section. Paul is retelling the story of Israel in such a way as to insist that even the negative side of 'election', the choice of those in whom God's power and wrath would be displayed, had strongly positive intent, just as in chapter 7. And that positive intent is then starting to bubble up from beneath the surface of the story. Paul cannot keep it down at this point. It breaks through: that in the accomplishment of this purpose God would make known the riches of his glory for the vessels of mercy, whom he prepared in advance for glory ... including gentiles among 'those whom he called' – which is, as we saw, a standard way of denoting God's people.[550]

The three main features of 9.6–29 to which I call attention for present purposes, then, are these. First, Paul has retold the story of Israel in such a way that, apart from the surprising inclusion of gentiles as 'returning exiles' in 9.24–6, it would be hard for a well-taught second-Temple Jew to object. Second, however, within the telling of this story Paul has highlighted certain features. He has laid stress on the 'call' which is 'not by works';[551] on the 'hardening' for the purpose of a worldwide proclamation. These then prepare the way for the surprising twist in the narrative at 9.24, grafting (as it were) the wild olive branch of 'gentile inclusion' into the cultivated olive of Israel's own narrative, and doing so in such a way as to leave the gentile Christians themselves fully aware that their status as such has nothing to do with any special virtue in being gentiles and everything to do with the surprising mercy of the God of Israel. That, of course, is precisely the point Paul will develop in chapter 11. And all of this, third, is shaped around the notion that Israel is to be seen as the Messiah's people according to the flesh, sharing his 'casting away' for the sake of the world.

By the end of 9.29, then, Paul has reached the point where God's judgment, precisely upon Israel itself, has produced the paradox that constituted the problem in 9.1–5. God's whittling down of Israel to a small 'remnant', though exactly in line with what the prophets had foretold, has gone far further than a zealous Pharisee would bear to contemplate: that the Messiah has come, and Israel as a whole has rejected him (both in rejecting Jesus himself and in rejecting the apostolic gospel about him). Meanwhile, though Paul has only given one explicit mention of the fact in verse 24, gentiles have been 'called', in line with an extended reading of Hosea 2 in which the rejected northern kingdom serves to represent the wider community of non-Israelites. Verses 24–6 of Romans 9 thus stand in relation to verses 27–9 somewhat as 10.20 does in relation to 10.21, quoting the two halves of Isaiah 65.1:

[550] 'call': see above, and e.g. 9.12: 'not of works but of the one who called'.

[551] Jewett 2007, 600 notes, following several commentators, that in 9.25 Paul has changed the *erō* of LXX Hos. 2.25 to *kalesō*, reversing the clauses in order to do so. Clearly the 'call' was a crucial theme at this point.

gentiles called alongside Jews (9.24–6)	Israel cut down to a remnant (9.27–9)
God revealed to gentiles not looking for him (10.20)	Israel disobedient and contrary (10.21)

In other words – and this is exactly how Paul sums it up in 9.30—10.4 – gentiles, who were not looking for Israel's God, or for the status of membership within his covenant people, have discovered both; while Israel itself, zealous for God and eager for covenant status, has failed to recognize 'the Messiah, who is God over all, blessed for ever'. Israel has thereby failed also to acknowledge, and submit to, 'the righteousness of God', the covenant plan which contained at its heart the darkness of Calvary as well as the bright light of God's presence and ongoing purposes. Indeed, as Romans 1—8 should have made clear, the cross of Jesus the Messiah is actually, for Paul, the place where both the righteousness of God and the love of God are most deeply on display (5.6–11). We should not be surprised, then, at these themes coming together here in just this fashion.

I propose, then, to repeat, that 9.6–29 is best read in three interlocking ways. First, in terms of the Jewish context, it is *a largely non-controversial Jewish presentation of election*, with hints of surprises but nothing more. Second, to an unsuspecting non-Jewish reader it is *a deliberately contentious account of God's justice displayed in ways which the gentile moralist might well think peculiar*, but which is designed to affirm the Jewish doctrine of election, not to undermine it, and to show the gentiles who will be directly addressed in 11.11–32 that their place in the narrative is precisely one of surprising inclusion into Abraham's family and its ongoing history. Third, in and through both of these it is a *christologically formed retelling of Israel's narrative*, drawing on themes developed earlier in the letter in such a way as to highlight God's purpose to save the world through the 'handing over' of the Messiah, Israel's representative, an event which could only come about as the focal point and intentional climax of the divine plan *for Israel itself to experience the covenantal 'casting away' which was, itself, the strange purpose of election.*

In case anybody doubts this – I am sometimes accused of optimism, but at this point I will be realistic – we may note, before turning explicitly to chapter 11, that when Paul sums up the present state of things he does so in exactly this manner: 'by their trespass, salvation has come to the nations; their trespass means riches for the world, their impoverishment means riches for the nations; their casting away means reconciliation for the world'.[552] Paul does not there elaborate exactly what he means, but he appears to be summing up something he has previously said (just as in referring to Jesus' death in 5.12–21 he is referring back to the earlier, fuller accounts in 3.24–6, 4.24–5 and 5.6–11). And the place he appears to have said it is in the long, and biblically anchored, account of election and its

[552] 11.11, 12, 15. See below.

purpose in 9.6–29, focused particularly on the bit that has made so many liberal theologians so alarmed: the potter and the pot, the 'what if God', the revelation of wrath and the making known of God's power. In other words, when in chapter 11 Paul states in a brief form something he apparently thinks he has said already about Israel's 'trespass', 'stumbling', 'casting away' and 'hardening', it is this interpretation of chapter 9 to which he is referring. And, to put the same point the other way round, chapter 11 confirms a *cruciform*, and *redemptive*, reading of the story of Israel's strange elected history in chapter 9.

These references also take us back helpfully, within the larger flow of thought of the letter, to Romans 2. There, the 'wrath' of God was to be poured out against all human unrighteousness and wickedness, the Jew first and also the Greek. But in sketching that picture at that point, Paul also built into his narrative the note of God's *makrothumia*, his 'great-heartedness' or 'patience', and God's 'kindness', delaying the final out-pouring of wrath so that more will reach repentance.[553] This, too, will be a keynote of his resolution of the question in Romans 11, though again not in the way often imagined.

We turn, then, to Romans 11 itself. What is Paul to make of it all?

(e) All Israel Shall Be Saved: Romans 11.1–32

(α) Introduction to Romans 11

We now move to the passage which, by common consent among many commentators, balances out the one we have just studied. This is where the whole argument had been heading all along.

9.1–5 11.33–6
9.6–29 **11.1–32**
9.30–3 10.18–21
10.1–4 10.14–17
10.5–13
10.9

Ahead, the virgin snow: no-one has come this way before. Behind, the only track his stumbling footprints. Questions now are real; his own; not mere rhetorical devices, but driven by the thought, *you can't stay here*. The path must carry on; must lead from tragedy to hope; but hope now wears a human face, that died, and lives. So that's the meaning? 'What will their acceptance be, but life from death?'

[553] 2.4; cf. 2 Pet. 3.9 (and nb. this is the passage about which the author comments that 'our beloved brother Paul' has written, 3.15); Wis. 11.23. The motif of God's patience is traditional: Wis. 15.1; Sir. 18.11; *P. Man.* 7; *4 Ezra* 7.74, 134.

This might have been the counsel he had given to young Onesimus: when you return, be sure you don't look down on those who've come a different route. God has imprisoned all, so all may now receive an equal mercy. It is the advice, or rather the stern warning, that he now gives to the Roman audience, largely gentile (and specifically addressed as such in 11.13). As I have suggested, they have been in view from the start, objecting on apparently moral grounds to the ancient Israelite doctrine of election, only to discover that it was that doctrine which came to its head in the Messiah himself. The attempt to get the messianic result without the underlying theology of election is the story of many theological wrong turns over the last two millennia.

This is the point at which we must firmly resist, on cast-iron exegetical grounds, the suggestion of Krister Stendahl and others: that Paul is asserting that God has now changed his plans.[554] The whole point of chapters 9 and 10 has been to *deny* that God had changed his plans, and to say, instead: this is in fact what had been planned, promised and envisaged all along, even though nobody in Israel (certainly not Saul of Tarsus!) had ever seen it like that before. After all, nobody in Israel had imagined a crucified Messiah. Paul has rethought the doctrine of election around the Messiah, and is now reworking Israel's vision of the future on the same basis. In doing so he has been careful precisely *not* to allow anyone to say that he has invented a new 'doctrine of election'. Verses 6–29 of chapter 9 are, as we have seen, a standard Jewish presentation, save only the intruding note about gentiles in verse 24. But the point is that 'the plan of God', in most Jewish thought, led up to the Messiah and no further. Those second-Temple Jews who believed that a Messiah would come had various overlapping ideas about what he would do. But apart from the strange vision in *4 Ezra* 7, written a generation after Paul and, more importantly, some time after the disaster of AD 70, most people simply assumed that with the Messiah God's perfect world would be ushered in, with Israel in particular rescued, vindicated, sharing his worldwide rule. So, granted that Paul believes Jesus to be the Messiah, and granted that things have not worked out at all like that, something must be said about this new and unexpected post-messianic situation. But what? To stop at the end of chapter 10, however well grounded that might have been in Isaiah and Deuteronomy, would hardly be satisfactory – especially in view of what he takes to be the situation in Rome. So Paul, out on his own, tramps off into uncharted territory, exploring what might now be said if this was truly how the covenant had been fulfilled, how Israel's election had played itself out. This is where eschatology must be freshly envisaged in the light of the reworking, through Messiah and spirit, of monotheism and election themselves.

If the covenant and the election were to be understood on the basis of the Messiah and his death, what then? That is the question, I suggest, which dominated his mind as he explored the previously unimagined problem of

[554] Stendahl 1976, 28.

an eschatology inaugurated by a crucified Messiah and not yet completed. And among the key elements of Romans 11 which have themselves not been highlighted, I mention for the moment only one: that whereas earlier in the letter Paul affirmed the role of Israel as the people called to be God's instruments in the plan of world salvation (2.17–24), so in this passage – perfectly consistently with 9.30–1! – he places *gentile Christians* in the equivalent position. What has happened to the Jews has been instrumental in their salvation; now, in turn, what is happening to them is happening for the sake of Israel (11.11–14, 30–1). This theme, pregnant with significance for the meaning of the passage as a whole, has not received the attention it deserves.

The main divisions of chapter 11, like those of its balancing chapter 9, are not particularly difficult to discern. The questions which Paul asks in verses 1 and 11 set the terms, and he appears to take a deep breath at verse 24 before plunging into verses 25–32. Within verses 11–24 many have discerned a smaller shift of direction, either at verse 17 or, as I prefer, at verse 16.[555] As we have done with Romans 9—11 as a whole, starting at the centre point and working outwards, I propose to begin here too at the middle, with 11.13–15, working outwards to 11.11–12 and 11.16–24, which tell a very similar story, before adding 11.1–10. We shall then review the whole of 11.1–24 before proceeding at last, with proper awe, to the 'mystery' of 11.25–32. The reason for this is partly to be sure we are paying attention to the way Paul has written the chapter, but also to be sure that when we arrive at 25–32 we do so with as full as possible an awareness of what has been said so far.

(β) The Centre: 11.13–15

We begin, then, at the centre:

11.1–10 11.25–32

11.11–12 11.16–24

11.13–15

At the heart of 11.1–32, and at the climax of this central mini-section, we find the statement which most obviously echoes things that Paul has said elsewhere about the Messiah. Here is the whole central passage:

> Now I am speaking to you gentiles. Insofar as I am the apostle of the gentiles, I celebrate my particular ministry, so that, if possible, I can make 'my flesh' jealous, and save some of them. If their casting away, you see, means reconciliation for the world, what will their acceptance mean but life from the dead?[556]

[555] See Aletti 2012, 139–71, and the discussion of options in Jewett 2007, 668, 671f. Keck 2005, 262 proposes, unusually, that the first section continues to v. 12.

[556] 11.13–15.

This, I suggest, is central to the appeal which Paul is making throughout the chapter. To put it in christological shorthand, relating back as Paul clearly intends to the advance statement in 9.5: if 9.6–29 expounds what it means that Israel is the Messiah's people 'according to the flesh', and if 9.30—10.13 expounds what it means that God has renewed the covenant in the faith in the one who is 'the same lord of all' (10.12), 11.1–32 now expounds what it means that Israel is called to be part of the people of the risen Messiah, who is 'God over all, blessed for ever'.[557] If Paul has been determined to rethink Israel's election in the light of Jesus the Messiah, it is only to be expected that he would make such a move as this as he explains what this will mean eschatologically.

We need to be clear just how striking 11.15 really is in its evocation of earlier language in Romans about Jesus and his redemptive work.[558] Here we have

> If their casting away means reconciliation for the world
> (*ei gar hē apobolē autōn katallagē kosmou*)
> What will their acceptance mean but life from the dead?
> (*tis hē proslēmpsis ei mē zōē ek nekrōn*)

The last time we met language like that, it was in the triumphant christological summary in 5.10, in a similar *a fortiori* argument:

> When we were enemies, we were reconciled to God through the death of his Son
> (*ei gar echthroi ontes katēllagēmen tō theō dia tou thanatou tou hyiou autou*)
> how much more, having already been reconciled, shall we be saved by his life?
> (*pollō mallon katallagentes sōthēsometha en tē zōē autou*)[559]

Chapter 5 has a good claim to be the driving heart, not only of chapters 1—8, but of the whole epistle. We should not, in other words, be surprised at the echo. What is striking, though, is to find this christological emphasis here: if Israel has embodied the *casting away* of the Messiah, Israel will now find a way to share his *resurrection* as well.[560] And the word Paul uses for the way by which they will get there is *proslēmpsis*, 'acceptance'. Like

[557] This places a question beside Keck's proposal (2005, 228f.) that the punctuation and meaning of the final clause in 9.5 is as it were independent of the larger context.

[558] Here I repeat, but also amplify, material from Wright 1980 ['Messiah and People of God'], 181f., 1991 [*Climax*], 247f., and esp. 2002 [*Romans*], 681–3, and hope to respond to Jewett 2007, 674 n. 70, who suggests that my proposal lacks a basis. At 681 Jewett notes the parallel with 5.10–11 (which is the 'basis' in question), but turns aside to the theme of 'global reconciliation' in the Roman civic cult, which is indeed important but should not obscure the interconnections of Paul's own writing. Bell 1994, 111f. (and 2005, 247f.) objects to my proposal on the grounds that 'Israel's casting aside is quite different to the casting aside of the Messiah', since the one happens because of disobedience but the other through obedience. That is actually the point and the paradox: Paul is treating Israel precisely as the Messiah's people *according to the flesh*, the place where the Adamic and messianic identities are held together.

[559] For the theme of 'reconciliation', *katallagē*, cf. too 2 Cor. 5.19; Col. 1.19f.

[560] This is exactly the point made by Hays 1989a, 61: 'What Paul has done . . . is to interpret the fate of Israel christologically . . . Israel undergoes rejection for the sake of the world, bearing suffering vicariously.' I should perhaps stress that this is a significantly different interpretation from that of Barth 1936–69, 2.2.278f. (followed cautiously by Cranfield 1979, 556), for whom Israel's 'stumble' was the handing over of Jesus to crucifixion, through which event 'reconciliation' was effected.

apobolē, this is a general word in 'secular' use,[561] presumably because Paul does not want at the moment to commit himself to more technical language about either element of the narrative. But the overall point should be clear: in order to discern how to move forwards within the uncharted theological territory in which he finds himself, the one clear signpost is that if Israel, as the Messiah's people, have lived through the historical equivalent of his crucifixion, being 'cast away for the reconciliation of the world', then *we should expect some equivalent of the resurrection.* This expectation grounds and sustains the hope held out in chapter 11. The Messiah is Israel's representative, summing up his people in himself, so that what is true of him is true of them. That was part of the reason why Paul said what he did in 9.5. Paul has worked out, earlier in the letter, what it means that all who belong to the Messiah inherit the blessings promised to Abraham. Now he is working out what it means that the Messiah's own people according to the flesh are just that, 'his own people according to the flesh'. And, at the heart of this, he has *endorsed not only Israel's election but also the purpose of that election in bringing about worldwide salvation.* This takes us back, in Romans, to 2.17–24; and, in Israel's own scriptures, to Genesis 12 and Isaiah 49. Paul is neither denying the election of Israel as the focal point of God's worldwide saving plan nor reducing it to a secondary place. He is interpreting it in the light of the Messiah's death, in order to find a way forward to an equally reinterpreted eschatological hope. He is not abandoning traditional Jewish eschatology. He is redefining it, too, around the Messiah.

He has not yet said what all this will mean. We would be rash to suppose that by *zōē ek nekrōn* he means 'resurrection' here in a simple sense, corresponding to 8.10–11, in other words their own future bodily resurrection. That, to be sure, might be involved. The case is often made. According to this view, there will be a large-scale conversion of Jews, perhaps of all Jews then alive (or even of all Jews who have ever lived, by some means or other), either at the time of the general resurrection or (as it would appear from the present passage) immediately prior to that event. The resurrection, in turn, as we know from 1 Thessalonians 4 and 1 Corinthians 15, was expected at the time of Jesus' final 'appearing' and the great cosmic renewal spoken of in Romans 8.18–26. But there are strong reasons to resist this interpretation of 11.15.

First, 'life from the dead' is of course what Paul describes as the effect of baptism itself. Those who are baptized are 'dead to sin and alive to God'.[562] Since what the present passage envisages is presently unbelieving Jews joining the 'remnant' of which Paul himself is a part, that might well be his meaning. Such Jews, coming for baptism, would be a fresh revelation of this 'life from the dead'.

Second, more specifically, this is the language Paul uses of himself as a Jew in his 'dying to the law' and 'living to God'. This is what it meant for

[561] *apobolē* = 'throwing away' or 'loss' (see Jewett 2007, 680 nn. 141–3); *proslēmpsis* = 'accepting back' or 'welcome' (Jewett 2007, 681).

[562] Rom. 6.11.

him, already a member of Abraham's family according to the flesh, to come to belong to the Messiah: 'I through the Torah died to Torah, that I might live to God; I am crucified with the Messiah – nevertheless I am alive, yet not I, but the Messiah who lives in me.'[563]

Third, again more specifically, Paul speaks of 'life from the dead' in Romans 4 in relation to Abraham's promised family. In 4.17, as is often noted, he indicates that God is both the one who 'raises the dead' and the one who 'calls into existence things that do not exist'. This is often taken as a reference to those who move from unbelief to faith, first the Jews (being raised from their 'dead' state within Abraham's family) and then the gentiles who are, as it were, created out of nothing. Such Jews, coming from death to life, are regular Messiah-people, not yet physically raised from the dead but brought, like Paul in the passage just mentioned, through the 'death with the Messiah' to a new 'life with God' – just as the 'children' promised to Abraham in Genesis 15 were ordinary children, born through the gift of life to his and Sarah's 'good-as-dead' bodies (4.18–21), not children who had been born, died and then been raised from the dead in that sense.

Fourth, Paul is here, in any case, at a particular point in the spiral argument of the letter, and is talking here about a *national*, corporate, 'casting away' and 'receiving back'.

It is, then, not only possible but probable that in 11.15 Paul is saying that when, in the present time, during the course of his gentile mission and as a result of the 'jealousy' this has aroused, more of his '[kinsfolk according to the] flesh' come to believe in and confess Jesus as the risen Messiah and lord, this will be a further sign to the whole body of Messiah-people of God's power to raise the dead, with all the excitement and celebration that would evoke. He might also mean that the arrival of more Jewish Messiah-believers would impart something of a new lease of life to the *ekklēsia*, a new dimension which a mostly gentile community would lack.

Whether some such explanation is on target, one thing is sure: verse 15 *explains* verse 14 (*gar*), and must then somehow be correlated with 'and save some of them'. It is not meant to be a new, different or larger point. The new term *proslēmpsis* must refer back to *kai sōsō tinas ex autōn*: it is the 'saving some of them', in other words, that is picked up by the 'what will their acceptance mean'. This would not of itself rule out the possibility that Paul had in mind two different (though related) events, first the steady coming-to-faith of 'some' Jews during the course of his own gentile ministry as a result of 'jealousy', and second a larger-scale conversion of Jews at the time of, or as the signal for, the general resurrection. But what he has written up to this point gives no suggestion whatever of the latter, which has to be read back into the present passage, if at all, from verses 25–7, to which we shall come later on. The high probability then seems to be that whenever one or more Jews become 'jealous', and turn in faith to the God

[563] Gal. 2.19–20.

who has now revealed his covenant plan and purpose in the Messiah (10.1–13), that event ought to be understood by the church, particularly its gentile members, not as a peculiar or even unwelcome event but as another bit of 'resurrection', to be celebrated as such. As in 2 Corinthians 3, where Paul has to *argue* that his ministry is a revelation of 'glory' (which is, at first sight, bizarre; arguing that glory has been revealed is rather like arguing that the sun has risen – either you can see it or you can't; but Paul's point is that it is the hidden glory of God seen in the face of Jesus the suffering Messiah, and that the apparent invisibility is due to the blind eyes of the observers), so here Paul has to *argue*, against those who would see the coming-to-faith of more Jews as unnecessary and undesirable, that such an event is part of inaugurated eschatology: 'life from the dead', happening here and now.

When we place verse 15 into the context of verses 13 and 14, which it is designed to explain, we see more clearly what is going on. The whole of chapters 9—11 is aimed rhetorically at a gentile audience, trying to get them to see that what has happened to God's ancient people was all along part of the divine plan, and that they themselves, so far from 'replacing' Israel in that plan, should count themselves fortunate to be incorporated into it.[564] Now Paul makes explicit what was implicit before, and homes in on the point of the whole section:

> [13]Now I am speaking to you gentiles. Insofar as I am the apostle of the gentiles, I celebrate my particular ministry, [14]so that, if possible, I can make my 'flesh' jealous (*hina parazēlōsō mou tēn sarka*), and save some of them.[565]

He is talking about the *salvation* of 'some of them', some of the presently unbelieving Jews. This relates directly, of course, to the question he raised in his agonized prayer of 10.1: How will God *save* them? According to 10.2–13, he will do it by renewing the covenant, as foretold by Moses himself in Deuteronomy 30, a passage drawn on by other second-Temple Jews for exactly this purpose. Paul's interpretation of it is that the covenant is renewed in and for those who confess that Jesus is lord and believe that God raised him from the dead: such people, whether Jew or gentile (10.12), will be both 'justified' and 'saved'. When therefore he speaks of 'saving some of them' here in 11.14, we are bound to conclude that this is what he has in mind, not because Paul is after all the apostle to the Jews as well as the gentiles (we remember, as Paul undoubtedly did, the division of labour in Galatians 2.7–9), but because his gentile ministry itself will 'make them jealous' and thus 'save some of them'.[566]

[564] So, rightly, Keck 2005, 275: 'Inclusion ... is *not* replacement' (italics original).

[565] 11.13–14.

[566] Baker 2005, 170–3 proposes that there is no causal connection between 'making them jealous' and 'saving some of them', since *parazēlōsō* really means 'stirring up zeal', which would lead away from faith in Jesus, not towards it. He is right that the translations have had to add 'so' (NEB) or 'thus' (NRSV) to make the point; Paul's text simply reads 'so that I may make my flesh jealous and save some of them.' But I find it impossible thus to separate the two halves of v. 14, where *ei pōs* introduces both verbs, with the thought leading easily on to 'save', and with 'some of them' indicating a positive relationship with 'make ... jealous'. Had Paul been intending (why?) to make *some* 'jealous' in the sense of 'angry, stirred to zeal',

The word 'some' seems to imply a small ambition. Why not all of them? Is that not what he will go on to say in 11.26? But the 'some' here corresponds to the realistic conclusion to 1 Corinthians 9.22: I became all things to all people, so that I might by all means save *some*. One or two manuscripts of the latter passage could not resist making Paul say what the demands of rhetoric might have suggested, 'so that I might by all means save *all*', *tois pasin gegona panta, hina pantōs pantas sōsō.*[567] But Paul does not say that, there or here.

That is an important first comment. But two other things stand out. First, the means by which Paul will 'save some of them' is through their *jealousy*. This is the motif which goes back to Deuteronomy 32.21, quoted in 10.19: 'I will make you jealous with a non-nation.'[568] In other words, God will – as Moses warned! – bring in people who are not from Israel, people who will then share 'the sonship, the glory, the covenants' and so on, and who will thus make Israel itself realize the result of turning away from God, failing to submit to his righteousness and refusing to believe in the messianic good news. The note of 'jealousy', in other words, echoes back through chapter 9, in particular in 9.4–5. This is the force of what has happened throughout Romans so far: Israel's vocation and privilege has been focused on the Messiah, and has then, 'in him', been given to all who believe, to the Jew first and also to the Greek. That then drives the lament of 9.1–5. Paul has already located this initially surprising phenomenon (Jews missing out, gentiles coming in) on the map of ancient prophecy (9.30–3; 10.14–21). Now he interprets it, in this light, to mean that his own ministry among the gentiles has a deeper, secondary purpose. It is not simply about bringing gentiles into Abraham's single, believing family. It is 'to make my flesh jealous and so save some of them'.

It has been speculated that this 'making my flesh jealous' may have been part of the point of the Collection to which Paul devoted so much time and effort, and whose final stages are envisaged in 15.25–28. Perhaps he thought that, by bringing money from gentile churches to help the poor Messiah-community in Jerusalem, this would stir up 'jealousy' among the non-Messiah-believing Jerusalemites. That seems to me somewhat more convoluted than the programme envisaged in 11.11–14, though a connection is not impossible. Others have speculated that the proposed mission to Spain was designed with this 'jealousy' in mind: if people from the ends of the earth, as Spain was considered to be, were to hail Israel's Messiah and join the community of his followers, maybe this would be the trigger for a larger-scale 'jealousy' and so a larger-scale 'salvation', and perhaps even the *parousia* itself. This has sometimes been linked with the idea of the 'pilgrim-

and to bring *others* to faith and salvation, I think he would have written the sentence quite differently. See too 11.31, where the *hina* implies the same kind of connection.

567 The western tradition of MSS. (DFG latt), and 33, have *pantas* for *tinas* (Did[pt]. Cl. and 33 add *tous* before *pantas*). Note too the next verse which begins *panta de poiō*. See the fuller note by Robertson and Plummer 1914 [1911], 193; Fee 1987, 422.

568 See the full study of Bell 1994.

age of the nations to Zion', though it is striking that Paul makes virtually no use of that tradition, no doubt because he sees the whole Zion tradition itself radically redrawn around the Messiah.[569] Here too I think we must be cautious, though in view of what Paul actually says in 11.13–14 we must allow that both the Collection and the planned Spanish mission, being key elements in Paul's gentile apostolate, must have been part of what he had in mind. I suspect, though, that Paul is not only thinking of his own *future* gentile-apostleship work, but of that which he had already accomplished: 'I magnify my ministry' need not refer only to things still unaccomplished. It refers more naturally to things he *has* already done, as in 15.15–21:

> [15]But I have written to you very boldly at some points, calling things to your mind through the grace which God has given me [16]to enable me to be a minister of King Jesus for the nations, working in the priestly service of God's good news, so that the offering of the nations may be acceptable, sanctified in the holy spirit.
>
> [17]This is the glad confidence I have in King Jesus, and in God's own presence. [18]Far be it from me, you see, to speak about anything except what the Messiah has accomplished through me for the obedience of the nations, in word and deed, [19]in the power of signs and wonders, in the power of God's spirit. I have completed announcing the good news of the Messiah from Jerusalem round as far as Illyricum. [20]My driving ambition has been to announce the good news in places where the Messiah has not been named, so that I can avoid building on anyone else's foundation. [21]Instead, as the Bible says,
>
> People who hadn't been told about him will see;
> People who hadn't heard will understand.

It is in this light that we must read 11.15, with its promise not only of a different future for presently unbelieving Israel, but of a greater future for the gentile Messiah-people as a result:

> If their casting away, you see, means reconciliation for the world, what will their acceptance mean but life from the dead?

This makes more explicit what was hinted at in 11.12, 'how much more will their fullness mean!'. Granted, this is all still quite deliberately vague. Paul is not spreading out a detailed map of what is going to happen next; he is cautiously pointing ahead in the dark towards uncharted territory. This is how his reimagined eschatology comes about.

From all this there emerge two points of particular relevance for our present study. First, Paul has given a fresh and positive role to the newly converted gentile believers. Their very existence will be the means of making his 'flesh' jealous and bringing some of them to salvation. In other words, the gentile Messiah-people are now, themselves, *elect for the sake of others*. Israel was elect for the sake of the world; that election has been focused on the Messiah; gentile believers have come to share in the Messiah's life and identity; so now, with complete consistency though with daring innovation,

[569] For the proposal, see e.g. Aus 1979; Bell 1994, 337–46 (including discussion of Aus, 345f.). This is a modification of the earlier theory of Munck 1959 [1954]; see ch. 16 below. Note the important response of e.g. Cranfield 1979, 766–8; Best 1984, 21f.: Paul cannot have been ignorant of the many other lands to east, north and south which remained unevangelized.

Paul declares that *gentile believers* now play a role, simply by being who they are, in an entirely new and previously unimagined phase of the divine eschatological purpose. Just as Israel had to be reminded of a still-controversial point, that the ancient scriptures themselves saw their own election as being for the sake of God's saving purposes for the wider world (and that those same scriptures saw them as having failed in that elective purpose[570]), so gentile Christians now need to be reminded that their own status, as the new and surprising addition to God's covenant family, is not for their own sake, but so that through their very existence, now, God will confront his ancient people with the challenge: Look, strangers are inheriting your promises; are you not jealous? We are back once more with the older brother in Luke 15.

Throughout, as in chapter 9, Paul insists that this is not a change of plan on God's part. It is the new, further, surprising, unexpected revelation of a previously unthought-of mystery – unthought-of because the question to which it was the answer, or at least *an* answer, had never been asked, could never have been asked, prior to this moment.

Second, when Paul speaks here of 'making my flesh jealous', *hina parazēlōsō mou tēn sarka*, flattened out in so many translations into 'my fellow Jews' or some such,[571] we should hear once again the resonances of chapter 7, filtered through 9.4 ('my brothers, my kinsfolk *kata sarka*, according to the flesh') and 9.5 ('of their race, *kata sarka*, according to the flesh, is the Messiah'). We recall the sequence of 7.5—8.11:

> 5For when we were living **in the flesh** (*hote gar ēmen en tē sarki*), the passions of sins which were through the law were at work in our limbs and organs, causing us to bear fruit for death . . .
>
> 14We know, you see, that the law is spiritual. I, however, am **made of flesh** (*sarkinos eimi*), sold as a slave under sin's authority. 15I don't understand what I do. I don't do what I want, you see, but I do what I hate. 16So if I do what I don't want to do, I am agreeing that the law is good.
>
> 17But now it is no longer I that do it; it's sin, living within me. 18I know, you see, that no good thing lives in me, that is, **in my human flesh** (*en tē sarki mou*). For I can will the good, but I can't perform it. 19For I don't do the good thing I want to do, but I end up doing the evil thing I don't want to do. 20So if I do what I don't want to do, it's no longer 'I' doing it; it's sin, living inside me . . .
>
> So then, left to my own self I am enslaved to God's law with my mind, but to sin's law **with my human flesh** (*tē de sarki*).
>
> 1So, therefore, there is no condemnation for those in the Messiah, Jesus! 2Why not? Because the law of the spirit of life in the Messiah, Jesus, released you from the law of sin and death.
>
> 3For God has done what the law (being weak **because of human flesh** (*dia tēs sarkos*)) was incapable of doing. God sent his own Son **in the likeness of sinful flesh** (*en tō homoiōmati tēs sarkos hamartias*), and as a sin-offering; and, right there **in the flesh** (*en tē sarki*), he condemned sin. 4This was in order that the right and proper verdict of the law could be fulfilled in us, as we live **not according to the flesh** (*ou kata sarka*) but according to the spirit.

570 Rom. 2.17–24.

571 So RSV. cf. NRSV 'my own people'; NJB 'my own blood-relations'; REB 'those of my own race'.

> [5]Look at it like this. People whose lives are **determined by human flesh** (*hoi gar kata sarka ontes*) focus their minds on **matters to do with the flesh** (*ta tēs sarkos phronousin*), but people whose lives are determined by the spirit focus their minds on matters to do with the spirit. [6]**Focus the mind on the flesh** (*to phronēma tēs sarkos*), and you'll die; but focus it on the spirit, and you'll have life, and peace. [7]The mind **focused on the flesh** (*to phronēma tēs sarkos*), you see, is hostile to God. It doesn't submit to God's law; in fact, it can't. [8]Those who are **determined by the flesh** (*hoi de en sarki ontes*) can't please God.
>
> [9]But you're **not people of flesh** (*hymeis de ouk este en sarki*); you're people of the spirit (if indeed God's spirit lives within you; note that anyone who doesn't have the spirit of the Messiah doesn't belong to him). [10]But if the Messiah is in you, the body is indeed dead because of sin, but the spirit is life because of covenant justice. [11]So, then, if the spirit of the one who raised Jesus from the dead lives within you, the one who raised the Messiah from the dead will give life to your mortal bodies, too, through his spirit who lives within you.

The parallel sometimes observed between *autos egō* in 7.25 and the same phrase in 9.3 appears, after all, to be more significant than might have been imagined.[572] Once again, Paul is not making the *identical* point in 9—11 to that which he made in chapter 7. He is not simply repeating himself in somewhat different terms. He is moving on, up to the next level of the spiral of argument, to say that what was worked out on the ground plan of chapters 7 and 8 is now being implemented one floor above. We already observed an interesting family resemblance between 9.30—10.4 and 7.7—8.4. Now we discern a further similarity, in that the problem to be addressed is highlighted in terms of 'flesh', and the solution is seen in terms of 'resurrection':

> What the Torah could not do in that it was 'weak because of **the flesh**', God has done . . . so you are not in the flesh, you are in the Spirit . . . and God will give **life** to your mortal bodies through his Spirit.
>
> . . . so that I may make '**my flesh**' jealous, and so save some of them; for if their casting away means life for the world, what will their acceptance be if not **life from the dead**?

So what does Paul mean this time round? Apparently this: just as God, through the Messiah, has dealt with the problem of 'flesh', because of which the Torah produced 'sin' (chapter 7), so he has now dealt with the further problem of Israel's 'descent according to the flesh' (9.8), because of which the Torah produced the zeal for 'their own righteousness' (9.31; 10.3). Thus, just as the divine solution to the original problem resulted in 'resurrection' (8.9–11), so the fresh configuration leads to a fresh divine solution (11.15): a 'resurrection', in terms of their being 'received back again' (*proslēmpsis*), welcomed back into the one people of God, the single family of Abraham.

Here is Paul's central answer to the question, What now? The template of the Messiah's redemptive work, as set out in chapters 7 and 8 (which is itself drawing further conclusions from the earlier argument of chapters 3 and 4, not to mention the very similar material in Galatians), provides the answer

[572] See Wright 2002 [*Romans*], 628.

to the question which had to be faced at the end of chapter 10. The Messiah himself has 'revealed' the 'mystery' of God's plan, not only the plan that led to the messianic events of Jesus' death and resurrection but the plan that now leads forwards, pointing into the otherwise unknown future for gentile and Jew alike. And part of the clue, again with echoes back to the end of Romans 2, is that the very existence of gentile Messiah-believers, receiving mercy from the God of Israel, has an unexpected but crucial significance in the divine purpose. This is a further sign of the eschatological redefinition of election. Those who are 'in the Messiah', even as gentile newcomers, are now themselves bearers of the promise and the purpose for what is still to come. This is at the heart of Paul's reimagined eschatology.

(γ) 11.11–12

We pull the camera back this time from 11.13–15, and consider the passages on either side. First, 11.11–12:

11.1–10 | **11.11–12** | 11.13–15 | 11.16–24 | 11.25–32

Here, in the sequence of thought of Paul's actual letter (as opposed to the way we are coming at it, working outwards from the middle) we find the second key question of the chapter. If Paul asked at 11.1, in effect, whether *any* Jews at all could be saved, and gave a strong 'yes, of course' (see below), he here asks whether any *more* Jews can be saved. 'Have they tripped up in such a way as to fall completely?' We must remind ourselves constantly (despite the shrill chorus of those who want to find here a grand statement about 'the scope of salvation') that Paul is not after all writing a systematic treatise, but a *letter* to a *largely gentile church* in Rome, where he strongly suspects that some are tempted to say that God has finished with the Jews, so that from now on Jesus' people will consist of gentiles only. Paul is, in other words, *opposing* any idea of 'replacing' the ancient people of God with a new gentile body. The irony of much recent study of Romans 11 is that while Paul is attacking what with hindsight we may see as an early form of Marcionism, of 'replacement' theology, people who expound his attack on that viewpoint find themselves accused of 'supersessionism' or, yes, 'replacement' or 'substitution' theology.[573] Paul's whole point is to say, *Yes: Jews can still be saved.* If he had wanted to say, 'Well, no, at the moment Jews can't be saved, but they all will be at the end,' he would have written

[573] Stowers 1994, 313 suggests that Barrett's exegesis here is controlled by 'the narrative of gentile Christianity's supersession of the Jews as the people of God'. One does not have to agree with everything Barrett says to find this charge extraordinary. Bell 1994, 3f. suggests that 'behind' my own view there lies 'the theory that the Church has taken on Israel's role, and Israel is disinherited'. Let the present chapter, and book, serve as the answer: my view is that, for Paul, *the crucified and risen Jesus of Nazareth is Israel's Messiah.* All else follows from this.

11.11–24 very differently, or perhaps not at all. Such a view would not have functioned as a warning against present gentile arrogance.

We spoke a moment ago of the parallels between 11.15 and Romans 5, and verse 11b offers another one. In 5.12–21 the trespass of Adam caused the problem that was then overcome by the rescue-operation of the Messiah. Here it is the 'trespass' of *Israel*, acting out (exactly in as in 5.20 and 7.7–12) that primordial Adamic 'stumble', but with remarkably different results. Here is Adam's 'trespass' in chapter 5:

> 17For if, by the **trespass** of the one (*tō tou henos paraptōmati*), death reigned through that one, how much more will those who receive the abundance of grace, and of the gift of covenant membership, of 'being in the right', reign in life through the one man Jesus the Messiah.[574]

And then, immediately, a further explanation:

> 18So, then, just as, through the **trespass** of one person (*di' henos paraptōmatos*), the result was condemnation for all people, even so, through the upright act of one person, the result is justification – life for all people.[575]

And then, almost at once, the placing of Torah (and hence of Israel) on this Adamic map:

> 20The law came in alongside, so that the **trespass** might be filled out to its full extent (*hina pleonasē to paraptōma*). But where sin increased, grace also superabounded . . .[576]

In terms of Romans 5—8, this is part of the 'problem': Israel, clinging to Torah for dear life (7.10), found that, through the presence of sin, the only result was death. That 'problem' is then addressed in 8.1–11, clearing the way for the 'new exodus' and 'inheritance' of 8.12–30.

But in terms of Romans 9—11, the *paraptōma* of Israel can now be seen in a different light. Israel's acting out of Adam's 'trespass' *has itself had redemptive consequences*, and, in addition, the next stage of Israel's journey will have a 'so much more' flavour to it:

> Have they tripped up in such a way as to fall completely? Certainly not! Rather, by their **trespass** (*tō autōn paraptōmati*), salvation has come to the nations, in order to make them jealous. 12If their **trespass** means riches for the world (*ei de to paraptōma autōn ploutos kosmou*), and their impoverishment means riches for the nations, how much more will their fullness mean![577]

There is only one explanation for this, and it is the spectacular one we glimpsed when we glanced ahead to the present passage from 9.6–29. Israel's 'fall' is precisely the fall of *the Messiah's people according to the flesh*. It therefore, remarkably, shares something of the redemptive quality of the

[574] 5.17.
[575] 5.18.
[576] 5.20.
[577] 11.11–12.

Messiah's crucifixion.[578] Paul says as much in summing up the whole argument towards the close of the chapter: 'you [gentiles] have now received mercy *through their disobedience*'.[579] That, indeed, linking back to 11.11–12, is a further sign that the 'mystery' revealed in 11.25–6 is not a new idea, discontinuous with the rest of the chapter, but is the new idea which is being expounded all the way from 11.11 to 11.32.[580]

Here, moreover, is a further unexpected meaning to Paul's representative claim in Galatians 2.19, *Christō synestaurōmai*, 'I am crucified with the Messiah'. Nowhere else has Paul even hinted at this fuller redemptive significance of the 'stumble' of Israel. Now at last we see where his sharp-edged, and often controversial, 'doctrine of election' in Romans 9 was going. This was never an abstract 'doctrine of predestination', attempting to plumb the mysteries of why some people (in general, without reference to Israel) hear and believe the gospel and others do not. Paul never encourages speculation of that sort. Rather, it was a way of saying, very specifically, that the fact of Israel's election (starting with the choice and call of Abraham) had always been there to deal with the sin of the world; that Israel's election had always involved Israel being narrowed down, not just to Isaac and then to Jacob, but to a *hypoleimma*, a 'remnant', a 'seed'; and that this 'remnant' itself would be narrowed down to a single point, to the Messiah himself, *who would himself be 'cast away' so that the world might be redeemed.* The point of 'election' was not to choose or call a people who would somehow mysteriously escape either the grim entail of Adam's sin or the results it brought in its train. It was not – as in some low-grade proposals! – about God simply choosing a people to be his close friends. The point was to choose and call a people through whom the sin of humankind, and its results for the whole creation, might be brought to the point where that sin, and those results, could at last be defeated, condemned, overcome. Hence the line that runs, in Romans, from 3.24–6 to 8.3–4 and on to 10.3–4, backed up by the summaries in 5.6–11 and 5.12–21. Here is the faithfulness of the Messiah, which discloses, unveils, *apocalypticizes*, the righteousness of God, God's covenant faithfulness.

Where has this brought us? Deuteronomy 32, a vital passage for Paul not least in Romans, spoke of God's 'degenerate children' as having 'dealt falsely with him'.[581] What Paul has shown, through the long-range outworking of the Messiah's death and resurrection, is that *even that falsehood has redounded to God's glory and the work of salvation*. This is not something other than what he was saying in 3.2–3. The Israelites were 'entrusted' with God's oracles, but if some proved unfaithful, that cannot nullify God's faithfulness, for God will be true even if every human is false. In other words, God will work *through Israel* for the salvation of the world, even though

[578] The idea of others sharing in the Messiah's sufferings, and of those extended 'messianic' sufferings having positive consequences, is of course not new in Paul: see e.g. 2 Cor. 4.7–15; Col. 1.24.

[579] 11.30.

[580] So e.g. Wagner 2010, 429: Paul 'only states plainly what he has been arguing all along'.

[581] Dt. 32.5.

Israel as a whole will turn away. What's more, indeed, God will work *through Israel's large-scale turning away* for the salvation of the world! This, Paul is saying, is what has now been accomplished. The glimpses of chapters 9—11 which could be seen in the questions of 3.1–9 have finally yielded up their secrets. Only when Romans is understood as a tightly composed symphonic whole can its various parts be understood.

For Paul, therefore, this is the key to, and the guarantee of, a further turn in the road, a new possibility, the possibility and indeed the promise that Israel has not after all 'stumbled so as to fall'. The disbelief, the rejection of the Messiah, the failure to acknowledge and submit to 'God's righteousness' in the electing purpose from Abraham onwards and all the way to the Messiah, and even the futile attempts of some of Paul's contemporaries to stand in the way of the gentile mission – all this has in fact turned out for 'the salvation of the nations'. Their 'trespass', he repeats with a different metaphor, has meant 'riches for the world' and their loss (*hēttēma*) has meant 'riches for the nations'.[582] What then will their *plērōma* mean?

As with *apobolē* and *proslēmpsis* in 11.15, so with *plērōma* here in 11.12: it is not at all clear what exactly Paul has in mind, and he probably intended it that way. Eschatology, even messianically revised eschatology, is all about peering ahead into the darkness, believing in certain clear fixed points but not being able to say what exactly will happen next. He is not going to make any predictions about whether God will save a myriad of his presently unbelieving fellow Israelites, or somewhat less; only (a) that he will save 'some', in other words considerably more than at present, (b) that this will count as a 'fullness', *plērōma*, and (c) that this will be the full extension of the small but growing 'remnant' of which he, Paul, is himself a part. But here, though this is not so often noticed, Paul hints at something else, something beyond even the *plērōma* or the *proslēmpsis* of his kinsfolk according to the flesh: there will be a 'how much more' in terms of benefits for the gentiles as well. Just as the Messiah's death won great blessings, but his resurrection even more so (5.10), so if Israel's 'diminution' has brought blessings to the world, their 'fullness' will mean something more, something Paul does not name except in the language of resurrection (11.15), which as we have seen itself remains, perhaps deliberately, ambiguous if evocative.

It thus appears that 11.12 draws together *both* the 'Adamic' parallel, whereby Israel acts out Adam's trespass, *and* the christological one, whereby Israel acts out the Messiah's death and resurrection. This, I suggest, contains Paul's basic answer to the new eschatological question that he faces in Romans 11. It fits exactly with the rhetorical thrust of the whole section, aimed at potentially cynical or even 'anti-Jewish' gentile Messiah-believers in Rome. The call of gentiles now places those ex-pagan believers into a

[582] *hēttēma* is very rare: according to LSJ, it is only found elsewhere in Isa. 31.8 LXX; 1 Cor. 6.7, with the meaning 'an utter loss' (see e.g. Keck 2005, 269). It is cognate with the more frequent *hēttaomai*, which (BDAG 441) has the sense of 'be defeated', as (for instance) in losing a race, or 'be treated worse'. Stowers 1994, 312–16 builds too much on the idea of 'losing a race': see, rightly, Wagner 2002, 267f. n. 155.

position, not of easy-going privilege, but of awesome responsibility. As with 'the Jew' in 2.17, they are the ones through whom God will now accomplish his remaining purposes. They are not there for their own sake, but so that God may work through them. This is part of the call to humility which emerges in 11.17–24, arguably the rhetorical climax of the chapter.

Paul's reference to Israel's *paraptōma* ties in with yet another theme from chapter 9. At the end of that chapter, as Paul is summing up the results of the strange election-narrative, he refers back to the well-known Isaianic passage about the stumbling stone:

> They have stumbled over the stumbling stone, 33as the Bible says,
> Look: I am placing in Zion a stone that will make people stumble,
> a rock that will trip people up;
> and the one who believes in him will never be put to shame.[583]

As we noted before, the 'stone' seems to have converging interpretations: *both* Torah *and* Messiah. But the point now is the *divine purpose* in the 'stumbling'. Here, at the end of the long account of the strange and apparently negative election – election in order to be pared down to the bone – we find a statement which emerges on the other side of the central account of the Messiah and the new covenant (10.1–13) in terms of the *divinely intended stumble* of Israel. Thus when Paul sums up Israel's failure in 11.11 with the words 'through their tripping up (*paraptōma*)' we can see where his line of thought in chapter 9 was heading. The word *paraptōma* came to have the technical sense of 'trespass', 'wrongdoing', as in classical Greek it had the metaphorical sense of 'blunder', 'going off course'. But its basic sense of 'false step', 'slip', 'stumble' could easily be recalled.[584]

If there is a *felix culpa* theology in the New Testament, it is perhaps at this point. Not the sin of Adam, about which there was nothing *felix*, not even in the long prospect of 'such a great redeemer'. If I have understood Paul, he would have said that the one who was from all eternity 'equal with God', the 'image of the invisible God, the firstborn of all creation', would have appeared anyway 'when the time had fully come', not then to redeem, but to rule gloriously over the completed creation.[585] However, granted the sin of humankind and the consequent corruption and decay of creation, the creator God called Abraham and his family so that through them the problem could be dealt with, *so that he might himself deal with the problem by coming as Abraham's seed, coming in person as Israel's representative Messiah*. And Paul's point throughout chapters 9—11 is that this divine redeeming action, for which Israel's election was the necessary means, both in the original choice and in the outworking, down to the remnant, casts its light around it, so that the history of the redemption-bearing people is also redemptive,

[583] 9.32b–33.

[584] cf. BDAG 770 ('offence, wrongdoing, sin') as against LSJ 1322 ('false step, slip, blunder', with resonances of 'falling from the right way').

[585] On the whole 'Scotist' christology herein implied, see now the important book of van Driel 2008. I am grateful to Prof. Ivor Davidson for this reference.

even though it is the Messiah, not Israel, in whose flesh 'sin is condemned' (8.3). If there is such a thing as *Heilsgeschichte*, it is only because at its heart it is *Verdammungsgeschichte*, the story of how the condemnation of the world was borne by Israel's Messiah, so that the world could be rescued. If there is a salvation history, it is only because the radically new thing that God did in the middle of history gives, at last, the meaning which that history would otherwise lack. The laying of the 'stumbling stone' in Israel, then, was itself part of the plan that the world might be redeemed precisely through Israel's 'casting away'. Paul, as so often, is here advancing the argument of 11.11–24 by invoking a theme he had mentioned earlier.

(δ) 11.16–24

All this brings us back to the main thrust of Romans 11. Having begun with the central verse 15 (with its contextualizing introduction, 11.13–14), and having then looked back at 11.11–12, we now come to the passage which immediately follows:

11.1–10				11.25–32
	11.11–12		**11.16–24**	
		11.13–15		

Here we have the much discussed 'olive tree' picture (11.16b–24), introduced by a different metaphor: the first-fruits and the whole lump (11.16a):

> If the first fruits are holy, so is the whole lump;
> If the root is holy, so are the branches.

Much ink has been spilt on the precise referent of Paul's two metaphors here, though part of the point of using picture-language is after all to be evocative and not mathematically precise. Does the 'first fruits' refer to the Messiah, risen from the dead, as in 1 Corinthians 15.20? Would the point then be that the Messiah, being himself a Jew, is the start of the 'remnant' of which Paul speaks in 11.1–6? Or does it refer to the remnant itself, the comparatively small group which, based on grace (11.6), has no reason not to get much bigger? Perhaps he means both. And as for the 'root' and the 'branches': since he says 'root' and not 'tree' (that comes later), does he mean Abraham? Or God? Or, again, the Messiah? Or the remnant?[586]

Fortunately for our purposes a decision on these much-debated issues is not necessary – though the 'olive tree' image does provide some clarity, since the 'remnant' would seem to be Jewish branches that, by grace (11.5–6), find themselves in the 'tree', and can hardly therefore be the root itself. Paul's thrust in both images is actually clear: the 'lump' and the (currently broken off) 'branches' are both ways of speaking of presently 'unbelieving'

[586] I have held various positions on these questions in the past (cf. e.g. Wright 2002 [*Romans*], 683f.). I trust one is allowed to change one's mind from time to time.

or 'hardened' (11.7) Jews, and of insisting in both cases that such people are 'holy' – not in the sense that they are already 'sanctified' in the full sense,[587] but in the sense of 1 Corinthians 7.14, where both an unbelieving spouse, and the children from such a mixed marriage, are 'holy'.[588] It is possible, and seems to me now likely, that in the two metaphors of verse 16 he arrives at the same conclusion by a different path, with the 'first fruits' being the 'remnant' as in 11.1–7 (with the Messiah not far away, but not foregrounded) and the 'root' being the patriarchs (to whom God had made the promises which remain the source of nourishment for gentile Christians as well as Jews, as in Romans 4).[589] The main difference between the images, though, is that the picture of the olive tree allows more metaphorical and even allegorical development: the 'tree' itself is the important thing, with some branches being broken off and others being grafted in. The main aim, throughout the entire section, is to say, 'Don't boast over the branches' (verse 18); 'Don't get big ideas about it' (verse 20); 'You mustn't . . . think too much of yourselves' (verse 25). Jews who are at present unbelieving are still part of the people 'according to the flesh' to whom the creator God made great and unbreakable promises. They are to be respected, and gentiles who have come to believe in the Jewish Messiah have no business to act superior to them. God is not finished with them; they have not been 'replaced' or 'disinherited' or 'substituted'. *God has already brought plenty of them to faith in their own Messiah; we can now understand the reasons why they were 'hardened' in the first place; so God will undoubtedly want to bring plenty more to faith, too.* That is the emphasis of the 'olive tree' picture.[590]

The analogy with the unbelieving spouse is instructive. Paul is *not* saying that presently unbelieving Jews are, or will be, necessarily saved, any more than he was saying in 1 Corinthians that an unbelieving spouse, however much 'sanctified' by the believing one, was automatically saved. If he had believed that about his fellow (but unbelieving) Jews, he could have saved

[587] As e.g. Rom. 6.19; 1 Cor. 6.11; 1 Thess. 4.3; etc.

[588] On which see e.g. Fitzmyer 2008, 299–301, and esp. Thiselton 2000, 527–33, with a history of interpretation.

[589] This is substantially the position of Fitzmyer 1993, 587, referring to others also. I find it significant that when the 'root' is mentioned again in v. 18 it is to warn against boasting: it isn't you that supports the root, but the root that supports you. This, in context, implies that the 'root' is the foundation of ethnic Israel, i.e. the patriarchs (cf. v. 28), rather than either God or the Messiah (though Bell 2005, 276 is right to point out messianic resonances in the word 'root': e.g. Isa. 11.10; 53.2).

[590] Nanos 2010a, 339f., begins by warding off readings which 'proclaim the supplanting of Israel by the church, the conflation of Israel with the church and especially that Christian gentiles are grafted into Israel, which the tree is understood to represent . . . In essence, "Israel" in this sense functions as a metonym for "Christianity."' This seems to me a way of ruling out what Paul is actually saying, in line with Rom. 1—4, Gal., etc., that Christian faith is the way in which gentiles join the family of Abraham. Nanos may well be right, here and at 372, to say that later generations have used the passage in ways which do not reflect Paul's intention, but to say that the 'tree' is not Israel (340f.) seems to me, as to most exegetes, straightforwardly wrong; he tacitly recognizes this when he then asserts that the allegory is itself 'broken' (369) or 'inadequate' (371), and 'does not sit well with the surrounding allegories and arguments' (373). Nanos's regular usage of 'Israelite' to mean 'Jew' (despite 9.6b) seems itself designed to ward off what most see as Paul's natural meaning. His earlier thesis (Nanos 1996), that the 'weak' in Rom. 14 are non-Christ-believing Jews in whose synagogues the Christ-believing gentiles are worshipping, has won little support.

himself a lot of heartache: 9.1–5 would be beside the point, and the exposition of 'salvation' in 10.2–13, in answer to the prayer of 10.1, would be irrelevant. His point is not 'so they are automatically saved'. His point, here and throughout the section, is that they are not automatically *not* saved. That is the rhetorical thrust of the entire chapter, and in a measure of the whole of chapters 9—11.

Paul, after all, knew what the atmosphere in Rome would be like. He had lived and worked in pagan cities for most of his life, as a hard-line young Jew in Tarsus and later as a travelling missionary for the Messiah. He knew, few better, what gentiles thought about Jews. He knew that a largely gentile church would need little encouragement to turn its nose up at the synagogue down the street, especially if the Jews had earlier been banished from town and had only recently been allowed back.[591] Once again we insist: he was not writing a treatise on soteriology, however much earnest expositors in older traditions try to turn Romans 1—4 into such a thing, and however much earnest expositors in newer traditions try to turn Romans 11 into such a thing. He was writing a letter: aware of a likely problem, and doing his best to nip it in the bud.

He therefore builds up his argument carefully. Having established that there was indeed a remnant of believing Jews (11.1–6), he has now said, vaguely but evocatively, that since we can glimpse, through a christological lens, the reason for what God has done, we can also expect a similarly christologically shaped 'fullness', a 'receiving back', a glorious future in which many more Jews will be 'saved', so that it will be like 'life from the dead' (11.11–15). All this, though exciting and evocative, is I think deliberately vague and arm-waving.[592] He is deliberately not saying precisely what this 'fullness' will look like. His aim is simply 'to save some'. But the 'olive tree' picture is a way of moving from these generalizations to very specific instructions. That is why verse 16 is linked with a *de* rather than a *gar*: it is not a further explanation of what has just been said, but a conclusion now to be drawn from it. God, he now says, is certainly capable of grafting 'broken branches' – Jews at present 'in unbelief' (11.23) – back into the 'tree' which is after all their own native plant. Indeed, this is a far more 'natural' thing for God to do, he says, than his grafting in of you gentiles! So do not indulge in a kind of theological inverted snobbery, imitating the 'boasting' of 2.17–20 which was ruled out at 3.27.

So what is the 'olive tree'? It is, of course, a metaphor for Israel itself. Israel as an olive tree is a familiar biblical image, often in a positive and attractive sense.[593] The whole point of the image is that there is – just as in Galatians 3! – a *single* family; a family rooted in the patriarchs and the promises God made to them; a family from which, strangely, many 'natural

[591] See the discussions and different views in e.g. Das 2007, ch. 4; Esler 2003b, ch. 4. My case here does not depend on this particular reconstruction, but it would certainly fit well (see Wright 2002 [*Romans*], 406–8).

[592] Wagner 2002, 271f.: 'somewhat cryptic'; 298 'rather fuzzy'.

[593] Pss. 1.3; 52.8; 128.3; Hos. 14.6.

branches' have been broken off, but into which many 'unnatural branches' have been grafted.[594] This is the family Paul has been talking about, on and off, throughout the letter, not least in chapter 4. This is the people into which some gentiles have surprisingly been brought and from which some Jews have, equally surprisingly, opted out, as in 9.30—10.13. There ought to be no further question about this: Paul is talking about the ancient people of God, now radically reconfigured around the Messiah. As one of America's scholarly elder statesmen put it in a recent commentary,

> Clear, of course, is Paul's insistence that by faith Christian gentiles are *incorporated into Israel* ... Paul probably understands the gentiles 'coming in' [as in 11.25] as their entering the people of God ... As Paul sees it, gentiles abandon their religion when they accept the gospel (1 Thess 1:9–10), but observant Jews who accept it do not change religions but reconfigure the religion they already have. Together both groups constitute something new, a new 'people' united by a shared conviction about the Christ-event as God's eschatological act.[595]

'Incorporated into Israel': yes, precisely. There are not two 'peoples of God', one for gentiles to be incorporated into and one for Jews to remain within. The 'olive tree' can mean nothing else; and that should alert us as to the way the whole chapter is running.[596] An even older statesman put it like this:

> From what have the unbelieving Jews been cut off? It cannot be that they have been cut off from the Jewish people considered as an ethnic entity: they are still Jews. The branches broken off ... , then, are those Jews, and they are the majority, *who have refused to be part of the true Israel*, the remnant that has believed in Christ. The olive in 11:17 stands for the community of Christian believers, the Church, at first composed of Jewish Christians of the root of Abraham ... through their acceptance of the gospel the gentiles have been engrafted into the people of God, the olive tree. And this olive tree ... is continuous with the root of Abraham ...[597]

Keck and Davies do not appear to be saying exactly the same thing. Keck sees believing gentiles as being incorporated into 'Israel'; Davies appears to restrict the phrase 'true Israel' to the believing Jewish remnant, though he like Keck sees the olive as a single tree into which the believing gentiles have been grafted. Jewett has yet a third angle of vision on the same reality:

[594] Nanos 2010a, 354 suggests that Paul is making a distinction between branches being 'broken' (*ekklaō*, as in 11.17, 19, 20) but still as it were loosely attached, and 'cut off' (*ekkoptō*, as in 11.22, 24, expressing the more severe threat to the 'wild branches' if they begin to boast). There may be a hint of a distinction here, but there are four problems with the proposal as it stands: (a) v. 19 suggests that the 'breaking' has made room for gentile ingrafting; (b) Paul parallels the fate of the 'natural branches' with the possible fate awaiting boastful gentiles (v. 21) (as Nanos sees, 364, 368, leading him to suggest that Paul's metaphor 'goes awry here', and that (369) 'the tree allegory ... is itself broken'); (c) when he says 'you too will be cut off' (v. 22), the 'too' (*kai*) indicates that 'cutting off' is basically the same fate which the 'natural branches' have already suffered; (d) Paul envisages the 'grafting in' of gentiles as equivalent to what the 'broken branches' will experience if they do not remain in unbelief (vv. 23f.).

[595] Keck 2005, 276, 279, 286 (my italics).

[596] So too (perhaps surprisingly) Bell 2005, 297: 'The primary reference of the olive tree has to be Israel ... It is into the olive tree of Israel that Gentile Christians have been grafted.'

[597] Davies 1984, 154f. (my italics).

> ... the basis for acknowledging the continued priority of Israel is that it provided the vehicle by which the holy, righteous community of the church came into the world ... Israel is the root and a Gentile believer is the branch.[598]

Does a gentile believer then become part of 'Israel'? If not, in what sense is he or she a branch now belonging to that root?[599]

All this amounts to the same overall point, which is very similar to that of Galatians 3. Abraham has one family, in which all believers share. The difference between the two epistles is this. In Galatians Paul is warning gentile believers that they must not try to become physically, ethnically, Jews. To do so would undermine that single family by insisting on an ethnic basis. In Romans he is warning gentile believers that they must not imagine that God cannot and will not bring more and more Jews back into what is, after all, their own proper family. That, too, would be to insist on an ethnic basis, only now a non-Jewish one rather than a Jewish one.

The question then, picking up Keck's way of putting it, is this: what does it mean to 'accept the gospel', and to 'reconfigure the religion they already have'? Paul has already answered those questions in Romans 3.21—4.25 and 10.1–13. Here he simply summarizes it: 'if they do not remain in unbelief, they will be grafted back in' (11.23).

Paul's use of this picture is relatively clear. But we should not miss the overtones of some of the biblical passages that stand behind the 'olive tree' picture, and one in particular. Jeremiah 11 resonates closely with Paul's meaning in certain respects. It is worth glancing at its key elements:

> The word that came to Jeremiah from YHWH: Hear the words of this covenant, and speak to the people of Judah and the inhabitants of Jerusalem. You shall say to them, 'Thus says YHWH, the God of Israel: Cursed be anyone who does not heed the words of this covenant, which I commanded your ancestors when I brought them out of the land of Egypt ...'
>
> And YHWH said to me, Proclaim all these words in the cities of Judah, and in the streets of Jerusalem: Hear the words of this covenant and do them. For I solemnly warned your ancestors when I brought them up out of the land of Egypt, warning them persistently, even to this day, saying, Obey my voice. Yet they did not obey or incline their ear, but everyone walked in the stubbornness of an evil will. So I brought upon them all the words of this covenant, which I commanded them to do, but they did not.[600]

This seems to be a clear echo of the covenantal threats in Deuteronomy 27—9. Indeed, Jeremiah 11.3 is more or less a quotation of Deuteronomy 27.26, which Paul himself uses in Galatians 3.10. When Jeremiah then says 'so I brought upon them all the words of this covenant', this indicates clearly that Jeremiah supposes that the curses of Deuteronomy have now fallen on the people – as Paul himself strongly implies both in Galatians and (by his

[598] Jewett 2007, 683.

[599] Hill 2001, 1103 roundly declares that 'there is no possibility here that Paul is referring to the church as ("spiritual") Israel'. Cf. too Nanos 2010a, 360: 'The gentiles join Israelites in the worship of the One God ... but they are not Israel, nor are they grafted into Israel.' He does, however, say (371) that believing gentiles are 'adopted ... into the family of God' (or 'God's larger family', 376) but without explaining the difference, and the relation, between this 'family' and 'Israel'.

[600] Jer. 11.1–4, 6–8.

use of Deuteronomy 29, 30 and 32) in the present section. The prophet then receives and passes on a long catalogue of Israel's misdemeanours, whereupon YHWH warns Jeremiah against even praying for the people any more, because he has no intention of listening.[601] (That, of course, resonates faintly but poignantly with Paul's mention of prayer in 9.3 and 10.1.) Then comes the devastating oracle, referring back to those earlier, happier days for the olive tree:

> YHWH once called you, 'A green olive tree, fair with goodly fruit'; but with the roar of a great tempest he will set fire to it, and its branches will be consumed. YHWH of hosts, who planted you, has pronounced evil against you, because of the evil that the house of Israel and the house of Judah have done . . .[602]

The prophet then finds himself 'like a lamb led to the slaughter', discovering that the people have been saying something similar about him:

> I did not know that it was against me that they devised schemes, saying, 'Let us destroy the tree with its fruit, let us cut him off from the land of the living, so that his name will no longer be remembered!'[603]

But he continues, none the less, with his work of uttering devastating oracles.[604]

Paul's use of the 'olive tree' picture appears to pick up where Jeremiah's leaves off. Jeremiah had the tempest ripping off branches and consuming them. But Paul, who like Jeremiah has been following the covenantal narrative of Deuteronomy, has a further word to speak. Yes, branches have been broken off, and other things have followed, but this is not the end of the story:

> [17]But if some of the branches were broken off, and you – a *wild* olive tree! – were grafted in among them, and came to share in the root of the olive with its rich sap, [18]don't boast over the branches. If you do boast, remember this: it isn't you that supports the root, but the root that supports you.
>
> [19]I know what you'll say next: 'Branches were broken off so that I could be grafted in.' [20]That's all very well. They were broken off because of unbelief – but you stand firm by faith. Don't get big ideas about it; instead, be afraid. [21]After all, if God didn't spare the natural branches, there's a strong possibility he won't spare you.
>
> [22]Note carefully, then, that God is both kind and severe. He is severe to those who have fallen, but he is kind to you, provided you continue in his kindness – otherwise you too will be cut off. [23]And they, too, if they do not remain in unbelief, will be grafted back in. God is able, you see, to graft them back in. [24]For if you were cut out of what is by nature a wild olive tree, and grafted, contrary to nature, into a cultivated olive tree, how much more will they, the natural branches, be grafted back into their own olive tree.[605]

601 11.14–15.

602 11.16–17.

603 11.19.

604 11.20–3.

605 11.17–24.

This famous passage has caused much discussion, but it is not really as complex as it has sometimes appeared. Two preliminary points may help.

First, Paul is just as much aware as modern commentators, perhaps more, that the process he is describing is 'contrary to nature'.[606] He may have been a town- and city-dweller rather than a countryman, but he knows perfectly well that the normal practice is to graft a cultivated shoot on to a wild stock, rather than the other way round, so that the energy of the wild stock will be channelled into the fruit-bearing cultivated stock. He deliberately describes the process outlined here as *para physin*, 'against nature' (verse 24). He is, after all, inching his way forwards into new territory. In the nature of the case, from his point of view at least, God has never done anything like this before.

Second, we do not need to be certain what situation Paul envisaged in Rome in order to understand what he is saying here. Enough to know, as we said before, that the normal Roman view of the Jews was disdainful or dismissive at best and angrily prejudiced at worst.[607] What is more, if Paul did indeed have a sense that the situation in the middle east was getting worse, as we suggested when looking at 1 Thessalonians 2, it will have been important to address this head on in case people in Rome, including gentile Messiah-followers, should begin to think of 'the Jews' in a still more negative way. But the urgent appeal he launches throughout this passage clearly indicates his belief that gentile Messiah-believers in Rome are already being tempted to suppose that 'the Jews' have been cut off for good. Perhaps some had even been quoting Jeremiah (a piece of shameless and unproveable mirror-reading; if others can guess what texts Paul's opponents had been quoting, why shouldn't I, just this once?). There you are, they were perhaps saying, those unbelieving Jews have broken the covenant, they have been cut off for ever. The tree is being destroyed with its fruit. Paul, happy as ever to pick up a scriptural challenge, will come back presently to the question of the covenant, and show what Jeremiah and others did with it.[608] First, though, he develops the picture of the olive tree in his own way, to devastating effect.

This moves in three steps. If we take it slowly we will see what he has in mind.

To begin with, the present situation and the danger of misinterpreting it (11.17–18). Branches have been broken off, and gentiles, wild olive

[606] See the discussion in Jewett 2007, 683–5; Nanos 2010a, 355–8: ancient husbandry was more complex than earlier commentators realized.

[607] See Wagner 2002, 274 n. 178: it is not clear whether Paul knew of existing tensions in Rome or whether a situation was 'simply imagined by Paul on the basis of his experience elsewhere'. On normal pagan anti-Jewish prejudice see Stern 1974–84; 1976. Nanos 2010a, 355 is surely correct to say that 'presumption toward Israelites who are not Christ-believers is a special problem that Paul fears is present among the members of the nations in Christ in Rome'. See too e.g. Wiefel 1991.

[608] 11.27, quoting Jer. 31.33f.: see below.

shoots,[609] have been grafted in among the remaining ones,[610] 'sharing the root of the olive with its rich sap'. That highlighting of the benefit of being grafted in, and of the goodness which is still in the original olive itself, shows the direction of Paul's argument. Sure enough, he proceeds with a warning against the danger of forgetting just this, and of ignoring the relationship they have to the olive. 'Don't boast: or, if you do, remember that the root is supporting you, not the other way around.'

So far, so good. As in Galatians, the gentile Messiah-believers have come to belong to the tree which is Abraham's family. This would make no sense unless Paul, here as elsewhere, is narrating the gentile believers into the story of Israel. They are part of that single family: neither the beginning of a new family in which Jews are not welcome (as Paul is afraid some Roman Messiah-followers may think); nor even a brand new family into which a few of Abraham's old family happen to have been included; but *the same family* which began with Abraham. Here is a challenge for the various large narratives which have been superimposed on Paul in recent years: so-called 'apocalyptic', for instance, which envisages God sweeping away all that had gone before and starting something totally new. What Paul says here is totally consistent with the revised election we studied throughout chapter 10 above – and, more important, fully in line with all the relevant passages earlier in Romans, such as 2.25–9, 3.21—4.25 and not least the great narrative of redemption in chapters 6—8.

Second, then, he explores the possible objection that 'the (new) branches' might raise to what he is saying, and explains, revealingly, why that objection would be ill-founded (11.19–21). 'Branches were broken off so that I might be grafted in': in other words, God's purpose was to include gentiles, and those other branches have been broken off as though to make room for the new ones. That, taken as it stands without Paul's further serious modification, might be seen as the beginning of a real 'supersession', not indeed of 'Jews' by 'gentiles' but of 'Jews' by 'gentile Christians'; and it would leave the gentile Messiah-followers still as it were in the driving seat. They would constitute the new reality, the leading edge of the movement. Paul accepts the premise, that branches have indeed been broken off and others grafted in, and that there may even have been some causal connection between these two events. That, after all, is what he was saying in 11.11–15: by their trespass, salvation has come to the nations. But his acceptance of this, for the sake of argument as it were (*kalōs*; 'all right: put it like that if you want'[611]), allows him to point up *how and why* this has happened, and to

[609] This seems to be the meaning, though the rare word *agrielaios* refers to an actual tree, not a branch or a collection of branches.

[610] *en autois*; not, then, 'in their place' or 'instead of them' but 'among them'. This, presumably, cannot mean 'among the ones that were broken off' (as, strangely, Davies 1984, 356 n. 6; Nanos 2010a, 358f. links this with his theory that the 'broken' branches are not actually broken *off*), but 'among the branches, some *others* of which were broken off'; see Cranfield 1979, 567; Dunn 1988b, 661; Bell 2005, 298. Hence the *syn* in *synkoinōnos* in 11.17, corresponding to Eph. 2.11–22: gentile Messiah-believers are now fellow branches with the existing Jewish Messiah-believers.

[611] Jewett 2007, 687 discusses the various nuances of the word; cf. too Donaldson 1993, 85.

pose the challenge which removes any sense of new-found superiority. 'They were broken off *because of unbelief* (*tē apistia*), but you stand firm *by faith* (*tē pistei*).' This is a critical addition to the argument. Commentators may have forgotten what Paul said in 10.6–13, but Paul himself has not. The whole problem of Romans 9—11 arises simply because 'the natural branches', or many of them, have not 'had faith', have not believed in Jesus' resurrection and lordship (10.6–13).[612] But this means that the Roman church needs to be warned, in the rather strong terms of verses 20–1: Don't get big ideas about all this; instead, be afraid. God is quite capable of applying the same treatment to you as he did to the 'natural branches'. Paul seems to be addressing, not individuals, but the whole church in Rome: if you substitute boasting for faith, replacing an identity found only in the Messiah with an ethnic 'identity' of your own, you too will be cut off (11.22).[613]

Third, then, 'the kindness and severity of God' (11.22–4). Here Paul has come back to the foundation of his discourse, which is not about branches, nor about nations and peoples, but primarily about God. He will not take this discussion forward except in those terms, and with those terms he will evoke the entire train of thought from the start of the letter. In particular, as with 2.4–5 and 9.21–2,[614] he is grappling with the issue of God's patience, and the situation that results when people either do or do not make appropriate use of the breathing space created by the divine forbearance. He has already said, in one of those earlier passages, that God's 'kindness' is meant to lead to repentance (2.4b). Now he says that it is meant to lead to *faith*. Branches were broken off because of unbelief; but you, he says, stand fast through faith (11.20). That is why, as we just saw, gentile Messiah-people must 'remain in his kindness, otherwise you too will be cut off', while 'they' (presently unbelieving Jews), 'if they do not remain in unbelief, will be grafted back in'.

This is the key point: *if they do not remain in unbelief*. Paul is not talking, and has never been talking, about a 'grafting back in' which can be accomplished by a route other than the faith he was so careful to spell out in 10.6–11.[615] There is less of a fashion now for postulating a *Sonderweg*, an 'alternative route' to salvation which bypasses what Paul calls 'faith' (always linked

[612] cf. too of course 3.2; 9.30–3; 10.18–21.

[613] Nanos 2010a, 370 n. 65, is wrong to suggest that I have reduced this threat to that of temporary discipline: see Wright 2002 [*Romans*], 686. See Haacker 2003, 91 on Paul's careful balance between personal 'assurance' as in Rom. 8.38f. and the necessary warning of e.g. 1 Cor. 10.12.

[614] cf. 3.26, stressing God's forbearance (*anochē*).

[615] Jewett 2007, 692 skates quickly over the point, criticizing Käsemann (1980 [1973], 310f.) for 'reify [ing] the doctrine of grace and rely[ing] on doctrinal instruction to evoke faith', which, Jewett declares, 'places those who think they have the right understanding of doctrine on the pedestal of honor and power, thus leaving the prejudices of Gentiles as well as Jews untouched'. This seems unfair to Käsemann, who like Jewett insists on the point being 'God is able', *dynatos*. Jewett's real problem seems to be that, in pressing towards some kind of universalism, he is unwilling to admit, as does Käsemann (310), that Paul's hope for unbelieving Israel 'certainly also here remains tied to grace and faith'. Jewett thus appears to allow his sociological honour/shame scheme to trump Paul's theological framework of grace and faith.

directly to the revelation of God in the gospel of Jesus). Paul is clear, as he has been all along. 'All who call upon the name of the Lord will be saved,' and what that means has been stated unambiguously in chapter 10.

He adds a note (verse 24) to the effect that this will pose no horticultural problems. The tree is already thoroughly miraculous, and God can do yet more. But this allows him to finish the section with the message he wants the Roman church to hear above all else: 'how much more will they ... be grafted back into their own olive tree'.

Both halves of this are important. On the one hand, the 'how much more', echoing the similar, albeit deliberately imprecise, statement in 11.12: it will be much easier for God to bring Jews back in than it was to bring gentiles in from the outside. Any suggestion that it is now difficult for God to do anything further with Jewish people must therefore be thrown out from the start. On the other hand, it is *their own olive tree, tē idia elaia*. Paul knew that the standing temptation for gentile Messiah-believers would be to regard the 'tree', which one must think of as in some sense 'the people of Abraham defined around the Messiah', as now somehow *their own*, instead of the natural property of Abraham's physical descendants. Not so, he says: it is 'their own'. He has come back to where he started: 'They are Israelites, and *theirs* are the sonship, the glory' and so on. The *hōn*, 'theirs', in 9.4 corresponds directly to *tē idia elaia*, 'their own olive tree', in 11.24. This is the truth of which a zealous snatching at 'their own righteousness' (*tēn idian dikaiosynēn*, 10.3) was a distorted parody. This is what Paul wants gentile Messiah-followers in Rome to grasp. The 'tree' into which they have been grafted remains Israel's, the single 'tree' of Abraham and his seed. Israel's covenant narrative, however much it has had to be retold in biblically dark tones as in 9.6–29, remains the divinely intended, and never rescinded, plan of salvation. That was the point of 3.1–9, and it is the point of 11.16–24 as well.

Without going very far down the route of mirror-reading or guessing as to historical context, and indeed without getting into needless complexity, I think we can see what Paul has in mind. Indeed, since this is more or less the rhetorical climax of the letter, coming as it does at the strategic moment within the third of the four great sections, we can now see what he has in mind in Romans as a whole. He is facing, more or less, the opposite problem to the one he had faced in Galatia. There, ex-pagan Messiah-believers were being pushed towards getting circumcised and becoming 'children of Abraham according to the flesh'. Here, Paul has a shrewd suspicion that in Rome he will find ex-pagan Messiah-believers whose local culture is pushing them towards a view of Judaism, and of the unbelieving Jews who embody it, as beyond the pale, possessing as it were a tangential relationship to Jesus but having turned aside from him, and leaving the way clear for this new movement, apart from its earliest members, to consist of gentiles only.[616] That was, more or less, what Marcion taught in Rome, within a

[616] Jewett 2007, 686 speaks anachronistically of 'anti-Semitism', but the basic point is correct.

hundred years of this letter. It was a popular message. Paul did not need special prophetic gifts to see the danger just a little way down the road.

This question is so different from those that have haunted Christian–Jewish discussions for at least the last seventy years in the western world that it is easy now to miss what Paul is saying.[617] The key question is not, Are the various religions equally valid ways to a distant deity? Nor is it, How can Christians affirm the 'civil rights' of Jewish people in the Post-holocaust world? The question Paul addresses follows on from the apparent failure of Israel described in 9.30—10.13. It comes, as we saw, in two stages: first (11.1–10), can any Jews at all be saved? and second, as in 11.11–24, can any *more* Jews be saved? 'Salvation' here, exactly as set out in 10.1–13, is correlated with the Messiah, and with the faith that believes his resurrection. In our own day, one runs the risk of being stigmatized as anti-Jewish if one even suggests that Jesus was and still is Israel's Messiah, who still longs for his own 'flesh' to accept him as such. For Paul – the irony would not be lost on him if he could listen in to our late-modern, postmodern or even post-liberal debates – the real anti-Jewish position would be the opposite: the suggestion that the messianic death and resurrection of Jesus, and his world-wide rule as *kyrios*, should be seen as a fine religious option for gentiles but off limits for Jews; the suggestion, in other words, that Jews are 'all right as they are', and should not under any circumstances be presented with the ancient messianic claim that Jesus' followers made, and still make, on the basis of nothing more nor less than his resurrection from the dead.

The olive tree picture militates against the idea that Paul is here speaking of a large-scale or last-minute re-entry of Jews by a kind of automatic divine fiat. First, he insists (11.23) that such re-entry will be for those 'who do not remain in unbelief', which relates directly to 10.6–13. Many, if not most these days, have tried to align this to the *parousia*.[618] This appears to avoid the suggestion of a *Sonderweg* for Israel, because the Israel that is to be saved in the end will thereby no longer 'remain in unbelief', but accept Jesus as Messiah when he is revealed to them. But it also avoids the currently unwelcome idea, which is nevertheless precisely what Paul says in 11.11–15, that the gentile mission itself will make Jews 'jealous' and so save some of them *in the present time*. But this postponement of the 'grafting back in' to the *parousia* hardly fits with the point Paul is eager to ram home throughout the chapter. Such a postponement would not relate to his specific warning to the gentile Christians in Rome. He introduces this warning as it were eyeball to eyeball in 11.13, and engages sharply with objections through the rhetorical second person singular in 11.17–24. The latter passage is focused on 11.18: 'Don't boast.' And this relates directly to the opening of the following passage, to which we will presently turn: 'You mustn't get the wrong idea and think too much of yourselves.' If this is the point Paul wishes to get across in 11.1–24 – that gentile Christians must realize that God can and

617 Sievers 1997 offers a helpful account of discussions in Roman Catholic circles.

618 e.g. Hofius 1990.

will re-graft presently unbelieving Jews into the 'olive tree' by means of bringing them to faith (11.23) – then it makes no sense for him suddenly to say, in effect, that in point of fact no Jews will come to faith until the *parousia*. How would that support his warning and exhortation? It would allow Christian gentiles in Rome to shrug their shoulders, to turn their backs on Jews for the present – which is the very opposite of what Paul is so eager to stress.[619]

Of course, if we approach Romans 9—11 as though it is primarily a treatise either about soteriology or about theodicy, we may easily be led into thinking that Paul is now saying 'all will be saved' (or at least 'all Jews will be saved'), on the one hand, or 'God will do the decent thing in the end' on the other. But if Paul is writing a *specific letter*, into this *specific situation*, it is vital that he should be talking, not about some sudden future event, but about the sort of things he mentioned in 11.14 ('and save some of them'), and about the consequent imperative ('don't boast'). And those relate, not to some postponed last-minute rescue, but to his own continuing ministry. He is, after all, seeking support for his Spanish mission, and his explanation for his apostolic practice in 10.14–17 and here as well must be read as part of his description of the kind of mission he is hoping the Roman church will unite in affirming.

What then about 'the Deliverer coming from Zion' in 11.26? We shall come to that presently. First, though, we need to look back to the opening of chapter 11. Here Paul sets out some of the key categories in terms of which he will then make his emphatic final statement.

(ε) 11.1–10

We return, then, to the beginning of the chapter:

11.1–10 11.11–12 11.13–15 11.16–24 11.25–32

The start of chapter 11, as we have suggested, is the point at which Paul is out on his own. If the prophecies of Deuteronomy 32 and Isaiah 65 have come so worryingly true, as at the end of chapter 10, what is to happen next? Can it be – as a cursory reading of 9.30–3 and its balancing 10.18–21 might suggest – that God's elective purposes have now simply switched from Abraham's physical family to a gentile-only family defined by Messiah-faith?

If this is a new question, Paul is determined to answer it as far as possible by reference to lines of thought, and not least biblical exposition, which he has already established. It is important to track the close links and echoes

[619] There are also theological puzzles about the now-popular 'all saved at the *parousia*' reading of 11.26a: see below, 1231–52.

between this opening paragraph and the whole of 9.6—10.21. Though this is new territory, the way forward into it is not to forget all that has gone before and to try something new, but to build on the strength of what has already been said.

The answer to the question, whether God has forsaken his people, is, 'Of course not' – and the argument of chapter 9 has in fact already made this clear, in the crucial verse 9.24: 'us whom he called, not only from Jews but also from gentiles'. *Not only from Jews*: in other words, certainly from Jews! This already shows that the 'Israel' that in 9.31 'pursued the law of righteousness but did not attain to that law', was already a *subset* of Abraham's physical family. It denotes 'the majority of Jews', 'Israel as a whole', but with key exceptions, namely, those who have believed, who have 'submitted to God's righteousness' and so, surprisingly, have 'attained to Torah' in the sense then clarified in 10.6–13. That is why there were two 'Israels' in 9.6b. So here in 11.1–6, the first part of this first sub-section, Paul insists that he himself is the obvious exception to any suggestion that 'God has rejected his people'. Echoing 1 Samuel 12.22, where the choice of the Benjaminite Saul as king reflected the fact that YHWH had not forsaken his people, so the calling of Saul of Tarsus can be advanced to the same end.[620] Paul is thus not simply a one-off, random example of the fact that Israel as a whole has not been cut off; his own case provides scriptural resonances which reinforce the point.[621] Paul is himself an 'Israelite', the word used already in 9.4, and now resonating also with the second 'Israel' meaning in 9.6b.[622]

The explanation he offers is rooted in the later narratives of the monarchy: there is a 'remnant'. More autobiographical hints emerge: there is excellent reason to suppose that Saul of Tarsus had modelled himself on Elijah and/or Phinehas, the great exemplars of 'zeal', and that what had happened on the Damascus Road had sent him off to complain to Israel's God that everything had gone horribly wrong, much as Elijah had gone off to complain to God about Ahab's threats following the victory over the prophets of Baal.[623] And the answer to Elijah is the answer to Saul of Tarsus, now becoming Paul the Apostle: there is still a remnant, a *leimma*. That, picking up the *hypoleimma* of 9.27,[624] is Paul's summary word to refer to God's

[620] The multiple echoes here are fascinating (and go beyond those proposed by e.g. Wagner 2002, 221, 224): (a) as the Benjaminite Saul persecuted the anointed but not yet enthroned David, so Saul of Tarsus persecuted the one he now regards as Messiah; (b) as Samuel interceded for Israel (1 Sam. 7.5, and esp. 12.19–25, with 12.22 quoted here), so Paul intercedes, and with similar promises and warnings, in 9.3; 10.1. The echoes of 'YHWH will not forsake his people' take us to Ps. 94 [LXX 93].14 and Jer. 31.37. Haacker 2003, 88 suggests an echo of Jdg. 20—1 when the tribe of Benjamin had to recover from being reduced to 600 men. Jewett (2007, 653, 655) refers to Elijah, too, as a Benjaminite; I am aware of no evidence for this, and the northern focus of his work, together with his home town of Tishbe in Gilead in northern Transjordan (1 Kgs. 17.1), makes it seem very unlikely.

[621] Against e.g. Dunn 1988b, 635; Esler 2003a, 293f., who insists that Paul is here expressing 'ethnic pride' (the older view of e.g. Dodd 1959 [1932], 184, reflected in the NEB: 'has God rejected his people? I cannot believe it! I am an Israelite myself . . .' This misses the scriptural echoes (as in the previous note), resulting in Dunn confessing that he cannot see the point of the reference to Benjamin.

[622] cf. too Phil. 3.5: *ek genous Israēl.*

[623] See *Perspectives* ch. 10.

[624] Where he quotes Isa. 10.22f. [21f. MT/EVV] in conjunction with Hos. 2.1 [1.10 MT/EVV].

statement that he has 'left for himself (*katelipon emautō*) seven thousand', which in turn was the answer to Elijah's overstated claim that he was 'left alone' (*kagō hypeleiphthēn monos*). The idea of the 'remnant' is thus rooted not only in written prophecy, but in the narrative of Israel. Elijah, the prophet of 'zeal',[625] is firmly told that God has provided a loyal remnant.

Yes, says Paul, and it is the same in the present time. Not all of 'Israel' have been disobedient and contrary: some have believed and confessed.[626] But this is '*according to the election of grace*'; that is the vital interpretative addition to the story. The first place Paul will find to stand, from which he can move cautiously forward into unexplored territory, is the place already marked out in his narrative of Israel in 9.6–13. As with Jacob and Esau, so now, the 'purpose of God in election' (9.11) will be established, 'not of works, but of the one who calls' (9.12). It is sometimes suggested that Romans 11 contradicts Romans 9. But here, as Romans 11 gets under way, we find Paul building on exactly the foundation he had laid two chapters before. As he does so, rubbing in the point in verse 6 ('if by grace, no longer by works, or grace would no longer be grace') what he says resonates strongly also with the description of Abraham's family in chapter 4.[627] At this point, he has not moved an inch from what he has already said about that family in chapters 1—4, or from the exposition of new-covenant salvation in 10.1–13.

The point of this 'remnant', then, is significantly different from the 'remnant' we find in some Jewish thinking roughly contemporary with Paul. There, the 'remnant' was the small number who had remained faithful Torah-observant Jews while everyone else fell away: a small number, in other words, who in Paul's terms in 9.30—10.3 had stuck with the pursuit of 'the law of righteousness', had pursued this law 'by works' and had believed themselves to have succeeded in sustaining 'their own righteousness'. This is precisely what Paul is here denying in insisting that it is 'by grace, no longer by works', as in chapter 4. *His theology of the 'remnant' is radically different from, say, that of Qumran.*[628] And this idea of a remnant chosen by grace then enables him to move forwards. Instead of a small number that looks like getting even smaller, this is a small number that looks like the start of something much bigger. That is the point of 11.11–15.

That, then, is the thrust of 11.1–6. But the fact that there is now a 'remnant according to the election of grace' then generates an important distinction: on the one hand, the 'election' or 'remnant' (including Paul himself); on the other hand, 'the rest', *hoi loipoi*. This is what he outlines in 11.7–10, where he returns to the question of Israel's 'search', or pursuit, as he had

[625] Immediately before the passage he quotes here (1 Kgs. 19.10b, 14b) we find Elijah's great protestation of 'zeal': 'I have been very zealous for YHWH, the God of hosts' (v. 10a, repeated at 14a). This resonates with Paul's own claim to 'zeal' in Gal. 1.13f., Phil. 3.6; and with his comment about those who (like his own former self) have 'a zeal for God', but not according to knowledge (Rom. 10.2).

[626] Did Paul see *apeithounta kai antilegonta* (10.21, quoting Isa. 65.2) as a kind of double opposite for the 'belief and confession' of 10.9f.?

[627] 4.4–6 and esp. 4.13–17, focused on 4.16: *ek pisteōs hina kata charin.*

[628] Details in Wright 2002 [*Romans*], 676.

described it in 9.30–1, 10.3 and 10.20 (*ho epizētei Israēl*, 'that which Israel sought'). I am inclined to punctuate verse 7 with a double question mark. The normal reading has a question followed by an answer: 'What then? Israel did not obtain what it was looking for; but the elect obtained it.' Perhaps, however, we should read, 'What then? Did Israel not obtain what it was looking for? Well, the elect obtained it.'[629] This is not merely a matter of style. Without that second question mark, Paul would appear to be making a distinction between 'Israel' and 'the chosen ones', leaving the word 'Israel' apparently denoting *simply* the company of those who did not obtain that which had been sought. With the second question mark, the distinction is between one 'Israel' and another, exactly as in 9.6b ('not all who are of Israel are Israel', *ou pantes hoi ex Israēl, houtoi Israēl*). 'Did Israel not obtain it? Well, the chosen ones did' – in other words, 'the chosen ones', *hē eklogē*, are the *positive* answer to the question, the 'Israel' that *did* obtain it, the second 'Israel' of 9.6b. Paul is here repeating, in a new form, the point he made in 9.31 and 10.3: Israel as a whole was looking for something but did not find it. There the contrast was with the gentiles who were finding something without looking for it; here the contrast is with 'the remnant' of Jews, the 'Israel' who, like Paul himself, have found it, albeit by grace not 'works'. 'The chosen company', *hē eklogē*, the second 'Israel', with Paul in their midst, are carrying forward the purposes and promises of God. They are the 'first fruits' of the much larger 'lump', as in 11.16a.

This brings us to the question: What then about 'the rest'? – the question which, one way or another, becomes crucial for much of the remainder of the chapter. From verse 7b through to verse 10 Paul explains, quoting once more from the law, the prophets and the Psalms (this, as usual, is surely not an accident, but an indication of a solemn statement), what has happened to 'the rest'. This is not, in other words, a bit of new or extraneous polemic against those who hold the position he once held himself. What has happened was foretold, and explained, in Israel's own traditions.

The basic claim is that 'the rest' have been 'hardened' (*epōrōthēsan*, verse 7b). It is important to understand what this means, and how the language of 'hardening' works, both in Paul's Jewish world and in his own thought. Obviously this has particular relevance for understanding 11.25, but we must do our best to set some parameters before we get there, rather than allow an assumed reading of that later verse to drive the present one.

The idea of 'hardening' is found at a similar point in 2 Corinthians 3. There, Paul is explaining the reason why Moses put a veil over his face: 'the sons of Israel' were not to be allowed to look at 'the end of what was being abolished', a cryptic way of referring both to the gradually fading glory of Moses' face following his encounter with God and to the ultimate 'end' or 'goal', the final future glory of which Moses' glory was a foretaste (3.13). Paul explains this by saying that in the case of the Israelites, 'their minds

[629] Elsewhere in Rom. *ti oun* as an opening question is followed by a second question: 3.9; 6.15. Cf. too *ti oun eroumen*, likewise regularly followed by a second question: 4.1 (see *Perspectives*, 579–84); 6.1; 7.7; 9.14, 30 (which should perhaps be re-examined in this light); cf. 1 Cor. 10.19.

were hardened', *epōrōthē ta noēmata autōn* (3.14). What is more, he says that this same condition, symbolized by the veil, persists to his own day: the equivalent of the hardening of the mind is that 'a veil lies over their heart' (3.15). This continuing condition of unbelieving Israel is only changed by the spirit-given freedom which enables one to gaze at 'the glory of the lord', at the one who 'has shone in our hearts to produce the light of the knowledge of the glory of God in the face of Jesus the Messiah' (3.16–18; 4.6). This happens 'whenever one turns to the lord': 3.16 quotes Exodus 34.34, and explains it in terms of the spirit. In other words, the hardening of the mind, or the veiling of the heart, is the continuing condition which is only to be transformed by the spirit's revelation of God's glory in the face of Jesus – in other words, through what Paul elsewhere refers to in terms of the 'call' of God and the work of the gospel of Jesus, resulting in Messiah-faith.

The two other references to 'hardening' in Romans are in very similar passages, in chapters 2 and 9. The word is different, using the *sklērotēs* root rather than *pōrōsis*, but the concept is closely aligned. In chapter 2, 'hardening' is what happens when God's judgment was already deserved but when God, in his patience and forbearance, provided a stay of execution to allow people to repent – and they refused:

> [2]God's judgment falls, we know, in accordance with the truth, on those who do such things. [3]But if you judge those who do them and yet do them yourself, do you really suppose that you will escape God's judgment? [4]Or do you despise the riches of God's **kindness**, forbearance and **patience**? Don't you know that God's **kindness** is meant to bring you to repentance? [5]But by your **hard**, unrepentant heart (*kata de tēn sklērotēta sou kai ametanoēton kardian*) you are building up a store of anger for yourself on the day of anger, the day when God's just judgment will be unveiled – [6]the God who will 'repay everyone according to their works'.[630]

The repetition of 'God's kindness' here in verse 4 (*chrēstotēs* and then *to chrēston*) is echoed in 11.22 (*chrēstotēs* no fewer than three times), and in a very similar context. Similarly, the notion of God's 'patience' here (*makrothymia*) is picked up in 9.14–23, precisely the other passage where the notion of 'hardening' plays a part:

> [17]For the Bible says to Pharaoh: 'This is why I have raised you up, to show my power in you, and so that my name may be proclaimed in all the earth.' [18]So, then, he has mercy on the one he wants, and he **hardens** (*sklērunei*) the one he wants.
>
> [19]You will say to me, then, 'So why does he still blame people? Who can stand against his purpose?' [20]Are you, a mere human being, going to answer God back? 'Surely the clay won't say to the potter, "Why did you make me like this?"' [21]Doesn't the potter have authority over the clay, so that he can make from the same lump one vessel for honour, and another for dishonour? [22]Supposing God wanted to demonstrate his anger and make known his power, and for that reason put up **very patiently** (*en pollē makrothymia*) with the vessels of anger created for destruction, [23]in order to make known the riches of his glory on the vessels of mercy, the ones he prepared in advance for glory – [24]including us, whom he called not only from among the Jews but also from among the gentiles?

[630] Rom. 2.2–6.

As we have already noted, in Romans 2 'God's kindness' is meant to lead to 'repentance', and in Romans 11 it is meant to lead to 'faith'. At the same time, God's 'hardening' of someone's heart appears to be a summary way of saying what is happening to Pharaoh in verse 17, quoting Exodus 9.16: God has raised him up, or 'made him stand', to reveal his power and announce his name in all the world. But this is what is then picked up in 9.22–4, with Paul's 'what if': in the events of exile and restoration, the 'potter and clay' moments spoken of by the prophets, *God is doing with Israel what he did with Pharaoh*, and indeed what he did with the 'hard and impenitent hearts' of chapter 2. That is, he is exercising great patience in order to make a space for something new to happen, but meanwhile 'hardening' those who, like the arrogant would-be judge in chapter 2, and Pharaoh in 9.17–18, persist in holding God's saving purposes at bay.[631] And the interesting parallel with 1 Thessalonians 2.16 makes its own point: this is the regular second-Temple Jewish theme of people using a time-interval to 'fill up the measure of their sins'.[632]

The point of Romans 11.7b is then to draw out the full meaning of this situation. 'The elect obtained it'; that is what Paul has insisted in 9.24 and 11.1–6, and presumably in the inclusion of Jews within the scheme of new-covenant salvation in 10.4–13. But 'the rest were hardened': they were, in other words, in the condition of resisting God's saving purpose, stumbling over the stumbling stone (9.32–3), and remaining 'ignorant of God's righteousness' (10.3). This, he insists, is precisely what scripture envisaged.

The scriptures in question begin with a quote from the Torah, namely Deuteronomy 29.4: 'But to this day YHWH has not given you a mind to understand, or eyes to see, or ears to hear.'[633] Deuteronomy 29 is of course part of the long warning about the 'curse', immediately preceding the crucial chapter 30 which Paul has set at the centre of his carefully constructed argument (10.6–8). God, declares Moses in prophesying the time of 'curse' and 'exile', has not given Israel a heart to know, or eyes to see, or ears to hear, up to this very day, despite the fact that Israel had seen all his wonders in Egypt.[634] In Deuteronomy, this condition will characterize Israel *up to the point where the covenant is renewed in chapter 30*. Even though Paul's judgment on his fellow (though unbelieving) Jews sounds harsh, he has been careful to couch it in terms which, in their original narratival context, are rooted in the covenantal scriptures and pointing forwards to the moment of covenantal resolution and rescue. Paul's reworked eschatology has not left the home base of monotheism and election.

The next reference is to Isaiah 29.10 ('God has poured out upon you a spirit of stupor', *pneuma katanyxeōs*), which links with the Deuteronomy reference by means of the regular Isaianic theme of unseeing eyes and

[631] See Jewett 2007, 586.

[632] Above, 1153–5.

[633] LXX 29.3.

[634] On all this, see Watson 2004, 436; Seifrid 2007, 670.

unhearing ears.[635] This is the condition which, in the book of Isaiah as a whole, describes Israel as it is apart for the rescuing work of God described in terms of the unveiling of his righteousness, the revelation of his glory and not least the work of the servant. Finally, Paul quotes from the Psalms ('Let their table become a snare and a trap, and a stumbling block and a punishment for them'): the original passage invokes the divine curse on those (presumably within Israel itself) who are opposed to the righteous and devout.[636] We should probably see this as an oblique reference to the 'table-fellowship' which non-Messiah-believing Jews, and also some Jewish Messiah-people, would try to restrict on ethnic grounds, as in Galatians 2.11–15 and 4.17. The reference to the 'stumbling block' picks up not only 9.32–3 (and thereby looks on also to 11.11–12), but also 1 Corinthians 1.23 and Galatians 5.11. The second couplet of this quotation ('Let their eyes be darkened so that they can't see, and make their backs bend low for ever') echoes the Isaiah prophecy about the unseeing eyes.

Let us put it delicately: if Paul had wanted to say that the condition of 'the rest' was not really that bad, that they could stay like that for a while and all would nevertheless be well in the end, that this was a temporary situation which would all come right eventually, he has gone about it in a very strange way. We should not read too much into the 'for ever' (*dia pantos*) in the last line, but we do not need to.[637] The entire passage from the second half of verse 7 through to verse 10 indicates that 'the rest', those who at present are not in the 'remnant', the *eklogē charitos*, are in the condition summarized by Deuteronomy 32 as well as 29. Paul aligns this condition with the 'hard and impenitent hearts' that refuse to use God's kindness as a chance for repentance in chapter 2, and the 'hardened' ones of chapter 9, those whom God has patiently put up with while developing his plan to make his power and his name known in all the world. The wider context of Romans 11 should leave us in no doubt that this is precisely the seam of thought into which Paul is here tapping once more – and, even, that it was *because* he wanted to get to *this* point in *this* way that he set up the previous categories, in chapter 9 especially, in the way that he did. Of course, the biblical quotations, especially that from Deuteronomy, hint that the condition of 'the rest' is by no means necessarily permanent. If someone is in the position described in Deuteronomy 29, they can always move forwards to Deuteronomy 30. That

[635] cf. Isa. 6.9f., and e.g. 42.18–20 with 42.7; 43.8.

[636] Ps. 68.23f.; cf. 15.3, quoting 68.10. Cf. too Rom. 3.10–18! And Ps. 35.8 (36.2 qu in Rom. 3.18).

[637] Jewett 2007, 664f. suggests that the probable meaning is 'continually' (cf. REB 'unceasingly') rather than (with RSV, NRSV, NEB, KNT) 'for ever'. Keck 2005, 267f. warns against the possible overtones of 'for ever'; see too Cranfield 1975, 1979, 2.552 and other lit. cited there; Dunn 1988b, 643f. See however Wright 2002 [*Romans*], 678: 'As the next passage will make clear, Paul does not suppose that any particular ethnic Jews are subject to this condemnation; there is always room for them to come to faith. The perpetual condemnation ... lies upon the rejection of the crucified Messiah, not upon this or that person who has acquiesced in that rejection ... judgment must be judgment if grace is to be grace.'

is what Paul has described in Romans 10.[638] But they also indicate that there is no hope for those who stay in that condition and do not move forward into the covenant renewal which has now taken place in the Messiah and is being implemented through the spirit.

(ζ) Romans 11.1–24: What Does Paul Envisage?

It is time to summarize our findings from the first twenty-four verses of the chapter, before proceeding to the final main section:

11.1–10				11.25–32
	11.11–12		**11.16–24**	
		11.13–15		

What then, according to 11.1–24, did Paul think was going to happen next, and on what grounds? I have argued above that, just as the centre of 9—11 as a whole is the christologically focused 10.1–17, so the centre of 11.1–32, that is, 11.13–15, is likewise essentially christological, echoing the 'reconciliation' theme in 5.10 as well as the 'Adamic' passages in 5.15–21, and leading, here as there, to the promise of 'life' (5.10, 21). I have suggested that this is the longer outworking of Paul's stated theme in the programmatic 9.5 (and, behind that, 1.3–4): Israel is 'the Messiah's people according to the flesh', and it is 'my flesh' that Paul seeks to 'make jealous', and some of whom he hopes to save (11.15). This 'jealousy' flows naturally from 9.30–1 (Israel is missing out, gentiles are coming in) and especially 10.18–21, focusing on Deuteronomy 32.21 (10.19).[639] This, to look back again, relates to 9.4–5: Paul's list of Israel's privileges summarizes what he has ascribed to the Messiah, and thence to his people, in Romans 3—8. Further back again, one might relate the 'jealousy' to 2.25–9, with its radical redefinition of *ho Ioudaios* and its mention of 'law-keeping uncircumcised people'.

But if the motif of 'jealousy' is natural as well as scriptural, because of gentiles coming in to the single Abrahamic family, Paul's use of it here is not only positive, pointing to the goal of salvation. He also uses it to remind the gentiles in Rome of what he had said back in 1.16: the gospel is *Ioudaiō te prōton kai Hellēni*, 'to the Jew first, and also, equally, to the Greek'. The present section maintains that careful balance. Paul never diminishes the 'also, equally'. That is what generates the 'jealousy'. But his renewed emphasis here, to the gentile Christians who seem to have needed it, is 'to the Jew

[638] Hill 2001, 1103 is wrong to suggest that 'the "mystery" revealed in 11:11–32 does not follow *logically* from 1:1—11:10' (his italics). Paul has carefully set up the category of the 'remnant according to grace' in such a way as to argue for its considerable increase. It is interesting that Hill sees vv. 11–32, and not just vv. 25–32, as revealing the new 'mystery', since vv. 11–24, as we have seen, do not themselves support the majority interpretation of vv. 25–32.

[639] We may note the immediately preceding verse, Dt. 32.20: They are a perverse generation, children in whom there is no faithfulness (*huioi, hois ouk estin pistis en autois*). This is precisely Paul's analysis of the problem in 11.20, 23.

first'.[640] His key move, transforming the 'jealousy' from negative into positive, is to indicate that even his own 'gentile apostolate' has Jewish salvation as its intended by-product. He 'glorifies' his particular ministry (11.13) – but not for its own sake. This is where the gentile Messiah-people discover that the 'elect' are the people *through whom*, not only *for whom*, God will work his saving purposes. When Paul sees gentiles believing the gospel, he thinks, 'Perhaps this will make my flesh jealous *and save some of them*' (11.14b). In terms of the entire flow of the letter, and not least of 9.1—11.10, this statement must be correlated with 10.1–13, where Paul prays for 'their' salvation and explains how this 'salvation' will be accomplished, going on in 10.14–17 to speak of the apostolic ministry as the necessary instrument of this faith-focused covenant renewal. However paradoxical it may seem, *Paul's own gentile mission will be the means*, or at least *a* means, *by which this prayer will be answered.* This, however counter-intuitive to many today, and perhaps also to many in Paul's own day, is at the heart of his argument.

That, at any rate, is Paul's hope, stated in realistic terms. He knows that most of his fellow Jews still resist the gospel message, even though he knows of many who, like himself, have come to recognize Jesus as Messiah after themselves previously being 'hardened'.[641] That is the point of 11.1–6: there is a 'remnant', *and this is the kind of remnant that can be expanded indefinitely.* As in 1 Corinthians 9.22, the 'some' in 11.14 is not an anticlimax: it is the Pauline mixture of certain hope and sober realism. That is to say: the 'lump' and the 'branches' of 11.16 are emphatically not beyond the reach of God's salvation. God has not abandoned the Jewish people; their 'tripping up' (11.11) does not mean that they have 'fallen completely', that no more Jews can ever be part of the second 'Israel' of 9.6b.

That is the main point he wants to get across, throughout the chapter, to the potentially anti-Jewish Roman Christians. But the 'salvation' for which he prays in relation to presently unbelieving Jews (10.1) will still depend on faith (10.6–13; 11.23). The main thrust of Paul's argument is firmly against anyone (gentile Christians, clearly) who might say 'God has cut them off, so God cannot and will not graft them back in'. The gospel remains 'to the Jew first'. The door is always open for them to return, and Paul's own gentile apostolate is itself part of the paradoxical means by which it will happen. But if Paul knew that there would come a time when some might say 'Very well: so you are saying that all Jews will after all be saved in the end,' all the evidence suggests that he would have rebutted that suggestion with equal force.

All this, then, points forward to the crucial little passage 11.25–7. This is where many controversies have clustered, much like seagulls round a fishing boat.

[640] The Jew-and-gentile point is repeated in 2.1–11; 3.21—4.25; and esp. 9.24; 10.4–13.

[641] See e.g. the list in Rom. 16, which includes various of his own kinsfolk (16.7; 11 – and possibly more: Prisca and Aquila (16.3) are said in Ac. 18.2 to be Jewish). Cf. too Col. 4.10f.

(η) 'All Israel Shall Be Saved': 11.25–7

The final section of 11.1–32 consists of verses 25–32.

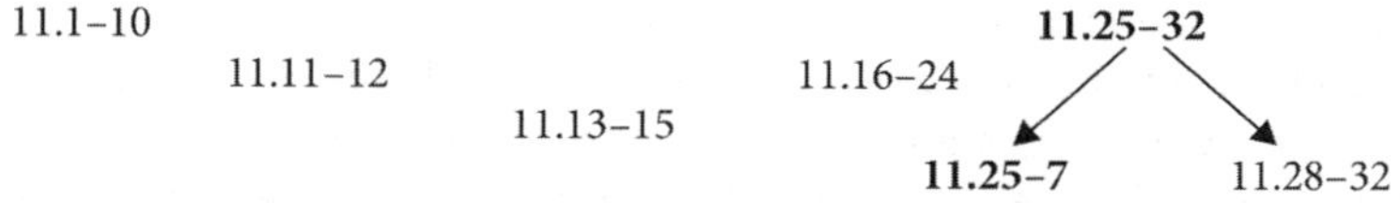

As so often in Paul, a dense opening statement (in this case, 11.25–7) is followed up with explanatory remarks (11.28–32) which draw the point to a sharp rhetorical conclusion. We note the obvious but often ignored rule: the dense opening statement means what the later verses say it means! With this in mind, we plunge into the all-important verses 25–7. I have translated them like this:

> [25]My dear brothers and sisters, you mustn't get the wrong idea and think too much of yourselves. That is why I don't want you to remain in ignorance of this mystery: a hardening has come for a time upon Israel, until the fullness of the nations comes in. [26]That is how 'all Israel shall be saved', as the Bible says:
>
> The Deliverer will come from Zion,
> and will turn away ungodliness from Jacob.
> [27]And this will be my covenant with them,
> whenever I take away their sins.

Faced with this, a majority of exegetes today have held Paul to be saying, basically, four things. First, he announces a new 'mystery', in addition to what has already been said and perhaps even trumping or contradicting some of it.[642] Second, the content of this 'mystery' is that the 'hardening' on the majority of 'Israel' is only temporary, and that it will in the end be removed, allowing those formerly 'hardened' to come to be saved in a large group. Third, this large group will be added to the presently existing Jewish 'remnant', this total (and totally Jewish) group being what Paul means by 'all Israel'. Fourth, the *parousia* of Jesus will be the time when, and perhaps also the means by which, this will happen.

There are of course variations. Some see the 'mystery' as consisting in the whole train of thought from verse 11, a position with which I am sympathetic for reasons that will become apparent. Some see the 'salvation' as being effected through 'faith', as in 11.23, even if this 'faith' is a sudden thing, occurring at the *parousia* itself; others insist that it must be a fresh act of powerful divine grace, without any correlated human activity, even 'faith' itself. Even granted the Jews-only view of 'all Israel', there are plenty of options: all Jews who have ever lived? All Jews alive at the time? Most but not all? And so on.

[642] Jewett 2007, 695 transfers the word 'mystery' into its English equivalent, speaking of the 'mysterious, future salvation of all Israel'. This is to use semantic slippage to point away from what Paul is actually saying.

I wish to argue, not for the first time, against all four of these points. However unpopular this case is, exegetical arguments, rooted in the assumption that Paul has built up a subtle and sustained argument over three chapters to this point (and, indeed, over all eleven chapters so far!), must be allowed a hearing.

1. First, on the 'mystery'. It is highly unlikely that when Paul says 'I do not want you to remain in ignorance of this mystery' he is referring to a *new* 'mystery', a secret piece of wisdom or doctrine which he is about to reveal.[643] For a start, the *gar* indicates that verse 25 is continuing to explain what has just gone before; it is not a new point, but a further drawing out of what was said in 11.16–24. For another thing, the purpose clause (literally, 'so that you may not be wise beyond yourselves'), which interestingly anticipates the similar appeal in 12.3, picks up exactly the thrust of the 'olive tree' picture and of 11.11–24 as a whole, repeating and amplifying the warning but not introducing anything new. Joachim Jeremias argued a generation ago that what we have here is not, as is often imagined, an 'apocalyptic speculation', but a combination of 'paraenesis' and 'warning against arrogance'.[644] Nils Dahl agrees:

> Paul introduces this statement as the disclosure of a revealed mystery. Yet the solution draws the conclusion of the preceding arguments. We should probably not think of a sudden, unmediated revelation granted to Paul but rather of a mystery hidden in Scripture until its explanation was unveiled.[645]

This is exactly right: what Paul says here summarizes, and draws out the significance of, the whole previous section from verse 11, rather than adding something substantially new.[646] The passage warns against gentile arrogance; well, he has already issued that warning, coming at the question from various angles from 11.13 onwards and sharpening the point in verses 17–24 with the rhetorically forceful second person singular. The passage speaks of a 'hardening' of Israel (except for the remnant); well, he has already spoken about that in 11.7, building on the 'hardening' passage in 9.14–23. The passage speaks of gentiles 'coming in' as a result of what has happened to most Jews; well, he explained in 11.11–15 that the Jews' 'stumble' had led to gentile inclusion, that the Jews' *apobolē* had resulted in the world's *katallagē* (11.15). Every element in verse 25 is thus simply a summary of what has gone before. Likewise, the possibility of restoration for Jews at

[643] e.g. Bruce 1963, 221. Jewett 2007, 698 unsurprisingly reports that 'efforts to specify the precise source of this oracle have not been successful': another case of hunting in the dark for a black cat that wasn't there anyway. On the emphatic nature of this opening, see e.g. Jeremias 1977, 195.

[644] Jeremias, ibid.; see too Ridderbos 1975 [1966], 358: 'One is not to think here of a special revelation he received, an esoteric secret, but of the insight he has into the realization of God's counsel . . .' Contra e.g. Wolter 2011, 427, who suggests that Paul can only solve the puzzle he faces when he speaks the language of apocalyptic ('apokalyptisch redet').

[645] Dahl 1977, 152, citing the background in the Scrolls for the use of 'mystery' as something present in scripture but only recognized by inspired interpreters; he compares Eph. 5.32.

[646] Of course, one could then argue the other way, and suggest that 11.11–24 is hinting all along at what we now find in 11.25–7; but one cannot then use the dense 11.25b–26a, interpreted in a particular way, to avoid what is said at more length in the earlier passage.

present 'hardened', of their sins being taken away, as in the combined scriptural quotations of 11.26b–27, is held out in the generalized terms of verses 12, 14 and 15, and becomes the key subject in 11.23–4, at the climax of the 'olive tree' allegory and the lead-in to the present short passage. The biblical citations are therefore likewise a summary of what has been said already. In particular, the notion of God's 'covenant' with Israel, so emphatically stressed in verse 27 with the combined quotation from Jeremiah 31 and Isaiah 27, looks back to the great exposition of the renewed covenant in 10.6–13, where Deuteronomy 30 was highlighted, and picks up from the implied promise in 11.8, where Paul quoted the immediately preceding chapter, Deuteronomy 29. The entire section from 9.6 onwards stands under the question of whether God has kept his word. The 'mystery' of Romans 11, in fact, is *the entire sequence of thought from 11.11 onwards*, building on the whole argument of 9.6—11.10, and drawn together in a single statement (11.25–7) at the start of its final sub-section. And this 'mystery' is rooted in the christology of the earlier chapters.

We would be wrong, in any case, to suppose that when Paul speaks of a 'mystery' he must necessarily be talking of a 'new doctrine' which is to be added on to those already taught.[647] Paul is obviously well aware that the word could be used in that fashion, but in several of his own uses he seems to mean something different, something more like a penetrating insight gained through a combination of scripture and reflection on the gospel.[648] The gospel itself, after all, was for Paul a 'revelation', not just in that Jesus had appeared to him in person on the road to Damascus but in that when it was proclaimed it 'unveiled' the righteousness of God.[649] In 1 Corinthians he writes of having proclaimed God's mystery to them simply by speaking of Jesus and his crucifixion.[650] When he speaks of himself as a 'household manager for God's mysteries', he means much the same;[651] and there may be more than a touch of irony, as he explains to the Corinthians, eager for 'special effects', the very down-to-earth gospel which he not only preaches but also embodies. To be sure, there may well be all kinds of heavenly secrets into which some may be able to peer.[652] But again and again they are all focused, for Paul, on the Messiah himself.[653] Indeed, to suppose that

[647] As suggested by e.g. Bockmuehl 1997 [1990], 170–5, speaking (174) of a 'hitherto unreleased piece of eschatological intelligence'.

[648] See Bockmuehl 174f.: 'The catalyst (as in many Jewish examples) is a Biblical meditation sparked by a problem of current concern: and the answer thus obtained is described as a mystery, i.e. a gift of revelation.' Whether we describe this as 'charismatic exegesis' (discussed by Bockmuehl 175 n. 88) does not affect his, or my, point. Bockmuehl is right to say that Paul 'couches new disclosures in fully traditional language and Biblical reasoning' (174), but this is precisely what he has done in 11.11–24, which does not predict the large-scale End-Time 'salvation of Jews' favoured by the majority.

[649] Rom. 1.17; 3.21.

[650] 1 Cor. 2.1f. This is reinforced a few verses later when he refers to 'speaking God's hidden wisdom in a mystery', again related directly if paradoxically to the cross (2.7f.).

[651] 1 Cor. 4.1.

[652] 1 Cor. 13.2; 14.2.

[653] e.g. Eph. 1.9f.; Col. 1.26f., summing up the great poem in 1.15–20 and explaining that the 'mystery' which has been revealed among the nations is 'the Messiah in you as the hope of glory'; cf. 2.2.

there might be a 'mystery' which was *not* centred upon the Messiah would have called into question some of Paul's most central beliefs. A 'mystery' for him was not a different thing, a separate category of knowledge from 'ordinary' Christian truth. The term became, rather, a way of flagging up the fact that some aspect of the gospel conveyed (a) a startling perspective on reality which other worldviews would not have imagined, (b) a perspective which would transform the faithful beholder and (c) a perspective which would join up the dots in the otherwise opaque eschatological plan of God.

This might include the *parousia*, but from the passages just cited it need not. Granted, of the two other passages in which Paul declares, after a long discussion, that he is now revealing a 'mystery', one of them has to do with the *parousia*, but as the previous discussion indicates this is by no means necessary. About the Messiah, yes; about the *parousia*, not necessarily. In 1 Corinthians 15.51, sometimes cited as an example of Paul telling a 'new doctrine', the 'mystery' which Paul solemnly announces is not in fact a completely different truth from the one he has been explaining for the preceding fifty verses (that is, the future bodily resurrection based on the resurrection of Jesus himself). It is a new angle of vision on the *same* point, explaining (as in 1 Thessalonians 4.15–17, using different imagery) what will happen to those who are left alive. But that leads Paul back, through the quotation of Isaiah 25.8 and Hosea 13.14 in 1 Corinthians 15.54–5, to the very point he made nearly thirty verses earlier, in verse 26: 'Death is the last enemy to be destroyed.' The 'mystery' here, in other words, is the result, not of a new revelation of a special doctrine quite different from anything hitherto spoken of, but of a particular, scripturally rooted, angle of vision which takes the hearers back, in more clarity and depth, to what had already been said. I suggest that in Romans 11 the combined quotation in verses 26 and 27 has much the same effect: taking the hearers' minds back to the points he was making around forty verses earlier, that is, in 10.1–13. 'This will be my covenant with them, whenever I take away their sins' (11.27) answers to, and deepens, the exposition of Deuteronomy 30.

The other similar passage makes the point more graphically. Ephesians 3 grows out of the programmatic 1.8–10 and the summing up of the gospel's effects in 2.11–22. In the latter passage, we find a viewpoint not unlike that of Romans 11: the coming together of Jews and gentiles in the single family of God, as both a tell-tale sign of God's plan to unite all things in the Messiah and a warning sign to the principalities and powers. Thus:

> 1[8]Yes, with all wisdom and insight [9]he has made known to us the secret (*mystērion*) of his purpose, just as he wanted it to be and set it forward in him [10]as a blueprint for when the time was ripe. His plan was to sum up the whole cosmos in the Messiah – yes, everything in heaven and on earth, in him.
>
> 3[2]I'm assuming, by the way, that you've heard about the plan of God's grace that was given to me to pass on to you? [3]You know – the secret purpose that God revealed to me, as I wrote briefly just now? [4]Anyway ...

When you read this you'll be able to understand the special insight I have into the Messiah's secret (*mystērion*). [5]This wasn't made known to human beings in previous generations, but now it's been revealed by the Spirit to God's holy apostles and prophets. [6]The secret is this: that, through the gospel, the gentiles are to share Israel's inheritance. They are to become fellow members of the body, along with them, and fellow-sharers of the promise in the Messiah Jesus.

[7]This is the gospel that I was appointed to serve, in line with the free gift of God's grace that was given to me. It was backed up with the power through which God accomplishes his work.

[8]I am the very least of all God's people. However, he gave me this task as a gift: that I should be the one to tell the gentiles the good news of the Messiah's wealth, wealth no one could begin to count. [9]My job is to make clear to everyone just what the secret plan (*mystērion*) is, the purpose that's been hidden from the very beginning of the world in God who created all things. [10]This is it: that God's wisdom, in all its rich variety, was to be made known to the rulers and authorities in the heavenly places – through the church! [11]This was God's eternal purpose, and he's accomplished it in the Messiah, Jesus our lord.

What Paul describes as a *mystērion* in Ephesians 3 is what he has spent half the previous chapter spelling out in detail, namely the coming together of Jews and Gentiles in a single body. This is not a *new* point, then, but a drawing of attention to the depth and power, to the heaven-and-earth nature, the fresh revelation, of the point just made. Much western scholarship has exemplified a characteristically protestant tendency to allow eschatology to trump ecclesiology, and so to prefer the 'mystery' of 1 Corinthians 15 (the future resurrection) to that of Ephesians 3 (the polychrome people of God). But part of Paul's point – in both letters, actually, and then especially in Romans itself! – is that ecclesiology (the fresh and full understanding of the Jewish doctrine of election in the light of Jesus the Messiah and of the spirit) is correlated all through with eschatology, similarly understood. The balance of our own present chapter and the previous one should make this point, but for the moment we simply note that the 'mystery' of Ephesians 1 and 3 (holding 2.11–22 in the middle), and the parallel passages in Colossians and indeed in the ending of Romans itself,[654] are not tell-tale indications of a different kind of theology to what we find in the 'main letters'. They are, rather, characteristically Pauline expressions of the belief that the central gospel events themselves reveal the secret, age-old plan of God the creator, the plan for 'the fullness of the times', for the 'but now' moment,[655] through which God would bring together all things in heaven and on earth and, in particular, would unite Jews and gentiles in a single body. There is every reason, therefore, to reject the idea that in Romans 11.25 Paul is putting forward a fresh 'revelation' which will state a new point out beyond, in addition to and perhaps even in contradiction to what he has said already.

This way of understanding the 'mystery' language here already hints at a very different reading of 11.25–7 from that of the majority. Before we can get to that, however, we must turn to the second point. What does he mean by

[654] Col. 1.26f.; 2.2, both of which look back to what has already been said in 1.15–20; Rom. 16.25, on which see Wagner 2002, 164f. n. 140; 271 n. 166.

[655] See Gal. 4.4.

saying that 'a hardening has come for a time upon Israel, until the fullness of the nations comes in'?

2. The normal view (to repeat) is that this 'hardening' (*pōrōsis*), clearly referring to 11.7 ('the rest were hardened', *hoi de loipoi epōrōthēsan*), is a temporary condition imposed on Israel (upon all, that is, except the 'remnant', such as Paul himself, who have already come to faith in the Messiah), which will then be removed through the events spoken of in verses 26 and 27, allowing 'the rest' to join 'the remnant' in coming to this same faith and so to the same salvation.[656] (The other view, still very popular, that sees a 'salvation' for 'the rest' apart from faith in the Messiah, is ruled out by verse 23, as well as 10.1–13 – as well as by 1.16–17, 3.21—4.25, and by Paul's earlier emphasis against there being any *prosōpolēmpsia*, 'respect of persons', with God.[657] Such a 'salvation for all Jews' would leave unsaved gentiles in the position of complaining against God for unfairness after all – and, according to Paul in Romans 4 and Galatians 3, they would have Abraham championing their cause.)

Let us be quite clear. Paul sees, in Romans 11 and in the parallel in 2 Corinthians 3, that there is indeed a possibility of this 'hardening' being removed. The whole point of 11.11–24 is that Jews who are at present in the category of 'the rest' who are being 'hardened' can indeed be made 'jealous' and so aroused to faith in the Messiah and to the salvation held out in 10.1–13. They can at any time, in other words, move from Deuteronomy 28 to Deuteronomy 30, to the covenant of heart-circumcision, to the Torah-keeping which consists of faith (10.6–9). This is what Paul means when he says, in 2 Corinthians 3.16, 'when one turns to the lord, the veil is removed'. That had happened to Paul himself, by his own account the most zealous of them all, and Paul looked for it to happen again and again *during the course of*, and indeed provoked by, his gentile apostolate. There is no sense, then, that the category of 'the rest' who are presently 'hardened' is a fixed number from which there can be no further movement. That is precisely what Paul is arguing against. But the 'unhardening' happens precisely 'when one turns to the lord'; or, in Romans, 'if they do not remain in unbelief'.[658]

[656] Harink 2003, 180–4, finds the phrase 'coming to faith' indicative of an individualistic understanding of 'faith' as something 'voluntary and self-moved', as opposed to Paul's being 'radically interrupted, accosted, captured, and commissioned in an apocalypse of the risen lord'. This, he says, leads to a failure to read God's relationship to Israel apocalyptically, 'that is, as a relationship in which God is the sovereign actor who interrupts and lays hold of Israel for his own purposes'. The present discussion should give the lie to the latter charge (and cf. e.g. Watson 2007 [1986], 329 n. 45). To the former, I refer to what has been said in ch. 10 above about 'faith' as the result of the spirit-driven 'apocalypse' in the gospel; and, in Rom. 9—11 itself, to 9.32; 10.4, 9–13, 14, 16, 17; and perhaps above all 11.20 and 23. The phrase 'coming to faith' may evoke, for some, an individualistic or voluntaristic self-caused fideism; I have used it heuristically, to summarize these and similar Pauline passages. Here as elsewhere W. S. Campbell 2008, 149–51 has followed Harink into an unnecessary ditch. See further below.

[657] So, rightly, Cosgrove 1997, 32, with many others including e.g. Sanders 1978, 183; Wagner 2002, 298 n. 238, against Stendahl, Gager, Gaston, and many others including now, it seems, Jewett 2007, 701f. For 'respect of persons', see 2.11 and discussion above.

[658] This is 'individualistic' (see Wagner 2002, 279 n. 194) only, but exactly, to the extent that *tinas* in 11.14 should be understood thus: individuals but precisely members of ethnic Israel who become, by faith, part of the second 'Israel' of 9.6.

By the same token, the notion of 'hardening', as we have seen it developed in chapters 2 and 9, and as Paul expresses it again in 2 Corinthians 3, does not of itself encourage the idea that this 'hardening' is a temporary condition *to be followed by an automatic unhardening*. The idea 'that this malady will ultimately be overcome'[659] is so firmly fixed in recent exegetical tradition that it, ironically, has itself formed such a hard crust on the reading of the passage that it may take a miracle to break through. One might invoke something Markus Bockmuehl says in a different context: 'Perhaps this is yet another instance where less is known than is confidently asserted.'[660] Much as we might like to hope for a sudden universal unhardening, this is simply not how the notion of 'hardening' itself functions. As we saw, the 'hard and impenitent heart' of 2.4–5 was what came about when the 'kindness' of God, meant to lead to repentance, was refused, so that the 'hardening' was the prelude, not to a sudden mercy despite the lack of repentance, but to judgment. This is cognate with the ancient biblical idea (not least in the Abraham-narrative and its exodus-promise) of a nation's sins being 'filled up' to the point where judgment was the only remaining possibility.[661] Similarly, the hardening of Pharaoh's heart, which in the narrative of 9.14–23 was then applied to the 'vessels of wrath' at the time of God's whittling down of Israel to a remnant, was not a temporary state which would then be reversed, but rather a condition brought about through the mysterious combination of human hard-heartedness and divine purpose. This, as we saw, Paul interpreted as the result of Israel's being 'the Messiah's people according to the flesh', with the Messiah's crucifixion inscribed into their history as it was into Paul's own very being.[662]

To repeat: Paul is not saying that all those presently 'hardened' are bound to remain in that condition. On the contrary. That is the position he fears the gentile Christians in Rome may adopt, and he is arguing against it, all the way from 11.11 to 11.32. Indeed, it is partly in order to argue against that position that he has constructed this seriously dense and densely serious section of the letter. Presently hardened Jews can at any time, he insists, be 'made jealous', and can thereby be brought to Messiah-faith and so to salvation. But we must not, in our eagerness to agree with him on this subject, overaccept the point and over-exegete the passage. The 'until' clause ('until the fullness of the nations comes in') does indeed provide a temporal marker, but it is not a marker which of itself can tell us what happens to the 'hardened' part of Israel once that time is reached. The majority view among recent exegetes has been to read the 'until' as indicating the time after which the 'hardening' will be lifted, and all 'the rest', suddenly unhardened, will be

[659] Jewett 2007, 700.

[660] Bockmuehl 1997 [1990], 174.

[661] Gen. 15.16; cf. again Mt. 23.32, and above, 1153f., on 1 Thess. 2.16.

[662] Again, Gal. 2.19f.; 6.17.

saved (with or without faith).[663] But Paul does not say this, and we must not without warrant lurch after such an understanding.

On the contrary. Insofar as there is a 'hardening', it is because the alternative is swift judgment, as in 1 Thessalonians 2.14–16. If that judgment is delayed, it is because of God's kindness and forbearance. But the proper response to that kindness and forbearance is not to tax it further, not to presume upon it continuing until a time when the 'hardening' is removed automatically, but to use the time thus created, the breathing space as judgment is delayed, for repentance (2.4) and faith (11.23). I am not aware of any occurrence of the quite widespread biblical theme of 'hardening' which envisages such a phenomenon as leading to anything other than eventual judgment.[664] (At this point someone will say, 'Ah, but that's where Paul is different.' But it begs the question to offer Romans 11.25–7 as evidence.)

Paul does not, in 11.11–32, spell out his view of what will happen to those who do not use this breathing space appropriately. But 11.7–10 tells its own story, as of course do 9.1–5 and 10.1. If, after all, Paul really did believe that those at present 'hardened' would sooner or later be rescued by a fresh divine act (perhaps sooner, if he did indeed expect the *parousia* in a short time), then why the tears? Why the unceasing anguish of heart? Why the heartfelt prayer for 'their' salvation, and the careful exposition of what it would take to bring that about (10.1–13)?[665] The only possible answer to this would be the exegetically fantastic one: that *up to the point of writing Romans* Paul has had this unceasing sorrow and anguish of heart, but *now that he has thought the matter through afresh*, or perhaps indeed has received a sudden divine revelation between the writing of verses 24 and 25 of Romans 11, through which he has discovered the new 'mystery' of Romans 11.25–7, he sees that actually he need not have been so concerned.[666] And that, as we have seen, would indeed be a fantasy. It is ruled out absolutely both by the extremely careful rhetorical planning and structuring of this whole section, and by the fact that 11.25 is closely linked to, and does not appear to offer a new view over against, all that has preceded it.[667] If the majority view were correct, Paul ought really to have told Tertius, his scribe, to throw away these three chapters and start again. And, actually, with that, he should have told him to scrap the whole letter. A good deal of chapters 2, 3 and 4 would have to go as well.

[663] Jewett 2007, 662 quotes Cranfield 1979, 549 approvingly in relation to the 'provisional character of the hardening'.

[664] cf. 2 Thess. 2.6–12, where the idea of 'restraint', though not the same as here, likewise means a delay in eschatological judgment.

[665] Jewett 2007, 698 sees this point clearly but cannot resolve it. See Schreiner 1998, 618: 'it is unlikely ... that the hardening to which Paul refers is reversible', except in the case of those who by grace come to believe.

[666] A version of this is offered by e.g. Schnelle 2005 [2003], 351.

[667] Starling 2011, 156 suggests that 'Israel' in 11.26 cannot mean 'the church' because this would be against the whole drift of the previous paragraphs. This is extraordinary: to look no further, the 'olive tree' of 11.17–24 clearly envisages the single community of God's people in which believing Jews and believing gentiles are both full members.

Exegesis, then, tells heavily against the majority view, of a present 'hardening' which will suddenly be removed. This is not to say that *apo merous* in 11.25 cannot be temporal ('for a time'), as opposed to partitive ('in part'), i.e. 'a hardening has come upon *a part* of Israel'.[668] Such a temporal meaning, though, would not point to a sudden last-minute 'unhardening'. The anguish of 9.1–5, and the heartfelt prayer of 10.1, are best explained, indeed perhaps can only be fully explained, if we assume that Paul thinks the 'hardening' will eventually give way to final judgment.[669] That gives just as much of a sense of time-lag: 'for a while'. But it is in my judgment far more likely that Paul is here referring to the 'hardening' coming upon *one part* of Israel, as in 11.1–7, especially verse 7.[670] This, as we have seen, was for a purpose: with the 'remnant' on the one hand and Paul's gentile mission on the other, not only will gentiles continue to 'come in', but the 'remnant' itself will become very much larger, moving towards an eventual 'fullness' (verse 12). The gentiles, too, will have their 'fullness' as they come in (verse 25): just as there was a 'fullness of time' at which God would act, so there is a 'fullness of persons', the completion of God's plan of worldwide salvation. That is the process of the gentile mission, which has been in view since 10.14–18, and which plays its key part in the argument of chapter 11 at verse 14. And that mission, Paul has already said in 11.14, is *the means by which God is making 'his flesh' jealous and so saving some of them*. Hence the two 'fullnesses' are related.

3. That, I propose, is how we should read 11.26a: *kai houtōs pas Israēl sōthēsetai*, 'and in this way "all Israel shall be saved"'. At this point an exegete arguing my present case may well feel like Paul as he quotes Elijah: 'I'm the only one left!'[671] It is not true, of course. There may not be seven thousand, but there might be seven or more out there who have not ... well, perhaps we had better not complete that sentence; anyway, if this is a Pauline remnant, as opposed to an Essene one, there might yet be more to come.[672] So strong has the majority view been that it has simply been assumed, not usually argued, (a) that this refers to a *new* event over and above anything yet described, (b) that 'all Israel' here can only refer to Jews,

[668] The alternative partitive reading, 'a partial hardening' (REB; cf. Gaston 1987, 143, 'there were only some things that Israel did not understand'), misses the point: in view of 11.1–10, being 'partly hardened' would make as much sense as being 'partly pregnant'. Wagner 2002, 278 translates 'a partial insensibility', but I do not think he intends the same view as Gaston.

[669] In parallel with 1 Thess. 2.14–16, though the referent may be different; see above, 1151–6.

[670] The phrase is temporal in Rom. 15.24; partitive (or 'quantitative') in Rom. 15.15; 2 Cor. 1.14; 2.5. See Bell 1994, 128 with other refs. Bell thinks that *apo merous* must go with *pōrōsis* rather than either *gegonen* (Cranfield's choice: 1979, 575, which I followed in Wright 2002 [*Romans*], 688) or with *Israēl*, which I now strongly prefer (with e.g. Keck 2005, 279). Paul is evoking, as the chiasmus of chs. 9—11 reaches its conclusion, the division within 'Israel' adumbrated in 9.6.

[671] 11.3, quoting 1 Kgs. 19.10, 14.

[672] cf. e.g. Whiteley 1964, 97f.; Glombitza 1964–5; Giblin 1970, 303; Jeremias 1977; Martin 1981, 134f.; Ponsot 1982; Aageson 1986, 284f.; Chilton 1988 (cf. too Chilton 2004, 234: Paul was aiming 'to include all the gentiles ... within an Israel now defined by faith alone'); and, a notable back-up for the list, Barth 1936–69, 2.2.300 (and behind him Irenaeus, Calvin and many others). Others are noted by Moo 1996, 721; Jewett 2007, 701 n. 73. See too the partial agreement from Donaldson, Keck (by implication), Niebuhr, and Wagner, noted below.

(c) that this may therefore refer to a mode of salvation other than that described in 10.1–13 or envisaged in 11.14, 23, and (d) that this will take place at the *parousia*.

The last of these points (d) will be dealt with presently when we look at the scriptural quotations in 11.26b–27 and challenge the fourth common assumption (that Paul is here thinking of something which happens at the *parousia*). The third (c) (a different mode of salvation) had its peak period of popularity a decade or two ago, at the climax of the post-holocaust reaction, and now seems to be in decline, though not without powerful advocates.[673] Most of those who now take 11.26a to refer to a future event, perhaps at the *parousia*, take Paul's point and link this to faith in Jesus, often suggesting a parallel with the sudden revelation through which Paul himself became convinced that Jesus had been raised and was Israel's Messiah.[674] But to assess this we must look more closely at (a) and (b).

(a) First, does verse 26a describe a *further* event, in addition to and subsequent to what has already been described, or does it describe, from a different and ironic point of view, the *same* event which Paul has been speaking of in 11.11–15 and 11.16–24? The first option – a further event – has regularly been allowed to pass unchallenged because of English translations which have rendered *kai houtōs* as 'and so'.[675] This, though accurate in its way, has allowed slippage: Paul's Greek means 'and in this way', or, as I have translated it, '*that is how* "all Israel shall be saved"'. But the English 'so'[676] can also mean 'then', which *houtōs* does not normally permit but which the majority view has assumed to be correct.[677] In this view, *first*, the fullness of the gentiles coming in, *then, after that, subsequently*, a new event involving the salvation of 'all Israel' as a different body.

Part of the argument against this majority reading has already been provided. If this were the case, why is Paul in such anguish? If Paul has known

[673] e.g. now Jewett 2007, 701. It is extraordinary to see the normally precise Jewett declaring that 'all' in 'all Israel' 'does not lend itself to the expression of exceptions'; one need only glance at mSanh. 10.1–3 to see the obvious counter-example, with three substantial paragraphs listing (and in some cases disputing) categories of people who might have been thought to be 'all Israel' but who will not inherit the coming age. The frequent OT phrase 'all Israel' makes the point (e.g Ex. 18.25; Dt. 1.1; 5.1; 13.11; 29.2; 31.11; 34.12; Josh. 3.7; 1 Sam. 3.20; 7.5; 25.1; 2 Sam. 8.15; 1 Kgs. 8.62; 12.1; 18.19; 1 Chr. 9.1; 18.14; 29.21; 2 Chr. 12.1; 29.24; Dan. 9.11): these regularly refer to the great bulk of the people, without at all implying 'every single individual'.

[674] e.g. Hofius 1990, 36f.; Jewett 2007, 701; Wolter 2011, 432 and many others.

[675] RSV and NRSV follow KJV, RV: 'and so all Israel will be saved'; NEB is shameless in its paraphrase, 'when that has happened, the whole of Israel will be saved'; REB goes an inch further with 'once that has happened . . .'. Contrast e.g. NJB: 'and this is how all Israel will be saved'.

[676] In German, *so* is consequential, not temporal. But the 1967 edition of the Luther translation has *alsdann*, 'then' or 'thereupon', which makes exactly the wrong point.

[677] van der Horst 2006, 176–80 and Jewett 2007, 701 produce various possible exceptions in which *houtōs* has a temporal sense; not all of them are to my mind convincing, though they succeed in putting a question mark beside the absolute non-temporal meaning indicated in e.g. BDAG 741f. and stressed by Fitzmyer 1993, 622f. See too Bell 2005, 259f. Davies 1984, 347 n. 36 sees *houtōs* as the equivalent of *tote*, 'then', which even the putative exceptions (he mentions Jn. 4.6) hardly warrant; see too e.g. Hofius 1990, 33–5. Schreiner 2001, 477 n. 14 (and 481) says that he is not suggesting that *kai houtōs* is temporal, only that the context reveals a temporal sequence. That is precisely what is at issue. A good deal of this was already well addressed by Jeremias 1977, 198.

all along that all his fellow Jews will eventually be saved – especially if, as the majority suppose, he envisages this at the *parousia* and expects that event in the near future – then why is there such a problem? Actually, however, the regular meaning of *houtōs* provides a rebuttal of (a) above: Paul gives no indication that he is talking about a *further* event, but rather gives every indication that this process in 11.25 – the hardening of Israel *apo merous*, and the use of the time thus created for the fullness of the gentiles to come in – *is the means by which* God is saving 'all Israel'.

The distinction between reading *houtōs* as an indication of time and an indication of manner effects a serious shift. If we read it as temporal, it opens up a forward perspective in the text: 'and *then*, something new will happen, namely the salvation of "all Israel", as scripture says . . .'. But if we read it as an indication of manner, it looks back: 'and *that*, the entire sequence of 11.11–24, summed up in 11.25, is *how* "all Israel" will be saved'. But this brings us to the all-important phrase itself.

(b) The apparent strength of the majority case on 11.25–7 is undoubtedly that the word 'Israel', elsewhere in this discussion, appears to refer to Jews and only Jews. Is it possible to gain any more precision at this point?

It is. Paul, as we have seen, has very carefully structured the entire three-chapter sequence. And he opens the account, the great historical narrative in which his theological point is displayed, with a clear distinction: not all those who are 'of Israel' are in fact 'Israel' (*ou gar pantes hoi ex Israēl houtoi Israēl*) (9.6b). That distinction hangs over the rest of the discussion like a puzzling question mark: who then are 'Israel', if not all Abraham's physical children are to qualify? Already this ought to alert us to the fact that *pas Israēl* in 11.26, close to the balancing point with 9.6 in the rhetorical architecture of the whole section, is not likely to mean 'all Abraham's physical children'.[678]

But (it will be objected) in 9.6–13 there is indeed a process of selection from *within* Abraham's physical family, a narrowing down which will continue through 9.14–29; but that still implies that 'Israel' is going to designate a subset of Abraham's physical children, rather than including gentiles. Not so. The all-important verse 9.24 indicates otherwise: 'we whom he called' is specifically broadened to include 'not only from Jews but also from gentiles'. And the 'call' here is the same technical term that we see in 9.7 and 9.12: 'in Isaac shall your seed be *called*', *klēthēsetai*, and 'not of works but of the one who *calls*', *tou kalountos*. 9.24, in fact, indicates already what is then picked up in 9.30 and 10.19–20: gentiles have found *dikaiosynē*, have even found God himself (10.20: 'I was found by those who were not looking for me'). This is the meaning of 10.6–13 as well. The Deuteronomic covenant renewal, Israel's great hope, has been fulfilled in and for all, Jew and gentile alike, who confess Jesus as *kyrios* and believe that God raised him from the dead. It would be absurd to say that, though believing gentiles are now

[678] See Keck 2005, 280: 'In 9.6 . . . [Paul] distinguishes the phenomenon "Israel" in history . . . from the Israel that will be saved on the day of salvation. This Israel may also be the olive tree into which the *plērōma* of the gentiles have been grafted, joining the regrafted Jews.'

numbered among the Deuteronomic new-covenant members, the ones whom God 'called', the ones who in turn, as in Joel, 'call on the name of the lord', the ones who, back in 2.25–9, 'fulfil the law', have their uncircumcision reckoned as circumcision, and are given the name *Ioudaios* – that these ones are not after all to be classified also as 'Israel', Abraham's seed. This, too, is already foreshadowed in the densely programmatic 9.5: the Messiah is 'of their race according to the flesh' and also 'God *over all*, blessed for ever', picked up dramatically in 10.12, *ho gar autos kyrios pantōn*, 'for the same lord is lord of all'. Gentile believers hail Israel's Messiah as 'lord'; Paul says they have found what Israel was looking for.

This is the evidence that must be set alongside the fact that the regular meaning of 'Israel' in chapters 9—11 is 'all, most or at least some Jews'. Leaving aside the distinction in 9.6, there are seven such references.[679] But the line of thought throughout the whole letter has all along indicated the possibility of a *polemical redefinition* even of this noble term for God's people.[680] We have already studied the relevant passages: 2.25–9, with its redefinition of 'circumcision' and even 'Jew', and chapter 4 as a whole, with its radical redefinition of Abraham's family, the discussion from which, in effect, chapter 9 then picks up the threads. The parallels in Philippians 3.2–11 ('we are the circumcision', 3.3), and especially Galatians, make the point strikingly. Galatians 6.16, as we saw, uses the phrase 'the Israel of God' to refer to the whole family of Abraham, Jewish Messiah-believers and gentile Messiah-believers alike.[681] We note again, as we did above, the interesting reference to 'Israel according to the flesh' in 1 Corinthians 10.18. Paul is there expounding the exodus-narrative, in order to apply it to the Jew-plus-gentile *ekklēsia* in Corinth to whom he has said that 'our fathers' were under the cloud and passed through the sea. In teaching the *ekklēsia* to think of itself as the people who tell this story as their own and learn to live within it, Paul's reference to 'Israel *kata sarka*' is revealing. Had he wished to reserve the word 'Israel' to mean 'Jews and Jews only', he would hardly have needed to add the qualifying phrase. This then coheres with the tripartite division of the human race in 10.32: Jews, Greeks, and the *ekklēsia tou theou*, the church of God. Clearly Paul has not settled on a single designation for the Messiah-people. But, equally clearly, he constantly refers to that people in ways which indicate what his explicit argument in Romans 2—4, in 2 Corinthians 3, in Galatians as a whole and in Philippians 3 all make clear: that in

[679] 9.27 (twice), 31; 10.19, 21; 11.2, 7.

[680] See esp. Cosgrove 1997, 23, insisting that the burden of proof here rests on those who would argue for what he calls 'national Israelism'. Donaldson 1997, 236–47 argues that Paul sees gentile converts as 'proselytes to a reconfigured Israel', so that 'Gentiles "in Christ" are ... members of Abraham's family; thus gentiles share in righteousness and salvation by becoming full members of a redefined Israel' (247). See the discussion in Wagner 2002, 293. Donaldson, however, distances himself from my own reading (345f. n. 41; 354f. n. 29), which may mean that I had not made myself fully clear. I was not (and am not) saying that, for Paul, the present situation (with only a small number of converts) is all that there is; rather, Paul is arguing from that present fact to the certainty that there will be many more, a future 'fullness'.

[681] See above 1145–51. In that case, as in the present one, the conclusion can only be resisted by ignoring the argument of the rest of the letter.

Israel's Messiah, Jesus, the one God has fulfilled the ancient Israelite hope, expressed by Torah, prophets and Psalms alike, by bringing the nations of the earth to belong to Abraham's people. Paul is acutely aware of the many painful paradoxes that go with this belief, but he will not draw back from it.

What is more, as we saw in examining 11.11–24, the whole context, particularly the 'olive tree' metaphor, encourages the reader to regard believing gentiles and believing Jews – and especially a lot more of the latter – as part of the same 'tree', which as we have seen many who remain unsure about the referent of 11.26 are happy to see as in some sense 'Israel'. This is the point where Ross Wagner, in his full and detailed study of Romans 9—11, agrees strongly with me on the redefined meaning of 'Israel', though not on the mode and timing of the final inclusion of ethnic Jews:

> This view [that 'all Israel' may include believing gentiles] is certainly a plausible inference from Paul's language of the gentiles 'coming in', particularly when it is heard in conjunction with the olive tree metaphor, where Gentile 'branches' are grafted into the 'root', which is Israel . . . For Paul, 'Israel' will be a complete entity only when 'the fullness of the gentiles' comes in and 'the Redeemer' comes from Zion to take away 'Jacob's' sins.[682]

I note in particular Wagner's point about the gentiles 'coming in' while part of Israel is 'hardened': what are they 'coming in' to, if not 'Israel', especially once more in the light of the olive tree? This makes it more difficult than people usually imagine to insist that the 'Israel' in verse 25, since it only refers to Jews, must be determinative for the 'all Israel' in verse 26.[683] Instead, what we have, in line with verse 19, is an 'Israel' simultaneously emptied (in part) by the exclusion of 'broken branches' and refilled by the inclusion of 'wild olive branches'. If that was what Paul means in verses 17–24 – and it seems uncontroversial – then we could gloss verse 25b–26a as follows, with the italicised portion imported from 11.11–15 and 11.23–4:

> A hardening has come upon part of 'Israel', until the fullness of the gentiles has 'come in' to that same 'Israel', *causing a much greater number of those presently 'hardened' to become 'jealous' and to swell the present small 'remnant' to a 'fullness' out of all proportion to its present diminution*; and that is the means by which, in the traditional phrase, '*All* Israel shall be saved.'

All Israel! A polemical redefinition indeed, making perfect sense in view of the repeated 'all' in 10.4, 11 and 13, and anticipating the 'all' of 11.32.[684]

[682] Wagner 2002, 278f.

[683] Against, it seems, Wagner himself (2002, 237 n. 65). The idea that 'entering in' is a pre-Pauline expression reflecting Jesus-tradition about the kingdom (e.g. Cranfield 1979, 576; Käsemann 1980 [1973], 313; Dunn 1988b, 680; Moo 1996, 718) seems to me a way of ignoring the rather obvious link to the 'olive tree' (note the 'grafting in' of vv. 17, 19, 23, 24, and remember the *gar* of v. 25; Jewett 2007, 700 considers this link 'less likely' without saying why), and thence to the idea of 'Israel' (Jewett 701: 'the eschatological church containing the predestined number of Jews and gentiles'). I am for some reason reminded of Schweitzer's famous remark about fetching water from a distance in a leaky bucket to water a garden which already has its own flowing stream (though he was making a different point).

[684] See Niebuhr 2010, 43ff.: the expression 'Israel' has been given new semantic content through 'those who call on the name of the lord' (which for Paul is focused on the Christ-event) in 10.13. On this point see esp. Rowe 2000.

Indeed, if 'come in' is taken in that sense of 'coming in' to the olive tree, to Israel,[685] the normal argument swings round 180 degrees: instead of saying 'Israel in verse 25 is ethnic, so it must be in verse 26 as well', we ought to say 'Israel in verse 25 consists of the whole people of God, within which many Jews are presently "hardened" *but into which many gentiles are being incorporated*, so "all Israel" in verse 26 must reflect that double existence.'[686]

First, then, there is the situation Paul faces when writing the letter:

ISRAEL

most Jews currently hardened | small but growing remnant | gentiles brought in

which leads to the future he envisages:

ALL ISRAEL

hugely increased 'remnant', through jealousy/faith | fullness of gentiles

The 'all' in 'all Israel' here is in my judgment best understood as a typically Pauline (and characteristically cryptic) note of redefinition, in line with the other such points elsewhere, not least Galatians 6.16.

There is every possibility, therefore, that *pas Israēl* in Romans 11.26 is just such another polemical redefinition, picking up the phrase which may have already been current: 'All Israel has a share in the age to come'. Just as the rabbis redefined that phrase so that it excluded Sadducees, and other Jews deemed to be beyond the pale,[687] so Paul has redefined it to include (1) Messiah-believing Jews – himself, all others already in that category and, he hopes, a much larger number who come to be 'jealous' and so to believe,[688] and (2) Messiah-believing gentiles ('to the Jew first, and also equally to the Greek'). But it excludes, as the rabbis' own 'all Israel' excluded those who were deemed outside, those Jews who, despite being given a space of time by God's patience and kindness, have stumbled over the stumbling stone and have not picked themselves up, have not become 'jealous' in the way

[685] See too Keck 2005, 279: the 'coming in' refers to 'their entering the people of God'.

[686] This shows, too, that Donaldson's objections (1997, 346f.) to my proposal miss the point: Paul does indeed envisage that the present 'some of them' in 11.14, which forms the background to 11.23f. and so to 11.25f., will become significantly more than at present, justifying the exalted (though deliberately vague) language of 11.11–15. No 'significant semantic shift' is required between vv. 25 and 26. Schreiner 2001, 477 speaks for the majority: in 11.25 'hardening is ascribed to "Israel" and salvation to "Gentiles".' That is exactly wrong: 'hardening' is ascribed to *part of Israel*, and what is ascribed to gentiles is 'coming in'. I hope it is clear that my argument for reading 'all Israel' in this way is not based on, but merely parallel to, my reading of Gal. 6.16 (against Eastman 2010, 385 n. 63). Nor is it 'against the context' of 11.25; it is in line with it (against most commentators; e.g. Bell 2005, 260; Reinbold 2010, 403).

[687] mSanh. 10.1.

[688] Wagner 2002, 279 n. 194, argues that the 'massive turning of Jews to Christ' will be '*as a result of* and *subsequent to* the entrance of the full number of gentiles' (his italics). But the 'as a result of' is dependent on 11.11–15, especially 11.14, and there Paul is clearly talking about the ongoing effect of his own ministry, not something which will happen as a distinct, later event. Most who see the large-scale final turning of Jews to the Messiah here envisage that this will be the result, not of gentiles coming in and their becoming jealous, as in 11.11–15, but of the *parousia* (e.g. Seifrid 2007, 673).

Deuteronomy 32 described, have not been provoked by Paul's own gentile apostolate, have not come to believe and confess in the way Deuteronomy 30 indicated, have not 'submitted to God's righteousness' (10.3), have not availed themselves of God's circumcision of the heart, have not joined in the renewal of the covenant and have not grasped at the divine fulfilment of the Abrahamic promises. To be sure, Paul locates this multiple failure ultimately in the inscrutable purposes of Israel's God. But he also lays all these charges at the door of his contemporaries.

This is not what most exegetes in the modern western tradition have wanted to hear. But it is what Paul wanted to say. Just as 'the wrath of God' in 1 Thessalonians 2.16 may refer, not to the judgment of the last day, but to an event or events within concrete history, so the saving of 'all Israel' may refer here, as in 11.14 and the surrounding verses, to actual concrete 'turnings' in which more and more of Paul's fellow kinsfolk will no longer 'remain in unbelief' (11.23).

We may note in particular, in concluding this point, that it is very close to what Ed Sanders argued thirty years ago, in an exposition which has not, I think, had its proper impact on subsequent discussion. Though Sanders continues to take 'Israel' as meaning 'Jews', he emphatically rejects 'two-covenant theology', as proposed by Mussner, Stendahl and others.[689] 'There is only one olive tree', he writes, 'and the condition of being a "branch" is "faith", for the Jew just as much as for the Gentile.'[690] The simplest reading of 11.13–36, he concludes, is this:

> The only way to enter the body of those who will be saved is by faith in Christ; the mission to the gentiles will indirectly lead to the salvation of 'all Israel' (that is, 'their fullness') [at this point Sanders adds a footnote: 'this supposes that *plērōma* in 11:12, *tinas* in 11:14 and *pas* in 11:26 mutually interpret one another']; thus at the eschaton God's entire plan will be fulfilled and the full number of both Jews and gentiles will be saved, and saved on the same basis . . .[691]

This holding together of the 'fullness' of verse 12, the 'save some of them' of verse 14 and the 'all Israel' in verse 26 is crucial. Paul is not offering two different routes for Jews, the first through 'jealousy' during the course of his ministry (and presumably, since by now Paul was used to the fact that he might die before the final End, during the course of other people's ministries) and the second through sudden fresh revelation at the *parousia*. How, in any case, would the latter escape the charge either of arbitrariness, if all Jews alive at the time were to be converted as Paul had been by a sudden revelation of Jesus (what about those who had died in the meantime?), or of partiality, if this applied retrospectively to all Jews who had ever lived (if God was going to do that for them, what about the scrupulous fairness of Romans 2.1–11, 3.27–30, and 10.6–13?), or indeed of coercion, if it were to

[689] Sanders 1983, 192–5.

[690] Sanders 1983, 195.

[691] Sanders 1983, 196. Sanders goes on to say that he thinks Paul's views would have changed if he could have seen all that has happened in the time since he wrote.

be automatic, with no room for the response of faith? And how would such an assertion support the warnings of 11.17–24 and especially 11.25? But if, when Paul says 'all Israel', he is envisaging a large, 'full' accumulation of a far greater number than at present, but by essentially the same means of 'jealousy' at the success of the gentile mission, then the passage holds together both in itself and with the rest of chapters 9—11, not least the central and vital 10.1–17.

4. All this brings us back to the fourth and final point of contention. What about the biblical citations which follow immediately upon 11.26a? Do they not state clearly that Paul is thinking both of the *parousia* and of a large-scale last-minute conversion of Israel, in the sense of presently unbelieving and 'hardened' Jews?

No. We note, as a preliminary point, that even if verses 26b and 27 did refer to such a thing, the implication would be, against the drift of the post-Stendahl 'two-covenant' reading, that Paul would still suppose that presently unbelieving Jews needed to have their 'ungodliness' removed, to have their 'sins' forgiven. But it is not only the two-covenant theory that is ruled out here. Paul's combination of quotation, allusion and echo, including his interesting modification of Isaianic passages in particular, indicates that he is *describing* the same event as in 11.14 (the possibility that presently unbelieving Jews will be made jealous and will come to faith and so to salvation), and that he is *connoting* the larger picture which he has already set out in 10.6–13, namely the fulfilment of the Deuteronomic 'new covenant', as interpreted further in Isaiah and, by echoing implication, Jeremiah. The 'covenant' which is cited here in verse 27 ('and this will be my covenant with them', *kai hautē autois hē par' emou diathēkē*), the first actual mention of *diathēkē* since 9.4 though it has been implicit underneath the argument all along, is not a separate 'covenant' to the one Paul has expounded in Romans 2.26–9, 4.1–25 and now in the present section, particularly 10.6–13. It is certainly not a 'covenant' which God has made with the Jewish people behind the back of the Messiah and of Abraham himself, to whom was promised, and to whom has now been given, a worldwide family. That would be dangerously close to the position against which Paul argues throughout Galatians, especially in chapter 3, and which has been firmly ruled out in 9.30—10.21. The covenant in question is precisely the covenant *through which sins will be forgiven*, which for Paul can only mean the covenant in which God has at last accomplished the purpose for which he called Abraham in the first place. It is the covenant through which, as in Deuteronomy 30, the 'curse' is lifted at last; the covenant through which, as in Isaiah 27 and Jeremiah 31, Israel's sins are forgiven.

It is worth looking at those two passages in more detail.[692] Isaiah 27 follows the sequence which predicts Israel's redemption, climaxing in resurrection.[693] The chapter picks up the theme of Israel as YHWH's vineyard, first

[692] On all this see esp. Wagner 2002, 280–98.

[693] 26.19; cf. *RSG* 116–18.

heard in chapter 5. The picture is not developed as smoothly here as in that earlier chapter, but the image of God's people as a tree recurs again and again, first in terms of the promise of blessing:

> Jacob shall take root, Israel shall blossom and put forth shoots, and fill the whole world with fruit[694]

but later in terms of continuing judgment:

> when its boughs are dry, they are broken; women come and make a fire of them. For this is a people without understanding; therefore he that made them will not have compassion on them, he that formed them will show them no favour.[695]

It is just possible that Paul has had this picture of the tree, restored and judged by God, in his mind as he developed his parallel image of the 'olive tree' with its branches. Whether or not that is so, his apparent quotation of a verse in between those two would fit nicely. The MT of the passage is translated thus in the NRSV:

> By expulsion, by exile you struggled against them; with his fierce blast he removed them in the day of the east wind. Therefore by this the guilt of Jacob will be expiated, and *this will be the full fruit of the removal of his sin*: when he makes all the stones of the altars like chalkstones crushed to pieces, no sacred poles or incense altars will remain standing.[696]

Paul, however, seems to have the Old Greek in mind: instead of 'this will be the full fruit of the removal of his sin', the Greek has *kai touto estin hē eulogia autou, hotan aphelōmai tēn hamartian autou*, 'and this will be his blessing, whenever I remove his sin'. Paul is echoing that final phrase, substituting *autōn*, 'their', for *autou*, 'his', and placing it at the end of the clause, and making 'sins' plural for singular. Thus, in the Isaiah passage, God's eschatological actions of mercy and judgment, like God's kindness and severity in Romans 11, stand on either flank, textually and theologically, of the forgiveness of sin, which in context means the removal of Israel's continuing idolatry. This fits well with the Deuteronomic context of Paul's own critique of his fellow Jews, in which he understands their refusal to believe the gospel, to 'submit to God's righteousness', in terms of the age-old idolatry predicted by Moses and pointed out by the prophets.

The forgiveness of sins is of course the ultimate blessing of the 'new covenant' predicted by Jeremiah.[697] Paul echoes this theme in the one other passage (2 Corinthians 3) where he speaks of the present 'hardening' of

[694] 27.6.

[695] 27.11. The LXX bears little relation here to the MT.

[696] 27.8–9. The italicized clause (MT *wezeh kol-periy hasir chatta'thō*) has come out quite differently in the Greek, and it is this to which Paul is alluding: see below.

[697] So e.g. Dahl 1977, 153. Wagner 2002, 290 is right to correct me for saying in an earlier article (Wright 1995 ['Romans and the Theology of Paul'], 61 = *Perspectives* ch. 7, 120) that Paul is *quoting* Jer. here, but he misses the key point: Jer. 31.34 (LXX 38.34) speaks of God forgiving iniquity and sin. Rom. 11.27, affirming that God's covenant will consist of his forgiving his people's sins, while at one level obviously quoting Isa. 59.21 and 27.9, at another level resonates powerfully with Jer. 31.33–4.

non-Messiah-believing Jews and where, as we saw, he speaks of Messiah-believers in terms very similar to those in Romans 2.25–9 and 7.4–6. According to Jeremiah,

> The days are surely coming, says YHWH, when I will make a new covenant with the house of Israel and the house of Judah. It will not be like the covenant that I made with their ancestors when I took them by the hand to bring them out of the land of Egypt – a covenant that they broke, though I was their husband, says YHWH. But this is the covenant that I will make with the house of Israel after those days, says YHWH: I will put my law within them, and I will write it on their hearts; and I will be their God, and they shall be my people. No longer shall they teach one another, or say to each other, 'Know YHWH', for they shall all know me, from the least of them to the greatest, says YHWH; for I will forgive their iniquity, and remember their sin no more.[698]

Paul is not quoting directly from this passage in Romans 11.27. But the way in which Jeremiah, here as elsewhere, picks up the Deuteronomic picture (God placing his law within his people and writing it on their hearts) resonates with Romans 2 and 7 as well as with 2 Corinthians 3. More particularly, it goes exactly with Paul's exegesis of Deuteronomy 30 in Romans 10.6–10. When, therefore, he declares that 'this will be my covenant with them, whenever I take away their sins', we would be right to hear the strong echo of Jeremiah 31 alongside or within the quotation from Isaiah 27. That in turn strongly reinforces a reference to Deuteronomy 30 in the sense which Paul has understood it in Romans 10.

This sends us back to Paul's primary biblical reference in these verses, which is from Isaiah 59. Here there is no problem in establishing the quotation; the difficulty is rather the reverse: why has Paul not quoted the whole passage, which is so germane to his purpose throughout these chapters? The answer may well be that Paul, here as elsewhere, was content to strike a note and let it resonate, intending indeed to refer to the whole passage but in haste to bring in also the other element, of the forgiveness of sin, which was found in the promises of restoration in Isaiah 27 and Jeremiah 31. Here, in any case, is the full Isaiah passage in question. Following a chapter in which the prophet has complained about the absence of justice (*mishpat*, *krisis*) and righteousness (*tsedaqah*, *dikaiosynē*), and has declared that Israel's transgressions are many, and that they testify against them, the prophet declares that YHWH himself will act, unveiling his own righteousness:

> YHWH saw it, and it displeased him that there was no justice. He saw that there was no one, and was appalled that there was no one to intervene; so his own arm brought him victory, and his righteousness upheld him. He put on righteousness like a breastplate, and a helmet of salvation on his head; he put on garments of vengeance for clothing, and wrapped himself in fury as in a mantle. According to their deeds, so will he repay; wrath to his adversaries, requital to his enemies; to the coastlands he will render requital. So those in the west shall fear the name of YHWH, and those in the east, his glory; for he will come like a pent-up stream that the wind of YHWH drives on.

[698] Jer. 31[LXX 38].31–4. The final clause in LXX is *kai tōn hamartiōn autōn ou mē mnēsthō eti.*

> And he will come to Zion[699] as Redeemer, to those in Jacob who turn from transgression, says YHWH. And as for me, this is my covenant with them, says YHWH: my spirit that is upon you, and my words that I have put in your mouth, shall not depart out of your mouth, or out of the mouths of your children, or out of the mouths of your children's children, says YHWH, from now on and forever.[700]

This whole passage is clearly very congenial to Paul: the revelation of God's righteousness, resulting in judgment and mercy, in the renewal of the covenant, in the gift of the spirit, in the words (*rhēmata*) in the mouth – all of this takes us back once more to 10.1–13, and makes us insist once more that Paul is here reaffirming what was said there, rather than trying out a different 'solution', an alternative way of salvation.[701] I do not think his switching, after 'this is my covenant with them',[702] to Isaiah 27 and (by implication) Jeremiah 31, has anything to do with a backing off from what Isaiah 59 goes on to say; rather the reverse. He is taking Isaiah 59 for granted, but is building in a further element, namely, that some in 'Israel' are presently under judgment but that their sins can be forgiven, and that this message is urgently needed by those at present 'hardened'.

At the same time, he has transformed Isaiah 59.21, so that instead of the Redeemer coming *on behalf of* Zion, he is coming *from* Zion. (Paul has elsewhere, of course, taken texts about the coming of YHWH and made them into texts about the coming of Jesus, as we saw earlier.) This change from *on behalf of* to *from* cannot be accidental. I suggested elsewhere that it could be an echo of another Isaianic passage, the promise of the Torah and God's word flowing out *from* Zion in order to bring judgment and peace to the nations of the world.[703] It might also be an echo of the blessing of Moses which ends (33.28–9) with the salvation of Israel: in 33.2 we read that 'the Lord comes from Sinai', *Kyrios ek Sina hēkei*.[704] A third option is Psalm 14.7:

> O that deliverance for Israel would come from Zion!
> (LXX *tis dōsei ek Siōn to sōtērion tou Israel*)
> When YHWH restores the fortunes of his people,

[699] MT *wuba ltsiyon go'el*; LXX *kai hēxei heneken Ziōn ho rhuomenos*. Why LXX has *heneken* instead of merely *eis* is not clear, but the result, MT's 'to Zion' and LXX's 'on behalf of Zion', is what Paul then radically adjusts: see below.

[700] Isa. 59.15b–21.

[701] Though the 'spirit' is not mentioned explicitly in Rom. 10, there is good reason to conclude that Paul understands the spirit's work when he quotes Joel 2.32 [LXX 3.5] in 10.13; and the parallels with Rom. 2.26–9 point in the same direction. See above, 1164–6.

[702] *kai hautē autois hē par' emou diathēkē*, the identical words in LXX Isa. 59.21 to Paul's quote in 11.27a.

[703] Isa. 2.3 (=Mic. 4.2): *ek gar Ziōn exeleusetai nomos kai logos kyriou ex Ierousalēm*. See Wright 1991 [*Climax*], 250f. Wagner 2002, 292 draws attention to Seitz 1993, 72, who points out that in this Isa. passage the gentile nations come in to Zion first, followed (Isa. 2.5) by 'the house of Jacob' in 2.5. Donaldson 1997, 329 n. 66 says, against my proposal, that 'nothing in Rom 11:25–26 parallels Isa 2:2–3, where God's word goes out from Zion to the gentiles'; but that depends on the prior assumption that Paul is here speaking of the *parousia*. If he is speaking (as in 10.14–21; 11.11–15) of a gentile mission whose reflex will be to 'make my flesh jealous' and so save some of them, it fits rather well: see below.

[704] cp. the similar use in *1 En.* 1.4: cf. Wright 2002 [*Romans*], 692 n. 463.

> Jacob will rejoice; Israel will be glad.[705]

Perhaps it is all three. The combination of Deuteronomy, Isaiah and the Psalms (Torah, prophets and writings once more) would not be unknown in Paul, to say the least. The effect, anyway, is the same: he has transformed a promise about something that God will do *for* Zion into a promise about something which God will do *through* or *from* Zion. It is quite true, as Terry Donaldson has argued (against his own earlier view), that Paul makes almost no use of the theme of 'the pilgrimage of the nations to Zion', which might at first sight seem strange granted his 'inclusive' vision and apostolate.[706] But the reason, I believe, now emerges, and forms a key element in Paul's redefinition of Jewish eschatology around Jesus and the spirit. If, as we have seen throughout this Part of the book, Paul sees Jesus and the spirit as constituting the renewed temple, the place where and the means by which Israel's God has returned as he had promised, then it would make no sense to undo this powerful theology by reinstating the earthly Jerusalem as the place to which the nations should go to find salvation (or, indeed, by translating it into a heavenly Jerusalem, a concept with which Paul was familiar but which is not relevant to the present discussion).[707] On the contrary: salvation is coming *from* Zion *to* the nations. Paul is not reinscribing the older centripetal tradition,[708] but nor is he abandoning the old belief that when Israel's God finally acted to fulfil his promises to his people the gentile nations would come under his rule, whether for rescue or ruin.[709] Rather, he is transforming the tradition into a centrifugal movement: the Redeemer now comes, with the gospel, *from* Zion to the world, and as a reflex (exactly as in 11.11–15) will 'banish ungodliness from Jacob'.[710] Paul has already stated in these chapters that he understands his own commission as the apostle to the gentiles to be the fulfilment of the

[705] Ps. 14 [LXX 13].7; the NRSV has turned the question in MT and LXX into the expression of a wish. Ps. 53.6 (suggested by Donaldson 1997, 329 n. 66) prays for salvation to come 'from Zion', but it is there salvation for Israel only.

[706] Donaldson 1993, 92; 1997, 101f.; against Donaldson 1986. The connection is assumed by e.g. Hays 1989a, 162.

[707] For the heavenly Jerusalem see Gal. 4.26. Some of the later rabbis transferred the ultimate 'pilgrimage' to the heavenly Jerusalem: e.g. bBB 75b (ascribed to R. Jochanan, a late third-century teacher).

[708] See e.g. Davies 1974, 217, using language which has now become politically incorrect though correctly Pauline: 'The life "in Christ" is the life of the eschatological Israel, an Israel, which, through Christ, transcends the connection with the land and with the Law attached to that land.'

[709] Donaldson 1993, 92 suggests that an inversion of the sequence 'Israel – gentiles' would mean 'the abandonment of the foundation of the tradition itself', since in that tradition the salvation of gentiles is the *consequence* of their seeing 'the redemption of Israel and the glorification of Zion'. This ignores Paul's central point, especially in 10.4–13: in the events concerning the Messiah, and in the outpouring of the spirit, Paul sees precisely the fulfilment of Israel's ancient hope. It is as a consequence of *that* that gentiles are now coming in. Moo's reply to Donaldson (1996, 684), that Paul's quote from Isa. 59.20f. is immediately adjacent to Isa. 60.1–7, one of the most important 'pilgrimage to Zion' texts, is well taken; but Paul is radically recasting the tradition around the Messiah, not simply echoing it. For earlier debates on this issue, e.g. between Stuhlmacher and Zeller, see Sanders 1983, 199f.

[710] 'Ungodliness' here echoes God's 'justification of the ungodly' in 4.5; Paul sees 'Jacob' in the same position as the pagans. On the transformation of the 'pilgrimage' tradition cf. Dunn 1988b, 680–2, though with some differences from my treatment here.

Isaianic promise of the herald announcing God's kingdom (10.15, citing Isaiah 52.7), and that this same ministry to the nations is designed, he has already said, to make 'his flesh' jealous and so save some of them. All this would fit exactly with the two lines of Isaiah 59 as Paul has adjusted them in Romans 11.26b. This, then, will be God's covenant: yes, the spirit and the word, as in Isaiah 59 and as in Romans 10, but more particularly the forgiveness of sins. 'Hardened' Israel cannot be affirmed in its present condition. Rather, the Israel that at the moment is still in the position of Deuteronomy 27—9 (as in 11.8) needs to be brought forwards into Deuteronomy 30. And that means Messiah-faith.

The complex of quotations in verses 26 and 27 thus have no specific reference to the *parousia*. True, Paul can use the verbal equivalent of the noun *ho rhuomenos*, 'the Deliverer', when referring to Jesus' return and his delivering of his people from the wrath to come.[711] But that does not mean that whenever he uses a cognate word he must always be referring to the 'second coming'.[712] In fact, there are good arguments for suggesting that it is God himself who is coming to deliver his people, not Jesus specifically, even though as we have seen elsewhere Paul cannot now speak of God without thinking of Jesus, or vice versa.[713] Perhaps once more, as in 11.11–15, Paul is deliberately leaving the prediction imprecise. What matters is that scripture will be fulfilled, the sin-forgiving covenant will be enacted and God's word will not have failed (9.6a).

What is particularly telling is the exact form of the quotation from Isaiah 27 at the end of 11.27, *hotan aphelōmai*, '*whenever* I take away' their sins. The natural reading of this is not to refer to one single action, a unique, one-off saving event at the end of all things, but to an indefinite future possibility. It could of course mean 'whenever it may be that I perform that single action', but it could equally mean 'at whatever time, however frequently repeated, people "turn to the lord and have the veil removed"', as in 2 Corinthians 3.15.

The point of it all – the thrust of this passage within the actual argument of Romans 11, as opposed to any grander scheme of soteriology or salvation history – is once again to insist, not upon a grand, large-scale last-minute conversion of all Jews (which would not have been relevant to the theme Paul is here stressing; if that was what was intended, the gentile Christians in Rome could have shrugged their shoulders and waited for God to do that in his own time) but upon what we might call the saveability of Jews within the *continuing* purposes of God. And this in turn is because Paul wants to be sure that the gentile Christians in Rome have really understood *grace*: all who are saved are saved by God's grace, and that means that ethnic origins, whether Jewish or gentile, generate no claim in themselves. That is the point of verses 20 and 23–4 in particular: gentile Christians

[711] 1 Thess. 1.10.

[712] Against e.g. Bell 2005, 267.

[713] See e.g. Fitzmyer 1993, 624f.; Keck 2005, 281f.; Wagner 2002, 297; Sanders 1983, 194. The normal *parousia* view is reaffirmed in Jewett 2007, 704.

'stand fast', not because they are gentiles (the temptation which Paul is warding off) but because they are Messiah-faith people. Likewise, when they are faced with the cultural pressure to dismiss the Jews as hopelessly cut off from God for ever, they must continually remind themselves that, following their 'casting away', such unbelieving Jews are now just as open to grace, just as able to be 'received back', as were the gentiles themselves – indeed, more so, since the 'olive tree' from which they have been cut out is still 'their own olive tree' (verse 24).

This then points to the final emphatic conclusion.

(θ) Disobedience and Mercy for All: 11.28–32

The last five verses of this section explain what has just been said and draw the argument of the letter so far to a rhetorically satisfying conclusion:

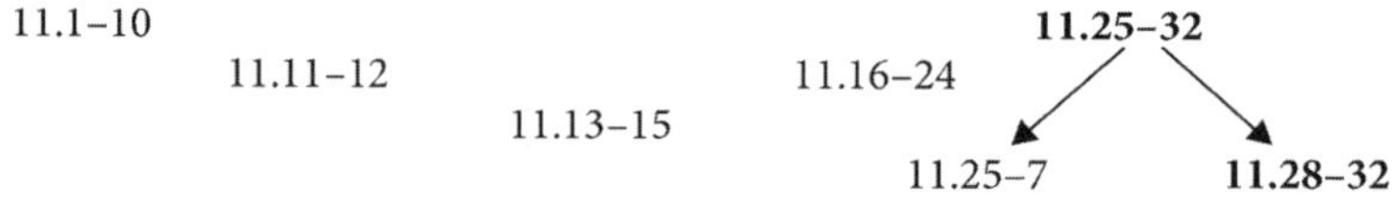

Once more we remind ourselves that Paul is here emphasizing what the potentially proud gentile Messiah-believers in Rome need to hear. The Jews who are at present 'hardened' are not to be seen as automatically outside the saving purposes of God. Here is the mystery of 'election' and its reframing by Paul in the light of the gospel:

> [28]As regards the good news, they are enemies – for your sake! But as regards God's choice they are beloved because of the patriarchs. [29]God's gifts and God's call, you see, cannot be undone. [30]For just as *you* were once disobedient to God, but now have received mercy through *their* disobedience, [31]so *they* have now disbelieved as well, in order that, through the mercy which has come *your* way, they too may now receive mercy. [32]For God has shut up all people in disobedience, so that he may have mercy upon all.

Every word here is important, but among the most important is the word 'now' towards the end of verse 31 ('they too may *now* receive mercy'). Some early scribes found this puzzling, and either omitted it or changed it to 'later', but the strong probability is that this is what Paul said.[714] To repeat: he is not talking of a *subsequent* mercy for presently 'hardened' Jews. He is

[714] So, cautiously, Metzger 1994 [1971], 465; more strongly, Jewett 2007, 694: 'it is difficult to conceive that [the MSS with the extra *nyn*] gratuitously added a third reference to "now"'. See too e.g. Seifrid 2007, 677 (the *nyn* is to be preferred as *lectio difficilior*). It seems to be the case that not all the scholars who favour the addition of the extra *nyn* appreciate the weight it gives to the reading of the whole passage in which Paul envisages the salvation of 'all Israel' as something to be achieved within the present dispensation, rather than as something only to be accomplished in a sudden last-minute divine action, perhaps at the *parousia*.

referring to *a continuing possibility* that 'some of them' (11.14) will be made 'jealous' and so provoked into faith and salvation.[715]

The final verse, 32, is strongly reminiscent of Galatians 3.22, indicating that Paul has not actually said anything radically new at this point, but rather has worked out more fully, and in a different polemical context, the theology of God's people and of the work of the Messiah which he stated some years earlier. The way he put it there was

> Scripture shut up everything together under the power of sin, so that the promise – which comes by the faithfulness of Jesus the Messiah – should be given to those who believe.

The connection of mercy with faith/faithfulness is made explicit in that passage; in the light of 11.23 we should suppose that it is implicit in the present context as well. Paul is not discussing, or proposing, the issue of 'universalism' which has haunted twentieth-century theological discussions.[716] Again, had he thought his way into such a position, he could have dried his tears and stopped being so sorrowful about 'his kinsfolk according to the flesh' (as well as scrubbing out – as some recent interpreters have tried to do! – passages like Romans 2.1–16). He is talking about *all people*, 'the Jew first and also the Greek', the 'all' over whom the Messiah is 'God' (9.5) and 'lord' (10.12). Perhaps only those who have lived in societies split down the middle can appreciate how that 'all' sounded in Paul's world – the early Christian world – where 'Jew and gentile' were the key categories. To allow his 'all' to resonate instead in the echo-chambers of the modern western world, with its quite different theological and soteriological questions, is mere anachronism.

Israel according to the flesh has thus found its history and eschatology shaped according to the messianic pattern, the christological pattern. *Israel has followed the Messiah through his 'casting away', and now is invited to join him also in his 'receiving back'*: the pattern of cross and resurrection is etched into Israel's history, as Israel's election itself is discerned, in the light of the Messiah himself, to be something significantly different from anything imagined either by devout Jews on the one hand or by anti-Jewish pagans on the other. From Paul's point of view, Israel's election was from the start the act of God for the redemption of the world; but Israel, itself in need of that redemption, could not be 'faithful' or obedient to God's vocation (3.2). The 'faithfulness' of the Messiah, as Israel's representative,

[715] See the strong, almost sermonic, words of Barth 1936–69, 2.2.305: 'The second *nyn* in v. 31, which is well established critically, seems to be rather out of place because the demonstration of the divine mercy towards the Jews, of which the verse speaks, is after all still future . . . But [the mercy shown to the gentiles in the present] is the means of divine mercy for the Jews too, so that in this sense the latter is already present.' This rules out 'the relegation of the Jewish question into the realm of eschatology' – which is, ironically, what one version of the present 'majority' reading of Rom. 11 succeeds in doing. If what Paul meant in 11.25f. was a salvation at the *parousia*, the second *nyn* in 11.31 should have read *hysteron* – as indeed we find in one or two MSS. The 'majority' view appears to have some early scribal antecedents. Dunn 1988b, 677 is undecided on the textual matter, and says (687) that if the *nyn* is there it highlights the 'eschatological imminence' of this final phase. This is a way of resisting its actual force.

[716] cf. e.g. Bell 2005, 264f., and many commentators e.g. Jewett 2007.

accomplished that worldwide redemption. If Israel according to the flesh is now, for the most part, 'hardened', Paul sees this as the necessary placing of them in the same category as gentiles, that is, all alike utterly dependent upon God's mercy, with nobody able to claim any kind of 'favoured nation clause'.

Thus for the moment, in 11.28, they are 'enemies because of you' – a radical way of putting what Paul had already said in 11.11, 12 and 15. The Jewish people as a whole have disbelieved, and as a result the word has gone out to the gentiles, just as Deuteronomy and Isaiah had said would happen. But this does not mean that God now regards unbelieving Jews as automatically *dis*qualified. That has been the main point Paul is stressing ever since 11.11. They remain 'beloved', not in the sense of 'automatically saved', but in the same sense that they are 'holy' in 11.16, corresponding to the 'holiness' of the unbelieving spouse in 1 Corinthians 7. They are, in other words, well within distance of God's call to faith, because of the patriarchs. Verse 28b ('beloved because of the patriarchs') seems to allude not only to 9.6–13, and behind that to chapter 4, but also perhaps to the 'root' of the tree, or even the tree itself, in 11.15b–24. The family to which unbelieving Jews still belong is, in other words, the physical family of Abraham, Isaac and Jacob, and the promises to them have not been taken back. Paul echoes the same theme in 15.8, where, summing up his gospel message one more time, Paul declares that the Messiah's faithful servant-work was undertaken 'on behalf of God's truthfulness' and 'to confirm the promises to the patriarchs', with the result that 'gentiles would glorify God for his mercy' – a very similar point to the present passage, and one which strikingly confirms our reading of the whole of chapter 11. Verse 28 is then further explained by the great statement of God's faithfulness: God's spiritual gifts, and God's 'call', are irrevocable (29). God will not say to Abraham that his physical children used to be welcome in his true family but will be no longer. Again, the 'call' resonates with the same term in 9.7, 12 and 9.24: God has 'called' both Jews and gentiles, and that call is not to be rescinded.[717]

The pair of verses which follow, 11.30–1, explain further in a balanced doublet. You (gentiles) were formerly disobedient to God, but now have received mercy; so they have now disbelieved, so that they too may now receive mercy. That is clear. What is not immediately clear is how to take the extra clauses Paul has inserted into this balanced statement:

30: Gentile disobedience	mercy to gentiles (in relation to Jewish disobedience)
31: Jewish disobedience	mercy to Jews (in relation to mercy to gentiles)

[717] Jewett 2002, 708 rightly interprets 'call' here as specifically relating to Jews (comparing 9.7, 11 [*sic*: presumably 12], 24, 25, 26), even though in 9.24–6 the relevant verb is applied precisely 'not only to Jews but also to gentiles', and despite its use elsewhere (Phil. 3.14; 2 Thess. 1.11). Once again we remind ourselves that Paul's aim here is to stress to gentile Christians God's continuing concern for the Jewish people.

It is possible to arrange the sentence as a chiasm:

A You were disobedient
B You received mercy
C in relation to their disobedience
C They too have now disobeyed
B in relation to your mercy
A So that they too may now receive mercy.[718]

The problem with this is the sense: in what way did the Jews disobey 'in relation to your mercy'? (The translation 'in relation to' reflects the ambiguity of the datives in both instances.) Verse 30 is clearly summing up one element in 11.11–15: God has used the Jewish 'stumble' or 'casting away' as the means of showing mercy to the gentiles. There are strong reasons, then, for taking verse 31 as a summary of the other side of the coin, again as in 11.11–15: the mercy shown to gentiles will be the means of making Jews 'jealous' and so bringing mercy to them as well. These two verses, in fact, go so closely with 11.11–15 that we see once again the high probability that in 11.25–7 Paul is not introducing a new or different scheme, but simply drawing out the full meaning of the one he has been expounding all along.[719] I am inclined therefore to go with those commentators and translators who render verse 31 to the effect: 'so they have now disbelieved as well, in order that, through the mercy which has come your way, they too may now receive mercy'.

This then leads naturally into the final verse of the argument (11.32): God has shut up all people in disobedience, so that he may have mercy upon all. All must come the same way. Paul has now applied this to the gentile Messiah-followers in Rome, to warn them away from a kind of inverted ethnic pride. There is no room for arrogance of any kind. All have been shut up in the prison house of 'disobedience', so that all who find themselves in God's family will know that they have come there by mercy alone. Paul knows this through the cross and resurrection of the Messiah, and the fresh understanding of the covenant which he has received through that great event. He has now worked it out with passion and rhetorical skill. This is Paul's ultimate revision of the second-Temple eschatology with which he had grown up. No longer would ethnic Israel look for a time when the nations of the world would come flocking in to Zion. The 'pilgrimage of the nations' had been turned inside out: now the apostolic mission would go 'from Zion' into the whole world, as in 10.14–17, and the fruits of that mission would make Paul's fellow Jews 'jealous' and provoke them out of their unbelief. This is reflected of course in Paul's theological explanation for the Collection: the nations have shared in the Jews' spiritual blessings, so it is

[718] See e.g. Dunn 1988b, 687f., following Wilcken and others, and followed now by Moo 1996, 734f., Schreiner 1998, 627f., Jewett 2007, 710.

[719] At first sight the 'so that' clause in v. 31 might look a little odd in the Greek, but there are other examples of similar constructions: e.g. 2 Cor. 2.4; Gal. 2.10; Col. 4.16, all of which have the *hina* delayed until after words which belong to the clause which it governs.

right and proper that they should minister to their earthly needs.[720] There is a sense in which not only 11.11–32, but the whole of chapters 9—11, form the 'mystery' which Paul sums up in 11.25–7: this is the fresh reading of scripture, rethought around the Messiah, which has issued in a fresh understanding of the hope of Israel. Without leaving the home base of Israel's scripture-rooted doctrine of election, Paul has retold the historical and eschatological narrative, weaving it into a pattern which is at once totally unexpected and totally shaped around the Messiah. That is how he worked.

(ι) The End and the Beginning: 11.33–6 and 9.1–5

9.1–5 **11.33–6**
9.6–29 11.1–32
9.30–3 10.18–21
10.1–4 10.14–17
10.5–13
10.9

In the end we glimpse the beginning. This most carefully constructed section of this most carefully constructed letter is held in balance between those most characteristic Jewish expressions, lament and praise: like many psalms, the section opens with the one and closes with the other.[721] The famous opening – great sorrow, endless pain, a prayer rising unbidden to his lips that he might himself be cast off if only that would rescue his fellow Jews – finds expression in the list of precious gifts to which Paul's kinsfolk are heirs. The famous conclusion – the unsearchable riches and inscrutable ways of God – finds expression in a paean of praise in which phrase after phrase resonates with the scriptures while also picking up themes in which the Jewish wisdom tradition overlapped with the speculations of the wider world, especially that of the Stoics. Paul is doing again what he does best: expounding the ancient faith of Israel, rethought and reimagined around Jesus and the spirit, in such a way as to take every thought captive to obey the Messiah.

It is curious, then, that the sorrowful doxology of 9.5 and the glorious doxology of 11.33–6 have both been subject to the comment that they do not concern Jesus. Many commentators still divide 9.5 so that, while the Messiah is 'of their race according to the flesh', it is 'God over all' who is 'blessed for ever, Amen'.[722] We saw in an earlier chapter that this is in fact by far the less likely reading, and in the present section we have seen that chapters 9—11 as a whole are in fact predicated precisely on a *christological* reading both of Israel's strange pathway – the fall and rise of many in Israel, as old Simeon put it! – and of the way by which Israel and the gentiles alike will come to salvation. *Ho gar autos kyrios pantōn*: the same lord is lord of

[720] Rom. 15.27.

[721] See e.g. Grieb 2010, 396.

[722] See the discussion in Wright 2002 [*Romans*], 629–31; Jewett 2007, 566–9; and above, 707–9.

all, for 'all who call on the name of the lord will be saved.' And the 'lord' in question, at the heart of the section in 10.9–13, is the Jesus to whom Paul ascribes biblical texts referring to YHWH. The Jewish Messiah according to the flesh, who is God over all, blessed for ever: that is the advance statement, not just of one theme to be woven into the ongoing discussion, but of the theological principle around which Paul will construct his revised eschatology, and of the hermeneutical principle in the light of which he will re-read those great texts from Deuteronomy, Isaiah, the Psalms and elsewhere.

By the same token, many have seen significance in the fact that Jesus is not mentioned in 11.33–6. Without going into details (this is after all a chapter on eschatology, not a commentary on Romans) we may beg to differ. By this stage in the argument, as we saw in relation to 11.11–15, christology has been woven into the very fabric of Paul's thought. It is the key to everything. When he celebrates the depth of the riches and the wisdom and knowledge of God, he knows very well that the Messiah is the place where one may find all the hidden treasures of wisdom and knowledge.[723] When he asks 'who has known the mind of the Lord?', he is well capable of answering his own question by saying 'We have the mind of the Messiah.'[724] And when he concludes 'for from him, through him and to him are all things', the prayer which had itself been reformed around the Messiah echoes closely just underneath: there is one God, the father, from whom are all things, and we to him, and one lord Jesus, the Messiah, through whom are all things, and we through him.[725] As Ed Sanders put it,

> By the time we meet him in his letters, ... Paul knew only one God, the one who sent Christ and who 'raised from the dead Jesus our lord' ... There should be no hard distinction between 'theocentric' and 'christocentric' strains in Paul's thought.[726]

We began this section by pointing out that it was all about God. Paul himself has told us that this means it is all about Jesus. Jesus was the reason for, and the eventual focus of, the opening lament. Jesus, the Messiah, was the *telos nomou*, the goal towards whom the whole narrative of Torah had been moving until at last it arrived at the covenant renewal of Deuteronomy 30, which Paul naturally interpreted in terms of the climactic events of Jesus' resurrection and enthronement. Jesus, as Israel's representative, was the one whose saving death and resurrection provided the pattern which enabled Paul to glimpse the astonishing 'mystery' that, instead of Israel being redeemed and the nations coming in to see what all the fuss was about, the gentiles would be redeemed so that the Jewish people might become jealous and come back into the 'tree' which was their own tree in the first place. Structurally, thematically, theologically, even rhetorically, Jesus the Messiah

[723] Col. 2.3.

[724] 1 Cor. 2.16.

[725] 1 Cor. 8.6. See above, 661–70.

[726] Sanders 1983, 194, cf. 41f.

is the central clue to Paul's view of God, of God's people and of God's future for the world. Romans 9—11, framed as it is between lament and praise, encapsulates exactly that inaugurated and reshaped eschatology which completes the triple account of Paul's theological vision.

7. Conclusion: Hope and Its Consequences

(i) Introduction: Paul's Revised Hope

Our sketch of Paul's theology is complete. He has rethought monotheism, election and eschatology – and their complex interrelationships! – in the light of Jesus the Messiah and of the spirit, and of the ancient scriptures which he regards as having found their 'yes' in Jesus. This is the coherent centre of his theological thought, upon which he draws in all kinds of situations to make points and develop arguments which deal with many different topics but which all relate coherently to this centre. I have come to see Paul's letters not so much as themselves the means by which he was developing his thought – that, I think, is a back-projection from our modern book-based academic culture – as small windows on to a larger, richer and denser world of belief and life, of exegesis and prayer, of faith and love and, yes, hope. The modern historian, reading Paul, is in the position of someone who discovers a few old family photograph albums. One could stay on safe ground and treat them as accidental combinations of individual snapshots. Or one could try to reconstruct the story of the family whose albums they were. The minimalist option, to deny the possibility of knowing anything outside what Paul actually says, is always open. But that would purchase the 'certainty' of a strictly limited positivistic account at the high price of ignoring the much more interesting and complex world from within which these texts emerged and of which they do indeed give us tantalizing glimpses. I have tried here to see what happens if we follow up, and join up, those glimpses, starting from the hypothesis that Paul's thought remained that of a first-century Pharisee who believed that the one God had fulfilled his ancient promises through his son and his spirit. I submit that this hypothesis has been more than fully demonstrated, resulting both in a much larger coherent centre to Paul's thought than has normally been supposed and in a rather different arrangement of the topics with which he was most concerned.

In particular, we have seen in the present chapter that Paul did indeed transform the hope of Israel. He took that hope, to which he had clung as a young and zealous Pharisee, and thought through what it meant to say, as he found himself compelled to say, that this hope both *had been fulfilled* through Jesus, in his kingdom-establishing death and resurrection, and the life-transforming spirit, and *would yet be fulfilled* in the second coming of Jesus and in the work of that same spirit to raise all the Messiah's people from the dead. Jews had lived for many generations with different kinds of 'now and not yet' combinations, the most obvious being the 'now' of having returned geographically from Babylon and the 'not yet' of the still unfulfilled prophecies of Daniel 9, Isaiah 40—55 and the rest. Having a hope of that shape, inaugurated but not consummated, was a typically second-Temple Jewish position.[727] Paul shifted – or rather, Paul believed that God had shifted – those now-and-not-yet hopes on to a different level. The hope remained profoundly Jewish, for all that Paul faced outwards as he proclaimed it, outwards to the world where a new kind of eschatology had been making its way into popular consciousness. The hope may well have developed as Paul taught it (and for every 'snapshot' we have in his letters we have to assume hundreds if not thousands of hours of teaching, explanation, scripture study, argument and prayer), but though Paul explains more about this hope in Romans than he does anywhere else there is no fundamental change, except in his own perspective (that he realizes, by the time of Philippians and 2 Corinthians, that he may not live to see the End himself). The hope remained the Jewish hope: the resurrection of the dead, as the centrepiece of the renewal of all creation, the flooding of God's world with justice and joy. It was transformed by the belief that this had already happened in and through Jesus, and in and through those in whom the spirit now dwelt, and that the still-future aspects of this hope would happen by exactly the same means. And that meant, of course, that hope was confirmed as such: 'Hope in turn', wrote Paul, 'does not make us ashamed, because the love of God has been poured out in our hearts through the holy spirit who has been given to us.'[728] The resurrection of Jesus remained, for Paul, the sure anchor of the entire future hope; the spirit was the *arrabōn*, the down-payment, the guarantee of the full 'inheritance'.[729]

(ii) The Effect of Paul's Theology

The threefold picture of Paul's theology which we have now completed takes its place within the overall argument of the present book in two ways. First, this theology is what Paul believed his churches needed to embrace, and to engage with, if the central symbol of their worldview, the unified and holy community itself, was even to exist, let alone to flourish. Second, this way of understanding Paul's central vision of God, God's people and God's future holds together, and enables us to make sense of, the many major debates which have swirled around 'Pauline studies' over the last century or so.

[727] cf. e.g. Watson 2004, 137: 'In spite of the historical realities of exile and return, the post-exilic writings in [the Book of the Twelve Prophets] are testimonies precisely to the deferral of a fulfilment which so often seems near at hand but never actually arrives.'

[728] Rom. 5.5.

[729] Rom. 8.23; 2 Cor. 1.22; Eph. 1.14.

First, my overall case in Part II of this book was that when we study the worldview which Paul attempts to inculcate in his converts we find that its central symbol is the united and holy community itself; but that this community was equipped with none of the symbolic markers (circumcision, food laws, sabbath, ethnic identity and endogamy, allegiance to the Jerusalem Temple) which gave Jewish communities in the Diaspora such a comparatively solid basis for their continuing common life. My overall case in Part III has been that Paul's theology, the prayerful and scripture-based exploration of the foundational Jewish themes of monotheism, election and eschatology, was designed to supply this lack, thus elevating something which (with hindsight) we now call 'theology' to a position, in terms of a community and its worldview, which it never previously possessed and which it still does not possess outside Christianity itself. First-century Jews engaged in the study of Torah because Torah not only supplied the community's boundary-markers but also brought its students into the presence of God – a belief which gained in importance for those who lived at a distance from the Temple itself. First-century pagan philosophers discussed questions to do with the gods as a matter of intellectual curiosity on the one hand and inner personal exploration or development on the other, but these questions were never required to play anything like the role that Christian theology had to take on from the start. For Paul, reflecting on God, God's people and God's future was the vital activity that enabled him to address urgent pastoral and practical questions in his communities, not least to do precisely with their unity and holiness.[730] In Paul's hands, 'theology' was born as a new discipline to meet a new challenge.

Paul's teaching seems to have been aimed at enabling his converts to continue this theological work for themselves. He does not supply all the answers, even to the comparatively few questions he addresses. What he does is to teach his hearers to think theologically: to think forward from the great narrative of Israel's scriptures into the world in which the Messiah had established God's sovereign rule among the nations through his death and resurrection, inaugurating the 'age to come', rescuing Jews and gentiles alike from the 'present evil age', and establishing them as a single family which was both in direct continuity (through the Messiah himself) with the ancient people of Abraham and in radical and cross-shaped discontinuity with Abraham's physical family and its traditions. The radical newness which had come about, the new life and energy in which Paul's converts found themselves caught up, was to be understood as the effect of the covenant renewal and new creation which had come about as the one God of Israel had revealed himself in dynamic action in and as Jesus the Messiah on the one hand and the spirit on the other. Only if the little churches of Asia, Greece and Rome had matured to that point in their thinking would they be able to be true to their vocation to remain united, to live with the radical holiness demanded by this new creation, and in both of these things to bear

[730] The importance of unity and holiness as the reconfiguration of second-Temple themes was explored particularly by Newton 1985.

witness to the pagan world around. Theology is what Paul used to bring depth and stability to the worldview of his churches.

Second, this vision of Paul's theology enables us, I believe, to draw together the strong points of the many different schools of Pauline interpretation that have emerged over the last century as scholarship has struggled to come to terms with this most powerful and enigmatic first-century activist and thinker. To begin with, we have firmly laid to rest the suggestion, influential ever since F. C. Baur, that Paul abandoned his Jewish framework of thought whether for ideological reasons (because it was legalistic and 'earthly') or for pragmatic ones (because it was irrelevant and incomprehensible to his gentile converts). On the contrary. The fact that Paul insisted on welcoming gentiles into God's people without circumcision had nothing to do either with an ideological rejection of 'Judaism' as the wrong sort of religion or with the pragmatic reflection that a 'law-free' gospel (there's a slippery shorthand term if ever I saw one) would attract more converts. He remained a deeply Jewish thinker, not least precisely at those points where he carved out a new path on the basis of the crucified and risen Messiah and the covenant-renewing spirit. What he did with these two foundational ideas was both anchored in the Jewish scriptures and aimed at producing and sustaining a kind of fulfilled Judaism, the kind Paul saw prophesied in Genesis, Deuteronomy, Isaiah, Jeremiah, Ezekiel and the Psalms. In fact, it was precisely because he remained a Jewish thinker that he engaged with the wider world. If that seems like a paradox, it is only because so much history-of-religions work has screened out, before the discussion even began, the possibility of such a thing, of a Jewish thinker with a message for the world (though that, of course, is what books such as the Wisdom of Solomon purported to be and to offer). As we saw in chapter 4, great harm is done to our understanding of Paul if we make 'religion' the catch-all category.

Paul engaged with the thought-forms of his day, pagan as well as Jewish. If his arguments seem to interact with Stoic thinking and expression, that is probably because he meant them to do so. But that does not mean that the best available analysis of what he was doing must be a semi-Jewish kind of Stoicism, any more than the best analysis could ever be that he was some sort of a gnostic.[731] Debates will no doubt continue over whether Paul was in fact a good or a loyal Jew (see chapter 15 below). Much the same question was raised in the first century, by no means only about Paul: many Jewish groups and teachers asked it of one another, and this came to a height first in the Roman/Jewish war of AD 66–70 and then in the bar-Kochba revolt in the 130s. Was bar-Kochba the Messiah, or was he leading Israel astray? Akiba, noblest of rabbis, believed that bar-Kochba was the Messiah, and he suffered for it. Paul, apostle to the pagans, believed that the crucified Jesus was the Messiah, and he suffered for it. But of Paul's *intention* to be a good, loyal member of Abraham's family there should be no doubt. What, after

[731] See ch. 14 below. It is remarkable, looking back, to see how strong the 'gnostic hypothesis' was in the years of Bultmannian dominance (notably in the works of W. Schmithals). Its demise marks a victory for sheer history.

all, was a loyal Jew supposed to do if he believed he had discovered (or, better, that God had revealed) the Messiah?

But if Paul was, and remained, a basically Jewish thinker, what *sort* of Jewish thinker was he? We shall return to these questions in chapter 15 below, but a brief summary at this point is in order. Was he a rabbi who happened to believe that he now knew the name of the Messiah? Was he an apocalyptist who believed that God had broken into the world in a fresh way, sweeping everything else off the table in order to establish something quite new? Was he the promoter of a 'salvation history' in the form of a smooth, untroubled narrative which had now reached its destination? He was none of these, though each has a point to make. He was (by his own self-description) a Messiah-man; but nothing in Judaism had prepared him or anyone else for what a Messiah-man might look like if the Messiah had been crucified. Paul had to work that out from scratch, and some of his sharpest theological expressions occur when we can see him doing exactly that. Galatians 2.15–21 is perhaps the most obvious of many possible examples. And in this working-out we see that, for Paul at least, one could not simply add this Messiah on to the end of an existing structure of thought, a new final chapter which would leave everything else as it was already. Everything would change. Nothing less than death and resurrection would be involved, right through the pattern of thought as well as the life of the believer. A new form of Torah-obedience was required and enabled (from the heart, but not involving such central Torah-observances as circumcision!); a new sort of 'apocalypse' had happened and was happening (the unveiling of Jesus as Messiah, both in the gospel events themselves and in the ongoing gospel proclamation); salvation there was, and history there was, but they no longer related to one another as once Paul might have imagined (the history was as much a damnation history as a salvation history, and both had reached their *telos* with the Messiah). The events concerning the Messiah, and the proclamation of those events, were at the centre of the paradox: these shocking, tradition-overturning, radically new events were *the things that Israel's God had promised all along*.

Underneath all of this was Paul's radical sense, rethought in every detail around the Messiah and the spirit: this was what the covenant with Abraham had always envisaged. The covenant *entailed* God's providential ordering of Israel's history. But, because the covenant was made with one branch of Adamic humanity, the covenant also, through the secondary provision of Torah, *entailed* God's 'No' to any suggestion that Israel could be affirmed as it stood. That is the plight of Romans 7; and that is why the covenant also *entailed* the bursting-in of the Messiah upon a Jewish world that was looking in the wrong direction for the wrong thing, though perhaps, in some cases at least, at the right time. Covenant theology, in the sense we have expounded it in relation to Galatians 2—4 and Romans 2—4 and 9—11, offers a rich, scriptural framework within which the proper emphases of what has recently called itself 'apocalyptic' and what in the past has sometimes called itself 'salvation history' can be retained and enhanced, despite the process of *metanoia* through which both must pass if they are to arrive at that destination. The covenant, as far as Paul was concerned, always envisaged God's call of Israel *for the sake of the nations*. Paul believed that it was the covenant in this sense that had been fulfilled in the death and resurrection of the Messiah, and that was being implemented through his own apostolic mission.

For Paul the rabbi, the prospect is more bleak. By Paul's own judgment, the zeal for Torah which characterized him and his colleagues in the Pharisaic movement was what had led them in the wrong direction. When he claimed that faith in Jesus as the risen lord was the true Torah-fulfilment of which Deuteronomy 30 had spoken (Romans 10.6–8), his mode of arguing the point, and the many other points that followed from it, bore no resemblance to anything we find in the Mishnah, let alone the Talmud. He can still line up scriptural quotations from Torah, prophets and writings. He can allude here and there to traditions of interpretation which are paralleled in various rabbinic texts. But Israel's Torah is now playing, at best, second fiddle to the new revelation which has taken place. The role which the rabbi assigned to Torah – the mode of YHWH's presence, the guide of his people – was, for Paul, taken rather obviously by Jesus and by the spirit. Torah does indeed continue to play a role, and a varied and subtle role, in Paul's thought. But it has been radically reshaped, like everything else, around the new self-revelation of Israel's God.

Paul, then, was a Jewish thinker for the gentile mission; a covenant thinker who drew together Israel's sense of historical tradition and the apocalyptist's dream of a totally fresh revelation. In particular, he combined, in a way that western theology has struggled to do, the sense (a) that the one God would call the whole world to account, and that this 'forensic' judgment could be brought forward into the present and (b) that this God had redefined his people, in the act of rescuing them from their sins and thus from the present evil age, in, through and around the Messiah. Paul allowed 'forensic' and 'participationist' categories to interact in his thinking. Indeed, we may doubt whether he would have recognized our 'categories' as neat, separate packages. Each emphasis took its place in relation to the other in a complex dance which should never have been separated. 'Justified *in the Messiah*', with the Messiah's death and resurrection 'reckoned' to those who are 'in him', and with *pistis* as the badge which demonstrates that those in whose heart the spirit has worked by means of the gospel really are Messiah-people – that is how this combination works. It is always possible, of course, for theologians and preachers to oversimplify in this way or that, to take a few elements of what Paul says and arrange them in a pattern that may satisfy for a while. But this regularly involves leaving out – or, indeed, striking out! – some elements, a verse here, a passage there. We have tried in these three chapters, particularly the central chapter 10, to indicate that the division which Schweitzer saw between 'law-court' language and 'being in

Christ' language is a divide not in the mind of Paul but in the eye of the (modern) beholder, and that the stand-off between expositions that have favoured one and marginalized the other is unhelpful and misleading. Again, I have proposed the category 'covenantal' as a heuristic label to denote the combination of the two, taken together with the other features mentioned in the previous paragraphs, and to locate the whole complex of thought where it belongs, which is with Paul's fresh messianic understanding of God's purposes *with, for and especially through* Israel. There may be better labels, but 'covenantal' still has merit. It highlights, in particular, Paul's great emphasis: that everything, in the last analysis, comes back to the question of God. And among all the other things which one might say, and which Paul does say, about God, this stands out as one of the main clues to Paul's theology, and hence to the strengthening of his worldview and the energizing of his mission: that God is, and has been, faithful.

(iii) Paul's Theology and His Three Worlds

With this vision of Paul's theology, we are at last in a position to see how he related to the three worlds he inhabited. As to his native Judaism: his critique was not that it was bad, shabby, second-rate, semi-Pelagian or concerned with physical rather than spiritual realities. His critique was eschatological: Israel's God had kept his promises, but Israel had refused to believe it. The Messiah had come to his own, and his own had not received him. Had Paul read John's prologue he would have nodded at that point, and muttered 'I wrote three whole chapters about that.' Of course, Paul's reimagining of the Jewish theology of God, God's people and God's future created many points of potential confrontation. But as with Qumran, where the community believed that the one God had secretly re-established his covenant with them, leaving the rest of Israel behind the game, so with Paul. He believed that the sun had risen, while most of his fellow Jews were insisting on keeping the bedroom curtains tight shut. We shall explore this, not least in relation to his fresh readings of scripture, in chapter 15.

With regard to the Greek world of popular religion and philosophy, Paul's radically revised monotheism, election and eschatology gave him a robust intellectual platform from which to critique, by implication and sometimes head on, the philosophies of the time, not least Stoicism.[732] But his real target was the popular culture: many gods, many lords and many idols, clamouring for allegiance and dehumanizing any who gave it. Paul may have been aware, too, of an implicit clash between his gospel and the mystical religions of the Orient, though this does not lie on the surface of his text. He did not derive his message or his practice from such sources, though he may have been aware that his vision of Christian initiation (for instance) was in a sense upstaging the 'mysteries'. I see him rather, as Luke

[732] On 1 Cor. 4 see Hays 2005, 19–21.

saw him in Athens, with his spirit grieved at a city full of idols, ready to debate more serious perspectives when given the chance. But at the level of hope, as we said earlier, there was no contest. The only hope in the ancient world was either for the smile of 'Fortuna' or for an escape to the Elysian fields. Paul held, taught and lived a hope which outflanked those options, because he believed in a God who was creator and judge, neither of which beliefs featured prominently in greco-roman religion or philosophy. We shall explore all this in chapters 12 and 13.

Perhaps the most striking thing about Israel's hope in its fresh Pauline expression was its undesigned coincidence with the realized eschatology of the Augustan age. It just so happened, as we saw in chapter 5, that Paul was telling Israel's story, from Abraham to the Messiah, in a world caught up in Rome's story, from the Trojan Wars to Augustus. When Paul spoke of the *parousia* or the *epiphaneia* of Jesus, he was writing for hearers who applied those words to a very different incarnate divinity. As we reflect on the full sweep of Paul's reworked Jewish theology, we should not be surprised that, like Genesis, Isaiah and Daniel before him, he told and lived the story of the creator God, of God's people and of God's future plans in a world where pagan empire was claiming to provide all the 'future' anyone could want. Our next chapter, introducing the final Part of this book, will therefore examine Paul's clash with the world of Roman empire.

This is after all a good place to begin as, with Paul's worldview and theology spread out before us, we now locate him within the wider world of his day. The patience of filter and focus will enable us to screen out the mass of details we have studied, and to zoom in on the question of, so to speak, What St Paul Really Did. The flocks of unruly birds, beating their wings around the bush, now gather into one. Only when we place him historically, culturally and intellectually within the multiple overlapping worlds we studied in Part I will we see the concentrated focus of his life and work. Paul's eschatological vision of the Messiah's victory (past and future), of the work of the spirit, and of the consequent new creation, had brought him to the place given matchless expression by Gerard Manley Hopkins:

> And for all this, nature is never spent;
> There lives the dearest freshness, deep down things.
> And though the last lights off the black west went,
> Oh, morning, at the brown brink eastward springs;
> Because the Holy Ghost over the bent
> World broods with warm breast, and with ah! Bright wings.[733]

This is the bird, perched and ready, in which all the others are concentred and gathered.

[733] Hopkins, 'God's Grandeur'.

集中 *ShūChū*

Concentration

Collection at a middle point.
Mindful concentration
As our flights of fancy converge,
Vagaries homing in,
Ruffled feathers of distraction,
Flocks of unruly birds
Beating their wings around the bush
Now gather into one. . . .

A rallied psyche
Nestles down. Zeroing in.
Density of thought.

Statio Benedict once named
The pause between two tasks;
A habit to break a habit,
An action brought to mind,
The moment we collect ourselves
In from the blurred edges.
Patience of filter and focus.
Screening out. Zooming in.

Bird perched and ready.
Concentred and gathered.
Our utmost presence.

Micheal O'Siadhail

PART IV

PAUL IN HISTORY

INTRODUCTION TO PART IV

This Part of the book began life, partly in my head and partly in rough draft, as the concluding sections of each of the three chapters that now form Part III. A glance back at the size of those three chapters, especially chapter 10, will explain why I decided against that earlier plan, but it may help if the reader remembers the original intention in what follows. The point was simply this: I wanted to explore the ways in which the main emphases of Paul's theology, his revised monotheism, election and eschatology, would relate to the three worlds in which he lived, those of the Jews, the Greeks and the Romans. Having explored those worlds in (I hope) their own terms in Part I, and having now set out Paul's worldview and theology as best I can, I return to those worlds in order to complete the essentially historical task of placing Paul within this complex and multi-dimensional map. Mindful, too, of the need to help the reader maintain a sense of location within a complex book, I have set these out here in the reverse order to that in which we met them in Part I. Here at least the book has a deliberately chiastic structure, with the chapters in this section balancing those in Part I, as set out in the diagram in the Preface.

The third of Micheal O'Siadhail's poems explains what is going on in this final section. We saw the birds hovering overhead, symbolic of the divine presence watching over Israel and its history, in chapter 2; we then studied Athene's owl in chapter 3, the cock which Socrates owed to Asclepius in chapter 4, and the Roman eagle in chapter 5. Philosophy, religion and empire were three of the main themes of the greco-roman world to which Paul believed himself called to go as the apostle of Israel's God and his Messiah. I then suggested, in Parts II and III, that Paul saw Jesus himself as the mid-point of the world – of all creation, all space, time and matter. As with the Japanese characters *Shū*, 'collection', and *Chū*, 'medium', so with their combination into *ShūChū*, 'concentration': the birds on the tree are now brought together, gathered into one. The density of Paul's thought – the fact that so many themes converge, home in, and nestle down at this point – is what makes him both fascinating and frustrating as a subject of study. I hope that by laying out these different elements in this way, and attempting to show the way they belonged together in Paul's own mind and (not least) in his actual life and work, we may be able to collect ourselves in from the blurred edges and arrive at some preliminary conclusions about where Paul belonged as a figure of first-century history.

We have long left behind the false antithesis of trying to place him, historically, as either a 'Jewish' thinker or a 'Greek' one. That either/or reflected nineteenth-century Hegelian Protestantism far too closely to be of much use as a historical tool. It lacked, in any case, important nuancing in terms of widely differing Jewish positions and equally wide divergencies in Paul's Greek, and indeed Roman, worlds. I hope this final Part of the book will serve as a pointer to the far more complex and interesting task of fresh exploration which now awaits.

But only a pointer; because, if we are not to write another five hundred pages by way of conclusion, we must ourselves now do quite a lot of filtering and focusing, of screening out and zooming in. It would be possible, on the basis of Parts II and III, to set off on a much larger exploration of where Paul belongs in relation to empire, religion, philosophy and ultimately to his own original Jewish context. Possible, perhaps, but not desirable or practical in the present setting. What I offer instead is some sharply focused proposals, in brief dialogue with selected debating partners, designed to stimulate further reflections, whether historical, philosophical, theological, exegetical or practical.

Changing the metaphor (the reader may perhaps be relieved to know that the birds will be migrating elsewhere from now on), the aim is to set up four spotlights, each trained on the apostle but from significantly different angles. Spotlights sometimes distort, sometimes cast peculiar shadows, and sometimes dazzle both subject and viewer. But it is better to have four of them than the single bright light, from whichever angle, that has all too often been fashionable. Having placed them in position in chapters 12, 13, 14 and 15, we will hope in the final chapter to see Paul more clearly as he goes about his apostolic tasks.

Chapter Twelve

THE LION AND THE EAGLE: PAUL IN CAESAR'S EMPIRE

1. Introduction

Every step Paul took, he walked on land ruled by Caesar. Every letter he wrote was sent to people who lived within Caesar's domain, who paid taxes to Caesar and whose civic leaders were eager to impress on them how lucky they were to enjoy the peace and prosperity that the Caesars had brought to their region. Paul himself declared that he had long wanted to visit Rome, Caesar's capital city; according to Acts, the way he got there was as a prisoner under guard, being looked after by Caesar's soldiers until Caesar himself would hear his case.[1] Was Caesar insignificant for Paul? Hardly.

But was that 'significance' merely a matter of trivial outward circumstances, or of inner meaning? One could claim that the internal combustion engine and the invention of tarmac have been 'significant' for Christian work in the western world over the last century, in that most ministers drive cars to get to church, to visit parishioners and even, in some cases, to attend remedial courses on the Bible and theology. But that is hardly 'significant' in the same way that it would be if the same ministers came to believe that their cars were polluting the planet, that covering acres of countryside with tarmac was destroying the natural habitats of other species and that the gospel of Jesus demanded a campaign against cars and roads as we know them.

So what sort of 'significance' might Caesar have for Paul? Was Caesar's world merely the backdrop, the assumed and taken-for-granted setting in which Paul went about telling everyone within earshot about Jesus? Or did that message, the communities it generated and the worldview that Paul inculcated within them, have at least an implicit 'significance' of the second sort? Might there be other options? As we noted before, the wave of enthusiastic Caesar-investigation which swept up the surprised beach of New Testament Studies in the 1990s may perhaps have overreached itself, as scholarly enthusiasms sometimes do, and it is time for a sober appraisal.[2] Was it a freak, or was it rather a sign that the tide is coming in?

[1] Rom. 1.9–15; Ac. 25.11f.; 27.1—28.16.

[2] See my earlier essays, now in *Perspectives* chs. 12, 16 and 27; and, among recent discussions, that of Barclay 2011, chs. 18, 19. Since Barclay critiques my own work directly, arguing that the Roman empire was 'insignificant' to Paul, I take him here as my main conversation partner. The most recent vol. of *New Documents* (Llewelyn and Harrison 2012, esp. 25–9, 55–86) contains some important documents and discussions in this whole area; I am grateful to Peter Rodgers for alerting me to this. Among recent works, Fantin 2011 is closer to my perspective, and Harrill 2012 closer to Barclay's.

This is not, to be sure, the way in which scholars used to approach the possible relationship between Paul's gospel and Caesar's world. In earlier days of history-of-religions research, it was sometimes suggested that the reason Paul used titles like 'son of god' and (occasionally) 'saviour' for Jesus, and the reason he spoke of a 'gospel' at all, was because these were the categories familiar to his audience, precisely because of the various Caesar-cults which had been spreading around the Mediterranean world, particularly in the eastern provinces where Paul travelled and worked. Paul, according to this theory, quickly abandoned any Jewish categories as being irrelevant to his pagan audience, and borrowed themes and ideas from their own culture in order to make Jesus relevant. Some still assume that any suggestion of 'significance', of an overlap of meaning between Paul's language about Jesus and first-century Roman language about Caesar, must mean *derivation* of that kind. But, as I have argued in various places, there is all the difference in the world between *derivation* and *confrontation*. It will be clear by this stage in the book that I do not think for a moment that what Paul said about Jesus and his gospel was *derived* from popular language about Caesar, or indeed about the many 'gods' and 'lords' of popular religion (on which, see the next chapter). If we are talking about derivation, it ought to be clear that Paul's fundamental ideas came from his native Jewish world, radically rethought around the crucified and risen Messiah and the gift of the spirit. But that leaves the question wide open as to whether he sometimes shaped his language and expressions deliberately in such a way as to *confront* the claims that one might hear in popular pagan culture with the very different claim that he himself was making. ('Confrontation' can of course cover many things, from friendly engagement to downright rejection, with all stages in between.)[3]

To the question of possible confrontation between Paul and the Roman empire there have been, broadly, three different kinds of reply. First, some have argued that Paul was actually an enthusiast for the Roman empire. If one starts from the most obviously relevant passage, Romans 13.1–7, where Paul declares that 'the powers that be are ordained of God', it is possible to suggest that Paul saw the Roman empire as not only essentially benign, but as actually serving to advance the gospel, by its good government, its new roads, its proper concern for justice and so on. From this perspective Paul, himself a Roman citizen, was quite happy with the civic and imperial structures the way they were, and sought only to use them appropriately in his otherwise completely different work of telling people about Jesus and encouraging the faithful in their discipleship.[4]

[3] See my early statement in Wright 1997 [*What St Paul*], ch. 5, esp. 79f.

[4] See e.g. Blumenfeld 2001: Paul celebrates the unity which Rome has brought to the world, and seeks to preserve and enhance it. This view has at least some echoes in the approach of e.g. Tertullian (e.g. *Apol.* 30–2; in *Ad Scap.* 2 he suggests that the Roman empire will last as long as the world), though Tertullian is also clear that the emperor remains firmly subordinate to the one God (e.g. *Apol.* 33.3). In the modern period a version of this was expressed by Ramsay n.d., 124–7, 130–41; there is a hint of it, though significantly qualified, in Dodd 1958 [1920], 44–50.

The mirror-image of this is the view made popular recently by Richard Horsley and others, who have suggested that Paul's essential message was one of social and political protest in which the arrogance and brutality of 'empire' was the main target. Horsley himself sometimes writes as though Paul was not even really interested in 'theology' as such, but was rather seeking to subvert the rule of Rome and challenge its claim to hegemony.[5] Anyone advocating a position like this will find Romans 13.1–7 to be an embarrassing counter-example; some have regarded it as a mere *ad hoc* comment about the rulers of whom Paul was aware at the time when he wrote the letter, others have boldly declared the passage to be a later insertion into the text, and other similar strategies have been attempted.[6] Some of us have tried to offer a modified and nuanced version of Horsley's position, in which an implicit critique of Rome and Caesar would be integrated within (rather than set over against) Paul's 'theology', and to point out that in Paul's Jewish world there is no necessary incompatibility between (a) the affirmation that the creator God intends there to be human authorities and (b) the sharp critique of what those authorities actually do. But the polarizations of our own day, both between 'theology' and 'politics' on the one hand and between pre-packaged 'left-wing' and 'right-wing' political assumptions on the other, have made it difficult for this even to be heard, let alone understood.[7]

A third answer is to suggest that the only 'significance' that Rome and Caesar had for Paul was like the 'significance' of the cars and the road for those who use them without asking awkward questions. Paul, on this account, had bigger fish to fry. He was indeed concerned to turn people away from the idols of their world, but the battles he was fighting at that level had to do with supernatural and 'spiritual' forces, not with the political realities which would, in any case, come and go from one culture to another. Today it was Rome; yesterday it might have been Babylon, Greece, Egypt or Syria; tomorrow it might be somebody else; but the gospel of Jesus was the same, and its cosmic reach and power made the petty princelings of this world about as significant as the pebbles in the road to one who drives over them on urgent, perhaps divine, business.[8]

The material I set out in chapters 2 and 5 above offers, I believe, some fresh ways forward towards a more nuanced view of the whole topic. Three factors in particular emerge which must be taken seriously in any ongoing discussion.

[5] See e.g. Horsley and Silberman 1997; Horsley 2004a; 2004b; Elliott 1994; 2008; Crossan and Reed 2004; Kahl 2010, etc. This movement shades off into various postmodern and postcolonial readings: cf. e.g. Stanley 2011; Marchal 2012.

[6] See the outline of options, and discussion, in Jewett 2007, 780–803.

[7] See *Perspectives* ch. 12, e.g. 188–200; and Wright 2002 [*Romans*], 716–23.

[8] See now e.g. Bryan 2005; Kim 2008. The position of Barclay 2011, ch. 19, is more nuanced (despite its title, 'Why the Roman Empire Was Insignificant to Paul'), and will be discussed below (1307–19). The suggestion (Miller 2010) that the imperial cult was less important than is sometimes thought in Paul's world seems to me insupportable (see ch. 5 above).

1. First, Paul draws explicitly on the rich Jewish tradition we studied in chapter 2, going back deep into scripture but finding various fresh expressions in his own period, in which Israel celebrated the belief that one day it would, as a nation, rule over the nations of the world.[9] This belief was sometimes, though not always, focused on the coming king who would embody that national vocation in himself. Even in Paul's own day, when the power of Rome must have appeared all but unconquerable to most of its subjects, this ancient Israelite belief found expression in sources as diverse as Philo and 1 Maccabees, joining up with the widespread aspiration for eventual freedom, a liberty in which the long years of 'continuing exile' would be over at last, and the dispersed tribes eventually regathered.

Within this Jewish world we find, in fact, precisely the two strands that have regularly been perceived in Paul. On the one hand, there is a tradition going back at least as far as Jeremiah according to which the present exile and slavery is the result of Israel's own covenant-breaking, idolatry and sin, and the present pagan rulers are therefore doing the will of Israel's God, even though they themselves would not see it like that.[10] The proper response, therefore, is for God's people to be good citizens under the pagan rulers in the present time, only standing out against the regime when fundamental principles are at stake.[11] This is the position of Daniel 1—6: Daniel and his companions were high-ranking civil servants, working for the king, and the only fault that could be found in them was that they continued to give unique allegiance to their own God.[12] They reminded emperors of the sovereignty of 'the God of heaven', and warned them of impending judgment, which then came to pass.[13] But, just as Jeremiah urged the exiles to seek the welfare of the pagan city, Daniel and his friends continued to work, as we would say, 'within the system'.

On the other hand, the warnings of judgment can escalate until they result in a different kind of narrative, where pagan empire reaches its arrogant height and is finally overthrown by the one true God in an act of judgment which will, *ipso facto*, bring his own people not only into freedom at last after their exile, but into their own long-promised world sovereignty. This results in a very different message from the command to settle down and seek the welfare of Babylon. Instead, in a diverse range of texts, the people are commanded to leave Babylon in a hurry and to avoid contracting uncleanness as they do so;[14] the final world-empire becomes ever more

[9] The word 'nation' itself is tricky because of modern assumptions about what constitutes such a thing. We use the word heuristically to denote that which is spoken of in the Psalms and prophets in terms of 'the nations' on the one hand and the people of the one God on the other.

[10] cf. e.g. Isa. 45.1–13.

[11] Jer. 29.4–7. Cp. *Mt. Pol.*, where at one moment Polycarp is refusing to swear by the 'genius' of Caesar (9.3) and at the next is offering to discuss the faith with the proconsul, since, he says, 'we have been taught to render honour . . . to princes and authorities appointed by God' (10.2).

[12] cf. esp. Dan. 6.5.

[13] e.g. Dan. 4.19–27; 5.17–28.

[14] Isa. 48.20; 52.11; cf. Zech. 2.6–13; Rev. 18.4.

shrill and monstrous until its sudden overthrow;[15] and, in the terrifying sustained oracle in Jeremiah 50 and 51, we find an unrelenting prophecy of Babylon's destruction, which even suggests that Israel itself will become the weapon through which the true God will smash nations and kingdoms.[16]

This widespread double-effect picture, held together in the same books (not least in Daniel itself), is not inconsistent. It is not as though the prophets were unable to make up their minds whether they thought the pagan empires were good, requiring unquestioning submission, or bad, requiring implacable opposition. That is the kind of sterile antithesis common in contemporary political (and theopolitical) discussions, as though one had to be either an out-and-out Constantinian or an out-and-out Anabaptist (I know that Constantine was more complicated than people normally imagine, and that Anabaptism, too, is far from monochrome; but the stereotypes will serve for the moment). The two biblical positions belong in fact within the same *narrative*: (i) at the moment, God has given the pagan rulers sovereignty, and Israel must navigate its way to a seeking of the welfare of the city which does not compromise its ultimate loyalty, but (ii) the time will come when God will overthrow the wicked pagans, not only rescuing Israel but setting it up as the new, alternative world kingdom. Eschatology is all: the key question is, 'what time is it?' As we saw in chapter 7, once you understand the story, the apparently different positions make sense.

A classic expression of this twofold belief is found in the Wisdom of Solomon, roughly contemporary with Paul:

> Listen therefore, O kings, and understand;
> learn, O judges of the ends of the earth.
> Give ear, you that rule over multitudes,
> and boast of many nations.
> For your dominion was given you from the Lord,
> and your sovereignty from the Most High;
> he will search out your works and inquire into your plans.
> Because as servants of his kingdom you did not rule rightly, or keep the law,
> or walk according to the purpose of God,
> he will come upon you terribly and swiftly,
> because severe judgment falls on those in high places.[17]

This particular complex Jewish narrative is where we should start if we are to understand Paul's vision of pagan empire – or rather, Paul's vision of the divine purpose in relation to pagan empire.

2. Second, we must emphasize once more the point made in chapter 5 above: the remarkable growth of the complex and variegated phenomena which we loosely summarize as 'imperial cult' in precisely the places where Paul was working.[18] When Paul wrote to the Corinthians about 'many gods,

[15] Dan. 7.8, 11, 19–22.

[16] cf. esp. Jer. 51.20–3, with echoes of the Messiah's role in Pss. 2.9; 110.5f.

[17] Wis. 6.1–5. The whole book expounds this point, not least through the retelling of the exodus-narrative in chs. 10—19.

[18] Against the minimalist reading of Miller 2010.

many lords' (8.5), he could not have forgotten, and would not expect them to forget, the imperial temple that had recently been built at the west end of the forum.[19] When he reminded the Thessalonians that they had 'turned to God from idols, to serve a living and true God, and to wait for his son from heaven', he no doubt had plenty of pagan divinities in mind, but would hardly have been able to ignore the claims of divine sonship which, echoing the beliefs about Hercules on the one hand and the claims made by Alexander on the other,[20] were now being advanced energetically by the one who claimed to be *divi filius*. We shall come back to this presently. However various and differentiated the local cults may have been by which Greece and Asia Minor gave honour to Rome and to its chief citizen in particular, such cults had burgeoned in the decades immediately before Paul's work, and were continuing to do so in his own day, not least in the cities where he preached and taught. This is the context in which we may remind ourselves of the famous words of Adolf Deissmann a century or so ago:

> It must not be supposed that St. Paul and his fellow-believers went through the world blindfolded, unaffected by what was then moving the minds of men in great cities. These pages [of his book, *Light from the Ancient East*], I think, have already shown by many examples how much the New Testament is a book of the Imperial age. We may certainly take it for granted that the Christians of the early Imperial period were familiar with the institutions and customs that the Empire had brought with it ... [Deissmann then adds some examples of small and recondite points, and concludes] If such superficial details were known among the people, how much more so the deification of the emperor, with its glittering and gorgeous store of the very loftiest terms employed in worship, compelling every monotheistic conscience to most powerful reaction! ... Thus there arises a polemical parallelism between the cult of the emperor and the cult of Christ, which makes itself felt where ancient words derived by Christianity from the treasury of the Septuagint and the Gospels happen to coincide with solemn concepts of the Imperial cult which sounded the same or similar.[21]

Though we shall see that this last judgment needs to be nuanced, the overall picture should not be doubted.

3. Third, we must note – as an antidote to the easy-going assumptions of post-Enlightenment western thought! – that there are many varieties of 'political' comment and action. The increasing polarization of American social, political and cultural life, on the one hand, and the continuing implicit class-based polarization of British politics, on the other, easily deceive English-speaking readers into supposing that one must be entirely 'for' this party and 'against' that one, and that anyone who is serious about such matters must hold the party line on all debated issues. But, as post-colonial studies have repeatedly shown, there are all kinds of options open to subject peoples. They can go along with the regime that is oppressing them; they may find that it does indeed bring some benefits to them and

[19] On the counter-imperial relevance of this passage see Fantin 2011, 225–31.

[20] Alexander originally claimed distant descent from Hercules, and hence from Zeus, but by 331 BC he had begun to claim direct sonship, through a kind of dual parentage (so Bosworth in *OCD* 59).

[21] Deissmann 1978 [1908], 340–2.

their families. Things are frequently complex, and by no means always polarized. But this does not mean that subject peoples do not retain some deep awareness that the foreign regime remains foreign, ultimately oppressive and undesirable. Equally, those who are passionately opposed to an oppressive regime may be divided in terms of how to express and embody that opposition. The notion of 'hidden transcripts' has become popular: one can say a good deal without actually saying it. The trouble with this, of course, is that, as with conspiracy theories, the more something is hidden the more one begins to suspect its presence, putting the historian in the awkward situation of treating the absence of evidence as itself constituting evidence. However, such an argument need not be entirely speculative. If a text gives at least some indications of a subversive approach, then other related passages can be brought into play, with due caution and without allowing political imagination to run riot.[22]

The task before us, then, is to take someone like Paul, with his background as a Pharisaic Jew as described in chapter 2 above, to imagine him facing the world described in chapter 5 above, and then to develop that picture in the light of his new worldview and theology as set out in Parts II and III above. That will form the context for a fresh examination of the key texts, and for a brief debate with one current controversialist.

2. Empire in Relation to Paul's Worldview and Theology

What, then, must be said as we think back through Parts II and III of the present book with the question of 'Paul and Empire' before our minds? The first and most obvious point, coming straight out of chapters 6 and 10, is that for Paul the gospel of Jesus the Messiah created and sustained a particular *community*. For Paul, those who were *en Christō* constituted a 'people', a family of 'brothers and sisters', with mutual ties and obligations indicated by the word *koinōnia*. Their allegiance to Jesus as *Christos* and *kyrios*, and to one another within this 'fellowship', was their primary identity. This community, astonishingly in the ancient world as in the modern, was by its very nature composed of people of all sorts on an even footing: Jews and non-Jews, rich and poor, slave and free, male and female. This remarkable unity across otherwise universal dividing-lines was balanced by an equally remarkable insistence on firm boundaries to do with belief and behaviour. There were plenty of questions as to where precisely those boundaries were to be located (much of 1 Corinthians deals with questions of that sort), but nobody doubted that such boundaries existed. Paul assumed, then, as a matter of worldview, sustained by his detailed theology, that those *en Christō* were a distinct family, and were to live as such.

This already constituted a challenge to most social and cultural groups in the ancient world, and not least to the assumptions which sustained the

[22] On 'hidden transcripts' see the seminal work, now widely discussed, of Scott 1990.

Roman empire itself. Groups of people gathering in unusual combinations, binding themselves in allegiance to a god, a cause, an ideal, were already regarded as a threat to the established social, cultural and political order. We have our own contemporary examples: after September 11, 2001, many airlines adopted a policy of forbidding passengers to cluster together at one point in the cabin. The risk of sudden terrorist action meant that three or four old friends, sitting for long hours at different points in the plane, were not allowed to meet up for a drink by the galley. That regulation is understandable, however apparently absurd in its actual operation. So, too, it is understandable that in many cities of the ancient world the authorities would look with suspicion on any groups who met together behind closed doors, especially when the people concerned did not in other respects belong to the same segments of society. What, people would wonder, might they be up to? And when the empire itself was attempting to unite people in allegiance to Caesar and Rome across ethnic divisions (though not across the divisions between slave and free or male and female), we should not be surprised that the early Christians encountered suspicion and hostility not only from local and transnational authorities but also from neighbours.

The central symbol of Paul's worldview, therefore (the united and holy community), already constituted a challenge both to the implicit assumptions of communities in the ancient world and, more specifically, to the empire of Rome. While Paul's churches remained small – we have frustratingly little information about actual numbers, but in most cases we can safely assume communities of a few dozen at most in towns and cities which numbered in the tens or hundreds of thousands – the impact will have been marginal, and the consequent threat small.[23] But by the end of Paul's life, which we assume to have been in the 60s under Nero, the Christians in Rome at least were sufficient in number to be used as scapegoats for civic disaster. Though other reasons may have been given as well (non-worship of traditional gods being the obvious one), the fact that they were known as a group with its own strong and non-traditional identity will have meant that from the very beginning the Christians, simply by being what Paul believed they were, will have raised eyebrows, then hackles, then suspicions. Before we even mention state cults, emperor-worship and the like, we should reckon that what Paul assumed as a matter of worldview about the

[23] Population estimates for the ancient world are notoriously problematic. It is normally regarded as plausible to reckon on between 100,000 and 300,000 for cities like Antioch and Ephesus, and roughly a million for Rome, not counting slaves who might have numbered about the same again. A similarly plausible guess for the whole Roman empire at the death of Augustus, remaining relatively stable for at least a century thereafter, puts the figure at about 54 million (again, not including slaves). As for the church, even if we give Luke the benefit of the doubt for the 3000 converted at Pentecost, the 5000 shortly after that, and many more thereafter (Ac. 2.41; 4.4; cf. 5.14; 6.7; 9.35; 11.21; 13.48), we might still conclude that by the time of Paul's death the total number of Christians in the Roman empire might be at most between 10,000 and 20,000, mostly concentrated in Palestine and Syria, with cities like Ephesus having churches of a few dozen, and Rome itself a scattering of house-churches with, at the most, a total of one or two hundred members (as reflected in Rom. 16). See M. H. Crawford in *OCD* 1223; Stark 1996; 2006, 64–70. Jewett (2007, 61f.) disagrees, suggesting that the Roman church might have numbered several thousand in Rome by 64, spread over 'dozens of groups' of which Paul (in Rom. 16) identifies only five.

followers of Jesus, and what he taught about the redefinition of the Jewish doctrine of election, set him and his communities on a collision course not only with the empire but with many deep-rooted assumptions in the normal civic life of the ancient world.

If that was so in relation to the central symbol of Paul's worldview, it was even more so in relation to the central narrative. As we saw in chapter 7, Paul's narrative world, the story he assumed and which he wanted his communities to assume as their own, was consciously global and cosmic. It spoke of the one creator God, of a single human race and of the focusing of that human race on to Abraham and his family. This essentially Jewish narrative – already a challenge to other visions of the human project! – carried with it the ambiguities we noticed a moment ago in relation to the nations and empires of the world. On the one hand, Jews in exile and/or dispersion were to accept that the rulers of the world were *both* appointed to their tasks by the one creator God *and* accountable to that God for the way they carried them out. The calling of the people who gave allegiance to that God was therefore to work for the good of the people and nation where they found themselves. On the other hand (as we saw, you need a narrative worldview in order to understand how these two things fit together), precisely because that God would call the nations to account, there would come a time when the arrogant pagan rulers would finally be judged, and when the people of the one God would themselves receive global sovereignty instead. The Jewish story which Paul assumed as basic thus carried with it *both* the injunction to patience and civic virtue in the present *and* the hope for a very different future in which the present rulers would be called to account – and would be replaced with God's own people.

But when Paul told that story, and assumed it at the core of his worldview, it took a new form. Something fresh, totally unexpected, had happened. At the worldview level, as we saw in chapters 7 and 8, he believed that with the Messiah's death and resurrection the new reality for which Israel had longed had at last dawned, even though it did not look like what he, or anyone else, had expected. To the question 'what time is it?', he assumed at the level of worldview, and argued at the level of theology (chapter 11 above), that the long-awaited eschaton had arrived. 'The resurrection of the dead' had already happened – in the person of the Messiah. For Paul this could only mean that Jesus himself was already enthroned as the world's true lord. The tension of 'now' and 'not yet' which has regularly been seen as characteristic of his vision of Christian living is if anything even more important in terms of his vision of Jesus as world ruler. Obviously there was still a 'not yet', and Paul was aware of it with every beating he endured, every minute he spent in prison, every time he looked out on a world still full of idolatry, tyranny, wickedness and death. But, equally obviously from his writings, there was a 'now' that had not been there before. 'The Messiah has to go on ruling, you see,' he wrote to the Corinthians, 'until "he has put all his enemies under his feet".' Jesus was, in other words, *already* ruling the world, as the Psalmist had promised, even though that rule still awaited its final triumph.[24] As with everything else to do with the future Jewish hope, Paul believed *both* that it had already arrived *and* that it was yet to arrive. If this was true for his view, say, of resurrection itself, it was every bit as true for his vision of the divine purpose for the pagan empires of the world. As a Pharisaic Jew, he had believed *both* that the nations were already under the strange providential rule of the one God (so that one should live peacefully under pagan rule for the time being), *and* that the one God would sooner or later bring about the great cosmic change through which his people would be ruling the world instead. The tension between the two halves of this belief constituted, broadly, the dividing-line between what can loosely be called the school of Hillel and the school of Shammai, with the Hillelites content to live at peace under the rule of pagan empire, and to practise their *halakah* in private, and the Shammaites convinced that it was time for the great revolution. After 135, of course, the Hillelite option was the only viable one left, the narrative of hope having died what seemed to be a final death.[25]

Paul the apostle now told the story differently. The great revolution *had already occurred* in the death and resurrection of Israel's Messiah. But precisely because there was a 'not yet' about this, as well as the obvious 'now', elements of what we may heuristically call the Hillelite position still remained. Jesus was already the world's true lord; but 'the powers that be' were still ordained by God. The apparent tension between 1 Corinthians 15.20–8 and Romans 13.1–7, which we shall explore in a minute, is the necessary eschatological tension generated by the way Israel's story had reached its unexpected climax with the crucifixion and resurrection of the Messiah. The narrative of Paul's worldview, then, and the answers to the worldview questions, particularly 'what time is it?', placed him at a new point on the worldview-map in relation to the old challenges of pagan empire and what to do about it. This new point did not correspond to anything we know from the post-135 rabbis, who had in effect given up the struggle for the kingdom of heaven and, with it, the idea of an ongoing narrative that would lead to the overthrow of pagan power. (If anything, Paul's viewpoint is closer, though still with many significant differences, to the inaugurated eschatologies of Qumran on the one hand and bar-Kochba on the other.) Nor does this new Pauline position correspond to anything we know in the normal church-and-society discussions of the post-Enlightenment western world, where left-wing Christians are eager to subpoena Paul in favour of their Marxist agendas and right-wing Christians are eager to quote Romans 13 in favour of governments doing whatever they think they need to do (dropping bombs on people, for instance). For Paul, inaugurated eschatology precipitated a new mode of the Pharisaic/Jewish political challenge. And if the 'not yet' indicated that there was still a sense

[24] 1 Cor. 15.25, quoting Ps. 110.1. On the idea of a rule which is firmly inaugurated but awaiting consummation see esp. *JVG* 467–72, and Wright 2011a [*Simply Jesus*], ch. 9.

[25] See above, ch. 2, on Hillel and Shammai. For the situation after 135, cf. *NTPG* 199f.

of 'living peacefully under the world's rulers', the 'now' indicated that something new had none the less happened. The Messiah 'rises up to rule the nations'; it had already happened, and Paul was there to announce it and to make it a reality.[26] This cannot be other than politically subversive, even though the nature of that subversion will not map on to the models we have assumed. But of one thing we can be sure. Daniel 7 had spoken of a sequence of four monsters. Everyone in the 160s BC would have identified the fourth monster as Syria. Everyone in the first century AD would have identified it as Rome. For someone steeped in the Jewish apocalyptic tradition, as Paul was, it would have been impossible to imagine that Rome was 'insignificant'.[27]

There is a second way in which the narrative Paul believed himself and his communities to be inhabiting produced a clash with Rome and its empire. This took place at the level both of worldview and of theology. Paul understood the nascent church to be living within a long story, that of Israel itself. After many apparent disasters and wrong turns, this story had finally been brought, by a massive ('apocalyptic'!) act of fresh divine grace, to the decisive and climactic fulfilment which had been envisaged from the beginning and which, despite ongoing disappointments, had been promised repeatedly thereafter. Israel's long history had at last reached its royal conclusion, even though nobody had imagined that the Messiah would himself be crucified and raised from the dead to attain his enthronement. But, as we saw in chapter 5, at exactly the same point in time the Roman world was being taught to understand its own history in a new way, which corresponds uncannily to this strange, and now strangely fulfilled, Jewish narrative. Horace, Livy and above all Virgil had celebrated the rise of Augustus as the unexpected royal climax to the long history of republican Rome, producing a new world order of peace, justice and prosperity.[28] The clash of narratives already visible in the book of Daniel, and in works dependent on it such as *4 Ezra*, developed in the late 60s and early 130s into actual open warfare. But it also developed in another direction, in the writings of Paul, into a theological account in which the decisive battle had already been fought and won.[29] There cannot, in the last analysis, be two parallel eschatological narratives of world domination. Either the history of Rome provides the true story, with Christian faith content to shelter, as a 'permitted religion', under its banner. Or the history of Israel, climaxing in the crucified and risen Messiah, must be seen as the true story, with that of Rome, however much under the overarching divine providence, as at best a distorted parody of the truth. As Nebuchadnezzar had learned the hard way, human kingdoms are indeed the gift of heaven's God, but heaven's God will judge human rulers for exercising their delegated rule with arrogance and self-aggrandisement.

[26] Rom. 15.12.

[27] On Barclay's comments about 'apocalyptic' and 'politics' in relation to 2 Thess. 2 see below, 1290 and esp. n. 53.

[28] See above, 219–312.

[29] 1 Cor. 2.8; Col. 2.15; see below.

As Paul told and retold the long story of the creator God and his chosen people, reaching its shocking climax in the crucified Messiah, he can hardly have been unaware, in a world where Virgil at least had already become a school-text, of the powerful alternative narrative that Rome was offering to the world. For someone who believed what Paul believed, Rome could never simply be the insignificant backdrop for his work, a kind of socio-cultural wallpaper. Rome offered a long and powerful story of a divinely appointed city, nation and culture from which had emerged the *divi filius* himself, bringing peace and justice and world domination. Paul told the long and evocative story of a divinely appointed people from whom, despite their many failures and tragedies, there had emerged the *theou hyios* himself, bringing peace and justice and claiming worldwide allegiance. When it came to long stories which eventually arrived at a surprising but world-transforming royal conclusion, Paul's story of Israel and its Messiah had only one competitor. Thus, while in terms of Daniel 7 Rome would be seen as the fourth monster, in terms of its own imperial narrative it would appear as the sole rival to the story of Israel. Either way, Rome could hardly be insignificant for Paul. It was not simply the present vehicle for the kind of dark powers that were always, from the Jewish point of view, active through pagan empires. It offered such a stark set of parallels to the narrative of Paul's gospel that it was bound to appear not just as one empire among many – the one which happened to be around at the time, so to speak – but as a strikingly specific parody of the message of Jesus and the community of his followers.

Of course, for Paul as for Jesus himself, the very notion of empire, of 'world domination', had itself been deconstructed by the cross and remade, in a quite different form, in the resurrection. Jesus was indeed to be hailed as the world's true sovereign, even though the mode of that sovereignty was now revealed as the sovereignty of love. This means, too, that the holy war which formed the 'now' of bar-Kochba's inaugurated eschatology, and might have been seen as the imminent future at Qumran, was replaced for Paul by the 'warfare' he describes in Ephesians 6. That, too, we must explore more fully in a moment, together with the new kind of paradoxes which then result.[30]

It is inevitable, then, that the worldview through which Paul looked at all of reality, with its central symbol of the people of God renewed *en Christō*, its central Israel- and Messiah-shaped narrative and its decisive inaugurated eschatology, would come into conflict with the worldview of empire as expressed by Roman writers, architects, tax-collectors and military commanders. Neither was making limited claims which would allow for the free operation of the other. Sooner or later they would be forced into a direct confrontation for which, perhaps, the strange incident which caused

[30] Protests are sometimes lodged against any idea of universal dominion, as though Paul ought really to have embraced a kind of radical egalitarian anarchy (e.g. Marchal 2012). One may of course take that view, but it is impossible to find it in Paul's texts.

Claudius to expel Jews from Rome may have been at least a foretaste.[31] But there remains one element of Paul's theology which we have not yet considered. Paul was, at least in his own estimation, a monotheist of the Jewish variety. His remarkably mature proto-trinitarian vision of the one God, which we explored in chapter 9, was itself bound to come into conflict with the claims of the new civic and imperial cults. There are, he wrote, many 'gods' and many 'lords', but 'for us' – and the 'us' is hugely significant as an ecclesial marker both against the pagan world and against the Jewish world that did not accept Jesus as Messiah – there is 'one God, the father ... and one lord, Jesus the Messiah.' As we saw, this was a deliberate rewriting of the central Jewish confessional prayer, the *Shema*, and it carried with it not only the stunning christological redefinition of the one God – discovering Jesus himself to be at the heart of monotheism! – but also the clear intent of upstaging all other 'gods' and 'lords' who might claim the attention of the Corinthians. And in Corinth, a city proud to be Roman, sporting new imperial shrines, celebrating Rome and Caesar with games and festivals, Rome could not have been insignificant. Of course there were plenty of other 'gods' and 'lords' as well. But nobody in Corinth would have missed the point. Those who followed the one God, one lord were to regard all other claimants to those words as a sham. Historically speaking, that must have included Rome and Caesar, not as an insignificant addition to a much larger pantheon, nor as merely the present holders of an imperial power whose real significance lay in the dark forces which it happened, for the moment, to embody, but as a central target of Paul's implied polemic.[32]

I suggest therefore that the inner logic of Paul's own worldview and theology, seen as the messianic redefinition of his second-Temple Jewish worldview, cannot but have brought him into conflict, whether implicit or explicit, with the claims, the narrative and the policies of the Roman empire. It remains vital, however, to see all this within the framework of Paul's distinctive (and, again, messianic) *eschatology*, with its all-important 'now/not yet' shape and balance. It will not do to ask simply whether Paul was 'for' or 'against' either the generalized idea of 'empire' or the Roman empire in particular. Like other Jews, he believed that the one God had appointed human authorities and intended that they should be obeyed. Like other Jews, he believed that the one God would hold such authorities to account. Unlike most other Jews,[33] *he believed that this holding-to-account had already happened, and that Israel's Messiah was already installed as the true ruler of the world.* As in other areas of his thinking, he was therefore precipitated into a new, unmapped territory in which it would be easy to be misunderstood, in his world as indeed in ours. If, as I believe, Paul was articulating a deeply counter-imperial theology, it was not of the type with which, as a hard-line Pharisee, he would previously have been familiar. If, as I believe, he was articulating a deeply monotheistic belief in the divine appointment of

[31] cf. *NTPG* 354f., on Suet. *Claud.* 25.4.

[32] On the well-known question of 'Jesus as lord' as against 'Caesar as lord' see now Fantin 2011.

[33] Again, we might make an exception here for the short-lived bar-Kochba revolt.

human rulers, frail and fallible though they remained, this was not simply identical with the view that had led Jeremiah to tell the exiles to seek the welfare of Babylon. Both sides of his previous Jewish belief about politics and empire had been radically rethought around the Messiah.

Up to this point I have been content with an outline argumentative strategy. I have suggested that there is a massive *prima facie* probability that, granted what Paul believed and granted what Rome claimed, the two would necessarily come into conflict. But history cannot work with 'must-have-been's alone. What has been said so far has been necessary in order that we may attune our ears to the overtones of what Paul actually says. Without these chambers of resonance, we might easily miss the point. So, then, with the echo chamber properly and historically constructed, we turn to the texts themselves.

3. Jesus Is Lord, and Therefore ...

(i) Who Are the 'Rulers', and What Has Happened to Them?

The rulers, as I said, had already been called to account. They had been judged, found wanting and held up to public ridicule:

> [God] blotted out the handwriting that was against us, opposing us with its legal demands. He took it right out of the way, by nailing it to the cross. He stripped the rulers and authorities of their armour, and displayed them contemptuously to public view, celebrating his triumph over them in him.[34]

This is, of course, part of a letter written from prison. Paul was in no danger of an over-realized eschatology, of imagining that the rulers and authorities had been rendered actually harmless. He was still chained up (4.3). Nevertheless, the remarkable statement in the second sentence above (verse 15) is framed within a larger discourse in which the new world has come to pass and the old one is to be regarded as irrelevant. Human traditions and 'the elements of the world' are things that threaten to take you captive, declares Paul, but if you are in the Messiah you are already fulfilled in him, because he is 'the head of all rule and authority' (2.10). His death and resurrection, and your incorporation into those events through baptism, mean in particular that neither the commands nor the accusations of the Jewish law have any claim upon you (2.13, 16–19, 20–3). But, though the warnings seem to be slanted against the dangers of being lured into some kind of Jewish way of life, at bottom they are rooted in the cosmic vision of chapter 1. It was not simply the demands of the Jewish law that had been nailed to the cross. It was the rulers and authorities themselves, the powers that, by crucifying Jesus, had supposed they were getting rid of such a nuisance, only to find that they had signed their own death warrant:

[34] Col. 2.14–15.

> We do, however, speak wisdom among the mature. But this isn't a wisdom of this present world, or of the rulers of this present world – those same rulers who are being done away with. No: we speak God's hidden wisdom in a mystery. This is the wisdom God prepared ahead of time, before the world began, for our glory.
>
> None of the rulers of this present age knew about this wisdom. If they had, you see, they wouldn't have crucified the lord of glory.[35]

That passage makes it impossible to imagine that when Paul speaks of 'powers' or 'rulers' he is referring *only* to so-called 'spiritual' forces. We might draw the same conclusion from a tiny phrase often overlooked in this connection: when Paul speaks contemptuously of 'so-called "gods", whether in heaven or on earth', the latter phrase, 'on earth', can only in his day refer to the Caesars.[36] Paul can think of the Olympians on the one hand, and know that they are a fiction; of Caesar on the other hand, and know that his theological claims are false. (His political claims were as strong as his legions.) To this extent, the very ordinary human who hides within the apparently divine status is parallel to the unpleasant little demons who hide behind the imposing facade of the fictitious pagan pantheon.[37] This is not the place to enter into the complex debates about the apparent interplay between human 'powers' and non-human 'powers', except to note that, like many in his world, Paul would not have made the sharp and absolute distinction between them that we are inclined to do. Just as he sees *daimonia* at work behind and within the official pagan 'deities',[38] so he recognizes the presence and power of unseen forces behind and within the actual humans who wield power in the obvious and immediate sense.[39] Three of his great, sweeping panoramas indicate that he bundles them all up together:

> I am persuaded, you see, that neither death nor life, nor angels nor rulers, nor the present, nor the future, nor powers, nor height, nor depth, nor any other creature will be able to separate us from the love of God in King Jesus our lord.[40]

> This was the power at work in the king when God raised him from the dead and sat him at his right hand in the heavenly places, above all rule and authority and power and lordship, and above every name that is invoked, both in the present age and also in the age to come. Yes: God has 'put all things under his feet', and has given him to the church as the head over all.[41]

> He is the image of God, the invisible one,
> the firstborn of all creation.
> For in him all things were created,
> in the heavens and here on the earth.

[35] 1 Cor. 2.6–8.

[36] 1 Cor. 8.5.

[37] 1 Cor. 10.20f.

[38] As in 1 Cor. 10.20.

[39] To this extent I agree with the careful analysis offered by Barclay 2011, 384f.; see below. On this whole topic the major work is still that of Wink 1984.

[40] Rom. 8.38f.

[41] Eph. 1.20–2.

> Things we can see and things we cannot,
> – thrones and lordships and rulers and powers –
> all things were created both through him and for him.[42]

Two points emerge here of relevance for our question. First, as to the *identity* of the 'rulers'. They clearly *include* all human authorities, from Caesar on his throne, giving himself 'divine' status, right down to the lowliest local administrator. But precisely by including them in a much larger array of 'powers' this way of speaking thereby *relativizes* all such rulers. 'Every name that is invoked': in eastern Asia Minor there was one name in particular that was invoked in Paul's day, and he knew it and so did his readers. Of course, by implicitly placing Caesar within a long list of other types of ruler and power Paul is demoting him, cutting him down to size. He is one among many. But this was itself a polemical point. In a world where an absolute monarch was busy drawing all other powers to himself, where statues and coins dressed him up as Zeus, Poseidon or some other lofty Olympian, to place Caesar by implication as one among many was already a calculated snub. It is much the same – ironically, in view of the way the passage has often been read – with Romans 13.1–7. When Caesar is being granted divine honours, to say that 'there is no authority except from God, and those that exist have been put in place by God' is to deny the very claim that Caesar is making.[43] The creator, who has made humans in his image so that they might reflect his authority into the world, intends that there should be human authorities, but insists that they should hold office only at his behest and subject to his scrutiny. This is, so far, the classic Jewish position we observed earlier.

Second, however, we note what Paul is saying *about* these authorities, including the most powerful human ones. They are now, whether they know it or not, subject not only to the instituting and judging authority of the one God, but also to the rule of the Messiah. That which was promised in Psalms 2 and 110, and many other Jewish texts, has already come to pass. Everything has already been 'put under his feet'. That which was created through him and for him, as in Colossians, has been placed in subjection under him, as in Ephesians. If we ask how this has happened, Colossians highlights the cross as the moment when the rulers and authorities were cut down to size, publicly shamed for their arrogance, and Ephesians highlights the resurrection and ascension as the means by which Jesus has been installed as the one and only human to whom all things are now subject. If we ask why this was necessary – why, granted the goodness of the original creation, including all authorities, the 'powers' would then need to be 'reconciled', as in Colossians 1.20, or defeated in the Messiah's triumph, as in 2.15 – Paul gives no direct answer, but he clearly believes that the created powers have rebelled against the creator, and have arrogated to themselves

[42] Col. 1.15f.

[43] Rom. 13.1. We might compare the remarkable Jn. 19.11. See again the nuanced statement in Tert. *Apol.* 30–3.

powers which they have now been eager to use against the creator's will. That is why, in another relativizing move, he insists that the real, ultimate enemy is not any human being or structure, but the dark anti-creational forces that stand behind them and use them as puppets in their nefarious purposes:

> The warfare we're engaged in, you see, isn't against flesh and blood. It's against the leaders, against the authorities, against the powers that rule the world in this dark age, against the wicked spiritual elements in the heavenly places.[44]

That is why the battle to which the apostle and his congregations are called is not a matter of ordinary human resistance or revolution, as in the violent insurgency which formed one Jewish tradition all the way from the Maccabees to bar-Kochba. Paul believed in a different kind of warfare, requiring a different kind of armour: truth as a belt, justice as a breastplate, the gospel of peace for shoes, faith for a shield, salvation as a helmet and God's word as a sword.[45] This corresponds closely to another passage in which, as we shall see, Paul dismisses the arrogant claims of empire as so much empty boasting, and goes on to insist that followers of the Messiah live already in the new day which is dawning:

> We daytime people should be self-controlled, clothing ourselves with the breastplate of faith and love, and with the helmet of the hope of salvation; because God has not placed us on the road to fury, but to gaining salvation through our lord Jesus the Messiah.[46]

This shift in perspective – the cutting down to size of pompous imperial pretensions, and the insistence on a different kind of battle altogether – is entirely consonant with the classic 'apocalyptic' passage in 1 Corinthians 15, where Paul stresses that the 'last enemies' over whom the Messiah must win the final victory are not (shall we say) Babylon, or Syria, or even Rome, but 'sin' and 'death' themselves:

> He has to go on ruling, you see, until 'he has put all his enemies under his feet'. Death is the last enemy to be destroyed . . .
>
> The 'sting' of death is sin, and the power of sin is the law. But thank God! He gives us the victory, through our lord Jesus the Messiah.[47]

And this in turn points to the redefinition of the messianic battle which we find in the gospels. To allow Rome, or any other empire, to set the agenda so firmly that it becomes 'the' enemy is to fail to see the real enemies hiding behind the glitter of armour and the point of a spear. 'Don't be afraid', says Jesus, 'of those who kill the body, and after that have nothing more they can

[44] Eph. 6.12.
[45] Eph. 6.14–17.
[46] 1 Thess. 5.8.
[47] 1 Cor. 15.25f., 56.

do'. Instead, 'fear the one who starts by killing and then has the right to throw people into Gehenna'.[48]

The trouble is, of course, that in the split-level worldview of western modernism it is difficult to make this point without people getting the (other) wrong end of the stick. Oh, we will be told, so you're saying that Paul isn't interested in Caesar after all, but only in 'spiritual' forces? Some will be eager to 'hear' something like this, others disappointed; but it is not at all what I am saying – and, more to the point, not at all what Paul is saying. If I can risk an analogy which will itself be anathema to some, we are told from time to time that 'it isn't guns that kill people, it's people that kill people'; but that sharp antithesis is called into question by the statistics which suggest that in a country with many guns more people will kill one another than in a country with few. In the same way, it would be wrong to say that it isn't empires that destroy human life, it's the demons that stand behind them. Yes, we may want to say: in the last analysis, empires may indeed become stupid puppets operated by demonic forces; but it remains the case that dark forces operate *through* arrogant tyranny – just as, Paul would be quick to add, they operate also through chaotic anarchy. That is the problem of politics, ancient and modern.[49] And it is not resolved by one-sided analyses.

Where does this leave us? With a sharper and clearer understanding of how the two-sided Jewish vision of political reality – rulers created by the one God and called to account before him – was given new depth, focus and above all chronological timing by Paul as a result of what he believed about the Messiah. Ancient Israel sang of the enthronement of the Messiah over the warring and squabbling kings of the earth; Paul believed that this enthronement had already happened. The prophets (and even, in some readings, the Pentateuch) had spoken of the coming king who would rule the nations; Paul believed that the king had come, and was already ruling. This cannot be 'spiritualized', as some might wish to do, without making a mockery – almost a gnostic mockery! – of the entire Jewish framework of thought. There is, however, a radical difference. The victory which Paul believes has already taken place has been effected not through the Messiah leading a military operation, as in the line from Judas Maccabaeus to Simon bar-Kochba, but through his paradoxical and shameful death on a Roman cross, and his subsequent resurrection and exaltation. Because of this, Paul recognizes that the victory which the Messiah's followers must now implement is not the transfer of ordinary political and military power from one group to another, but the transformation of that power itself into something different altogether, something in fact much more powerful. The greatest power in and beyond all creation, as he says at the end of his greatest chapter, has now been unveiled in action, and it remains the one thing that can withstand all other powers. For Paul, its nature and its name was Love.

[48] Lk. 12.4f. (par. Mt. 10.28f.). See *JVG* 454f., and the larger discussion of 446–63.

[49] A classic example is the debate between Agrippa and Maecenas, advising Augustus, in Dio Cassius *Hist.* 52.

(ii) The Apocalyptic, and Therefore Political, Triumph of God

With all this in mind, we turn to the two letters where the case for an implicit anti-Roman polemic is clearest. It may or may not be significant that, Romans itself excepted, they are the two letters addressed to cities geographically closest to the capital: Thessalonica and Philippi.[50]

The two letters to the Thessalonians are, of course, known for their 'apocalyptic' mode of expression. This is sharpest in the second letter, causing those who wanted to keep Paul and 'apocalyptic' at arm's length from one another to assign it to a different hand. But with the proper re-emphasis on 'apocalyptic' as part of Paul's context – for all the misunderstandings which have swirled around that term! – it ought to be time for a reconsideration. And with the equally proper emphasis in recent studies on the essentially 'political' meaning of 'apocalyptic' language in the Jewish world of the second-Temple period, we ought to be able to say, of both the Thessalonian letters, not only that they belong firmly within the overall Pauline corpus but that we ought to expect them to be engaged, at some level or other, precisely with the 'political' world of the day. Just as we learn, as a matter of genre, that in the poetry of the Psalms a reference to smoke coming out of God's nostrils does not intend a flat, literal meaning; that when Jesus says he is a 'door' he does not mean he is made of wood; and that when Genesis says the world was made in six days it is not referring to six periods of twenty-four hours, so we have learned (or we should have done), as a matter of genre, that 'apocalyptic' language in Paul's world was regularly employed as a coded way of speaking about the rise and fall of great world powers. Daniel, after all, is the book which stands most obviously at or near the head of the genre, and when Daniel wrote about four monsters coming up out of the sea he was not writing a script for a fantasy horror movie. We know how Daniel was being read in the first century, and it is clear that he was talking about actual empires, and the actual overthrow of the last and most terrible of them.[51]

So when we read 2 Thessalonians 2, we ought not to imagine that this is simply a wild 'apocalyptic' fantasy about some great coming event, totally discontinuous with present socio-political reality. As I have often said, it is clear that 'the day of the lord' in this passage cannot be 'the end of the world'; if it were, neither Paul nor the Thessalonians would expect to be informed of such a thing by letter. Rather, we seem to be in the realm (a) of major and important socio-political events which (b) can best be referred to through 'apocalyptic' language:

> Now concerning the royal presence of our lord Jesus the Messiah, and our gathering together around him, this is our request, my dear family. Please don't be suddenly blown off course in your thinking, or be unsettled, either through spiritual influence, or through a word, or through a letter supposedly from us, telling you that the day of the lord has already arrived.

[50] On Roman presence and influence in northern Greece cf. above, 330–3.

[51] See once more above, 117–39.

> Don't let anyone deceive you in any way. You see, it can't happen unless first the rebellion takes place, and the man of lawlessness, the son of destruction, is revealed. He is the one who sets himself against every so-called god or cult object, and usurps their role, so that he installs himself in God's temple, and makes himself out to be a god.[52]

It is ironic that this passage has played less of a role in discussions of 'Paul and politics' than it should have done – no doubt because of the prejudice against Pauline authorship which, as I said, was based almost entirely on an older anti-apocalyptic viewpoint which, like Marcion (and Bultmann!) with Romans 8.18–26, wanted to cut out or marginalize all such traces of 'Jewish' thought-forms. But once we have recognized Paul as a thoroughly 'apocalyptic' thinker, and once we recapture the sense that 'apocalyptic' itself was a major carrier of social and political critique, then there should be no question as to what is going on here.[53] Paul is reminding the Thessalonians that for evil finally to be eradicated from God's world it must be brought to full height, must be concentrated at one point and must be dealt with there. In the world of the first century, to speak of someone who insists on his own superiority to other gods and cult objects, installs himself in their place in temples and particularly in the Temple in Jerusalem, and gives himself out to be a god, is clearly to refer to the Roman emperor. This, of course, creates other puzzles, since the obvious candidate for someone doing what is here described is Gaius Caligula, whose failed attempt to have his statue installed in the Jerusalem Temple took place in AD 40, shortly before his death in 41 – long before, on any credible chronology, Paul the apostle ever visited northern Greece. The best guess, then, is that Paul, keenly aware (like the whole Jewish world) of that crisis and what it meant, was peering into the foggy future with the aid of apocalyptic imagery, and using Gaius and his megalomaniac plan as an image, a template, for what would surely come one day. Some other tyrant would try the same trick, or at least another grab at divine power for which Gaius's crazy plan would serve as an appropriate metaphor. Just as it would be silly to insist that this passage must be taken as an exact literal prediction of what will take place (think of the wings and the claws on *4 Ezra*'s eagle!), so it would be equally silly to think that the passage can therefore be 'spiritualized', and bear no relation to actual empires and their actual blasphemies, or to Rome in particular. A wise first-century reader of this text would know both that it certainly referred to Rome, and to Caesar, and also that it was seeing Rome, and Caesar, as the lens through which 'the mystery of lawlessness' itself (verse 7) could be glimpsed, working itself up to full height and thus being fully fitted for the judgment to come. Behind Rome, then, to be sure, stands the satan (verse 9); but this,

[52] 2 Thess. 2.1–5.

[53] Against e.g. Barclay 2011, 380 n. 58, who admits that 2 Thess. 2 appears to be an exception to his case, but says that the passage's register 'is very different from the undisputed Pauline texts' and that it 'appears to refer to a future apocalyptic event, not a present political reality'. The latter antithesis is puzzling, revealing a surprisingly unhistorical usage of 'apocalyptic' (see e.g. Portier-Young 2011). The point about a different register is dubious in the light of the numerous 'apocalyptic' passages in other letters; and, in any case, every single Pauline letter has many unique elements (think, for instance, of the 'allegory' in Gal. 4, with its contrast of the heavenly and earthly Jerusalems).

though again relativizing Rome (Rome/Caesar is not divine, and Rome/Caesar is not the satan), nevertheless provides as sharp a political critique of Rome/Caesar as any Jew could imagine. The point where Rome/Caesar takes on divine status is the point where Rome/Caesar is most obviously acting as satan's puppet.[54]

This clear and 'apocalyptic' reference to Rome sends us back to 1 Thessalonians with a sense that the strong implications we observed earlier in the present chapter might well find expression here too. It has often been pointed out that Paul's references to the *parousia* of Jesus can themselves be seen as an upstaging of the *parousia* of Caesar, either arriving for a state visit to a colony or returning home after a victorious campaign.[55] But the more explicit reference to the boasting of Rome here comes in 1 Thessalonians 5.3:

> When people say, 'Peace and security!', then swift ruin will arrive at their doorstep, like the pains that come over a woman in labour, and they won't have a chance of escape.

That will be 'the day of the lord', coming like a midnight robber; but those who belong to Jesus are living by a different clock, and for them the sun is already up.[56] But who is it that proclaims 'peace and security'? A wealth of evidence, including coins, points in one rather obvious direction: this was a standard boast of the Roman empire.[57] Again, Paul is doing two things simultaneously. First, he is cutting the boasters down to size, as though one might say 'I gather there are some people going about saying "peace and security"...' He will not dignify them with a full and explicit attack, but there should be no doubt in our minds, as there was none in the Thessalonians', as to the identity of 'some people' here. Second, then, he is declaring that in any case the proud tyrants of this world, with their global protection rackets ('do what we say and you'll be nice and safe'), are part of the old order of things, the night-time world which will be swept away when the new day, which has already dawned in Jesus, bursts at last upon the drunk and sleepy citizens of darkness.[58] This is obviously the same picture we found in 1 Corinthians 2, where 'the rulers of this world', who all unknowingly had crucified the lord of glory, are 'being done away with', destined to be abolished. Both pictures look back to the older Jewish visions of great world kingdoms whose power is taken from them when the one God judges the world and exalts his own people to sovereignty instead.[59]

We can be sure that 2 Thessalonians 2 is referring, 'apocalyptically' and politically, to the blasphemous boasts of the Roman emperors. We can be morally sure that 1 Thessalonians 5 is referring, dismissively and thereby all

[54] On 2 Thess. 2 see now esp. J. R. Harrison in Llewelyn and Harrison 2012, 73–5.

[55] See above, 1082–5; and *RSG* 213–19.

[56] 1 Thess. 5.2, 4f.

[57] See, recently, Weima 2012.

[58] 5.4–7.

[59] 1 Cor. 2.6; cf. e.g. Ps. 2; Dan. 7; Wis. 6.1–8.

the more powerfully, to the imperial boast of 'protection' which the inhabitants of northern Greece would know only too well. What about the other letter to northern Greece, the short and stunning letter to Philippi?

We need once more to remember the context as we set it out in chapter 5, and to recall that Philippi had been the site of one of the key battles in the civil war from which Augustus had eventually emerged as the winner. Augustus had claimed to bring peace and prosperity to the whole Roman world, rescuing it from its apparent slide into chaos; his accession was hailed as 'good news'; his successors were acclaimed variously as 'saviour' and 'lord'.[60] This language would be, quite literally, common coin in northern Greece, and especially in a city some of whose members at least were Roman citizens, part of the old colonial families. Whether citizens or not, all residents of Philippi and the surrounding areas would be reminded on a regular basis, by festivals and games, by statues and temples, by coins, inscriptions and public proclamations, just how fortunate they were to be living in Caesar's world.

That is the echo chamber within which we should try to 'hear' Paul's climactic warning and triumphant statement of hope:

> You see, there are several people who behave as enemies of the cross of the Messiah. I told you about them often enough, and now I'm weeping as I say it again. They are on the road to destruction; their stomach is their god, and they find glory in their own shame. All they ever think about is what's on the earth.
>
> We are citizens of heaven, you see, and we're eagerly waiting for the saviour, the lord, King Jesus, who is going to come from there. Our present body is a shabby old thing, but he's going to transform it so that it's just like his glorious body. And he's going to do this by the power which makes him able to bring everything into line under his authority.[61]

We leave to one side the question as to who Paul is describing, and weeping over, in verses 18 and 19. The point is that, even if they might actually be Jews, or people claiming to be Christians, Paul is describing them in language a first-century Jew might regularly use of pagans. Their horizon is bounded by *ta epigeia*, 'what's on the earth'. This sets him up for the contrast with the Christian identity: 'We are citizens of heaven', *hēmōn gar to politeuma en ouranois*. As I have argued elsewhere, this does *not* mean 'so we are looking forward to leaving earth behind and going to heaven itself'. The language of citizenship does not work that way, as anyone in Philippi could have told you; to be a citizen of Rome did not mean that one day you would leave Philippi and go back to live in Rome itself. A colony of citizens constituted a centripetal movement, not a centrifugal one. And if the language of citizenship, of belonging to a *politeuma*, already suggests a contrast between the ultimate loyalties of the Christian and the ultimate loyalties of the Roman, this is sharpened to a point by Paul's description of Jesus in this

60 On the language of 'saviour' and 'salvation' from Augustus to Hadrian, see now B. Bitner in Llewelyn and Harrison 2012, 76–85.

61 Phil. 3.18–21.

passage. Instead of Caesar coming from Rome to rescue a beleaguered colony, Jesus will come from heaven to transform the world, and particularly to give new bodies to his own people. He is the *sōtēr*, the saviour; he is the *kyrios*, the lord; he is *Christos*, the Messiah, the Jewish king destined to be lord of the whole world.[62]

Paul rubs this in by echoing Psalm 8.7, as he does in 1 Corinthians 15. The psalm, read by both Paul, Hebrews and some of their Jewish contemporaries in a messianic sense, spoke of the destiny of the human being, the 'son of man', as a kind of extension of the mandate of Genesis 1:

> You have made him a little lower than God, and crowned him with glory and honour. You have given him dominion over the works of your hands; you have put all things under his feet.[63]

Paul thus contrasts the true *politeuma*, destined to come into being on earth as in heaven, with the merely earthly one; he hails Jesus as the Messiah promised in scripture, destined to rule the whole world; he gives him the titles 'saviour' and 'lord'.[64] He speaks of his coming from heaven, as he did in 1 and 2 Thessalonians in the passages just studied. It requires, I suggest, a particular sort of deafness to suggest that he intends no allusion to Caesar.[65]

This conclusion is powerfully supported by the passage which some see as the very heart of all Paul's theology, and which on any showing is one of the most remarkable pieces of early Christian writing. Philippians 2.6–11 has of course been studied intensively, and we do not need to do more than allude to the work of others.[66] Three points only need to be made here.

First, we observe particularly the overall *narrative* of the passage. It is not simply a matter of Paul declaring that Jesus is to receive the homage from every creature in heaven, on earth and under the earth – though that already makes its own powerful statement.[67] It is a matter of Jesus coming to that universal sovereignty by a particular route. And the pattern of the narrative, with the Messiah setting off on a dark and horrible task, accomplishing it, and therefore receiving supreme exaltation, is the pattern by which, since at

62 On *kyrios* as an imperial title used by e.g. Tiberius and Nero see Foerster in *TDNT* 3.1054f., with Oakes 2001, 171f.; Fantin 2011, 193, 196–202.

63 Ps. 8.5f., keeping the singular 'him' and 'his' (for NRSV 'them' and 'their'), which is how Paul, following the LXX, evidently took it. Cp. 1 Cor. 15.27; Heb. 2.6–8. Did Paul, here and in 1 Cor. 15, intend also an allusion to Dan. 7?

64 See not least Oakes 2001, 138–47, 160–5; e.g. 141: 'the link between saving and power was a central element in Roman Imperial ideology'.

65 Barclay 2011, 379 suggests that 'modern hearers may find an echo of "Rome" in this text, with the noise of "the Roman empire" dominating their sensory perception'. He suggests that when Paul listened to his world 'he heard rather different sounds'. We should perhaps turn the point around: (a) the Philippians would undoubtedly have their sensory perceptions well attuned to the rhetoric of Rome and its empire (see Oakes 2001, 174: 'Imperial ideology was all around'); (b) if Paul had wanted them not to think of those well-known realities he would have done well not to use the language he did in fact use when speaking here of Jesus and his present and future reign.

66 And, indeed, to my own previous expositions – though in the major one, that of *Climax* ch. 4, I managed to ignore the Caesar-overtones entirely.

67 Phil. 2.10 (not 2.11 as in Barclay 2011, 379).

least the time of Alexander the Great, kings and emperors caused their own stories to be told. Though it may be doubted whether verses 6–8, the story of incarnation, servanthood and death, would remind anyone of the stories of people coming to imperial power by means of great trials, there should be no question about the force of the 'therefore' in verse 9: this is a narrative of imperial legitimation, and would be readily recognized as such. *This* is how Jesus has attained the position of *kyrios*. Powerful and detailed arguments have been advanced that most Philippian hearers of this letter would hear echoes of Caesar more strongly than echoes of any other possible contender.[68] The parallels with 3.20–1 are strong, meaning that at least on a second hearing of the letter people would pick up the even clearer Caesar-reference here as well. The passage speaks of universal authority being granted for a specific and narratable reason, by the proper authority. It is this narrative, telling the story of Jesus so that it echoes and upstages the story of Caesar, that lies at the heart of the claim to detect a subversive echo of Caesar in this passage.

But there is more. In verse 9 Jesus is given 'the name which is over all names'. As Peter Oakes has pointed out,

> The giving of the names *Augustus* and *Pater Patriae* was a vital part of the process of accession of an emperor. These names were exclusive to the Emperor in this period, clearly distinguishing him from any co-regent ... In Roman political terms, in the Julio-Claudian period, the 'name above every name' could only belong to the Emperor himself.[69]

This 'name' was, of course, *kyrios*, which in Paul's world (as we saw in chapter 9) was the regular Septuagintal rendering for the untranslatable YHWH. As with some of Paul's other key terms – *euangelion* comes to mind – we find a remarkable confluence between a biblical allusion and an imperial one.[70] We should not imagine that only one 'side' of this double allusion was intended, or would be heard. Here, as in 3.20, *kyrios* was a Caesar-title now applied to Jesus.

Third, in particular, we note the quotation from Isaiah 45.23 in verse 10. It is taken from a passage where the prophet is issuing one of his scathing denunciations of the great pagan empire of Babylon. Beside the imperial idols, who are incapable of saving anyone or anything, YHWH announces himself as the only God, 'a righteous God and saviour' (LXX *dikaios kai sōtēr*), to whom all the ends of the earth should turn to be saved.[71] This ties 2.9–11 more tightly still to 3.20–1, and indicates that Paul is consciously drawing on the scriptural themes not just of YHWH's universal sovereignty

[68] See esp. Oakes 2001, 147–74.

[69] Oakes 2001, 170.

[70] See my essay in *Perspectives* ch. 6. See also Bauckham 2008/9, 197 n. 37: 'Paul's christological monotheism must have had anti-imperial force and this is a key passage for recognizing that' (citing also Bockmuehl 1998; A. Y. Collins 1999; Hellerman 2005). See too Bauckham 2008/9, 145f., tracing the counter-imperial force of christological monotheism through into subsequent centuries.

[71] Isa. 45.21f. The idea of YHWH as 'saviour' is prominent in Isa.: e.g. 43.3, 11; 45.15; 49.26; 60.16; 63.8.

but also of him as the true God, the one and only 'saviour', in explicit contrast to the idolatrous pretensions of pagan empire. Once again – to put the point negatively – if Paul had wanted not to draw the Philippians' attention to the possible parallels between the Messiah and the emperor, he went about it in a very strange way. His echoes are as strong as they would be for someone in Germany in the 1930s who referred to the leader of a new movement – or indeed to Jesus! – as 'Der Führer'. (The Nazis actually forbade the use of the word, unless in compounds, except in reference to Hitler himself.) It would not have been much of a defence to claim that when you used the word you heard rather different sounds.

There is an interesting tail-piece to this brief consideration of Philippians 2.6–11. In the immediate sequel, Paul urges his hearers to 'work at bringing about your own salvation', since 'God himself is the one who's at work among you'.[72] This talk of working at one's own salvation has naturally sent shivers down many a protestant spine, since at first glance it appears to undermine 'justification by faith alone'. But that is not at all what Paul is talking about. 'Salvation', *sōtēria*, was what Caesar offered to those who gave him allegiance. The Philippians, believing that Jesus was the only one at whose name every knee should bow, were faced with the task of working out, in the practical details of everyday life within Caesar's world, what it would mean, what it would look like and feel like, to explore the *sōtēria* which Jesus offered instead.[73] Paul gives them some pointers, but in a short letter he can hardly do more than provide suggestions. He is, however, confident that the one true God is at work among them, so that they will be able to understand their own variety of 'salvation', just as they must learn the meaning of their own variety of *politeuma*, 'citizenship'.

Before assessing the overall contribution of the Thessalonian and Philippian letters, we should at least raise again the question I raised some years ago in relation to Philippians 3. When Paul in 3.18 urges his hearers to 'join together in imitating me' (*symmimētai mou ginesthe*), following the 'pattern of behaviour' which he has laid down, what exactly does he have in mind? It could of course be a general command, more or less identical in content to what he says in 4.9 ('these are the things you should do: what you learned, received, heard and saw in and through me'). It could simply be a reference to the specific contrast he then draws between verses 18–19 and verses 20–1: instead of living for the belly, and for earthly things, one should live as a citizen of heaven, knowing that the present body will be transformed to be like the Messiah's glorious body. That exhortation – remember the future resurrection, so treat your body accordingly! – corresponds quite closely to 1 Corinthians 6.12–14. But it is interesting that, in another parallel with 1 Corinthians, Paul's command to imitate him comes after a long section in which he has been describing his own pattern of life: 'Copy me', he says, 'just as I'm copying the Messiah' (1 Corinthians 11.1),

[72] Phil. 2.12f.

[73] cf. 1.28.

though he has not there been speaking of the Messiah as an example. The specific aspect of his own behaviour which he wants the Corinthians to copy is the fact that he is 'not seeking his own advantage, but that of the many' (10.33), in other words, his giving up of his own rights, as the Messiah had done, for the sake of the gospel (9.1–27). In that whole section (1 Corinthians 8.1—11.1) he applies that principle in detail to the challenges faced by the church in relation to idol-temples and the sacrificial meat which made its way from them into the open market: the 'strong' are to be prepared to give up their 'rights' if exercising them would cause the 'weak' to 'stumble' (8.13; 10.24, 28).[74] We might conclude from this parallel between Philippians 3.17 and 1 Corinthians 11.1 that, in addition to the obvious behavioural questions indicated by a surface reading of Philippians 3.18–21, Paul may have something else in mind.

In particular, I have wondered – it is hard to make this more than a question, and the point would only work if everything I have said about Philippians so far in this chapter were to be accepted – whether Paul has in mind more specifically the example he is setting in his autobiographical story (3.4–11, with verses 12–16 as a development of that). Here, as in 1 Corinthians 9, he is talking about the fact that he has given up his own 'rights'; only, whereas in that case it was his 'rights' as an apostle, in the present case it concerns his advantages as a Jew. He lists his Jewish privileges, and then declares that he has reckoned all this gain to be loss because of the Messiah. He is, he declares, choosing the fellowship of the Messiah's sufferings, including conformity to his death, so that he may eventually attain to the resurrection of the dead.

It has often been noticed that this section exhibits parallels to the poem of 2.6–11, with the difference that now it is Paul who is, as it were, not regarding his Jewish privileges as something to exploit.[75] The parallel extends in quite a rich way: the Messiah, in not regarding his equality with God as something to exploit, did not give it up; he merely did the totally unexpected thing, and became obedient unto death. That is why he has been exalted. Now Paul, reckoning his Jewish privileges as something not to be exploited, nevertheless clings to the Jewish Messiah, and embraces that very Jewish belief in suffering as the way to vindication, in the hope of the very specifically Jewish (and indeed Pharisaic) blessing of resurrection. This passage, in fact, looks in two directions: back to 2.6–11 and on to 3.20–1.

For that reason I have come to see it as possible – no more than that, but no less – that when Paul urges his hearers to join in imitating him he has something more in mind than simply the avoidance of sensuality (3.18–19). What I have proposed in the past, and mention again as a possibility worth exploring, is that we should read chapter 3 as a kind of sustained hint. His hearers are not Jews. They cannot 'imitate him' in abandoning, or radically reinterpreting, Jewish privileges in the way he has done. They do, however,

[74] cf. Rom. 14.13–21.

[75] For this reading of 2.6, see Wright 1991 [*Climax*], ch. 4, now accepted by many commentaries.

have certain civic privileges. We do not know how many of them, if any, were Roman citizens, but the city as a whole (like many in Paul's day) took pride in its Roman culture. Paul is not telling them they should not do that. He goes on in the next chapter to say that they are to ponder 'whatever is true, holy, upright, pure, attractive, of good reputation, virtuous, praiseworthy'. He is not (in that sense) a dualist. As with the crowds in Lystra, who switched in an instant from worshipping Paul to stoning him, and as with the bystanders on Malta, who switched the other way by seeing him first as a dangerous criminal and then as a god, some readers of Paul have tended to make him either entirely 'pro-Roman' or entirely 'anti-Roman'. This, as I have said many times (to the dismay of readers on either side of our modern political spectrums, and to the deaf ears of some critics who have assumed that when I say Paul had a counter-imperial gospel I mean that he was a modern Marxist or anarchist born out of due time), is shallow. There are many varieties of qualified support, and many varieties of qualified critique.[76] What we might suggest in Philippians 3 is precisely that: qualified critique. Paul's hearers must work out 'their own salvation' for themselves, but as they do so he will give them his own example of giving up rights and privileges as a model, and let them work it out from there. It may, after all, be safer to make such a hint than to write a letter explaining in detail precisely what he thinks about the blasphemous claims of Caesar.[77]

What then might we conclude from this brief look at the Thessalonian and Philippian letters, in the light of our earlier consideration of 1 Corinthians, Ephesians and Colossians? That Paul warned his hearers against the blasphemous claims that Rome and its chief citizen had made and were still making: certainly. That he constantly relativized all human claims to absolute power, and ascribed that to Jesus instead: of course. That, like Daniel or the Wisdom of Solomon, he spoke both of the divine appointment of pagan rulers and also of the divine judgment they would have to face: naturally. So far, this corresponds to what many second-Temple Jews might have said,

[76] As Barclay 2011, 378 n. 55 rightly points out – though I resist his suggestion there that I have offered a 'flat reading of vocabulary parallels'.

[77] I have suggested before that this could be the meaning of the otherwise strange 'safe for you' (*hymin de asphales*) in 3.2. The widely varying meanings of *asphalēs* make it impossible to be sure. Barclay's objection, that no commentary takes the line I have done (2011, 380 n. 59) is curious: if exegetes were only allowed to recycle ideas already available, biblical research would be pointless. Nor do I think that my suggestion here would mean that Paul is 'shading the gospel' (381). It is true, as Barclay points out, that plenty of people, including Philo and Josephus, spoke out against various aspects of imperial rule, up to and including emperor-worship (Barclay 381f.), but that does not mean that Paul, writing to a small congregation already suffering persecution, might not decide to use hints rather than direct statements. Tacitus's harsh remarks about Roman rule (*Agric.* 30.1—32.4, in the speech of Calgacus) are hardly a precedent for what someone like Paul might have thought he could get away with or what might be safe for his hearers. Barclay's suggestion (382 n. 63) that under Roman rule one could always appeal to superior magistrates, and ultimately to the emperor himself, and then to the example of previous emperors, seems impossibly naive precisely in the light of Tacitus's attack. The fact that Paul and others did sometimes do this hardly implies that there was a smooth-running and carefully impartial system which he could confidently recommend to his hearers: Paul was himself a high-profile case and he may have gambled on that ensuring him a safe passage (though cf. Ac. 27.42f.!). Warning people that a time may come to abandon civic status or privilege does not necessarily mean that the entire system is already as bad as it could be.

with the sole exception of the name of Jesus. But for Paul there was something different, something which generates what we can only call a primitive Christian theopolitics, a radical mutation of the Jewish view of pagan empire exactly in line with Paul's radical mutation of Jewish theology as a whole. For Paul, the long-awaited new day had dawned. Judgment had already been passed and executed; the rulers and authorities had already been mocked and humiliated on the cross. Death itself, the last weapon of the tyrant, had been defeated. The 'rulers of this age' were therefore to be seen as part of the night which was now coming to an end, part of the old world order which was already in process of being dismantled, its power defeated by the superior power of divine love.

Paul was therefore advocating something much more subtle than either a 'pro-Roman' or an 'anti-Roman' stance as commonly imagined (not least, today, by those who hope he will be 'anti-Roman' in order that he may be 'anti-empire' in the way they want to be 'anti-empire'). His Jesus-based eschatology has modified both halves of the traditional Jewish stance. In line with Jeremiah's 'seek the welfare of the city' (and the top-flight civil service jobs of Daniel and his friends), Paul urges his hearers to be good citizens, to make sure that their public behaviour matches up to the gospel, to be good neighbours, to do good to all.[78] In particular, as we shall see, he urges them to obey the governing authorities, to submit to the law, to pay their taxes.[79] But there is a difference. In Jeremiah's Babylon, the Babylonian authorities reigned supreme. Jews in exile believed that their one God was somehow still in charge, but they also believed – at any rate, those who listened to Jeremiah or who read Deuteronomy believed – that they were there in exile precisely because of their sin, and that only when the redemption arrived would their situation be alleviated. Paul believed that this new moment had already come. As far as Jeremiah is concerned, there might be many hours of darkness still to come. Paul balances his command to obey the authorities with a reminder that the night is far gone and the day is already dawning.[80]

The second half of the traditional Jewish stance was the promise that one day YHWH would call pagan rulers (and Jewish rulers as well, of course) to account. That had happened from time to time in history, and the book of Daniel sees the madness of Nebuchadnezzar and the fall of Belshazzar as examples of it, looking back like all such events to the judgment on Pharaoh and Egypt at the time of the original redemption.[81] But the Jews of the second-Temple period still looked for a greater day, for the moment when the Fourth Beast itself would be judged and condemned once and for all. The scheme (in Daniel 2 and 7) of four kingdoms followed by God's own kingdom does not envisage that there will then be another decline, and a further sequence of four, or five, on and on for ever. This will be a once-for-

78 Phil. 1.27; Rom. 12.14–18; Gal. 6.10 (cf. Eph. 4.28); 1 Thess. 5.15; cf. 1 Tim. 6.18.

79 Rom. 13.1–7; see below.

80 Rom. 13.11–14; 1 Thess. 5.1–11.

81 Nebuchadnezzar: Dan. 4; Belshazzar: Dan. 5; Pharaoh: Ex. 14—15, cp. Wis. 10—19. The exodus remains the model in Revelation's vision of the coming judgment on Rome.

all event. For the second-Temple Jews, that event lay in the future. *For Paul, it lay in the past.* The claim is unmistakeable. God, he says, even now leads us in his triumphal procession in the Messiah; this God has celebrated his victory over the rulers of this age, and whatever they may do in the meantime, 'in all these things we are completely victorious through the one who loved us'.[82] For Paul, as for the gospels, the Messiah is *already* reigning – and it is the unity and holiness of the church that demonstrates that fact to the puzzled and possibly angry continuing rulers and authorities.[83] This, he says, is the sign that signifies the coming final destruction of the arrogant powers of the world, but the sign to the Messiah's followers that their ultimate rescue is at hand. The apostle's sufferings, in particular, are the sign that the new world is being born; they are like a smell which some perceive as the smell of death and others as the smell of life.[84]

What we find in Paul, therefore, is *the new form of the Jewish political paradox*. Instead of being in exile and seeking the welfare of the city, he is already living in the new day that has dawned with the Messiah. Instead of the long wait for the one God to judge sin, death and all human wickedness, judgment has already been passed. There is, as it were, a lightness of step about Paul's political critique: Jesus is already in charge, and every knee is to bow at his name. As we saw when examining Paul's worldview, he might have said: We are no longer in exile. We are members of the newly inaugurated family of renewed humans, looking for the day when the King will return and transform the world. In the meantime we must not make the mistake of giving credence to the blasphemous claims of Rome. The one God is sweeping away the rulers of the present age, not least (according to Daniel 7) the last great empire of the sequence of four, which Paul of course takes to be Rome. When that empire tells its own story in a way which parodies the true story of the one God, his people and his world, we cannot regard it as irrelevant or insignificant. There is much more to the gospel than opposition to empire, whether Rome's or anyone else's. But if Rome is at the moment giving every appearance of taking over the world, including its religion, it is Rome that will be the implicit target of the Pauline version of the ancient Jewish critique.

(iii) Rising to Rule the Nations

Paul's teaching and theology cannot, then, be reduced to some kind of 'anti-imperial' rhetoric. Nevertheless, it is noticeable that when he writes a letter to Rome itself he draws explicitly on biblical traditions, at key points in the letter, which together stake out the vital claim, at the very centre of his 'gospel', that the crucified and risen Jesus is the lord who claims the allegiance of the whole world. These biblical traditions go back to ancient Israelite

[82] 2 Cor. 2.14; Col. 2.15; Rom. 8.37.

[83] Eph. 3.10.

[84] Phil. 1.28; 2 Cor. 2.16.

polemic against paganism, and set out the hope that one day the people of the one God would themselves become the rulers of the world. In some cases they focus this hope on the coming king, who will draw together the promises of Psalm 2, Isaiah 11 and similar passages. The negative corollary of this is, of course, that any pagan king who launches a similar claim is being straightforwardly outflanked. Anyone writing a letter to Rome in the mid-50s AD must have known that there was indeed an emperor there whose predecessors had made that kind of claim (especially the arch-predecessor, Augustus, with his claims to bring peace, justice and prosperity to the whole world), and that the present emperor was well on the way to making that sort of claim himself, with the eager-to-please colonies and provinces in the very areas where Paul had worked being only too ready to support him.

Once again we must say it: if Paul had wanted not to make this point, he went about composing his greatest letter in a strange way. The opening of the letter, and the dramatic conclusion of its theological exposition, make claims about Jesus which must have raised eyebrows among its first hearers, perhaps even making some of them anxious or nervous:

> Paul, a slave of King Jesus, called to be an apostle, set apart for God's good news, which he promised beforehand through his prophets in the sacred writings – the good news about his son, who was descended from David's seed in terms of flesh, and who was marked out powerfully as God's son in terms of the spirit of holiness by the resurrection of the dead: Jesus, the king, our lord!
>
> Through him we have received grace and apostleship to bring about believing obedience among all the nations for the sake of his name. That includes you, too, who are called by Jesus the king.
>
> This letter comes to all in Rome who love God, all who are called to be his holy people. Grace and peace to you from God our father, and King Jesus, the lord.[85]

> Welcome one another, therefore, as the Messiah has welcomed you, to God's glory. Let me tell you why: the Messiah became a servant of the circumcised people in order to demonstrate the truthfulness of God – that is, to confirm the promises to the patriarchs, and to bring the nations to praise God for his mercy. As the Bible says:
>
> That is why I will praise you among the nations, and will sing to your name.
>
> And again it says,
>
> Rejoice, you nations, with his people.
>
> And again,
>
> Praise the Lord, all nations,
> and let all the peoples sing his praise.
>
> And Isaiah says once more:
>
> There shall be the root of Jesse,
> the one who rises up to rule the nations;
> the nations shall hope in him.
>
> May the God of hope fill you with all joy and peace in believing, so that you may overflow with hope by the power of the holy spirit.[86]

God's gospel; God's son; supreme power; worldwide allegiance from all nations; the ancient Israelite dream of all nations coming to worship the one

[85] Rom. 1.1–7; see, recently, Harrison 2011, 146–50.

[86] Rom. 15.7–13, quoting Ps. 18 [LXX 17].50; Dt. 32.43; Ps. 117.1; and, climactically, Isa. 11.10 in the LXX version (on this, see *RSG* 266f.). After this Paul turns to travel plans and final greetings.

God, and the more focused ancient vision of a coming king from David's line who would 'rise up to rule the nations'. From ancient times this Israelite hope was not just a vague dream of better times to come. It was the stubbornly maintained belief that, despite everything, Israel's God, the creator, would bring the nations under his rule. More often than not this belief involved the consequent belief that Israel's God would overthrow the present wicked rulers of those nations. Paul draws on exactly those aspirations in order to declare that it has happened at last. Jesus has been raised, and he is the true ruler of the nations, the one to whom Israel's God has promised that he would inherit the world. There is, of course, far more to Romans than this, but not less.

Nor are these passages merely rhetorical bookends at either side of a letter whose principal subject-matter is quite different. The great claims of Rome, especially under Augustus, to have brought salvation to the world and thereby to have instantiated justice and peace (and, indeed, to have discovered those two as divinities), inaugurating a golden age of prosperity – all this finds an echo in Romans, as Paul announces and develops his main theme. The 'gospel' of the 'son of God' provides the apocalyptic unveiling of the divine justice, through which salvation comes to all who believe (1.16–17); this results in 'peace' (5.1), and in the ultimate new world when the whole creation will be set free from its slavery to corruption (8.19–21). There is no need to develop this theme further. Either the point is made with these passages or it will never be heard at all. It is not, to repeat, that Paul is writing Romans simply to say 'anything Caesar can do, Jesus can do better'. But, on the way to saying all the other things he wants to say, he is cheerfully and, I suggest, quite deliberately outflanking the 'gospel' of the emperor with the gospel of Jesus. There is nothing implausible or outrageous in such a suggestion. Paul, by this stage, was a master of rhetorical possibilities, and it was not difficult for him to phrase what he wanted to say in such a way that it would serve several functions at the same time. Even journalists and preachers can do such things; why not an apostle?

In particular, I think it quite plausible that among the rhetorical goals Paul has in writing Romans 9 and 10 he may aim at a further outflanking move. As I argued in chapter 11, Romans 9.6—10.21 consists of a massive and spectacular retelling of the entire story of Israel, from Abraham to the present day – and, from another point of view, from Genesis to Deuteronomy, since Paul sees the promise of Deuteronomy 30 and the warning of Deuteronomy 32 both fulfilled in his own day. The strange, dark story of Israel – Abraham, Isaac and Ishmael, Jacob and Esau, Moses and Pharaoh, the prophets, the exile, the remnant ... and the Messiah, the *telos nomou*, the 'goal of the Torah', the one through whom 'the righteousness of God' was at last fulfilled: that is the story. A millennium-long narrative with a surprising and royal conclusion, leading to a new kind of empire in which the heralds of the king go off to tell the nations what has happened, to summon their allegiance (*pistis*), and, as Isaiah says, to welcome them in even though they were not expecting such a thing:[87] is it just coincidence that this mirrors rather exactly, in outline at least, the long story told by the writers of Augustus's day, starting with the founding fathers (not least the twins, Romulus and Remus), and leading through many strange episodes to the sudden new day in which the emperor would spread his realm far and wide, welcoming subjects and even new citizens from the ends of the earth?

Perhaps it is coincidence, though a very strange one. In any case, Romans 9—11 is of course 'about' much more than a coded upstaging of the great imperial narrative. But, even if one were to see this simply as a reflex, a side-swipe at an obvious but essentially trivial alternative narrative, one might pause; it is hardly so trivial in a letter to Rome itself. We do not know the precise causes of Nero's persecution of the Christians, a decade or so after Paul wrote this letter. We do not know whether Paul was killed as part of that crack-down, or at some other point. Nor was there systematic persecution of Christians for some generations after this point. But we do know that the Christians had acquired a reputation for being anti-social. And, granted the fact that many of them did not observe the Jewish taboos which sometimes occasioned pagan sneers, and worse, we must hypothesize that there was something about the small Roman church which would make people suspicious. In a world where loyalty to Caesar had become one of the major features of life, it could be that the Christians were 'working out their own salvation with fear and trembling', and coming to realize that, somehow or other, if Jesus was lord Caesar was not.

What then did Paul mean in the famous passage in Romans 13?

> Every person must be subject to the ruling authorities. There is no authority, you see, except from God, and those that exist have been put in place by God. As a result, anyone who rebels against authority is resisting what God has set up, and those who resist will bring judgment on themselves. For rulers hold no terrors for people who do good, but only for people who do evil.
>
> If you want to have no fear of the ruling power, do what is good, and it will praise you. It is God's servant, you see, for you and your good. But if you do evil, be afraid; the sword it carries is no empty gesture. It is God's servant, you see: an agent of justice to bring his anger on evildoers. That is why it is necessary to submit, not only to avoid punishment but because of conscience.
>
> That, too, is why you pay taxes. The officials in question are God's ministers, attending to this very thing. So pay each of them what is owed: tribute to those who collect it, revenue to those who collect it. Respect those who should be respected. Honour the people one ought to honour.[88]

By now it should be clear. This passage is not a comment on specifically Roman rule, either in general or at the time Paul was writing. It is not a way of saying, 'I have had a good look at the way the Romans are currently running the world, and it has my stamp of approval.' It is not, in other words, an *ad hoc* message which Paul might have altered in other circumstances.[89]

[87] Rom. 10.20 (cf. 9.30f.), quoting Isa. 65.1.

[88] Rom. 13.1–7. See Wright 2002 [*Romans*], 716–23. See recently Fantin 2011, 261–5.

[89] See e.g. Cassidy 2001, suggesting that by the time Paul writes Philippians he had changed his mind.

It is a classic piece of Jewish writing about how to live wisely under alien rule. It does not imply that the present system of government is perfect, any more than Jesus' response to Pilate in John 19.11 implies that Caesar and his minions are doing the right thing in sending him to his death. It merely states that the one God wants human authorities to run his world, and that the people of the one God should respect such authorities. However, as we see in Acts (which, whatever its actual historical value, certainly reflects this classic Jewish double-edged position), respect for authorities goes hand in hand with believing that they will be called to account by the one God – and with plenty of anticipated eschatology as the people of the one God do some calling to account in advance. The early church was clear that they should obey the true God rather than human authorities.[90] They were, however, prepared not only to obey those authorities under normal circumstances but also, when necessary, to remind them of their proper vocation.[91]

Romans 13.1–7 cannot therefore be pressed into service, as has so often been done, to make the point that Paul had no critique of empire in general or of Rome in particular. Certainly one could not make the parallel point about John's gospel on the basis of 19.11. There are three things, however, we should notice about the passage. The first is that the command to obey the authorities balances the command to avoid private vengeance in 12.19–21 (Romans 13.1–7 has often suffered from being detached from its context, but it means what it means precisely here). When Paul says in 12.19 (quoting Deuteronomy 32.35) that vengeance belongs to the one God, and then so soon afterwards that this creator God has given civic authorities the task of exercising vengeance (the same word) on wrongdoers, it is clear that the two go together. Anarchy encourages vigilante movements, as people take the law into their own hands, either from a general fear or from anger against perceived and unpunished offence or attack. The alternative is some kind of structure of authority; whether or not the authorities are doing their job, it is vital for normal human life, and particularly normal Christian life, that they are there and carry that responsibility. And, as with Daniel 6, the people of the one God must be found without blame except for that unique allegiance.

Second, in a world where rulers have been accustomed to claim divine honours, the statement that they hold their office as a vocation from the one God (13.1) constitutes a major demotion. We have already made this point, but it bears repetition.

Third, Paul's essentially Jewish, almost Jeremiah-like, exposition of how to live under alien rule is radically transformed, here as elsewhere, by his eschatology. When he says in 13.11–14 (as in 1 Thessalonians 5) that the night is almost done and the day is at hand, this does not mean that one can or should therefore sit light to ordinary social life, as in 12.14–18, or to civic obligations, as in 13.1–7. If what is coming to birth in the God-given new

[90] Ac. 4.19; 5.29.

[91] cf. e.g. Ac. 16.35–9; 23.1–11; 25.6–12; cp. 18.12–17; 19.35–41.

day is a world of love and justice, then it behoves followers of Jesus to live by, and in accordance with, that love and justice in the present, so as to be ready for the day when it comes. And, just as 13.1–7 needs chapter 12 as one part of its proper context, so it also needs chapters 14 and 15. Paul declares emphatically in 14.4, 7–12 that all will stand before the divine throne of judgment, and in 15.7–13 that the risen Messiah is the rightful ruler of the nations. It is when 13.1–7 is detached from its context and elevated into being a complete statement of 'Paul's view of earthly rulers' or 'Paul's political philosophy' or some such that problems arise.[92] Within the framework of chapters 12—15 as a whole it plays its limited role, just as it articulates the limited and temporary role of earthly rulers within the creator's purposes.

There remains one letter to be considered.[93] Galatians has become controversial recently because of three different, but possibly convergent, proposals about the previously unimagined importance of Rome for the situation and for Paul's argument. Now that it is becoming more widely accepted, on the basis of archaeology and topography in particular, that Galatians was written to churches in the south of the Roman province, where there were substantial Jewish communities,[94] the possibility emerges that one element in 'the problem of Galatia' may have been the social pressure of the newly burgeoning imperial ideology, including various cults. It is at least conceivable

(a) that ex-pagan Christians had been claiming the right accorded to the Jews not to take part in festivals or cult relating to Rome or Caesar;
(b) that questions had been asked, whether by suspicious neighbours or by local officials, as to whether these ex-pagan Christians could legitimately make such a claim;
(c) that local non-Christian Jews were anxious about their own status being in jeopardy if it was suspected that others were claiming it on different grounds;
(d) that pressure was being brought to bear on ex-pagan Christians to get circumcised in order to be 'legitimated' as 'proper Jews' and hence to be exempt from Roman ceremonies;
(e) that Paul regarded the attempt to have ex-pagan Christians circumcised as a step back to the 'old age' in terms of the Mosaic dispensation which had run its course with the arrival of the Messiah, and
(f) that he regarded facing persecution (in this case, most likely of pagan origin, for not joining in imperial celebrations) as part of the inevitable result of following the crucified Messiah;

[92] So, rightly, Jewett 2007, 786. Something similar might be said about the way people have treated the famous 'render unto Caesar' passage in Mk. 12.13–17 par. It means what it means within the overall proclamation of God's kingdom.

[93] I leave 1 Cor. out of consideration here, though a case has been made for a Roman cultic background to 1 Cor. 8—10: see Winter 2001, ch. 12; Fantin 2011, 225–31, 244–6.

[94] See above e.g. 808 with n. 109.

(g) that at least part of his polemic against 'another gospel' had to do with the 'gospel' of Caesar, then being assiduously propagated.[95]

This, obviously, would provide a radically different vision of the Galatian problem than any of the accounts that have been current in mainline scholarship, or for that matter the pre-scholarly readings of the letter going back to patristic times. It is not for that reason to be ignored. The fact that the suggestion can be made, and that attention has been drawn to the widespread local Roman cults and culture, at least opens up possibilities that must be considered. And for Galatians to acquire this kind of 'political' edge would sit well with the recent attempts to read the letter in terms of an 'apocalyptic' context – though, ironically, those who advocate such a thing, wishing to make a good show in the scholarly flesh, do not themselves observe the terms of first-century 'apocalyptic' by recognizing its political meaning.

This is not the place to enter into either an account of the varieties within this 'new look' on Galatians, or an exegetical, historical or theological investigation of their various possibilities. The whole thing may prove to be a red herring; or new modifications may be introduced, not least through fresh archaeological and similar investigations. The question seems to me at least worth serious consideration. For the moment we need only say this: it would not be surprising if one critical feature of life in Paul's churches was the question of how far one could go in taking part in Roman festivities and/or cult. In Corinth, the attempt by Jewish leaders to have Paul tried was dismissed by Gallio as a mere question of in-house Jewish law, thus effectively legitimating Christian practice and mission (and presumably granting the Christians the same religious exemptions as the Jews) in the province of Achaea.[96] We have no reason to suppose that similar judgments were made elsewhere, and every reason to imagine that the question of public allegiance to Rome and Caesar remained a smouldering ember for the Christians up to the time when it burst into full flame at the trial of Polycarp.[97]

4. Paul and Caesar: Conclusion

This, then, is my provisional conclusion – recognizing that this angle of vision on Paul is in comparative infancy in contemporary scholarship, and that a lot of work still needs to be done at every level from archaeology to exegesis, not least to integrate political ideas with philosophical and theological paradigms. Even without embracing the various proposals currently

[95] For different varieties of this hypothesis see e.g. Winter 1994, ch. 7; 2002a; Hardin 2008; Kahl 2010. The proposals of Mark Nanos (e.g. Nanos 2002a) have some analogy to this line of thought, as does the brief analysis by Griffith-Jones 2004, 222–4, of the situation in Antioch. The early versions of this proposal are helpfully discussed by Witherington 1998, 447–9.

[96] Ac. 18.12–17; see e.g. Winter 1999; see discussion in e.g. Haenchen 1971, 540f.; Schnabel 2012, 763f.

[97] See *NTPG* 346–8.

on the table for reading Paul as a 'counter-imperial' theologian, there is enough evidence to make a *prima facie* case, not indeed that he was a modern Marxist born out of due time, but that he saw the gospel of Jesus the Messiah as upstaging, outflanking, delegitimizing and generally subverting the 'gospel' of Caesar and Rome. 'When they say, "peace and security" ...': Paul could see that the increasingly grandiose claims of Rome were departing from the sphere of appropriate governmental authority, which, granted the second-Temple Jewish models for living under alien rule, he might be expected to affirm. The Roman imperial rhetoric was entering instead the sphere of inappropriate and idolatrous claims. Those claims supported and undergirded a regime which, for all its mechanisms of justice, its roads, its postal service and other amenities, more than earned the right to be seen as the vicious eagle that, in *4 Ezra*, played the part of Daniel's Fourth Monster. Rome was the pagan empire on whose watch, and by whose command, 'the lord of glory' had been crucified. Rome was the city that told its own story in what must have seemed, to Paul, a remarkable parody of the gospel story of Abraham's family now fulfilled in David's risen son. Rome was not just one empire among others. It brought into concrete and climactic expression the many-sided phenomenon (which is after all an updated and demythologized way of saying 'the many-headed monster') of arrogant human rebellion against the creator, and of arrogant human construction of systems and cities that claimed to rule the creator's world. The builders of the new Babel had been thwarted, and Abraham's seed had accomplished what they could not.

Paul did not, however, advocate the normal sort of revolution. There can be little doubt that Saul of Tarsus would have done so, had he stayed in Jerusalem as a hard-line right-wing Pharisee through the 50s and on into the 60s and its disastrous war. The biggest revolution in his own political thought happened not simply because he believed that the Messiah had now come. That by itself might simply have meant, as bar-Kochba's followers believed, 'So the revolution has begun!' The much larger transformation came with the apocalyptic unveiling of the saving plan of Israel's God in the form of the *crucified* Messiah. The eschaton had not simply been inaugurated; it had been *reshaped*. A different fulfilment; a different kind of victory; a different kind of political theology.

This did not mean, for Paul, a backing off from confrontation and challenge. Far from it. It simply meant that the confrontation now took a different mode, corresponding to the cross by which the powers had already been judged and held up to contempt:

> We put no obstacles in anybody's way, so that nobody will say abusive things about our ministry. Instead, we recommend ourselves as God's servants: with much patience, with sufferings, difficulties, hardships, beatings, imprisonments, riots, hard work, sleepless nights, going without food, with purity, knowledge, great-heartedness, kindness, the holy spirit, genuine love, by speaking the truth, by God's power, with weapons for God's faithful work in left and right hand alike, through glory and shame, through slander and praise; as deceivers, and yet true; as unknown, yet very well known; as dying, and look –

we are alive; as punished, yet not killed; as sad, yet always celebrating; as poor, yet bringing riches to many; as having nothing, yet possessing everything.[98]

Yes, we are mere humans, but we don't fight the war in a merely human way. The weapons we use for the fight ... are not merely human; they carry a power from God that can tear down fortresses! We tear down clever arguments, and every proud notion that sets itself up against the knowledge of God. We take every thought prisoner and make it obey the Messiah ...[99]

A different kind of revolution. A different kind of 'subversion' – and, Paul would have said, a more powerful and effective one.

This was not, then, an escape into pietism, as today's eager quasi-Marxists might allege. That is the route taken by the second-century gnostics; Paul would not have faced riots, imprisonment and the threat of death if all he had been doing was teaching people an apolitical and dehistoricized spirituality.[100] Paul's vision of the kingdom, its present reality and future consummation, remained emphatically this-worldly. It was not about humans escaping the life and rule of earth by being taken away to heaven in the future, or by anticipating that with a detached spirituality in the present. It was about the transformation, not the abandonment, of present reality.

The problem for today's interpreter is, of course, the difficulty of conceiving of a Christian political standpoint which is neither compromised nor dualist. Too often we have seen churches affirm 'the powers that be' in a way which effectively muzzles the church's witness; too often we have seen churches so afraid of all worldly power that they retreat into private huddles. The post-Enlightenment world has squashed all options into the two boxes of a 'Constantinian' compromise and an 'Anabaptist' detachment – not that the historical settlement under, and after, Constantine was the kind of thing people often imagine, any more than the historic Anabaptist position was so straightforward, either. Just as Paul's soteriology does not fit into the easy either/or of sixteenth-century antitheses, so his vision of the powers of the world and the power of the risen Messiah does not fit easily into the political categories of western modernity. As with questions of justification, so with questions of Paul and politics: we need twenty-first-century answers to first-century questions, not nineteenth-century answers to sixteenth-century questions.

This is in fact one of the major points on which John Barclay and I agree, though one might not instantly realize that from his account of my work. Since he has done me the honour of detailed exposition and critique, it may be appropriate here to sketch briefly some of the key points at issue.[101]

First, Barclay and I agree that whatever Paul may or may not have thought about the Roman empire, and its cults of 'Rome' and the imperial

[98] 2 Cor. 6.3–10.

[99] 2 Cor. 10.3–5.

[100] On which, see *RSG* 534–51 and esp. 548–50; and Wright 2006b [*Judas*], 41–53.

[101] Barclay 2011, ch. 19; ch. 18 is also relevant, setting out the ground of Roman religion and the emperor, much as in my chs. 4 and 5 above. Refs. to Barclay in what follows are to this book. I am grateful to Christoph Heilig for discussion of the following points.

family, any such reflections will have been located within the wider world of pagan religion and society, not as an isolated or independent entity.[102] It was partly to make this point that I wrote chapters 4 and 5 above in the way I did. Insofar as New Testament scholarship (including some of my own earlier and shorter writings) has not made this point, no doubt out of over-enthusiasm for a possible 'imperial critique' in early Christianity, the balance clearly needs to be restored, and this can now be done. It is also good to see Barclay's acknowledgment that, until the recent burst of enthusiasm, New Testament scholars had 'generally underestimated the importance of specifically Roman politico-religious features for the life of the first Christians'.[103]

Second, Barclay and I agree that whatever Paul may have thought about Rome, it does him no justice at all to place him on a flattened-out scale of being 'for' or 'against' Roman rule.[104] This is precisely what I have tried to argue in all my previous essays on the topic, doing my best (perhaps not always successfully) to show how the typically Jewish 'positive' understanding of human authorities as created and intended by the one God (Romans 13.1–7; Colossians 1.15–17) can sit perfectly well alongside a sharp, and equally typically Jewish, critique of actual authorities, especially if they move towards some kind of self-divinization.[105] Barclay himself is happy to propose 'highly differentiated evaluations of Roman power' in the juxtaposition of Romans 8.31–9 and 13.1–7, which is more or less what I meant by suggesting that Romans 13 carries an implicit 'nevertheless' in its apparent and superficial contrast with what I see as the implied subversion in Romans 1.3–7, 15.7–13, and elsewhere.[106] The assumption that we might be able to map Paul's implicit engagement (or lack thereof) with Rome by using modern political categories, resulting in 'supportive' passages like Romans 13 (or Colossians 1) which might then appear to be at loggerheads with other more apparently 'critical' passages (such as Philippians, or Colossians 2!), is precisely what I have tried to resist.

Third, Barclay and I emphatically agree that, whatever Paul may or may not have said about Rome, his entire worldview stood over against the entire ancient pagan system of religion and power, resulting in 'a thorough rejection of the mental and practical fabric of these symbolic structures' and predicating instead 'a new reality which has restructured the co-ordinates of existence'.[107] Barclay describes this in sharp, almost strident, language:

[102] Barclay notes (370) that, unlike some other recent writers, I have tried to make this point clear.

[103] Barclay 366.

[104] Barclay 367, 374, 376, 378 n. 55 (the alternatives of 'support' or 'subversion'), 384 (the danger of superimposing a modern political analysis), 386 ('neither simple opposition nor obedience').

[105] Indeed, a strong case can be made for seeing Col. 1.15–20 as encoding just such a critique: see e.g. Walsh and Keesmaat 2004, 79–95.

[106] Barclay 385. It is good to find that Barclay is happy to see these passages as expressing an evaluation of *Roman* power, despite the fact that the word 'Rome' does not occur in them.

[107] Barclay 361.

> It is this radical, totalising stance which made Christianity so 'intolerant' of alternative perspectives, since the 'truth', centred on Christ, exposed every alternative as at best an illusion, at worst a demonic insurgency ... This new ideology did not just challenge Caesar's divine claims, it offered a radical alternative to the structures of Roman religion and thus of Roman civilisation as a whole. In the words of Keith Hopkins, 'Christianity subverted the whole priestly calendar of civic rituals and public festivals on which Roman rule in the provinces rested. Christianity was a revolutionary movement.' Paul has a good claim to be the founding ideologue of that revolution ...[108]

Ironically, of course, one might take this paragraph to indicate a fairly dualistic account of Paul's worldview, which I do not think Barclay intends. Use of language like 'totalising', 'intolerant', 'ideology' and 'ideologue' does run the risk of appearing to locate Paul within a thoroughly late-modern framework. This simply shows how difficult it is to think into the thought-forms of other cultures and, as Barclay says later, to show how Paul was able 'to traverse the political conditions of the Roman world at a "diagonal"'.[109] But this is clearly what he and I are both trying to do.

What then of Barclay's specific criticisms? He reframes the issues into four, beginning with what he calls 'Pauline Epistemology', by which he seems to mean something quite like what I mean by 'worldview'.[110] Here he claims that whereas we, looking at the ancient world, perceive the imperial cult 'as an insidious expression of Roman hegemony', Paul's interpretative frame 'may have been different from our late-modern modes of historical interpretation and ideological analysis'.[111] Indeed it may, but it is hardly our current modes of interpretation and analysis that placed new imperial temples at visually strategic points in the cities of Paul's world, or displayed Caesar on coins and statues in the guise of one or other of the ancient pantheon. The more we think precisely into Paul's world, rather than our own, and the more we locate Paul (as we have tried to do in the main Parts of this book) within his own transformed-Jewish world, the more these things loom large, rather than fading quietly into the general background of pagan culture. We remind ourselves of Deissmann's line, quoted earlier, about Paul and his colleagues not going about blindfold. Barclay seems to me to be here following Martyn into the trap of supposing that 'apocalyptic' means the sweeping away of all previous visions of reality, including that of second-Temple Judaism, whereas as I argued in chapter 2, and then in Parts II and III in relation to Paul himself, we should really see 'apocalyptic', in both its Jewish and Pauline contexts, as all about the fresh revelation of Israel's God and particularly the exposé of the folly and blasphemy of pagan

[108] Barclay 362, quoting Hopkins 1999, 78. This 'totalising stance' is naturally resisted by those who hope to find Paul an ally in the project of postmodern pluralism (e.g. Marchal 2012).

[109] Barclay 385.

[110] 'Epistemology' properly denotes the study of, or a theory about, the nature or grounds of knowledge, but what Barclay is talking about here is 'the terms in which [Paul] viewed [his world]' (Barclay 375), which is a subtly but significantly different thing. Barclay here follows a famous article by Martyn 1997b, 89–110.

[111] Barclay 374.

power.[112] The more we study Paul's worldview – including his 'apocalyptic epistemology' – the more we should expect *both* (as Barclay suggests) that 'the political is for [Paul] enmeshed in an all-encompassing power-struggle which covers every domain of life',[113] *and* that, from within that 'apocalyptic' worldview, he would point specifically to the last great pagan empire, the final 'monster' to arise, now to be confronted by Israel's Messiah, as (for instance) in *4 Ezra*'s reading of Daniel 7. I agree that Paul might not wish to dignify Rome by responding to its grandiose claims in its own terms. This may be one reason why he does not name it specifically when making the critical and subversive comments we have already examined. But this points on to the question of coded language, to which we shall return presently.

It is from within Barclay's first main point that we must understand what he means by saying that the Roman empire was 'insignificant' to Paul. He denies that Paul's theology was 'apolitical' or 'spiritualized'. Rather, he sees Paul bundling up the 'powers', envisaging them as 'encompassing, permeating, enmeshing, infiltrating, and corrupting the political' arena.[114] Thus

> for him the 'political' is fused with other realities whose identity is clarified and named from the epistemological standpoint of the Christ-event. In this sense the Roman empire is not significant to Paul *qua the Roman empire*: it certainly features on his map, but under different auspices and as subservient to more significant powers.[115]

I agree with the premise (the 'powers' as penetrating the 'political' sphere, which is 'enmeshed in larger and more comprehensive force-fields'[116]), but not the conclusion. But this brings us to Barclay's fuller statement:

> Paul . . . reframes reality, including political reality, mapping the world in ways that reduce the claims of the imperial cult and of the Roman empire to comparative insignificance . . . From Paul's perspective, the Roman empire never was and never would be a significant actor in the drama of history: its agency was derived and dependent, co-opted by powers (divine or Satanic) far more powerful that [*sic*] itself. There was nothing significant about it being Roman – nothing new, nothing different, and nothing epoch-making . . . Rome did not rule the world, or write the script of history, or constitute anything unique.[117]

It is this proposal that I am challenging.

[112] Barclay 384 n. 70 indicates that he does indeed follow Martyn up to a point, though in a more nuanced fashion: over against what he sees as my placing of Paul 'in ideological continuity with the biblical/Jewish tradition of monotheistic critique of paganism', he says 'I would place stronger emphasis on the new division of the cosmos created by the Christ-event . . . which strongly reshapes and reapplies the biblical categories themselves.' This supports his statement in the text that 'Paul sees no significant differences between Romans and Greeks, only a categorical distinction between the *kosmos* and the *kainē ktisis* which was created by the cross.' I have, however, argued not just for 'ideological continuity' but for radical modification; and I have suggested that there are good reasons to think that Paul, while certainly lumping Romans, Greeks and everybody else together as part of the *kosmos* which is challenged by the new creation, still sees Rome as playing a specific role precisely at the moment of eschatological and apocalyptic crisis. See below.

[113] Barclay 376.

[114] Barclay, in private correspondence dated 9 September 2012: see his pp. 374, 376, 379, 386.

[115] Barclay 385.

[116] Barclay 384.

[117] Barclay 386.

I agree that for Paul what ultimately mattered were the 'powers' which operated in and through all kinds of organizations and systems. I agree that he saw them as a defeated rabble, led in the Messiah's triumphal procession. I agree that when he saw Roman temples, statues and coins he did not simply see Rome, but rather the powers, of whatever sort (but particularly 'death') that were at work through Rome. But I contend that he nevertheless saw these powers coming together and doing their worst precisely in and through Rome itself. I believe that he (like Josephus, at the very point where he, too, cleverly conceals this meaning) almost certainly saw Rome as the final great empire prophesied by Daniel. I submit that the way Paul lines up his arguments in several key passages indicates that he saw in the claims of Rome, and particularly of its emperor, an extraordinary parallel to, and parody of, the claims of Jesus. In no previous empire, after all, had 'gospel', 'son of god' and so on come together at the climax of a centuries-long narrative which now claimed world rulership and the possession of, and distribution rights over, freedom, justice and peace. Paul undoubtedly believed that 'the powers', however we describe them, were at work in Rome, providing the real energy and identity behind statues and soldiers, armies and temples, and even Caesar himself. But that simply shows just how *significant* Rome itself, uniquely and shockingly, really was for Paul. To use the language of Revelation, when Paul looked at the Roman empire he glimpsed the face of the Monster.

Rome did indeed constitute something unique, and importantly so. It was in Rome, and its imperial pretensions, that the 'powers' came together and did their worst. And that 'worst' was reflected directly in the almost uncanny parallels not only between Roman imperial language and the (biblically based) language of Paul's gospel, but also between the Roman imperial *narrative* and the (biblically based) narrative which Paul believed had reached its climax in Jesus. Here, it seems, we meet yet another moment in the ongoing struggle between 'apocalyptic', in the sense proposed by J. L. Martyn and others, and what I have argued is the true first-century Jewish meaning of the term. Barclay, offering a skilfully nuanced and modified version of Martyn, envisages an 'apocalyptic' event in which all previous 'powers' are simply set aside. I am following what I take to be a first-century understanding in which all previous narratives – the story of 'the powers' as well as of Israel! – come to their shattering and transformative climax. And just as Jesus is no mere cipher for Israel's narrative, but the very son of the covenant God, so Rome is no mere irrelevant or insignificant political entity, but the final Monster in whom precisely the power of 'death' itself has been unleashed on to that 'son of God'. The cross is at the centre of it all. Mark highlights this by having a *Roman* centurion, at the foot of the *Roman* cross, declaring that Jesus is 'son of God'.[118] Paul highlights the same thing, I have argued, by deliberately allowing his biblically based statements of

[118] Mk. 15.39.

Jesus and his gospel to resonate with, and so to subvert, the climactically blasphemous claims of Rome and Caesar.

My disagreement here with John Barclay is in one sense oblique. We agree about a great deal. We are much closer to one another than either of us is to those out on the flanks: those, on the one hand, who envisage Paul's gospel as being entirely 'apolitical', and those on the other who think his message consisted of a non-theological call to revolution. To that extent I wonder, from time to time, whether (like Käsemann attacking Stendahl when his real target was perhaps Cullmann!) Barclay's actual target might be writers like Richard Horsley or Neil Elliott – not to mention Marcus Borg and Dominic Crossan – who often give the appearance of offering a more explicitly non-theological counter-imperial analysis. No matter: I am happy to soak up the attack and, I hope, neutralize it.[119]

Barclay's second point concerns Paul's supposedly 'political' vocabulary. He is quite right, of course, to say that using similar vocabulary for Jesus to that which was in use for Caesar does not necessarily imply a direct critique. By itself, the use of a word like *basileus*, 'king', for earthly rulers and for Jesus, or even for God the father, does not imply a direct conflict.[120] The question arises, however, not so much from isolated technical terms as from the things which are said about them in their various contexts. By itself the word *kyrios* could mean all sorts of things, but when Paul speaks of Jesus as the one who claims worldwide allegiance for the sake of his name we have moved into a different area. The word 'president' is used in the United States of America not only for the elected head of state but for the senior official in thousands of businesses, colleges, golf clubs and other organizations. This causes neither confusion nor confrontation. But if a new group were to arise, claiming that they were the rightful heirs of the whole country and that their leader was its true ruler, and referring to that leader as 'President', the word would spring to life in a rather different way.

In particular, Barclay seems to me to ignore completely the point about the *narrative* in, for instance, Philippians 2.6–11. This has to do, not with a mere single word, but with the entire story about the way in which Jesus has attained to world sovereignty, with every knee bending at his name. Barclay's reading of Philippians as a whole proceeds by picking off individual verses and declaring that this or that word or phrase does not necessarily indicate an opposition to Rome. But it is the actual argument of the letter, and the way in which the terms both about civic life and about Jesus himself

[119] Whether such a judgment would do justice to any of those just named is another matter. Horsley at least has frequently written dismissively about 'theology' as the thing from which a post-Stendahl sociocultural reading of Paul would free us. See Horsley 2004b, etc.; Crossan and Reed 2004; Elliott 2008; Borg and Crossan 2009.

[120] As e.g. 1 Tim. 2.2 with 6.15 (Barclay 378, quoting the use of this in Tert. *Apol.* 30—3). Barclay also refers (377) to Ac. 17.7 ('another king'), and says, rightly, that this is Luke's construction of how some people were hearing 'Paul'; though why he thinks that Luke considers this a mistaken construction, in view of Ac. 1.1–11 and 28.31, is not clear to me. Nor is the language of *basileus* foreign to Paul: Barclay notes the cognate terms in 1 Cor. 15.24f., and we should add the use of similar language in Rom. 5.17–21, as well as the fresh evaluation of 'royal' significance in *Christos* itself (above, ch. 10: and cf. e.g. Rom. 15.12).

build up and reach their climaxes in 2.10–11 and 3.20–1, that force the implicit antithesis upon our attention. The idea that it is modern scholars who are reading an echo of Rome into the text because 'the noise of "the Roman empire" [is] dominating their sensory perception' is remarkable.[121] The Roman empire has done anything but dominate scholars' sensory perceptions until very recently, and the extent to which it is now making a come-back is due, not to an ideological desire to invent such things, but to the archaeological and historical evidence.

Nor will it do to contrast my reading of Paul here with the second-century evidence. In the *Martyrdom of Polycarp*, the crunch comes not so much with a general charge of 'atheism', but with the question of whether or not he will say 'Caesar is lord' (*Kyrios Kaisar*), or swear by his 'genius' (*tychē*).[122] The proconsul then tries it the other way round: will Polycarp 'revile Christ'? No, comes the famous reply:

> For eighty-six years I have been his servant, and he has done me no wrong; so how can I blaspheme my king who saved me?[123]

Kirsopp Lake is correct: 'the antithesis to Caesar is clearly implied'.[124] A *basileus* who is also a *sōtēr*: this is what Caesar claimed, and this is what the Christians claimed about Jesus. This does not of course prove of itself that when Paul, writing to a highly Romanized city, spoke of Jesus as *sōtēr*, as *kyrios* and as *Christos*, and declared that he had the power to submit all things to himself in line with ancient messianic prophecy, he intended a similar antithesis, but it certainly strengthens what was already, in my judgment, a high probability.[125]

As always, individual words mean what they mean within the wider context, and the context of the key passages in Paul's letters points strongly, I have argued, in the direction of implicit confrontation.[126] To Barclay's point that the main charge against the early Christians was failure to worship any of the regular gods, and that the question of imperial worship was secondary, one must reply that though of course worshipping Caesar (or not) was a special case of the more general refusal, it is obvious that the trials of people like Polycarp do not pick out any other specific divinities, for instance the gods peculiar to the town or city in question. Yes, the Christian

[121] Barclay 379.

[122] *Mt. Pol.* 8.2; 9.2.

[123] *Mt. Pol.* 9.3 (my tr.).

[124] Loeb ad loc.

[125] Phil. 3.20f.; see above.

[126] It is interesting that in *The Acts of Paul*, cited by Barclay 377, Nero's cupbearer Patroclus, whom Paul had raised from death after the manner of the story of Eutychus in Ac. 20.9–12, declares before Nero that Christ Jesus is 'the king of the ages', who will 'destroy all kingdoms under heaven' (Elliott 1993, 386). This is the language of apocalyptic, specifically of Daniel. Assuming the work to be a second-century fiction, the passage nevertheless bears witness to the persistence of a Daniel-based vision of Jesus' world-wide and counter-imperial kingdom.

refusal to worship the gods in general mattered; but Caesar was always the particular case.[127]

This brings us to Barclay's third challenge, the question of 'coded language' and 'reading between the lines'. Barclay is right that I have not until recently used the category of 'hidden transcripts' as set out by James Scott and picked up by Richard Horsley and others.[128] It is of course extremely difficult to track, let alone to map, the question of hidden meanings of whatever sort, even in contemporary texts, never mind ancient ones – though I note that Barclay himself clearly thinks he can do this in relation to Josephus, tracking not only what he meant in his overt statements (no reticence about authorial intent there!) but also his allusions, his differences of tone, his backing off from possible bluntness:

> He never attacks Roman religion directly, and what he says in criticism of the Greeks is safely allied to that Roman perception which contrasted Greek 'decadence' to their own 'frugality'. Perhaps Josephus could not afford to be as blunt as his Christian successors, but perhaps he did not wish to be. The result is a finely-composed apologetic, in which ears differently attuned may hear – or may entirely miss – some of its subtler polemical undertones.[129]

If Barclay can make this sort of statement about Josephus, I do not see why others should not in principle offer the same kind of analysis of Paul. Nor will it do for someone who can see so clearly into the inner workings of Josephus's mind to raise an eyebrow at the attempt to discern 'authorial intent' in Paul, as though we all knew such a thing to be forbidden by the not-so-hidden transcripts of postmodern ideology.[130] In particular, Barclay's fine-tuned analysis of Josephus's clever avoidance of direct criticism of Roman religion provides quite a close model for what I think was going on with Paul, and demonstrates that there is more than one context in which one might wish to hint at things, to be guarded in what was said explicitly. That is why Barclay's question about Paul being able to speak quite openly of Rome when necessary (in Romans 1.7, 15, and in reference to 'Caesar's household' in Philippians 4.22) is beside the point: Paul was not there making any particular criticism.[131] That brings us back again to the nature of coded critique, which Barclay is so good at recognizing in Josephus but so

[127] This tells also against Kim 2008, 60–4.

[128] Barclay 382, citing Horsley 2004a; Elliott 2008; Kahl 2010.

[129] Barclay 344 (the conclusion of his ch. 17, 'Snarling Sweetly: A Study of Josephus on Idolatry').

[130] Barclay 370, 378: I see the raised eyebrow, and the implicit claim to the high ground of postmodern uncertainty, when he says 'Wright … is confident that he can detect not only what "must have been heard" in Paul's letters, but also what Paul himself intended,' and contrasts this by speaking of 'those hermeneutically less committed to (or confident about) authorial intention …'. Barclay does not include himself in the latter group, but the way the sentence is framed strongly implies an authorial intent to raise doubts in the reader's mind about my apparent over-confidence. To this I reply that, like everyone proposing an hypothesis, I am stating it as clearly as I can while testing it against the evidence. To Barclay's positive point there, that even those who question the search for 'intention' may look at the larger literary context, I reply, Precisely: it is, again and again, the larger literary context (e.g. the whole narrative of Phil. 2) which establishes the meaning of the otherwise isolated terms in question.

[131] Barclay 375.

unwilling to recognize in Paul. His general point, that Paul would not wish to elevate Rome to the position of being *the* target of gospel polemic, is I think correct; but that accords well with my point, that Paul does seem to be clearly implying a reference to Roman imperial rhetoric in the passages we studied above. Perhaps it is worth making the point, albeit necessarily anecdotally and autobiographically, that there are many occasions when people in public life have to make speeches or give lectures on politically sensitive topics, and have to make a decision as to whether to go into great detail or just send a signal. Sometimes you have to choose: either you must lay out the whole topic at length, carefully ruling out misunderstandings and being sure to strike the right balance, or you must say something short and necessarily cryptic, which those with ears to hear may take away and ponder. I think Paul was good at both, but often employed the latter.

The parallels Barclay draws with Philo, Josephus and especially Tacitus will hardly stand up as counter-evidence to this.[132] Yes, Philo could openly challenge Caligula's divine claims; Josephus could declare the imperial cult to be useful neither to the one God nor to human beings, and could criticize Roman governors; Tacitus could be scathing in his denunciation (in the mouth of a British leader) of what Rome got up to in the name of 'peace'.[133] The nuanced and historically sensitive reading for which Barclay rightly pleads elsewhere seems suddenly to have deserted him: neither Philo, Josephus nor Tacitus are in a position anything like that of the ragamuffin apostle, a strange, wandering Jewish jailbird, writing to small and quite possibly muddled groups of people. Some of his hearers might well take fright at a direct and frank statement of everything Paul believed about Caesar and Rome. Some might waver in their allegiance and find themselves reporting to the authorities that Paul and his communities believed that there was 'another king, namely Jesus'. Better to be oblique; not necessarily (as I have suggested on other occasions) in case his letters were detected by the authorities, but perhaps because he was anxious, as a pastor writing or speaking to his flock might well be anxious, about people getting the wrong end of the stick, and either seizing too enthusiastically upon, or taking fright at, what to the wrong ears might sound like a literal call to arms.[134] If Barclay can say 'perhaps' in relation to Josephus's subtle intentions, perhaps we

[132] Barclay 381.

[133] Philo *Leg.* 357; Jos. *Ap.* 2.75; Tac. *Agric.* 30.5 (the full speech is at 30.1—32.4, not 30.3—31.2 as Barclay 382). There is a good deal more going on in the Tacitus passage than meets the eye.

[134] It will not do, then, to draw attention to the reference to believers from Caesar's household (Phil. 4.22) as though this disproved the theory about coded messages. In any case, the believers in question are not of course in Philippi, but in the city from which the letter is being written (which I think was Ephesus). What is more, though Paul was not assuming, as was Josephus, a wide and diverse public audience (so, rightly, Barclay 382f.), there may well have been potential diversity of different sorts even in the small groups he would envisage listening to the letters. I know the difference between a radio broadcast and a private meeting; but even in a private meeting there are plenty of occasions when one chooses one's words carefully and settles on coded language as the best option. Paul's letters were not straightforwardly 'public discourse', but nor were they exactly 'private'. Outsiders could and did come into Christian assemblies (cf. 1 Cor. 14.23). A letter designed to be read in different assemblies, and no doubt read aloud several times in the same assembly, becomes potentially more 'public' with each reading.

can say it too in relation to Paul – and indeed, despite his and others' objections, in relation to Philo, who was himself capable, when he judged occasion demanded it (which was not all the time), of coded critique.[135]

Josephus, of course, supplies another interesting example, at exactly the point where I have suggested that Paul, too, might be expected to single out the Roman empire not just as one miscellaneous bit of pagan nonsense among others but as the highly significant 'fourth empire' within Daniel's scheme. Josephus recounts in considerable detail Daniel's interpretation of the great statue in Nebuchadnezzar's dream, but when he comes to the punch-line he suddenly draws back:

> And Daniel also revealed to the king the meaning of the stone, but I have not thought it proper to relate this, since I am expected to write of what is past and done and not of what is to be; if, however, there is anyone who has so keen a desire for exact information that he will not stop short of inquiring more closely but wishes to learn about the hidden things that are to come, let him take the trouble to read the Book of Daniel, which he will find among the sacred writings.[136]

The excuse is plainly a smokescreen. As Marcus notes in the Loeb edition,

> Josephus's evasiveness about the meaning of the stone which destroyed the kingdom of iron ... is due to the fact that the Jewish interpretation of it current in his day took it as a symbol of the Messiah or Messianic kingdom which would make an end of the Roman empire.[137]

In case there is any doubt on the matter, we find Josephus doing exactly the same thing when we come to the climax of the book, Daniel chapter 7. Having retold in considerable detail the splendid tale of Daniel in the lions' den (Daniel 6), he turns aside, first to describe Daniel's wonderful fortress at Ecbatana, and second to hail Daniel as unique among the prophets in that he not only prophesied the future but fixed the time at which these things

[135] See Goodenough 1967, 21–41. Barclay 381 n. 62 cites Barraclough 1980, 491–506 as a refutation of Goodenough. Barraclough, however, is more nuanced than Barclay implies. He agrees (492) that Philo in the relevant text (*Somn.* 2.90–109) 'views the Romans critically', though like Barclay on Paul Barraclough ascribes this to a more general 'anti-Gentile' feeling. He concedes (492f.) that *Somn.* 2.48, 53, 55, 57, 62 does indeed 'suggest Roman practice and claims', allowing that this may be an instance (in his view, a rare one), where 'the Romans are clearly indicated in a context generally aimed at Gentile arrogance'. He admits that *Jos.* 79 would take on a deeper meaning when read the way Goodenough proposes (496), though offering a nuanced argument for an alternative reading. He agrees with Goodenough's conclusion that Philo presents Joseph as according with the hellenistic ideal of kingship (499), though he offers contextual and linguistic arguments against a coded allusion to the Roman prefect of Alexandria (500). In particular, he concedes (501f.) that the *De Somniis* 'contains the criticism of Flaccus that came to full expression in his express work on that figure', though Flaccus is not named in *Somn.* We might compare *Somn.* 2.123, where Philo mentions knowing 'one of the ruling class' (*andra tina oida tōn hēgemonikōn*) who had tried to stop the Jews keeping the sabbath; the fact that commentators disagree over who this was shows well enough that Philo, though on other occasions capable of being blunt, could sometimes also be oblique, and no doubt with good reason. Goodenough may well have overstated his case, but when modified his underlying point remains valid. Barclay's implied either/or, in which people must always be *either* blunt *or* oblique but never both, does not fit Philo, or Josephus; or Paul.

[136] *Ant.* 10.210.

[137] Loeb ad loc.

would come to pass.[138] Then, without any explanation, he skips over Daniel 7 entirely and begins his exposition of chapter 8 and, more briefly, of the rest of the book (including the prophecy of the Roman empire and its laying waste of the Temple in Jerusalem).[139] To have expounded Daniel 7 at all would, of course, have led Josephus into the same problem he so carefully avoided in relation to chapter 2, since as we know from various texts, not least *4 Ezra*, the passage was being read in the first century in terms of the divine overthrow of the last great pagan kingdom and its replacement with the sovereignty of the chosen people, led by the Messiah. If Josephus can be reticent about such things in his context, having in mind no doubt one part at least of his wide intended audience; if he can be blunt when he wants and cryptic when he wants; then, *mutatis mutandis* – and there are of course plenty of *mutanda* – so can Paul.

The most obvious example of a coded, apocalyptic work which almost everyone now thinks was intended as a direct subversion of Rome and its blasphemous claims is the book of Revelation. And, like Paul, Revelation never once names Rome explicitly. The signs are obvious: the city set upon seven hills, ruling the kings of the earth and welcoming merchants from around the world, leaves no choice.[140] But the word 'Rome' does not appear. And Revelation provides another interesting point, too. The book never cites scripture explicitly; there are no quotation-formulae, no references to 'as it says in the prophet Isaiah'. But the book is soaked in Israel's scriptures from start to finish, and it makes excellent sense to study these quotations and allusions as such. This provides at least a partial answer to Barclay's comment about my use of Hays's criteria for detecting allusion and echo.[141] He is right of course that since Paul does quote the scriptures explicitly it makes sense to look for other allusions and echoes as well. But Revelation shows that this can be done even in the absence of explicit quotations. And in my view the hints in Paul about the pretensions and claims of Rome and Caesar are sufficiently strong to justify, again *mutatis mutandis*, a similar investigation.

Barclay's fourth and final point is his own exposition of Paul's political theology. As I have indicated, I agree with him that we must avoid modernizing analyses; that Paul allowed (what I see as) his implicit critique of the claims of Rome and Caesar to remain on the edge, as a strong implication of what he was saying, rather than according those claims the respect and dignity of a full-on treatment on their own ground. 'At the deepest level', writes Barclay, 'Paul undermines Augustus and his successors not by confronting them in their own terms, but by reducing them to bit-part players in a drama scripted by the cross and resurrection of Jesus.'[142] Up to a point, yes;

[138] *Ant.* 10.264–7.

[139] *Ant.* 10.276; there are textual problems at this point but Marcus, in the Loeb ad loc., is happy to support this reading.

[140] Rev. 17.9, 18; 18.11–13.

[141] Barclay 380.

[142] Barclay 386f.

and that is partly, I think, why Paul does not name his target specifically. I am glad that Barclay does at least agree that 'Paul undermines Augustus and his successors'. But I do not think this means that, as in Barclay's title, 'the Roman Empire was Insignificant for Paul', even if Barclay modifies this to 'comparative insignificance'.[143] Granted, in Paul's retrieval and reframing of Jewish apocalyptic language and imagery, as for instance in Romans 5—8 and 1 Corinthians 15, the ultimate powers that are ranged against the creator and his creation are 'sin' and 'death', the latter being the 'final enemy' to be destroyed at the conclusion of the Messiah's already-inaugurated reign. But the fact that the Messiah in Revelation already possesses 'the keys of death and hell' does not prevent John the Seer from placing Messiah and Caesar, gospel and empire, in antithetic parallelism for much of his book, greatly of course to the detriment of the latter.[144] Just because pretensions of empire are radically cut down to size in the Christian versions of Jewish apocalyptic, that does not mean that they are unimportant or insignificant.

On the contrary, Rome appeared as the specific and focused instantiation of what 'the powers' were all about. Only Rome could claim a worldwide 'obedient allegiance' at the time of Paul's writing. Only of Caesar did people tell the glowing narrative of how he had come to be hailed as *kyrios* or *sōtēr*. Only of Augustus's empire did poets sing of a story hundreds of years old now arriving at its royal climax and bringing justice, peace and prosperity to the world. These were the claims that were etched in marble, stamped on coins and celebrated in public festivals in precisely the world where Paul announced Jesus as lord, where he spoke of the gospel-shaped and gospel-revealed new world of justice and peace. However much Paul believed that Caesar's claims had been overturned in the fresh apocalypse of the cross, they remained the public and powerful manifestation of the powers that had ruled the world. Herodotus told the story of the Greeks' triumph over the Persians, which created space for the remarkable flowering of fifth-century Athenian culture. But no Greek of the time would say, in any sense, that the Persian empire was therefore 'insignificant'.

The key to it all, then, as to so much else, is to understand the Jewish context from which Paul came, and then to understand the nature of the change in Paul's Jewish understanding caused by his belief in the crucified and risen Messiah. In terms of the present book, this means starting with chapter 2 above, and rethinking the questions of power and politics in the light of Parts II and III.

I have argued above that Paul's context will have given him the classic Jewish view. First, earthly powers, not themselves divine, were nevertheless instituted by the one God who intended that his world should be governed by humans. Second, all such earthly powers would one day be called to account, and judged strictly for their frequent arrogance, blasphemy and tyranny. I have then argued that we can see in Paul a decisive eschatological

[143] Barclay 386 (see the discussion above).

[144] See Rev. 1.18; and the implicit but generally acknowledged contrast in chs. 5, 12—14, 19.

modification of both halves of this position. First, he reaffirmed (in line with most other Jews of his day) that all earthly powers were indeed created by the one God, and he added (as the specifically Christian modification of this) that they were created in, through and for the Messiah himself; they were, that is, intended to serve *his* purposes. Paul did not follow this through in the explicitly revolutionary way some might like, at least in his extant writings, but the position was a coherent modification of his starting-point. Second, he saw that the coming judgment of the one God *had already taken place*, with the result that 'the powers' had already been led in shame behind the Messiah in his triumph (however paradoxical this must have seemed, as Paul wrote from prison!). The Messiah himself was already ruling the world, and would go on reigning until the 'last enemy', death itself, was defeated.[145]

When Paul places Rome and Caesar on this cosmic map he is indeed cutting them down to size. He is mocking their own global and cosmic boasts. But this does not mean they are insignificant, either to him or to his hearers. Just as Paul has given, in his major theological expositions, the foundation for what later became known as Christian theology, so he has given, by clear implication, the foundation for what might be called a Christian political vision: neither Marxist nor neo-conservative, neither Constantinian nor Anabaptist, neither 'left' nor 'right' in our shallow modern categorizations, but nuanced and differentiated in quite other (and still very Jewish) modes. In a world where many were eagerly worshipping Caesar and Rome, Paul not only reaffirmed the Jewish monotheism which undermined all such self-serving and tyranny-supporting blasphemies, but also offered repeated hints that the specific claims of this emperor and this empire fell significantly within those larger categories. In a world where many, not least many pious and zealous Jews, were eager for military revolution and rebellion against Rome, Paul insisted that the crucial victory had already been won, and that the victory in question was a victory won not *by* violence but *over* violence itself. Perhaps the only way one can keep that balance is by strong hints, by poetry, by language all the more powerful because, like some modern plays, it leaves the relevant character just a little off stage. 'Neither death nor life, nor angels nor rulers . . . nor any other creature will be able to separate us from the love of God in King Jesus our lord.' The power and pretensions of Rome are downgraded, outflanked, subverted and rendered impotent by the power of love: the love of the one God revealed in the crucified and risen Jesus, Israel's Messiah and Caesar's lord.

[145] 1 Cor. 15.26.

Chapter Thirteen

A DIFFERENT SACRIFICE: PAUL AND 'RELIGION'

1. Introduction

My first visit to Germany was in the spring of 1976. I was there for the initial meeting of the joint seminar organized by the Theology Faculty in Oxford and the Faculty for Protestant Theology in Bonn. Among the many insights which that week provided me, one has particular relevance to the present chapter.

The opening paper, given by Antonius Gunneweg, a senior Old Testament scholar from the Bonn faculty, was entitled 'Religion oder Offenbarung: Zum hermeneutischen Problem des Alten Testaments', i.e. 'Religion or Revelation? Concerning the Hermeneutical Problem of the Old Testament'.[1] The question was posed in terms of the standard protestant assumption, strengthened through the theology of Karl Barth: 'religion' was something humans did to try to gain favour with God, whereas 'revelation' was what happened when God, as an act of free grace, chose to unveil his love or his purposes to humans.[2] Seen from this point of view, Christianity was not a 'religion' at all, since it was about divine grace rather than human effort, and the question was whether the Old Testament shared this character, or whether it had to be seen as the Jewish version of the human effort to please God, or even to know him.

It would be interesting to map this discussion on to the larger German debates of the twentieth century: for instance, Deissmann's insistence that Paul himself was an archetypal *homo religiosus* against Käsemann's insistence that it was precisely against *homo religiosus* that Paul's ultimate polemic was directed. That remains a task for another time. The particular insight came with the response by Professor James Barr, who had recently moved to Oxford from Manchester. He pointed out that in England the word 'religion' carried few if any of the negative connotations presupposed in the German title of the paper. In England, 'religion' meant, more or less, 'what some people do on Sunday mornings', with a penumbra of assumptions about ethical standards and personal piety (perhaps with a dash of

[1] Subsequently published as Gunneweg 1977.

[2] On Barth's polemic against 'religion', and the following of this by Martyn 1997a and b, see on the one hand the sharp comments of Ashton 2000, 23–5 (on Ashton's own larger construct see below) and, on the other hand, Griffiths 2005, 674f. Griffiths's conclusion ('it may reasonably be doubted that a concept of religion usable for Christian thought can be salvaged') refers to the modern concept of 'religion', not to the first-century *religio* which is my theme in the present chapter.

what might be called 'mysticism'). People might not wish to join in, but neither they nor the worshippers perceived 'religion' as a bad or dangerous thing (unless the mysticism got out of hand).

Times have changed, of course. We have more recently had Richard Dawkins and his ilk telling us that 'religions' are bad both for their practitioners and for society as a whole; a kind of turbo-charged and politicized version of the continental protestant position.[3] There has also grown up in some evangelical, fundamentalist and similar circles a sense that 'religion' is what happens in boring mainline churches while they themselves are enjoying something quite different: a living relationship with God, perhaps, rather than an outward form. Those, too, are issues to be addressed elsewhere, but they locate the subject of the present chapter in relation to the varied uses of the word in contemporary thought, with a warning against importing into a historical study the assumptions and prejudices of a much later age. This chapter addresses the question, in parallel with the previous chapter: what happens when we try to locate the Paul we have studied in Parts II and III within the picture we sketched in chapter 4? I intend, in other words, to investigate here the relation of Paul to *first-century* 'religion', as discussed in that earlier chapter, rather than to 'religion' as that term has been understood since at least the eighteenth century.

This is all the more complicated in that several works which have discussed Paul in terms of 'religion' have not made this distinction clear. Locating the study of early Christianity within university and college 'Departments of Religion' has had a massive, if mostly hidden, impact on the way in which the subject is perceived, carrying the implication that we all know what 'religion' is – and that, for instance, it has little or nothing to do with politics or 'real life'. When the traditional subject-matter of early Christianity is put into the box we now call 'religion', various things happen.[4]

A classic example is Ed Sanders's *Paul and Palestinian Judaism*, whose telling subtitle was 'A Comparison of Patterns of Religion'. Sanders's work constituted a quantum leap forward in method as well as content, but by firmly labelling his project as a study of 'patterns of religion' he did three things which I believe are together responsible for what seem to me significant distortion.[5]

1. Sanders used, without any discussion, an implicit definition of 'religion' which belongs in the eighteenth rather than in the first century. He treats

[3] e.g. Dawkins 2006.

[4] Most discussions of 'religion' in relation to Paul bypass the question of actual terminology, since Paul seldom, even including Acts and the Pastorals, uses Greek words which correspond to the Latin *religio*: cf. *deisidaimōn/-monia* (Ac. 25.19; 17.22); *eusebeia/-beō/-bēs* (1 Tim. 2.2; 3.16; 4.7, 8; 6.3, 5, 6, 11; 2 Tim. 3.5; Tit. 1.1 / Ac. 17.23; 1 Tim. 5.4 / Ac. 10.2, 7); *thrēskeia* (Ac. 26.5; Col. 2.18). What follows is therefore not an attempt to exegete things Paul himself *says* about 'religion', even in C1 terms, but an attempt to place him on the map of what the greco-roman world of his day meant by *religio*.

[5] I use the word 'Judaism' in this discussion because it is the term Sanders (like most others) uses, despite the caveats I discussed above at xxivf., 82, 89. Ashton 2000, 27 offers some critical comments on Sanders which dovetail with what I say here.

'religion' as denoting the entire system of what something like 'Christianity' or 'Judaism' is, how it functions and what it claims to accomplish. Though he screens out certain questions,[6] he nevertheless includes within 'religion' all sorts of things which in the ancient world would have been seen as part of 'philosophy' or even 'theology'. This – as, indeed, with Deissmann – distorts the evidence. The rather basic telescope of 'religion', in this sense, is incapable of seeing some of the most important stars in the Pauline sky.[7]

2. Sanders nevertheless imports 'Christian' categories into his analysis. Though he declares that his aim is 'to compare an entire religion, parts and all, with an entire religion, parts and all', 'considered and defined on their own merits and in their own terms', he sets up his categories on surprisingly 'Christian' grounds. Even his general statement that 'the term "pattern" points toward the question of how one moves from the logical starting point to the logical conclusion of the religion'[8] implies that a 'religion' is about the making of such a journey, which might perhaps be seen as an essentially Jewish perception (grounded in the patriarchal wanderings, the exodus and the return from exile) and may also translate into Christianity in terms of a 'journey' from sin to salvation. But most ancient 'religion' did not have such a 'logical starting point' or 'logical conclusion' – or, if one could see such a thing, it was an abstract reflection, the sort of thing a Cicero might go home and write a book about, rather than part of the religion itself. In particular, Sanders subsumes 'soteriology' under the larger category of 'religion'.[9] He rightly sees that some religions, including at least some branches of ancient Judaism, are not concerned with 'soteriology' and its correlated doctrines (sin, a future life and so on) in the way that he takes early Christianity to be, but he goes ahead anyway with his basic categories of 'getting in and staying in': 'the way in which a religion is understood to admit and retain members', he says, 'is considered to be the way it "functions"'.[10]

This, I suspect, is what lies at the root of the radical rejection of Sanders in much conservative Protestantism, and to this extent at least the protest is justified. This is not because Sanders has 'got Judaism wrong'; no doubt he has oversimplified, as we all do, but his basic perception of Jewish practice as a response to the grace implicitly embodied in the covenant is substantially correct. Rather, the protest is justified for two reasons, one which the

[6] Such as 'speculative questions as how the world was created; when the end will come; what will be the nature of the afterlife; the identity of the Messiah; and the like' (Sanders 1977, 17).

[7] e.g. the failure, in both Deissmann and Sanders, to see the difference between 'someone being in Christ' and 'Christ being in someone' – a distinction important to Paul but inconsequential from the point of view of 'religion'. Sanders tellingly admits that how the experience of 'being in Christ' related to the experience of 'being in Israel' 'is more opaque to research than is thought', and concedes that the method of his book is not up to the task: 'we must be content with analyzing how religion appears in Jewish and Pauline thought' (549).

[8] Sanders 1977, 17.

[9] ibid.: 'A pattern of religion thus has largely to do with the items which a systematic theology classifies under "soteriology".'

[10] ibid.

critics of the 'new perspective' have glimpsed and one which, I think, they have not.

The one they have glimpsed is that, despite his insistence that Judaism is a religion of grace (that too, of course, may be seen to be a 'Christianizing' judgment; who said 'grace' was that important, if not the early Christians, especially Paul?), he has by his very categories made 'Christianity' into a kind of 'religion', at the very moment when conservative Protestants were eagerly distancing themselves, after the manner of Antonius Gunneweg or even Karl Barth, from any such thing. The knee-jerk reaction against the 'new perspective' thus assumes that Sanders (like others, such as the present writer), so far from discovering that Judaism was a religion of grace, was sneakily transforming Christianity into a religion of works – indeed, into a 'religion', which in those terms must *ex hypothesi* be about 'works'. Sanders's attempt to rescue Judaism from that charge has thus rebounded. Instead of making Judaism much more like Christianity, he has (some people suppose) made Christianity much more like Judaism, or at least the 'Judaism' of standard protestant polemic. Though the terms here are inexact, there is an important point trying to get out: the category 'religion', as used by Sanders, necessarily distorts the actual subject-matter of Paul's letters. And also, perhaps, second-Temple Judaism itself – though not in the ways Sanders's conservative critics have usually imagined.

The second reason why the protest is justified, one not glimpsed by the opponents of the 'new perspective', is not simply because this analysis may well distort Paul himself, and perhaps also ancient Judaism, but also because it is simply not true that the way a religion 'functions' has to do with the way in which it 'is understood to admit and retain members'. For most 'religions' in the eighteenth-century sense, and certainly most 'religion' in the first-century sense, the 'functioning' of the religion in question had little if anything to do with the way in which members were admitted and retained. Even the ancient mysteries, with their elaborate initiation rituals, were about a lot more than that. It looks as though Sanders has assumed, no doubt from a Christian and even Pauline standpoint, that something like 'conversion' ('getting in') looms large on the one hand, and that one may justifiably think of the ordinary daily practice of 'religion' in terms of 'staying in'. But most 'religion' in the ancient world was not about 'conversion', and most practitioners of ancient 'religion' were not concerned with 'staying in' anything very much, except, in a loose sense, in the *polis* whose gods were being worshipped or invoked.[11] Israel's scriptures do indeed issue stringent warnings about individuals being 'cut off from among their people' for certain behaviour, and equally stringent warnings about the nation as a whole being sent into exile for persistently breaking the covenant. The

[11] See Stowers 2001, 91f.: 'an Egyptian who became a citizen of a Greek *polis* changed religious practices and adopted a whole range of cultural and social relations, but we do not call this "conversion".' Something like 'conversion', Stowers notes, was sometimes envisaged in relation to the struggles of the soul after virtue. But this was (a) about philosophy, not 'religion', and (b) about the individual's own progress, not about 'getting into' or 'staying in' a community.

idea of 'staying in' may thus be seen as a Jewish category, though not I think one which many first-century Jews (Qumran perhaps excepted) sat about discussing at length or in detail. But in the wider pagan world, though we have evidence of people being ejected from this or that city (especially Rome) because they were trying to import an alien religion or a dangerous philosophy, the idea of 'staying in' is not a category that would naturally suggest itself within the world of first-century 'religion'.

There is a further irony in Sanders's account. By focusing his study of Paul on 'getting in and staying in', he all but ignored the elements of Paul's thought, and more important his actual life and the lives of his churches, which might properly have been investigated under the heading of 'religion': for instance, baptism and the Lord's Supper, neither of which does he treat in any detail. Sanders has, in fact, tried to discuss Paul's *theology* as though it were *religion,* and has left 'religion' itself to one side. The present chapter is in part an attempt to remedy this deficiency.

3. Again as a result of all this, Sanders screens out eschatology from his account of both Judaism and Christianity, except insofar as both hold a view about the ultimate end. (Even that, he says, 'need not be a decisive point for the pattern of religion'.)[12] Eschatology, in the early Christian sense of the belief in a single purpose of the one God which, long awaited, had now been fulfilled or at least inaugurated, is precisely one of the things which the eighteenth-century analysis of 'religion' screened out (perhaps because the Enlightenment had its own eschatology, in which world history was reaching its great climax with the work of Voltaire, Rousseau and Thomas Jefferson). By *comparing* Paul and Judaism in terms of 'patterns of religion', he makes it impossible to see that the early Christians, like at least the Qumran sect in one way and the followers of bar-Kochba in another, were claiming that Israel's God had inaugurated or was inaugurating his long-promised purposes and that they themselves were in the vanguard of this new movement. Since placing Paul in that world of first-century Jewish eschatology is arguably one of the most important things one should do with the apostle, it is not surprising that subsequent scholarship has found Sanders's account of Paul significantly lop-sided. Indeed we might paraphrase Sanders's own famous summary of Paul's position *vis-à-vis* Judaism: *this is what we find wrong in Sanders's account of Paul: it is not Christianity.*[13] Or not quite.

My criticisms of Sanders are parallel to those offered by John Ashton, a Johannine scholar who in retirement has turned his attention to Paul.[14]

[12] Sanders 1977, 17. This is perhaps the biggest single difference between Sanders and Schweitzer, to whom he is in many other ways very close.

[13] See Sanders 1977, 552. I hasten to add that there is much in Sanders's account, not least his conclusion (543–56), which is admirable and helpful. His final sentence (555f.) is not only exactly right but calls into question any suggestion that his project could be a complete account of Paul: 'In his letters Paul appears as one who bases the explanations of his gospel, his theology, on the meaning of the death and resurrection of Jesus, not as one who has fitted the death and resurrection into a pre-existing scheme, where they take the place of other motifs with similar functions.'

[14] Ashton 2000 (subsequent refs. to Ashton are to this work); on Schweitzer and Sanders cf. 149–51.

Ashton's own account of 'the religion of Paul the Apostle' is not (as he and I both take Sanders's account to be, in practice if not in theory) an attempt to do theology by other means. Ashton firmly pushes to one side the long tradition in which Paul has been mined for answers to the questions of Christian systematic theology, not least post-Reformation protestant dogmatics, and proposes instead that Paul can be explained in terms of his 'religious experience'.

One might suppose that this was another way of turning back to Schweitzer, but Ashton includes Schweitzer in his critique, suggesting that though Schweitzer was in theory writing about Paul's 'mysticism' he was in fact still portraying Paul as a thinker following a logical train of thought rather than a mystic struggling to put the ineffable into words.[15] The latter is the route Ashton himself takes. He proposes that the apostle should be seen in terms of the cross-cultural religious category of 'shaman', and that what happened to Paul on the road to Damascus involved him in a kind of death-and-rebirth experience out of which the most important features of his writings can be explained.[16] Ashton is aware that calling Paul a 'shaman' will not be to everyone's taste, and suggests that such people might think of it as a metaphor.[17]

There is much to admire in Ashton's bold and innovative proposal, not least his polymathic range of cultural reference. But there are two serious problems with it in terms of a first-century historical account. First, the category of 'religious experience' to which Ashton appeals, though it does indeed have some purchase on certain 'shamanistic' traditions ancient and modern, does not have very much to do with what the first-century world thought of as 'religion'. Apart, that is, from the mystery religions; and it is no surprise that Ashton, though submitting to the scholarly consensus that Paul did not derive his ideas from there, nevertheless tries to hold the category open as having 'convergent resemblances', 'coincidental' features which, though they may not provide geneological parentage for Paul's experience, offer significant parallels.[18] The category of 'religious experience' itself, however, as expounded by Ashton (and as played off against 'theology'), cannot but strike the reader as a re-run of Schleiermacher's project, to exalt 'feeling' over dogma. It is no surprise that Ashton comes down very hard on Karl Barth.[19]

This may simply mean that once again the post-Enlightenment category of 'religion' includes things which first-century *religio* did not, and vice versa. Ashton is clear that he is reading Paul against the apparent grain of what he himself says. He does not accuse the apostle of 'rationalizing' his

[15] Ashton 144, 149.

[16] Ashton 10f., 135, etc.

[17] Ashton 39f., 59, 214. I am reminded of a cartoon in which a bishop, consoling a Mother Superior about the death-watch beetle in the convent roof, suggests that 'it may help to think of it as a metaphor'.

[18] Ashton 14–16, 244.

[19] Ashton 24f., 60, including some hard words too about Martyn 1997a and his (ab)use of the category 'apocalyptic' as a stark alternative to 'religion'.

feelings into a theological argument, as Räisänen and others have done, but his study amounts to the same thing.[20]

Second, though Ashton claims to be offering a key to explain Paul, he never in fact deals with most of Paul's major themes, such as the righteousness of God, justification by faith, Messiahship, incarnational christology and so forth. When offering exegesis of particular passages, he never attempts to show how they fit within the larger context of a letter or chapter. Thus, for instance, to present Romans 8.23–30 as though it were not the climax of a lengthy, sustained and essentially *theological* argument is simply to misread it.[21] In particular, he declares from the outset that it is impossible to understand what Paul says simply in terms of modifications of Jewish belief, and that this justifies one in looking elsewhere – without ever showing that he has grasped the way in which second-Temple Jews, of any variety, actually thought and acted.[22] His treatment of the spirit, clearly central to his thesis, remains flawed by his failure to give attention to the specifically biblical and Jewish context through which Paul interpreted his remarkable 'experiences'. All this means that when Paul does give a vivid statement of 'dying and rising', as in Romans 6 or Galatians 2.19–20, Ashton does not see how the passages in question actually work. However vivid the statement in the latter passage ('through the law I died to the law, that I might live to God. I have been crucified with the Messiah. I am, however, alive – but it isn't me any longer, it's the Messiah who lives in me'), it cannot be an appeal to a unique experience which Paul alone has had, since his whole point is to say that this 'dying and rising' is what has happened to all Jews who have come to be 'in the Messiah'. If Peter in Antioch, or the 'agitators' in Galatia, had been able to say, 'Well, Paul, you have indeed had remarkable shamanistic experiences, but you mustn't expect us to have had them too, so what you say is irrelevant,' Paul would have been wasting his breath.[23]

Ashton's project thus remains frustrating, however fascinating in some respects. As an attempt to 'explain' Paul, it clearly fails. As an attempt to explore his 'religious experience', in the basically modern sense of that phrase (however many ancient shamanistic parallels one might find – not that Ashton finds very many), it belongs more within an account of 'psychology', or even 'psychology of religion', rather than 'religion' itself in any first-century sense.[24]

[20] e.g. Ashton 28, 138, where he declares, of 2 Cor. 3.18 and related passages, that 'most of this is, strictly speaking, nonsense'; 216–24, where he deconstructs Rom. 7.13–25 on the grounds that as it stands it is self-contradictory. It is one thing for Ashton to say that he finds bodily resurrection incredible (82), but any historical account of Paul's thought must factor in, as a central element, the fact that Paul firmly believed it. Cf. too Räisänen 1986 [1983]; 2008.

[21] Ashton 138–41.

[22] Ashton 10f.

[23] See above, 852f., 858f.

[24] Ashton claims (4f.) that his interest is slightly different from this, which explains why he only has one passing reference to Theissen 1987 [1983]; but it seems to me that this is where his project more naturally belongs.

The 'inner' or 'experiential' side of things is doubtless important in its own way. When Paul speaks about the 'heart', its secrets and its beliefs, he is indeed referring to the deep wellsprings of human imagination, intention and intuition in a way that cannot be reduced to terms of a process of rational thought moving from first intellectual principles to final intellectual conclusions. However, Ashton's polemic against 'theology' is unconvincing (and might cause some to turn the author's own analytic method back on him).[25] The point for which I have been arguing throughout this book is that Paul did indeed think through, articulate and teach a coherent *theology*, which was indeed 'a modification of Jewish belief' in the light of the crucified and risen Messiah and the gift of the spirit; and that Paul urged his communities to learn how to think these things through, not as a displacement activity when faced with ineffable experiences, but as their grasping of the reality of Israel's God and his purposes, the reality within which they would be able to live. Without 'theology' in the sense we have explored it in Part III of this book, Paul had reason to suppose that the new worldview he was doing his best to inculcate would not be able to stand firm. As we shall see in a moment, Paul's own revised and rethought 'religion' had the same goal in mind.

The need for 'theology', not just as a set of dogmas to be taught and learned but as a task for the whole church, is the reason why Paul speaks in various places of the *mind* being renewed, as well as the heart. There is no good historical, theological or indeed religious reason to reduce the former to the latter, to say that what may appear to be theological argument is in fact the complex and contradictory musings of someone who has had a profound and largely ineffable religious experience. Ashton's account is, not least, highly individual-centred; one would scarcely guess, reading him, just how important for Paul was the unity, and the common life, of the community of the Messiah's people. We may agree that Paul's whole life, including all his 'experiences' of whatever kind, was part of a seamless whole from which his intellectual arguments cannot be split off. But this does not justify privileging these 'experiences' over his actual arguments. Nor, in particular, does this help us very much in locating Paul within his own world, where 'religion' meant something very different from that aspect of nineteenth-century thought to which Ashton implicitly appeals.

A very different account of primitive Christian religion has been offered by Gerd Theissen. Theissen is much more alert than Sanders to the question of what 'religion' actually is, though he, writing with one eye on the contemporary world of interested agnosticism, produces a definition which tries to include both the eighteenth century and the first: 'Religion', he writes, 'is a cultural sign language which promises a gain in life by corresponding to an

[25] See the refrain of 'religion therefore not theology': Ashton 25–8; 45; 121, 125, 126, 162f., 213, 234, 244. To say that '"salvation", like "grace", is a word that has had all the blood drained out of it by theology', so that 'the religious concept of salvation is – can only be – a metaphor' (158f.) makes one wonder what 'theology' Ashton has been reading. To say that 'people are not turned into converts by theological arguments, certainly not by arguments hurled precipitately at them by a stranger from abroad' (163) may have some truth in it, but seems a gross caricature of Luke's (or anybody's) picture of Paul.

ultimate reality'.[26] Theissen's exposition of the first element of this, the 'cultural sign language', is perhaps the most important part for our purposes. Religion, he says, is a *semiotic* phenomenon: it operates with a system of 'signs' which 'guide our attention, bring our impressions together coherently, and link them with our actions'. Humans cannot survive without such systems: 'only in a world interpreted in this way', he declares, 'can we live and breathe.'[27] This sign-system characteristically tells stories, often now referred to as 'myths' (whether or not they are deemed to have historical value); it engages in 'rites', patterns of behaviour which 'take on symbolic surplus value'; and it assumes some kind of 'ethics'. A sign-system will develop its own semiotic grammar in which its characteristic motifs are woven together in a more or less organized way, providing the unique character which differentiates it from other sign-systems. Such systems, Theissen points out (as we have done in Part I), are part of a larger culture. 'Religions are socio-cultural sign systems,' he says. 'Therefore they are historical: they come into being and pass away, split up and get mixed up. They are closely bound up with the history of those groups which hand them down.'[28] Quite so. Theissen then suggests that changes within the system are brought about above all by 'charismatics', with Jesus as the obvious example.

Much of this analysis, in these general terms, applies to what the first century understood by 'religion', and indeed offers an analysis which implicitly challenges the shrunken use of that word in modern western thought. We might question the inclusion of 'ethics', however, which in the first century (except for the Jewish world) was the province, not of 'religion', but of 'philosophy'. Similar points could be made about Theissen's analysis of religion as something 'which promises a gain in life'; here he, like Sanders, does seem to be leaning, though more gently, in the direction of a very generalized soteriology which may not in fact be true to the first century (again, with the possible exception of the mystery religions).

Throughout his book, Theissen uses a powerful and evocative running metaphor. His initial exposition of it alerts us to the two purposes of his book. Primitive Christian religion, he says,

> is a sign language – a 'semiotic cathedral' – which has been erected in the midst of history: not out of stones but out of signs of various kinds. Like all churches and cathedrals, it too has been designed throughout by human beings, built by human beings, and is used and preserved by human beings. But just as one cannot understand the Gothic cathedrals unless one hears and sees them as a hymn of praise to God in stone, so too one cannot understand this semiotic cathedral if one forgets that those who built it once erected it as a great hymn of praise and thanks for the irruption of a transcendent reality.[29]

[26] Theissen 1999, 2.

[27] ibid. Theissen refers to Cassirer 1944 for the argument that a human is *animal symbolicum*, an animal that transforms the world into a home by a system of interpreted signs.

[28] Theissen 1999, 6.

[29] Theissen 1999, 17f. 'Irruption of transcendent reality' sounds like a demythologized reference to a Jewish-apocalyptic, or perhaps even Barthian, belief. Many religions build 'semiotic cathedrals' which have little to do with 'transcendent reality', let alone the idea of its 'irruption' into the present world.

He then imagines 'secularized visitors' to such a 'cathedral' having a conversation with those who want to join in the hymn of praise. What is there, he asks, to stop both sets of visitors talking to one another about their points of view, and entering into a rational conversation about the cathedral? Here is Theissen's apologetic hope:

> The sketches of a theory of primitive religion presented here seek to make such a conversation possible – a conversation about the mysterious sign world of primitive Christian religion. For some, this is part of looking after monuments, and looking after monuments is a very noble affair. But I should add that for me, a concern with primitive Christian religion involves more than being curator of a monument.[30]

His book, then, is both a historical analysis of 'primitive Christian religion', including obviously that of Paul, and an attempt to engage with the 'secularized visitors' who may be looking around this 'semiotic cathedral' as curious tourists. From my perspective, I can only applaud the attempt to bring these two purposes together, though I worry that it may have caused Theissen, like Sanders, to push too much 'theology', and indeed 'ethics', into 'religion', and thus to make harder any real attempt to locate the early Christians, not least Paul, within the actual 'religious' world of their day.

Theissen's specific proposals, as they relate to Paul (his book covers 'primitive Christianity' as a whole), form a good introduction to the similar though not identical proposals that I shall advance in the present chapter. Anyone who studies the history of primitive Christian religion, he says, picking up his controlling metaphor once more,

> can follow the origin of a new religious sign system or, to use another image, the building of a semiotic cathedral. Its building material consists of signs in three different forms: a narrative sign language consisting of myth and history; a prescriptive sign language consisting of imperatives and evaluations; and a ritual sign language consisting of the primitive Christian sacraments of baptism and eucharist ... [The ritual sign language] is often underestimated, because only a few texts in the New Testament relate to the primitive Christian rites. But it is of great importance: the whole sign system of a religion is concentrated in its rites.[31]

This seems to me correct, as does Theissen's observation that the 'rites' in question are independent of space and time, giving a means by which ordinary space and time can be structured and hence by which humans can experience them as a different sort of time; they are freed from everyday purposes; they serve to ward off chaos and anxiety.[32] And his exposition of the 'rites' in question, both the central ones and the other peripheral elements which we shall also examine below, leads to his final conclusion, which is where he comes closest (though without saying so) to what we saw in chapter 4 to be true of 'religion' in the ancient pagan world: 'the sign world of primitive Christianity was plausible to its inhabitants because its

[30] Theissen 1999, 18.

[31] Theissen 1999, 121.

[32] Theissen 1999, 121f. He says 'the eternal' where I would say 'a different sort of time'.

axioms contributed towards forming a community'.[33] He returns at the end to his controlling image: this semiotic 'cathedral' can still be visited by secular tourists who would leave without saying a prayer, but he would be delighted if such visitors could at least understand why prayer was the main purpose of constructing the cathedral in the first place.[34] This is a moving apologia, all the more so for the way it determinedly puts everything into language which makes no unnecessary 'Christian' demands upon the hypothetical secularized reader.

My purpose is rather different. I want now, with these two recent forays into the study of Paul's 'religion' in mind, to offer an alternative one, overlapping much more with Theissen than with Sanders. But I want to go considerably further than Theissen in two or three particulars, and to propose a way of understanding Paul within the 'religious' world of his day which shows how the implicit clash of *political* allegiance and culture we studied in the previous chapter was, hardly surprisingly, focused in and symbolized by an implicit clash of *religious* allegiance and culture. This will, of course, prepare for the third element, in which we shall study, in the next chapter, the implicit engagement of Paul with the wider world of *philosophy*.

2. Paul among the Religions

(i) Introduction

We saw in chapter 4 that, according to Cicero at least, the religion of the Roman world was divided up principally into (a) ritual (especially sacrifice, but also the various festivals according to the various sacred calendars), (b) the taking of auguries and (c) the searching of sacred books such as the Sibylline Oracles. The ancient myths, contained in Homer and the great poets, contributed to these as a backdrop, providing occasional aitiological explanations and reminding this or that city of its ancient heritage and traditions. The purpose of *religio*, watched over carefully by the various orders of priesthood who overlapped considerably with the magistrates and other civic hierarchy, was to bind the gods and the city together, to consolidate the *pax deorum* and, in one memorable phrase, to continue social policy by other means. The culture was soaked in divinities, and 'religion' was the way of bringing that to tangible and effective expression. 'Religion', we remind ourselves, was not a way of teaching people how to behave; for that you might go to the philosophers. It was not in itself a way of deciding actual policy, except for the occasional intervention from augury or oracles, though it frequently guided the ways in which policies reached on other grounds were carried out (for instance, in the timing of a battle). It was innately conservative, in that it emphasized the ultimate good of civic peace

[33] Theissen 1999, 303. This is then expounded at 303–5.

[34] Theissen 1999, 306f.

and harmony and offered the means by which that could be maintained, since the gods were themselves deemed to be part of the overall social fabric. Within this, as we saw, the 'mystery' religions offered a more individualized deepening of personal spirituality and a more focused and definite future hope.

At first sight, and especially for those wearing protestant spectacles, it might appear that Paul had nothing whatever to do with any of this.[35] As we saw in the earlier chapter, the early Christians did not offer animal sacrifice (or, if some still did in the Jerusalem Temple, it was never seen as part of Christian obligation); there was no developed must-get-it-right liturgy (consider the different early forms of Last Supper traditions and even of the Lord's Prayer itself!); there was no equivalent of the ancient sacred calendars. The early Christians did not inspect the entrails of birds, or observe them in flight, with a view to discerning divine purpose or favour; they did not consult books of oracles. Their use of Israel's scriptures was of quite a different order from the way their pagan neighbours 'used', or at least presupposed, Homer and the poets. They did not order their lives around the harmony of the local *polis*, or take any responsibility for it. They had no priestly hierarchy. They did not believe that 'the gods' had any real existence, and so took no trouble to learn their names and be sure they pronounced them properly when they prayed. When Paul knew that Epaphroditus had been healed, he regarded it as a sign of the mercy of the one God, not as meaning that he now owed a cock to Asclepius. When he used the language of 'mystery', it was to speak of something which used to be hidden but was now in principle revealed to all the world. This is, broadly speaking, the reason for the verdict that many have reached, that earliest Christianity, including that of Paul, was in first-century terms not a 'religion'. That verdict was shared by their contemporaries, who saw them as 'atheists' – a term which now, to some, indicates a tough-minded resolve not to be taken in by religious superstition, but which then carried a profound anti-social stigma. 'Atheists' were, by definition, people who were not playing their part in keeping the gods and the city together, in sustaining the multi-faceted social and civic harmony upon which all else depended. They posed an implicit threat to social stability and security.

And yet. When we put together the question raised by chapter 4 above with the worldview-analysis we offered in Part II, we find a significantly different picture, which does in my view justify the use of the word 'religion', albeit in a sense redefined, as everything else was for Paul, around Jesus himself. Paul used the *language* of sacrifice, to correspond to a reality which, though it did not involve the killing of animals, certainly involved realities of space, time and matter. He believed in divine guidance, though he did not go to Delphi or anywhere similar to seek it. He used Israel's sacred scriptures, not in the way Cicero and his colleagues might have used the

[35] For what follows, cp. the similar account in Stowers 2001, 85–7. Stowers emphasizes the way in which 'normal' religion was bound up with agricultural productivity and hence the prosperity of the community. For the normal 'protestant' position, cp. the work of E. A. Judge, discussed in ch. 4 above.

Sibylline Oracles, nor in the way they thought of Homer and the poets, but nevertheless in a way which spoke of the ancient sources and traditions of life upon which he was drawing afresh and with which he intended to stand in at least some continuity. Certain ancient narratives in particular – we shall look at the role of the exodus-story presently – were foundational not only for his thinking but for certain things which he and his communities *did*. And, in particular (here this chapter links arms closely with the previous one), there were various things that Paul and his followers did which he regarded as binding them closely not only to one another but to the one God, one lord whom they worshipped. If a 'religion' in the ancient world was the system of signs, including myths and rites, by which people were 'bound' together (assuming the link of *religio* with *religare*)[36] as a civic unity in which gods and humans both shared, the whole of Part II above provides evidence that Paul saw the common life of those *en Christō* as precisely that: a united community, whose *politeuma* was in the heavenly places, and whose complex unity was both expressed in and powerfully reinforced by the radically new kind of sacrifice, the very different kind of celebration, the attention to ancient scriptures, the prayers and particularly the special and symbolic 'rites' of baptism and eucharist.

From this binding together all kinds of other results followed. These showed that, for Paul at least, those who belonged to the Messiah were a new kind of *polis*, a non-geographical and non-ethnic *polis* to be sure, but nevertheless a real community of actual human beings stretching across space and, it seems, back through time as far as those Paul refers to as 'our fathers', the exodus generation, and 'our father' Abraham himself. When, in other words, we put the eighteenth-century definitions of 'religion' firmly to one side and ask ourselves about the first-century definition instead, we find that Paul was indeed teaching, operating and living within something we might very well call *religio*, however much it had been redefined. This *religio* was bound to appear as a radical variation on that of his Jewish contemporaries. We find, in particular, this *religio* was the means by which Paul believed that the one God who had made himself known in and through the one lord, and was active by the one spirit, was 'binding' this single community to himself, much as the *religio* of Rome was supposed to bind gods and mortals together in a single theopolitical harmony. When we look at Paul and his communities with first-century eyes, these conclusions are, I submit, unavoidable.

This, for instance, is part of what the remarkable appeal to unity in Philippians 2.1–4 is all about. The appeal is, of course, backed up by a succinct statement of what others might call (though Paul did not) the Christians' foundation 'myth', namely the story of Jesus himself. And it issues in what, again, others might call an 'ethic'. Religion by another name?

[36] See above, 247 n. 5.

(ii) Baptism: the Jesus-Shaped Exodus

My main quarrel with Theissen's stimulating account of primitive Christian religion is that he does not give nearly enough space to exploring the exodus-story as the key backdrop to several features of Paul's implied 'religion'. He is aware of it, of course, but ironically it seems to function for him more as Homer might have functioned for an educated Roman, as a distant source of themes and imagery rather than the founding 'myth' in a fuller sense. But perhaps the best place to begin a brief treatment of baptism as 'religion', complementing what was said earlier in other contexts, is with the passage where Paul most obviously sees it in relation to the binding together of the single community in fellowship with the one God, one lord and one spirit:

> Now about things relating to the spirit's work, my brothers and sisters, I don't want you to remain ignorant. You know that when you were still pagans you were led off, carried away again and again, after speechless idols. So I want to make it clear to you that nobody who is speaking by God's spirit ever says 'Jesus be cursed!'; and nobody can say 'Jesus is lord!', except by the holy spirit.
>
> There are different types of spiritual gifts, but the same spirit; there are different types of service, but the same lord; and there are different types of activity, but it is the same God who operates all of them in everyone. The point of the spirit being revealed in each one is so that all may benefit . . .
>
> Let me explain. Just as the body is one, and has many members, and all the members of the body, though they are many, are one body, so also is the Messiah. For we all were baptized into one body, by one spirit – whether Jews or Greeks, whether slaves or free – and we were all given one spirit to drink.[37]

'When you were still pagans': the word here is *ethnē*, 'nations', but the context (a description of 'pagan' worship) makes it clear that Paul is giving the word a 'religious' colouring – and contrasting that with something similar but different. Instead of the ecstatic utterance of pagan worship, there is an ecstatic utterance of Christian worship, and you can tell the difference because the one will reject Jesus and the other will hail him as *kyrios*, lord. The work of the holy spirit is precisely to bind the worshipper to the Messiah in glad allegiance. The one God, spoken of as we saw before in three different ways, shares in the common life of this new community, and the community shares in the life of the divine: the same spirit, the same lord, the same God, operating all these things in everyone. This is precisely what *religio* meant in the ancient world of Paul's day – except that it is now all reorganized around Jesus.

The whole passage is of course about the *unity* of the 'body', where the 'body' consists of all the baptized. The frequently observed parallel between Paul's use of 'body' metaphors and the same imagery in Stoic political thought is likely to have been at least in the back of Paul's mind, and with similar intent.[38] He is talking, however, about a new 'body', a new kind of

[37] 1 Cor. 12.1–7, 12–13.

[38] See Lee 2006.

civic community, in which precisely the normal distinctions by which civic life was marked – ethnic and social groupings – were now irrelevant. But in the front of Paul's mind, as we can see from a similar train of thought two chapters earlier, is the ancient narrative of the exodus, the 'myth' (in that sense) by which the 'religious' act of baptism means what it means:

> I don't want you to be ignorant, my brothers and sisters, that our fathers were all under the cloud and all went through the sea. They were all baptized into Moses in the cloud and in the sea. They all ate the same spiritual food and drank the same spiritual drink. They drank, you see, from the spiritual rock that followed them, and the rock was the Messiah.[39]

The double use of water in this passage – the water of the Red Sea through which the Israelites passed and the water which flowed from the rock for them to drink in the desert – is easily the best explanation for the otherwise initially puzzling double reference in chapter 12 (we were all baptized . . . and given one spirit to drink). The Messiah's people, for Paul, are thus the *new-exodus* people, formed as was ancient Israel into 'a people' by the *redeeming action* of the one God on their behalf and by the *sovereign and holy presence* of the one God in their midst, leading them in the pillar of cloud and fire and sustaining them on their journey. And baptism, it here becomes clear, is indeed (to use the old theological language) the 'outward and visible' sign of entry into the Messiah's people, defining them just as surely as the crossing of the Red Sea defined the people whom Abraham's God brought out of Egypt. The emphasis on differentiated unity in the rest of the chapter merely underscores the basic point: that the 'religious' act of baptism, resonating with the ancient 'myth' of exodus now reworked around Jesus and the spirit, 'binds' the baptized to the one God and constitutes them as an actual, not merely a theoretical or 'invisible', community. Paul is already aware, as later ecclesiastical theorists would be aware, of the sharp problems, both theological and pastoral, which follow from that affirmation. That is (one of the reasons) why he writes 1 Corinthians 10. But already, even with this one short passage, we find his 'religion' taking shape.

It is, however, a religion into which one *enters*, in a way that was basically not true for Roman religion, with the mysteries as the obvious exception. The ancient Romans had various ceremonies marking the entry of a young citizen upon adult life and responsibilities, but so far as I am aware there was no rite that a native-born Roman needed to go through in order to 'belong' to the divine-and-human solidarity of the community, or that a foreigner coming in needed to submit to before being able to join in the 'religious' festivals in which the civic life of the city was celebrated and sustained. The *polis* was not a 'mystery'. One can see, from this absence of any formal parallel, how easily earlier generations of scholars were led to postulate that there must therefore have been 'derivation' at this point, not from civic religion, but from the mystery religions themselves. They, after all, specialized in 'initiation' ceremonies, leading to membership in a kind of inner

[39] 1 Cor. 10.1–4.

family which shared sacred meals and gave mutual encouragement to follow a particular way of life. But, despite the continuing sense among some that the 'disproofs' of such derivation – which have been substantial – cannot really have meant quite what they said, there are in fact no links between Paul's view of baptism and the actual 'mystery religions' for which we have evidence.[40]

Has Paul then 'derived' his view of baptism from Jewish 'washings' such as proselyte baptism? Not obviously. Does he indicate an analogy between baptism and circumcision? Yes, to some extent; Paul makes that point in Colossians 2.11–12, though it does not appear loadbearing for any large elements of his argument, and Paul develops the idea of baptism there in terms of the death and resurrection of Jesus (as in Romans 6, for which see below), whereas circumcision has only a tenuous link to such ideas.[41] Does it trace back to John the Baptist? Yes, certainly. But John the Baptist himself was looking back to a much more obvious derivation, to which Paul alludes over and over again: the exodus.

John's baptism symbolically evoked the exodus. That cannot have been accidental. Israel's God, he believed, was calling out a new, renewed people, and he would himself shortly appear in person in their midst. Baptism, most obviously, involves going through water; that is the link Paul makes in 1 Corinthians 10.1. Baptism involves setting the slaves free; that is the link he makes in Romans 6, where it takes its place as part of a much larger redrawn exodus-narrative. Baptism invokes the gift and the presence of the spirit, as in the exodus the living presence of YHWH accompanied the people out of Egypt and came to dwell in the tabernacle, the forerunner of the Jerusalem Temple. Only when we bring the Exodus-story out from the shadows of a mythological background and place it in the full spotlight can we understand where Paul's idea of 'initiation', of *entering* the community, comes from. Jews and gentiles, slave and free, and (as in Galatians 3.28) male and female: all alike need to be baptized if they are to belong, to be part of *Christos*. They are to become people in whom the spirit now dwells: living temples. The reason the first Christians, Paul included, needed a rite of initiation, which the mainstream pagan *religio* lacked, was not because they were inventing a new mystery religion, but because they believed that the new exodus had occurred, and with it *kainē ktisis*, new creation. Sanders was right to see that 'getting in' was hugely important for Paul and his churches, and indeed right to see that the model for this in the Jewish world was the mighty covenantal act of the one God in the exodus. Ironically, he failed to draw out the fact that the reason Paul needed to highlight 'getting in', not only with baptism but with his whole theology of justification, was

[40] Theissen 1999, 129, 344f. is a good example: see below. For the standard 'disproofs', see e.g. Wedderburn 1987a; 1987b; Wagner 1967 [1962]. See not least Betz 1994, proposing that there are analogies between Pauline baptism and the hellenistic world, but that Pauline baptism is ultimately derived, in a complicated way, from Judaism (though Betz does not see the underlying exodus-narrative and its significance).

[41] On circumcision see e.g. Bernat 2010; Thiessen 2011.

not that he was constructing a new religion as it were in parallel with Judaism, but because he believed that the one God had at last done the new thing he had promised, and that the radical nature of this new thing demanded a fresh start for all. The difference between Paul and his own native context had to do with eschatology, not with a critique of, or a parallel attempt at, 'religion'. What Paul believed about the people of God, on the basis of what he believed about Jesus, demanded that he teach and practise the rite of baptism; not that Paul, if his Corinthian disclaimer is any indication, seems to have done much baptizing himself.[42]

'Getting in', then, was not a general religious category for which Paul had his own local variation. It was not even a category that first-century Jews were much bothered about. The cases of proselytes, and of converts like Aseneth in the famous novella, are much discussed by scholars because they seem to offer partial parallels to the idea of Christian 'conversion', but in the last analysis they are a blind alley. To judge both from second-Temple literature and from the rabbis, 'getting in' was not a big question. They did not even view the exodus that way; why should they have? If Paul went back to it, as clearly he did, it was because *the idea of 'getting in', in the form we know it in Paul, including its significant place among other ideas, was itself a Christian innovation*, necessitated by the unexpected and shocking unveiling of God's age-old plan in the death and resurrection of the Messiah. As with Paul's use of biblical expressions which just happened to have Caesar-resonances, so here it is quite possible, perhaps even likely, that when Paul, developing his exodus-based theology, spoke of people 'entering into' *Christos*, and so on, he may have had a sense of confrontation. He may, also, have had a sense that the transformation of character which he believed happened by the work of the spirit through the gospel had some analogies with the soul-struggles described by some philosophers. But he derived his theology of 'getting in', as symbolized in baptism, from his reinterpretation of the exodus in the light of Jesus.

The essentially 'religious' character of the rite is highlighted earlier in 1 Corinthians by Paul's emphasis on the *name* of Jesus the Messiah. (We recall the vital importance, in pagan religion, of getting the name right when addressing or invoking a god.)

> Well! Has the Messiah been cut up into pieces? Was Paul crucified for you? Or were you baptized into Paul's name? I'm grateful to God that I didn't baptize any of you except Crispus and Gaius, so that none of you could say that you were baptized into *my* name.[43]

And the point of being baptized into this name is intimately linked with the Messiah's cross:

[42] 1 Cor. 1.13–17.

[43] 1 Cor. 1.13–15.

> This is the point, you see: the Messiah didn't send me to baptize; he sent me to announce the gospel! Not with words of wisdom, either, otherwise the Messiah's cross would lose its power.[44]

This is further linked to the new sense of community identity – again, founded on the holiness expected of exodus-people – which for the Corinthians was so difficult to understand and for Paul so necessary to emphasize:

> But you were washed clean; you were made holy; you were put back to rights – in the name of the lord, King Jesus, and in the spirit of our God.[45]

The close analogies with the other passages noted above make it highly likely that this is indeed a reference to baptism, drawing out its implications, as one might expect from an exodus-concept, in terms of holiness on the one hand and 'justification' on the other, and all in the 'name' of Jesus. And this connection helps, I suggest, to understand why Paul came to regard baptism as a 'washing'.[46] Here too there is a biblical background,[47] and the likelihood is that Paul is not so much thinking of specific second-Temple Jewish 'washings', but rather (a) of the exodus itself as a passage through water and (b) of the prophetic promise of personal and covenantal renewal, bringing these two together to form a powerful symbol of leaving behind the old life of slavery and sin and being renewed by the spirit.

Behind it all, of course, stand the strange words of Jesus himself, subsequently interpreted by the earliest church in the light of the events which swiftly followed. He had spoken cryptically of 'a baptism' with which he had to be baptized, and it was obvious with hindsight that this referred to his death.[48] The confluence of those words, and those events, with the dramatic work of John the Baptist by which the start of Jesus' public career had been signalled, and with the fact that Jesus' death and resurrection had taken place precisely at the time of the Passover, meant that myth, history and prophetic symbolism rushed together with explosive force. In the new world that Jesus' followers believed had been launched by his resurrection and the gift of his spirit, baptism retained the meaning it seems already to have had during Jesus' public career – identification with his kingdom-movement – and to have deepened its resonance with the exodus on the one hand and with his death on the other. Already by the time Paul was writing to Corinth, less than twenty-five years after those events, he could let down the pail of this or that argument into that overflowing, over-determined well of meaning and draw out whatever he needed. And what he mostly needed

[44] 1 Cor. 1.17.

[45] 1 Cor. 6.11.

[46] cf. Eph. 5.26; Tit. 3.5; 2 Pet. 1.9.

[47] e.g. Ezek. 36.25, in a context with which Paul is very familiar (e.g. Rom. 2.25–9), and which also involves the promise of the spirit.

[48] Mk. 10.38; Lk. 12.50. See *JVG* 572f., with Hengel's comment about the extreme improbability of such obscure sayings being invented by the post-Easter church, which was not reticent or oblique in speaking of and interpreting Jesus' death.

were ways of reminding his congregations of the two things which we saw in Part II to be central to the entire symbolic system of his worldview: the *unity* of the *ekklēsia*, and its *holiness*.

This is, one might say, the rebirth not just of a community, not just of the individuals within it, but of the very notion of 'religion' itself. Paul had no time for, no truck with, the pagan religion all around him. But he practised, and explained, a rite by which, he believed, people of every sort were brought into solidarity with the one God through the one lord, and were made temples of the one Spirit; a rite with its meaning derived from a millennium-old narrative and having the effect of binding together a particular community and shaping its communal life. Any intelligent Roman, hearing all this, would say: this is *religio* all right, though it is quite different from anything we have imagined or experienced in our world.

Exactly this sense of exodus-shaped freedom from slavery, and of solidarity with the Messiah in his new life, is what we find in the other classic Pauline passage on baptism:

> Don't you know that all of us who were baptized into the Messiah, Jesus, were baptized into his death? That means that we were buried with him, through baptism, into death, so that, just as the Messiah was raised from the dead through the father's glory, we too might behave with a new quality of life. For if we have been planted together in the likeness of his death, we shall also be in the likeness of his resurrection . . .
>
> . . . So don't allow sin to rule in your mortal body, to make you obey its desires. Nor should you present your limbs and organs to sin to be used for its wicked purposes. Rather present yourselves to God, as people alive from the dead, and your limbs and organs to God, to be used for the righteous purposes of his covenant. Sin won't actually rule over you, you see, since you are not under law but under grace.
>
> What then? Shall we sin, because we are not under law but under grace? Certainly not! Don't you know that if you present yourselves to someone as obedient slaves, you really are slaves of the one you obey, whether that happens to be sin, which leads to death, or obedience, which leads to final vindication? Thank God that, though you were once slaves to sin, you have become obedient from the heart to the pattern of teaching to which you were committed. You were freed from sin, and now you have been enslaved to God's covenant justice . . .[49]

The passage goes on, exploring the 'slave/free' contrast further and further, and pointing forwards to the classic 'exodus'-passage in Romans 8.12–25, which we studied at some length earlier. We should be in no doubt that, for Paul, baptism gained its meaning from two primary poles around which it revolved: the exodus on the one hand, and the death and resurrection of Jesus on the other. Paul regarded it as the God-given means by which people would 'get in' to the new solidarity, the new humanity whose primary characteristic was that it had been freed from sin by death and resurrection, and whose primary obligations therefore now included holiness and, as in 1 Corinthians and elsewhere, unity. This is *religio*. Paul's version.

[49] Rom. 6.2–5; 12–18.

(iii) The Living Sacrifice

The language Paul uses in Romans 6 points to another feature which again we are bound to see as a kind of *religio* manqué. The Christians offered no animal sacrifices. But Paul was not shy of using the language of sacrifice, and even priesthood, to express the primary obligation of those *en Christō*, namely, the obligation to 'present' one's body, one's whole self to the one God. This primary obligation was the principal thing that had to be done over and over again, just as animal sacrifice was done in both the pagan and the Jewish worlds as the means by which the gods and humans could live together in harmony, solidarity and in community, and in particular the means by which the normal agricultural basis for human life would be blessed and assured of continuity and fruitfulness. The word 'present', *paristēmi/parastanō*, used in the passage just quoted from Romans 6 when Paul is speaking of 'presenting' one's body to God for his purposes, has a wide range of meaning. But it can also be used much more specifically as a technical term for the 'presenting' of a sacrifice.[50] That is just what we find a few chapters later:

> So, my dear family, this is my appeal to you by the mercies of God: offer [*parastēsai*] your bodies as a living sacrifice, holy and pleasing to God. Worship like this brings your mind into line with God's.[51] What's more, don't let yourselves be squeezed into the shape dictated by the present age. Instead, be transformed by the renewing of your minds, so that you can work out what God's will is, what is good, acceptable and complete.
>
> Through the grace which was given to me, I have this to say to each one of you: don't think of yourselves more highly than you ought to think. Rather, think soberly, in line with faith, the true standard which God has marked out for each of you. As in one body we have many limbs and organs, you see, and all the parts have different functions, so we, many as we are, are one body in the Messiah, and individually we belong to one another.[52]

This passage, set at the head of the final section of Paul's most carefully planned and carefully balanced letter, underlines precisely the points that have been made already in relation to baptism. This is 'religion' all right – sacrifice, worship and the knitting together thereby of the single community in fellowship one with another and not least with the God who is being worshipped. We in the modern west, most of whom have seldom seen an animal being killed, let alone killed within a religious ritual, let alone had to do such a thing ourselves, will no doubt find it as difficult to think our way into the shock and drama of Paul's opening metaphor here as we do to appreciate the enormity of his telling the Corinthian Christians that they were the temple of the living God. Sacrifice happened all the time in Paul's day, in

[50] e.g. Diod. Sic. 3.72; Jos. *War* 2.89; *Ant.* 4.113.

[51] The tr. here is an attempt at the controversial *logikē latreia*, on which see e.g. Jewett 2007, 729f.: the phrase 'signals the desire to set claim to a broad tradition of Greco-Roman as well as Jewish philosophy of religion. In place of the *latreia* of the Jewish cult (9.4) or the worship of finite images in Greco-Roman cults (1.23), Paul presents the bodily service of a community . . . as the fulfilment of the vision of worship that would be truly reasonable.'

[52] Rom. 12.1–5.

every city in the greco-roman world. One was never far away either from an animal about to be killed or from the smell of a recently sacrificed animal being cooked and eaten. The *polis* was bound together by such things, just as individuals were bound thereby to the specific gods with whom they were hoping to do business.

The business of those *en Christō* was the business of the new age, of the new creation for which the mind needed to be renewed; and for that the body, the whole public person, had to be offered to the one God. The death that had taken place in baptism, as in Romans 6, had been matched by the resurrection to new life. The newly alive body belonged to God, was to be offered to God, was to be available for worship and work in the new projects that were now beginning. Once again Paul emphasizes the unity of the family, both in the passage quoted and in the more specific exhortations which follow. That is what *religio* is meant to generate, as much now in the new creation, *mutatis mutandis*, as was supposed to be the case in the cities and towns of the old.

It is perhaps worth saying, as well, that just as we in the modern west do not instantly resonate to the metaphor of animal sacrifice, so those of us who belong to churches of the Reformation may need to distance ourselves, in reading Paul, from one of that movement's key assumptions: that 'sacrifice' was itself 'something humans did to earn favour with God' – in other words, part of the 'works-righteousness' which Luther assumed to be the target of Paul's polemic. In particular, as a special case and second-order problem within that, the Reformers stressed in their eucharistic theology what Paul and the author to the Hebrews both stress, that the death of Jesus was a single, unrepeatable event,[53] so that any attempt to make it happen again, through 'the sacrifice of the Mass', ran the immediate risk of humans trying to do all over again what Jesus had already done uniquely, offering a blasphemous insult to 'the finished work of Christ'. The eucharistic liturgy many of us Anglicans knew from childhood spoke of the 'one, perfect and sufficient sacrifice, oblation and satisfaction', making it clear beyond cavil that, whatever the officiant was doing in presiding at the service, he was *not* attempting to sacrifice Christ all over again.[54] Our concern here is not with the accuracy of those assessments of late medieval Catholicism, but with the legacy of such polemics within the protestant movements that have shaped contemporary biblical scholarship. Paul seems blithely innocent of any problem at this point. Of course, the 'sacrifice' of which he speaks in Romans 12.1 is to take place in the context of 'the mercies of God'; but he would almost certainly have said that about the entire Jewish sacrificial system. He would, I think, have made a Sanders-like response to the whole question: everything the scriptures commanded in terms of sacrificial cult, as indeed lawkeeping in general, was a matter of response to the covenant love and mercy of the one God. True, pagans spoke and wrote as though

[53] cf. e.g. Rom. 6.9f.; Heb. 9.26–8; 10.12–14.

[54] It was always 'he' in the Church of England, until the first women priests were ordained in 1994.

their sacrifices might bend the ear of this god, or twist the arm of that one; but that was not Paul's view of Israel's cult, and in using the language of 'religion' in the way he did he gave no hostages to the fickle fortunes of later theological debates.

Once you let a metaphor out of its hutch, of course, it can meet other metaphors and do what metaphors do best, at least in Paul: get together in new formations and generate further offspring. We noted in an earlier chapter Paul's fresh use of temple-imagery in relation to the church, and to individual Christians. That is obviously another spoke from the same wheel. But Paul can also speak of his own work in explicitly sacrificial terms:

> I have written to you very boldly at some points, calling things to your mind through the grace which God has given me to enable me to be a minister of King Jesus for the nations, working in the priestly service of God's good news, so that the offering of the nations may be acceptable, sanctified in the holy spirit.[55]

> Yes, even if I am to be poured out like a drink-offering on the sacrifice and service of your faith, I shall celebrate, and celebrate jointly with you all. In the same way, you should celebrate, yes, and celebrate with me.[56]

We should not miss the point of the last line in that second passage – in the letter to Philippi especially, where as we saw in the previous chapter Paul seems to be specially conscious of the Roman imperial context. 'Celebrate' in Paul's world did not just mean 'feel happy', or 'open a bottle of champagne when you pass the exam'. Celebration meant festivals; it meant processions; it meant garlands of flowers, street parties, games and athletic contests (Paul has just referred in the previous verse to the 'race' that he has been running). And celebration meant, above all, sacrifice: at the height of the event the participants would end up in the temple of whichever god was playing host to the festivities, and there animals would be slaughtered and offered up, with all the trimmings, including libations of wine poured on top of the sacrifice. Paul sees the active faith of the Philippian Christians as being like that. There is a celebration going on (he says it again and again in this letter), and at the heart of it their Jesus-shaped *pistis* is both the sacrifice (*thysia*) and service (*leitourgia*, the word from which we get 'liturgy'). This is what the Jesus-festival looks like. If he, Paul, is called to face martyrdom right now, his death will be like the drink-offering poured out on top of it all, and that should simply increase the level of celebration. The lavish nature of Paul's developed metaphor reflects the lavish way in which he had taken the most central event of daily, weekly and annual pagan *religio* and made it serve the cause of the Messiah.

In particular, the metaphor does what it does within the strong and repeated call in Philippians for the unity and solidarity of the church. Philippians 2.1–4, as we saw earlier, is one of the most remarkable appeals for unity, resonating back into chapter 1.27–30 and on into 2.12–18 as a

[55] Rom. 15.15f.

[56] Phil. 2.17f.

whole. This sacrifice is part of what happens when the little community, facing persecution, is learning to 'work out its own salvation', to realize (as a pagan community might believe about its own divinities, not least at times of festival and sacrifice) that 'God himself is the one who's at work among you' (2.13). Even in what appears at first glance to be a random metaphor, then, Paul is still working with the assumption that 'religion' is what strengthens and unites the *polis* – with the difference that the *polis* in question consists of the Messiah's people, those whose *politeuma* is 'in the heavens' against the day when heaven and earth are brought together at last (3.20–1). Exactly the same effect is created when he returns to the metaphor in the closing of the letter, as he thanks the Philippians for the gift they had sent him. 'It's like a sacrifice', he says, 'with a beautiful smell, a worthy offering, giving pleasure to God.'[57] Mutual generosity within the *koinōnia* of the Messiah's people, in other words, functions as part of the God-given means by which the community is bound together (in this case, the apostle and this particular church) with God himself both taking the initiative and being delighted with the result. This is the emphatically Christian version of the *religio* by which, through sacrifices, a community in the Roman world would have hoped to strengthen the bonds, both human and divine, that held them together.[58]

The first of the two passages quoted above, from Romans 15, has a slightly different flavour. Its primary allusion is not to pagan festivities, but to the regular procession of Jews from the far-off lands of the Diaspora, coming to Jerusalem for the great Jewish festivals. Here, in other words, Paul is adapting *Jewish* 'religion', exactly in line with the eschatological vision which he already articulated in (among other passages) Romans 10. Now that we are living in the moment of covenant renewal promised in Deuteronomy 30, the passage is saying, it is time for people (such as Paul himself) to be sent out to tell the world about Israel's Messiah, in fulfilment of Isaiah's prophecies. And, just as in those same prophecies people would stream into Jerusalem from all directions to worship the one God, so Paul is now heading for Jerusalem with the money that he has collected to help the impoverished believers there. Paul seems to see this particular ministry, which has involved a good deal of labour and (as we see in 2 Corinthians) heart-searching and careful explanation, within the metaphor of priesthood and sacrifice. If in Philippians 2 he is to be the drink-offering on the sacrifice, here the gentile Christians are the sacrifice and he is the priest who is presenting them at the altar. This whole picture, we should remind ourselves, is a *metaphor*. Paul has not reinscribed Jerusalem as the centre of the earth, and the basic movement of his mission is centrifugal, not centripetal, as the systematic exposition of Romans 10 indicates. But the metaphor is too good to pass up.

[57] Phil. 4.18.

[58] See the careful and subtle way in which 2 Cor. 8 and 9 indicate the same stitching together of divine and human 'gifts' for the good of the whole community.

Once again we are witnessing what we might call *religion reborn*. If this metaphor of 'birth' reminds us of babies, it is perhaps appropriate to think of the old rule about not throwing babies out with the bathwater. Paul has rejected pagan religion in all its works and ways. But 'religion' itself – centred upon the celebratory offering of sacrifice, through which humans and the divine presence are bound together in the solidarity of one community and its consequent fruitfulness – is something Paul sees fulfilled and transformed in and through Jesus. Jewish 'religion' was, for him, a signpost pointing forwards to this new reality. Pagan 'religion' was a parody of it, distorting it in line with the distorted and dehumanizing pseudo-divinities of the pagan pantheon. But 'religion' itself: if Paul had wanted to warn his hearers against it, he would have done better not to speak in these ways of the true sacrifice, the new priesthood, the drink-offering poured out on top of the celebratory sacrifice.

All depended, of course, on the one sacrifice which Paul believed had been offered when Jesus gave up his life in obedience to the Father's will. The sacrificial nature of Jesus' death, itself related initially (it seems) to the fact that Jesus died at Passover-time and spoke of his death in relation to that Passover and to the 'new covenant' promised by Jeremiah, does not fall neatly into an easy systematic package of ideas, either in Paul or in other early Christian writers (though many of them know it and use related notions).[59] Faced with corruption in the church, Paul uses the Passover theme as a way of saying that the corrupting element is like yeast which works its way through the lump of dough. Being Passover-people, they must get rid of the yeast:

> Don't you know that a little yeast works its way through the whole lump of dough? Cleanse out the old yeast, so that you can be a new lump, the yeast-free lump you really are. It's Passover-time, you see, and the Passover lamb – the Messiah, I mean – has already been sacrificed! What we now have to do is to keep the festival properly: none of the yeast of the old life, and none of the yeast of depravity and wickedness, either. What we need is yeast-free bread, and that means sincerity and truth.[60]

The Messiah, then, is the Passover sacrifice, and his followers must think through what that means for their whole life. That, we may suspect, is the original and controlling sacrificial image for the death of Jesus, but it is by no means the only one. Paul refers to Jesus as the sin-offering;[61] as the *hilastērion*, the place and means of propitiation;[62] and, in a memorable passage, an offering with which God is properly delighted:

> So you should be imitators of God, like dear children. Conduct yourselves in love, just as the Messiah loved us, and gave himself for us, as a sweet-smelling offering and sacrifice to God.[63]

[59] cf. e.g. Heb. 9.11—10.18; 1 Pet. 1.19; 1 Jn. 2.2; 4.10; Rev. 5.6, 9f.

[60] 1 Cor. 5.6–8.

[61] Rom. 8.3 (see Wright 1991 [*Climax*], ch. 11); perhaps 2 Cor. 5.21. See above, 898, 900.

[62] Rom. 3.24–6.

[63] Eph. 5.1f.

That passage, too, grows out of the command to unity, and goes on at once to speak of the need for holiness. 'Religion' in general was all about the unity of the community; first-century Jewish 'religion', always with exodus and Temple in mind, was all about holiness. Paul scoops up the whole package, reshapes it around the Messiah, and sets the lively metaphors scampering around in celebration.

(iv) The Breaking of Bread

Everything we have said so far about exodus, baptism and sacrifice comes into new focus when Paul speaks of the 'breaking of bread', the eucharist. The intense little passages in which he addresses two particular problems associated with the church's regular celebratory meal are scarcely enough to provide a full 'Pauline theology of the eucharist'. They nevertheless tell us enough to see that, for Paul, this shared meal was (a) anchored firmly in the exodus-story, the Passover-narrative, which had found a strange new fulfilment in Jesus, (b) understood as the intimate sharing of life and presence between the lord and his people and (c) designed to express the unity, solidarity and holiness of the community. This is a classic piece of Pauline rethinking and reworking of *religio*. It is a Jewish tradition focused on Jesus, resulting in a rite which upstages the sacrificial meals of pagan worship, and must not be confused with them – and certainly must not imitate the social hierarchy embodied in such pagan meals – but yet can be spoken of by analogy with them. This is a subtle but vital point.

The first element here – the exodus-context – we have already noted. Paul, warning the Corinthians not to behave like the Israelites in the wilderness, aligns the crossing of the Red Sea with baptism, and the wilderness feedings with the eucharist. 'They were all baptized into Moses in the cloud and in the sea,' he says. 'They all ate the same spiritual food and drank the same spiritual drink.'[64] This then sets up the argument against the immoral behaviour which characterized the wilderness generation and which threatens to characterize the Corinthians as well (10.6–13). It is not least for that reason that, despite allowing Christians to eat any meat sold in the marketplace (8.8; 10.25–7), Paul insists that they must not go into idol-temples and share in the meals that take place there. This, he says, is to put the sharing of the Messiah's life in direct competition with the sharing of the life of the *daimonia* who hide out within the hollow sham of idolatry, like petty criminals squatting in an empty but echoing mansion.

The fact that he can make this parallel speaks volumes for what he thinks is actually taking place at the eucharist:

> Therefore, my dear people, run away from idolatry. I'm speaking as to intelligent people: you yourselves must weigh my words. The cup of blessing which we bless is a sharing in the Messiah's blood, isn't it? The bread we break is a sharing in the Messiah's body, isn't

[64] 1 Cor. 10.2f.

> it? There is one loaf; well, then, there may be several of us, but we are one body, because we all share the one loaf.[65]

This 'sharing' in the Messiah's body and blood is conceived not only on the model of the 'sharing' which was taking place at pagan meals, but also on the model of the 'sharing' which Israel, from the time of the exodus through to Paul's own day, believed was happening 'in the altar', a reverent periphrasis for the one God himself:

> Consider ethnic Israel. Those who eat from the sacrifices share in the altar, don't they? So what am I saying? That idol-food is real, or that an idol is a real being? No: but when they offer sacrifices, they offer them to demons, not to God. And *I don't want you to be table-partners with demons.* You can't drink the cup of the lord and the cup of demons. You can't share in the table of the lord and the table of demons. Surely you don't want to provoke the lord to jealousy? We aren't stronger than him, are we?[66]

Here, as often in Paul, 'sharing' can be expressed as *koinōnia*. Those who 'share in the altar' in ethnic Israel are *koinōnoi tou thysiastēriou*, 'sharers of the altar'; being 'table-partners with demons' is *koinōnoi tōn daimoniōn*, 'sharers of demons'. Alternatively, in speaking of 'sharing in the table', whether of the lord or of demons, Paul uses *metechein*, which points in much the same direction. The point in either case has to do with *a sharing of common life*. As in ethnic Israel those who eat the sacrificial meat offered in the Temple are sharing in the very life of Israel's God, who has promised to meet with his people at that altar; as in pagan sacrificial meals those who eat the sacrifices suppose themselves to be sharing in the very life of Zeus, Athene or whoever (whereas, in Paul's analysis, they are actually sharing in the sordid and squalid life of the *daimonia*); so those who share 'the table of the lord' are actually sharing the lord's own life. If this were not so, there would be no competition, no provoking to jealousy.[67] The first element we noted (the exodus-context) thus leads Paul directly and naturally to the second element (the intimate sharing of life and presence between the lord and his people). That is the context within which Paul makes his appeal for the third element, the unity, solidarity and holiness of the community. Not only are idol-temples themselves off limits for Paul's churches. The meat itself is part of God's good creation, and can be eaten without any problem by those who know it to be just that; but if a fellow Christian is going to be wounded in conscience at the sight of a believer eating idol-food, that believer must abstain.[68]

This discussion of the eucharist, brought into 1 Corinthians 10 almost incidentally as part of Paul's distinction between giving permission to eat

[65] 1 Cor. 10.14–17.

[66] 1 Cor. 10.18–22.

[67] The theme of 'provoking to jealousy' is a further exodus-reference, picking up Dt. 32.21 as in Rom. 10.19. The whole passage (Dt. 32 in general, and 32.10–21 in particular), is significant: it recounts the tale of the wilderness wandering, as Paul does in 1 Cor. 10, and accuses the Israelites of provoking YHWH to jealousy by worshipping *daimonia*. See Hays 1989a, 94.

[68] 10.28f.; cf. 8.7–13.

idol-meat and warning against going into idol-temples, prepares the way for the direct discussion of the meal itself in chapter 11. All this takes place, of course, within the sequence of arguments for the unity of the church which stretches back to the opening of the letter and leads on to the great climax in chapters 12 (the 'body of the Messiah'), 13 (the poem about love) and 14 (order, rather than chaos, in public worship). This time the particular aspect of unity that seems under threat is the unity of rich and poor within the one fellowship. There may be more than that going on in the rather dense introduction (11.17–22), but not less, and it is beside our present purpose to enquire further.[69] When the *ekklēsia* assembles to celebrate the Lord's Supper, everyone seems to be bringing their own food, which means that those with plenty are well fed while those who have nothing are shamed (11.22). The similarity between this situation and many social occasions in the ancient world, at which distinctions of class and wealth were strongly marked, is all too obvious, and flies in the face of Paul's entire vision of the one church, the central symbol of its own worldview.

The crucial verse for our purposes is 11.29, where Paul declares that if people eat and drink 'without recognizing the body' they are eating and drinking judgment on themselves. What is this 'body', and what does it mean to recognize it? The context provides a strong argument in favour of taking the 'body' as the united community, the Messiah's single family. The introduction in 11.17–22 highlights the inappropriate social divisions that were tarnishing the gatherings, and the conclusion to the chapter in 11.33–4 addresses the same point ('treat one another as honoured guests by waiting for each other'). It is not unimportant, as well, that the next chapter focuses on the *ekklēsia* as 'the body of the Messiah' in the sense of the single unity containing many different 'members'. All this strongly suggests that in the crucial verse 11.29 Paul has in mind the importance of 'recognizing the body' in the sense of 'recognizing that we who eat and drink this meal are a single body', as he had already said in 10.17 ('there may be several of us, but we are one body, because we all share the one loaf'). The 'unworthiness' of which he speaks in verse 27 ('anyone who eats the bread or drinks the cup of the lord in an unworthy manner will be guilty of the body and blood of the lord') must then refer, in the present instance, to the kind of selfish or snobbish behaviour described in verses 17–22, though no doubt Paul would have said the same about any other kind of 'unworthiness'.

As often, however, Paul says slightly more by way of grounding for this point than might at first be thought necessary. As he does so, he gives us a window right into the heart of the 'religion', in the firmly first-century sense, which he took for granted:

> This, you see, is what I received from the lord, and handed on to you. On the night when the lord Jesus was betrayed, he took bread, gave thanks, broke it, and said, 'This is my body; it's for you! Do this as a memorial of me.' He did the same with the cup after supper, and said, 'This cup is the new covenant in my blood. Whenever you drink it, do this as a

[69] See above, ch. 6, esp. 427–9.

> memorial of me.' For whenever you eat this bread and drink the cup, you are announcing the lord's death until he comes.[70]

This gives further content to what we already noted in relation to 1 Corinthians 10, where the exodus-context provides a strong indication that Paul sees the Lord's Supper, if not exactly as a Passover meal, nevertheless closely related to it.[71] As with everything else in Paul, this has been reframed by, and rethought around, the death of Jesus; the theme of *koinōnia* in the previous chapter, where the eating and drinking was seen as a real participation in the life of the lord, may indicate that the 'memorial' (*amamnēsis*) here is much more than simply an aid to the memory. Paul sees the eucharistic action as part of inaugurated eschatology, looking both back and forwards. You are announcing the lord's death, he says, until he comes (verse 26). The present time, given its particular meaning by being the 'present' which follows from *this* 'past' and anticipates *this* 'future', is the time of the lord's 'presence', the time when he is 'announced'. As in the argument of the previous chapter, where the reality of sharing with the lord would precipitate a direct conflict if one were also to share with *daimonia*, so here the reality of the 'memorial' and the 'announcement' are what give special force to the warning which follows:

> It follows from this that anyone who eats the bread or drinks the cup of the lord in an unworthy manner will be guilty of the body and blood of the lord. Everyone should test themselves; that's how you should eat the bread and drink the cup. You see, if you eat and drink without recognizing the body, you eat and drink judgment on yourself. That's why several of you are weak and sick, and some have died. But if we learned how to judge ourselves, we would not incur judgment. But when we are judged by the lord, we are punished, so that we won't be condemned along with the world.[72]

Here again Paul has said somewhat more than he needs for his central argument. His main point is that if the eucharist is a real sharing in the lord and his death, then anything which fragments the unity of the lord's single 'body' is a crime against the lord himself.[73] But once again he frames this within a larger eschatological picture. There is a final judgment coming, but just as for Christians the verdict has already been announced in the death of the Messiah, so any 'judgment' that is still to happen because of the continuing sin even of Christians must be brought forward from the future into the present. This is part of Paul's larger picture of eschatology and judgment, and it reminds us that for Paul the element of *religio* was always framed within such a picture.[74]

The eucharist thus clearly functions for Paul as a *rite*, complete with traditional words; as *a rite in which a 'founding myth' was rehearsed*, though in this case the 'founding myth' was an actual event which had occurred not

[70] 1 Cor. 11.23–6.

[71] cf. also of course 1 Cor. 5.7.

[72] 1 Cor. 11.27–32.

[73] cp. 1 Cor. 8.12.

[74] On present and future 'judgment' see above, e.g. 1049f., 1080f. On this point cf. 1 Cor. 4.1–5.

long before; as *a rite in which the worshippers share the life of the divinity being worshipped*, though the divinity in question is a human being of recent memory; as *a rite dependent on a prior sacrifice*, albeit the very strange one of the crucifixion of that same human being; as *a rite which should bind the community together*, so that signs of disunity during the rite are a contradiction of its inner meaning; as *a rite which, if thus performed in the wrong way, will have bad consequences for that community*. Once again: any pagan who heard and grasped what Paul was saying here would conclude from each of these components, and particularly from their striking and dense combination, that this was indeed part of a *religio*, even though it was quite unlike anything that had been imagined before. In the same way, any Jewish onlooker would see that the traditions of Israel, particularly the narrative of the exodus, had provided the framework for Paul's understanding. But, again, no Jew before the time of Jesus had imagined anything quite like this.[75]

The truly remarkable thing, for anyone disposed to object to this argument (perhaps on the grounds that we had assumed that Paul had rejected 'religion' outright), is that as we saw with his astonishing christology he can clearly take these foundational points for granted. He assumes not only that the eucharist is central to the worshipping life of the Corinthians, but that it already has all these features. It has included from the beginning the narrative framework both of the events which led to Jesus' death ('on the night when [he] was betrayed'), of the meal he celebrated at that moment and of the words he spoke. Paul 'received' this 'from the lord', and he 'handed it on' to the Corinthians (11.23). This, as in 15.3, is the language of 'tradition', which once again has been deeply suspect in protestant circles but seems to be no problem to Paul. The theological and cultural sensitivities of the sixteenth century on the one hand and the modern period on the other should not prevent us from drawing the strictly historical conclusion that, in terms of the first century, what Paul was describing was a new, surprising but still recognizable type of *religio*.

(v) Prayer

Paul's description of the eucharist provides a rare glimpse of how his churches might have prayed. This is not the place to go into the early history of eucharistic liturgies. But it does seem likely that the public rehearsal of Jesus' last meal, and of the words he spoke on that occasion, already formed part of their public worship. The fact that other early eucharistic liturgies may be significantly different (we naturally think of *Didache* 9—10) is neither here nor there. What matters for our purposes is that Paul assumed that his communities would have a common life in which prayer

[75] cf. 1QSa 2.20f., where the Messiah will bless the bread and wine; but there is of course no sense there that the community would be sharing in his life and death.

played a central role. In his world, communities which prayed together were bound together, and binding together was what *religio* meant and did.

The other signs of formal or semi-formal words of prayer in Paul are well known. We have already referred to the apparent revision of the *Shema* in 1 Corinthians 8.6, and I have suggested that Paul's new wording was in use not just as a theological formulation but, like its prototype, as a regular prayer: an invocation of the one God, one lord and a statement of exclusive personal loyalty to this divinity. There is also the fascinating, if to us frustrating, Aramaic cry of *Marana tha*, 'Our lord, come!', best explained as an already traditional element among Jesus' first followers in Palestine and remaining, untranslated, in the worshipping life of otherwise Greek-speaking churches.[76] This is paralleled by the cry of *Abba* which, again, Paul assumes to be normal among those in whom the Spirit has been at work through the gospel of Jesus.[77] This is obviously far too tiny a sample to admit of any generalizations, but we are bound to notice that the prayers in question consist of words, names or titles of God or Jesus. Perhaps one of the reasons for the preservation of the Aramaic form was that sense, common to religion in antiquity, that it was after all important to be accurate in the words with which one invoked the deity. Once again, even though Paul's *religio* was quite unlike anything else of the time, a *religio* it remained.

The glorious and potentially chaotic worshipping life of the church as we suddenly glimpse it in 1 Corinthians 14 makes the same ultimate point from a different angle. Paul was well aware that the phenomenon of ecstatic speech, 'glossolalia' (speaking in tongues) and related experiences, were common in the 'religious' world of his day. That is why he needs to issue a warning about apparently ecstatic speech which ends up cursing Jesus.[78] Thus, whereas in some circles today 'speaking in tongues' is regarded as something which marks Christians off from other religions, perhaps even something which marks off specially mature Christians from other members of the church, for Paul it was something which was paralleled and well known in very different settings. Like the eating and drinking in the eucharist, at that level of generality the Christians were doing the same thing as their neighbours, up to the point at which one might ask what it all meant.

That is why, again, when Paul is discussing this particular 'religious' phenomenon of tongues, and the related phenomena of interpretation, prophecy and so on, the emphasis is on *unity*. The whole church must be 'built up' by what is said.[79] 'God is the God, not of chaos, but of peace,' he declares; so 'everything should be done in a seemly fashion, and in proper order'.[80] Not for Paul the romantic protestant dream of a holy anarchy with the worshippers simply doing and saying what comes naturally or spontaneously. That

[76] 1 Cor. 16.22, on which see Thiselton 2000, 1347–52.

[77] Rom. 8.15; Gal. 4.6. Whether or not this is a hint at the use of the Lord's Prayer is impossible to say.

[78] 1 Cor. 12.2f.

[79] 1 Cor. 14.4, 5, 12, 26.

[80] 1 Cor. 14.33, 40.

retrojection of a much later cultural imperative is every bit as anachronistic as the retrojection into Paul's day of elaborate liturgies or ecclesial hierarchies. Paul, in any case, expects public worship to include psalm-singing and 'teaching', as well as 'revelations', 'tongues' and 'interpretations'.[81] There are to be formal moments as well as informal, and the latter are not to lapse into chaos. Again, we do not need to pursue this in any detail, but just to note the point: anyone in Paul's wider cultural context who read 1 Corinthians 14 would know that Paul was talking about one aspect of what they would call *religio*. Paul and his communities would know it too. Worship and invocation were part of the first thing for which Cicero used that word.

(vi) Discerning the Way

The other two things for which Cicero used the word *religio* are also paralleled in Paul, though again in radically different mode. For Cicero, the other two aspects were the taking of auguries and the consultation of ancient oracular texts. Paul did not, of course, use divination, or consult the entrails (or the flight-paths) of birds. He did not expect to be guided, or warned, by a sudden clap of thunder. But he believed that the divinity he invoked guided him, at least when he particularly needed it. Whatever we think of the historical value of Acts, it is noticeable that there are several moments when specific words from the lord give order and direction to Paul's life, from his conversion itself through to the angelic encouragement he received shortly before the shipwreck.[82] It is equally noticeable that there are several moments when we might have expected such things but none appear. Paul, Silas and Timothy go wandering off northwards through Asia Minor without knowing quite where they are going. The only guidance, for a while, is negative: they are forbidden to preach here, prevented from going there.[83] Many of Paul's decisions about where to go next, and when to move on, seem to have been taken on what we might think of as purely pragmatic or common-sense grounds, not least when he was being physically threatened or attacked and deemed it prudent to leave town in a hurry. If Paul urged his hearers to learn how to think things through, to develop a wise Christian mind, it was something he had had to do himself.[84] Certainly Luke has made no attempt to portray the apostolic mission in terms of constant 'supernatural' guidance, though that kind of 'intervention' does happen from time to time.

In Paul's own writings this kind of guidance seems at best oblique. He has long been intending to go to Rome, but things have got in the way. His journeyings have been planned on the basis of his overall understanding of

[81] 1 Cor. 14.26.

[82] cf. Ac. 9.3–6 (cf. 22.6–11; 26.13–20), 12, 15–17; 11.27–30; 13.1–3; 16.7–10; 18.9–11; 19.21; 21.10–14; 23.11; 27.23–6.

[83] Ac. 16.6f.

[84] See above, 1095–1128.

God's work in and through him, not *ad hoc* because of particular sudden impulses – even if some might accuse him of such a thing.[85] God would use combinations of circumstances both to encourage him and to nudge him in a particular direction.[86] There might be occasional moments of 'revelation', but these are conspicuously rare.[87] As often as not, Paul sees the divine hand only in retrospect.[88] For the present, the attempt to discern divine intent carries a 'maybe' about with it. *Maybe*, he writes to Philemon about Onesimus, *this is the reason he was separated from you*. To believe in providence often means saying 'perhaps'.[89]

All this might seem to lead to the paradoxical conclusion that Paul was less certain of the divine will, on a day-to-day basis, than his pagan counterparts. No doubt he would have said 'than his pagan counterparts *thought they were*', but the contrast is still interesting. This is balanced, however, not only by the sense that those who 'present their bodies' and have their minds renewed, as in Romans 12.1–2, are in fact being led by the spirit, even though it may not seem so clear at the time, but also in particular by the solid grounding Paul claims both in Israel's scriptures and in the events concerning Jesus. We shall look at Paul's relation to the scriptures in chapter 15; for him, they were far more than any oracle, Sibylline or otherwise. True, he once describes them as 'God's oracles', but that has a special connotation in the context of one particular argument.[90] True, his own writings sometimes give hints of an 'oracular' style, though in my judgment the passages sometimes described as fresh oracles, unattached by any reasoning to the rest of the surrounding argument, are nothing of the kind.[91] He saw the scriptures as much more than a rag-bag of sayings and cryptic wisdom, 'oracles' waiting to be decoded and applied randomly to this or that situation. They told the story of the one God, his world and his people, in such a way (Paul believed) as to lead the eye not only up to Jesus but on beyond, all the way to the expanding apostolic mission. What Paul thus loses by comparison with his pagan contemporaries in terms of augury, he more than makes up through the scriptures.

In particular, the recent events concerning Jesus provided Paul with a clear sense of how his own life and calling were to be shaped. This is evident from his extended apostolic apologia, and from his regular invocation of the Jesus-story in one way or another.[92] The scriptures, together with the (usually implicit) story of Jesus as their proper if shocking fulfilment, thus take the place, within his *religio*, of the combination of augury, oracles and

[85] Rom. 1.13; 15.14–33; 1 Cor. 16.5–9; 2 Cor. 1.23—2.4. For the accusation: 2 Cor. 1.17–22.

[86] 2 Cor. 7.5–16; 1 Thess. 2.17—3.10.

[87] Gal. 2.1f. (cf. Ac. 11.27–30); cf. e.g. Ac. 16.8.

[88] e.g. Phil. 1.12–18.

[89] Philem. 15.

[90] Rom. 3.2; cf. *Perspectives*, ch. 30.

[91] See Aune 1983, discussed by Ashton 2000, 189. The best known example is Paul's statement about 'all Israel' in Rom. 11.25–7 (see Ashton 2000, 192f.), on which see above, 1231–52.

[92] 2 Cor. 2.14—6.13; Phil. 2.6–11; cf. e.g. 1 Cor. 11.1.

sacred books.[93] Once again, they are radically different sorts of things. But if an intelligent pagan, talking to Paul about his life, his thought and his worldview, were to hear him speaking about the things we have just listed, the conclusion might be reached that, though this was a very odd sort of *religio*, that was none the less what it was.

3. Paul and 'Religion': Conclusion

The point is now made and can be summed up briefly. When we look at Paul's worldview (Part II) and theology (Part III) in the light of the world of 'religion' we studied in chapter 4, we see both radical dissimilarity and perhaps surprising similarity. The differences are obvious, and would have been obvious to Paul's communities and their neighbours. Not only did the Christians not join in with the pagan religious customs, they did not have their own version (as did the Jews) of the most central 'religious' activity, namely animal sacrifice. But Paul was not shy about using the language and thought-forms of the *religio* of his day in relation to the activities which, as we saw, formed central elements of his praxis. Once we back off from the debates of the last two centuries in which the word 'religion' in its modern sense has played such a key role, often being muddled up with protestant fears about 'works-righteousness', and locate Paul instead within his own world, there is nothing to lose and everything to gain by recognizing that he, his communities and their neighbours would have seen the central praxis of the early Christians as itself a form of *religio*. All the marks are there.

Above all, we have noticed that the things which Paul's communities most characteristically did as part of their worship were seen by Paul, just as Jewish and pagan *religio* was seen by those who took part in it, as underlining and strengthening the unity of the community in question. Pagan *religio* bound together the *polis* and the gods in a single family. Paul believed in the one God, one lord of his revised Jewish monotheism, with the one spirit being poured out on all who shared this faith; and the 'religious' things he and his communities did, especially baptism and eucharist, constituted a similar binding together of the community both in itself and within the life of this single divinity. This was not, of course, a subtle attempt by Paul or his communities to put the one God in their debt, as anxious theologians have sometimes imagined. Part of what Paul believed about this one God was that, in Jesus, he had put the whole world in his debt, completely and for ever. That is why one of Paul's central motifs is gratitude. It is also why

[93] We may compare and contrast Josephus, who (as part of his explanation for his own changing sides during the war) claims that he had been given special insight, through dreams, into the contemporary fulfilment of ancient scriptural prophecies (*War* 3.350–4). For Paul, the crucial fulfilment had already happened in the events concerning Jesus. Both cases involved a claim about the fulfilment of scriptural prophecies of universal sovereignty. For Josephus, at least on the face of his account, this was now passing to Rome. For Paul, it had already passed to Israel's Messiah.

he seems to have turned the whole notion of debt on its head: the debt of love is the only form he permits.[94]

All this opens up the possibility of future scholarly projects in relation to the historical comparison between the *religio* (in the first-century sense) of Paul and his communities and that of other first-century communities. Such a project would need to be clear, however, as the projects we discussed at the start of the present chapter were not entirely clear, about two things. First, *religio* in this sense stands in relation to 'theology' somewhat as the steering wheel of a car stands in relation to the map. They are not the same thing, and cannot be collapsed into one another. But they need each other. Without theology, *religio* might wander aimlessly all over the place. Without *religio*, theology might remain an abstract exercise. Second, if we were to study Paul's *religio* in more detail, not least as a 'comparative' exercise, we would need to be clear that a vital part of his 'theology', built into his *religio* at every point, is *eschatology*. Paul did not see himself as setting up, founding, or taking part in a 'religion' which was in itself 'superior' to other 'religions'. Seeing things that way, ironically, often begins in relativism and ends in supersessionism. Paul believed that the one God who had made the world had acted in a radical new way, in fulfilment of his promises to Israel. That, as we have seen – over against those who assume that 'apocalyptic' automatically means the death of all 'religion' – resulted in a new world, a new worldview and a new theology, which were expressed in what we might call *eschatological religion*: communal and personal activities which celebrated the radically new action of the one God, and which bound together the community of his worshippers with one another and with that God himself.

That multiple binding together is all-important, and Paul refers to it with one of his most important words. At the heart of the eschatological religion, both in its sense of the presence of the one God and in its innermost response to that one God, and working itself out immediately in the mutual bonding of Jesus' followers, was what he called *agapē*, love. That, as we saw in our previous chapter, was part of what constituted the implicit challenge of the Christian gospel to the powers that ruled the world, not least through their own types of 'religion' and their own offers of 'salvation'. It was also closely bound up with the other vital engagement between Paul and his wider environment: the question of philosophy.

[94] Rom. 13.8. This whole topic needs further consideration for which the present volume, sadly, leaves no room.

Chapter Fourteen

THE FOOLISHNESS OF GOD: PAUL AMONG THE PHILOSOPHERS

1. Introduction

Somewhere among historical novels waiting to be written is a fresh account of the fictitious but potentially illuminating meeting between Paul and Seneca.[1] The distinguished Roman is slightly senior in age. But the wandering apostle, with his endless travels, imprisonments, beatings and sleepless nights, might be mistaken for the older man. It is the year 63. Nero has been on the throne for nine years. Seneca, whose relationship with his former pupil has cooled to the point of mutual disfavour, has left the court and is devoting himself to philosophical contemplation in such time as remains, knowing full well what normally happens to ex-courtiers. Paul, meanwhile, has arrived in Rome as a prisoner and is awaiting trial. He, too, does not expect to live very long. He had earlier invited the Jewish elders in Rome to hear his account of the gospel, and has now, while still under house arrest, taken to inviting non-Jewish intellectuals to discuss their views with him.[2] Seneca, intrigued, decides to accept, and the two men spend the day explaining their own beliefs and exploring one another's. It is the kind of scenario that Seneca himself, or indeed Cicero, might easily have written up as a dialogue, following the Socratic model to which all ancient philosophy looked back.

Fiction can sometimes function as a microscope, enabling us to see some of the undoubted facts of the day in three dimensions. But the 'facts' of Paul's engagement with the philosophical world of his day are themselves elusive, at least initially. When we ask, as we must in this chapter, how the Paul we have come to know might have responded to the philosophical world of his day, we might be forgiven for thinking that he would sweep it all away with a single wave of the hand:

> The word of the cross, you see, is madness to people who are being destroyed. But to us – those who are being saved – it is God's power. This is what the Bible says, after all:
>
> I will destroy the wisdom of the wise;
> the shrewdness of the clever I'll abolish.
>
> Where is the wise person? Where is the educated person? Where is the debater of this present age? Don't you see that God has turned the world's wisdom into folly? This is how

[1] As we saw in ch. 3, a collection of short letters between the two men, now regarded as spurious, was known by the time of Jerome and Augustine; see 220 above.

[2] Ac. 28.17–28 describes the meeting with Jewish leaders; the invitation to pagans is part of my hypothetical fiction.

> it's happened: in God's wisdom, the world didn't know God through wisdom, so it gave God pleasure, through the folly of our proclamation, to save those who believe. Jews look for signs, you see, and Greeks search for wisdom; but we announce the crucified Messiah, a scandal to Jews and folly to Gentiles, but to those who are called, Jews and Greeks alike, the Messiah – God's power and God's wisdom. God's folly is wiser than humans, you see, and God's weakness is stronger than humans.[3]

Another fine rhetorical flourish announcing the folly of all human rhetoric! Perhaps, though, this is more than a simple dismissal; as usual, Paul writes at more than one level. God's folly, he goes on to say, creates its own new genres of 'wisdom':

> We do, however, speak wisdom among the mature. But this isn't a wisdom of this present world, or of the rulers of this present world – those same rulers who are being done away with. No: we speak God's hidden wisdom in a mystery. This is the wisdom God prepared ahead of time, before the world began, for our glory.[4]

That, in a measure, is the story of the two letters to Corinth: a firm denial that Paul's gospel owes anything to human wisdom, coupled with a careful construction of an alternative 'wisdom' which, hidden for long ages, has now been revealed. We see the same thing in one of his central discussions, when he dismisses 'knowledge' of the merely human sort. It puffs you up, he says, but love builds you up. Thus:

> If anybody thinks they 'know' something, they don't yet 'know' in the way they ought to know. But if anybody loves God, they are 'known' – by him.[5]

This trumping of human knowledge by divine knowledge, and by the 'love' that is the proper name for the latter, recurs as a theme in the exquisite poem of chapter 13:

> Love never fails. But prophecies will be
> abolished; tongues will stop; and knowledge, too,
> be done away. We know, you see, in part;
> we prophesy in part; but, with perfection,
> the partial is abolished . . .
> For at the moment all that we can see
> are puzzling reflections in a mirror;
> then, face to face. I know in part, for now;
> but then I'll know completely, through and through,
> even as I'm completely known. So, now,
> faith, hope, and love remain, these three; and, of them,
> love is the greatest.[6]

There is, then, an *epistemological* revolution at the heart of Paul's worldview and theology. It isn't just that he now knows things he did not before; it is,

[3] 1 Cor. 1.18–25.
[4] 1 Cor. 2.6f.
[5] 1 Cor. 8.1–3.
[6] 1 Cor. 13.8–13.

rather, that *the act of knowing* has itself been transformed. This has been an important sub-theme in some recent writing on Paul, but it has not always, in my judgment, been explored to the full, or necessarily helpfully.[7] Ordinary human wisdom, ordinary human knowledge, is not just cancelled. It is taken up into something at one level similar and at another level radically different. Paul's name for the new 'something' is *agapē*, love.[8]

The warnings against ordinary human wisdom – again, perhaps Paul is here saying more than one thing at a time – are repeated in Colossians 2:

> Watch out that nobody uses philosophy and hollow trickery to take you captive! These are in line with human tradition, and with the 'elements of the world' – not the king. In him, you see, all the full measure of divinity has taken up bodily residence. What's more, you are fulfilled in him, since he's the head of all rule and authority.[9]

And the new wisdom is once again spelled out in terms both of Jesus and of *agapē*:

> I want their hearts to be encouraged as they're brought together in love. I want them to experience all the wealth of definite understanding, and to come to the knowledge of God's mystery – the Messiah, the king! He's the place where you'll find all the hidden treasures of wisdom and knowledge.
>
> I'm saying this so that nobody will deceive you with plausible words . . .[10]

Colossians, indeed, is where we find the fullest exposition anywhere in Paul of a cosmic vision, shaped out of the 'wisdom' traditions of scripture on the one hand and around Jesus himself on the other. To this we shall return.

Has Paul then rejected all the wisdom, understanding and insight of the pagan world? Not at all. Just as the person with true 'knowledge' is able to eat any meat sold in the market, whatever its provenance,[11] so those who belong to the Messiah are able to recognize, celebrate and learn from all kinds of good qualities in the wider world:

> For the rest, my dear family, these are the things you should think through: whatever is true, whatever is holy, whatever is upright, whatever is pure, whatever is attractive, whatever has a good reputation; anything virtuous, anything praiseworthy.[12]

Paul can say much the same thing, when in more combative mood, by using the metaphor of military strategy. The intellectual weapons that are used against him are not simply to be broken and thrown away. They can be turned to positive use:

[7] The famous article of J. L. Martyn on 'Epistemology at the Turn of the Ages', now in Martyn 1997b, 89–110, raises important questions but should not be deemed to have settled them for ever.

[8] On the idea of an epistemology of love cf. *NTPG* 62–4, and the development of the theme in e.g. Middleton and Walsh 1998, ch. 7; Walsh and Keesmaat 2004, ch. 7.

[9] Col. 2.8–10. For the complex meanings in this passage see above, 992–5.

[10] Col. 2.2–4.

[11] 1 Cor. 10.23–6. In 8.7–10 Paul describes this 'knowledge' (spelled out in 8.4–6) as *gnōsis*.

[12] Phil. 4.8.

> Yes, we are mere humans, but we don't fight the war in a merely human way. The weapons we use for the fight, you see, are not merely human; they carry a power from God that can tear down fortresses! We tear down clever arguments, and every proud notion that sets itself up against the knowledge of God. We take every thought prisoner and make it obey the Messiah.[13]

Paul is not, in other words, speaking about an accidental or unreflective use of this or that motif taken from his surrounding culture. He is well aware of ideas and worldviews 'out there', of their present ambiguous status and of how they might relate to his own beliefs. Even if in his letters we do not see the head-on confrontation with philosophical teachers and their arguments that we might surmise had often taken place, Paul had clearly thought through the issues involved, both the specific questions and topics and the meta-question of what his overall approach should be. The purpose of the present chapter is to probe cautiously forward into the things he does say in the letters, looking for signs of that wider engagement which, from these hints, we may guess stands behind them. We are, in fact, inching our way towards the kind of discussion which Paul might have had with Seneca.

As we do so, we leave behind, hopefully for ever, the sterile antithesis which has dogged the footsteps of Pauline scholarship ever since F. C. Baur squashed Paul, and the rest of early Christianity, into the two boxes demanded by his Hegelian ideology. Not only are the labels 'Judaism' and 'hellenism' dangerously anachronistic, as we saw earlier. Not only do we now know that Paul's 'Jewish' world was firmly and irrevocably part of wider 'hellenistic' culture, which itself was anything but monolithic. Much scholarship is now well aware that ignoring these problems produces gross and distorting historical oversimplification. The deeper problem is that those two labels, with their apparent but pseudo-historical validation, have been used to designate two competing ideologies, setting up a Procrustean bed on which different thinkers can be placed and to whose shape they can be fitted by a process of philosophical, cultural and not least historical torture. The protests against all this have increased in recent years, though even those who have voiced them have not, I think, seen all the ramifications of following through a genuinely historical investigation.[14]

However, just because we reject the ideologically shaped antithesis proposed by Baur and his followers, we are not at liberty to ignore the historically grounded evidence for the *real* antithesis which manifested itself at the time. We cannot, for instance, simply ignore the Maccabaean literature, or *4 Ezra*. We cannot pretend that the Roman–Jewish war of 66–70, or the great revolt of 132–5, were simply outbreaks of ordinary anti-imperial revolution, though of course they were that as well. As we have seen, most Jews in the first century thought of themselves as significantly different from their non-Jewish neighbours; most non-Jews recognized this significant difference, which showed up in a variety of ways; and many Jewish thinkers and writers

[13] 2 Cor. 10.3–5.

[14] See esp. Meeks 2001 and Martin 2001.

of the time brought this to articulation in a range of writings, in a variety of different genres and styles, expressing and urging what they saw as a specifically Jewish worldview. Of course these matters are complex, and these writings are part of a multi-faceted culture, interwoven with ideas from 'outside'. The antithesis that many Jews perceived, and that many non-Jews recognized as well, bears little relation to the Hegelian pair of 'isms' that have dominated scholarship for so long. All this can be seen in Philo and Josephus, or indeed in the Wisdom of Solomon, which we looked at in this connection at the end of chapter 3. It will not do to recognize and reject the nineteenth-century distortions and then to pretend that the first century was simply a flat landscape on which various odd people did various odd and interlocking things. To go in that direction would, in fact, be to impose another ideology – that of late-modern or postmodern relativism – in place of the Hegelian one. As usual, it is the Jewish evidence that will suffer most on that new Procrustean bed.

In particular, what will be lost is the sense of a *narrative*: the story of 'freedom', Jewish style, going back (as in the Wisdom of Solomon) to the exodus but stretching forward towards the real 'return from exile'.[15] This sense of belonging within an immense and liberating story can be seen across much second-Temple literature, with its *only* significant non-Jewish parallel being, as we saw, the imperial narrative told by Horace, Livy and above all Virgil.[16] It is history, not ideology or theology, that will protest against any treatment of Paul and his world that fails to take account of this irreducible, and irreducibly Jewish, element of the picture.

Since Paul, as we have seen, shared this story and the typical Jewish self-perceptions that went with it (seeing them transformed around the Messiah but not abandoned), we should expect to understand his engagement with the wider world of his day by loose analogy with books like the Wisdom of Solomon, with the significant differences occasioned by his particular messianic belief. Thus, just as we saw the engagement of Wisdom with many varieties of contemporary philosophy, borrowing from Plato, rejecting Epicureanism, parallel in some respects with Stoicism, but underneath it all continuing to tell the story of Israel's God, his people and his world, so – *mutatis mutandis*, of course – we might expect to find Paul doing something similar.

How might we expect to map such engagement? Obviously one can start by noting similarities and parallels of all sorts. There is nothing wrong with that. But in a book such as the present one we have the chance to stand back and look at the larger picture. When we do, it is hard to suppose that Paul himself would not have had great respect for some of the thinkers we studied in chapter 3. It is too easy to assume that, as a zealous Pharisaic Jew, he would simply sweep them all away as so much *skybala*, trash. Certainly that is not what he seems to be saying in some of the key passages: *whatever* is

[15] See above, 139–63.

[16] See above, 299–312.

true, holy and so on is what one should think about, wherever it may be found. Paul of course believed that he had been given insight into all things, all wisdom, through the divine *pneuma*, the spirit of the Messiah.[17] This kind of wisdom already made the 'wisdom of the world' look like foolishness to him.[18] But precisely because this spirit was the spirit of the one God who had made the whole world Paul expected that there might be points of overlap, of congruence.[19] He would indeed regard it as his right and calling to 'take every thought prisoner and make it obey the Messiah', but there were plenty of thoughts out there which, he might have judged, would be ready servants if only they were bought up and employed within the right household. Not only thoughts; methods. How this plays out we must explore presently.

The parallels and similarities, then, matter. They have been surveyed reasonably thoroughly, in articles and monographs with particular focus, especially and naturally in the area of ethics, in relation to Paul's pastoral language and so forth.[20] But what is required, on a loose analogy to the programme Sanders articulated in relation to the task of comparing 'patterns of religion', is to look at one entire picture in its own terms, and compare it with another entire picture again in its own terms. (I suggested in the previous chapter that Sanders did not in fact achieve this goal, but the aim is laudable.) We must now, therefore, attempt to place the Paul we observed in Parts II and III alongside the philosophical world we sketched in chapter 3, and see what happens – and how, if at all, the implicit engagement between the two pictures came to actual expression in his letters. We are thus using the 'logic' of scientific method to work from the known (the worlds of the philosophers and of Paul) to the unknown (the potential engagement between them), in order to form hypotheses which will then be tested against the actual evidence of the letters themselves.

2. Paul's Questions to the Philosophers

(i) Introduction

There are, naturally, two ways of approaching this challenging task. One can set out the philosophers' agenda in their own terms and see what Paul might have said to them. Or one might set out Paul's worldview and theology, and see what the philosophers might have said to him. I shall go by the first road, starting with the first-century philosophy we examined in chapter 3, and asking, in the light of Parts II and III, what Paul might have said in response. Some of the second possibility will be glimpsed as well on the way, and will lead us to certain questions that arise from within the dominant

[17] 1 Cor. 2.15f.

[18] 1 Cor. 1.18—2.16.

[19] See the point made by Udo Schnelle, quoted above at 1116, esp. n. 307.

[20] See e.g. Malherbe 1987; 1989a and b.

traditions of Paul's time. It is a matter of some surprise that even those who have written on, say, Paul and the Stoics in recent years have not approached the subject in this holistic way.[21]

The philosophers, as we saw, divided their investigations into three: physics, ethics and logic. 'Theology', already named as a topic by the time of Plato, was subsumed under 'physics'; it was part of 'what there was', what the 'nature' of the whole world might be. The three topics were closely related: the question of how to behave, individually and socially ('ethics'), was directly related to the analysis of the world, which included an analysis of what it meant to be human ('physics'). 'Logic' was a matter of understanding and employing an epistemology that was coherent with the results of both 'physics' and 'ethics'. These three topics formed the playing-fields on which the different schools did battle over particular issues.

If we are to give Paul free rein to address the philosophers, everything we know about him suggests that before getting into details, either on the three main topics or the proposals of the different schools, he would want to challenge the basic tripartite scheme itself. He himself does indeed have a view about 'what there is' and how it has come to be, and about the nature and role of humans within that. But for him the crucial question of 'theology' is not one sub-topic of investigation within that, but forms the much larger world within which 'physics' itself (not that he calls it that) ought to be located. Paul, in other words, remains a traditional Jew, believing that the one God of Abraham is not an item within the cosmos to be investigated like everything else, but the one 'from whom, through whom, and to whom are all things'.[22] He would, in other words, want to take the idea of 'god' out of the category of 'physics' in which pagan philosophy had placed it, seeing such placing as itself a failure to realize who the one God actually was. This single move already implies a radical change not only in 'physics', where 'the gods' had been located, but in 'ethics' and 'logic' as well, which were closely integrated with that basic analysis. Unless Paul was to break with his Jewish tradition entirely, 'ethics' would never be, for him, simply a matter of discerning the 'nature' either of the world, or of humans, and trying to live in accordance with it, though it would always involve that as well. It would always involve a direct address, a command, from the one God who is not *part* of the cosmos, nor yet detached from it, but remains in sovereign and dynamic relation with it.

Nor will Paul agree with the philosophers about 'logic'. For him, epistemology would never be simply a matter of learning how to translate the miscellany of information that arrives through the senses into a coherent and wise account of the world. The one God of Abraham is a god of *revelation* – not that 'revelation' ('apocalypse' in Greek) is antithetical to knowledge gained by observation of the world, since the one god is also the world's creator. Like God himself, Jesus is not simply one person about

[21] For the work of T. Engberg-Pedersen see below.

[22] Rom. 11.36. Yes, some philosophers said things like that too, but Paul understood that statement, and followed through its implications, in a typically Jewish way.

whom one might know certain things. He is the one in whom the very treasures of knowledge itself are hidden.

So Paul, after the manner of the annoying student who starts asking awkward questions before the lecture has properly begun, would almost certainly want to raise a question about the initial three-part division of the subject itself. He would want to privilege 'theology', in the sense we described earlier in the book, ahead of all the other topics, and to revise the meaning of the questions themselves, let alone the answers one might give, in that light.

I have said all this as a hypothesis: what Paul 'would have done', working outwards from what we know of his worldview and theology towards what we know of the philosophy of his day. But this is not merely imagination or guesswork. The supporting evidence is close at hand:

> ... We know that 'We all have knowledge'. Knowledge puffs you up, but love builds you up! If anybody thinks they 'know' something, they don't yet 'know' in the way they ought to know. But if anybody loves God, they are 'known' – by him.[23]

> However, at that stage you didn't know God, and so you were enslaved to beings that, in their proper nature, are not gods. But now that you've come to know God – or, better, to be known *by* God – how can you turn back again to that weak and poverty-stricken line-up of elements that you want to serve all over again?[24]

This is precisely a revision of the *epistemological* order: instead of humans acquiring knowledge of a variety of things within the whole cosmos, gods included, there is 'one God' who takes the initiative. God's 'knowing' creates the context for human 'knowing'; and the result is not a 'knowledge' such as one might have of a detached object (a tree, say, or a distant star). The result, to say it again, is love, *agapē*.

This suggests strongly that Paul would want to line up the three subjects of the philosophers with 'logic' (suitably reworked) at the head. Granted, 'how we know things' is a function of 'that which is known'. When we 'know' a musical theme, or a sibling, or a street in the town, we mean something different by the word 'know' in each case, and the means by which we gain that knowledge will be different, too. But if the overriding 'knowledge' is the knowledge which the one God has of the world, and of all its inhabitants, everything else will be seen in a new light as a result.

All this might have been said by a devout Jew (say, the author of the Wisdom of Solomon), though I am not aware that anyone said it quite that sharply before Paul. But there is a second element to the implicit challenge he would throw down to the philosophers. What has happened in and through Jesus the Messiah has resulted in a new sort of *knowledge* commensurate with the new *world* that has now been launched:

> From this moment on, therefore, we don't regard anybody from a merely human point of view. Even if we once regarded the Messiah that way, we don't do so any longer. Thus, if

[23] 1 Cor. 8.1–3, leading to Paul's 'revised *Shema*' (above, 661–70).

[24] Gal. 4.8f.

> anyone is in the Messiah, there is a new creation! Old things have gone, and look – everything has become new![25]

This passage has frequently been invoked in the service of various programmes, from Rudolf Bultmann's rejection of 'the historical Jesus' to J. Louis Martyn's 'apocalyptic'.[26] Paul is clearly revising the question of 'how we are to know anything or anyone at all' in the light of the 'new creation' which he believes has come about through the death and resurrection of the Messiah. (The specific point at issue in the larger context is how Paul's apostleship is to be understood; the Corinthians are assessing him in terms of the old creation, and Paul is insisting that everything must now be looked at in the light of the new one.) There is therefore a double epistemological shift which Paul would bring to the fore, prior to any discussion of specific points. Everything – 'physics', 'ethics' and even 'logic' itself – is to be seen in the light of the one God and of the new creation ushered in by the risen Messiah.

We must therefore look more closely, first, at the question of epistemology. What might Paul say on the topic designated by the philosophers as 'logic'?

(ii) 'Logic' and Epistemology

The wise owls of Athens were adept at peering into the darkness and seeing what others could not. But Paul was aware, partly because of Israel's scriptures and their vision of the one God, and partly because of what he believed about the Messiah, both that the darkness was deeper than had been thought and that a new day had already dawned which enabled one to see things that were previously invisible – including, remarkably, the one God himself, revealed in his 'image'.[27] Both of these – the deeper darkness and the new dawn – are important if we are to understand his epistemology and the way it related to, and in some respects challenged, the views of his contemporaries.

First, the deeper darkness. For Paul, this was not simply a matter of being led astray either by sense-perceptions or by the surface-level whims and passions of ordinary human life. It was a blindness of a different sort:

> However, if our gospel still remains 'veiled', it is veiled for people who are perishing. What's happening there is that the god of this world has blinded the minds of unbelievers, so that they won't see the light of the gospel of the glory of the Messiah, who is God's image.[28]

[25] 2 Cor. 5.16f.

[26] See Martyn's article (above, n. 7).

[27] 2 Cor. 4.1–6; Col. 1.15f.

[28] 2 Cor. 4.3f.

> You must no longer behave like the Gentiles, foolish-minded as they are. Their understanding is darkened; they are cut off from God's life because of their deep-seated ignorance, which springs from the fact that their hearts are hard. They have lost all moral sensitivity, and have given themselves over to whatever takes their fancy . . .[29]

> There was a time when you were excluded! You were enemies in your thinking, and in wicked behaviour.[30]

And, in the fullest statement of this type:

> The anger of God is unveiled from heaven against all the ungodliness and injustice performed by people who use injustice to suppress the truth. What can be known of God, you see, is plain to them, since God has made it plain to them. Ever since the world was made, his eternal power and deity have been seen and known in the things he made. As a result, they have no excuse: they knew God, but didn't honour him as God or thank him. Instead, they learned to think in useless ways, and their unwise heart grew dark. They declared themselves to be wise, but in fact they became foolish. They swapped the glory of the immortal God for the likeness of the image of mortal humans – and of birds, animals and reptiles . . . They swapped God's truth for a lie, and worshipped and served the creature rather than the creator, who is blessed for ever, Amen . . . Moreover, just as they did not see fit to hold on to knowledge of God, God gave them up to an unfit mind, so that they would behave inappropriately . . .[31]

This last passage introduces more complications. Paul is not simply stating that unbelievers have 'darkened' or blinded minds. He is providing a kind of historical aetiology for that condition, dependent for its full force on echoes of Genesis 3. Nor is he saying that the first humans knew God by observation of the created world but that since the Fall this has not been the case. He seems to be saying *both* that people still do have a basic knowledge of God *and* that everybody covers this up and learns distorted patterns of thought which result in, and are then in turn intensified by, distorted patterns of behaviour. It is no part of our purpose here to unravel all the mysteries of this paragraph in Romans 1. We have looked at those elsewhere.[32] What matters is Paul's overall point, throughout these various passages: the problem of true knowledge is not merely that appearances deceive, or that people make wrong inferences, but rather that human rebellion against the one God has resulted in a distortion and a darkening of the knowledge that humans have, or still ought to have. Paul would want to say to the philosophers that wisdom is not simply a matter of learning to see, like the owls, in ordinary darkness. It is a matter of the one God piercing the darkness and bringing new light, the light of new creation, and at the same time opening the eyes that have been blinded by 'the god of this world' so that they can see that light.

That is why his basic exhortation in Romans 12, balancing the devastating analysis in chapter 1 of the distorted mind and behaviour, has to do with

[29] Eph. 4.17–19.

[30] Col. 1.21.

[31] Rom. 1.18–23, 25, 28.

[32] Above, 764–71; and see Wright 2002 [*Romans*], 428–36.

eschatological renewal: 'Don't let yourselves be squeezed into the shape dictated by the present age', he says.

> Instead, be transformed by the renewing of your minds, so that you can work out what God's will is, what is good, acceptable and complete.[33]

This in turn is cognate with what he says about the 'mind of the flesh' and the 'mind of the spirit' in Romans 8:

> People whose lives are determined by human flesh focus their minds on matters to do with the flesh, but people whose lives are determined by the spirit focus their minds on matters to do with the spirit. Focus the mind on the flesh, and you'll die; but focus it on the spirit, and you'll have life, and peace. The mind focused on the flesh, you see, is hostile to God. It doesn't submit to God's law; in fact, it can't. Those who are determined by the flesh can't please God.
>
> But you're not people of flesh; you're people of the spirit . . .[34]

If the problem has to do with the unrenewed 'mind', the 'mind of the flesh', then the solution – the way to see again after all this darkness – is for the spirit to perform a work in the mind as much as in the heart or the body:

> The spirit, you see, searches everything, yes, even the depths of God. Think of it this way: who knows what is really going on inside a person, except the spirit of the person which is inside them? Well, it's like that with God. Nobody knows what is going on inside God except God's spirit. And we haven't received the spirit of the world, but the spirit that comes from God, so that we can know the things that have been given to us by God.
>
> That, then, is what we speak. We don't use words we've been taught by human wisdom, but words we've been taught by the spirit, interpreting spiritual things to spiritual people.
>
> Someone living at the merely human level doesn't accept the things of God's spirit. They are foolishness to such people, you see, and they can't understand them because they need to be discerned spiritually. But spiritual people discern everything, while nobody else can discern the truth about them! For 'Who has known the mind of the lord, so as to instruct him?' But we have the mind of the Messiah.[35]

This is of course an extraordinary claim: to have privileged access to the mind of the one God himself, through the Messiah. But it might appear to raise a further problem for Paul, which we must examine briefly.

The claim in 1 Corinthians 2 might appear to create a kind of private epistemological world. Paul might be taken to be referring to an inner sanctum of spirit-given 'knowledge', which would cut off the possessor from all ordinary human knowledge, and also cut off the non-possessor from any access to the gospel. Paul, however, clearly does not believe this. In fact, he sees it the other way round: as far as he is concerned, *the closed, private world is the dark and dangerous 'natural world' where most people live.* To this extent, and to this extent only, his epistemology could be seen on the

[33] Rom. 12.2.

[34] Rom. 8.5–9.

[35] 1 Cor. 2.10–16.

analogy with Plato's famous picture of the Cave.[36] The people in the cave are restricted in their knowledge because all they can see is a distorted set of shadows and reflections. The ones who turn to the light and come out of the cave can then see everything clearly, including the things that were producing the flickering images they could see before. Paul believed that when his powerful gospel was proclaimed it opened people's eyes to the reality not only of the one God and his Messiah but also to the realities of the rest of the world, including those areas where they would have obligations and duties. Precisely because the God in whom Paul believed was the one God of creation, as we shall see in more detail in a moment, he believed that knowledge of this God – or rather, as he himself puts it, being known by this God – opened a person's eyes to see *the whole world* as it truly was.

No doubt Paul would recognize that the people he calls 'unspiritual' or 'merely human' would think that it was they who were seeing the world truly. Paul would expect them to repay his compliment and suggest that it was actually Paul and others like him who were living in a world of private fantasy. That might, as well, be Paul's own verdict on (for instance) the adherents of the mystery religions. But what Paul believed about what the philosophers called 'physics' – namely, that there was one God who had made the whole world through his second self, the one whom Paul knew as Jesus the Messiah – meant that knowledge of this one God and one lord, in a mind renewed by the one true spirit, provided an unrivalled knowledge of the world as it really was. Just as the philosophers linked logic to physics, and both to ethics, so Paul's epistemology reflected exactly his vision of divinely created reality.

This accords completely with the position we find in Israel's scriptures; and indeed Paul regarded those scriptures, when read properly in the light of the Messiah,[37] as a major source of real knowledge. Of course, his way of reading them was controversial in his day and is controversial still today. But few will question that he regarded scripture, rightly interpreted, as giving him the solid basis from which to work. And scripture itself spoke of the creator God as knowable through his creation. Thus, even though Paul undoubtedly accorded a special status to scripture, we should not see that as standing over against the revelation in creation, but actually as pointing to it, intertwined with it, and celebrating its fulfilment and redemption.[38] That is how Paul's creational monotheism worked.

Once the premises of knowledge are established, however, Paul was only too ready to engage in the kind of logical argument which characterized the philosophers of his day. Within that new knowledge, and as a clear sign that it did not cancel out ordinary knowledge of the world but rather took it up within itself, Paul could and did use some of the regular rhetorical tools that

[36] Plato, *Rep.* bk. VII.

[37] As opposed to the blindfolded reading of those 'whose minds are hardened' as in 2 Cor. 3.14f.; see above, 980–4.

[38] e.g. Ps. 19 etc., quoted by Paul in Rom. 10.18. On the fulfilment and redemption of creation cf. of course Rom. 8.18–25.

were employed as ways of poking and prodding at ideas and themes to be sure they were in good order. Ever since Socrates engaged in 'dialogues' whose aim was to probe deeper into the things people said and make them clarify or modify what they meant, the various schools had used the tools of logic to move from the things that could be taken as known to other things that might follow from them. As we saw, the 'diatribe' style, reproducing the kind of question-and-answer format of public disputation, was one such tool, designed to make sure that a subject was being thought through thoroughly. Paul used it sparingly, but it is noticeable that he employed it particularly when, for instance in parts of Romans, he was probing deeper into some of the densest areas of his theology – particularly the question of the fate of Israel.[39]

I would not myself build too much on this one way or another. Paul's use of the 'diatribe' does not mean, on the one hand, that he was smuggling in Stoic logic by the back door or, on the other hand, that he was simply being inconsistent, leaning on a stick he had himself declared to be broken. His claim to understand – indeed to possess! – 'the mind of the Messiah' was not a claim that he and his congregations now knew everything there was to know, and had no need to think things through. Rather, his claim was that his, and their, human minds were being transformed by the spirit so that they were able at last to understand the full, deep truths about the world. But for that one needed to think clearly, which is where the 'diatribe' could help.

This is not the place to follow up the point in any detail. Suffice it to say that his deployment of this tool serves as a reminder of how he understood knowledge itself. Someone who has access to privileged and incontrovertible information, fresh from a divine source, does not argue. The Pythia at Delphi spoke in hexameters; she did not normally use words like *gar*, *oun*, *dioti* and the other regular connectives by which logicians mounted their case. Argument is what happens when, starting from a given point, one wishes not simply to inform one's hearers of divine truth but to convince them of other truths, other aspects of truth, which follow from those first premises. Paul is quite capable of appealing to basic truths that do not need arguing – the gospel events of Jesus' death and resurrection, for instance, and their unveiling of the *dikaiosynē* and *sophia* of the one God. His regular use of the tools of argument shows that, for him, the understanding and wisdom he wishes his hearers to possess must mesh with their understanding of everything else. He is not inviting them to share a small, private world. He is helping them to think through public truth.

Paul would therefore wish to say to the philosophers of his day that, though their aim of thinking everything through and proceeding by logical steps from the known to the unknown was right and proper, they were always in danger of being trapped in the darkness from which they claimed to be able to free others. Above all, his *eschatological* vision meant that as far

[39] On the 'diatribe' see above, 222, 224, 453, 458.

as he was concerned the night was already nearly over, and those who belonged to the Messiah were able to see clearly things which were still puzzling to everybody else. The owls of Athens might claim to see in the dark, but once the new day was dawning a new kind of seeing would be available.

(iii) 'What There Is': Paul's Comments on 'Physics'

The second category of ancient philosophical investigation is the large and many-sided topic of 'physics': what there is in *physis*, nature. As we saw in the introductory remarks to this chapter, for Paul this did not include 'god' or 'the gods', because the one God was the creator of the world, not part of it. Though he never discusses head on the question of how the world came to be, every time he gets near the question, in pursuit of a different theme, it is clear what his answer would be. He assumes the ancient Jewish view that the world is the creation of the one God, and that therefore it is not to be identified with that God (as in pantheism) nor to be seen as the disastrous handiwork either of blind chance (the Epicurean view) or of a malevolent subsidiary deity (as in some gnostic systems). But Paul has gone a step further than this Jewish view. He has taken the ancient scriptural theme of 'wisdom' as the divine assistant in creation, and has construed this dramatically in terms of Jesus himself – or rather, we should say, in terms of the mysterious one, the second self of the one God, who became human *in and as* Jesus of Nazareth. We have already explored this in chapter 9, and need only refer to the two most obvious texts in which Paul does not advance a theory about *how* the one God made the world except to say that he did it in, through and for his image-bearing son:

> There is one God, the father,
> from whom are all things, and we live to him and for him;
> and one lord, Jesus the Messiah,
> through whom are all things, and we live through him.[40]

Through whom are all things; that is the point, the thing that marks out Paul from his Jewish neighbours on the one hand (who, even if they thought of 'wisdom' as the handmaid of the one God, did not think of this figure as an actual human being) and his pagan conversation partners on the other. This is then amplified dramatically in the great poem of Colossians 1:

> He is the image of God, the invisible one,
>   the firstborn of all creation.
> For in him all things were created,
>   in the heavens and here on the earth.
> Things we can see and things we cannot,
>   – thrones and lordships and rulers and powers –
> all things were created both through him and for him.[41]

[40] 1 Cor. 8.6; see above, 661–70.

[41] Col. 1.15f.

This is dramatic enough as an account of creation and its purpose. But there is more: Paul believes that in this same Jesus the *new* creation has now come into being:

> He is the start of it all,
> firstborn from realms of the dead;
> so in all things he might be the chief.
> For in him all the Fullness was glad to dwell
> and through him to reconcile all to himself,
> making peace through the blood of his cross,
> through him – yes, things on the earth,
> and also the things in the heavens.[42]

It is this robust version of the Jewish monotheistic doctrine of creation that underlies Paul's equally robust affirmation that the present world of space, time and matter is itself good. That is why marital union is good in itself (1 Corinthians 7), why all meat is good in itself, even if offered to an idol (1 Corinthians 8, 10), why all time, all days, are basically the same in the sight of the one God (Romans 14.5). Here we see the *creational* element of Paul's inaugurated eschatology. One might have imagined that, if the new creation had already been launched, everything about the old one would become not only irrelevant but somehow shabby, tarnished, shown up as in some sense actually evil, so that Paul would be advocating escape. Not at all. For Paul the old creation has, of course, been relativized. It no longer assumes cultural, or even cultic, significance. But it remains good, and can be enjoyed if received with thanksgiving.[43] The new world, already launched with Jesus' resurrection, reaffirms the essential goodness of the old one even as it relativizes its ultimate significance. As with the biblical texts on which he drew, Paul understood the entire created order not as a static entity to be observed but as part of a *narrative*, a narrative which had now, he believed, entered its long-awaited new phase.

His pagan interlocutors might well not have understood this point. The Stoics, of course, believed in a great coming conflagration after which the world would start up all over again; but, as we shall see later, that is not at all the same as what Paul was talking about in his vision of new creation. And it was this vision that, I suggest, would have been at the heart of what he might have wanted to say to them when discussing 'physics'.

This *eschatological* version of *creational monotheism* was deeply embedded in Paul's thinking, emerging in various classic passages such as Romans 8 or 1 Corinthians 15. It frames the account he gives of two of the major topics of philosophy, and of ancient 'physics': what it means to be human, and what account we should give of death. Clearly, he believes that humans are made in the image of the creator, and that this like everything else is to be *renewed* through the action of Messiah and spirit.[44] This gives a more

[42] Col. 1.18–20.

[43] Rom. 14.6; 1 Cor. 10.30.

[44] Rom. 8.29; Col. 3.10; cf. 2. Cor. 4.4–6.

precise focus, and again a narrative framework, to the widespread ancient belief that humans stood in some close relationship to the divine. As for death, Paul would firmly have agreed with the Wisdom of Solomon, which opposed the Epicurean proposal, and insisted that death was not after all the end of the person concerned, but that the creator looked after the souls of the dead (or at least the righteous dead) until the time of his fresh 'visitation'.[45] And Paul's vision of new creation, including bodily resurrection, was of course significantly different from the various other ancient visions, whether Platonic or Stoic or whatever, of what might happen at individual death.[46] Death as we know it was for Paul an intruder into the good creation, and it had now been defeated.

All this means that Paul conceived of the relationship between the world and the divine – one of the most significant features of any worldview! – in a significantly different way from any of his non-Jewish philosophical contemporaries. He might have had some sympathy for Plato's belief that one ought to look through and beyond the material world to the transcendent truths that might be glimpsed there as if behind a veil, but he would have had none at all for the way some of his contemporaries were interpreting the Platonic tradition to the effect that the material world was essentially a bad place from which one ought to long to escape. He might have recognized in Aristotle's argument for a 'prime mover' an analogy at least to his own view that creation provided a good reason to believe in a creator, but would certainly have rejected the dry, impersonal vision of this creator in favour of the personal and compassionate divinity of Israel's scriptures, the God of Exodus, of Isaiah, of the Psalms, who had now been made known more specifically in and as Jesus the Messiah. He would have insisted, against the Epicureans, that the one God was not far removed from the world, but was present and active within it. He would certainly have made the point that, though the world was indeed on a journey, so that one could tell its story, that story was destined to end not in the ultimate dissolution of its entire atomic structure but in the complete new creation, which would put all wrongs to right at last. But the presence and activity of the one God within creation was not, as in Stoicism, a matter of a divine *pneuma* or fiery presence animating everything, so that 'the divine' was present everywhere because everything was already 'divine'. The God in whom Paul believed was present to and within the world, and especially to and within human beings, but was not contained within the world or humans. Rather, he was present *alongside*, and in a sense *over against*, the world and humans, guiding, calling to account, challenging and enabling. He was present, supremely and shockingly, in Jesus himself, a human of recent memory; and he was present in a special way, different on the one hand from his presence in Jesus but different on the other hand from his presence everywhere else, in those who were now indwelt by 'the spirit of Jesus'. Such people were *pneumatikoi*,

[45] Wis. 3.7; see above, 241, and *RSG* 167f.

[46] See *RSG* ch. 2.

'spirit-animated' people, as opposed to the merely *psychikoi*, humans whose inner principle was the *psychē*, the ordinary human life rather than the Jesus-shaped divine life.[47]

To say all this clearly was, we may suppose, as hard for Paul as it is for us. To approach the frontier between the human and the divine is also to approach the borders of language. This problem emerges, for instance, when he talks about 'the divine spirit bearing witness with our spirit',[48] and the problem is only slightly alleviated when he talks instead about the divine spirit residing in a person's 'heart'.[49] The questions English-language exegetes sometimes ask, as to whether 'spirit' should have a capital letter or not, indicating the divine spirit rather than the human one, shows well enough that there is fluidity of thought at this point. And this fluidity is found not only at the interrelation, in specifically Christian terms, between the divine spirit (or the spirit of Jesus) and the human spirit. It is found at the interrelation between this very specific and restricted use of *pneuma* and the one that was popular in the world of Paul's Stoic contemporaries, for whom the fiery divine 'breath' indwelt everything and everyone, irrespective of their beliefs or style of life.[50] If we ask why Paul would choose such a well-known word and give it a significantly different meaning, we may suspect that the answer would lie in the scriptural explanations that had been given, from the earliest days of the Christian movement, for the strange phenomenon of people finding themselves given new energy, a new sense of direction and above all a strong sense of the personal presence of Jesus, experienced in the way one might expect to experience the presence of the one God himself. Paul seems to have chosen to go on using this potentially confusing word because of these roots, believing that what he and the other followers of Jesus were experiencing was the inauguration of the promised new covenant.[51]

Paul believed, in particular, that the whole world was being called to account by the one God. It was neither moving ahead randomly towards dissolution, nor was it heading for a cosmic conflagration in which the fiery *pneuma* already operative within it would transform everything else into fire and then start it all up once more. Paul's eschatology, in other words, was quite different from the vision both of the Epicurean and of the Stoic. His worldview at this point, as elsewhere, was basically Jewish, assuming that the one God who had made the world was responsible, as creator, for putting it right – that is, for judging and remaking it. This God had promised, in the scriptures, to do exactly that. And, as we saw in chapter 11, and in line with the rest of his worldview and theology, Paul had rethought this vision of eschatological judgment around Jesus himself, Israel's Messiah and

[47] cf. esp. 1 Cor. 2.14f. On the meaning of *pneumatikos* see below.

[48] Rom. 8.16.

[49] e.g. Gal. 4.6; cf. Rom. 2.29 etc.

[50] This, indeed, may be the explanation of why, from early on, Christians referred to the 'spirit' of which they were speaking as 'the *holy* spirit'.

[51] For the biblical and Jewish roots of Paul's spirit-language see above, 709–28.

hence the one through whom, as in Psalm 2, the One God would call the nations to account. If Jesus' resurrection thus declared to the world that he was indeed Israel's Messiah, it also, *ipso facto*, announced him as judge.[52]

Paul's implicit engagement with the philosophers on the question of 'physics' was therefore, unsurprisingly, a variation on the position that might have been taken by some of his Jewish contemporaries. It is, in this respect, not unlike that of the Wisdom of Solomon. There, too, the rulers of the world were to be held to account before the one God. There, too, the ancient story of God's rescue of his people from Egypt was retold both as foundation myth and as paradigm. Paul had thought through, and was both arguing and living, a specifically Christian variation on this: in Jesus, the rulers had already been judged; the new exodus had already taken place; and a family had been brought into being indwelt by the divine 'wisdom' that had been active in creation and in the story of Israel, and that had now come to dwell fully in Jesus and in his spirit-led people. This is how he puts it in Colossians:

> We are instructing everybody and teaching everybody in every kind of wisdom, so that we can present everybody grown up, complete, in the king . . . I want their hearts to be encouraged as they're brought together in love. I want them to experience all the wealth of definite understanding, and to come to the knowledge of God's mystery – the Messiah, the king! He is the place where you'll find all the hidden treasures of wisdom and knowledge.[53]

His vision of the cosmos, therefore – his answer to the philosophical debates about 'physics' – was characterized through and through by *agapē*: the outflowing love which led the creator God to make a world in the first place, the radical love which led the Messiah to die and now the uniting love which bound together all those who had embraced the Messiah in faith and hope. This vision of reality led naturally, as did the 'physics' of his contemporaries, to the third question: how then should humans behave?

(iv) 'Ethics'

The difference between Paul's ethics and those of his philosophical contemporaries can be summed up easily. They believed that once one had discovered and understood ('logic') what the world was, how it worked and what human beings actually were ('physics'), it was the task of humans to live in accordance with that, rather than against its grain ('ethics'). Paul believed that *the world had been renewed in the Messiah*; that those who were themselves 'in the Messiah' had also been renewed as image-bearing human beings; and that the task of such people was to live in accordance with the *new* world, rather than against *its* grain. Since for Paul, as we saw, this

[52] All this, of course, corresponds very well to the short summary of what Luke supposed Paul might have said in Athens: Ac. 17.22–31 (on which see Rowe 2011).

[53] Col. 1.28; 2.2f.

renewal did not mean the abolition of the good creation but rather its transformation and fulfilment (that, of course, is part of the meaning of the resurrection), and since the renewal had been *inaugurated within the ongoing flow of history* rather than arriving complete all at once, there is a natural and considerable overlap between what Paul saw as living in accordance with the new creation and what his contemporaries saw as living in accordance with the world as they knew it. For Paul, the renewal of *the existing creation* was just as important as *the renewal* of the existing creation. Without the second, one would be trapped in a world of inevitable entropy. Without the first, the idea of new creation would collapse into some kind of gnosticism. We should not therefore be surprised to find all kinds of parallels between Paul's 'ethics' and those of his contemporaries, even though again and again Paul has *framed* his account of proper Christian behaviour in a quite different way. Any account of Paul and his philosophical contemporaries will want to clarify both the differences and the similarities.[54]

1. First, the differences. This is how Paul makes his characteristic appeal: on the basis of the new identity of the Christian, who has in baptism shared the dying and rising of the Messiah, and must live in accordance with the new world which has broken in already upon the continuing old one:

> We died to sin; how can we still live in it? Don't you know that all of us who were baptized into the Messiah, Jesus, were baptized into his death? That means that we were buried with him, through baptism, into death, so that, just as the Messiah was raised from the dead through the father's glory, we too might behave with a new quality of life ... So don't allow sin to rule in your mortal body, to make you obey its desires. Nor should you present your limbs and organs to sin to be used for its wicked purposes. Rather, present yourselves to God, as people alive from the dead, and your limbs and organs to God, to be used for the righteous purposes of his covenant.[55]

> Don't let yourselves be squeezed into the shape dictated by the present age. Instead, be transformed by the renewing of your minds, so that you can work out what God's will is, what is good, acceptable and complete.[56]

> The body is not meant for immorality, but for the lord, and the lord for the body. What's more, God raised the lord; and he will raise us, too, through his power ...
>
> Or don't you know that your body is a temple of the holy spirit within you, the spirit God gave you, so that you don't belong to yourselves? You were quite an expensive purchase! So glorify God in your body.[57]

> There are several people who behave as enemies of the cross of the Messiah ... They are on the road to destruction; their stomach is their god, and they find glory in their own shame. All they ever think about is what's on the earth.
>
> We are citizens of heaven, you see, and we're eagerly waiting for the saviour, the lord, King Jesus, who is going to come from there. Our present body is a shabby old thing, but he's going to transform it so that it's just like his glorious body ...[58]

[54] On Paul's 'ethics' within his eschatology see 1101–28.

[55] Rom. 6.2–4, 12–13.

[56] Rom. 12.2.

[57] 1 Cor. 6.13f., 19f.

[58] Phil. 3.18–21.

> That [old] way of life is decaying, as a result of deceitful lusts. Instead, you must be renewed in the spirit of your mind, and you must put on the new humanity, which is being created the way God intended it, displaying justice and genuine holiness.[59]

> So if you were raised to life with the king, search for the things that are above, where the king is seated at God's right hand! Think about the things that are above, not the things that belong on the earth. Don't you see: you died, and your life has been hidden with the king, in God! When the king is revealed (and he is your life, remember), then you too will be revealed with him in glory.
>
> So, then, you must kill off the parts of you that belong on the earth ... [there follows a double list, of sexual sins on the one hand and sins of the tongue on the other] ... You have stripped off the old human nature, complete with its patterns of behaviour, and you have put on the new one – which is being renewed in the image of the creator, bringing you into possession of new knowledge.[60]

> ... you should continue more and more to behave in the manner that you received from us as the appropriate way of behaving and of pleasing God. You know, of course, what instructions we gave you through the lord Jesus. This is God's will, you see: he wants you to be holy, to keep well away from fornication. Each of you should know how to control your own body in holiness and honour, not in the madness of lust like Gentiles who don't know God ... Anyone who rejects this, then, is not rejecting a human command, but the God who gives his holy spirit to you.[61]

This is only the small tip of a large iceberg. Passage after passage in Paul gives evidence of the same frame of reference: the creator God has renewed the world through Jesus, and is renewing you by his spirit, so your bodies in the present must be brought into line with their future resurrected identity – not as an effort after the impossible, but as the making real of the new identity already given in baptism.[62] The people who have experienced the new exodus must learn, as the people of the first exodus did not entirely learn, what it means to be both free from Egypt and the dwelling-place of the living God.[63] That combination of rescue from slavery and new-temple theology characterizes Paul's thinking at point after point, providing the strong narrative framework which underlies and gives direction to the general standards on which he insists and the particular commands he addresses to the young churches. Paul has a rich, complex but coherent vision of what has happened in the Messiah, both cosmically (generating a whole new world which now sits uncomfortably alongside the continuing old one) and personally for those who belong to him. That, for instance, is why suffering is so important for Paul: it is the sign that one is indeed living at that dangerous fault-line. At point after point what he says about personal life ('ethics') reflects exactly what he says or implies about the cosmos ('physics'). He knows about both, and so do the young churches, because

[59] Eph. 4.22–4.

[60] Col. 3.1–10.

[61] 1 Thess. 4.1–8.

[62] It is commonly supposed that Rom. 6 does not share the vision of Eph. 1 and Col. 2—3, according to which the baptized are *already* 'raised with the Messiah'; but this is a misapprehension. See Wright 2002 [*Romans*], 538.

[63] 1 Cor. 10.1–10; Rom. 8.12–17.

their understanding has been enlightened by the spirit so that they can see what remains opaque to the rest of the world, and can think clearly and appropriately about it all ('logic').

We might expect that Paul and his churches, as exodus-people, would set themselves to keep Torah; and the answer is that they do and they don't. We shall come to that in the next chapter. There is a sense in which Messiah and spirit together accomplish, in and through believers, 'what the Torah could not do', producing the same result – the transformation of character into a genuine God-reflecting humanness and the 'life' which results – but by a different route. That is what Paul hints at in various passages, such as Romans 2 and 2 Corinthians 3.[64] But the implicit difference between him and his philosophical contemporaries is not that he has a particular lawcode to follow, given by the God of Israel, and they do not. Nor is the difference to be found in any suggestion that Paul believed in a more or less instantaneous conversion while those in the philosophical tradition looked for a steady process of moral transformation. That, actually, represents a point of similarity, as we shall see in a moment. The implicit difference is both in his *framing perspective*, which as we saw is that of a new-creation eschatology that has been fulfilled in Jesus the Messiah and is now being energized by the divine *pneuma*, and more specifically in the *character* which has been glimpsed in Jesus, both in himself and particularly in his dying and rising.[65] As I have argued elsewhere, Paul does indeed teach what we may call a virtue ethic. He believes in moral progress, and in the hard work required to make it happen. He has, as it were, taken the classical tradition of 'virtue', all the way from Plato and Aristotle to Cicero and beyond, and has reworked it into a Christian key.[66] But at the head of his list of virtues he regularly places *agapē*, the 'love' which he has seen revealed in the Messiah. Like other early Christian moralists he adds three other virtues which, like *agapē* itself, were more or less unknown in the world of paganism: patience, chastity and humility. About these things we do not need here to speak in any detail, except to draw attention to these as striking differences of content, corresponding to the radical differences of framing, between Paul and his pagan philosophical contemporaries.[67]

2. Second, then, the similarities. As we have noted, because for Paul the new creation is the renewal of the existing world, not its abandonment and replacement, there is a good deal of overlap between the behaviour he expects of Jesus' followers and the behaviour that many pagan moralists would have urged. We noted at the start of the chapter Paul's positive and encouraging exhortation to think about anything that is true, holy, upright,

[64] Rom. 2.25–9; 2 Cor. 3.3–18.

[65] cf. Eph. 4.21 and Phil. 2.6–11, with the discussion above, 1097f., 1115–20.

[66] See Wright 2010 [*Virtue Reborn/After You Believe*], *passim*. On 'moral formation' in Paul see now Thompson 2011.

[67] See *Virtue Reborn/After You Believe*, esp. chs. 5, 6, 7. On the four early Christian 'virtues' unknown to the ancient pagan world (patience, chastity, humility and love) see Blackburn 2008 [1994], 381, discussed in *Virtue Reborn* 114, 214–20 (= *After You Believe* 131f., 248–55).

pure, attractive, of good reputation, virtuous or praiseworthy. True, he balances this with the command to copy *him* (as opposed to copying the world around) in matters of specific behaviour. But the open invitation to contemplate all that is good or worthwhile in the wider non-Christian environment is a clear hint that we should expect overlap; and this is what we find. He can appeal to general and widely known beliefs of what is 'good' or 'evil'. Christian standards are by no means purely discontinuous with those of everyone else.[68] In the same passage, he urges the Roman Christians to celebrate with those who are celebrating, and to mourn with the mourners. There may be some celebrations from which the Christians will hold back, but Paul wants to emphasize the call to be, basically, good neighbours.[69]

In particular, Paul anticipates the second-century apologists in wanting the followers of Jesus to make a good impression on the society around them. They are not to be awkward or snooty; they must not give the appearance of thinking themselves superior.[70] 'Think through', he says, 'what will seem good to everyone who is watching', and if possible live at peace with everyone.[71] They are to 'behave wisely towards outsiders', or 'in a way that outsiders will respect', buying up every opportunity to do good to all, and to speak a fresh, clear word in answer to any challenge. They are to give no occasion for sneers or grumbles, for instance by not paying bills on time.[72] Though their primary obligation of care is to fellow Christians, if they get the chance to be of benefit to others they should take it eagerly.[73]

This, I suggest, is the context within which we should understand the 'household codes', lists of guidelines for husbands and wives, parents and children, masters and slaves.[74] These are emphatically for a community which is living out an eschatology inaugurated but not yet consummated. Paul treads a fine line (some would say he loses his balance here, and/or that the passages in question thereby demonstrate a non-Pauline authorship) between challenging followers of Jesus to live counter-culturally, being radically different from those around, and merely accommodating to the prevailing cultural mores.[75] Paul is well aware of likely charges that might be brought against followers of Jesus: people might well say that they were socially, culturally or politically subversive in ways which were not in fact a reflection of the gospel. He is determined that his communities will order their common lives, not least their family lives, in such a way that the only things people will find to say against them will be to do with their basic allegiance to Jesus. Many writers today seem to expect that all morality will be reduced to the liberal ideals of western society in the early years of the

[68] Rom. 12.9.

[69] Rom. 12.15.

[70] Rom. 12.16.

[71] Rom. 12.17f.

[72] Col. 4.5f.; 1 Thess. 4.11f.

[73] Gal. 6.10; 1 Thess. 3.12; 5.15; this is probably part of the meaning, too, of Eph. 2.10.

[74] See too above, 1108.

[75] The key passages are Eph. 5.21—6.9; Col. 3.18—4.1.

twenty-first century, and then to complain that the early Christians ought to have said this more clearly than they seem to have done. This has made it harder for us to understand, let alone to appreciate, Paul's agenda. It is, however, often noted that he significantly modifies the expectations of his day, not least by emphasizing the obligations of husbands to wives, parents to children and masters to slaves (not just the subservience of those wives, children and slaves), by adding 'in the lord' at various points, and, in the case of Ephesians 5, building a remarkable theology of marriage on the model of the Messiah himself and his death. Even when Paul is saying things which are similar to what one might have heard in the moralism of his day, he regularly adds another dimension which subtly and profoundly changes the whole mood and impact.[76]

The point seems to be, above all, that he believes in the *rehumanizing* power of the gospel of Jesus. The gospel is not meant to make people odd or less than fully human; it is meant to renew them in their genuine, image-bearing humanness. We should expect, then, to find that standards emphasized in the finest contemporary philosophers would be echoed by Paul. We can find plenty of shrewd and wise words about drunkenness, sexual misbehaviour, anger and violence, lying and deceit, honesty and hard work in Cicero, Seneca or Epictetus, as well as in Paul. The many parallels here would only be surprising to someone who supposed that Paul derived everything from Torah on the one hand and the teaching of Jesus on the other, and indeed that those two sources would themselves be completely discontinuous with pagan moralism. Such assumptions would be straightforwardly invalid. But, as with 'parallelomania' in other spheres, so here: it will not do simply to amass a list of places where Paul can be matched in his moral teaching by Epictetus, Musonius Rufus or whoever. (Or indeed the other way round, first expounding the Stoics and then finding parallels in Paul![77]) The point is that Paul thinks he has found a way to the genuine humanness which the philosophers have glimpsed but cannot actually attain. One might highlight, for example, his insistence towards the end of Philippians that he has learned how to be *autarkēs*, 'content' in the sense of being self-sufficient. The state of *autarkeia* was a favourite virtue with Cynics and Stoics as well as (perhaps more obviously) Epicureans. The latter sought that state through retiring from the world and learning to be content, like the gods as they imagined them, in a quiet and happy detachment.[78] The Cynics and Stoics sought this same state through training themselves not to need the usual pleasures of life and to make do with whatever circumstances came their way.[79] Paul is at this point closer to the Stoics, but again the claim to have arrived at this particular goal is framed in a specifically Christian way:

[76] For suggestions down this line cf. e.g. Maier 2005.

[77] e.g. Engberg-Pedersen, on whom see below.

[78] See Epicurus in Diog. Laert. 10.130.

[79] e.g. *SVF* 3.67.3; 3.68.5. Socrates was seen as *autarkēs*: Diog. Laert. 2.24.

> I'm not talking about lacking anything. I've learnt to be content [*autarkēs*] with what I have. I know how to do without, and I know how to cope with plenty. In every possible situation I've learned the hidden secret of being full and hungry, of having plenty and going without, and it's this: I have strength for everything in the one who gives me power.[80]

Paul is affirming the goal; but he is also claiming that the best way to arrive at it is through following Jesus, hard though that road will be. He does not, however, affirm either the Epicurean goal of *ataraxia*, an untroubled life, or the Stoic/Cynic goal of *apatheia*, the state in which one no longer feels suffering. Paul has plenty of troubles, and plenty of suffering, and accepts them not only as the natural and necessary concomitant of his calling, and indeed of following the crucified Jesus, but also as the lens through which true knowledge is glimpsed. The philosophers suppose one may come to true knowledge by avoiding suffering; Paul, by embracing it. There are places where his road enables him to link arms with the philosophers, but their respective journeys began in different places, and they will eventually come to a parting of their ways. They are, after all, heading for the city of *eudaimonia*, and he for the city of the crucified and risen Messiah.[81] Once again, Paul's underlying theology of *renewed humanity in the Messiah* explains this easily. He has not derived his moral framework from the surrounding philosophies, but he is happy to recognize that at many points the Christian is called to walk the path of genuine humanness that others have sketched before – and perhaps to do so more effectively.

All this demands, I think, that we read certain Pauline texts in at least a bifocal fashion. One obvious passage in which Paul appears to be echoing several pagan moralists is Romans 7, where Paul joins a long line from Aristotle onwards in complaining (through the medium of the first person singular, the 'I', which like many exegetes I understand as a rhetorical ploy rather than actual autobiography) that 'I don't do the good thing I want to do, but I end up doing the evil thing I don't want to do.'[82] This is the classic problem of *akrasia*, 'weakness of will'.[83] It has been proposed that Paul, here and perhaps elsewhere, is claiming as a major point that being 'in Christ' enables one to attain the self-mastery at which the philosophical schools, especially Stoicism, were aiming. There is a sense in which I agree with this, but only in the following way.

Romans 7.7–25, and indeed on into 8.1–11, is primarily an argument about Israel's Torah; that, as I have argued elsewhere, is the referent of *nomos* throughout, puzzling though that may initially seem in some passages. As part of Paul's large-scale retelling of the exodus-story, between the slaves going through the water to find freedom in chapter 6 and their 'inheriting' of the promised new creation in chapter 8, the Passover-people must

[80] Phil. 4.11–13.

[81] Paul is not interested in *eudaimonia* as such, and the attempt to suggest he is is one of the many ways in which Engberg-Pedersen misunderstands him: see below.

[82] Rom. 7.19.

[83] See Wright 2002 [*Romans*], 549–72; and e.g. Keener 2009, 93f. with classical references.

come to Mount Sinai, where they discover the strange truth about Torah, as we set it out in our chapters 7, 10 and 11 above: Torah was given with a deliberately negative intent, to highlight 'sin' and make it appear 'very sinful indeed'.[84] Paul will then go on to show that 'God has done what the law . . . was incapable of doing' (8.3): that in the Messiah and by the spirit the one God has given the 'life' which Torah could not, because it was 'weak because of human flesh' – in other words, because the raw material the Torah was working on, namely the people of Israel, was, like everyone else, incapable of obedience and so of finding the life which Torah promised (7.10).

But that larger framework of argument is just that, a framework. Simply to offer that analysis of the passage would be almost (though not quite) as inadequate as identifying it as part of Paul's spiritual autobiography and leaving it at that. I do think that there is a sense in which the passage as I have outlined it functions as a kind of autobiography, but *not* because 'that's how it felt at the time'. Philippians 3.4–6, as has often been pointed out, makes it clear that it was not at all how it felt for Paul the 'zealous' Jew. Rather, this is a *retrospective theological* autobiography: this is how Paul, as a man 'in the Messiah', now analyzes *what in fact was going on*, even though at the time he neither felt it like this nor saw it like this. But this, too, is only part of the complete analysis that must be offered. Paul, like the mature Mozart, was quite capable of writing several different musical lines to be sung at the same time, and we must not be put off by the spiritual heirs of the Austrian Emperor who complained that there were 'too many notes'.[85] The crucial point for the present chapter is that Paul has carefully and deliberately set out his retrospective theological analysis of the plight of the devout Jew under Torah *in terms of the well-known dilemma of the pagan moralists.*

This is, if you like, the negative corollary of the positive point made a moment ago, that when Paul saw what life in the Messiah was really like in terms of renewed humanity it was bound to overlap with what non-Christian moralists had glimpsed as the way to behave. This was entailed by Paul's belief in creational (and now eschatological) monotheism: if humanity was really being restored in and through Messiah and spirit, one would not expect the result to be out of step at every point with the best that the rest of the human race had seen. So now, as the negative side of the same point, Paul is making it clear, as he does at many points in Romans, that *the Jew is also in Adam*; that when Torah arrives in Israel, Israel recapitulates the sin which is common to all humankind (5.20; 7.7–12); and that, as a result, the state of Israel under Torah is simply the Jewish version (heightened, made more ironic, sharpened up to the point of great lament) of the plight of an Aristotle complaining of *akrasia* (and analyzing it microscopically), or an Ovid observing wryly that *video meliora proboque, deteriora*

[84] Rom. 5.20; 7.13; cp. Gal. 3.19, 21f.

[85] Shaffer 1985 [1980], 37. To be fair to Emperor Joseph, the words are put into his mouth by the scheming Count Orsini-Rosenberg.

sequor.[86] This is itself, to be sure, part of Paul's argument about the state of Israel under Torah, but it indicates well enough that Paul is fully aware of the pagan tradition in question, and that his overall argument is designed to deal with that problem as well. He is, after all, describing 'all' in Romans 5.12–21, from which the whole of the rest of chapters 5—8 grows; the salvation highlighted in chapter 8 is not specific to ethnic Israel. We cannot flatten out Paul's argument into simply a coded way of speaking about self-mastery, promising that the Christian will be able to attain it where the pagan could not, but nor can we ignore the fact that this dimension is contained within his larger argument, as the journey from Durham to York is contained within the journey from Edinburgh to London.

Much of Romans is in fact multi-dimensional, which is what makes that letter so inexhaustible in both reference and resonance. But there is one other passage in particular which comes up for discussion in a similar way to chapter 7. In Romans 2, Paul speaks twice of non-Jews who, somehow or other, 'keep the law'. I have argued elsewhere that in these passages Paul has non-Jewish *Christians* in mind; the echoes of other passages where that is the case, combined with the actual drift of the argument, make that in my view overwhelmingly likely. But what I may have missed before is the possibility, again, of multiple resonance.[87]

Take, first, the well-known passage at the end of the chapter, which we have discussed more than once before, and which most agree is a cryptic reference to non-Jewish Christians:

> Meanwhile, if uncircumcised people keep the law's requirements [*dikaiōmata*], their uncircumcision will be regarded as circumcision, won't it? So people who are by nature uncircumcised [*hē ek physeōs akrobustia*, literally 'the by nature uncircumcision'], but who fulfil the law, will pass judgment on people like you who possess the letter of the law and circumcision but who break the law ... The 'Jew' is the one in secret; and 'circumcision is a matter of the heart, in the spirit rather than the letter. Such a person gets 'praise', not from humans, but from God.[88]

The last two verses are echoed in Romans 7.4–6 and 2 Corinthians 3.6, where it is clear that Paul is talking about Christians, calling to mind as well the 'new covenant' theme in which the law is written on the heart by the spirit.[89] This in turn links up with the 'circumcision of the heart', itself a new-covenant blessing, promised in Deuteronomy 30 and elsewhere.[90] There should be no doubt that the 'uncircumcised lawkeepers' of Romans 2.26–9, who are nevertheless 'circumcised in heart', are gentile Christians as described more fully later in the letter and elsewhere.[91]

[86] Arist. *Nic. Eth.* 7; Ovid *Met.* 7.20f. ('I see the better, and I approve it, but I follow the worse').

[87] See Wright 2002 [*Romans*], 440–3, 448–50; and *Perspectives*, ch. 9.

[88] Rom. 2.26–9.

[89] 2 Cor. 3.3, echoing Ezek. 11.19; 36.26.

[90] Dt. 30.6 (cf. 10.16); cf. Jer. 31.33; Ezek. 36.26f. (in 36.27 one of the results is that the people concerned will walk in God's *dikaiōmata*).

[91] It is no argument against this to suggest that in ch. 2 Paul is only concerned to prove all humans sinful. His argument is much more many-sided than that: see again *Perspectives*, chs. 9 and 30.

It is at first sight harder to make the same case for Romans 2.12–16, but I persist in thinking that it should be done:

> Everyone who sinned outside the law, you see, will perish outside the law – and those who sinned from within the law will be judged by means of the law. After all, it isn't those who *hear* the law who are in the right before God. It's those who *do* the law who will be declared to be in the right!
>
> This is how it works out. Gentiles don't possess the law as their birthright; but whenever they do what the law says, they are a law for themselves, despite not possessing the law. They show that the work of the law is written on their hearts. Their conscience bears witness as well, and their thoughts will run this way and that, sometimes accusing them and sometimes excusing, on the day when (according to the gospel I proclaim) God judges all human secrets through King Jesus.[92]

Paul has been addressing the pagan moralist in 2.1: 'anyone, whoever you are, who sits in judgment'. This is someone who hears the tale of moral disintegration Paul has outlined in 1.18–32 and joins Paul in condemning such behaviour. Not so fast, says Paul: you are in fact doing all this yourself, in one way or another. The Jewish moralist may be included here as well – the point is arguable either way, which probably means that Paul is being deliberately ambiguous – but certainly the pagan moralist is an obvious target. Paul's main point, the climax to which the first ten verses of the chapter lead and from which the next five verses (quoted above) then follow as an explanation, is that 'God shows no partiality' (2.11). The way this will work out, he says here, is that the Jewish law will be the standard for Jews, while non-Jews will perish (Paul does not even say 'will be judged') 'outside the law'. What counts – this is the point here – is 'doing the law': *hoi poiētai nomou dikaiōthēsontai*, 'the doers of the law will be justified'.[93]

This leaves Paul with an obvious question. If 'doing the law' is what counts, how can any gentiles do it, since they, being gentiles by birth (as they are 'uncircumcised by birth' in 2.27), do not possess it? His answer is cryptic, and the reason for this is similar to the reason for the complexity of chapter 7: he is saying two things at once.

First, he is anticipating what he says in 2.26–9. There will come a time when gentiles will be incorporated into the 'new covenant' promised in scripture, and as a result they will have 'the work of the law written on their hearts'. The echoes of 2 Corinthians 3.3, and behind that of Jeremiah and Ezekiel, are clear, and the close similarity of Romans 2.26–9 makes this highly likely. Though by 'nature' (*physei*) they do not possess the law,[94] they 'do the things of the law'.[95]

Second, however, he is indicating by sidelong reference that *this new covenant fulfilment of the law by gentiles will be the true fulfilment of the proper*

[92] Rom. 2.12–16.

[93] 2.13, a verse which understandably startles those who have been taught from the cradle that Paul believes one cannot be 'justified' by doing the law.

[94] 2.14, similar to *hē ek physeōs akrobustia* in 2.27.

[95] *ta tou nomou poiousin*, parallel to *ta dikaiōmata tou nomou phylassē* in 2.26 and *ton nomon telousa* in 2.27.

aspirations of the pagan moralist. The way Paul has described this strange 'lawkeeping' is such as to send echoes out into the world of philosophical moralism, especially that of the Stoics, which spoke of a doing of law 'by nature', and of people being 'a law to themselves'.[96] Paul is saying, in effect, Very well: you, the pagan moralist whom I have been addressing since 2.1, may well believe that it is possible for someone like yourself to keep the law 'by nature', and to 'be a law to yourself'. I agree – but the way in which you will accomplish that will be, as I will explain later, through your coming to have the divine law written on your heart. That is the only way you will really be 'a law to yourself'.

If this double-edged interpretation of a tricky passage is accepted, we might reach the following conclusion. Paul, as well as being a clever writer (Romans reminds us of that on every page), is well aware of the theories, aspirations and expressions of the moral world of first-century paganism. He will not declare this world bankrupt; only impotent. As in chapter 7, with which chapter 2 has some interesting links, he picks up the highest aspirations of the moralist, the 'unknown gods' of their ethical worlds, and proposes to announce to them the thing after which they had been ignorantly aspiring. The clear echoes of Stoicism in the present passage, then, are not a sign that Paul has simply scooped up some Stoic language and incorporated it without much reflection into an argument about something else. They are certainly not an indication that he supposes (against the grain of 1.18—3.20 as a whole) that there are actually some pagan moralists out there who, without faith in Jesus or new-covenant membership, really do 'keep the law' in such a way as to be 'justified'.[97] The echoes of Stoicism are there because Paul is addressing the pagan moralist in his own terms, almost teasingly. Your ideal of being a law to yourself, he says, is, as it stands, a mirage; but it can become a reality. Follow the Ariadne's thread of this letter and you'll find the way out into the light.

I have argued in this section that if we imagine Paul posing questions, and alternative interpretations, to the three main categories of pagan philosophy, logic, physics and ethics, he would do so not in a head-on fashion, declaring it all to be worthless, but in the oblique fashion of someone seeing a genuine striving after accuracy and clarity of thought, truth of description of the world, and uprightness of life. With these, Paul has no quarrel. His quarrel is with the fact that the aspiration always fails to meet its goal – and that he believes that the one God, the creator, who has made himself known through Jesus the Messiah, has opened eyes and minds, has unveiled his complex but coherent truth in a way never before imagined and has given a quite new *pneuma* into the hearts of his people so that, in fulfilling his ancient promises of covenant renewal, he would also fulfil the deepest and highest aspirations of all human hearts. Paul has expressed this belief in a variety of ways, but particularly in those lists of virtues (and they really *are*

[96] See Jewett 2007, 213f.; and e.g. Gathercole 2002b.

[97] Against e.g. Dodd 1959 [1932], 61f.

'virtues', in the sense that they must be intentionally chosen, practised and perfected in the power of the spirit; they will not 'happen automatically', bypassing the will, choice and effort of those concerned) where we recognize a good deal from the wider world of late antiquity but still notice key elements that are unique. I have already mentioned them: patience, humility, chastity and above all *agapē*, love. 'Of them all, love is the greatest.'

There was a good reason why no pagan moralist had ever said that, and it was the same reason why it was central for Paul. It had to do with Jesus. Ultimately, Paul does not have a quarrel with pagan philosophy, just as one does not have a quarrel with a jigsaw that is hard to do because fifty or more pieces are missing, so that those attempting the puzzle are reduced to joining together pieces that do not really belong. Just as Paul is not trying to invent a new 'religion', so he is not trying to 'construct a philosophy' as such, though as we have seen his version of early Christianity is in some ways more like a philosophical school than anything else known at the time. Paul is proclaiming Jesus himself, and discovering as he does so that all the treasures of wisdom and knowledge find their key in him. Put him in the middle of the picture, he is saying, and all your aspirations after wisdom and right living will fit together at last. In the course of expounding, teaching and defending the message of the crucified and risen Messiah of Israel, the lord of the world, he is aware that if this message is true it will catch up within itself all other glimpses of truth from whatever source, and sometimes his language reflects that.

He therefore provides, in terms of a 'logic', a 'physics' and an 'ethic' reshaped around the gospel of Jesus, the larger framework within which what he says about 'politics' and 'religion' make the sense they do. Like the Wisdom of Solomon, he confronts the sceptics and the Epicureans with the news of Psalm 2: the one God will judge the wicked nations through his Messiah. Unlike Wisdom, Paul knows who the Messiah is, and his death and resurrection has reshaped the confrontation itself. Like Wisdom, Paul tells again the story of the world, and of Israel, in terms of 'wisdom' as the secret power by which it all happened, leading at last to the great exodus through which God's people are rescued and the wicked pagan empire overthrown. The all-powerful Word has leapt down from heaven, not now to deal out death but to take on death itself in single combat and to emerge victorious.[98] Paul's Jesus-shaped rethinking of the exodus-narrative enables him to radicalize the message of Wisdom, transforming its confrontation into an invitation, its portrait of 'wisdom' personified into an actual person and its engagement with the philosophies of its day into a new synthesis. The one God is the creator of heaven and earth, not simply a divine element within everything. Stoic pantheism will not do. But the one God is not far from any one of us, and 'we are also his offspring': no room for Epicureanism, then, and meanwhile the highest 'religious' aspirations of the

[98] cf. Wis. 18.15.

Stoic may find a new home.[99] One may indeed suppose, with the Academic or the Sceptic, that there isn't enough evidence to go on; but the one God has called the world to account, as the Psalms and prophets always said he would, through his appointed agent, the Messiah; and of this he has given assurance to all, by raising him from the dead.

They mocked in Athens, and they mock still. Take away the resurrection, and the picture falls apart. Paul knew that as well as they did. But the power of Paul's gospel, then and now, to change lives, to fulfil the aspirations of ancient philosophy as well as the dreams of Israel, provides at least in part the sign that this was indeed a 'wisdom' that could be imparted to the 'mature', even though it might appear folly to everyone else:

> My speech and my proclamation were not in persuasive words of wisdom, but in transparent proof brought home powerfully by the spirit, so that your faith might not be in human wisdom but in God's power.[100]

This was Paul's answer to the philosophies of his day. You could not fit the Jewish worldview into the non-Jewish, let alone the Jewish-but-scandalous message of Jesus into the pagan systems. The danger with announcing that one is going to transcend the Judaism/Hellenism divide is that it sounds like a typical Enlightenment attempt to gain a god's-eye view from which all differences cease to be noticeable, whereas for Paul the scriptures of Israel, and the God of Israel, could not thus be flattened out. But do it the other way – allow the gospel to state the terms, and let everything else find a home within it – and there will be not only wisdom but also power:

> Jews look for signs, you see, and Greeks search for wisdom; but we announce the crucified Messiah, a scandal to Jews and folly to Gentiles, but to those who are called, Jews and Greeks alike, the Messiah – God's power and God's wisdom. God's folly is wiser than humans, you see, and God's weakness is stronger than humans.[101]

3. Paul and the Stoics in Recent Study

(i) Introduction

As we saw in chapter 3, no single philosophical tradition dominated Paul's world. As in our own day, when bits and pieces of various ideas swirl around in popular culture, clashing, combining or simply co-existing in cheerful incoherence, so there is no reason to suppose that Paul's audience, even in a single city, let alone across the Mediterranean world, would be monochrome in its assumptions about how to think clearly, what the world consisted of, and how humans should behave. The same small town might easily include adherents of any or all of the four major schools (Plato's

[99] We might compare, for instance, the 'Hymn of Cleanthes'; or indeed the noble prayer of Epictetus (above, 226f.).

[100] 1 Cor. 2.4f.

[101] 1 Cor. 1.22–5.

Academy, Aristotle's Lyceum, the Stoics and the Epicureans), or who held in their minds an unsorted amalgamation of different elements from all of them. There might also be serious Sceptics, denying that any certainty was possible about such matters, or others who simply shrugged their shoulders and didn't bother with hard questions. As we have seen, this variety of thought and belief was mapped loosely on to the two equally overlapping worlds of 'politics' and 'religion'. A confused and confusing world.

We can nevertheless be reasonably confident that a popular-level Stoicism was widespread in the worlds which Paul visited and to which he wrote. As we saw when looking at characters like Epictetus, the 'official' pantheism of the school left plenty of room for people to continue worshipping the gods and praying to them as though they were in some sense 'other' than themselves, not simply the ultimate form of the fiery *pneuma* which pervaded all things and all people. At the popular level, Stoicism provided a conveniently flexible way of viewing the world, giving plenty of good advice on how to behave in a wide variety of situations (first-century Stoics were nothing if not practical) and offering encouragement and fortitude to face the problems and troubles of ordinary life. Seneca himself, Paul's great contemporary, was among other things a popularizer determined to make the guidance of philosophy available to ordinary people.[102] It was in any case harder to be an Epicurean: to do it properly, you had to have the means to escape to your peaceful haven and to live a quiet life without having to work too hard. Stoicism, by contrast, seemed to have something for everybody (though it tended to be the upper classes who studied and tried to practise it). It is fair to assume, therefore, that when Paul was writing to a city like Corinth or Ephesus, and quite possibly the smaller towns as well, he would expect his hearers to be familiar with some of the basic concepts of Stoicism, and to 'hear' things that he said within that context – much as today, with western culture still basically Epicurean or at least Deist, people 'hear' the word 'god' as referring to a distant, detached being, and 'ethics' or 'morality' as 'a set of rules designed to stop us having fun'.

The possibility of 'hearing' what Paul was saying with first-century Stoic ears has been explored by various recent writers. Paul's ethics, obviously, are a natural place to look.[103] His language about the divine *pneuma* is another obvious place. We may in the end conclude that the main sources for what he says about the spirit are (a) the scriptures and (b) the actual experience of the first Christians, but he must have known that for many of his hearers the word *pneuma* denoted the ultimately divine identity at the heart of all things, the hot breath that would eventually consume all things.[104] When he speaks of the church as the body of the Messiah, he was almost certainly aware that this was an image used by some Stoics to talk about the universal family of humankind, as well as by others to refer to

[102] See Ross 1974, 117. I owe this reference to Lee 2006, 200.

[103] See e.g. Thorsteinsson 2010. The most important recent contribution in this area is that of Rabens 2010.

[104] See e.g. Martin 1995. For Engberg-Pedersen see below.

what we still sometimes call the 'body politic' of a particular civic community.[105] Some have suggested that Paul's vision of the eschaton, particularly the great scene in Romans 8.18–25, might have been heard on analogy with the Stoic vision of the coming great conflagration, after which all things would start up once more.[106] Whether Paul himself would have intended such echoes, granted the sources of his language in the Jewish apocalyptic traditions and their reshaping around the Messiah and his resurrection, we may doubt, but it is always possible that some of his hearers might have seen what he was doing as in some ways parallel to that well-known Stoic theme.

Some of Paul's own main themes, of course, cut right across the founding principles of all the main philosophies, Stoicism included. His vision of joy is radically different from the Epicurean vision of pleasure, and his embrace of suffering constitutes a major difference between him and both Epicureanism and Stoicism. His belief in the God of Israel as both radically other than the world and yet intimately involved with it cannot be caught in the categories either of the Porch or of the Garden. And his vision of the ultimate goal of human life is also radically different from theirs, both in its actual content and in the fact that it is not a vision of self-discovery or self-improvement at all. It is, rather, a matter of displacing the 'self' from the centre of the picture and placing the Messiah, and his death and resurrection, there instead:

> . . . so that my profit may be the Messiah, and that I may be discovered in him, not having my own covenant status defined by Torah, but the status which comes through the Messiah's faithfulness: the covenant status from God which is given to faith. This means knowing him, knowing the power of his resurrection, and knowing the partnership of his sufferings. It means sharing the form and pattern of his death, so that somehow I may arrive at the final resurrection from the dead.[107]

Likewise, Paul's vision of the living presence of the one God, one lord, resulting in him seeing the church and the individual Christian to be 'temples' on the shocking analogy with the Jerusalem Temple itself, might be thought to have some analogies with the Stoic doctrine of the indwelling of the *pneuma* or the *logos*. But for Paul there are radical differences in both source (the biblical view of God's tabernacling presence), content (the *pneuma* as a divine gift, not an automatic human possession) and goal (holiness and unity in the present, resurrection in the future). And the ultimate scandal remained the cross itself. Any self-respecting Greek or Roman with even a smattering of the noble philosophical traditions would be horrified at the idea that the ultimate revelation of the one true God might be the ugly judicial lynching of a young Jew. Any attempt to bring Paul together with his philosophical contemporaries must factor in these stumbling-blocks from the start. Paul was not a first-century moralizing philosopher

[105] See e.g. Lee 2006.

[106] See below for this view in Engberg-Pedersen; and above, 215f.

[107] Phil. 3.8–11.

who happened to hold, on the side as it were, a few strange views about Jesus, and about the meaning and effect of his death and resurrection. These were, for him, the very centre. If we are to compare different schemes of thought with one another we must compare centres with centres, not one person's centre with another person's periphery.

(ii) Beyond the Engberg-Pedersen Divide?

(a) Exposition

When we think of present scholarship on Paul and the Stoics, one name emerges from the pack like a marathon runner out in the lead. The lively and engaging style of the Danish scholar Troels Engberg-Pedersen has opened up apparent new possibilities in an area which many in the previous generation had all but ignored. Even those who had worked in this field may well sense that Engberg-Pedersen's proposals go far beyond their more modest offerings. One recent commentator calls him 'one of the very best Pauline scholars in the world', claiming that his most recent book is 'intellectually exciting, timely and controversial'.[108] Those claims will themselves be controversial, but there is no doubt that Engberg-Pedersen has at the very least raised questions with which any serious historical account of Paul must come to terms. That is the justification for including a detailed discussion of his work at this point, now that we have laid the ground for it with our own exposition of Paul in relation to his philosophical contemporaries.

Out of Engberg-Pedersen's many works, the central statements of his thesis about Paul are found in his 2000 book, *Paul and the Stoics*, and in the follow-up volume, *Cosmology and Self in the Apostle Paul*, whose subtitle *The Material Spirit* tells its own story.[109] Engberg-Pedersen comes to Paul as a lifelong student of ancient philosophy; if there is a danger of 'parallelomania' for him, it is that he reads Paul looking for parallels to the Stoics, rather than (like many New Testament scholars) the other way round. I hope that my own treatment of the sources, in chapter 3 and here, will enable us to keep a proper balance.

Engberg-Pedersen emphasizes that Paul is not a philosopher, nor particularly a Stoic. He argues, however, that Paul drew freely on the philosophical traditions of his time, not least the Stoic traditions, in commending to his congregations the way of life he believed was best. He states at the outset of *Paul and the Stoics* that he intends to explore Paul's 'worldview' within a social-historical context, aiming (as we said just now) to see Paul as a whole and Stoicism as a whole, not just to examine detached motifs.[110] He intends, he says, to build up a picture of Paul's entire 'form of life and symbolic

[108] J. Barclay, quoted on the cover of Engberg-Pedersen 2010.

[109] In what follows I shall refer to *Paul and the Stoics* (Engberg-Pedersen 2000) as *PS*, and to *Cosmology and the Self* (Engberg-Pedersen 2010) as *CS*.

[110] *PS* 1f.

world'.[111] This sounds much like the aim we set ourselves in Part II of the present book, though Engberg-Pedersen goes about it in a very different way. He says that his work stands in line with the 'new perspective' of Ed Sanders and Heikki Räisänen, and one can see some similarities while observing considerable differences, not least with Sanders's detailed analysis of Jewish thought, which Engberg-Pedersen does not attempt. He claims to be part of a movement which is rescuing Paul from the 'protestant' tradition,[112] and indeed from 'theology' as a whole.[113] His approach, he emphasizes, is 'naturalistic and not theological', because to read with theological intent is to lose 'the historical-critical edge'.[114] There is a sense, reading him, that he is doing to the European theological tradition what the ancient Cynics did to the establishments of their day: as self-styled 'dogs', they barked and yapped at the hollow pretensions of the rich and the respectable.[115] I don't know that the theological traditions themselves are either rich or respectable these days, but reading Engberg-Pedersen reminds one of the sharp critique and calculated disdain of a Diogenes, barking at the theological interpretations of Paul which he perceives as irrelevant to the real issues.

In particular, and in line with a collection of essays he himself edited, Engberg-Pedersen claims repeatedly that it is time to go, and that he himself is going, 'Beyond the Judaism/Hellenism Divide'. This means rescuing Paul from the sterile pseudo-antitheses of nineteenth-century ideologically driven scholarship, and presenting the apostle as someone who was able to draw freely on both Jewish and non-Jewish traditions, combining his 'apocalyptic' worldview, which remained important, with major themes and motifs from the non-Jewish world, and particularly from the world of Stoicism. Engberg-Pedersen allows that Paul did thus still have a double source of ideas, but denies that we have to choose between them, as though trying to make Paul *either* a 'Jewish' *or* a 'hellenistic' thinker. His basic argument in the earlier volume, amplified from a different angle in the later one, is that Paul is basically operating within the essential structure of Stoic ethics, so that even if Paul speaks of 'God' and 'Christ' where the Stoic speaks of rationality and reason, 'it is the same basic structure that holds together Stoic ethics and Paul's comprehensive theologizing'.[116]

There are two tools of thought which Engberg-Pedersen himself uses throughout and which deserve comment because of their radical influence on his whole project. The first is what he calls 'philosophical exegesis', which means that 'the interpreter applies categories of interpretation that make sense philosophically, whether in an ancient or a modern context'.[117]

[111] *PS* 21.

[112] *PS* ix.

[113] *PS* 1: his work will be 'from a different perspective than the traditional, theological one'. The comma seems just as important here as the famous comma at the end of 1 Thess. 2.14 (see above, 1152f.).

[114] *PS* 2; cf. 29, 30, 43.

[115] See above, 229f.; and *JVG* 66–74.

[116] *PS* 47.

[117] From the blurb on the back cover of *CS*.

As philosophers themselves might say, it all depends what you mean by 'making sense'; to judge from Engberg-Pedersen's actual practice, what this means is that categories of interpretation which do not 'make sense' include much of Paul's 'apocalyptic' Jewish context. Instead, he brings to the text the categories he has culled from ancient Stoicism on the one hand and from contemporary cultural analysts, particularly Foucault and Bourdieu, on the other. The question of whether this itself 'makes sense' in terms of an historical analysis of Paul is one to which we must return.

The second tool of thought, which works closely with this, is the category developed by the late Bernard Williams, that of ideas and beliefs which constitute 'a real option for us'.[118] This, to be frank, is more of a problem. It is not simply that the question of what constitutes 'a real option for us' might conceivably be more open than Engberg-Pedersen allows (see below). It is not even a question of who 'we' or 'us' might actually be. He says at one point that 'scholars ought to ... make clear to themselves and their readers exactly where and how their own existential interest is involved in their professional scholarly work', and he claims to have done this himself. But he also says, in a blunt footnote, 'Of course, very much hangs on who the "we" are.' It does indeed, thinks the reader; but Engberg-Pedersen's note then concludes, 'I shall not address that question.'[119]

But these confusions, and the perception even of a certain subterfuge, is still not the deepest problem. The deepest problem is this: what is this notion of a 'real option' doing within an *historical* analysis of Paul and the *historical* relation he might or might not have had to *historical* Stoicism? It hardly makes sense for Engberg-Pedersen, in the name of historical criticism, to strain out the gnat of theological readings and then swallow the camel of a loosely formulated 'real option for us'. Unless I am much mistaken, it is the task of the historian to get inside the mind of, and be able to expound the thought of, people whose worldviews, mindsets, aims, motivations, imaginations, likes and dislikes are significantly different from our own at, potentially, every point. I have a feeling that Aristotle said something just like that. Indeed, when characters in history look similar to ourselves, we may be in danger of then projecting our own worldviews on to them, so that all we hear is the echo of our own voices bouncing back off the distant historical wall. This has demonstrably happened in the discipline, as for instance in Barth's claim that, when the Reformers were reading Paul, the barrier between the sixteenth and the first centuries disappeared, leaving Paul speaking directly to the new situation.[120] A similar problem occurred when the great Ronald Syme envisaged the rise and rule of Augustus by analogy with the great tyrannies of the mid-twentieth century. Analogies

[118] *PS* 16f., referring to Williams 1985, 160f. He emphasizes the idea throughout 17–24 and returns to it at various stages, developing it in *CS* in terms of things which are 'defensible' (e.g. 2f. 6, 193) though again without explaining what his grounds are for wanting to 'defend' a first-century idea rather than simply, as a historian, to expound it, or indeed what one might be 'defending' it against.

[119] *PS* 26, 309 n. 35.

[120] Barth 1968 [1933], 7.

may help, but they may also deceive us into thinking we 'know' more than we do.[121]

In the present case, what seems to be driving Engberg-Pedersen's adoption of this method is a sort of missionary accommodation, which I suspect he would shun if it were attempted in other directions. He seems to envisage the kind of Procrustean slimming-down of New Testament proclamation that we associate with some aspects of early twentieth-century scholarship:

> We may think, indeed we should think, that Paul's belief in the story of the Christ event, in the direct form in which he understood it, was false. But we may let ourselves be stimulated by the *kind* of 'theologizing' that we find in Paul to think that we should ourselves adopt the same kind: one that attempts to tease out the meaning for human beings of the Christ event in a manner that makes immediate sense philosophically and in that way presents the special shape of the Christ-believing form of life as a real option to one's contemporaries.[122]

It gradually becomes clear, of course, what the criterion is for deciding whether something is a 'real option' for us or not: philosophical analysis will insert the surgeon's knife between the bits of Paul that we want to keep and the bits we do not – the latter being precisely 'theology', which we must avoid lest we lose our historical-critical edge! What must be stripped away, it seems, is the full-on 'apocalyptic' understanding of Paul's gospel. 'Anthropology' and 'ethics', then, are fine, and can be liberated from 'theology' and even (despite the second book) 'cosmology'.

This, as Engberg-Pedersen recognizes, is very close to Bultmann's 'demythologizing' programme, and though he distances himself from Bultmann in some ways it is not clear to me that he has dealt with the problems this parallel inevitably raises.[123] In fact, Engberg-Pedersen's statement of his misgivings at treating as 'historical' something which seems strange to us looks to me like an abandonment of historical method altogether:

> Scholars often speak of Paul's idea here [he is discussing 'participation in Christ'] as if it made immediate sense and indeed was more or less readily acceptable to us. But it is not. On the contrary, it looks as if it is very far from constituting a real option for us. That also means, however, that it is very difficult to develop, *even as part of doing one's existentially neutral, historical work*, what it at all meant to Paul. Since it appears so strange to us, one really cannot feel sure that one has got it sufficiently right for it to be possible to develop it further and combine it with other similar ideas. A shared level of discourse is lacking. But that is just another way of saying that one cannot recur to a shared field of 'phenomena' to fill it in. By contrast, with the 'anthropological' and 'ethical' ideas with which we shall be centrally concerned, there is far more of an initial likelihood that we do share Paul's level

121 Above, ch. 5, on Syme and Augustus. I note again (as above, ch. 7 n. 28) Lewis 1964, vii: when we meet a word we don't recognize, we look it up, but when we meet one we recognize whose meaning has in fact changed, we wrongly imagine we know what the author was talking about.

122 *PS* 304 (the last paragraph of the book). The previous two pages build up to this, with the argument that 'one type of language that Paul uses, the substantive one, does not constitute a real option for us, whereas the other, cognitive one does' (303).

123 See *PS* 18f., and frequently.

of discourse. And so the road is open to a 'phenomenological' reading that presupposes that, at least tentatively.[124]

We might comment that this use of 'philosophical exegesis' in search of things that might be a 'real option' for us already seems to be a lot more 'critical' than 'historical': more bark than bite, perhaps. It constitutes a radical application of the method known as *Sachkritik*, by which the expositor claims to be able to 'correct' certain strands of someone's thoughts in line with 'more central' elements. This already presupposes that the interpreter understands how a train of thought 'ought to work' better than the person, two thousand years ago, who was thinking it – something which in other fields, with less at stake, one might regard as far-fetched. It is one thing to ponder the question of how to communicate – and, it seems, to commend – first-century ideas to one's contemporaries. But it is strange to find someone whose basic discipline is ancient philosophy complaining that if certain ancient ideas are not 'real options' for us we ought to be anxious as to whether we can even describe them properly. That is certainly not what Bernard Williams had in mind. It would make it hard to write about any ideas other than those with which we already felt sympathy. This is the dilemma, of course, of dyed-in-the-wool 'method actors', who can only play particular parts by identifying themselves completely with the characters concerned and then 'acting naturally', as opposed to the traditional acting in which one thinks through how such a person would behave and then behaves in that way.

Engberg-Pedersen seems, in fact, to be making a historiographical mistake: treating the distinction between ideas that are a 'real option' for us, and ideas that are not, as an index to the *historical* analysis of Paul's mind. He believes (it seems) that Paul's anthropological and ethical ideas are a 'real option', whereas his theological and 'apocalyptic' ones are not; therefore *Paul's anthropological and ethical ideas are deemed to constitute the real centre of his thought*. 'I like this, or at least I can resonate with it, therefore it must be what Paul really meant.' Of course, Engberg-Pedersen never puts it as baldly as that, though he sometimes comes quite close; and he does say, repeatedly, that 'apocalyptic' ideas continued to be important for Paul. But again and again he claims to have uncovered, and to be expounding, that which was *actually* central for the apostle. There are thus serious questions to be asked, even before we get to the subject-matter itself.

Engberg-Pedersen's two books, ten years apart, present different but, we are assured, complementary aspects of Paul's thought. That thought is, in both cases, expounded in the light of Stoic parallels, and with the underlying thesis that, in getting 'beyond the Judaism/Hellenism divide', Paul's most fundamental ideas were derived from ... Stoicism.

The first book, *Paul and the Stoics*, concentrates on the pattern of conversion, for which Engberg-Pedersen has an elaborate model. He offers a 'cognitive' or 'ethical' reading of this conversion-model: what counts is what

124 *PS* 27f.: my italics.

one *knows* or *thinks*, and how one then behaves as a result. The model indicates a conversion from an initial state of self-centredness, via a call or fresh vision, whether of 'God' or the *logos* or 'reason'. This conversion results in a new state of being in which one is open to others and ready for 'altruism'.[125] Such a conversion, whether in Paul or in the philosophical tradition, is a complete change, with no turning back; once it has happened, it is 'all or nothing', with no dithering half measures, no 'already/not yet'.[126] Paul has already left the fleshly body behind; he is 'disengaged from the body', perhaps because something – we do not know what – had 'happened in his body' when he was converted.[127] Engberg-Pedersen applies this model first to the Stoics (using Cicero's *Ends* Book III as the key text) and then to Philippians, Romans and Galatians. 'It may be hoped', he says, 'that readers of Paul will intuitively feel that the ... model captures something that is reasonably central in Paul's thought world.'[128] One may be surprised that a philosopher would appeal to intuitive feelings rather than to argument. As the two books proceed one learns not to be so surprised.

The second book, *Cosmology and Self in the Apostle Paul*, expounds what Engberg-Pedersen takes to be the 'physical pattern' which corresponds to, and underlies, the cognitive and ethical themes explored in the first book. Here, following Dale Martin (to whom the book is dedicated), he emphasizes the 'physical' nature of the *pneuma* of which Paul speaks so frequently. Whereas in Platonism the word *pneuma* denoted a non-material reality, in Stoicism all reality was in some sense or other 'physical' or 'material', and the *pneuma*, as we saw in chapter 3, was thought of as the fiery divine substance which indwelt all reality, all persons, and the cosmos itself. Engberg-Pedersen expounds several themes in Paul in terms of this 'material' rather than 'immaterial' *pneuma*, producing striking and challenging results. Again and again he insists that what Paul is saying is not 'metaphorical', but 'literal'. When, for instance, Paul was preaching, or even writing letters, he believed that this 'material *pneuma*' was being passed from him to his hearers. We may be puzzled by the word 'cosmology' as it appears in the title of the book, and frequently inside it, since Engberg-Pedersen is not talking about Paul's view of the *kosmos*, but about his overall theory of human life. This is where the focus is placed on the 'self', since as with the previous volume Engberg-Pedersen is concerned with the vision of 'self' in both Paul and Stoicism, which comes to the fore in a striking chapter comparing Epictetus with Paul. This is in my view one of the most successful of Engberg-Pedersen's analyses, and should be factored in to subsequent studies of this important area.

The book's final flourish is an exposition, and application to Paul and the Stoics, of Pierre Bourdieu's concept of 'habitus', which attempts, after the

[125] The model is expounded in *PS* ch. 2, and summarized at 175f. and in *CS* 176–8. 'Altruism': e.g. *PS* 56 and frequently.

[126] *PS* 8, 70f., and frequently.

[127] *CS* 2f., 121f., 144.

[128] *PS* 40.

manner of Clifford Geertz or Charles Taylor, to provide a larger concept which will include the multiple aspects of social and material culture – what I have continued to refer to as 'worldview'. Whether or not we are convinced by Engberg-Pedersen's application of this to Paul, it remains in my judgment a potentially fruitful route to explore.

(b) Critique

I have already commented on some of the issues raised by Engberg-Pedersen's own explanation of his method. We may begin this critique by pointing out some quite serious peculiarities – the more serious because, as a philosopher, Engberg-Pedersen might be expected to be clear in his use of key terms and sharp in his mounting of arguments. Sadly, he is neither. To begin with, his more recent book is marred by the constant use of 'metaphorical' and 'literal' to mean 'abstract' and 'concrete'. However common this is in popular discourse, it is bound to breed confusion in a serious discussion, especially when there is also discussion of actual metaphors. One hesitates to make the point again, but it seems necessary: the fact that a word is used 'metaphorically' tells us nothing whatever about whether the entity to which it refers is 'material' or 'non-material', and the fact that a word is used 'literally' likewise tells us nothing about the physicality or otherwise of its referent. One can use a metaphor to refer to a concrete object, and one can speak literally about abstract, non-material entities.[129] It would have been much clearer to use 'concrete' and 'abstract', allowing 'metaphorical' and 'literal' to do their proper job of explaining how particular words refer to things rather than what sort of things they are referring to.

One may more readily excuse an idiosyncratic use of 'worldview' and 'cosmology', since these terms are both in use today in a variety of senses. But it would have been good to see some recognition that there is a lively debate about 'worldview', going back to Geertz (who is cited but not engaged with) and continuing through Taylor and others, and to know where Engberg-Pedersen would situate himself in terms of the 'worldview elements' which I and others have highlighted.[130] These are after all cognate with his stated (but as yet unfulfilled) aim of mapping the symbolic world of Paul and his contemporaries. As for 'cosmology', it is strange to find it used like this:

[129] Random examples of worrying passages: 'the author [of Wisdom of Solomon] starts out thinking in Stoic terms, [but] he aims to add a Platonist perspective – meaning an immaterial one – literally on top of the Stoic picture' (23); 'baptism and pneuma hang intrinsically together and they generate the one physical body to which all baptized believers belong when in a wholly literal sense they are "in Christ"' (69); also 96f., 174f. and frequently. Speaking of Paul's language of having died with Christ, he says 'But try to take it literally. What it then means is that Paul now lives as being filled up by Christ . . . who is both literally dead and literally alive (in heaven)' (162). Paul would be surprised to know that Christ was 'literally dead'.

[130] e.g. *NTPG* Part II, applied in *JVG*; and in the present vol., Part II.

> On the one hand, there is a basically metaphorical or, if not metaphorical, then at least cognitive way of understanding Paul's language. On the other hand, there is a non-metaphorical, concrete and basically physical – or as I shall call it, cosmological – way of understanding that language.[131]

Engberg-Pedersen also speaks of Paul 'drawing on his cosmology of the *pneuma*', and speaks of his belief in various stages in Christian identity being 'thoroughly cosmological'.[132] Since none of these uses have anything directly to do with 'cosmology' as normally understood, one is bound to wonder whether a better term might have been found.

This brings us to two old friends: 'apocalyptic' and 'salvation history'. In both cases Engberg-Pedersen's usage is idiosyncratic. As regards 'apocalyptic', he shares with some other New Testament scholars today the (bad) habit of using the word without regard for the actual 'apocalyptic' traditions from Daniel through to *4 Ezra*, which as we saw in chapter 2 have little to do with the kind of 'end-of-the-world' fantasy imagined by some, and plenty to do with the *metaphorical* investing of space–time events with their *theological* significance.[133] He speaks, as some scholars of second-Temple Judaism used to do, of the 'pessimism' of 'apocalyptic' (as opposed to the supposed 'optimism' of the Stoics), and can talk of a fresh reading of 2 Corinthians 4 and 5 which 'removes it fairly drastically from the level of operation of ordinary "apocalyptic" writings'.[134] He gives no sign, however, that he understands the traditions that emerge in these 'apocalyptic' writings, or the theological and political freight they carry, as set out for instance in chapter 2 above.

When it comes to 'salvation history', Engberg-Pedersen first uses the phrase to refer to the 'history' which moves *forward* from the time of Jesus to the ultimate end, a use which so far as I know is unique to himself; and he then uses the same phrase to refer (is this, too, unique?) to the Stoic sense of time moving forwards towards the final conflagration.[135] When he subsequently uses the term in the more normal sense – to denote some kind of historical sequence between the divine promise to the patriarchs and the coming of the Messiah – he suggests that Paul 'felt forced to try to construct a picture also of God's dealings with mankind (or at least with the Jews) *before* Christ, as these dealings were witnessed to in the Jewish scripture'.[136] Nobody who understands the place of Adam, Abraham, Moses and so on within the Jewish world of Paul's day could speak of Paul 'constructing' such a thing as though *de novo*, or indeed of him being 'forced' to do so.

[131] *CS* 1.

[132] *CS* 156, 164.

[133] Unsurprisingly, Engberg-Pedersen (*CS* 248 n. 5) is enthusiastic about Adams 2007, which enables him to hold on to his 'literal' reading of 'apocalyptic', which in turn facilitates his judgment that such material is not a 'real option' for us. See the discussion above, 163–75.

[134] *CS* 94f., 50.

[135] *CS* 21.

[136] *CS* 12. Paul then, he says, 'added Adam to his salvation historical scheme' (*CS* 13).

These all place road-blocks in the way of an easy understanding, not to mention appropriation, of Engberg-Pedersen's main theses. There is a particular theological (or perhaps even 'cosmological') irony which emerges from these verbal peculiarities: the very thing that, we may surmise, compels him to say that Paul's 'apocalyptic' thought does not constitute a 'real option' for us is its concrete vision of the future; but he replaces it with the 'material *pneuma*', which then offers a remarkably concrete vision of baptism, preaching and so on, which many will find equally hard to understand, let alone adopt for themselves. If 'real options' are what count, we may wonder what has happened, in the second of Engberg-Pedersen's books, to the central criterion by which the first was organized.

As for exegesis itself, Engberg-Pedersen's marginalization of Paul's subtle and complex Jewish world leaves him at a considerable disadvantage. He is reduced to forcing ideas and themes into texts and then making them central, as with his insistence that Philippians 3.4–11 is really all about the *pneuma* even though the word never occurs.[137] Despite saying that it is important 'to stay closer to the immediate level of the text itself' in respect of Galatians 2, one would never know from his discussion what the chapter was basically about.[138] If one is going to bark at the tradition, it helps to know your target. To say, of Romans 7, that 'the whole point of Paul's account seems to lie in making his readers themselves experience the experiences of the self that he is recounting', and that 'Paul is, as it were, trying to make his readers convert in exactly the self-generating and pneumatic way that he has elsewhere described for his own case' is simply to fail to read the text. However controversial Romans 7 may be, this can hardly be its 'whole point'. Engberg-Pedersen, perhaps realizing this, resorts to breathtaking subjectivism:

> I can imagine that this reading will be roundly rejected by scholars. I can only reply that I have a strong sense that exactly here we are extremely close to Paul's own understanding of what is going on in this text. If he were present, he would have nodded.[139]

This is neither exegesis nor history.

What, then, of Engberg-Pedersen's main proposals? His account (in the first volume) of conversion in Paul and the Stoics is, frankly, so generalized that it is hardly of any use in understanding either Paul or Cicero (his main source for Stoicism at this point), let alone comparing them. It would not be difficult to apply exactly the same model to the appeal of the Wisdom of Solomon (building on Proverbs and elsewhere), where the rulers of the

[137] *CS* 41–5, 147, 151. I agree of course that the spirit, mentioned in Phil. 3.2, is implicit in the passage thereafter: see above, 1164 for the same phenomenon in Rom. 10.13. When it comes to words, one simply cannot treat Paul's *gar* (normally translated 'for', i.e. introducing an explanation) as if it were 'contrastive' (*CS* 245 n. 41). Precisely if Paul is the careful philosophical thinker Engberg-Pedersen wants him to be, he would not use key logical terms to mean their opposite.

[138] *CS* 157–62 (qu. from 161). 'A process of Foucauldian subjectification' (159) cannot compensate for a clarification of why Paul and Peter were disagreeing at Antioch.

[139] *CS* 168f.

world lack the true wisdom, and persecute the righteous, but are urged to acquire this divine wisdom so that they can learn the ways of the creator. One could apply it to the teaching of Torah in numerous works from the second-Temple period and then from the rabbis. One could certainly apply it to texts from Qumran. Further afield, I am no expert in Buddhism, but I see no reason why it might not be applied to the transition from being unenlightened to a state of enlightenment. It is hard to see, then, that it adds much to our grasp of what Paul, or the Stoics, were all about.

There is another problem with the model. How do we know it applied to the Stoicism with which Paul was familiar? Cicero's book *De Finibus* is Engberg-Pedersen's primary source here; but Cicero elsewhere portrays himself as an Academic, not a Stoic, and when he puts Stoic arguments into someone else's mouth in dialogues (in this case, 'Cato') we may, or we may not, be hearing what a Stoic of the first century BC would actually have said. We would hardly trust a report by Josephus of someone else's position to be an accurate view of 'what Jews believed' even in his own day; and Cicero was writing a century before Paul, half a world away, and putting words into someone else's mouth. Even granted all that, we may note that 'conversion', in the sense that Engberg-Pedersen wants to find it, is hardly the central topic of discussion in the *De Finibus* itself, just as one may read hundreds of pages in Seneca, Paul's contemporary who certainly was a Stoic, without finding a passage to which Engberg-Pedersen's model actually applies.

In fact, Cicero and Seneca themselves undermine one of Engberg-Pedersen's central claims, that both for Paul and for Stoicism 'conversion' is an 'all or nothing' moment in which one leaves the old life behind for ever.[140] To be sure, someone wanting to become a philosopher would have to turn away from previous worldviews and commitments and take up the new challenge. Such a moment – as we see, for instance, with Dio Chrysostom – would indeed be like a conversion. But though the challenge to such a transformation is always there underneath the writings of those we have studied in chapter 3, it is not a major feature. Rather, we find on every page of Cicero and Seneca, and the others, advice about how to move forwards, how to deal with this moral problem or that bad habit, how to deepen the commitment one already has. That, of course, is what 'virtue', whether in the Platonist or the Aristotelian tradition, was all about. To be sure, one had to make a start. But habits, by definition, are not acquired overnight; and virtue is, by definition, a habit. That is why, as Engberg-Pedersen sees, a certain amount of Paul (not as much as he imagines, but a certain amount) and a good deal of Stoic writing consists of *paraenesis*, exhortation. Those who have made a start need to make progress, to move forwards beyond the level they have already attained. It is not, then, all in place at conversion.

Faced with all this, it comes as no surprise to find a leading expert on ancient Stoicism describing Engberg-Pedersen's project as 'impressive but

[140] *PS* 8f., 38, 70f., etc.

... wholly misguided'.[141] Perhaps this is why Engberg-Pedersen issues an appeal to 'enlightened' modern scholars and philosophers: they, he supposes, are the ones who will understand his point.[142]

In the same way, though of course Paul does describe in more than one place the change that happened in his own life (Galatians 1 and 2 and Philippians 3 come to mind, and one might also invoke the account of rescue from sin and death in Ephesians 2.1–10), it is by no means clear that this is *the* major theme of his writing and teaching. Of course, he believes in conversion, in people 'turning from idols to serve a living and true God'.[143] But that is as it were the starting-point which he can then take for granted, rather than the main focus of his theology. In addition, whenever Paul does speak of that transition, in his own life or that of others, the point is never that everyone ought to have some such transition for (as it were) its own sake. The point is always *Jesus*: 'I calculate everything as a loss, because knowing Messiah Jesus as my lord is worth far more than everything else put together!'[144] Whether Paul would have recognized a Stoic 'conversion' (even supposing that the Stoics he knew were prepared to think or speak in such a way) as the same kind of thing as having one's life revolutionized by the powerful message of the Jesus-gospel we may well doubt.

In any case – and here is one of the most curious things about Engberg-Pedersen's account of 'conversion' – it is not at all the case that the transition in Paul's life was from a life centred upon self alone to a life opened out to others. Yes, of course, as 'a man in the Messiah' he believed in and experienced the primary quality of *agapē* (which is not the same as 'altruism', the word Engberg-Pedersen prefers). But he began, as he tells us in the same 'conversion' passages in Galatians and Philippians, very much within the solidarity of ethnic Israel. His whole pre-conversion identity was, in that sense, *corporate*. In fact, as with Qumran, even though it would be wrong to see the transition as being from 'corporate' to 'individual' there was nevertheless something 'individual' about the process of one person leaving that old 'corporate' identity in order then to be joined to a different one (however much, as again in both Qumran and Paul, the subsequent 'different one' was held to be the true identity to which the old one had pointed). And, on the other pole of the supposed comparison, Engberg-Pedersen admits that the Stoics, once thoroughly 'converted' to their new way of life, were actually thoroughgoing individualists. As we know from the whole Aristotelian tradition which they had adapted, 'virtue' in ancient philosophy was basically an individual pursuit.[145] Engberg-Pedersen claims that Stoics were just as 'community-oriented' as Paul, but when he faces the question directly he has to admit that this was at best skin deep:

141 Brennan 2005, 231, quoted modestly by Engberg-Pedersen at *CS* 249 n. 10.

142 *PS* 26.

143 1 Thess. 1.9.

144 Phil. 3.8.

145 See the discussion in Wright 2010 [*Virtue Reborn/After You Believe*] 176f./204f.

> None of these Stoics [Seneca, Epictetus, Musonius Rufus, Dio Chrysostom], however, went so far as ever to consider practising Stoicism as a communitarian project. Their Stoicism remained more or less 'individualistic'. Some of them, it is true, had contact with the group of senators in Ist-century Rome who constituted a 'Stoic opposition' to the emperors. Here we do see some reflection of the political potential in Stoicism. But to speak of a communitarian project of the kind envisaged directly by Zeno and indirectly by Chrysippus would be wrong.[146]

Engberg-Pedersen explains this on the basis that all these Stoics were from the upper class. They would not have been prepared to leave that level of society to live a common life in accordance with their philosophy. This alone speaks volumes for the difference between Paul and the Stoics: 'Not many of you', writes the apostle to the Corinthians, 'were nobly born'.[147] But then, casting about for an exception to his rule about Stoic individualism, Engberg-Pedersen alights on – Paul himself:

> Do we not find any attempt in Paul's day to practise Stoicism as a communitarian project? Yes. With all the necessary qualifications: Paul's own community-creating project is just such an attempt.[148]

Once again the reader – never mind the historian or the exegete – has a sharp intake of breath. According to the model of 'conversion' which is supposedly the pattern that unites Paul and the Stoics, one begins with an isolated self and ends with a community. Paul, for certain, began with one sort of community and ended with another. The Stoics began as members of the upper classes, a strong and tightly knit community if ever there was one, and ended as individualists. How can this 'model' make any sense? And how can we cite Paul, in the middle of an argument such as this book is advancing, as an example of the other pole of comparison?

Engberg-Pedersen's more recent book focuses on the 'material *pneuma*'. He attempts to understand Paul's many references to it (and hints about it) in terms of a strict Stoic 'materiality' as opposed to the Platonic 'non-material' understanding which he rightly sees has been characteristic of much later Christian understanding.[149] Despite the word 'cosmology' in the book's title, he never discusses Paul's major theme of 'new creation', or indeed the creational theology underlying it. Nor does he ever address – astonishingly in two books about Paul and the Stoics – the difference between a scripturally based Jewish monotheism (and Paul's variations on

[146] *PS* 78.

[147] 1 Cor. 1.26.

[148] *PS* 78.

[149] See *CS* 14–19. Here, as elsewhere, Engberg-Pedersen notes that other scholars contrast Paul's Jewish and 'apocalyptic' context for understanding the *pneuma* with a 'philosophical' one (on Martin: 16–18; on Barclay, 208f. n. 12), but says that one should not regard this as a dichotomy, after the manner of earlier 'pro-Jewish, . . . pro-Christian, anti-philosophical' treatments (16). His response is that 'a Stoic-like, philosophical understanding of the Pauline pneuma is what fits the evidence best' (18), and that 'there is no intrinsic contrast between such a picture and Hebrew Bible and "apocalyptic" understandings of God and eschatology' (18f.). This claim stands or falls with Engberg-Pedersen's exposition of resurrection, on which see below.

that theme) and the flexible pantheism of first-century Stoicism. These, one might have thought, would be basic to any project such as the one proposed. Instead, he turns at once, in his more recent book, to a topic which was undoubtedly central for Paul: resurrection.[150]

Perhaps the most startling thing in the whole book is the phrase 'Paul's Stoic resurrection'.[151] Stoics, like all other ancient non-Jews known to us, did not believe in 'resurrection', that is, in the possibility that someone who was bodily dead might become bodily alive again. All sorts of other post-mortem possibilities were canvassed across the ancient world, but, as many writers in many traditions (including Stoics) declared whenever the question came up, 'resurrection' as such was not among them.[152] What then does Engberg-Pedersen mean by suggesting that Paul's resurrection is 'Stoic' in its basic orientation?

His principal move is to align two passages in 1 Corinthians 15, and to read the latter in the light of the former. First we find Paul describing different sorts of bodies which are to be found in the cosmos as a whole:

> Not all physical objects have the same kind of physicality. There is one kind of physicality for humans, another kind for animals, another for birds, and another for fish. Some bodies belong in the heavens (*sōmata epourania*), and some on the earth (*sōmata epigeia*); and the kind of glory appropriate for the ones in the heavens is different from the kind of glory appropriate for the ones on the earth. There is one kind of glory for the sun, another for the moon, and another for the stars, since the stars themselves vary, with different degrees of glory.[153]

The key phrase here is *sōmata epourania*, 'heavenly bodies'. In context, this clearly refers to astral objects (sun, moon and stars, with the stars then further distinguished from one another) as opposed to objects on the earth. But Engberg-Pedersen seizes upon this and uses it as the key to interpret the second member of Paul's next pairing:

> That's what it's like with the resurrection of the dead. It is sown decaying, and raised undecaying. It is sown in shame, and raised in glory. It is sown in weakness, and raised in power. It is sown as the embodiment of ordinary nature (*sōma psychikon*), and raised as the embodiment of the spirit (*sōma pneumatikon*). If ordinary nature has its embodiment (*ei estin sōma psychikon*), then the spirit too has its embodiment (*estin kai pneumatikon*).[154]

Engberg-Pedersen thus brings these together:

> ... human beings are 'sown', that is, lead their lives to begin with ... as physical and sensible beings of 'flesh and blood'... ; eventually, however, they will be raised to a glorious state of eternal life that is connected with heaven and, one suspects, with the heavenly

[150] *CS* ch. 1 (8–38).

[151] *CS* 98.

[152] For full details, both of the meaning of 'resurrection' and of ancient non-Jewish views of life beyond death, see *RSG*, esp. ch. 2 (32–84); on Seneca's view of death, 54 (with refs.).

[153] 1 Cor. 15.39–41.

[154] 1 Cor. 15.42–4.

> *bodies.* Basically, then, Paul is relying on a single, straightforward contrast between an earthly kind of body connected with death and a heavenly kind of body connected with eternal life.[155]

Note the tell-tale 'one suspects'. This is precisely what Paul does *not* say, and what the flow of his thought neither requires nor implies. Indeed, the passage as a whole, and the meaning of 'resurrection' as a whole, positively rule out this move. As Engberg-Pedersen sees, the contrast of the *psychikos* person with the *pneumatikos* goes back to an earlier passage in the letter, where both categories of persons are just that, persons, not one category of ordinary people and another of stars in the sky.[156] But what Engberg-Pedersen is eager – too eager – to affirm is that when Paul said 'resurrection' he did not mean what everyone else, Jew and non-Jew alike, meant by that term in the first century. He meant 'a body dwelling in heaven':

> It seems that [Paul] must have had a more precise idea in mind when he contrasts a 'psychic body' with a 'pneumatic' one. This suggests that the contrast was *already* contained in the basic contrast he drew in the second set of premisses between 'earthly bodies' and 'heavenly bodies'. A 'psychic' body belongs *on earth* as exemplified by the 'earthly bodies' mentioned in 15:39; and a 'pneumatic' one belongs *in heaven* as exemplified by the 'heavenly bodies' mentioned in 15:41. Or to be even more precise: a 'pneumatic body' *is* a heavenly body like the sun, moon and stars.[157]

This is precisely what Paul is not saying in this passage, but this reading enables Engberg-Pedersen then to claim (a) that Paul is following 'apocalyptic' literature in seeing 'those who are being saved' as stars in heaven, and (b) that the reason he describes these people, in this future state, as 'pneumatic' is because he is thinking of the specifically Stoic *pneuma*, through which 'heavenly bodies that are situated at the top of the hierarchical *scala naturae* are distinctly made up of pneuma'.[158] Both of these claims are groundless. First, though some Jewish writers (taking the simile in Daniel 12.2–3 as a literal prediction) did imagine the righteous after death to be like stars in the sky, this was not the mainstream Jewish (Pharisaic) 'resurrection' view, and it is specifically not what any early Christians, especially Paul, understood by 'resurrection'.[159] Second, and crucially, *Paul does not envisage 'resurrection' as meaning 'being in heaven'*. Engberg-Pedersen is here simply repeating a view which, however widespread in contemporary western Christianity, is none the less a radical misunderstanding of first-century beliefs. The word 'resurrection', for Paul and all other early Christians, was never a fancy way of speaking of 'going to heaven'. It was always and only about the renewal of actual bodily life – which meant bodily life in

[155] *CS* 27 (italics original).

[156] 1 Cor. 2.14f.; *CS* 28.

[157] *CS* 28 (italics original).

[158] *CS* 20. He adds 'as we saw in the texts from Cicero'; but *de Nat. De.* 2, which he discussed at *CS* 20, does not mention 'spirit', but rather 'aether'. He discusses the relationship between *pneuma* and 'aether' at 213 n. 39, but despite his best efforts to align the two they seem to remain subtly different.

[159] cf. *RSG* 110–12, 344–6. Cp. *2 Bar.*, on which cf. *RSG* 161f.

a recreated cosmos (see below).[160] Paul never, in fact, actually speaks of the dead 'going to heaven'. The closest he comes is when he says that his desire is 'to leave all this and be with the Messiah'.[161] When he speaks of heavenly citizenship, it is not because he is looking forward to going to heaven. He is looking forward to the Messiah coming *from* heaven to change the present body into a glorious body like his own.[162] Missing this point leads Engberg-Pedersen into a whole stream of misunderstandings which we do not need to describe in detail.[163]

There are two crucial points which Engberg-Pedersen misses in this account of 1 Corinthians 15, which is the foundation of his whole second volume.[164] First, throughout this chapter Paul is building on Genesis 1, 2 and 3, in order to give an account of *new creation*, rooted in Jewish-style creational monotheism. This is where some genuine 'cosmology' would have helped: there is all the difference in the world between Paul's retrieval of Jewish creational monotheism and the pantheistic vision of the Stoics. As elsewhere in such comparisons, two views may keep one another company for part of the journey. Paul's allusion to the *pnoē zōēs* ('breath of life') from Genesis 2.7 is a case in point, alongside the Stoic *pneuma* which is itself the 'divine' force in all things. It is perfectly possible that Paul, expounding a biblically rooted vision of new creation, is deliberately picking up ideas from other worldviews and making them serve his purpose, or showing how their best insights point beyond themselves to a fuller reality than they had envisaged. That kind of tactic is what he declares as his regular practice in his programmatic statement in 2 Corinthians 10.4–5. But all the signs are that in this chapter, as elsewhere, he is consciously and deliberately expounding scripture in the light of Jesus, not expounding Stoicism in the light of some vague background 'apocalyptic' ideas.

The second crucial point is noted by Engberg-Pedersen, but he waves it away in a strange footnote.[165] The distinction Paul makes between *sōma psychikon* and *sōma pneumatikon* is specifically not a distinction between what the two 'bodies' are *composed of* – *psychē* on the one hand, *pneuma* on the other. It is a distinction between what the two 'bodies' are *animated by*: again, either *psychē* or *pneuma*. This vital distinction between *composition* and *animation* has been badly obscured in the popular mind by translations in the RSV tradition, which have, astonishingly, rendered *sōma psychikon* by 'physical body' and *sōma pneumatikon* by 'spiritual body', thus strongly

[160] See *RSG passim*, and e.g. *Surprised by Hope* chs. 1–3 and 10.

[161] Phil. 1.23.

[162] Phil. 3.20f. Engberg-Pedersen *CS* 56 fails to see this point in expounding the passage.

[163] See e.g. *CS* 12, 43, 46, 50, 147, 162f., 181. At 88, discussing 2 Cor. 12.1–5, he suggests that the 'third heaven' was the highest, but this is very unlikely (see Gooder 2006).

[164] On 1 Cor. 15 see the full account in *RSG* 312–61.

[165] *CS* 217 n. 73, where he (a) says correctly that I read 'pneumatic' as meaning 'animated by' and not 'composed of' [spirit], (b) says that this reminds him of an article by Crouzel 1976 and then (c) comments 'This is pure Bultmann.' Crouzel must speak for himself; the question is not who else has said this. The meaning of *pneumatikos* has nothing to do with Bultmann, but with lexicography, and my reading of the passage can hardly be said to be Bultmannian.

evoking a Platonic dualism between a 'material' body and a 'non-material' body, feeding a widespread misconception that Paul, the earliest Christian writer, did not believe in bodily resurrection. At least Engberg-Pedersen and I can agree that such a reading is totally unwarranted. For a start, *psychē* is normally translated 'soul'; it is a word one might use, or echo, within Platonism if one wanted to stress that something was *non*-material, not that it was 'physical'. But does the Stoic version of 'physical' really help – help, I mean, in terms of understanding what Paul is saying?

The argument now goes much deeper. I have set out this point elsewhere, but since it is so often misunderstood (or, as in this case, waved away airily) it is important to repeat the historical basis.[166]

First, philology. As the grammarians have pointed out, Greek adjectives ending in *-ikos* tend to refer to ethical or functional meanings. If you want adjectives that refer to the stuff of which something is made, they tend to be the ones that end in *-inos*.[167]

Second, parallel usage, not least among philosophers and doctors. Aristotle, speaking of wombs that are 'swollen with air', uses the phrase *hysterai pneumatikai*, and nobody supposes that he thought the wombs were *made of* something called *pneuma*.[168] Galen quotes the third-century BC writer Erasistratus who uses *pneumatikē* to refer to the left ventricle of the heart, the one that *conveys* the *pneuma*, not one that is *composed* of it.[169] Similarly, the first-century BC writer Vitruvius speaks of a machine that is 'moved by wind', a *pneumatikon organon*, and we do not imagine that he took the machines to be *made* of wind.[170] Following the Aristotle reference, the word can be active, referring for instance, almost as a transferred epithet, to *pneumatikos* wine, i.e. wine that causes the stomach to fill with flatulence.[171] The adverb *pneumatikōs* can be used in the sense of 'in one breath'.[172] There are no uses in Liddell and Scott which support the meaning which Engberg-Pedersen (in company with many over the last century) wants to find in 1 Corinthians 15.[173]

Third, classic exegesis. The International Critical Commentary on 1 Corinthians declares that

> Evidently, *psychikon* does not mean that the body is made of *psychē*, consists entirely of *psychē*: and *pneumatikon* does not mean it is made and consists entirely of *pneuma*. The

[166] See *RSG* 347–56, esp. 350–2.

[167] Moulton and Turner 1908–76, 2.359, 378. Generalizations across ancient Greek usage are risky, but this one seems to be backed up by the lexicographical detail (below).

[168] Arist. *Hist. An.* 584b22.

[169] Gal., *On the Usefulness of Parts* 6.12; cp. *Placita Philosophorum* 4.5.7.

[170] Vitr. 10.1.1; cp. Gal. *Anim. Pass.* 2.3, *pneumatika mēchanēma.*

[171] Arist. *Pr.* 955a35.

[172] Hermog. *Inv.* 4.1.

[173] An exception might be Philo *Abr.* 113; but there *pneumatikē* (modifying *ousia*, 'nature') is linked, not contrasted, with *psychoeidous*, 'soul-like'.

> adjectives mean 'congenital with,' 'formed to be the organ of' … The *pneuma* … is … the future body's principle of life.[174]

In my earlier treatment I quoted other commentaries, too, both German and English, to the same effect.[175] To these should be added the careful and thorough treatment of Thiselton, who after laying out several different options argues forcefully that Paul is simply not here talking about the *composition* of the new body, but 'the transformation of character or pattern of existence effected by the Holy Spirit'.[176] All this simply rules out Engberg-Pedersen's view of resurrection in Paul, and with it all talk of believers being 'torn out of the world' in order to be situated 'in a cosmologically imagined heaven of pneumatic, heavenly bodies'.[177] This is an idea found nowhere in Paul. It is deeply inimical to his thought.

Engberg-Pedersen's treatment of the resurrection leads directly to a similar treatment of Paul's vision of new creation. This, he declares, is to be understood on the basis of the Stoic doctrine of *ekpyrōsis*, the coming 'conflagration'. Though he professes that he is not making Paul out to be a Stoic, he certainly makes him sound like one:

> … the physical pneuma … will also eventually *literally* make believers gain 'victory' over any opposing cosmological forces whether on earth or in the sublunary sphere of heaven. They will be transformed and carried away from the earth, which will itself be transformed at the conflagration by God's powerful love.[178]

This, it seems, is the result of Engberg-Pedersen's much-heralded 'dissolution' of the contrast between Jewish (or 'apocalyptic') ideas and Stoic ones: the Stoic ones win every time.[179] He argues that to understand Paul's vision of the ultimate end we should put together the cosmic vision of Romans 8 with the warning about 'fire' in 1 Corinthians 3. But this is radically mistaken. Both passages have their origins in Paul's own language and imagery, taken from his biblical sources.

Romans 8, in particular, belongs where it does not as a detached statement about some future cosmic transformation but as the carefully planned climax of the entire sequence of thought from chapter 1 onwards, looking back particularly to Romans 4 (where Abraham is promised that he will 'inherit the world'), Romans 5.12–21 (where the rule of sin and death is replaced by the worldwide rule of grace, of righteousness and even of God's people) and Romans 8.12–17 (where the people are described in terms reminiscent of the exodus journey towards the 'inheritance', which now turns out to be the renewed cosmos that is set free from its 'slavery to decay'). In

[174] Robertson and Plummer 1914 [1911], 372.

[175] Conzelmann 1975 [1969], 283; Witherington 1995, 308f.

[176] Thiselton 2000, 1275–81, here at 1279. Thiselton (1278) also quotes Barrett 1971a [1968], 372 ('the new body animated by the Spirit of God') and Wolff 1996, 407 ('a body under the control of the divine Spirit').

[177] *CS* 97.

[178] *CS* 96 (italics original).

[179] cf. *CS* 212 n. 35.

particular, the passage turns on the messianic promise of Psalm 2, that the coming king would have the nations for his 'inheritance'. This is a million miles away from anything to do with the pantheistic doctrine of *ekpyrōsis*, in which the inner divine fire eventually takes over all the other elements to purify them so that the world may begin all over again. It is radically different not only in content, but also in its sense of chronology: for the Stoic, the 'conflagration' will happen again and again in an endless cycle, while for Paul the one God is moving his creation towards its one and only goal. This relates directly to the radical difference, which Engberg-Pedersen never discusses, between Stoic pantheism (which is itself of course a form of monotheism) and the Jewish-style *creational* monotheism which Paul has developed in the light of the Messiah and the spirit.

As for 1 Corinthians 3.10–17, and the image of a coming fire which will burn up rubbish and purify what is left, the loose analogy with the Stoic conflagration is only skin deep. The Stoic theory is of the fiery *pneuma* that already inhabits everything and that will eventually work its way outwards to consume all other elements. This seems to be taken 'literally' by the Stoics, certainly if we are to believe Engberg-Pedersen's repeated, and repeatedly italicized, use of that word. Paul's image, however, is clearly a metaphor, and makes use of the idea of a building, specifically a temple, which will be destroyed by fire, leaving its precious metal and jewels purified and intact. Yes, Paul could at this point have been glancing across the market-place to where a group of Stoic philosophers was arguing about this or that. He could have been saying 'Fire, is it? All right, let me tell you about the true divine fire that is coming one day.' But his type of fire comes from somewhere else (it does not start out as an inner fiery substance, but is sent upon the 'building' from elsewhere); it performs a different function (it does not reduce all other elements to fire, but destroys some and purifies others); and it reaches a different goal (it does not leave the world ready to begin all over again, but provides the condition of salvation, by destroying that which cannot last and by enhancing that which can and will). A different fire; a different purpose.

I have spent considerable time on these two books by Engberg-Pedersen because they address a question which seems to me of central importance for our whole subject: how did the Apostle to the Gentiles relate to the dominant philosophy of his day? Because of their industry and learning these works may already be seen as benchmarks for addressing this topic. But they proceed in such a misleading fashion that a marker needs to be put down, instead, to the effect that though the issues are important this is not the way to find the answers. It is important that from time to time the theological traditions submit themselves to sharp critique, to hearing the point the barking dogs are making. But they need to be on target.

We could, no doubt, say much more. It would be important, for instance, to note that whereas Engberg-Pedersen constantly speaks of cognitive awareness, of knowledge, as the centre of what Paul thinks is important,

Paul himself explicitly deconstructs that notion by saying that (a) what matters is God's knowledge of us, not ours of him, and (b) knowledge will puff you up, but love builds you up.[180] That same motif characterizes Paul's radical revision of Aristotelian virtue-theory: the goal is not *eudaimonia*, but the Messiah himself, and the primary character-strength required in the present if one is stretching forward to that future is again *agapē*, love. All this is basic to Paul's actual and implicit engagement with the philosophical world of his day, but there is no sign that Engberg-Pedersen has got inside such questions.

Nor is there any sign that he has really understood the world of first-century Jews, their stories, their symbols, their political realities and aspirations and the way their literature addressed such matters. He works with a one-dimensional cardboard cut-out called 'apocalyptic' which bears little relation to the texts or movements we actually know, let alone the way they were reworked in early Christianity. Nor has he really understood some of the key issues at stake in current Pauline scholarship. He claims to have followed Sanders and Schweitzer in overcoming the divide between 'justification' and 'participation', but since he never discusses the former and only briefly treats the latter, and since in any case Sanders and Schweitzer did not overcome that divide at all but rather set it all the more firmly in stone, we are no further forward.[181]

In particular, his claim throughout, in these books and elsewhere, to have gone beyond 'the Judaism/Hellenism divide', is not made good. Yes, the nineteenth-century constructs which used those labels were damaging to scholarship (and to wider culture and European civilization), and we must avoid all that. But this does not mean that there was no difference in the first century between Jews and non-Jews, or between their respective symbolic worlds, characteristic narratives and so on. Of course, each side of that 'divide' could be further subdivided, the Jews into different strands and parties, fluid and flexible but producing variations on some central themes, and the non-Jews into different philosophical, religious, political and many other strands, schools, cultures and sub-cultures. No doubt, as with Philo in one way and the Wisdom of Solomon in another, there were many points, probably many more than we know, at which the Jewish worlds and the non-Jewish worlds bumped into one another, coming away like two cars after a brief encounter in the parking lot, with someone else's paint still showing. Sometimes it undoubtedly went far deeper than that. I have myself suggested, earlier in this chapter, that Paul, at various points in his writings, may well have done quite deliberately what he says in 2 Corinthians 10, that is, pick up ideas from outside the Jewish world and make them serve the gospel. But to collapse the Jewish world, in all its rich variety, into the word 'apocalyptic', as Engberg-Pedersen does, and then at every point to subsume

180 cf. e.g. *PS* 62.

181 See *CS* 150, with 242f. n. 27.

it, in Paul's thought and writing, under a reinscribed Stoicism, is without historical or exegetical warrant.

Nor, therefore, does he get near the heart of Paul. Despite his claim to 'cover all of it', to make Paul coherent, to expound 'the heart of Paul's worldview' and so on,[182] what we have here, ironically, is Hamlet without the prince; or perhaps one should say the Prince of Denmark without the king, the queen and the travelling players. What else can we say when someone, setting out ostensibly to expound and explain what Paul was really all about, sweeps aside the notion of 'salvation' as irrelevant, because it belongs to Paul's theological discourse and is therefore not a matter of direct concern in a supposed analysis of what was really central for him?[183] And what about the cheerful and cavalier Cynic-style dismissal of most of the major *topoi* of Pauline studies? When trying to solve the problem of one of Paul's key terms, says Engberg-Pedersen,

> One may wonder . . . whether there is any likelihood of progress until one decides to place in parenthesis to begin with the whole gamut of traditional theological concepts: soteriology, christology, justification, grace, works, etc.[184]

This is, of course, exactly what he said he would do at the start of his first book: investigate Paul while bracketing out 'theology', concentrating instead on his 'worldview', 'cosmology' and so on. And his two books really do carry out this agenda: the topics he lists in that remarkable quotation never come on stage, except to make brief guest appearances in the extended (but idiosyncratic) exegesis in *Paul and the Stoics*. It is as risky to reconstruct the train of thought of a contemporary as it is of an ancient writer, but a plausible hypothesis might run as follows: (a) that Engberg-Pedersen, coming (one imagines) from a tradition of Danish Lutheranism, has supposed from the start that what really matters to Paul is conversion, while sensing that the theological structures that have been built around that have failed in some way (coherence?); (b) that he has studied ancient and modern philosophy and found that it offers 'real options' which Paul, as he stands, did not; (c) that he has constructed a conversion-model which he can then 'find' in Stoic writers on the one hand and in Paul on the other; then, (d) that, armed with the Stoic notion of the 'material *pneuma*', he has done his best to re-read Paul in that light, again bracketing out most of his central theological concepts: *et voilà*, we have passed beyond the Judaism/Hellenism divide. What has actually happened, however, is that we have passed beyond a divide which Engberg-Pedersen has himself invented and operated: the divide between what he finds to be a 'real option', which is a version of Stoic anthropology, ethics and *pneuma* and which, with a little help from modern philosophy and cultural studies as well, he attempts to read into Paul, and

[182] *CS* 75f., 139, 89f., 137.

[183] *PS* 39.

[184] *CS* 245 n. 42. We note in particular the total absence of the cross, so central for Paul, from the books under discussion.

what he finds to be not a 'real option', which is most of the things that most readers of Paul have supposed, on good exegetical and historical grounds, to constitute the very heart of his thought. Yes, we need to do worldview-studies. Yes, we need to put Paul in his wider social, cultural, political contexts (what happened to the political in Engberg-Pedersen's treatment, I wonder?). Yes, we may well have a lot to learn from people like Bourdieu about how to understand humans in their full cultural environment. I have tried in the present book to do all or at least most of that. But I have concluded, on the basis of the worldview-studies of Part II, that Paul *needed to rethink his theology* if the worldview he was developing and inculcating was to remain stable and coherent. Hence Part III. And that exposition of both worldview and theology, I submit, is still waiting to be explored in terms of the hypothetical meeting between Paul and Seneca, or between Paul and Epictetus,[185] or between Paul and Dio Chrystostom or anyone else for that matter. The present chapter is only the beginning of that kind of hypothetical engagement. I hope it will stimulate others to take matters further.

4. Conclusion

We have now examined the three overlapping and interlocking worlds to which the Apostle to the Gentiles found himself sent at the behest of the God of Israel and his crucified and risen Messiah. These worlds did not, of course, present themselves as tidy wholes, any more than the politics, religion and philosophy of our own day appear in neat packages. The combination of long hindsight on the one hand and scarcity of source material on the other enables us to imagine that we 'see' a more coherent picture than would have appeared to the apostle as he trudged into yet another bustling city and set about finding a place to ply his trade. There is however some value, at least heuristically, in setting out his hypothetical and perhaps actual engagement with these three 'worlds', if only because much scholarship has tended to concentrate on one to the exclusion of the others, or has confused them in some way. I hope that these three chapters have at least set up signposts towards more work that could and should be done.

I note in particular, as something I might have hoped to cover had there been more space, that though I have delved a little way into the overlap between 'politics' and 'religion' – specifically, in relation to the phenomena we think of as imperial cults – and though I have tried to insist that the 'religious' element in ancient philosophy (including what the philosophers would have called 'theology') matters in both those worlds, I have not tried to do the same between philosophy and politics. It would be a task well worth doing to plot out the ways in which the various philosophies of Paul's day generated and sustained political systems and regimes, both formally and informally, and also movements of opposition or revolution, and to

[185] Engberg-Pedersen's chapter (*CS* ch. 4, 106–38) is an interesting start, granted all the caveats of my present discussion. See too e.g. Huttunen 2009.

enquire whether we might learn anything at that level about how Paul might have engaged with those worlds – or whether, as some have suggested, he would rise above it all and concentrate on higher things. I shall try, in the final chapter of this book, at least to sketch some ways in which the total project to which he was called involved a freshly conceived integration of things that, to his contemporaries, might have been thought of as 'political', 'religious' and 'philosophical', but which for Paul will have appeared as parts of a coherent, and Messiah-shaped, whole.

Paul did not, then, derive his key ideas from his non-Jewish environment, but nor can his relationship with that environment be labelled simply 'confrontation'. It is far more subtle. He did not, indeed, take over his main themes from the worlds of non-Jewish politics, religion or philosophy, but nor did he march through those worlds resolutely looking the other way and regarding them as irrelevant. Nor did he say they were all completely wrong from top to bottom. When he says that all the treasures of wisdom and knowledge are hidden in the Messiah, he does not mean, as did some who believed that all truth was contained in the Bible, that one could throw all other books away. Tracking, plotting and assessing the many lines and levels of his engagement with his complex non-Jewish world is a task awaiting further attention.

The logic of this Part of the book, mirroring that of the first Part, ought now I hope to be clear. Paul began as a Jew, and went out from there into the world of non-Jewish ideas, religions and political systems. He firmly believed that he was called to be the Apostle to the Gentiles; and, with that historical starting-point in mind, we have gone back through those systems, practices and ideas, looking for the ways in which the Paul we have come to know in Parts II and III would have engaged, and did in fact engage, with those aspects of non-Jewish culture.

He was not, however, Apostle to the Jews. Any effect his ministry might have on his own 'kinsfolk according to the flesh' he saw simply as a reflex of his primary task.[186] Nevertheless, it was an important reflex, resulting in some of his sharpest arguments. So, having sketched briefly some of the ways in which his primary ministry might have worked out on the ground, we come back to the question which inevitably haunts all studies of Paul's theology, not least the kind of argument we mounted in Part III of the present book. What were the main lines of Paul's reflex engagement – if we may call it that – with his own flesh and blood?

[186] Rom. 11.11–16: see above, 1206–22.

Chapter Fifteen

TO KNOW THE PLACE FOR THE FIRST TIME: PAUL AND HIS JEWISH CONTEXT

1. Introduction

As we retrace our explorations through Paul's world, we return at last to the place where it all began, namely the first-century Jewish world. There is, however, an inevitable asymmetry between this chapter and the previous three. When we looked at Paul and the Roman empire in chapter 12, at Paul and the late-antique religious world in chapter 13 and at Paul and the pagan philosophers in chapter 14, we were examining how the Paul whose worldview and theology we had explored in Parts II and III related to the worlds in and to which he was, by his own account, a missionary. His call was to be the apostle to the non-Jewish nations. He came with a Jewish message and a Jewish way of life for the non-Jewish world. He did not see himself as founding or establishing a new, non-Jewish movement. He believed that the message and life he proclaimed and inculcated was, in some sense, the fulfilment of all he had believed as a strict Pharisaic Jew. He understood himself to be taking his native way of life, admittedly in a radically transformed version, into the wider world. He was not, then, the apostle *to* the Jews, however much time he spent in Jewish contexts. He was, in his own eyes at least, the apostle *from* the Jews to the rest of the world. His engagement with his own contemporary Jewish world was therefore of a different order from his engagement with the other worlds where we have tried to locate him.

One of the central arguments of this whole book, after all, is that Paul remained stubbornly and intentionally a deeply Jewish thinker. That claim might be challenged, both in his day and in ours. But I have argued that the full sweep of his theological understanding can best be understood, not as a random or pragmatic amalgamation of bits and pieces from his native heritage and his hellenistic culture, strung together with whatever string would hold it firm while he pressed home a particular point, but as the structurally and scripturally coherent reworking of the central themes of the Jewish heritage, monotheism, election and eschatology, articulated in such a way as to make and sustain the claim that this is the way to a full and genuine human life. There is no point trying, at this late stage, to develop these arguments once again; Parts II and III of the book must speak for themselves. Nor is there any point, therefore, in trying to structure the present chapter on the rough model of the previous three. The question of 'Paul and the Jewish world', or however we want to phrase it, remains a different *sort* of question from 'Paul and empire', 'Paul and religion' or 'Paul and philosophy'. As far as Paul was concerned, he had a mission *to* those worlds, a mission which (to repeat) had come *from* the world of the first-century Jews.[1] All that he had to say in relation to the latter world was therefore, as it were, by way of reflex from his primary task.

I have argued that all this has little to do with 'religion' and a great deal to do with 'eschatology'. To say this might appear to have a superficial analogy with the generalized Barthian and indeed protestant protest against 'religion' as such, which drives the analyses of Käsemann, Martyn and others; but actually my point is different and deeper. It is *not* the case that Paul opposes something called 'Judaism' because it is a 'religion', whereas he was advocating something different (whether 'eschatology', 'faith' or anything else). That is a classic form of western supersessionism: 'the Jews were clinging to "religion", but Paul was offering something different and better'. Nor is it the case, despite regular suggestions in contemporary writing (not least that which has followed E. P. Sanders in comparing 'patterns of religion' in Paul and 'Judaism'), that Paul was advocating or modelling a new sort of 'religion' which he considered (for some reason) superior to other forms of 'religion', especially Judaism. Paul was simply not concerned very much with 'religion' as such, whether for or against. That is a distraction. That very lining-up of the question, either in terms of 'religion versus eschatology' or in terms of 'one sort of religion against another', *is itself part of the problem introduced by modern western scholarship*, determined as it has been to make 'religion' central by some means or other. Paul's critique of his fellow Jews was not centrally or primarily a critique of either their 'religion' in general or any features of it in particular.

What mattered, rather, was his belief that *Jesus of Nazareth was Israel's Messiah*. More precisely and importantly, that *the crucified and risen Jesus of Nazareth was Israel's Messiah and the world's true lord*. Every single thing we know about Paul, particularly from his own writings, makes the sense it makes on the basic Jewish assumption that when the Messiah appeared he would bring about the fulfilment of God's ancient promises to Israel. And the clash with those of his fellow Jews who did not believe that Jesus was Israel's Messiah came precisely on the level not of 'religion' but of *messianic eschatology*: he believed that the Messiah had come, and had inaugurated the long-awaited new age, and they did not. At this point, and to this extent, Paul was standing on exactly the same ground as Akiba a century later, confronting the critics who told him he was wrong to suppose that Simeon ben-Kosiba was 'the son of the star'. To this we shall return.

[1] This is to make a similar point, at this level of generality, to Nanos 2010b, though our perspectives then naturally diverge. The essay of Frey 2007 brings the German discussion of the topic forward from an older polarization, and an essentially non- or anti-Jewish Paul, towards the more complex but historically coherent position of Paul as still emphatically Jewish – which then simply sets the stage for the real questions to begin.

The shock to the system, of course, came not simply with a clash of claims about a particular messianic claimant, but with the claim that a *crucified* man was the Messiah. The otherwise unthinkable notion of a crucified Messiah was forced on Paul and the other early Jesus-followers by Jesus' resurrection, which compelled them to take seriously the messianic claim which otherwise the crucifixion would have falsified. Jesus had neither defeated the pagans in battle, nor rebuilt the Temple, nor established a visible new empire of justice and peace; on the contrary, he seemed not only to have failed in any such messianic tasks but to have been cursed by God in the process. The resurrection transformed this perception, offering divine confirmation of the title Pilate had placed above Jesus' head on the cross, and awakening echoes in Israel's scriptures to which implicit appeal was made in some of the earliest Christian confessions.[2] The resurrection confirmed what Pilate had caused to be written about Jesus' head on the cross: King of the Jews. However paradoxical, however shocking, however previously unthinkable, this was what Paul firmly believed, and this belief generated the entire shape and content of his life's work. When we place Paul within his own Jewish context, this is what stands out far above everything else.

Insofar as Paul would have had anything much to say about comparing one ancient 'religion' with another (as opposed to our modern attempts to compare the things *we* call 'religions'), he would undoubtedly have regarded the basic comparison as being between the Jewish 'religion' and the multiple varieties of pagan 'religion'. On that question he would have had no choice. If Paul had been asked to 'compare' the two, he would undoubtedly have noted the pure Jewish monotheism; the underpinning covenantal narrative; the single sanctuary; the high valuation of humans and hence of moral standards; and, not least, the extraordinary and still unsurpassed Jewish hymnbook. All these, he would have said, showed up the complex and messy life of ancient paganism as a shabby muddle. But the point of course was not that Paul had looked out at the world of 'religions' and chosen one of them. That, again, is a very modern idea. Paul was born a Jew, and believed that the Jewish way of life and view of life were above all *true*. There was indeed one creator God, the God of Abraham, of the exodus, of the Psalms, of the prophets, of the long-awaited future hope. And there was one true way to be human, the way of faithful and wise obedience to this one God. Had Paul wished to 'compare religions', then – even supposing he would have understood the question! – he would have regarded it as a no-brainer. The Jewish way of life and worship would win every time.

But Paul was not 'comparing religions', either before or after what happened to him on the Damascus Road. When he began to speak in the synagogues and elsewhere about the Jesus who had appeared to him on the road, he was not 'advocating' a new 'religion'. Nor was he saying, 'Up to now you've had a "religion", but I've got something different to offer.' He was

[2] e.g. Rom. 1.3–4; 1 Cor. 15.3–8: see above, e.g. 518, 525, 555.

declaring that the God whom the Jews had worshipped all along, the God made known in their scriptures, had done at last what he had promised, and that with that divine action a new world order had come into being. Paul's theology and mission were rooted in and defined by this *christologically inaugurated eschatology*. In Jesus, the End had arrived in the Middle, and everything was different as a result. But it was a difference – and Paul insisted on this strongly and fiercely – which (with hindsight of course) one ought to see as having been intended all along. The one God had not suddenly changed his mind, his plans or his ultimate purposes. The one God had acted suddenly, shockingly and unexpectedly – just as he had always said he would. And just as, again with hindsight, Paul could see made sense if this God really was righteous in his dealings with the whole world.

This meant, inevitably, that Paul stood in a complex and ambiguous relation to those of his Jewish contemporaries who did not believe that Jesus of Nazareth had been raised from the dead, and who therefore had no reason to believe that he was Israel's Messiah. To tell such people about Jesus was not Paul's primary task, though the evidence, from his letters as well as Acts, strongly suggests that in Asia and Greece he normally began in synagogues and only moved out into lecture-halls or near equivalents when he had to.[3] No: his main message, as he reminds the Thessalonians, was the deeply Jewish one, that pagans should turn from idols to worship the true and living God.[4] Anything he might have to say to his Jewish contemporaries who did not believe in Jesus he would say by way of reflex from that primary vocation. Anything he might say *about* such people, when addressing pagan converts, he would say (as in Galatians, Philippians and Colossians) by way of explanation and warning. Much of what has often been considered central to Paul's theology, especially his teaching on justification and the law, comes into these categories: when Paul spoke to pagans, as he did most of the time, he spoke, not about justification, but about the one God and his son, Jesus. 'Justification' came in as and when he had to explain to converts that they were indeed full members of the single family God had promised to Abraham, irrespective of circumcision and the other traditional marks of Jewish identity.[5] And the critique of his compatriots who refused to believe in Jesus – a critique whose obverse was heart-stopping grief – grew directly out of the same eschatology. The tide had turned in the affairs of Israel; Paul was taking it at the flood. Those who omitted to do so would for ever remain in shallows and in miseries.

Paul understood, from his own earlier life, the motivations and intentions that drove non-Jesus-believing Jews to oppose the message altogether. From his experience of early debates among Jesus-believing Jews – not least the incident at Antioch and the conference at Jerusalem – he understood, too, the intentions and motivations of those Jesus-believing Jews who took the view that converted pagans should take on full Jewish identity by becoming

[3] See below, 1484–1504 on Paul's missionary strategy.

[4] 1 Thess. 1.9f.

[5] 'Justification' could of course be mentioned in passing, as in e.g. 1 Cor. 6.11.

circumcised. All these we have discussed already, at some length. We must now probe a little deeper into this particular interface, into some of the key questions that have swirled around the question of 'Paul and the Jews' – itself, of course, a potentially misleading way of putting it, granted that Paul spoke of himself as a Jew, an Israelite, a Hebrew of Hebrews and so on.[6] Hence the subtitle of this chapter: Paul and *his* Jewish context.

We must stress again, being aware of today's political and cultural pressures, that Paul had no intention of 'founding a new religion'.[7] He did not see himself as setting up something called 'Christianity' as opposed to something called 'Judaism'. The field of 'ity's and 'ism's belongs in the ideologically slanted world of western modernity, not in the world of second-Temple Jews and their pagan neighbours. Paul knew only of the God of Israel and his promised return to set his people free and claim the nations as his own. As we saw in chapter 2, Paul had been living in the great multifaceted narrative shaped by Israel's scriptures, longing for the moment of covenant renewal, of 'return from exile', of the fulfilment of Deuteronomy, Isaiah, the Psalms and so much besides. He believed that all this had been accomplished in and through Jesus; that it was coming true, and would come fully true, through the spirit. What else could he do but obey? How else would he see himself and other believers but as members of Abraham's single, renewed family?

This means that we must recognize some recent slogans for what they are. When people talk, as they often do these days, of 'replacement' theologies in which something called 'the church' *replaces* something called 'the Jews', or 'Israel';[8] when people talk, as they sometimes do, of 'substitution' theologies, in which 'the church' (again!) has *substituted* for 'Israel' or 'the Jews' in the divine plan;[9] when they refer to a position in which 'the church' has *displaced* 'Israel'; when they talk, above all, of that unfortunate word 'supersession', in which 'the church' – and often the *gentile* church at that – has *superseded* 'the Jews' or 'Israel'[10] – there we are witnessing something which, while it may have been true of much later generations, was not and could not have been true for Paul. For Paul it was dazzlingly clear. Either Jesus was Israel's Messiah or he was not. *Tertium non datur*. There was no suggestion of Jesus being a 'Christian Messiah' as opposed to a 'Jewish' one

[6] A 'Jew': Ac. 21.39; 22.3; Gal. 2.15; 'Israelite': Rom. 11.1; 2 Cor. 11.22; 'of the race of Israel': Phil. 3.5; 'Hebrew': 2 Cor. 11.22; Phil. 3.5. On Rom. 2.28f.; 1 Cor. 9.20 see below.

[7] Against e.g. Betz 1979, 320, who sees Paul announcing 'the establishment of a new religion'. Correctly e.g. Bird 2012, 23: 'Paul never intended to set up a new religious entity.'

[8] Nanos 2010a and elsewhere.

[9] See the various discussions in Bell 1994; 2005.

[10] Harink 2003, ch. 4; W. S. Campbell 2008 (see below). We are now even offered something called a 'post-supersessionist interpretation' of one Pauline passage: see Rudolph 2011 (the phrase occurs, as a description of the book, on the back cover). The implicit claim to a new periodization of scholarship begs a good many questions. A different, and arguably more helpful, line is taken by Longenecker 2007, who argues for what we might call a 'benign' Pauline 'supersessionism' over against the toxic alternatives of 'replacement' and the increasingly discredited 'two-covenant' theory. But I suspect that the 's'-word will retain its pejorative overtones, as e.g. in Rudolph 2011, 211. On the whole set of questions see the survey in Zetterholm 2009, 129–63.

– a strange modern notion, accidentally encouraged by Christians themselves deJudaizing their message and with it their christology.[11] But if Jesus really was Israel's Messiah, then no first-century Jew could have supposed for a minute that following him was an *option* that one might take up or not. There would be no room for saying, 'Well, some of us think Jesus is Messiah and some of us don't, so let's not worry about it.' To reject the Davidic king would be to follow Jeroboam the son of Nebat into drastic and dangerous rebellion.

What has happened, I think, is that modern historians have looked back on Paul and his teaching through a complex set of spectacles. We have looked at him, first, in the light of the second, third and fourth centuries, where 'the church', though still incorporating many Jews, became, and was sometimes seen as, a mostly non-Jewish phenomenon.[12] We have looked at those centuries themselves not only through the tearful misted-up spectacles of post-holocaust western thinkers, but through the distorting lenses of post-Enlightenment historians of something called 'religion'. We have then relentlessly substituted sociological/religious categories for eschatological ones, Christian eschatology being one of the things the Enlightenment wanted to ignore. The question has then become: was Paul a 'supersessionist' – that nasty, dangerous thing which the modern western 'church' has supposedly endorsed – or was he something else, and if so what? But this is a false perception. The 's'-word, and the other terms that sometimes do duty for it, arise only when we allow the modernist displacement of first-century eschatological belief to lure us into imagining that first-century Jewish rejection of claims about Jesus was basically a clash of 'religions'. That itself, ironically enough, constitutes a capitulation to an essentially paganizing movement, denying the original *Jewish* perception (of God's kingdom coming on earth as in heaven) and allowing it to be 'superseded' by the all-too-easy pagan assumption that what was 'really' going on was a choice between systems; between societies; between 'religions'. Many of the great Jewish writers on Paul of earlier generations rejected this way of looking at things: much as they continued to disagree with Paul's basic claims, they realized that in his own mind he was following the consistent, and in itself deeply Jewish, line of 'fulfilment'.[13] But to suppose, as many writers now do, that because we can prove that Paul said 'lots of positive things about Judaism' he cannot therefore have held any critique of his own former position, or advanced any claim about a recent and transformative

[11] See Novenson 2014. Once one realizes that for Paul messianic belief and christological belief are one and the same (see above, 643–709 with 815–36), it becomes very strange to say that there might be a future 'messianic' event which Jews would not have to acknowledge 'in expressly christological terms' (Pawlikowski 2012, 172).

[12] Jews continued, however, to be a fertile source of new believers in Jesus as Messiah: see Stark 1996, ch. 3.

[13] See e.g. Klausner 1943, 591: Paul 'considered his teaching as true Judaism, as the fulfilment of the promises and assurances of authentic Judaism'; so too Sandmel 1978, 336; Schoeps 1961 [1959], 237.

messianic fulfilment, is to fail to understand how Judaism itself – to risk the generalization! – normally operates.[14]

At the same time, the polemic in question has borrowed unwarranted energy from the sneering negativity of contemporary western anti-ecclesiasticalism. Particularly in the world of academic biblical studies, in which contempt for the institutional church is a recurring epidemic (and in some Anabaptist circles, in which rejection of a supposedly 'Constantinian' church is a badge of honour), the phrase 'the church' regularly connotes power and privilege, arrogant self-importance and a disregard for minorities. And, of course, non-Jewish membership. (This is reinforced, with further irony, in the modernist assumption that conversion is undesirable, thus making evangelism among Jews politically incorrect, despite Romans 11.11–24, and leaving 'messianic Jews' high and dry as an embarrassment to both 'sides'.) That then skews the terms of the debate: either Paul did, or he did not, substitute 'the church', with all those overtones, for 'Israel'! Now, of course, nothing that we would even begin to recognize as 'the church' of today's western world was thinkable in Paul's day, or indeed for several generations afterwards. Scholars who would be quick to spot anachronisms in other contexts often seem curiously blind to an obvious one here.

This is not, of course, to deny that churches of all sorts, in the last half-millennium at least, have indeed had a rotten track record as regards 'the Jews', and on many other questions too. Just as military generals are the people most likely to say what a horrible and disgusting thing war is, so those who have been leaders in institutional churches are the most likely to agree with the charges of folly, corruption, arrogance and sin. Within that, of course, some foolish or wicked would-be Christian rhetoric has fuelled the fires, literal as well as metaphorical, of what was basically and always an essentially *pagan* rejection of the Jewish way of life, its monotheism, its Torah, its sense of community. But if we allow this proper awareness and perception of ecclesial mistakes to cloud our historical judgment of what Paul thought he was doing, or if we allow it to force us into the false polarization of different 'types of religion' in our modern sense or even in Paul's ancient one, we are guilty of just as much anachronism as the so-called 'old perspective' was when it projected its rejection of medieval Catholicism back on to Paul's rejection of the 'works of Torah'.

What has happened, in short, is this. We have looked back through post-Enlightenment and post-holocaust spectacles at teachers like Chrystostom in the fourth century or indeed Luther in the sixteenth. We have then looked at Paul in the light of them. Then we have tried to decide whether Paul was, or was not, guilty of the sins which the modern west has come to associate with 'the church' and its elbowing of 'the Jews' out of the picture. This is not a recipe for doing history. And history is what this book is basically about.

[14] This criticism applies to several of the essays in Bieringer and Pollefeyt 2012a.

When we approach the question historically, everything looks remarkably different. Take the movements a century or more either side of Paul. Think of Qumran, where the scrolls bear witness to a sect which saw itself as 'Israel' while 'Israel' as a whole was apostate. The covenant had been renewed! This was what the prophets had foretold! The exile was over – at least in principle, with this group as the advance guard of the coming new day. All that, uncontroversially, is what the leaders and members of the sect believed.[15] Was this 'replacement theology'? Was it 'substitution'? Was it even 'supersession'? One could use words like that, but that was not of course how the sect saw itself, and the words would carry none of today's negative overtones. Such words evoke, and belong within, static, non-eschatological systems. The whole point, for the Damascus Document, 4QMMT and many other scrolls, was that the long narrative of Israel's strange and often tragic history had reached its appointed goal. Torah and prophets had foretold a coming time of renewal, a righteous remnant ... was it unJewish, or anti-Jewish, to claim that this was now happening? Of course not. It might be wrong. It might be a false hope. Time would tell. But it was not, in any sense we should consider meaningful today, 'supersessionist'.[16] How could claiming that Israel's God had finally kept his promises be anything other than a cause for Jewish celebration?

Or consider the rise of bar-Kochba, a century after Paul's day. Once again, the dark forces of paganism closed in. The new emperor forbade Jewish practices and threatened to obliterate the nation and its historic, theologically central capital.[17] What was a loyal Jew to do? Some were calculating that the renewed 'exile' following Jerusalem's destruction (starting with AD 70) had lasted nearly seventy years. Perhaps *this*, after all, would be the fulfilment of Jeremiah's well-known prophecy?[18] Some believed that the emerging young leader, Simeon ben-Kosiba, really was Israel's Messiah, the son of the star. Others sharply disagreed, either because their calculations were different or because they had already decided, following the earlier disaster, that piety was now superseding politics. What was to be done? Those who, like Akiba himself, seen by many as the greatest rabbi of the time or perhaps ever, believed that ben-Kosiba was the Messiah, had no choice. They had to follow him and try to make the revolution happen – facing down the sceptics and scoffers with the challenge to faith and hope and military revolt. If Israel's God was at last sending his promised deliverer, it would hardly be 'supersessionist' to rally to his cause and to scorn the Hillelite rabbis who now wanted to study Torah rather than work for the kingdom. This was not a matter of 'replacing' or 'displacing' something

[15] As an obvious example: CD 2.14—4.12.

[16] Thus, though I see the point made by Levenson (1993, x) in saying that early Christian 'supersessionism' is simply a variation within what was happening in the Jewish world anyway, I prefer not to use the word. It is more appropriate for the kind of schemes proposed in the middle and late C20 by those who see 'Judaism' as a 'religion', and Paul as the 'apocalyptic' thinker who opposed all 'religion' as such.

[17] See further *NTPG* 165f.; and above, 619f.

[18] Jer. 25.11; see above, 142.

called 'Israel' and substituting something else. If ben-Kosiba was the Messiah, then his followers constituted the renewed Israel. That was Akiba's position, and he died for it.[19]

Paul belongs exactly on this map. He believed that Israel's God had renewed the covenant through the Messiah, Jesus. He might, of course, have been wrong. He would no doubt have said that the Qumran sectarians had been wrong to suppose that covenant renewal was taking place with them. The post-135 rabbis declared that Akiba and his colleagues had been wrong to back bar-Kochba. They all might have been wrong; but not unJewish, or anti-Jewish. Or 'supersessionist' – except in an historical sense shorn of all its pejorative overtones. All of them, Paul included, believed in the divine purpose according to which God would act in judgment and mercy. Isaiah had spoken of trees being cut down, and a new shoot springing up in their place. John the Baptist had spoken of the axe being laid to the roots of the tree, of God creating children for Abraham from the very stones.[20] This is the prophetic language of judgment and renewal. It is the kind of thing that second-Temple Jews believed in and hoped for.

Of course any such claim would be contentious. Different groups might well accuse one another of disloyalty, of misreading the signs and the scriptures. That is what the writers of the Scrolls thought about the Pharisees.[21] The Pharisees may well have returned the compliment. It is certainly what the Pharisees' putative successors, the rabbis, thought about the Sadducees, and continued to think about them long after the last Sadducee perished in Jerusalem's great disaster. It is certainly what many Jewish groups thought about one another during those last tragic years of AD 66–70: rival parties, each supposing themselves to be the chosen few, anathematized and even killed one another. When revolution is in the air, fuelled by scriptural promises on the one hand and social problems on the other, you will always get competing claims, and they will often couch themselves in the language of 'true Israel', like the many 'true Marxist' groups of the last hundred years and the small but dangerous 'Real Irish Republican Army' of our own day. The Jewish world that was ready to explode in that way was the world in which Saul of Tarsus had gone off to Damascus to stop the blaspheming Jesus-followers in their tracks – and the world in which Paul the apostle went about claiming that Israel's God had raised Jesus from the dead.

Ah but, say the self-styled anti-supersessionists (not to mention the 'post-supersessionists'): Paul's message was different. He was bringing in uncircumcized gentiles, so by creating a non-Jewish 'church' he was doing something no other Jewish groups had done. Neither Qumran, nor Akiba, nor anyone in between, had envisaged a 'renewed covenant' which would

[19] As with almost everything else in the period, doubt has been cast on the historical value of the (much later) traditions about Akiba; but the point I am making, about the shape and effect of a disputed claim about messianic eschatology, remains valid even if the 'history' were to be disproved. See now e.g. Friedman 2004; Yadin 2010.

[20] Isa. 6.13; 10.33—11.3; Mt. 3.9f./Lk. 3.8f.

[21] See above, 81.

include non-Jews and thereby displace Jews. Paul, of course, never speaks about 'displacement'. The closest he gets to it – in Romans 11.17 – is a debating point which he uses to warn precisely against gentile arrogance.[22] What he says – and he is careful always to ground this in some of the most fundamental biblical texts – is that Israel's God always intended and promised that when he fulfilled his promises to Israel then the rest of the world would be renewed as well, and that this is what was now happening through the gentile mission. *The extension to non-Jews of renewed-covenant membership was itself, Paul insisted, one part of deep-rooted Jewish eschatology.*

Of course, Paul knew where the real stumbling-block lay. Any suggestion that the Jewish people could simply continue as they were without any transformation, that the one God would vindicate them as they stood, came face to face with the fact of the crucified Messiah. The cross, for Paul, was not simply an isolated incident, the mechanism of a detached 'atonement'. It was where the whole narrative had been going all along. It spoke volumes to him, personally and (so he believed) representatively, about the way in which the Israel-shaped divine purpose was to be understood. This is where Paul's view of the 'remnant' is significantly different from anything we find in Qumran. For the Damascus Document, the 'remnant' was the small group from within Israel who remained faithful, who embraced an ultra-strict observance of Torah, while the remaining Jews were outside. For Paul, his own position and that of other Jesus-believing Jews was not that they had somehow clung on, not that through their 'zeal' they were the last remaining genuine Israelites, but that they had 'died' with the Messiah and come through to a new life the other side of that 'death'. And in the new world of that 'resurrection' they found themselves sharing this messianic life with all those marked out by Messiah-faith. That, Paul insisted, was what God had all along promised to Abraham. The Qumran community saw itself as the *yahad*, the 'one community'. That is how Paul saw the single community of Jews and gentiles who shared Messiah-faith.

Paul was not shy of explaining all this by referring to himself. That is why the study of what happened to him on the road to Damascus – or rather, of what he said about what happened to him on the road to Damascus – is of theological, and not merely biographical, interest.

2. Conversion, Call or Transformation?

We might, I suppose, have discussed this question right at the start. But it is really only now, with a fuller understanding of Paul's theology, that we can appreciate what he says about the Damascus Road event. This might lead us into many complex by-paths, not least of the psychology of Paul's 'religious

[22] See above, 1217, on Rom. 11.17.

experience', about which many unproveable theories have been advanced.[23] But our focus here must be on Paul's own view of what happened.

The current controversy over how to describe or label the Damascus Road event was begun by Krister Stendahl as part of his protest against envisaging Paul in modern western Christian categories.[24] His point, in retrospect, was obvious: that the word 'conversion', which the church for many centuries has used to describe the Damascus Road event, carries seriously anachronistic connotations. All the regular contemporary meanings of the word take us in wrong directions.[25] There are many recent studies of the issue; this is not the place to review them, and for our present purposes I offer my own tripartite reflections on how the word is used.[26]

The word 'conversion' can be used, first, to denote the moment when an adherent of one 'religion' (in the modern sense) abandons it and embraces another: as, say, if a Muslim were to become a Buddhist, or vice versa. That usage is almost unknown in the ancient world, because 'religions' in our modern sense were themselves, as we have seen, unknown, with the exception of those who joined one or other of the 'mystery religions', and even that should not, perhaps, be thought of as 'converting', since one did not *abandon* any of the regular divinities in order to add Mithras, or Isis, to one's personal portfolio.[27] The closest to 'conversion' one might come, ironically, is the phenomenon of a non-Jew 'converting', abandoning pagan deities, and embracing the Jewish life.

To imagine that this change of 'religions' was what happened to Paul on the road to Damascus is not only anachronistic. It implies that he moved,

[23] See the account in e.g. Segal 1990, 285–300; on wider psychological issues in Paul, Theissen 1987 [1983].

[24] See Stendahl 1976.

[25] Dictionary definitions, in any case, only take us so far. The 10th edition of Merriam-Webster's *Collegiate Dictionary* (1998) gives, as the meaning relevant to present discussion, 'an experience associated with a definite and decisive adoption of religion', which tells us more about the basically secular stance of the dictionary than about actual usage, since many modern Christians would describe their conversion as a move *from* 'religion' to something else, e.g. 'faith'. The 3rd edition of Merriam-Webster's *New International Dictionary* (1993) offers the general 'change from one belief, view, course, party, or principle to another', and then, more specifically, 'the bringing over or persuasion of a person to the Christian faith', followed by another general meaning ('a change of one's feelings or one's point of view from a state marked by indifference or opposition to one of zealous acceptance') and then, more specifically again, 'such a change in one's religious orientation marked also by a concomitant change in belief', which is still quite vague. The relevant section in the *Oxford English Dictionary* has 'the bringing of anyone over to a specified religious faith, profession, or party, esp. to one regarded as true, from what is regarded as falsehood or error', and then more specifically 'the turning of sinners to God; a spiritual change from sinfulness, ungodliness, or worldliness to love of God and pursuit of holiness'. These are all very blunt instruments when it comes to describing first-century phenomena, including Paul's moment on the Damascus Road.

[26] See the important discussion in Chester 2003, 3–42; Bird 2010, 17–43 (esp. 18–24 on the problem of definition); also Dickson 2003, 8f. and elsewhere, and e.g. McClendon and Conniry 2000.

[27] The classic study remains that of Nock 1961 [1933]. Nock also discusses the quasi-'conversion' of those who embraced a particular philosophy. Fredriksen 2010, 239f. rightly insists that where 'religion' was an innate, not a detachable, aspect of identity, 'conversion' was 'tantamount to changing one's ethnicity'. Conversion to Judaism, she says, 'was understood by ancient contemporaries as forging a political alliance, entering the Jewish *politeia*, and … assuming foreign laws and traditions'. Such people turned their backs on the local gods, disrupting the fundamental relations between gods and humans.

quite consciously, from something we might call 'Judaism' to something we might call 'Christianity'. Not only did Paul not put it like that. We can say firmly that he *would not have* put it like that.[28] For him, as we have seen throughout this book, belonging to the Messiah's people meant what it meant within a thoroughly Jewish frame of reference. That was Stendahl's main point, and the evidence is strongly on his side.[29]

The large-scale abandonment of 'religion' in the modern western world has given rise to a second meaning of 'conversion' (the one given in the Merriam-Webster *Collegiate Dictionary*[30]). In this case, an atheist or agnostic, for whom the world of 'religion' as a whole has been a closed book, enters a believing and practising community, often through a personal experience of the sudden disclosure of previously unimagined non-material realities. Various stock phrases, which should not be pressed for precise meaning, are used to denote such a moment (I use the 'Christian' phrases, because they are well known; equivalent terms no doubt exist for someone who becomes , say, a Muslim): 'coming to faith'; 'getting religion'; 'discovering Jesus as one's personal saviour'; 'being born again'; 'accepting Christ into one's heart and life'; 'joining the church', and so on. Such a moment is often characterized by a sense of inner renewal, an awareness of the presence and love of God and the living person of Jesus, and the birth of desires for prayer, scripture, Christian fellowship and a transformed life. When people have spoken of the 'conversion' of Paul, this is the kind of image that has often been conjured up. Clearly there are problems here, since such previously non-religious 'converts' hardly provide a model for the devout Pharisee Saul of Tarsus.

This then leads to a third current meaning. Many modern western 'converts' to Christianity have had some background in what they then come to regard as the 'formal religion' of official Christianity. Then, like Martin Luther and many others, they have had a new experience of God's grace and personal love which they contrast sharply with all they had known before. 'Conversion' then carries the connotations of moving from 'religion' to 'faith', from formal membership and outward ritual observance to a living inner reality. This experience has sustained the fiction that Paul himself moved from 'religion' to 'faith', and that he looked 'back' on something called 'Judaism' as the former – 'the wrong kind of thing' – because he had discovered the latter. Not only has our entire exposition of his thought called this framework (and with it the recent variation that calls itself an 'apocalyptic' reading) into question. Had Paul thought in this way, we would not have expected to see him practising and teaching what look very

[28] See e.g. Roetzel 2009, 407: 'Neither [Paul] nor Acts ... refers to this radical turning in Paul's behaviour as a repudiation of one religion for another, which for a 1st-cent. Jew like Paul would imply turning away from the true God to idolatry.'

[29] Stendahl himself, however, is rightly criticized by e.g. Peace 1999, 29 (cited in Chester 2003, 155) on the grounds that his rejection of 'conversion' as a description of what happened to Paul depends on a modern western notion of 'conversion', when his whole point was to warn against modern western conceptions.

[30] cf. n. 25 above.

like the elements of a 'religion' within his Jesus-and-spirit framework (chapter 13 above). But this (mis)reading has provided the context for a standard 'old perspective' view not only of what happened on the Damascus Road but of 'justification by faith' itself. Such modern western converts, having previously assumed that 'religion' was a matter of impressing God by good works, have discovered through 'conversion' that what mattered was not their work for God but God's loving rescue of them. It has then been easy and natural for people to imagine that this was how it was for Saul of Tarsus: trying to earn God's favour by good deeds, and then coming to realize that what mattered was divine grace and answering faith. All this is well known, and has formed the staple diet of many a sermon, many a system. This meaning of 'conversion', however, is severely anachronistic in Paul's case. That, too, was part of Stendahl's point, and it stands near the heart of the so-called 'new perspective': Saul of Tarsus was not trying to earn his own salvation by hard moral effort and needing to learn about previously unknown quantities called 'grace' and 'faith'. As we have seen, something very different was going on.[31]

Stendahl basically pointed out that these essentially modern visions of 'conversion' implied a deep devaluation of second-Temple Judaism, and of Pharisaism in particular. They caricature Saul of Tarsus as a cross between a Deist and a Pelagian, trying to please a distant deity by unaided moral effort – a picture which does no justice to the theology, or the piety, of a devout Pharisee. That is why, instead of 'conversion', Stendahl proposed 'call': what happened to Paul on the Damascus Road was not so much (he said) a matter of turning, or being turned, away from one 'religion', or indeed from one particular god, and embracing, or being embraced by, another one. It was a matter of a fresh, and admittedly surprising, 'call', in the sense of 'vocation', from the one God whom Paul continued to worship, and who was now commissioning him to tell the non-Jewish peoples about him. Stendahl thus put a high value on *continuity* between Saul of Tarsus and Paul the apostle: the same God, the same 'religion', the same overall narrative, but just a new task.

Paul does indeed speak of God's 'call' in this connection:

> But when God, who set me apart from my mother's womb, and called me by his grace, was pleased to unveil his son in me, so that I might announce the good news about him among the nations – immediately I did not confer with flesh and blood. Nor did I go up to Jerusalem to those who were apostles before me . . . [32]

Since this is, on my reckoning, the only time Paul refers explicitly to what *happened to him or in him* on the Damascus Road (as opposed to his simply

[31] The debate on these matters can be seen to advantage in the dialogue between e.g. Kim 2002; Dunn 2008 [2005], ch. 15 (orig. 1997).

[32] Gal. 1.15–17.

'seeing' Jesus), it is all we have to go on.[33] There is nothing about repentance and faith; nothing about finding his heart strangely warmed; nothing about replacing 'works' with 'faith'. There is a 'call', like that of the ancient prophets; the one God is 'unveiling his son' not 'to me' but 'in me', which is explained in terms of what this God wanted to do *through* Paul, namely, to send the good news to the nations. There is the tell-tale hint, mentioning 'those who were apostles before me': what happened to Paul, by this unique account, was his call and commission to be an apostle, or rather *the* 'apostle to the nations'. One sort of activity stopped (persecuting the church); another began (announcing God's son to the nations).

The two passages in which he refers briefly to the same event in terms of his own seeing of the risen Jesus also relate directly to his apostolic vocation. 'I've seen Jesus our lord, haven't I?' he asks rhetorically, by way of reminding the Corinthians of his apostolic qualification (1 Corinthians 9.1). 'Last of all', he says, adding his own recollection to the church's official Easter tradition, 'he appeared even to me' (1 Corinthians 15.8). And this, as he goes on to say, is what has constituted him as an 'apostle'.

In the latter passage, however, he does speak as well about the radical transformation which this 'appearing' had effected in him:

> Last of all, as to one ripped from the womb, he appeared even to me.
>
> I'm the least of the apostles, you see. In fact, I don't really deserve to be called 'apostle' at all, because I persecuted God's church! But I am what I am because of God's grace, and his grace to me wasn't wasted. On the contrary, I worked harder than all of them – though it wasn't me, but God's grace which was with me.[34]

Here we see the note which Paul emphasizes in Galatians, again and again: grace. 'God called me by his grace' (Galatians 1.15). Stendahl was right to this extent: when Paul speaks of Jesus appearing to him, the result is the particular commission he received, the particular task that was laid upon him. To that extent, 'grace' might be thought of in terms of a fresh divine power at work, not so much *upon* him (as in the normal 'conversion' model) as *through* him. Paul, after all, speaks elsewhere of the divine 'grace' not simply in connection with justification or salvation but in connection with his apostolic vocation.[35] But the context (the ripping from the womb, the previous persecution, the fact that 'I am what I am because of God's grace') implies that there was more to it than simply the life of Jewish devotion taking a new and unexpected vocational turn. Paul did not regard his previous self as a *tabula rasa*, waiting in faith and hope and then being given an important new task. (One might think of the mother of Jesus in such a fashion, but the song which Luke puts on her lips indicates that she, too, came to

[33] I have argued elsewhere that, despite strong advocacy, we should not see 2 Cor. 4.1–6 or 12.1–5 as references to that event: cf. *RSG* 384–8. Few now regard Rom. 7.7—8.11 as a description of Paul's conversion, though it still has its place as a retrospective analysis of the transition from being 'under the law' when 'in the flesh' to being 'in the spirit' and finding thereby a new fulfilment: see above, 892–902.

[34] 1 Cor. 15.8–10. See *RSG* 382–4.

[35] Rom. 1.5; 15.15f.; perhaps also 12.3; 1 Cor. 3.10; Gal. 2.9; Eph. 3.2, 7; cf. Col. 1.25.

her vocation with a clear agenda already in place.[36]) Paul was actively – zealously, he says in Galatians 1.14 and Philippians 3.6 – persecuting the new messianic movement. And he seems to have seen this not simply as something which he then profoundly regrets in the light of his subsequent beliefs. He speaks of it as a kind of quintessential sin, acting in direct opposition to what the one God of Israel had now done. It was not simply 'religion'. It was full-scale rebellion. It represented, from Paul's Messiah-and-spirit perspective, a radical misconstrual of Israel's God, Israel's scriptures and Israel's purpose. This, as we saw towards the end of chapter 9, was part of his gospel-driven awareness of just how bad and profound 'the problem of evil' actually was.

What then about the larger context of his statement in Galatians? Does this not imply that he had formerly belonged to something called 'Judaism', but was now part of something else? The answer is 'yes' and 'no', but mostly 'no':

> You heard, didn't you, the way I behaved when I was still within 'Judaism'. I persecuted the church of God violently, and ravaged it. I advanced in Judaism beyond many of my own age and people; I was extremely zealous for my ancestral traditions.
>
> But when God . . .[37]

Another classic case of deceptive words – which is why I put the first occurrence of 'Judaism' in inverted commas. Our inclination is to hear such words as denoting 'religions' in our modern sense. But the word *ioudaismos*, like other such formations in Paul's day, points in a different direction. Such words denoted, not the life and practice of a 'religion', but the active and energetic defence and promotion of a way of life.[38] That was what Paul had been doing: not simply 'being a Jew', but violently defending the Jewish way of life against what he saw as apostasy and paganization. He has not abandoned his Jewish roots and meanings, but simply gained a radical new insight into them. As far as he was concerned, the 'God' of whom he spoke in verse 15 is the same as the 'God' he thought he was serving all along. The subtle way he explains what had happened to him stresses the continuity, not the discontinuity, between the person he had now become and the rich and deep ancestral traditions for which he had formerly been 'zealous':

> But when God, who set me apart from my mother's womb, and called me by his grace, was pleased to unveil his son in me, so that I might announce the good news about him among the nations – immediately I did not confer with flesh and blood. Nor did I go up to Jerusalem to those who were apostles before me. No; I went away to Arabia, and afterwards returned to Damascus.[39]

[36] Lk. 1.46–55.

[37] Gal. 1.13–15; we discuss the sequel immediately below.

[38] See Mason 2007; and the notes on this topic above, xxivf., 82, 89.

[39] Gal. 1.15–17.

The way he explains what had happened to him makes the point. His 'call' echoes those of the prophets, and particularly that of the 'servant' in Isaiah 49.1. And his reaction – to go off to 'Arabia' before returning to Damascus – resonates with the reaction of the prophet Elijah after he, too, had been stopped in his 'zealous' tracks.[40] If Paul had wanted to say that what had happened on the road to Damascus had turned him away from his Jewish heritage and traditions, he went about it in a very strange way.

For Paul, then, what happened on that day was indeed his 'call'. But this, too, may be heard anachronistically – a possibility which I think Stendahl did not take fully on board. Clearly, Paul had in mind the 'call' of the ancient prophets. But for him 'call' became almost a technical term, not just for 'vocation' in the sense of a divine summons to a particular task, but for the effect of *the gospel itself* on a person. 'Those he marked out in advance, *he also called*; *those he called* he also justified' (Romans 8.29). Here the 'call' is the best shorthand Paul can find – at a moment of high and dramatic clarity, where he was not likely to choose words at random – to denote the complex event which he elsewhere describes in terms of the transformational work of gospel and spirit.[41] To be sure, this language, too, cannot be reduced to terms of 'conversion' in either of the two senses noted above. It regularly has to do with the purpose *for which* someone is 'called'.[42] But for Paul it clearly *includes* the sense, which he elsewhere explores in more detail, of a fresh and transformative divine work in which the person concerned is not merely redirected but revolutionized.

That is clearly what happened to Paul. The late Alan Segal, perhaps the most thorough and sensitive Jewish writer on Paul in modern times, allows for Stendahl's point but insists that both in ancient and even in modern terms 'Paul was both converted and called'.[43] Thus

> The primary fact of Paul's personal experience as a Christian is his enormous transformation, his conversion from a persecutor of Christianity to a persecuted advocate of it. To read Paul properly, I maintain, one must recognize that Paul was a Pharisaic Jew who converted to a new apocalyptic, Jewish sect and then lived in a Hellenistic, gentile Christian community as a Jew among gentiles. Indeed, conversion is a decisive and deliberate change in religious community, even when the convert nominally affirms the same religion.[44]

Segal here correctly identifies what I see as the least unhelpful category in this context: 'transformation'. Nor was this simply a matter of a gradual change. It came about, for Paul, through something he describes in the vivid terms of death and resurrection. When he states dramatically in Romans

[40] See 1 Kgs. 19.1–18, which Paul echoes again at Rom. 11.3f.; cf. *Perspectives*, ch. 10. On Paul's echoes of Isa. here see esp. Ciampa 1998.

[41] See above, 952f. We might compare e.g. 1 Cor. 1.9; 7.15–24; Gal. 1.6; 1 Thess. 2.12; 2 Thess. 2.14; and cp. *klēsis*, the cognate noun ('call') in e.g. 1 Cor. 1.26.

[42] e.g. Rom. 9.12; Gal. 5.13; Eph. 4.1, 4; Col. 3.15; 1 Thess. 4.7; 2 Thess. 1.11.

[43] Segal 1990, 6.

[44] Segal 1990, 6f. The idea that Paul 'converted' from one type of Judaism to another is firmly endorsed by e.g. Frey 2007, 321.

6.2–11 that baptism means dying and rising with the Messiah, we cannot suppose that this was, for him personally, a mere abstract idea or ideal. And when he sets out in Philippians 3 the stark contrast between his present and former life it does indeed look for all the world like the kind of change we might want to call 'conversion'.[45] Segal uses, though Paul himself does not, the language of 'rebirth' to describe this, insisting that Paul is here describing his own 'experience' in order then to 'generalize' this in application to the whole Christian community. This is consonant with Segal's emphasis all through: Paul, having himself been 'converted' in a dramatic and convulsive way, came to believe that this was how the whole new movement should be defined.[46]

There is more than a grain of truth in this, but also I believe a mistake. For Paul what mattered was not that he, Paul, had had a particular kind of 'experience', but that *Israel's Messiah had been crucified and been raised.* Paul was not the kind of evangelist who insists that everyone should 'experience' things in the same way that he or she has done.[47] He was the kind of teacher who wanted people to work out, to think through and then to live out, what had *in fact* happened to the Messiah and what therefore had *in fact* happened to them through baptism into the Messiah. 'Calculate yourselves', he says, 'as being dead to sin, and alive to God in the Messiah, Jesus.'[48] Segal gently but regularly implies that some Jews might have come to faith in Jesus as Messiah in less convulsive ways. Paul, however, insists on the non-negotiable 'transformation' which consisted of the cross itself, not as a private spiritual experience but as the public messianic event to which one was joined in baptism.

This comes to a head at the conclusion of the long introduction to Galatians. The drama of the 'Antioch incident' in 2.11–14, and the high rhetoric of Paul's reported rebuke to Peter in 2.15–21, can obliterate for the modern reader the sense of continuity with the earlier material, and particularly with Paul's brief account of his 'call' in 1.15–16. But I think we should see 2.19–20 as in a sense forming a 'circle' with that earlier passage and indeed a conclusion to one of the main themes of the first two chapters. The subtext of those chapters is that Paul's own character and apostolate have been challenged and undermined. From the very first verse ('My apostleship doesn't derive from human sources! Nor did it come through a human being. It came through Jesus the Messiah, and God the father who raised him from the dead') he is telling his own story in order to explain in no uncertain terms that his apostleship and gospel are the real thing. I suggest that the cleverly crafted rhetorical transition to the first person singular in 2.18 is designed to round off his own story and simultaneously to focus on what will be a main emphasis in the body of the letter.

[45] On Phil. 3 see above, 984–92.

[46] Segal 1990, 141; cf. e.g. 129.

[47] Gaston 1987, 139f. suggests that Paul's problems arose because others had not shared 'his revelation in Damascus'.

[48] Rom. 6.11.

He is, after all, about to make the Messiah's crucifixion the backbone of the letter (Galatians 3.1, 13; 4.5; 5.24; 6.12, 14). Thus, when he speaks in 2.19–20 of his own co-crucifixion, and his own messianic new 'life' the other side of that, he is not saying 'I have had this experience; you should have it too'. He is saying, rather, 'this is what it means *for everyone* that Israel's Messiah was crucified and raised'. He will not speak about such things in the third person, as though detaching himself clinically from the drastic thing that has happened to the Messiah and therefore to Israel. But nor should we mistake his first-person description for a mere 'record of his own experience'. That would have been useless in the implied rhetorical situation. Peter could have responded, as I think Alan Segal might like him to have done, 'Well, Paul, that's how it was for you, but of course for many of us believing in Jesus as Messiah hasn't been like that,' and the conversation would have been at a shoulder-shrugging impasse. The whole point of what Paul says, even though he switches from first person plural in verses 15 and 16 ('*We* are Jews by birth, not "Gentile sinners". But *we* know that a person is not declared "righteous" by works of the Jewish law ... that is why *we* too believed in the Messiah ...') to the first person singular in verse 18 ('If *I* build up once more the things which *I* tore down, *I* demonstrate that *I* am a lawbreaker'), is that *all this is true for Peter as well, and for all other Jewish Messiah-believers*. The 'I' makes this vivid, and has the function in the larger unit of completing the explanation of Paul's own apostolic call that he began in 1.13, but the underlying point is to do with the Messiah himself, whose death and resurrection are the effective signals for the 'transformation' which is both 'call' and 'conversion' and much besides:

> Through the law I died to the law, so that I might live to God. I have been crucified with the Messiah. I am, however, alive – but it isn't me any longer, it's the Messiah who lives in me. And the life I do still live in the flesh, I live within the faithfulness of the son of God, who loved me and gave himself for me.[49]

The Messiah's cross; the Messiah's faithfulness; the Messiah's life; the Messiah's love. For Paul, the divine 'call' on the road to Damascus meant being grasped by and incorporated into all of those Israel-redefining realities. And those messianic events, as far as Paul was concerned, meant the same thing for Peter and Barnabas and the 'certain persons' who 'came from James' (2.12), if only they would realize it. Paul was not projecting his own 'experience'. He was unpacking the meaning of the messianic events.

When we look into the depths of what Paul has said in this sharp and dramatic passage we realize that several aspects even of our modern meanings of 'conversion' are in fact contained within it, albeit themselves in a transformed sense. Paul has not switched from one 'religion' to another; rather, the Messiah's death and resurrection have redefined, in a moment of unveiled truth, the goal and meaning of the whole Jewish way of life. Paul has not stopped believing in the one God whose 'grace' is proclaimed right

[49] Gal. 2.19f.

across Israel's scriptures; he has seen that grace in personal action in the Messiah, and now sees those scriptures in an entirely new light. He has always invoked the one God in personal prayer, and he continues to do so; he has not (that is) been 'converted' in some modern sense, from having no belief in or awareness of a supreme deity to having such a thing for the first time. But he now knows this one God as the one who sent the son, and the one who sends the spirit of the son (Galatians 4.4–7). At the heart of all this, however, is the theme which millions of 'conversions' ancient and modern have in common: a sense of overwhelming love. That is why, for Paul, the deepest and most intimate element in 'conversion' led directly to 'call':

> If we are beside ourselves, you see, it's for God; and if we are in our right mind, it's for you. For the Messiah's love makes us press on. We have come to the conviction that one died for all, and therefore all died. And he died for all in order that those who live should live no longer for themselves, but for him who died and was raised on their behalf.[50]

We might want to call this messianic love the 'objective reality' to which Paul appeals, again and again. Certainly he resists all attempts to reduce matters to his own subjective interiority. But of course the notion of 'love' itself resists precisely this objective/subjective alternative.[51] What happened to Paul on the road to Damascus contained at its core, he insists, a *personal meeting* involving a real 'seeing' of the risen Jesus; a *cognitive awareness* that the resurrection had declared Jesus to be Israel's Messiah, and that his death and resurrection were the Israel-redefining and world-claiming events for which Israel had longed; and a *personal transformation* such as love regularly effects, in which the heart itself was, in biblical language, 'circumcised', enabled at last to love the one God with a spirit-given love, and thus to keep the *Shema* itself.[52] A call: in a sense. A conversion: in a sense. What happened to Paul, personally and convulsively, was what through the Messiah's death and resurrection had happened to the world as a whole, as he says in Galatians 6.14, and more specifically to Israel as a whole, resulting in the mission to the nations. God's Israel-purpose was fulfilled, and was transformed in fulfilment. Paul believed that this transformation, and this fulfilment, had been effected *in* him and was being effected *through* him. And all this happened through the revelation of Jesus on the road to Damascus.

3. Paul and Jewish 'Identity'

(i) Introduction: the Question of 'Identity'

All this brings us back, from a new angle and with considerably more weight of exegesis behind us, to a question which surfaced as far back as

[50] 2 Cor. 5.13–15.

[51] See above, 1356 on the 'epistemology of love'.

[52] Rom. 2.29; 5.5; 8.28.

chapters 6 and 8. The question to which I refer, that of Paul's 'identity', has acquired an air of sharp and sometimes unpleasant controversy, not least because contemporary discussions of 'identity' have become central in several areas of public discourse. Discussing 'who Paul was' or 'who Paul thought he was' thus becomes a way of addressing these matters from another angle, just as discussing his doctrine of justification becomes a way of addressing other issues in some parts of today's church. Much is at stake as a result, and as usual it is often historical exegesis that comes off worst.

The question, anyway, can be put like this: in what sense, if any, did Paul still think of himself, or describe himself, as 'a Jew'?[53] Did he embrace that 'identity', try to modify it, distance himself from it, or what? And, as part of that, did he continue to do what 'a Jew' might be expected to do, namely keep Torah? If so, granted there were many views in his day on what 'keeping Torah' actually involved, in what way and to what extent did he do this? Did he perhaps still *claim* to keep Torah but with less strictness than in his previous life as a Pharisee? Did he do things himself, and teach others to do them, which some or most Jews of his day would have regarded as either compromising Torah-observance or abandoning it altogether? Or what?

At first sight the answer might be obvious. Paul was still, physically, the same person he had always been. His parents were still his parents, even if (one of many things on which we have no information) they had disowned him. Among those over whom he grieves bitterly in Romans 9.1–5 are undoubtedly people near and dear to him. He was still a Hebrew, an Israelite, of the seed of Abraham and the tribe of Benjamin, as he insists in a couple of passages.[54] If in Galatians he could use himself as an example of what happens to every person who is baptized into the death and resurrection of the Messiah, in Romans he can still use himself as an example of someone of Israelite stock who is firmly and solidly a member of the 'remnant', one of Abraham's physical family who also belongs to Abraham's 'family of promise'.[55] In one interesting little passage he appears to speak of himself as part of the 'we' which constitutes the Jewish people insofar as they are 'in the wrong'.[56] And in one famous passage, reporting his sharp exchange with

[53] On the fashionable language of 'identity' see the remarks of Dunn 1999, 176, pointing out the danger of anachronism – dangers not avoided in my view by e.g. W. S. Campbell 2008. Considerable nuancing on 'identity' in Paul's world is now provided by the detailed analysis of Sechrest 2009, 21–109 (and e.g. 141, 163, pointing out that the notion of 'identity' is itself in flux), though the word 'race' and its cognates, used throughout, might themselves be thought loaded. The question of Paul's Jewish identity in current debate received a solid foundation in Niebuhr 1992. The work of Johnson Hodge 2007 makes a further significant contribution, though she ends up opting for the largely discredited view of Gaston and Gager.

[54] Rom. 11.1; 2 Cor. 11.22; cf. Sechrest 2009, 41–5.

[55] Rom. 9.8.

[56] Rom. 3.5; some, however, dispute whether the 'we' here means 'we Jews', or is a more general statement. Cf. Sechrest 2009, 151f. The point emerges again, with similar puzzles, at 3.9.

Peter at Antioch, he declares, 'We are Jews by birth, not "Gentile sinners".'[57] All this seems fairly conclusive at first glance.[58]

But then the doubts begin. Would Paul's Jewish contemporaries have considered him a 'Jew'? This is not just about things that he believed. Many Jews no doubt believed many strange things, including the identification of strange people as 'Messiahs'. But Jews then as now have seldom made niceties of 'belief' the main criterion. The question would have been, what was he *doing*, or perhaps not doing? Paul admitted people to Abraham's family without requiring the covenant sign of circumcision. Paul spoke of the 'temple', referring not now to the shrine in Jerusalem but to the fellowship of Jesus-followers and even to individuals among them. Paul treated the Messiah-faith 'family' *as* an extended family, insisting on people 'marrying within' that family in the way he would previously have insisted on Jewish endogamy. Paul does not seem to have bothered about the sabbath, regarding it as something that Messiah-followers could observe or not as they chose.[59] All this must have raised not only eyebrows but also hackles among the Jewish populations in the Diaspora.

Notoriously, Paul went further. He shared table-fellowship with non-Jews who were Messiah-believers. If that caused problems even for Peter and Barnabas, as it seems to have done (we can hardly suppose that Paul invented the awkward 'Antioch incident' out of thin air), we can be sure that it would have caused serious problems for the young Saul of Tarsus.[60] He advised the Messiah-people in Corinth to accept dinner invitations from anyone and everyone, and to eat unquestioningly what was provided, the only exception being if someone's conscience was still 'weak' at the thought of eating idol-meat.[61] Not only, then, did he advocate eating with uncircumcised and even with unbelieving gentiles, but on an apparently straightforward reading of the relevant passages (we shall discuss them further in a moment) he advocated, in principle, eating their non-kosher food,

[57] Gal. 2.15. The word here translated 'by birth' is *physei*: literally 'by nature'. This was his and Peter's 'given', their starting-point.

[58] So e.g. Nanos 2012, 106, 129.

[59] The question of whether he continued to 'observe' the Jewish calendar, and if so in what sense, remains a moot point in view of discussions of Gal. 4.9 and e.g. 1 Cor. 16.8f.: see Hardin 2008, 120f. (against e.g. Thiselton 2000, 1329f.). Hardin's caution here, allied to his reading of the letter as a warning against Roman imperial celebrations, scarcely warrants Rudolph's claiming him as an ally (2011, 211, referring to Zetterholm 2009, 127–63, who however never mentions Hardin). Paul's reference to Pentecost in 1 Cor. 16 proves little: a modern atheist might well say 'I will see you after Easter' with no implication that they believed in Jesus' resurrection or that they would be in church to celebrate it.

[60] See above, 93f.; 854. When people scratch around for counter-examples (i.e. Jews content to eat with gentiles) they have to make do with strange possibilities: Rudolph 2011, 127 offers the story of Judith (Jdth. 12.17–19), which is bizarre. Judith brought her own food to the meal she shared with Holofernes, the Assyrian general she was planning to kill. Perhaps Judith would have said, if asked, 'To the Assyrians I became as an Assyrian (though not eating their food), that I might kill an Assyrian.' The other example regularly cited, *Let. Arist.* 128–69 (Rudolph 127–9), does indeed show that exceptional circumstances might permit eating together, provided the food was kosher, but this remains, and was seen to be at the time, an exception to the normal rule. Undoubtedly there was a wide range of actual practice in the Diaspora, but the evidence for *amixia*, a taboo on commensality, is not confined to pagan slurs (*pace* e.g. Fredriksen 2010, 249).

[61] 1 Cor. 10.25–30.

on the scriptural grounds that 'the earth and its fullness belong to the lord'.[62] Since it is clear from the discussions in both 1 Corinthians 8—10 and Romans 14—15 that Paul considered himself emphatically among the 'strong' who were happy to see the world this way, as opposed to the 'weak' who still had scruples (to whom he none the less deferred where appropriate), it would appear not only that Paul was advising gentile Christians in Corinth to eat non-kosher food but that he was happy to do so himself, and that he was happy to see other 'Jewish Christians' following this pattern. And at this point some today might say, as some of his contemporaries certainly did, that he had stopped being a 'Jew' altogether. He had abandoned the most basic markers of Jewish identity.[63]

So is that how he saw himself, too? Once more there are signals pointing in this direction. However we punctuate 1 Thessalonians 2.14–15, Paul is certainly distancing himself from 'the Judaeans' he there describes.[64] However we read Romans 10.1–3, Paul is certainly grieving over, and praying for, those of his kinsfolk who 'have a zeal for God' which is 'not based on knowledge'. He recognizes, as one who has known it from both sides, that the gospel of the crucified Messiah is 'a scandal to Jews'.[65] He lists all the remarkable privileges and symbols of status which he had as a devout and zealous Pharisaic Jew, and then declares that they are all *skybala*, a word whose more polite translations include 'dung'.[66]

Above all, there is Galatians 2. Right after saying 'We are Jews by birth, not "Gentile sinners"', Paul proceeds with a radical *but* of redefinition: 'But we know that a person is not declared "righteous" by works of the Jewish law, but through the faithfulness of Jesus the Messiah.'[67] Then, in the most dramatic of redefinitions (in a passage we have studied many times already but which remains strangely absent from the discussions of those who want to claim that Paul remained a 'Torah-observant' Jew), he says, 'Through the

62 1 Cor. 10.26, quoting Ps. 24.1.

63 On the nature of intra-Jewish polemic see Rudolph 2011, 38f., 52.

64 See above, 1151–3.

65 1 Cor. 1.23; Gal. 5.11. It is interesting that neither of these texts is even mentioned by W. S. Campbell 2008 or Rudolph 2011. Tomson 1990 mentions Gal. 5.11 but does not discuss this specific point.

66 Phil. 3.4–6, 8. For Rudolph 2011, 45f. to say that Paul here 'indirectly points up the importance of Jewishness', while obviously true at one level, is bizarre: (a) Paul is saying, as strongly as possible, that these identity-markers no longer matter; (b) in his list of previous status-markers Paul includes his zealous church-persecution, which presumably he now regarded not simply as 'less important' than his new faith but as something horrible and shameful (despite Dunn 2008 [2005], 481); (c) Rudolph appears to think that if we can somehow say that Jewishness is still 'important' this will enable his thesis of a Torah-observant Paul to be salvaged. Campbell 2012, 45 n. 25 (and see his other writings cited by Rudolph 2011, 45f.) suggests that in using *skybala* 'Paul does not intend to "trash" his Jewish attributes', which is odd considering that 'trash' would be another possible, if mild, translation of the word. He is disingenuous in quoting Bockmuehl 1998, 207f. in support of the interpretation of 'food scraps for dogs', an interpretation Bockmuehl discusses and rejects on the grounds that 'the reference is to that which is thrown away because it is filthy and objectionable'.

67 Gal. 2.16 (see above, 856f.). For the avoidance of doubt, in the previous sentence there is no Greek verb corresponding to 'are': Paul wrote *hēmeis physei Ioudaioi*, 'we by-nature Jews'. The question is therefore open as to whether the subsequent passage implies 'but no longer', or 'no longer in the same sense'. See Sechrest 2009, 168f. (Paul leaves this identity behind; cf. too 141); Hays 2000, 236 (Paul affirms the continuing 'Jewish' identity in order to build differently upon it).

law I died to the law, so that I might live to God,' explaining that this has come about through his co-crucifixion with the Messiah. How much clearer do things need to be?

I can understand people who are rightly concerned for Christian–Jewish relations today struggling with this text. I can understand people trying to imagine that it was maybe a rhetorical overstatement.[68] What I cannot understand is people trying to make an argument that Paul was in some sense a Torah-observant Jew but not even mentioning this major piece of counter-evidence.[69] Nor can I understand someone suggesting that for Paul to recognize Jesus as Messiah 'did not mean any repudiation of the Torah'.[70] If 'dying to something' is not repudiating it, Paul's words have no meaning.[71]

What Paul says in the rhetorically charged 'I' of Galatians 2.19–20, he repeats in the second person plural in the massively significant Romans 7.4–6. 'You too died to the law through the body of the Messiah ... now we have been cut loose from the law; we have died to the thing in which we were held tightly.'[72] Rather than dodge the implications of Philippians 3 and the *skandalon* texts, then, we are bound, as historical exegetes, to see them within a framework which can include passages from Galatians and Romans whose central role in key arguments can hardly be gainsaid.

I have argued above that the central reason for Paul's sharp statements about no longer being under Torah were not to do with comparative religion, but with *messianic eschatology*: the Messiah had come, had died and been raised, and the whole world had been transformed, 'Israel' included. That is more or less exactly what Paul says in Galatians 6.14. I suggested in chapter 9 that this gave Paul the basis not just for an eschatological deduction ('we are now in a new time in which Torah is no longer relevant') but for an actual critique: Israel under Torah turned out to be just as 'Adamic' as the rest of humanity. Within this again we may now glimpse a further level of critique, which for Paul was more specifically autobiographical.

Paul seems to have seen the violent actions of his earlier days not just as a case of mistaken 'zeal', though it was that as well. He seems to have seen those actions as embodying something quintessential about the way a would-be Torah-observant Pharisaism, and beyond that perhaps Israel as a whole, had taken a drastically wrong turn. To repeat: this did not mean, for Paul, that there was anything wrong *with being Jewish*, or with God's call to

[68] See e.g. Nanos 2002a, 321: the Galatians 'knew the character of the speaker and the nature of the subject to be out of keeping with his words, and thus the intentions of the writer to be other than what he actually said'. Paul is certainly capable of irony, but claims like this are skating complex pirouettes on very thin historical ice.

[69] Gal. 2.19 is not in the index of Tomson 1990; W. S. Campbell 2008; Rudolph 2011. As W. S. Campbell himself says (2008, 133), 'we cannot bypass those passages where there is a clear witness to the contrary'.

[70] Pawlikowski 2012, 170.

[71] See Sanders 1983, 177: 'dying to the law' is 'the language of conversion in the sense of abandonment ... One gives something up in order to accept something else.'

[72] Rom. 7.4–6, too, is missing from the treatments of Tomson, Campbell and Rudolph.

Israel.[73] Paul saw his earlier persecution of the Jesus-followers not simply as a bit of misguided youthful exuberance but as a symptom of a drastically wrong construal of what it meant to be genuinely Jewish. His renewed-Jewish self rejected, on the basis of the Jewish Messiah and the fresh reading of Israel's scriptures which his death and resurrection evoked, the praxis which as a young Pharisee he had believed to be required by his Jewish Torah-faithfulness. Thus the critique of Israel in Romans 2.17–24, 7.7–25 and 9.30—10.21 does not imply that there is 'anything wrong with being Jewish'. Paul rules that out explicitly, again and again. What is 'wrong' is that Paul's kinsfolk according to the flesh 'have a zeal for God' which, he says, 'is not based on knowledge' (10.2). Granted the reference to 'zeal', linking this passage to Galatians 1.13–14 and Philippians 3.6, this looks very much like an autobiographical hint, which joins up with reflections elsewhere on his persecuting activity.[74]

This critique of violent 'zeal', we may note, would place Paul on the same page, in this respect, as Josephus. Josephus attributes the disaster of AD 66–70 to the hotheaded violence of the 'zealots'.[75] He accuses the violent rebels of other things, too: breaking the law and defiling the Temple, which is different from anything Paul says about his former self (though it reflects the charges brought against him in Acts[76]). But the general point is still important. If Josephus could point the finger at violent 'zeal' as a dramatic distortion of true Jewish loyalty, it is hardly making Paul 'anti-Jewish' to point out that he does the same. This would then strengthen the view that in Galatians, Philippians and Colossians, as we noted in chapter 10, Paul can use ironic language to say that a would-be Jewish life which refuses to recognize Jesus as Messiah is turning itself into the same kind of 'religion' as was evident in the world around.

What then did Paul say about himself in relation to 'Jewishness' and connected topics? The evidence is set out earlier in this book, and here we can simply summarize. Of first importance, as I have argued all through, was Paul's solid and carefully worked out belief that, in the messianic events concerning Jesus, Israel's God had been faithful to the covenant promises to Abraham. This is of course routinely denied by the modern traditions (mostly German and American) that see Galatians as *opposing* an Abraham-based covenant theology. That position really does sail close to the wind of saying that Paul is rejecting something called 'Judaism'. But I believe there should be no doubt that Paul was indeed affirming that what God had promised to Abraham he had fulfilled in the Messiah. Of course, Paul did

[73] W. S. Campbell 2008, 149–51, suggests that I have projected a modern conversion-scheme back on to Paul, thus ignoring the 'continuity' between Paul and his Jewish world and creating instead a sort of anti-Judaism. This is a bizarre misrepresentation. Campbell himself projects contemporary categories ('difference', 'otherness', 'diversity', etc.) back on to Paul, which is why he is forced to ignore several key passages in the letters in order to try to make his case.

[74] 1 Cor. 15.9, reflected further in Eph. 3.8; 1 Tim. 1.13, 15.

[75] See *NTPG* 170–81; and e.g. Jos. *JW* 5.442f., with e.g. Hengel 1989 [1961], 16, 183–6, citing many other passages. I am grateful to Jessiah Nickel for discussion of these.

[76] cf. Ac. 21.21, 28; 24.5f.

what many other Jewish groups of the time were doing, namely, redrawing the boundaries of Abraham's family.[77] But making Abraham and his family central was about as Jewish-affirming a thing to do as Paul could have done, and redrawing the boundaries simply meant that Paul was, to that extent, just another typical second-Temple Jew.

In particular, Paul insists – it is the main theme of Galatians 3 – that Abraham has *one* family, not two or more. This is a radically Jewish thing to say, and it completely rules out any suggestion that Abraham might have a 'covenant' family consisting of Jews (whether Christian or not) and another one of those 'in Christ'.[78] We have seen the same, again and again, in relation to Romans 2.25–9, where Paul insists on the goodness and God-givenness of circumcision and 'the commandments' and then insists, in line with Deuteronomy and Jeremiah, that the place where these things really matter is the heart. So far, so Jewish – though of course Paul then opens things up so that the physically 'uncircumcised' can be part of this 'renewed-heart' people too, exactly as in Romans 4, Romans 10 or Galatians 3.[79] Similar things could be said about 2 Corinthians 3 and Philippians 3.2–11, which as we have seen elsewhere are deeply and radically *Jewish* in what they say and how they say it, *including* the sharp internal critique which is such a regular feature of Jewish life in the modern as in the ancient world.[80]

We have seen the results of all this in chapter 11 above. Paul can refer to spirit-led, Messiah-believing gentiles and Jews together as 'the Jew'; 'the circumcision'; and even on occasion as 'Israel' (suitably redefined: 'Israel of

[77] Rom. 4 and Gal. 3 make it very difficult to say, as does Fredriksen 2010, 244, that gentile Jesus-believers 'are adopted not into Israel's family, but into God's' so that 'God, not Abraham, is their "Abba",' and so while Jewish and gentile Jesus-believers share the same heavenly father *kata pneuma* they remain distinct *kata sarka*. This, it seems to me, is exactly what Paul is denying.

[78] e.g. Campbell 2012, 53, claiming that 'Paul does not argue for a single family of Abraham's descendants but for a plurality of families' – precisely the opposite of what Paul says in Gal. 3.16–29! Campbell seems to find this hard to sustain, however (49f., suggesting that 'whilst the covenant in the NT in relation to the inclusion of gentiles is necessarily a christological category, it cannot be used ecclesiologically'; what happened to *en Christō* and similar ecclesiological formulations, which Paul uses in exactly this connection?). He refers to Beker 1980, 96; but though Beker does suggest (wrongly) that Paul refers to a twofold 'seed' in Rom. 4.13, 16, 18 (*sperma* is in fact always singular here) he also rightly insists that Paul's emphasis in Rom. 4 is on 'the unity of Jew and Gentile in the one church' and that in Gal. 'Christ as the singular seed is the one in whom all are one'.

[79] I am surprised that Sechrest 2009, 152 n. 3 resists the idea that 2.25–9 refers to gentile Christians. Her suggestion that because in 2.26 Paul uses *phylassō* for 'keeping' the law he must be referring to 'Jewish obedience' (a) rests on far too slight an exegetical base, Paul's only other use of the verb being Gal. 6.13 and (b) seems to ignore the fact that the subject of the verb here is precisely *un*circumcised people. She cites Moo 1996, 170 n. 21, but Moo's main point is to stress the vague generality of most of the relevant words. Moo's own attempt (171) to have his cake and eat it at this point demonstrates the difficulties of Sechrest's position here, as also that of Rudolph 2011, 54. Rudolph's suggestion (73f.) that Rom. 2.25–7 shows that the distinction of 'circumcision' and 'foreskin', and hence of 'Jew' and 'Gentile', even 'in Christ', remains 'fundamental in Paul's thought' is breathtaking, granted that the whole point of the passage is that 'their uncircumcision will be counted as circumcision' (2.26) and that the *Ioudaios* is not the one with outward circumcision but the one 'in secret', 'in spirit not letter' (2.28f.). So far from this passage supporting a view of Paul as Torah-observant in Rudolph's sense, it counts heavily against it.

[80] cf. again Rudolph 2011, 38f., discussing contemporary differences between 'orthodox' and 'ultra-orthodox' Jews; cf. 52: 'Intra-Jewish sectarian polemic . . . abounds in modern times', often using sharp and overstated rhetoric.

God' in Galatians, 'all Israel' in Romans).[81] In particular, as again we have seen in plenty of places, he develops an explicitly Deuteronomic vision of what it means, granted the renewal of the covenant and the end of exile, to 'fulfil Torah', to 'do the law', to 'observe the commandments'. He can speak of 'the law of faith'. One of the most decisive moments in the whole of Romans is where he expounds Deuteronomy 30 in terms of confessing Jesus as lord and believing that God raised him from the dead, and this draws together, as we have seen, a large number of other passages in which he hints, this way and that, at the same thing. Again and again the point is that *gentiles can do this as well, while remaining uncircumcised.* And the upshot of it all is that if one were to accuse Paul of no longer observing Torah, he would roundly declare that though he had come out from under the rule of Torah, 'dying to it' by being co-crucified with the Messiah, the spirit-driven life in the Messiah *was in fact the true Torah-observance*, the thing towards which Deuteronomy had been pointing all along. It led, not least, to the deep and heart-felt keeping of the *Shema*: one God, therefore one people of God.[82] It was vital to Paul to see the Messiah's cross blocking the way to any perpetuation of the world of Torah-observance in which he had grown up and been active. But, as he suggests in Romans 8.1–11, with resurrection and spirit a new form of Torah-observance had emerged to which he was utterly committed and in which he believed uncircumcised gentile believers had a full share. To speak of this, as some want to, as the 'erasure' of something called 'Jewish identity' would have made no sense to Paul. If the Messiah has come, and if in and through him Israel's God has acted dramatically to fulfil his promises to Abraham and to do for Israel and the world what they could not do for themselves, then to cling to the old ways of Torah-observance and to something called 'Jewish identity' as though it had value in itself quite apart from the purposes and promises of Israel's God (an idea the more popular today because of the postmodern imperative to celebrate 'identity', 'difference' and so on) would be, from Paul's point of view, like the young son insisting on staying immature rather than growing up (Galatians 4.1–7). It would be like the bridegroom returning from the wars to find that the bride preferred the careful life of distant engagement to the prospect of actual marriage. It would be like keeping the candles burning and the curtains tight shut even though the sun was coming up on a spring morning. Paul might have added, as Josephus effectively did, that to do that was to risk burning the house down. Eschatological messianism (or if you prefer messianic eschatology) is what counts, a vision rooted in the Jewish world, only comprehensible as a scripturally based variation on first-century visions of what it meant to be a loyal Israelite. How could it be 'anti-Jewish' to claim that the Messiah had been raised from the dead and was the lord of the world? Paul would have scorned all attempts to construct, or to cling to, something called 'Jewish identity' apart from the one

[81] Rom. 2.29; Phil. 3.3; Gal. 6.16; Rom. 11.26.

[82] Rom. 3.30; Gal. 3.16–20.

'identity' which mattered: that of being Messiah-people. That is what all the key discussions are about, whether in Romans or Galatians, in Philippians or Ephesians.

(ii) 'Like a Jew to the Jews'?

But what about 1 Corinthians? Is it not there that he speaks of a 'rule in all the churches' according to which Jews must stay as observant Jews while gentiles must observe such commandments as pertain to them? And might that not blow the lid off the whole argument I have presented?

The passage in question comes within the discussion of marriage in 1 Corinthians 7. Paul is arguing that in the present time of urgency or distress one should not rush to change one's social or cultural circumstances. His main point, to which he will return, is to advise for the present against either hasty marriage or hasty divorce (7.26–8). This is the particular application of a more general principle:

> This is the overriding rule: everyone should conduct their lives as the lord appointed, as God has called them. This is what I lay down in all the churches. If someone was circumcised when he was called, he shouldn't try to remove the marks. If someone was uncircumcised when he was called, he shouldn't get circumcised. Circumcision is nothing; uncircumcision is nothing; what matters is keeping God's commandments![83]

Like most exegetes, I have in the past taken verse 19 as a deliberate irony.[84] Paul knew as well as anyone that circumcision was itself one of the 'commandments', and here he was saying that it was irrelevant! Put this together with Romans 2.26–9 or Romans 10.5–13 and it makes excellent rhetorical sense: Paul has a larger vision of 'keeping God's commandments', which now transcends the questions of 'Torah-observance' as seen through the eyes of the zealous Pharisee. The verbal flourish reminds me of that great Christian leader James Houston banging on the table and saying, 'We must forget "evangelicalism" and concentrate on the gospel!' Forget circumcision – and keep the commandments!

A case has, however, been made for quite a different reading. Some have insisted that here Paul establishes a universal rule: that Jesus-believing Jews *should continue to be completely Torah-observant*, and that Jesus-believing gentiles should observe the Noachide commandments which some later rabbis regarded as the gentiles' equivalent of Torah. Peter Tomson, in particular, has set up this interpretation as the yardstick by which to interpret other passages, notably 1 Corinthians 9.19–23 (to which we shall come presently).[85] But this is gross over-exegesis. Granted that Paul can use the words

[83] 1 Cor. 7.17–19.

[84] See e.g. Dunn 2008 [2005], 336f.

[85] Tomson 1990, 270–4; cf. too Tomson 1996, 267–9. Tomson is followed once more by Rudolph (2011, 205, 210) (appealing to Bockmuehl 2000, 170f.) and declaring that 'this *rule* serves as a principal literary context for interpreting Paul's nomistic language in 1 Cor 9:19–23' (205, italics original).

'circumcision' and 'uncircumcision' to refer metonymically to 'Jews' and 'gentiles' respectively, he is here talking quite literally about the state of the male member. What he says to a Jewish Messiah-believer is not 'you must observe Torah exactly as you always have done', but 'you shouldn't even think about having the operation to reverse your circumcision' (as some hellenizers had done in the Maccabaean period[86]), just as he says to gentile Messiah-believers what he says in Galatians: 'don't even think about getting circumcised'. For someone to 'remain in the state in which they were called' (his summary of the 'rule' in verse 24) has nothing to do with 'continuing to observe Torah in the same way', or indeed with gentiles taking upon themselves the Noachide commands. Paul firmly expects gentile converts to live 'no longer like the gentiles' in relation, particularly, to sexual morality; that is, he does not insist that *they* should continue to follow their previous practices![87] Paul does not say, in other words, what some dearly wish he had said, namely that 'Jews and gentiles should each stick to their respective ways of life.' Nor does he say, more specifically, that 'Jews are to remain practising Jews and not live as gentiles.'[88] Indeed, when Paul said to Peter that he had been 'living like a gentile' in Galatians 2.14, this was not a criticism. It was, for Paul, part of 'the truth of the gospel'. To take 1 Corinthians 7.19 as an injunction to keep the whole law in a 'normal' pre-gospel Jewish way is to fly in the face of Paul's major statements about the law elsewhere, and to risk building up once more things that had been torn down.

All this brings us to the passage which has proved particularly contentious in these discussions:

> I am indeed free from everyone; but I have enslaved myself to everyone, so that I can win all the more. I became like a Jew to the Jews, to win Jews. I became like someone under the law to the people who are under the law, even though I'm not myself under the law, so that I could win those under the law. To the lawless I became like someone lawless (even though I'm not lawless before God, but under the Messiah's law), so that I could win the lawless. I became weak to the weak, to win the weak. I have become all things to all people, so that in all ways I might save some. I do it all because of the gospel, so that I can be a partner in its benefits.[89]

There are not too many Pauline passages where we can say, without hesitation, what the 'natural' meaning is, but here I believe it is clear. Paul understood himself to possess what in our jargon we might call a new 'identity' – the word is slippery, but it is hard to think of a better one – in which his previous 'identity' as a 'Jew', as one 'under the law', had been, to say the least, drastically modified. It no longer defined who he was, and what he

[86] 1 Macc. 1.15; cf. Jos. *Ant.* 12.241.

[87] Eph. 4.17; 1 Thess. 4.5; cf. 1 Cor. 6.11. This may overlap with the Noachide commands, but I see no evidence that this was Paul's reason for insisting on this dramatic change.

[88] Tomson 1996, 267; Rudolph 2011, 210.

[89] 1 Cor. 9.19–23. The classic treatment remains that of Chadwick 1954–5, who describes v. 22 ('all things to all people') as 'perhaps as serious as any passage in the Pauline corpus' (274). For recent discussions cf. e.g. Schnabel 2004, 953–60; Sandnes 2011.

could and could not do. For the sake of his missionary strategy, and that alone, he 'became like a Jew to the Jews'.

The 'like' is missing in a few manuscripts, but whether or not it is present the point remains stark. *Being a 'Jew' was no longer Paul's basic identity.* He backs it up: for the sake of his mission 'to the people who are under the law', that is, the Jewish people, he became *like* someone under the law, even though that was not now 'who he was' at the deepest level.[90] This fits completely with what he says elsewhere: 'you died to the law'; 'now we have been cut loose from the law'; 'through the law I died to the law'; 'now that faithfulness has come, we are no longer *hypo paigagōgon*, under the "pedagogue", the "babysitter"' – in other words, the 'law' that looked after Abraham's family during its period of minority.[91]

This reading of 1 Corinthians 9 has come under sustained attack. Peter Tomson applied drastic textual surgery to the whole passage, eliminating the 'like' (*hōs*) in 'like a Jew', on the flimsiest of manuscript evidence, and cutting out the entire phrase 'even though I'm not myself under the law' on almost equally shaky grounds.[92] David Rudolph has drawn back from such blatant attempts to force the passage not to say what it clearly does say, but he too avoids what most have seen as its basic thrust.[93] His tactic is to suggest that there were different levels of Jewish lawkeeping in Paul's day, as there are today; that Paul knew very well that the strict way he himself had kept the Torah as a Pharisee was not the way many of his Jewish contemporaries 'kept Torah'; that he was content to use various tactics of accommodation and compromise which would still have been regarded as in some sense faithful Torah-observance; and that this is reflected in Paul's language:

> The expression *tois hypo nomon* ('those under the law') would thus refer to 'Pharisees'... It follows that Paul's statement 'I myself am not under the law' need not imply that Paul ceased to be a Torah-observant Jew. It would only mean that he stopped living according to Pharisaic or particularly strict standards of Torah observance as a consistent lifestyle.[94]
>
> It should be remembered that in a society where it was normative for Jews to be law observant, *if a Jew referred to other Jews as 'under the law', it would have likely had the*

[90] See e.g. Hays 1997, 153: Paul is now 'transcending all cultural allegiances'.

[91] Rom. 4.4, 6; Gal. 2.19; 3.25.

[92] Tomson 1990, 277–9, using (among other things) the tenuous argument that as the church became more anti-Jewish such things were more likely to be added. The anti-Jewish textual surgery for which we have evidence (i.e. that of Marcion) tended to cut things out rather than put things in; and in any case, as Metzger points out (1994 [1971], 493), it is easy to see how a copyist's eye might have skipped from one occurrence of *hypo nomon* to the other. See too Thiselton 2000, 701.

[93] Rudolph 2011, 153 (against Tomson's surgery); but cf. the title of Rudolph's monograph, *A Jew to the Jews*, which does imply something similar.

[94] Rudolph 2011, 158f., cf. 198–200.

> *connotation 'under the law in a particularly fervent way'*, perhaps comparable in meaning to 'zealous for the law' . . .[95]

This seems to me fantastically unlikely in view of Paul's other uses of 'under the law', not least in Galatians and Romans.[96] There is no evidence that Paul was using coded language to make an *inner-Jewish* distinction at this point. One can hardly imagine such a reading even being dreamed of except when the text in question presents such an apparently solid block – a stumbling-block, one might say – in the path of the Pauline reinterpretation many seem determined to press upon us.

Another writer to explore alternative ways of reading 1 Corinthians 9 is Mark Nanos. He too seeks to avoid what I have seen as the 'natural' meaning of the text, though he goes about it in a quite different way from Rudolph. In a recent article, he sets up something he calls 'the traditional conceptualization of Paulinism', which he explains as 'privileging of gentileness, freedom from Torah and Jewish identity', and proceeds to castigate the 'Paul' of this model.[97] Such a Paul, according to Nanos's reading of this passage, 'adopts a highly questionable way of life', 'is deceitful and hypocritical', 'subverts his own teaching', thereby adopts 'an ineffective bait and switch strategy', follows 'absolutely contrary behaviour' involving 'flip-flopping', demonstrates 'moral bankruptcy' and reveals a Paulinism (and thus a Christianity) which has 'a serpent-like guile at its very heart'.[98] Any converts that result, Nanos declares,

> will adopt this chameleon-like expedient behaviour thereafter on the same terms, that is, only in order to trick other Jews. That creates a spiral of duplicity, with long-range deleterious results for their psychological and spiritual as well as social well-being should they remain 'Christians' after finding out the truth.[99]

All this leads to a peroration where Nanos's description of the supposed 'Paulinism' begins to remind me of Richard Dawkins's description of the God of the Bible. The charges against this 'Paul', he says, are:

> moral dishonesty, hypocrisy, misrepresentation, trickery, inconsistency, subversion of principles for expedience, and practical shortsightedness.[100]

[95] Rudolph 2011, 196 (italics original). Rudolph draws the parallel with contemporary Jewish language for the 'ultra-orthodox' (the *haredim* or *frum*) as opposed to the *masorti* ('traditional'). He proposes (197) that Paul either coined or borrowed the phrase 'under the law' to refer 'to the *haredim* or *frum* of his day'. Rudolph supports this with a reference to Paul's comment about 'the "extremely religious" . . . among the Gentiles he sought to win' (Ac. 17.22), but this is hardly to the point: Paul was not distinguishing particularly scrupulous Athenian pagans from any others, but making a (sarcastic?) comment about pagan religiosity as a whole.

[96] So e.g. Sechrest 2009, 156: this is the basis of her monograph's title, *A Former Jew*.

[97] Nanos 2012, 108.

[98] Nanos 2012, 108f., 114f. This is the potential charge to which Chadwick 1954–5 responds.

[99] Nanos 2012, 120.

[100] Nanos 2012, 139.

All these Nanos undertakes to eliminate with his own theory as to what the text means. Paul was not, he says, talking about what he *did*, but only what he *said*. This is a 'rhetorical adaptability' which 'did not include the adoption of conduct representing his various audiences' convictional propositions, but not his own'.[101] Thus

> I propose that instead of 'behaving like' according to the model of lifestyle adaptability, this language [i.e. 1 Corinthians 9.19–23] signifies how Paul *reasons like* and *relates* his convictions *like*, how he *engages like*, how he rhetorically meets people where they are, according to their own world-views and premises. Paul *reasons* with, *relates* to, or *engages* Jews as/like (in the manner of) a Jew, and so on. In this rhetorical, discursive sense Paul could actually *become like* – or even *become* – *everything to everyone*.[102]

This means knowing how to communicate effectively and respectively. It provides, says Nanos, the right approach for today's Jewish–Christian dialogue. Such a dialogue

> seeks to understand the other on their own terms, and to successfully explain one's own premises and world-view in cross-culturally intelligible terms in order to advance mutual respect and beneficial relationships going forward. These are goals to which one can hardly object.[103]

Even those undisturbed by split infinitives may nevertheless feel uneasy at this sentence. Was Paul *really* modelling and advocating such a remarkably postmodern agenda? If that was all Paul was doing, and was known to be doing, why (as Nanos himself sees) would anyone object? As Paul himself said in a different context, 'if I were still pleasing people, I wouldn't be a slave of the Messiah', or 'If I am still announcing circumcision, why are people still persecuting me? If I were, the scandal of the cross would have been neutralized.'[104] But object they did; we can hardly suppose that Paul received the 'forty lashes less one' over and over again for speaking (as many Jews were able to do) in cross-culturally intelligible terms.[105] In any case, Nanos seems to forget, in looking at these five verses in 1 Corinthians 9, the role they play in the discourse as a whole (the unit in question is commonly agreed to run from 1 Corinthians 8.1 to 11.1). Paul's whole point is that he is modelling behaviour in which one *gives up one's rights* for the sake of others. He has enslaved himself, he says. In what way does Nanos's Paul 'enslave himself' by engaging in cross-culturally intelligible dialogue? How would that provide a model for the larger appeal Paul is making, that though the Christian of whatever background is free to eat food of whatever sort, this is a 'right' which must be given up if it causes someone else to

[101] Nanos 2012, 123.

[102] Nanos 2012, 130 (italics – and everything else – original).

[103] Nanos 2012, 139.

[104] Gal. 1.10; 5.11.

[105] 2 Cor. 11.24 (cf. Dt. 25.3). Rudolph 2011, 204 n. 128 discusses the reasons for this punishment, concluding that we cannot be certain (on later rabbinic traditions relating to such floggings see mMakk. 3.1–8).

stumble? The ultimate model for this, as with the similar argument in Philippians 2.1–11, is of course Jesus himself, which is why Paul concludes the whole section by urging them to 'copy me, just as I'm copying the Messiah'.[106] Nanos's rhetorically adaptable Paul is not giving up anything. He is just behaving like a civilized modern western dialogue partner.

Paul's overriding concern, throughout the section, does of course include the desire to avoid giving offence. 'Be blameless', he says, 'before Jews and Greeks and the church of God, just as I try to please everybody in everything, not pursuing my own advantage, but that of the great majority, so that they may be saved.'[107] This actually looks like a further summing up of exactly what he had said in 9.19–23, and the claim of 'trying to please everybody' is clearly an old habit, since it had occasioned the slur to which he responded in Galatians 1.10. So must we after all say that Paul was either wicked (in the way Nanos has so graphically described) or just stupid, unable to realize that people would see through his 'flip-flopping' behaviour?

Emphatically not. Nanos, like many others, has simply misrepresented the case. He seems to have no idea of what the thrust of Paul's gospel actually was. He describes Paul as 'seeking to convince fellow Jews as well as Gentiles to turn to Jesus as the one representing the ideals and promises of Torah', who would naturally therefore 'uphold the quintessential basis of that message, that is, he would observe Torah'.[108] But where did this idea come from, that the point of Jesus was that he represented Torah? Yes, Paul does say in Romans 10 that the Messiah is the *telos nomou*, the 'goal of Torah', and he expounds Deuteronomy 30 to exactly this effect. But Paul does not see Torah simply as a set of commands, a lifestyle. He sees it, as Josephus saw it, as Daniel saw it, as Qumran saw it, as a *narrative*; a narrative that was straining forward to an explosive dénouement; a narrative that, in Paul's case, had reached that dénouement in the Messiah. And with the Messiah all things are different, not least because 'through the law I died to the law, so that I might live to God'. Paul was not, as Nanos's hypothetical Paul seems to have been, trying to persuade people to adopt 'propositional values which he believes to be superior'.[109] He was telling them that the crucified and risen Jewish Messiah was the lord of the world – an essentially Jewish message, a message incomprehensible except in solidly biblical and Jewish terms, and yet a message whose explosive quality transcended polite cross-cultural dialogue by as much as a Shakespeare soliloquy transcends 'Twinkle, twinkle, little star'. Nanos has tried to put the wind of Paul's gospel into the bottle of postmodern morality, and it will not fit. The true Paul was not offering 'superior' propositions or a 'better' way of life, to be argued

[106] 1 Cor. 11.1.

[107] 1 Cor. 10.32f.

[108] Nanos 2012, 106f. In a footnote he tries again: 'How much sense would it make for Paul to proclaim Jesus to demonstrate the righteous ideals of Torah and to be its goal . . . if at the same time Paul . . . degraded Torah . . .?'

[109] Nanos 2012, 119.

for within a 'comparative religion' framework. He was offering eschatological messianism.

Nanos, in fact, has carefully bracketed out the apocalyptic and eschatological claim which alone makes sense of Paul's behaviour and of his claim in this passage. Of course, if Paul was teaching a lifestyle, or inculcating a series of propositions, he might well be accused of such gross inconsistency as to constitute a moral failure.[110] But if he believed that Jesus was Israel's Messiah through whom 'the world has been crucified to me and I to the world', how was he supposed to live?

If he simply went on keeping Torah, insisting that continuing Torah-observance was mandatory for Jewish converts, he could not have said what he did to Peter in Galatians 2.14. Peter, like Paul himself, had been 'living like a gentile' in the sense of sharing open table-fellowship; that was demanded, Paul believed, by 'gospel truth'. But if Paul, 'living like a gentile' (in other words, sharing table-fellowship with non-Jews and also sharing their food, including meat that might have been offered to idols), then went into a new town and visited the synagogue community, he would of course be tactful. If he refused to behave Jewishly in that context, on the grounds that he believed in a new kind of Torah-fulfilment altogether, the message he would have communicated would have been that he was teaching a totally non-Jewish faith and practice. That, of course, was the garbled news that, according to Acts, had made its way back to Jerusalem.[111] But for Paul this was a travesty. His message, and the life of his communities (to say it yet again) remained essentially Jewish, making claims which only made the sense they made within a Jewish worldview, as a new dramatic variation on themes common in much second-Temple Jewish life. He believed that in Jesus Israel's Messiah had arrived, ushering in the new age for which Torah and prophets had longed, fulfilling God's promises to Abraham. One would hardly make that point to one's fellow Jews by openly flouting what was seen as normal Torah-observance. Hence: 'to the Jews I became like a Jew, to win Jews'. Of course, Paul believed that the radical fulfilment of the promises had resulted in a new kind of Torah-obedience in which, though some things had been intensified (praying the *Shema*, for instance!), others were set aside.[112] But one would not even gain a hearing for the essentially Jewish 'good news' about the Messiah if one began by openly flouting Torah. Could he explain, at a first meeting, all that he had in his head, which eventually came out in the subtle but deeply satisfying exposition in Romans? Of course not – any more than he was going to be able to explain it to the angry crowd in Jerusalem, who had heard rumours about him that corresponded more than a little to the unpleasant charges which Nanos

[110] Ancient pagan philosophers, not least Cynics, were sometimes accused of being too flexible: see Mitchell 1991/2, 133–6, citing esp. Plut. *Mor.* 96F–97; Keener 2005, 80f.

[111] Ac. 21.21, 28.

[112] The continuities are rightly stressed by Fredriksen 2010, 251f.: 'the insistence that none other than the god of Israel be worshiped' was 'defining; it was non-negotiable; it was uniquely Jewish'. To this extent she is correct to say that Paul's gospel was not 'Law-free'.

heaps on the head of what he sees as traditional 'Paulinism'.[113] So he would 'become like a Jew to the Jews', with the 'like' indicating behaviour, presumably in relation to food and probably sabbath. The potential charge of inconsistency only works *from within a framework that has bracketed out eschatological messianism before it starts.* Of course, a synagogue member might say to Paul, 'But didn't I hear that in your last town you were eating all kinds of food – and with uncircumcised gentiles, too?' Faced with that question, Paul could no doubt explain himself, perhaps in language we would recognize from Galatians. Or if Paul were in Corinth, regularly sharing in the common meals of the church, and a Jewish family invited him to dinner, he would eat kosher food with them. Would they at once accuse him of hypocrisy? Would he have done better to have brought his own pork sandwiches? What good would that have done? Ironically, Nanos is precisely failing 'to understand the other on their own terms'. He is insisting on putting things in *his* own terms, producing the alternative of either a grossly caricatured and culpable 'Paulinism' or the equally spurious 'Paul' of a neutered cross-cultural dialogue. If Nanos's picture of the apostle were correct, the paragraph might have finished 'I've become some things to some people, so that by some means I may be inoffensive and inclusive to all.' Much more satisfactory for the early twenty-first century, perhaps. But a lot less like Paul.[114]

The details may then be cleared up. There is a sense, of course, in which Paul is indeed a 'Jew'. But he has already declared in Galatians 2.15–21 that this is not his basic 'identity' (if we must use that language). There should be no problem as to what he means here. When he goes to the synagogues, as he seems to have done in city after city, of course he behaves in accordance with normal Jewish practice. (We should not dismiss the account in Acts; had Paul not gone to synagogues he would not have received the synagogue punishment, and the fact that he received it more than once shows that he continued to regard himself as in some sense 'belonging'.) Nothing in the gospel tells him not to follow Jewish practice in these circumstances. If he

[113] On the relevant Acts passages see e.g. Barrett 1998, 1012f. Barrett sees the ambiguity of the situation, not least of Paul's vow in Ac. 21.20–6. But he too, like Nanos, raises questions of consistency (though he ascribes the problem to Luke rather than Paul), suggesting that, by taking the vow, Luke's 'Paul' was trying 'to suggest something that was not true, namely that he too . . . was regularly observant of the Law as understood within Judaism', a point which Barrett suggests is not covered in 1 Cor. 9. This I think subtly misrepresents the point. In Ac. 21.24 James says that if Paul performs the vow everyone will know that the accusations against him (that he teaches Jews to abandon Moses, etc., as in v. 21) are false, and 'that you too are behaving as a law-observant Jew should'. What should have been the response from one who believed that the gospel was 'for the Jew first'? 'Do this and we will know you are loyal to Torah; don't do it and everyone will believe you have torn up the scriptures!' Faced with that loaded and dangerous alternative, Paul would unhesitatingly choose the former, since everything he believed was predicated on the assumption that the law and the prophets were fulfilled in the Messiah. Let those who have never faced tricky and potentially life-threatening political/religious situations, abounding in distorted questions and false alternatives, refrain from casting the first stone.

[114] On Paul's dilemma here see esp. Hays 1997, 179: 'Paul's policy of accommodating himself to the standards of various reference groups will work only so long as those groups are not actually trying to live together. Alternatively, this strategy might work if everyone else within the church would adopt Paul's policy of evangelical flexibility so that all were willing to adapt themselves to one another and to the needs of the church's mission. That . . . is precisely the goal of Paul's exhortation.'

doesn't, he might as well not show up at all – thereby undermining 'to the Jew first'. Likewise, he then behaves as though (despite Galatians 2.19 and Romans 7.4) he is after all 'under the law'; again, that seems to include synagogue discipline.[115] How easy it would have been simply never to turn up, to be regarded as if anything an *apikoros*, a traitor, an ex-Jew. But the gospel is 'to the Jew first and also equally to the Greek'. I suspect all this would be second nature to real cross-cultural missionaries. Charges of inconsistency are bound to arise, but the inconsistency here is in the eye of the beholder. Paul is claiming to be consistent to the *nomos Christou*, the 'Messiah's law' of Galatians 6.2 according to which one must 'carry each other's burdens'; this, I think, is the meaning of *ennomos Christou*, 'under the Messiah's law', in this passage as well.[116] Here, as in 1 Corinthians 7.19 (and in other passages like Galatians 4.21), we should undoubtedly hear a gentle irony: if you want to be under a 'law', try this one! Nor should we try to bend the unusual phrase Paul uses when he says 'even though I'm not lawless before God' to make it an affirmation of full Torah-observance. The Greek is literally 'not being lawless of God', *anomos theou*, and does not naturally cash out as a direct reference to the 'law of God'.[117]

Paul's statement that he 'became weak' to the 'weak' is easily explained in terms of 1 Corinthians 8.9–13, and here we come upon an interesting point: the 'winning' of which he speaks here cannot simply be to do with primary evangelism.[118] 'The weak', here and in Romans 14—15, are Christians who still harbour scruples on certain issues, and whose consciences must be respected.[119] Paul is speaking not only as an evangelist but as a pastor. His task is not only to evangelize but to bring people to what we might call messianic maturity.[120] The strategy he here outlines is part of that larger whole.

Like the dog that refused to bark in the night, there is one category missing in Paul's list.[121] He does not say 'to the strong I became strong, that I

[115] If there is a distinction between 'Jews' and 'those under the law', it might be natural to assume that the latter phrase refers to God-fearers or proselytes (see e.g. Witherington 1995, 212; Hays 1997, 153f., suggesting also that the category might have been introduced for the sake of being able to clarify his own position of not being himself 'under the law'); or that the *Ioudaioi* were Judaeans, while 'those under the law' were Diaspora Jews (e.g. Horsley 1998, 131).

[116] See e.g. Stanton 2003, 173f.: 'under Christ's jurisdiction'; Fitzmyer 2008, 371: 'Christian love, which springs from faith . . . constitutes "the law of Christ" . . . but it is only "law" in a wholly analogous sense. It is the way Christ exercises his lordship over those who are called to him.'

[117] Rudolph 2011, 160 is disingenuous in asking what *nomos theou* means here, since that is not the phrase Paul uses. He backs up his interpretation (that Paul is clarifying that his evangelistic association with gentile sinners 'should not be interpreted as a neglect or abandonment of "God's law"') with a reference to Thiselton 2000, 704. But, while Thiselton agrees that Paul is guarding against antinomianism, he is also clear that Paul is opposed to the 'misuse' of the law 'as a means of establishing a false security which distracts people from God's grace in Christ', and cannot therefore be said to support Rudolph's point at all.

[118] See Witherington 1995, 204 n. 4 *ad fin*.

[119] The attempt of Nanos in his various writings to suggest that the 'weak' are in fact Jews who do not believe in Jesus has met with little success.

[120] Col. 1.28, etc.; cf. e.g. 1 Cor. 14.20.

[121] Actually, there are others too: he does not say 'to the Greeks I became a Greek', and despite Chadwick 1954–5, 261, 263 he does not say 'a Gentile to the Gentiles'.

might win the strong'. Perhaps he thought that four categories were enough (the Jews, those under the law, the lawless and the 'weak'). Perhaps he subsumed the 'strong' under the 'lawless', though this seems unlikely. Perhaps, then, the answer is that Paul saw himself firmly as already among the 'strong'. The position he is articulating is in fact precisely *the 'strong' position*, as he would have seen it. And the 'strength' in question has nothing to do with moral courage or a tough personal character. It has everything to do with the firmness of the conviction that in Jesus the crucified Messiah Israel's God had made himself fully and finally known. Paul could not *become* 'strong'; he was 'strong' already. That indicates clearly enough that the other categories he mentions, even the category 'Jew' in its normal sense of a synagogue-obedient, Torah-observant people, are 'identities' he could 'identify with' as need arose, without being defined by them. This was not, we may be sure, an easy position, or one lightly espoused. Romans 9.1–5 makes it clear that this cannot be the case, and Acts 21 shows how easy it was for things to go horribly wrong. But that, too, is the point of 1 Corinthians 9 as a whole. Paul is asking the Corinthians to be prepared to abandon their 'rights' for the sake of the gospel. That is what he does on a regular basis. And 'becoming a Jew' means, for him, putting on hold his 'right' to live in a new way, not indeed *anomos theou* but definitely *ennomos Christou*. What neither Tomson nor Rudolph nor Nanos seem able to grasp is that for Paul something radically new had happened, something which was at the same time the radical fulfilment of Israel's ancient hopes. Paul would only appear inconsistent to one who was looking, not through the spectacles of eschatological messianism, but through the distorting lens of comparative religion; or perhaps, one who was looking from the point of view of this or that faction, when Paul's carefully considered pattern of behaviour corresponded to the tactics well known in the ancient world for those who, like Paul, were determined to avoid such factionalism.[122] His consistency was that of announcing and following the crucified Messiah, knowing him to be 'a scandal to Jews and folly to Gentiles'.[123] That earlier statement in 1 Corinthians, in fact, foreshadows the controversial passage we have been discussing, and in doing so points on to the final question of this section. Did Paul then think of 'belonging to the Messiah' as constituting a different sort of reality or 'identity', distinct from 'Jews' and 'gentiles' alike?

(iii) A 'Third Race'?

Among the other buzz-words which the debate about Paul's Jewish 'identity' has generated, the notion of a 'third race' – the followers of Jesus as a new corporate entity, distinct from both 'Jews' and 'gentiles' – has been

[122] See esp. Mitchell 1991/2, 147–9.

[123] 1 Cor. 1.23.

both canvassed and attacked in the last generation. This brings the discussion of 'identity' into sharp focus.

Some, like Ed Sanders, have seen it as obvious that Paul viewed 'the church' as a 'third entity'. Sanders denies that Paul would have been happy with the phrase 'third race' itself, but what he affirms comes close to the same thing:

> In very important ways the church was, in Paul's view and even more in his practice, a third entity. It was not established by admitting Gentiles to Israel according to the flesh ... but by admitting all, whether Jew or Greek, into the body of Christ by faith in him. Admission was sealed by baptism, most emphatically not by circumcision and acceptance of the law ... The rules governing behaviour were partly Jewish [Sanders has especially sexual ethics in mind here], but not entirely, and thus in this way too Paul's Gentile churches were a third entity. Gentile converts definitely had to separate themselves from important aspects acceptable to observant Jews, whether Christian or non-Christian. Christian Jews would have to give up aspects of the law if they were to associate with Gentile Christians. Paul's view of the church, supported by his practice, against his own conscious intention [Sanders seems here to be referring to his earlier suggestion that Paul would have been horrified at the idea of a 'third race'], was substantially that it was a third entity, not just because it was composed of both Jew and Greek, but also because it was in important ways neither Jewish nor Greek.[124]

This is a fascinating and seminal passage. Three comments are necessary. First, it should be clear from the rest of the passage that when Sanders refers to 'Paul's Gentile churches' he does not mean 'gentile-only' churches, but 'churches composed of both Jews and non-Jews but on gentile territory'. Second, I find Sanders's argument here so strong that it is not clear to me why he then doubts that Paul would have thought of a 'third race' (especially when we define 'race' carefully: see below). Third, however, I do think Paul would have objected to the bald statement that the new entity was in important ways 'neither Jewish nor Greek'. It depends, of course, what you mean by 'Jewish', but our old friend Romans 2.29 would indicate that for Paul anyone who was 'in the Messiah' and indwelt by the spirit could be called *Ioudaios*. Such people were worshipping Israel's God, and at least some aspects of their behaviour (avoiding idolatry and *porneia*) were to be ordered accordingly. If there is such a thing as a 'third race', the genetic link it possesses with one of its contributory components is quite different from the link it has with the other one.

The suggestion of a 'third race' has provoked strong reactions. The editors of a recent collection of essays on 'Paul and Judaism', discovering that one of their contributors actually believes more or less what Sanders had argued thirty years ago, describe this in the shocked tones of an elegant lady discovering that her favourite nephew is going to marry a chorus girl. 'Bird', they say, 'actually thinks that the new group of Jesus believers could be conceived of as a third race.'[125] In the same vein, Rudolph declares that what he

[124] Sanders 1983, 178f. The reference to Paul's supposed rejection of 'third race' is at 173.

[125] Bieringer and Pollefeyt 2012b, 10. The implication seems to be: How did that man get in here without a postmodern wedding garment?

calls 'the consensus reading', according to which Paul belonged to 'the "third entity" church', reinforces the view that Pauline Christianity 'was an anti-Jewish movement', leading 'to the delegitimisation of Jewish existence and to the erasure, or displacement, of Jews from the church'.[126] This kind of rhetorical overplaying of the hand does historical exegesis no good. Rudolph, Nanos and many others are reacting obviously and naturally to the bitter experience of Jewish people in Europe and elsewhere for many generations, but one cannot decide first-century meanings that way, any more than one can force Paul to adjudicate a debate between Luther and Calvin. This so-called 'post-supersessionist' position, however, is itself well on the way to becoming a new 'consensus'. The protests that have been raised against it (pointing out that when Paul faced potential anti-Judaism in Rome he did it by arguing that Jewish people *could and would* return, in faith, to 'their own olive tree', in other words, that the real 'anti-Judaism' would be to *deny* Jews a place in the messianic company of Abraham's worldwide family) have fallen on deaf ears. This is not what people want to hear.[127] But, as with questions of Pauline doctrinal teaching, it will not do to highlight features of a much later, and totally different, world and use them as Procrustean beds to force Paul into shape. That merely reproduces the worst features of a former ecclesiastical control to which historical exegesis rightly objected. History matters.

The phrase 'third race' is not of course found in the New Testament. The nearest we get is 1 Peter 2.9 ('you are a chosen race [*genos eklekton*], a royal priesthood; a holy nation; a people for God's possession'). 'Third race' itself first appears in the second-century writers Clement of Alexandria and Aristides.[128] Actually, in the Syriac texts of Aristides, which some consider superior to the Greek one, the Christians are a *fourth* group, after 'barbarians, Greeks and Jews'.[129] The point being made in these and similar texts has to do primarily with *worship*: the Christians worship in a different manner from Jews and Greeks alike.[130] The idea of the Christians as a different kind of entity then becomes a familiar theme as the second century progresses towards the third. By the time the Pseudo-Cyprianic *De Pascha* was written, some time in the 240s, it can simply state that 'we Christians are the third race'. The tone and context suggest that by then the phrase was well known.[131] Tertullian records it being used contemptuously by an angry

[126] Rudolph 2011, 211.

[127] See Bird 2012, 20f.

[128] Clem. *Strom.* 6.5.41.6; Aristides *Apol.* 2.2. See the discussion in Sechrest 2009, 13f.

[129] See D. F. Wright 2003, 134. In the Syriac the ref. is to Arist. *Apol.* 15. See further Richardson 1969, 22f.

[130] So D. F. Wright 2003, 135f. The wider issues are discussed further in Buell 2005, arguing that early Christians 'used ethnic reasoning', with 'the vocabulary of peoplehood and human difference', to legitimize 'various forms of Christianness as the universal, most authentic manifestation of humanity' (2).

[131] Ps-Cyprian *De Pascha Computus* 17 [= Ogg 1955, 16], qu. in D. F. Wright 2003, 136. According to *Ep. Diog.* 1.1, Christians are 'a new breed [*genos*] of humans', who neither worship the gods of the Greeks nor follow the superstition [*deisidaimonia*] of the Jews. In 5.17 it states that Christians are attacked as 'foreigners' (*allophyloi*, which in the LXX denotes 'Philistines') by Jews and persecuted by Greeks. *Mt. Pol.* speaks of the Christians as a 'race', though not a 'third' one (3.2; cf. 14.1; 17.1). Cf. Sechrest 2009, 14.

crowd.[132] We should note that the idea emerged when it was bound to be seen as ridiculous and counter-intuitive, as this tiny group of mostly uneducated people presumed to behave, and particularly to worship, in a unique way. At that level, the claim was clearly true: nobody else in the ancient world was doing it that way.

A strong case can be made, following Sanders and others, for seeing Paul himself as advocating, if not the phrase 'third race' itself, nevertheless something approaching it. Sechrest concludes 'that Pauline theology constructs a change in religious belief and practice as a change in ethno-racial identity'.[133] The evidence for this is scattered across several sections of the present book. It is already present when Paul speaks in Galatians 3 of Abraham's single family, his 'heirs', marked out by Messiah-faith. A good deal of what we argued in chapter 10, and in the last section of chapter 11, is heading in this direction. But the notion comes into full view, quite sharply, in two or three key passages. The first is the one with which we closed the previous subsection:

> Jews look for signs, you see, and Greeks search for wisdom; but we announce the crucified Messiah, a scandal to Jews and folly to Gentiles, but to those who are called, Jews and Greeks alike, the Messiah – God's power and God's wisdom. God's folly is wiser than humans, you see, and God's weakness is stronger than humans.[134]

This spectacular little passage compresses a great deal into epigrammatic form. Above all it emphasizes something often neglected in the relevant discussions: that the focus of Paul's life and work is not a 'system', not a 'religion', not an attempt to forge a new social reality in and of itself, but a *person*: the crucified Messiah. All else is defined in relation to him. Any attempt to water down the 'scandal' that this posed for Jews, or the 'folly' that it presented to Greeks, is a large step away from Paul.

This opening statement in 1 Corinthians already means that those who belong to the Messiah are defined, are given an 'identity' if we must use the term, that is (a) rooted in Israel's Messiah, and hence in that sense inalienably 'Jewish', but (b) *redefined* around the *crucified and risen* Messiah and hence in that sense inalienably 'scandalous' to Jews. Rooted and redefined: continuity and discontinuity. Those are the classic marks of Paul's thought and life. And those are the ways in which he thought of the Messiah's people. They remain Abraham's family: 'our fathers', he says to the mostly gentile Corinthian Christians, came out of Egypt with Moses. The Corinthians used to be 'Gentiles' but are now no longer (12.2). But for Jews, like Paul, the rule is: 'I am crucified with the Messiah'. Scandalous. A third entity.

That is why we should not be surprised at the cognate language used, almost artlessly, at the end of the long discussion of chapters 8—10:

[132] Tert. *Scorp.* 10.

[133] Sechrest 2009, 15.

[134] 1 Cor. 1.22–5.

> So, then, whether you eat or drink or whatever you do, do everything to God's glory. Be blameless before Jews and Greeks and the church of God, just as I try to please everybody in everything, not pursuing my own advantage, but that of the great majority, so that they may be saved. Copy me, just as I'm copying the Messiah.[135]

This is reflected precisely in the sharp conclusion to Galatians:

> God forbid that I should boast – except in the cross of our lord Jesus the Messiah, through whom the world has been crucified to me and I to the world. Circumcision, you see, is nothing; neither is uncircumcision! What matters is new creation. Peace and mercy on everyone who lines up by that standard – yes, on God's Israel.[136]

We discussed the last phrase at length in chapter 11. The point here is the combination of elements found in the two passages from 1 Corinthians: a tripartite division (circumcision, uncircumcision, new creation), rooted in the Messiah and his cross (rather than in any 'inclusive' sociological experimentation for its own sake). And Paul's claim throughout Galatians is that this is what Israel's scriptures always promised, even though nobody had seen it like this until the messianic events burst in upon the unready world, including the unready Jewish world.

There is then no reason to resist the 'natural' reading of 1 Corinthians 10: Jews, Greeks and the church of God, a threefold reality.[137] Paul has prepared for this tripartite understanding of humanity, as we saw, by identifying the Corinthian church with the exodus generation (10.1) and by insisting that they are the people who pray the *Shema* in its new form (8.6). At the same time he can speak of 'ethnic Israel' in 10.18, drawing an analogy from 'their' practice to what is true of the Messiah's people, and thus necessarily differentiating between the two groups. I submit that it is only the extreme Post-holocaust reluctance to say anything like this that has prevented writers on Paul from drawing the obvious conclusion: he saw the people of the crucified Messiah as having a Messiah-shaped identity which marked them off from Jew and Greek alike. Thiselton catches the balance of Paul's thought:

> In 10:1–22 Paul has stressed the continuity of the Church with Israel; the phrase **the Church of God** in this context calls attention at the same time to a discontinuity, as if to imply that 'the people of God' are partly redefined, although not in exclusivist terms since their roots and basis of divine promise and covenant remain in continuity with Israel's history.[138]

We should note – a point usually missed – that the very idea of a 'third race' *itself presupposes a deeply Jewish way of looking at the world.* Nobody else divided the world into 'Jew' and 'gentile', or 'Jew' and 'Greek' (for Paul,

[135] 1 Cor. 10.31—11.1.

[136] Gal 6.14–16. The connection is made by Sechrest 2009, 156.

[137] Fitzmyer 2008, 403 (following Lindemann) points out that this is the earliest instance of 'the church of God' seen as an entity over against Jews and Greeks.

[138] Thiselton 2000, 795 (bold type original). See too e.g. Mitchell 1991/2, 258: 'As in 1:18–31, Jews and Greeks should be understood as separate from the church – which is now the primary identity of all Christians.'

'Greek' of course often did duty for 'gentile'). You only say 'third race' if you are starting with, and in a measure reinscribing as well as transcending, that basic duality. The idea of a messianically formed and shaped new entity cannot therefore be seen as a non- or anti-Jewish idea, however much inevitable tension there would be between those Jews who did not believe in Jesus and those who did. Qumran itself held an embryonic 'third entity' view of itself, marked out against the wicked world of paganism but also, necessarily, against the majority of Jews. I submit, therefore, that though Paul himself does not use the phrase 'third race', and though we have to be careful to anchor 'race' to its ancient rather than its modern use and connotations, something like that idea is not only Pauline but retains a quintessential, if characteristically paradoxical, Jewish character and flavour.[139]

Of course, the Greeks themselves also regularly divided the world into 'Greeks' and 'barbarians'. Paul reflects that usage on more than one occasion.[140] We should not be surprised, then, that the Syriac version of Aristides sees the Christians as a *fourth* race, after barbarians, Greeks and Jews. To that extent, an originally if paradoxically Jewish idea was being extended into new contexts. But its Jewish DNA is still clearly visible.

Paul makes it clear, in fact, that though this strange new thing – is it a religion? is it a social grouping? is it a philosophy? is it a sect? – is significantly and explicably different from both 'Jews' and 'Greeks', its character remains fundamentally Jewish. Hence the *Ioudaios* in Romans 2.29 and the *peritomē* in Philippians 3.3. Hence the creational ethic, especially in relation to sexual behaviour. Hence, above all, the fulfilment of the promises in Torah itself. And hence, particularly, the 'olive tree' in Romans 11.

Here I part company with Sechrest, who in other respects I have found helpful. She suggests that for Paul the church is a '*completely new* ethnosocial particularity'.[141] Sechrest is here reacting against Caroline Johnson Hodge, who uses a different kind of tree, that of the Jewish 'family tree' into which gentiles are grafted as a subordinate bough.[142] But the reaction goes, I think, a shade too far. Paul insists that even when (Jewish) branches are cut off from the olive tree it remains 'their own olive tree'.[143] Once any branches, whether Jewish or gentile, are firmly in the tree, they are, for Paul, on an absolutely equal footing, and must learn to live as such. That is part of the point of Romans 14 and 15. But the way they get there, and the account that one must give of that process, retains an important differentiation, which finally gives the lie to all the slurs about 'supersession', 'erasure' and the rest. Abraham is the father of uncircumcised believers, says Paul, and also of the circumcised 'who are not merely circumcised but who follow

[139] The modern and ancient views of ethnic identity are carefully and distinctly analysed by Sechrest 2009, chs. 2 and 3.

[140] e.g. Rom. 1.14; cf. too esp. Col. 3.11, where he sets aside no fewer than four antithetical pairs (Greek and Jew, circumcised and uncircumcised, barbarian and Scythian, slave and free) in order to say once more that the Messiah is what matters, 'everything and in everything'.

[141] Sechrest 2009, 210 (my italics).

[142] Johnson Hodge 2007, 143.

[143] Rom. 11.24.

the steps of the faith which Abraham possessed while still uncircumcised'.[144] All this has come about, making Abraham the father of a single multinational family, because of the God in whom he believed, 'the God who gives life to the dead and calls into existence things that do not exist'.[145] I have said it before, and emphasize it here: for Paul, when a Jew believes in 'the one who raised from the dead Jesus our lord' (Romans 4.24) this constitutes an act of 'resurrection', whereas when a gentile believes Paul sees that event as an act of 'new creation'.[146] True, the 'ethno-social particularity' which results from this double miracle is new. No such community had existed before, but this one does now. But it is part of Paul's constant argument, particularly in Romans 9—11, that the new particularity *is the very thing God promised to Abraham in the first place*. It may be 'completely new' in terms of actual space–time–matter reality. But Paul insists that it is not a novelty in the divine purposes. The olive tree has existed ever since Abraham; God always intended to include gentiles within it. That was part of the original promise.[147] The real radical discontinuity, for Paul, was between the 'former life' of the gentiles and their new membership. For the Jew, like himself, what mattered was 'I am crucified with the Messiah; I am, however, alive'. This may seem like splitting hairs, but for Paul it was vital. The discontinuity is essential. But so is the continuity. Without that, as Paul saw clearly, a high road would be open to gentile arrogance.

But Paul's answer to that problem, as we saw in Romans 9—11, was not to say that 'Jews are all right as they are'. It was to insist that, when a gentile believes the gospel, that person is incorporated into the same *essentially Jewish* olive tree; and that presently disbelieving Jews could be brought back into 'their own olive tree' – 'if they do not remain in unbelief'.[148] For Paul, there was only one olive tree, because there was only one God; and the divine purposes, though wise beyond human imaginings, were fully revealed in Israel's Messiah, the crucified and risen Jesus of Nazareth. The 'identity' of the Messiah's people was thus grounded, like everything else in Paul's thought, in the faithfulness of Israel's God.

4. Paul and Israel's Scriptures

(i) Introduction

This brings us at last to a question which hovers over all discussions of Paul, and which in the last generation has surfaced in several new ways. (This was

[144] Rom. 4.12.

[145] Rom. 4.17.

[146] Wright 2002 [*Romans*], 498.

[147] To this extent I agree with Fredriksen 2010, 251 n. 52: 'Precisely in and through its ineradicable Jewishness, Paul's gospel brings the good news of universal redemption' – even if she and I would disagree as to how that general statement plays out in practice.

[148] See above, 1161, 1213–21, 1236, 1245.

only to be expected, granted all the different 'perspectives' that have appeared: the way we understand Paul's use of scripture is always directly linked to the way we understand the larger contours of his writing.) As with all the topics in this final Part of the present book, there is no space for the substantial discussion that might draw together all the threads from our previous discussion. But we must at least give a brief summary.[149]

Hardly anyone will doubt that Paul knew Israel's scriptures well, and that he used them freely and frequently in some (though not all) of his letters. But there the ways divide. Did he know them by heart, or did he have to look up texts when he needed to quote something? Did he think of them in the Hebrew, or in the Septuagint, or both? If so, in which form(s) of the text(s)? Did he care about accuracy, or was he content to quote freely and give a general sense? Was he aware of the larger context of the passages he quoted, or was he just, in the modern sense, proof-texting?[150] How does his use of scripture compare with the complex uses we find in the very diverse Jewish literature of the second-Temple period and on into the rabbis? Large monographs have been devoted to detailed exploration of one or more of these questions. There is no sign of consensus, but rather of a healthy if confused multi-layered discussion.[151]

This is not the place for a history of research. But we may note that some of the older discussions were relentlessly left-brain in their analytic method, studying the precise formulae with which Paul introduced quotations, the exact text-forms he was using and the microscopic details of syntax and vocabulary.[152] As the greatest first-century teacher himself said, however, 'you should have done these, without neglecting the others'.[153] And the 'others' in this case have been making a come-back in the last thirty years, with a sweeping initial victory for a right-brain analysis, followed – as is usual in such debates, whether about philosophy, physics or pharmaceutical engineering – by an alarmed left-brain reaction, and a continuing, but not always mutually attentive, dialogue.[154]

[149] See too *Perspectives*, ch. 32. The recent vol. of essays edited by Porter and Stanley (2008) contains some important work, e.g. DiMattei 2008 (though I think my study of Jewish narratives in ch. 2 above would challenge some of what he says); Fisk 2008, who concludes (185) that 'it does not appear unreasonable to think that many of those who first read or heard [Romans] would have enjoyed considerable prior, and ongoing, exposure to a number of the scriptural passages Paul cites'.

[150] This, famously, is Sanders's view of two of Paul's key quotations on 'righteousness' and 'faith', i.e. Gen. 15.6 and Hab. 2.4 (see e.g. Sanders 1978, 483f.). I have heard Sanders say, more than once, that Paul, wanting to link 'righteousness' and 'faith', ran through his mental concordance to find passages that made the connection, came up with two of them, and dropped them into the arguments of Galatians and Romans. This is one of several points where, I believe, Sanders failed to carry through his own programme of reading Paul in the light of second-Temple Judaism.

[151] Among the most impressive: Wilk 1998; Wagner 2002; Watson 2004. Since my name, too, begins with 'W' I hope that the present section can contribute, however briefly, to the further development of their work.

[152] e.g. Ellis 1957.

[153] Mt. 23.23.

[154] On the 'right-brain' and 'left-brain' methods, see above all McGilchrist 2009; in relation to NT studies: Wright 2012b ['Imagining the Kingdom'], 396–8.

The right-brain come-back was the work of Richard B. Hays. In *Echoes of Scripture in the Letters of Paul*, Hays took several key Pauline texts and argued that when Paul quoted scripture he intended to evoke, and hoped his listeners would pick up, the larger context of the often very short quotations.[155] Hays built on contemporary work in the field of intertextuality, exploring ways in which one may attain methodological control not just when studying actual quotations but when listening for 'echoes'. Hays, who had already written a powerful and provocative monograph on the implicit narratives underlying some key Pauline texts, came to Paul's use of scripture from a totally different angle from that of the earlier atomistic studies.[156] He insisted not only on reading individual verses in the light of their own larger Pauline contexts, but on reading the passages Paul quotes in the light of theirs – and understanding both these larger wholes, Paul's entire arguments and the entire arguments of biblical passages, within a sophisticated theological and narratival framework. Much earlier study of Paul's use of scripture assumed a more or less standard (and often protestant) shape and content to Paul's theology, only questioning how Paul had gone about backing this up, or trying to 'prove' it, with scriptural quotations – as though Paul was really, after all, writing an older version of the Westminster Confession, replete with biblical references as 'scripture proofs'. Hays offered instead a big picture in which Paul was working with whole books and sections of books, scooping up the narrative theology of Israel's scriptures, reshaping it around Jesus and the spirit and retelling it as the undergirding narrative for the nascent church. The difference between Hays and much that had gone before is the difference between Adam Smith's *The Wealth of Nations* and the balance-sheet of a manufacturing company.

Maybe, replied the critics, but you still have to balance the books, and when you do so you may find that Smith got some things significantly wrong. Among those who have challenged Hays's reading, Christopher Stanley has developed an alternative and effectively 'minimalist' account of Paul's use of scripture.[157] According to Stanley, Paul's audiences, being composed largely of gentiles, and not well-educated ones at that, would have been very unlikely to pick up what we may think we discern as biblical 'echoes'. This means that we must assume Paul's purpose in quoting scripture to be quite different from the sophisticated and often quite subtle intertextual meanings proposed by Hays. Instead, we should conclude that his quotations were mainly for rhetorical effect, demonstrating to his audience that he knew ancient texts which, so he claimed, supported his position. In a world where such an appeal might carry weight, that is all, for the most part, that we should suppose Paul to be doing. In fact, says Stanley at one point, Paul was relying on the fact that his audience did not know the

[155] Hays 1989a.

[156] Hays 2002 [1983]: this work also ignited the continuing debate on *pistis Christou*, arguing strongly for 'faith[fulness] *of* Christ' rather than 'faith *in* Christ' as the Pauline meaning.

[157] Stanley 1992 and 2004. Stanley has energetically co-ordinated continuing study and debate, collected now in two volumes: Porter and Stanley 2008; Stanley 2012.

texts; otherwise they would have spotted the points at which he was playing fast and loose with them.[158] Stanley is not the only one to make that kind of suggestion.[159]

This is not the place to engage with Stanley in any detail, or indeed with the many other writers whose diverse work fills the symposia he has edited or co-edited. The idea of Paul adding rhetorical verisimilitude to an otherwise bald and unconvincing theological narrative might seem appealing for a short while. But closer study of what he is actually saying in the letters, where (as we have seen throughout this book) his whole case is that the one God of Israel has acted freshly and decisively in Jesus, gives it the lie. Scripture is *part of this story*, not merely the 'authoritative' witness to, or proof of, ideas or exhortations which are otherwise freestanding. In any case, if I may quote my recent article on the subject, 'reducing Paul's compositional options to the limits of hypothetical reader-incompetence is an example of that left-brain rationalism, allied to a hermeneutic of suspicion, from which biblical studies has suffered for too long'.[160] Most writers, like artists in other fields, put a good deal more into a composition than the first audience will pick up. In any case, Paul's letters were hardly meant to be read once and once only; and the context for further readings would inevitably have included discussion between audience, reader and local leadership, and above all teaching, in which the teaching of the scriptures must have been prominent if not central. Paul certainly assumed that his letters would be read within the context of local church life, to which they would contribute and from which further readings of them would gain. Local scripture-teaching would help people begin to grasp what was going on; the letters themselves would direct the development of that local teaching, as new converts, eager to discover more both about Jesus and about their own new 'identity', realized they needed to spend time with Genesis, Deuteronomy, Isaiah and the rest.[161]

This relates, too, to the smaller-scale but important point about individual words and the resonances they might produce. Ernst Käsemann, famously, questioned whether Paul could have intended a bilingual pun in Romans 2.29, where he describes someone as *Ioudaios* and declares that such a person gains 'praise' from God. 'Praise' is *epainos* in Greek, but Paul would know that the name *Judah* was the Hebrew word for 'praise'. This, says Käsemann, 'would hardly have been intelligible to the Roman community'.[162] But even if we suppose the Roman church(es) to be composed almost entirely of gentile converts with no synagogue background, one might still suppose that someone would point out, sooner or later, what Paul was doing. If even this is challenged (though it should not be), the point still stands: writers often put things in their works simply because they

158 Stanley 2004, 135.

159 cf. e.g. Dunn 1993, 185, on Gal. 3.16f.: 'Paul could just about hope to get away with it.'

160 *Perspectives*, 549.

161 So e.g. Watson 2004, 43 n. 30: ('audience recognition is desirable but not essential'); 127f. n. 1.

162 Käsemann 1980 [1973], 77.

feel like it, whether or not anyone will get the point. The recent discovery of a hidden but powerful meaning within C. S. Lewis's *Narnia* stories is a case in point.[163] Paul would have been quite capable of allowing a particular resonance to sit patiently, like an unopened letter, waiting to be discovered. Martin McNamara, a Targumic expert, has it right: 'At times, particularly in moments of heightened tension, Paul seems to have written from the abundance of his own mind rather than from what his readers would be expected to know.'[164]

My case, here as elsewhere, is simple in outline. First, as to method: we should assume, unless strong evidence to the contrary is provided, that Paul's *use* of Israel's scriptures was at least broadly consonant with what he believed about the *relation* of ancient Israel to the Messiah and his people. The older 'proof-text' view, and the more recent 'rhetorical effect' view, have regularly assumed that for Paul the scriptures were simply a repository of supposedly authoritative divine oracles from which one could draw support *for an exposition which was basically about something else*, or something at least significantly different. These views are part of a view of Paul's gospel in which he sees Jesus as the solution to the generalized plight of humanity, with the story and the scriptures of Israel as simply a detached backdrop. The further one goes down that road (the road that leads to Marcion), the more one might come to see the scriptures as part of the problem rather than part of the solution, so that one might suppose that Paul only delved back into them when forced to do so by his opponents. What one says about Paul's use of scripture thus regularly reflects a larger picture of Paul's relation to ancient Israel as a whole. This is why, methodologically, the present brief discussion comes where it does in the book: one can only get at this question in the light of an overall account.

Granted this principle, and the account I have given of Paul in Parts II and III of this book, I propose that Paul's understanding of Israel's scriptures should have as its basic framework the *covenant narrative of Israel* as we explored it in chapter 2 and again, in relation to Paul himself, in chapter 7. Paul does a thousand different things with scripture, but the broad base from which one ought to start is his belief, expounded throughout the present book, that in Jesus and in the fresh work of the divine spirit Israel's God had brought to its climax the extraordinary, and often dark and disastrous, story of Abraham and his family. God had made solemn covenantal promises to Abraham; Paul believed they were now fulfilled. God had promised Abraham a single worldwide family, inheriting not just the land but the whole world; that was now being accomplished in the reign of Israel's Messiah and the spirit-driven mission of his followers. What was more, God had brought his people out of Egypt, rescuing them from slavery, and the prophets had promised over and over that he would do it again, rescuing his

[163] See the remarkable, and utterly convincing, work of Ward 2008, demonstrating that the seven *Narnia* books deliberately embody the seven characteristic moods associated in the medieval period with the seven 'planets' – Mercury, Venus, Mars, Jupiter, Saturn, the sun and the moon.

[164] McNamara 1978, 36.

people from the continuing 'exile' from which Daniel 9 and many other texts had prayed to be released. Paul believed God had now accomplished those promises. The entire 'Book of the Twelve', the powerful shorter prophetic texts upon which Paul drew for some of his key themes, was, like the great narrative from Genesis to 2 Kings, a story in search of an ending:

> In spite of the historical realities of exile and return, the post-exilic writings in the collection are testimonies precisely to the deferral of a fulfilment which so often seems near at hand but never actually arrives.[165]

In particular, I believe that we can see, far above the normal wrangling about 'Paul and the Torah' (did Paul think the law was a good thing or a bad thing – as if one could expect a sensible answer from such a question!), a reading of Torah itself, the 'Five Books' and particularly the first and last of them, which maps on to other second-Temple 'readings' such as that, implicitly at least, of Josephus. The more we leave behind the dreamland of an atomized reading of Torah, dividing it into sources and strata, and wake up instead to a holistic account in which we might discern a larger narrative line from the start of Genesis to the close of Deuteronomy, the more we find Paul there ahead of us, up and about and retelling the story so that the close of Deuteronomy – the great covenant renewal of chapter 30, followed by the dark warning of chapter 32 – does indeed show us the place to which the story of Abraham had been pointing all along. That is what is going on in Romans 9.6—10.21. Not to glimpse that Torah-shaped narrative line is to miss the full force of Paul's statement that the Messiah is the *telos nomou*, the goal, aim, ultimate fulfilment, of Torah.[166]

Similarly, if we fail to spot the way in which Paul is working with key texts from the Psalms and prophets, filling in the single narrative line with multiple hints of messianic fulfilment, we are actually deJudaizing as well as dehistoricizing his view of his own work and the vocation of his churches. When he declares that 'we are heirs of God, and fellow heirs (*klēronomoi*) with the Messiah' (Romans 8.17), we should cast our minds back to Psalm 2, evoked already in Paul's affirmation of Jesus as the Davidic 'son of God' in 1.4, and reflect on the promise made to this 'son', the promise which gave specific focus to the initial promise to Abraham: 'Ask of me, and I will make the nations your heritage (*klēronomia*), and the ends of the earth your possession.' The line which begins with Abraham thus reaches forward to the Messiah, and thence out to embrace the world:

> The Messiah became a servant of the circumcised people in order to demonstrate the truthfulness of God – that is, to confirm the promises to the patriarchs, and to bring the nations to praise God for his mercy. As the Bible says:
>
> That is why I will praise you among the nations,
> and will sing to your name.
>
> And again it says,
>
> Rejoice, you nations, with his people.

[165] Watson 2004, 137; the whole section (129–48) is full of suggestive insight.

[166] See above, 704, 1179; and my earlier statement of this position in Wright 1991 [*Climax*], 241–4.

And again,
> Praise the Lord, all nations,
> and let all the peoples sing his praise.

And Isaiah says once more:
> There shall be the root of Jesse,
> the one who rises up to rule the nations;
> the nations shall hope in him.[167]

Torah, prophets and writings combine to tell *the single story* which, despite all its disasters and disappointments, has reached its fulfilment.

If the story stretches forwards from Abraham to David, to the promised return from exile and the 'new exodus', and ultimately not only to the Messiah himself but to the extension of his rule across the world, then it also stretches back behind Abraham to Adam himself. Romans 5.12–21 is of course the classic passage, but we should not miss the point. Adam is not merely an example, or (as it were) a detached primal sinner. Genesis itself links Adam to Abraham through the words of command to the former and vocation to the latter.[168] The Psalms, by implication at least, link Adam to the Messiah, through Psalm 8 in which the image-bearing vocation of Genesis 1 is repeated in relation to the 'son of man', a phrase whose residual indeterminacy cannot mask its use, in the first century at least, in relation to the long-awaited king.[169] So when Paul strings together Adam and the Messiah in 1 Corinthians 15.20–8, drawing in Psalm 110.1 as well by means of its own echo of Psalm 8.6 ('he has put all his enemies under his feet' being picked up by 'he has put all things in order under his feet'), these are not just 'proof-texts'. Nor can one say that, because of the unsophistication of the Corinthian audience (a point which could itself be challenged), Paul cannot actually intend to shower them with Genesis and the Psalms, and perhaps Daniel as well, in quite this way.[170] Paul is expounding his central *messianic eschatology*, the point of which is precisely that the scriptural narrative is fulfilled in the new creation which *has* happened in Jesus' resurrection and *will* happen through his messianic reign.

The main problem with 'Paul and scripture' comes, of course, as one subset of the question of 'Paul and the law'. That, too, as I argued towards the end of chapter 10, can only be understood within the narrative framework of Paul's reading of Israel's story and the strange way that story was brought to its conclusion in the Messiah.[171] But it still, of course, leaves all kinds of loose ends awaiting further attention. These need to be addressed properly in a commentary, or a string of articles, but as a starting-point for such a larger exercise I offer here a brief encounter with what, on anyone's assessment, must count as one of the most creative and innovative books ever

[167] Rom. 15.8–12 (the summing up of the whole letter), quoting Ps. 18.49/2 Sam. 22.50; Dt. 32.43; Ps. 117.1; and, climactically, Isa. 11.10.

[168] See above, 783–95.

[169] See Ps. 8.4; cf. 80.17 [MT 80.18], where 'the son of man you made so strong for yourself' seems to refer to the king.

[170] An echo of Dan. 2.44 is detected by some (e.g. Fitzmyer 2008, 572) in 15.24.

[171] On the 'narrative roles' of Torah cf. Hays 2005, 85–100 (orig. 1996a); and above, ch. 7.

written about Paul and scripture: Francis Watson's *Paul and the Hermeneutics of Faith*.[172]

(ii) Hermeneutics, Faith and the Faithfulness of God

Watson's book, which deserves full and careful study, is a brilliant attempt to do three things. First, he is determined to understand Paul as a subtle and intelligent reader of scripture. The apostle is not a purveyor of proof-texts or random references. He sees scripture, particularly the Five Books of Moses, as an entirety with which one must wrestle. Watson recognizes that one cannot simply dismiss Paul's exegesis by saying that he reads like a rabbi, not like a modern historically conscious exegete. Nor can one say that Paul only dives into scripture when forced to by his opponents.[173] Paul believes that it is a central part of Christian faith to be not only a reader of scripture but one who is *changed* by that reading.[174]

Second, Watson provides a rich historical context for Paul by comparing his reading of key texts with other readings of the same texts from the same second-Temple period: Wisdom, *Jubilees*, Philo, Josephus, Baruch, *4 Ezra* and not least Qumran. He thus brings Paul into critical dialogue with several other readings and styles of reading – not that Paul knew any of those texts, except perhaps the Wisdom of Solomon, but that they were so to speak theological cousins, tracing their lineage to the same stock though now expressing it differently.

Third, Watson has a particular case to argue about the way Paul read Torah in particular. Paul, he argues, discerned a 'duality' within Torah itself, hearing two 'voices' and trying to do them both justice.[175] He eschews older expressions of a similar polarity, as though Paul were opposing two abstract 'systems' such as 'promise' on the one hand and 'law' on the other. The two 'voices' Paul hears are in the text of Torah itself, and Paul does his best, according to Watson, to honour both of them in their proper way:

> In reading the Torah, Paul chooses to highlight two major tensions that he finds within it: the tension between the unconditional promise and the Sinai legislation, and the tension between the law's offer of life and its curse. These are tensions between *books*: Genesis and Exodus, Leviticus and Deuteronomy.[176]

[172] Watson 2004. Subsequent references are to this book unless otherwise noted. As the reader will detect (Watson, xii, 376 n. 34), the present remarks are part of a much more long-running conversation.

[173] Watson 17.

[174] Watson ix.

[175] Watson 54f.

[176] Watson 22 (italics original). (Already a note of generalization creeps in: the first half of Exodus is in fact about God's action in liberating his people in fulfilment of the Abrahamic promise.) Cf. 524: 'Paul's reading and the others all register the discrepancy between the patriarchal narratives of Genesis and the Sinai revelation narrated in Exodus. The discrepancy can be overcome by projecting the law back into Genesis, or it can be used to assert the absolute significance of the promise: in either case, it is the same textual phenomenon that generates the divergent readings.'

> ... there does appear to be a distinction between a reading of the Torah that lays all possible emphasis on the promise to Abraham of unconditional divine saving action, worldwide in its scope, and a reading centred upon the demand emanating from Sinai for specific forms of human action and abstention.[177]

> Paul's antithetical hermeneutic claims to have uncovered a deep tension within the law itself, between an 'optimistic' voice that assumes that its commandments can and should be obeyed, and a 'pessimistic' voice that holds that this project of bringing righteousness into human life is doomed to failure.[178]

> Texts that Paul has cited – 'there is no one righteous, not even one', 'the one who is righteous by faith shall live' – encapsulate the double-edged testimony of scripture as a whole.[179]

Watson's underlying purpose in all this is clear. Over against any suggestion that Paul first came to believe in something called 'righteousness by faith' and then went looking for scriptural texts to prove it, he is claiming 'that Paul's doctrine ... is an exercise in scriptural interpretation and hermeneutics':

> Paul seeks to persuade his readers that this language and conceptuality is generated by scripture, which thereby bears witness to its own fundamental duality. In its prophetic voice, scripture speaks of the (positive) outcome of God's future saving action; in the voice of the law, it speaks of the (negative) outcome of the human action that the law itself had previously promoted. This dual scriptural testimony is fundamental to the Pauline hermeneutics of faith.[180]

There is thus 'a deep faultline within scripture itself', an 'inner-scriptural antithesis'. Scripture contains 'darkness and light', though these are not to be located at the point where Paul's hypothetical interlocutors would have seen them, in other words at the border between Israel and the gentiles, but rather 'at the border between God and humankind'.[181] Paul 'heard two voices ... contending with one another like Esau and Jacob in their mother's womb'.[182]

In all this, Watson is advancing a variety of claims. He proposes that the 'works/faith' antithesis is, in its original context, a shorthand for a disagreement between Paul and other Jews (including some Messiah-believers) as to what their shared scriptures were 'really' about. He maps this disagreement on to the larger disagreements, among pre-Christian second-Temple Jews in general, as to how one should (scripturally) understand the relationship of divine and human agency.

177 Watson 29: Watson is careful here to affirm also a double reading of Luther, right on some things and wrong on others.

178 Watson 66. I find this use of 'optimism' and 'pessimism' unhelpful: the readings in question have nothing to do with the prior attitude of the reader.

179 Watson 73.

180 Watson 76.

181 Watson 162, 331, 168.

182 Watson 341. At 520 these have become 'a plurality of voices'.

The question that occurs to a contemporary reader at this point is whether, and to what extent, Watson is saying something so very different from the older protestant exegesis of which he himself has been critical in the past but to (some aspects of) which he seems to have returned. He is rightly critical of elements within, and some exponents of, the so-called and pluriform 'new perspective', but this certainly does not mean that he is merely offering an exegetically and historically sophisticated version of the old one.[183] He can sometimes appear to speak cavalierly of the post-Sanders mood in which, he says, 'a veto has been imposed on the supposition that the commandments could have been understood as the way to life in Second Temple Judaism'.[184] (It all depends whether one is talking of present justification or final justification ... as we saw in chapters 2 and 10 above.)[185] The question is focused for me by the memory of C. H. Dodd's comment on Romans 10.5 and 6. Dodd, patronizing as ever, congratulates Paul on having anticipated the nineteenth-century higher criticism in separating out the 'prophetic spirit' of Deuteronomy from the 'hard and mechanical' ceremonial righteousness of Leviticus.[186] Dodd's breathtaking arrogance is a million miles from Watson's careful and historically sensitive reading. But some might wonder whether Watson has done enough to explain how, in the last analysis, his reading of what Paul actually meant is significantly different.

Before Watson gets to the Torah proper, he offers a detailed and complex analysis of Paul's use of Habakkuk 2.4, a text I might have discussed much earlier in the present book but have saved for this moment. Habakkuk, argues Watson, and this text in particular, were far from being a random selection on Paul's part. Indeed, he makes a strong case that this book, and this text, were already being regarded in Paul's Jewish world as in some sense a summary of the entire message of the 'Book of the Twelve' prophets.[187] Watson argues in particular that Paul's quotation of this text at the end of Romans 1.17 must be seen as controlling the meaning of the whole verse, over against commentators who, he says, are misled by the method of sequential exposition and fail to realize that what Paul means by 'the righteousness of God is revealed through faith for faith' in the first half of the verse must be determined by 'the righteous by faith shall live' in the

[183] See his remarks on Sanders at e.g. Watson 13, 16. I believe he is wrong, however, to speak of the gulf between the Reformers and Paul as the 'fundamental dogma' of the 'new perspective': that perceived gulf was the result, not the foundation, of early 'new perspective' work.

[184] Watson 323.

[185] cf. Watson 329: 'The Leviticus text makes life conditional on law observance. This is fully compatible with assumptions about the covenant, the divine mercy, and Israel's separation from the nations.' This is, I think, more or less what Sanders meant by 'covenantal nomism'. When therefore Watson concludes that 'The dichotomies that have been set up in this area should be dismantled,' it seems to me we need more nuancing: which dichotomies, and set up by whom?

[186] Dodd 1959 [1932], 177: 'It shows real insight on Paul's part that he should have recognized (without the aid of modern criticism) that there is a *stratum* in the Pentateuch which goes deeper than the bald legalism of other parts, and comes very near in spirit to Christianity' (italics original).

[187] Watson 87, 101, 120.

second half.[188] The Habakkuk quotation thus functions as a test: unless we expound 'the righteousness of God' in such a way that the prophetic quotation will support it, we are misreading Paul.

Put like that, it is hard to disagree. But when we get to specifics, I think disagreement is inevitable. Before we get there, however, I want to raise some questions about Watson's overall argument, not least in relation to his major thesis about Paul finding 'two voices' within Torah itself.

Watson has I think raised exactly the right question in exactly the right way. Until it is proved to the contrary, we should assume that Paul's reading of Israel's scriptures belongs on the map of second-Temple readings as a whole, albeit with significant variations because of the specifics of his own theological standpoint. And until it is proved to the contrary we should indeed regard Paul as a sophisticated and nuanced reader of Torah, prophets and Psalms, able to work with the larger wholes of entire books and groupings of books, not simply with isolated texts. Watson's thinking through of these two issues ought to shift future discussions, both of 'Paul and scripture' and of 'Paul and Torah', on to entirely new levels. Reviewers are too ready with the phrase 'ground-breaking', but Watson's book richly deserves it.

It will come as no surprise, though, that I find Watson's account focused far too much on scripture as 'normative' and far too little on scripture as 'narrative'. When Watson speaks of scripture as 'normative' for Paul he regularly seems to move to abstractions: it is 'normative saving truth', speaking of a 'proper relationship to God' or an 'ordained way to salvation'.[189] There are times when the summaries of Paul's message sound almost Bultmannian, which it seems is less of a problem for Watson than it would be for me: 'In the light of God's life-giving action in Christ', he writes, 'the law discloses the limits and limitations of a human action that intends the life that the law itself conditionally offers.'[190] What I miss here is the sense of all scripture, including Torah, as Israel's historical and prophetic *narrative*, the story which Saul of Tarsus and his contemporaries believed ought to have been continuing but which seemed to have ground to a frightening, and theologically challenging, halt.

My puzzle here is that at several points Watson does recognize this (despite his denial of an essentially narrative element in Paul, as we saw in chapter 7).[191] He sees that the Book of the Twelve implied an ongoing narrative which was not getting anywhere.[192] He sees, in line with Richard Hays, that Paul has a sense of the scriptural narrative as a whole, not simply of disconnected fragments upon which one might draw – though he then says that 'the construal of scripture that will emerge [from his treatment] is less smoothly linear, more fractured, than Hays' reference to unfailing

[188] Watson 53.

[189] Watson 26, 179 n. 14, 124, 163, 189.

[190] Watson 465.

[191] See above, 462.

[192] Watson 137, 140f.

divine faithfulness might suggest'[193] – an echo, there, of the normal so-called 'apocalyptic' critique of anything approaching 'salvation history', though I do not recognize in Hays's work, any more than in my own, anything that might be called smooth or linear. He speaks of 'the unfolding narrative of the Pentateuch', later glossed in terms of the unfolding of 'the story of God's covenant with Israel', as standing over against any idea of a 'canon within the canon' or 'a proto-Marcionite rejection of the law'.[194] He notices, in particular, the so-called Deuteronomic view of history, according to which the covenant set out in Deuteronomy 27—30 is inscribed in Israel's history right through to Paul's own day (though he never, perhaps surprisingly, tackles what might be thought to be the clearest example, that of 4QMMT).[195] But none of these points about an underlying narrative is allowed to influence the overall reading. Perhaps it is going too far to say that I find in Watson, as Watson finds in Paul's reading of Torah, two voices in unresolved tension with one another: the dominant one, which is of two principles which stand side by side in unresolved opposition, and the recognized but undeveloped one, which is of a narrative in which, as I shall presently suggest, that opposition is not only resolved but strangely fulfilled. Just as I suspect that Watson has missed a trick by not seeing how Paul integrates these themes (so that, for instance, the unfinished narrative of the Twelve Prophets is in fact held within the still-unfinished prophetic narrative of Torah itself), it is possible that I have missed one in my reading of Watson himself. But I simply do not see how the covenantal narrative, which he acknowledges, fits in with the sharp and abiding antithesis which is his central theme.[196] In particular, Watson never deals head on with Paul's reading of texts which seem, to me at least, to speak clearly not of a 'second chance', but of *covenant renewal.* Without explicit narrative, eschatology itself collapses into different abstract schemes.[197]

The other thing, cognate with this, which I miss at a general level in Watson's account is a sense of the fuller socio-political second-Temple context. Watson knows very well that second-Temple Jews were not simply sitting around discussing abstract systems of 'salvation'. He sees that 'there is no incompatibility between "national" and "transcendent" eschatologies'.[198] But we never get the sense that the texts he is studying, including the letters of Paul, emerge from a politically turbulent and dangerous world in which

[193] Watson 23.

[194] Watson 163 n. 61; 185.

[195] Watson 433, 455–60; for the whole theme, see above, 124–6, and *Perspectives* ch. 21.

[196] On the covenant narrative see e.g. Watson 433, 455, 460f.

[197] See e.g. Watson 335, where Rom. 10.5–8 is discussed in terms of 'the law's project', 'the continuing practice of the law as the way to righteousness and life', 'Moses' principle' which 'places a specific human praxis in the foreground' as opposed to 'the divine praxis' and so on. Granted, the point for Watson here is that God has acted in Christ to bring the law to an end and so to inaugurate something new, and to that extent he is postulating some kind of eschatological narrative (rather like that of Sanders: God has acted in Christ, so the law must be wrong). What the second-Temple texts that use Dt. 30 emphasize, however, is not a different system but the renewal of the covenant.

[198] Watson 484.

the overriding questions were not, in the modern sense, 'how will we be saved', but rather, 'What is going on?' 'What is Israel's God up to?' 'How is he going to rescue us from our present plight?' 'What are we waiting for and how can we help it come about?' and 'What should we be doing in the mean time?'[199] Watson is right to criticize others for ignoring 'the theological ferment of Second Temple Judaism', with all its different 'competing claims to articulate authentic Jewish scriptural tradition'.[200] But one might be forgiven for drawing the conclusion that this theological ferment was really 'about' different systems of 'salvation' in a modern western sense (complete with abstract discussions of 'divine and human agency'), rather than the very this-worldly 'rescue' for which, demonstrably, many of Paul's contemporaries were looking. The multiple readings of scripture in Paul's day were not merely part of a theological ferment but also part of what we might, with equally dangerous anachronism, call religious, philosophical and especially political ferment. And all this pushes us back to the question, raised sharply by *4 Ezra* and many others: what about the divine *righteousness*? How is Israel's God going to be faithful to his promises?

I have argued at length, earlier in this book, that Paul was well aware of the complex but coherent controlling narratives of second-Temple Judaism (as explored in chapter 2), and that he made fresh and creative use of them (as set out in chapter 7). My point now is that this is reflected exactly, and again coherently, in his use of scripture. He reads the early chapters of Genesis, as did some others, in terms of something going wrong early on which the call of Abraham would (somehow) put right. That is why, having expounded the covenant with Abraham in Romans 4, he can stand back and sum up the picture in terms of Adam and the Messiah in Romans 5. And as for Abraham himself, any 'exemplary' role he may have for Paul – one can see at least something of that in Romans 4.18–25 – is subsumed under the far more important theme, that of the establishment in Genesis 15 of the covenant to which God has now been faithful. Here Watson is absolutely right, I believe, to oppose atomistic readings of Paul's quotations. Paul is not just grabbing texts at random.[201] But he never sees the underlying covenantal theme which provides Paul's real framework. When he says that, for Paul, 'the crucial question is whether his thesis about righteousness by faith can produce a plausible and persuasive reading of scripture',[202] I sense this to be the wrong way round. Paul is digging deeper and deeper underneath the headlines of his argument and demonstrating that what he has said about justification is itself the product of the covenant God made with

[199] I have suggested elsewhere that Josephus's celebrated account of the different Jewish 'philosophies' was in fact a translation into abstract categories (predestination, free will and so on) of realities which were much more politically focused (will we be passive in God's coming action, or will he act *through* us?). See e.g. *NTPG* 181f., 200f.; *RSG* 175–81.

[200] Watson 26 n. 52.

[201] See e.g. Watson 40–2. At 72 he says that Paul 'gradually assimilates the language of Genesis 15.6 into his own discourse'; if I am right, Rom. 4 as a whole is an exposition of Gen. 15 as a whole, with 15.6 as its centre and key.

[202] Watson 42.

Abraham. Thus, though Watson is right to show that Paul avoids the regular ploy of treating Abraham as a 'pious example', the patriarch still remains an 'example', only this time of 'faith'.[203] Again, Watson also recognizes that Paul sees Abraham as the one to whom the worldwide promise was made. 'Both God and Abraham are understood in terms of the universal future that is entailed in their relationship.'[204] But, as before, I do not see this insight woven into the main fabric of Watson's argument.

When it comes to Leviticus and Numbers, Watson makes a fascinating case for seeing the famous Leviticus 18.5 ('the one who does these things shall live in them') as a summary of this entire strand of Torah.[205] He also proposes, interestingly, that Numbers, though not quoted directly, stands behind Romans 7, with its account of the judgment of death brought by Torah on the rebellious Israelites in the wilderness.[206] Yet I cannot resist pointing out that if we were looking for passages which come close to Watson's proposal that Paul finds 'two voices' in the Torah, Romans 7 is *the* obvious candidate. Here is the *nomos tou theou*, the 'law of God', in which 'I' delight; and here is another *nomos*, at war with the first one, leading me captive to the *nomos* of sin and death. Might this not be the quintessential statement of Watson's point? The 'other law' of Romans 7.23, whatever it is, is doing what Paul says Torah itself was doing, or rather what 'sin' was doing *through* Torah, in 7.7–12 and especially 7.13. Might this not be the point where Paul agrees, however ironically, with Watson's 'two voices' theory?[207]

But the point is then, of course, that this tension is *resolved* – in the renewal of the covenant. One cannot criticize a book as rich and dense as Watson's for the passages it misses out; but I was surprised none the less by the absence of Romans 8.1–11. There, explicitly resolving the problem of Romans 7, Paul speaks of the *dikaiōma* of the law being fulfilled, and contrasts 'the mind of the flesh', which does not and cannot submit to God's law, with 'the mind of the spirit', which presumably can and does. This is exactly cognate with our old friend Romans 2.25–9, where Paul speaks of a 'fulfilment of the law' on the part of uncircumcised gentiles.[208]

[203] See Watson 218: 'Abraham exemplifies the way of life enabled by a divine speech-act in which unconditional divine saving action is announced'; 220: 'Abraham exemplifies a righteousness without works . . .'.

[204] Watson 269.

[205] Watson 315–29.

[206] Watson 356–80.

[207] Watson 376 expresses regret that something like this view, expounded by him in an undergraduate essay, 'continues to mislead' his former tutor (see Wright 1991 [*Climax*], 198). I can set his mind at rest: I changed my mind completely about the entire drift of Rom. 7 in the late 1970s, and any resonances of my, or indeed his, earlier views are undesigned coincidences.

[208] Watson 352f., n. 57 wrestles with the problem (for his view) that 2.27–9 uses 'distinctively Christian terminology', appearing to describe 'his anonymous righteous Gentiles as though they were Christians', whereas for Watson it would be more appropriate if one could show that 'these obedient Gentiles retrospectively turn out to be an unreal hypothesis'. This is, I think, an unnecessary problem, as the resolution of the narrative in 10.5–8 will show (see below).

All this comes to a head in the treatment of Deuteronomy. Watson, as I said before, sees from time to time that the book offers, and was seen by some second-Temple thinkers to offer, a large-scale narrative which was used to interpret Israel's ongoing life right up to Paul's day and beyond. The sequence of exile and restoration, with a *continuing* exile as in Daniel 9, is firmly inscribed in various second-Temple readings of the 'covenantal' chapters of Deuteronomy 27—30. Here as elsewhere the implicit *narrative* is the vital thing: Moses warns that, after an initial period of blessing, Israel will commit sin and be punished with exile (27—9). The promise that after that there will come a dramatic renewal and restoration is not, as Watson says, a 'second chance'.[209] Paul, drawing on this passage and referring to the speaker not as Moses but as 'the righteousness of faith', is not correcting 'Moses' over-optimistic claim' about such a 'second chance',[210] an idea not found in the text but only in Watson's reading (from which the themes of covenant, exile, restoration and renewal have at this point been all but eliminated). He is speaking of a new moment, picked up later by Jeremiah and Ezekiel, in which God will at last circumcise the hearts of his people so that they will love him from the heart. The transformation at that point will not only be in the people, however, but in the effect of their hearts being renewed: they will now be able, in some sense or other, to keep Torah.

This is not 'optimistic'. Indeed, as I said earlier, it seems to me that such categories are fundamentally misleading (as though Leviticus 18.5 were after all representing a kind of proto-Pelagianism). Deuteronomy 30 has no sense of 'perhaps things will turn out all right after all'. It is all about a fresh divine action, resulting in a radical change in human character, which in turn results in a new sort of Torah-fulfilment. And that, as I have argued in chapter 11 above, is exactly what Paul is talking about in Romans 10.

Here, I believe, is the deepest clue to Paul's reading of Torah. As in Watson's summary of Baruch, 'the entire history of Israel is already contained *in nuce* within the Torah itself'.[211] When we add Deuteronomy 32 into the picture, as Paul does in Romans 10.19, the same point must be made. Just as Josephus spoke of Deuteronomy 32 as a prophecy of events, some of which had come to pass and some of which were coming to pass in his own day, so Paul saw this climactic chapter not simply as a poem from the distant past but as a prediction of the reality he was himself facing in the unbelief of his fellow Jews.[212] It will not do to say simply that Deuteronomy's central section (chapters 5—26) contains laws to guide Israel's life within the land, while according to chapters 27—34 'Israel's future under the law is a future under the law's curse'.[213] As the parallels in 4QMMT and Baruch make clear, resonating with the many other sources which indicate belief in a continuing exile according to a Deuteronomic scheme, the ultimate curse of the

[209] Watson 433, 438f., 471.

[210] Watson 439.

[211] Watson 463.

[212] Jos. *Ant.* 4.303, not discussed by Watson (see above, 130f.).

[213] Watson 426.

law is exile itself, and exile is to be undone in the great renewal of Deuteronomy 30.

Thus Romans 9.6—10.21, which presents a strong claim to be considered as the central point of Paul's reading of Israel's scriptures, demands to be understood as a messianically reshaped reading of Torah itself, into which the prophets and Psalms have also been woven. The narrative runs from Genesis to Deuteronomy, from Abraham (9.7) to the Song of Moses (10.19), taking in the events of the exodus on the one hand and the central command of Leviticus on the other. Its central claim is *telos nomou Christos*, the Messiah is the goal of the law.[214] The Messiah is the point to which the long-drawn-out narrative of Torah (including the covenantal exile) had been heading all along; through him, Deuteronomy 30 has been fulfilled at last. And with that a new kind of Torah-fulfilment, hinted at throughout Romans, has been opened up. I have expounded all this elsewhere.[215] As with many other points in this short review of Watson's remarkable book, I am in full agreement with him that for Paul Deuteronomy makes it clear that Israel will indeed go into exile.[216] But Watson never sees, or at least never develops, the equally important point, that for Paul *the renewal spoken of in Deuteronomy 30 has already happened through the Messiah*. This is precisely what gives Romans 9—11 the combined sense of celebration and tragedy: Deuteronomy 30 has happened, but Deuteronomy 32 is still true of unbelieving Israel. One way or another, the point remains: this is a reading of the whole of Torah. Watson's invitation, to join him in an exploration of Paul's reading of entire books and sequences of books, and to do so in implicit dialogue with other second-Temple Jewish readers of the same texts, is right on target. This ought indeed to be the agenda. But I believe it will result in a very different reading of Paul's use of scripture from that which he offers.

What then happens to the demand of Leviticus? Is it swallowed entirely in the fulfilment of Deuteronomy 30, so that Romans 10.6–8 catches up Leviticus 18.5 and says 'and this is how it's done'? In a sense, yes. But in another sense, no. Precisely because Deuteronomy 32 is still true of Paul's unbelieving contemporaries, we must link it with the earlier statements of the failure of Israel in Romans 9.30—10.4. In that tricky passage 9.31 Paul declares, not that Israel did not attain 'righteousness' because she pursued it by 'law', but that Israel did not attain 'the law' because she pursued it 'by works'.[217] And this is where our earlier exposition of the strange purpose of Torah comes to our help. As in Romans 5.20 and 7.13, and perhaps especially Galatians 3.22, *the divinely planned negative role of Torah was itself one moment in the larger narrative*. Here is my alternative proposal to Watson's 'two voices in the text': what Paul discerns are *two moments in Israel's*

[214] Against Watson 332.

[215] Above, chs. 10, 11.

[216] Watson 415.

[217] Watson 333 suggests that it would have been clearer if Paul had written 'did not attain to righteousness', though he concedes that Paul was also making a subtly different point.

covenantal narrative, two moments which have now strangely, but as Paul believes providentially, overlapped. The Messiah has inaugurated Deuteronomy 30, the covenant renewal, and with it a kind of 'attaining to Torah' of which Saul of Tarsus had never dreamed.[218] But unbelieving Israel was still attempting to 'attain Torah' by the route of 'works', by – in other words – an inevitable reading of Leviticus 18.5. This is part of what Paul means when he says that they have 'stumbled over the stumbling stone', placed there by God himself. The 'two voices' are not two alternative ways of operating, two competing systems of salvation. They are – insofar as Paul would be happy with this language at all – the voice that says 'Israel is my servant, in whom I will be glorified', and the voice that says 'Israel too is in Adam'. Paul believed that the two strands met in the Messiah's cross – which, strangely, seems not to feature much in Watson's analysis. This is why, as Watson sees so clearly, one cannot give an account of 'Paul's use of scripture' as though it were an incidental side-feature, a decorative motif on the outside of his thought and expression. How Paul reads scripture is both a symptom of and a signpost towards the deepest realities of his understanding of the gospel, indeed of God himself.

In particular, Paul's reading of Torah, so far from being either arbitrary or atomistic, reflects a widespread second-Temple sense that after the long 'exile' Deuteronomy 30 would at last come true, even if (as in 4QMMT) most Israelites remained oblivious to it. The sharp antithesis which Watson sees in Paul's reading is there, but it is held within the partly resolved and partly unresolved covenant narrative. It is not the case that Paul wants his contemporaries to 'keep reading', on past Deuteronomy 30, seen as a 'second chance' which remains unattainable, to the new moment of Deuteronomy 32.[219] The point is not, as Watson suggests, to move 'beyond the conditional logic of the blessing and the curse to a final insight into the unconditional basis of divine saving action'.[220] That is to swap Paul's specific messianic claim for a general and abstract theological principle, and here of all places that is inappropriate. Paul's claim is that, in the Messiah, the goal of Torah, the point towards which the entire narrative from Genesis had been straining, has after all been reached, and that with the Messiah the great covenant renewal predicted in Deuteronomy 30 has come about (and, yes, this is in fact a matter of unconditional divine saving action; you get the general principle within the specific historical action). It is not simply that 'God has chosen to act differently', as though God might arbitrarily decide to change course in midstream. The whole of Romans 9—11 argues against that idea. What God has done in the Messiah, however shocking or surprising, and whatever puzzles and problems arise as a result, is what (Paul now believes) God had always intended to do. This, indeed, is part of

[218] Against Watson 505, who suggests that Paul is fundamentally rewriting Dt. 30 and in effect neutralizing the fact that otherwise it would stand alongside (the normal reading of) Lev. 18.5. To see what is going on here we urgently need the whole of Rom. 7.1—8.11.

[219] Against Watson 473.

[220] Watson 473.

what Paul understands by the righteousness, or the covenant faithfulness, of God.

All of which brings us back to Romans 1.16–17, and to the quotation from Habakkuk 2.4. This is clearly a key text for Paul. He quotes it not only at this strategic junction but also at the heart of one of the densest bits of Galatians (3.11). It may function as a further index of his way of reading scripture:

> I'm not ashamed of the good news; it's God's power, bringing salvation to everyone who believes – to the Jew first, and also, equally, to the Greek. This is because God's covenant justice is unveiled in it, from faithfulness to faithfulness. As it says in the Bible, 'the just shall live by faith.'

A tendentious translation, of course, as all attempts are. These two verses offer a headline for what is to come; and, as journalists know, headlines are often compressed beyond comprehensibility, and need to be understood in the light of the smaller print below. Thus I have translated *dikaiosynē theou* as 'God's covenant justice', but many, including Francis Watson, read it, as Luther did, as denoting the righteous status which counts before God, the 'righteousness' which consists of faith. Likewise, I have translated *ek pisteōs eis pistin* as 'from faithfulness to faithfulness', but many, including Watson, regard this as a double reference to the 'faith' of the believer, not (as I suppose) to the faithfulness of God on the one hand and of the believer on the other. And I have translated the quotation of Habakkuk 2.4, *ho de dikaios ek pisteōs zēsetai*, as 'the just shall live by faith', whereas a long tradition, discussed in considerable detail by Watson, takes 'by faith' to modify 'the just', rendering the phrase as 'the one who is righteous by faith shall have life', or some such. About these things, as someone has said, we do not now need to speak in detail.[221]

The point we do need to pick up here, however, is Watson's bold claim that the meaning of *dikaiosynē theou apokalyptetai ek pisteōs eis pistin* is to be calibrated according to the meaning of the Habakkuk quotation which follows it immediately. As he rightly says, we should prefer a reading of the whole verse which can make sense of the interdependence of its parts.[222] But can we be so sure that any of the 'parts' are as secure as Watson supposes – even granted that his discussion of the Habakkuk passage, as used in Paul and Qumran in particular, runs to well over a hundred pages?[223]

I think not. For a start, I pick up clues in Watson's own reading of the original context of Habakkuk. As he rightly says,

> While Habakkuk is also concerned with a specific enemy, the book focuses not on the Chaldeans *per se* but on the theological problem that they exemplify: the problem of the

[221] I have, of course, discussed them all in Wright 2002 [*Romans*], 424–6.

[222] Watson 52. At 43 he goes further: the citation, he says, 'actually *generates* its antecedent. This prophetic text is the matrix from which Paul's own assertion derives' (italics original). This bold thesis, about the origin of Paul's doctrine of justification itself, deserves much fuller discussion.

[223] Watson 33–163 (three substantial chapters).

> continuing non-occurrence of divine saving action. That alone is the issue which the prophet hopes to resolve as he awaits the divine word upon his watchtower.[224]

Quite so. But what Watson does not appear to see is that this issue of the apparent non-occurrence of divine saving action is precisely what is often referred to in terms of the question of God's *faithfulness* and/or *righteousness*. The two English terms 'faithfulness' and 'righteousness' overlap at this point, neither catching all the nuances of the various possible Hebrew and Greek terms they try to represent, but this hardly matters: the whole point is, *what is God up to at this time of crisis?* How and when will he act, as we know he must, in faithfulness to his covenanted promises to his people? And – a further wrinkle, but an important one – at this time of waiting, who are to be accounted the true people of God? If the whole world is being shaken to bits, how can we tell who God's people really are?[225] This is the question of 'God's righteousness', whether in Isaiah 40—55, Daniel 9, *4 Ezra* or elsewhere.

Watson, however, frames the discussion of *dikaiosynē theou* in terms, more or less, of the older debate between Bultmann, who saw 'the righteousness of God' as the 'righteousness' of the believer, and Käsemann, who saw it as 'God's salvation-creating power'.[226] He rightly notes the strong points of Käsemann's theory, particularly the parallels between 'the righteousness of God' in Romans 1.17 and 'the power of God' in verse 16 and 'the wrath of God' in verse 18, and points out that Käsemann was then at a loss as to how to read *ek pisteōs eis pistin*. If 'God's righteousness' really did mean 'God's saving power', Watson comments, it would have been better for Paul to clinch the sentence by quoting a passage like Psalm 98.2, where the revelation of God's own 'righteousness' before the nations is placed in direct parallel to the making known of his salvation.[227] Watson, however, insists that 'the righteousness of God' must be attached tightly to 'by faith', *ek pisteōs*, since otherwise the Habakkuk quotation is making the wrong point. But Käsemann's reading of *dikaiosynē theou* is not in fact the only, or even the most (biblically) natural, alternative to that of Luther, Bultmann or indeed Watson himself. The meaning Käsemann was anxious to screen out – anything to do with God's covenant with Israel, and his faithfulness to that covenant – is precisely the centre of concern for Habakkuk, for *4 Ezra*, and as I have argued at length above, for Paul himself. Faced with catastrophic events in which it appeared that God's faithfulness was called radically into question, how was God in fact going to be faithful – and who were to be regarded as his faithful people at such a time? It is this *double* question to which the prophet is given an answer in 2.4, and it is this *double* answer

[224] Watson 141f.

[225] As I said in Wright 2009 [*Justification*], 157 [UK edn.], 182 [US edn.], my first hint of trying to understand Hab. 2.4 in its larger context came as a gift from my friend Peter Rodgers, for whose continuing support I remain grateful.

[226] Watson 49f.

[227] D. A. Campbell 2008, in a characteristically brilliant and provocative piece, argues that Paul does in fact echo this psalm here.

which Paul is evoking in Romans 1.17 – as also in 3.21—4.25, and climactically in 9.6—10.21.

In fact, the complex textual evidence suggests that God's own 'righteousness' or 'faithfulness' may have been the more natural subject of Habakkuk 2.4 in the first place. The Septuagint, translating Habakkuk 2.4, renders the Hebrew *be'emunathō* ('in/by *his* faith/faithfulness') as *ek pisteōs mou* ('on the basis of *my* faithfulness'). This either shows that the original Hebrew text itself read *be'emunathi* ('by/in *my* faith/faithfulness'), an easy orthographic slippage, or that the Greek translator found that to be in any case the more natural meaning.[228] Certainly there is no reason, faced with the last clause of Romans 1.17, (a) to insist that one can take it only as a reference to human faith, and then (b) to insist in consequence upon a hitherto unheard-of meaning for the well-known biblical phrase *dikaiosynē theou*. To reverse the kind of argument Watson uses here: if when Paul wrote 'the righteousness of God' he was referring to a human quality which counted as 'righteousness' in God's sight, he would have done better not to back it up with a verse which, in the Greek Bible at least, was seen as referring to God's own 'faithfulness'.

In any case, the wider context in Habakkuk is not only about the theological and practical confusion of ignorant armies clashing by night. It contains a particular question to which 2.4 might be thought to be the answer. In 1.13, the prophet appeals to YHWH as the judge who ought to be settling a lawsuit:

> Your eyes are too pure to behold evil,
> and you cannot look on wrongdoing;
> why do you look on the treacherous,
> and are silent when the wicked swallow
> those more righteous than they?

As with other 'more righteous than . . .' phrases in the Hebrew scriptures, the proper way to read this is not as a moral contrast *per se* ('these people have more credit in the moral bank than those ones') but as an implied lawcourt scenario: these people are in the right, and those ones are in the wrong![229] God is supposed to be the judge, and if the case came to court he would – he must! – find in favour of us, the beleaguered and oppressed, and hence against the treacherous and wicked. We confidently expect a positive verdict; they can be sure of a negative one. That is a key element in the prophet's complaint. He wants *justice*; he wants justification – that is, he wants the case to be decided in Israel's favour (and in favour of the true Israelites, perhaps, as against the 'proud' of 2.4a). The righteous judge is

[228] See the discussion in Watson 153f., allowing that the notion of divine faithfulness is indeed a plausible meaning though eventually deciding that the reference is to human faithfulness. As is well known, the verse is also quoted in Heb. 10.38, where the MSS vary between *ho de dikaios mou ek pisteōs zēsetai*, the same without the *mou*, and the same with *ek pisteōs mou* instead of *mou ek pisteōs*. If this adds anything (apart from confusion) to the debate about Rom. 1, it may be the point that for some scribes at least the notion of God's own faithfulness was a natural way to read *pistis* here.

[229] Against Watson 150; see above, 796–9, on e.g. Gen. 37.26; 1 Sam. 24.17.

under obligation to settle the case that way; Israel's covenant God is under obligation to settle the case *Israel's* way. If and when God acts in covenant faithfulness, then, his people will be vindicated: the 'righteousness' of God will result in the 'righteousness' of his people.[230] That, together with the *eschatological* use of Habakkuk in the second-Temple period, is the larger context in which Habakkuk 2.4 must be read in Paul.[231] And it shows, among other things, that references to God's righteousness and human righteousness, so far from cancelling one another out, belong firmly together. God is the righteous judge, the faithful covenant-maker: his people will be declared 'righteous', covenant members, at the last, and this is anticipated in the present. Ironically, so far from Habakkuk providing a solid fixed point from which one can reason back to a historically surprising and innovatory meaning of *dikaiosynē theou* earlier in the verse, the normal historical meaning of that phrase enables the potential ambiguities present in the Habakkuk passage to point forward to Paul's fuller exposition of *both* the faithfulness of God *and* the faith of humans in 3.21—4.25.

This then underscores a reading of Paul's references to *dikaiosynē theou*, in 1.17a and elsewhere, in terms of God's own 'righteousness', his faithfulness to the covenant, as I expounded it in chapter 10 above. As Richard Hays argued many years ago, this is in any case strongly supported by Paul's use of Psalm 143 (LXX 142) in Romans 3.20 and Galatians 2.16. Granted, Paul only quotes 143.2 ('no one living is righteous before you'), but that verse depends directly on verse 1 ('answer me in your righteousness') which in turn looks on to verse 11 ('in your righteousness bring me out of trouble').[232] When, immediately afterwards, Paul declares that the divine *dikaiosynē* has been unveiled (3.21), and goes on to explain this in unambiguous terms to do with God's own 'righteousness' (3.25–6), we should be in no doubt that he has this theme in mind. Once more, the righteousness of

[230] The LXX translator of Hab. 1.13 omitted the closing *mimmennu*, 'rather than they', flattening the idiom into a straight moral contrast; but the answer of 2.4 indicates that the word was original, and was intended in this sense.

[231] For what it is worth, the Qumran commentary on Hab. 1.13 provides an explicit lawcourt scenario, though a human one rather than God's: 'Its interpretation concerns the House of Absalom and the members of their council, who kept silent when the Teacher of Righteousness was rebuked, and did not help him against the Man of the Lie, who rejected the Law in the midst of their whole Council' (1QpHab. 5.9–12, tr. García Martínez and Tigchelaar).

[232] Hays 1980, reprinted in Hays 2005, 50–60. Watson, in his sole discussion (67) of this psalm, does not in my view succeed in his attempt to avoid the implications which Hays draws. He sees that in the psalm God's righteousness is identified with God's mercy, and that in Rom. 3.4f. God's own righteousness is in question. But he is wrong (except at the merely grammatical level) to say that Hays's argument demonstrates *Käsemann's* understanding: Käsemann, as we saw, screens out the vital theme of covenant faithfulness, which is precisely what Hays highlights as the proper meaning of the subjective genitive reading on which, against Bultmann (and Watson) they agree. Watson's plea, that we must understand 'the righteousness of God' by way of texts *actually cited* in Rom. (his italics), prompts the reflection that the whole of Rom. 1—4 is heading for the discussion of Gen. 15 in ch. 4, where the covenant is established, the covenant to which God (so Paul argues) has now been faithful. Watson finds himself compelled to see Paul's use of 'righteousness of God' as a fresh coinage, a gloss on Hab. 2.4, referring to the human righteousness which is valid before God. We are not then entirely surprised when (71, 75f.) he gives in my view a less than adequate account of Rom. 3.25f., where God's own righteousness is clearly the central topic.

Israel's God is correlated with human righteousness (or the lack thereof).[233] The verse Paul quotes, coming poignantly at the end of 1.18—3.20, functions both as a plea against the judgment that might by now be supposed inevitable and, by its echo of verse 1, as a plea for God's covenant faithfulness to bring about the desired rescue. The whole thought is once more very close to that of Daniel 9.

That in turn then offers a natural way of understanding the otherwise troublesome *ek pisteōs eis pistin* in 1.17. As the opening verses of chapter 3 make clear, Paul is working with the whole notion of the divine faithfulness, truthfulness, righteousness and justice, just as he is in Romans 9 and 10.[234] These terms are not mutually exclusive, but rather mutually defining and interlocking. I have argued elsewhere that Paul sees the covenant plan, to which Israel's God will remain faithful, as requiring a faithful Israelite, and that in 3.21–6 that is what is provided – in the 'faithfulness' of the Messiah (anticipating the theme of the Messiah's 'obedience' in 5.12–21).[235] This provides a natural, if rich, understanding of 3.22: God's covenant faithfulness is revealed through the faithfulness of Jesus the Messiah for the benefit of all who believe/are faithful (*dia pisteōs ... eis pantas tous pisteuontas*). This in turn looks back easily enough to the dense, headlining phrase in 1.17: God's righteousness is revealed, on the basis of the faithfulness of God, for the benefit of those who have faith.[236] Whichever option we then choose for the interpretation of Habakkuk 2.4 as read by Paul, the whole prophetic context as set out above will support the entire range of Paul's theme as he explains how Israel's God has been faithful to the covenant by establishing, through the Messiah, an Abrahamic people whose only defining characteristic is *pistis*.

In answer to the question some might then ask, whether Paul in quoting Habakkuk 2.4 sees Jesus himself as 'the righteous one', my answer – at this point like Watson! – is that this is probably a bridge too far.[237] Certainly nobody could guess that from the context of Romans 1.1–17. When Paul does eventually unveil 'the righteousness of God through the faithfulness of the Messiah' in 3.22 the latter is, as it were, subsumed under the former: the point is (3.25) that 'God put Jesus forth'. The Messiah's faithfulness is the living embodiment of the divine covenant faithfulness. But it is that divine faithfulness, called into question for Habakkuk by the Chaldean invasion (and for *4 Ezra* by the destruction of Jerusalem), and for Paul's contemporaries by the shocking events of the gospel itself, to which the apostle is referring in 1.17.[238]

[233] One might also compare *Pss. Sol.*, e.g. 2.6–21; 8.4–8, 23–32; 9.1–7; 10.5.

[234] See *Perspectives* ch. 30. See too Rom. 15.8.

[235] See again *Perspectives* ch. 30.

[236] This double use is paralleled in Philo *Abr.* 273, where God is faithful to faithful Abraham.

[237] See the earlier arguments of Hays 1989b (reworked in Hays 2005, 119–42); Campbell 1994; and Watson 50–2.

[238] There is no space here for what would naturally follow at this point, namely a discussion of the use of Hab. 2.4 in Gal. 3.11. That must wait for a future commentary.

I thus end up almost diametrically opposite to Francis Watson when it comes to Paul's use of Habakkuk – though paying warm tribute to him for the creative and helpful way in which he has raised both this question and that of Paul's overall reading of Torah itself. I do not think that Habakkuk 2.4 must be read in terms of a human 'righteousness' which consists in, or comes by, faith; I do not think that this or any other reading of the verse must be allowed to determine how we read Romans 1.17a. So far from the prophet providing a fixed point around which the meaning of *dikaiosynē theou* must be reconfigured, the wider usage of the phrase and its cognates, and associated ideas in Romans, creates a massive presumption in favour of taking it to refer to the divine 'righteousness' in the sense of 'faithfulness to the covenant'. When we return to Habakkuk with this in mind we find a close match both in the prophet's own situation and in the re-reading of his work in the second-Temple period.[239] Israel's God is in the right, and through the gospel he has brought into being a covenant people as he always promised to Abraham. Paul reads Israel's scriptures as a vast and complex narrative, the story of the faithful creator, the faithful covenant God, the God who in Israel's Messiah kept his ancient promises and thereby created a people marked out by their *pistis*, their own gospel-generated faith or faithfulness. The scriptures do not so much bear witness, for Paul, to an abstract truth ('the one God is faithful'). They *narrate* that faithfulness, and, in doing so, invite the whole world into the faithful family whose source and focus is the crucified and risen Messiah.

5. Conclusion

A Jew like no other. Yes, perhaps. An anomalous Jew: from one point of view, yes. A renegade Jew? Not if you believe that Jesus was Israel's Messiah. An Israelite indeed – though with enough rhetorical guile to harangue the Galatians one minute, tease the Corinthians the next, and set before the Romans a *text* like no other, a document only comprehensible as coming from the very heart of the Jewish world and yet opening up vistas never before imagined there or anywhere else. Paul insisted that his primary self-definition was not, in fact, simply that of being Jewish. His primary self-understanding was that he was a Messiah-man. He was *en Christō*, and conversely the Messiah lived in him, so that Paul and all other Messiah-people had 'the Messiah's mind'. These extraordinary claims, only comprehensible from within the Jewish world, nevertheless split that world open at the seams. They are those of a man who has burnt his boats. Like those who followed David to Adullam's cave, there was no way back to the court of Saul. Like those who hailed bar-Kochba as Messiah, you could not then say that you were actually a Hillelite at heart, so please could you just study and practise Torah in private and let the Romans have Jerusalem and run the

[239] Still important here is the work of Strobel 1961, not discussed by Watson.

world if that's what they wanted. Either this man is the king, in which case Israel, and in a measure the world, is now to be seen and defined in terms of his reign. Or we are of all people most to be pitied.

But the 'identity' of which Paul was aware, and the project to which he found himself called and compelled – for which the phrase 'apostle to the nations' was his own shorthand – was then inevitably more than simply 'religious'. It was more than 'having a faith', or indeed a hope. At every point in the present Part of this book we have seen that Paul has something important to say to the worlds of politics, 'religion', philosophy and now the multi-faceted first-century Jewish world as well. This is not a mere accidental by-product of a 'mission' which was really 'about' something else. The fulfilled-Jewish identity of Paul, which we have tried in this chapter to map, requires all the categories we have explored so far – theology, worldview, culture, politics, religion, philosophy, the Jewish world itself – and perhaps more again. I suspect, in fact, that our late-modern discourse will struggle to provide us with categories adequate to express what Paul thought he was doing. But in our final chapter, to which we now turn, we must do our best to find some.

Chapter Sixteen

SIGNS OF THE NEW CREATION: PAUL'S AIMS AND ACHIEVEMENTS

1. Introduction

It was a turbulent and dangerous century. Imperial power had once again reared its frightening head. People looked this way and that for help, only to discover that pragmatists and ideologues alike could change sides, and change shape, overnight. Some were content to keep their heads down and hope for the best. Those who cherished the ancient longing for a new time, a new and redemptive *kind* of time, were losing faith in historical 'progress', and searched fiercely not just for a hope to which they could cling but for a course of action to which they could commit themselves and summon others. For many Jewish people, trapped as so often between warring powers, the question was not so much how to think about it all (though that was vital too) but rather, what was to be *done*? Marx, though partly discredited, could still be invoked: the point was not simply to interpret the world, but to change it.

For one such thinker and doer, who like Saul of Tarsus claimed the historic tribal name of Benjamin, this meant not only some version of the ancient messianic hope, but a hope which would redeem the past as well as the present:

> In every era the attempt must be made anew to wrest tradition away from a conformism that is about to overpower it. The Messiah comes not only as the redeemer, he comes as the subduer of Antichrist. Only that historian will have the gift of fanning the spark of hope in the past who is firmly convinced that *even the dead* will not be safe from the enemy if he wins. And this enemy has not ceased to be victorious.[1]

It is not enough, in other words, simply to tell the old stories and to rely on 'progress' to take us where we need to go. We look for a different sort of moment, a transformation not only *in* time but *of* time itself.

That was the vision of Walter Benjamin, who wrote those words as the Nazis closed in on him in his unsafe Parisian exile in 1940.[2] Disgusted at the way Stalin's Russia had made peace with Hitler's Germany, calling into question the whole Marxist project he had earlier embraced, he escaped to Spain, but it was no good. Terrified that the Gestapo were hard on his heels,

[1] Benjamin 1968 [1940], 255.

[2] The clearest commentary known to me is that of Löwy 2005.

he committed suicide. In an eerie parallel with Dietrich Bonhoeffer, from whom in other respects he was so different, this seminal thinker bequeathed words with a peculiar, haunting poignancy. Even when modernist Jews give up believing in God, they may still find themselves hoping for a coming moment that might redeem even the past:

> We know that the Jews were prohibited from investigating the future. The Torah and the prayers instruct them in remembrance, however. This stripped the future of its magic, to which all those succumb who turn to the soothsayers for enlightenment. This does not imply, however, that for the Jews the future turned into homogenous, empty time. For every second of time was the strait gate through which Messiah might enter.[3]

This is not the moment to embark on a detailed discussion of one of the most fascinating minds of the twentieth century. But Benjamin offers a reminder that the ancient Jewish vision, in which the Messiah and the redemption of history have played such an important role, has to do not simply with 'spirituality' or 'religion', not with an escapist salvation in which the rest of the world ceases to matter, but with the challenge to action in the world itself. As Benjamin's friend Hannah Arendt put it,

> We can no longer afford to take that which was good in the past and simply call it our heritage, to discard the bad and simply think of it as a dead load which by itself time will bury in oblivion. The subterranean stream of Western history has finally come to the surface and usurped the dignity of our tradition. This is the reality in which we live. And this is why all efforts to escape from the grimness of the present into nostalgia for a still intact past, or into the anticipated oblivion of a better future, are vain.[4]

Arendt and Benjamin, in the extreme conditions of the mid-century crisis, understood the urgency of present action. One can neither wait to let 'progress' take care of things, nor escape into an alternative world. Something has to be *done*, and done *now*. What we need, declared Arendt, is

> a new guarantee which can be found only in a new political principle, in a new law on earth, whose validity this time must comprehend the whole of humanity while its power must remain strictly limited, rooted in and controlled by newly defined territorial entities.[5]

One does not have to fill in too many gaps to see that this is essentially a *Jewish* vision: a world at one, with human authorities necessary but firmly under limitation. The 'newly defined territorial entities' are beside the point here. One only has to think of the Balkans or the middle east, two generations on, to shudder at the implications. But the point is, for Benjamin as well as Arendt, that one cannot go on as before. This is the moment for action. Now is the acceptable time. Now is, or might be, the day of salvation.

[3] Benjamin 1968 [1940], 264.

[4] Arendt 1968 [1950], preface of 1950 (*ad fin.*). Earlier in the same preface she writes: 'This book has been written against a background of both reckless optimism and reckless despair. It holds that Progress and Doom are two sides of the same medal; that both are articles of superstition, not of faith.'

[5] Arendt, ibid.

This reminder, and its obvious echoes of that earlier representative of the tribe of Benjamin, sends us back from the twentieth century to the equally turbulent and dangerous first century. What happens when we stand back from the last four chapters, from (that is) our account of Paul's explicit and implicit engagement with the worlds of politics, religion and philosophy, and with the Jewish world of his own upbringing?

Many books on Paul's thought conclude with an account of his eschatology, or ecclesiology, or ethics. We have located each of these elsewhere, but it is not for that reason alone that the normal endings are inappropriate here. I have argued that Paul's theology is what it is, and means what it means, not only in relation to his wider social, philosophical, cultural/religious and political worlds, and especially that of ancient Judaism, but more particularly in relation to the worldview through which he had come to see all of reality. The symbols, praxis and stories which formed the spectacles he wore and which he taught his churches to wear, together with the strongly implicit answers he gave to the key worldview questions, all point to an integration of life, thought, work, prayer and not least the building and maintaining of communities. That integrated whole, his many-sided life-project, is what we must now try briefly to describe.

Paul's theology itself plays its own role within that integration. This 'theology' was not simply the elegant organization of the central elements of Jewish belief, reworked around Messiah and spirit. It was the beating heart which ensured that the lifeblood of prayer and God-given energy was animating the whole project. What a recent writer has described in terms of the relationship between political power and the philosophical enterprise can and should be said, *mutatis mutandis*, about the still more complex relationship in Paul between worldview and theology on the one hand, and between that worldview/theology combination itself and the wider contexts, Jewish and non-Jewish, on the other:

> Whether despotic or populist, political rulers have sought to conscript philosophical voices in order to claim ideological validation, solicit prestige or adorn propaganda. Reciprocally, academic mandarins, speculative thinkers and intellectual publicists have felt drawn to charismatic leaders ... [Thinkers may possess] a deeply entrenched nostalgia for enactment, for the realization of otherwise inert doctrines and proposals, the translation of word into deed. Aspirations to performative fulfilment haunt the thinker; the plaudits of the sage flatter the tyrant. Seneca is close to Nero; Machiavelli is fascinated by Cesare Borgia; Sartre is an apologist for the barbarism of Mao.[6]

To see Paul as the philosopher who provided the ideological validation for the worldwide rule of Jesus would hardly capture the whole of his thought, but it would possess more than a grain of truth, and one regularly screened out. Paul was precisely not an isolated, detached thinker. That is why the isolated thinkers in the western academic tradition have had such difficulty with him, seeing confusion in his pastoral skill and contradiction in his subtle paradoxes. He was a man of action, of performative fulfilment. He was

[6] Steiner 2013.

both thinker and doer, regarding his thinking as itself a form of worship, and his doing, too, as a sacrificial offering through which to implement the already-accomplished achievement of the Messiah. He was an integrated whole: razor-sharp mind and passionate heart working together.

If in the present chapter, then, we turn at last to his 'doing', this is not to replace theory with practice, still less ideology with pragmatism. For Paul, the 'doing' was the ultimately important thing, precisely because at the heart of his thinking lay the goal of new *creation*. Since Paul believed that this new creation had already begun in the resurrection of the Messiah, this could not, by definition, remain a mere idea. If it was true, it had to become what we might call a historical reality. Hence the preaching of the gospel, the planting and pastoring of churches, the confrontation with authorities and not least the writing of letters. I want in this chapter to argue that Paul's practical aim was the creation and maintenance of particular kinds of communities; that the means to their creation and maintenance was the key notion of reconciliation; and that these communities, which he regarded as the spirit-inhabited Messiah-people, constituted at least in his mind and perhaps also in historical truth a new kind of reality, embodying a new kind of philosophy, of religion and of politics, and a new kind of combination of those; and all of this within the reality we studied in the previous chapter, a new kind of Jewishness, a community of new covenant, a community rooted in a new kind of prayer. Call this practical ecclesiology, or indeed missiology, if you like; but whereas those phrases might be taken today to imply the mere pragmatics of a theory already thought through, for Paul there was always a complex give-and-take between the impulse and imperative of the gospel and the stubborn realities of communities and individuals.

That is why it matters, providentially he might have said, that what we have from him are precisely letters, not treatises. His writings, from Romans to Philemon, embody in their own situational purposes the overall aim, not of communication merely, but of community. The authority the lord had given him, he said, was for building up, not for tearing down.[7] His writing was a form of *doing*: he was concerned, not to explain the world or indeed the church, but to change it. Central to his whole life was the word 'now', often preceded with the contrast-sharpening 'but'. *But now . . .*

This integrative vision, as the previous chapter and indeed the whole book has made clear, was an essentially Jewish perception of reality. It is no accident that, in the book whose review I quoted a moment ago, the particular place where the attempted confluence of politics and philosophy was happening was the German Third Reich. When the Nazis were constructing a newly integrated form of would-be philosophically grounded community, they found anti-semitism to be an ideological necessity, not merely a pragmatic desideratum. There could not be two chosen peoples. There could not, in particular, be two *histories*: the Jewish history had to be erased, by the burning of the Torah as well as by the killing of its devotees, in order

[7] 2 Cor. 13.10.

that the fresh Nazi story of Germany could stand on its own new feet.[8] Hence the anguished discussion, in twentieth-century continental philosophy and consequent debates to this day, on the question of just how deeply committed to the Nazi cause was the towering philosopher of the day, Martin Heidegger.

Indeed, part of the task of New Testament scholarship in the twenty-first century, it seems to me, is the long overdue liberation of exegesis and theology, and actually of early Christian history itself, from the dark gravitational pull of the whole post-Enlightenment European philosophical and political matrix, of which Heidegger was and is a central symbol, and which has sucked the past – including the New Testament! – into its orbit and forced it to reflect its flickering ideological 'light' rather than shining with its own proper beams. History – to state the obvious, but sometimes the obvious things get ignored – ought always to be liberating, freeing the past from the tyranny of the present. And for that one needs always to *think in different ways*. As fully fledged historians have long been aware, if the past is indeed a 'foreign country' where 'they do things differently',[9] the historian is by definition one who learns to live there as a respectful guest, rather than insisting on speaking loudly in his own language to drown out the strange local babble and behaving according to his own customs irrespective of local tradition and taboo. To say this is not of course to revert to a naive realism, but to grapple, as I argued in an earlier book, with the application to historical method of a properly *critical* realism, fully aware of the postmodern critique of all external knowledge but equally aware that to cut off that access is to collapse into a clever-sounding solipsism.[10]

The historical study of Paul, which I have attempted in this book, will therefore in itself constitute a move towards liberation from at least three paradigms that have arguably continued to pull historical exegesis out of shape. F. C. Baur forced upon the material his rigid and anachronistic analysis of the two 'isms', Juda*ism* and Hellen*ism*, the latter to be preferred over the former. Bultmann took this forward; his geographical and ideological proximity to Heidegger himself showed themselves in developing a previously implicit ideological commitment (interpreting the core of early Christianity in essentially non- or even anti-Jewish ways on the pretext of a supposedly 'Pauline' gospel with 'Judaism' as its foil). The would-be and self-styled 'apocalyptic' school (which, despite its ideological opposition to historical progression, is now rather proud of its three-generational lineage) has superimposed upon Paul, the apostle of hope, the despairing negativity of his twentieth-century Benjaminite cousin. All these – to revert to the image I used in the opening chapter – are forms of *slavery*, captivity, in which words, thoughts and documents from the first century have been

[8] See particularly Confino 2012. The parallel between this and the proposals of today's neo-'apocalyptic' interpreters of Paul is, or should be, a matter of concern.

[9] cf. Hartley 1997 [1953], 5.

[10] The subject is of course far more complex than this, and much discussed among contemporary historians (cf. e.g. Bentley 2006); see further *NTPG* ch. 4.

compelled to make ideological bricks with less and less historical straw. Like other forms of liberation, of exodus, the task of freeing a genuinely historical exegesis from these and other forms of captivity is itself pregnant with Jewish narrative and hope, which Baur, Bultmann and the neo-'apocalyptists' have routinely marginalized. Among many ironies here, the self-description of the slave-masters has been that of 'historical criticism', supposedly seeking to use history to awaken Christianity from its pre-Enlightenment dogmatic slumbers. But in reality, again and again, not least in the present fad for a supposedly Benjaminite 'apocalyptic' of sheer negativity towards the past, it is 'theology', in the form of post-Enlightenment ideologies of one kind or another, that has kept its boot firmly on the neck of an enslaved history.

Part of the irony of all this is that Walter Benjamin's own frustrated denunciation of various types of mid-twentieth-century Marxism itself constituted a form precisely of inner-*Jewish* debate. Marx himself, of course, had offered a secularized, Hegelian version of the Jewish story of liberation. That story, with its two basic elements, is seen in the truly 'apocalyptic' early Jewish books like Daniel, *1 Enoch* and *4 Ezra*, for all their various differences. First there is the long and dark historical sequence, to be understood within the Deuteronomic and Danielic framework as the time of covenant disaster but also, in consequence, as the time of divine patience and providence, inviting an answering patience from those who clung to promises that showed no present sign of coming true. Second, there is the sudden (messianic) moment when the God of Israel would act in fresh and shocking ways to turn everything upside down and introduce the new era of liberation, whether through the exaltation of 'one like a son of man', the arrival of a great white bull or the emergence from the forest of the Lion of Judah, confronting the horrible pagan eagle. This new 'apocalypse' would happen, not like a slow dawn eventually reaching full day, but as a shockingly new and radical event. It would, nevertheless, be the true and long-awaited fulfilment of the ancient scriptural and covenantal promises.

If we bring that picture forward nineteen centuries or so, but take God out of it, we find Karl Marx. For Marx, the rejection of God necessarily put more weight (as one would expect from the Enlightenment's latent Epicureanism) on the *process* itself. The revolution, when it came, would not be the result of a new irruption from outside (there being no *deus ex machina* to perform such a trick) but the sudden eruption from within of a social volcano whose pressure had been building up below the surface. Marx therefore had a much higher view of the long historical sequence, the historical process, than was held by his first-century apocalyptic ancestors. Their belief in an overall divine providence, and in ancient promises that had yet to be fulfilled, did not lead, as some today imagine such beliefs would necessarily lead, to a Hegelian theory of immanent progress in which history would arrive, under its own steam and without human agency, at the liberating or messianic conclusion. The ancient apocalyptists were not process theologians. Their God remained sovereign over, not contained within, the dark and puzzling years of waiting, of exile. And within that strange sovereignty human decisions and actions, for good or (more often) for ill, had a vital role to play.

But if Marx was thus significantly different from his ancient semi-predecessors, he was ironically on the same page as the very different (but equally Epicurean) post-Enlightenment Social Darwinist thinkers who believed in a 'progress' through which 'enlightenment', in the form of gradual social amelioration, would spread throughout human society. The late nineteenth century saw liberal theologians offering a version of this narrative, bringing 'God' back into the picture (theology, like nature, abhors a vacuum) as the inner driving force within that 'progress'. But, whether officially atheist or would-be theist, all such theories effectively deified the process itself. That, of course, is why they, like the Third Reich in its turn, were necessarily anti-Jewish. As Hegel had said, Judaism was the wrong *kind* of 'religion'. From the Enlightenment perspective, it was a category mistake. 'Religion', as redefined in the eighteenth century, was not *supposed* to be about race and territory – which of course meant that the Nazi ideology would not be recognized as a false religion until it was too late. But Judaism continued to remind the world of a God who remained sovereign over, and different from, the world of creation, including the world of history. The power of Karl Barth's protest against the 'smoothly progressing' liberal theology of the early 1900s came precisely from his retrieval of this essentially Jewish and biblical insight.

But to use Barth, as some have done, as a way of saying 'No!' to *all* pre-apocalyptic history is to be true neither to ancient Jewish theology, including that of the 'apocalyptists' themselves, nor to Jesus, nor to Paul, nor even (though this is not my present point) to Barth himself. And to invoke the tragic figure of Walter Benjamin to this effect, though appealing to those among today's exegetes who make a virtue out of imposing modern categories on to ancient history,[11] is again to fail to understand the early Jewish world, or Paul as the exponent of its most remarkable mutation, or again Benjamin himself.

Benjamin, after all, was reacting against the perceived bankruptcy of various forms of mid-century Marxism. This is what happens (we might say

[11] An example of this is in Harink 2010. Harink begins by dismissing any attempt to see the gospel within its larger historical context, and perhaps not surprisingly ends by exalting Barth on Romans and dismissing commentaries such as those of Jewett and the present author, saying that 'Wright, as much as Jewett, presents us with a contextualized gospel in Paul' (295). This is part of Harink's recurring accusation, that I articulate a 'progressive salvation-history' which enables people today to locate themselves within a further ongoing history, contrasting with his view of Barth, who (says Harink) writes his commentary 'within that singular time of the gospel' (299) – a very odd claim, in view of Barth's clear and obvious contextualization within the world of early twentieth-century continental history and thought, and indeed in view of the partial parallel between Barth's 'No' and the revolutionary programme of Marxism. Somehow, apparently, an 'apocalyptic' theologian can think Paul's thoughts after him with no *historical* effort: rejecting 'history' as a dangerous irrelevance, corrupting the pure inbreaking 'apocalypse', such a person has privileged access to the inner meaning of ancient documents and is absolved from any need to engage in historical exegesis.

with the temerity of comfortable hindsight!) when you put your faith in a different kind of god, in this case the god of Marxist 'process', and it lets you down. That was why Benjamin called for a plague on both the houses, the Marxist dream of 'progress' and the Nazi dream of an evolved super-race. Their diabolical pact in 1940 destroyed all sense that 'history' might be 'going somewhere' in and of itself (as though Hitler and Stalin were just the unthinking tools of an invisible dialectical or mythological 'process'!), that it might, without outside help, produce not only a new age of freedom and justice but a new world in which the wrongs of the past would somehow themselves be righted. Benjamin, clinging to the vestiges of Jewish hope as expressed in the Psalms and Isaiah, saw no chance of that hope arriving through the ways he, and many of his contemporaries, had imagined. The only hope then would be for a totally new 'messianic moment' – remembering that for Benjamin the Messiah was not to be a human individual, but a corporate identity, a people that would seize the moment and *act* to bring about the great redemption.

All this may seem remote from normal discussions of the apostle Paul. And yet it is very close to him – close in the way that two paths might be close, and even parallel, though separated by a high wall or a narrow but fast-flowing river. Paul must be contextualized, as we have tried to contextualize him, in the turbulent Jewish world of the mid-first century, where, as in the twentieth, the swirling currents of empire, history, hope and messianic redemption were sweeping people this way and that, shaping and reshaping culture as well as theory, action as well as thought. (To claim that we must contextualize someone is not to claim that they are the passive victim of their circumstances, that they are incapable of saying something startling and fresh!) That first-century Jewish world is where, for all their sharp differences, there lived people like Josephus and the author of *4 Ezra*. That is where we find the Scrolls. That is the world of Judas the Galilean in the generation before Paul, and of Simeon ben-Kosiba in the century after him. Unless we locate Paul on that map, we have snatched him out of his own world, like God snatching up Ezekiel by a lock of his hair, in order to relocate him in a very different one where, though he may still prophesy, he will not be at home. Those who have used Benjamin and other twentieth-century thinkers to interpret Paul ought at least to have this going for them, that they are trying to see him in three dimensions, not merely as the teacher of a timeless soteriology; though sometimes even there Benjamin has been made to stand simply for apocalyptic discontinuity. What he (and Arendt) had given up, however, was not the ancient Jewish hope for the world-rectifying messianic moment. What they had given up was the Hegelian and Marxist caricature of that hope.

But Walter Benjamin stood on the other side of that deep river, of that high wall. First, he was trying to reconceive the question of Jewish existence, and of the Jewish (messianic?) vocation, *etsi Deus non daretur*. His proposal leant on pillars that could not sustain it. Even Saul of Tarsus, trusting in the

God of Israel, was hoping that violent acts of 'zeal', purifying the holy people, would hasten the coming of the kingdom – a vision which Benjamin might have understood, even if he did not share its motivation. Equally, and decisively, Benjamin was still looking *ahead* to the messianic moment, the time when even the dead would find their ancient wrongs righted. Paul the apostle was looking *back* to what he believed was the true messianic moment, when the resurrection of the crucified Jesus demonstrated that the creator God had launched exactly that long-awaited project. The two Benjaminites are separated not only by nearly two millennia but by theology and eschatology. For Walter, all one could now hope for was a messianic moment of action, without visible antecedent. For Paul, the Messiah had come, fulfilling (however paradoxically) the long-deferred covenantal promise.

Paul was thus able to reclaim and retrieve Israel's long history, not of course as a nineteenth-century story of an immanent progress, a smooth self-propelled upward journey into the light, but as the story of promises kept at last, of genuine anticipations of the coming kingdom, of a covenant faithfulness which would result, as Deuteronomy had warned and as Daniel had confessed, in devastating destruction and exile but also in the sudden and surprising covenant renewal spoken of by Moses and the prophets. The faithfulness of God had been displayed at last, and the whole argument of Romans depends on the fact that this revelation was *not* simply a blinding flash without a context. Yes: God's covenant justice had been displayed 'quite apart from the law'; but 'the law and the prophets bore witness to it'. When Paul explained what he meant by that last phrase it became clear that he was referring principally to the covenant which God had made with Abraham.[12] To deny this in Paul's day meant taking a large step towards Marcion. To deny it in the twentieth or twenty-first century means perpetuating the myth of a non- or even anti-Jewish 'Christianity', as we see abundantly in the flagship work of the new 'apocalyptic' movement, Martyn's commentary on Galatians.[13]

The entire enterprise of contemporary 'apocalyptic' readings of Paul got off on the wrong foot, in fact, when Käsemann picked up from the climate of the times (a further irony) the notion that perhaps 'apocalyptic' meant a totally new revelation which would take up all the hermeneutical space available, leaving no room for anything that went before. Benjamin's famous invoking of Klee's *Angelus Novus*, the angel that sees all previous 'history' as a heap of rubbish,[14] might of course trigger some memories of the Paul of Philippians 3, gazing on his privileged past (including his Benjaminite tribal descent) and declaring it all to be *skybala*. But the analogy is only skin deep. Paul's whole point (Philippians 3.3) is that *we are the circumcision*, and that the ancient hope of Israel – the Messiah and resurrection itself, God's dealing with the fate even of the dead, the thing for which

[12] Rom. 3.21 in the context of 3.21—4.25 as a whole.

[13] Martyn 1997a: see *Interpreters*.

[14] See Löwy 2005, 60–8, with the picture at 61.

Walter Benjamin longed! – has now been accomplished. Paul is therefore living in the messianic moment, and urging his hearers to see themselves that way, too. 'The right time is now! The day of salvation is here!'[15] Käsemann, determined for reasons of his Lutheran theology to rule out any notion of the covenant, lest it turn Paul's faith back into a Jewish work, or into a feature of bourgeois religiosity (which for Käsemann amounted to much the same thing), appealed to a notion of 'apocalyptic' which the ancient apocalyptists themselves would never have recognized but which has continued to be popular in the late-modern western world. In doing so he tacitly admitted, what we might have guessed from Benjamin himself, that his 'apocalyptic' was actually not so very different from the 'gnosticism' it had displaced in his reconfiguration of Bultmann's theory of Christian origins. For Bultmann, gnosticism had been at least the step-mother of early Christianity; for Käsemann 'apocalyptic' was the mother. This might, on the surface, have implied a welcome step towards a more explicitly Jewish history-of-religions context. But Käsemann and his more recent followers have been careful to screen out precisely the themes where we see Paul's fulfilled-Jewish vision at its most obvious: Messiahship, the Abrahamic covenant, the faithfulness of the one God.

The answer to all this is not to abandon history but to do it better. Nor does this mean, of course, that whereas all others come with 'presuppositions', we British empiricists are simply reading 'history' with an uncluttered mind! This is why I spent some time at the start of this project articulating the method of 'critical realism' in relation to history itself. And this is why, in the first Part of this book, I spent considerably more time sketching out, not indeed a projection of my own time and culture on to Paul's world, but that world itself, as far as a critically realist historiography can glimpse it, in its own terms.

When we see Walter Benjamin in relation to the ancient Jewish world, he reminds me, not of Paul, but of those who found themselves in despair after the failure of the bar-Kochba revolt. They had calculated the times: nearly seventy years from the destruction of AD 70, and perhaps (who could tell?) nearly 490 years from whichever starting-point Daniel 9 might have had in mind. They had longed for the messianic moment, the great redemption, the time when the ancient martyrs would be raised from the dead to enjoy their long-awaited vindication. And it had come to nothing. This offers the best and most likely explanation for the rise of second-century Jewish gnosticism: everything that has gone before is worthless; history is a pile of rubble; scripture itself must be read upside down with the heroes and villains changing places; and the god of creation is a wicked and deceitful god, not to be trusted.[16] Gnosticism believes in the failure, not the faithfulness, of Israel's God. The collapse of the bar-Kochba revolt was, of course, quite different from the Molotov-Ribbentrop pact which precipitated Benjamin's despair in 1940. But, *mutatis mutandis*, the apostle Paul would have looked

[15] 2 Cor. 6.2.

[16] On gnostic origins see Smith 2005.

at both of them, the disappointed Jews of the 130s and of the 1930s, and would have grieved that they could not recognize the true messianic moment as having already arrived in Jesus of Nazareth.

Ironically, it was the resurrection that made the difference. It is hard, sometimes, to probe beneath the surface of Benjamin's elusive writing and discern what exactly he had in mind in speaking of even the dead being at risk from the new tyrants, in hoping still for a redemption in which their ancient wrongs would be put right. The resurrection of Jesus, as the historical and transphysical new life of the crucified Jesus,[17] had been screened out of much German theology long before Käsemann, and had long since come to function merely as a metaphor for the rise of faith in the crucified one. But this, as with Benjamin from his secular standpoint, pushed all the weight of expectation on to the future. And when that future failed to arrive on time (the secular echo of the 'delayed *parousia*'!), despair set in.[18] The apostle Paul, from the tribe of Benjamin, spoke precisely of the messianic event which had *already* declared God's judgment against all the forces of evil and God's vindication of his suffering people. His kinsman, nearly two millennia later, was operating with the same overall set of questions, but with significant and quantifiable elements radically altered or even missing.

Walter Benjamin thus provides not only a highly illuminating partial analogy to the apostle, but also a highly illuminating partial explanation for the rise, and continuing recent popularity, of the so-called 'apocalyptic' school of interpretation. But the analogy to Paul remains only partial, and the parts that are omitted are the central features of Paul's own thought: the long-awaited return and continuing presence of Israel's God; resurrection; the inauguration of messianic time; the reappropriation of the now-fulfilled covenant promises. What both the Benjaminites do for us is to remind us that we cannot interpret these rich, dense and often dark themes without paying attention to their entire historical setting, however paradoxical it may be to say that of Walter Benjamin himself. We cannot, in other words, shrink them to debates about 'Paul and the law' or alternative readings of a disembodied, westernized 'soteriology'. They demand, at least, to be seen in their full political, religious, philosophical and cultural settings. That is what this book has been trying to do.

What I propose in this final chapter, then, is an outline of Paul's aims and indeed his achievements, but on a broader canvas than is normally allowed. I cherish the hope that the final volume in this series will deal more directly, in summary of the whole, with the question of early Christian missiology. One of the reasons I do not see the series as a 'New Testament Theology' is that theology itself, in the New Testament, is not an end in itself, but (as I argued in Part III) is the vital, non-negotiable and central ingredient in the healthy life of the community of Jesus' followers. Just as the principal and

[17] On 'transphysical' see *RSG* 477, 606f., 612, 678f.

[18] Is it any wonder that the 'myth of the delayed *parousia*', and the equally mythical crisis it supposedly caused in the second-generation church (see *NTPG* 459–64), dominated German New Testament scholarship, and its offshoots, in the second half of the twentieth century?

ultimate goal of all historical work on J. S. Bach ought to be a more sensitive and intelligent performance of his music, so the principal and ultimate goal of all historical work on the New Testament ought to be a more sensitive and intelligent practice of Christian mission and discipleship. It is clearly impossible to open up that huge topic at this stage of the present book. What we can and must do instead is to draw together the threads of the whole argument in such a way as to round off our picture of Paul and point on to the larger issues of early Christian mission, and indeed of theological and historical integration.

2. Paul in Several Dimensions: the Ministry of Reconciliation

The Benjaminite reflections offered above point us back to the larger context of Paul's life and work which we sketched in Part I and revisited in chapters 12, 13, 14 and 15. It is important now to insist that when we think about Paul's aims and intentions – the practical outflowing of his worldview, as in the theoretical model sketched in *NTPG* Part II and in chapter 6 above – we see them in this larger framework, resisting all attempts to squash them into something smaller.

I have in mind in particular the normal modern western meanings of words like 'mission' and 'evangelism'. There has of course been a good deal of discussion as to what these words mean, and no agreement is in sight. Both words are labels which different groups stick on different activities which for whatever reason they believe they ought to undertake (or, in the case of some relativists, believe they ought not to undertake). The meanings shift with the activities. But the whole picture of 'what Paul was doing' has in my view been radically pulled out of shape by the two main drivers of modern western Christianity, and our study of Paul in his first-century context should go some way at least towards suggesting a larger and more integrated picture.[19]

First, there was the long period of the middle ages, in which Christian sights were firmly fixed on 'going to heaven' (with as little time as possible spent en route in purgatory). To be sure, there were many who believed in the importance of doing things in the present world too, whether like St Francis they wanted to transform the world from below or like some popes they wanted to impose a different sort of transformation from above. But even the Crusades, insofar as we can retrieve the motivation of those who organized or took part in them, had an eye towards an otherworldly reward. And – providing Marx with such legitimacy as his famous jibe possesses! – the promise of heavenly bliss was indeed, for the great majority, a drug to

[19] The massive and important survey of Paul's mission in Schnabel 2004, Part V remains a vital resource, even though he does not attempt to integrate the different dimensions of Paul's multi-faceted work in the way I am proposing. Other recent bibliography on Paul's missionary theology and message is given by Porter 2011, 171 n. 9.

dull the pain of ordinary life.[20] This focus on an essentially Platonic 'spiritual heaven', discontinuous with this world and only related to it by the tangential mechanism of soul-saving and soul-making, has for a millennium radically distorted the western Christian hold on resurrection itself, the central claim and belief of the early Christians.[21] Its effect on perceptions of Paul as 'missionary' or 'evangelist' has been to focus attention on Paul as a 'soul-winner'. However disruptive the sixteenth-century Reformation may have been, and however many social, cultural and political factors must be taken into account in any proper account of it, its effect on the reading of Paul was not to change this basic perception of his ultimate aim ('heaven' as the goal, something which Paul never says, and 'the soul' as the thing that might or might not go there, another thing which Paul never says). The effect of the Reformation was, instead, simply to alter the terms and conditions on which this kind of 'salvation' might be found. Hence the stress on a particular reading of 'justification'. Within such a context, to ask questions about Paul's 'mission' or 'evangelism' would be to enquire how he went about collecting inhabitants for this future 'heaven'. And his missionary strategy would be seen as the way in which, whether deliberately or accidentally, he set about doing this.

To this western picture – which as anyone who has read this book to this point will be well aware does scant justice both to Paul and to 'justification'! – the Enlightenment added its own extra spin. God and the world were to be sharply separated. Not only was the Christian destined for a completely different world; he or she had no business, *quā* Christian, trying to alter the course of the present one. A Platonist eschatology combined with an Epicurean polity: with God removed from the world, humans had to run it themselves, and any suggestion that the kingdom of God might have to do with theocracy, with things happening at God's behest 'on earth as in heaven', was dangerous heresy. Many atheists insisted on this division in order to keep the rumour of God from spoiling the secular paradise; many Christians, to keep the filth of the present world from spoiling the spiritual one. Within this context, Paul's 'mission' and 'evangelism' could not, by definition, have had anything to do with the rise and fall of empires, with speaking the truth to power or calling rulers to account. Any proposal along such lines would be countered with Jesus' gnomic sayings, 'Give Caesar back what belongs to Caesar' and 'My kingdom is not of this world', and indeed with Paul's brief point about civil obedience in Romans 13. The uncomfortable suggestion that 'on earth as in heaven' might mean what it said, or that when Matthew's risen Jesus claimed to possess all authority on earth as well as in heaven he meant what he said, has been easily swatted away within the post-Enlightenment world, both Christian and non-Christian.[22] Here we see

[20] Marx 2012 [1843–4], 5: 'Religion is the sigh of the oppressed creature, the heart of a heartless world, and the soul of soulless conditions. It is the opium of the people.'

[21] See *RSG, passim*; and Wright 2008 [*Surprised by Hope*]. For a similar protest in the Jewish world cf. Levenson 1993.

[22] cf. Mt. 22.21 and par.; Jn. 18.36; Rom. 13.1–7; Mt. 6.10; and esp. 28.18.

the seed-bed of the various alternative modern ideas about 'apocalyptic'. God is basically absent, certainly not providing a hidden hand for 'history'. Anything he does will have to be a sudden 'invasion' from outside. This has little to do with first-century Jewish ideas, but plenty to do with modern philosophical and cultural strands.

Reformation and Enlightenment combine, too, to change the terms of Paul's aims in relation to 'religion'. As we saw in chapters 4 and 13, that slippery word has had various meanings, and it is today almost unusable without constant explanation and qualification. Protestants have regularly regarded 'religion' as consisting of 'things humans do to please God' (often without noticing that 'pleasing God' is itself a Pauline category!), and so have played off 'religion' against the supposed higher reality of 'faith'. This has then been projected back on to 'Judaism', as though the ultimate target for Paul's polemic was *homo religiosus*; this ties up with the regular usage among atheists, who use 'religion' to mean 'superstition'. For tolerant post-Enlightenment thinkers, all 'religions' are good; for intolerant ones (and certain types of Protestant), bad. Within that framework, the question of Paul's aims looks different: was Paul trying to propagate 'religion', or to offer something else in its place? Confusion continues – worse confounded by contemporary muddles about 'religion and politics', and indeed *both* among those who see 'Judaism' as the 'wrong' type of religion and Christianity as the 'right' type *and* among those who see 'Judaism' as a 'religion' and therefore the wrong type of thing altogether.

All these divisions and confusions make it difficult to get back to Paul's aims and intentions, but this is where history itself comes into its own. In Part I we mapped the philosophical, religious and political world of Paul's day, and in the present Part we have been locating the Paul of Parts II and III within that larger, more confusing world. (Again we must insist: this has nothing to do with reducing Paul and his gospel to terms of their context, and everything to do with the fresh impact Paul had in proclaiming a gospel which was folly to Greeks and scandalous to Jews. To understand the folly, and the scandal, you have to understand the Greek and Jewish worlds of the day, rather than imagining that they correspond straightforwardly to elements in today's church or world.)

A further step, beyond the scope of the present volume, would have been to map, as well, the numerous ways in which the worlds of greco-roman philosophy, religion and politics impinged on one another. We have, of course, done a bit of that. We have noticed at various points the interplay of first-century 'religion' and 'politics', both Jewish and pagan. We have said less about the philosophical justifications for particular styles of government, or conversely the effect which living under various types of polity may have had on philosophical thought. Nor have we explored very deeply the interplay between 'religion' and 'philosophy' themselves, though we may have said enough to indicate various ways forward. It would also have been good to delve more deeply into the multiple and complex ways in which other Jews in Paul's day navigated the same larger worlds that he did, and the different proposals they came up with – proposals which of course included violent revolution, philosophical reflection, messianic movements and the formation of new communities, in addition to a proto-rabbinic withdrawal from the world into Torah-piety. First-century Jews, like twenty-first-century ones, were concerned with much more than just a set of ideas or theories. Once more: not just to interpret the world, but to change it.[23] All this must be taken, if not as read, at least as a set of signposts to tasks that demand more attention. But what we can do now, however briefly, is to sketch the equivalent complex integration in the case of Paul himself.

My proposal is that Paul's aims and intentions were, from our point of view, multi-dimensional. When he engaged in 'mission' and 'evangelism'; when he laboured as a pastor and teacher; when he worked with his hands to earn his own living; when he travelled restlessly, prayed without stopping, languished in prison; when, in particular, he wrote letters – what did he think he was doing? What, indeed, was he doing *without thinking about it*, since by now these 'aims' were part of his worldview, part of the spectacles through which he viewed the world? What were the aims and intentions about which, had he been challenged, Paul would have been momentarily puzzled in the way that a baseball player would be puzzled if asked why he had hit the ball and started running? What questions would have elicited the equivalent of the answer, 'That's just how the game is played'?

My proposal here is not entirely new, nor would it be credible if it were. But approaching it this way may reveal new aspects of a well-known perspective, and indeed bring us back to the task we set ourselves at the outset, that of drawing history and theology themselves closer together. My proposal is that Paul's aims and intentions can be summarized under the word *katallagē*, 'reconciliation'. I mean this at several interlocking levels.[24]

The risk with this proposal is that it will collapse back into one of the shrunken versions of Paul's task I mentioned earlier. 'Be reconciled to God; be reconciled to one another.' Paul did indeed say and do things that could be summarized like that, and at least once he used that kind of summary himself. But putting it like that might imply that his aims and intentions could be comfortably placed in the sedate living-room of late-modern western Christianity without moving any of the other furniture. And that, granted our argument so far, would be remarkable to the point of ridicule.

The danger is that one might quite easily speak about the 'reconciliation' of humans both with God and with one another in terms of the normal western 'gospel' and its immediate implications – that is, without regard either for Paul's insistence on the fulfilment of the promises to Abraham or for the larger impact his founding of messianic communities would have within the complex greco-roman world. That would leave chapters 2—5 and

[23] Marx 1932 [1845], no. 11.

[24] At the formal level, a focus on 'reconciliation' echoes the earlier proposal of e.g. Martin 1981; cf. too e.g. Stuhlmacher 1977, 1999, 320f.; Marshall 2007, 98–137 (I am grateful to Michael Bird for the latter references); Porter 2011. But the material content I propose below goes, I think, into wider territory.

12—15 of the present book simply as interesting decoration around the border, whereas my whole point, and I think Paul's whole point, is that his gospel left nothing on the outside. What we call 'philosophy', 'religion' and 'politics', and Paul's engagements with them, were not interesting side-effects, by-products spinning off the edge of his 'main' task like wood-shavings from a joiner's workshop which could then be used for kindling or animal bedding. For Paul, everything grew in the field of God's new world. His gospel was rooted in Jewish creational monotheism; his gospel proclaimed that in Jesus the Messiah a whole new creation, a new cosmos, had come to birth; his gospel (so he believed) articulated the truth about the world, about its creator, about all human life; those who believed this gospel formed the community in which that truth came to life. His gospel of reconciliation, in other words, was not 'about' something other than what we have separated out and labelled as 'politics', 'religion' and 'philosophy'. For him, 'reconciliation' *included* them all, indeed reconciled them all. His essentially Jewish, or if you like fulfilled-Jewish, way of looking at the whole world brought into a fresh unity that which, in non-Jewish eyes (then and now!) might be seen as different or indeed competing aspects of life. Thus, reversing the movement of historical (and poetical) astronomy, what first we guessed as stars – separate spheres such as 'philosophy', 'politics' or 'religion' – Paul now knew as points, pinpricks in a dome behind which there shone a single, greater light, the light of the gospel itself. 'New creation' for him was not just an arm-waving phrase, a hyperbolic description of the radical change of life that happened when someone was 'in the Messiah'. No:

> If we are beside ourselves, you see, it's for God; and if we are in our right mind, it's for you. For the Messiah's love makes us press on. We have come to the conviction that one died for all, and therefore all died. And he died for all in order that those who live should live no longer for themselves, but for him who died and was raised on their behalf.
>
> From this moment on, therefore, we don't regard anybody from a merely human point of view. Even if we once regarded the Messiah that way, we don't do so any longer. Thus, if anyone is in the Messiah, there is a new creation! Old things have gone, and look – everything has become new!
>
> It all comes from God. He reconciled us to himself through the Messiah, and he gave us the ministry of reconciliation. This is how it came about: God was reconciling the world to himself in the Messiah, not counting their trespasses against them, and entrusting us with the message of reconciliation. So we are ambassadors, speaking on behalf of the Messiah, as though God were making his appeal through us. We implore people on the Messiah's behalf to be reconciled to God. The Messiah did not know sin, but God made him to be sin on our behalf, so that in him we might embody God's faithfulness to the covenant.
>
> So, as we work together with God, we appeal to you in particular: when you accept God's grace, don't let it go to waste! This is what he says:
>
> I listened to you when the time was right,
> I came to your aid on the day of salvation.
>
> Look! The right time is now! Look! The day of salvation is here![25]

[25] 2 Cor. 5.13—6.2.

There are many passages in Paul that stake a claim to sum up what he thought he was doing, but this one trumps most of them – not least because in 2 Corinthians he has been forced to articulate afresh precisely 'what he thought he was doing', and this passage is one of its climaxes. Being 'beside ourselves' or 'in our right mind', being overmastered by a love which makes us act in a different way, seeing everything in a new light, claiming that a new world has been born, claiming even to be embodying the divine covenant faithfulness – this sounds like someone who, challenged to the core by distressing and disconcerting opposition, whips off his worldview-spectacles and describes the lenses. *This is how I look at the world; this is how the things I do make sense within that worldview.* What I do is me; for that I came. This is one of Paul's central statements, if not *the* central statement, of his aims and intentions.[26]

The whole thing is framed in terms not of an escapist soteriology or piety but precisely of *new creation*. 'If anyone is in the Messiah, there is a new creation' – or, more literally (since as often Paul skips unnecessary words): 'If anyone in Messiah, new creation.' The newness is the messianic newness, that for which Walter Benjamin longed without realizing that his distant cousin had already proclaimed it. Paul believed himself to be standing on the threshold of new creation, the fresh reality for which the creation itself had been on tiptoe with expectation. But he was not just a spectator. He was called to do and say things through which new creation *was happening already*: each personal 'new creation', through Messiah-faith and baptism, was another signpost to the larger 'new creation' of which the Psalms and the prophets had spoken. Other passages in 2 Corinthians show that he was thinking in these terms, of a whole new world coming to birth with the arrival of renewed and transformed humans. He is jealous over the church and anxious that, like Eve, the bride may be tricked into a second fall:

> I arranged to marry you off, like a pure virgin, to the one man I presented you to, namely the Messiah. But the serpent tricked Eve with its cunning, and in the same way I'm afraid that your minds may be corrupted from the single-mindedness and purity which the Messiah's people should have.[27]

Paul could only write like that if he really did believe that his apostolic work was an advance project for the ultimate new creation itself. He was in the business, not of rescuing souls from corrupting bodies and a doomed world, but of transforming humans as wholes, to be both signs of that larger new creation and workers in its cause. That is one of the reasons why the church mattered to Paul: ecclesiology was a signpost to cosmology. New covenant; new creation. That is the sequence of thought which underlies 2 Corinthians 3, 4 and 5.

In saying even this we meet at once an opposite danger to those we already noted. If Paul is seen as a practical new-creation man, one might

[26] cf. too e.g. 1 Cor. 9.16f.: 'Woe betide me if I *don't* announce the gospel!'

[27] 2 Cor. 11.2f.; cp. the image of the 'new husband' in Rom. 7.1–6.

then cast him simply in the role of a glorified social worker on the one hand or a global politician on the other. If we say that he was aiming to generate and sustain communities which would not only point to, but actually be an advance part of, the coming renewed world, nervous western theologians might imagine that we were moving away from 'the gospel', the message about the love of God, about vindication at the coming judgment and so on. Anything but. The key passage we quoted from 2 Corinthians 5 is rooted in the statement a few verses earlier that all will stand before the Messiah's judgment seat (5.10), and begins as we saw with a glorious statement of 'the Messiah's love' in dying for all (5.14–15). This results in the fundamental appeal that people should be 'reconciled to God' (5.20), which Paul spells out more fully in the summary statement of the whole gospel in Romans 5.6–11. All is based once more on the death of Jesus, dying for all (2 Corinthians 5.14–15), made 'to be sin on our behalf' (5.20). None of this is lost if we draw attention as well to the larger framework of the passage, and to Paul's larger, and integrated, aims and intentions there expressed.

That larger framework includes, of course, Paul's dramatic statement that in the Messiah 'God was reconciling *the world* to himself' (5.19). This is closely cognate not only with the negative statement in Galatians 6.14, that through the cross 'the world has been crucified to me and I to the world', but also with the positive statement of Colossians 1, that the entire cosmos which was made through God's son in the first place has now been reconciled by his crucifixion.[28] Not for the first time, 2 Corinthians is very close to Colossians, and here both affirm the cosmic scope of what God did in the Messiah, within which of course the personal or 'individual' message of the gospel finds its full and proper place. As in Colossians 1.23, Paul believed that the gospel had, in some strange sense, already been preached to every *creature*, *ktisis*, under heaven. Every creature: nothing is left out. No wonder all creation groans, having heard this word and longing for its fulfilment. This leads to another tell-tale, almost throwaway, line: Paul explains his vocation in terms of being the servant of this (cosmic) gospel.

It already appears, then, that Paul did not see himself as simply snatching souls out of the world's wreck in order to populate a Platonic heaven.[29] In the light of Paul's statements in various places about his hope for the whole creation, we should take seriously what he says about God reconciling 'the world' to himself. Paul does not mean by this the kind of easy-going universalism that has been popular in some theological circles. His letters make that quite clear. Nor does he suppose that through his gospel the world's rulers will suddenly come to their senses and – among many other things! – stop persecuting him. His 'cosmic' claims are made in the teeth of the

[28] Col. 1.15–20, on which see above, 670–7.

[29] I was surprised that Bockmuehl 2011 (in Perrin and Hays 2011) would suppose that when I have said this sort of thing before I meant to rule out any kind of 'going to heaven' at all. I have long held and taught that for Paul, as for other early Christians and for those Jews who believed in resurrection, some kind of intermediate state should be postulated between bodily death and bodily resurrection, which we can perfectly well call 'heaven' while noting that normally the early Christians did not use that term in that way. See my remarks in Perrin and Hays 2011, 231–4, and Wright 2008 [*Surprised by Hope*], *passim*.

apparent evidence, evidence he parades before the Corinthians on either side of the passage under present discussion.[30] The Messiah's victory is always deeply paradoxical during the present age. There is no suggestion that the world has started on a smooth and steady upward path to utopia, or that the church itself is now launched into a triumphant development. But nor will the churches which come into being through Paul's announcement of the Jesus-focused good news of the creator God be mere accidental and temporary collections of individuals each of whom happens to have responded to that gospel. They will be signs and foretastes of the new world that is to be, not least because of their unity across traditional boundaries, their holiness of life, their embracing of the *human* vocation to bear the divine image, and particularly their suffering. As in Romans 8, the renewal of humans is the prelude to, and the means of, the renewal of all creation.

Paul's work both as an evangelist and as a pastor and teacher was therefore in the service of the unity and holiness of the church, as we saw in Part II. But the unity and holiness of the church was itself in the service of this larger aim. 'If anyone is in the Messiah, there is a new creation!' And with that new creation, as we saw in chapter 14, there went a new mode of knowing:

> From this moment on, therefore, we don't regard anybody from a merely human point of view. Even if we once regarded the Messiah that way, we don't do so any longer.[31]

As I argued in chapter 14, this did not mean that Paul lived in a private world, a fantasy-land where he and others might claim to see things with no public reality. For Paul, the point was that the new creation launched with Jesus' resurrection was the *renewal* of *creation*, not its abolition and replacement; so that the new-creation mode of knowing was a deeper, truer, richer mode of knowing *about the old creation as well*. And with that deeper knowing came all sorts of consequences, which we have tried to plot in the preceding chapters.

In particular, the communities which came into being through the gospel were to embody that new world in the ways which our disjointed categories have separated out. They were indeed to be a kind of philosophical school, teaching and modelling a new worldview, inculcating a new understanding, a new way of thinking. They were to train people not only to practise the virtues everyone already acknowledged but also to develop some new ones, and with all that to find a new way to virtue itself, the transformed mind and heart through which the creator's intention would at last be realized. They were indeed, despite their lack of priests, sacrifices and temples, to be a new kind of 'religion': to read and study their sacred texts and to weave them into the beginnings of a liturgical praxis. In that worship, they believed, heaven and earth came together, God's time and human time were fused and matter itself was transfigured to become heavy with meaning and

[30] cf. 2 Cor. 4.7–12; 6.4–13; cf. 11.22–33.

[31] 2 Cor. 5.16; see above, 1361f.

possibility. These communities were indeed, despite their powerlessness or actually because of it, on the way to becoming a new kind of *polis*, a social and cultural community cutting across normal boundaries and barriers, obedient to a different *kyrios*, modelling a new way of being human and a new kind of power. There, too, the second letter to Corinth leads the way, though arguably all that Paul was doing in his famous power/weakness contrasts in that letter was picking up and developing what Jesus had already said. And done.[32] If we do not recognize Paul's churches as in some sense philosophical communities, religious groups and political bodies it is perhaps because we have been thinking of the modern meanings of such terms rather than those which were known in Paul's world.

My point, anyway, is that the worldview we studied in Part II and the theology we examined in Part III were designed by Paul with this larger new creation in mind. He saw the church as a *microcosmos*, a little world, not simply as an alternative to the present one, an escapist's country cottage for those tired of city life, but as the prototype of what was to come. That is why, of course, unity and holiness mattered. And, because this *microcosmos* was there in the world it was designed to function like a beacon: a light in a dark place, as again Jesus had said. The new way of being human, the new way in which 'philosophy', 'religion' and 'politics' were all scooped up together and transcended in a renewed-Jewish messianic way of life, was bound to be threatening to those who lived by other philosophies, religions and political arrangements. Hence the inevitability of suffering. But it was also supposed in equal measure to be compellingly attractive. Paul was an evangelist, and he knew of others who were called to that task, but there is surprisingly little evidence that he wanted his communities to be energetically outgoing in their own propagation of the faith. Enough for the moment, it seemed, that they should be ... united, and holy.

Everything we have said so far points to one conclusion which is obvious as soon as you see it but perhaps surprising in the present context. A place of reconciliation between God and the world; a place where humans might be reconciled to one another; a *microcosmos* in which the world is contained in a nutshell as a sign of what God intends to do for the whole creation; a new sort of *polis* in which heaven and earth come together, where a quite new sort of 'religion' takes place, where the hidden springs of wisdom are at last laid bare; a community which celebrates its identity as the people of the new exodus: all this means – as we might have guessed from his various comments – that Paul's aims and intentions could be summed up as the vocation to build and maintain *the new temple*.[33] Some of Paul's Jewish contemporaries had seen the dispersal of Jews and their culture around the world as a sign of a new world order. Similarly, Paul saw the dispersed 'temple' – small groups meeting in villages and cities with the living presence of the creator God in their midst by the spirit – as the sign of creation at last

[32] cf. e.g. 2 Cor. 12.9f.; 13.1–4; cf. e.g. Mk. 10.35–45.

[33] cf. 1 Cor. 3.10–17 (see above, 355–7, 391f.). I am grateful to Jamie Davies for the brainstorming session in which this point emerged.

transformed. That, as I argued earlier, is one of the hidden but important themes within the rich, dense chapter we know as Romans 8.

It is also here in 2 Corinthians 5. *God was reconciling the world to himself in the Messiah* (5.19). This evocative clause might be taken as referring simply to what God was doing *through* the Messiah. But the near-parallel in Colossians 1.19 ('in him all the Fullness was glad to dwell, and through him to reconcile all to himself') suggests that this was part of Paul's larger temple-imagery, part of that theme of YHWH's return to Zion which we saw in chapter 9 to be at the heart of his view both of Jesus and of the spirit. (We recall, too, that in Colossians 1.27 he envisaged individual churches as places where the Messiah was in the midst as a signpost to the eventual glory of the new creation.[34]) And of course 2 Corinthians 5 stands on the shoulders of 2 Corinthians 3 and 4, where Paul vigorously expounds the 'new covenant' of Jeremiah 31 in terms of an ultimate fulfilment of what happened after Moses' intercession over Israel towards the end of the book of Exodus. Exodus ends, despite the sin of the golden calf, with the Shekinah coming to dwell in the newly made wilderness tabernacle, thus completing a circle with the implicit 'temple' of all creation in Genesis 1, and anticipating the construction of the Temple in Jerusalem and its filling with the divine presence (1 Kings 8.10–13). Paul picks up that whole theme and sees the goal of the new exodus as being the arrival of the divine glory through the Messiah and the spirit:

> All of us, without any veil on our faces, gaze at the glory of the lord as in a mirror, and so are being changed into the same image, from glory to glory, just as you'd expect from the lord, the spirit.
>
> We don't proclaim ourselves, you see, but Jesus the Messiah as lord, and ourselves as your servants because of Jesus; because the God who said 'let light shine out of darkness' has shone in our hearts, to produce the light of the knowledge of the glory of God in the face of Jesus the Messiah.[35]

For Paul, then, 'evangelism' was not just about soul-rescuing, and 'mission' was not just about the wider advancement of Christian understanding. Paul's apostolic task was, so to speak, tabernacle-construction, temple-building. That is clear already in 1 Corinthians 3. In other words, he saw his vocation in terms of bringing into being 'places' – humans, one by one and collectively – in which heaven and earth would come together and be, yes, *reconciled*. 'God was reconciling the world to himself in the Messiah': the Messiah is the new temple where heaven and earth meet, reconciled through his sacrifice. Paul's vocation was to announce that this had happened, to 'name the Messiah' after the manner of a herald proclaiming a new sovereign (see below) and so to extend this temple-shaped mission into the rest of the world. This was his equivalent of those sudden biblical

[34] See *Perspectives* ch. 23.

[35] 2 Cor. 3.18; 4.5f.

glimpses of pagans flocking to Jerusalem to worship the true God.[36] This time, however, the Shekinah was going out into the world (this turning of the Jewish hope inside out explains Paul's missionary strategy, as we shall see in a moment), so that in every place there would be a sign that heaven and earth had come together indeed, that the creator and the cosmos were reconciled at last.[37]

Every single Christian would be a living example of this ('if anyone is in the Messiah, there is a new creation'). But whereas much western understanding has seen the individual as the goal, Paul sees individual Christians as signs pointing to a larger reality. He describes his own mission vividly in verse 20: 'We implore people on the Messiah's behalf', he writes, 'to be reconciled to God.' He longs to see the heaven-and-earth event, the temple-event, happening once more. The Messiah's sacrificial death has already occurred (verse 21a), a gift of love for the whole world (verses 14–15), and the 'temple' can now be the place of reconciliation. Paul's 'aim', the worldview-level understanding of his own role in the midst of it all, drawing on the servant-imagery from Isaiah, was that he was called, as an apostle, to embody God's faithfulness to the covenant. 'The faithfulness of God' was not simply to be a main theme of Paul's teaching. It was to be the hidden inner meaning of his life – and, as befits a follower of the crucified Messiah, particularly of his suffering.[38]

The larger reality to which this points, the new creation itself, is to be symbolized by *the whole church, united and holy*. The new temple is to be the place to which all nations will come to worship the God of Abraham, Isaac and Jacob. That is Paul's vision in the theological climax to Romans (15.7–13, on which see below), and it was the practical state of affairs for which he worked tirelessly and about which he wrote in letter after letter. The reconciliation of Jew and Greek, particularly, was obviously near the heart of Paul's aim. Despite efforts that are still made to suggest that they remained quite separate in his mind (see chapter 15 above), the force of his repeated denials cannot be gainsaid: 'there is no distinction'; 'there is no distinction between Jew and Greek'; 'neither circumcision nor uncircumcision matters'; 'there is no longer Jew or Greek'; 'circumcision is nothing; neither is uncircumcision'.[39] Yes, of course, Paul was aware that existing differences still had to be navigated with wisdom and humility. That is what he does from one angle in Romans 11, from another in Romans 14. But all this is in the service of the larger vision, from which he would not step back even for a moment. It was the vision of a new temple, a new house of praise, where songs originally sung in the shrine in Jerusalem would arise from hearts and mouths in every nation:

[36] Isa. 2.2–4; 66.18; Mic. 4.1–3; Zech. 2.11; 8.20–3; 14.16.

[37] This, too, was seen in the early church as scripturally promised: cf. e.g. Mal. 1.5, 11, 14.

[38] 2 Cor. 5.21 (see above, 874–85), with 4.7–12 and 6.3–10.

[39] Rom. 3.22; 10.12; 1 Cor. 7.19; Gal. 3.28; 6.15.

Welcome one another, therefore, as the Messiah has welcomed you, to God's glory. Let me tell you why: the Messiah became a servant of the circumcised people in order to demonstrate the truthfulness of God – that is, to confirm the promises to the patriarchs, and to bring the nations to praise God for his mercy. As the Bible says:

> That is why I will praise you among the nations,
> and will sing to your name.

And again it says,

> Rejoice, you nations, with his people.

And again,

> Praise the Lord, all nations,
> and let all the peoples sing his praise.

And Isaiah says once more:

> There shall be the root of Jesse
> the one who rises up to rule the nations;
> the nations shall hope in him.[40]

All this creates a vantage point from which we can see, in a far more integrated fashion than normal, the various elements of Paul's work which belonged to the 'aims and intentions' at the heart of his worldview. 'The ministry of reconciliation', which includes 'the message of reconciliation' (2 Corinthians 5.18, 19), is his own shorthand for activities which we observe, both in his letters and in the pages of Acts, as characteristic symptoms of deeper motivations. When we understand them all in the light of the temple-vision we have just briefly expounded they attain a rich and multi-faceted coherence.

In particular, we may note various features which are often left isolated but which come together under this rubric. His teaching in 1 Corinthians 8—10 and Romans 14—15 about *adiaphora* and how to handle the questions related to that topic; his high-voltage polemic in Galatians about gentiles not needing to become physically Jewish; his cooler but no less effective argument in Romans about gentile Christians not despising the other 'branches'; his knocking of heads together in the faction-ridden church in Corinth; his constant plea in Philippians for a deep and rich unity – all these bespeak a settled aim, to bring about through teaching and example the single united family which God had promised to Abraham and had accomplished through the Messiah. The 'Collection' of money from gentile churches to take to impoverished Jewish Christians in Jerusalem and Judaea no doubt started as a bright idea, but once it had taken root it deserves to be seen, in worldview terms, at least as an 'intention', flowing from the 'aim' of Jew/gentile unity in the Messiah.

[40] Rom. 15.7–12, quoting Ps. 18.49 (= 2 Sam. 22.50); Dt. 32.43; Ps. 117.1; Isa. 11.1, 10. Torah, prophets and writings round off the biblically rooted vision of the whole letter.

True, when he cautiously explains in 2 Corinthians the fact that on his forthcoming visit he will expect to find the money already collected, he does not go into any detail about what we might call the 'ecumenical' purpose of it all, except in the most general terms:

> Through meeting the test of this service you will glorify God in two ways: first, because your confession of faith in the Messiah's gospel has brought you into proper order, and second, because you have entered into genuine and sincere partnership (*koinōnia*) with them and with everyone. What's more, they will then pray for you and long for you because of the surpassing grace God has given to you.[41]

Why he does not spell out more fully the underlying symbolic as well as practical reasons for the Collection, we can only guess. Perhaps it was because of the strained relationships with some Jerusalem-based Christians implied in 11.22 and the surrounding passages. Perhaps it was because of an earlier sense of implicit competition between the supporters of Paul and Peter, as reflected in 1 Corinthians 1—4. However, since Paul does not mention here, either, the fact of the Jerusalem Christians' impoverished state, but takes it for granted, perhaps he is also taking for granted the theological and symbolic significance which emerges in the fuller account in Romans 15:

> Now, though, I am going to Jerusalem to render service to God's people there. Macedonia and Achaea, you see, have happily decided to enter into partnership (*koinōnia*) with the poor believers in Jerusalem. They were eager to do this, and indeed they owe them a debt. If the nations have shared in the Jews' spiritual blessings, it is right and proper that they should minister to their earthly needs. So when I have completed this, and tied up all the loose ends, I will come via you to Spain . . .[42]

Here again we have the theme of *koinōnia*, which we have seen ever since the start of this book to be a key term for Paul, flagging up his sense not only of a purpose pragmatically shared but also of an aim and goal on which the Messiah's people agree and for which they covenant to work together. And since what Paul here says about the theological and symbolical purpose of the Collection coheres so closely with the aim of reconciliation which we have already seen to run through so much of his writing, we can be sure that this was not an afterthought, an extra idea which had not previously occurred to Paul, but was rather deep within his own motivational pattern. If the goal of 'reconciliation' thus belongs in Paul's worldview as one of his key *aims*, we may suggest that the Collection, which by the time of 2 Corinthians is a project that Paul and his audience both take for granted, should itself be classified in worldview terms as an *intention*, something which,

[41] 2 Cor. 9.13f.

[42] Rom. 15.25–8. The clause about 'tying up the loose ends' is one of the few places where I have indulged not just in paraphrase but in swapping a now incomprehensible ancient metaphor ('sealed to them this fruit' is what Paul wrote) for a modern one which performs a similar task in its context. See Jewett 2007, 932: 'To seal the fruit of the Jerusalem offering is . . . to guarantee its delivery against theft and embezzlement . . . His explanation says in effect, "when I am completely finished with this matter," I will be free to fulfill the long-standing plan to visit Rome.'

though in principle detachable from the 'aims', has now become so closely identified with one of those 'aims' as now itself to be taken for granted. The only remaining questions are then, Will the money be ready when I come?[43] and, Will they accept it when I give it to them?[44]

I have argued in chapter 11 against the suggestion that Paul was hoping to bring about, through delivering the Collection in Jerusalem, some kind of large-scale last-minute conversion of Jews, and perhaps even the *parousia* itself.[45] Had that been his expectation (showing how generous the gentiles were being and so 'making my flesh jealous', and so forth), he would hardly have been telling the Romans that once he had delivered the money he was coming to see them on the way to Spain. By the same token, I do not think that he regarded his proposed Spanish mission as a kind of final act of missionary work, completing some biblical itinerary so that *then*, perhaps by taking yet more money to Jerusalem, he would bring about either that large-scale Jewish conversion, or the *parousia*, or both.[46] Such suggestions stem partly from the continuing notion of an 'imminent *parousia*' itself, and partly from an attempt first to read between the lines both of Romans 11 and of Romans 15 and then to join up those imagined in-between lines. Granted that all essays in Pauline interpretation involve some reading between the lines of his dense and allusive prose, in this case both halves of the proposal are in my view unwarranted. Paul did not think the *parousia* would necessarily happen at once, and he certainly was not trying to provoke or hasten it by his missionary work.

So what was his strategy, then? Why did he go where he went? Why did he not go elsewhere? What did he mean by 'finding myself with no more room in these regions', that is, in the east (Romans 15.23)? Did he think that by going to Spain he was completing some biblical or prophetic trajectory, or was this simply a pragmatic decision?[47]

There is no doubt that Paul did have ancient prophecy in mind when thinking about his journeys. 'People who hadn't been told about him will see,' he says, quoting Isaiah 52.15 in Romans 15.21; 'people who hadn't heard will understand.' He is making a very specific point here, namely that his 'intention' has been 'to announce the good news in places where the Messiah has not been named, so that I can avoid building on anyone else's foundation'.[48] A cryptic hint, of course; but we are almost certainly correct to see this as a reference at least to Peter. If Peter has founded the church in

[43] cf. 1 Cor. 16.1–4 with 2 Cor. 8.10–12, 24; 9.3–5.

[44] cf. Rom. 15.31.

[45] See e.g. Munck 1959 [1954]. Munck's view is given a fresh if modified airing by e.g. Kim 2011.

[46] e.g. Aus 1979, supported now by Jewett 2007, 924. Plenty of other scholars have taken a similar view: e.g. Sanders 1983, 193 and elsewhere.

[47] The question of Paul's geographical strategy is raised by Schnabel 2004, 1320, but he remains cautious as to whether it can be answered; see too Schnabel, 1481. I find it strange that Kim 2011, 23 can gloss Rom. 15.19 as Paul having fully preached the gospel 'in the Eastern hemisphere of the *oikumene*': that would surely have meant at least Parthia, if not India and the lands beyond.

[48] Rom. 15.20.

Rome, Paul has tried to go elsewhere; and he is only really going to Rome now, it appears, in order to use it as the natural staging-post for Spain.[49]

This suggests, incidentally but importantly, that by this time the division of labour agreed in Galatians 2.1–10 had broken down, if only for practical reasons. Peter had clearly not stuck to the agreement to go only to Jews, and all the signs are that Paul had regularly been speaking in synagogues in the Jewish Diaspora, not merely to non-Jews. Indeed, the message he insists on in writing to Rome is that the gospel is 'to the Jew first, and also, equally, to the Greek'.[50] Though it is undoubtedly the case that this advance statement is preparing the gentile audience for the dénouement in chapter 11 (the warning against gentile Christians presuming upon their new status and looking down on the 'broken branches' of unbelieving Jews), a good case can be made for seeing it as a statement of actual missionary policy. Paul is explaining to the Roman audience how his gospel actually works, not only so that they will apply it to their own situation but so that they will support him, presumably financially, in the next stage of his own mission in which this policy would be carried out once more.[51] The picture in Acts, of course, is just this: Paul preaches first in synagogues and only then, having been thrown out, turns to gentile audiences.[52] Older scholarship often rejected this as unhistorical on the basis, not least, of Galatians 2.1–10, and particularly on the ideological basis, latent still in the DNA of much scholarship, that Paul had 'translated' the original 'Jewish' message into a 'gentile' one, swapping the idea of a royal or scripturally warranted Messiah for a Jesus-shaped version of the *kyrios*-cults of the wider ancient world. Such a 'Paul' would have had no particular reason to go into a synagogue in the first place. We have said enough in chapter 9 and elsewhere, I trust, to refute that notion quite thoroughly. Paul's gospel was a *Jewish* message for the *non-Jewish* world – something which classic history-of-religions analyses found difficult to grasp – for the very good reason that he believed the God of Israel to be the God of the whole world, and Israel's Messiah to be the world's true lord. If we allow our vision of his missionary methods and practice to be shaped by this foundational theological insight we will see that there is no reason for doubting the basic pattern we find in Acts. Indeed, as Ed Sanders pointed out thirty years ago, if Paul had not gone on attending synagogues he would not have continued to receive the standard,

[49] 15.23f.; there is an apparent tension between this statement and that in Rom. 1.8–15, where Paul ends up saying that he is eager to preach the gospel 'to you, too, in Rome'. I take this latter phrase as a generic statement of Paul's wider ministry; he has already explained, with slightly heavy-handed tact, that he hopes 'to share with you some spiritual blessing to give you strength; that is, I want to encourage you, and be encouraged by you, in the faith you and I share' (1.11f.). Jewett 2007, 134 is right: the apparent contradiction disappears on closer inspection, esp. of 1.13.

[50] Rom. 1.17; cf. 2.9, 10.

[51] When Paul speaks of the Roman church 'sending him on' to Spain (15.24), the word he uses, *propemphthēnai*, almost certainly carries the connotation of support either in money or in kind: see Jewett 2007, 925f. This is without prejudice to Jewett's own theory (see Jewett 1988).

[52] e.g. Ac. 13.5; 13.14–52; 14.1–6; 17.1–5, 10–14; 18.4–7; 19.8–10.

and horrible, synagogue punishment of 'forty lashes less one'.[53] He went on going to the synagogue; and, when he did, the things he said and did (or perhaps the things he was believed to have said and done elsewhere) provoked serious punishment. Had the older paradigm been correct, he could have spared himself the trouble. He saw his work being, as he says, to the Jew first and also to the Greek.

We may safely assume, from the way Romans is structured, that he intended his audience to gather that this was to be his continuing practice in the ongoing mission to Spain as well. This raises an odd question. Older commentaries used to assume that since there were plentiful Roman settlements in Spain,[54] and since the Jewish Diaspora had spread alongside the Roman one, there were plenty of Jews there already. Josephus and others strongly imply that by this stage there were Jews in every possible place around the world, but this has not been verified by archaeological remains.[55] Jewett quotes Romans 1.14 to the effect that Paul declares his indebtedness to both Greeks and barbarians in order to link his missionary plans to a Spain which was, he says, 'stubbornly resistant to greco-roman culture', but if this was really the case why would Paul's indebtedness to *Greeks* lead to a mission there?[56] And when, two verses later, summarizing his main theme, Paul speaks of the gospel being God's power for salvation 'to the Jew first, and also, equally, to the Greek' (1.16), we may reasonably

[53] 2 Cor. 11.24; see Sanders 1983, 192: 'He kept showing up, and obviously he submitted to the thirty-nine stripes. He undoubtedly thought that those who judged him deserving of punishment were wrong, but had he wished he could have withdrawn from Jewish society altogether and thus not have been punished.' See too e.g. Frey 2007, 304.

[54] e.g. Käsemann 1980 [1973], 383; Black 1973, 177.

[55] cf. the general statements in Jos. *Ap.* 2.282; *War* 2.398; 7.43; *Ant.* 14.115 (citing Strabo to the same effect); see too Philo *Flacc.* 45f.; *Sib. Or.* 3.271, and Augustine's citing of Seneca similarly in *Civ. Dei* 6.11. (Contrast Just. *Dial.* 117, claiming that Mal. 1.11 is not fulfilled by the Jews, because there are in fact nations where they have never dwelt, whereas Christians are already to be found in every possible location.) Cf. too Ac. 2.5, speaking of 'devout Jews from every nation under heaven' gathering in Jerusalem at Pentecost. A Jewish presence in Spain is challenged by Jewett 2007, 924, citing the eight-page article of Bowers 1975 and the single-page piece by Thornton 1975 under the rubric 'as the recent studies have shown'. Thornton adds little on this point except to stress the paucity of archaeological evidence (see also e.g. Cranfield 1975, 1979, 769 n. 1). Bowers (396, 400) plays down the first-century evidence of a Palestinian amphora on Ibiza; even if this is evidence primarily of trade, such trade regularly, in the wider Mediterranean world, generated immigration. He also plays down Josephus's report (*War* 2.183) that Caligula banished Herod Antipas to Spain, where he died (in *Ant.* 18.252 Jos. has changed this to Lyons in Gaul; this is sometimes resolved, e.g. by Hoehner 1980 [1972], 262, through postulating a different 'Lyons', Lugdunum Convenarum, on the Spain/Gaul frontier). Granted, banishing a Jewish king to a place does not necessarily mean that there was already a Jewish community there, but nor can this be ruled out. The testimony of Strabo and Seneca, as well as Josephus and Philo, though generalized, would make it strange to think there were no Jews in Spain at all. Bowers tries to clinch his case (402) by claiming that in Rom. 10.14–21 Paul says that the Jewish people have all now heard the good news, so that a Spanish mission cannot be aimed at any more Jews. This rests on a misunderstanding: (a) 10.14–18 is about *gentiles* hearing the gospel; (b) 10.18 is in any case an argument from the revelation in the natural world as in Ps. 19.4, not in the preaching of the gospel; (c) Paul does not mention Jewish reactions to the gospel until 10.19, and then only in terms of Isa. and Deut., not in terms of places where he himself has preached. This is not to deny (Bowers 400) that the later substantial Jewish population in Spain will have been the result of forced migrations after the disasters of 70 and 135.

[56] Jewett 2007, 924 (wrongly citing Rom. 1.15). Thornton 1975 stresses the paucity of Greek inscriptions in Spain at this period.

wonder why he would speak thus, in a passage acknowledged to be thematic for the whole letter, if the purpose of that letter were to solicit support for a mission to a territory where no Jews were to be found. We may therefore take it that Paul at least believed that there were significant Jewish communities in Spain.

But why Spain itself? It was, of course, the limit of the known world – though we may suppose that Paul's travel plans would be far more likely to take him towards the eastern shore of Spain in the first instance, rather than going on through the Pillars of Hercules and up the western side of the peninsula. He might in any case have been planning to travel to Spain mostly on land, perhaps cutting corners by sea voyages but taking in the north-west coast of Italy and the southern coast of Gaul.[57] However, the voyage from Ostia, Rome's port, to Tarraco in north-eastern Spain was regularly accomplished in four days; with Spain as a highly important centre of Roman activity there was a regular brisk traffic, and Paul may well have hoped to make straight for Tarraco itself, where the massive new temple to Augustus dominated the city, easily visible to incoming ships.[58] But, to repeat, why Spain at all?

It is not easy to be sure how Paul's mental map might have worked, but Isaiah repeatedly mentions 'coastlands far away' and 'the ends of the earth' as places where the good news will be proclaimed, and it is a fair guess – especially considering that he quotes Isaiah when talking about these plans – that he had passages like this in mind.[59]

One such passage appends a string of place-names:

> For I know their works and their thoughts, and I am coming to gather all nations and tongues; and they shall come and shall see my glory, and I will set a sign among them. From them I will send survivors to the nations, to Tarshish, Put, and Lud – which draw the bow – to Tubal and Javan, to the coastlands far away that have not heard of my fame or seen my glory; and they shall declare my glory among the nations. They shall bring all your kindred from all the nations as an offering to YHWH ... to my holy mountain Jerusalem, says YHWH.[60]

These places are not all straightforward to locate, to say the least. We have no means of knowing whether Paul, reading Isaiah, would have been able to place them on a map either. Tarshish, famous in the Bible as the place to which Jonah was trying to flee instead of going obediently to Nineveh, has been located both in north Africa, on the coast of the Red Sea, and even as a synonym for 'Tarsus', Paul's birthplace; but a majority now see it as 'Tharsis' in southwestern Spain.[61] Put seems to be in Africa; Josephus

[57] This was the pattern, according to Ac. 20.1–16, of the last trip around the Aegean.

[58] On Tarraco cf. Schnabel 2004, 1277f., with other refs. The city, a Roman colony since 45 BC, was the capital of the province of Hispania Citerior. On Tiberius's permission for the temple of Augustus cf. Tac. *Ann.* 1.78.

[59] Isa. 11.11, 12; 24.15; 41.1, 5; 42.4, 10, 12; 49.1; 51.5; 59.18; 60.9; 66.19.

[60] Isa. 66.18–20.

[61] cf. Jon. 1.3; cp. Ps. 72.10; and cf. Elat 1982, with e.g. Hdt. 4.152.

identifies it with Libya.[62] Libya has also been suggested as the location of Lud, though it is now less favoured; an alternative would be to see it as a form of 'Lydia', on the west coast of Asia Minor, but yet another possibility is to place it on the east African coast south of Egypt.[63] Tubal is most likely to be found in eastern Asia Minor, perhaps in the area of Cilicia, Paul's own home region. The word 'Javan' is probably cognate with 'Ionia', originally designating the coastlands and islands of western Asia Minor; by the time of Daniel 8.21 it means, more or less, 'Greece', which is how some modern translations render it.[64] Any attempt, therefore, to make Isaiah 66 correspond to Paul's travels has to stretch the point more than a little: even supposing 'Lud' to be Lydia, which would allow Paul's known journeys to intersect with three out of the five, hoping to add Tarshish in an eventual Spanish journey, it still leaves 'Put' unaccounted for, and also, if it is after all in Africa, 'Lud'. Isaiah 66 thus hardly matches what we know of either Paul's actual journeys or his future plans.[65]

This raises, however, another major question when we are examining his 'aims': why did Paul not mention north Africa at all? Was he planning to return from Spain along the north African coast? If not, why not – granted that the whole coastline was dotted with greco-roman towns and cities, some of considerable culture and antiquity, many if not most with thriving Jewish populations? Did he suppose that someone else – not Peter presumably, but one of the other apostles – had already been travelling westwards from Egypt, founding churches as he went? We do not know. Nor do we have any idea what Paul would have thought about the lands to the east, regions for which his own starting-point, Antioch in Syria, would have been the gateway. If, as Richard Bauckham has argued, James in Jerusalem was seen as holding the geographical centre, not simply the eastern edge, of the new messianic movement, how did Paul view the other half of that missionary outreach?[66] Does it even matter?

It might do – if we supposed that Paul actually saw the world through spectacles in which his own call to action, the deep-rooted 'aim' in his worldview, was to convert the whole world, or at least representatives of the whole world, before the *parousia*. Certainly Paul sees the entire cosmos as already having heard, in some sense or other, the good news of the Messiah's resurrection and of the triumph of the creator God through him. Certainly he sees himself as the servant of that good news, not only of some

[62] Jos. *Ant.* 1.132f.

[63] cf. Jer. 46.9; Ezek. 30.5, both suggesting an African location; but the Akkadian *Luddu*, referring to Lydia, may be a better clue; so e.g. Walker 2000. But others, such as Sadler 2009, insist on an African location (though not Libya), possibly in the region of today's Somaliland.

[64] e.g. NRSV.

[65] Scott 1995 proposed, on the basis of this text and the 'table of nations' in Gen. 10, that Paul saw himself called to the 'sons of Japheth'. This has not found much favour in subsequent discussion (though cf. e.g. Frey 2007, 302f.; Rosner 2011, 161f. I agree with Rosner (161) that 'the glory of God informs the ambitious itinerary of Paul's missionary journeys', and that Paul clearly echoes Isa. 66.18–21 in Rom. 15, but I do not think that this means that he has retained a Jerusalem-centred view.

[66] Bauckham 1995b.

small part of it. But the sweeping statement of a north-westerly trajectory, from Jerusalem as far round as Illyricum, tells a very different story from the converting-the-world narrative.[67] This is Paul *on his way to Rome*, even if, as he finally plans his visit, he insists that Rome is actually a staging-post for Spain. Or at least, this is a Paul deliberately announcing the name of Jesus in places where the Roman empire and culture ran deep; but that would have been true, as well, in central north Africa, and as we have seen Paul never mentions that as a possible further missionary field. The closest we get is Titus in Crete, and that is an outpost of Greece, not an outcrop of Africa.[68]

My proposal, then, is that in some of the scholarly discussion an imagined eschatology has ousted an actual political engagement. It is not the first time such a thing has happened. The suggestion that Paul was eager to get converts from 'the ends of the earth' in time for, and perhaps in order to hasten, the *parousia* has, as we have seen, serious problems of its own. But it does not in any case fit with Paul's own actual statements of his present achievements and future intentions. If we add up the key sites of his mission: Galatia, Ephesus, Philippi, Thessalonica and Corinth, and add to that list Illyricum (Romans 15.19), Rome itself and the Roman cities of Spain, what we are looking at is not a trawl of the whole created order, but the establishment of messianic communities in the very places where Caesar's power was strongest.[69] Granted, Caesar's power was also strong in Alexandria (in Egypt) and in Carthage (in 'Africa' proper: roughly modern Tunisia). But a glance at the map indicates the priorities, even supposing that Paul imagined the north African seaboard still to be virgin territory. He had travelled the central heartlands of the Roman empire, and it was now time to head for the city at the very heart itself, and to go on from there to the key western outpost of Rome's wide domains. If we want to understand Paul's 'aims', this is where to look.[70]

This strategy may, of course, have been partly pragmatic. Paul as a Roman citizen could travel freely in that world, or at least more freely than non-citizens, appealing where necessary to the Roman order and the local magistrates, even if they did not understand what he was talking about. But I propose, in the light of chapters 5 and 12 above, that Paul did indeed conceive of his mission and vocation, not simply, as he says tactfully to the

[67] This does not mean that Paul continued to regard Jerusalem (as he had probably done before) as the centre of the earth (e.g. Ezek. 5.5; 38.12; and cf. e.g. Frey 2007, 302f.). Jerusalem remains important, but not that important; and the idea of a circle from Jerusalem to Illyricum (Rom. 15.19) places Jerusalem on the rim of the circle, not at its centre.

[68] cf. Tit. 1.5. The global vision implied by Ps. 72.10 – Tarshish in the west, 'Sheba and Seba' in the south and east – seems to have played no role in Paul's strategy.

[69] This point is made from different angles by writers such as White 1999, 130–2 (132: 'the physical specificity of his obligation as Christ's ambassador was probably inspired by the boundaries of the Roman Empire'); Crossan and Reed 2004, 354–6; Magda 2009, 52f. The question of whether Paul did in fact reach Spain (as probably implied by *1 Clem.* 5.6) cannot be settled either way. 2 Tim. 4.9–21, sometimes cited as evidence of further travels after an initial arrival at Rome, provides very shaky foundations for any historical reconstruction.

[70] On the question of how to understand the 'political' dimension of Paul's thought and action, see ch. 12 above.

Romans, to announce the Messiah in places where he has not yet been named (Romans 15.20), but to do so in the places where another *kyrios*, another world ruler, another *basileus*, *was* being named and was being worshipped as the one and only sovereign. Those references to 'above every name that is named' are not there by accident.[71] This in turn reinforces my view that the heart of Paul's gospel is not 'here's how to be saved', or 'get on board before the *parousia*', but *Jesus is lord*. The ends of the earth would hear this in due time. Perhaps it is a shame that nobody invented a legend in which one might say of Paul, rather than of Jesus, 'And did those feet in ancient time walk upon England's mountains green?', even if the implied answer would again be, 'No, actually.' But the point was to name the Messiah, to announce him as lord, in the culture-forming places, the cities to and from which all local or international roads ran.

This explains, I think, the otherwise strange suggestion that Paul had 'no room' for further work in the east. Many had not heard the gospel; most had not responded to it in faith. But Jesus had been announced there as *kyrios*: Paul's work was that of a herald, a *kēryx*, one who announces a *kērygma*.[72] All this in turn reinforces my claim, throughout this book, that Paul's theology and gospel remained fundamentally *Jewish*, a biblically rooted message about the Jewish Messiah who was the world's true lord and who therefore had to be proclaimed as such to the non-Jewish world.[73]

Why then did Paul concentrate on the Roman world in this really rather narrow sense? A second level of pragmatism suggests itself: not only could Paul travel relatively easily in the world where he could claim *civis Romanus sum*, but he knew that new ideas and beliefs would flow out along the trade routes from the great centres to the far-flung interior. The reason he could write to Philemon about Onesimus in Colosse is that he had met them both, and been responsible for the conversion of both, but not in the small inland town of Colosse itself, which he had not visited. Most likely he met them both in Ephesus. The wild northern lands of Moesia, Sarmatia and the rest might similarly be reached from Philippi and Thessalonica; Gaul, perhaps even Britain, from Italy and Spain. Stick to the Roman roads and cities, and the trade routes will do the rest. But I suggest another, more obviously Jewish, exegetical and theological reason for his concentration on the Roman heartlands.

Paul, like his mid-century Jewish contemporaries, undoubtedly knew the great four-kingdom prophecies of Daniel 2 and 7. He would have had no

[71] Eph. 1.21; Phil. 2.9–11.

[72] The noun *kēryx* is found in the Paulines only in 1 Tim. 2.7; 2 Tim. 1.11. The abstract *kērygma* is at Rom. 16.25 and, perhaps more importantly, 1 Cor. 1.21; 2.4; 15.14. But the verb *kēryssō* appears to be among Paul's favourite terms to describe the activity he saw as basic to his calling: Rom. 10.8, 14, 15; 1 Cor. 1.23; 9.27; 15.11, 12; 2 Cor. 1.19; 4.5; 11.4 (twice); Gal. 2.2; 5.11; Phil. 1.15; Col. 1.23; 1 Thess. 2.19, and 1 Tim. 3.16; 2 Tim. 4.2. Kim 2011 discusses Paul as 'herald' but not in the sense I am taking it.

[73] This proposal gives shape and depth to the much vaguer suggestions of Magda 2009, ch. 4. She argues, rightly in my view, that 'Paul works from Roman geography both incidentally and consciously' (82), but suggests that this is at least in part because, as a native of Tarsus and a student of Stoicism there he had been 'taught to be a cosmopolitan' (83). Nobody who drew on Ps. 2 or Isa. 11 needed a Stoic to teach them that Israel's God claimed the whole world through the anointed Davidic king.

difficulty in decoding the fourth kingdom as Rome. Like *4 Ezra*, though with a very different lion to stand against the eagle, he will have identified Rome as the leading edge of opposition to the suddenly inbreaking kingdom of God. If, according to Daniel 7, the vindication of the human figure, whom one must assume Paul would construe messianically, meant that 'the people of the saints of the most high' were now receiving the kingdom, there was no point in announcing that kingdom out in the deserts of Arabia or the far-off uplands of Scythia.[74] Whatever else we may think about the representation of Paul in Acts, here it is spot on: Paul ends up in Rome, boldly announcing the kingdom of God and the sovereignty of Jesus the Messiah, with no one stopping him.[75] If we are in any historically grounded sense to see Paul as an 'apocalyptic' thinker, this is what such a claim might mean: that with the sudden arrival (and crucifixion and resurrection) of Israel's Messiah, the dark night of successive world empires was over and the new day had begun, the day in which that Messiah would call those empires, and particularly the final one, to account. If we understand this aright, we should actually have predicted that Paul, as the herald of the freshly revealed divine faithfulness in the Messiah, was most likely to concentrate his efforts on 'naming the Messiah' in the key places where a very different name had been 'named'.[76]

All this means that the 'ministry of reconciliation' which Paul cites as his central vocation is not simply about reconciling individuals to the one God, or about bringing such individuals together into the single family of the church. These tasks remain vital and central, but they are designed both to point beyond themselves and to be the means of that to which they point, namely, the reconciliation of the whole creation to its creator – which involves, as always, rescuing it from the rule of usurpers. This hypothesis points on to a wider thesis about the Pauline integration of themes, strands and cultural overtones which theology and exegesis have often separated out but which, I suggest, Paul himself held firmly together.

3. Integration and Reconciliation

All we have said so far means that we must postulate a thorough integration, in the 'aims and intentions' section of Paul's own mindset, between what we have seen as the Jewishly rooted gospel of the Messiah and what we have seen as the political engagement between Paul's gospel and Caesar's empire. An integration, in fact, which, granted the long years in which scholars have

[74] The widespread fashion for understanding Paul's reference to a journey to Arabia in Gal. 1.17 as an early evangelistic effort is I think unwarranted. As I have argued elsewhere (see *Perspectives* ch. 10), I see that trip as part of his role-modelling of Elijah in 1 Kgs. 19, not an early mission trip. The reference to hostility from the Nabatean king (2 Cor. 11.32), often invoked in support, is irrelevant, relating to the city of Damascus itself rather than to lands further south (see e.g. Schnabel 2004, 1032–45; Magda 2009, 101).

[75] Ac. 28.31.

[76] cf. Rom. 15.20 with Eph. 1.21; Phil. 2.9–11.

seen them as completely distinct, might even be seen as a 'reconciliation', though if I am right Paul would never have seen (what we call) 'politics' and (what we call) 'theology' as separable in the first place. The political engagement we have sketched in chapter 12, in other words, was not simply a distant or occasional 'implication' of a mission which was at its heart 'about' something else (either dehistoricized 'conversions' or a hasty pre-*parousia* collection of representative gentiles). As in the famous paragraph in Mark 10.35–45, where James and John are put in their place by Jesus' radical redefinition of power itself, at the heart of which lies the claim that 'the son of man didn't come to be waited on; he came to be the servant, to give his life "as a ransom for many"', we find the (Isaianic) good news of Jesus and his death at the heart of the (equally Isaianic) proclamation that Israel's God is sovereign over the nations and their idols.[77] When Paul, summarizing his missionary strategy in Romans 15, quotes the same section of Isaiah, we may confidently propose that he has in mind the same complex integration. At the level of worldview or mindset, so deep that he now took it for granted, Paul aimed to announce Jesus as lord right across Caesar's principal domains, to make it clear that the Messiah had been vindicated and that at his name every knee would bow – even if at the moment this was more or less bound to lead to persecution, prison and death.

Paul's aims have a kind of holy boldness about them, a *parrhēsia*, a freedom of speech. Just as he could confidently if cheekily remind the Philippian magistrates that they should have treated a Roman citizen like him very differently, so he could confidently speak and live for Jesus as the ultimate lord over against the now hugely overblown pretensions of Rome, and particularly of Caesar himself. The tension between those two appeals – the one capitalizing on Roman citizenship, the other challenging the pretensions of Caesar – is more apparent (especially on the two-dimensional spectrum of late-modern western politics) than real. No biblically literate Jew – think of the book of Daniel! – would have had any difficulty reconciling the two. The one sovereign God wants human rulers to establish order, but will hold them to account when they abuse that vocation and divinize themselves. Paul's double position – Roman citizen, apostle of the Messiah – fits exactly within the inaugurated-eschatological version of that complex belief. Placing Paul within his actual historical context, as we have tried to do in this book, enables us to make sense of his underlying aims in a way which an abstracted 'Paul', seeking only to save a few more souls or to precipitate the *parousia*, or indeed to announce an ahistorical 'apocalypse', cannot do.

This also helps us to integrate the other two dimensions of his wider context. The ultimate symbol of his worldview – the church itself, its unity and holiness – was to be expressed in an actual outward fashion which, though startlingly unlike anything the ancient world knew as 'religion' (no sacrifices, no stone-and-timber temples, no priestly hierarchy), nevertheless retained vestiges of something we may call 'religion'. As the old 'religions'

[77] cf. Mk. 10.45, quoting Isa. 53.10–12.

reflected the old social order, with magistrates doubling as priests and vice versa, so this new quasi-religion, as we explored it in chapter 13, reflected the new social order in the Messiah, where neither Jew nor Greek, slave nor free, male nor female had any privilege, all being one in the Messiah. Navigating what that meant, managing the puzzles which arose and sorting out the chaos that sometimes resulted occupied a fair part of Paul's letters, much more in fact than is taken up with christology or justification, though each of those key 'doctrines' is of course umbilically linked to the central symbol. Again, what Paul wanted to see as the result of all his labours was cross-culturally united *worship*; and unless we are to deny that 'worship' is in some sense a fundamentally 'religious' activity, which seems absurd, certainly in Paul's world, we must conclude that he was indeed concerned not only to integrate his essentially Jewish gospel with his implicit subversion of the claims of Caesar but also to accomplish something to which Israel's scriptures had pointed, and something which Caesar had tried to achieve in his way, namely a *cult* in which the one God would be worshipped by people of every kind and kin. 'Religion', in this rather severely redefined sense, is integrated with everything else Paul was trying to do.

We see this in a fleeting but significant moment in the same passage in Romans 15 where Paul gives us a glimpse of his mature missionary strategy. He is, he says,

> a minister of King Jesus for the nations, working in the priestly service of God's good news, so that the offering of the nations may be acceptable, sanctified in the holy spirit.[78]

This sudden flash of sacerdotal language may well be linked to the passage in Isaiah we looked at before, where the prophet speaks of people from every nation flocking towards Jerusalem so that they may see the divine glory which will be revealed there:

> I am coming to gather all nations and tongues; and they shall come and shall see my glory, and I will set a sign among them ... they shall bring all your kindred from all the nations as an offering to YHWH, on horses, and in chariots, and in litters, and on mules, and on dromedaries, to my holy mountain Jerusalem, says YHWH, just as the Israelites bring a grain offering in a clean vessel to the house of YHWH. And I will also take some of them as priests and as Levites, says YHWH.[79]

For Paul, of course, the divine glory had already been unveiled, not in the Jerusalem Temple but in Jesus and the spirit. The geographical focus has therefore shifted, resulting in a centrifugal mission rather than a centripetal one. This is a further aspect of his reworked, or indeed inside-out, Jewish eschatology. But the point remains: the nations will themselves constitute

[78] Rom. 15.16. The phrase 'the offering of the nations' means 'the offering which consists of the nations', not 'the offering which the nations will offer': see below. A recent study of the passage is that of Gibson 2011, though I want to go further than him in various ways.

[79] Isa. 66.18–21.

the new sacrifice, to be brought in worship to the one God.[80] We saw above that though Paul was probably not following the list of locations in the same passage – Tarshish, Put, Lud, Tubal and Javan – as a blueprint for his own geographical strategy, he may well have had the underlying point in mind, modified by his sense that Rome, the last great world empire, had to be the focus of his messianic announcement. In the same way, he was not following Isaiah's Jerusalem-centred agenda, but was transferring to the new eschatological situation the same idea of priestly service with non-Jewish nations as the offering.[81] The passage in Isaiah goes on to speak of the new heavens and the new earth in which 'all flesh shall come to worship before me, says YHWH'.[82] Paul had established, earlier in Romans, that the entire world was now the 'inheritance' of the Messiah and his people, as indeed had been promised to Abraham.[83] He now drew together, in a fresh configuration, several elements of older Jewish worldwide hope: the message reaching to the coastlands, the nations coming in pilgrimage with sacrifices, financial contributions being sent to Jerusalem, the worldwide announcement of Israel's God as the ultimate sovereign.[84] As with every other element of his theology, so it was with his mission strategy (at least as he articulated it in Romans; we have no means of knowing how long this idea had been forming in his mind, and his response to the charge of vacillation in 2 Corinthians 1.15–22 may indicate that the current plan was fairly recent). The crucified and risen Messiah, and the outpoured spirit, meant here as elsewhere a transformed and transforming fulfilment of the Isaianic promises. Paul clearly saw himself not only as a 'herald' but also as a 'prophet'; but the ancient prophetic agenda had been transposed into the startling new key required by the gospel.

All this – the establishment and maintenance of communities in which this Jewish Messiah-message brought to birth a quasi-empire rivalling Caesar's and a quasi-cult to give it expression – provided a fresh and previously unimagined coherence of gospel, politics and religion. In a world where *collegia* were carefully regulated, sometimes suppressed and often under suspicion, there is no way that the communities called into being by Paul's

[80] For 'the offering of the Gentiles' as an objective genitive, 'the offering which consists of the Gentiles', rather than 'the offering which the Gentiles are making', see Fitzmyer 1993, 712; Moo 1996, 890.

[81] For the possibility that Paul may have had some kind of Roman map in mind see Jewett 2007, 912f. I agree with Magda 2009, 82 that Paul was working consciously in terms of Roman geography, though her explanation for this in terms of philosophy (a cosmopolitan vision picked up from Stoics in Tarsus) rather than politics (the vocation to name Jesus as lord in Caesar's domains) seems to miss the point. Paul knew the difference between the worldwide biblical vision of e.g. Isa. 11 and Ps. 2 on the one hand and pantheistic globalism on the other.

[82] Isa. 66.22f.

[83] Rom. 8.17–30; 4.13.

[84] The 'Collection' was not a Christian version of the Jewish 'temple tax', or a levy imposed by the 'mother church': so, rightly, e.g. Fitzmyer 1993, 722. It owes much more to the needs of 'the poor' (cf. Gal. 2.10). However, Paul cannot have been ignorant of the ironic overtones of the plan he was now implementing.

gospel could have been seen as politically irrelevant.[85] But there is one final element. Paul also knew that he had to think through, and to teach, a coherent and integrated vision of the one God and his world which would serve and sustain that already large and complex whole in the way that the great philosophies had served in relation to their wider world. Here again I regret that space has forbidden the study of integrative models in the greco-roman world itself. I would like to have explored more fully the ways in which someone like Cicero actually integrated, in thought as well as practice, the worlds of politics, religion and philosophy, in each of which he was a prominent participant. But we can at least see the way in which *Paul* integrated them. His implicit and sometimes explicit engagement with the great philosophical systems, particularly that of the Stoics, retaining his Jewish integrity but doing his best to 'take every thought prisoner and make it obey the Messiah', has been explored in chapter 14. What we now glimpse is that this engagement is itself part of a wider reconciliation or integration.

How did this work? The slogan 'all truth is God's truth' is a modern coinage, but Paul would have agreed with it whole-heartedly, just as he was prepared to say that all food was God's food: the earth and its fullness belong to the lord.[86] Paul's vision of *physics*, as we saw, was of an integrated cosmos in which heaven and earth, meant to work together, had *come* together in Jesus the Messiah and were united afresh, through the spirit, in the lives and especially the worship of those who belonged to the Messiah. His understanding of *ethics*, rooted in Jewish creational monotheism, was that of a genuinely human existence in which the new creation was coming to birth. He affirmed the goodness of the original creation (hence the strong emphasis on classic Jewish sexual ethics, the key point where Paul insisted that gentile converts should renounce gentile ways) while insisting that the death and resurrection of the Messiah had dealt with the sin, corruption and death that was distorting and destroying the old creation. His understanding of *logic* itself, the basis and process of knowledge, was transformed into a new kind of knowing, a cross-and-resurrection-based knowledge in which the renewed and transformed mind of Romans 12.2, 'the mind of the Messiah' as in 1 Corinthians 2.16, could and should reach out and grasp the realities of the new world as well as understanding, from that perspective, the real truths about the old one. All this we have explored quite fully already. Here we note that the categories into which scholarship has necessarily divided Paul's complex world are themselves reconciled and integrated in multiple and overlapping ways in his writings.

Much of this has not normally even been mentioned, far less investigated, in works on 'Pauline theology'. But unless we are to give a severely

[85] On 'clubs' in the Roman world, see e.g. Stevenson and Lintott 2003. Augustus passed a law regulating *collegia* (*ILS* 4966); Trajan forbade their formation in Bithynia (Pliny, *Ep*., 10.34). This does not mean that Paul expected followers of Jesus to engage in what today would be called 'political activity' (see, of course, Rom. 13.1–7); the mere formation and maintenance of such associations constituted a challenge to all other social orders.

[86] 1 Cor. 10.26.

shrunken account of that great but elusive reality it is vital that we see the 'theology', escaping on Jewish wings from the category of 'physics' where it had previously belonged in the world of the non-Jewish philosophers, as itself proposing a new and larger category of understanding, an all-embracing vision of reality, incorporating but far transcending the philosophies even of a Cicero or a Seneca. We might suggest, in particular, that Paul's dramatic account of the reworking, through Messiah and spirit, of monotheism, election and eschatology enabled that Jewish framework to do at last what by itself it seemed incapable of doing: taking on the wider world, challenging its puzzled moralists and outflanking its wisest sages. What Paul says about the inability, and the surprising new fulfilment, of Torah in Romans 7 and 8 turns out to be true at a deeper and richer level in relation to the entire body of ancient Jewish thought about God, Israel and the future. Paul's vision in Romans 8 of creation renewed offers the reality to which the new-creation visions of Isaiah and the Psalms bore witness. One might even say that the Stoic hypothesis about the periodic world-renewing fire, though from Paul's perspective quite muddled and mistaken, nevertheless bore oblique witness to the same reality, much as the pagan moralists bore witness to the notion of a genuinely human existence, even though it remained beyond their reach.

Romans 8, as we said before, is from one angle all about *temple*-theology, and the temple is perhaps the most haunting symbol for Paul's underlying missionary aims. The spirit has come to 'indwell' God's people, to lead them, as the fire and cloud and the wilderness tabernacle led ancient Israel, to the inheritance. And the inheritance itself, the entire renewed creation, is the reality to which the original Temple pointed, just as the creation-story itself in Genesis 1 is in fact a 'temple'-vision, God making a heaven-and-earth house for himself in which he would place, at its heart and as the climax of creation itself, the humans who would be his image-bearers, his royal priesthood, summing up the worship of creation and reflecting his wise order into his world. 'Those he called according to his purpose' are marked out 'to be shaped according to the model of the image of his son'. Paul's vision in Romans 8.17–30 of renewed humans as the stewards (under God) of renewed creation, the messianic 'inheritance', reflects both Psalm 2.8 and Romans 4.13. It speaks of the true inheritance both of Abraham and of the Davidic king, going far beyond the original 'garden', far beyond one piece of territory in the middle east, out and away along the roads that had appeared at Rome's behest when the time had fully come, now carrying the apostle from Jerusalem as far round as Illyricum, pointing him on to Rome itself and, beyond that again, to the farthest outposts of Caesar's empire. Paul's aim was to be the *temple-builder for the kingdom*, planting on non-Jewish soil little communities in which heaven and earth would come together at last, places where the returning glory of Israel's God would shine out, heralding and anticipating the day when God would be all in all.

To that end he announced Jesus as the crucified and risen lord. His evangelistic efforts fulfilled over and over the commission he could not escape even if he had wanted to (1 Corinthians 9.16–17). He saw the strange power of the gospel-announcement do its work again and again, even though it was obviously folly to Greeks and a stumbling-block to Jews. Lives were transformed by it: believing hearts, confessing lips, renewed minds. Much modern western Pauline theology has stopped there, but Paul did not. He saw, not least because of his utter rootedness in Israel's scriptures as well as his thorough immersion in the non-Jewish world of his day, that such transformed lives had to be transformed in relation to their entire culture, which we here have summarized under politics, religion and philosophy but which could have been extended into all possible categories of human life.[87]

The lives that were thus to be transformed in relation to that wider culture would, in the nature of the case, in the nature of the 'image-bearing' vocation now renewed in the Messiah, be transform*ing*. They were to shine like lights in a dark place, indicating that there was a different way to be human, a renewed and renewing way, a way patterned upon the Messiah himself, empowered through his spirit. In particular, this new way of being human was to be modelled by the apostle. 'Copy me, just as I'm copying the Messiah.'[88] With that we are touching bedrock. Among Paul's deepest aims was to be someone who could say that with utter integrity.

When therefore we speak of Paul aiming to generate and sustain communities in the Messiah that were both united and holy, we are not intending to refer to the often disheartened ecumenism or embattled ethics that come to many minds when they hear such words today. We are speaking of a larger reality altogether, which Paul had at the back of his mind whether he was faced with Euodia and Syntyche in Philippi, with Philemon and Onesimus in Colosse, or – looking more widely – with the Paul-party, the Peter-party and perhaps the Christ-party in Corinth, the proto-Marcionite gentile Christians in Rome, or the would-be Jewish gentiles in Galatia. We are speaking about the foundation, through the spirit-empowered announcement of Jesus crucified and risen, of a community which from one point of view would be seen as a 'philosophy', from another as a *koinōnia*, a partnership, from another as a new if strange kind of 'religion', and from yet another as a new *polis*, a socio-cultural entity giving allegiance to a different *kyrios*. All these and more are encompassed in Paul's (very Jewish) vision of the Messiah's people. His worldview demanded no less; his theology sustained no less. All of these were, in his mind, truths which already existed in the Messiah and were to be brought about by the tireless labour of himself and his colleagues, the apostolic work in which he was privileged to share, the work through which the divine purpose for Israel itself was being fulfilled, taking the news of the one God, the creator, the covenant God, to the ends of the earth, and calling forth in every place the pure sacrifice of praise.

[87] One obvious area deserving of much fuller treatment is economics, on which see the important recent work of Longenecker 2010.

[88] 1 Cor. 11.1.

It was because of that large vision, inadequately summed up in our modern language of unity and holiness, that Paul aimed to plant such churches in Caesar's territory. It was because of that hope, inaugurated but very far indeed from realized, that he went on teaching the young churches not only what to think but more importantly *how* to think. It was because of that purpose that he insisted (in 1 Corinthians 11) that corporate worship should not only be properly ordered but should model an integration, a reconciliation, which challenged the social and cultural divisions in the world outside. Only when we glimpse the way in which the new reality that was called into being by the gospel confronted the larger worlds in which Paul lived, and outflanked them at their own game with the essentially Jewish message about the crucified and risen Messiah, can we understand not only the coherence but the massive importance of his theology.

Paul's theology, after all, was not a matter of sorting out abstract categories, helpful though that can sometimes be for clarifying what is going on. It was not a matter of fine-tuning precisely what someone needed to believe *about* salvation in order to be saved. It was the larger reality to which all his scripture-soaked reflection was pointing and from which all his energetic missionary and pastoral activity – including letter-writing! – was directed: a reality in which hard thinking and glad worship were integrated, reconciled and united. This has been a book about Paul's theology, but it has been impossible to give a proper account of it without locating it firmly within, and showing its dynamic purposes in relation to, the multiple Jewish and greco-roman worlds in which Paul lived and worked and in which his gospel produced its dramatic and – to use the fashionable language! – 'apocalyptic' effects.

All of this brings us back at last to the way in which different categories have been imposed upon the apostle in our own day. It will surprise nobody that I want to suggest an integration, a reconciliation, here as well – precisely because I think Paul himself would not have recognized as separate 'categories' the various labels and headings, together with the texts which are said to embody them, into which his thought has been divided in the last few generations. This is where we return briefly to Paul's distant cousin and his friends in the embattled world of the mid-twentieth century.

What Walter Benjamin, Hannah Arendt and others were longing for in the dangerous and turbulent Europe of the 1930s and 1940s was a new moment. A messianic moment: a 'now' time in which neither the shallow promises of 'progress' nor the equally shallow despair of 'doom' would hold sway. Arendt, as we saw, spoke explicitly of the need for 'a new law on earth', operating through strictly limited political powers. These longings, which grew directly out of a deeply Jewish vision of reality that had seen through the threadbare heresy of mainstream Marxism, can be mapped quite well on to the longings and aspirations of many in the world of second-Temple Judaism. The question, What is to be *done*, was every bit as vital and urgent then as in recent continental history. It was the question asked by Saul of Tarsus, and answered in zealous and violent action.

But it will not do – either as an account of Benjamin and his friends, or as an account of second-Temple Jewish hopes! – to abstract from such complex situations an idea called 'apocalyptic' in which one simply renounces 'progress' as a heap of rubble and announces the arrival of a new day unattached to anything that has preceded it. That, as we saw, is in fact what some were doing in the 1930s, saying a sharp *No* to the past, to the *religious* past, to the *specifically Jewish* religious past. When Benjamin and others longed for the messianic moment, and refused the false hopes of Hegelian or Marxist determinism, they were not rejecting the ancient Jewish vision of a world set right, of promises awaiting fulfilment. They were rejecting, rather, spurious routes to such a goal. It is therefore shallow and ultimately ridiculous to hold them up as bearing witness to something one might call 'apocalyptic' in the sense of a rejection of history, of ancient promises. No second-Temple Jews, so far as we know, held anything remotely like a Hegelian or a Marxist theory about the smooth progress of history to an eventually full-flowering goal. But that certainly did not mean that they rejected the idea of a covenant history, a Deuteronomic and Danielic narrative, in which the redemptive or messianic goal remained up ahead. Of course, part of the point of that biblical narrative, understood in the way we mapped it in chapter 2, was precisely that for much of the time the story was travelling through darkness. Exile, punishment, disaster and shame seemed to be the norm as the monsters came up out of the sea and made war against God's holy people. To collapse an ancient *Heilsgeschichte* into a modernist or determinist doctrine of 'progress', and then to reject it on those grounds, is like imagining that when Paul said 'beware of dogs' in Philippians 3.2 he was warning against four-footed canine companions. The fact that some people in the 1930s did indeed advocate a 'salvation history' which was really the totalitarian wolf dressed up in biblical sheep's clothing cannot justify an equal and opposite (and equally shallow) reaction – especially from historical critics, which is what Käsemann, the apostle of the modern 'apocalyptic' movement, manifestly claimed to be.

But this means that the way stands open to a full and thorough reconciliation of a *genuine* 'apocalyptic', such as might be recognized in the first century, with a *genuine*, and equally recognizable, salvation history. Both are there in Deuteronomy 27—32. Both are there, retrieving Deuteronomy, in Daniel. Both are there, retrieving them both and much besides, in the New Testament and not least in Paul. And both come together in what I have called, using a relatively infrequent word as a shorthand (as indeed do those who speak of 'apocalyptic' and 'salvation history'!), as Paul's essentially *covenant* theology. The meaning and implications of all this are explained throughout the present book.[89] My point here is simply that, at every level, the study of Pauline theology ought to effect reconciliation, even between categories that he himself would not have recognized as distinct entities.

[89] It should not be necessary once more to say that a 'covenant' theology does not mean that Paul absolutized the *Mosaic* dispensation. The point of Gal. 3 is precisely that he appeals over the head of Moses to Abraham himself.

The covenantal framework goes further in its capacity to integrate. It easily incorporates both the sense of ancient promises and turbulent intermediate histories and the sense of a sudden irruptive and unexpected (and yet predicted) new messianic moment. It thereby gives birth to, and explains the mutual relationships between, what have been separated out as 'justification' (or 'forensic') categories and 'participatory' (or 'incorporative', or even 'mystical') categories. Here we are at the familiar fault-line with Schweitzer, Sanders and now Douglas Campbell on the one side and the continuing Lutheran and other protestant exegesis on the other. Again, however, the sharp division is unsustainable, whether on historical, exegetical or theological grounds. Both 'juridical' and 'participatory' categories depend entirely, in Paul, on a fresh messianic reading of scripture. Both have to do with the creation through the gospel of the single faith-characterized family whose identity is 'in the Messiah' and who already, in their baptism, hear the verdict 'righteous' that had been pronounced over Jesus himself in his resurrection. It is as unjustifiable to caricature 'justification' as a soteriological form of Arianism, and so to dismiss it in preference for some kind of incorporative and perhaps apocalyptic system, as it would be to caricature Paul's incorporative language as a form of self-serving early catholic ecclesiasticism and so to privilege the message of free grace and justification instead. Such shadow-boxing may have considerable relevance to movements and debates in the western church over the last few hundred years, but they bear no relation to what Paul was talking about. (That sentence might itself be thought a form of shadow-boxing. The arguments in question are discussed elsewhere.[90])

In particular, there is no need to perpetuate the battle between things that call themselves the 'new perspective' or the 'old perspective' on Paul. Both were, in any case, misleading in their singularity: there are many 'new perspectives' on the loose by now, and a good many significantly different 'old perspectives' as well. Insofar as the 'new perspective' ran the risk of collapsing into 'sociology' or 'comparative religion', it of course needed to be rethought theologically to take account of, and to give the central place to, Paul's emphases on the divine act in the cross of the Messiah and its appropriation by faith. Insofar as the 'old perspective' continued to base itself on a caricature of ancient Jewish beliefs, forcing old Jewish texts as well as Paul himself to give answers to questions they were not asking while ignoring the ones they were faced with, it of course needed to be rethought theologically to take account of, and give a central place to, the Jewish and Pauline emphases on the surprising and freshly revelatory divine act in fulfilling the covenant with Abraham and completing (balancing both meanings of *telos* in Romans 10.4!) the covenant with Moses. But I hope that the discussion in this book has given a quite new set of angles of vision – perspectives, I almost said – on the false either/or of the last generation. Protests are often necessary, even if sometimes overstated. Reactions are sometimes

[90] See *Interpreters*.

appropriate, even if sometimes shrill or merely nostalgic. Fuller integration, fuller reconciliation, is always the Pauline aim, and I hope we have gone a good way towards achieving it.

Finally, I trust we have held in proper balance the historical analysis of Paul in relation to the complex worlds of his day. We have indeed gone way beyond an older, Hegelian, 'Judaism/Hellenism divide', though not in the way some others have tried to do. Indeed, I have insisted, with much recent scholarship, that the idea of those 'isms' themselves is deeply misleading: first, in describing them as quasi-religious movements; second, in suggesting or implying that they were not overlapping and interpenetrating; and particularly third, in attaching an evaluative scheme to them. The original nineteenth-century privileging of 'Hellenism' has of course naturally bred an equal and opposite reaction in a somewhat frantic philo-Judaism. Now the discussion is often reduced to postmodern and even moralistic confusion, as different schools scramble over one another to claim the last bit of high moral ground left in a rootless world, that of identifying with a supposed victim. This is no way to do history. That is why I have found myself compelled to provide a fresh multi-layered historical account in Part I, even though that account is itself of necessity short and insufficiently nuanced. And it is from within this fresh account that I believe we can see in proper perspective the true nature of Paul's theology as a fresh Messiah-and-spirit reworking of the central Jewish beliefs, and with that can reconcile the warring parties in the Pauline debates of the last generations.

I am conscious, in writing all this, that if I were to try to summarize what I have said in this chapter so far, and to do so in Pauline language, I might end up writing something like the letter to the Ephesians. I trust this will not be counted against me for unrighteousness. Even if, on other grounds, we were fully convinced that Paul did not and could not have written the letter, most agree that it was at least written by someone close to him, consciously developing and imitating him, drawing deeply on several aspects of his other writing to produce a general, overall summary of his teaching. The cosmic vision of chapter 1 frames the soteriological statement of 2.1–10 and the carefully matching ecclesiological statement of 2.11–22; these in turn give rise to the statement of Paul's aims in 3.1–13. The unity and holiness of the church, which I have argued on other grounds lies at the heart of Paul's version of the early Christian worldview, comprises 4.1—6.9, leaving only the striking statement of spiritual warfare and the concluding exhortation to prayer, to which, along with Paul's own prayer in 3.14–21, I shall come presently. The 'temple'-theme, explicit in 2.20–2, is arguably under the surface in much of the letter, already indicated by the plan for heaven and earth to come together (1.10); and the political and cultural aim of it all is explicit in 3.10, where the rulers and authorities are confronted with the new reality, an assembly composed of people from every nation. If the Paul who had already written Galatians and 1 Corinthians, and would shortly write Philippians, Colossians and Philemon, to be followed by 2 Corinthians and above all Romans, were in prison in Ephesus, and were to decide to write a circular to be sent to all the churches in the region, adopting the somewhat florid Asiatic style but incorporating much of his basic teaching in summary form, it is easy to imagine Ephesians as the result. If, having written Colossians as well, Paul were to send 'Ephesians' by the same messenger, to be delivered to the church in nearby Laodicea, he might well refer to 'Ephesians' as 'the letter to Laodicea'.[91] Like most things in ancient history, this hypothesis remains unprovable, putting six and six together and making fifteen. But twelve out of fifteen isn't bad. A lot better than imposing a nineteenth-century liberal protestantism on Paul and then declaring that Ephesians doesn't fit.

So where does this leave us? We have discussed the aims and intentions of Paul in relation both to his explicitly stated plans and his self-description as having been entrusted with the 'ministry of reconciliation'. This, I have suggested, is ultimately a temple-vision: Paul believed that the one God was establishing his presence by his spirit in all the world, and that it was his vocation to call into being, through the gospel, communities where that would be a reality. But since that reality is all about reconciliation, between God and the world, God and humans, and not least humans with one another, the large-scale cosmic vision cannot help being earthed at every point in the actual life, and the actual human tensions, of actual churches and individuals. That is where we began, with Paul's utter determination to bring Philemon and Onesimus together as brothers in the Messiah. That, in a sense, is where we should end.

We explored in chapter 1, in a bit of *sensus plenior* folly, the possibilities of seeing Philemon and Onesimus as playing the roles of History and Theology, first one way and then the other. My hope in bringing this book to a close is that I have said enough to hold Paul up as an excellent point of reference for exactly that larger reconciliation. History, and exegesis as a branch of history, have for too long been isolated from Theology, and the mutual suspicions and recriminations between the two are far-reaching and deeply damaging.

I have argued, in particular, that a *historical* study of Paul and his communities, and the worldview which Paul does his best to inculcate in his communities (Part II), necessarily required that Paul would develop what we must call his *theology*, as a quite new sort of discipline, consisting of scripture-based, communal and prayerful reflection and teaching on God, God's people and God's future. Without this theology, Paul believed, the central worldview-symbol of a united and holy church would be a far-off fantasy. Subsequent church history amply bears this out: when theology is distorted, or displaced altogether, unity and holiness are compromised, and sometimes are thought not even to matter. But to allow this theology to be detached from history, either in general or, in particular, from the actual historical exegesis of texts written by Paul and the other early Christians, is

[91] As I suggested in Wright 1986b [*Col. and Philem.*], 160, following Lightfoot and Caird.

to alter quite radically the character of that theology itself. The present book has approached the task of this greater reconciliation from the side of history, attempting to place Paul in his actual (if complex) historical setting and offering a historical/exegetical account of his writings and especially of his newly minted 'theology' itself. I hope that 'theologians', accustomed to waiting a long time to see if any theologically useful crumbs might fall from the exegete's table – to see if any good thing might come out of an exegetical Nazareth! – might find, perhaps to their surprise, that this account of Paul is theologically fruitful, both in offering a new hypothesis as to how and why the discipline of 'Christian theology' actually began and in proposing fresh lines of investigation about its central topics: christology, pneumatology, soteriology, eschatology and several other 'ologies' besides. All this is merely to say that the multiple reconciliations I have in mind point forward to all kinds of tasks, not least in relation to the still wider divisions between church and academy. The study of Paul has suffered because of these many divisions. It would be good if the process could be reversed, with the study of Paul becoming the instrument of their reconciliation.

4. Conclusion: Exalted Manna

All this suggests that we look, in conclusion, at 'What St Paul Really Did' in terms of the praxis which remained his deepest and most constant 'aim'. If we are to paraphrase Paul's very soul, to study his heart in its pilgrimage to the promised inheritance, to catch his deepest aims and intentions at the moment when, by his own account, the divine breath was groaning in him and the Heart-Searcher himself was listening to the resultant inarticulate desires, we must recognize in him a kind of tune which all things hear and fear, the deep and constant gospel-inspired activity which, in form as well as in substance, might have seemed folly to Greeks and a scandal to Jews. We have at several points noticed Paul's prayers, not simply as pious attachments to the outside of his theological or practical teaching but as their very heart. This is the place to end, and perhaps to begin.

The breathtaking renewed *Shema* of 1 Corinthians 8.6 is the obvious first example. The christologically revised prayer of the Jewish people forms the theological heart of highly practical teaching: one God, the father; one lord, Jesus the Messiah, and all things coming *from* the father and *through* the lord.[92] As Wayne Meeks saw thirty years ago, that revised monotheism – in the form, appropriately, of a prayer – stood at the heart of Paul's sociocultural vision.[93]

The fulsome doxologies belong here as well, not simply as pious accessories to arguments that are 'about' something else, but as appropriate summaries of what the argument has been about all along. The natural example

[92] See above, 661–70.

[93] See Meeks 1983, 164–70.

here is the framing of Romans 9—11 between the opening doxology of 9.5 and the closing one of 11.33–6, both of which shine their searchlights into the heart of that extraordinary passage, meeting and crossing at the centre where 'if you profess with your mouth that Jesus is lord, and believe in your heart that God raised him from the dead, you will be saved ... for there is no distinction between Jew and Greek, since the same lord is lord of all, and is rich towards all who call upon him', since 'all who call upon the name of the lord will be saved'.[94] The prayerful invocation of the *kyrios*, who in the Septuagint is clearly YHWH and in Romans 10 is clearly Jesus, is the point where the painful prayer of 9.1–5, with its closing and initially puzzling doxology, meets the exultant celebration of 11.33–6. If you believe that the one God, the world's creator, is in fact the faithful covenant God – and that is the whole point of Romans 9—11 and in a measure of everything Paul said and wrote – then the most appropriate way to write about this God is not in abstract discourse but in prayer and praise. Here Paul lets down the Christian plummet, sounding heaven and earth, bringing together the constant prayer life of ancient Israel with the renewed prayer life of the Messiah's people, forming in his writing as well as in his church-planting a temple in which heaven appears in the ordinary world and humans made of dust are promised their well-dressed new life.

The same could be said of Ephesians 3.14–21, which delves deep into the gospel in which the divine *love* is the main theme and comes up with one of the most sustained and extraordinary invocations ever written:

> Because of this, I am kneeling down before the father, the one who gives the name of 'family' to every family that there is, in heaven and on earth. My prayer is this: that he will lay out all the riches of his glory to give you strength and power, through his spirit, in your inner being; that the Messiah may make his home in your hearts, through faith; that love may be your root, your firm foundation; and that you may be strong enough (with all God's holy ones) to grasp the breadth and length and height and depth, and to know the Messiah's love – though actually it's so deep that nobody can really know it! So may God fill you with all his fullness.
>
> So: to the one who is capable of doing far, far more than we can ask or imagine, granted the power which is working in us – to him be glory, in the church, and in the Messiah Jesus, to all generations, and to the ages of ages! Amen.

This is temple-language; it is (incipiently) trinitarian language; it is cosmic language; it is the language of faith and hope, and above all of love. It draws together monotheism, election and eschatology. It forms the beating heart of the united and holy community which is, for Paul, the central worldview-symbol, the sign to the powers that Jesus is lord (3.10–11). This, in the gentle language of later poetry, is softness, and peace, and joy, and love, and bliss. When Paul tells his hearers to 'pray constantly', and says that he is doing so himself, it is this sort of constant celebration and intercession he seems to have in mind, reflecting of course the regular sacrifice and incense

[94] Rom. 10.9, 12f.

offered in the Temple itself.[95] As with so much Jewish prayer, it is the prayer of hope offered amid the ruins of the present: Paul in prison, struggling as in Ephesians 6.10–20 with the 'principalities and powers', aware as ever of 'battles outside and fears inside',[96] nevertheless reaches out in a prayer which expresses and encapsulates the centre of his richest thought. The inevitable sadness and frustration of the 'not yet', well known to all who work in the church, is always to be balanced, in prayer and hope, with the 'already', the 'now' of the gospel. For that to happen in prayer, there must be theology; for it to happen in theology, there must be prayer.

Not just any prayer, and not just any theology. At the heart of it all, shaping thought and firing devotion, there is 'the love of God in the Messiah, Jesus our lord' (Romans 8.39). If the crucified and risen Messiah himself was, astonishingly, the place where heaven and earth met, the true temple, the start of the new creation; if those indwelt by the spirit were themselves enabled to keep the *Shema*, responding to the sovereign and self-giving love of God by loving him from the heart in return, fulfilling the ancient vision of Deuteronomy at the same time as discovering a depth of heaven-and-earth relation at which the most discerning of the pagan philosophers could only guess; if these things were so, then the glad celebration of that love provided the deepest 'aim' of all, the central act of worship which for Paul had long ceased to be a matter of choice or decision and had become a matter of mindset, the deepest habit of the heart. 'The Son of God loved me and gave himself for me.' 'The Messiah's love makes us press on.' 'The love of God has been poured out into our hearts through the holy spirit who has been given to us.' 'God demonstrates his own love for us: the Messiah died for us while we were still sinners.' 'Who shall separate us from the Messiah's love?' 'Neither death nor life ... nor any other creature will be able to separate us from the love of God in the Messiah, Jesus our lord.'[97] The past is redeemed, as well as the present and the future; this messianic moment has to do neither with 'progress' nor with 'doom'. New creation is here, to be glimpsed in praise and intercession, worked for in apostolic vocation, and above all known in love.

This is the language of prayer, and it is therefore also the language of theology: of the new thing we call 'Christian theology' which Paul fashioned out of ancient Jewish elements glimpsed anew through Messiah and spirit. Old praise dies unless you feed it, said Herbert. The renewed praise of Paul's doxologies takes its place at the historically situated and theologically explosive fusion of worlds where Paul stood in the middle, between Athens and Jerusalem, between the kingdom of God and the kingdoms of the world, between Philemon and Onesimus, between history and theology, between exegesis and the life of the church, between heaven and earth. Collection at a middle point. This is language forged and fashioned in the shape of the

[95] 1 Thess. 5.17; cf. Rom. 1.9; 1 Thess. 1.3; 2.13; similarly, Rom. 12.12; Eph. 6.18; Phil. 4.6; Col. 4.2. On prayer as the equivalent of Temple-worship cf. e.g. Ps. 141.2; Dan. 9.21.

[96] 2 Cor. 7.5.

[97] Gal. 2.20; 2 Cor. 5.14; Rom. 5.5, 8; 8.35, 39.

cross, *both* as the decisive apocalyptic event in which the covenant faithfulness of the creator God was unveiled once and for all *and* as the character-shaping truth which was now carved into world history and into the hearts and lives of all those 'in the Messiah', all those with Messiah-faith. For Paul, prayer and theology met in his personal history, as in the once-for-all history of the crucified and risen Messiah. Paul's 'aims', his apostolic vocation, modelled the faithfulness of God. Concentred and gathered. Prayer became theology, theology prayer. Something understood.

FULL BIBLIOGRAPHY OF WORKS REFERRED TO IN PARTS I–IV

Abbreviations

1. Stylistic Shorthands

ad fin.	at the end
ad loc.	at the [relevant] place
alt.	altered
b.	born
bib./bibliog.	bibliography
bk.	book
c.	circa
cf.	confer
ch(s).	chapter(s)
C*n*.	*nth* century
com.	commentary
contra	against
cp.	compare
d.	died
ed(s).	edited by
edn(s).	edition(s)
e.g.	for example
esp.	especially
et al.	and others
etc.	et cetera
f.	and the following (verse, page or line)
fl.	flourished
foll.	following
fr./frag.	fragment(s)
Gk.	Greek
Heb.	Hebrew
ib./ibid.	the same place
id./idem	the same person
introd.	introduction/introduced by
ital.	italics
loc. cit.	in the place cited
mg.	margin
MS(S)	manuscript(s)

n.	(foot/end)note
nb.	note well
n.d.	no date
orig.	original/originally
pace	with all due respect to different opinion
par(r).	parallel(s) (in the synoptic tradition)
passim	throughout
pt.	part.
pub.	published
qu.	quoting/quoted
R.	Rabbi
ref(s).	reference(s)
rev.	revision/revised by
sc.	presumably
sic	thus (acknowledging an error in original)
subsequ.	subsequent
s.v(v).	under the word(s)
tr.	translation/translated by
v(v).	verse(s)
vol(s).	volume(s).

2. Primary Sources

ADPB	*The Authorised Daily Prayer Book of the United Hebrew Congregations of the British Commonwealth of Nations*, tr. S. Singer. New edn. London: Eyre & Spottiswoode, 1962.
Ael. Arist.	Aelius Aristides (*Orat.=Oration*)
Aesch.	Aeschylus (*Ag.=Agamemnon*; *Eumen.=Eumenides*; *Pers.=Persians*)
ANF	*The Ante-Nicene Fathers*, ed. A. Roberts, J. Donaldson et al. 10 vols. Buffalo: The Christian Literature Publishing Company, 1887.
Apuleius	Apuleius (*Met.=Metamorphoses*)
Arist.	Aristotle (*De An.=De Anima*; *Hist. An.=Historia Animalium*; *Nic. Eth. =Nichomachean Ethics*; *Pol.=Politics; Pr.=Problems)*
Aristides	Aristides (*Apol.=Apology*)
Aristoph.	Aristophanes (*Birds=The Birds*; *Ecclesiaz.=Ecclesiazousae*; *Frogs=The Frogs*)
Aug.	Augustine (*Civ. Dei=City of God*)
Aulus Gellius	Aulus Gellius (*Noct. Att.=Noctes Atticae*)
AV	Authorized ['King James'] Version
Calpurnius Siculus	Calpurnius Siculus (*Ecl.=Eclogues*)
Cic.	Cicero (*Amic.=De Amicitia; Att.=Epistulae ad Atticum; De Div.=De Divinatione; De Leg.=De Legibus; De Nat. De.=De Natura Deorum; Ends=De Finibus Bonorum et Malorum; Har. Resp.=De Haruspicum Responsis; Part. Or.=De Partitionibus Oratoriae; Phil.=Philippicae*)
Clem.	Clement of Alexandria (*Strom.=Stromata*)

Danby	H. Danby, *The Mishnah, Translated from the Hebrew with Introduction and Brief Explanatory Notes*. Oxford: Oxford University Press, 1933.
Diels, *Vorsokr.*	H. A. Diels, *Die Fragmente der Vorsokratiker*. 6th edn. 3 vols. Hildesheim: Weidmann, 1951–2 [1903].
Digest	*The Digest of Justinian*. 4 vols., ed. A. Watson. Philadelphia: University of Pennsylvania Press, 1985.
Dio Cassius	Dio Cassius (*Hist.=Historia Romana*)
Dio Chrys.	Dio Chrysostom (*Orat.=Oration*)
Diod. Sic.	Diodorus Siculus
Diog. Laert.	Diogenes Laertius (*Lives/Vit. Philos.=Lives and Opinions of Eminent Philosophers*)
Dionysius of Halicarnassus	(*Ant. Rom.=Roman Antiquities*)
Ep. Diog.	*Epistula ad Diognetum*
Epict.	Epictetus (*Disc.=Discourses*; *Ench.=Encheiridion*)
Eurip.	Euripides (*Hippol.=Hippolytus*)
EV(V)	English Version(s) of the Bible
Gal.	Galen (*Anim. Pass.=Passions of the Soul*)
GM/T	F. García Martínez and E. J. C. Tigchelaar, *The Dead Sea Scrolls Study Edition*. 2 vols. Leiden: Brill, 1997–8.
Hdt.	Herodotus
Heraclit.	Heraclitus (presocratic philosopher) (*Ep.=Epistles*)
Hermog.	Hermogenes (*Inv.=On Finding*)
Hesiod	Hesiod (*Op.=Works and Days*)
Hippolytus	Hippolytus (*Ref. Omn. Haer.=Refutation of All Heresies*)
Homer	Homer (*Il.=Iliad*; *Od.=Odyssey*)
Hor.	Horace (*Ep.=Epistles*; *Epod.=Epodes*; *Carm.=Carmen Saeculare*; *Od. =Odes*; *Sat.=Satires*)
Ign.	Ignatius of Antioch (*Eph.=To the Ephesians*)
Inscr. Cos.	*The Inscriptions of Cos*, ed. W. R. Paton and E. L. Hicks. Oxford: Oxford University Press, 1891.
Iren.	Irenaeus (*Adv. Haer.=Adversus Haereseis*)
Jer.	Jerome (*De Vir. Ill.=De Viris Illustribus*)
Jos.	Josephus (*Ap.=Against Apion*; *War=The Jewish War*; *Ant.=Jewish Antiquities*)
JosAs	*Joseph and Aseneth*
Just.	Justin Martyr (*Apol.=Apology*; *Dial.=Dialogue with Trypho*)
Juv.	Juvenal (*Sat.=Satires*)
LAB	*Liber Antiquitatum Biblicarum* (=Pseudo-Philo)
Livy	T. Livy, *History of Rome* (*Praef.*='Preface')
Lucan	Lucan (*Bell. Civ.=Bellum Civile*)
Lucr.	Lucretius (*De Re. Nat.=De Rerum Natura*)
LW	*Luther's Works*. Minneapolis: Fortress; St Louis: Concordia. 1957– .
LXX	Septuagint version of the Old Testament
Macrobius	Macrobius (*Sat.=Saturnalia*)
Martial	Martial (*Epig.=Epigrams*)
MT	Masoretic Text (of the Hebrew Bible)

Mt. Pol.	*Martyrdom of Polycarp*
NH	Nag Hammadi
NPNF	*The Nicene and Post-Nicene Fathers*, ed. P. Schaff et al. 1st series: 14 vols; 2nd series: 13 vols. Buffalo: The Christian Literature Publishing Company, 1886–98.
NT	New Testament
NTA	*New Testament Apocrypha*, ed. E. Hennecke and W. Schneemelcher. 2 vols. London: SCM Press, 1963–5 [1959–64].
OGI	*Orientis Graeci Inscriptiones Selectae*, ed. W. Dittenberger. 2 vols. Hildesheim: Olms, 1960 [orig.: Leipzig: Hirzel, 1903–5].
Origen	Origen (*De Princ.=De Principiis*)
OT	Old Testament
Ovid	Ovid (*(Ep. ex) Pont.=Epistulae ex Ponto*; *Fast.=Fasti*; *Met.= Metamorphoses*; *Trist.=Tristia*)
Paus.	Pausanias (*Descr. Graec.=Description of Greece*)
Philo	Philo of Alexandria (*(De) Spec. Leg.=De Specialibus Legibus; Dec.=De Decalogo; Flacc.=In Flaccum; Fug.=De Profugis (or, De Fuga et Inventione); Leg.=Legum Allegoriae; (Migr.) Abr.=De Migratione Abrahami; De Mut. Nom.=De Mutatione Nominum; Omn. Prob. Lib.=Quod omnis probus liber sit; (De) Praem.=De Praemiis et Poenis; Post.=De posteritate Caini; Quaest. Gen.=Quaestiones in Genesin; Quis rer.=Quis rerum; (De) Somn.=De Somniis; Spec.=De Specialibus Legibus; Virt.=De Virtutibus; Vit. Cont.=De Vita Contemplativa; Vit. Mos.=De Vita Mosis*)
Philostr.	Philostratus (*Apoll.=Life of Apollonius of Tyana*; *VS=Vitae Sophistarum*)
Pind.	Pindar (*Ol.=Olympian Odes*; *Pyth.=Pythian Odes*)
Plato	Plato (*Apol.=Apology*; *Crat.=Cratylus*; *Phaedr.=Phaedrus*; *Protag.=Protagoras; Rep.=Republic*; *Tim.=Timaeus*)
Pliny	Pliny the Elder (*NH=Natural History*)
Pliny	Pliny the Younger (*Ep.=Epistulae*)
Plut.	Plutarch (*Alex.=Life of Alexander*; *Ant.=Life of Antony*; *Comm. Not.=de Communibus Notitiis*; *Mor.=Moralia*; *Peric.=Life of Pericles*; *Them.=Themistocles*; *Tranq.=De Tranquillitate Animi*)
Porphyry	Porphyry (*De Antr. Nymph.=De Antro Nympharum*)
Ps-Phil.	Pseudo-Philo, *Liber Antiquitatum Biblicarum*
RG/Res Gest.	*Res Gestae Divi Augusti*
SB	H. L. Strack and P. Billerbeck, *Kommentar zum Neuen Testament aus Talmud und Midrasch*. 6 vols. Munich: C. H. Beck, 1926–56.
Sen.	Seneca the Younger (*Ben.=De Beneficiis; Clem.=De Clementia; De Prov.=De Providentia; Ep.=Epistles; Ep. Mor.=Moral Epistles; N.Q.=Naturales Quaestiones*)
Suet.	Suetonius (*Aug.=Augustus; Calig.=Caligula; Claud.=Claudius; Dom. =Domitian; Gal.=Galba; Iul.=Julius Caesar; Ner.=Nero; Tib.=Tiberius; Vesp.=Vespasian*)
Tac.	Tacitus (*Agric.=Agricola*; *Ann.=Annals*; *Dial.=Dialogue on Oratory*; *Hist. =Histories*)
Tert.	Tertullian (*Ad Scap.=Ad Scapulam; Apol.=Apology; De Anim.=De Anima; Scorp.=Scorpiace*)

Val. Max.	Valerius Maximus
Vell. Pat.	Velleius Paterculus (*Hist.=Compendium of Roman History*)
Virg.	Virgil (*Aen.=Aeneid*; *Ec.=Eclogues*; *Georg.=Georgics*)
Vitr.	Vitruvius

3. Secondary Sources, etc.

AB	Anchor Bible
ABD	*Anchor Bible Dictionary*, ed. D. N. Freedman. 6 vols. New York: Doubleday, 1992.
ABRL	Anchor Bible Reference Library
AGJU	*Arbeiten zur Geschichte des antiken Judentums und des Urchristentums*
BDAG	*A Greek–English Lexicon of the New Testament and Other Early Christian Literature*. 3rd edn., rev. and ed. Frederick W. Danker, based on W. Bauer's *Griechisch–Deutsch Wörterbuch*, 6th edn., and on previous English edns. by W. F. Arndt, F. W. Gingrich, and F. W. Danker. Chicago and London: University of Chicago Press, 2000 [1957].
CD	Karl Barth, *Church Dogmatics* [ET of *KD*]. Edinburgh: T&T Clark, 1936–69.
DJD	*Discoveries in the Judaean Desert*
ESV	English Standard Version
Exp. T.	*Expository Times*
FS	Festschrift
HGBK	N. T. Wright, *How God Became King: The Forgotten Story of the Gospels*. San Francisco: HarperOne; London: SPCK, 2012.
IBC	Interpretation: A Bible Commentary for Teaching and Preaching
ICC	International Critical Commentary
IGR	*Inscriptiones Graecae ad res Romanas pertinentes*, ed. R. Cagnat et al. Paris, 1911–27.
ILS	*Inscriptiones Latinae Selectae*, ed. H. Dessau. Berolini, 1892–1916.
JB	Jerusalem Bible
JSJSup	Journal for the Study of Judaism Supplements
JSNTSup	Journal for the Study of the New Testament Supplements
JSOTSup	Journal for the Study of the Old Testament Supplements
JSPL	*Journal for the Study of Paul and His Letters*
JVG	N. T. Wright, *Jesus and the Victory of God* (vol. 2 of Christian Origins and the Question of God). London: SPCK; Minneapolis: Fortress, 1996.
KD	Karl Barth, *Kirchliche Dogmatik*
KJV	King James ['Authorized'] Version
KNT	N. T. Wright, *The Kingdom New Testament*. San Francisco: HarperOne, 2011 [US edn. of *NTE*].
KRS	G. S. Kirk, J. E. Raven and M. Schofield, eds., *The Presocratic Philosophers: A Critical History with a Selection of Texts*. 2nd edn. Cambridge: Cambridge University Press, 2007 [1957].
LCL	Loeb Classical Library (various publishers, currently Cambridge, MA and London: Harvard University Press).

LS	C. T. Lewis and C. Short, *A Latin Dictionary*. Oxford: Clarendon Press, 1996 [1879].
LSJ	H. G. Liddell and R. Scott, *A Greek–English Lexicon*, 9th edn. by H. S. Jones and R. McKenzie, with suppl. by P. G. W. Glare and A. A. Thompson. Oxford: Oxford University Press, 1996 [1843].
NA (25)	Nestle-Aland *Novum Testamentum Graece* (25th edn.)
NEB	New English Bible
NIB	*The New Interpreter's Bible*. 12 vols. Nashville: Abingdon, 1994–2002.
NIV	New International Version
NJB	New Jerusalem Bible
NovTSup	Novum Testamentum Supplements
NP	'new perspective' (on Paul)
NRSV	New Revised Standard Version
NTE	N. T. Wright *The New Testament for Everyone.* London: SPCK, 2011 [UK edn. of *KNT*].
NTPG	N. T. Wright, *The New Testament and the People of God* (vol. 1 of Christian Origins and the Question of God.). London: SPCK; Minneapolis: Fortress, 1992.
OCD	*The Oxford Classical Dictionary*, eds. S. Hornblower and A. Spawforth. 3rd edn. Oxford: Oxford University Press, 1996.
ODCC	*The Oxford Dictionary of the Christian Church*, ed. E. A. Livingstone. 3rd edn. Oxford: Oxford University Press, 1997.
OTP	*The Old Testament Pseudepigrapha*, 2 vols., ed. J. H. Charlesworth. New York: Doubleday, 1983, 1985.
REB	Revised English Bible
RSG	N. T. Wright, *The Resurrection of the Son of God* (vol. 3 of Christian Origins and the Question of God). London: SPCK; Minneapolis: Fortress, 2003.
RSV	Revised Standard Version
RV	Revised Version
SB	H. L. Strack and P. Billerbeck, *Kommentar zum Neuen Testament aus Talmud und Midrasch*. 6 vols. Munich: C. H. Beck, 1926–56.
SBL	Society of Biblical Literature
SVF	*Stoicorum Veterum Fragmenta*, ed. H. von Arnim. 4 vols. Leipzig: Teubner, 1903–24.
TDNT	*Theological Dictionary of the New Testament*, ed. G. Kittel and G. Friedrich. 10 vols. Grand Rapids: Eerdmans, 1964–76.
WUNT	Wissenschaftliche Untersuchungen zum Neuen Testament

A

PRIMARY SOURCES

1. Bible

Biblia Hebraica Stuttgartensia, ed. K. Elliger and W. Rudolph. 5th edn. Stuttgart: Deutsche Bibelgesellschaft, 1997 [1967].

Septuaginta: Id est Vetus Testamentum Graece iuxta LXX interpres, ed. A. Rahlfs. 2 vols. in 1. Stuttgart: Deutsche Bibelgesellschaft, 1979 [1935].

Novum Testamentum Graece, ed. B. Aland, K. Aland, J. Karavidopoulos, C. M. Martini, and B. M. Metzger. 27th edn., revised. Stuttgart: Deutsche Bibelgesellschaft, 1993 [1898].

The Holy Bible with the Books Called Apocrypha: The Revised Version with the Revised Marginal References. Oxford: Oxford University Press, n.d. [1898].

The Holy Bible, Containing the Old and New Testaments with the Apocryphal/Deutero~canonical Books: New Revised Standard Version. New York and Oxford: Oxford University Press, 1989.

The New Testament for Everyone. Tr. Tom Wright. London: SPCK, 2011 (US edn.: *The Kingdom New Testament.* San Francisco: HarperOne).

2. Other Jewish Texts

The Mishnah, Translated from the Hebrew with Introduction and Brief Explanatory Notes, ed. and tr. H. Danby. Oxford: Oxford University Press, 1933.

The Babylonian Talmud, ed. I. Epstein. 36 vols. London: Soncino, 1935–8.

The Minor Tractates of the Talmud, ed. A. Cohen. 2 vols. London: Soncino, 1965.

Midrash Rabbah, tr. and ed. H. Freedman and M. Simon. 2nd edn. 10 vols. London: Soncino, 1951 [1939].

Pesikta Rabbati, ed. M. Friedman. Vienna: Kaiser, 1880.

Pirḳê de Rabbi Eliezer, tr. and ed. Gerald Friedlander. New York: Hermon Press, 1965.

(For other rabbinic literature, and details of Targumim, etc., cf. Schürer 1.68–118.)

The Old Testament Pseudepigrapha, ed. J. H. Charlesworth. 2 vols. Garden City, NY: Doubleday, 1983–5.

The Apocryphal Old Testament, ed. H. F. D. Sparks. Oxford: Clarendon Press, 1984.

The Authorised Daily Prayer Book of the United Hebrew Congregations of the British Commonwealth of Nations, tr. S. Singer. New edn. London: Eyre & Spottiswoode, 1962.

Josephus: *Works*, ed. H. St. J. Thackeray, R. Marcus, A. Wikgren and L. H. Feldman. 9 vols. LCL, 1929–65.

Philo: *Works*, ed. F. H. Colson, G. H. Whitaker, J. W. Earp and R. Marcus. 12 vols. LCL, 1929–53.

Qumran: *Discoveries in the Judaean Desert*, ed. D. Barthélemy et al. 39 vols. Oxford: Clarendon Press, 1955–2002.

——, *Die Texte aus Qumran*, ed. E. Lohse. Darmstadt: Wissenschaftliche Buchgesellschaft, 1964.

——, *The Dead Sea Scrolls. Hebrew, Aramaic, and Greek Texts with English Translations*, ed. J. H. Charlesworth. 10 vols. Tübingen: Mohr; Louisville: Westminster John Knox Press, 1994–.

——, tr.: F. García Martínez, *The Dead Sea Scrolls Translated: The Qumran Texts in English*. Leiden: Brill, 1994.

——, tr.: G. Vermes, *The Dead Sea Scrolls in English*. 4th edn. London: Penguin, 1995 [1962].

3. Other Early Christian and Related Texts

Apostolic Fathers: *The Apostolic Fathers*, ed. and tr. J. B. Lightfoot. 5 vols. London: Macmillan, 1889–90. Reprint: Peabody, MA: Hendrickson, 1989.

——, *The Apostolic Fathers*, ed. and tr. Kirsopp Lake. 2 vols. LCL, 1965.

——, *Early Christian Writings*, tr. Maxwell Staniforth, introd. and ed. A. Louth. London: Penguin, 1987 [1968].

——, *The Apostolic Fathers*, 2nd edn., tr. J. B. Lightfoot and J. R. Harmer, ed. and rev. Michael W. Holmes. Leicester: Apollos; Grand Rapids, MI: Baker, 1989.

Aristides, *Apol.*: *The Apology of Aristides on Behalf of the Christians. From a Syriac Ms Preserved on Mount Sinai*, ed. with introd. and tr. with an appendix containing the main portion of the original Greek text, by J. A. Robinson. Texts and Studies I.i. 2nd edn. Cambridge: Cambridge University Press, 1893.

Augustine, *City of God: De Civitate Dei Libri XXII*, ed. B. Dombart and A. Kalb. Stuttgart: Teubner, 1981.

——, tr. in *NPNF*, 1st ser., 2.1–511.

——, *City of God*, tr. H. Bettenson. Harmondsworth: Penguin, 1972.

Hippolytus: in *ANF* 5.9–259.

Irenaeus: in *ANF* 1.309–578.

Jerome, *Liber de Viris Illustribus*, in *PL* 23.602–719.

Justin: in *ANF* 1.159–306.

——, *The Writings of Justin Martyr and Athenagoras*, tr. M. Dods, G. Reith, and B. P. Pratten. Edinburgh: T&T Clark, 1870.

——, *St. Justin Martyr: The First and Second Apologies*, tr. and introd. L. W. Barnard. New York and Mahwah, NJ: Paulist Press, 1997.

Nag Hammadi texts: *The Nag Hammadi Library in English*, ed. J. M. Robinson. Leiden: Brill; San Francisco: Harper & Row, 1977.

New Testament Apocrypha, ed. E. Hennecke and W. Schneemelcher. 2 vols. London: SCM Press; Philadelphia: Westminster Press, 1963–5 [1959–64].

——, *The Apocryphal New Testament: A Collection of Apocryphal Christian Literature in an English Translation Based on M. R. James*, ed. J. K. Elliott. Oxford: Clarendon Press, 1993.

Origen: in *ANF* 4.223–669.

Tertullian: in *ANF* 3.1—4.166.

——, *Apology* and *De Spectaculis*, tr. T. R. Glover, with Minucius Felix, *Octavius*, tr. G. H. Rendall. LCL, 1931.

4. Pagan Texts

Aelius Aristides, *Panathenaic Oration*, etc., ed. C. A. Behr. 4 vols. LCL, 1973–86.

Aeschylus, tr. and ed. H. Weir Smyth and H. Lloyd-Jones. 2 vols. LCL, 1956–7 [1922–6].

Apuleius: *Apuleius, the Golden Ass, or Metamorphoses*, tr. and ed. E. J. Kenney. London: Penguin, 1998.

Aristophanes, ed. J. Henderson. 4 vols. LCL, 1998–2002.

Aristotle, *De Anima*: *On the Soul*, ed. W. S. Hett. LCL, 1936.

——, *Nicomachean Ethics*, ed. H. Rackham. LCL, 1926.

——, *The Ethics of Aristotle*, tr. J. A. K. Thomson. Harmondsworth: Penguin, 1955.

——, *Historia Animalium*, ed. A. L. Peck and D. M. Balme. 3 vols. LCL, 1965–91.

——, *Politics*, ed. H. Rackham. LCL, 1932.

——, *Problems*, tr. R. Mayhew. 2 vols. LCL, 2011.

——, *The Complete Works of Aristotle*, ed. J. Barnes. 2 vols. Princeton: Princeton University Press, 1984.

Augustus, *see under* Velleius Paterculus.

Callimachus, *Hymns and Epigrams*, tr. G. R. Mair. LCL, 1921.

Cassius Dio: see Dio Cassius.

Cicero, *De Finibus Bonorum et Malorum*, tr. H. Rackham. LCL, 1914.

——, *De Natura Deorum*: *Cicero: The Nature of the Gods*, tr. H. C. P. McGregor. London: Penguin, 1972.

——, *De Natura Deorum* and *Academica*, ed. H. Rackham. LCL, 1933.

——, *De Re Publica, De Legibus*, tr. C. W. Keyes. LCL, 1928.

——, *Tusculan Disputations*, tr. J. E. King. LCL, 1927.

——, *Epistulae ad Atticum*, tr. D. R. Shackleton Bailey. 4 vols. LCL, 1999.

——, *De Amicitia* and *De Diviniatione*, tr. W. A. Falconer. LCL, 1923.

——, *Philippicae*, tr. D. R. Shackleton Bailey. 2 vols. LCL, 2010.

——, *De Haruspicum Responsis*, tr. N. H. Watts. LCL, 1923.

Dio Cassius: *Dio's Roman History*, tr. H. B. Foster and E. Cary. 9 vols. LCL, 1914–27.

Diodorus Siculus, tr. C. H. Oldfather et al. 10 vols. LCL, 1933–67.

Diogenes Laertius, *Lives of Eminent Philosophers*, tr. R. D. Hicks. 2 vols. LCL, 1925.

Dionysius of Halicarnassus, *Roman Antiquities*, tr. E. Spelman and E. Cary. 7 vols. LCL, 1937–50.

Epictetus: *The Discourses as Reported by Arrian, the Manual, and Fragments*, ed. and tr. W. A. Oldfather. 2 vols. LCL, 1978–9.

Epicurus: *Epicurea*, ed. H. Usener. Dubuque, Iowa: Reprint Library, n.d. [1887].

——, *Letters, Principal Doctrines, and Vatican Sayings*, tr. and ed. R. M. Geer. Indianapolis: Bobbs-Merrill, 1964.

Euripides: *Euripides*, tr. and ed. D. Kovacs. 5 vols. LCL, 1994–2002.

Galen, *Animae Passiones*, in *Galeni Scripta Minora* I, ed. J. Marquardt. Leipzig: Teubner, 1884.

——, *On the Usefulness of the Parts of the Body*, tr. M. T. May. Ithaca: Cornell University Press, 1968.

Heraclitus (presocratic philosopher): in Diels, *Vorsokr.* 1.67.
Hermogenes, *On Finding*, ed. H. Rabe. Leipzig: Teubner, 1913.
Herodotus, *The Persian Wars*, tr. A. D. Godley. 4 vols. LCL, 1989.
Hesiod, *Works and Days*, ed. with Prolegomena and Commentary by M. L. West. Oxford: Clarendon Press, 1978.
Homer, *The Iliad*, tr. A. T. Murray, rev. W. F. Wyatt. 2 vols. LCL, 1999 [1924–5].
——, *The Odyssey*, tr. A. T. Murray, rev. G. E. Dimock, 2 vols. LCL, 1995 [1919].
Horace: *The Satires of Horace*, ed. A. Palmer. London: Macmillan, 1885.
——, *Horace: Satires and Epistles; Perseus: Satires*, tr. and ed. N. Rudd. Rev. edn. London: Penguin, 1987 [1973].
——, S. Lyons, *Horace's Odes and the Mystery of Do-Re-Mi.* Oxford: Oxbow Books, 2007.
——, *Odes and Epodes*, tr. and ed. N. Rudd. LCL, 2004.
——, *Satires, Epistles, Ars Poetica*, tr. H. R. Fairclough. LCL, 1926.
Hyginus: *Fables*, ed. and tr. J.-Y. Boriaud. Paris: Les Belles Lettres, 1997.
Juvenal: *Juvenal and Persius*, tr. G. G. Ramsay. LCL, 1920.
——, *Juvenal. The Sixteen Satires*, tr. and introd. P. Green. London: Penguin Books, 1974 [1967].
Livy, *History of Rome*, tr. A. C. Schlesinger et al. 14 vols. LCL, 1919–59.
Lucan: *The Civil War*, tr. J. D. Duff. LCL, 1928.
Lucretius, *De Rerum Natura*, tr. W. H. D. Rouse, rev. M. F. Smith. LCL, 1992 [1975].
Marcus Aurelius: *Marcus Aurelius*, ed. and tr. C. R. Haines. LCL, rev. edn. 1930 [1916]
Martial: *The Epigrams*, tr. J. Michie. London: Penguin, 1978 [1973].
——. *Epigrams*, tr. D. R. Shackleton Bailey. 2 vols. LCL, 1993.
Ovid, *Fasti*, tr. J. G. Frazer. LCL, 1931.
——, *Metamorphoses*, tr. F. J. Miller. 2 vols. LCL, 1916.
——, *Tristia* and *Ex Ponto*, tr. A. L. Wheeler. LCL, 1924.
Pausanias, *Description of Greece*, tr. and ed. W. Jones. 5 vols. LCL, 1918–35.
Philostratus, *The Life of Apollonius of Tyana*, tr. F. C. Conybeare. 2 vols. LCL, 1912.
——, *Lives of the Sophists*, tr. W. C. Wright. LCL, 1921.
Pindar, *Odes*, etc., tr. J. Sandys. LCL, 1938.
Placita Philosophorum (Pseudo-Plutarch), ed. H. Diels, *Doxographi Graeci*, Berlin 1879, p. 273.
Plato, *Cratylus, Parmenides, Greater Hippias, Lesser Hippias*, ed. H. N. Fowler. LCL, 1926.
——, *Euthyphro, Apology, Crito, Phaedo, Phaedrus*, tr. H. N. Fowler. LCL, 1914.
——, *Laches, Protagoras, Meno, Euthydemus*, ed. W. R. M. Lamb. LCL, 1924.
——, *Laws*, tr. R. G. Bury. 2 vols. LCL, 1926.
——, *Lysis, Symposium, Gorgias*, tr. W. R. M. Lamb. LCL, 1925.
——, *Politicus, Philebus, Ion*, tr. H. N. Fowler and W. R. M. Lamb. LCL, 1925.
——, *Platonis Res Publica*, tr. J. Burnet. Oxford: Clarendon Press, 1902.
——, *The Republic*, tr. P. Shorey. LCL, 1935.
——, *Timaeus, Critias, Cleitophon, Menexenus, Epistles*, tr. R. G. Bury. LCL, 1929.
——, *The Collected Dialogues, Including the Letters*, ed. E. Hamilton and H. Cairns. Princeton, NJ: Princeton University Press, 1963 [1961].
Pliny the Elder, *Natural History*, tr. H. Rackham et al. 10 vols. LCL, 1938–62.
Pliny the Younger: *C. Plini Caecili Secundi Epistularum Libri Decem*, ed. R. A. B. Mynors. Oxford: Oxford University Press, 1963.
——, *The Letters of the Younger Pliny*, tr. and introd. B. Radice. London: Penguin, 1963.
Plutarch, *Lives*, tr. B. Perrin. 11 vols. LCL, 1914–26.

——, *Moralia*, tr. F. C. Babbitt et al. 16 vols. LCL, 1927–69.

Polybius, *Histories*, tr. W. R. Paton et al. 6 vols. LCL, 1922–7.

Porphyry, *De Antro Nympharum*, ed. A. Nauck. Leipzig: Teubner, 1886.

Quintilian, *Institutio Oratoria*, tr. H. E. Butler. 4 vols. LCL, 1920–2.

Seneca, *Apocolocyntosis* (with Petronius, *Satyricon*), tr. W. H. D. Rouse and E. H. Warmington. LCL, 1969 [1913].

——, *Apocolocyntosis*, ed. P. T. Eden. Cambridge: Cambridge University Press, 1984.

——, *Moral Essays*, tr. J. W. Basore. 3 vols. LCL, 1928–35.

——, *Epistulae Morales*, tr. R. M. Gummere. 3 vols. LCL, 1917–25.

Suetonius: *C. Suetoni Tranquili Opera*, vol. 1. *De Vita Caesarum Libri VIII*. Ed. M. Ihm. Stuttgart: Teubner, 1978 [1908].

——, *Suetonius*, tr. J. C. Rolfe. 2nd edn. 2 vols. LCL, 1997–8 [1913–14].

——, *Suetonius. The Twelve Caesars*, tr. R. Graves. London: Penguin, 1957.

Tacitus, *Annals*: *Cornelii Taciti Annalium ab Excessu Divi Augusti Libri*, ed. C. D. Fisher. Oxford: Clarendon Press, 1906.

——, *Tacitus. The Annals of Imperial Rome*, tr. M. Grant. London: Penguin, 1956.

——, *Histories*: *Cornelii Taciti Historiarum Libri*, ed. C. D. Fisher. Oxford: Clarendon Press, n.d.

——, *Tacitus. The Histories*, tr. K. Wellesley. London: Penguin, 1964.

——, *Agricola, Germania, Dialogus*, tr. M. Hutton and W. Peterson; rev. R. M. Ogilvie, E. H. Warmington, and M. Winterbottom. LCL, 1970 [1914].

——, *Histories and Annals*, tr. C. H. Moore and J. Jackson. 4 vols. LCL, 1925–37.

Valerius Maximus, *Memorable Doings and Sayings*, tr. D. R. Shackleton Bailey. LCL, 2000.

Velleius Paterculus, *Compendium of Roman History*, and the *Res Gestae Divi Augusti*, tr. F. W. Shipley. LCL, 1924.

Virgil, *Eclogues, Georgics, Aeneid and the Minor Poems*, tr. H. R. Fairclough, rev. G. P. Goold. 2 vols. LCL, 1999 [1916–18].

Vitruvius, *On Architecture*, tr. F. Granger. 2 vols. LCL, 1931–4.

B

SECONDARY LITERATURE

Ageson, J. W. 1986. 'Scripture and Structure in the Development of the Argument in Romans 9—11.' *Catholic Biblical Quarterly* 48:265–89.

Achtemeier, P. J. 1996. 'The Continuing Quest for Coherence in St. Paul: An Experiment in Thought.' Pp. 132–45 in *Theology and Ethics in Paul and His Interpreters: Essays in Honor of Victor Paul Furnish*, eds. E. H. Lovering and J. L. Sumney. Nashville: Abingdon.

Ackroyd, Peter R. 1968. *Exile and Restoration: A Study of Hebrew Thought of the Sixth Century BC*. London: SCM Press.

Adams, E. 1997a. 'Abraham's Faith and Gentile Disobedience: Textual Links between Romans 1 and 4.' *Journal for the Study of the New Testament* 65:47–66.

——. 1997b. 'Historical Crisis and Cosmic Crisis in Mark 13 and Lucan's *Civil War*.' *Tyndale Bulletin* 48.2:329–44.

——. 2000. *Constructing the World: A Study in Paul's Cosmological Language*. Edinburgh: T&T Clark.

——. 2002. 'Paul's Story of God and Creation: The Story of How God Fulfils His Purposes in Creation.' Pp. 19–43 in *Narrative Dynamics in Paul: A Critical Assessment*, ed. B. W. Longenecker. Louisville: Westminster John Knox Press.

——. 2006. 'The "Coming of God" Tradition and Its Influence on New Testament Parousia Texts.' Pp. 1–19 in *Biblical Traditions in Transmission: Essays in Honour of Michael A. Knibb*, eds. C. Hempel and J. M. Lieu. Leiden: Brill.

——. 2007. *The Stars Will Fall from Heaven: Cosmic Catastrophe in the New Testament and Its World*. London: T&T Clark.

Agamben, G. 2006. *The Time That Remains: A Commentary on the Letter to the Romans*. Stanford, CA: Stanford University Press.

Agosto, E. 2003. 'Paul and Commendation.' Pp. 101–33 in *Paul in the Greco-Roman World: A Handbook*, ed. J. P. Sampley. Harrisburg, PA: Trinity Press International.

Alcock, S. E. 1989. 'Roman Imperialism in the Greek Landscape.' *Journal of Roman Antiquities* 2:5–34.

——. 2001. 'The Reconfiguration of Memory in the Eastern Roman Empire.' Pp. 323–50 in *Empires: Perspectives from Archaeology and History*, eds. S. E. Alcock et al. Cambridge: Cambridge University Press.

Aletti, J. N. 1993. *Epître aux Colossiens*. Paris: Cerf.

——. 2010 [1992]. *God's Justice in Romans: Keys for Interpretating the Epistle to the Romans*, tr. P. M. Meyer. Rome: Gregorian and Biblical Press.

——. 2012. *New Approaches for Interpreting the Letters of Saint Paul: Collected Essays. Rhetoric, Soteriology, Christology and Ecclesiology*. Rome: Gregorian and Biblical Press.

Algra, K. 2003. 'Stoic Theology.' Pp. 153–78 in *The Cambridge Companion to the Stoics*, ed. B. Inwood. Cambridge: Cambridge University Press.

Allen, L. C. 1970. 'The Old Testament Background of (ΠΡΟ) ΟΡΙΖΕΙΝ in the New Testament.' *New Testament Studies* 17:104–8.

Allison, D. C. 1985. *The End of the Ages Has Come: An Early Interpretation of the Passion and Resurrection of Jesus*. Philadelphia: Fortress.

——. 1994. 'A Plea for Thoroughgoing Eschatology.' *Journal of Biblical Literature* 113:651–68.

——. 1998. *Jesus of Nazareth: Millenarian Prophet*. Minneapolis: Fortress.

——. 1999. 'Jesus and the Victory of Apocalyptic.' Pp. 126–41 in *Jesus and the Restoration of Israel: A Critical Assessment of N. T. Wright's* Jesus and the Victory of God. Downers Grove, IL.: InterVarsity Press.

——. 2005. *Resurrecting Jesus: The Earliest Christian Tradition and Its Interpreters*. London; New York: T&T Clark.

——. 2007a. 'Day of the Lord.' Pp. 46–7 in *The New Interpreter's Dictionary of the Bible*, vol. 2, eds. K. D. Sakenfeld et al. Nashville: Abingdon.

——. 2007b. 'Eschatology of the NT.' Pp. 294–9 in *The New Interpreter's Dictionary of the Bible*, vol. 2, eds. K. D. Sakenfeld et al. Nashville: Abingdon.

——. 2009. *The Historical Christ and the Theological Jesus*. Grand Rapids: Eerdmans.

——. 2010. *Constructing Jesus: Memory, Imagination, and History*. Grand Rapids: Baker Academic.

Ando, C. 2000. *Imperial Ideology and Provincial Loyalty in the Roman Empire*. Berkeley; Los Angeles; London: University of California Press.

——. 2008. *The Matter of the Gods: Religion and the Roman Empire*. London: University of California Press.

Arendt, H. 1968 [1950]. *The Origins of Totalitarianism: New Edition with Added Prefaces*. Orlando: Harvest Books (Harcourt).

Arnold, C. 1995. *The Colossian Syncretism: The Interface between Christianity and Folk Belief in Colosse*. Tübingen: Mohr.

Arzt-Grabner, P. 2001. 'The Case of Onesimus: An Interpretation of Paul's Letter to Philemon Based on Documentary Papyri and Ostraca.' *Annali di Storia dell'esegesi* 18:589–614.

——. 2003. *Philemon*. Göttingen: Vandenhoeck & Ruprecht.

——. 2004. 'Onesimus *Erro*: Zur Vorgeschichte des Philemonbriefes.' *Zeitschrift für die Neutestamentliche Wissenschaft* 95(1):131–43.

——. 2010. 'How to Deal with Onesimus? Paul's Solution within the Frame of Ancient Legal and Documentary Sources.' Pp. 113–42 in *Philemon in Perspective: Interpreting a Pauline Letter*, ed. D. F. Tolmie. Berlin: De Gruyter.

Ashton, J. 2000. *The Religion of Paul the Apostle*. New Haven and London: Yale University Press.

Asurmendi, J. M. 2006. 'Baruch: Causes, Effects and Remedies for a Disaster.' Pp. 187–200 in *History and Identity: How Israel's Later Authors Viewed Its Earlier History*, eds. N. Calduch-Benages and J. Liesen. Berlin: De Gruyter.

Athanassiadi, P., and M. Frede, eds. 1999. *Pagan Monotheism in Late Antiquity*. Oxford: Oxford University Press, Clarendon Press.

Atkins, Robert. 2010. 'Contextual Interpretation of the Letter to Philemon in the United States.' Pp. 205–21 in *Philemon in Perspective: Interpreting a Pauline Letter*, ed. D. F. Tolmie. Berlin: De Gruyter.

Audi, R., ed. 1999 [1995]. *The Cambridge Dictionary of Philosophy*. Cambridge: Cambridge University Press.

Aune, David E. 1983. *Prophecy in Early Christianity and the Ancient Mediterranean World*. Grand Rapids: Eerdmans.

——. 1992. 'Eschatology (Early Christian).' Pp. 594–609 in *Anchor Bible Dictionary*, vol. 2, ed. David N. Freedman. New York: Doubleday.

Aus, R. 1979. 'Paul's Travel Plans to Spain and the "Full Number of the Gentiles".' *Novum Testamentum* 21:232–62.

Austin, J. L. 1975. *How to Do Things with Words*. 2nd edn., eds. J. O. Urmson and Marina Sbiś. Cambridge, MA: Harvard University Press.

Avemarie, F. 2000. 'Review of K. Yinger, *Paul, Judaism and Judgment According to Deeds*.' *Journal of Theological Studies* 50:271–4.

Bachmann, M. 2008 [1999]. *Anti-Judaism in Galatians? Exegetical Studies on a Polemical Letter and on Paul's Theology*. Grand Rapids: Eerdmans.

——. 2012. 'Paul, Israel and the Gentiles: Hermeneutical and Exegetical Notes.' Pp. 72–105 in *Paul and Judaism: Crosscurrents in Pauline Exegesis and the Study of Jewish–Christian Relations*, eds. R. Beiringer and D. Pollefeyt. London: T&T Clark.

Badenas, R. 1985. *Christ the End of the Law: Romans 10.4 in Pauline Perspective*. Sheffield: JSOT Press.

Badiou, A. 2003. *Saint Paul: The Foundation of Universalism*. Stanford, CA: Stanford University Press.

Baker, M. 2005. 'Paul and the Salvation of Israel: Paul's Ministry, the Motif of Jealousy, and Israel's Yes.' *Catholic Biblical Quarterly* 67:469–84.

Balzer, K. 2001. *Deutero-Isaiah: A Commentary on Isaiah 40—55*. Minneapolis: Fortress.

Barclay, J. M. G. 1987. 'Mirror-Reading a Polemical Letter: Galatians as a Test Case.' *Journal for the Study of the New Testament* 31:73–93.

——. 1988. *Obeying the Truth: A Study of Paul's Ethics in Galatians*. Studies of the New Testament and Its World. Edinburgh: T&T Clark.

——. 1991. 'Paul, Philemon and the Dilemma of Christian Slave-Ownership.' *New Testament Studies* 37:161–86.

——. 1996. *Jews in the Mediterranean Diaspora from Alexander to Trajan (323 BCE — 117 CE)*. Edinburgh: T&T Clark.

——. 2002. 'Paul's Story: Theology as Testimony.' Pp. 133–56 in *Narrative Dynamics in Paul: A Critical Assessment*, ed. B. W. Longenecker. Louisville: Westminster John Knox Press.

——. 2004 [1997]. *Colossians and Philemon* (New Testament Guides, vol. 12). London: Continuum.

——. 2006. '"By the Grace of God I Am What I Am": Grace and Agency in Philo and Paul.' Pp. 140–57 in *Divine and Human Agency in Paul and His Cultural Environment*, eds. J. M. G. Barclay and S. J. Gathercole. London: T&T Clark.

——. 2010. 'Approaching Romans 9—11 from the Wisdom of Solomon.' Pp. 91–109 in *Between Gospel and Election: Explorations in the Interpretation of Romans 9—11*, eds. F. Wilk and J. R. Wagner. Tübingen: Mohr.

——. 2011. *Pauline Churches and Diaspora Jews*. Tübingen: Mohr.

Barclay, J. M. G., and S. J. Gathercole, eds. 2006. *Divine and Human Agency in Paul and His Cultural Environment*. London: T&T Clark.

Barker, M. 1992. *The Great Angel: A Study of Israel's Second God*. London: SPCK.

——. 2004. *Temple Theology: An Introduction*. London: SPCK.

Barnett, P. W. 1993. 'Opponents of Paul.' Pp. 644–53 in *Dictionary of Paul and His Letters*, eds. G. F. Hawthorne, R. P. Martin, and D. G. Reid. Downers Grove, IL.: InterVarsity Press.

Barraclough, R. 1980. 'Philo's Politics, Roman Rule and Hellenistic Judaism.' Pp. 417–553 in *Aufstieg und Niedergang der Römischen Welt*, vol. II.12.1. Berlin: De Gruyter.

Barram, M. 2011. 'Pauline Mission as Salvific Intentionality: Fostering a Missional Consciousness in 1 Corinthians 9:19–23 and 10:31—11:1.' Pp. 234–46 in *Paul as Missionary: Identity, Activity, Theology, and Practice*, eds. T. J. Burke and B. S. Rosner. London: T&T Clark.

Barrett, A. A. 1989. *Caligula: The Corruption of Power*. London: B. T. Batsford Ltd.

Barrett, C. K. 1947. *The Holy Spirit and the Gospel Tradition*. London: SPCK.

——. 1971a [1968]. *A Commentary on the First Epistle to the Corinthians*. 2nd edn. London: A&C Black.

——. 1971b [1957]. *A Commentary on the Epistle to the Romans*. London: A&C Black.

——. 1973. *A Commentary on the Second Epistle to the Corinthians*. London: A&C Black.

——. 1976. 'The Allegory of Abraham, Sarah, and Hagar in the Argument of Galatians.' Pp. 1–16 in *Rechtfertigung: Festschrift für Ernst Käsemann zum 70. Geburtstag*, eds. J. Friedrich, W. Pöhlmann, and P. Stuhlmacher. Tübingen: Mohr.

——. 1982. *Essays on Paul*. London: SPCK.

——., ed. and introd. 1987 [1956]. *The New Testament Background: Selected Documents*. Rev. edn. London: SPCK.

——. 1998. *Acts 15—28*. London: T&T Clark.

Barth, K. 1936–69. *Church Dogmatics*. Edinburgh: T&T Clark.

——. 1968 [1933]. *The Epistle to the Romans*, tr. Edwyn C. Hoskyns. Oxford: Oxford University Press.

Barton, J. 2011 [1988]. *People of the Book? The Authority of the Bible in Christianity*. 3rd edn. London: SPCK.

Barton, S. C., ed. 2007. *Idolatry: False Worship in the Bible, Early Judaism and Christianity*. London: T&T Clark.

Bassler, J. M. 1982. *Divine Impartiality: Paul and a Theological Axiom*. Chico, CA: Scholars Press.

——., ed. 1991. *Pauline Theology, Volume 1: Thessalonians, Philippians, Galatians, Philemon*. Minneapolis: Augsburg Fortress.

Bauckham, R. J. 1981. 'The Worship of Jesus in Apocalyptic Christianity.' *New Testament Studies* 27:322–41.

——. 1993. *The Climax of Prophecy: Studies on the Book of Revelation*. Edinburgh: T&T Clark International.

——. 1995a. 'James and the Jerusalem Church.' Pp. 415–80 in *The Book of Acts in Its First Century Setting*, eds. Richard J. Bauckham and Bruce W. Winter. Grand Rapids: Eerdmans.

——. 1995b. 'James at the Centre.' *European Pentecostal Theological Association Bulletin* 14:22–33.

——. 2001. 'Apocalypses.' Pp. 135–87 in *Justification and Variegated Nomism, Volume 1: The Complexities of Second Temple Judaism*, eds. D. A. Carson, Peter T. O'Brien, and M. A. Seifrid. Tübingen: Mohr.

——. 2008/9. *Jesus and the God of Israel: 'God Crucified' and Other Studies on the New Testament's Christology of Divine Identity*. Milton Keynes: Paternoster (2008); Grand Rapids: Eerdmans (2009).

Beacham, R. 2005. 'The Emperor as Impresario: Producing the Pageant of Power.' Pp. 151–74 in *The Cambridge Companion to the Age of Augustus*, ed. K. Galinsky. Cambridge: Cambridge University Press.

Beale, G. K. 1989. 'The Old Testament Background of Reconciliation in 2 Cor 5—7 and Its Bearing on the Literary Problem of 2 Corinthians 6:14—7:1.' *New Testament Studies* 35:550–81.

——. 1999. 'Peace and Mercy upon the Israel of God. The Old Testament Background of Galatians 6,16b.' *Biblica* 80:204–23.

——. 2004. *The Temple and the Church's Mission: A Biblical Theology of the Dwelling Place of God*. Downers Grove, IL: InterVarsity Press.

——. 2008. *We Become What We Worship: A Biblical Theology of Idolatry*. Downers Grove, IL: IVP Academic.

Beard, M. 2007. *The Roman Triumph*. Cambridge, MA: The Belknap Press of Harvard University Press.

Beard, M., and J. A. North, eds. 1990. *Pagan Priests: Religion and Power in the Ancient World*. Ithaca, NY: Cornell University Press.

Beard, M., J. North, and S. Price. 1998. *Religions of Rome, Vol. 1: A History*. Cambridge: Cambridge University Press.

Beckwith, R. T. 1980. 'The Significance of the Calendar for Interpreting Essene Chronology and Eschatology.' *Révue de Qumran* 38:167–202.

——. 1981. 'Daniel 9 and the Date of Messiah's Coming in Essene, Hellenistic, Pharisaic, Zealot and Early Christian Computation.' *Révue de Qumran* 40:521–42.

——. 1996. *Calendar and Chronology, Jewish and Christian: Biblical, Intertestamental and Patristic Studies. AGJU*, vol. 33. Leiden: Brill.

Beker, J. C. 1980. *Paul the Apostle: The Triumph of God in Life and Thought*. Philadelphia: Fortress.

Bekken, P. J. 2007. *The Word Is Near You: A Study of Deuteronomy 30:12–14 in Paul's Letter to the Romans in a Jewish Context*. Berlin: De Gruyter.

Belayche, N. 2011. '*Hypsistos*: A Way of Exalting the Gods in Graeco-Roman Polytheism.' Pp. 139–74 in *The Religious History of the Roman Empire: Pagans, Jews and Christians*, eds. J. A. North and S. R. F. Price. Oxford: Oxford University Press.

Bell, R. H. 1994. *Provoked to Jealousy: The Origin and Purpose of the Jealousy Motif in Romans 9—11*. Tübingen: Mohr.

——. 2005. *The Irrevocable Call of God: An Inquiry into Paul's Theology of Israel*. Tübingen: Mohr.

Benjamin, W. 1968 [1940]. *Illuminations*, ed. H. Arendt, tr. H. Zohn. New York: Schocken Books.

Benko, S. 1984. *Pagan Rome and the Early Christians*. Bloomington and Indianapolis: Indiana University Press.

Bentley, M. 2006. 'Past and "Presence": Revisiting Historical Ontology.' *History and Theory* 45 (October):349–61.

Berger, P. L., and T. Luckman. 1966. *The Social Construction of Reality: A Treatise in the Sociology of Knowledge*. Garden City, NY: Doubleday.

Bernat, D. A. 2010. 'Circumcision.' Pp. 471–4 in *The Eerdmans Dictionary of Early Judaism*, eds. J. J. Collins and D. C. Harlow. Grand Rapids: Eerdmans.

Best, E. 1972. *The First and Second Epistles to the Thessalonians*. London: A&C Black.

——. 1984. 'The Revelation to Evangelize the Gentiles.' *Journal of Theological Studies* 35(1):1–30.

Betjeman, J. 1982. *Uncollected Poems*. London: John Murray.

Bett, R. 2010. *The Cambridge Companion to Ancient Scepticism*. Cambridge: Cambridge University Press.

Betz, H.-D. 1973. '2 Cor 6:14—7:1: An Anti-Pauline Fragment?' *Journal of Biblical Literature* 92(1):88–108.

——. 1979. *Galatians: A Commentary on Paul's Letter to the Churches in Galatia*. Philadelphia: Fortress.

——. 1994. 'Transferring a Ritual: Paul's Interpretation of Baptism in Romans 6.' Pp. 84–118 in *Paul in His Hellenistic Context*, ed. T. Engberg-Pedersen. Edinburgh: T&T Clark.

Bickerman, E. J. 1979. *The God of the Maccabees: Studies on the Meaning and Origin of the Maccabean Revolt*. Leiden: Brill.

Bieringer, R. 1987. '2 Kor 5,19a und die Versöhnung der Welt.' *Ephemerides Theologicae Lovanienses* 63:295–326.

Bieringer, R., and D. Pollefeyt, eds. 2012a. *Paul and Judaism: Crosscurrents in Pauline Exegesis and the Story of Jewish–Christian Relations*. London: T&T Clark.

——. 2012b. 'Prologue: Wrestling with the Jewish Paul.' Pp. 1–14 in *Paul and Judaism: Crosscurrents in Pauline Exegesis and the Study of Jewish–Christian Relations*, eds. R. Bieringer and D. Pollefeyt. London: T&T Clark.

Bird, M. F. 2006. *Jesus and the Origins of the Gentile Mission*. London: T&T Clark.

——. 2007. *The Saving Righteousness of God: Studies on Paul, Justification and the New Perspective*. Milton Keynes: Paternoster.

——. 2008a. 'Tearing the Heavens and Shaking the Heavenlies: Mark's Cosmology in Its Apocalyptic Context.' Pp. 45–59 in *Cosmology and New Testament Theology*. London: T&T Clark International.

——. 2008b. *Introducing Paul: The Man, His Mission and His Message*. Downers Grove, IL: IVP Academic.

——. 2009a. *Are You the One Who Is to Come? The Historical Jesus and the Messianic Question*. Grand Rapids: Baker Academic.

——. 2009b. *Colossians and Philemon*. Eugene, OR: Cascade Books.

——. 2010. *Crossing Over Sea and Land: Jewish Missionary Activity in the Second Temple Period*. Peabody, MA: Hendrickson.

——. 2012. 'Salvation in Paul's Judaism?' Pp. 15–40 in *Paul and Judaism: Crosscurrents in Pauline Exegesis and the Study of Jewish–Christian Relations*, eds. R. Bieringer and D. Pollefeyt. London: T&T Clark.

Bird, M. F., and P. M. Sprinkle, eds. 2009. *The Faith of Jesus Christ: Exegetical, Biblical and Theological Studies*. Milton Keynes: Paternoster.

Black, M. 1973. *Romans*. London: Oliphants.

Blackburn, S. 2008 [1994]. *The Oxford Dictionary of Philosophy*. 2nd edn. rev. Oxford: Oxford University Press.

Blackwell, B. C. 2011. *Christosis: Pauline Soteriology in Light of Deification in Irenaeus and Cyril of Alexandria*. Tübingen: Mohr.

Blaschke, A. 1998. *Beschneidung: Zeugnisse der Bible und verwandter Texte*. Tübingen: Francke Verlag.

Bloom, J. J. 2010. *Jewish Revolts against Rome, A.D. 66–135: A Military Analysis*. Jefferson, NC: McFarland.

Blumenfeld, B. 2001. *The Political Paul: Justice, Democracy and Kingship in a Hellenistic Framework*. Sheffield: Sheffield Academic Press.

Bock, D. L. 1999. 'The Trial and Death of Jesus in N. T. Wright's *Jesus and the Victory of God*.' Pp. 101–25, 308–10 in *Jesus and the Restoration of Israel: A Critical Assessment of N. T. Wright's* Jesus and the Victory of God, ed. Carey C. Newman. Downers Grove, IL: InterVarsity Press.

Bockmuehl, M. N. A. 1997 [1990]. *Revelation and Mystery in Ancient Judaism and Pauline Christianity*. Grand Rapids: Eerdmans.

——. 1998. *The Epistle to the Philippians*. London: A&C Black.

——. 2000. *Jewish Law in Gentile Churches: Halakhah and the Beginning of Christian Public Ethics*. London: T&T Clark.

——. 2001. '1QS and Salvation at Qumran.' Pp. 381–414 in *Justification and Variegated Nomism, Volume 1: The Complexities of Second Temple Judaism*, eds. D. A. Carson, Peter T. O'Brien, and Mark A. Seifrid. Tübingen: Mohr.

——. 2011. 'Did St. Paul Go to Heaven When He Died?' Pp. 211–31 in *Jesus, Paul and the People of God: A Theological Dialogue with N. T. Wright*, eds. N. Perrin and R. B. Hays. Downers Grove, IL: InterVarsity Press; London: SPCK.

Boer, R. 2010. *Secularism and Biblical Studies*. Sheffield: Equinox.

Borg, M. J., and J. D. Crossan. 2009. *The First Paul: Reclaiming the Radical Visionary behind the Church's Conservative Icon*. San Francisco and London: HarperCollins and SPCK.

Boring, M. E. 2007. 'Household Codes.' Pp. 905–6 in *The New Interpreter's Dictionary of the Bible*, vol. 2, eds. K. D. Sakenfeld et al. Nashville: Abingdon.

Bornkamm, G. 1971 [1969]. *Paul*. London: Hodder & Stoughton.

Botha, P. J. J. 2010. 'Hierarchy and Obedience: The Legacy of the Letter to Philemon.' Pp. 251–71 in *Philemon in Perspective: Interpreting a Pauline Letter*, ed. D. F. Tolmie. Berlin: De Gruyter.

Bourdieu, P. 1977 [1972]. *Outline of the Theory of Practice*. Cambridge: Cambridge University Press.

Bousset, W. 1970 [1913]. *Kyrios Christos: A History of Belief in Christ from the Beginnings of Christianity to Irenaeus*, tr. John E. Steely. Nashville: Abingdon.

Bowers, W. P. 1975. 'Jewish Communities in Spain in the Time of Paul the Apostle.' *Journal of Theological Studies* n.s. 26(2):395–402.

Bowersock, G. 1973. 'Syria under Vespasian.' *Journal of Roman Studies* 63:133–40.

Boyarin, D. 1994. *A Radical Jew: Paul and the Politics of Identity*. Berkeley: University of California Press.

——. 2012. *The Jewish Gospels: The Story of the Jewish Christ*. New York: New Press.

Boyce, M. 1991 [1975]. *A History of Zoroastrianism*. Leiden: Brill.

Bradshaw, P. F. 2004. *Eucharistic Origins*. Oxford: Oxford University Press.

Brauch, M. T. 1977. 'Perspectives on "God's Righteousness" in Recent German Discussion.' Pp. 523–42 in *Paul and Palestinian Judaism: A Comparison of Patterns of Religion*, ed. E. P. Sanders. London: SCM Press.

Brennan, T. 2005. *The Stoic Life: Emotions, Duties, and Fate*. Oxford: Clarendon Press.

Brent, A. 1999. *The Imperial Cult and the Development of Church Order: Concepts and Images of Authority in Paganism and Early Christianity before the Age of Cyprian*. Leiden: Brill.

Briggs, A. 2011. *Secret Days: Code-Breaking in Bletchley Park*. London: Frontline Books.

Broadie, S. 2003. 'The Sophists and Socrates.' Pp. 73–97 in *The Cambridge Companion to Greek and Roman Philosophy*, ed. D. Sedley. Cambridge: Cambridge University Press.

Brooke, G. J. 2000. 'Reading the Plain Meaning of Scripture in the Dead Sea Scrolls.' Pp. 67–90 in *Jewish Ways of Reading the Bible*. Oxford: Oxford University Press.

Brown, W. P. 1999. *The Ethos of the Cosmos: The Genesis of Moral Imagination in the Bible*. Grand Rapids: Eerdmans.

Bruce, F. F. 1963. *The Epistle of Paul to the Romans: An Introduction and Commentary*. London: Tyndale Press.

——. 1977. *Paul: Apostle of the Free Spirit*. Exeter: Paternoster.

Brunschwig, J., and D. Sedley. 2003. 'Hellenistic Philosophy.' Pp. 151–83 in *The Cambridge Companion to Greek and Roman Philosophy*, ed. D. Sedley. Cambridge: Cambridge University Press.

Bryan, C. 2000. *A Preface to Romans: Notes on the Epistle in Its Literary and Cultural Setting*. Oxford: Oxford University Press.

——. 2005. *Render to Caesar: Jesus, the Early Church, and the Roman Superpower*. New York: Oxford University Press.

Bryan, S. M. 2002. *Jesus and Israel's Traditions of Judgment and Restoration*. Cambridge: Cambridge University Press.

Buell, D. K. 2005. *Why This New Race? Ethnic Reasoning in Early Christianity*. New York: Columbia University Press.

Bultmann, R. 1910. *Der Stil der paulinischen Predigt und die kynisch-stoische Diatribe*. Göttingen: Vandenhoeck & Ruprecht.

——. 1951–5. *Theology of the New Testament*, tr. Kendrick Grobel. London: SCM Press; New York: Scribner's.

——. 1954. '"The Bible Today" und die Eschatologie.' Pp. 402–8 in *The Background of the New Testament and Its Eschatology: In Honour of Charles Harold Dodd*, eds. W. D. Davies and D. Daube. Cambridge: Cambridge University Press.

——. 1957. *History and Eschatology: The Presence of Eternity*. New York: Harper & Brothers, Harper Torchbooks/Cloister Library.

——. 1958. *Jesus Christ and Mythology*. New York: Scribner's.

——. 1960. *Existence and Faith*, ed. Schubert M. Ogden. Living Age Books. New York: World Publishing, Meridian.

——. 1967. *Exegetica*. Tübingen: Mohr.

——. 1995 [1924]. 'The Problem of Ethics in Paul.' Pp. 195–216 in *Understanding Paul's Ethics*, ed. B. S. Rosner. Grand Rapids: Eerdmans.

Burke, T. J. 2006. *Adopted into God's Family: Exploring a Pauline Metaphor*. Downers Grove, IL: InterVarsity Press.

Burkert, W. 1985 [1977]. *Greek Religion*. Cambridge, MA: Harvard University Press.

——. 1987. *Ancient Mystery Cults*. Cambridge, MA: Harvard University Press.

Burnett, A. 1983. 'Review of R. Albert, "Das Bild des Augustus auf den frühen Reichsprägungen. Studien zur Vergöttlichung des ersten Princeps".' *Gnomon* 55:563–5.

Burney, C. F. 1925. 'Christ as the APXH of Creation.' *Journal of Theological Studies* 27:160–77.

Burridge, R. A. 2007. *Imitating Jesus: An Inclusive Approach to New Testament Ethics*. Grand Rapids: Eerdmans.

Burton, E. de W. 1921. *A Critical and Exegetical Commentary on the Epistle to the Galatians*. Edinburgh: T&T Clark.

Byrne, B. 1979. *'Sons of God' – 'Seed of Abraham': A Study of the Idea of the Sonship of God of All Christians in Paul against the Jewish Background*. Rome: Biblical Institute Press.

——. 1996. *Romans*. Collegeville, MN: Liturgical Press.

Byron, J. 2003. *Slavery Metaphors in Early Judaism and Pauline Christianity: A Traditio-Historical and Exegetical Examination*. Tübingen: Mohr.

——. 2004. 'Paul and the Background of Slavery: The Status Quaestionis in New Testament Scholarship.' *Currents in Biblical Research* 3:116–39.

Cadwallader, A. H., and M. Trainor, eds. 2011. *Colossae in Space and Time: Linking to an Ancient City*. Göttingen: Vandenhoeck & Ruprecht.

Caird, G. B. 1956. *Principalities and Powers: A Study in Pauline Theology*. Oxford: Oxford University Press.

——. 1976. *Paul's Letters from Prison*. Oxford: Oxford University Press.

——. 1980. *The Language and Imagery of the Bible*. London: Duckworth.

Calduch-Benages, N., and J. Liesen, eds. 2006. *History and Identity: How Israel's Later Authors Viewed Its Earlier History*. Berlin: De Gruyter.

Callahan, A. D. 1993. 'Paul's Epistle to Philemon: Toward an Alternative *Argumentum*.' *Harvard Theological Review* 86:357–76.

Calvin, J. 1960 [1559]. *The Institutes of the Christian Religion*. Vol. 2. ed. John T. McNeill, tr. Ford Lewis Battles. Philadelphia: Westminster Press.

——. 1961 [1552]. *Concerning the Eternal Predestination of God*. London: James Clarke.

Campbell, D. A. 1994. 'Romans 1:17 – a *Crux Interpretum* for the ΠΙΣΤΙΣ ΧΡΙΣΤΟΥ Debate.' *Journal of Biblical Literature* 113:265–85.

——. 2005. *The Quest for Paul's Gospel: A Suggested Strategy*. London: T&T Clark.

——. 2008. 'An Echo of Scripture in Paul, and Its Implications.' Pp. 367–91 in *The Word Leaps the Gap: Essays on Scripture and Theology in Honor of Richard B Hays*, eds. J. R. Wagner, C. K. Rowe, and A. K. Grieb. Grand Rapids: Eerdmans.

——. 2009. *The Deliverance of God: An Apocalyptic Rereading of Justification in Paul*. Grand Rapids: Eerdmans.

——. 2011. 'Galatians 5.11: Evidence of an Early Law-Observant Mission by Paul?' *New Testament Studies* 57(3):325–47.

Campbell, W. S. 2008. *Paul and the Creation of Christian Identity*. London: T&T Clark.

——. 2012. 'Covenantal Theology and Participation in Christ: Pauline Perspectives on Transformation.' Pp. 41–60 in *Paul and Judaism: Crosscurrents in Pauline Exegesis and the Study of Jewish–Christian Relations*, eds. R. Beiringer and D. Pollefeyt. London: T&T Clark.

Cancik, H. 1999. 'The Reception of Greek Cults in Rome: A Precondition of the Emergence of an "Imperial Religion".' *Archiv für Religionsgeschichte* 1(2):161–73.

Capes, D. B. 1992. *Old Testament Yahweh Texts in Paul's Christology*. Tübingen: Mohr.

——. 2004. 'YHWH Texts and Monotheism in Paul's Christology.' Pp. 120–37 in *Early Jewish and Christian Monotheism*, eds. L. T. Stuckenbruck and W. E. S. North. London: T&T Clark.

——. 2007. 'Pauline Exegesis and the Incarnate Christ.' Pp. 135–53 in *Israel's God and Rebecca's Children: Christology and Community in Early Judaism and Christianity. Essays in Honor of Larry W. Hurtado and Alan F. Segal*, eds. D. B. Capes, A. D. DeConick, H. K. Bond, and T. A. Miller. Waco: Baylor University Press.

Capes, D. B., A. D. DeConick, H. K. Bond, and T. A. Miller, eds. 2007. *Israel's God and Rebecca's Children: Christology and Community in Early Judaism and Christianity. Essays in Honor of Larry W. Hurtado and Alan F. Segal.* Waco: Baylor University Press.

Carleton Paget, J. 1996. 'Jewish Proselytism at the Time of Christian Origins: Chimera or Reality?' *Journal for the Study of the New Testament* 62:65–103.

Carroll, R. P. 1992. 'Israel, History of (Post-Monarchic Period).' Pp. 567–76 in *Anchor Bible Dictionary*, vol. 3, ed. David N. Freedman. New York: Doubleday.

Carson, D. A. 2001a. 'Introduction.' Pp. 1–5 in *Justification and Variegated Nomism, Volume 1: The Complexities of Second Temple Judaism*, eds. D. A. Carson, Peter T. O'Brien, and Mark A. Seifrid. Tübingen: Mohr.

——. 2001b. 'Summaries and Conclusions.' Pp. 505–48 in *Justification and Variegated Nomism, Volume 1: The Complexities of Second Temple Judaism*, eds. D. A. Carson, Peter T. O'Brien, and Mark A. Seifrid. Tübingen: Mohr.

——. 2004. 'The Vindication of Imputation: On Fields of Discourse and Semantic Fields.' Pp. 46–78 in *Justification: What's at Stake in the Current Debates*, eds. M. Husbands and D. J. Treier. Downers Grove, IL: InterVarsity Press.

Carson, D. A., P. T. O'Brien, and M. A. Seifrid. 2001–4. *Justification and Variegated Nomism: Vol. 1: The Complexities of Second Temple Judaism; Vol. 2: The Paradoxes of Paul.* Tübingen: Mohr; Grand Rapids: Baker Academic.

Casey, M. 1991. *From Jewish Prophet to Gentile God: The Origins and Development of New Testament Christology*. Cambridge: Cambridge University Press.

——. 1998. 'Review of *Jesus and the Victory of God* by N. T. Wright.' *Journal for the Study of the New Testament* 69:95–103.

Cassidy, R. J. 2001. *Paul in Chains: Roman Imprisonment and the Letters of St. Paul.* New York: Crossroad.

Cassirer, E. 1944. *Essay on Man*. New Haven: Yale University Press.

Cassuto, U. 1961–4. *A Commentary on the Book of Genesis*. 2 vols. Jerusalem: Magnes Press.

——. 1961. *The Documentary Hypothesis and the Composition of the Pentateuch*, tr. I. Abrahams. Jerusalem: Magnes Press.

Catchpole, D. 2004. 'Who and Where Is the "Wretched Man" of Romans 7 and Why Is "She" Wretched?' Pp. 168–80 in *The Holy Spirit and Christian Origins: Essays in Honor of James D. G. Dunn*, eds. G. N. Stanton, B. W. Longenecker, and S. C. Barton. Grand Rapids: Eerdmans.

Chadwick, H. 1954–5. '"All Things to All Men" (1 Cor. IX.22).' *New Testament Studies* 1:261–75.

Champlin, E. 2003. *Nero*. Cambridge, MA: The Belknap Press of Harvard University Press.

Chapman, D. W. 2008. *Ancient Jewish and Christian Perceptions of Crucifixion*. Grand Rapids: Baker Academic.

Charlesworth, J. H., ed. 1983. *The Old Testament Pseudepigrapha*. Vol. 1, *Apocalyptic Literature and Testaments*. Garden City, NY: Doubleday.

——., ed. 1985. *The Old Testament Pseudepigrapha.* Vol. 2, *Expansions of the 'Old Testament' and Legends, Wisdom and Philosophical Literature, Prayers, Psalms and Odes, Fragments of Lost Judaeo-Hellenistic Works.* Garden City, NY: Doubleday.

——. 1992a. 'From Messianology to Christology: Problems and Prospects.' Pp. 3–35 in *The Messiah: Developments in Earliest Judaism and Christianity*, ed. J. H. Charlesworth. Minneapolis: Fortress.

——., ed. 1992b. *The Messiah: Developments in Earliest Judaism and Christianity.* Minneapolis: Fortress.

Chesnutt, R. D. 2003. 'Covenant and Cosmos in Wisdom of Solomon 10—19.' Pp. 223–49 in *The Concept of the Covenant in the Second Temple Period.* Leiden: Brill.

Chester, A. 2007. *Messiah and Exaltation: Jewish Messianic and Visionary Traditions and New Testament Christology.* Tübingen: Mohr.

——. 2012. *Future Hope and Present Reality. Volume 1: Eschatology and Transformation in the Hebrew Bible.* Tübingen: Mohr.

Chester, S. J. 2003. *Conversion at Corinth: Perspectives on Conversion in Paul's Theology and the Corinthian Church.* London: T&T Clark.

Childs, B. S. 2001. *Isaiah: A Commentary.* Louisville: Westminster John Knox Press.

Chilton, B. D. 1988. 'Romans 9—11 as Scriptural Interpretation and Dialogue with Judaism.' *Ex Auditu* 4:27–37.

——. 2004. *Rabbi Paul: An Intellectual Biography.* New York: Doubleday.

Choksy, J. K. 1999. 'Zoroastrianism.' Pp. 755–7 in *Late Antiquity: A Guide to the Postclassical World*, ed. G. W. Bowersock, P. Brown, and O. Grabar. Cambridge, MA: The Belknap Press of the Harvard University Press.

Churchill, T. W. R. 2010. *Divine Initiative and the Christology of the Damascus Road Encounter.* Eugene, OR: Pickwick.

Ciampa, R. E. 1998. *The Presence and Function of Scripture in Galatians 1 and 2.* Tübingen: Mohr.

——. 2007. 'Deuteronomy in Galatians and Romans.' Pp. 99–117 in *Deuteronomy in the New Testament: The New Testament and the Scriptures of Israel*, eds. S. Moyise and M. J. J. Menken. London: T&T Clark.

Clark, A. J. 2007. *Divine Qualities: Cult and Community in Republican Rome.* Oxford: Oxford University Press.

Clements, R. E. 1965. *God and Temple.* Oxford: Blackwell.

——. 1984. 'Monotheism and the Canonical Process.' *Theology* 87:336–44.

Cohen, S. J. D. 1979. *Josephus in Galilee and Rome: His Vita and Development as a Historian.* Leiden: Brill.

——. 2011. 'The Letter of Paul to the Galatians.' Pp. 332–44 in *The Jewish Annotated New Testament: New Revised Standard Version*, eds. A.-J. Levine and M. Z. Brettler. New York: Oxford University Press.

Cohick, L. H. 2011. 'Citizenship and Empire: Paul's Letter to the Philippians and Eric Liddell's Work in China.' *Journal for the Study of Paul and His Letters* 1(2):137–52.

Coleiro, E. 1979. *An Introduction to Virgil's Bucolics with an Edition of the Text.* Amsterdam: Humanities Press.

Collins, A. Y. 1999. 'The Worship of Jesus and the Imperial Cult.' Pp. 234–57 in *The Jewish Roots of Christological Monotheism: Papers from the St. Andrews Conference on the Historical Origins of the Worship of Jesus*, eds. C. C. Newman, J. R. Davila, and G. S. Lewis. Leiden: Brill.

Collins, J. J. 1987. 'Messianism in the Maccabean Period.' Pp. 97–109 in *Judaisms and Their Messiahs at the Turn of the Christian Era*, eds. J. Neusner, W. S. Green, and E. S. Frerichs. Cambridge: Cambridge University Press.

——. 1993. *Daniel*. Minneapolis: Fortress.

——. 2000a. *Between Athens and Jerusalem: Jewish Identity in the Hellenistic Diaspora*. Grand Rapids: Eerdmans.

——. 2000b. 'Eschatologies of Late Antiquity.' Pp. 330–7 in *Dictionary of New Testament Background*, eds. C. A. Evans and S. E. Porter. Downers Grove, IL: InterVarsity Press.

——. 2010a. 'Eschatology.' Pp. 594–7 in *The Eerdmans Dictionary of Early Judaism*, eds. J. J. Collins and D. C. Harlow. Grand Rapids: Eerdmans.

——. 2010b [1995]. *The Scepter and the Star: The Messiahs of the Dead Sea Scrolls and Other Ancient Literature*. New York: Doubleday.

Collins, J. J., and A. Y. Collins. 2008. *King and Messiah as Son of God: Divine, Human and Angelic Messianic Figures in Biblical and Related Literature*. Grand Rapids: Eerdmans.

Collins, J. J., and D. C. Harlow, eds. 2010. *The Eerdmans Dictionary of Early Judaism*. Grand Rapids: Eerdmans.

Collins, K. J. 2004. 'The Doctrine of Justification: Historic Wesleyan and Contemporary Understandings.' Pp. 177–202 in *Justification: What's at Stake in the Current Debates*, eds. M. Husbands and D. J. Treier. Downers Grove, IL: InterVarsity Press.

Collins, R. F. 1999. *First Corinthians*. Collegeville, MN: Michael Glazier/Liturgical Press.

——. 2009. 'Servant of the Lord, The.' Pp. 192–5 in *The New Interpreter's Dictionary of the Bible*, vol. 5, eds. K. D. Sakenfeld et al. Nashville: Abingdon.

Confino, A. 2012. 'Why Did the Nazis Burn the Hebrew Bible? Nazi Germany, Representations of the Past, and the Holocaust.' *The Journal of Modern History* 84(2), June:369–400.

Conzelmann, H. 1960 [1953]. *The Theology of Luke*, tr. Geoffrey Buswell. London, NY: Faber, Harper & Row.

——. 1975 [1969]. *1 Corinthians: A Commentary on the First Epistle to the Corinthians*, tr. James W. Leitch. Hermeneia. Philadelphia: Fortress.

Cook, M. 2011. 'The Letter of Paul to the Philippians.' Pp. 354–61 in *The Jewish Annotated New Testament*, eds. A.-J. Levine and M. Z. Brettler. Oxford: Oxford University Press.

Corley, J. 2006. 'The Review of History in Eleazar's Prayer in 3 Macc 6:1–15.' Pp. 201–29 in *History and Identity: How Israel's Later Authors Viewed Its Earlier History*, eds. N. Calduch-Benages and J. Liesen. Berlin: De Gruyter.

——. 2009. 'Sirach.' Pp. 285–94 in *The New Interpreter's Dictionary of the Bible*, vol. 5, eds. K. D. Sakenfeld et al. Nashville: Abingdon.

Cosgrove, C. H. 1997. *Elusive Israel: The Puzzle of Election in Romans*. Louisville: Westminster John Knox Press.

Countryman, L. W. 1988. *Dirt, Greed and Sex: Sexual Ethics in the New Testament and Their Implications for Today*. Philadelphia: Fortress.

Cousar, C. B. 2009. *Philippians and Philemon*. Louisville: Westminster John Knox Press.

Cranfield, C. E. B. 1975, 1979. *A Critical and Exegetical Commentary on the Epistle to the Romans*. 2 vols. Edinburgh: T&T Clark.

Crook, J. A. 1996. 'Political History, 30 B. C. to A. D. 14.' Pp. 70–112 in *Cambridge Ancient History*, vol. 10, eds. A. K. Bowman, E. Champlin, and A. Lintott. Cambridge: Cambridge University Press.

Crossan, J. D. 1991. *The Historical Jesus: The Life of a Mediterranean Jewish Peasant.* San Francisco: Harper.

Crossan, J. D., and J. L. Reed. 2004. *In Search of Paul. How Jesus's Apostle Opposed Rome's Empire with God's Kingdom: A New Vision of Paul's Words and World.* San Francisco: HarperSanFrancisco.

Crouzel, H. 1976. 'Geist (Heiliger Geist).' Pp. 490–545 in *Reallexicon für Antike und Christentum*, vol. 9. Stuttgart: Anton Hiersemann.

Cullmann, O. 1962 [1951]. *Christ and Time: The Primitive Christian Conception of Time and History*, tr. Floyd V. Filson. London: SCM Press.

——. 1963 [1957]. *The Christology of the New Testament.* Rev. edn., tr. Shirley C. Guthrie and Charles A. M. Hall. London: SCM Press; Philadelphia: Westminster Press.

——. 1967 [1965]. *Salvation in History.* London: SCM Press; New York: Harper & Row.

Cummins, S. A. 2007. 'Divine Life and Corporate Christology: God, Messiah Jesus, and the Covenant Community in Paul.' Pp. 190–209 in *The Messiah in the Old and New Testaments*, ed. S. E. Porter. Grand Rapids: Eerdmans.

Cupitt, D. 1991. *What is a Story?* London: SCM Press.

Dahl, N. A. 1941. *Das Volk Gottes: Eine Untersuchung zum Kirchenbewusstsein des Urchristentums.* Oslo: Jacob Dybwad.

——. 1974. *The Crucified Messiah and Other Essays.* Minneapolis: Augsburg.

——. 1977. *Studies in Paul: Theology for the Early Christian Mission.* Minneapolis: Augsburg.

——. 1991. *Jesus the Christ: The Historical Origins of Christological Doctrine.* ed. D. H. Juel. Minneapolis: Fortress.

——. 1992. 'Messianic Ideas and the Crucifixion of Jesus.' Pp. 382–403 in *The Messiah: Developments in Earliest Judaism and Christianity*, ed. J. H. Charlesworth. Minneapolis: Fortress.

Danby, H. 1933. *The Mishnah, Translated from the Hebrew with Introduction and Brief Explanatory Notes.* Oxford: Oxford University Press.

Danker, F. W. 1982. *Benefactor: Epigraphic Study of a Graeco-Roman and New Testament Semantic Field.* St Louis: Clayton.

Das, A. A. 2007. *Solving the Romans Debate.* Minneapolis: Fortress.

Davies, G. I. 1991. 'The Presence of God in the Second Temple and Rabbinic Doctrine.' Pp. 32–6 in *Templum Amicitiae: Essays on the Second Temple Presented to Ernst Bammel*, ed. William Horbury. Sheffield: Sheffield Academic Press.

Davies, P. R. 1977. 'Hasidim in the Maccabean Period.' *Journal of Jewish Studies* 28:127–40.

Davies, P. R., and B. D. Chilton. 1978. 'The Aqedah: A Revised Tradition History.' *Catholic Biblical Quarterly* 40:514–46.

Davies, W. D. 1974. *The Gospel and the Land: Early Christianity and Jewish Territorial Doctrine.* Berkeley: University of California Press.

——. 1980 [1948]. *Paul and Rabbinic Judaism.* 4th edn. Philadelphia: Fortress.

——. 1984. *Jewish and Pauline Studies.* London: SPCK; Philadelphia: Fortress.

Davis, C. J. 1996. *The Name and Way of the Lord.* Sheffield: JSOT Press.

Dawkins, R. 2006. *The God Delusion.* London: Black Swan.

de Boer, M. C. 1988. *The Defeat of Death. Apocalyptic Eschatology in 1 Corinthians 15 and Romans 5.* Sheffield: Sheffield Academic Press.

——. 1989. 'Paul and Jewish Apocalyptic Eschatology.' Pp. 169–90 in *Apocalyptic and the New Testament: Essays in Honor of J. Louis Martyn*, eds. J. Marcus and M. L. Soards. Sheffield: Sheffield Academic Press.

——. 2011. *Galatians: A Commentary*. Louisville: Westminster John Knox Press.

de Vos, Craig S. 2001. 'Once a Slave, Always a Slave? Slavery, Manumission and Relational Patterns in Paul's Letter to Philemon.' *Journal for the Study of the New Testament* 82:89–105.

Deines, R. 2001. 'The Pharisees between "Judaisms" and "Common Judaism".' Pp. 443–504 in *Justification and Variegated Nomism, Volume 1: The Complexities of Second Temple Judaism*, eds. D. A. Carson, Peter T. O'Brien, and Mark A Seifrid. Tübingen and Grand Rapids: Mohr and Baker Academic.

——. 2010. 'Pharisees.' Pp. 1061–3 in *The Eerdmans Dictionary of Early Judaism*, eds. John J. Collins and Daniel C. Harlow. Grand Rapids: Eerdmans.

Deissmann, A. 1978 [1908]. *Light from the Ancient East: The New Testament Illustrated by Recently Discovered Texts of the Graeco-Roman World*. Grand Rapids: Baker Book House.

Derrett, J. D. M. 1988. 'The Functions of the Epistle to Philemon.' *Zeitschrift für die Neutestamentliche Wissenschaft und die Kunde der Ältesten Kirche* 79:63–91.

di Lella, A. A. 2006. 'Ben Sira's Praise of the Ancestors of Old (Sir 44–49): The History of Israel as Paraenetic Apologetics.' Pp. 151–70 in *History and Identity: How Israel's Later Authors Viewed Its Earlier History*, eds. N. Calduch-Benages and J. Liesen. Berlin: De Gruyter.

Dickson, J. P. 2003. *Mission-Commitment in Ancient Judaism and in the Pauline Communities*. Tübingen: Mohr.

Dillon, J. T. 2004. *Musonius Rufus and Education in the Good Life*. Lanham, MD: University Press of America.

DiMattei, S. 2008. 'Biblical Narratives.' Pp. 59–93 in *As It Is Written: Studying Paul's Use of Scripture*, eds. S. E. Porter and C. D. Stanley. Atlanta: Society of Biblical Literature.

Dodd, B. J. 1998. 'The Story of Christ and the Imitation of Paul in Philippians 2—3.' Pp. 154–61 in *Where Christology Began: Essays on Philippians 2*, eds. R. P. Martin and B. J. Dodd. Louisville: Westminster John Knox Press.

Dodd, C. H. 1946. *The Bible Today*. Cambridge: Cambridge University Press.

——. 1958 [1920]. *The Meaning of Paul for Today*. London: Fontana.

——. 1959 [1932]. *The Epistle of Paul to the Romans*. London: Collins/Fontana.

Donaldson, T. L. 1986. 'The "Curse of the Law" and the Inclusion of the Gentiles: Galatians 3.13–14.' *New Testament Studies* 32.

——. 1990. 'Proselytes or "Righteous Gentiles"? The Status of Gentiles in Eschatological Pilgrimage Patterns of Thought.' *Journal for the Study of the Pseudepigrapha* 7:3–27.

——. 1993. '"Riches for the Gentiles" (Rom 11:12): Israel's Rejection and Paul's Gentile Mission.' *Journal of Biblical Literature* 112:81–98.

——. 1997. *Paul and the Gentiles: Remapping the Apostle's Convictional World*. Minneapolis: Fortress.

Donfried, K. P. 1984. 'I Thessalonians 2:13–16 as a Test Case.' *Interpretation* 38:242–53.

Douthat, R. 2012. *Bad Religion: How We Became a Nation of Heretics*. New York: Free Press.

Downing, F. G. 1998. *Cynics, Paul and the Pauline Churches*. London, NY: Routledge.

——. 2000. *Making Sense in (and of) the First Christian Century*. Sheffield: JSOT Press.

Downs, D. J. 2006. 'Paul's Collection and the Book of Acts Revisited.' *New Testament Studies* 52:50–70.

Duff, T. 1999. *Plutarch's Lives: Exploring Virtue and Vice*. Oxford: Clarendon Press.

Dunn, J. D. G. 1975a. *Jesus and the Spirit: A Study of the Religious and Charismatic Experience of Jesus and the First Christians as Reflected in the New Testament*. London: SCM Press.

——. 1975b. 'Romans 7.14–25 in the Theology of St. Paul.' *Theologische Zeitschrift* 31:257–73.

——. 1978. 'The Birth of a Metaphor – Baptized in Spirit.' *Expository Times* 89:77–8; 134–8; 173–5.

——. 1980. *Christology in the Making: A New Testament Inquiry into the Origins of the Doctrine of the Incarnation*. London: SCM Press; Philadelphia: Westminster Press.

——. 1982. 'Was Christianity a Monotheistic Faith from the Beginning?' *Scottish Journal of Theology* 35:303–36.

——. 1988a. *Romans 1—8*. Waco: Word Books.

——. 1988b. *Romans 9—16*. Waco: Word Books.

——. 1990. *Jesus, Paul and the Law: Studies in Mark and Galatians*. London: SPCK.

——. 1992. 'The Justice of God: A Renewed Perspective on Justification by Faith.' *Journal of Theological Studies* n.s. 43:1–21.

——. 1993. *A Commentary on the Epistle to the Galatians*. London: A&C Black.

——. 1995. 'The Colossian Philosophy: A Confident Jewish Apologia.' *Biblica* 76:153–81.

——. 1996. *The Epistles to the Colossians and to Philemon: A Commentary on the Greek Text*. Grand Rapids: Eerdmans.

——. 1998. *The Theology of Paul the Apostle*. Grand Rapids: Eerdmans.

——. 1999. 'Who Did Paul Think He Was? A Study of Jewish Identity.' *New Testament Studies* 45(2):174–93.

——. 2002. 'The Narrative Approach to Paul: Whose Story?' Pp. 217–30 in *Narrative Dynamics in Paul: A Critical Analysis*, ed. B. W. Longenecker. Louisville: Westminster John Knox Press.

——. 2008 [2005]. *The New Perspective on Paul*. Grand Rapids: Eerdmans.

——. 2009 [1987]. *The Living Word*. 2nd edn. Minneapolis: Fortress.

——. 2010. *Did the First Christians Worship Jesus? The New Testament Evidence*. London: SPCK.

Dunne, J. A. 2013. 'Cast Out the Aggressive Agitators (Gl 4:29–30): Suffering, Identity and the Ethics of Expulsion in Paul's Mission to the Galatians.' In *Sensitivity to Out-siders: Exploring the Dynamic Relationship between Mission and Ethics in the New Testament and Early Christianity*, ed. J. Kok, T. Nicklas, D. Roth, and C. M. Hays. Tübingen: Mohr.

Eastman, S. G. 2006. '"Cast Out the Slave Woman and Her Son": The Dynamics of Exclusion and Inclusion in Galatians 4.30.' *Journal for the Study of the New Testament* 28 (3):309–36.

——. 2007. *Recovering Paul's Mother Tongue: Language and Theology in Galatians*. Grand Rapids: Eerdmans.

——. 2008. 'Imitating Christ Imitating Us: Paul's Educational Project in Philippians.' Pp. 427–51 in *The Word Leaps the Gap: Essays on Scripture and Theology in Honor of Richard B. Hays*, eds. J. R. Wagner, C. K. Rowe, and A. K. Grieb. Grand Rapids: Eerdmans.

——. 2010. 'Israel and the Mercy of God: A Re-Reading of Galatians 6.16 and Romans 9—11.' *New Testament Studies* 56:367–95.

Eco, U. 1979. *The Role of the Reader: Explorations of the Semiotics of Texts*. Bloomington, IN: Indiana University Press.

Egger-Wenzel, R. 2006. 'The Testament of Mattathias to His Sons in Macc 2:49–70. A Key-word Composition with the Aim of Justification.' Pp. 141–9 in *History and Identity: How Israel's Later Authors Viewed Its Earlier History*, eds. N. Calduch-Benages and J. Liesen. Berlin: De Gruyter.

Ehrenberg, V., and A. H. M. Jones. 1976 [1955]. *Documents Illustrating the Reigns of Augustus and Tiberius*. Oxford: Oxford University Press.

Eisenbaum, P. 2009. *Paul Was Not a Christian: The Original Message of a Misunderstood Apostle*. San Francisco: HarperOne.

Elat, M. 1982. 'Tarshish and the Problem of Phoenician Colonisation in the Western Mediterranean.' *Orientalia Lovaniensia Periodica* 13:56–69.

Elliott, J. H. 1995. 'The Jewish Messianic Movement: From Faction to Sect.' Pp. 75–95 in *Modelling Early Christianity: Social-Scientific Studies of the New Testament in Its Context*, ed. P. F. Esler. London: Routledge.

Elliott, J. K. 1993. *The Apocryphal New Testament: A Collection of Apocryphal Christian Literature in an English Translation*. Oxford: Clarendon Press.

Elliott, N. 1994. *Liberating Paul: The Justice of God and the Politics of the Apostle*. Maryknoll, NY: Orbis.

——. 2008. *The Arrogance of Nations: Reading Romans in the Shadow of Empire*. Minneapolis: Fortress.

Ellis, E. E. 1957. *Paul's Use of the Old Testament*. Edinburgh: Oliver & Boyd.

Elsner, J. 1991. 'Cult and Sculpture: Sacrifice in the Ara Pacis Augustae.' *Journal of Roman Studies* 81:50–61.

Engberg-Pedersen, T. 2000. *Paul and the Stoics*. Edinburgh: T&T Clark.

——., ed. 2001. *Paul beyond the Judaism/Hellenism Divide*. Louisville: Westminster John Knox Press.

——. 2010. *Cosmology and Self in the Apostle Paul: The Material Spirit*. Oxford: Oxford University Press.

Eshel, H. 2010. 'Bar Kokhba Revolt.' Pp. 421–5 in *The Eerdmans Dictionary of Early Judaism*, eds. J. J. Collins and D. C. Harlow. Grand Rapids: Eerdmans.

Eskola, T. 2001. *Messiah and the Throne: Jewish Merkabah Mysticism and Early Christian Exaltation Discourse*. Tübingen: Mohr.

Esler, P. F. 1994. *The First Christians in Their Social Worlds: Social-Scientific Approaches to New Testament Interpretation*. London: Routledge.

——. 1998. *Galatians*. London, NY: Routledge.

——. 2001. 'I Thessalonians.' Pp. 1199–212 in *The Oxford Bible Commentary*, eds. J. Barton and J. Muddiman. Oxford: Oxford University Press.

——. 2003a. *Conflict and Identity in Romans*. London: Routledge.

——. 2003b. 'Social Identity, the Virtues, and the Good Life: A New Approach to Romans 12:1—15:13.' *Biblical Theology Bulletin* 33:51–63.

Evans, C. A. 1997. 'Aspects of Exile and Restoration in the Proclamation of Jesus and the Gospels.' Pp. 299–328. In *Exile: Old Testament, Jewish, and Christian Conceptions*, ed. James M. Scott. Leiden: Brill.

——. 2008. 'John the Baptist.' Pp. 345–51 in *The New Interpreter's Dictionary of the Bible*, vol. 3, eds. K. D. Sakenfeld et al. Nashville: Abingdon.

Evans, C. A., and P. W. Flint, eds. 1997. *Eschatology, Messianism and the Dead Sea Scrolls*. Grand Rapids: Eerdmans.

Evans, C. A., and S. E. Porter, eds. 2000. *Dictionary of New Testament Background: A Compendium of Contemporary Biblical Scholarship*. Downers Grove, IL: InterVarsity Press.

Fantin, J. D. 2011. *The Lord of the Entire World: Lord Jesus, a Challenge to Lord Caesar?* Sheffield: Sheffield Phoenix Press.

Fatehi, M. 2000. *The Spirit's Relation to the Risen Lord in Paul: An Examination of Its Christological Implications*. Tübingen: Mohr.

Fee, G. D. 1987. *The First Epistle to the Corinthians*, ed. F. F. Bruce. The New International Commentary on the New Testament. Grand Rapids: Eerdmans.

——. 1994. *God's Empowering Presence: The Holy Spirit in the Letters of Paul*. Peabody, MA: Hendrickson.

——. 1995. *Paul's Letter to the Philippians*. Grand Rapids: Eerdmans.

——. 2007. *Pauline Christology: An Exegetical-Theological Study*. Peabody, MA: Hendrickson.

——. 2009. *The First and Second Letters to the Thessalonians*. Grand Rapids: Eerdmans.

Feeney, D. 2007. *Caesar's Calendar: Ancient Time and the Beginnings of History*. Berkeley and Los Angeles: University of California Press.

Fine, S., and J. D. Brolley. 2009. 'Synagogue.' Pp. 416–27 in *The New Interpreter's Dictionary of the Bible*, vol. 5, eds. K. D. Sakenfeld et al. Nashville: Abingdon.

Fishbane, Michael. 1988 [1985]. *Biblical Interpretation in Ancient Israel*. Oxford: Oxford University Press.

Fishwick, D. 1987. *Études Préliminaires aux Religions Orientales dans l'Empire Romain 108*. Vol. 1.1–2, *The Imperial Cult in the Latin West: Studies in the Ruler Cult of the Western Provinces of the Roman Empire*. Leiden: Brill.

Fisk, B. N. 2001. *Do You Not Remember? Scripture, Story and Exegesis in the Rewritten Bible of Pseudo-Philo*. Sheffield: Sheffield Academic Press.

——. 2008. 'Synagogue Influence and Scriptural Knowledge among the Christians of Rome.' Pp. 157–85 in *As It Is Written: Studying Paul's Use of Scripture*, eds. S. E. Porter and C. D. Stanley. Atlanta: Society of Biblical Literature.

Fitzmyer, J. A. 1993. *Romans: A New Translation with Introduction and Commentary*. New York: Doubleday.

——. 2000. *The Letter to Philemon*. New York: Doubleday.

——. 2007. *The One Who Is to Come*. Grand Rapids: Eerdmans.

——. 2008. *First Corinthians: A New Translation with Introduction and Commentary*. New Haven: Yale University Press.

Fletcher-Louis, C. H. T. 1999. 'The Worship of Divine Humanity as God's Image and the Worship of Jesus.' Pp. 112–28 in *The Jewish Roots of Christological Monotheism: Papers from the St. Andrews Conference on the Historical Origins of the Worship of Jesus*, eds. C. C. Newman, J. R. Davila, and G. S. Lewis. Leiden: Brill.

Flusser, D. 1988. *Judaism and the Origins of Christianity*. Jerusalem: Magnes Press.

——. 1996. 'Die Gesetzeswerke in Qumran und bei Paulus.' Pp. 395–403 in *Geschichte – Tradition – Reflexion: Festschrift für Martin Hengel zum 70. Geburtstag. Bd 1: Judentum*, eds. Hubert Cancik, Hermann Lichtenberger, and Peter Schäfer. Tübingen: Mohr.

Forbes, C. 2003. 'Paul and Rhetorical Comparison.' Pp. 135–71 in *Paul in the Greco-Roman World: A Handbook*, ed. J. P. Sampley. Harrisburg, PA: Trinity Press International.

Fossum, J. 1989. 'Colossians 1.15–18a in the Light of Jewish Mysticism and Gnosticism.' *New Testament Studies* 35:183–201.

Fowden, G. 1999. 'Religious Communities.' Pp. 82–106 in *Late Antiquity: A Guide to the Postclassical World*, eds. G. W. Bowersock, P. Brown, and O. Grabar. Cambridge, MA: The Belknap Press of the Harvard University Press.

Fowl, S. E. 1990. *The Story of Christ in the Ethics of Paul: An Analysis of the Function of the Hymnic Material in the Pauline Corpus*. Sheffield: Sheffield Academic Press.

——. 1998. 'Christology and Ethics in Philippians 2:5–11.' Pp. 140–53 in *Where Christology Began: Essays on Philippians 2*, eds. R. P. Martin and B. J. Dodd. Louisville: Westminster John Knox Press.

——. 2005. *Philippians*. Grand Rapids: Eerdmans.

France, R. T. 1971. *Jesus and the Old Testament*. London: Tyndale.

——. 2002. *The Gospel of Mark: A Commentary on the Greek Text*. Grand Rapids: Eerdmans.

Fredriksen, P. 2007. 'Mandatory Retirement: Ideas in the Study of Christian Origins Whose Time Has Come to Go.' Pp. 25–38 in *Israel's God and Rebecca's Children: Christology and Community in Early Judaism and Christianity. Essays in Honor of Larry W. Hurtado and Alan F. Segal*, eds. D. B. Capes, A. D. DeConick, H. K. Bond, and T. Miller. Waco: Baylor University Press.

——. 2010. 'Judaizing the Nations: The Ritual Demands of Paul's Gospel.' *New Testament Studies* 56:232–52.

Free Presbyterian Church of Scotland. 1970. *The Confession of Faith; the Larger and Shorter Catechisms; with the Scripture Proofs at Large, Together with the Sum of Saving Knowledge*. Inverness: The Publications Committee of the Free Presbyterian Church of Scotland.

Fretheim, T. E. 2007. 'God, OT View of.' Pp. 603–18 in *The New Interpreter's Dictionary of the Bible*, vol. 2, eds. K. D. Sakenfeld et al. Nashville: Abingdon.

Frey, J. 2007. 'Paul's Jewish Identity.' Pp. 285–321 in *Jewish Identity in the Greco-Roman World*, eds. J. Frey, D. R. Schwartz, and S. Gripentrog. Leiden: Brill.

Friedenreich, D. M. 2011. 'Food and Table Fellowship.' Pp. 521–4 in *The Jewish Annotated New Testament*, eds. A.-J. Levine and M. Z. Brettler. Oxford: Oxford University Press.

Friedman, S. 2004. 'A Good Story Deserves Retelling – the Unfolding of the Akiva Legend.' *Journal for the Study of Judaism* 2:55–93.

Friesen, S. J. 1993. *Twice Neokoros: Ephesus, Asia and the Cult of the Flavian Imperial Family*. Leiden: Brill.

——. 2001. *Imperial Cults and the Apocalypse of John: Reading Revelation in the Ruins*. Oxford; New York: Oxford University Press.

——. 2005. 'Satan's Throne, Imperial Cults and the Social Settings of Revelation.' *Journal for the Study of the New Testament* 27(3):351–73.

——. 2009. 'Paul and Economics: The Jerusalem Collection as an Alternative to Patronage.' Pp. 27–54 in *Paul Unbound: Other Perspectives on the Apostle*, ed. M. D. Given. Peabody, MA: Hendrickson.

Fuller, M. E. 2006. *The Restoration of Israel*. Berlin: De Gruyter.

Funk, R. W. 1967. 'The Apostolic *Parousia*: Form and Significance.' Pp. 249–68 in *Christian History and Interpretation: Studies Presented to John Knox*, eds. W. R. Farmer, C. F. D. Moule, and R. R. Niebuhr. Cambridge: Cambridge University Press.

Furnish, V. P. 1968. *Theology and Ethics in Paul*. Nashville: Abingdon.

——. 1972. *The Love Command in the New Testament*. Nashville: Abingdon.

——. 1984. *II Corinthians*. Anchor Bible. New York: Doubleday.

——. 1990. 'Paul the Theologian.' Pp. 19–34 in *The Conversation Continues: Studies in Paul and John in Honor of J. Louis Martyn*, eds. R. T. Fortna and B. R. Gaventa. Nashville: Abingdon.

Gager, J. G. 1983. *The Origins of Anti-Semitism*. Oxford: Oxford University Press.

Galinsky, K. 1996. *Augustan Culture: An Interpretive Introduction*. Princeton: Princeton University Press.

——., ed. 2005. *The Cambridge Companion to the Age of Augustus*. Cambridge: Cambridge University Press.

García Martínez, F., and E. J. C. Tigchelaar. 1997. *The Dead Sea Scrolls Study Edition. Vol. 1: 1Q1—4Q273*. Leiden: Brill.

——. 1998. *The Dead Sea Scrolls Study Edition. Vol. 2: 4Q274—11Q31*. Leiden: Brill.

Garnet, P. 1977. *Salvation and Atonement in the Qumran Scrolls*. Tübingen: Mohr.

Gärtner, B. 1965. *The Temple and the Community in Qumran and the New Testament*. Cambridge: Cambridge University Press.

Gasparro, G. S. 2011. 'Mysteries and Oriental Cults: A Problem in the History of Religions.' Pp. 276–324 in *The Religious History of the Roman Empire: Pagans, Jews and Christians*, eds. J. A. North and S. R. F. Price. Oxford: Oxford University Press.

Gaston, L. 1987. *Paul and the Torah*. Vancouver: University of British Columbia Press.

Gathercole, S. J. 2000. 'The Critical and Dogmatic Agenda of Albert Schweitzer's *The Quest of the Historical Jesus*.' *Tyndale Bulletin* 51:261–83.

——. 2002a. *Where Is Boasting? Early Jewish Soteriology and Paul's Response in Romans 1—5*. Grand Rapids: Eerdmans.

——. 2002b. 'A Law Unto Themselves: The Gentiles in Romans 2.14–15 Revisited.' *Journal for the Study of the New Testament* 85:27–49.

——. 2006a. 'The Doctrine of Justification in Paul and Beyond: Some Proposals.' Pp. 219–41 in *Justification in Perspective: Historical Developments and Contemporary Challenges*, ed. B. L. McCormack. Grand Rapids: Baker Academic.

——. 2006b. *The Preexistent Son: Recovering the Christologies of Matthew, Mark, and Luke*. Grand Rapids: Eerdmans.

——. 2010. 'Election.' Pp. 571–3 in *The Eerdmans Dictionary of Early Judaism*, eds. J. J. Collins and D. C. Harlow. Grand Rapids: Eerdmans.

Gaventa, B. R. 1998. *First and Second Thessalonians*. Louisville: John Knox Press.

——. 2003. *The Acts of the Apostles*. Nashville: Abingdon.

——. 2007. *Our Mother Saint Paul*. Louisville: Westminster John Knox Press.

——. 2008. 'From Toxic Speech to the Redemption of Doxology in Paul's Letter to the Romans.' Pp. 392–408 in *The Word Leaps the Gap: Essays on Scripture and Theology in Honor of Richard B. Hays*, eds. J. R. Wagner, C. K. Rowe, and A. K. Grieb. Grand Rapids: Eerdmans.

——. 2010. 'On the Calling-Into-Being of Israel: Romans 9:6–29.' Pp. 255–69 in *Between Gospel and Election: Explorations in the Interpretation of Romans 9—11*, eds. F. Wilk and J. R. Wagner. Tübingen: Mohr.

Gazda, E. K., and D. Y. Ng. 2011. *Building a New Rome: The Imperial Colony of Pisidian Antioch (25 BC–AD 700)*. Ann Arbor, MI: Kelsey Museum of Archaeology.

Geertz, C. 2000 [1973]. *The Interpretation of Cultures*. 2nd edn. New York: Basic Books.

Getty, M. A. 1988. 'Paul and the Salvation of Israel: A Perspective on Romans 9—11.' *Catholic Biblical Quarterly* 50:456–69.

Giblin, C. H. 1970. *In Hope of God's Glory: Pauline Theological Perspectives*. New York: Herder.

Gibson, R. J. 2011. 'Paul the Missionary, in Priestly Service of the Servant-Christ (Romans 15.16).' Pp. 51–62 in *Paul as Missionary: Identity, Activity, Theology, and Practice*, eds. T. J. Burke and B. S. Rosner. London: T&T Clark.

Gignilliat, M. 2007. *Paul and Isaiah's Servants: Paul's Theological Reading of Isaiah 40—66 in 2 Corinthians 5.14—6.10*. London: T&T Clark.

Gilbert, M. 1997. *The Last Pages of the Wisdom of Solomon*. Dublin: Irish Biblical Association.

——. 2006. 'The Origins According to the Wisdom of Solomon.' Pp. 171–85 in *History and Identity: How Israel's Later Writers Viewed Its Earlier History*, eds. N. Calduch-Benages and J. Liesen. Berlin: De Gruyter.

Gill, C. 2003. 'The School in the Roman Imperial Period.' Pp. 33–58 in *The Cambridge Companion to the Stoics*, ed. B. Inwood. Cambridge: Cambridge University Press.

Gilliard, F. 1989. 'The Problem of the Anti-Semitic Comma between 1 Thessalonians 2:14 and 15.' *New Testament Studies* 35:481–502.

Ginzberg, L. 1937 [1909]. *The Legends of the Jews*. 14th edn., tr. H. Szold. Philadelphia: Jewish Publication Society of America.

Glombitza, O. 1964–5. 'Apostolische Sorge: Welche Sorge treibt den Apostel Paulus zu den Sätzen Röm. xi 25ff.?' *Novum Testamentum* 7:312–18.

Golding, W. 1995. *The Double Tongue*. London: Faber & Faber.

Goldingay, J., and D. Payne. 2006. *A Critical and Exegetical Commentary on Isaiah 40—55*. Edinburgh: T&T Clark.

Goldstein, J. A. 1987. 'How the Authors of 1 and 2 Maccabees Treated the "Messianic" Promises.' Pp. 69–96 in *Judaisms and Their Messiahs at the Turn of the Christian Era*, eds. J. Neusner, W. S. Green, and E. S. Frerichs. Cambridge: Cambridge University Press.

——. 1995. 'The Judaism of the Synagogues (Focusing on the Synagogue of Dura-Europos).' Pp. 109–57 in *Judaism in Late Antiquity*, ed. J. Neusner. Leiden: Brill.

Gooch, P. W. 1997. *Reflections on Jesus and Socrates: Word and Silence*. New Haven: Yale University Press.

Goodenough, E. R. 1953–68. *Jewish Symbols in the Graeco-Roman Period*. New York: Pantheon.

——. 1967. *The Politics of Philo Judaeus*. Hildesheim: Olms.

Gooder, P. R. 2006. *Only the Third Heaven? 2 Corinthians 12.1–10 and Heavenly Ascent*. London: T&T Clark.

Goodman, M. 1994. *Mission and Conversion: Proselytizing in the Religious History of the Roman Empire*. Oxford: Oxford University Press.

Gordon, R. 1990. 'Religion in the Roman Empire: The Civic Compromise and Its Limits.' Pp. 233–55 in *Pagan Priests: Religion and Power in the Ancient World*, eds. M. Beard and J. A. North. Ithaca, NY: Cornell University Press.

——. 2011. 'Ritual and Hierarchy in the Mysteries of Mithras.' Pp. 325–65 in *The Religious History of the Roman Empire*, eds. J. A. North and S. R. F. Price. Oxford: Oxford University Press.

Gorman, M. J. 2001. *Cruciformity: Paul's Narrative Spirituality of the Cross.* Grand Rapids: Eerdmans.

——. 2004. *Apostle of the Crucified Lord: A Theological Introduction to Paul and His Letters.* Grand Rapids: Eerdmans.

——. 2009. *Inhabiting the Cruciform God: Kenosis, Justification, and Theosis in Paul's Narrative Soteriology.* Grand Rapids: Eerdmans.

——. 2011. 'Justification and Justice in Paul, with Special Reference to the Corinthians.' *Journal for the Study of Paul and His Letters* 1(1):23–40.

——. 2013. 'Paul and the Cruciform Way of God in Christ.' *Journal of Moral Theology* 2 (1):64–83.

——. 2014. *Becoming the Gospel: Paul, Participation and Mission.* Grand Rapids: Eerdmans.

Gosling, J. C. B. 1990. *Weakness of the Will.* London: Routledge.

Gowan, D. E. 1977. 'The Exile in Jewish Apocalyptic.' Pp. 205–23 in *Scripture in History and Theology: Essays in Honor of J. Coert Rylaarsdam*, eds. A. E. Merrill and T. W. Overholt. Pittsburgh: Pickwick.

Grabbe, L. L. 1979. 'Chronography in Hellenistic Jewish Historiography.' *Society of Biblical Literature Seminar Papers* 17.2:43–68.

——. 1992. *Judaism from Cyrus to Hadrian.* Minneapolis: Fortress.

——. 2003. 'Did All Jews Think Alike? "Covenant" in Philo and Josephus in the Context of Second Temple Judaic Religion.' Pp. 251–66 in *The Concept of the Covenant in the Second Temple Period*, eds. Stanley E. Porter and Jacqueline C. R. de Roo. Leiden: Brill.

Gradel, I. 2002. *Emperor Worship and Roman Religion.* Oxford: Oxford University Press.

Grant, R. M. 1988. *Greek Apologists of the Second Century.* Philadelphia: Westminster Press.

Greenblatt, S. 2011. *The Swerve: How the Renaissance Began.* London: The Bodley Head.

Grieb, A. K. 2006. '"So That in Him We Might Become the Righteousness of God" (2 Cor 5:21): Some Theological Reflections on the Church Becoming Justice.' *Ex Auditu* 22:58–80.

——. 2010. 'Paul's Theological Preoccupation in Romans 9—11.' Pp. 391–400 in *Between Gospel and Election: Explorations in the Interpretation of Romans 9—11*, eds. F. Wilk and J. R. Wagner. Tübingen: Mohr.

Griffith-Jones, R. 2004. *The Gospel According to Paul: The Creative Genius Who Brought Jesus to the World.* San Francisco: HarperSanFrancisco.

——. 2012. '"Keep up Your Transformation within the Renewal of Your Mind": Romans as a Therapeutic Letter.' Pp. 137–60 in *Experientia II*, eds. C. Schantz and R. Werline. Atlanta: Society of Biblical Literature.

Griffiths, P. J. 2005. 'Religion.' Pp. 672–5 in *Dictionary for Theological Interpretation of the Bible*, ed. K. J. Vanhoozer. Grand Rapids: Baker Academic; London: SPCK.

Grosby, S. E. 2002. *Biblical Ideas of Nationality: Ancient and Modern.* Winona Lake, IN: Eisenbrauns.

Gundry, R. H. 1980. 'The Moral Frustration of Paul before His Conversion: Sexual Lust in Romans 7.7–25.' Pp. 228–45 in *Pauline Studies: Essays Presented to Professor F. F. Bruce on His 70th Birthday*, eds. Donald A. Hagner and Murray J. Harris. Exeter: Paternoster; Grand Rapids: Eerdmans.

——. 2004. 'The Nonimputation of Christ's Righteousness.' Pp. 17–45 in *Justification: What's at Stake in the Current Debates*, eds. M. Husbands and D. J. Treier. Downers Grove, IL: InterVarsity Press.

Gunneweg, A. 1977. 'Religion oder Offenbarung: Zum hermeneutischen Problem des Alten Testaments.' *Zeitschrift für Theologie und Kirche* 74:151–78.

Günther, R., and R. Müller. 1988. *Das goldene Zeitalter: Utopien der hellenistisch-römischen Antike*. Leipzig: Kohlhammer.

Gurtner, D. M. 2009. *Second Baruch: A Critical Edition of the Syriac Text*. New York; London: T&T Clark.

Haacker, K. 1971–2. 'War Paulus Hillelit?' Pp. 106–20 in *Das Institutum Judaicum der Universität Tübingen in den Jahren 1971–72*. Tübingen: Mohr.

——. 1975. 'Die Berufung des Verfolgers und die Rechtfertigung des Gottlosen. Erwägungen zum Zusammenhang zwischen Biographie und Theologie des Apostels Paulus.' *Theologische Beiträge* 6:1–19.

——. 2003. *The Theology of Paul's Letter to the Romans*. Cambridge: Cambridge University Press.

Haenchen, E. 1971. *The Acts of the Apostles*. Oxford: Blackwell.

Hafemann, S. J. 1988. 'The Salvation of Israel in Romans 11:25–32: A Response to Krister Stendahl.' *Ex Auditu* 4:38–58.

——. 1995. *Paul, Moses and the History of Israel: The Letter/Spirit Contrast and the Argument from Scripture in 2 Corinthians 3*. Tübingen: Mohr.

——. 2000a. *2 Corinthians: The NIV Application Commentary*. Grand Rapids: Zondervan.

——. 2000b. 'Roman Triumph.' Pp. 1004–8 in *Dictionary of New Testament Background*, eds. C. A. Evans and S. E. Porter. Downers Grove, IL: InterVarsity Press.

Hahn, S. W. 2009. *Kinship by Covenant: A Canonical Approach to the Fulfillment of God's Saving Promises*. New Haven and London: Yale University Press.

Halpern-Amaru, B. 1997. 'Exile and Return in Jubilees.' Pp. 127–44 in *Exile: Old Testament, Jewish, and Christian Conceptions*, ed. James M. Scott. Leiden: Brill.

Hanson, A. T. 1957. *The Wrath of the Lamb*. London: SPCK.

——. 1974. *Studies in Paul's Technique and Theology*. London: SPCK.

Haran, M. 1995 [1978]. *Temples and Temple Service in Ancient Israel*. Winona Lake, IN: Eisenbrauns.

Hardin, J. K. 2008. *Galatians and the Imperial Cult*. Tübingen: Mohr.

Harink, D. K. 2003. *Paul among the Postliberals*. Grand Rapids: Brazos.

——. 2010. 'Time and Politics in Four Commentaries on Romans.' Pp. 282–312 in *Paul, Philosophy and the Theopolitical Vision*, ed. D. Harink. Eugene, OR: Cascade Books.

Harmon, M. S. 2010. *She Must and Shall Go Free: Paul's Isaianic Gospel in Galatians*. Berlin: De Gruyter.

Harrill, J. A. 1999. 'Using the Roman Jurists to Interpret Philemon: A Response to Peter Lampe.' *Zeitschrift für die Neutestamentliche Wissenschaft* 90(1):135–8.

——. 2009a. 'Philemon.' Pp. 497–9 in *The New Interpreter's Dictionary of the Bible*, vol. 4, eds. K. D. Sakenfeld et al. Nashville: Abingdon.

——. 2009b. 'Slavery.' Pp. 299–308 in *The New Interpreter's Dictionary of the Bible*, vol. 5, eds. K. D. Sakenfeld et al. Nashville: Abingdon.

——. 2012. *Paul the Apostle: His Life and Legacy in Their Roman Context*. Cambridge: Cambridge University Press.

Harrington, D. J. 1973. 'Interpreting Israel's History: The *Testament of Moses* as a Rewriting of Deut 31—34.' Pp. 59–70 in *Studies on the Testament of Moses*, ed. G. W. E. Nickelsburg. Cambridge: Society of Biblical Literature.

Harrington, D. J., and J. F. Keenan. 2010. 'Paul and Virtue Ethics: Building Bridges between New Testament Studies and Moral Theology.' Lanham, MD: Rowman & Littlefield.

Harris, M. J. 1991. *Colossians and Philemon*. Grand Rapids: Eerdmans.

Harrison, J. R. 1999. 'Paul, Eschatology and the Augustan Age of Grace.' *Tyndale Bulletin* 50 (1):79–91.

——. 2002. 'Paul and the Imperial Gospel at Thessaloniki.' *Journal for the Study of the New Testament* 25(1):71–96.

——. 2011. *Paul and the Imperial Authorities at Thessalonica and Rome. A Study in the Conflict of Ideology*. Tübingen: Mohr.

Hartley, L. P. 1997 [1953]. *The Go-Between*, ed. D. Brooks-Davies. London: Penguin.

Hatina, T. R. 1996. 'The Focus of Mark 13:24–27: The Parousia, or the Destruction of the Temple.' *Bulletin of Biblical Research* 6:43–66.

——. 2002. *In Search of a Context: The Function of Scripture in Mark's Narrative*. Sheffield: Sheffield Academic Press.

Hay, D. M., ed. 1993. *Pauline Theology, Volume 2: 1 and 2 Corinthians*. Minneapolis: Fortress.

Hay, D. M, and E. Elizabeth Johnson, eds. 1995. *Pauline Theology, Volume 3: Romans*. Minneapolis: Fortress.

Hays, R. B. 1980. 'Psalm 143 and the Logic of Romans 3.' *Journal of Biblical Literature* 99:107–15.

——. 1983. *The Faith of Jesus Christ: An Investigation of the Narrative Substructure of Galatians 3:1—4:11*. SBL Dissertation Series. Chico, CA: Scholars Press.

——. 1985. '"Have We Found Abraham to Be Our Forefather According to the Flesh?" A Reconsideration of Rom. 4:1.' *Novum Testamentum* 27:76–98.

——. 1989a. *Echoes of Scripture in the Letters of Paul*. New Haven: Yale University Press.

——. 1989b. '"The Righteous One" as Eschatological Deliverer: Hermeneutics at the Turn of the Ages.' Pp. 191–215 in *Apocalyptic and the New Testament: Essays in Honor of J. Louis Martyn*, eds. J. Marcus and M. L. Soards. Sheffield: JSOT Press.

——. 1996a. 'The Role of Scripture in Paul's Ethics.' Pp. 30–47 in *Theology and Ethics in Paul and His Interpreters: Essays in Honor of Victor Paul Furnish*, eds. E. G. Lovering and J. J. Sumney. Nashville: Abingdon.

——. 1996b. *The Moral Vision of the New Testament: A Contemporary Introduction to New Testament Ethics*. San Francisco: HarperSanFrancisco.

——. 1997. *First Corinthians*. Interpretation Commentaries. Louisville: John Knox Press.

——. 2000. 'The Letter to the Galatians: Introduction, Commentary, and Reflections.' Pp. 181–348 in *The New Interpreter's Bible*, ed. L. E. Keck. Nashville: Abingdon.

——. 2002 [1983]. *The Faith of Jesus Christ: The Narrative Substructure of Galatians 3:1—4:11*. 2nd edn. Grand Rapids: Eerdmans.

——. 2005. *The Conversion of the Imagination: Paul as Interpreter of Israel's Scriptures*. Grand Rapids: Eerdmans.

Hayward, C. T. R. 1999. 'Sirach and Wisdom's Resting Place.' Pp. 31–46 in *Where Shall Wisdom Be Found? Wisdom in the Bible, the Church and the Contemporary World*, ed. S. C. Barton. Edinburgh: T&T Clark.

Hayward, R. 1991. 'Sacrifice and World Order: Some Observations on Ben Sira's Attitude to the Temple Service.' Pp. 22–34 in *Sacrifice and Redemption: Durham Essays in Theology*, ed. Stephen W. Sykes. Cambridge: Cambridge University Press.

Hegel, G. W. F. 1837/1928. *Vorlesungen über die Philosophie der Geschichte*. In Sämtliche Werke, vol. 11. Stuttgart: Frommans Verlag.

——. 1991 [1821]. *Elements of the Philosophy of Right*. Cambridge: Cambridge University Press.

Hellerman, J. H. 2005. *Reconstructing Honor in Roman Philippi: Carmen Christi as Cursus Pudorum*. Cambridge: Cambridge University Press.

Hengel, M. 1974. *Judaism and Hellenism: Studies in Their Encounter in Palestine during the Early Hellenistic Period*, tr. John Bowden. London: SCM Press.

——. 1976. *The Son of God: The Origin of Christology and the History of Jewish-Hellenistic Religion*, tr. John Bowden. Philadelphia: Fortress.

——. 1979. *Acts and the History of Earliest Christianity*, tr. John Bowden. Philadelphia: Fortress.

——. 1983. *Between Jesus and Paul: Studies in the Earliest History of Christianity*, tr. John Bowden. London: SCM Press.

——. 1989 [1961]. *The Zealots: Investigations into the Jewish Freedom Movement in the Period from Herod 1 until 70 A.D.*, tr. by D. Smith. Edinburgh: T&T Clark.

——. 1991. *The Pre-Christian Paul*, tr. John Bowden, in collaboration with Roland Deines. London: SCM Press; Philadelphia: Trinity Press International.

——. 1992. 'Christological Titles in Early Christianity.' Pp. 425–48 in *The Messiah: Developments in Earliest Judaism and Christianity*, ed. J. H. Charlesworth. Minneapolis: Fortress.

——. 1995. *Studies in Early Christology*. Edinburgh: T&T Clark.

——. 2006. *Studien zur Christologie: Kleine Schriften IV*, ed. C.-J. Thornton. Tübingen: Mohr.

Henze, M. 2010. 'Baruch, Second Book of.' Pp. 426–8 in *The Eerdmans Dictionary of Early Judaism*, eds. J. J. Collins and D. C. Harlow. Grand Rapids: Eerdmans.

Héring, J. 1966 [1962]. *The First Epistle of Saint Paul to the Corinthians*, tr. A. W. Heathcote and P. J. Allcock. London: Epworth Press.

Herman, G. 1987. *Ritualised Friendship and the Greek City*. Cambridge: Cambridge University Press.

Hester, J. D. 1968. *Paul's Concept of Inheritance*. Edinburgh: Oliver & Boyd.

Hezser, C. 2005. 'Review of David Instone-Brewer, *Traditions of the Rabbis from the Era of the New Testament: Prayer and Agriculture*.' *Journal of Jewish Studies* 56.2:347–9.

Hickling, C. J. 1975. 'St Paul the Writer.' Pp. 85–96 in *St Paul: Teacher and Traveller*, ed. I. Bulmer-Thomas. London: The Faith Press.

Hiebert, P. G. 2008. *Transforming Worldviews: An Anthropological Understanding of How People Change*. Grand Rapids: Baker Academic.

Hiers, R. H. 1992. 'Day of the Lord.' Pp. 82–3 in *Anchor Bible Dictionary*, ed. D. N. Freedman. New York: Doubleday.

Hill, C. C. 2001. 'Romans.' Pp. 1083–108 in *The Oxford Bible Commentary*, eds. J. Barton and J. Muddiman. Oxford: Oxford University Press.

Hock, R. F. 1980. *The Social Context of Paul's Ministry: Tentmaking and Apostleship*. Philadelphia: Fortress.

——. 2003. 'Paul and Greco-Roman Education.' Pp. 198–227 in *Paul in the Greco-Roman World: A Handbook*, ed. J. P. Sampley. Harrisburg, PA: Trinity Press International.

Hoehner, H. W. 1980 [1972]. *Herod Antipas: A Contemporary of Jesus Christ*. Grand Rapids: Zondervan.

——. 2002. *Ephesians: An Exegetical Commentary*. Grand Rapids: Baker Academic.

Hoff, M. C. 1996. 'The Politics and Architecture of the Athenean Imperial Cult.' Pp. 185–200 in *Subject and Ruler: The Cult of the Ruling Power in Classical Antiquity (Festschrift D. Fishwick)*, ed. A. Small. Dexter, MI: Thompson-Shore.

Hofius, O. 1990. '"All Israel Will Be Saved": Divine Salvation and Israel's Deliverance in Romans 9—11.' *Princeton Seminary Bulletin* 11:19–39.

Holland, P. 1994. *The Oxford Shakespeare: A Midsummer Night's Dream*. Oxford: Oxford University Press.

Holowchak, M. A. 2008. *The Stoics: A Guide for the Perplexed*. London/New York: Continuum.

Honderich, T. 1995. *The Oxford Companion to Philosophy*. Oxford: Oxford University Press.

Hood, J. B. 2013. *Imitating God in Christ: Recapturing a Biblical Pattern*. Downers Grove, IL: InterVarsity Press.

Hooke, S. H. 1958. *Myth, Ritual and Kingship: Essays on the Theory and Practice of Kingship in the Ancient Near East and in Israel*. Oxford: Clarendon Press.

Hooker, M. D. 1959. *Jesus and the Servant: The Influence of the Servant Concept of Deutero-Isaiah in the New Testament*. London: SPCK.

——. 1959–60. 'Adam in Romans I.' *New Testament Studies* 6:297–306.

——. 1971. 'Interchange in Christ.' *Journal of Theological Studies* n.s. 22(2):349–61.

——. 1972. 'On Using the Wrong Tool.' *Theology* 75:570–81.

——. 1973. 'Were There False Teachers in Colossae?' Pp. 315–31 in *Christ and Spirit in the New Testament: Essays in Honour of Charles Francis Digby Moule*, eds. B. Lindars and S. S. Smalley. Cambridge: Cambridge University Press.

——. 1975. 'In His Own Image?' Pp. 28–44 in *What about the New Testament? Essays in Honour of Christopher Evans*, eds. Morna D. Hooker and Colin Hickling. London: SCM Press.

——. 1990. *From Adam to Christ: Essays on Paul*. Cambridge: Cambridge University Press.

——. 2000. 'The Letter to the Philippians: Introduction, Commentary, and Reflections.' Pp. 467–549 in *The New Interpreter's Bible*, vol. 11, eds. L. E. Keck et al. Nashville: Abingdon.

——. 2002. '"Heirs of Abraham": The Gentiles' Role in Israel's Story. A Response to Bruce W. Longenecker.' Pp. 85–96 in *Narrative Dynamics in Paul: A Critical Assessment*, ed. B. W. Longenecker. Louisville: Westminster John Knox Press.

——. 2008. 'On Becoming the Righteousness of God: Another Look at 2 Cor 5:21.' *Novum Testamentum* 50:358–75.

——. 2013. 'Conformity to Christ.' *Theology* 116(2):83–92.

Hopkins, K. 1999. *A World Full of Gods: Pagans, Jews and Christians in the Roman Empire*. London: Phoenix.

Horbury, W. 1998. *Jewish Messianism and the Cult of Christ*. London: SCM Press.

——. 2003. *Messianism among Jews and Christians: Biblical and Historical Studies*. London: T&T Clark.

——. 2012. 'Jewish Imperial Thought and Pauline Gospel.' Unpublished paper delivered at Annual Meeting of SNTS. Leuven.

Horrell, D. G., ed. 1999. *Social-Scientific Approaches to New Testament Interpretation*. Edinburgh: T&T Clark.
——. 2002. 'Paul's Narratives or Narrative Substructure? The Significance of "Paul's Story".' Pp. 157–71 in *Narrative Dynamics in Paul: A Critical Assessment*, ed. B. W. Longenecker. Louisville: Westminster John Knox Press.
——. 2005. *Solidarity and Difference: A Contemporary Reading of Paul's Ethics*. London: T&T Clark.
Horsley, R. A. 1998. *1 Corinthians*. Nashville: Abingdon.
——. 2004a. *Hidden Transcripts and the Arts of Resistance: Applying the Work of James C. Scott to Jesus and Paul*. Atlanta: Society of Biblical Literature.
——. 2004b. *Paul and the Roman Imperial Order*. Harrisburg, PA: Trinity Press International.
——. 2009. *Revolt of the Scribes: Resistance and Apocalyptic Origins*. Minneapolis: Augsburg Fortress.
Horsley, R. A., and N. A. Silberman. 1997. *The Message of the Kingdom: How Jesus and Paul Ignited a Revolution and Transformed the Ancient World*. New York: Grossett/Putnam.
Howard, G. 1967. 'Notes and Observations on the "Faith of Christ".' *Harvard Theological Review* 60:459–65.
——. 1969. 'Christ the End of the Law: The Meaning of Romans 10:4ff.' *Journal of Biblical Literature* 88:331–8.
——. 1970. 'Romans 3:21–31 and the Inclusion of the Gentiles.' *Harvard Theological Review* 63:223–33.
——. 1979. *Paul: Crisis in Galatia. A Study in Early Christian Theology*. Cambridge: Cambridge University Press.
Hübner, H. 1984 [1974]. *Law in Paul's Thought*, tr. J. C. G. Greig. Edinburgh: T&T Clark.
Huby, J. 1957 [1940]. *Saint Paul. Épître aux Romains. Traduction et Commentaire*. Paris: Beauchesne.
Hultgren, A. J. 2010. *Paul's Letter to the Romans: A Commentary*. Grand Rapids: Eerdmans.
Humphrey, E. M. 2000. *Joseph and Aseneth*. Sheffield: Sheffield Academic Press.
——. 2007. 'Esdras, Second Book of.' Pp. 309–13 in *The New Interpreter's Dictionary of the Bible*, vol. 2, eds. K. D. Sakenfeld et al. Nashville: Abingdon.
Hurtado, L. W. 1984. 'Jesus as Lordly Example in Philippians 2:5–11.' Pp. 113–26 in *From Jesus to Paul: Studies in Honour of Francis Wright Beare*, eds. P. Richardson and J. C. Hurd. Waterloo, Ontario: Wilfrid Laurier University Press.
——. 1988. *One God, One Lord: Early Christian Devotion and Ancient Jewish Monotheism*. Philadelphia: Fortress.
——. 1999a. *At the Origins of Christian Worship: The Context and Character of Earliest Christian Devotion*. Carlisle: Paternoster.
——. 1999b. 'Jesus' Divine Sonship in Paul's Epistle to the Romans.' Pp. 217–33 in *Romans and the People of God: Essays in Honor of Gordon D. Fee on the Occasion of His 65th Birthday*, eds. S. K. Soderlund and N. T. Wright. Grand Rapids: Eerdmans.
——. 2003. *Lord Jesus Christ: Devotion to Jesus in Earliest Christianity*. Grand Rapids: Eerdmans.
——. 2005. *How on Earth Did Jesus Become a God? Historical Questions about Earliest Devotion to Jesus*. Grand Rapids: Eerdmans.

——. 2006. *The Earliest Christian Artifacts: Manuscripts and Christian Origins*. Grand Rapids: Eerdmans.

——. 2010. 'Monotheism.' Pp. 961–4 in *The Eerdmans Dictionary of Early Judaism*, eds. J. J. Collins and D. C. Harlow. Grand Rapids: Eerdmans.

Husbands, M., and D. J. Trier. 2004. *Justification: What's at Stake in the Current Debates*. Downers Grove, IL: InterVarsity Press.

Huttunen, N. 2009. *Paul and Epictetus on Law: A Comparison*. London: T&T Clark.

Instone-Brewer, D. 1992. *Techniques and Assumptions in Jewish Exegesis before 70 CE*. Tübingen: Mohr.

——. 2004. *Traditions of the Rabbis from the Era of the New Testament, Volume 1: Prayer and Agriculture*. Grand Rapids: Eerdmans.

Jacobson, J. 1996. *A Commentary on Pseudo-Philo's* Liber Antiquitatum Biblicarum *with Latin Text and English Translation*. Leiden: Brill.

Jenkins, D. E. 2002. *The Calling of a Cuckoo: Not Quite an Autobiography*. London: Continuum.

Jeremias, J. 1969. 'Paulus als Hillelit.' Pp. 88–94 in *Neotestamentica et Semitica: Studies in Honour of M. Black*, eds. E. E. Ellis and M. Wilcox. Edinburgh: T&T Clark.

——. 1977. 'Einige vorwiegend sprachliche Beobachtungen zu Röm 11, 25–36.' Pp. 193–205 in *Die Israelfrage nach Röm 9—11*, ed. L. de Lorenzi. Rome: Abtei von St Paul vor den Mauern.

Jewett, R. 1971. *Paul's Anthropological Terms: A Study of Their Use in Conflict Settings*. Leiden: Brill.

——. 1986. *The Thessalonian Correspondence: Pauline Rhetoric and Millennial Piety*. Philadelphia: Fortress.

——. 1988. 'Paul, Phoebe, and the Spanish Mission.' Pp. 142–61 in *The Social World of Formative Christianity and Judaism*, eds. J. Neusner, P. Borgen, E. S. Frerichs, and R. Horsley. Philadelphia: Fortress.

——. 2002 [1970–1]. 'The Agitators and the Galatian Congregation.' Pp. 334–47 in *The Galatians Debate: Contemporary Issues in Rhetorical and Historical Interpretation*, ed. M. D. Nanos. Peabody, MA: Hendrickson.

——. 2007. *Romans*. Minneapolis: Fortress.

Johnson, A. 2009. 'Sanctify, Sanctification.' Pp. 96–101 in *The New Interpreter's Bible Dictionary*, vol. 5, eds. K. D. Sakenfeld et al. Nashville: Abingdon.

Johnson, A. R. 1967. *Sacral Kingship in Ancient Israel*. Cardiff: University of Wales Press.

Johnson, E. E. 1989. *The Function of Apocalyptic and Wisdom Traditions in Romans 9—11*. Atlanta: Scholars Press.

Johnson, E. E., and D. M. Hay. 1997. *Pauline Theology, Volume 4: Looking Back, Pressing On*. Atlanta: Scholars Press.

Johnson, L. T. 1986. *The Writings of the New Testament: An Interpretation*. London: SCM Press.

——. 2001. *The First and Second Letters to Timothy: A New Translation with Introduction and Commentary*. New York: Doubleday.

Johnson, M. V., J. A. Noel, and D. K. Williams, eds. 2012. *Onesimus Our Brother: Reading Religion, Race and Culture in Philemon*. Minneapolis: Fortress.

Johnson, S. 1941. 'Notes and Comments.' *Anglican Theological Review* 23:173–6.

Johnson Hodge, C. E. 2007. *If Sons, Then Heirs: A Study of Kinship and Ethnicity in the Letters of Paul*. New York: Oxford University Press.

Jonas, H. 1963 [1958]. *The Gnostic Religion: The Message of the Alien God and the Beginnings of Christianity*. 2nd edn. Boston, MA: Beacon Press.

Jones, A. 2003. 'The Stoics and the Astronomical Sciences.' Pp. 328–44 in *The Cambridge Companion to the Stoics*, ed. B. Inwood. Cambridge: Cambridge University Press.

Jones, C. P. 1971. *Plutarch and Rome*. Oxford: Clarendon Press.

Judge, E. A. 1960. *The Social Pattern of Christian Groups in the First Century*. London: Tyndale (= 2008b, ch. 1).

——. 1960/1. 'The Early Christians as a Scholastic Community.' *Journal of Religious History* 1, 2:5–15; 125–37 (= 2008a, ch. 34).

——. 1968. 'Paul's Boasting in Relation to Contemporary Professional Practice.' *Australian Biblical Review* 16:37–50 (= 2008b, ch. 2).

——. 2008a. *The First Christians in the Roman World: Augustan and New Testament Essays*, ed. J. R. Harrison. Tübingen: Mohr.

——. 2008b. *Social Distinctives of the Christians in the First Century*, ed. D. M. Scholer. Peabody, MA: Hendrickson.

——. 2012. 'What Makes a Philosophical School?' Pp. 1–5 in *New Documents Illustrating Early Christianity*, vol. 10, eds. S. R. Llewelyn and J. R. Harrison. Grand Rapids: Eerdmans.

Kahl, B. 2010. *Galatians Re-Imagined: Reading with the Eyes of the Vanquished*. Minneapolis: Fortress.

Kaiser, O. 2006. '"Our Fathers Never Triumphed by Arms . . ." The Interpretation of Biblical History in the Addresses of Flavius Josephus to the Besieged Jerusalemites in Bell. Jud. V.356–426.' Pp. 239–64 in *History and Identity: How Israel's Later Writers Viewed Its Earlier History*, eds. N. Calduch-Benages and J. Liesen. Berlin: De Gruyter.

Kaminsky, J. S. 2007. *Yet I Loved Jacob: Reclaiming the Biblical Concept of Election*. Nashville: Abingdon.

Kammler, H.-C. 2003. 'Die Prädikation Jesu Christi als Gott und die paulinische Christologie. Erwägungen zur Exegese von Röm 9,5b.' *Zeitschrift für die Neutestamentliche Wissenschaft und die Kunde der Älteren Kirche* 94:164–80.

Kampen, J. L. 1988. *The Hasideans and the Origin of Pharisaism: A Study in 1 and 2 Maccabees*. Atlanta: Scholars Press.

——. 2007. 'Hasidim.' Pp. 739–40 in *The New Interpreter's Dictionary of the Bible*, vol. 2, eds. K. D. Sakenfeld et al. Nashville: Abingdon.

Kärkkäinen, V.-M. 2012. *The Holy Spirit: A Guide to Christian Theology*. Louisville: Westminster John Knox Press.

Käsemann, E. 1964 [1960]. *Essays on New Testament Themes*, tr. W. J. Montague. London: SCM Press.

——. 1968. 'A Critical Analysis of Philippians 2:5—11.' *Journal for Theology and Church [= God and Christ: Existence and Province]* 5:45–88.

——. 1969 [1965]. *New Testament Questions of Today*, tr. W. J. Montague. London: SCM Press.

——. 1971 [1969]. *Perspectives on Paul*, tr. Margaret Kohl. London: SCM Press.

——. 1980 [1973]. *Commentary on Romans*, tr. and ed. Geoffrey W. Bromiley. Grand Rapids: Eerdmans.

——. 2010. *On Being a Disciple of the Crucified Nazarene*, eds. R. Landau and W. Kraus. Grand Rapids: Eerdmans.

Kautzsch, E. 1910. *Gesenius' Hebrew Grammar*. Rev. and ed. A. E. Cowley. Oxford: Clarendon Press.

Keck, L. E. 1984. 'Paul and Apocalyptic Theology.' *Interpretation* 38(July):229–41.

——. 2005. *Romans*. Nashville: Abingdon.

Kee, H. C. 1980 [1973]. *The Origins of Christianity: Sources and Documents*. London: SPCK.

Keener, C. S. 1993. *The IVP Bible Background Commentary: New Testament*. Downers Grove, IL: InterVarsity Press.

——. 2005. *1—2 Corinthians*. Cambridge: Cambridge University Press.

——. 2009. *Romans: A New Covenant Commentary*. Eugene, OR: Cascade Books.

——. 2012. *Acts: An Exegetical Commentary*. Grand Rapids: Baker Academic.

Keesmaat, S. C. 1999. *Paul and His Story: (Re)Interpreting the Exodus Tradition*. JSNT Supplement Series. Sheffield: Sheffield Academic Press.

Kenny, A. 1986. *A Stylometric Study of the New Testament*. Oxford: Clarendon Press.

——. 2010. *A New History of Western Philosophy*. Oxford: Oxford University Press.

Kiley, M. 1986. *Colossians as Pseudepigraphy*. Sheffield: JSOT Press.

Kim, S. 1981. *The Origin of Paul's Gospel*. Tübingen: Mohr.

——. 1993. 'Jesus, Sayings of.' Pp. 474–92 in *Dictionary of Paul and His Letters*, eds. G. F. Hawthorne, R. P. Martin, and D. G. Reid. Downers Grove, IL: InterVarsity Press.

——. 1997. '2 Cor. 5:11–21 and the Origin of Paul's Concept of "Reconciliation".' *Novum Testamentum* 39:360–84.

——. 2002. *Paul and the New Perspective: Second Thoughts on the Origin of Paul's Gospel*. Grand Rapids: Eerdmans.

——. 2008. *Christ and Caesar: The Gospel and the Roman Empire in the Writings of Paul and Luke*. Grand Rapids: Eerdmans.

——. 2011. 'Paul as an Eschatological Herald.' Pp. 9–24 in *Paul as Missionary: Identity, Activity, Theology, and Practice*, eds. T. J. Burke and B. S. Rosner. London: T&T Clark.

Kimelman, R. 1988–9. 'The Daily 'Amidah and the Rhetoric of Redemption.' *Jewish Quarterly Review* 79:165–97.

King, K. L. 2003. *What Is Gnosticism?* Cambridge, MA: The Belknap Press of Harvard University Press.

Kipling, R. 1927. *Rudyard Kipling's Verse: Inclusive Edition, 1885–1926*. London: Hodder & Stoughton.

Kirk, G. S., J. E. Raven, and M. Schofield. 1983 [1957]. *The Presocratic Philosophers: A Critical History with a Selection of Texts*. 2nd edn. Cambridge: Cambridge University Press.

Kirk, J. R. D. 2008. *Unlocking Romans: Resurrection and the Justification of God*. Grand Rapids: Eerdmans.

Klassen, W. 1992. 'Love (NT and Early Jewish).' Pp. 381–96 in *Anchor Bible Dictionary*, vol. 4, ed. D. N. Freedman. New York: Doubleday.

Klauck, H.-J. 2000 [1995/6]. *The Religious Context of Early Christianity*. Edinburgh: T&T Clark.

Klausner, J. 1943. *From Jesus to Paul*. New York: Macmillan.

Kleiner, D. E. E. 2005. 'Semblance and Storytelling in Augustan Rome.' Pp. 197–233 in *The Cambridge Companion to the Age of Augustus*, ed. K. Galinsky. Cambridge: Cambridge University Press.

Kloppenborg, J. S. 2008. 'Love in the NT.' Pp. 703–13 in *The New Interpreter's Dictionary of the Bible*, vol. 3, eds. K. D. Sakenfeld et al. Nashville: Abingdon.

Knibb, M. A. 1976. 'The Exile in the Literature of the Intertestamental Period.' *Heythrop Journal* 17(3):253–79.

——. 1987. *The Qumran Community*. Cambridge: Cambridge University Press.

Knox, J. 1935. *Philemon among the Letters of Paul*. Chicago: University of Chicago Press.

Koch, D. A. 1986. *Die Schrift als Zeuge des Evangeliums: Untersuchungen zur Verwendung und zum Verständnis der Schrift bei Paulus*. Tübingen: Mohr.

Koch, K. 1972 [1970]. *The Rediscovery of Apocalyptic: A Polemical Work on a Neglected Area of Biblical Studies and Its Damaging Effects on Theology and Philosophy*, tr. Margaret Kohl. London: SCM Press.

Koenig, J. 2000. *The Feast of the World's Redemption: Eucharistic Origins and Christian Mission*. Harrisburg, PA: Trinity Press International.

Koester, H. 1982a [1980]. *Introduction to the New Testament*. Vol. 1, *History, Culture and Religion of the Hellenistic Age*. Philadelphia: Fortress; Berlin: De Gruyter.

——. 1982b. *Introduction to the New Testament*. Vol. 2, *History and Literature of Early Christianity*. Philadelphia: Fortress; Berlin: De Gruyter.

——. 1990. *Ancient Christian Gospels: Their History and Development*. London: SCM Press; Philadelphia: Trinity Press International.

Kraemer, R. S. 1998. *When Aseneth Met Joseph: A Late Antique Tale of the Biblical Patriarch and His Egyptian Wife, Reconsidered*. Oxford: Oxford University Press.

Kramer, W. G. 1966. *Christ, Lord, Son of God*, tr. B. Hardy. London: SCM Press.

Kreitzer, L. J. 1987. *Jesus and God in Paul's Eschatology*. Sheffield: JSOT Press.

——. 1993. 'Eschatology.' Pp. 253–69 in *Dictionary of Paul and His Letters*, eds. G. F. Hawthorne, R. P. Martin, and D. G. Reid. Downers Grove, IL: InterVarsity Press.

——. 1996. *Striking New Images: Roman Imperial Coinage and the New Testament World*. Sheffield: Sheffield Academic Press.

Kruse, C. G. 1993. 'Call, Calling.' Pp. 84–5 in *Dictionary of Paul and His Letters*, eds. G. F. Hawthorne, R. P. Martin, and D. G. Reid. Downers Grove, IL: InterVarsity Press.

Kugler, R. A. 2001. 'Testaments.' Pp. 189–213 in *Justification and Variegated Nomism, Volume 1: The Complexities of Second Temple Judaism*, eds. D. A. Carson, Peter T. O'Brien, and Mark A. Seifrid. Tübingen: Mohr.

Kumitz, C. 2004. *Der Brief als Medium der* agapē: *Eine Untersuchung zur rhetorischen und epistolographischen Gestalt des Philemonbriefes*. Frankfurt am Main: Peter Lang.

Kümmel, W. G. 1974 [1929]. *Römer 7 und die Bekehrung des Paulus*. Munich: Kaiser.

Küng, H. 1964 [1957]. *Justification: The Doctrine of Karl Barth and a Catholic Reflection*, tr. T. Collins, E. E. Tolk, and D. Grandskou. London: Burns & Oates.

Kwon, Y.-G. 2004. *Eschatology in Galatians: Rethinking Paul's Response to the Crisis in Galatia*. Tübingen: Mohr.

Lacocque, A. 1979 [1976]. *The Book of Daniel*. London: SPCK.

Ladd, G. E. 1974a. *The Presence of the Future: The Eschatology of Biblical Realism*. Grand Rapids: Eerdmans.

——. 1974b. *A Theology of the New Testament*. Grand Rapids: Eerdmans.

Lampe, P. 1985. 'Keine "Sklavenflucht" des Onesimus.' *Zeitschrift Für die Neutestamentliche Wissenschaft und die Kunde der Älteren Kirche* 76:135–7.

——. 2003 [1987]. *From Paul to Valentinus: Christians at Rome in the First Two Centuries*, tr. Michael Steinhauser. London: T&T Clark.

Lane, A. N. S. 2006. 'A Tale of Two Imperial Cities: Justification at Regensburg (1541) and Trent (1546–1547).' Pp. 119–45 in *Justification in Perspective: Historical Developments and Contemporary Challenges*, ed. B. L. McCormack. Grand Rapids: Baker Academic.

Lang, B. 2004. 'On the "The" in "the Jews".' Pp. 63–70 in *Those Who Forget the Past: The Question of Anti-Semitism*, ed. R. Rosenbaum. New York: Random House.

Lawrence, J. D. 2006. *Washing in Water: Trajectories of Ritual Bathing in the Hebrew Bible and Second Temple Literature*. Atlanta: Society of Biblical Literature.

——. 2010. 'Washing, Ritual.' Pp. 1331–2 in *The Eerdmans Dictionary of Early Judaism*, eds. J. J. Collins and D. C. Harlow. Grand Rapids: Eerdmans.

Leary, T. J. 1992. 'Paul's Improper Name.' *New Testament Studies* 32(3):467–9.

Lee, A. H. I. 2005. *From Messiah to Preexistent Son: Jesus' Self-Consciousness and Early Christian Exegesis of Messianic Psalms*. Tübingen: Mohr.

Lee, M. V. 2006. *Paul, the Stoics, and the Body of Christ*. Cambridge: Cambridge University Press.

Lenowitz, H. 2001 [1998]. *The Jewish Messiahs: From the Galilee to Crown Heights*. New York: Oxford University Press.

Leon, H. J. 1995 [1960]. *The Jews of Ancient Rome*. New introd. Carolyn A. Osiek. Peabody, MA: Hendrickson.

Levenson, J. D. 1993. *The Death and Resurrection of the Beloved Son: The Transformation of Child Sacrifice in Judaism and Christianity*. New Haven: Yale University Press.

——. 2012. *Inheriting Abraham: The Legacy of the Patriarch in Judaism, Christianity, and Islam*. Princeton: Princeton University Press.

Levin, B. 1983. *Enthusiasms*. New York: Crown Publishers Inc.

Levine, A.-J. 2011. 'Bearing False Witness: Common Errors Made about Early Judaism.' Pp. 501–4 in *The Jewish Annotated New Testament*, eds. A.-J. Levine and M. Z. Brettler. Oxford: Oxford University Press.

Levison, J. R. 1988. *Portraits of Adam in Early Judaism: From Sirach to 2 Baruch*. Sheffield: Sheffield Academic Press.

——. 1997. *The Spirit in First-Century Judaism*. Leiden: Brill.

——. 2009. *Filled with the Spirit*. Grand Rapids: Eerdmans.

——. 2010. 'Adam and Eve.' Pp. 300–2 in *The Eerdmans Dictionary of Early Judaism*, eds. J. J. Collins and D. C. Harlow. Grand Rapids: Eerdmans.

Lewis, C. S. 1952. *The Voyage of the Dawn Treader*. London: Macmillan.

——. 1954. *English Literature in the Sixteenth Century Excluding Drama*. Oxford: Clarendon Press.

——. 1955 [1942]. *The Screwtape Letters*. London: Fontana.

——. 1960 [1942]. *A Preface to* Paradise Lost. London: Oxford University Press.

——. 1961. *An Experiment in Criticism*. Cambridge: Cambridge University Press.

——. 1964. *The Discarded Image: An Introduction to Medieval and Renaissance Literature*. Cambridge: Cambridge University Press.

Lichtenberger, H. 2006. 'Historiography in the Damascus Document.' Pp. 231–8 in *History and Identity: How Israel's Later Authors Viewed Its Earlier History*, eds. N. Calduch-Benages and J. Liesen. Berlin: De Gruyter.

Lietzmann, D. H. 1971. *An die Römer*. Tübingen: Mohr.

Lieu, S. 1999. 'Manichaeism.' Pp. 555–6 in *Late Antiquity: A Guide to the Postclassical World*, eds. G. W. Bowersock, P. Brown, and O. Grabar. Cambridge, MA: The Belknap Press of the Harvard University Press.

Lightfoot, J. B. 1868. *St Paul's Epistle to the Philippians: A Revised Text with Introduction, Notes and Dissertations*. London: Macmillan and Co.

——. 1876. *St Paul's Epistles to the Colossians and to Philemon*. 2nd edn. London: Macmillan.

——. 1904. *Notes on Epistles of St Paul from Unpublished Commentaries*. London: Macmillan.

Lightstone, J. 2006 [1984]. *Commerce of the Sacred: Mediation of the Divine among Jews in the Graeco-Roman Diaspora*. New edn. New York: Columbia University Press.

Lim, T. H. 2007. 'Deuteronomy in the Judaism of the Second Temple Period.' Pp. 6–26 in *Deuteronomy in the New Testament: The New Testament and the Scriptures of Israel*, eds. S. Moyise and M. J. J. Menken. London: T&T Clark.

Lincicum, D. 2010. *Paul and the Early Jewish Encounter with Deuteronomy*. Tübingen: Mohr.

Lincoln, A. T. 1990. *Ephesians*. Word Biblical Commentary, vol. 42. Waco: Word Books.

——. 2002. 'The Stories of Predecessors and Inheritors in Galatians and Romans.' Pp. 172–203 in *Narrative Dynamics in Paul: A Critical Assessment*, ed. B. W. Longenecker. Louisville: Westminster John Knox Press.

Lindemann, A. 2000. *Der Erste Korintherbrief*. Tübingen: Mohr.

Litwa, M. D. 2012. *We Are Being Transformed: Deification in Paul's Soteriology*. Berlin: De Gruyter.

Lizza, R. 2011. 'Leap of Faith: The Making of a Republican Front-Runner.' *New Yorker*, 15 and 22 August, 54–63.

Llewelyn, S. R., ed. 1998. *New Documents Illustrating Early Christianity, Volume 8*. Grand Rapids: Eerdmans.

Llewelyn, S. R., and J. R. Harrison, eds. 2012. *New Documents Illustrating Early Christianity, Volume 10*. Grand Rapids: Eerdmans.

Loewe, R. 1981. '"Salvation" Is Not of the Jews.' *Journal of Theological Studies* 22:341–68.

Logan, A. H. B. 2006. *The Gnostics: Identifying an Early Christian Cult*. London: T&T Clark.

Lohse, E. 1971 [1968]. *Colossians and Philemon*, tr. W. R. Poehlmann and R. J. Karris. Philadelphia: Fortress.

Long, A. A. 2003. 'Roman Philosophy.' Pp. 184–210 in *The Cambridge Companion to Greek and Roman Philosophy*, ed. D. Sedley. Cambridge: Cambridge University Press.

——. 2006. *From Epicurus to Epictetus: Studies in Hellenistic and Roman Philosophy*. Oxford: Oxford University Press, Clarendon Press.

Long, A. A., and D. N. Sedley. 1987. *The Hellenistic Philosophers, Volume 1: Translations of the Principal Sources with Philosophical Commentary*. Cambridge, UK; London; New York: Cambridge University Press.

Longenecker, B. W. 1990. 'Eschatology and the Covenant: A Comparison of 4 Ezra and Romans 1—11'. Unpublished doctoral dissertation, Durham University.

——. 1991. *Eschatology and the Covenant in 4 Ezra and Romans 1—11*. Sheffield: Sheffield Academic Press.

——. 1998. *The Triumph of Abraham's God: The Transformation of Identity in Galatians.* Edinburgh: T&T Clark.

——. 2002a. *Narrative Dynamics in Paul: A Critical Assessment.* Louisville: Westminster John Knox Press.

——. 2002b. 'Narrative Interest in the Study of Paul: Retrospective and Prospective.' Pp. 3–18 in *Narrative Dynamics in Paul: A Critical Assessment*, ed. B. W. Longenecker. Louisville: Westminster John Knox Press.

——. 2002c. 'Sharing in Their Spiritual Blessings? The Stories of Israel in Galatians and Romans.' Pp. 58–84 in *Narrative Dynamics in Paul: A Critical Assessment*, ed. B. W. Longenecker. Louisville: Westminster John Knox Press.

——. 2007. 'On Israel's God and God's Israel: Assessing Supersessionism in Paul.' *Journal of Theological Studies* n.s. 58:26–44.

——. 2009. 'Socio-Economic Profiling of the First Urban Christians.' Pp. 36–59 in *After the First Urban Christians: The Social-Scientific Study of Pauline Christianity Twenty-Five Years Later*, eds. T. D. Still and D. G. Horrell. London: T&T Clark.

——. 2010. *Remember the Poor: Paul, Poverty, and the Greco-Roman World.* Grand Rapids: Eerdmans.

——. 2012. 'Salvation History in Galatians and the Making of a Pauline Discourse.' *Journal for the Study of Paul and His Letters* 2(2):1–24.

Longenecker, R. N. 1990. *Galatians.* Dallas: Word Books.

——., ed. 2005. *Contours of Christology in the New Testament.* Grand Rapids: Eerdmans.

Löwy, M. 2005. *Fire Alarm: Reading Walter Benjamin's 'On the Concept of History'.* London, NY: Verso.

Lucas, J. R. 1976. *Freedom and Grace.* London: SPCK.

Lundquist, J. M. 2008. *The Temple of Jerusalem: Past, Present and Future.* Westport, CT: Praeger Publishers.

Luther, M. 1970 [1520]. *Three Treatises.* Philadelphia: Fortress.

——. 1971 [1516]. *Luther: Lectures on Romans*, tr. and ed. W. Pauck. Philadelphia: Westminster Press.

Lutz, C. E. 1947. 'Musonius Rufus, "The Roman Socrates".' *Yale Classical Studies* 10:3–147.

Lyons, S. 1996. *The Fleeting Years: Odes of Horace from the Augustan Age of Rome.* Stoke-on-Trent: Staffordshire University Press.

——. 2007. *Horace's Odes and the Mystery of Do-Re-Mi.* Oxford: Oxbow Books.

Macaskill, G. 2007. *Revealed Wisdom and Inaugurated Eschatology in Ancient Judaism and Early Christianity.* Leiden: Brill.

McClendon, J. W., and C. J. Conniry. 2000. 'Conversion.' Pp. 135–6 in *The Oxford Companion to Christian Thought*, ed. A. Hastings. Oxford: Oxford University Press.

Maccoby, H. 1986. *The Mythmaker: Paul and the Invention of Christianity.* London: Weidenfeld & Nicolson.

McConville, J. G. 1986. 'Ezra-Nehemiah and the Fulfillment of Prophecy.' *Vetus Testamentum* 36:205–24.

McCormack, B. L. 2004. 'What's at Stake in Current Debates over Justification? The Crisis of Protestantism in the West.' Pp. 81–117 in *Justification: What's at Stake in the Current Debates*, ed. M. Husbands and D. J. Treier. Downers Grove, IL: InterVarsity Press.

——. 2006a. '*Justitia Aliena*: Karl Barth in Conversation with the Evangelical Doctrine of Imputed Righteousness.' Pp. 167–96 in *Justification in Perspective: Historical Developments and Contemporary Challenges*, ed. B. L. McCormack. Grand Rapids: Baker Academic.

——., ed. 2006b. *Justification in Perspective: Historical Developments and Contemporary Challenges*. Grand Rapids: Baker Academic.

MacDonald, N. 2003. *Deuteronomy and the Meaning of Monotheism*. Tübingen: Mohr.

——. 2004. 'The Origin of "Monotheism".' Pp. 204–15 in *Early Jewish and Christian Monotheism*, ed. L. T. Stuckenbruck and W. E. S. North. London: T&T Clark International.

McGilchrist, I. 2009. *The Master and His Emissary: The Divided Brain and the Making of the Western World*. New Haven and London: Yale University Press.

McGowan, A. T. B. 2006. 'Justification and the *Ordo Salutis*.' Pp. 147–66 in *Justification in Perspective: Historical Developments and Contemporary Challenges*, ed. B. L. McCormack. Grand Rapids: Baker Academic.

McGrath, A. E. 1986. *Iustitia Dei: A History of the Christian Doctrine of Justification*. Cambridge: Cambridge University Press.

McGrath, J. F. 2009. *The Only True God: Early Christian Monotheism in Its Jewish Context*. Urbana, Chicago and Springfield, IL: University of Illinois Press.

McGrath, J. F., and J. Truex, comp. 2004. 'Early Jewish and Christian Monotheism: A Select Bibliography.' Pp. 235–42 in *Early Jewish and Christian Monotheism*, ed. L. T. Stuckenbruck and W. E. S. North. London: T&T Clark International.

McKnight, S. 1991. *A Light among the Gentiles: Jewish Missionary Activity in the Second Temple Period*. Minneapolis: Augsburg Fortress.

McLaren, J. S. 2005. 'Jews and the Imperial Cult: From Augustus to Domitian.' *Journal for the Study of the New Testament* 27(3):257–78.

McNamara, M. 1978. '"*To de (Hagar) Sina Oros Estin en Tē Arabia*" (Gal. 4:25a): Paul and Petra.' *Milltown Studies* 2:24–41.

MacRae, G. 1987. 'Messiah and Gospel.' Pp. 169–85 in *Judaisms and Their Messiahs at the Turn of the Christian Era*, eds. J. Neusner, W. S. Green, and E. Frerichs. Cambridge: Cambridge University Press.

Madeline, L., ed. 2008. *Correspondence: Pablo Picasso and Gertrude Stein*. London: Seagull.

Magda, K. 2009. *Paul's Territoriality and Mission Strategy*. Tübingen: Mohr.

Maier, H. O. 2005. 'A Sly Civility: Colossians and Empire.' *Journal for the Study of the New Testament* 27(3):323–49.

Malherbe, A. J. 1986. *Moral Exhortation, A Greco-Roman Sourcebook*. Philadelphia: Westminster Press.

——. 1987. *Paul and the Thessalonians: The Philosophic Tradition of Pastoral Care*. Philadelphia: Fortress.

——. 1989a. 'Greco-Roman Religion and Philosophy and the New Testament.' Pp. 3–26 in *The New Testament and Its Modern Interpreters*, eds. E. J. Epp and G. W. MacRae. Atlanta: Scholars Press.

——. 1989b. *Paul and the Popular Philosophers*. Minneapolis: Fortress.

——. 2000. *The Letters to the Thessalonians: A New Translation with Introduction and Commentary*. New Haven: Yale University Press.

Malina, B. J. 1993. *The New Testament World: Insights from Cultural Anthropology*. Rev. edn. Louisville: Westminster John Knox Press.

Malina, B. J., and J. H. Neyrey. 1996. *Portraits of Paul: An Archaeology of Ancient Personality.* Louisville: Westminster John Knox Press.

Manson, T. W. 1962a. 'Appendix 1. ΛΟΓΙΑ in the Greek Versions of the OT.' Pp. 87–96 in *Studies in the Gospels and Epistles.* Manchester: Manchester University Press.

——. 1962b. 'Appendix 2. ΛΟΓΙΑ in N. T. ' Pp. 87–104 in *Studies in the Gospels and Epistles.* Manchester: Manchester University Press.

Marchal, J. A., ed. 2012. *Studying Paul's Letters: Contemporary Perspectives and Methods.* Minneapolis: Fortress.

Marcus, J. 1986a. 'The Evil Inclination in the Letters of Paul.' *Irish Biblical Studies* 8:8–21.

——. 1986b. *The Mystery of the Kingdom of God.* Atlanta: Scholars Press.

——. 1989. 'The Circumcision and the Uncircumcision in Rome.' *New Testament Studies* 35:67–81.

Marsden, G. M. 2006 [1980]. *Fundamentalism and American Culture.* New York: Oxford University Press.

Marshall, I. H. 1993. 'The Theology of Philemon.' Pp. 175–91 in *The Theology of the Shorter Pauline Letters*, eds. K. P. Donfriend and I. H. Marshall. Cambridge: Cambridge University Press.

——. 1999. 'Romans 16:25–27 – an Apt Conclusion.' Pp. 170–84 in *Romans and the People of God: Essays in Honor of Gordon D. Fee on the Occasion of His 65th Birthday*, eds. S. K. Soderlund and N. T. Wright. Grand Rapids: Eerdmans.

——. 2002. 'Response to A. T. Lincoln: The Stories of Predecessors and Inheritors in Galatians and Romans.' Pp. 204–14 in *Narrative Dynamics in Paul: A Critical Assessment*, ed. B. W. Longenecker. Louisville: Westminster John Knox Press.

——. 2007. *Aspects of the Atonement: Cross and Resurrection in the Reconciling of God and Humanity.* London: Paternoster.

——. 2008. 'Lord's Supper.' Pp. 695–700 in *The New Interpreter's Dictionary of the Bible*, vol. 3, eds. K. D. Sakenfeld et al. Nashville: Abingdon.

Martin, D. B. 1995. *The Corinthian Body.* New Haven: Yale University Press.

——. 2001. 'Paul and the Judaism/Hellenism Dichotomy: Toward a Social History of the Question.' Pp. 29–61 in *Paul beyond the Judaism/Hellenism Divide*, ed. Troels Engberg-Pedersen. Louisville: Westminster John Knox Press.

Martin, R. P. 1981. *Reconciliation: A Study of Paul's Theology.* London: Marshall, Morgan & Scott.

——. 1997 [1967]. *A Hymn of Christ: Philippians 2:5–11 in Recent Interpretation.* 3rd edn. Downers Grove, IL: InterVarsity Press.

Martin, R. P., and B. J. Dodd, eds. 1998. *Where Christology Began: Essays on Philippians 2.* Louisville: Westminster John Knox Press.

Martyn, J. L. 1997a. *Galatians: A New Translation with Introduction and Commentary.* Anchor Bible, vol. 33a. New York: Doubleday.

——. 1997b. *Theological Issues in the Letters of Paul.* Nashville: Abingdon.

Marx, K. 1932 [1845]. *Theses on Feuerbach.* Moscow: Marx-Engels-Lenin Institute.

——. 2012 [1843–4]. *Critique of Hegel's 'Philosophy of Right'.* Chicago: Aristeus Books.

Mason, A. 2000. 'Dispensationalism.' Pp. 169–70 in *The Oxford Companion to Christian Thought*, ed. A. Hastings. Oxford: Oxford University Press.

Mason, S. 1994. 'Josephus, Daniel and the Flavian House.' Pp. 161–91 in *Josephus and the History of the Greco-Roman Period: Essays in Memory of Morton Smith*, eds. F. Parente and J. Sievers. Leiden: Brill.

——. 2001. *Flavius Josephus: Translation and Commentary, Volume 9: Life of Josephus.* Leiden: Brill.

——. 2007. 'Jews, Judaeans, Judaizing, Judaism: Problems of Categorization in Ancient History.' *Journal for the Study of Judaism* 38:457–512.

Mason, S., and L. H. Feldman, eds. 1999. *Flavius Josephus: Translation and Commentary, Volume 3: Antiquities 1–4* . Leiden: Brill.

Matera, F. J. 1999. *New Testament Christology*. Louisville: Westminster John Knox Press.

——. 2012. *God's Saving Grace: A Pauline Theology*. Grand Rapids: Eerdmans.

Matlock, R. Barry. 1996. *Unveiling the Apocalyptic Paul: Paul's Interpreters and the Rhetoric of Criticism*. Sheffield: Sheffield Academic Press.

May, A. S. 2004. *'The Body for the Lord': Sex and Identity in 1 Corinthians 5—7*. London: T&T Clark.

Meadors, E. P. 2006. *Idolatry and the Hardening of the Heart*. New York: T&T Clark.

Meeks, W. A. 1982. '"And Rose Up to Play": Midrash and Paraenesis in 1 Corinthians 10:1–22.' *Journal for the Study of the New Testament* 16:64–78.

——. 1983. *The First Urban Christians: The Social World of the Apostle Paul.* New Haven: Yale University Press.

——. 1986a. 'A Hermeneutics of Social Embodiment.' *Harvard Theological Review* 79:176–86.

——. 1986b. *The Moral World of the First Christians*. Philadelphia: Westminster Press.

——. 1991. 'The Man from Heaven in Paul's Letter to the Philippians.' Pp. 329–36 in *The Future of Early Christianity: Essays in Honor of Helmut Koester*, ed. B. Pearson. Minneapolis: Fortress.

——. 1993. *The Origins of Christian Morality: The First Two Centuries*. New Haven: Yale University Press.

——. 1996. 'The "Haustafeln" and American Slavery: A Hermeneutical Challenge.' Pp. 232–53 in *Theology and Ethics in Paul and His Interpreters: Essays in Honor of Victor Paul Furnish*, eds. E. H. Lovering and J. L. Sumney. Nashville: Abingdon.

——. 2001. 'Judaism, Hellenism and the Birth of Christianity.' Pp. 17–27 in *Paul beyond the Judaism/Hellenism Divide*, ed. T. Engberg-Pedersen. Louisville: Westminster John Knox Press.

Meggitt, J. J. 1998. *Paul, Poverty and Survival*. Edinburgh: T&T Clark.

——. 2002. 'Taking the Emperor's Clothes Seriously: The New Testament and the Roman Emperor.' Pp. 143–69 in *The Quest for Wisdom: Essays in Honour of Philip Budd*, ed. C. E. Joynes. Cambridge: Orchard Academic.

Meilander, G. 2011. 'Christian Theology: Ethics.' Pp. 576–88 in *The Blackwell Companion to Paul*, ed. S. Westerholm. Oxford: Blackwell.

Mellor, R. 1975. ΘΕΑ ΡΩΜΑ: *The Worship of the Goddess Roma in the Greek World*. Göttingen: Vandenhoeck & Ruprecht.

Mendels, D. 1992. *The Rise and Fall of Jewish Nationalism*. Grand Rapids: Eerdmans.

——. 1996. 'Pagan or Jewish? The Presentation of Paul's Mission in the Book of Acts.' Pp. 431–52 in *Geschichte - Tradition - Reflexion: Festschrift für Martin Hengel zum 70. Geburtstag. Bd 1: Judentum*, eds. H. Cancik, H. Lichtenberger, and P. Schäfer. Tübingen: Mohr.

Metzger, B. M. 1973. 'The Punctuation of Rom. 9:5.' Pp. 95–112 in *Christ and Spirit in the New Testament: In Honour of Charles Francis Digby Moule*, ed. Barnabas Lindars and Stephen S. Smalley. Cambridge: Cambridge University Press.

——. 1994 [1971]. *A Textual Commentary on the Greek New Testament*. 2nd edn. London and New York: United Bible Societies; Stuttgart: Deutsche Bibelgesellschaft.

Meyer, B. F. 1989. *Critical Realism and the New Testament*. Princeton Theological Monograph Series, vol. 17. Allison Park, PA: Pickwick.

Meyer, M. W., ed. 1987. *The Ancient Mysteries: A Sourcebook*. New York: Harper & Row.

Meyer, P. W. 1990. 'The Worm at the Core of the Apple: Exegetical Reflections on Romans 7.' Pp. 62–84 in *The Conversation Continues: Studies in Paul and John in Honor of J. Louis Martyn*, eds. R. T. Fortna and B. R. Gaventa. Nashville: Abingdon.

Middleton, R. J. 2005. *The Liberating Image: The Imago Dei in Genesis 1*. Grand Rapids: Brazos Press.

Middleton, R. J., and B. J. Walsh. 1998. *Truth Is Stranger Than It Used to Be: Biblical Faith in a Postmodern Age*. Downers Grove, IL: InterVarsity Press.

Mikalson, J. D. 2010 [2005]. *Ancient Greek Religion*. Chichester: Wiley-Blackwell.

Mildenberg, L. 1984. *The Coinage of the Bar-Kokhba War*. Aarau: Sauerländer Verlag.

Millar, F. 2002. 'The Emperor, the Senate and the Provinces.' Pp. 271–91 in *Rome, the Greek World, and the East, Volume 1. The Roman Republic and the Augustan Revolution*, eds. H. M. Cotton and G. M. Rogers. Chapel Hill: University of North Carolina Press.

Miller, C. 2010. 'The Imperial Cult in the Pauline Cities of Asia Minor and Greece.' *Catholic Biblical Quarterly* 72:314–32.

Minear, P. S. 1971. *The Obedience of Faith*. London: SCM Press.

Mitchell, M. M. 1991/2. *Paul and the Rhetoric of Reconciliation: An Exegetical Investigation of the Language and Composition of 1 Corinthians*. Louisville: Westminster John Knox Press.

Mitchell, S. 1993a. *Anatolia: Land, Men and Gods in Asia Minor, Volume 1: The Celts in Anatolia and the Impact of Roman Rule*. Oxford: Clarendon Press.

——. 1993b. *Anatolia: Land, Men and Gods in Asia Minor, Volume 2: The Rise of the Church*. Oxford: Clarendon Press.

——. 1999. 'The Cult of Theos Hypsistos between Pagans, Jews and Christians.' Pp. 81–148 in *Pagan Monotheism in Late Antiquity*, eds. P. Athanassiadi and M. Frede. Oxford: Clarendon Press.

Mitchell, S., and P. van Nuffelen, eds. 2010. *One God: Pagan Monotheism in the Roman Empire*. Cambridge: Cambridge University Press.

Mitchell, S., and M. Waelkins, eds. 1998. *Pisidian Antioch: The Site and Its Monuments*. London: Duckworth with the Classical Press of Wales.

Moberly, R. W. L. 2004. 'How Appropriate Is "Monotheism" as a Category for Biblical Interpretation?' Pp. 216–34 in *Early Jewish and Christian Monotheism*. London: T&T Clark International.

——. 2009. *The Theology of the Book of Genesis*. Cambridge: Cambridge University Press.

Moessner, D. 1989. *Lord of the Banquet: The Literary and Theological Significance of the Lukan Travel Narrative*. Harrisburg, PA: Trinity Press International.

Montefiore, C. G., and H. Loewe, comp. 1974 [1938]. *A Rabbinic Anthology*. New York: Schocken Books.

Moo, D. J. 1996. *The Epistle to the Romans*. Grand Rapids: Eerdmans.

——. 2004. 'Israel and the Law in Romans 5—11: Interaction with the New Perspective.' Pp. 185–216 in *Justification and Variegated Nomism, Volume 2: The Paradoxes of Paul*, eds. D. A. Carson, P. T. O'Brien, and M. A. Seifried. Grand Rapids: Baker Academic.

——. 2008. *The Letters to the Colossians and to Philemon*. Grand Rapids: Eerdmans.

Moore, G. F. 1927. *Judaism in the First Centuries of the Christian Era: The Age of the Tannaim*. Cambridge, MA: Harvard University Press.

Morales, R. J. 2010. *The Spirit and the Restoration of Israel*. Tübingen: Mohr.

Morgan, G. 2006. *69 A.D.: The Year of Four Emperors*. Oxford: Oxford University Press.

Morgan, R. 1973. *The Nature of New Testament Theology: The Contribution of William Wrede and Adolf Schlatter*. London: SCM Press.

——. 1998. 'Incarnation, Myth, and Theology: Ernst Käsemann's Interpretation of Philippians 2:5–11.' Pp. 43–73 in *Where Christology Began: Essays on Philippians 2*, eds. R. P. Martin and B. J. Dodd. Louisville: Westminster John Knox Press.

Most, G. W. 2003. 'Philosophy and Religion.' Pp. 300–22 in *The Cambridge Companion to Greek and Roman Philosophy*, ed. D. Sedley. Cambridge: Cambridge University Press.

Motyer, J. A. 1993. *The Prophecy of Isaiah*. Leicester: InterVarsity Press.

Moule, C. F. D. 1957. *The Epistles of Paul the Apostle to the Colossians and to Philemon*. Cambridge: Cambridge University Press.

——. 1964. 'The Judgment Theme in the Sacraments.' Pp. 464–81 in *The Background of the New Testament and Its Eschatology: In Honour of Charles Harold Dodd*, eds. W. D. Davies and D. Daube. Cambridge: Cambridge University Press.

——. 1977. *The Origin of Christology*. Cambridge: Cambridge University Press.

Moulton, J. H., and N. Turner. 1908 [1906]–76. *A Grammar of New Testament Greek*. Edinburgh: T&T Clark.

Moyise, S. 2010. *Paul and Scripture: Studying the New Testament Use of the Old Testament*. Grand Rapids: Baker Academic.

Müller, P. 2012. *Der Brief an Philemon*. Göttingen: Vandenhoeck & Ruprecht.

Munck, J. 1959 [1954]. *Paul and the Salvation of Mankind*, tr. Frank Clarke. London: SCM Press; Richmond, VA: John Knox Press.

Murphy, F. J. 2005. *The Structure and Meaning of Second Baruch*. Atlanta: Scholars Press.

——. 2010. 'Biblical Antiquities (Pseudo-Philo).' Pp. 440–2 in *The Eerdmans Dictionary of Early Judaism*, eds. J. J. Collins and D. C. Harlow. Grand Rapids: Eerdmans.

Murphy-O'Connor, J. 1978. 'I Cor. 8.6: Cosmology or Soteriology?' *Révue Biblique* 85:253–67.

——. 1991. '2 Timothy Contrasted with 1 Timothy and Titus.' *Révue Biblique* 98:403–18.

——. 1995. *Paul the Letter-Writer: His World, His Options, His Skills*. Collegeville, MN: Liturgical Press.

——. 1998 [1980]. *The Holy Land: An Oxford Archaeological Guide from Earliest Times to 1700*. 4th edn. Oxford: Oxford University Press.

Murray, O. 2001 [1986, 1988]. 'Life and Society in Classical Greece.' Pp. 198–227 in *The Oxford Illustrated History of Greece and the Hellenistic World*, eds. John Boardman, Jasper Griffin, and Oswyn Murray. Oxford: Oxford University Press.

Mussner, F. 1974. *Der Galaterbrief*. Freiburg: Herder.

Nanos, M. D. 1996. *The Mystery of Romans*. Minneapolis: Fortress.

——. 2002a. *The Irony of Galatians: Paul's Letter in First-Century Context*. Minneapolis: Fortress.

——., ed. 2002b. *The Galatians Debate: Contemporary Issues in Rhetorical and Historical Interpretation*. Peabody, MA: Hendrikson.

——. 2010a. '"Broken Branches": A Pauline Metaphor Gone Awry? (Romans 11:11–24).' Pp. 339–76 in *Between Gospel and Election: Explorations in the Interpretation of Romans 9—11*, eds. F. Wilk and J. R. Wagner. Tübingen: Mohr.

——. 2010b. 'Paul and Judaism: Why Not Paul's Judaism?' Pp. 117–60 in *Paul Unbound: Other Perspectives on the Apostle*, ed. M. D. Given. Peabody, MA: Hendrickson.

——. 2011. 'The Letter of Paul to the Romans.' Pp. 253–86 in *The Jewish Annotated New Testament: New Revised Standard Version*, eds. A.-J. Levine and M. Z. Brettler. New York: Oxford University Press.

——. 2012. 'Paul's Relationship to Torah in Light of His Strategy "to Become Everything to Everyone" (1 Corinthians 9.19–23).' Pp. 106–40 in *Paul and Judaism: Crosscurrents in Pauline Exegesis and the Study of Jewish–Christian Relations*, eds. R. Bieringer and D. Pollefeyt. London: T&T Clark.

Naugle, D. K. 2002. *Worldview: The History of a Concept*. Grand Rapids: Eerdmans.

Naylor, J. 2010. 'The Roman Imperial Cult and Revelation.' *Currents in Biblical Research* 8 (2):207–39.

Neill, S. C., and N. T. Wright. 1988 [1964]. *The Interpretation of the New Testament, 1861–1986*. 2nd edn. Oxford: Oxford University Press.

Neiman, S. 2002. *Evil in Modern Thought: An Alternative History of Philosophy*. Princeton: Princeton University Press.

Neumann, K. J. 1990. *The Authenticity of the Pauline Epistles in the Light of Stylostatistical Analysis*. Atlanta: Scholars Press.

Neusner, J. 1973. *From Politics to Piety*. Englewood Cliffs, NJ: Prentice-Hall.

——. 1985. *Genesis Rabbah: The Judaic Commentary to the Book of Genesis: A New American Translation*. Atlanta: Scholars Press.

——. 2004. *The Idea of History in Rabbinic Judaism*. Leiden: Brill.

Neusner, J., W. S. Green, and E. Frerichs, eds. 1987. *Judaisms and Their Messiahs at the Turn of the Christian Era*. Cambridge: Cambridge University Press.

Newman, C. C. 1992. *Paul's Glory-Christology: Tradition and Rhetoric*. Leiden: Brill.

Newman, C. C., J. R. Davila, and G. S. Lewis, eds. 1999. *The Jewish Roots of Christological Monotheism: Papers from the St. Andrews Conference on the Historical Origins of the Worship of Jesus*. Leiden: Brill.

Newton, M. 1985. *The Concept of Purity at Qumran and in the Letters of Paul*. Cambridge: Cambridge University Press.

Neyrey, J. H. 1990. *Paul, in Other Words: A Cultural Reading of His Letters*. Louisville: Westminster John Knox Press.

Neyrey, J. H., and Eric C. Stewart. 2008. *The Social World of the New Testament: Insights and Models*. Peabody, MA: Hendrickson.

Nickelsburg, G. W. E. 1972. *Resurrection, Immortality and Eternal Life in Intertestamental Judaism*. Cambridge, MA: Harvard University Press.

——. 1981. *Jewish Literature between the Bible and the Mishnah*. Philadelphia: Fortress.

Nicklas, T. 2008. 'The Letter to Philemon: A Discussion with J. Albert Harrill.' Pp. 201–20 in *Paul's World*, ed. S. E. Porter. Leiden: Brill.

Niebuhr, K.-W. 1992. *Heidenapostel aus Israel: Die Jüdische Identität des Paulus nach Ihrer Darstellung in Seinen Briefen*. Tübingen: Mohr.

——. 2010. '"Nicht alle aus Israel sind Israel" (Röm 9,6b): Römer 9—11 als Zeugnis paulinischer Anthropologie.' Pp. 433–62 in *Between Gospel and Election: Explorations in the Interpretation of Romans 9—11*, eds. F. Wilk and J. R. Wagner. Tübingen: Mohr.

Nock, A. D. 1961 [1933]. *Conversion: The Old and the New in Religion from Alexander the Great to Augustine of Hippo*. London: Oxford University Press.

Nordling, J. G. 1991. 'Onesimus Fugitivus: A Defense of the Runaway Slave Hypothesis in Philemon.' *Journal for the Study of the New Testament* 41:97–119.

——. 2004. *Philemon*. St Louis: Concordia.

North, J. A. 2011. 'Pagans, Polytheists and the Pendulum.' Pp. 479–502 in *The Religious History of the Roman Empire: Pagans, Jews and Christians*, eds. J. A. North and S. R. F. Price. Oxford: Oxford University Press.

Norton, J. D. H. 2011. *Contours in the Text: Textual Variations in the Writings of Paul, Josephus and the Yahad*. London: T&T Clark.

Novenson, M. 2012. *Christ among the Messiahs: Christ Language in Paul and Messiah Language in Ancient Judaism*. New York: Oxford University Press.

——. 2013. 'Paul's Former Occupation in *Ioudaismos*.' In *Galatians and Christian Theology: Justification, the Gospel, and Ethics in Paul's Letter*, eds. M. W. Elliott, S. J. Hafemann, and N. T. Wright. Grand Rapids: Baker Academic.

——. 2014. *The Grammar of Messianism*. Oxford: Oxford University Press.

Nowell, I. 2009. 'Tobit, Book of.' Pp. 612–17 in *The New Interpreter's Dictionary of the Bible*, vol. 5, eds. K. D. Sakenfeld et al. Nashville: Abingdon.

Oakes, P. 2001. *Philippians: From People to Letter*. Cambridge: Cambridge University Press.

——. 2005. 'Re-Mapping the Universe: Paul and the Emperor in 1 Thessalonians and Philippians.' *Journal for the Study of the New Testament* 27(3):301–22.

——. 2009. *Reading Romans in Pompeii: Paul's Letter at Ground Level*. London: SPCK.

O'Brien, P. T. 1991. *Commentary on Philippians*. Grand Rapids: Eerdmans.

——. 1993. 'Fellowship, Communion, Sharing.' Pp. 293–5 in *Dictionary of Paul and His Letters*, eds. G. F. Hawthorne and R. P. Martin. Downers Grove, IL: InterVarsity Press.

——. 2004. 'Was Paul a Covenantal Nomist?' Pp. 249–96 in *Justification and Variegated Nomism, Volume 2: The Paradoxes of Paul*, eds. D. A. Carson, P. T. O'Brien, and M. A. Seifrid. Grand Rapids: Baker Academic.

O'Donovan, O. M. T. 2002. 'Response to N. T. Wright.' Pp. 194–5 in *A Royal Priesthood: The Use of the Bible Ethically and Politically. A Dialogue with Oliver O'Donovan*, eds. C. Bartholomew et al. Carlisle: Paternoster.

——. 2005. *The Ways of Judgment*. Grand Rapids: Eerdmans.

Ogg, G., tr. and ed. 1955. *Pseudo-Cyprian,* De Pascha Computus. London: SPCK.

Ogilvie, R. M. 1986. *The Romans and Their Gods*. London: The Hogarth Press.

O'Neill, J. C. 1980. *Messiah: Six Lectures on the Ministry of Jesus*. Cambridge: Cochrane Press.

——. 1995. *Who Did Jesus Think He Was?* Leiden: Brill.

Onesti, K. L., and M. T. Brauch. 1993. 'Righteousness, Righteousness of God.' Pp. 827–37 in *Dictionary of Paul and His Letters*, eds. G. F. Hawthorne, R. P. Martin, and D. G. Reid. Downers Grove, IL: InterVarsity Press.

Ortlund, D. C. 2012. *Zeal Without Knowledge: The Concept of Zeal in Romans 10, Galatians 1, and Philippians 3*. London: T&T Clark.

O'Siadhail, M. 2010. *Tongues*. Tarset, Northumberland: Bloodaxe Books.

Osiek, C. 2000. *Philippians, Philemon*. Nashville: Abingdon.

Oss, D. A. 1989. 'The Interpretation of the "Stone" Passages by Peter and Paul: A Comparative Study.' *Journal of the Evangelical Theological Society* 32:181–200.

Padwick, C. E. 1930 [1929]. *Temple Gairdner of Cairo*. London: SPCK.

Passaro, A. 2006. 'Theological Hermeneutics and Historical Motifs in Pss 105–106.' Pp. 43–55 in *History and Identity: How Israel's Later Authors Viewed Its Earlier History*, eds. N. Calduch-Benages and J. Liesen. Berlin: De Gruyter.

Pawlikowski, J. T. 2012. 'A Christian–Jewish Dialogical Model in Light of New Research on Paul's Relationship with Judaism.' Pp. 163–73 in *Paul and Judaism: Crosscurrents in Pauline Exegesis and the Study of Jewish–Christian Relations*, eds. R. Bieringer and D. Pollefeyt. London: T&T Clark.

Peace, R. V. 1999. *Conversion in the New Testament: Paul and the Twelve*. Grand Rapids: Eerdmans.

Pearson, B. A. 1971. 'I Thessalonians 2:13–16: A Deutero-Pauline Interpolation.' *Harvard Theological Review* 64:79–94.

Peirce, C. S. 1958. *Collected Papers VII*. Cambridge, MA: Harvard University Press.

Pennington, J. T., and S. M. McDonough, eds. 2008. *Cosmology and New Testament Theology*. London: T&T Clark.

Perkins, P. 2001. *Abraham's Divided Children: Galatians and the Politics of Faith*. Harrisburg, PA: Trinity Press International.

Perriman, A. 2010. *The Future of the People of God: Reading Romans Before and After Western Christendom*. Eugene, OR: Cascade Books.

Perrin, N. 2010. *Jesus the Temple*. London: SPCK.

Perrin, N. and R. B. Hays, eds. 2011. *Jesus, Paul and the People of God: A Theological Dialogue with N. T. Wright*. Downers Grove, IL: InterVarsity Press; London: SPCK.

Pervo, R. I. 2009. *Acts: A Commentary*. Minneapolis: Fortress.

Petersen, D. L. 1995. *Zechariah 9—14 and Malachi: A Commentary*. Louisville: Westminster John Knox Press.

Petersen, N. R. 1985. *Rediscovering Paul: Philemon and the Sociology of Paul's Narrative World*. Philadelphia: Fortress.

Phua, R. L.-S. 2005. *Idolatry and Authority: A Study of 1 Corinthians 8.1—11.1 in the Light of the Jewish Diaspora*. London: T&T Clark.

Pickett, R. 1997. *The Cross in Corinth: The Social Significance of the Death of Jesus*. Sheffield: Sheffield Academic Press.

Piper, J. 2002. *Counted Righteous in Christ: Should We Abandon the Imputation of Christ's Righteousness?* Wheaton, IL: Crossway Books.

——. 2007. *The Future of Justification: A Response to N. T. Wright*. Wheaton, IL: Crossway Books.

Pitre, B. 2005. *Jesus, the Tribulation, and the End of the Exile: Restoration Eschatology and the Origin of the Atonement*. Tübingen: Mohr; Grand Rapids: Baker Academic.

Platt, V. 2011. *Facing the Gods: Epiphany and Representation in Graeco-Roman Art, Literature and Religion*. Cambridge: Cambridge University Press.

Pleket, H. W. 1965. 'An Aspect of the Imperial Cult: Imperial Mysteries.' *Harvard Theological Review* 58:331–47.

Poirier, J. C. 2008. 'The Measure of Stewardship: *Pistis* in Romans 12:3.' *Tyndale Bulletin* 59 (1):145–52.

Polaski, S. H. 1999. *Paul and the Discourse of Power*. Sheffield: Sheffield Academic Press.

Ponsot, J. 1982. 'Et Ainsi Tout Israël Sera Sauvé: Rom., XI, 26a.' *Révue Biblique* 89:406–17.

Porter, A. L. 2009. 'Temples, Leontopolis and Elephantine.' Pp. 509–10 in *The New Interpreter's Dictionary of the Bible*, vol. 5, eds. K. D. Sakenfeld et al. Nashville: Abingdon.

Porter, J. R. 1965. 'The Legal Aspects of the Concept of "Corporate Personality" in the Old Testament.' *Vetus Testamentum* 15:361–80.

Porter, S. E. 2011. 'Reconciliation as the Heart of Paul's Missionary Theology.' Pp. 169–79 in *Paul as Missionary: Identity, Activity, Theology, and Practice*, eds. T. J. Burke and B. S. Rosner. London: T&T Clark.

Porter, S. E., and C. D. Stanley, eds. 2008. *As It Is Written: Studying Paul's Use of Scripture*. Atlanta: Society of Biblical Literature.

Portier-Young, A. E. 2011. *Apocalypse Against Empire: Theologies of Resistance in Early Judaism*. Grand Rapids: Eerdmans.

Powell, M. A. 1993 [1990]. *What Is Narrative Criticism?* London: SPCK.

Price, S. R. F. 1984. *Rituals and Power: The Roman Imperial Cult in Asia Minor*. Cambridge: Cambridge University Press.

——. 1996. 'The Place of Religion: Rome in the Early Empire.' Pp. 812–47 in *Cambridge Ancient History*, vol. 10, eds. A. K. Bowman, E. Champlin, and A. Lintott. Cambridge: Cambridge University Press.

——. 1999. *Religions of the Ancient Greeks*. Cambridge: Cambridge University Press.

——. 2001 [1986, 1988]. 'The History of the Hellenistic Period.' Pp. 309–31 in *The Oxford Illustrated History of Greece and the Hellenistic World*, eds. John Boardman, Jasper Griffin, and Oswyn Murray. Oxford: Oxford University Press.

——. 2011. 'Homogeneity and Diversity in the Religions of Rome.' Pp. 253–75 in *The Religious History of the Roman Empire: Pagans, Jews, and Christians*. Oxford: Oxford University Press.

Prior, M. 1989. *Paul the Letter-Writer: And the Second Letter to Timothy*. Sheffield: Sheffield Academic Press.

Puerto, M. N. 2006. 'Reinterpreting the Past: Judith 5.' Pp. 115–40 in *History and Identity: How Israel's Later Authors Viewed Its Earlier History*, eds. N. Calduch-Benages and J. Liesen. Berlin: De Gruyter.

Punt, J. 2010. 'Paul, Power and Philemon. "Knowing Your Place": A Postcolonial Reading.' Pp. 223–50 in *Philemon in Perspective: Interpreting a Pauline Letter*, ed. D. F. Tolmie. Berlin: De Gruyter.

Quinton, A. 1995. 'Romanticism, Philosophical.' Pp. 778 in *The Oxford Companion to Philosophy*, ed. T. Honderich. Oxford: Oxford University Press.

Rabens, V. 2010. *The Holy Spirit and Ethics in Paul: Transformation and Empowering for Religious-Ethical Life*. Tübingen: Mohr.

Rainbow, P. A. 1991. 'Jewish Monotheism as the Matrix for New Testament Christology: A Review Article.' *Novum Testamentum* 33(1):78–91.

Räisänen, H. 1986 [1983]. *Paul and the Law*. Philadelphia: Fortress.

——. 2008. 'A Controversial Jew and His Conflicting Convictions.' Pp. 319–35 in *Redefining First-Century Jewish and Christian Identities: Essays in Honor of Ed Parish Sanders*, ed. F. E. Udoh. Notre Dame: University of Notre Dame Press.

Ramsay, W. M. n.d. *St. Paul the Traveller and the Roman Citizen*. London: Hodder & Stoughton.

Rankin, D. 1995. *Tertullian and the Church*. Cambridge: Cambridge University Press.

Rapske, B. M. 1991. 'The Prisoner Paul in the Eyes of Onesimus.' *New Testament Studies* 37:187–203.

Rawlinson, A. E. J. 1930. 'Corpus Christi.' Pp. 225–44 in *Mysterium Christi: Christological Studies by British and German Theologians*, eds. G. K. A. Bell and D. A. Deissmann. London: Longmans, Green & Co.

Reasoner, M. 1999. *The Strong and the Weak: Romans 14.1—15.13 in Context*. Cambridge: Cambridge University Press.

Reid, D. G. 1993. 'Principalities and Powers.' Pp. 746–52 in *Dictionary of Paul and His Letters*, eds. G. F. Hawthorne, R. P. Martin, and D. G. Reid. Downers Grove, IL: InterVarsity Press.

Reif, S. C. 2006. 'The Function of History in Early Rabbinic Liturgy.' Pp. 321–39 in *History and Identity: How Israel's Later Authors Viewed Its Earlier History*, eds. N. Calduch-Benages and J. Liesen. Berlin: De Gruyter.

Reinbold, W. 2010. 'Zur Bedeutung des Begriffes "Israel" in Römer 9—11.' Pp. 401–16 in *Between Gospel and Election: Explorations in the Interpretation of Romans 9—11*, eds. F. Wilk and J. R. Wagner. Tübingen: Mohr.

Reinmuth, E. 2006. *Der Brief des Paulus an Philemon*. Leipzig: Evangelische Verlagsanstalt.

Reiser, M. 1997. *Jesus and Judgment: The Eschatological Proclamation in Its Jewish Context*, tr. Linda M. Maloney. Minneapolis: Fortress.

Renwick, D. A. 1991. *Paul, the Temple, and the Presence of God*. Atlanta: Scholars Press.

Reumann, J. 2008. *Philippians: A New Translation with Introduction and Commentary*. New Haven: Yale University Press.

Reumann, J., J. A. Fitzmyer, and J. D. Quinn. 1982. *'Righteousness' in the New Testament: 'Justification' in the United States Lutheran–Roman Catholic Dialogue*. Philadelphia: Fortress.

Revell, L. 2009. *Roman Imperialism and Local Identities*. Cambridge: Cambridge University Press.

Richards, E. R. 2004. *Paul and First-Century Letter-Writing: Secretaries, Composition and Collection*. Downers Grove, IL: InterVarsity Press.

Richardson, G. Peter. 1969. *Israel in the Apostolic Church*. Cambridge: Cambridge University Press.

——. 1996. *Herod: King of the Jews and Friend of the Romans*. Columbia, SC: University of South Carolina Press.

Richardson, J. S. 2008. *The Language of Empire: Rome and the Idea of Empire from the Third Century BC to the Second Century AD*. Cambridge: Cambridge University Press.

——. 2012. *Augustan Rome 44 BC to AD 14: The Restoration of the Republic and the Establishment of the Empire*. Edinburgh: Edinburgh University Press.

Richardson, N. 1994. *Paul's Language about God*. Sheffield: Sheffield Academic Press.

Ricks, C., ed. 1999. *The Oxford Book of English Verse*. Oxford: Oxford University Press.

Ridderbos, H. N. 1975 [1966]. *Paul: An Outline of His Theology*, tr. J. R. de Witt. Grand Rapids: Eerdmans.

Riesenfeld, H. 1982. 'Faith and Love Promoting Hope: An Interpretation of Philemon v. 6.' Pp. 251–7 in *Paul and Paulinism: Essays in Honour of C. K. Barrett*, eds. M. D. Hooker and S. G. Wilson. London: SPCK.

Riesner, R. 2000. 'A Pre-Christian Jewish Mission?' Pp. 211–50 in *The Mission of the Early Church to Jews and Gentiles*, eds. J. Ådna and H. Kvalbein. Tübingen: Mohr.

Ripley, J. J. 2010. 'Aqedah.' Pp. 355–7 in *The Eerdmans Dictionary of Early Judaism*, eds. J. J. Collins and D. C. Harlow. Grand Rapids: Eerdmans.

Rives, J. B. 2007. *Religion in the Roman Empire*. Oxford: Blackwell.

Roberts, J. J. M. 1987. 'Yahweh's Foundation in Zion (Isa 28:16).' *Journal of Biblical Literature* 106:27–45.

——. 2009. 'Temple, Jerusalem.' Pp. 494–509 in *The New Interpreter's Dictionary of the Bible*, vol. 5, eds. K. D. Sakenfeld et al. Nashville: Abingdon.

Robertson, A. and A. Plummer. 1914 [1911]. *A Critical and Exegetical Commentary on the First Epistle of St Paul to the Corinthians*. 2nd edn. Edinburgh: T&T Clark.

Robinson, J. A. 1904 [1903]. *St Paul's Epistle to the Ephesians: A Revised Text and Translation with Exposition and Notes*. London: Macmillan.

Robinson, J. A. T. 1952. *The Body: A Study in Pauline Theology*. London: SCM Press.

——. 1976. *Redating the New Testament*. London: SCM Press.

——. 1979. *Wrestling with Romans*. London: SCM Press.

Röcker, F. W. 2009. *Belial und Katechon: Eine Untersuchung zu 2 Thess 2,1–12 und 1 Thess 4,13—5,11*. Tübingen: Mohr.

Roetzel, C. J. 2003. *Paul – a Jew on the Margins*. Louisville: Westminster John Knox Press.

——. 2009. 'Paul, the Apostle.' Pp. 404–21 in *The New Interpreter's Dictionary of the Bible*, vol. 4, eds. K. D. Sakenfeld et al. Nashville: Abingdon.

Rogerson, J. W. 1970. 'The Hebrew Conception of Corporate Personality: A Re-Examination.' *Journal of Theological Studies* 21:1–16.

Rosner, B. S. 1990. 'Moses Appointing Judges: An Antecedent to 1 Cor 1—6?' *Zeitschrift für die Neutestamentliche Wissenschaft* 82:275–8.

——. 1994. *Paul, Scripture and Ethics: A Study of 1 Corinthians 5—7*. Leiden: Brill.

——. 2003. 'Paul's Ethics.' Pp. 212–23 in *The Cambridge Companion to St Paul*, ed. J. D. G. Dunn. Cambridge: Cambridge University Press.

——. 2011. 'The Glory of God in Paul's Missionary Theology and Practice.' Pp. 158–68 in *Paul as Missionary: Identity, Activity, Theology, and Practice*, eds. T. J. Burke and B. S. Rosner. London: T&T Clark.

Ross, G. M. 1974. 'Seneca's Philosophical Influence.' Pp. 116–65 in *Seneca*, ed. C. D. N. Costa. London: Routledge & Kegan Paul.

Rowe, C. K. 2000. 'Romans 10:13: What Is the Name of the Lord?' *Horizons in Biblical Theology* 22:135–73.

——. 2005a. 'New Testament Iconography? Situating Paul in the Absence of Material Evidence.' Pp. 289–312 in *Picturing the New Testament*, eds. A. Weissenrieder, F. Wendt, and P. von Gemünden. Tübingen: Mohr.

——. 2005b. 'Luke-Acts and the Imperial Cult: A Way through the Conundrum?' *Journal for the Study of the New Testament* 27:279–300.

——. 2009. *World Upside Down: Reading Acts in the Graeco-Roman Age*. Oxford: Oxford University Press.

——. 2011. 'The Grammar of Life: The Areopagus Speech and Pagan Tradition.' *New Testament Studies* 57:31–50.

Rowland, C. C. 1996. 'Apocalyptic Mysticism and the New Testament.' Pp. 405–30 in *Geschichte - Tradition - Reflexion. Festschrift für Martin Hengel zum 70. Geburtstag. Bd 1: Judentum*, eds. H. Cancik, H. Lichtenberger, and P. Schäfer. Tübingen: Mohr.

Rowland, C. C., and C. R. A Morray-Jones. 2009. *The Mystery of God: Early Jewish Mysticism and the New Testament*. Leiden: Brill.

Rowley, H. H. 1964 [1950]. *The Biblical Doctrine of Election*. London: Lutterworth.

Rudolph, D. J. 2011. *A Jew to the Jews: Jewish Contours of Pauline Flexibility in 1 Corinthians 9:19–23*. Tübingen: Mohr.

Rüpke, J. 2007 [2001]. *Religion of the Romans*. Cambridge: Polity Press.

——. 2011. 'Roman Religion and the Religion of Empire: Some Reflections on Method.' Pp. 9–36 in *The Religious History of the Roman Empire: Pagans, Jews and Christians*, eds. J. A. North and S. R. F. Price. Oxford: Oxford University Press.

Russell, D. A. 1973. *Plutarch*. London: Duckworth.

Rüterswörden, U. 2006 [1994–5]. '*Sāmaʿ*.' Pp. 253–79 in *The Theological Dictionary of the Old Testament*, vol. 15, ed. G. J. Botterweck. Grand Rapids: Eerdmans.

Ryan, J. M. 2005. *Philippians and Philemon*. Collegeville, MN: Liturgical Press.

Sacks, J. 2011. *The Great Partnership: God, Science and the Search for Meaning*. London: Hodder & Stoughton.

Sadler, R. S. 2009. 'Put.' Pp. 691–2 in *The New Interpreter's Dictionary of the Bible*, vol. 4, eds. K. D. Sakenfeld et al. Nashville: Abingdon.

Sailhamer, J. H. 1992. *The Pentateuch as Narrative: A Biblical-Theological Commentary*. Grand Rapids: Zondervan.

Salles, R. 2009. 'Chrysippus on Conflagration and the Indestructibility of the Cosmos.' Pp. 118–34 in *God & Cosmos in Stoicism*, ed. R. Salles. Oxford: Oxford University Press.

Sampley, J. P. 2002. 'The First Letter to the Corinthians: Introduction, Commentary, and Reflections.' Pp. 771–1003 in *The New Interpreter's Bible*, eds. L. E. Keck et al. Nashville: Abingdon.

——., ed. 2003a. *Paul in the Greco-Roman World: A Handbook*. Harrisburg, PA: Trinity Press International.

——. 2003b. 'Paul and Frank Speech.' Pp. 293–318 in *Paul in the Greco-Roman World: A Handbook*, ed. J. P. Sampley. Harrisburg, PA: Trinity Press International.

Sanday, W., and A. C. Headlam. 1902 [1895]. *A Critical and Exegetical Commentary on the Epistle to the Romans*. 5th edn. Edinburgh: T&T Clark.

Sanders, E. P. 1977. *Paul and Palestinian Judaism: A Comparison of Patterns of Religion*. London: SCM Press; Philadelphia: Fortress.

——. 1978. 'Paul's Attitude toward the Jewish People.' *Union Seminary Quarterly Review* 33:175–87.

——. 1983. *Paul, the Law and the Jewish People*. London: SCM Press; Philadelphia: Fortress.

——. 1990. 'Jewish Association with Gentiles and Galatians 2:11–14.' Pp. 170–88 in *The Conversation Continues: Studies in Paul and John in Honor of J. Louis Martyn*, eds. Robert T. Fortna and Beverley R. Gaventa. Nashville: Abingdon.

——. 1992. *Judaism: Practice and Belief, 63 BCE — 66 CE*. London: SCM Press.

——. 2007. 'God Gave the Law to Condemn: Providence in Paul and Josephus.' Pp. 78–97 in *The Impartial God: Essays in Biblical Studies in Honor of Jouette M. Bassler*, eds. C. J. Roetzel and R. L. Foster. Sheffield: Sheffield Phoenix Press.

——. 2008a. 'Comparing Judaism and Christianity: An Academic Autobiography.' Pp. 11–41 in *Redefining First-Century Jewish and Christian Identities: Essays in Honor of Ed Parish Sanders*, ed. F. E. Udoh. Notre Dame: University of Notre Dame Press.

——. 2008b. 'Did Paul's Theology Develop?' Pp. 325–50 in *The Word Leaps the Gap: Essays on Scripture and Theology in Honor of Richard B. Hays*, eds. J. R. Wagner, C. K. Rowe, and A. K. Grieb. Grand Rapids: Eerdmans.

——. 2009. 'Paul between Judaism and Hellenism.' Pp. 74–90 in *St Paul among the Philosophers*, eds. J. D. Caputo and L. M. Alcoff. Bloomington, IN: Indiana University Press.

Sandmel, S. 1962. 'Parallelomania.' *Journal of Biblical Literature* 81:1–13.

——. 1978. *Judaism and Christian Beginnings*. New York: Oxford University Press.

Sandnes, K. O. 2011. 'A Missionary Strategy in 1 Corinthians 9.19–23?' Pp. 128–41 in *Paul as Missionary: Identity, Activity, Theology, and Practice*, eds. T. J. Burke and B. S. Rosner. London: T&T Clark.

Sänger, D. 2010. '"Er wird die Gottlosigkeit von Jacob entfernen" (Röm 11,26): Kontinuität und Wandel in den Israelaussagen des Apostels Paulus.' Pp. 121–46 in *Between Gospel and Election: Explorations in the Interpretation of Romans 9—11*, eds. F. Wilk and J. R. Wagner. Tübingen: Mohr.

Schäfer, P. 1972. *Die Vorstellung vom Heiligen Geist in der rabbinischen Literatur*. Munich: Kösel-Verlag.

——., ed. 2003. *The Bar Kokhba War Reconsidered*. Tübingen: Mohr.

Schechter, S. 1961 [1909]. *Aspects of Rabbinic Theology: Major Concepts of the Talmud*. New edn. Introd. L. Finkelstein. New York: Schocken Books.

Scheid, J. 1990. *Romulus et Ses Frères: Le Collège des Frères Arvales, Modèle du Culte Public dans la Rome des Empereurs*. Rome: Ecole Française de Rome.

——. 2005. 'Augustus and Roman Religion: Continuity, Conservatism, and Innovation.' Pp. 175–93 in *The Cambridge Companion to the Age of Augustus*, ed. K. Galinsky. Cambridge: Cambridge University Press.

——. 2009 [2001]. 'To Honour the *Princeps* and Venerate the Gods: Public Cult, Neighbourhood Cults, and Imperial Cult in Augustan Rome.' Pp. 275–99 in *Augustus*, ed. J. Edmondson. Edinburgh: Edinburgh University Press.

Schmidt, R. 1982. 'Exil I. Altes und Neues Testament.' Pp. 707–10 in *Theologisches Realenzyklopädie*, vol. 10, eds. G. Muller, H. Balz, G. Krause. Berlin: De Gruyter.

Schmidt, T. 1919. *Der Leib Christi (Sōma Christou): Eine Untersuchung zum urchristlichen Gemeindegedanken*. Leipzig: Deichert.

Schnabel, E. J. 2004. *Early Christian Mission*. Downers Grove, IL: InterVarsity Press.

——. 2009. 'Pharisees.' Pp. 485–96 in *The New Interpreter's Dictionary of the Bible*, vol. 4, eds. K. D. Sakenfeld et al. Nashville: Abingdon.

——. 2012. *Acts*. Grand Rapids: Zondervan.

Schnelle, U. 1983. *Gerechtigkeit und Christusgegenwart: Vorpaulinische und paulinische Tauftheologie*. Göttingen: Vandenhoeck & Ruprecht.

——. 2001. 'Transformation und Partizipation als Grundgedanken paulinischer Theologie.' *New Testament Studies* 47:58–75.

——. 2005 [2003]. *Apostle Paul: His Life and Theology*, tr. M. E. Boring. Grand Rapids: Baker Academic.

Schoeps, H.-J. 1961 [1959]. *Paul: The Theology of the Apostle in the Light of Jewish Religious History*, tr. H. Knight. London: Lutterworth.

Schofield, M. 2003a. 'The Pre-Socratics.' Pp. 42–72 in *The Cambridge Companion to Greek and Roman Philosophy*, ed. D. Sedley. Cambridge: Cambridge University Press.

——. 2003b. 'Stoic Ethics.' Pp. 233–56 in *The Cambridge Companion to the Stoics*, ed. B. Inwood. Cambridge: Cambridge University Press.

Scholem, G. 1971. *The Messianic Idea in Judaism, and Other Essays on Jewish Spirituality*. New York: Schocken Books.

Schrage, W. 1995. *Der erste Brief an die Korinther. 2. Teilband, 1 Kor 6,12—11,16*. Solothurn; Düsseldorf; Neukirchen-Vluyn: Benziger.

Schreiner, T. R. 1998. *Romans*. Grand Rapids: Baker Academic.

——. 2001. *Paul: Apostle of God's Glory in Christ*. Downers Grove, IL: IVP Academic.

——. 2010. *Galatians (Exegetical Commentary on the New Testament)*. Grand Rapids: Zondervan.

Schrenk, G. 1964 [1935]. '*Dikē* etc.' Pp. 178–225 in *Theological Dictionary of the New Testament*, vol. 2, ed. G. Kittel. Grand Rapids: Eerdmans.

Schürer, E. 1973–87. *The History of the Jewish People in the Age of Jesus Christ (175 B.C.—A. D. 135)*. Rev. and ed. G. Vermes, F. Millar, and M. Black. Edinburgh: T&T Clark.

Schwartz, D. B. 2012. *The First Modern Jew: Spinoza and the History of an Image*. Princeton: Princeton University Press.

Schwartz, D. R. 1992. *Studies in the Jewish Background of Christianity*. Wissenschaftliche Untersuchungen zum Neuen Testament, vol. 60. Tübingen: Mohr.

——. 2007. '"Judaean" or "Jew"? How Should We Translate IOUDAIOS in Josephus?' Pp. 3–27 in *Jewish Identity in the Greco-Roman World/Jüdische Identität in der Griechisch-Römischen Welt*, eds. J. Frey, D. R. Schwartz, and S. Gripentrog. Leiden: Brill.

Schweitzer, A. 1912. *Paul and His Interpreters: A Critical History*, tr. W. Montgomery. London: A&C Black.

——. 1925 [1901]. *The Mystery of the Kingdom of God*, tr. W. Lowrie. London: A&C Black.

——. 1931. *The Mysticism of Paul the Apostle*. London: A&C Black.

——. 1954 [1906]. *The Quest of the Historical Jesus: A Critical Study of Its Progress from Reimarus to Wrede*, tr. W. B. D. Montgomery. London: A&C Black.

——. 1968 [1930]. *The Mysticism of Paul the Apostle*, tr. William Montgomery, with a preface by F. C. Burkitt. London: A&C Black; New York: Seabury Press.

Scott, J. C. 1990. *Domination and the Arts of Resistance: Hidden Transcripts*. New Haven: Yale University Press.

Scott, J. M. 1993a. '"For as Many as Are of Works of the Law Are under a Curse" (Gal 3:10).' Pp. 187–221 in *Paul and the Scriptures of Israel*, vol. 112, eds. C. A. Evans and J. A. Sanders. Sheffield: JSOT Press.

——. 1993b. 'Paul's Use of Deuteronomistic Tradition.' *Journal of Biblical Literature* 112:645–65.

——. 1993c. 'Restoration of Israel.' Pp. 796–805 in *Dictionary of Paul and His Letters*, eds. G. F. Hawthorne, R. P. Martin, and D. G. Reid. Downers Grove, IL: InterVarsity Press.

——. 1995. *Paul and the Nations: The Old Testament and Jewish Background of Paul's Mission to the Nations with Special Reference to the Destination of Galatians.* Tübingen: Mohr.

——., ed. 1997a. *Exile: Old Testament, Jewish and Christian Conceptions.* Supplements to the Journal for the Study of Judaism, vol. 56. Leiden: Brill.

——. 1997b. 'Exile and the Self-Understanding of Diaspora Jews in the Greco-Roman Period.' Pp. 173–218 in *Exile: Old Testament, Jewish, and Christian Conceptions*, ed. James M. Scott. Leiden: Brill.

——. 2005. *On Earth as in Heaven: The Restoration of Sacred Time and Sacred Space in the Book of Jubilees.* Leiden: Brill.

Scott, K. 1929. 'Plutarch and the Ruler Cult.' *Transactions and Proceedings of the American Philological Association* 60:117–35.

——. 1932a. 'The Elder and Younger Pliny on Emperor Worship.' *Transactions and Proceedings of the American Philological Association* 63:156–66.

——. 1932b. 'Humor at the Expense of the Ruler Cult.' *Classical Philology* 27:311–28.

Scroggs, R. 1966. *The Last Adam.* Oxford: Blackwell.

——. 1989. 'Eschatological Existence in Matthew and Paul: *Coincidentia Oppositorum.*' Pp. 125–46 in *Apocalyptic and the New Testament: Essays in Honor of J. Louis Martyn*, eds. J. Marcus and M. L. Soards. Sheffield: JSOT Press.

Searle, J. R. 1969. *Speech Acts: An Essay in the Philosophy of Language.* Cambridge: Cambridge University Press.

——. 1979. *Expression and Meaning: Studies in the Theory of Speech Acts.* Cambridge: Cambridge University Press.

Sechrest, L. L. 2009. *A Former Jew: Paul and the Dialectics of Race.* London: T&T Clark.

Sedley, D. N. 2003. 'The School, from Zeno to Arius Didymus.' Pp. 7–32 in *The Cambridge Companion to the Stoics*, ed. Brad Inwood. Cambridge: Cambridge University Press.

Seebass, H., and C. Brown. 1978 [1971]. 'Righteousness, Justification.' Pp. 352–77 in *The New International Dictionary of New Testament Theology*, vol. 3, ed. C. Brown. Exeter: Paternoster.

Seesengood, R. P. 2010. *Paul: A Brief History.* Chichester: Wiley-Blackwell.

Segal, A. F. 1977. *Two Powers in Heaven: Early Rabbinic Reports about Christianity and Gnosticism.* Leiden: Brill.

——. 1984. '"He Who Did Not Spare His Own Son": Jesus, Paul and the Akedah.' Pp. 169–84 in *From Jesus to Paul: Studies in Honour of Francis Wright Beare*, eds. G. P. Richardson and J. C. Hurd. Waterloo, Ontario: Wilfrid Laurier University Press.

——. 1990. *Paul the Convert: The Apostolate and Apostasy of Saul the Pharisee.* New Haven and London: Yale University Press.

——. 2003. 'Paul's Jewish Presuppositions.' Pp. 159–72 in *The Cambridge Companion to St Paul*, ed. J. D. G. Dunn. Cambridge: Cambridge University Press.

Seifrid, M. A. 1992. *Justification by Faith: The Origin and Development of a Central Pauline Theme.* Supplements to *Novum Testamentum*, vol. 68. Leiden: Brill.

——. 1994. 'Blind Alleys in the Controversy over the Paul of History.' *Tyndale Bulletin* 45:73–95.

——. 2000. *Christ, Our Righteousness: Paul's Theology of Justification.* Leicester: Apollos.

——. 2001. 'Righteousness Language in the Hebrew Scriptures and Early Judaism.' Pp. 415–42 in *Justification and Variegated Nomism, Volume 1: The Complexities of Second Temple Judaism*, eds. D. A. Carson, P. T. O'Brien, and M. A. Seifrid. Tübingen: Mohr.

——. 2004. 'Luther, Melanchthon and Paul on the Question of Imputation: Recommendations on a Current Debate.' Pp. 137–52 in *Justification: What's at Stake in the Current Debates*, eds. M. Husbands and D. J. Treier. Downers Grove, IL: InterVarsity Press.

——. 2007. 'Romans.' Pp. 607–94 in *Commentary on the New Testament Use of the Old Testament*, eds. G. K. Beale and D. A. Carson. Downers Grove, IL: InterVarsity Press.

Seitz, C. R. 1993. *Isaiah 1—39*. Louisville: John Knox Press.

Sevenster, J. N. 1961. *Paul and Seneca*. Leiden: Brill.

——. 1975. *The Roots of Pagan Anti-Semitism in the Ancient World*. Leiden: Brill.

Shaffer, P. 1985 [1980]. *Amadeus*. London: Penguin.

Shaw, G. 1983. *The Cost of Authority*. London: SCM Press.

Sherk, R. K. 1969. *Roman Documents from the Greek East: Senatus Consulta and Epistula to the Age of Augustus*. Baltimore: Johns Hopkins University Press.

——. 1984. *Translated Documents of Greece and Rome, Volume 4: Rome and the Greek East to the Death of Augustus*. Cambridge: Cambridge University Press.

Sherwin-White, A. N. 1969 [1963]. *Roman Society and Roman Law in the New Testament*. 3rd edn. Oxford: Oxford University Press.

Sievers, J. 1997. '"God's Gifts and Call Are Irrevocable": The Interpretation of Rom 11:29 and Its Uses.' *SBL Seminar Papers 1997*:337–57.

Sire, J. W. 2004. *Naming the Elephant: Worldview as a Concept*. Downers Grove, IL: InterVarsity Press.

Skarsaune, O. 2002. *In the Shadow of the Temple: Jewish Influences on Early Christianity*. Downers Grove, IL: InterVarsity Press.

Skinner, J. 1910. *A Critical and Exegetical Commentary on Genesis*. Edinburgh: T&T Clark.

Slater, W. J., ed. 1991. *Dining in a Classical Context*. Ann Arbor, MI: University of Michigan Press.

Smallwood, E. M. 1967. *Documents Illustrating the Principates of Gaius, Claudius and Nero*. Cambridge: Cambridge University Press.

——. 2001. *The Jews under Roman Rule: From Pompey to Diocletian: A Study in Political Relations*. Leiden: Brill.

Smith, C. 2003. *Moral, Believing Animals: Human Personhood and Culture*. New York: Oxford University Press.

——. 2010. *What Is a Person?: Rethinking Humanity, Social Life, and the Moral Good from the Person Up*. Chicago: University of Chicago Press.

Smith, C. B. 2005. *No Longer Jews: The Search for Gnostic Origins*. Grand Rapids: Baker Academic.

Smith, D. E. 2003. *From Symposium to Eucharist: The Banquet in the Early Christian World*. Minneapolis: Fortress.

Smith, J. K. A. 2009. *The Devil Reads Derrida: And Other Essays on the University, the Church, Politics, and the Arts*. Grand Rapids: Eerdmans.

Smith, R. L. 1984. *Micah—Malachi*. Word Biblical Commentary, vol. 32. Waco: Word Books.

Smith, R. R. R. 1987. 'The Imperial Reliefs from the Sebasteion at Aphrodisias.' *Journal of Roman Studies* 77:88–138.

——. 1990. 'Myth and Allegory in the Sebasteion.' *Journal of Roman Studies Supplement* 1:89–100.

Snodgrass, K. R. 1986. 'Justification by Grace – to the Doers: An Analysis of the Place of Romans 2 in the Theology of Paul.' *New Testament Studies* 32:72–93.

Soards, M. 1987. 'Käsemann's "Righteousness" Reexamined.' *Catholic Biblical Quarterly* 49:264–7.

Söding, T. 2001. 'Verheissung und Erfüllung im Lichte paulinischer Theologie.' *New Testament Studies* 47:146–70.

Soskice, J. M. 1985. *Metaphor and Religious Language*. Oxford: Clarendon Press.

Stanley, C. D., 1992. *Paul and the Language of Scripture: Citation Technique in the Pauline Epistles and Contemporary Literature*. Cambridge: Cambridge University Press.

——. 2004. *Arguing with Scripture: The Rhetoric of Quotations in the Letters of Paul*. New York: T&T Clark International.

——., ed. 2011. *The Colonized Apostle: Paul through Postcolonial Eyes*. Minneapolis: Fortress.

——., ed. 2012. *Paul and Scripture: Extending the Conversation*. Atlanta: Society of Biblical Literature.

Stanton, G. N. 2001. 'Galatians.' Pp. 1152–65 in *The Oxford Bible Commentary*, eds. J. Barton and J. Muddiman. Oxford: Oxford University Press.

——. 2003. 'The Law of Christ: A Neglected Theological Gem.' Pp. 169–84 in *Reading Texts, Seeking Wisdom: Scripture and Theology*, eds. D. F. Ford and G. N. Stanton. Grand Rapids: Eerdmans.

——. 2004. *Jesus and Gospel*. Cambridge: Cambridge University Press.

Stark, R. 1996. *The Rise of Christianity: A Sociologist Reconsiders History*. Princeton: Princeton University Press.

——. 2006. *Cities of God: The Real Story of How Christianity Became an Urban Movement and Conquered Rome*. New York: HarperSanFrancisco.

Starling, D. I. 2011. *Not My People: Gentiles as Exiles in Pauline Hermeneutics*. Berlin: De Gruyter.

Steck, O. H. 1967. *Israel und das gewaltsame Geschick der Propheten. Untersuchungen zur Überlieferung des deuteronomistischen Geschichtsbildes im Alten Testament, Spätjudentum und Urchristentum*. Neukirchen-Vluyn: Neukirchener Verlag.

——. 1968. 'Das Problem theologischer Strömungen in nachexilischer Zeit.' *Evangelische Theologie* 28:445–58.

——. 1993. *Das apokryphe Baruchbuch: Studien zu Rezeption und Konzentration 'kanonischer' Überlieferung*. Göttingen: Vandenhoeck & Ruprecht.

Stein, R. 2001. 'Review of *Jesus and the Victory of God* by N. T. Wright.' *Journal of the Evangelical Theological Society* 44:207–18.

Steiner, G. 1996. *No Passion Spent: Essays 1978—1996*. London and Boston: Faber.

——. 2013. 'How Private a Nazi? Review of Yvonne Sherratt, *Hitler's Philosophers* (Yale University Press, 2012).' *The Times Literary Supplement*, 22 February, 5.

Stendahl, K. 1976. *Paul among Jews and Gentiles*. Philadelphia: Fortress.

——. 1995. *Final Account: Paul's Letter to the Romans*. Minneapolis: Fortress.

Stern, M. 1974–84. *Greek and Latin Authors on Jews and Judaism*. Jerusalem: Israel Academy of Sciences and Humanities.

——. 1976. 'The Jews in Greek and Latin Literature.' Pp. 1101–59 in *Compendia Rerum Iudaicarum Ad Novum Testamentum*. Vol. 2, *The Jewish People in the First Century: Historical Geography, Political History, Social, Cultural and Religious Life and Institutions*, eds. S. Safrai and M. Stern. Philadelphia: Fortress.

Stettler, C. 2000. *Der Kolosserhymnus: Untersuchungen zu Form, traditionsgeschichtlichem Hintergund und Aussage von Kol 1,15–20*. Tübingen: Mohr.

Stevenson, G. S., and A. W. Lintott. 2003. 'Clubs, Roman.' Pp. 352–3 in *Oxford Classical Dictionary*. 3rd edn., eds. S. Hornblower and A. Spawforth. Oxford: Oxford University Press.

Still, T. D. 2011. *Philippians and Philemon*. Macon, GA: Smith & Helwys.

Stone, M. E. 1990. *Fourth Ezra: A Commentary on the Book of Fourth Ezra*. Minneapolis: Augsburg Fortress.

Stowers, S. K. 1981. *The Diatribe and Paul's Letter to the Romans*. Chico, CA: Scholars Press.

——. 1986. *Letter Writing in Greco-Roman Antiquity*. Philadelphia: Westminster Press.

——. 1994. *A Rereading of Romans: Justice, Jews, and Gentiles*. New Haven: Yale University Press.

——. 2001. 'Does Pauline Christianity Resemble a Hellenistic Philosophy?' Pp. 81–102 in *Paul beyond the Judaism/Hellenism Divide*, ed. T. Engberg-Pedersen. Louisville: Westminster John Knox Press.

Strack, H. L., and P. Billerbeck. 1926–61. *Kommentar zum Neuen Testament aus Talmud und Midrasch*. Munich: C. H. Beck.

Strobel, A. 1961. *Untersuchungen zum eschatologischen Verzögerungsproblem, auf Grund der spätjudisch-urchristlichen Geschichte von Habakuk 2,2 ff.* Leiden: Brill.

Stroup, G. W. 1981. *The Promise of Narrative Theology*. London: SCM Press.

Stuckenbruck, L. T., and W. E. S. North, eds. 2004. *Early Jewish and Christian Monotheism*. London: T&T Clark International.

Stuhlmacher, P. 1966. *Gerechtigkeit Gottes bei Paulus*. Göttingen: Vandenhoeck & Ruprecht.

——. 1975. *Der Brief an Philemon*. Einsiedeln/Neukirchen-Vluyn: Benziger/Neukirchener-Verlag.

——. 1977. *Historical Criticism and Theological Interpretation of Scripture: Towards a Hermeneutics of Consent*, tr. Roy A. Harrisville. Philadelphia: Fortress; London: SPCK.

——. 1986 [1981]. *Reconciliation, Law and Righteousness: Essays in Biblical Theology*, tr. E. Kalin. Philadelphia: Fortress.

——. 1999. *Biblische Theologie des Neuen Testaments. Band 2: Von der Paulusschule bis zur Johannesoffenbarung. Der Kanon und Seine Auslegung*. Göttingen: Vandenhoeck & Ruprecht.

Suggs, M. J. 1967. '"The Word Is Near You": Romans 10:6–10 within the Purpose of the Letter.' Pp. 289–312 in *Christian History and Interpretation: Studies Presented to John Knox*, eds. W. R. Farmer, C. F. D. Moule, and R. R. Niebuhr. Cambridge: Cambridge University Press.

Sumney, J. L. 1999. *'Servants of Satan,' 'False Brothers,' and Other Opponents of Paul*. Sheffield: Sheffield Academic Press.

Swartley, W. M. 2006. *Covenant of Peace: The Missing Peace in New Testament Theology and Ethics*. Grand Rapids: Eerdmans.

Syme, R. 1939. *The Roman Revolution*. Oxford: Oxford University Press.

Talmon, S. 1987. 'Waiting for the Messiah: The Spiritual Universe of the Qumran Covenanters.' Pp. 111–37 in *Judaisms and Their Messiahs at the Turn of the Christian Era*, eds. J. Neusner, W. S. Green, and E. S. Frerichs. Cambridge: Cambridge University Press.

Taylor, C. 2007. *A Secular Age*. Cambridge, MA: The Belknap Press of Harvard University Press.

Taylor, J. E. 2006. 'Baptism.' Pp. 390–5 in *The New Interpreter's Dictionary of the Bible*, vol. 1, eds. K. D. Sakenfeld et al. Nashville: Abingdon.

——. 2010. 'Therapeutae.' Pp. 1305–7 in *The Eerdmans Dictionary of Early Judaism*, eds. J. J. Collins and D. C. Harlow. Grand Rapids: Eerdmans.

Terrien, S. 2000. *The Elusive Presence: Toward a New Biblical Theology*. Eugene, OR: Wipf and Stock.

Theissen, G. 1982. *The Social Setting of Pauline Christianity: Essays on Corinth*, ed. and tr. John H. Schutz. Philadelphia: Fortress.

——. 1987 [1983]. *Psychological Aspects of Pauline Theology*, tr. John P. Galvin. Edinburgh: T&T Clark.

——. 1999. *A Theory of Primitive Christian Religion*. London: SCM Press.

Thielman, F. 1989. *From Plight to Solution: A Jewish Framework for Understanding Paul's View of the Law in Galatians and Romans*. Leiden: Brill.

——. 1994. *Paul and the Law: A Contextual Approach*. Downer's Grove, IL: InterVarsity Press.

——. 1995. 'The Story of Israel and the Theology of Romans 5—8.' Pp. 169–95 in *Pauline Theology, Volume. 3: Romans*, eds. David M. Hay and E. Elizabeth Johnson. Minneapolis: Fortress.

——. 2005. *Theology of the New Testament: A Canonical and Synthetic Approach*. Grand Rapids: Zondervan.

Thiessen, M. 2011. *Contesting Conversion: Genealogy, Circumcision, and Identity in Ancient Judaism and Christianity*. Oxford: Oxford University Press.

Thiselton, A. C. 1980. *The Two Horizons*. Exeter: Paternoster.

——. 1992. *New Horizons in Hermeneutics: The Theory and Practice of Transforming Biblical Reading*. London and New York: HarperCollins.

——. 2000. *The First Epistle to the Corinthians: A Commentary on the Greek Text*. Grand Rapids: Eerdmans; Carlisle: Paternoster.

——. 2007. *The Hermeneutics of Doctrine*. Grand Rapids: Eerdmans.

——. 2009. *The Living Paul: An Introduction to the Apostle and His Thought*. London: SPCK.

Thompson, J. W. 2011. *Moral Formation According to Paul: The Context and Coherence of Pauline Ethics*. Grand Rapids: Baker Academic.

Thompson, M. B. 1991. *Clothed with Christ: The Example and Teaching of Jesus in Romans 12.1—15.13*. Sheffield: Sheffield Academic Press.

Thornton, T. C. G. 1975. 'St. Paul's Missionary Intentions in Spain.' *Expository Times* 86 (4):120.

Thorsteinsson, R. M. 2006. 'Paul and Roman Stoicism: Romans 12 and Contemporary Stoic Ethics.' *Journal for the Study of the New Testament* 29:139–61.

——. 2010. *Roman Christianity and Roman Stoicism: A Comparative Study of Ancient Morality*. Oxford: Oxford University Press.

Thrall, M. E. 1994, 2000. *A Critical and Exegetical Commentary on the Second Epistle to the Corinthians*. Edinburgh: T&T Clark.

Tilling, C. 2012. *Paul's Divine Christology*. Tübingen: Mohr.

Tobin, T. H. 2004. *Paul's Rhetoric in Its Contexts: The Argument of Romans*. Peabody, MA: Hendrickson.

Tomson, P. J. 1990. *Paul and the Jewish Law: Halakha in the Letters of the Apostle to the Gentiles*. Assen: Van Gorcum; Minneapolis: Fortress.

——. 1996. 'Paul's Jewish Background in View of His Law Teaching in 1 Cor 7.' Pp. 251–70 in *Paul and the Mosaic Law*, ed. J. D. G. Dunn. Tübingen: Mohr.

Towner, P. H. 1993. 'Households, Household Codes.' Pp. 417–19 in *Dictionary of Paul and His Letters*, eds. G. F. Hawthorne, R. P. Martin, and D. G. Reid. Downers Grove, IL: InterVarsity Press.

——. 2006. *The Letters to Timothy and Titus*. Grand Rapids: Eerdmans.

Trebilco, P. R. 1991. *Jewish Communities in Asia Minor*. Cambridge: Cambridge University Press.

——. 2004. *The Early Christians in Ephesus from Paul to Ignatius*. Tübingen: Mohr.

Tuckett, C. M. 2000. 'Paul, Scripture and Ethics: Some Reflections.' *New Testament Studies* 46:403–24.

Turcan, R. 1996. *The Cults of the Roman Empire*, tr. Antonia Nevill. Oxford: Blackwell.

van der Horst, P. W. 2006. *Jews and Christians in Their Graeco-Roman Context*. Tübingen: Mohr.

van Driel, E. C. 2008. *Incarnation Anyway: Arguments for Supralapsarian Christology*. New York: Oxford University Press.

van Unnik, W. C. 1993. *Das Selbstverständnis der jüdischen Diaspora in der hellenistisch-römischen Zeit*. Leiden: Brill.

VanderKam, J. C. 1997. 'Exile in Apocalyptic Jewish Literature.' Pp. 89–109 in *Exile: Old Testament, Jewish, and Christian Conceptions*, ed. James M. Scott. Leiden: Brill.

Vanhoozer, K. 2010. *Remythologizing Theology: Divine Action, Passion and Authorship*. Cambridge: Cambridge University Press.

——. 2011. 'Wrighting the Wrongs of the Reformation? The State of the Union with Christ in St. Paul and Protestant Soteriology.' Pp. 235–59 in *Jesus, Paul and the People of God: A Theological Dialogue with N. T. Wright*, eds. N. Perrin and R. B. Hays. Downers Grove, IL: InterVarsity Press; London: SPCK.

VanLandingham, C. 2006. *Judgment and Justification in Early Judaism and the Apostle Paul*. Peabody, MA: Hendrickson.

Vermes, G. 1973. *Jesus the Jew: A Historian's Reading of the Gospels*. London: Collins.

——. 1997. *The Complete Dead Sea Scrolls in English*. Harmondsworth: Penguin.

——. 2009. *Searching for the Real Jesus*. London: SCM Press.

——. 2010. *Jesus in the Jewish World*. London: SCM Press.

Vermeylen, J. 2006. 'The Gracious God, Sinners and Foreigners: How Nehemiah 9 Interprets the History of Israel.' Pp. 77–114 in *History and Identity: How Israel's Later Authors Viewed Its Earlier History*. eds. N. Calduch-Benages and J. Liesen. Berlin: De Gruyter.

Vernezze, P. T. 2005. *Don't Worry, Be Stoic: Ancient Wisdom for Troubled Times*. Lanham, MD: University Press of America.

Vielhauer, P. 1966. 'On the "Paulinisms" of Acts.' Pp. 33–51 in *Studies in Luke-Acts: Essays Presented in Honor of Paul Schubert*, eds. L. E. Keck and J. L. Martyn. Nashville: Abingdon.

von Rad, G. 1962 [1957]. *Old Testament Theology: The Theology of Israel's Historical Traditions*, tr. D. M. G. Stalker. Edinburgh and London: Oliver & Boyd.

Waaler, E. 2008. *The Shema and the First Commandment in First Corinthians: An Intertextual Approach to Paul's Re-Reading of Deuteronomy*. Tübingen: Mohr.

Wacholder, B. Z. 1975. *Essays on Jewish Chronology and Chronography*. New York: Ktav.

Wagner, G. 1967 [1962]. *Pauline Baptism and the Pagan Mysteries: The Problem of the Pauline Doctrine of Baptism in Romans 6:1–11 in the Light of Its Religious-Historical Parallels*. Edinburgh: Oliver & Boyd.

Wagner, J. R. 2002. *Heralds of the Good News: Isaiah and Paul 'in Concert' in the Letter to the Romans*. Leiden: Brill.

——. 2010. '"Not from the Jews Only, but Also from the Gentiles": Mercy to the Nations in Romans 9—11.' Pp. 417–31 in *Between Gospel and Election: Explorations in the Interpretation of Romans 9—11*, eds. F. Wilk and J. R. Wagner. Tübingen: Mohr.

Wagner, J. R., C. K. Rowe, and A. K. Grieb, eds. 2008. *The Word Leaps the Gap: Essays on Scripture and Theology in Honor of Richard B. Hays*. Grand Rapids/Cambridge: Eerdmans.

Walker, L. L. 2000. 'Lud, Ludim.' P. 827 in *The Eerdmans Dictionary of the Bible*, ed. D. N. Freedman. Grand Rapids: Eerdmans.

Wall, R. W. 1993. *Colossians & Philemon*. Downers Grove, IL: InterVarsity Press.

Wallace-Hadrill, A. 1986. 'Image and Authority in the Coinage of Augustus.' *Journal of Roman Studies* 76:66–87.

——. 2008. *Rome's Cultural Revolution*. Cambridge: Cambridge University Press.

Wallis, I. G. 1995. *The Faith of Jesus Christ in Early Christian Traditions*. Cambridge: Cambridge University Press.

Walsh, B. J., and S. C. Keesmaat. 2004. *Colossians Remixed: Subverting the Empire*. Downers Grove, IL: IVP Academic.

Walsh, B. J., and J. R. Middleton. 1984. *The Transforming Vision: Shaping a Christian World View*. Downers Grove, IL: InterVarsity Press.

Walton, J. H. 2001. *The NIV Application Commentary: Genesis*. Grand Rapids: Zondervan.

——. 2003. 'The Imagery of the Substitute King Ritual in Isaiah's Fourth Servant Song.' *Journal of Biblical Literature* 122:734–43.

——. 2009. *The Lost World of Genesis One*. Downers Grove, IL: InterVarsity Press.

Ward, M. 2008. *Planet Narnia: The Seven Heavens in the Imagination of C. S. Lewis*. Oxford: Oxford University Press.

Ware, J. P. 2011 [2005]. *Paul and the Mission of the Church: Philippians in Ancient Jewish Context*. Grand Rapids: Baker Academic.

Waterfield, R. 2009. *Why Socrates Died: Dispelling the Myths*. London: Faber and Faber.

Waters, G. P. 2004. *Justification and the New Perspective on Paul: A Review and Response*. Phillipsburg, NJ: Presbyterian & Reformed.

——. 2006. *The End of Deuteronomy in the Epistles of Paul*. Tübingen: Mohr.

Watson, D. F. 1993. 'Diatribe.' Pp. 213–14 in *Dictionary of Paul and His Letters*, eds. G. F. Hawthorne, R. P. Martin, and D. G. Reid. Downers Grove, IL: InterVarsity Press.

Watson, F. B. 1986. *Paul, Judaism and the Gentiles: A Sociological Approach*. Cambridge: Cambridge University Press.

——. 2002. 'Is There a Story in These Texts?' Pp. 231–9 in *Narrative Dynamics in Paul: A Critical Assessment*, ed. B. W. Longenecker. Louisville: Westminster John Knox Press.

——. 2004. *Paul and the Hermeneutics of Faith*. London: T&T Clark.

——. 2007 [1986]. *Paul, Judaism and the Gentiles: Beyond the New Perspective*. Rev. and expanded edn. Grand Rapids: Eerdmans.

Watts, R. E. 1999. '"For I Am Not Ashamed of the Gospel": Romans 1:16–17 and Habakkuk 2:4.' Pp. 3–15 in *Romans and the People of God: Essays in Honor of Gordon D. Fee on the Occasion of His 65th Birthday*, eds. S. K. Soderlund and N. T. Wright. Grand Rapids: Eerdmans.

——. 2000 [1997]. *Isaiah's New Exodus in Mark*. Grand Rapids: Baker Academic.

Weatherly, J. A. 1991. 'The Authenticity of I Thessalonians 2.13–16: Additional Evidence.' *Journal for the Study of the New Testament* 41:79–98.

Wedderburn, A. J. M. 1985. 'Some Observations on Paul's Use of the Phrases "in Christ" and "with Christ".' *Journal for the Study of the New Testament* 25:83–97.

——. 1987a. *Baptism and Resurrection: Studies in Pauline Theology against Its Graeco-Roman Background*. Tübingen: Mohr.

——. 1987b. 'The Soteriology of the Mysteries and Pauline Baptismal Theology.' *Novum Testamentum* 29(1):53–72.

Weima, J. A. D. 1993. 'Gal. 6:11–18: A Hermeneutical Key to the Galatian Letter.' *Calvin Theological Journal* 28:90–107.

——. 2010. 'Paul's Persuasive Prose: An Epistolary Analysis of the Letter to Philemon.' Pp. 29–60 in *Philemon in Perspective: Interpreting a Pauline Letter*, ed. D. F. Tolmie. Berlin: De Gruyter.

——. 2012. '"Peace and Security" (1 Thess 5.3): Prophetic Warning or Political Propaganda?' *New Testament Studies* 58:331–59.

Weinstock, S. 1971. *Divus Iulius*. Oxford: Clarendon Press.

Wells, K. B. 2010. 'Grace, Obedience and the Hermeneutics of Agency.' Unpublished doctoral dissertation, Durham University.

Wendland, E. 2010. '"You Will Do Even More Than I Say": On the Rhetorical Function of Stylistic Form in the Letter to Philemon.' Pp. 79–111 in *Philemon in Perspective: Interpreting a Pauline Letter*, ed. D. Francis Tolmie. Berlin: De Gruyter.

Wengst, K. 1987 [1986]. *Pax Romana and the Peace of Jesus Christ*. London: SCM Press.

West, M. 1999. 'Towards Monotheism.' Pp. 21–40 in *Pagan Monotheism in Late Antiquity*, eds. P. Athanassiadi and M. Frede. Oxford: Clarendon Press.

Westerholm, S. 2004. *Perspectives Old and New on Paul: The 'Lutheran' Paul and His Critics*. Grand Rapids: Eerdmans.

White, J. L. 1999. *The Apostle of God: Paul and the Promise of Abraham*. Peabody, MA: Hendrickson.

White, M. J. 2003. 'Stoic Natural Philosophy (Physics and Cosmology).' Pp. 124–52 in *The Cambridge Companion to the Stoics*, ed. B. Inwood. Cambridge: Cambridge University Press.

Whiteley, D. E. H. 1964. *The Theology of St. Paul*. Philadelphia: Fortress.

Wiefel, W. 1991. 'The Jewish Community in Ancient Rome and the Origins of Roman Christianity.' Pp. 85–110 in *The Romans Debate: Revised and Expanded Edition*, ed. K. P. Donfried. Peabody, MA: Hendrickson.

Wilcken, R. L. 2003. *The Christians as the Romans Saw Them*. Rev. edn. New Haven: Yale University Press.

Wilk, F. 1998. *Die Bedeutung des Jesajabuches für Paulus*. Göttingen: Vandenhoeck & Ruprecht.

——. 2010. 'Rahmen und Aufbau von Römer 9—11.' Pp. 227–53 in *Between Gospel and Election: Explorations in the Interpretation of Romans 9—11*, eds. F. Wilk and J. R. Wagner. Tübingen: Mohr.

Wilk, F., and J. R. Wagner, eds. 2010. *Between Gospel and Election: Explorations in the Interpretation of Romans 9—11*. Tübingen: Mohr.

Williams, B. 1985. *Ethics and the Limits of Philosophy*. London: Collins Fontana.

Williams, M. 2004. 'Being a Jew in Rome: Sabbath Fasting as an Expression of Romano-Jewish Identity.' Pp. 8–18 in *Negotiating Diaspora: Jewish Strategies in the Roman Empire*, ed. J. M. G. Barclay. Edinburgh: T&T Clark.

Williams, M. A. 1996. *Rethinking 'Gnosticism': An Argument for Dismantling a Dubious Category*. Princeton: Princeton University Press.

Williams, S. K. 1980. 'The Righteousness of God in Romans.' *Journal of Biblical Literature* 99 (2):241–90.

——. 1989. 'The Hearing of Faith: ΑΚΟΗ ΠΙΣΤΕΟΣ in Galatians 3.' *New Testament Studies* 35:82–93.

——. 1997. *Galatians*. Nashville: Abingdon.

Williamson, H. G. M. 1985. *Ezra, Nehemiah*. Dallas: Word Books.

Willitts, J. 2005. 'Isa 54,1 in Gal 4,24b–27: Reading Genesis in Light of Isaiah.' *Zeitschrift für die Neutestamentliche Wissenschaft* 96(3):188–210.

Wilson, C. 2008. *Epicureanism at the Origins of Modernity*. Oxford: Clarendon Press.

Wilson, R. McL. 2005. *Colossians and Philemon*. London/New York: T&T Clark.

Wilson, T. A. 2007. *The Curse of the Law and the Crisis in Galatia: Reassessing the Purpose of Galatians*. Tübingen: Mohr.

Wink, W. 1984. *The Powers*. Vol. 1, *Naming the Powers: The Language of Power in the New Testament*. Philadelphia: Fortress.

——. 1986. *The Powers*. Vol. 2, *Unmasking the Powers: The Invisible Forces That Determine Human Existence*. Philadelphia: Fortress.

——. 1992. *The Powers*. Vol. 3, *Engaging the Powers: Discernment and Resistance in a World of Domination*. Minneapolis: Fortress.

Winter, B. W. 1994. *Seek the Welfare of the City: Christians as Benefactors and Citizens*. Grand Rapids: Eerdmans.

——. 1999. 'Gallio's Ruling on the Legal State of Early Christianity (Acts 18:14–15).' *Tyndale Bulletin* 50:213–24.

——. 2001. *After Paul Left Corinth: The Influence of Secular Ethics and Social Change*. Grand Rapids: Eerdmans.

——. 2002a. 'The Imperial Cult and Early Christians in Pisidian Antioch (Acts XIII 13–50 and Gal VI 11–18).' Pp. 67–75 in *Actes du 1er Congrès International sur Antioche de Pisidie, Collection Archéologie et Histoire de L'Antiquité*, ed. T. Drew-Bear, M. Tashalan, and C. M. Thomas. Lyon: Université Lumière-Lyon.

——. 2002b [1997]. *Philo and Paul among the Sophists: Alexandrian and Corinthian Responses to a Julio-Claudian Movement*. Grand Rapids; Cambridge, UK: Eerdmans.

Winter, S. B. C. 1987. 'Paul's Letter to Philemon.' *New Testament Studies* 33:1–15.

Wischmeyer, O. 2006. 'Stephen's Speech before the Sanhedrin against the Background of the Summaries of the History of Israel (Acts 7).' Pp. 341–58 in *History and Identity: How Israel's Later Authors Viewed Its Earlier History*, eds. N. Calduch-Benages and J. Liesen. Berlin: De Gruyter.

Wise, M. O. 2003. 'The Concept of a New Covenant in the Teacher Hymns from Qumran (1QHa x-Xvii).' Pp. 99–128 in *The Concept of the Covenant in the Second Temple Period*, eds. S. E. Porter and J. C. R. de Roo. Leiden: Brill.

——. 2010. 'Crucifixion.' Pp. 500–1 in *The Eerdmans Dictionary of Early Judaism*, eds. J. J. Collins and D. C. Harlow. Grand Rapids: Eerdmans.

Witherington III, B. 1994. *Paul's Narrative Thought World: The Tapestry of Tragedy and Triumph*. Louisville: Westminster John Knox Press.

——. 1995. *Conflict and Community in Corinth: A Socio-Rhetorical Commentary on 1 and 2 Corinthians*. Grand Rapids: Eerdmans.

——. 1998. *Grace in Galatia: A Commentary on St Paul's Letter to the Galatians*. Edinburgh: T&T Clark.

——. 2004. *Paul's Letter to the Romans: A Socio-Rhetorical Commentary*. Assisted by D. Hyatt. Grand Rapids: Eerdmans.

——. 2007. *The Letters to Philemon, the Colossians and the Ephesians. A Socio-Rhetorical Commentary on the Captivity Epistles*. Grand Rapids: Eerdmans.

Witte, M. 2006. 'From Exodus to David – History and Historiography in Psalm 78.' Pp. 21–42 in *History and Identity: How Israel's Later Authors Viewed Its Earlier History*, eds. N. Calduch-Benages and J. Liesen. Berlin: De Gruyter.

Wittgenstein, L. 1958. *Philosophical Investigations*, tr. G. E. M. Anscombe. New York: Macmillan.

——. 1967. *Zettel*, ed. and tr. G. E. M. Anscombe, ed. G. H. von Wright. Oxford: Blackwell.

Wolff, C. 1996. *Der erste Brief des Paulus an die Korinther*. Leipzig: Evangelische Verlagsanstalt.

Wolter, M. 2008. 'Von der Entmachtung des Buchstabens durch seine Attribute. Eine Spurensuche, ausgehend von Röm 2,29.' Pp. 149–61 in *Sprachgewinn. Festschrift für Günter Bader*, eds. H. Assel and H.-Ch. Askani. Berlin, Münster: Lit Verlag.

——. 2010. 'The Letter to Philemon as Ethical Counterpart of Paul's Doctrine of Justification.' Pp. 169–79 in *Philemon in Perspective: Interpreting a Pauline Letter*, ed. D. F. Tolmie. Berlin: De Gruyter.

——. 2011. *Paulus: Ein Grundriss seiner Theologie*. Neukirchen-Vluyn: Neukirchener Verlagsgesellschaft.

Wolterstorff, N. 1995. *Divine Discourse*. Cambridge: Cambridge University Press.

Woolf, G. 2001. 'Inventing Empire in Ancient Rome.' Pp. 311–22 in *Empires: Perspectives from Archaeology and History*, eds. S. E. Alcock, T. N. D'Altroy, K. D. Morrison, and C. M. Sinopoli. Cambridge: Cambridge University Press.

Wright, A. T. 2005. *The Origin of Evil Spirits: The Reception of Genesis 6:1–4 in Early Jewish Literature*. Tübingen: Mohr.

Wright, D. F. 2003. '"A Race Apart"? Jews, Gentiles, Christians.' *Bibliotheca Sacra* 160:131–41.

Wright, N. T. 1978. 'The Paul of History and the Apostle of Faith.' *Tyndale Bulletin* 29:61–88.

——. 1980. 'The Messiah and the People of God: A Study in Pauline Theology with particular reference to the Argument of the Epistle to the Romans.' Unpublished doctoral dissertation, Oxford University.

——. 1986a. '"Constraints" and the Jesus of History.' *Scottish Journal of Theology* 39:189–210.

——. 1986b. *The Epistles of Paul to the Colossians and to Philemon*. Leicester: InterVarsity Press; Grand Rapids: Eerdmans (= *Col. and Philem.*).

——. 1991. *The Climax of the Covenant: Christ and the Law in Pauline Theology*. Edinburgh: T&T Clark; Minneapolis: Fortress (= *Climax*).

——. 1992. *The New Testament and the People of God*. Christian Origins and the Question of God, vol. I. London: SPCK; Minneapolis: Fortress (= *NTPG*).

——. 1995. 'Romans and the Theology of Paul.' Pp. 30–67 in *Pauline Theology, Volume 3: Romans*, eds. David M. Hay and E. Elizabeth Johnson. Minneapolis: Fortress.

——. 1996. *Jesus and the Victory of God*. Christian Origins and the Question of God, vol. II. London: SPCK; Minneapolis: Fortress (= *JVG*).

——. 1997. *What St Paul Really Said*. Oxford: Lion; Grand Rapids: Eerdmans.

——. 1999. *The Way of the Lord*. London: SPCK; Grand Rapids: Eerdmans.

——. 2002. 'Romans.' Pp. 393–770 in *The New Interpreter's Bible*, vol. 10, ed. L. E. Keck. Nashville: Abingdon.

——. 2003. *The Resurrection of the Son of God*. Christian Origins and the Question of God, vol. III. London: SPCK; Minneapolis: Fortress (= *RSG*).

——. 2004. 'An Incompleat (but Grateful) Response to the Review by Markus Bockmuehl of *The Resurrection of the Son of God*.' *Journal for the Study of the New Testament* 26 (4):505–10.

——. 2005a. *Paul: Fresh Perspectives* (US title *Paul in Fresh Perspective*). London: SPCK; Minneapolis: Fortress (= *Fresh Perspectives*).

——. 2005b. 'Resurrecting Old Arguments: Responding to Four Essays.' *Journal for the Study of the Historical Jesus* 3(2):187–209.

——. 2006a. *Evil and the Justice of God*. London: SPCK; Downers Grove, IL: InterVarsity Press.

——. 2006b. *Judas and the Gospel of Jesus: Have We Missed the Truth about Christianity?* London: SPCK; Grand Rapids: Baker.

——. 2008. *Surprised by Hope*. London: SPCK; San Francisco: HarperSanFrancisco.

——. 2009. *Justification: God's Plan and Paul's Vision*. London: SPCK; Downers Grove, IL: InterVarsity Press (= *Justification*).

——. 2010. *Virtue Reborn* (US title *After You Believe*). London: SPCK; San Francisco: HarperOne.

——. 2011a. *Simply Jesus: Who He Was, What He Did, Why It Matters*. London: SPCK; San Francisco: HarperOne.

——. 2011b [2005]. *Scripture and the Authority of God: How to Read the Bible Today*. 2nd edn. San Francisco: HarperOne (UK edn. London: SPCK, 2013).

——. 2012a. *How God Became King: The Forgotten Story of the Gospels*. San Francisco: HarperOne; London: SPCK.

——. 2012b. 'Imagining the Kingdom: Mission and Theology in Early Christianity.' *Scottish Journal of Theology* 65(4):379–401.

——. 2013. *Pauline Perspectives*. London: SPCK; Minneapolis: Fortress (= *Perspectives*).

——. 2014. *Paul and His Recent Interpreters*. London: SPCK; Minneapolis: Fortress (= *Interpreters*).

Wright, R. B. 1985. 'Psalms of Solomon: A New Translation and Introduction.' Pp. 639–70 in *The Old Testament Pseudepigrapha, Volume 2*, ed. James H. Charlesworth. Garden City, NY: Doubleday.

Wyschogrod, M. 1983. *The Body of Faith: Judaism as Corporeal Election*. New York: Seabury Press.

Yadin, A. 2010. 'Akiba (Akiva).' Pp. 315–16 in *The Eerdmans Dictionary of Early Judaism*, eds. J. J. Collins and D. C. Harlow. Grand Rapids: Eerdmans.

Yarborough, O. L. 1985. *Not Like the Gentiles: Marriage Rules in the Letters of Paul*. Atlanta: Scholars Press.

Yeung, M. W. 2002. *Faith in Jesus and Paul: A Comparison with Special Reference to 'Faith That Can Move Mountains' and 'Your Faith Has Healed/Saved You'*. Tübingen: Mohr.

Yinger, K. L. 1999. *Paul, Judaism and Justification According to Deeds*. Cambridge: Cambridge University Press.

Young, F., and D. F. Ford. 1987. *Meaning and Truth in 2 Corinthians*. London: SPCK.

Zanker, P. 1988. *The Power of Images in the Age of Augustus*. Ann Arbor, MI: University of Michigan Press.

——. 2010. *Roman Art*. Los Angeles, CA: J. Paul Getty Museum.

Zeller, D. 1984. *Der Brief an die Römer*. Regensburg: Verlag Friedrich Pustet.

Zetterholm, M. 2009. *Approaches to Paul: A Student's Guide to Recent Scholarship*. Minneapolis: Fortress.

Ziesler, J. A. 1972. *The Meaning of Righteousness in Paul*. Cambridge: Cambridge University Press.

Zimmerli, W. 1978. *Old Testament Theology in Outline*. New York: Continuum.

Zimmermann, R. 2007. 'Jenseits von Indikativ und Imperativ: Entwurf einer "impliziten Ethik" des Paulus am Beispiel des 1. Korintherbriefes.' *Theologische Literaturzeitung* 132:259–84.

INDEX OF ANCIENT SOURCES

Page numbers in bold print indicate key discussions of frequently referred-to passages in Paul's letters.

1. Old Testament

Nb.: Where verse numbers of EVV differ from MT or LXX, the EV is followed

Genesis

1 102, 165, 191f., 406, 446, 476, 486, 561, 675, 1010, 1060, 1293, 1455, 1493, 1509
1—3 561, 686, 1052, 1117, 1400
1—12 752
1.1 673, 675
1.1-26 622
1.2 78, 168
1.26 439, 686
1.26-8 438, 640, 686, 908
1.26-31 787
1.28 439, 785, 1010
2 106, 438, 446, 476, 486, 705
2.2 559f.
2.2f. 102
2.7 1400
2.21 498
3 440, 438, 476, 486, 762f., 787, 849, 1072, 1363
3.5 686
3.6 786
3.16 786
3.17 787
3.22 686
4.1-16 895
4.26 703
5.3 439
5.29 787
6 133, 476, 740, 742, 763, 871
6.2 694
6.2-4 476
9.1-9 787
10 1501
11 740, 763, 849
11.30 1137
12 121, 366, 527, 791, 848, 861, 1199
12.1 366
12.2f. 785
12.3 85, 121, 366, 827, 861, 1006
12.7 366
12.10-16 94
12.10-20 788
13 869
13.14 911
13.15 366, 869
13.16 121
15 121, 124, 363, 366, 422, 498, 527, 529, 788, 795, 848-50, 861f., 868, 873, 876, 928, 971-3, 996, 1002f., 1005, 1007, 1013, 1139, 1153, 1200, 1461, 1469
15.1 1003
15.1-6 789
15.5 121
15.6 88, 848, 972, 1450, 1461
15.7-11 789f.
15.7-21 131
15.12 498
15.12-16 789
15.12-21 498, 789
15.13 527, 657
15.13-16 876
15.16 1112, 1153, 1237
15.17-21 789
15.18 119, 121, 366
16.2f. 1135
16.3 786
16.10 786
17 786, 795, 848, 853, 868f., 1002
17.1-8 790
17.1-14 790
17.2 785

Genesis (*continued*)
17.5 784, 1004, 1006
17.6 785
17.8 366, 785, 869
17.10f. 121, 848
17.11 790
17.13 790
17.19 790
17.21 790
17.25f. 1134
18 684, 861
18.8 861
21.9 1136
21.10 1136
21.12 827
21.19 1135
22 697, 786f., 791, 848, 902, 905f.
22.1–3 904
22.7–18 904
22.16–18 785, 788
24 869
24.7 366, 869
26.3f. 785
26.4 366
26.24 785
28.3 785
28.10–22 96
28.13 366
28.14 911
34.1–31 1154
35.11 786
35.11f. 786
35.12 366
37—50 688
37.26 1468
38 799
38.26 798, 945
41.37–43 688
41.38 721
47.27 786
48.3f. 786
49 827
49.1 147
49.10 120
49.24 668

Exodus
1.7 786
2 795, 802
2.23f. 791
2.23–5 876
2.24 1056
3 795, 802
3.1–6 100
3.2 356
3.6–8 791
3.8 366
3.13–15 100, 657, 1076
3.16f. 791
4 657
4.22 128, 424, 959, 1070
4.22f. 658, 694, 874
6 795, 802
6.2–8 791, 1076
6.5 1056
6.6 845
9.16 1227
12.12f. 791
12.23–7 791
12.40 527
13.21f. 356, 714
14—15 1298
14.19 714
15 736
15.1–18 623
15.13 845
18.13–27 980
18.25 1240
19.4–6 805
19.6 80, 487, 506
19.18 356
20.24 100
21 15
21.2–6 14
21.6 13
23.2 948
23.2f. 937
23.6 948
23.6–9 937
23.7 948
23.22 85
23.31 119, 285
26.1 97
29.45 888
29.45f. 714, 716
29.46 97
31.1–3 721
31.1–11 103
31.2 103
31.18 981
32 740, 1189
32—4 97
32—40 677, 716
32.1–35 744
32.13 786
32.15 981
33 1189
33—4 679
33.12–23 678
33.19 679, 1185
34.5–9 100
34.6 651
34.6f. 1076
34.30 505
34.34 726, 1226
35.31 721
40 106, 189, 712, 716, 1091
40.34f. 678, 1052
40.34–8 98
40.38f. 1052

Leviticus
18 506, 973, 1167
18.5 506, 515, 532, 865, 1014, 1171, 1173, 1462–5
19.15 937, 948
19.18 1119
23f. 149
25 149
25.10 149
25.39–41 13
25.46 13
26 149, 152, 161, 176
26.1–13 149
26.1–45 928
26.9 786
26.11 1021

26.11f. 355, 558, 714, 1041
26.12 637
26.14–33 149
26.33 149
26.34f. 150
26.40–5 150
26.41 148, 923, 1076
26.44f. 1165

Numbers
5.3 714
11.17 105, 721
11.25 721
14.1–4 657
14.20–3 1052
14.21 191, 679
15.30 898
15.30f. 744
15.37–41 84
16.41–50 101
24 131, 827
24.7 120
24.14 147
24.17 84, 104
25 421
25.1–18 744
25.6–8 88
25.7–13 84
25.11 88
25.12 1013
25.12f. 88, 849
25.13 96
27.18 721
35.34 714

Deuteronomy
1.1 1240
1.6—3.29 118
1.10f. 786
1.17 948
3.15–20 1106
4 143
4.7 153
4.7f. 182
4.25–31 126, 146
4.29 153, 725
4.30 147
4.37 860
5—26 1463
5.1 1240
6 705
6.3 366
6.4f. 662, 664
6.6 724
6.9 90
6.10–25 118
6.15 714
7.8 845, 860
7.12—8.20 928
7.13f. 786
7.21 714
8.1 786
8.7 502
8.17 1171
9 1178
9.4 502, 1077, 1171f.
9.4–7 1171
9.10f. 981
10.15 860
10.16 148, 424, 923, 984, 1076
10.17 663, 806, 948, 1087
11.20 90
11.24 119
11.26–8 928
12.5 96, 98
12.11 98, 100
13.5 845
13.11 1240
14.1f. 874
14.23 96, 98, 100
15 15
15.6 120
15.12–18 14
15.15 15, 845
15.17 13
16.2 96, 98
16.18–20 937, 948
17.8 96, 98
17.12 744, 898
18.6 96, 98
21.8 845
21.23 407
23.3 157
24.17 937, 948
24.18 845
25.1 937
25.3 1438
26—9 125
26.2 96, 98
26.5–9 118
26.16—28.68 928
26.19 120
27 526, 1166
27f. 1055
27—9 1215, 1251, 1463
27—30 118, 124, 143, 146, 149f., 162, 176, 185, 502–4, 514, 1165, 1460, 1463
27—32 182, 929, 1512
27—34 1463
27.19 937, 948
27.26 526, 1215
28 149, 178, 1166, 1236
28f. 139, 142, 761
28.1 120
28.4 786
28.10–13 120
28.13 126
28.15–68 143
28.25 120
28.33 151
28.37 154
28.43 120
28.45–68 1034
28.49–52 156
28.51 151
28.63 786
29 150, 868, 1216, 1227f., 1233
29.2 1240
29.4 1227
29.12 143
29.14 143
29.19 143
29.19–29 1034
29.20–8 143
29.27 143
29.28 156

Deuteronomy (*continued*)
29.29 143, 156
30 120, 124–6, 139, 143, 144, 146f., 149, 152f., 156f., 161f., 176, 185, 188, 196, 362, 408, 424, 499, 501f., 504, 506, 513–15, 532, 703f., 759, 815, 823, 864, 867, 892, 910, 925, 931, 1008, 1036, 1065, 1072, 1077, 1089, 1159f., 1164f., 1166f., 1171–4, 1179, 1201, 1216, 1227f., 1233f., 1236, 1245f., 1248, 1251, 1257, 1263, 1301, 1342, 1379, 1433, 1439, 1454, 1460, 1463–5
30.1f. 1165
30.1–3 125f.
30.1–5 120
30.1–20 1054
30.2f. 154, 725
30.3 155
30.3–5 143, 159
30.5 786
30.6 143, 424, 725, 759, 867, 923, 984, 1076, 1379
30.7 85, 120, 143, 149
30.11–14 152, 1173
30.12f. 867
30.12–14 1173
30.14 725, 1163, 1174
30.15f. 515
30.15–20 515, 936
30.16 120, 786, 901
30.19 156
30.19f. 515
31 143
31—3 143
31.11 1240
32 77, 117f., 130f., 143, 156, 162, 170, 399, 501, 503f., 669, 744, 874, 897, 1165, 1208, 1216, 1222, 1228, 1245, 1301, 1345, 1454, 1463–5
32.4 668
32.4–42 1034
32.5 131, 1208
32.6–14 131
32.7–43 118
32.10f. 77
32.10–21 1345
32.11 156
32.15–18 131, 668
32.17 421
32.19–35 131
32.20 1077, 1229
32.21 156, 533, 704, 1077, 1180, 1202, 1229, 1345
32.31 668
32.35 669, 1303
32.36 1054
32.39 669
32.43 669, 1054, 1300, 1455, 1495
33 143, 1165
33f. 155
33.2 156, 705, 871
33.6–25 131
33.29 1003
34.9 721
34.12 1240

Joshua
3.7 1240
10.12–14 138
18.1 96
19.51 96
21.2 96
22.9 96
24.2–13 118

Judges
3.10 721
6.34 721
11.29 721
13.25 721
14.6 721
14.19 721
15.14 721
18.31 96
20f. 1223

1 Samuel
1.3 96
1.24 96
2.2 668
3.20 1240
3.21 96
4.3 96
7.5 1223, 1240
11.5–11 721
12.19–25 1223
12.22 1223
16.13 721, 829
17 829
18.6–9 829
24.12–15 798
24.17 798, 945, 1468
25.1 1240

2 Samuel
7 99, 119, 148, 190
7.1–17 99
7.2 358
7.5f. 358
7.8 558, 715
7.10–14 190
7.12f. 103
7.12–14 715, 1062
7.12–17 121
7.14 558, 637, 694, 1041
8.15 1240
19.43 829
20.1 829
21.17 119
22.2 668
22.29 119
22.50 1455, 1495
23.3 668

1 Kings
3 675
3.5–14 103
3.9–12 103
3.15 103
3.16–28 103
4 103
4.21 285
4.21–4 119
5 103
8 106, 189, 716, 1052
8.10f. 98
8.10–13 1493
8.11 1053
8.15–21 99
8.27 100, 1022
8.29 100
8.29f. 365
8.32 937
8.35 365
8.38 365
8.44 365
8.48f. 365
8.62 1240
8.62–6 102
9.3 100
10 1053
10.24 1053
11.13 96, 98
11.30f. 829
11.36 100, 119
12.1 1240
12.16 829
14.2 96
14.21 96, 98
15.4 119
17.1 1223
18.17f. 1155
18.19 1240
18.20–40 84
19 1504
19f. 88
19.1–18 1423
19.10 84, 88, 1224, 1239
19.11f. 356
19.14 88, 1224, 1239

2 Kings
6.15–19 1083
8.19 119
17.7–20 125
23.12 267

1 Chronicles
5.19 1139
9.1 1240
16.8 703
16.18 366
17.13 694
18.14 1240
22.1 96
28.1—29.22 103
28.2 560
29.10–12 192
29.21 1240
30.1–12 103

2 Chronicles
1.7–13 103
2—7 103
2.6 100
2.12 103
2.13–16 103
5.14 1053
6.20f. 365
7.1 1053
7.12 96
9 1053
9.23 1053
12.1 1240
12.13 96
19.6f. 948
19.7 806, 1087
20.7 366
21.7 119
26.16–21 100
29.24 1240
36.21f. 142

Ezra
1.1–4 1050
3.11 1151
9 119, 132, 802, 996
9.6–9 151
9.6–15 119

Nehemiah
1.8f. 120
1.9 96
9 119, 132, 143, 151, 996
9.6–38 119
9.8 366
9.17 657
9.20 105
9.36f. 151

Job
1.6 694
2.1 694
4.17 798
26 628
28 152
29.14 947
32.2 798
34.11 938, 1087
34.19 1087
38—41 628
38.4—39.30 152
38.7 694
40.8—41.26 152
41.4 13

Psalms
1.3 1213
2 119, 128, 138, 240–2, 366, 410, 488, 533, 544, 563, 659, 694, 700f., 720, 730, 734, 741, 767, 818f., 821, 829, 849, 868, 906, 1023, 1050, 1053–4, 1062, 1064f., 1091, 1286, 1291, 1300, 1371, 1382, 1403, 1454, 1503, 1507
2.1 190
2.1–6 172
2.1–11 1054
2.2 819

Psalms (*continued*)
2.6 819
2.6f. 99
2.7 692, 694, 700, 818, 1062
2.7f. 241, 533, 658
2.7–9 482, 702, 1064
2.8 121, 622, 868, 911, 1509
2.8f. 366
2.9 1058, 1275
2.9–12 819, 821, 832
2.10 660
2.12 694
3.4 99
5.7 365
7.9–10 1056
8 518, 521, 561, 640, 734, 736, 821f., 1050, 1064, 1126, 1455
8.3 480
8.3–8 440
8.4 1455
8.5 686
8.5f. 686, 1293
8.5–8 486
8.6 639–41, 821, 1455
8.6f. 1092
8.7 686, 736, 1293
9.8f. 113
9.11 98
11.4 365
14.7 99, 1249f.
15 100
17.8 77
18.2 668
18.6 365
18.6–9 99
18.7 99
18.10 99
18.43–9 120
18.49 1455, 1495
18.50 1300
19 452, 628, 895, 1017, 1163, 1180, 1365
19.1 489
19.4 1174, 1499
19.5 819
20.2f. 99
22 1160
22.27 366, 1058
24 639f.
24.1 393, 403, 475, 564, 639, 668–70, 1429
24.3f. 669
24.3–6 100
24.5 669
24.7–10 99, 670
26.1 799
26.8 98
27.4 99
28.2 99, 365
28.4 1087
29.9 99
33.5 191
33.8f. 629
35.8 1228
35.24 1056
36.2 1228
36.7 77
40.10–12 1056
42f. 99
42.6 365
43.3 98
43.3f. 365
44 902, 906f.
44.20–2 635
44.23 635
44.24 635
44.26 635
46.4 102
46.4f. 98
48.1–3 98
48.9 99
50.2 99
50.6 1056
50.23 96
51 744
51.4 844
51.7 96
52.8 1213
53.6 99, 1250
57.1 77
57.3 99
61.4 77
62.2 668
62.12 938, 1087
63.2 99
63.7 77
65.1f. 99
65.3 96
66.4 1058
67.3f. 1058
67.4 916
68 820
68.10 1228
68.16–18 98
68.17 871
68.23–4 1152, 1228
68.32 1058
68.35 99
69.9 820
72 137, 410, 1054
72.8 119, 285, 366, 1006
72.8f. 1064
72.8–11 366, 815, 1058
72.10 1500, 1502
72.13 1006
72.19 190, 1053
73 741
73.17 99
74 741
74.1–11 799
74.2 98
74.18–23 799
76.2 98
77 109
78 118, 137
78.35 668
78.38 96
78.60 96
78.68 98
78.70–2 118
79 109
79.1 98
79.8f. 96
80 109
80.8–19 794
80.11 119
80.17 1455

82.1–8 113
82.2 937, 948
83.6–8 1185
83.7 1139
84.1 98
84.1–12 100
84.11 1151
86.9 1058
87.2 98
88 452, 631, 741
89 109, 137, 182, 631, 701, 741, 1045
89.25 119, 285, 366, 1006
89.26f. 658, 694, 818
91.4 77
93.2 484
93.5 100
94.12f. 979
94.14 1223
95.5 480
95.11 561
96 188, 741, 1053
96.6 99
96.10–13 482, 916, 926
97.6 1056
97.8 99
98 188, 741, 1053
98.2 1467
98.7–9 482, 916, 1044
99.2 99
99.6 703
99.9 100
100.3 480
100.4 100
102.16 190
102.22 1058
104 628
104—7 1045
104.27–33 191
105 118, 137
105.1 703
105.10f. 366
105.44 366
106 118f., 137
106.20 677, 1189
106.30–1 88
106.31 849
106.47 120
107.43 113
110 518, 521, 693, 734, 737, 820, 1065f., 1286
110.1 639, 736, 820f., 1064, 1280, 1455
110.1f. 832
110.2 99
110.5–7 821, 832, 1064, 1275
111.6 121, 366
115.3–8 743
115.4–8 376
116 636f.
116.4 99, 703
116.13 703
116.17 703
116.18f. 99
117.1 1058, 1300, 1455, 1495
118 356
118.20 100
118.22 1065
118.22f. 356, 1179
119 895, 1017
119.64 189, 191
122 98
124.5 1151
126 151
127.6 1151
128.3 1213
132 119, 560f.
132.8 560, 1022
132.13f. 98, 1022
132.13–18 560
132.14 102, 358
132.17 119
134.3 99
135 119
135.15–18 376, 743
135.21 98, 106, 358, 1022
136 119, 631
137 631f.
138.2 365
138.8 480
139.6–9 152
141.2 96, 1518
143 996, 1469
143.1 995
143.2 969, 995, 1469
147.2 120
147.20 182, 840
148.5f. 629
148.14 629
150.1 100

Proverbs
3.19 673
8 103, 191, 483
8.22 484, 673
8.22–31 103
8.30 484
16.6 96
17.15 948
18.5 937, 948
24.12 938, 1087
24.23f. 948
28.21 948
30.4 152

Ecclesiastes
5.8 937, 948
12.14 1087

Isaiah
1.9—4.2 1185
2 192, 1058
2.2 147
2.2f. 105
2.2–4 195, 1053, 1056, 1059, 1494
2.3 1249
2.5 1249
2.10 704
2.12 1050
2.19 704
2.21 704
5.1–7 794
5.23 948
6 189, 489, 1052
6.1–5 98
6.3 189, 489, 1053, 1093
6.5 100

Isaiah (*continued*)
6.9f. 1228
6.13 1185, 1416
8.14 704, 1065, 1179
9.2–7 1054
9.6f. 120
9.7 366
10 810
10.2 937, 948
10.5–19 1050
10.13 157
10.22 1185, 1223
10.33—11.3 1416
11 128, 172, 192, 399, 544, 563, 631, 734, 745, 752, 819f., 1057, 1300, 1503, 1507
11.1 1495
11.1–4 1044
11.1–10 105, 366, 410, 482f., 702, 740, 820, 1057, 1093
11.1–16 1054
11.2 721
11.3–5 832
11.4 366, 372, 1084
11.5 372
11.6–9 1044
11.8f. 191
11.9 988, 1093
11.10 120, 699, 820, 1212, 1300, 1455, 1495
11.11 105, 1500
11.12 1500
12.4 703
13 165, 171
13.6 1050
17.10 668
22.5 1050
23.13 762
23.15 142
24.15 1500
25.6–9 736, 756, 1053, 1057
25.8 736, 756, 1234
26.4 668
26.21 99
27 1233, 1246–9, 1251
27.6 147
27.9 96, 1247
28.16 703f., 1065
29.10 1227f.
30.29 668
31.4–5 105
31.5 77
31.8 1209
32.15 972
33.21 102
34 151
34.4 169
37.18f. 376
38.7f. 138
39.1–7 762
40 1091
40—55 119, 151, 161, 190, 242, 534, 629–31, 669, 673, 681f., 705, 734, 749, 761, 770, 772, 796, 811, 846, 882, 913, 928, 998f., 1026, 1071, 1259, 1467
40—66 655, 683, 696, 736, 802, 882
40.1 119
40.1–11 107
40.3 1045
40.4 153
40.5 189, 679, 681
40.8 682
40.9 44, 681, 915
40.10 681
40.12–26 681
40.13 704
40.19f. 376
40.28 632
41.1 1500
41.5 1500
41.8 119, 682
41.10 1056
41.14 654
41.27 915
42 544, 811, 906
42.1 721
42.1–4 366, 682
42.1–9 682, 1054
42.3–6 1057
42.4 1500
42.6 366, 882, 1026
42.6f. 805
42.6–9 803
42.7 1228
42.8 681
42.10 1500
42.10–12 366
42.12 1500
42.18–20 1228
42.19 682
42.21 803
43.2 681
43.3 1294
43.4 860
43.8 1228
43.10 682
43.11 1294
43.14f. 654
43.22 1026
44.6 654
44.8 668
44.9–20 376
44.24 654
44.26 682
44.28 142
45 681, 683, 702, 810
45.1–6 1050
45.1–13 1274
45.2 153
45.3 810
45.4 810
45.14 1053
45.15 1294
45.20–5 681, 803
45.21f. 1294
45.23 681–3, 688, 702, 704, 1294
46.1—47.15 681
46.12–13 803
46.13 681, 846
48.11 681
48.12 1026

48.16 696, 721
48.20 1274
49 811, 905f., 1000, 1057, 1199
49.1 564, 1026, 1423, 1500
49.1–6 416, 682
49.1–13 682
49.3 564
49.3–9 558
49.4 564, 905
49.5f. 805, 1057
49.6 113, 811, 905
49.6f. 366, 882
49.7 884
49.8 557, 564, 637, 881f., 1062
49.12 882
49.13 119, 558
49.18 702
49.26 1294
50 902, 905f.
50.1 1010
50.4–9 682
50.10 682
51 906
51.1 1056
51.1–3 906, 1137
51.1–6 804
51.2 119, 1026
51.3 119
51.4–6 906
51.5 682, 846, 1056, 1500
51.7f. 1056
51.8 846
51.12 119
52 715, 837, 1051, 1091, 1174, 1192
52.4f. 714
52.5 812
52.5–8 813
52.7 44, 372, 410, 416, 564, 715, 915, 1251
52.7–10 682
52.7–12 107, 1051, 1137
52.10 366
52.11 355, 558, 637, 714, 1041, 1274
52.12 714
52.13 683
52.13—53.12 682, 915
52.15 366, 820, 1497
53 813, 850, 906, 1137, 1160, 1174, 1192
53.1 416, 682
53.2 1212
53.5f. 885
53.10 999
53.10–12 1505
53.11 999
53.12 1192
54 151, 682, 1137–9, 1150
54.1 1137f., 1150
54.5 1138, 1150
54.5–8 1010
54.10 849, 882, 1013, 1138, 1150
54.17 1056
55 113, 682, 1053, 1174
55.1 368, 1138
55.1–5 366
55.3 119, 882, 999, 1138
55.11 681f., 1174
55.12 482
56.4 882
56.6 882
56.6–8 1053, 1057
59 1248f., 1251
59.15–21 804, 1249
59.17 372, 1127
59.18 938, 1500
59.20f. 358, 1250
59.21 882, 1247, 1249
60.1f. 190
60.1–7 1250
60.1–16 366
60.3 113
60.3–7 1057
60.6 915
60.9 1500
60.13 105
60.16 1294
61.1 696, 721, 915
61.1–7 366
61.1–11 1054
61.6 487
61.8 882
61.10 372, 947
63.1–9 1054
63.8 1294
63.9 860
63.11 105, 721
64.1 679
65 1222
65f. 113
65.1 1180, 1193, 1302
65.2 1161, 1180, 1224
65.17–18 192
65.17–25 740, 756, 1093
65.23 564, 905
66 1501
66.1 100, 561
66.5 704
66.15 356, 704
66.18 1494
66.18–21 105, 366, 1057, 1500f., 1506
66.18–23 1053
66.19 1500
66.22 1093
66.22f. 1507

Jeremiah

1 416
2.11 1189
3.16 787
3.17 105, 1056
4 169
4.4 148, 424, 923, 984, 1076
4.23–8 169
4.27f. 170
5.28 948
7.12 96
9.22f. 1143
9.24 704, 988
9.25f. 923, 984
9.26 148, 424, 1076
10.1–5 376

Jeremiah (*continued*)
11 1215
11.1–4 1215
11.3 1215
11.6–8 1215
17.9 768
17.10 938, 1087
20.7 169, 896
21.14 938
23.3 787
23.24 102
24.7 888
25.11f. 142, 1415
26.6 96
27.6–11 1050
29.4–7 1274
29.7 279, 380
29.10 142
29.13f. 126
30.3 157
30.20 85
31 151, 503, 867, 892, 981, 1139, 1233, 1246, 1248f., 1493
31.3 860
31.9 128, 658, 694
31.20 128
31.31–4 981, 1248
31.31–7 1095
31.33 724, 867, 923, 1076, 1379
31.33f. 1217, 1247
31.37 1223
32.19 938, 1087
32.39f. 923, 1076
33.23–6 119
36.1–4 169
46.9 1501
46.10 1050
49.6 157
50f. 1275
50.15 1087
50.29 1087
51.20–3 1275
51.45 714

Lamentations
2.15 99

Ezekiel
1 415
5.5 1502
7.7 1050
7.10 1050
8—11 105
10f. 189
10.1–22 1051
10.4 1053
11.19 724, 923, 981, 1076, 1379
11.22f. 1051
12.23 1050
13.5 1050
18.30 938
20.5–44 119
20.34 1041
20.41 1041
21.25 1050
22.4 1050
23 119
30.3 1050
30.5 1501
33.20 938
34.23f. 682
34.24 714
34.25 1013
34.30 714
35.10 105
36 503, 812, 815, 837, 867, 892
36f. 192
36.11 787
36.16–38 1095
36.20 812
36.20–8 812
36.25 1337
36.26 724, 867, 981, 1379
36.26–8 923, 1076, 1379
36.28 714, 888
37 714, 720
37—48 192
37.4–14 972
37.15–28 1053
37.23 714
37.26 1013
37.27 355, 558, 714, 1021, 1041
38.12 1502
40—8 1051
43 677, 712
43.1–9 1051
44.7 923, 984, 1076
44.9 923
47.1–12 102
48.35 105, 1051

Daniel
1—6 1274
1.8–12 93
2 117, 119f., 130, 132, 133, 142, 159, 170f., 192, 294, 356, 631, 1298, 1317, 1503
2.31–5 284
2.31–45 299
2.34f. 120, 1065, 1179
2.35 356
2.44 356, 1455
2.44f. 120, 631, 1065, 1179
2.48 688
3 630f.
3.28f. 631
3.30 688
4 1298
4.19–27 1274
5 1298
5.17–28 1274
5.18 631
5.21 631
5.23 631
5.29 688
6 630f., 1303, 1316
6.5 1274
6.10 365
6.26f. 631
7 117, 119f., 130, 133, 142, 159, 169–71, 284, 294, 549, 627, 631, 685, 693, 799,

980, 1050, 1063–5, 1090, 1281f., 1291, 1293, 1298f., 1310, 1316f., 1503f.
7.8 1275
7.9 690
7.11 1275
7.13f. 120, 631
7.14 506, 1064
7.18 120, 284, 506, 631, 1027, 1064, 1090
7.19–22 1275
7.22 120, 506, 922, 980, 1027, 1064, 1090
7.26f. 631
7.27 120, 506, 980, 1027, 1064, 1090
8.21 1501
8.23 1154
9 87, 117, 119f., 123, 136, 140, 142f., 145f., 150f., 156, 160, 162, 170, 178, 294, 561, 632, 745, 761, 772, 799f., 802, 840, 846, 928f., 996, 1055, 1159, 1259, 1454, 1463, 1467, 1470, 1482
9.2 142
9.4f. 800
9.4–19 119
9.7 800, 1055
9.8 1055
9.11 800, 1240
9.11f. 1055
9.11–13 143, 1055
9.14 800, 1055
9.15f. 800, 1055
9.15–19 144
9.16 1055
9.18 800, 1055
9.21 1518
9.22–7 144
9.24 96, 133, 142
9.25–7 120
9.26 692
9.27 148
12 163
12.2 1060, 1102
12.2f. 163, 1399

Hosea
1f. 1010
1.10 976, 1053
1.10f. 1053
2 1185, 1193
2.1 1010, 1084, 1223
2.16–19 1010
2.23 1010, 1053
2.25 1184, 1193
11.1 128, 694, 860, 874, 976
13.14 1234
14.6 1213

Joel
1.15 1050
2.11 1050
2.27 703
2.28 917
2.28–32 703, 972, 1078, 1166
2.31 704, 1050
2.32 703f., 867, 917, 953, 1077, 1164, 1166, 1249
3 169
3.1 169
3.14 169, 1050
3.20f. 169
3.21 98

Amos
5.12 937, 948
5.18 1051
5.18–20 1050
5.26f. 104
9.2f. 152
9.11 190

Obadiah
15 1050

Jonah
1.3 1500
2.4 365

Micah
1.2 365
1.2–3 99
3.7–8 721
4 192
4.1 147
4.1–3 1053, 1056, 1494
4.2 1249
5.1–8 120

Habakkuk
1.12 668
1.13 1469
2 489
2.4 865, 973, 1450, 1458, 1466–71
2.13f. 191
2.14 489, 1053, 1093
2.20 365

Zephaniah
1.7 1050
1.14 1050

Haggai
2.4f. 721
2.5 105
2.7 105, 1057

Zechariah
1.12 142
2.4f. 105
2.5 192
2.6–13 1274
2.10f. 105, 1057
2.11 1494
3.8 682
4.6 721
7.5 142
7.12 721
8 1058
8.20–3 195, 1053, 1057, 1494

Zechariah (*continued*)
9.9f. 633
9.10 119, 285
10.6–12 1053
10.8 787
13.9 1061
14.1 1050
14.5 704, 706, 1084
14.5–9 705
14.8 102
14.9 633, 641, 1061
14.16 1494
14.16–19 1053, 1057

Malachi
1.2 860
1.5 1056, 1494
1.11 1494, 1499
1.14 1056, 1494
2.4f. 849
2.5 1013
2.9 948
3.1 1045
3.1f. 106
3.1–4 189
3.2 1051
4.5 1050

2. Apocrypha

Tobit
1.10f. 93
3.3f. 154
3.6 154
3.11f. 365
4.13 1119
4.15 1119
12—14 154
13.1f. 154
13.5 154
13.9 154
13.11 154, 1058
13.16 154
14.4–7 154f.
14.5 155, 877
14.5–7 1058

Judith
4.3 158
5.5–21 121
5.19 158
8.18f. 158
9.8 100
9.11–14 623
10—12 93
12.17–19 1428

Additions to the Book of Esther
C.26 (=14.17) 93

Wisdom of Solomon
1—5 436
3.7 1369
3.7f. 183
3.8 922, 980, 1090
4.16 922
4.20—5.23 183
5.5 660
5.15 1060
5.18 1127
6 660
6.1–5 1275
6.1–8 1291
6.17–18 1119
7—9 152, 483, 693, 698
7.1–22 660
7.7—9.18 103
7.26 660
9 671f., 675
9.9–13 660
9.15 628
9.18 660
10—12 126
10—18 1051
10—19 101, 1298
10.9–12 1184
11.23 1112, 1195
12.23–7 640
13—19 126
13.1–19 766
14.17–21 346
14.22 346
15.1 1195
15.1–19 766
15.14–17 743
18.4 1057
18.14–16 717
18.15 1382
18.24 101
19.3–5 1154

Ben-Sirach
4.15 980, 1090
11.26 938
16.12–14 938
18.11 1195
19.20 107
24 99, 106f., 121, 152f., 157, 192, 483, 655, 672, 675, 698, 908
24.1 671
24.3 671
24.4 106
24.6–10 671
24.7 560
24.8–12 106
24.11 560
24.23 106, 671
24.25–9 106
31.15 1119
33.25–30 1108
33.31–3 1108
35.14f. 1087
35.19 1087
35.24 938
36.1–21 157f.
36.11 120
36.17 874, 976
36.18 560
44—50 106
44.19–21 1006
44.20f. 121
44.21 366, 815, 1005
45.7–12 101
45.23f. 88
45.24 849, 1013
45.24f. 121
45.25 106
48.1f. 88
48.1–11 84

49 121
49.11f. 103
49.12 106
50 90, 121, 157
50.5 106
50.5–7 98
50.11 101, 106
50.13 106
50.26 106
51.30 938

Baruch
1.11 279
2.11–15 622
2.24–35 152
3 672, 1167
3.6–8 152
3.14 152
3.29—4.4 152f.
5.2 947
5.7 153
5.9 801

1 Maccabees
1.11–15 91
1.15 1435
1.41–64 87
1.54 145
2 92, 123, 932
2.11f. 87
2.12 99
2.19–22 87
2.23–6 88
2.28 92
2.29–68 88
2.32–8 91
2.49–68 122
2.51–68 194
2.52 121
2.54 849
2.58 84
2.67 187
4.8–11 620
4.30–3 620
7.13 89
7.33 279
7.36–8 620
7.37 96
8.17–32 282
12.1–4 281
13.48 187
14 303
14.4f. 159
14.4–15 1061

2 Maccabees
1.24 21
1.24–9 620, 801
1.27 120
2.8 1053
2.18 120, 159
4.11–17 91
6.1–11 92
6.11 91
6.14 1154
6.18 93
6.18–31 444
6.21 444
7.1 93
7.9 1060
7.14 1060
7.19 86
7.23 1060
7.27–9 180
7.28f. 621
7.29 1060
7.35–8 621
8.12 1082
10.26 85
12.39–45 180
14.6 89
14.15 182
14.34 79
14.34–6 620
14.38 93

1 Esdras
1.57f. 142
4.58 365

3 Maccabees
1 355
1.16–19 562
2.1–20 122, 180, 620
2.14 100
2.16 98
2.33 446
3.3–7 93
3.4 93, 94
3.7 94
3.17 1082
6.1–15 122
6.28 874, 976
7.2–9 122

4 Maccabees
1.1 993
1.6 445
1.11 637
4.21 800
4.34 177
5.1—6.30 444
5.2 93
5.8f. 177
5.10 993
5.22 993
5.25f. 177
6.10 1113
6.15 444
6.28f. 637
7.7–9 993
9.23 395
13.9 395
15.3 1060
16.20f. 136
17.11–16 1113
17.20–2 637
18.10–19 136

3. Pseudepigrapha

Apocalypse of Abraham
27–9 156

2 Baruch
4.2–6 1138
14.13 178, 815, 1059
14.17–19 794
15.8 178
17.3 476
21—34 132

2 Baruch (*continued*)
21.8 877
21.19–25 133
21.23 164
23.4 133, 476
25.2–4 133
28.1 133
29.3–8 133
30.1–5 133
30.2–5 164
35—40 171
35—46 133
39.3–5 133
39.7 171
39.7—40.2 133
40.3 133, 171
44.4 806
44.11–15 178
47—52 133
48.42 476
51.8–12 163
53—74 133
53.3–11 133
54.15 476
54.19 476
56.5f. 476
56.5–8 133
56.10–13 133
57.1–3 133
59.4–11 132
60.1f. 134
61.1–8 134
62.1–8 134
63—6 134
67.6 134
68.3–7 161
68.5–7 156
69f. 134
70.9 134
72.2 528
72.2–6 134
73.1–6 134
75.1–5 134
78—86 134
83.3 134

1 Enoch
1—5 155
1—36 476
1.3–9 156, 170
1.4 1249
1.9 980
5.7 366, 1005
10.21 1058
14.13–24 98
22.3f. 164
42 166
57.3 1058
62.3 801
71.15 178, 1059
85—90 122f., 137, 161
89.11f. 122
89.16–19 122
89.73–7 155
90 192
90.1–5 155
90.9–14 123
90.20–42 155
90.23 156
90.24–7 155
90.28f. 1138
90.29 155
90.29–33 98
90.30 155
90.31–6 155
90.33 1058
90.37–8 123, 793
91.14 1058
93.9f. 155
93.11–14 152
95.3 980
95.7 802
103 143
104.2 980

Joseph and Aseneth 93f.
11.7–11 622

Jubilees
1.7–13 125
1.15–18 125
1.23 923, 984
1.23–5 976
1.27f. 98, 871
2.23 792
3.30f. 792
5.16 806
15.28–32 1185
16.26 792
16.28 125
17 904
17.3 1005
18 904
19.21 815
19.24f. 792
20.11–13 1185
22.9 1151
22.13 792
22.14 1005
22.15 801
22.16 93
24.11 125
24.29 922
32.19 1005
33.18 806
50.5 125

Testament of Abraham
1—4 980

Testament/Assumption of Moses
3.1–3 156
3.3 126
3.14 127
7.1 127
8.1–5 127
8.3 91
9.1–7 127
9.2 156
10 165, 170
10.1 156
10.1–10 127
10.8–10 163
12.4 127
12.9 127
12.13 127

Psalms of Solomon
1.2f. 83

2.2–4 83
2.6–21 1470
2.25–31 288
3.12 1060
4.14–25 83
7.1 98
7.6 98
8.1–34 83
8.4–8 1470
8.23–32 1470
8.32 801
9.1–7 1470
9.5 1087
9.8–11 127
10.5 1470
13.1 1060
17 1050
17.1–4 623
17.4 128
17.21 623
17.21–4 128
17.21–32 832
17.26 976, 1090
17.26–46 1058
17.29 1090
17.30–2 127f.
17.45f. 623
18 1050
18.1 623
18.3–7 128
18.4 694
18.5 623
18.7f. 832
18.10 623
18.10–12 138

Pseudo-Philo (*Liber Antiquitatum Biblicarum*)
9.3 170
11.5 172
19.1–16 126
26.1–3 1154
28.6–9 126

4 Ezra
3.4–27 132
3.5 793
3.7 476
3.10f. 793
3.13–15 793
3.15 793
3.20 793
3.23 793
3.26 793
4.5–8 152
4.26–32 132
4.30 476
4.36f. 877
5 171
6 742
6.9 178
6.53f. 793
6.55–9 622, 793, 976
6.58 874
7 1196
7.11 476, 793
7.12f. 178
7.24 185
7.26 1138
7.26–36 1112
7.29 692
7.33f. 801, 1112
7.35 801, 938
7.50 178, 1059
7.59 1005
7.74 1195
7.75 1093
7.77 185
7.112f. 178
7.129 156
7.134 1195
8.1 178
8.32f. 185
8.44 793
9.13 793, 801
9.20–2 794
10.25–8 1138
11 877
11f. 132, 170, 347, 1064
11.44 171, 877
12.10–12 284
12.10–35 156
12.11f. 170
12.32–4 171
13 132
13.1–3 356
13.8–11 356
13.13 1058
13.36 1138
13.45 156
14.6 156

3 Baruch
4.16 440
16.2 156

Testaments of the Twelve Patriarchs
T. Reuben
6.8f. 1119

T. Levi
3.2 1087
5.2 716
6.3–11 1154
14.1 552
14.4 1057
16.1—18.14 156
18.10–14 793
19.1–3 156

T. Judah
23.1—24.6 156

T. Issachar
5.2 1119
7.6 1119

T. Zebulun
5.1 1119
8.2 716
9.8 1058

T. Dan
5.7–13 802

T. Naphtali 156
4.3 161
8.3 801

Testaments of the Twelve Patriarchs (*continued*)

T. Gad
4.2 1119
4.7 1119
5.2f. 1119

T. Benjamin
3.3f. 1119
9.2 1058

Ezekiel the Tragedian
68–82a 627

4. Qumran

Damascus Document (CD)
1.1—2.1 123
1.3–11 151
1.7 126
2.12 759
2.14—3.12 771
2.14—4.12 1415
3.2 123
3.4–12 123
3.10f. 123
3.10–14 151
3.12–14 123
3.20 123, 189, 794
3.21—6.11 123
4.13—5.19 771
5.11–13 759
6.20f. 1119
7.4 759
7.15f. 104

1QH
2.18 923
4.15 794
4.37 802
6.12–19 192
8.20 759
10.18 984
11.37–8 148
13.5 1151
17.15 189
20.11f. 759
23.20 984

1QM
18.8 802

1QS
1.3 1119
1.9 1119
1.21–5 801
3.6 759
4.7 1060
4.18–21 972
4.23 189, 794
5.5 148, 759, 923, 984
5.8f. 148
5.21 96
6.18 96
8.5–10 98
8.6 922
9.3–7 96, 711
9.16 1119
9.21 1119
11.12 802

1QLit. Pr.
2.3–6 794

1QSa
2.20f. 1348

1QpHab
2.5–10 151
5.9–12 1469
7.11 185
8.1 185
11.13 923, 984
12.4f. 185

4QMMT
9–16 126, 185
10–17 147
18–32 124
27 185
27–32 185

4Q174 (=4QFlor.)
1.1–7 96
1.3–7 187
1.7 96
10–13 694
10–14 693

4Q177
185 923

4Q225 904

4Q246
2.1 694

4Q504
5–7 1165
5.6–14 1165

4QpPs37
3.1f. 794

11Q19 (=11QTemple) 98, 107
29.7–10 106
59 148f.

5. Josephus

Against Apion
2.35 93
2.47 993
2.66 91
2.73–7 177
2.75 1315
2.77 345
2.121–4 379
2.190–2 624
2.209–14 1119
2.282 1499

Jewish War
1.33 95
1.67–9 107
1.403 325
1.404 325
1.414 325

2.89 1339
2.118 84
2.119 993
2.183 1499
2.197 345
2.223–7 1154
2.382 282
2.386 282
2.398 1499
2.409f. 345
2.488 93
3.350–4 1352
3.399–408 130, 1065
4.324 101
4.605f. 282
5 163
5.161 296
5.212–18 101
5.222–4 296
5.376–419 129
5.395 159
5.412 129
5.415 129
5.419 129
5.442f. 1431
6 173
6.288–300 173
6.299 106
6.312–15 117, 130, 142, 294, 1065
6.399–408 294
7.43 1499
7.323 801
7.422–32 95

Jewish Antiquities
1.132f. 1501
2.108 801
3.80 1082
3.86–8 130
3.91 624
3.179–87 101
3.203 1082
4—10 84
4.43–50 130
4.113 1339
4.125 131
4.303 130f., 1463
4.314 131
4.320 131
9.55 1083
10.210 1316
10.264–7 1317
10.266–8 170
10.267 117, 294
10.276 1317
11.1–2 142
11.55 801
12.126 94
12.241 91, 1435
12.387f. 95
13.62–73 95
13.172 85
13.285 95
13.299f. 107
14.115 1499
14.185–267 278
14.301–23 278
15.298 325
15.339f. 325
15.363f. 325
15.380–425 296
16.27–65 121
18.11 993
18.252 1499
19.4 333
19.300–11 345
20.17–53 195
20.43–8 195
20.105–12 1154
20.236f. 95
23 84

6. Philo

De Decalogo
65 624

De Fuga et Inventione (or, *De Profugis*)
138–41 153

De Migratione Abrahami
89–93 91
92 923

De Mutatione Nominumi
223 993
236–8 153

De Posteritate Caini
83–8 153

De Praemiis et Poenis
82–4 153
85–8 173
94–7 120
127–72 148
153–61 148
163–72 148, 173

De Somniis
1.149 191
2.48 1316
2.53 1316
2.55 1316
2.57 1316
2.62 1316
2.90–109 1316
2.123 1316
2.127 993
2.180 153

De Specialibus Legibus
1.97 182
1.301 153
1.305 984
2.163 182
2.167 182
2.253 80, 83, 165

De Virtutibus
51–174 1119
183 153

De Vita Contemplativa 32

De Vita Mosis
2.117 101
2.288 131

Philo (*continued*)
In Flaccum
30f. 121
38f. 121
45f. 120, 1499
96 93

Legum Allegoriae
22 339
150f. 325
154 328
156 993
157 345
158 91
245 993
281–4 120
299–306 325
305 325
317 345
357 316, 345, 1315

Quaestiones in Genesin
2.62 684

Quis rerum
42 106
197 101

Quod Omnis Probus Liber Sit
88 993

7. Rabbinic Works

Mishnah
mBerakoth
1.5 84
2.5 84
3.3 90
5.1 89
7.2 387
9.2 411, 412
9.5 411

mSanhedrin
10.1 178, 186, 1059, 1244
10.1–3 1240
10.1–4 187, 929

mMakkot
3.1–8 1438

mEduyot
5.3 85

mAboth
1.2 90
1.11 157
1.12 194
3.2 95, 108
3.5 1140
4.1 1059

mAboth Zarah
1.3 277
1.4 175

mKerithoth
1.2 744, 898
2.6 898
3.2 744, 898

mTamid
7.4 639

mYadayim
3.5 85
4.4 156

Babylonian Talmud
bBerakoth
9.5 1059
61b 84, 619

bPesahim
108a 82

bSanhedrin
38a 627
97a 127
102a 742

bHagigah
14a 627

bMenahot
43b 1150
43b–44a 388

Palestinian Talmud
jBerakoth
9.14b 619
13b 1150

jKilaim
1.4 82

jTaanit
2.165a 106
68d 145

Tosefta
tBerakoth
6.18 388
7.18 1150
14b–15a 619
35a 639

tSotah
47b 86

Targumim, etc.
Genesis Rabbah
1.2 484
1.4 484
3.9 102
4.4 102
12.9 794
14.6 794
40.6 94
44.5 135
44.19 133

Targum of Jonathan on Isaiah
6.9–13 157

Sifre Deuteronomy
307–33 131

8. New Testament

Matthew
3.9f. 1416
5—7 760
5.12 1153
6.10 1485
10.23 167
10.28f. 1288
10.40 11
11.20–4 922
12.43–5 378
16.16 818
16.23 1179
16.27 1087
18.6f. 1179
19.16 164
19.28 980, 1090
21.28–32 1180
21.33–46 1180
21.35–6 1153
21.42 356, 1180
21.44 1179
22.1–14 1180
22.6 1153
22.21 1485
22.39 1119
22.44 693
23 195
23.15 194
23.21 106
23.23 1450
23.32 1237
23.32f. 1153
23.34 1153
23.37 1153
24.29 703
26.64 693
28.18 410, 1485

Mark
1.2f. 1045
6.14–16 828
7.1–23 760, 768
8.33 547
9.10 828
10.2–12 446
10.5–9 760
10.17 1069
10.18 164
10.22 1105
10.25–45 433
10.30 1069
10.35–45 700, 1492, 1505
10.38 1337
10.45 1505
12.1–12 125
12.10 1065
12.13–17 89, 1304
12.36 693
13 167
13.5–8 173
13.24 703
14.62 693
15.39 1311
16.19 693

Luke
1.6 1034
1.46–55 1422
1.68 654
2.21 425
2.25 143
3.8f. 1416
7.16 654
11.24–6 378
12.4f. 1288
12.50 1337
15 1204
15.19 14
15.31f. 1181
17.1 1179
18.18 164
19.41–4 1155
19.42–4 1155
19.44 654
20.42f. 693
22.28–30 1090
22.30 980
22.69 693
23.11 15
23.15 15
23.34 1168
24.21 654
24.39 492

John
1.1–18 672, 717
1.10f. 1180
1.14 1073
1.14–18 356
2.13–22 356
3.15f. 1069
3.16 1119
3.36 1069
4.6 1240
4.22 837
7.18 909
8.46 909
13—17 356
13.34f. 1119
15.16 774
16.2 250
16.3 1168
18.36 1485
19.11 1286, 1303
20.28 342

Acts
1.1–11 1312
1.6 110
1.9–11 356
2 356, 1164
2.1–4 356
2.5 1499
2.17–21 703, 1166
2.21 703
2.23 1192
2.33 1166
2.34–5 693
2.41 1278
2.42 11
3.13 1192
3.17 1168
4 172
4.2 551
4.4 1278
4.11 1065
4.19 1303
5 156

Acts (*continued*)
5.14 1278
5.29 1303
5.34 81
5.34–9 85, 86
6.7 1278
6.8—7.53 356
7 118, 1158
7.6 527
7.38 871
7.51 148, 923
7.52 1153
7.53 871
8.3 1153
9.1f. 1153
9.3–6 1350
9.3–9 34
9.4 828
9.12 1350
9.14 703
9.15–17 1350
9.21 703, 1153
9.27 854
9.30 205
9.35 1278
10.2 1321
10.7 1321
10.9–16 93
10.28 93
10.34 1087
10.41 1089
10.42 702, 1089
10.45 1166
11.3 93
11.4–10 93
11.21 1278
11.25 205
11.27–30 1350f.
12.15 828
13f. 268, 329
13.1–3 854, 1350
13.5 1498
13.14 364
13.14–52 1498
13.27 1168
13.42 364
13.42–52 854
13.44 364
13.45 1180
13.46 1069
13.48 1069, 1278
14.1–6 1498
14.1–20 854
14.8–20 356
15 63
15.1 855
15.5 81
15.21 364
16.1–3 362
16.6f. 1350
16.7–10 1350
16.8 1351
16.13 364
16.20f. 274
16.35–9 1303
17 213, 242, 356
17.1–5 1498
17.2 364
17.5–14 1153, 1155
17.6f. 274
17.7 1066, 1312
17.10–14 1498
17.16–34 356
17.18 238
17.22 250, 1321, 1371, 1437
17.23 1321
17.26 117
17.30f. 1066
17.31 343, 702, 767, 832, 1089
17.32 223
18.2 1230
18.4 364
18.4–7 1498
18.9–11 1350
18.12–17 1153, 1303, 1305
19.8–10 1498
19.21 1350
19.23–40 256
19.35–41 1303
20.1–16 1500
20.9–12 1313
20.16 364
21 359, 1443
21.10–14 1350
21.17 828
21.18—23.11 356
21.20–6 1441
21.21 1431, 1440
21.24 1441
21.28 1431, 1440
21.39 89, 1412
22.3 87, 89, 205, 1412
22.4f. 1153
22.6–11 34, 1350
22.16 703
22.22 1185
23.1–10 81, 1303
23.2 86
23.6 81, 84
23.9 828
23.11 1350
23.34 89
24.5f. 1431
25.6–12 1303
25.11f. 1271
25.19 1321
26.5 81, 84, 250, 1321
26.9–11 1153
26.12–19 34
26.13–20 1350
26.14 828
27.1—28.16 1271
27.9 1099
27.10f. 223
27.22 1099
27.23–6 1350
27.42–3 1297
28.17–28 1355
28.31 1312, 1504

Romans
1 448, 918, 1121f., 1363, 1468
1—3 757
1—4 38f., 779, 850f., 891, 903, 938, 974, 1011, 1164, 1167, 1469

1—8 779, 900, 938, 941f., 995, 1179
1.1 383, 411, 701
1.1–4 1062
1.1–6 523, 699, 915, 1300
1.1–17 1470
1.2 552
1.3 701, 817f.
1.3–5 201, 383, 477, 523, 533f., 555, 647, 661, 692, 694, 699f., 707, 768, 818, 820, 835, 844, 900, 905, 916, 943, 1158, 1164, 1229, 1410
1.3–7 1308
1.4 699f., 759, 939, 941, 950, 997
1.5 200f., 367, 383, 405, 684, 843, 911, 916, 944, 1066, 1421
1.6 701, 1026
1.7 443, 701, 1027, 1314
1.8 412, 436
1.9 701, 1518
1.9f. 252, 365, 383, 492
1.9–15 1271, 1498
1.11f. 1498
1.13 252, 1351, 1498
1.14 1448, 1499
1.15 1314
1.15–17 916, 920
1.16 383, 411, 544, 770, 811, 837, 887, 916, 932, 1002, 1072, 1174, 1229, 1499
1.16f. 477, 555, 699, 766, 887, 901, 916, 995, 1072, 1158, 1164, 1236, 1301, 1466
1.16–25 642
1.17 383, 502, 549, 641, 764, 767, 769, 865, 943, 1168, 1233, 1458, 1467f., 1470f., 1498
1.18 767, 769, 819, 1002, 1467
1.18–25 375f., 475, 490, 757, 769, 952, 1007, 1012, 1363
1.18–32 765f., 768f., 843, 1380
1.18—2.16 **764–71**, 811, 840, 927, 998, 1029
1.18—3.20 496, 739, 751, 766, 771, 921, 937, 1381, 1470
1.18—4.25 513, 764, 935
1.19f. 638
1.20f. 458, 492
1.20–5 640, 1122
1.21 770
1.23 677, 1189
1.24 492, 770
1.24–31 767
1.25 442, 754, 1091
1.28 492, 1122, 1363
1.31 549
1.32 755, 766, 936
2 506, 768, 770, 777, 812, 897, 938, 941, 954, 965, 977f., 1008, 1011, 1195, 1374, 1379
2—4 1242, 1262
2.1 744, 768, 1380f.
2.1–11 840, 843, 939, 954, 1024, 1072, 1245
2.1–16 496, 641, 751, 766, 900, 903, 935, 941, 958, 1085, 1088f., 1156, 1253
2.2 939
2.3–6 1112, 1191
2.4 1000, 1219, 1238
2.5 492, 767, 770, 1079f., 1191, 1219
2.5–11 936f.
2.5–16 553
2.7 939, 1029, 1037, 1069
2.7–10 1029
2.8 767
2.8f. 939
2.9 492, 837, 1498
2.9–11 933
2.10 837, 939, 1029, 1498
2.11 806, 841, 938, 1380
2.12 506, 843
2.12f. 936f., 939
2.12–16 768, 1089f., 1380
2.13 927, 940, 1037, 1088, 1380
2.14 1088, 1380
2.15 492, 770
2.16 521, 544, 549, 553, 702, 753, 767, 819, 832, 859, 935f., 977, 1079
2.17 397, 838, 888, 961, 1000, 1003, 1143
2.17–20 770, 811, 837–9, 841, 857, 893, 895, 998, 1213
2.17–24 364, 498, 506, 840, 921, 924, 1197, 1199, 1204, 1431
2.17–29 362, 770f., 921
2.17—3.8 429, 548, 1018
2.19 496
2.19f. 500
2.21–4 812
2.24 684, 812
2.25 492, 1432
2.25–9 362, 424, 502, 512, 527, 532, 703, 768, 810, 812f., 814, 836, 864, 867, 891f., 917, 921, 924f., 940, 958, 973, 980, 985, 1007, 1009f., 1020, 1029, 1089, 1148, 1166f., 1171, 1187f., 1218, 1229, 1242, 1248, 1337, 1374, 1379f., 1432, 1434, 1462
2.26 501, 513, 901, 922, 1146, 1432

Romans (*continued*)
2.26f. 512f., 544, 553, 839, 923, 1037, 1078, 1089, 1109, 1173, 1380
2.26–9 1249, 1379
2.27 725, 922, 940, 1107, 1115
2.28f. 362, 539, 553, 725, 1008, 1076, 1137, 1412
2.29 148, 492, 512f., 673, 759, 770, 936, 940, 960, 984, 986, 991, 993, 1090, 1107, 1146, 1166, 1370, 1426, 1433, 1444, 1448, 1452
3 525, 531, 641, 777, 813, 831, 836, 847, 857, 954, 1039
3f. 643, **836–51**, 954, 963, 965, 1029, 1161
3.1 837
3.1f. 497
3.1–4 498, 837, 841, 857
3.1–8 499f., 771, 836, 1055, 1209
3.1–26 830
3.1–31 836
3.2 836f., 864, 931, 978, 1027, 1253, 1351
3.2f. 830, 842f., 1000, 1208
3.3 838
3.3–7 641, 995f.
3.4f. 1469
3.5 767, 1427
3.7f. 859
3.9 767, 843, 937, 1225, 1427
3.10f. 859
3.10–18 1228
3.10–20 771
3.13–15 1225f.
3.16–18 1226
3.18 1228
3.19 1034
3.19f. 506, 509, 777, 840, 859, 865, 888, 933, 938, 947, 1019
3.20 507, 843, 884, 893, 897, 969, 995f., 1034, 1469
3.21 458, 552, 556, 641, 830, 843, 909, 943, 946, 991, 995, 997, 1002, 1005, 1088, 1168, 1182, 1233, 1469
3.21–3 840f., 845, 949
3.21–6 498, 528f., 549, 777, 839, 843, 883, 885–7, 903, 999, 1072, 1168, 1470
3.21–31 641, 841, 909, 935, 958, 991, 996, 1031
3.21—4.25 770f., 831, 840, 850, 885, 891, 900f., 921, 958, **995–1007**, 1019, 1072, 1088, 1167, 1169, 1176, 1218, 1236, 1468, 1481
3.21—8.39 754
3.22 531, 544, 641, 830, 836, 839, 845, 857, 859, 872, 931, 942, 997, 1027, 1470, 1494
3.23 486, 531, 641, 686, 888, 999
3.24 891, 944, 950f., 958, 988, 998, 1024
3.24f. 647, 795, 845, 851, 886, 958, 1001, 1024, 1194, 1208, 1343
3.25 998, 1469f.
3.25–6 1469
3.26 556, 647, 795, 844f., 847, 997f., 1001, 1343, 1469
3.27 847, 888, 922, 958, 1036, 1078, 1109, 1143, 1213
3.27–31 924, 1003f., 1168, 1178, 1245
3.27—4.25 846
3.28 847, 864, 1001, 1005
3.29 847
3.29–30 389, 641, 806, 864, 1001
3.30 79, 722, 867, 872, 1013, 1433
3.31 848, 909, 1002, 1037, 1078
4 363, 401, 422f., 498, 515, 531, 813, 847–50, 861, 868, 889, 901, 905, 928, 998, 1002, 1008, 1071, 1122, 1402, 1432, 1461
4.1 849, 1003f., 1006, 1225
4.1–25 841
4.2 1003, 1007, 1143
4.3–6 883, 963
4.3–12 19
4.4 643, 850, 1003, 1436
4.4–6 1224
4.5 850, 1004, 1006, 1188
4.6 1226
4.7f. 704, 849
4.9 643
4.9–12 362, 1004
4.9–17 973
4.10f. 963
4.11 544, 1002, 1167
4.11f. 924
4.12 363, 1004f., 1449
4.13 366, 467, 488, 533, 552, 622, 730, 815, 819, 849, 972, 1004, 1006, 1022, 1091, 1432, 1507, 1509
4.13–17 1224
4.14f. 973, 1006

4.15 507, 642, 859, 1019, 1037
4.16 1005, 1224, 1432
4.16f. 849, 924, 1006
4.17 552, 642, 1002–4, 1449
4.18 1432
4.18–21 952, 1012, 1200
4.18–25 849, 1007, 1461
4.19–21 1122
4.23–5 529, 552, 963
4.24 839, 1449
4.24f. 847, 903, 905, 944, 952f., 997, 1002, 1007, 1194
4.25 813, 1002, 1024, 1192
4.28 458
5 422, 476, 513, 525, 532, 696, 700, 721, 842f., 891, 927, 1091, 1461
5—8 38f., 439, 489, 530, 543, 779, 831, 851, 891, 899, 903, 921, 938, 951, 957f., 974, 996, **1007–26**, 1030f., 1126, 1318, 1379
5.1 383, 886, 888, 956, 1011, 1301
5.1f. 715
5.1–5 886, 958, 1019, 1141
5.1–11 530, 903, 1011, 1025
5.2 546, 886, 888, 1091
5.2–5 1116
5.3 722, 889, 1030
5.4f. 546, 722, 1030
5.5 492, 660, 722, 770, 886f., 889, 941, 1013, 1077, 1166, 1259, 1426, 1518
5.6–8 886
5.6–11 383, 529, 531, 845, 885–7, 999, 1024, 1119, 1194, 1208, 1490
5.6–21 **885–92**
5.8 1518
5.8f. 695
5.8–10 722, 886–8, 908
5.9 998
5.9f. 530, 556, 886–8
5.10 1198, 1229
5.10f. 500, 546, 888
5.12 889
5.12–14 859, 889
5.12–21 531, 535, 686, 769, 830, 843, 885f., 890f., 1009, 1014, 1194, 1207f., 1379, 1402, 1455, 1470
5.13 889
5.14–21 908
5.15–17 890
5.15–19 686, 845, 1229
5.16 939
5.17 367, 440, 467, 481, 485, 488, 531, 544, 558, 890, 931, 959, 1063, 1090, 1116
5.18 686, 889, 936, 939, 1131
5.18–21 890, 1312
5.19 686, 1490
5.20 500, 503, 507, 509, 511, 531f., 859, 870, 889, 891, 895–7, 910, 1014f., 1018f., 1033, 1177f., 1182, 1190, 1192, 1207, 1378, 1464
5.20f. 769, 1017, 1019
5.21 481, 545, 896, 1028, 1063, 1069, 1229
6 409, 422, 425, 440, 513, 659f., 951, 963, 970, 1103, 1105, 1326, 1335, 1339f.
6—8 530, 659, 661, 835, 886, 963, 1014, 1070
6.1–14 962
6.2 1009
6.2–5 1102, 1338, 1372
6.2–11 252, 422, 532, 990, 1102, 1105, 1424
6.3 1009
6.3–14 893
6.4 425, 441, 1009
6.4–8 827
6.5 963
6.6 425, 531, 893, 1009, 1016, 1018
6.6–11 20
6.8 963
6.8–11 1102
6.9 435
6.9f. 1340
6.11 19, 422f., 513, 531, 827, 951, 963, 1009, 1028, 1199, 1424
6.12–14 963, 1103, 1372
6.12–18 1338
6.12–23 481, 491, 723, 1014, 1063, 1078
6.13 938
6.14 513, 532, 1177
6.15 1225
6.16–20 938
6.16—7.1 558
6.17 492, 770, 1077
6.19 1212
6.21 1014
6.22 1069, 1106
6.23 545, 1069, 1106
7 422, 508, 520, 527, 532, 659, 755, 759, 878, 892, 894, 898, 970, 986, 1008f., 1012, 1015, 1034, 1073, 1171, 1262, 1377, 1394, 1462, 1509
7.1 1015
7.1–3 446, 892, 1009, 1016, 1078
7.1–6 511–13, 1009
7.1–22 660
7.1–25 769

Romans (*continued*)
7.1—8.4 764
7.1—8.11 463, **892–902**, 909, 1001, 1077, 1177, 1465
7.2f. 1009
7.4 532, 892, 1009, 1442
7.4–6 651, 703, 725, 769, 864, 892, 917, 924, 980, 1007, 1009, 1018, 1024, 1248, 1379, 1430
7.5 1141
7.5—8.11 1204
7.6 492, 512, 556, 886, 921, 1013, 1141
7.7 884, 1225
7.7–12 893f., 1010, 1014, 1207, 1378, 1462
7.7–25 394, 493, 503, 720, 751, 859, 1037, 1142, 1177, 1190, 1377, 1431
7.7—8.4 866, 1205
7.7—8.11 871, 1018, 1122, 1177f., 1421
7.8 896, 1010
7.8–11 508, 1014
7.10 506, 871, 894, 901, 936, 1020, 1037, 1207
7.11 493
7.12 511, 894
7.12–16 446
7.13 509–11, 532, 764, 894–7, 1019, 1033, 1178, 1182, 1378, 1462, 1464
7.13–20 870, 893, 895, 1016f.
7.13–25 1017, 1019, 1035, 1326
7.14–20 1016
7.14–23 510f., 894f.
7.17 1017–19
7.18 1019
7.19 1377
7.20 1017, 1019
7.21 1017f.
7.21–5 893, 1018
7.21—8.4 1177
7.22–5 1122
7.23 492, 994, 1462
7.24 511, 1019, 1190
7.25 492, 1205
7.26 660
7.39 446
8 422, 476, 479, 488, 513, 532f., 635, 657f., 660, 662, 671, 693, 695f., 700, 716, 718f., 721, 730, 747, 759, 762, 780, 819, 841, 848, 868, 900–3, 905, 939–41, 950, 954f., 957, 960, 1008, 1013, 1015, 1032, 1034, 1040, 1091f., 1109, 1127f., 1364, 1368, 1402, 1491, 1493, 1509
8.1 556, 900, 922, 926, 936, 939, 956, 958, 1020
8.1f. 659
8.1–4 **659–61**, 716, 900, 903, 1019
8.1–17 720
8.1–11 769, 900f., 903, 924, 941, 1020, 1037, 1142, 1167, 1207, 1377, 1433, 1462
8.2 871, 901, 936
8.3 507, 661, 671f., 698, 700f., 725, 895, 897, 900f., 939, 943, 1015f., 1024, 1034, 1182, 1211, 1343
8.3f. 383, 511f., 532, 660, 695, 900, 909, 941, 1177f., 1208
8.4 901, 936, 938, 1078, 1192
8.4–17 1030
8.5–8 703, 814, 922, 941, 951, 1020, 1029, 1037, 1123, 1364
8.5–11 357, 661, 723
8.6 871, 901, 1020
8.7–9 1078
8.9 956, 1020, 1029, 1141
8.9–11 422, 716, 720, 858, 917, 956, 1021–3, 1074, 1102, 1105, 1127, 1205
8.10 871, 901, 938, 940, 1019f., 1093
8.11 871, 894, 1020, 1062, 1093
8.12–14 1029
8.12–16 422, 440, 491, 723, 941, 951, 1012, 1105f., 1373, 1402
8.12–25 1005, 1338
8.12–30 1207
8.13 1030, 1117
8.14–17 659, 694f., 1022
8.15 528, 941, 956, 976, 1012, 1349
8.16 492, 1370
8.17 485, 701, 908, 911, 986, 1091f., 1454
8.17f. 488, 534, 819, 906
8.17–20 1050, 1064
8.17–25 165, 435, 868, 889, 1066
8.17–30 366f., 422, 440, 936, 1012, 1116f., 1507, 1509
8.18 1069
8.18–21 485, 546, 902
8.18–24 819, 1023, 1365, 1385
8.18–27 479, 486, 531, 888, 941, 1113, 1191, 1199, 1290
8.18–30 1011
8.19 941, 1092
8.19–21 440, 1301
8.19–26 61

8.20 488, 1092
8.21 409, 546, 1073, 1092
8.22–7 720
8.23 941, 959, 1066, 1078, 1094, 1259
8.23–30 1326
8.24 927, 1174
8.25 941
8.26f. 365, 443, 492, 960, 1013, 1066, 1127
8.27 770, 924, 1027, 1077
8.27f. 721f.
8.28 1013, 1025f., 1426
8.28–30 634, 721f., 919, 941, 959, 1024
8.29 439f., 485, 640, 694f., 908, 941, 952, 955, 1022f., 1126, 1368, 1423
8.30 489, 546, 959
8.31f. 697
8.31–5 695
8.31–9 530, 635, 722f., 885, 887, **902–8**, 924, 941, 958, 1008, 1011, 1308
8.32 903f., 907, 1192
8.33 905, 907, 938, 940, 1024
8.34 635, 693, 902, 939, 1024, 1066
8.34–9 476, 907
8.35 884, 1025, 1518
8.35–9 1025
8.36 906
8.37 899, 907, 1093, 1299
8.37–9 757
8.38f. 1219, 1285
8.39 907, 1518
9 422, 515, 705, 708, 878, 906
9f. 499, 1301, 1470
9—11 39f., 398, 495, 498–500, 514, 539, 703, 708, 747, 755, 776, 780, 895, 910, 924, 938f., 942, 965, 1007, 1011, 1015, 1018, 1026, 1032, 1071, 1128, 1132f., 1145, 1150, **1156–1258**, 1262, 1302, 1449, 1464f., 1517
9.1 492
9.1–5 368, 394, 397, 444, 708, 1012, 1020, 1162–4, 1175, 1193, 1202, 1213, 1238f., **1256–8**, 1427, 1443, 1517
9.2 1049
9.2–6 1226
9.3 539, 542, 1018, 1189, 1216
9.4 250, 769, 941, 1174, 1220, 1223
9.4f. 500, 941, 1012, 1202, 1204, 1229
9.5 524, 707–9, 817, 1198, 1253, 1256
9.6 638, 780, 924, 1157, 1181, 1184, 1188, 1223, 1242
9.6–9 906, 1166, 1176
9.6–13 1224, 1241
9.6–20 1184f.
9.6–29 533, 769, 839, 1162–4, 1172, 1176, **1181–95**, 1198, 1207, 1220
9.6—10.13 501, 823, 1172
9.6—10.21 463, 499, 1223, 1301, 1454, 1464, 1468
9.6—11.10 1233
9.7 827, 1072, 1187, 1254, 1464
9.8 1072, 1157, 1205, 1427
9.8f. 1157
9.10–13 1184, 1188
9.11 1157, 1224
9.12 1157, 1169, 1184, 1188, 1224, 1254, 1423
9.13 1157
9.14 499, 501, 1157, 1168, 1186, 1225
9.14–18 1189
9.14–23 1226, 1232, 1237
9.14–29 500, 1184, 1241
9.15 679, 1185, 1189
9.15f. 1150, 1157, 1184
9.17 684, 1157
9.17f. 1184, 1191, 1227
9.18 1150, 1157
9.19 393, 1157, 1184, 1186
9.20–3 393, 1191
9.20–9 1192
9.21 1157
9.21f. 1219
9.22 1157, 1190
9.22–4 1179, 1227
9.23 1150, 1157, 1190
9.24 1176, 1184f., 1187–90, 1193, 1223, 1227, 1241, 1254
9.24–6 925, 1185, 1187, 1193
9.25 1157
9.25f. 1010, 1053
9.26–9 1159, 1185, 1187, 1193
9.27 704, 1159, 1184, 1223
9.27–30 1176
9.29 704, 1184, 1187, 1193
9.30 533, 814, 906, 1179f., 1225, 1241
9.30–3 870, 925, 1019, 1035, 1162, 1164, **1176–81**, 1202, 1222
9.30—10.4 1016, 1178, 1194, 1205, 1224, 1464

Romans (*continued*)
9.30—10.13 533, 769, 895, 1001, 1025, 1177, 1181, 1183, 1188, 1198, 1214, 1221, 1224
9.30—10.21 1162, 1169, 1246, 1431
9.31 929, 1205, 1223, 1464
9.31f. 922
9.32 1161, 1179, 1236
9.32f. 356, 704, 1177–9, 1227f.
9.33 1065
10 185, 704, 706, 848, 910, 917, 922, 954, 1036, 1173, 1179, 1342, 1432, 1439, 1463
10.1 252, 368, 542, 1161, 1174, 1176, 1201, 1213, 1216, 1230, 1238f.
10.1–4 533, 1163, 1429
10.1–13 642, 707f., 924, 958, 1110, 1168, 1177, 1201, 1210, 1215, 1221, 1224, 1234, 1236, 1238, 1240, 1249
10.1–17 1164, **1165–76**, 1179, 1246
10.2 1161, 1169, 1224, 1431
10.2f. 929, 991, 1077, 1179
10.2–13 1176, 1213
10.3 1072, 1168, 1172, 1185, 1205, 1208, 1225, 1227, 1245
10.4 502, 544, 704, 708, 1035, 1159, 1163, 1172, 1192, 1208, 1236, 1243, 1513
10.4–13 641, 925, 1078, 1227
10.4–17 1175
10.5 506, 515, 865, 1173, 1458
10.5–8 1460
10.5–9 514
10.5–11 952
10.5–13 814, 1163f., 1174f., 1181, 1434
10.6 415, 704f., 708, 1167, 1171, 1458
10.6–8 161, 704, 867, 1072, 1165, 1173f., 1177, 1227, 1236, 1248, 1263, 1464
10.6–11 770, 937, 1077, 1219
10.6–13 661, 864, 892, 917, 922, 1161, 1219, 1221, 1223, 1230, 1233, 1241, 1245f.
10.7 704, 708
10.8 1173f., 1503
10.8–10 492
10.9 703–5, 708, 850, 944, 952, 1163f., 1173, 1517
10.9f. 953, 956, 1224
10.9–11 758, 887
10.9–13 383, 1167, 1236
10.11 887, 1077, 1159, 1179, 1243
10.12 1077, 1175, 1198, 1201, 1253, 1494
10.12f. 641, 703, 705–8, 1159, 1517
10.13 684, 703f., 867, 917, 953, 1164, 1166, 1243, 1394
10.13–15 956
10.14 708, 1163, 1503
10.14–17 1163, 1175, 1192, 1222, 1236, 1255
10.14–21 953, 1202, 1499
10.15 1251, 1503
10.15f. 410, 416, 564, 1174
10.16 944, 1180
10.17 394, 708, 1173
10.18 819, 1173, 1365
10.18–21 758, 1162–4, **1176–81**, 1222
10.19 501, 669, 1077, 1172, 1180, 1202, 1229, 1241, 1345, 1463f.
10.20 1193, 1225, 1241, 1302, 1504
10.21 1159, 1180, 1193, 1224
10.28f. 1345
10.31—11.1 394
11 806f., 1130, 1132, 1206, 1234, 1247, 1448, 1494, 1497
11.1 499, 542, 1197, 1206, 1412, 1427
11.1–6 394, 397, 1176, 1211–13, 1223f., 1227, 1230, 1239
11.1–10 1221, **1223–9**
11.1–14 1202
11.1–24 1221, **1229–31**
11.1–32 1162–4, 1182–4, **1195–1252**
11.3 1239, 1423
11.5 556, 1211
11.6 1169, 1184, 1211
11.7 1184, 1212, 1225, 1227, 1236, 1239
11.7–10 1189, 1224f., 1228, 1238
11.8 492, 1192, 1233, 1251
11.11 704, 1197, 1210, 1230, 1254
11.11f. 1161, **1206–11**, 1228
11.11–15 1189, 1197, 1213, 1218, 1221, 1224, 1232, 1240, 1243, 1250f., 1255, 1257, 1407

11.11–24 1207, 1211, 1221, 1232, 1236, 1241, 1243, 1414
11.11–32 1194, 1208, 1237, 1256
11.12 500, 1203, 1209, 1220, 1233, 1245, 1254
11.13 200, 397, 492, 1196, 1201, 1221, 1230
11.13–15 **1197–1206**
11.13–36 1245
11.14 539, 1200f., 1222, 1230, 1233, 1240, 1245f., 1253
11.15 409, 500, 888, 1161, 1198–1201, 1203, 1205, 1209, 1232f., 1254
11.16 1197, 1225, 1230, 1254
11.16–24 1197, 1206, **1211–23**, 1229, 1232, 1240
11.17 1197, 1217, 1417
11.17–24 540, 542, 1216, 1210, 1221, 1238, 1246
11.18 1212, 1217, 1221
11.19–21 1218
11.20 1212, 1236, 1251
11.21 903
11.22 1219, 1226
11.23 397, 1161, 1213, 1215, 1221f., 1230f., 1233, 1236, 1238, 1240, 1245, 1251, 1253
11.24 1197, 1219f., 1233, 1238, 1243, 1251f., 1448
11.25 1189, 1212, 1225, 1232, 1235, 1238f., 1241, 1244, 1246
11.25–7 1161, 1184, 1200, 1208, **1231–52**, 1255f., 1351
11.25–32 1197, 1231
11.26 358, 1175, 1202, 1234, 1239f., 1243–6, 1251, 1433
11.27 1177, 1233f., 1240, 1246f., 1248, 1251
11.28 1254
11.28–32 1231, **1252–6**
11.29 368, 1184, 1254
11.30f. 1254f.
11.30–2 1150, 1161, 1184, 1197
11.31 556, 1150, 1161, 1252f.
11.32 865f., 872, 1019, 1049, 1150, 1192, 1131, 1243, 1253, 1255
11.33 988
11.33–6 134, 639, 708, 1162–4, **1256–8**, 1517
11.34 704
11.36 101, 475, 1360
12 380, 556, 1115, 1121–3, 1126, 1156, 1304, 1363
12—16 398, 938, 1011, 1304
12.1 1340
12.1f. 27, 358, 478, 491, 723, 962, 1030, 1123, 1351
12.1–5 1339
12.2 250, 452, 478, 492, 556, 1069, 1072, 1364, 1508, 1101, 1124, 1372
12.3 1124, 1232, 1421
12.3–8 1123
12.9 430, 1375
12.9–15 1108
12.12 365, 1518
12.13 11, 443, 1027
12.14–18 1298, 1303
12.14—13.10 1097
12.15 1375
12.16 1375
12.17 639
12.17f. 1375
12.19 669, 1115
12.19–21 1156, 1303
13 1280, 1302, 1308, 1485
13.1 492, 1286, 1303
13.1–7 42, 379, 381, 639, 1115, 1272f., 1280, 1286, 1298, 1302–4, 1308, 1485, 1489, 1508
13.4 1156
13.8 1353
13.8–10 922, 1078, 1110, 1118
13.9 1119
13.10 431
13.11 562
13.11–14 553, 962, 1101, 1298, 1303
13.12 478, 1079
13.14 441, 1108
14 403, 667f., 988, 1115, 1136, 1494
14f. 11, 397, 1032, 1304, 1429, 1442, 1448, 1495
14.1 11, 564
14.1–12 1115
14.1—15.6 359
14.1—15.13 962, 1120
14.3 11
14.3–12 399
14.4 444, 1304
14.5 1123, 1368
14.5f. 363f., 492
14.6 393, 1368
14.6–17 359, 413
14.7 1106
14.7–12 702, 1304
14.8–9 879
14.9 668
14.10–12 544, 549, 553, 935, 1085, 1089, 1115

Romans (*continued*)
14.11 702, 704
14.13 1115
14.13–21 1296
14.14 475, 564
14.15 430
14.17 481, 663, 1063, 1097, 1114
14.17f. 668
14.18 639
14.19 1097
14.21 667
14.22 544
14.23 360
15 1027, 1342, 1496f., 1505f.
15.1–9 1105
15.1–13 401, 819
15.3 820, 1104
15.4 552
15.5 1104
15.6 706
15.7 11, 1104
15.7–13 399, 524, 556, 1300, 1304, 1308, 1494, 1494f.
15.8 1254, 1470
15.8f. 200, 368, 416, 504
15.8–12 1455
15.9 684, 704, 1150
15.9–13 201, 552
15.10 501, 669
15.11 704
15.12 120, 383, 533f., 817, 820, 835, 1281, 1312
15.13 413, 1097
15.14–33 1351
15.15 1239
15.15f. 1341, 1421
15.15–21 1203
15.16 11, 200, 358, 558, 1506
15.18 120
15.19 358, 1497, 1502
15.20 1497, 1503
15.21 1497
15.22 252
15.23 1497
15.23f. 8, 1498
15.24 1239, 1498
15.25f. 443, 1027
15.25–8 1202, 1496
15.27 11, 1256
15.30 252
15.31 1027
15.31f. 252, 443, 558
16 1278
16.1f. 386
16.2–6 201, 443
16.3 1230
16.4 492
16.7 648, 1230
16.11 1230
16.15 443, 1027
16.17–20 548, 1121
16.18 492, 770
16.20 372
16.23 379, 386
16.25 477, 1235, 1503
16.26 367, 405, 556, 843, 916

1 Corinthians
1 426f.
1—2 200
1—4 1496
1.2 443, 540, 684, 703, 1026f., 1166
1.3 701
1.4–7 412
1.8 553, 1079
1.8f. 834
1.9 11, 1026, 1423
1.10 492, 684
1.13 18
1.13–15 1336
1.13–17 1336
1.17 411, 425, 1337
1.18 383
1.18–25 522, 541, 917, 1355
1.18—2.16 236, 391, 1359
1.20 1069
1.21 544, 1503
1.22–5 1383, 1446
1.23 667, 817, 860, 1169, 1228, 1429, 1443, 1503
1.24 383, 1026
1.26 1026, 1397, 1423
1.30 881, 951
1.30f. 522
1.31 704, 888, 1143
2 414, 1291, 1364
2.1f. 1233
2.1–10 476
2.4 1503
2.4f. 383, 1383
2.6 1068f., 1291
2.6–8 372, 687, 756, 1285, 1355
2.7 552
2.7f. 1233
2.8 899, 911, 1068f., 1168, 1281
2.8f. 522
2.10–16 1364
2.14–16 1121, 1370, 1399
2.15 704
2.15f. 236, 1359
2.16 390, 492, 687, 704, 708, 1257, 1508
3 711, 715, 1080, 1402, 1493
3.1 432
3.7 711
3.10 1421
3.10–17 1074, 1403, 1492
3.12 391, 711
3.13 553, 978, 1080
3.16 357, 712, 1021
3.16f. 355, 391, 712, 1074
3.18 391, 1069
3.18–23 1121
3.20 704
4 391, 957, 965, 977, 984, 997, 1264
4.1 1233
4.1–5 936, 941, 977, 1347
4.2 497
4.4f. 553

4.5 549, 770, 936, 957, 977, 1090, 1115
4.6 1104
4.8 481, 544, 1063, 1090
4.9–13 432, 1117
4.14 258
4.16 394f., 1104
4.19f. 383
4.20 481, 1063
5 48, 446, 540, 927, 979
5.1 541, 639
5.1–5 1136
5.1–13 1118
5.3 978
5.4 383, 684
5.5 979, 1079
5.6–8 360, 1136, 1343
5.7 427, 1070, 1347
5.9–13 360
5.10 360
5.11 446
5.12f. 978
6 396, 927, 1112, 1114
6.1f. 443, 1027
6.1–3 1090
6.1–5 977, 979, 1115
6.2 922, 931
6.2f. 488, 549, 979
6.3 544
6.5 1090
6.6 1115
6.7 1209
6.9 481, 553, 819, 1121
6.9f. 366, 481, 758, 1063
6.9–11 1114
6.9–21 1118
6.10 819
6.11 684, 760, 979, 1212, 1337, 1411, 1435
6.12–14 1295
6.13f. 1112, 1372
6.18–20 409, 712
6.19 355
6.19f. 1074, 1112, 1372
7 639, 875, 1118, 1254, 1368
7.1–11 639
7.1–40 1118
7.5 372
7.6–16 432
7.8 1118
7.10f. 446
7.11 888
7.12–16 369, 446
7.14 1212
7.15–24 1423
7.16 437
7.17–19 1434
7.19 361, 513, 922, 1036, 1078, 1109, 1141, 1143, 1434f., 1442, 1494
7.20 1026
7.25–40 639, 1118
7.26 1069
7.26–8 1434
7.29–31 562, 1098
7.37 492
7.39 369, 444, 446
8 398, 403, 668, 701, 988, 1136, 1368
8—10 359, 377, 564, **661–70**, 733, 1104, 1120, 1304, 1429, 1495
8.1–3 643, 988, 1355, 1361
8.1–6 376, 663, 988
8.1—11.1 1296, 1438
8.3 664, 732, 1166
8.4 664
8.4–6 201, 275, 1356
8.5 664, 1285
8.6 359, 365, 429, 475, 535, 547, 649, 661, 664f., 670, 672, 674, 697f., 701, 707f., 723, 729, 733, 737, 773, 860, 909, 976, 988, 1257, 1349, 1367, 1447, 1516
8.7–10 1356
8.7–13 1120, 1345
8.8 359
8.9–13 1442
8.10 361
8.11 360
8.11f. 667
8.12 1347
8.13 13, 667, 1296
9 394, 420, 668, 1296, 1436–8, 1441, 1443
9.1 34, 1421
9.1–27 1296
9.16 411, 451
9.16f. 394, 1489, 1510
9.17 837
9.19–23 1434f., 1438
9.20 359, 542, 1412
9.20–2 1153
9.22 1202, 1230, 1435
9.23 411
9.24 1113
9.27 994, 1503
10 394, 396, 403, 421, 423, 427, 669, 963, 1022, 1070, 1078, 1103, 1150, 1187, 1334, 1345, 1347, 1368, 1447
10.1 416, 428, 1335, 1447
10.1f. 539
10.1–5 420, 503, 1334
10.1–10 543, 1373
10.1–13 662, 668
10.1–22 1144
10.2–3 1070, 1344
10.7 677
10.7–10 421
10.11 552, 662, 668, 670, 1070
10.12 1219
10.14 1120
10.14–17 1345
10.14–22 361, 372, 640
10.15–17 428
10.16 11
10.16f. 669
10.16–22 252, 669
10.17 394

1 Corinthians (*continued*)
10.18 11, 428, 539, 1147f., 1242
10.18–22 1345
10.19 1225
10.20 11, 421, 732, 1285
10.20f. 1285
10.20–2 734
10.22 669, 704
10.23 1120
10.23–6 1356
10.24 1296
10.25 669
10.25f. 444
10.25–30 1428
10.25—11.1 1120
10.26 359, 475, 564, 639, 670, 1429, 1508
10.27 854
10.27–30 360
10.28 1145, 1296
10.28f. 1345
10.30 1368
10.31f. 626
10.31—11.1 394, 1447
10.32 396f., 540, 1144, 1439
10.33 1296
11 1511
11.1 394, 1104, 1295f., 1351, 1439, 1510
11.2–16 875
11.22 1496
11.23–6 428, 1347
11.24 252
11.27–32 1347
11.29–32 553, 979
11.30 740
12 391, 426f., 430, 728, 1118, 1123
12—14 1120
12.1–3 426, 962
12.1–7 1333
12.2 416, 490, 539, 541, 1107, 1446
12.2f. 1349
12.3 544, 917, 953
12.4–6 723
12.4–11 426
12.6 919
12.11–13 723
12.12f. 426, 962, 1333
12.12–20 396
12.12–31 1123
12.14–26 426
12.27–31 426
13 391, 430, 439, 452, 1118–20
13.2 1233
13.8–13 553, 1118, 1355
13.12 988
14 391, 430, 1349f.
14.2 1233
14.4f. 1349
14.6 967
14.12 1349
14.14f. 492
14.19 492
14.20 567, 1121, 1442
14.22 544
14.23 1315
14.25 1053
14.26 1349f.
14.33 443, 1027, 1097, 1349
14.40 1349
15 426, 439, 476, 481, 486, 489, 519, 521, 523–5, 551, 668, 795, 817, 820f., 918, 926, 1066, 1080, 1092, 1094, 1117, 1161, 1199, 1235, 1287, 1293, 1318, 1368, 1398, 1400f.
15.1f. 411, 518
15.1–8 915
15.1–11 439
15.3 525, 879, 884
15.3f. 817
15.3–9 518, 555, 1410
15.3–11 648
15.8 1421
15.8–11 34, 1421
15.9 896, 1144, 1153, 1431
15.10 955, 1107
15.11 648, 1503
15.12 120, 1503
15.12–19 439
15.14 1503
15.17 71
15.18 120
15.20 1211
15.20–8 367, 439, 476, 479, 481, 535, 546, 665, 668, 670, 701, 706, 730, **733–7**, 756f., 820, 907f., 941, 1040, 1063f., 1080, 1114, 1280, 1455
15.21f. 439, 769, 821
15.22 503, 827, 1064
15.23 944, 1084
15.23–8 370, 481, 551, 639, 1063
15.24 481, 550, 1048, 1063, 1080, 1099, 1312
15.24f. 820
15.25 693, 1064, 1106, 1280
15.25f. 1287
15.25–7 518
15.26 1094, 1319
15.26–8 684
15.27 561, 640, 686, 737, 1050, 1064, 1293
15.28 550, 553, 665, 707, 737, 1093
15.29 427
15.29–34 418, 426, 439
15.35–49 439
15.39 491
15.39–41 1398
15.42–4 1398
15.42–9 438
15.45 492
15.45–9 1064

15.49 440
15.50 481, 492, 553, 819, 1063
15.50–7 762
15.51 1234
15.54 736, 756
15.54f. 1234
15.56 892, 1287
15.58 564, 905, 1107
16 1428
16.1 443, 1027
16.1–4 1497
16.5–9 1351
16.7–9 252
16.8f. 1428
16.12 492
16.15 443, 1027
16.17 1082
16.21 353
16.22 1349

2 Corinthians

1.1 443, 982, 1027
1.2 701
1.3f. 412
1.3–11 252
1.7 11
1.8 432
1.8–11 549
1.11 549
1.14 553, 1079, 1239
1.15–22 1507
1.15—2.13 713
1.17–22 1351
1.19 1503
1.20 17, 552, 557, 810, 1047, 1075
1.21 833f.
1.22 492, 972, 1094, 1259
1.23 492
1.23—2.4 1351
2.1–11 48
2.4 492, 1255
2.5 1239
2.5–11 1136
2.11 372, 548
2.14 252, 988, 1299
2.14—6.13 713, 724, 1351
2.16 1299
2.17—7.1 881
3 101, 414, 441, 502f., 507, 527, 532, 715, 724, 750, 871f., 892, 917, 921, **980–4**, 1007, 1010, 1013, 1020, 1023, 1075, 1091, 1139, 1201, 1225, 1237, 1242, 1247f., 1374, 1432
3f. **677–80**, 1021, 1489, 1493
3—6 879, 1023
3.1 724
3.1–3 724
3.1–6 513, 677, 814, 864, 883
3.2f. 492
3.3 727, 867, 981, 1379f.
3.3–6 984
3.3–18 1374
3.4f. 982
3.6 727, 923, 981, 984, 1379
3.7 1145
3.7–12 726
3.7—4.6 546, 677
3.9 984
3.12—4.6 699
3.13 1145, 1225
3.14 1033, 1226, 1365
3.15 492, 1226, 1251
3.15–18 726
3.16 1226, 1236
3.16f. 365, 984, 1226
3.18 406, 441, 983f., 1226, 1326, 1493
4 435, 636, 676, 679, 1073, 1393
4—6 441
4.1–6 1362, 1421
4.3f. 1362
4.3–6 679
4.4 406, 411, 414, 439, 640, 726, 1069
4.5 1503
4.5–6 441, 726, 880, 1073, 1368, 1493
4.6 34, 492, 636, 983f., 988, 1226
4.7 383
4.7–12 432, 1075, 1491, 1494
4.7–15 883f., 1208
4.7–18 1117, 1151
4.7—5.10 883
4.8–11 636
4.10 432
4.12 434
4.15f. 549
4.16 1075
5 20, 503, 675, 885, 1393, 1489, 1493
5.1–10 879
5.5 972
5.7 726
5.10 549, 553, 702, 880, 935, 938, 1087, 1089, 1490
5.11–21 20
5.11—6.2 564, **874–85**, 881
5.13–15 880, 1426
5.13—6.2 1488
5.14 431, 884, 1518
5.14f. 1490
5.15 880, 884
5.16 1491
5.16f. 20, 880, 1362
5.16–19 676
5.17 452, 477f., 676, 880, 1072, 1093, 1101, 1143, 1151
5.17—6.2 561
5.18 884, 888, 1495
5.19 9, 20, 884–6, 888, 1198, 1490, 1493, 1495
5.20 883, 885, 887f., 1490
5.20f. 882

2 Corinthians (*continued*)

5.21 20, 70, 558, 724, 881–4, 909, 951, 980, 1343, 1494
6 379, 557, 905
6.1 956
6.1f. 557, 882
6.1–10 882
6.2 408, 416, 637, 881f., 905, 997, 1062, 1482
6.3–10 432, 637, 884, 1151, 1307, 1494
6.3–13 1117, 1491
6.6 430
6.14 11, 444
6.14—7.1 369, 637, 713
6.15 544
6.16 355, 357f., 1021, 1146
6.16–18 1041, 1074
6.18 704
7.1 715
7.4 413
7.5 353, 1518
7.5–16 713, 1351
7.6 1082
7.7 1082
8—9 15, 429, 454, 1027, 1342
8.4 11, 443, 1027
8.9 688, 1105
8.10–12 1497
8.16 252
8.21 639
8.23 11
8.24 1497
9.1 443
9.3–5 1497
9.7 430
9.8 380
9.11f. 549
9.12 443
9.13 11, 411
9.13–14 1496
9.24 213
10 1404
10.1 449
10.3–6 369, 1307, 1357
10.4f. 206, 1400
10.5 201, 614, 988, 994
10.10 1082
10.10—11.15 548
10.17 704, 1143
11.2 651
11.2f. 1078, 1489
11.3 493, 548, 769, 834, 1121
11.4 648, 1503
11.12–15 547
11.14–15 372
11.15 1087
11.21–32 548
11.22 542, 1412, 1427
11.23–5 1151
11.23–33 70, 433, 1491
11.24 541, 1438, 1499
11.24–7 1153
11.29 667
11.32 1504
12.1–5 1400, 1421
12.1–10 413
12.4 1173
12.7–9 372
12.8–10 433
12.9 383
12.9f. 1492
12.15 492
13.1 1173
13.1–4 1492
13.4 383
13.10 1476
13.11 1097
13.12 443
13.13 11, 727

Galatians

1 452
1f. 462
1.1 701
1.1—6.15 1143
1.3 701
1.3–5 477, 525
1.4 452, 552, 556, 558, 718, 911, 969f., 1068f., 1072, 1101, 1143, 1145
1.6 1026, 1141, 1423
1.6–9 648, 1135
1.7 1145
1.8f. 1145
1.10 1438f.
1.11 411, 497
1.11–17 34
1.12 414
1.13 967, 1144, 1147, 1425
1.13f. 82, 86, 88, 200, 542, 1153, 1155, 1224
1.13–14 1431
1.13–15 1422
1.14 84, 1169, 1422
1.15 955, 1026, 1421f.
1.15f. 416, 1424
1.15–17 1420, 1422
1.16 200, 414, 1111
1.17 355, 1504
1.21 205
1.23 1153
1.24 416
2 853, 880, 954, 1429
2—4 498, 780, **851–79**, 965, 1011, 1028, 1262
2.1f. 1351
2.1–10 63, 355, 1498
2.2 416, 564, 905, 1503
2.3–5 361
2.5 390, 411
2.6 1028, 1087
2.7 200, 837
2.7–9 1149, 1201
2.8 919
2.9 11, 200, 355, 1028, 1421
2.9–10 454
2.10 1255, 1507
2.10–14 966
2.11 643

2.11–14 93, 359, 1135, 1228, 1424
2.11–21 853f., 1135
2.12 643, 854, 1425
2.13 854
2.14 853, 855, 1435, 1440
2.15 967–9, 1004, 1412, 1428
2.15f. 856, 968
2.15–21 20, 360, 388, 753, **852–60**, 909f., 920, 966f., 973, 988, 1031, 1262, 1424, 1441
2.15—4.11 643, 831, **966–76**, 1169
2.16 782, 857, 859, 967–9, 973, 1429, 1469
2.16–18 961
2.16–21 986
2.16—3.9 836
2.17 950, 969–71, 988, 1028
2.17f. 511, 753, 859, 872, 1037, 1171
2.17–21 564, 857, 894
2.18 859, 1424
2.19 188, 509, 531, 857, 1010, 1147, 1169, 1182, 1208, 1430, 1436, 1442
2.19f. 371, 408, 423, 450, 533, 695, 810, 827, 831, 852, 892, 963, 987, 1009, 1020, 1025, 1117, 1141, 1143, 1237, 1425
2.19–20 1200, 1326, 1424, 1430
2.19–21 394, 508f., 728, 753, 782, 857, 859, 866, 879, 1136, 1147
2.20 525, 530, 856, 857f., 865, 884, 906, 955f., 970, 988, 1010, 1069, 1140, 1518
2.21 363, 750, 857, 862, 869f., 1141
3 79, 363, 366, 388f., 401, 423, 498f., 528, 642, 831, 848, 857, 863, 889, 928, 971, 1005, 1017, 1139, 1188, 1213, 1215, 1432
3f. 38, 366, 508, 543, 730, 781, 853, 862
3.1 1425
3.1–5 759, 857, 860f., 971f.
3.1—4.7 1134
3.1—4.11 **860–79**, 971
3.2 544, 861
3.2–5 919, 1137
3.5 861, 971
3.6–9 389, 863, 972
3.6—4.7 642
3.8 827, 861, 867, 973, 1004, 1188
3.9 861, 973
3.10 1139, 1215
3.10–14 507, 526, 532, 862f., **863–8**, 870, 910, 969, 973
3.11 865, 973, 1466, 1470
3.12 506, 515, 1171
3.13 763, 863, 865, 1035, 1425
3.13f. 528, 851, 1139
3.14 467, 499, 504, 528, 642, 827, 832, 867, 971, 973f., 976, 1137
3.15–18 851, 862f., **868–70**
3.15–22 910
3.16 18, 831, 834, 869, 871f., 944
3.16f. 1452
3.16–20 1433
3.16–29 872, 875, 1432
3.17 527, 869f.
3.18 366, 642, 869f.
3.19 389, 509, 870f., 878, 891, 894f., 944, 1139, 1378
3.19f. 642f., 871f., 1033
3.19–22 862, 868, **870–3**
3.19–28 861
3.20 389, 663
3.21 506, 871, 1014, 1033, 1037, 1177, 1378, 1469
3.21—4.7 1023
3.22 509, 511, 544, 642, 753, 857, 866, 870–3, 878, 894f., 967, 969, 974, 1005, 1018f., 1033, 1139, 1253, 1464
3.23 527, 1139
3.23–6 975
3.23–9 423f., 544, 818, 862f., **873–6**, 974, 988, 1014, 1139, 1169
3.23—4.7 986
3.24 527, 833, 871, 1139
3.24–9 857, 871
3.25 1436
3.25f. 1469
3.25–9 1103
3.26 388, 658, 857, 874, 975
3.26–9 831, 833, 944, 962
3.27 388, 423f., 441, 642, 874, 962, 975, 1108
3.27–9 388f., 423f., 642, 861, 868
3.28 11, 388, 426, 539, 834, 975, 1150, 1335, 1494
3.28f. 695
3.29 366, 388, 528, 642, 861, 868, 908, 944, 972, 976, 1166
4 527, 662, 693, 696, 720f., 941, 950, 1032, 1290
4—6 1031, 1133–51

Galatians (*continued*)
4.1 366, 876, 908
4.1–3 1139
4.1–7 876, 972, 974–6, 1014, 1076, 1134, 1140, 1433
4.1–11 **656–9**, **876–9**, 988
4.3 878
4.3–7 527, 1070, 1426
4.3–11 718
4.4 383, 508, 528, 532, 552, 643, 658, 671f., 698, 700f., 873, 877, 1110, 1235
4.4f. 877
4.5 941, 1425
4.5–7 528, 695f., 974, 988
4.6 492, 694, 956, 1349, 1370
4.6f. 513, 528, 831, 861, 876, 878, 1022, 1137
4.7 366, 658, 833, 876, 976, 991, 1147
4.8 490, 1147
4.8f. 657, 1361
4.8–11 376, 878, 976
4.9 988, 1076, 1147, 1428
4.10 274, 364
4.11 564, 905, 1133
4.12–14 1145
4.12–20 1135
4.14 11
4.17 967, 1135, 1228
4.19 258
4.21 1136, 1442
4.21–31 923
4.21—5.1 1133f., 1136, 1148
4.25–7 355
4.26 1250
4.27 1150
4.29 1134, 1136f.
4.30 366, 1136
5 430, 662, 759, 927, 955, 1114
5f. 853, 1106
5.1 1133, 1139
5.2 1141
5.2–6 361, 1140f.
5.2–12 1135
5.3 1141, 1171
5.4 1141
5.5 927, 1095, 1140f.
5.6 361, 431, 1140f., 1144
5.8 1026
5.9 1136
5.10 1135f.
5.11 194, 541, 860, 1169, 1228, 1429, 1438, 1503
5.12 987
5.13 1026, 1423
5.13f. 1110
5.13–21 1118
5.14 1037, 1118f.
5.16 1030, 1142
5.16–26 448, 513, 758, 814, 1078
5.17f. 1141f.
5.18 1078
5.19–23 1106
5.19–25 1116
5.21 366, 481, 553, 819, 1063, 1095, 1114
5.22 413, 920, 1118
5.23 1037
5.24 445, 1117, 1142, 1425
6 1146
6.2 1078, 1110, 1146f., 1442
6.6 11
6.6–10 58
6.7 1121
6.8 1069
6.9 1107
6.10 380, 401, 449, 1147, 1298, 1375
6.11 353, 1142
6.11–17 1135, 1145
6.12 1135, 1142, 1148, 1425
6.13 1142, 1432
6.14 988, 1136, 1425f., 1430, 1490
6.14–16 478, 1142, 1447
6.15 361, 477, 539, 552, 1072, 1093, 1101, 1141, 1144f., 1147f., 1494
6.16 401, 1107, 1131, 1143, 1147–51, 1242, 1244, 1433
6.17 435, 541, 1151, 1237
6.18 492

Ephesians
1 1373, 1514
1—3 1099, 1234f.
1.1 443, 1027
1.2 701
1.3–14 412f., 561, 730
1.5 941
1.8–10 1234
1.9f. 1233
1.10 552, 555f., 559, 561, 715, 730, 1514
1.14 972, 1094, 1259
1.15 1027
1.18 492, 1026f.
1.19–23 383, 822
1.20 693, 919
1.20–2 1066, 1285
1.21 684, 731f., 1503f.
1.22 561, 640, 1050
2.1–3 771, 927
2.1–10 715, 1396, 1514
2.2 372, 1069
2.3 371, 492
2.8 57, 544, 953, 955
2.10 380, 1124, 1375
2.11–22 57, 79, 552, 864, 1218, 1234f., 1514
2.11—3.21 402
2.12 1043, 1145
2.13 556
2.14 715
2.14f. 1037
2.14–18 909f., 1097

2.15 892
2.15f. 729
2.17 715
2.19 1027
2.19–22 715, 729, 1514
2.22 358
2.30 1023
3 1234
3.1 200
3.1–13 1514
3.2 1421
3.2–11 1234f.
3.5 556, 1027
3.7 1421
3.7–10 383
3.7–12 252
3.8 200, 411, 1027, 1431
3.9–13 731
3.10 372, 556, 1299, 1514
3.10f. 911, 1517
3.13 252, 734
3.14–19 252
3.14–21 1514, 1517
3.17 358, 492, 716, 1021
3.17–19 431
3.18 1027
3.20 919
4 17, 729, 1118
4—6 1099
4.1 1026, 1423
4.1–3 728
4.1–16 430
4.1—6.9 1514
4.2–6 427
4.4 1026, 1423
4.4–6 728
4.9–10 415
4.12 1027
4.12f. 18, 834
4.13–16 728, 834
4.14 1121
4.14–16 1121
4.15 18, 834
4.16 1118
4.17 492, 1435
4.17–19 1363
4.17–24 1108
4.17—5.20 448, 927
4.18 492
4.21 832, 1374
4.22 1121
4.22–4 1373
4.23 492, 1121
4.24 441, 640
4.28 1298
4.30 1080
5 419, 1114, 1376
5.1 1104
5.1f. 1343
5.1–20 201
5.2 431
5.3 779, 1027
5.3–5 1092
5.5 366, 481, 553, 819, 1063, 1106f.
5.5–10 1114
5.6 767, 1121
5.7 379
5.10 1124
5.11–14 1102
5.16 562, 1069
5.17 1124
5.19 492
5.20 412
5.21–33 875
5.21—6.9 1108, 1375
5.23 383
5.25 431
5.26 1173, 1337
5.32 419, 1232
6 549, 1127, 1282
6.6 492
6.9 1087
6.10–17 372
6.10–20 448, 476, 549, 557, 732, 1518
6.11–19 1126
6.12 1287
6.13 1069
6.14–17 1287
6.17 1173
6.18 1027, 1518
6.18–20 252, 365

Philippians

1.1 443, 1027
1.2 701
1.3–5 412
1.4 413
1.5 11
1.6 18, 553, 940, 953–5, 957, 1029, 1079, 1156
1.7 1124
1.9 430
1.9–11 1119, 1121
1.10 553, 1079
1.12 411
1.12–14 435
1.12–18 1351
1.15 1503
1.15–18 548
1.17f. 435
1.21–3 986
1.23 1400
1.26 1082
1.27 380, 411, 492, 614, 1298
1.27f. 390
1.27–30 435, 1341
1.28 1295, 1299
1.29 953
1.29f. 1117
2 535, 663, 667, 680, 701, 704, 733, 843, 1105, 1314
2f. 449
2.1 11
2.1–4 11, 390, 394, 430, 728, 1104f., 1332, 1341
2.2 1124
2.5 392, 1104, 1121, 1124
2.5–8 685
2.6f. 989
2.6–8 531, 687, 689, 700, 879
2.6–11 394, 462, 517, 534, 649, 672, **680–9**, 737, 821, 1040,

Philippians (*continued*)
1104, 1293, 1295f., 1312, 1351, 1374
2.7f. 700
2.8 687f., 843, 890, 989
2.9 683
2.9–11 383, 533, 680, 684–6, 688, 706, 821, 1294, 1503f.
2.10 681, 1293
2.10f. 686, 702, 704, 1067
2.11 702, 707
2.12 1082, 1124
2.12f. 1295
2.12–18 1341
2.13 919, 1342
2.14–16 628, 1107
2.14–17 637
2.15 448, 547, 1111
2.16 416, 436, 553, 564, 905, 1079
2.17 358
2.17f. 1117, 1341
2.19–30 434
2.27 252
2.30 492
3 394, 750, 777, 891, 921, 954, 961, 991f., 997, 1011, 1024, 1242, 1295, 1424
3.2 548, 984f., 994, 1394
3.2f. 986, 993
3.2–8 362
3.2–11 362, 394, 462, 687, 782, 810, 830f., 965, **984–92**, 1007, 1037, 1104, 1169, 1242
3.2–16 564
3.3 250, 363, 539, 921, 960, 1012, 1076, 1107, 1143, 1146, 1148, 1166, 1187, 1433
3.4–6 86f., 200, 748, 989, 1429
3.4–8 542
3.4–11 987, 1296
3.5 81, 1145, 1223, 1412
3.5f. 82, 84, 929
3.6 84, 1034, 1153, 1155, 1169, 1224
3.7–11 371, 545, 931, 1020, 1169
3.8 986, 988, 1396, 1429
3.8f. 950
3.8–11 832, 1385
3.9 858, 892, 947, 955f., 988f., 996, 1035, 1172, 1294
3.9–11 1023
3.10 11, 383, 987f., 1117
3.11 987
3.12–14 1113
3.12–16 551, 1296
3.14 213, 1026, 1254
3.15 1124
3.15f. 1113
3.17 395, 1104, 1296
3.17–19 548, 1113, 1118, 1296
3.17–21 637
3.18 353, 1295
3.18–21 554, 641, 927, 1292, 1295f., 1372
3.19 1124
3.20 383, 1294
3.20f. 821, 908, 926, 1067, 1083, 1294, 1296, 1313, 1342, 1400
3.21 561
3.24 1024
4.2 1124
4.5 553
4.6 365, 1518
4.7 492, 1097
4.8 236, 381, 448, 639, 1116, 1356
4.9 395, 449, 1104, 1295
4.10 1124
4.10f. 412
4.10–20 1119
4.11 452
4.11–13 1377
4.13 492
4.15 11
4.18 1342
4.20 1160
4.21f. 1027
4.22 379, 1314f.

Colossians
1 189, 415, 535, 561, **670–7**
1.2 443, 701, 1027
1.3–5 412
1.4 1027
1.8 430, 758
1.11 383
1.12 365, 412, 1026f.
1.12–14 367, 674
1.13 481, 1063, 1068
1.13f. 1069
1.15 377, 406, 441, 640
1.15f. 1286, 1362, 1367
1.15–17 475, 547
1.15–20 201, 372, 380f., 649, 672, 1233, 1235, 1308, 1490
1.16–18 1067
1.18–20 1368
1.19 358
1.19f. 879, 908, 1198
1.21 1363
1.22 1111
1.23 411, 1503
1.24 1208
1.24f. 33, 434, 1117
1.24–9 637
1.25 1421
1.26 1027
1.26f. 1233, 1235
1.27 437, 547, 1075
1.28 1121, 1371, 1442
1.29 383, 919, 955, 1107
2 363, 424, **992–5**
2f. 1373
2.1–3 1181
2.2 1233, 1235
2.2f. 201, 1356, 1371
2.3 1257
2.4 1121

2.7 365, 412
2.8 200, 548, 1121
2.8–10 1356
2.8–23 548
2.9 358, 908, 992
2.9f. 675
2.11 148
2.11–13 252, 362, 425, 992, 1103
2.12 424
2.13–15 899, 910
2.13—3.17 1103
2.14f. 476, 523, 879, 892, 992, 1284
2.15 372, 756, 911, 927, 1068, 1281, 1299
2.16–19 993
2.18 250, 414, 492, 1321
2.20–3 993
3.1 10, 441, 693
3.1–4 489
3.1–11 1103, 1118, 1373
3.4 1083
3.4–7 201
3.5 445, 1030, 1107
3.5–11 927
3.6 767
3.9 1030
3.9–11 441
3.10 640, 1108, 1368
3.11 1448
3.12 1027
3.14 1119
3.15 492, 1026, 1097, 1104, 1423
3.15–17 365, 412
3.16 358, 717
3.17 684
3.18f. 875
3.18—4.1 1108, 1375
3.23 492
3.25 1087
4.2 412, 1518
4.2f. 365
4.5 562
4.5f. 1375
4.7–9 14
4.10f. 1230
4.11 481, 733, 1063
4.12 1121
4.16 1255
4.18 353

1 Thessalonians
1.1 701
1.3 412, 1518
1.4f. 918
1.5 383, 411, 953
1.6 395, 413, 1104
1.7 544
1.8–10 376, 436
1.9 1396
1.9f. 331, 490, 637, 918, 1214, 1411
1.10 767, 888, 1251
2 1151–6, 1190f., 1217
2.4 497, 837
2.8 492
2.10 544
2.11–16 638
2.12 481, 1026, 1423
2.13 544, 919, 953, 1518
2.14 395, 436, 1104, 1144, 1152
2.14f. 1429
2.14–16 1152, 1155, 1238f.
2.15 1152
2.16 864, 896, 1081, 1154, 1227, 1237, 1245
2.17—3.10 1351
2.18–19 372
2.19 1084, 1503
3.1–5 436, 1117
3.5 416, 564, 905
3.6 430
3.11–13 706
3.12 1375
3.13 704, 706, 1027, 1084, 1111
4 356, 1107, 1199
4.1–7 357, 1373
4.3 1212
4.3–5 1114
4.3–8 1118
4.4–6 927
4.5 1107, 1435
4.7 1026, 1423
4.9 430
4.9–12 401, 1118
4.11f. 1375
4.14 879
4.15 1084
4.15–17 1234
5 549, 1291, 1303
5.1–11 962, 1102, 1298
5.2 553, 1079, 1291
5.3 1097, 1291
5.4–7 1291
5.4–10 553
5.5 478
5.8 448, 549, 1102, 1127, 1287
5.10 879
5.13 1097
5.14 1107
5.15 380, 1298, 1375
5.17 1518
5.18 412
5.21 1121, 1124
5.23 492, 1084, 1111
5.24 1026
5.27 1027

2 Thessalonians
1.2 701
1.3 412
1.5 481, 1063
1.5–10 553, 1090
1.7 383, 704
1.8 944
1.9 704
1.10 544, 1027
1.11 1026, 1254, 1423
1.12 684, 704
2 1281, 1289–91
2.1 1084
2.1–5 1290
2.1–12 1081
2.2 492, 1079, 1081
2.2–12 553

2 Thessalonians (*continued*)
2.3 1121
2.5–8 550
2.6 117
2.6–12 1238
2.8 1083f.
2.8f. 373
2.10 1121
2.13f. 918
2.14 1026, 1423
3.1 436
3.6 684
3.6–13 1107
3.7 395, 1104
3.9 1104
3.17 353

1 Timothy
1.1 383
1.2 701
1.11 497, 837
1.12 412
1.13 1153, 1168, 1431
1.15 896, 1431
1.17 481, 1063
2.1 365
2.1f. 279
2.2 1312, 1321
2.3 383
2.7 1503
3.1 684
3.16 250, 943, 1321, 1503
4.4 393
4.7 1321
4.8 1321
4.10 383
5.4 1321
5.10 1027
6.3 1321
6.5 1321
6.6 1321
6.11 1321
6.12 1026
6.14 1083
6.15 481, 1063, 1312
6.17–18 380
6.18 1298

2 Timothy
1.2 701
1.3 412
1.5 358
1.7 383
1.9 1026
1.10 383, 1083
1.11 1503
1.14 358
1.18 1080
2.5 1113
2.12 1090
2.19 684
2.22 703
3.5 1321
3.6 994
4.1 481, 1063, 1083
4.2 1503
4.6 358
4.7–8 1113
4.8 213, 1080, 1083
4.9–21 1502
4.14 1087
4.18 481, 1063
4.20 379

Titus
1.1 1321
1.3 383, 497
1.4 383, 701
1.5 1502
2.10 383
2.13 383, 707f., 1083
3.4 383
3.5 1337
3.6 383

Philemon
1 19, 21
3 701
4–5 16, 412
5 443
5–7 19
6 11, 16, 18, 54, 833f.
8 15, 21
8–22 5
9 21
10 19
12 11, 13, 14, 19
13 15, 19, 411
14 13, 15
15 9, 13f., 555, 1191, 1351
16 10, 14, 19
17 10–14, 18
17–20 16, 54
18 9
19 353
20 13, 15, 21
21 12, 13, 15
25 492

Hebrews
1.3 693
1.13 693
2.2 871
2.6–8 1293
2.6–9 1050
3.7—4.11 561
4.15 909
7.26 909
8.1 693
9.11—10.18 1343
9.26–8 1340
10.12 693
10.12–14 1340
10.26 744
10.38 1468
11 1158
12.1f. 1113
12.3–11 979
12.22 1138
13.14 1138

James
1.26f. 249

1 Peter
1.17 1087
1.19 1343
2.4–10 356
2.5 487

2.7 1065
2.8 1179
2.9 487, 1445
2.11f. 203
2.18—3.7 1108
2.22 909
3.13–17 203
4.3–6 203
4.4f. 379
4.15 21
5.4 1083

2 Peter
1.9 1337
3.9 1195
3.13 358, 1093
3.15 1195
3.15f. 14

1 John
2.2 1343
2.28 1083
3.1 1119
3.2 1083
4.7f. 1119
4.7–12 1119
4.10 1343

Revelation
1.6 487
1.18 1318
2.23 1087
2.26 980
3.12 1138
3.21 1090
4.11 314
5.6 1343
5.9f. 165, 1343
5.9–14 651
5.10 487, 1090
5.13 709
6.12 703
6.17 703
8.7 703
12.10 899
13.11–17 321
14.1 703
17.9 1317
17.18 1317
18.4 1274
18.6 1087
18.11–13 1317
19.10 651
20.4 922, 980, 1090
20.6 487
20.12f. 1087
21f. 102, 1138
21.27 967
22.5 1090
22.8f. 651
22.12 1087

9. Christian and/or Gnostic Works

Aquinas
Summa Theologica
1a 774

Aristides
Apology on Behalf of the Christians
2.2 1445
15 1445

Augustine
City of God
6.5 217
6.10 251
6.11 1499

Letters
153.14 220

Retractiones
1.13 247

Clement of Alexandria
Stromata
6.5.41.6 1445

Clement of Rome
1 Clement
5.6 1502

Didache
9f. 1348

Ignatius of Antioch
To the Ephesians
1.3 15
2.1 15
6.2 15

Jerome
De Viris Illustribus
12 220

Justin Martyr
1 Apology
1.4.1 21
1.4.5 21
26 450

Dialogue with Trypho
50 684
56 684
117 1499

Martyrdom of Polycarp
3.2 1445
8.2 1313
9.2 1313
9.3 1274, 1313
10.2 1274
14.1 1445
17.1 1445

Odes of Solomon
11.1–3 923

Origen
De Principiis
3.5.6f. 735

Pseudo-Cyprian
De Pascha Computus
17 1445

Tertullian
Ad Scapulam
2 1272

Tertullian (*continued*)
Apology
3.5 21
21.1 277, 280
30.1 278
30–2 1272
30–3 1286, 1312
33.3 1272

De Anima
20 220

Scorpiace
10 1446

10. Pagan Sources

Aelius Aristides
Panathenaic Oration
26.32 315

Aeschylus
Agamemnon
160 259

Aratus
Phaenomena
100–14 298

Letter of Aristeas
16 624, 630
128–69 1428
132 624
139 93, 94, 379
227 1119

Aristophanes
Birds
301 197

Clouds 233

Frogs
353–71 263

Aristotle
De Anima
A4, 411a7 246

Historia Animalium
584b22 1401

Metaphysics
983.b.29 217

Nicomachean Ethics
7 738, 1379
8 4

Poetics
1449b.22–8 471

Politics
1.12f. 54

Aulus Gellius
Noctes Atticae
15.11.5 223

Calpurnius Siculus
Eclogues
1.42–8 339

Cicero
De Amicitia 4

De Divinatione
2.148 272

De Finibus Bonorum et Malorum 1395
3 214, 1391
3.1.3—2.5 231
3.4.15 231
3.9.31 214
3.12.40 231
3.15.48 215
3.21.69 221
3.21.72 215
4 231

De Haruspicum Responsis
18 252

De Legibus
2 247
2.12 271
2.13.36 263
2.30 272

De Natura Deorum
1.82 318
1.117 253
2 1399
2.8 253
2.9f. 318
2.28.72 247, 249
2.61 270
3.2.5 271
3.5 252

Epistulae ad Atticum
12.45.3 317
13.28.3 317
16.5.3 317

Philippicae
1.34 338
3.3–5 290

Dio Cassius
Historia Romana
52 1288
65.12 203
72.36.4 228

Dio Chrysostom
Oration
12.39–47 217
14 22
16.2 292
31.11 269
43.45.3 317
44.6.4 327
45.7.1 317
47.18f. 318
51.19f. 317
51.19.7 334

51.20.6–9 325
53.16.8 288
53.27.3 317
54.2.5 292
55.10a.2 334
56.30.3 295
57.8.3 336
58.2.8 336
59.28.3–4 332
61.35.3 339
62.14 292
62.14.2 332
63.9.4 292
67.4.7 314

Diodorus Siculus
34.1.2 94

Diogenes Laertius
Lives and Opinions of Eminent Philosophers
1.33 388, 1150
2.24 1376
3.27–9 233
6 230
6.46 230
6.60f. 230
6.69 230
7.23 215
7.40 198
7.88 214
7.89 214
7.89–97 214
7.124 218
7.125f. 214
7.135 217
7.137 214, 216
7.138f. 217
7.147–8 217
7.183 213
8.86–91 209

Dionysius of Halicarnassus
Roman Antiquities
7.72.15–18 268

Epictetus
Discourses
1.3.1–3 225
1.4.13–15 224
1.10.7–8 24
1.10.12f. 224
1.14.6 225
1.14.12–17 226
1.16.7f. 226
1.16.15–21 227
1.16.19 226
1.24.1f. 226
1.24.3–10 227
1.25.13 226
1.29.47 226
1.30.1 226
2.5.22 226
2.6.9 226
2.8.2 225
2.8.11f. 225
2.14.11–13 227
2.18.29 226
2.19.26f. 226
2.23.6 226
3.2.1–15 617
3.3.13 226
3.13.4f. 216
3.13.9 288
3.22 230
3.22.23f. 227
3.22.53f. 230
4.1.33–40 5
4.7.6 227
4.12.11 226

Encheiridion
53.1 218

Epistula ad Diognetum
1.1 1445
5 379

Euripides
Hippolytus
612 897

Galen
De Usu Partium
6.12 1401

Passions of the Soul
2.3 1401

Heraclitus
Epistles
4 101

Hermogenes
On Finding
4.1 1401

Herodotus
Histories
2.53 258

Hesiod
Works and Days
109–26 298

Hippolytus
Refutation of All Heresies
5.8.39 265

Homer
Iliad
1.188–222 197

Odyssey
4.354f. 306

Horace
Carmen Saeculare 272, 296
4.15.4–9 288
5 263
17–24 299

Epistles
2.1.15–17 323
2.1.26 263
2.1.255f. 288
2.1.258f. 288

Horace (*continued*)
Epodes
16 301
16.63–6 301

Odes
1.2.25–44 322
1.2.44–52 322
1.3.9–12 322
1.5.1–4 322
1.6 301
1.12 299
1.12.49–60 322
1.37 298
2.9 298
2.12 298
3.5.1–4 292
3.6.1–8 318
3.14 298
3.26.3–6 322
3.30 301
4.2 298
4.5 298
4.5.33–6 322
4.15 298
4.15.4–32 300

Inscriptions of Cos
391 1083

Justinian
Digesta
38.1–5 5

Juvenal
Satires
8.211–30 292

Livy
History of Rome
Preface, 7 288
1.7.9 288
1.55.1 269
4.19f. 303
4.20.7 318
4.32 303
4.34 303
4.35 303
5 256
5.13.4–8 253
5.23.10 249
5.41.8 288
5.52.1–3 256
7.2.2 253
8.6.9 288
8.9.10 288
22.10.9f. 261

Lucan
Bellum Civile
1.72–82 174
1.367–72 340
2.266–9 174
2.289–92 174
7.135–8 174
7.151–84 174

Lucretius
De Rerum Natura
1.1–49 212
1.565–9 212
1.716–829 212
1.931 249
1.1021–51 234
2.180–1 215
5.8–12 316
5.195–9 215
5.416–508 234
6.92–5 213
6.749–55 197

Macrobius
Saturnalia
1.24 xx

Martial
Epigrams
5.8.1 314
8.2.5f. 314
10.72.3 314

Ovid
Epistulae ex Ponto
1.7.43–6 320
1.7.49–52 320

Fasti
1.589 288
1.607–16 288
1.717f. 296
5 255
5.143–6 319
5.569–78 296
5.575 296
5.579f. 296
5.595 296

Metamorphoses
1.89–112 298, 301
4.55–166 471
7.20f. 1379

Tristia
1.5.77–84 320

Pausanias
Description of Greece
2.2.8—3.1 255

Philostratus
Life of Apollonius of Tyana
33 94

Vitae Sophistarum
481 237

Pindar
Fragments
54 261

Plato
Apology
20e–22e 262
38a 208

Cratylus
400e 259

Phaedo
118a 246

Phaedrus
265b 262
244a–245a 262
273c 259

Protagoras 738

Republic
2 (379a) 217
7 1365

Timaeus
28b 259

Pliny the Elder
Natural History
2.93f. 317
36.101f. 271, 295

Pliny the Younger
Epistulae
3.5 75
3.11 223
4.8 272
6.16 3
6.20 3
9.21 3
9.24 4
10.33f. 203
10.34 1508
10.96 4
10.96.7 202

Plutarch
De Communibus Notitiis
1065b 216
1067a 216

De Tranquillitate Animi
20 101

Life of Alexander
8.2 306
26.2–5 306

Life of Antony
24 319

Life of Gaius Marius
46.1 1150

Life of Pericles
32.1 233

Life of Pompey
24 266

Moralia
96F–97 1440

Themistocles
30 1083

Porphyry
De Antro Nympharum
6 266

Res Gestae Divi Augusti
1.1 316
1.7 288
2.13 288, 296
6 190
19.2 319
31—3 316
34 297

Seneca the Younger
Apocolocyntosis 219, 339

De Beneficiis
4.7f. 269
7.7.3 101
318–28 22

De Clementia
2.1.4 339

De Ira
1.20.4 338
3.36.1–3 218

De Providentia
6.7 224

Epistles
47.11 22
48 220
48.1f. 221
48.10 221
48.11 221
90.29 101
102 222

Moral Epistles
8.8 221
9.16 216
12.11 221
14.17 221
41.1f. 221
41.3 221
73.16 222

Naturales Quaestiones
3.27.1—30.8 216
3.29.1 216
3.29.5 216
3.30.8 216

Suetonius
Augustus
7.2 288
22 288
28 295
52 324
54f. 301
70 317
100.3 336

Caligula
22 337
22.2 338
27.3 337
30 338
50 337
60 292

Claudius
2 323
22 338
25.4 21, 1283
25.5 338

Suetonius (*continued*)
Domitian
13.1f. 314, 341

Gaius
22 332

Julius Caesar
88 317

Nero
10.1 339
21.3 292

Tiberius
26 337
59.1 336

Vespasian
4 170
4.5 293
23 314

Tacitus
Agricola
30.1—32.4 1315
30.3—31.2 1297
30.5 1315
30.6 284, 345

Annals
1.2 288
1.10 336
1.78 1500
2.43 290
4.19–20 303
4.32 303
4.34 303
4.35 303
4.37 337
4.37.3 336
4.38.1f. 336
12.54 337
15.44 379
15.59 223
15.62–4 219
15.71 223

Dialogue on Oratory
13 307

Histories
3.81 223
5.5.2 94
5.13 106, 170, 293

Valerius Maximus
3.2.4 304

Velleius Paterculus
Compendium of Roman History
2.125.1–3 292
2.126.1–4 302
2.126.3 288
36.1 286

Virgil
Aeneid
1.1–7 307
1.33 307
1.68 308
1.205f. 307
1.214–16 288
1.234 308
1.267f. 308
1.270–7 308
1.276–7 285
1.278f. 284, 308
1.282 308
1.286–90 308
1.289 322
1.293 288
2.293 270
2.293–5 308
3.12 308
3.148–50 270
4.229–31 284
4.274–6 308
4.625–9 308
4.630–705 308
6.780–803 309
6.781–4 308
6.781–853 284
6.818–20 309
6.847–53 309
7.607 288
7.609f. 288
8.11 308
8.39 308
8.370–406 310
8.635 310
8.652–62 310
8.671–713 310
8.714–16 288
8.714–22 310
8.731 310
9.642 308, 322
9.642–3 288
10.11–15 308
12.198 288
12.829–42 310
12.839–40 284
12.949 296

Eclogues
4 1043
4.4–17 304
4.5–8 297
4.52 305
9.47–9 317

Georgics
1.24–42 322
2.136–72 296
3.10–39 322
3.16 305
3.26–39 288, 305
4.560–2 305
4.562 322

Vitruvius
10.1.1 1401

INDEX OF MODERN AUTHORS

Aageson, J. W., 1239
Achtemeier, P. J., 617
Ackroyd, P. R., 139
Adams, E., 28, 167–75, 190, 370, 487f., 653, 769, 1007, 1049, 1393
Agamben, G., 42, 179, 552f., 556, 559, 561, 818, 835
Agosto, E., 453
Alcock, S. E., 304, 330, 332
Aletti, J. N., 992, 1162, 1183, 1197
Alexander, P., 146
Algra, K., 216, 218, 222
Allen, L. C., 700
Allison, D. C., 167, 170, 172–5, 178, 481, 531, 547, 1047, 1050, 1082, 1117
Ando, C., 247, 252–4, 256, 267, 269–71, 324
Arendt, H., 1474, 1480, 1511
Arnold, C., 992
Arzt-Grabner, P., 8–10, 21
Ashton, J., 1320f., 1324–7, 1351
Asurmendi, J. M., 153
Athanassiadi, P., 200f., 218, 247, 276
Atkins, R., 12
Audi, R., 206
Aune, D. E., 1061, 1106, 1126, 1351
Aus, R., 1203, 1497
Austin, J. L., 946
Avemarie, F., 937

Bachmann, M., 1130f., 1142, 1144–6, 1148f.
Badenas, R., 1166, 1172
Badiou, A., 42, 73, 1170
Baker, M., 1201
Balzer, K., 682
Barclay, J. M. G., xxii, 4, 8, 10, 12f., 16, 28, 50, 79, 89–95, 108, 149, 177, 180, 195, 200, 239, 344, 354f., 379, 400, 445, 462, 549, 614, 673, 775, 843, 853, 860, 864, 922f., 967, 1075, 1134, 1142, 1144, 1184, 1271, 1273, 1281, 1285, 1290, 1293, 1297, 1307–18, 1386, 1397
Barker, M., 95, 629, 684
Barnett, P. W., 548
Barraclough, R., 1316
Barram, M., 437
Barrett, A. A., 337
Barrett, C. K., 205, 265, 364, 663, 723, 766, 882, 972, 1134, 1166, 1177, 1179, 1206, 1402, 1441
Barth, K., 200, 425, 458, 569, 748, 757, 766, 774, 780, 808, 865, 913, 953, 1198, 1239, 1253, 1320, 1323, 1325, 1388, 1479
Barton, J., 869
Barton, S. C., 743
Bassler, J. M., xx, 768, 806, 938, 1087
Bauckham, R. J., 60, 155f., 355, 534, 619, 624–6, 629f., 633, 637, 647f., 651–4, 663, 665, 670, 673, 677, 680, 683–6, 697, 701f., 704, 730, 1294, 1501
Baur, F. C., 52, 56, 58, 63, 201, 646, 844, 1261, 1357, 1477f.
Beacham, R., 307, 319
Beale, G. K., 101f., 105, 181, 192, 356, 378, 743, 882, 1053, 1145, 1148, 1151
Beard, M., 247f., 265–72, 275f., 288f., 305, 313, 316f., 331, 335, 379
Beckwith, R. T., 123, 125, 127, 145
Beker, J. C., 40, 45, 462f., 568, 617, 1432
Bekken, P. J., 1165f., 1168
Belayche, N., 269

Bell, R. H., 921, 1144, 1156, 1159, 1180, 1198, 1202f., 1206, 1212, 1214, 1218, 1239f., 1244, 1251, 1253, 1412
Benjamin, W., 835, 1473f., 1478–83, 1489, 1511f.
Benko, S., 278
Bentley, M., 1477
Berger, P. L., 24, 25, 351, 463, 466
Bernat, D. A., 1335
Best, E., 1152, 1203
Bett, R., 231
Betz, H.-D., 369, 388, 404, 420, 610, 853, 1116, 1134, 1139, 1144, 1147, 1335, 1412
Bickerman, E. J., 620
Bieringer, R., 676, 1414, 1444
Billerbeck, P., 81, 894
Bird, M. F., 8, 17, 173, 195, 358, 405, 424, 475, 477, 673, 811, 836, 881, 915, 928, 934, 937, 946, 951f., 954, 956, 962, 992, 994, 1002, 1144, 1412, 1418, 1444f., 1487
Black, M., 702, 1499
Blackburn, S., 448, 1116, 1374
Blackwell, B. C., 546, 781, 1021
Blaschke, A., 91, 361
Bloom, J. J., 620
Blumenfeld, B., 1272
Bock, D. L., 140
Bockmuehl, M. N. A., 42, 96, 185, 359, 374, 414, 437, 449, 821, 986, 989f., 1096f., 1099, 1104, 1110, 1120, 1233, 1237, 1294, 1429, 1434, 1490
Boer, R., 72
Bond, H. K., 647
Borg, M. J., 7, 58, 1312
Boring, M. E., 1108, 1116
Bornkamm, G., 747
Botha, P. J. J., 6
Bourdieu, P., 24, 1388, 1406
Bousset, W., 458, 645, 647, 650, 694
Bowers, W. P., 1499
Bowersock, G., 343
Boyarin, D., 42, 648, 692, 695, 731, 922
Boyce, M., 738
Bradshaw, P. F., 427
Brauch, M. T., 796, 800, 841, 997, 1055
Brennan, T., 1396
Brent, A., 312
Briggs, A., 50
Broadie, S., 208
Brolley, J. D., 96
Brooke, G. J., 176
Brown, C., 796
Brown, W. P., 24, 101
Bruce, F. F., 86, 729, 1232
Brunschwig, J., 214f., 218, 234
Bryan, C., 898, 921, 1273
Bryan, S. M., 151, 160–2
Buell, D. K., 1445
Bultmann, R., 55, 67, 71, 141, 165, 167f., 222, 386, 405, 443, 457–60, 510, 613, 624, 645, 647, 649, 747, 748, 778f., 844, 882, 896, 991, 1016, 1098, 1290, 1389, 1400, 1467, 1469, 1477f., 1482
Burke, T. J., 950
Burkert, W., 247f., 257, 259f., 262–4
Burnett, A., 317
Burney, C. F., 673, 675
Burridge, R. A., 1098f., 1104f., 1120
Burton, E. de W., 764, 1144
Byrne, B., 440, 894, 921, 941
Byron, J., 12

Cadwallader, A. H., 35
Caird, G. B., 168–70, 457, 722, 756, 945, 985, 988, 991, 1515
Calduch-Benages, N., 117
Callahan, A. D., 8
Calvin, J., 774, 935, 950, 1239, 1445
Campbell, D. A., 31, 39f., 57, 568, 739, 748, 751, 757f., 765–7, 912, 967, 1011, 1031, 1039, 1085, 1120, 1467, 1470, 1513
Campbell, W. S., 808, 813, 985, 1129, 1236, 1412, 1427, 1429–32
Cancik, H., 268
Capes, D. B., 647, 670, 702, 704
Carleton Paget, J., 195
Carroll, R. P., 139f., 161
Carson, D. A., 139, 142, 160, 188, 802, 914, 929, 935, 1002
Casey, M. P., 140, 647f.
Cassidy, R. J., 1302
Cassirer, E., 1328
Cassuto, U., 785
Catchpole, D., 963
Chadwick, H., 1435, 1437, 1442

Champlin, E., 29, 254, 262, 292
Chapman, D. W., 407
Charlesworth, J. H., 81, 94, 123, 262, 622f. 817, 1119, 1154
Chesnutt, R. D., 101
Chester, A., 160, 817–20
Chester, S. J., 442, 1418f.
Childs, B. S., 682
Chilton, B. D., 904, 1239
Choksy, J. K., 738
Churchill, T. W. R., 649
Ciampa, R. E., 416, 905, 1165, 1171, 1423
Clark, A. J., 270, 290
Clements, R. E., 97, 630
Cohen, S. J. D., 63, 388, 1144
Cohick, L. H., 687
Coleiro, E., 304
Collins, A. Y., 327f., 694, 818, 977, 1294
Collins, C., 854
Collins, J. J., 123, 156, 171, 818, 964, 1043, 1044, 1090
Collins, K. J., 936
Collins, R. F., 682, 694, 977
Confino, A., 1477
Conniry, C. J., 1418
Conzelmann, H., 62, 552, 1402
Cook, M., 984
Corley, J., 107, 122
Cosgrove, C. H., 1236, 1242
Countryman, L. W., 446
Cousar, C. B., 8, 16, 984
Cowan, J. A., 63, 131
Cranfield, C. E. B., 506, 510, 700, 702, 704, 837f., 901, 943, 1016, 1025, 1032, 1060, 1086, 1198, 1203, 1218, 1228, 1238, 1243, 1499
Crofton, R. E., xxv
Crook, J. A., 323
Crossan, J. D., 7, 58, 312, 337, 466, 1273, 1312, 1502
Crouzel, H., 1400
Cullmann, O., 41, 458, 462, 468, 548, 553, 644, 780, 1312
Cummins, S. A., 405
Cupitt, D., 466, 474

Dahl, N. A., 37, 402, 624f., 817, 826, 1163, 1232, 1247
Danby, H., 90, 186, 870
Danker, F. W., 330
Das, A. A., 1213
Davies, G. I., 106
Davies, J. P., xxiii, 206, 994, 1492
Davies, P. R., 89, 904
Davies, W. D., 41, 89, 106, 646, 894, 1005, 1145, 1152, 1166, 1214, 1218, 1240, 1250
Davis, C. J., 704
Dawkins, R., 1321
de Boer, M. C., 40f., 58, 361, 366, 484, 781, 853, 857, 862, 866, 871, 874, 877, 919, 954, 970–2, 974, 1059, 1131, 1134, 1144, 1147, 1149
de Vos, C. S., 5
DeConick, A. D., 647
Deines, R., 80f., 83, 139, 184, 188
Deissmann, A., 312, 1276, 1322
Derrett, J. D. M., 15
di Lella, A. A., 121
Dickson, J. P., 1418
Dillon, J. T., 223
DiMattei, S., 1450
Dodd, B. J., 680, 1104
Dodd, C. H., 54, 60, 495, 499, 510, 766f., 836, 893, 1157, 1173, 1223, 1272, 1381, 1458
Donaldson, T. L., 86, 195, 537, 1053, 1058f., 1218, 1239, 1242, 1249f.
Donfried, K. P., 1152
Douthat, R., 142
Downing, F. G., 146, 230, 233
Downs, D. J., 58
Duff, T., 211
Dunn, J. D. G., 37, 42, 58, 140, 184f., 361, 385, 418, 424, 444, 460, 474f., 487, 495, 498, 510, 534, 626, 647–9, 663f., 686, 688, 704, 707, 825, 834, 836f., 847, 854, 869, 885, 893f., 919, 923, 925, 928, 930, 967, 972, 975, 985, 987–90, 992, 994, 1005, 1016, 1032, 1046, 1060, 1079, 1084, 1094, 1097–9, 1109, 1116, 1139, 1144, 1165, 1188, 1218, 1223, 1228, 1243, 1250, 1253, 1255, 1420, 1427, 1429, 1434, 1452
Dunne, J. A., 967

Eastman, S. G., 967, 1104, 1135–7, 1142, 1144, 1148, 1150, 1184, 1244
Eco, U., 462
Egger-Wenzel, R., 122

Ehrenberg, V., 328
Eisenbaum, P., 59, 541, 564, 611, 937, 1129
Elat, M., 1500
Elliott, J. H., 809
Elliott, J. K., 220, 1166, 1313
Elliott, N., 1273, 1312, 1314
Ellis, E. E., 1450
Elsner, J., 315
Engberg-Pedersen, T., 24, 37, 44, 64, 66, 168, 219, 227, 234, 385f., 404, 459, 1360, 1376f., 1384–6, 1386–1406
Eshel, H., 620
Eskola, T., 649
Esler, P. F., 442, 764, 809, 1131, 1213, 1223
Evans, C. A., 78, 139, 151, 153, 156, 158f., 161, 421

Fantin, J. D., 1271, 1276, 1283, 1293, 1302, 1304
Fatehi, M., 1166
Fee, G. D., xxi, 550, 638, 649, 663, 699, 710, 712f., 715f., 821, 901, 917, 935, 989, 1023, 1152f., 1202
Feeney, D., 271, 298, 301f., 310
Feldman, L. H., 129, 131
Fine, S., 96
Fishbane, M., 143, 150, 152, 176, 787
Fishwick, D., 333
Fisk, B. N., 126, 136, 1450
Fitzmyer, J. A., 8, 13, 15, 21, 395, 405, 518, 552, 663, 665, 700, 704, 735, 753, 764, 894, 904, 923f., 956, 977f., 1114, 1177, 1188, 1212, 1240, 1251, 1442, 1447, 1455, 1507
Fletcher-Louis, C. H. T., 106, 686
Flint, P. W., 139
Flusser, D., 81, 96
Forbes, C., 453
Ford, D. F., 625
Fossum, J., 674
Fowden, G., 738
Fowl, S. E., 988, 991, 1104, 1121, 1124
France, R. T., 167
Frede, M., 200f., 218, 247, 276
Fredriksen, P., 94, 619, 626, 1418, 1428, 1432, 1440, 1449
Frerichs, E., 135, 143
Fretheim, T. E., 629
Frey, J., 1409, 1423, 1499, 1501, 1502
Friedenreich, D. M., 93
Friedman, S., 1416
Friesen, S. J., 58, 312, 315, 325, 327–9, 331f., 334, 337–9, 341f.
Fuchs, E., 141
Fuller, M. E., 95, 151, 154, 158f., 162, 1514
Funk, R. W., 453
Furnish, V. P., 27, 503, 676, 688, 713, 834, 882f., 1097f., 1119

Gager, J. G., 401, 1129, 1136, 1427
Galinsky, K., xx, 248, 255, 268, 270, 288, 290, 295–9, 301, 303f., 307, 314, 316–23, 328, 331, 334
García Martínez, F., 96, 147–9
Garnet, P., 151
Gärtner, B., 96
Gasparro, G. S., 263
Gaston, L., 401, 1129, 1161, 1236, 1239, 1424, 1427
Gathercole, S. J., 166, 184, 549, 674, 775, 843, 927, 930, 1003, 1037, 1381
Gaventa, B. R., 257, 356, 399, 1154, 1187
Gazda, E. K., 328
Geertz, C., 24–6, 28, 59, 351, 418, 442f., 450, 456f., 463, 466, 1392
Getty, M. A., 1162, 1185
Giblin, C. H., 1239
Gibson, R. J., 1506
Gignilliat, M., 879, 883, 905
Gilbert, M., 126, 136
Gill, C., 614, 617
Gilliard, F., 1152
Ginzberg, L., 131, 904
Glombitza, O., 1239
Golding, W., 278
Goldingay, J., 682
Goldstein, J. A., 123, 146, 155, 159
Gooch, P. W., 209
Goodenough, E. R., 180, 1316
Gooder, P. R., 414, 1400
Goodman, M., 195
Gordon, R., 266, 273, 320, 322, 338, 341f.
Gorman, M. J., 19–21, 59, 377, 394, 402, 437, 517, 546, 650, 781, 857f., 881, 914, 946, 956–8, 963, 986, 1012, 1023, 1031, 1097, 1104
Gosling, J. C. B., 738
Gowan, D. E., 151, 154, 156, 158
Grabbe, L. L., 78, 145, 159

Gradel, I., 247, 268, 270, 273–5, 313, 316, 323, 327
Grant, R. M., 448
Green, W. S., 135, 143
Greenblatt, S., 212, 738
Greimas, A. J., 110, 487
Grieb, A. K., 73, 798, 881, 883, 1158, 1162, 1256
Griffith-Jones, R., 1121, 1305
Griffiths, P. J., 247, 1320
Grosby, S. E., 94
Gundry, R. H., 510, 881, 951
Gunneweg, A., 1320, 1323
Günther, R., 298
Gurtner, D. M., 132

Haacker, K., 86, 1219, 1223
Haenchen, E., 1305
Hafemann, S. J., 379, 724, 879, 883, 983, 1188
Hahn, S. W., 781, 851
Halpern-Amaru, B., 126
Hanson, A. T., 767, 836, 839
Haran, M., 95, 103
Hardin, J. K., 312, 325, 328, 336, 338f., 853, 1142, 1305, 1428
Harink, D. K., 41, 808, 810, 813, 926, 985, 1159, 1161, 1189, 1236, 1412, 1479
Harlow, D. C., 964
Harmon, M. S., 1137
Harrill, J. A., 8, 16, 1271
Harrington, D. J., 127, 131, 1115
Harris, M. J., 13, 18, 834
Harrison, J. R., 106, 284, 306, 312, 330, 339, 433, 488, 550, 1271, 1291f., 1300
Hartley, L. P., 1477
Harvey, A. E., 146
Hatina, T. R., 167
Hay, D. M., xx
Hays, R. B., xxv, 14f., 42, 110, 131, 361, 369, 405, 413, 416f., 421, 442, 447, 458, 462, 467, 478, 487, 501f., 505, 526, 537, 539–41, 552, 635f., 663, 669f., 735, 836, 842, 849, 859, 865–7, 870f., 874, 881, 902f., 906, 908, 919, 943, 950, 967, 969, 974f., 977, 979, 981, 995, 1045, 1096f., 1099, 1104, 1109, 1119f., 1129f., 1134f., 1137–9, 1142, 1144, 1150, 1167f., 1171, 1187, 1198, 1250, 1264, 1345, 1429, 1436, 1441f., 1451, 1455, 1459, 1469f., 1490
Hayward, C. T. R., 106, 560
Hayward, R., 792
Headlam, A. C., 1166
Hegel, G. W. F., 197f., 269
Hellerman, J. H., 534
Hengel, M., 58, 62, 76, 84–6, 136, 195, 205, 415, 645, 1170, 1479
Henze, M., 132
Héring, J., 552
Herman, G., 4f.
Hester, J. D., 1005
Hezser, C., 81
Hickling, C. J., 382
Hiebert, P. G., 24
Hiers, R. H., 1050
Hill, C. C., 1215, 1229
Hock, R. F., 386, 453
Hoehner, H. W., 419, 1499
Hoff, M. C., 330
Hofius, O., 1221, 1240
Holland, P., 471
Holowchak, M. A., 212
Honderich, T., 206
Hood, J. B., 1104
Hooke, S. H., 827
Hooker, M. D., xix, 19, 458, 467f., 610, 683, 769, 794, 821, 881f., 988–90, 992, 1104
Hopkins, K., 1309
Horbury, W., 120f., 135, 627, 649, 651, 692, 695, 746
Horrell, D. G., 19, 28, 42, 73, 312, 359, 367, 380, 387f., 390, 393, 397, 399, 401, 403, 405f., 417f., 428, 442–9, 457, 468, 562, 567, 613, 617, 639
Horsley, R. A., 57, 175, 312, 1273, 1312, 1314, 1442
Howard, G., 925
Hübner, H., 85f.
Huby, J., 835
Hultgren, A. J., 708, 748, 1088, 1160, 1168
Humphrey, E. M., 183, 622
Hurtado, L. W., 354, 619, 624, 626f., 647–50, 691, 694, 697, 1104
Husbands, M., 914
Huttunen, N., 1406

Instone-Brewer, D., 81, 84, 96, 176f., 387

Jacobson, J., 126
Jenkins, D. E., 445

Jeremias, J., 86, 1232, 1239f.
Jewett, R., 379, 492, 506, 510, 523, 697, 700, 704, 707, 716, 753, 762, 764, 768f., 820, 838, 841, 843–5, 849, 894, 896, 898, 901, 905f., 924, 948, 952, 996f., 1001f., 1005, 1010, 1016f., 1025, 1034, 1123, 1142, 1154, 1158, 1161f., 1165, 1168, 1172, 1184, 1187, 1189, 1193, 1197–9, 1214f., 1217–20, 1223, 1227f., 1231f., 1236–40, 1243, 1251–6, 1273, 1278, 1304, 1339, 1381, 1479, 1496–9, 1507
Johnson, A., 1105
Johnson, A. R., 827
Johnson, E. E., xx, 1184
Johnson, L. T., 58f., 415
Johnson, M. V., 12
Johnson, S., 1154
Johnson Hodge, C. E., 401, 1427, 1448
Jonas, H., 738
Jones, A., 216
Jones, A. H. M., 328
Jones, C. P., 211
Judge, E. A., 28f., 195, 203, 237, 249f., 290, 316, 418, 433, 544, 1331

Kahl, B., 329, 1273, 1305, 1314
Kaiser, O., 129
Kaminsky J. S., 91, 97, 769, 806, 811, 935, 1001, 1190
Kammler, H.-C., 707
Kampen, J. L., 89
Kärkkäinen, V.-M., 710
Käsemann, E., 41, 49, 54f., 82, 401, 410, 434, 460, 468, 480f., 552, 610, 674, 704, 780f., 783, 795, 802, 807f., 841, 844, 848, 882, 894f., 901, 922f., 946, 948, 990, 996, 1055, 1085, 1088, 1104, 1131, 1186, 1219, 1243, 1312, 1409, 1452, 1467, 1469, 1481–3, 1499, 1512
Kautzsch, E., 798
Keck, L. E., 612, 751, 893, 901, 924, 1160, 1162, 1167, 1172, 1179, 1181, 1186–9, 1191, 1197, 1201, 1209, 1214, 1228, 1239, 1241, 1244, 1251
Kee, H. C., 40, 1119, 1154
Keenan, J. F., 1115
Keener, C. S., 63, 78, 841, 879, 881, 883–5, 1377, 1440
Keesmaat, S. C., 635, 656, 718, 720, 876, 1023, 1308, 1356
Kenny, A., 60, 206
Kiley, M., 58
Kim, S., 86, 195, 649, 882, 1104, 1273, 1314, 1420, 1497, 1503
Kimelman, R., 177
King, K. L., 458, 628
Kipling, R., 26, 454, 538
Kirk, G. S., 208
Kirk, J. R. D., 409, 818, 901
Klassen, W., 1119
Klauck, H.-J., 252, 304, 312, 315, 318, 331, 337f., 341, 343
Klausner, J., 1413
Kleiner, D. E. E., 315
Kloppenborg, J. S., 429
Knibb, M. A., 151, 155
Knox, J., 8
Koch, D. A., 415
Koch, K., 61, 168
Koenig, J., 427
Koester, H., 50, 205, 266, 458
Kraemer, R. S., 622
Kramer, W. G., 817, 824, 832
Kreitzer, L. J., 279, 644, 737, 1046
Kruse, C. G., 918
Kugler, R. A., 143
Kumitz, C., 5, 7, 18
Kümmel, W. G., 510, 896, 1016
Küng, H., 913
Kwon, Y.-G., 974

Lacocque, A., 192
Ladd, G. E., 1047
Lampe, P., 8, 195
Lane, A. N. S., 956
Lang, B., xxi
Lawrence, J. D., 420
Leary, T. J., xxii
Lee, A. H. I., 649
Lee, M. V., 1333, 1384f.
Lenowitz, H., 115
Leon, H. J., 195
Levenson, J. D., 636, 643, 688, 697, 785f., 788f., 809, 889, 903, 905, 1170, 1415, 1485
Levin, B., 680
Levine, A.-J., 93
Levison, J. R., 710, 759, 792
Lewis, C. S., xv, 15f., 141, 466, 649, 777, 1389
Lichtenberger, H., 123f.
Liesen, J., 117

Lietzmann, D. H., 901, 1085, 1109
Lieu, S., 738
Lightfoot, J. B., 21, 220, 694, 1515
Lightstone, J., 91, 96
Lim, T. H., 126
Lincicum, D., 126, 663, 768, 1165, 1171
Lincoln, A. T., 56, 419, 495
Lindemann, A., 663, 1447
Lintott, A. W., 1508
Litwa, M. D., 781
Lizza, R., 1131
Llewelyn, S. R., 8–10, 1271, 1291f.
Loewe, R., 837, 1045
Logan, A. H. B., 458
Lohse, E., 7, 21
Long, A. A., 215f., 216, 231f.
Longenecker, B. W., 386, 456, 466, 468, 474f., 508, 524, 779, 928, 948, 1055, 1166, 1412, 1510
Longenecker, R. N., 649, 948, 967, 972, 1119, 1135, 1138f., 1144
Löwy, M., 1473, 1481
Lucas, J. R., 230
Luckman, T., 24f., 351, 463, 466
Lundquist, J. M., 97
Luther, M., 67, 69, 141f., 514, 569, 745, 747, 765, 774, 915, 1129, 1169, 1240, 1340, 1414, 1419, 1445, 1457, 1466f.
Lutz, C. E., 222
Lyons, S., 300, 322

Macaskill, G., 674
McClendon, J. W., 1418
Maccoby, H., 84, 645
McConville, J. G., 161
McCormack, B. L., 914, 925f., 935, 946, 950, 952
MacDonald, N., 619
McDonough, S. M., 370
McGilchrist, I., 1450
McGowan, A. T. B., 951f.
McGrath, A. E., 913
McGrath, J. F., 619, 649, 663
McKnight, S., 195, 811
McLaren, J. S., 324, 344
McNamara, M., 1453
MacRae, G., 820
Madeline, L., 54
Magda, K., 1502–4, 1507
Maier, H. O., 340, 1376
Malherbe, A. J., 19, 26, 56, 200, 434, 550, 613, 1099, 1152–4, 1156, 1359
Malina, B. J., xviii, 28, 401
Manson, T. W., 838
Marchal, J. A., 73, 1273, 1282, 1309
Marcus, J., 894, 922
Marsden, G. M., 1130
Marshall, I. H., 13, 428, 463, 475, 843, 1487
Martin, D. B., 44, 76, 647, 723, 1384, 1397
Martin, R. P., 680, 686, 1239, 1487
Martyn, J. L., 14, 26, 40f., 58, 141, 401, 405, 460, 484, 528, 542, 550, 552, 562, 748, 757, 766, 781, 783, 808, 851, 870f., 876, 878, 911, 924, 926, 954, 967, 972, 974, 985, 1069, 1130f., 1139, 1144, 1147, 1309–11, 1320, 1325, 1356, 1409, 1481
Marx, K., 181, 198, 737, 775, 1473, 1478f., 1484f., 1487
Mason, A., 1130
Mason, S., 63, 76, 82, 86, 117, 129, 131, 369, 775
Matera, F. J., 474
Matlock, R. B., 54, 553
May, A. S., 446
Meadors, E. P., 378
Meeks, W. A., xxi, 12, 25, 26, 37, 42, 44, 58, 76, 94, 238, 353, 355, 359, 374, 386f., 392f., 400–2, 405f., 414, 417f., 442, 474, 540, 565, 612, 625f., 647, 724, 776, 817, 1096, 1099, 1100, 1121, 1136, 1153, 1357, 1516
Meggitt, J. J., 294, 307, 312, 330, 334, 386
Meilander, G., 1110, 1116
Mellor, R., 289
Mendels, D., 78, 85, 94, 195, 450
Metzger, B. M., 11, 18, 156, 707, 985, 1252, 1436
Meyer, B. F., xviii
Meyer, M. W., 249, 263, 265
Meyer, P. W., 509
Middleton, R. J., 27f., 351, 843, 1356
Mikalson, J. D., 247
Mildenberg, L., 104
Millar, F., 294, 321
Miller, C., 1273, 1275
Minear, P. S., 397
Mitchell, M. M., 391, 426, 1440, 1443, 1447
Mitchell, S., 269, 276, 328, 333, 339, 342, 808

Moberly, R. W. L., 619, 630, 786
Moessner, D., 151
Montefiore, C. G., 1045
Moo, D. J., 8, 13, 17, 56, 841, 843, 898, 901, 921f., 928, 992, 994, 1001, 1058, 1187, 1239, 1243, 1255, 1432, 1507
Moore, G. F., 1059
Morales, R. J., 861
Morgan, G., 223, 293
Morgan, R., 59f., 141, 1104
Morray-Jones, C. R. A., 414
Most, G. W., 204, 217, 222, 235
Motyer, J. A., 558
Moule, C. F. D., 15, 17, 644, 649f., 825, 834, 979
Moulton, J. H., 994, 1401
Moyise, S., 613, 1166
Müller, P., 8
Müller, R., 298
Munck, J., 117, 195, 416, 1203, 1497
Murphy, F. J., 126, 156, 762
Murphy-O'Connor, J., 61, 352, 393, 453, 665, 686
Murray, O., 91
Mussner, F., 1144, 1245

Nanos, M. D., xxi, 359, 397, 541–3, 1130, 1134, 1144, 1186, 1212, 1214f., 1217–9, 1305, 1409, 1412, 1428, 1430, 1437, 1438, 1439–43, 1445
Naugle, D. K., 24
Naylor, J., 312, 314, 343
Neill, S. C., 779, 783
Neiman, S., 738
Neumann, K. J., 60
Neusner, J., 80, 94, 102, 135f., 143, 794
Newman, C. C., 105, 142, 650, 679, 691
Newton, M., 1108, 1260
Neyrey, J. H., xviii, 28, 370, 401, 418
Ng, D. Y., 328
Nickelsburg, G. W. E., 127, 139, 156
Nicklas, T., 8, 16
Niebuhr, K.-W., 86, 193, 1239, 1243, 1427
Nock, A. D., 238, 1418
Noel, J. A., 12
Nordling, J. G., 8, 10, 13, 18
North, J. A., 200, 247f., 265–72, 275f., 289, 313, 316f., 331, 335, 649
Norton, J. D. H., 176
Novenson, M., 183, 288, 369, 817, 824f., 855, 1413
Nowell, I., 154

Oakes, P., 26, 296, 329–31, 390, 435, 534, 687, 1293f.
O'Brien, P. T., 11, 914, 927–9, 937, 949, 954f., 985f., 988–91
O'Donovan, O. M. T., 456, 475, 482, 1099
Ogg, G., 1445
Ogilvie, R. M., 311, 332
O'Neill, J. C., 648, 695
Onesti, K. L., 796, 800
Ortlund, D. C., 1169
O'Siadhail, M., xxv, 348, 570, 606, 1266, 1269
Osiek, C., 8
Oss, D. A., 1179
Padwick, C. E., 411
Passaro, A., 118
Pawlikowski, J. T., 1413, 1430
Payne, D., 682
Peace, R. V., 1419
Pearson, B. A., 1152
Peirce, C. S., xviii
Pennington, J. T., 370
Perkins, P., 1136
Perriman, A., 762, 768, 1081
Perrin, N., 356, 1490
Pervo, R. I., 62,
Petersen, D. L., 706
Petersen, N. R., 7, 48, 463, 466, 921
Phua, R. L.-S., 377
Pickett, R., 406
Piper, J., 914, 957, 1031
Pitre, B., 173
Platt, V., 237
Pleket, H. W., 331, 335
Poirier, J. C., 497
Polaski, S. H., 6
Pollefeyt, D., 1414, 1444
Ponsot, J., 1239
Porter, A. L., 95
Porter, J. R., 827
Porter, S. E., 78, 1450f., 1484, 1487
Portier-Young, A. E., 139, 175, 346, 915, 1290
Powell, M. A., 456
Price, S. R. F., 91, 218, 247–9, 252, 265–72, 275f., 289, 312f., 315–17, 321, 323–7, 329, 331f., 334f.
Prior M., 61
Puerto, M. N., 121
Punt, J., 6

Quinn, J. D., 956
Quinton, A., 982

Rabens, V., 1100, 1384

Rainbow, P. A., 626
Räisänen, H., 509, 748, 755, 764, 1032, 1326, 1387
Ramsay, W. M., 1272
Rankin, D., 448
Rapske, B. M., 5, 8
Raven, J. E., 208
Rawlinson, A. E. J., 826
Reasoner, M., 397
Reid, D. G., 756
Reif, S. C., 82, 136
Reinbold, W., 1244
Reinmuth, E., 8
Reiser, M., 164
Renwick, D. A., 98, 101, 355, 1023
Reumann, J., 437, 449, 956, 989
Revell, L., 290, 314, 333
Richards, E. R., 453
Richardson, G. P., 1144f.
Richardson, J. S., 199, 281, 285, 288–90, 294, 296, 304f., 318, 321, 323
Richardson, N., 723
Richardson, P., 324
Ricks, C., 465
Ridderbos, H. N., 554, 1032, 1046, 1081, 1085, 1093f., 1096, 1098, 1109, 1111, 1118, 1144, 1232
Riesenfeld, H., 17
Riesner, R., 121, 195
Ripley, J. J., 903f.
Rives, J. B., 247, 251, 253, 255, 260, 265f., 269, 273–8, 313, 321, 338
Roberts, J. J. M., 99, 100f., 103
Robertson, A., 1202, 1402
Robinson, J. A., 419
Robinson, J. A. T., 60, 828, 892
Röcker, F. W., 550
Roetzel, C. J., 617, 775, 1419
Rogerson, J. W., 827
Rosner, B. S., 980, 1099, 1109, 1501
Ross, G. M., 1384
Rowe, C. K., 22, 63, 73, 312, 314, 353, 375, 406, 442, 566, 666, 703, 1066, 1164, 1175, 1243, 1371
Rowland, C. C., 414
Rowley, H. H., 806
Rudolph, D. J., 1412, 1428–30, 1432, 1434–8, 1442–5
Rüpke, J., 217, 247f., 252, 255, 268f., 271, 274, 276, 279, 312, 315f., 614
Russell, D. A., 211
Rüterswörden, U., 722, 890
Ryan, J. M., 8, 834

Sacks, J., 665, 742
Sadler, R. S., 1501
Sailhamer, J. H., 143
Salles, R., 216
Sampley, J. P., 453, 979
Sanday, W., 1166
Sanders, E. P., xx, 39–41, 57, 80f., 87, 93, 97, 114, 140f., 163, 185, 188, 193, 201, 312, 353f., 413, 415, 460, 509, 565, 617, 739, 747f., 750f., 755, 757, 766, 777, 779, 781, 823, 825, 852, 912, 927, 988, 1032, 1059f., 1085, 1088, 1108, 1144f., 1153, 1176, 1236, 1245, 1250f., 1257, 1321–4, 1327–30, 1335, 1340, 1359, 1387, 1404, 1409, 1430, 1444, 1446, 1450, 1458, 1460, 1497–9, 1513
Sandmel, S., 78, 750, 1413
Sandnes, K. O., 1435
Sänger, D., 1152
Schäfer, P., 104f., 620
Schechter, S., 179, 1045, 1063
Scheid, J., 249, 273, 308, 314, 318, 321, 336
Schmidt, R., 139
Schmidt, T., 826
Schnabel, E. J., 81, 321, 338, 1305, 1435, 1484, 1497, 1500, 1504
Schnelle, U., xix, 45, 385, 415, 419f., 492, 506, 626, 818, 925, 932, 944, 962, 1032, 1046, 1069, 1094, 1097, 1099, 1102, 1110, 1116f., 1121, 1123, 1144, 1157, 1172, 1238, 1359
Schoeps, H.-J., 193, 645, 1059, 1413
Schofield, M., 208, 214, 617
Scholem, G., 179
Schrage, W., 1148
Schreiner, T. R., 385, 492, 626, 779, 836, 840, 853, 859, 862, 865, 872, 874, 881, 896, 901, 913, 917, 927f., 943, 946, 952, 958, 962, 966, 968, 974, 991, 1001, 1032, 1045f., 1084, 1088, 1092, 1096, 1109, 1111, 1138f., 1142, 1144, 1166, 1238, 1240, 1244, 1255
Schrenk, G., 796

Schürer, E., 132, 135, 1059
Schwartz, D. B., 203
Schwartz, D. R., 80, 92, 775
Schweitzer, A., 31, 37–9, 55, 57, 165–8, 420, 434, 459f., 467, 779, 825, 875, 912, 950, 962, 1039, 1058, 1263, 1324f., 1404, 1513
Scott, J. C., 915, 1277, 1314
Scott, J. M., 131, 139, 144f., 149, 159, 179, 1501
Scott, K., 343
Scroggs, R., 27, 792
Searle, J. R., 946
Sechrest, L. L., 1427, 1429, 1432, 1437, 1445–8
Sedley, D. N., 57, 199, 214–16, 218, 234
Seebass, H., 796
Seesengood, R. P., 73, 445
Segal, A. F., 81, 86, 183, 613, 627, 685, 904, 1418, 1423–5
Seifrid, M. A., 124, 142, 153, 155, 157–60, 798, 914, 928f., 957, 988f., 1002f., 1169, 1227, 1244, 1252
Seitz, C. R., 762, 1249
Sevenster, J. N., 94, 220
Shaffer, P., 109, 1378
Shaw, G., 6
Sherk, R. K., 326f.
Sherwin-White, A. N., 280
Sievers, J., 1221
Silberman, N. A., 1273
Sire, J. W., 24
Skarsaune, O., 76, 78, 96, 407, 700
Skinner, J., 798
Slater, W. J., 395
Smallwood, E. M., 280, 339
Smith, C., 24
Smith, C. B., 1482
Smith, D. E., 427
Smith, J. K. A., 24, 28, 447
Smith, M., 193
Smith, R. L., 706
Smith, R. R. R., 340
Snodgrass, K. R., 936
Soards, M., 1055
Söding, T., 524
Soskice, J. M., 25
Sprinkle, P. M., 836
Stanley C. D., 14, 415, 613, 1273, 1450–2
Stanton, G. N., 326f., 1144, 1442
Stark, R., 449, 1278, 1413
Starling, D. I., 1053, 1172, 1185, 1238
Steck, O. H., 126, 139, 142, 151, 153, 156f., 162, 1165
Stein, R., 140
Steiner, G., 209, 1475
Stendahl, K., 468, 708, 780, 1129, 1145, 1160, 1162, 1196, 1236, 1245f., 1312, 1418–21, 1423
Stern, M., 195, 1217
Stettler, C., 673
Stevenson, G. S., 1508
Stewart, E. C., 28
Still, T. D., 17
Stone, M. E., 877
Stowers, S. K., 202, 222, 238, 453, 838, 841, 1167, 1186, 1206, 1209, 1323, 1331
Strack, H. L., 81, 894
Strobel, A., 1471
Stroup, G. W., 456
Stuckenbruck, L. T., 143, 649
Stuhlmacher, P., 764, 833, 882, 1250, 1487
Suggs, M. J., 1167
Sumney, J. L., 992
Swartley, W. M., 1097
Syme, R., 248, 289, 294, 634, 1388f.

Talmon, S., 151
Taubes, J., 42, 73
Taylor, C., 24, 28, 351, 1392
Taylor, J. E., 32, 874
Terrien, S., 97
Theissen, G., 1326–30, 1335, 1418
Thielman, F., 139, 158, 748, 1032
Thiessen, M., 82, 91–3, 195, 769, 775, 1335
Thiselton, A. C., 66, 251, 369, 377f., 391, 394f., 425, 428, 446, 457, 459, 552, 554, 664f., 712, 723, 735, 945f., 977, 979, 1098, 1114, 1144, 1212, 1349, 1402, 1428, 1436, 1442, 1447
Thompson, J. W., 1098f., 1107, 1115f., 1118f., 1128, 1374
Thompson, M. B., 1105
Thornton, T. C. G., 1499
Thorsteinsson, R. M., 22, 1384
Thrall, M. E., 369, 676, 688, 713, 834, 980, 1021
Tigchelaar, E. J. C., 96, 147–9, 1469
Tilling, C., 17, 651, 1025
Tobin, T. H., 153, 1162, 1166f., 1181, 1188

Tomson, P. J., 42, 359, 1099, 1429f., 1434–6, 1443
Towner, P. H., 415, 1108
Trainor, M., 35
Trebilco, P. R., 50, 149
Trier, D. J., 914
Truex, J., 619
Tuckett, C. M., 613, 1099
Turcan, R., 247, 251, 266f.
Turner, N., 994, 1401

van der Horst, P. W., 1240
van Driel, E. C., 1210
van Nuffelen, P., 276
van Unnik, W. C., 149, 193
VanderKam, J. C., 146, 151, 155f.
Vanhoozer, K., 38, 458, 914, 928, 935, 945f., 950
VanLandingham, C., 164
Vermes, G., 96, 147f., 185, 189, 647f., 794
Vermeylen, J., 119
Vernezze, P. T., 212
Vielhauer, P., 63
von Rad, G., 143

Waaler, E., 663, 668
Wacholder, B. Z., 145
Waelkins, M., 328
Wagner, G., 420
Wagner, J. R., 73, 415f., 702, 820, 1162, 1165, 1168, 1179, 1208f., 1217, 1223, 1236, 1239, 1242–4, 1246f., 1249, 1251, 1335, 1450
Walker, L. L., 1501
Wall, R. W., 14, 19, 834
Wallace-Hadrill, A., 253, 258, 289, 294, 297, 318, 331
Wallis, I. G., 842
Walsh, B. J., 27f., 351, 1308, 1356
Walton, J. H., 101f., 119, 192, 498, 560
Ward, M., 469, 1453
Ware, J. P., 195, 437
Waterfield, R., 208f., 246
Waters, G. P., 914, 1165
Watson, D. F., 222
Watson, F. B., 25, 70, 152, 462f., 466, 542, 613f., 748f., 849, 865, 921, 967, 1152, 1162, 1164, 1166, 1168, 1171–3, 1178, 1236, 1259, 1450, 1452, 1456–71
Watts, R. E., 865, 943, 1044
Weatherly, J. A., 1152
Wedderburn, A. J. M., 420, 827, 1335
Weima, J. A. D., 17, 1144f., 1147, 1291
Weinstock, S., 317, 327
Wells, K. B., 124, 148, 153
Wendland, E., 7
Wengst, K., 284
West, M., 276
Westerholm, S., 505, 626, 777
White, J. L., 1502
White, M. J., 28, 217, 614
Whiteley, D. E. H., 723, 1239
Wiefel, W., 1217
Wilcken, R. L., 278
Wilk, F., 882, 905, 1156, 1162, 1450
Williams, B., 1388, 1390
Williams, D. K., 12
Williams, M., 91
Williams, M. A., 458, 628
Williams, S. K., 29, 389, 802, 838, 919, 972, 995, 997, 1055, 1144
Williamson, H. G. M., 151
Willitts, J., 1137
Wilson, C., 212, 738
Wilson, R. McL., 8, 11, 13, 17, 21, 673f., 992f.
Wilson, T. A., 863
Wink, W., 756, 1285
Winter, B. W., 237, 380, 562, 1304f.
Winter, S. B. C., 8
Wischmeyer, O., 118, 122f., 136
Wise, M. O., 148, 407
Witherington III, B., 12, 60, 362, 395, 440, 462, 474, 669, 841, 853, 874, 972, 974, 977, 979, 992, 994, 1110, 1118, 1134f., 1137, 1139, 1144, 1305, 1402, 1442
Witte, M., 118
Wittgenstein, L., 554
Wolff, C., 1402
Wolter, M., 8, 16, 21, 385, 1033, 1046, 1098f., 1109f., 1119, 1148, 1152, 1184, 1232, 1240
Wolterstorff, N., 946
Woolf, G., 285, 304, 306, 333, 343
Wright, A. T., 632
Wright, D. F., 1445
Wright, R. B., 81, 127, 623,
Wyschogrod, M., 806, 1190

Yadin, A., 1416
Yarborough, O. L., 562
Yeung, M. W., 865
Yinger, K. L., 164, 936
Young, F., 625

Zanker, P., 257, 294, 296, 312, 315, 324, 329, 334
Zeller, D., 1176, 1250
Zetterholm, M., 1412, 1428
Ziesler, J. A., 928, 990
Zimmerli, W., 718
Zimmerman, R., 1099
Žižek, S., 42

INDEX OF SELECTED TOPICS

Nb.: since much of the book is expository, many topics are best tracked through their occurrences in key texts, for which see the Index of biblical and other references above.

Aaron, 101, 121, 130, 281, 740, 742, 878

Abduction, method, xviii

Abraham, 642f. and *passim*; allegory in Gal. 4, 1133–40; and exodus, 788; and faith, 643, 1122; and monotheism, 642f.; 'blessing' of, 1004; call of, 741, 775 (to rescue Adam, 138f., 776, 784–95, 850, 890f., 908, 1005f., 1455); covenant with, 788–90, 1262, 1453, 1461; family remodelled, 761, 1003, 1161; father of all, 1006f., 1449; main subject of Gal. 3, 860f.; not just an 'example', 1461f.; promises to, 772, 782, 838, 972–4, 1054, 1166, 1188, 1209; 'reward', 850, 1002–4; role in argument of Rom., 1002; 'seed' of, 868f., 1187f.; world made on account of, 794; messianic fulfilment, 1210

Absalom, rebellion of, 829

Academy (philosophical school), 206–11, 218, 230–2, 252, 318, 378, 568, 1383f., 1395; and evil, 738, 741

Acts, use of in Pauline study, 62f., 376f.; and Galatians, 63

Adam, 889; acted out by Israel, 1207f. (by Israel and Messiah, 1209f.); and Messiah, 1064, 1455; as 'first husband' in Rom. 7, 893, 1009; as origin of evil, 740, 742, 745, 762, 769; disobedience of, 890; in Pauline christology, 686, 734; linked to Sinai, 894, 1010; to be rescued through Abrahamic covenant, 783–95, 850, 889

Adiaphora ('things indifferent'), 358f., 398, 1038, 1120, 1136, 1495

'Age to come' (or 'new age'), 186f., 477f., 555–62, 1059f., 1068f.; birthpangs of, 1102

Agrippa (friend of Augustus), 1288

Akiba, Rabbi, 82f., 85, 145, 619f., 626, 634, 662, 745, 773, 827, 985, 1129f., 1261, 1409, 1415f.; 'two powers' teaching, 627

Akrasia, 1377f.

Alcibiades, 208, 263

Alexander the Great, 76, 687, 1294

'All Israel', *see* Israel

Allusions, biblical, on detecting, 13f.

Amixia, 93f., 854, 859, 1428

Anabaptist views, 1275, 1307, 1414

Anarchy, encouraging vigilantism, 1303

Angels, involved in law-giving, 871

'Anthropology', as category of Pauline thought, 778; played off against other ideas, 778f.; 'anthropological eschatology', 926f.; 'anthropological terms', 491f.

Antioch, situation in, 853–5, 966f.

Antiochus Epiphanes, 87, 104, 144, 625, 767

Anxieties, protestant, 115, 385, 421, 546, 955f., 1029, 1096f., 1129, 1331, 1340, 1352

Apatheia, 1377

'Apocalyptic', as (controversial) category in Paul, 39f., 781, 877f., 924, 1059, 1071f., 1143, 1182, 1289, 1393, 1486, 1512; and 'narrative', 460; not antithetical to 'political', 1290; actual referents of, 163–75;

signs and portents, 175f.; *see also* Theology, Pauline
Apostleship, 451, 563
Aqedah ('binding' of Isaac), 697, 786–8, 903f.; as basis for Israel's election, 904; relativized by Paul, 905
Arabia, visit to, 1504
Arendt, H., 1474, 1511
Areopagus address, 376f.
Aristotle, 54, 209–11, 738, 1378
Arminius, J., 953
Asclepius, 246, 251
Assurance, not dependent on subsequent spirit-led life, 1030
Ataraxia, 212, 1377
Athene, 1045
Athens, 197, and ch. 3 *passim*
'Atonement-theology', 897, 1070f.
Augustine (of Hippo), 744, 747
'Augustinian' approach to problem of evil, 748
Augustus, 272, ch. 5 *passim*, esp. 289–91, 295–8; 634, 687, 824f., 1300f.
Autarkeia, 214, 1376f.

Bach, J. S., 1484
Baptism, 417–27; 893, 962–4, 1014, 1103f., 1333–9
Bar-Kochba (Simeon ben-Kosiba), 82f., 85, 104, 115, 145, 619f., 625, 826f., 985, 1129, 1261, 1287, 1415f., 1471, 1480
Barth, Karl, 200, 748, 757, 766, 780, 913, 953, 1325, 1388, 1479
Barthian tradition of interpretation, 808, 1409
Battle, eschatological, 1054; redefined, 370f., 1126f.
'Being in Christ', as category of Pauline thought, 779; *see too* 'Incorporation' *and* Theology, Pauline
Benjamin, tribe of, 22, 86, 545, 775, 829, 987, 1145f., 1223, 1427, 1473, 1475, 1483
Benjamin, Walter, 835, 1473–5, 1478, 1480–3, 1489, 1511f.
Birthpangs, *see* 'Age to come'
Blair, T., 336, 1162
Boasting, eliminated by gospel, 847, 1000f., 1003, 1007, 1143, 1221
Body (*sōma*), 491
'Body of Messiah', *see* Messiah, body of
Bourdieu, P. 1391f., 1406
Brown, G., 336
Bultmann, R., 1389, 1478

Caesar, chs. 5, 12 *passim*; not ultimate ruler, 1065; falsity of divine claims, 1285; *see also* Augustus, Julius, etc.
Cain, 1015f.
Caligula, 291f., 1290, 1315
'Call', 918, 955, 959, 1026, 1183, 1188, 1193; Paul's own 'call', 1417–26
Calvin, Jean, 774
Cappadocian Fathers, 709f.
Celebration, 1341
Celibacy, within eschatological ethics, 1118
Character, *see* Virtue
Charismata, 1123f.
Chiastic structure of Rom. 9—11, 1162–4, 1183f.
Christology, early, ch. 9 *passim*, esp. e.g. 644f., 690f.; integrated with revised election, 1040; not controversial in early church, 648, 689, 709; 'subordinationist'?, 735f.; Pauline, 643–709
'Christos', meaning of, *see* Messiah; neither name nor title but 'honorific', 824
Christus Victor, in atonement-theology, 899
Chrysostom, 1414
Church, as primary worldview-symbol, 384f., 387f.; discipline within, 978, 1135; nature of, 1491f.; unity of, 30, 359f., 394–404, 540, 1340f., 1349f.; *see also* Single family; as correlate of monotheism, 642f., 687
Cicero, 218f., 231f., 256, 263f., 276, 318, 566, 1354, 1376, 1394f., 1508f.; on 'religions', 252f., 271f., 274
Circumcision, as covenant sign, 790; of heart, 923, 958, 1008, 1173, 1379f.; redefined through gospel, 361–3, 424f., 960, 984–7, 992, 1020, 1076, 1180, 1434f.
Claudius, emperor, 292, 1283
'Coherence' as criterion in theology, 617
Collection, 454, 1202f., 1255, 1495–7, 1507
Colossian heresy (hypothetical), 992
Colossians, as Pauline, 56–61
'Consistency' in theology, 617f.
Constantine, 1275, 1307

Continuing exile, *see* Exile, continuing
Conversion, 1395–7; meaning of, 1418–20; Paul's, 1417–26
'Corporate personality', 827
Covenant, as category in Paul, 40, 780–2; as larger unifying category, 846f., 875, 900f., 933, 1013, 1025, 1263f., 1512; distinguished from 'salvation history', 780; in Gal. 3, 862, 868; in Rom. 4, 996; in relation to 'law court' and 'righteousness', 795–804, 960f.; new/renewed covenant, 502, 724–7, 892f., 917, 1167, 1246, 1460, 1462; purpose, 804–15, 1072; with Abraham, 788–90; covenantal eschatology, 927–34; 'two-covenant' theory, 1175
Craig, P. P., 1146
Creation, goodness of, 627f., 639; and new creation, 190–2, 635f., 819, 1072, 1143; creational eschatology, 926; creational monotheism, 652f., 661f.; rescue of, 755
Critical realism, xviii, 51, 67
Croesus, 262
Cross, as central symbol, 20, 74, 406f.; victory over powers, 1068; at heart of eschatology as well as monotheism and election, 1071; meaning of, 844, 910f., 995–1007; revealing divine righteousness, 911; scandal of, 407, 688 (*and see* Scandal); redefining power etc., 1040
Crucified Messiah, *see* Messiah
Cruciformity, 1104, 1142
Culture, within worldviews, 34f.
Curse of Torah, 124f., 139, 143, 146–50, 161, 407, 467, 502, 507, 515f., 526f., 763f., 776, 788, 800, 823, 864–7, 923, 929, 931, 973, 996, 1034–6, 1055, 1139, 1165f., 1172, 1215, 1227, 1246, 1456, 1463, 1465; continuing in second-Temple period, 1165, 1215f., 1227
Cynics, 229f.

Daniel, as read in C1, 116f., 170f., 282f., 345f., 693; echoes in Paul? 1064f., 1090, 1293, 1311, 1455, 1503f.
Dating of Paul's letters, problem of, xix
David, King, 798f., 802, 1042, 1455, 1471; and Goliath, 828f.
'Day of YHWH', 1047, 1050; transformed into 'day of lord Jesus' etc., 1047, 1079–81
Death, as 'real/last enemy', 372, 760f., 1094, 1298, 1319; as 'power', 756; of Jesus, *see* Jesus, death of; not mentioned in Gal., 970
Deification, as category in Paul, 781, *and see* *Theōsis*
Deism, 632; as type of 'monotheism', 632
Democritus, 212
Demons, 251, 377f., 640, 732, 734, 743, 1285, 1345
Diaspora Judaism, 89f.; as 'colonial' movement? 120
'Diatribe' style, 222, 224, 453, 458, 1366
Diogenes, 1387
Dispensationalism, 1130
'Divine identity', 651f.
'Divinity' of Jesus, *see* Jesus, divinity of
Divorce, 445f.
Domitian, 817
Dualisms and 'dualities', 370f.
Dura-Europos, synagogue decoration, 159

Eighteen Benedictions, 84, 1149
Election, ch. 10 *passim*; meaning of, 182f., 566, 774f.; purpose of, 775f., 1015, 1190f.; question raised by revised monotheism, 772; redefined around Messiah, 815–911, esp. e.g. 846, 855, 860, 884, 891, 899, 902f., 907; around spirit, 912–1038, esp. e.g. 980f., 1018, 1023f., 1027; eschatological challenge of, 1128–1258 *passim*, esp. e.g. 1137
Eleusinian mysteries, 263f.
Eliezer ben Hyrcanus, 83, 167
Elijah, 81, 167, 1239, 1423, 1504
Elysian fields, hope for, 1043, 1265
Emperor and empire, cults of, 311–43, 730f., 1275f.; under Augustus, 321–35; in Rome, 321–4; in provinces, 324–35; under Tiberius, 336f.; under Caligula, 337f.; under Claudius, 338f.; under Nero, 339f.; effects of, 341–3; Jews permitted to pray *for* emperor, 315, 344; introducing 'sameness', 731
Empire, ch. 5 *passim*; alternative visions of, 381f.; 911; Jewish critiques, 1274; narrative of, 298–311, 383, 1265, 1281f., 1301,

1318, 1358; Paul's missionary strategy in relation to, 1501–4; target of Paul's polemic? 1273, ch. 12 *passim*; thriving on relativism, 634;
'End of the law', *see Telos nomou*
Endogamy, Jewish, 1035, 1260; Christian, 369, 444, 1074, 1428; *and see* Family identity
Enlightenment, influence on christology, 646f.
Ephesians, possible authenticity of, and prejudice against, 56–60, 556f.; as summary of Pauline theology, 1514f.
Ephesus, probable location of Paul writing Philemon, 7f.
Epictetus, 223–7, 1376, 1383f.; prayer of, 226f.
Epicurus and Epicureans, 211–13; and evil, 738, 741, 743, 775; as seen by rabbis, 186; default mode in modernism, 213; modern equivalents, 743; opposed by Wis. Sol. and Paul, 1369
'Epiphany', 1083
Epistemological revolution in Paul, 568f., 1355f., 1361f.
Esau, 1184f., 1188
'Eschatological monotheism', 633, 652f., 655, 689, 730
Eschatology, ch. 11 *passim*; growing from within monotheism, 1045; Pauline, sources of, 1047; development in? 1094; tells story and points forward, 1181; reworked around Messiah, 1190; alteration to Jewish counter-imperial hope, 1298f.; screened out by Sanders, 1324; different from Stoics and Epicureans, 1370; *see also* 'anthropological eschatology, creational eschatology, covenantal eschatology, final eschatology, Hope
'Eternal life' (*zōē aiōnios*), 163f., 1029, 1060, 1069, 1087, 1146
'Ethics', in ancient philosophy, 198; meaning of word, 1096; Pauline, 447f., 1030, 1095–1128, 1371–83 *passim*; use of scripture within, 1100; within eschatology, 1047f., 1112f.; and resurrection, 1112; and Torah, 1125; within theology, 1097; posing problems for Protestants, 1096; relation to 'physics', 1100
Eucharist, 427–9, 979, 1344–8
Evil, origin and nature of, 632; 'inclination', 769, 894; 'problem' of, 737–47; ultimate incomprehensibility of, 742; addressed within monotheism, 746; fresh vision of in Paul, 746f., 900; in Israel as well, 753; *see also* 'Plight and solution'
Exegesis, nature of, 48; as branch of history, 52f.
Exile, continuing, 139–63, 525, 867, 1165, 1463; basis in Daniel 9, 142f.; in rabbis, 156f.; in Josephus, 159; Deuteronomic warnings of, 792, 1464; objections to, 159–63; result of idolatry, 761; end of/restoration from, 1036, 1164, 1166, 1453f.
Existentialist ethics, 1106
Exodus, link with Abraham, 788
Exodus-theology, 14, 420–3, 428, 655–8, 662f., 674, 677, 718f., 845, 876–8, 976, 983, 1022; and monotheism, 657; 'new exodus', 718f., 802, 1013f., 1053, 1069f., 1076, 1105, 1140, 1334f., 1344f., 1373
'Experience', Paul's, 413f., 852f., 1326f., 1424f.; 'appeal to', 971

Fact-checkers, 1131
Faith, human, 839, 920, 997; as gift, 952; appropriate covenant badge, 406, 839f., 848f., 931, 968, 989, 991, 1001f.
Faithfulness, of Messiah, 836–51, 857, 967f.; *see also* Covenant; God
Family identity, as Jewish symbol, 94f., 367; renewed through Messiah, 545f.
Final eschatology, 936–42; vital role of spirit within, 940
Flesh (*sarx*), 491, 1020; mind of, 1109f.; Israel according to, 1204f.
Folly, allure of, 744
Food laws, 92
Forensic categories, *see* Law court imagery *and* Theology, Pauline
'Forensic eschatology', 934f.; blended with 'covenantal eschatology', 935; *see* Theology, Pauline
Forgiveness of sins, 1247f.
Freedom, Christian, 1123f.
Fruit of the spirit, *see* Spirit, fruit of

Galatia, situation in, 853
Gamaliel, 86
Gentiles, Paul's references to, 79 and *passim*; attracted to Judaism, 194f.; 'doing the law', 1089, though 'not under law', 865; included in new covenant, 931f.; narrated into Israel's story, 540f., 1149f., 1176f., 1187, 1214; leaving 'pagan' identity, 541; attaining 'righteousness', 1176f., 1194; now given a role in narrative, 1197, 1203f.
'German Christians', 757, 780
Glory, divine; in temple, 99f.; as rule over world, 1091–3; filling whole world, 189, 1052f., 1093; hope of, 1075, 1091; in christology, 679, 691, 1226; in suffering apostleship, 726; in groaning prayer, 1127
Glossolalia, 1349f.
Gnosticism, 458; origins of, 628, 1307, 1482; and evil, 742; road towards, 1065; not relevant to Col. 1, 674; to Col. 2, 993; to Gal. 4, 988
God, Israel's, *passim*; as creator and judge, 638–41; as 'father', 697f.; as 'heart-searcher', 721f.; as impartial, 1087; as judge, 702; as main subject of Rom. 9—11, 1157f.; as topic within 'physics', 1360; faithfulness of, *passim*, and e.g. 22, 77, 480, 537, 763, 772, 836–9, 879, 900, 910, 1071f.; patience of, 1195; plan not changed, 1196, but reaching fruition, 643; returning to judge and save, 761, *and see* YHWH, return of; 'righteousness' of, *see* Righteousness
Golden age, ancient hope for, 1043
Golden calf, 97, 677, 699, 725, 740, 744, 769, 786, 878, 897, 983, 1022, 1051, 1185, 1189, 1493
Goliath, 828f.
Gospel, meaning in Paul, 410f., 517f., 914–17; and 'new covenant', 917; and spirit, 952–4, 1028; as power, 917f.; in imperial language, 915, 1292; in Isaiah, 915
Guidance, divine, 1350f.

Hadrian, emperor, 625
Hagar, 1133f., 1139
Hamlet, 461
'Hard supersessionism', 806f.
'Hardening', 1191f., 1212, 1225f., 1227, 1236–9, 1251–4
Heart, corruption of, 768, 770; renewal of, 759, 923, 981f., 1076f.; *and see* Circumcision of heart
Hegel, G. W. F., 780, and influence, 1270, 1357f., 1477–9, 1512
Heidegger, M., 459, 1477
Heirs, *see* 'Inheritance'
Herbert, G., 1162, 1518
Hermeneutical gap, 66f.
Herod the Great, 81f., 84f., 104, 121, 160, 211, 281f., 320, 324f., 344
'Hidden transcripts', 1277, 1314
High priest, like Adam, 792
Hillel, 85, 187
Historian, task of, 48–51, 385, 1388, 1477; dangerous, 70; necessary but insufficient, 76; never neutral, 55f.
History and sociology, 385; and theology, 68–74; 1515f.
History of religions, 51f.
Hitler, Adolf, 634, 743, 1295
Holiness, 356f., 444f., 1026f., 1048, 1105
Holofernes, drunk and decapitated, 121, 158, 622f., 899, 1428
Homer, 197, 211, 250, 254, 258f., 306, 1330–3
Homo religiosus, in Käsemann's interpretation, 807, 1131, 1320, 1486
Hope, Jewish and pagan, 1043; realized and redefined, ch. 11 *passim*, esp. 1061–78, 1258f.; still future, 1078–95
Horace, 298–301, 322f.
Hospitality, 401
'Household codes', 58, 1108, 1375f.
Houston, James, 1434

Identity, Jewish, in Paul, 1426–49
Idolatry, 276f., 633, 639; continuing danger of, 668f., 743; effects of, 743f.
Idols, as non-existent, 640, 666
Ignatius of Antioch, 817
Image of God, 377f., 438–41, 486–9, 492f.; Messiah as, 406, 726
Imitation, of Messiah, 1104; of Paul, 1104, 1295f.; of both, 394, 1510
Impartiality of God, 1087
Imperial cult, *see* Empire

'Imputation', *see* Righteousness
Inaugurated eschatology, 942–4, 1046; divine purpose of time-lag, 1048f.; inaugurated judgment, 976–80; through the spirit, 1074–8
'Incorporation' into Messiah, 779, 825–35; and justification, 950f.; explaining puzzles in Gal. 3, 869; stemming from Jesus' resurrection, 827f.; as controlling category in key passages, 830f.; meaning of key phrases, 832–5; *and see* Theology, Pauline
'Indicative and Imperative', 1098f.
'Inheritance', 366f., 659, 730; as new creation, 635, 659; Messiah as 'heir', believers as 'fellow heirs', 1023; spirit as foretaste of, 971f., 974, 1075, 1094
'Interchange', 1104
Interpretatio Romana, *see* Syncretism
Isaac, 1185; 'binding' of, *see* Aqedah
Ishmael, 790, 1184, 1188
Israel, use of in Paul, 539f., 1145f., 1183; 'all Israel', 1243–5; as servant, 804f.; as true humanity, 794; calling, 495–505, 775, 1035; cruciform reading of history, 1195; faithlessness of, 838–40; future of, 1048, 1128–1258 *passim*; in Adam, 371, 503, 764, 769, 771, 895, 1014, 1017, 1207f., 1430; Messiah's people according to the flesh, 500; not just an example, 1186; polemical definitions of, 1146, 1242 (in Gal. 6.16, 1143–51; in Rom. 11, 1241f.); purpose of, 783–815, 898 (not thereby 'instrumentalized', 810f.); 'trespass' of, 1194; unbelief of, 1161, 1219f., 1236; story of, 495–505, 822f., 1158–61, 1172; 'true Israel', 815, 826, 1187
Iustitia, as Roman goddess, 170, 290

Jacob, 1185, 1188; taking role of Abraham in *Jubilees*, 792
James (brother of Jesus), 388, 526f., 643, 852, 854, 856, 869, 872, 966, 1425, 1501
Jealousy, motif in Rom. 11, 1201–4, 1244f., 1252f.
Jeroboam, 742, 1413
Jerusalem, apostles in, 853, 1028; conference, 967; fall of, 1154; new Jerusalem, 1137; Jerusalem above, 1138
Jesus, *passim*; condemned as pseudo-Messiah, 943; death of, 880, 886, 908f. (foundational for justification, 949, 998f.); divinity of, 644–709, esp. e.g. 644f., 709; resurrection of, 408, 1383, 1483; sinlessness of, 909; as 'last Adam', 734; as (Israel's) Messiah, 815–36, 905; as faithful Messiah, 836–51; as 'son of God', 657, 690–4; false polarization of Jesus' teaching and Paul's, 880; impact on early church, 649; *see too* Messiah
'Jewish supersessionism', 809f.
Jews, Judaeans, meaning of in general, 775, 922f.; in Paul, 538f., 1007f., 1020, 1145f.; 'Jewish background' an inappropriate category, 776
Josephus, view of Temple, 107; on Daniel, 117, 130, 293; on God changing sides, 129; to Rome as Titus's advisor, 293; on Dt. 32, 130f.
Joy, 354f., 413, 418, 430, 437, 481, 558, 668, 1259, 1385, 1517
Jubilee, 13, 91, 125, 144f., 149f., 178f., 261, 276, 560f.
Judah (patriarch), 797f., 802
Judaism, *passim*; modern meanings of, xxivf., 76, 82, 89, 443, 1422, 1477; anachronistic models, 1357; transformation of in second century, 115; attitudes to Roman empire, 730f.; attitude of Enlightenment towards, 645
Judas Maccabaeus, 167
Judas the Galilean, 1480
Judgment, 481, 976f.; final, 978, 1080, 1085f., 1088–90; shared by believers, 1090; anticipated and held back, 1115
Julius Caesar, 272, 280, 285–7, 824
Justification, 31f., 856, 858f., 925–1032, 1167, 1411; and 'assurance', 949; and baptism, 962–4; and 'incorporation', 950; and 'transformation', 957; and 'works of Torah', 184–7; as one competing element in Paul, 777; based on revised monotheism, 912; by works, 760; declarative verdict, 945; dependent on the *extra nos* of Jesus' death, 955; in relation to 'participation', 858; in relation to spirit, 912–1032; in relation to 'salvation', 887, 913, 927;

misleadingly 'expanded', 913f.; modernist parody of, 1087; moved from periphery to centre, 932, 964f.; new status of *dikaiosynē*, 945f.; of ungodly, 1004; full statement (but without forensic element) in Rom. 10, 1167

Kingdom of God, in Judaism, 84f.; in Paul, 480f., 733–7, 757, 772f., 1063f.; already inaugurated, 1066; and ethics, 1106, 1113f.; and Messiah, 1114

Koinōnia, 10f., 16–20, 251, 401, 1345, 1496, 1510; as challenge to empire, 252, 383f., 1277f., 1507f.

kyrios, *see* 'Lord'

Land of Canaan/Israel/Palestine, symbol of, 366f.; promises concerning, 787; 849f.; 972

Law, *see* Torah

Law court imagery and/or scenario, 777, 795–804, esp. 797f., 933f., 947, 976–8; *and see* Theology, Pauline

'Letter and spirit', 923f., 982f.

Lisbon earthquake, 738

Livy, 302–4

'Logic', in ancient philosophy, 198

'Lord' as Jesus-title, 670, 701–6, 1066, 1294; as Caesar-title, 1292, and ch. 5 *passim*

Love, for God, through spirit, 721f., 1013, 1023; for one another, 429–31, 1118–20, 1140; of God in death of son, 529, 696, 842, 860, 880, 885f., 902–8, 1025, 1093, 1489, 1517f.; of God for Jacob, 1186; of Messiah, 525, 1426; danger of word losing cutting edge, 1119f.; as ultimate power, 1319; only debt allowed, 1353; new form of knowledge, 1356; greatest virtue, 1382

Luther, Martin, 745, 747, 774, 1414, 1466

Maccabaean martyrs, 987; revolt, 87–9

Maecenas, 1288

Manicheism, 738, 754

Marcionite views, 754, 806, 862, 1017, 1206, 1220f., 1453, 1481

Marcus Aurelius, 204, 227–9

Mark Antony, 281, 287f., 317

Marx, Karl, 198, 775, 1478f., 1484

Mattathias, 87f., 92, 121, 184, 194

Mediator figures, use in christology, 649

Mercy, divine, 1111f., 1150, 1183, 1252

Messiah, 137f., 690; category treated as irrelevant but in fact central, 734f., 816–25, 1040, 1413; 'faithful', 836–51, 857, 871, 900, 910, 969, 997, 1208; already ruling, 561; as identity-marker of his people, 404–11, 543f.; as judge, 767f., 1085f.; as major theme of Romans, 1012; as model for divine purpose of election, 1192; as transforming previous Jewish thought-forms, 1262; as true Adam/human being, 736f., 908, 1050, 1064; as world-sovereign, 1050, 1053f.; body of, 396f., 426f., 825f., 834, 892, 1009f., 1346, 1384, 1430; central to Rom. 9—11, 1257f.; crucified, 667, 688, 1146, 1151; incorporative, 17f., 21f., 825–35; M. still royal (Davidic) title, 817–19; story of, 517–36; *see too* Jesus as Messiah

Messianic narrative, 822; prophecies, 692f.; victory, 820f.

Messianic time, 550–62, 1181f.

Messianic woes, 520, 884, 987, 1019, 1023, 1145, 1208, 1296; tribulation, 1117

Midsummer Night's Dream, A, 461, 468–73

Mind, Christian/renewed, 27, 567, 569, 1114, 1120f., 1364; Romans as therapy towards this end, 1121; unfit mind, 1122; link of mind and heart, 1122; in Rom. 7, 1122f.; and worship, 1123; in Phil., 1124

Mindset, *see* Worldview

Minerva, 197f.

Mirror-reading, problem of, 1128, 1217, 1220

Mission, in Paul, 436f., 549f., 1484–1504

Mithradates of Pontus, 199, 280

Mithraism, 266f.

Modernist moralizing, 12, 1170, 1182, 1195

Monotheism, ch. 9 *passim*, esp. 619f., 628f.; Jewish, basic to Paul, 37, 179f., 566, 569; creational and covenantal, 180f.; and Abraham, 642f.; and exodus-theology, 657; and evil, 181f., 737f., 739f.; and intermediary figures 624, 626, 632; and kingdom of God, 621, 631; and pagan empire, 631, 731f.; and structures of government, 627f.; and suffering, 621f., 634f.; and unity

of people, 641–3, 728f.; creational, 661f., 668f., 676; cultic, 652, 661f., 676; eschatological, 633, 652f., 655, 661f., 676, 689, 730; intensifies problems and regrounds hope, 632, 747; needed to fill gap left by Jewish symbols, 402; neglect in earlier scholarship, 624f.; not a bare belief but an agenda, 734; not controversial in earliest Christianity, 627; not in tension with high christology, 652; now irreducibly threefold, 727, 729; redrawn around Jesus, 644–709; redrawn around the spirit, 709–28; Stoic, 218
Moses, 677f., 791, 871–3, 982f., 1075, 1082, 1095, 1151, 1167, 1189, 1512
Mozart, W. A., 1018
Musonius Rufus, 203, 222f., 1376
'My Last Duchess', 464f.
Mystery, of Rom. 11, 1197, 1228f., 1231–5
Mystery religions, 263–7
'Mysticism', 414f.; Schweitzer's misleading term for 'being in Christ', 779, 1039f.; use by Ashton, 1325f.
Myths, ancient, well known throughout antiquity, 255; as part of worldviews, 456f.

Name of God, 99f., 684; 'name of the lord', calling on, 703, 1336
Narrative, *see* Story
Nero, 292f.
New age, *see* 'Age to come'
New covenant, *see* Covenant
New creation, 482, 635f., 1023, 1072, 1091–3, 1143, 1476f.; and 'public theology', 1100
New exodus, *see* Exodus-theology
'New Israel', 826
'New perspective' on Paul, 925, 1109, 1513; place of 'story' within, 460; G. Howard as harbinger of, 925; criticisms of, 1322–4
Nietzsche, F., 49
Noachide commands, 1434f.
Noah, as 'new Adam', 787

Obedience, of Messiah, 843, 889f.
Olive tree image, 1211–22, 1243
Onesimus, 5–22, 68–74, 465, 1503, 1515, 1518
Ordo salutis, 959f.; wrong to impose on Paul, 1030, 1088
Orpheism, 264
O'Siadhail, Micheal, xxivf., 1269
Ovid, 301, 1378f.

Paganism, classical, ch. 4 *passim*; attempting to deal with evil, 739; confronted by revised monotheism, 666, and chs. 12–14 *passim*
Parousia, 756, 1082–5; in relation to Caesar, 1082, 1085, 1289–93; to God at Sinai, 1082; to Paul's plans, 1501f.; myth of imminent or delayed *parousia*, 1098, 1483; possible reference in Rom. 11, 1221f.; problems with, 1231–52, esp. 1246f., 1251f.
Pastoral letters, debates over authenticity, 61f.
Paul, as coherent thinker, 568; as Jewish thinker, 611, 617, 1038; as pastor, 452, 568; as writer, 453f.; christology, not unique to him, 649; Damascus Road experience of, 611, 649; death of, 773; defence of apostleship, 724–6, 879f.; engagement with pagan world, chs. 12–14 *passim*, 613; letter-writing, reason for, 612f.; not 'anti-Jewish', 1155, 1187; Jewish identity, nature of, 1426–49; use of scripture, 613, 1449–56; theology, *see* Theology, Pauline
Pausanias, description of Corinth, 255
Persecution, of Paul, 1151
Pharaoh, 791, 1189, 1227
Pharisees, 80–90, 1189; theology of, 179–93; possible mission of, 194f.
Philemon, 5–22, 68–74, 465, 1503, 1515, 1518; as allegory for history and theology, 68–74
Philo, 1095; on Pharisees, 82f., 116; on keeping Torah, 91; on coming liberty, 120; coded political messages, 1315f.
Philosophy, ancient, ch. 3 *passim*; timeline, 244f.; four schools, 206f., 237f.; worldview of, 232–7; Jewish responses to, 238–43; Paul's engagement with, ch. 14 *passim*; topics in, 23
Phineas, 81, 135f., 167
'Physics', in ancient philosophy, 198
Pistis, meaning of, *see* Faith
Pistis Christou, *see* Faithfulness
Plato, 207–9

'Plight and solution', 739, 747–72
'Plight', revised through the cross, 752–6; through the resurrection, 756–8; through the spirit, 758–64
Pliny the Younger, 3–5, 9, 15, 453
Politeuma, 1292f., 1332, 1342
Politics, and Pauline theology, 42f., 1504f.; ch. 12 *passim*.
Polycarp, 1313
Pompey, 279–81, 286f.
Population estimates, 1278
Poseidon, 1286
Postmodern moralism, 53, 967, 1105, 1170, 1182, 1314, 1444; as illegitimate tool in historical research, 743, 810, 1439, 1441
'Powers', Paul's view of, 451f., 756f., 762f., 771; not to be played off against 'human sin', 771
Prayer, in Judaism, 365; as part of 'battle', 1127; that Paul might have prayed, 1189; as part of 'religion', 1348–50; as heart of Paul's theology, 1516–19; *see too Shema*
Pre-Pauline formulae, 523, 647, 844
'Present age', 1059f., 1069
Pride and Prejudice, 461, 463
Primitivism, fad for, 647; modifications in, 647
Providence, 1156
'Public theology', beginnings of, 614, 1100
Purity, 193
Pythagoras, 208
Pythagoreanism, 264
Pythia at Delphi, 278

Qumran, holding 'supersessionist' view, 809

Rabbis, indifferent to history? 136f.
Reconciliation, 20, 30, 74; as ultimate meaning of Paul's thought, 879, 888, 1487–1516
Redemption, as exodus-language, 1070
Reepicheep the Mouse, 16
Regeneration, not linked to justification in Paul, 954
Rehoboam, 828f.
Relativism, 1131
'Religion', in ancient world, 202f.; ch. 4 *passim*; in Greece, 258–63; in Roman world, 267–74; not involving 'belief', 276; not involving teaching morality, 276; in modern western world, 1320f., 1486; 'Departments of', 1321; as semiotic phenomenon, 1328; Paul in relation to, 1261, ch. 13 *passim*; Paul not 'comparing religions', 1409–11, or 'founding a new religion', 1412; religion swept away by 'apocalyptic'? 807f.; problems of terminology, 1129; concept reborn, 1338, 1343
Remnant, 1185, 1208, 1223f., 1230; different from Qumran, 1224
'Replacement theology', 1129, 1159, 1206, 1415
'Representation', in atonement-theology, 898; *see also* Incorporation
Resurrection, nature of in Paul, 1398–1402; as future hope, 1093f.; demonstrating Jesus' Messiahship, 1062; generating incorporative messianism, 828; in Judaism, 1060; Israel's equivalent to, 1198–1200; significance of within christology, 691f., 699f., 943; split into two, giving inaugurated eschatology, 1048, 1062; transforming view of 'plight', 756–8, 762; vital for Paul's whole theology, 408, 1383, 1483; worldview-marker, 409f.
Return of Jews to land, 1130
Return of YHWH, *see* YHWH, return of
Reynolds, F. M. B., 1146
Righteousness, of God, 795–804, 841, 881f., 1055f., 1158, 1168, 1208, 1249, 1467–9, *and see* Theodicy; correlated with divine truthfulness, judgment and glory, 995f.; not the same as 'righteousness' of believer, 946; as 'covenant faithfulness', 799–801 (as primary category, 804), 928, 935f.; as faithfulness to all creation, 801; cross as ultimate revelation of, 911; embodied in apostolic ministry, 879–85; 'imputed', 881–3, 914; in relation to Abraham, 848f.; of judge, as different from plaintiff or defendant, 799; of Israel before God, 799; problems of older debates, 801f., 841
Righteousness of humans, 856, 1141; of Israel, 1171f.; as 'right behaviour', 796f.

Romans, letter to, symphonic shaping of, 1011; not separate theological systems, 1011f.; *and see* Theology, Pauline
Romanticism, influence on christology, 646f.; on hermeneutics, 982f.; on ethics, 1106
Rome, cult of, 730f.; significance for Paul, 1305–19; *see too* Emperor
Rulers, 1067f., 1284–7

Sabbath, 91, 363f., 555–61
Sabinianus, correspondent of Pliny, 3–5, 20f., 453
Sacrifice, 898; language of, 1331; living, 1339–44
Salvation, different views of, 31, 113, 164f., 188, 742, 749, 754, 762, 770; in Rom. 10, 1174f.; relation to 'justification', 887f., 927; 'work out your own salvation', 1124, 1295–7; *see also* Theology, Pauline
'Salvation history', as category in Paul, 39f., 780, 924, 1071f., 1182; different meanings of, 783, 1393, 1512; not smooth and evolutionary, 1017; linked with 'damnation history', 129, 137, 780, 1211, 1262; *and see* Theology, Pauline
Sanders, E. P., revolution in understanding Paul, 748f.
Sarah, 788, 1133f., 1137–9
Saul, King, 798f., 802, 1223
Scandal, of cross, 407, 541–3, 667, 860, 1169, 1429, 1446; of particularity, 447, 889, 1170
Sceptics, 230f.
Scriptures, read as ongoing narrative, 175–7; Paul's reading of, 415f., 1449–71
Second Thessalonians, debates over authenticity, 61
'Seed', of Abraham, 1005; single, 388f., 642f., 868f., 1005, 1213
Seneca, 218–22, 566, 1354f., 1376, 1384, 1395, 1509; (fictitious) correspondence with Paul, 220
'Servant' of YHWH, 682, 906, 999f.
Sexual holiness, 201, 222, 277, 392, 445–7, 639, 641, 712, 1107, 1114, 1117f., 1125, 1435, 1448, 1508
Shakespeare, William, 473, 536, 680
Shammai, 85
Shekinah, 95, 106, 180, 189; *and see* Spirit
Shema prayer, 84, 411, 529, 619f., 624, 630, 706, 722–4, 727f., 733, 759, 772f., 814, 909, 1023, 1025, 1426, 1447, 1518; renewed version, 365, 403, 636, 662–8, 1150, 1283, 1349, 1516; anchoring unity and holiness, 666f.
Sibylline oracles, 262f.
Sin (*see also* Evil), as 'power', 372, 756, 843; nature of, 493, 742f.; not main subject of Gal., 970; problem of, 754, 760; within Israel too, 743, 871f.; lured on to Israel by Torah, 896; major topic in Rom. 7 but not 9—11, 1177;
Sinai, Mt, 981, 1014, 1139
Single divine plan, 499
Single family, central in Gal. 3, 388f., 863, 873–5, 968f., 1432; in Rom., 1213
Slavery, 32f., 54
Social Darwinism, 1479
'Social science', 28
Socrates, 198, 207–9, 246, 248, 262, 275, 433f., 1366
Solomon, 99, 103, 829, 1067
Solzhenitsyn, A., 54
'Son of God', 657f., 691–4; *see also* Jesus; as messianic title, 691f., 695f.; as 'Israel in person', 695f.; in relation to 'father', 697f.; in relation to resurrection, 699f.; as Caesar-title, 1272
Soteriology, as subset of 'election', xvi
Spain, Paul's hope to visit, 1498–1501
Spirit, holy, indwelling, 357f.; and faith, 952f.; and justification, 912–1032; and new exodus, 717–27; as foretaste/guarantee of inheritance, 972, 1259; as new Shekinah, 711–17, 725, 983, 1073, 1127, 1493f.; divine and human, 1370; doing what Torah could not, 1020, 1374; fruit of, 1117; present though not mentioned, 974, 1077, 1089, 1157, 1164, 1166, 1394; transforming work revealing nature of evil, 758f.; vital role in final eschatology, 940; within monotheism, 709–28; working through gospel, 1028; in Stoicism, 214, 1391
'Stewball', 465

Stoicheia ('elements'), 228, 239, 382, 480, 878, 976, 993, 1147

Stoics, 213–19; default mode in ancient world, 213; and evil, 738, 741, 775; and conflagration, 168, 216, 484, 1368, 1402f.; and self-mastery, 1016; might recognize Rom. 2, 1088, 1379–82; Paul's engagement with, 378, 1264, ch. 14 *passim*; as source of Paul's ideas? 1390f.

Story, as worldview-marker, ch. 7 *passim*; failure of denarrativized theology, 457–9; story essential in Paul's Jewish world, 458f.; interlocking narratives, 461–74, 521, 534; story of God and creation, 475–85; of humans (vocation, failure, rescue, reinstatement), 485–94; story of Israel (as yet unfinished), 109–14, 373, 495–505; story of Torah, 505–16; story of Messiah, 517–36; continuous story, 114; objections to, 140f.; story of Israel (biblical), 117–21; in second-Temple literature, 121–8; after AD 70, 128–35

Strabo, 199

'Substitution', in atonement-theology, 898

Suffering, 70, 355, 431f., 434f., 440f., 452, 479, 545, 557f., 621, 634–8, 682f., 721f., 724, 732, 773, 883, 889, 900, 902f., 906f., 953, 960, 1047, 1065, 1076, 1116f., 1296, 1299, 1373, 1377, 1385, 1491f., *and see* Messianic woes

'Supersessionism', 368, 784, 805f., 1129f., 1180, 1206, 1409, 1413, 1415f., 1431, 1448; three versions of ('hard', 'sweeping' and 'Jewish'), 806–10, 912f., 985f.; 'post-supersessionism', 1445

'Sweeping supersessionism', *see* Supersessionism

Symbolic praxis, as worldview-element, ch. 6 *passim*

Synagogue, Paul's visits to, 1440–2, 1498f.

Syncretism, varieties of, 216f., 268f., 275, 319f., 624, 630

Synergism, 181, 955f.

Tabernacle, wilderness, 677–9, 717–27, 1021f.

Tacitus, critical of Rome, 1315

Tamar, 797f., 802

Tarraco, 1500

Tarshish, 1500, 1507

Tarsus, 89f., 199, 205–7, 213, 237, 266, 307, 1213, 1500, 1503, 1507

Taurobolium, 265

Telos nomou, 'end of the law', 502, 533, 1172, 1454, 1513

Temple, Jerusalem, 95–108; microcosm of creation, 101–3; linked to Davidic house, 103f.; alternatives to, 107f.; draws together monotheism and election, 1041; taken by Romans, 744; Temple-theology in Paul, 355f., 391f., 679, 709–28, 729f,, 1021f., 1074f., 1492–5, 1509; threat to, 1290; in relation to 'new exodus', 714

Tertius, 1162, 1238

Tertullian, 279f.

Thales, 208, 246

Thanksgiving, as symbol, 412f.

Theodicy, 622, 802, 1186, 1222 *and see* Righteousness of God

'Theology', ancient meanings of, 216f.

Theology, Pauline, nature of, xvi, 26, 30f., 404, 609f., 614, 1166, 1259f., 1361, 1508f.; quest for coherence, 45f.; main categories monotheism, election, eschatology, 46f.; necessary to sustain worldview, 30, 565–7; new symbolic role, 352, 403, 565f.; as identity marker, 374; intended effect of, 1259–61; not really 'rabbinic', 1263; categories in scholarly analysis, 37–41; seven competing elements in analysis, 777–83, 965f.; categories not distinct in Gal., 851, 875f.; categories overlap throughout Romans, 891, 900f., 903, 997f., 999f., 1005f., 1008, 1010, 1024f., 1031f.; balance of covenantal and forensic, 961f.; of apocalyptic and covenant, 370; of apocalyptic and incorporative, 974–6; of apocalyptic and salvation history, 1038, 1071, 1262f., 1393; of juridical and participationist, 38, 529f., 1039, 1263f., 1513; all categories in 2 Cor. 3f., 984; in Phil. 3, 986, 988f.; unprecedented questions, 1160; ultimate coherence of, 1261, 1511–14

Theology, relation to history, 1515f.; to worldview, 609f., 625, 730, 1039; Jewish framework of, 610f.; reworked by Paul around Jesus and spirit, 612 and Part III *passim*

Theōsis ('divinization'), 546, 955, 1021–3, 1031; cruciform, 1023
'Third Race', 1443–9; itself presupposes Jewish worldview, 1447f.
Tiberius, 291
Time, fullness of, 552, 877; messianic, 550–62, 1181f.; overlap of, 1101
Torah, 90–5; within Pharisaism, 183; and soteriology, 851; arrival of, parallel to 'fall' in Eden, 894, 1014; as *paidagōgos*, 874, 910; curse of, 763f.; different roles of, ch. 7 *passim*, esp. 485; 847, 891, 1032–8; duality within? 1456–8; fulfilled, however paradoxically, 922, 1036f., 1078, 1109f., 1125; inevitable misuse of, 1034; narrative of, 485, 505–16, 823, 1033, 1125, 1454; paradoxes of, 720, 851–79 (esp. 861f., 870–4), 889, 892–902 esp. 895f., 909, 1002, 1005, 1014, 1018, 1179, 1456f.; Paul's view of, 755, 758, 1032–8, 1263; pointing ultimately to resurrection, 1037; purpose of, 1033f.; pursuing in wrong way, 1177f.; 'two Torahs in Israel', 86; 'under the law', 1436f.; works of, 995, 1183
Transformation, as category in Paul, 781, 956f., 1030; and justification, 957
Tribulation, *see* Messianic woes
Trinity, later doctrine of, 723
Triumphalism, ecclesial (Paul's rejection of), 731f.
Tübingen school, 56
Tychicus, 14

Unity of church, *see* Church, unity of

Velleius Paterculus, 302
Ventidius Cumanus, 1154
Vespasian, 293
Vesuvius, eruption of, 3
Virgil, xx, 231, 268, 284, 295–7, 301, 304–11, 321–3, 334, 345, 1281f., 1358
Virtue, 1395; in Pauline ethics, 1115f., 1373f., 1403f.

Warfare, spiritual, 732f.
Westminster Confession, 774
'Wisdom', search for, 380; of God, 629; and Torah, 671f.; needed for 'return from exile' in Baruch, 152f.; as mode of divine 'return', 106, 655, 671f., 696; in Paul's christology, 670–7, 696, 698; unveiling of previously hidden, 731; new kind of, 1356
Wisdom of Solomon, and ancient philosophy, 238–43; compared with Paul, 660f.
Wittgenstein, L., 554
Woes, *see* Messianic woes
'Word' of God, 629; *rhēma* in Rom. 10, 1173f.
Word-play, 21, 994f., 1452f.
Works of law, *see* Torah
Worldview, meaning of and relation to mindset and theology, xvi, 23–36, 63–6; 351f.; 565f., 609f., 625, 730, 1038f., 1309, 1391–3
Worship, within worldviews, 35f.; Paul's fundamental aim, 1506
Wrath, 174, 507, 554, 642, 760, 763–8, 771, 800, 811, 819, 837, 884, 997, 1005, 1029, 1037, 1086f., 1114, 1152–6, 1193, 1195, 1237, 1245, 1251, 1467

YHWH, presence of in Temple, 97–100; return of, 104–7, 189f., 653–6, 677f., 698f., 1044f., 1049, 1051f., 1073, 1493; in christology, 663f., 677f., 681, 698f., 705; in form of 'wisdom', 655; in pneumatology, 709–28, 1127

Zeal, 80–9, 92, 94, 108, 126, 136, 165, 178, 184, 193–6, 352, 364, 369f., 373, 395, 444, 564, 620f., 624f., 734, 850, 896, 929–31, 987–9, 1016, 1035, 1061, 1153–5, 1169, 1185, 1190, 1194, 1201, 1205, 1220, 1223f., 1263, 1378, 1481; as quintessential sin, 1422f.; critique of in Paul and Josephus, 1429–31
Zeno, 211, 213f.
Zerubbabel, 103, 105, 121
Zeus, emperors dressing as, 1286; non-existence of, 377, 743
Zion, pilgrimage of nations to, 1056–9, 1202f. (turned inside out, 1255); placing stone in, 1179; redeemer coming from, 1249f.
Zoroastrianism, 738